OVEN TEMPERATURES

To convert temperature from Fahrenheit to Celsius: subtract 32, multiply by 5, and divide by 9.
To convert from Celsius to Fahrenheit: multiply by 9, divide by 5, and add 32.

FAHRENHEIT	CELSIUS	GAS MARK	DESCRIPTION
250	120	½	very low
275	140	1	very low
300	150	2	low
325	160	3	low/moderate
350	175	4	moderate
375	190	5	moderately hot
400	200	6	hot
425	220	7	very hot
450	230	8	very hot

LENGTH

Exact conversion: 1 inch = 2.54 cm

IMPERIAL	METRIC
¼ inch	0.5 cm
½ inch	1 cm
1 inch	2.5 cm
6 inches	15 cm
1 foot (12 inches)	30 cm

SOME USEFUL DRY VOLUME MEASURE EQUIVALENTS

INGREDIENT	AMERICAN STANDARD	IMPERIAL WEIGHT	METRIC
Coarse salt	1 teaspoon	⅕ oz	5 g
	1½ teaspoons	¼ oz	8 g
	1 tablespoon	½ oz	15 g
Grated cheese	1 tablespoon	⅙ oz	5 g
	¼ cup	1 scant oz	20–25 g
Breadcrumbs	1 tablespoon	⅛ oz	4 g
	¼ cup	½ oz	16 g
All-purpose flour	1 tablespoon	¼ oz	8 g
	¼ cup	1 oz	30g
	½ cup	2½ oz	70 g
Granulated sugar	1 tablespoon	½ oz	15 g

BUTTER

American cooks often measure butter in sticks; use the following table to convert.

STANDARD U.S. MEASURE	IMPERIAL WEIGHT	METRIC
1 tablespoon	½ oz	15 g
2 tablespoons	1 oz	30 g
½ stick (4 tablespoons)	2 oz	60 g
1 stick (8 tablespoons)	4 oz	120 g

USEFUL EQUIVALENTS

All-purpose flour = plain flour

Kosher salt = coarse salt

Cornstarch = corn flour

Superfine sugar = caster sugar

Heavy cream = double cream

Light cream = single cream

Cheesecloth = muslin

Parchment paper = greaseproof paper

THE ESSENTIAL
New York Times
COOK
BOOK

THE ESSENTIAL
New York Times
COOK BOOK

Classic Recipes for a New Century

AMANDA HESSER

W. W. Norton & Company
New York • London

For information about permission to reproduce selections from this book,
write to Permissions, W. W. Norton & Company, Inc.,
500 Fifth Avenue, New York, NY 10110

For information about special discounts for bulk purchases, please contact
W. W. Norton Special Sales at specialsales@wwnorton.com or 800-233-4830

Manufacturing by Courier Westford
Book design by Iris Weinstein
Production manager: Julia Druskin
Digital production manager: Sue Carlson

Library of Congress Cataloging-in-Publication Data

Hesser, Amanda.
The essential New York Times cook book : classic recipes for a
new century / Amanda Hesser.—1st ed.
p. cm.
Includes bibliographical references and index.
ISBN 978-0-393-06103-1 (hardcover)
1. Cookbooks. I. New York times. II. Title.
TX714.H476 2010
641.5—dc22
2010033311

W. W. Norton & Company, Inc.
500 Fifth Avenue, New York, N.Y. 10110
www.wwnorton.com

W. W. Norton & Company Ltd.
Castle House, 75/76 Wells Street, London W1T 3QT

1 2 3 4 5 6 7 8 9 0

FOR TAD, WALKER, AND ADDIE

CONTENTS

ACKNOWLEDGMENTS

When I set out to write this cookbook, I had no idea how massive the *Times* 150-year-old food archive was or the fortitude I would need to navigate it. And I certainly didn't plan to test anything like 1,400 recipes.

I couldn't have done any of it without the help of Merrill Stubbs, whose research and cooking skills are limitless, and who has become like a sister—one with a happily complementary set of enthusiasms. She doesn't like making pastry dough; I love it. I hate chopping parsley; she finds it a gratifying challenge. When I was pregnant with twins and unable to stand, Merrill would set up a cutting board at my dining room table and bring me vegetables to chop. Once my twins were born, we'd take turns stirring pots and swinging the babies in their bouncy seats. We spent hundreds of weekends and evenings testing recipes, eating triumphant and failed dinners, and doing dishes late into the night.

My husband, Tad, a reluctant foodie, had the taxing job of tasting everything. He would like it to be made clear that he lobbied for the Mocha Cheesecake on page 756, and that the biscotti recipes, a cookie he despises for its "unfriendly" crunch, were included over his objections. There is no way in one short paragraph that I can amply thank him for all of his help—his laser-like editing, his tolerance for dinners consisting entirely of four kinds of crab cakes, his patience with my hare-brained scheme to take on this project while I had a full-time job, his heroic dishwashing, his willingness to cook dinner during the months (well, years) when I was actually writing the book, his infinite support and sweetness.

This was a true family affair. Our children, Walker and Addie, were raised on the recipes in this book: they got them first as purees, later as solids. They ate roast pigeon cut into tiny bits, spaghetti with sea urchin sauce, and île flottante before the age of two. They'll probably grow up to subsist entirely on junk food. My father-in-law, Dorie Friend, a long-time *Times* reader, worked on title ideas; Mary French, his girlfriend, helped perfect the Stewed Corn on page 271; our babysitter, Lorna Lambert, kept the trains running; and the entire Friend family served as open-minded and enthusiastic tasters.

As she has with my previous books, my sister, Rhonda Thomson, played a vital role in whipping this one into shape. She tested (and retested and retested) recipes for me, read proofs, and—using her expertise as a designer—weighed in on page layouts and fonts. Any time I saw them over the past few years, my mother, Judith Hesser, and my sister, Andrea Manella, were roped in to help me put together potential dishes for the book (there is now a rule that I'm no longer allowed to test recipes on family visits—OK, hot dogs for all!). And my brother, Dean, and sister-in-law, Leslie, let me hole up in their house in Pennsylvania for a week to write, during which time I managed to coax Dean into testing the Moscow Mule (page 20), Cheese Straws (page 79) and Pickled Shrimp (page 95). All great!

Any institution as old as the *New York Times* can seem like a crazy family filled with eccentric characters (the disguise-flaunting food critic Ruth Reichl; the peerless bon vivant R. W. Apple Jr.) and hidebound, idiosyncratic rules (its style book insists on calling a "lychee" a "lychee nut"), but I am grateful to have worked at such a remarkable place and to have had a chance to capture some of its history in this book. Among the dozens of people who helped me in ways small and large were Susan Chira, Alex Ward, Tomi Murata, Nancy Lee, Gerry Marzorati, Bill Keller, Jeff Roth, Linda Amster, Pat Gurosky, Nick Fox, Anne-Marie Schiro, Rick Flaste, Trish Hall, Andy Port, Michalene Busico, Mike Levitas, Joanna Milter, Phyllis Collazo, Michael Ryan Murphy, and Kathi Gilmore-Barnes.

This kind of project doesn't take a village, it takes a metropolis teeming with smart young recent college graduates. Among the many whom I will probably end up working for someday are Emily McKenna (who tested 150 recipes in a month, created the source list, and assisted in countless other valuable and thoughtful ways), Helen Johnston (who helped with recipe pairings, recipe categories, and menus), Jacqueline Barba (who proofread every recipe), Nicole Tourtelot, Alison Liss, Johanna Smith, Lauren Shockey,

Tabitha Schick, Adrienne Davich, Francesca Gilberti, and James Malloy.

Countless food writers, specialists, and historians contributed to my research. I am particularly grateful to Andy Smith, a professor at The New School in New York City; Anne Mendelson, the writer and food historian; and the Association for the Study of Food and Society, whose Listserv members have been extraordinarily generous with their time over the years.

I found many wonderful old cookbooks, including my copy of Craig Claiborne's *New York Times Cookbook*, at Bonnie Slotnick Cookbooks in Manhattan. One splendid new book that is especially thoughtful about the changes in American food and food journalism is David Kamp's *United States of Arugula*.

No cookbook should be published without a lot of friends and opinionated cooks weighing in. Early on, Nora Ephron suggested I write the book from a personal point of view rather than that of an arm's-length editor. My friends Esther Fein and Jennifer Steinhauer made sure this WASP included all the right Jewish foods; Jennifer also read proofs and kept on me like an army sergeant to finish the manuscript. Elizabeth Beier came up with the chronological recipe structure within chapters. And every time I saw Aleksandra Crapanzano, she'd whisper a new favorite *Times* recipe into my ear. I am also filled with appreciation for the dozens of friends, family, and neighbors who recommended recipes and tasted the various dishes that I forced upon them. And I am grateful to the hundreds of people (some of whom I know, most of whom I don't) on Twitter and Facebook, who readily answered questions about recipes like carne asada (p. 581), and about the material used for the book cover, and who contributed a huge number of excellent ideas for the food timeline in the introduction.

Thanks to Heather Schroder, my agent and

a great cook herself, who didn't press the mute button every time I called to complain about ten-step recipes and sinks full of dishes. W. W. Norton's Starling Lawrence, Jeannie Luciano, and Jill Bialosky had a great vision for this book and an understanding of the time it would take. Julia Druskin came up with the clean, timeless design and worked tirelessly to find an ingredient font that was both compact and vivid. Bill Rusin and Ingsu Liu came up with a cover that pleased everyone (not an easy task!). And Judith Sutton copyedited this manuscript with such precision and deftness I think her next job should be inspecting the Large Hadron Collider. She surely wanted to egg my house for the number of times I misspelled chiles. Or is it chilis?

I wrote much of this book underground on the 2/3 subway train and I am genuinely glad to live in a place where the MTA provides clean, well-lighted cars. If they'd put in WiFi too, I might actually have met my deadline.

This book, I hope, will serve as a monument to all the great food writers, home cooks, and chefs whose work has made the *Times* food sections a must-read for more than a century and strongly shaped the way we eat. I am particularly grateful to the many people who have generously allowed me to reprint their work here and to all the *Times* writers whose exceptional voices became part of our food culture: among the many, Jane Nick-erson, Juliet Corson, June Owen, Kiley Taylor, Jane Holt, Charlotte Hughes, Jean Hewitt, Nan Ickeringill, Raymond A. Sokolov, Mark Bittman, Marian Burros, Florence Fabricant, Patricia Wells, Molly O'Neill, Melissa Clark, Nancy Harmon Jenkins, R. W. Apple Jr., Suzanne Hamlin, Julia Moskin, Sam Sifton, Julia Reed, Jonathan Reynolds, Jason Epstein, John Willoughby, Chris Schlesinger, Joan Nathan, Toby Cecchini, William L. Hamilton, Matt Lee, Ted Lee, Jonathan Miles, Ruth P. Casa-Emillos, Denise Landis, Regina Schrambling, Christine Muhlke, Pete Wells, Kim Severson, Alex Witchel, Eric Asimov, Frank Prial, Howard Goldberg, Ed Levine, Bryan Miller, Mimi Sheraton, Oliver Strand, Peter Meehan, Maura Egan, Michael Pollan, Paul Greenberg, William Grimes, Jill Santopietro, Pierre Franey, and the great Craig Claiborne.

Last but definitely not least, I want to thank the thousands of newspaper readers from around the world who wrote to me to tell me their most beloved *Times* recipes. They sent thoughtful, multipart e-mails. They sent tattered decades-old clippings. They recounted how these recipes epitomized both periods and shifts in their lives. They wrote, directly and indirectly, about the community of food. Many of them also sent follow-up e-mails years later, wondering where the book was.

Here it is.

INTRODUCTION

This book began in 2004 over a lunch of Sri Lankan food at a restaurant in Manhattan's Theatre District. Susan Chira, a foreign correspondent and editor at the *New York Times*, was cultivating book projects by the paper's staffers. She asked me if I had any ideas. I had exactly none, but Susan is also into food, so we began talking about cookbooks. It occurred to me that of the many cookbooks containing recipes from the *Times*, the best known—the one on nearly all of my friends' mothers' kitchen shelves—was *The New York Times Cookbook* by Craig Claiborne. Still in print, it was originally published in 1961, nearly fifty years ago.

But, as Susan and I discussed, American cooking has seen monumental changes in the intervening decades. We discovered classic French food and then Italian, New American, Japanese, and Southeast Asian before looping back to France for a brief rendezvous with the bistro, and then on to the trattoria, tapas bar, and British butcher. We learned about seasonal cooking as well as local cooking, sustainable foods, and artisanal ingredients. We became vegetarians, pescatarians, vegans, and locavores. In 1961, there were lots of curious home cooks. Now there

are lots and lots of obsessed and well-informed foodies.

Before lunch was over, this book was in the works. Had I known then that it would take six years and entail cooking more than 1,400 recipes, I might never have gotten started.

During the course of this project, whenever I told someone I was writing a *New York Times* cookbook, they'd say, "Oh! You're updating Craig Claiborne's!" As soon as I said, "Well, no . . ." they'd frown. Claiborne's collection of more than 1,000 of his recipes was splendid and seminal; an instant best seller, it gave the *Times*'s food section an identity, not only as a source of great recipes but also as the leading voice in the food world, an arbiter of style. Yet Claiborne's book, for all its virtues, encompassed just a decade of years of his food coverage. The manuscript I'm working on, I'd tell those who asked, would be much broader in scope. It would include the most noteworthy recipes all the way from the 1850s, when the paper began covering food, to today. It would be a kind of 150-year flip book of American cooking.

Did I mention that it would *not* be an update of Claiborne's book?

To start, I crowd-sourced many of the recipes that *had* to be included by posting an "author's query" in the Wednesday Dining section and the Sunday *Magazine* asking readers to let me know their favorite *Times* recipes. The results were delightful: thousands of e-mails and letters poured in, with more than 6,000 recipes suggested. I learned about classics like Claiborne's Paella (a recipe that took him six years to perfect; see p. 309), Le Cirque's Spaghetti Primavera (a recipe so famous that three people claimed to have invented it; p. 314), and Forget-It Meringue Torte (a bouncy meringue cake that billows like a jib in the oven; p. 823).

The letters also contained passionate accounts of readers' relationships with dishes they had been cooking for decades. Readers wrote me about recipes that had held together their marriages, reminded them of lost youth, given them the cooking bug, and symbolized their annual family gatherings.

After much collating by my talented assistant (and now business partner) Merrill Stubbs, I had 145 single-spaced pages of recipe suggestions. The document, which is divided into recipe categories like soups, salads, beef, and cakes, sums up both what, exactly, we really love to eat—namely gazpacho, chicken, shrimp, salmon, crab cakes, meat loaf, chocolate cake, cheesecake, apple tarts, lemon desserts, and coffee cakes—and which writers' recipes seemed most inventive and easiest to make. I joked that I should call the book either

Chicken and Dessert or *Forever Bittman: The Best Recipes from the Recipe Writer We Love.*

Four of the top five most-recommended recipes were desserts, unsurprisingly; surprisingly, four of the five were more than twenty years old:

Purple Plum Torte (265 votes; p. 763)
David Eyre's Pancake (80 votes; p. 813)
Teddie's Apple Cake (37 votes; p. 752)
Chocolate Dump-It Cake (24 votes; p. 781—my mother's recipe and a terrific one, but surely a biased result, as I asked for the suggestions)
Ed Giobbi's Lasagna (23 votes; Lasagna on p. 342 edged it out)

WAYS TO USE THIS BOOK:

To reconnect with the dishes you grew up with.

To discover the joys of dishes you've never heard of—like Eldorado Petit's Fried Noodles with Garlic Mayonnaise (p. 324) and Huntington Pudding (p. 802).

As a compendium of the most well-known and influential recipes printed in the *New York Times*.

As a time machine, to travel back to when corn pancakes were chichi (1980s) and rum omelets were a dramatic dessert (nineteenth century).

As a gateway to culinary adventure: go ahead, try that Raspberry Bavarian Cream (p. 807) from 1910. It could be a new sleeper hit for your dinner parties.

As a weight for pressing terrines—its size and heft are just right.

WAYS NOT TO USE THIS BOOK:

For academic research—I'm not a food historian, so if you're really interested in the origin of Saratoga potatoes, do what I did and turn to Andrew F. Smith's *Oxford Encyclopedia of Food and Drink in America*, *America Cooks* by the Browns, and James Beard's *American Cookery*.

As a path to weight loss—if you dive in and start cooking, expect to be enjoying your share of butter. Don't get angry at an old recipe (or me); appreciate the past for what it is and balance heavier recipes with lighter dishes from the 2000s.

As a doorstop—though I admit it's heavy enough to serve as one.

I decided to test any recipe that was recommended by three or more people, which meant some 400 recipes stretching back to the late

1950s. Merrill and I devised menus of three to five recipes. A few days a week, she'd shop and we'd meet at my house after I got home from work. Then we'd cook for hours, usually sitting down to eat with my husband, Tad, around 10:30 p.m., at which point we'd all weigh in—Tad playing the Simon Cowell role—and then Merrill and I would make notes while Tad did the dishes. (Our sturdy twelve-year-old dishwasher survived two cycles a day during these years.) Once my twins were born, in 2006, they too were roped into the project—turns out, almost any recipe in this book can be pureed!

As we cooked our way through that stack, I discovered interesting shifts in the way *Times* readers have approached food. Desserts experi-

enced a major renaissance during the 1970s, as the writers served up ambitious cakes, extraordinarily sweet American pies, and a novel concept called the French tart. Pastry chefs then cut back on the sugar and moved away from these monolithic, Wayne Thiebaud–style desserts to heavily constructed individual servings. We ate a lot of duck in the 1990s and none at all in recent years. We discovered faki (p. 121), bobotie (p. 532), and baumkuchentorte (p. 747), then promptly forgot about them. We learned to cook pasta and sauce it properly, and to roast vegetables, but we left a lot of great Germanic foods like goulash and spaetzle by the curb. We tried and largely failed to adopt Chinese cooking at home.

There were a few writers who shall go nameless whose occasional recipe failed to meet basic standards of edibility. And there are surely readers who will scorn me for not including their favorites—or for not even locating their favorites. Seven people wrote in about clams possilipo, but though Merrill and I made dozens of searches, it remained lost in the archives, probably under a pile of chicken and dessert recipes. My hope is that revelatory reader-recommended recipes such as Cucumbers in Cream (p. 225) and Fontainebleau (p. 829) will make up for any gaps.

After the first year, as the pile of "yes" recipes grew, the book began taking shape. It wasn't going to be a dutifully comprehensive collection of recipes or a thoroughgoing history of American cooking. It was going to be an eclectic panorama of both high-toned masterpieces and low-brow grub, a fever chart of culinary passions. It was going to be by turns global and local, simple and baroque, ancient and prescient. A book, I am convinced, that will serve your every mood.

Two years, 400 post-day-job late-night recipe tests, and two babies later, the book's foundation was complete.

PHASE TWO: THE PREVIOUS 100 YEARS

Next project: the century of recipes that predated most of us. This time there were no readers or cooks to turn to, just a lot of reading and sleuthing to do in a lush if uncultivated playground. The *Times*'s vast nineteenth-century recipe

• Sugar, coffee, butter, and red meat are rationed during World War II.	—1940s—	
• Henri Soulé opens Le Pavillon in New York City and ushers in fancy French dining.	—1941—	
• Cake mixes hit the shelves, a half-century before Anne Byrn's *The Cake Mix Doctor.*	—1950s—	• Passenger jets make travel easier, giving Americans firsthand access to French cheese and wines.
• Pierre Franey becomes the chef at Le Pavillon.	—1952—	• Elizabeth David writes *French Country Cooking*—readers swoon over France.
• M. F. K. Fisher's books are collected in *The Art of Eating.*	—1954—	• Swanson comes out with a snazzy new concept: the frozen TV dinner.
• Tappan introduces a home version of Percey Spencer's microwave oven; it costs more than $1000 ($10,000 in today's money).	—1955—	
• The Federal Aid Highway Act is passed and the interstate highway system is established; food now is transported long distances as easily by truck as by rail.	—1956—	• The first Williams-Sonoma launches in California.
• Craig Claiborne is hired as the food editor at the *Times*; readers are introduced to chicken paprikash and leeks vinaigrette.	—1957—	
• Diet Rite is the first low-calorie soda.	—1958—	
• Joe Baum opens the Four Seasons in the Seagram Building on Park Avenue in New York City; the restaurant, designed by Philip Johnson and hung with paintings by Picasso and Miró, costs $4.5 million.	—1959—	
• Weight Watchers inspires millions of Americans to obsess over calories.	—1960s—	
• Reuben Mattus makes a high-butterfat ice cream, mixes in much less than the usual amount of air, and sells it as Häagen-Dazs.	—1960—	• Bill Niman starts raising cattle humanely in northern California, initiating a movement that will take three decades to gain significant traction.

Left events	Year	Right events
• André Soltner begins taking reservations at Lutèce; soon, they are impossible to get.	—1961—	• After taking nearly a decade to write it, Julia Child, Louisette Bertholle, and Simone Beck find a publisher for *Mastering the Art of French Cooking*; Americans discover their inner Francophiles.
• Anchor Steam Brewery becomes the first American microbrewery.	—1965—	
• High-fructose corn syrup production leaps forward; American food culture falls backward.	—1967—	• Robert Mondavi releases his first vintage of Fumé Blanc.
• Pink peppercorns, foie gras, Paul Bocuse, and Fernand Point become part of our vocabulary of nouvelle cuisine. • The decade of home-baked desserts.	—1970s—	• Turns out just about anything can be cooked in a Crock-Pot.
• Willy Wonka and his Oompa-Loompas tip vats of chocolate into the dreams of a generation of children.	—1971—	• Starbucks is launched in Seattle; becomes a chain in 1987; goes public in 1992. • Alice Waters dreams up Chez Panisse (and a food revolution).
• Dr. Robert Atkins's *Diet Revolution* is published; takes off twenty years later.	—1972—	• James Beard writes *American Cookery*, and Diana Kennedy writes *The Cuisines of Mexico*.
• Marcella Hazan writes *The Classic Italian Cookbook*.	—1973—	• Carl G. Sontheimer demonstrates the first Cuisinart at the Housewares Show in Chicago.
• Le Cirque opens; its regular patrons include Frank Sinatra, Princess Grace, Sanford I. Weill, Bill Blass, and Nancy and Ronald Reagan.	—1974—	• Chocolate curls are the dominant cake decoration.
• Mollie Katzen comes out with *The Moosewood Cookbook*, and the Silver Palate opens on Manhattan's Upper West Side.	—1977—	
• Robert Parker begins publishing *The Wine Advocate*; soon wineries quail at his name.	—1978—	
• Laura Chenel starts making European-style goat's milk cheese in California. • The new miracle tool: tongs. • Balsamic vinegar drugs us into thinking no salad can live without it. • Americans eat way too much oat bran.	—1980s—	• After an earlier flameout, frozen yogurt conquers the market by eliminating any traces of tangy yogurt flavor. • Sales of olive oil grow 72 percent in the second half of the decade. • California cuisine. • Raspberry coulis.

archive was largely user-generated and ran under the rubric "The Household." Readers submitted housekeeping tips, health remedies, and loads of recipes—it was like an online forum. None of this material seems to have been vetted by the editors, so readers were free to propagate a conviction that noses should be wiped by alternating left and right sides to prevent "deformity," or that anxious people should eat fatty foods because fat around the nerves "smooths them out." "The Household" format also inspired an inordinate number of nostrums for asthmatic canaries.

But food mattered—as the food historian Anne Mendelson has observed, the thinking of the day was, "If you don't have good food, you can't have good morality." Recipes were usually brief—almost Tweet-like in their shorthanded scope—and were composed in a paragraph form with ingredients listed in the order in which the writer remembered them. The general assumption was that you knew how to cook and bake, so no one needed to tell you what size cake pan to use or that you needed to butter it, or how to tie up a roast, or make a custard. Just make it already! Here are two examples:

Eccles Cake (1877)

Make a rich and delicate puff paste; roll it out thin, cut it round, using a bowl for that purpose; sprinkle each round with nicely washed currents

- Whole Foods Market brings natural foods to a supermarket setting in Austin, Texas.

—1980—

—1982—
- Wolfgang Puck and Ed LaDou create a phenomenon: the gourmet pizza made in a wood-fired oven.

- Martha Stewart, a caterer, writes *Entertaining*, then takes over the world.

- Nora Ephron writes *Heartburn*. Ex-husband, Carl Bernstein, gets heartburn.

—1983—

- Harold McGee makes it cool to be a geek in the kitchen with *On Food and Cooking*, providing riveting explanations of why mayonnaise breaks and how to temper chocolate.

—1984—
- Paul Levy and Ann Barr coin the term "foodie" in their *Official Foodie Handbook*.
- Marian Burros starts writing "Eating Well," the *Times*'s first health-related food column.

- Florence Fabricant gets New Yorkers obsessed with prosciutto.

—1985—

- The Slow Food organization is founded in Italy by Carlo Petrini.

—1986—

- Rick Bayless opens Frontera Grill in Chicago and publishes *Authentic Mexican*.

—1987—
- *Babette's Feast*.

- Laurie Colwin writes *Home Cooking*.

—1988—
- The sun-dried tomato gets used and abused.

- The *Times* declares fresh herbs trendy.

—1989—

- Fat-free craze; amazingly, no one loses weight!
- Sustainability becomes a buzzword for the food movement.
- Pan-Asian cooking is attempted and pretty much fails.

—1990s—
- Heritage breeds of vegetables, fruits, and even animals become chic.
- Architectural food.
- Sushi shifts from curiosity to obsession.
- People begin talking about seasonal cooking.

- Molly O'Neill begins writing for the *Times Sunday Magazine*.

—1992—

- Emeril Lagasse shakes food television with a single word, "Bam!"

—1993—
- Food Network is launched; now seen in 100 million American homes.
- Fresh mozzarella changes pizza forever.

- *The Mediterranean Diet* by Nancy Harmon Jenkins imports a new diet pyramid, in which meat is minimized and vegetables and grains are heralded.

—1994—

- *Big Night*.

—1996—
- Monsanto introduces genetically modified soybeans.

[*sic*], a little sugar, chopped lemon (only a small quantity of lemon), and nutmeg; wet the edges well, then place another round of paste on the top, pressing the edges neatly together; put in a hot oven and bake quickly.—Polly.

Crullers (1878)

One pint sour buttermilk, nearly the same white sugar, half pint butter and lard mixed, three eggs, one teaspoonful soda, flour to make a light dough; warm ingredients.

Among recipes for more proletarian johnny-cakes and tripe stew were recipes for granita, polenta, fruit cordials, and salads with nastur-

tium. Occasionally there were full-fledged food essays, articles debating what constituted good ice cream, treatises on table manners, surveys of the city's cattle and produce markets, and reported stories on olive oil production and its culinary uses. An 1852 story on a country dinner included this menu: roast potatoes, fricasseed chicken, bread, butter, cream pies, fritters, Pippin apples, and cracked butternuts. From this bountiful if erratic archive, the *Times* published its first cookbook in 1875.

These early recipes were dominated by the equivalent of today's "power users," with frequent contributions from such readers as Aunt Addie,

Mollie, and Bob the Sea Cook, whose recipes you'll find in the following pages. No one could outcook Aunt Addie: if you sent in a recipe for tomato soup, she'd raise you three tomato soups the following week. Mollie was hard-working and determined, if not the best recipe writer—measurements and techniques eluded her. And Bob the Sea Cook was an excellent storyteller, if occasionally sexist and racist. In a recipe for lobster and chicken curry, for which garlic must be peeled, he wrote, "If there are any ladies on board, make them do it."

Poring through the archives reminded me that food is like fashion, a business of recycling and tweaking. An 1895 story pointed to some changes in the layout of the kitchen, noting, "The ideal is converting the kitchen into a nearer similitude to the drawing room." In the 1980s, similarly, we embraced the "open kitchen." A 1879 recipe declared that baking beets was better than boiling them because it concentrates the sugars. More than 100 years later, I wrote about Tom Colicchio's method of baking beets in foil—to concentrate the sugars. "A Chafing Dish Frolic," a story from 1909, told you how to plan a cooking party for children. Nowadays, people throw cooking parties for adults.

Anthony Bourdain would have eaten well in

• AllRecipes.com, the world's largest food Web site, is founded by Tim Hunt in Seattle.	—1997—	• *The Joy of Cooking* is dramatically and controversially revised to exclude squirrel stew and include smoked tofu burgers.
• The *Times* creates the Dining Section and introduces color photos!		• Americans install professional stoves in their home kitchens (and two dishwashers if they're feeling fancy).
• Everyone is into French country cooking.	—1998—	• Fleur de sel downgrades the salt shaker.
• Crock-Pots successfully rebrand themselves as slow cookers.	—2000s—	• Bagged salad is a $2 billion industry.
• El Bulli gets noticed, and chefs around the world become obsessed with molecular gastronomy.	—2000—	• Prosecco takes off as Americans weary of the cost of Champagne.
• Foie gras is on every other menu.		• Anthony Bourdain shocks us with chef tales in *Kitchen Confidential*.
• Bottled water is the fastest-growing beverage category for the past decade.	—2001—	
• There are 3,100 farmers' markets in the United States, compared with just 100 in the 1960s.	—2002—	• Michael Pollan buys a cow and exposes the dark side of agribusiness for a story in the *Times Magazine*.
• Costco becomes the largest wine retailer in America.		
• The food memoir becomes a genre.	—2003—	• *101 Cookbooks* goes online, establishing a sophisticated tone for food blogs.
• The Microplane zester (originally a wood rasp) radically changes zesting citrus and grating cheese—really!		• *Times* food writers begin what the paper insists on calling "web-logging" :)
• La Caravelle closes after forty years—one of the last of the great French restaurants in New York City.	—2004—	• Meyer lemons abound.
• Sous-vide is all the rage.	—2005—	• The term "locavore" is used in the *Times*.
• E. coli outbreaks become a news staple.	—2006—	• "Food porn" is coined by Bill Buford in a *New Yorker* article.
• *Ratatouille* celebrates chefs, bistro cooking, and rats.	—2007—	• Banner year for smoked paprika and Brussels sprouts.
• Small batch coffee roasting creates a cult-like following.	—2008—	
• *Food, Inc.*, a documentary about the dark side of our industrialized food system, is nominated for an Oscar.	—2009—	• *Julie & Julia*, the movie about Julie Powell, the blogger, and Julia Child, the national treasure, is a hit.
• *Gourmet* folds after 68 years in print.		
• Jamie Oliver is awarded the TED Prize for his work fighting childhood obesity.	—2010—	• Specialty coffee bars proliferate in New York City.

the 1870s, which presented some extreme foods, including horse steak, brain fritters, starfish, roasted cat (Rôti de Chat), and braised lion with olives and oranges. This last dish was served as a special dinner at Restaurant Magny in New York. "When Mr. Lion was placed upon the table," a participant wrote, "there was a religious silence, which, however, only lasted for a few seconds, for at the first mouthful a murmur of approbation ran round the table, and the guests with one accord drank to the health of Mr. Cheret"—the hunter— "and M. Magny, coupling in their admiration the valiant lion-slayer and the clever artiste who had proved himself able to prepare such a delicious dish out of the flesh of this ferocious game, which is more frequently in the habit of eating others than of being eaten itself."

The first forty years of the twentieth century, however, were a culinary abyss. The *Times* moved away from reader recipes and toward uninspiring ones written by its staff for a column unpromisingly titled "Women Here and There" (which was later replaced by "Victuals and Vitamins"). Sheila Hibben, a *New Yorker* writer in the 1930s, was a prescient critic of the shift toward convenience cooking. In her 1932 book *The National Cookbook: A Kitchen Americana*, she wrote, "If the American housekeeper would only pay attention to how things taste, would study the materials of her own district, would become a virago even about fresh materials, how much happier everybody in her family would be!"

A year later, in the *Times*, she smartly observed, "Our forefathers knew about food and were proud of the knowledge, but with the passing of the pride of knowing came a new pride in not knowing— a singular phenomenon to be observed nowhere save in the United States of the last twenty years. For some inexplicable reason the young American woman of immediate postwar days got the idea into her head that not knowing how to make biscuit was the first step in sophistication, and,

as she took a good many steps in that direction, traditional American cooking was rapidly on the way to perishing from the face of the earth."

Yet even during this dark period the *Times* kept in touch with food culture. A 1903 story noted the trend for chop suey. In 1940, the paper wrote about a company that specialized in early mail-order food (fresh crab, pies, etc.), which was called "air shopping." There were stories about men who cooked, new cooking thermometers, roasting steak on oak planks, and one of my favorite inexplicable headlines: "Bad Cookery: Produces Results and Bad Ones."

Merrill listed the title of every recipe published during the long span between 1852 and 1960 so we could see which dishes were part of the vernacular and which were outliers. She created folders of all the variations on recipes like deviled crabs or orange ice, and then, as I extracted the prevailing techniques, I'd figure out which recipes to cook by looking for voice, interesting details, and ingredients and techniques that promised a successful outcome. I looked at the dozens of variations of such nineteenth-century staples as tomato soup, tripe *á la mode de Caen*, fritters, lemon pie, and Roman punch. There were a few once-popular recipes like whigs and graham gems (types of rolls) and all manner of terrapin (turtle) that felt too dated to include. Only once was there a dish I wanted to feature—charlotte Russe—but simply couldn't: all the recipes seemed stiff and bizarrely flavored.

More risky were the outliers, yet these were where the greatest rewards lay. And the only way to see what was what was to get in the kitchen and start cooking. This off-roading led to lacy Green Pea Fritters (1876; p. 270); sun-dried Tomato Figs (1877; p. 591); Spanish Fricco, a hearty beef and potato stew (1877; p. 506); bright and bracing Raspberry Granita (1898; p. 719); Raspberry Vinegar, a refreshing drink syrup (1900; p. 14); Chicken à la Marengo (1908; p. 453); and Green

Goddess Salad (1948; p. 176)—some of my favorite recipes in the book. It also led to a few belly flops, like silver cake (made with cream of tartar), which was as tough as a foam mat, and a vinegar pie that was more vinegar than pie.

Sharp-eyed readers may suspect that I slacked off during the 1940s and '50s, but if you could taste some of the recipes I made from this era, you would see that I am saving you from a world of hurt. I am sparing you the 1947 canapé that involved spreading peanut butter on toast, topping it with bacon, and finishing it under the broiler, and from the inglorious memory of the winter day in 1958 when Craig Claiborne ran recipes for turnip casserole, turnip soup, steamed white turnips, pureed rutabagas, and baked rutabagas. This is a cookbook, not Madame Tussaud's.

Another 400 recipes and another two years later—with my toddlers adapting to dinners of Roasted Squab with Chicken Liver Stuffing (p. 454), Ceylon Curry of Oysters (p. 391), and Fried Sweetbreads (p. 506)—the second pillar of research was in place.

THE FINAL PHASE

There were still 600 more recipes to test and the book to write. I turned back to the reader suggestions to make sure there were no glaring gaps. I did the same with the nineteenth-century list. I asked the food writers and editors at the *Times* for their suggestions, and then I spent a couple of days at the paper, digging into the Dining sections and *Magazine* food columns that had been published since I'd begun the project. Here I discovered extraordinary dishes like Stuck-Pot Rice with Yogurt and Spices (p. 351), Thomas Keller's Gazpacho (p. 146), and Tangerine Sherbet (p. 734), and I reimmersed myself in the more recent history of the *Times*'s food coverage.

After the 1950s, the *Times* food pages increasingly reflected not the way Americans were eating but the way Americans were going to be eating. Craig Claiborne arrived in 1957, at a time when Clementine Paddleford at the *New York Herald Tribune* was the city's leading food writer. "Craig ate Clem's lunch," Molly O'Neill, the longtime Sunday *Magazine* columnist said in a talk she recently gave about him. "Craig rode into town much younger, much cuter, a little exotic, and a true journalist." He knew what he liked to eat and, therefore, what everyone else should be eating: German stews and Southern desserts. "He defined food chic from almost the start of his work at the *Times*," Anne Mendelson, the food historian, said. As Claiborne grew into the job, he grew synonymous with it. He expanded his areas of interest to cover foreign cuisines with an unprecedented zeal, writing about osso buco and Dutch apple cake, Pakistani pigeons and pilau, tostones and tempura, génoise and buttercream.

Readers developed an intimate relationship with Claiborne: he was part reporter, part prophet, and part therapist. His number was listed in the phone book, and panicked readers didn't hesitate to call him from the stove. A friend of Florence Fabricant's once dialed him up when a scallop sauce wasn't reducing properly. "Boil the bejeezus out of it," Claiborne advised, and hung up. Nadine Brozan, a *Times* reporter, told me that people would offer her money to tell them what Craig was going to publish so they could stock up on the ingredients before the story ran and the shelves went bare.

In 1974, he teamed up with the well-known chef Pierre Franey for a Sunday cooking column. To write it, they'd get together at Claiborne's house in the Hamptons. Franey would cook and shout out measurements while Claiborne typed on his IBM Selectric. They also threw legendary parties there, one of them so packed with people that the deck collapsed.

As Claiborne's career was winding down, in 1983, he wrote about Alice Waters. The article served as a baton pass. When Claiborne went into retirement, taking with him chicken paprikash, crepes Suzette, and stuffed peppers, the food revolution was beginning. The *Times* amped up its food coverage and recipes, treating fads as news and recipes as gospel. Too many excellent writers have contributed to the paper's coverage to name them all here, but you'll find their work in the book. (And keep in mind that some of the greatest *Times* food writers—R. W. Apple, William Grimes, Frank Bruni, Ruth Reichl, Kim Severson, Eric Asimov, Mimi Sheraton, and Frank Prial among them—appear only occasionally here because they didn't write much about cooking.)

In the 1990s, Molly O'Neill's food column in the Sunday *Magazine* served as a springboard for chefs like Emeril Lagasse and new ingredients like kaffir lime leaves. O'Neill loved New York's lox shops as much as she adored fine dining, and she brought her omnivore's curiosity to the page, with love letters to pesto, riffs on granita, and an enduring love for French food. But perhaps the most influential column to run since Claiborne in his prime is Mark Bittman's "The Minimalist." It was the brainchild of Rick Flaste, who with Trish Hall created the *Times's* first full-fledged all-food section, Dining In/Dining Out. Bittman's column was originally supposed to be called "The Spontaneous Cook" and was going to focus on what you could cook with the ingredients you had in the fridge. It was planned for the new food section, but then the new section took three years to develop. When Flaste finally called, he told Bittman, "So you're doing this column and it's going to be really clever and really interesting and new and common and easy." Flaste told him to make the first one about red pepper puree, "the ketchup of the future." After Bittman wrote it, he told me, he thought, "OK, now I'm out of ideas. What am I going to do next?" He's been writing the column for thirteen years.

Seeking to do justice to all these developments, Merrill and I returned to the kitchen and started testing, and my sister, Rhonda, began re-testing recipes that needed minor tweaks. Eventually, finally, I sat down in front of my computer.

As I wrote, I tried to balance classics like Osso Buco alla Milanese (p. 535) and Chocolate Mousse (p. 820) with esoteric finds like Oriental Watercress Soup (p. 111), Charleston Coconut Sweeties (p. 683), and Tuna Curry (p. 435), a Sri Lankan dish that I included in honor of Susan Chira. I tried to trace the evolution of some currently popular dishes, like panna cotta, by highlighting the custards and creams—blancmange, pot de crème, crème brûlée—that preceded it. And when readers had expressed sufficient interest, I occasionally included variants of the same basic dish—you'll find two versions or more of boeuf bourguignonne, butternut squash soup, black bean soup, and gazpacho.

My test for whether or not to include a recipe was simple: after testing it, I'd ask myself, "Would I make this again?" And with 1,104 of the recipes, the answer was yes. I made the Raspberry Granita (p. 719) three times, baked Teddie's Apple Cake (p. 752) at least four times, and made the Stewed Fennel (p. 245) on easily a half dozen occasions. I also included a fair number of recipes from my own stories, not because I thought my work was so special, but because I could turn to them to fill in gaps, because I knew they worked—and because there was no one to stop me!

While there are some whoppingly time-consuming recipes in the book, there are also plenty of basics, like chicken broth and plain vinaigrette. There are recipes with lots of cream, butter, and booze, and a smaller number made with oil and herb infusions. The book isn't a one-stop-shopping, how-to-cook-everything compendium, but if you cook your way through it, you'll be more experienced than nearly anyone else. I'm certainly a much better cook than when I started this project: I've learned to braise meats in their own juices, poach scrambled eggs, combine molasses and lemon, bake bread in a Dutch oven, and make candy.

MY APPROACH TO THE RECIPES

Keep in mind that relatively few of these recipes originated in the *Times*—the paper is a way station for recipes, which pass through on their way from chefs and home cooks to readers. So the archive is a mish-mash of the traditional, the innovative, and everything in between.

Over 150 years, cooking styles and methods have changed.

- The main improvement has been intensity of flavor. Recipes are much more aggressively seasoned now, with layers of herbs and spices.
- Cayenne was the only chile-based heat up until about 1970; chiles, in many varieties, are now commonplace.
- Meats, especially chicken, cook nearly twice as fast as they did 100 years ago because animals are raised more quickly and exercise less, which renders their meat more tender.
- Egg yolks have either shrunk or lost their binding strength—old custard recipes that called for 3 yolks generally needed 5 to 6 "modern" egg yolks to set.

Sometimes I left the recipe language as it was, to preserve it. At other times—taking into account that many of the original recipes are available to the public on the *Times* website, should anyone want to see them—I completely rewrote the instructions because they were vague or confusing. And I added "Cooking Notes" where necessary for clarity. I also added serving suggestions for almost every recipe, drawing on other recipes in the book to offer up either complete menus or an array of complementary dishes.

In general, though, I made the decision to trust the reader. If there is too much dressing for the amount of greens you have, I expect you to figure out how to add a little at a time until the salad is properly dressed. I count on you to remember to always season a dish to taste rather than depending on a step that tells you to do so. And if you don't have the right size casserole dish for a gratin, I know you'll find some other dish and improvise.

My cooking axioms:

- Use fresh spices, good oil, and flaky noniodized salt.
- Low-fat dairy is not a dependable substitute.
- Add enough salt to your pasta water that it tastes like seawater.
- If a recipe calls for yogurt, use a whole-milk Greek yogurt like Fage (unless otherwise instructed). The recipe and your life will be better for it.
- Good ingredients are sometimes expensive. But if more people buy them, the prices will drop (at last, my economics degree proves useful).
- Use more salt and higher heat than you think is prudent when searing meats.
- Take cookies off the baking sheet within 2 minutes, no matter what the recipe says.
- Undermixing is always better than overmixing.
- I know this sounds batty, but no toasters and no teapots—they take up valuable counter and stove space. (Use your broiler for toasting and a pan to boil water.)

- Refrigerate your best oils and definitely don't store them near your stove.
- Use a meat pounder to crush garlic and spices.
- When it comes to pastry and bread doughs, remember you're the boss.
- Embrace the adventure of cooking odysseys like Paul Prudhomme's Cajun-Style Gumbo (p. 125), the humor of recipes like Turducken (p. 485), the majesty of desserts like the Gâteau de Crepes (p. 785), and the economy of dishes like Baked Mushrooms (p. 212).

The recipes in this book will turn out differently in your kitchen than they did in mine or than they did for the person who wrote up the recipe fifty years ago. Recipes are by nature inexact, because everyone works with different ingredients, tools, skills, and expectations. Be patient. Adapt. And if a typo turned teaspoons into tablespoons, try your best not to curse my name, but simply let me know (I can easily be found online).

CONCLUSION

I tried to make this a book that blended the *Times*'s best recipes with the interests and passions of its readers. I'm excited to have written a cookbook that is genuinely unlike any other—one that gathers up both modern and classic recipes, tells a story of American cooking, includes many surprises (early doughnuts, the forgotten oyster pan roast, and the best panna cotta recipe in the world), and, most of all, provides curious and savvy food lovers with a book that can be a lifetime kitchen companion.

As a lark, shortly before I handed the book in, I Tweeted to ask what people thought the title should be. I loved writer Andy Selsberg's response: *That Old Gray Lady Can Cook*. But the overwhelming favorite was *All the Food That's Fit to Eat*.

I thought that was apt. I hope you'll find it so, too.

THE ESSENTIAL

New York Times

COOK BOOK

1 ⌒ DRINKS, COCKTAILS, PUNCHES, AND GLÖGG

• Café au Lait (p. 9). —1856—

• The punch bowl is a fixture in bars. —1860s—

• Jerry Thomas, a prominent New York bartender, writes the seminal manual *How to Mix Drinks; or, The Bon-Vivant's Companion.* —1862—

• Summer fruit finds its way into cordials like the blackberry one on p. 11. —1870s—

 • Home winemakers send in recipes for wines made with ginger, elderberry, blackberry, currant, rhubarb, lemon, gooseberry, and even tomato.

• Recipes for brandied cherries, also known as Cherry Bounce (p. 13), appear regularly in the food pages.

• If you have a party, you probably serve Milk Punch (p. 10) or Roman Punch (p. 12). —1880—

• A *Times* writer describes eggnog as "a mixture of eggs, milk, sugar, spices, rum, brandy, and—headache." —1895—

• Raspberry Vinegar (p. 14), a potent and addictive fruit syrup best drunk with sparkling water. —1900—

• The *Times* runs a story on summer drinks such as Claret Cup (p. 12) and Champagne Cup (p. 14). —1901—

• Early sighting of hot cocoa with marshmallows. —1910—

• Prohibition becomes law. —1920—

• Prohibition ends—and with it go the joys of making moonshine. —1933—

• Jane Nickerson writes about drinks from New York's great bars, including the Pierre, the Waldorf-Astoria, and the Stork Club. —1940s—

• Iced coffee arrives (p. 17). The first Starbucks will open in Seattle thirty-one years later. —1940—

• The Martini (p. 35) as we know it, with gin as the main player. —1950s—

• Craig Claiborne publishes a recipe for an eggnog that's so thick it requires a spoon for consumption (p. 22). —1959—

• Frank Prial is named the first wine critic for the *Times*. —1972—

• Self-imposed Prohibition? Hardly any drinks make it into the food pages. —1980s—

 • College students everywhere indulge in too many Long Island iced teas.

• Jell-O shots are popularized, a new and exciting way to get drunk.

 • Dale DeGroff revives the showman bartender at New York City's Rainbow Room.

• Microbreweries open up around the country, revitalizing the art of beer making. —1990s—

 • Single-malt Scotch fuels Wall Street's bankers; bottled water fuels Hollywood.

• The word "mixologist" first appeared in the *Times* in 1966, and then not again until this year. —1999—

• Prosecco floods the mainstream with bubbly wine at prices a fraction of Champagne. Reims gasps. —2001—

• Hipster bartenders in the outer boroughs begin concocting their own bitters. —2002—

• Q Tonic, a naturally made upstart tonic water brand, is launched. —2006—

I

DRINKS, COCKTAILS, PUNCHES, AND GLÖGG

America has never settled the question of whether it's a wine- or beer-drinking nation, so our liquid preferences have always been a free-for-all. Wine for the erudite. Cocktails for the adventuresome. Beer for the mainstream.

Drinking habits were in the midst of an important shift when the *Times* started up in 1851. Punches, also called bowls, had been a staple of bars and saloons, where large batches would be mixed up in ceramic vessels and ladled out throughout the day. Although plenty of punch recipes showed up in the early issues of the *Times*, as a genre they were on their way out. At home, people used spirits and wine as a means to preserve fruits. The archives teem with homemade wines and sweet fruit-infused cordials particularly in the summer months, when fruit was plentiful and the only way to save it from the garbage heap was to turn it into jams or preserve it in alcohol.

Until the mid-nineteenth century, cocktails were a rag-tag assortment of drinks—slings, juleps, bumbos, toddies, fixes, sack-possets, and sangarees—each with its own fungible definition. But they were about to begin a long, inventive ride into the twentieth century with the help of people like Jerry Thomas, a New York

bartender and the cocktail's premier evangelist. Thomas wrote the first cocktail manual, *How to Mix Drinks, or The Bon-Vivant's Companion*, in 1862. In it and in later editions, the heady communal punch makes way for the neat solitary cocktail.

The *Times*'s food and drink coverage nearly came to a halt around 1910 (a decade before Prohibition), and by the time regular publication of recipes resumed in 1940, cocktails had a firm hold on Americans' attention. The Bloody Mary made its debut in the *Times* in 1948, and it has continued to enchant bartenders and food writers: variations on the trifecta of tomato, heat, and spirit have shown up every few years since. In recent years, there was the Peppar Tomato in 2000 (p. 31), which refined the drink by first making tomato water; the Bloody Paradise, also in 2000 (p. 30), which calls for grains of paradise, a rarified spice; and the Sir Francis Drake (p. 36), a peppy blend of Clamato juice, sherry, celery salt, horseradish, Tabasco, and lemon. Those searching for something less baroque found it in 2003 with The Bone (p. 34), which cut to the chase with just Tabasco, lime, and rye.

But the drink *Times* readers have long loved

most is eggnog. I've included the two best recipes: Craig Claiborne's boozy snowdrift and a version by Jeffrey Morgenthaler, a blogger, who discovered that if you skip all the technique—the separating of eggs, the whipping of cream—and just toss everything into a blender and buzz the hell out of it, you end up with a nog that's rich yet not overbearing.

Cheers!

RECIPES BY CATEGORY

CAFÉ AU LAIT

This was one of the first recipes published in the *New York Times* (which was then called the *New York Daily Times*). The recipe came in a letter to the editor: a reader, A.B.C., complaining about the excess of meat in people's diets, suggested café au lait for breakfast as an alternative to the popular "animal foods"—eggs, pork, and whatnot. A.B.C.'s advice anticipated Michael Pollan's thinking in his 2008 book *In Defense of Food: An Eater's Manifesto*.

The recipe, as you'll see from A.B.C.'s letter, is more a reference to a French ritual than a recipe. But it still works just fine.

———

ORIGINAL RECIPE

"It is often a wonder to us Americans how a Frenchman can live at so little expense, and still enjoy as good health as if he had meat daily. The fact is, we eat altogether too much animal food; and if anyone will try for a few months and eat meat only at dinner, I feel sure he will not desire to return to the strong diet. I was in France fifteen months, and ate nothing during that period for breakfast but *café au lait* (i.e., coffee to the milk,) for which I usually paid *four cents*. They have two methods of preparing it, as far as I learned. The popular manner is, first, to make a decoction of coffee as strong as possible with water. Then add as much of this to boiled milk as you wish, and sweeten."

SERVING SUGGESTIONS
Callie's Doughnuts (p. 621), Eggs à la Lavalette (p. 622)

JUNE 20, 1856: "A PALATABLE DIET FOR A MAN HARD-UP." A LETTER TO THE EDITOR SIGNED A.B.C.

—1856

LEMON SYRUP

You can use this syrup as a means to any number of pleasant ends: stir it into iced tea, spoon it over ice cream, sweeten mint tea and cocktails with it. I like it swirled into sparkling water. It may firm up in the fridge—use a strong spoon to scoop it out.

———

Grated zest of 3 lemons
Juice of 6 lemons, or as needed
4 cups sugar

1. Combine the lemon zest and juice. You should have about 1½ cups. Let stand overnight.
2. The next day, combine the juice and zest with the sugar in a medium saucepan. Stir over medium heat until the sugar is fully dissolved, but do not let the mixture boil. It will remain cloudy for a while, then will begin to foam and bubble, so it's difficult to see if the sugar is dissolved. To test it, spoon a little onto a plate, let cool, and taste it.
3. When all the sugar has liquefied, remove the syrup from the heat, let it settle, and then skim off any foam that has risen to the top. Strain into a container and refrigerate until ready to use. The syrup will keep for up to 2 months in the fridge.

MAKES 4 CUPS

VARIATION
Try it with Meyer lemons, blood oranges, or any other citrus, adjusting the sugar as desired.

SERVING SUGGESTIONS
'ino's Tuna with Black Olive Pesto Panini (p. 373), Blue Cheese Cheesecake (p. 61), Thai Beef Salad (p. 543)

JUNE 11, 1876: "THE HOUSEHOLD: RECEIPTS." RECIPE SIGNED K. L. H.

—1876

~ GINGER CORDIAL

The ginger gives this drink its subtle character, but it's the currants whose lush pink hue makes it look like an extract of orchids. I drank it chilled, over ice, quite happily. You could also top it with a splash of sparkling water—or why not prosecco?

———

A 2-ounce piece of fresh ginger

2 lemons

I heaping tablespoon blanched whole almonds

2¼ pounds fresh currants

32 ounces (I quart) brandy

2¼ cups sugar

I. There is no need to peel the ginger. Thinly slice it, then, using a mortar and pestle or a rolling pin, pound it to bruise it. Use a vegetable peeler to pare the zest from the lemons. Crush the almonds in a mortar and pestle or with a rolling pin.

2. Place the currants in a large bowl and crush them with a potato masher. Leaving the stems in is OK—it's too tedious to remove them. Add the ginger, lemon zest, almonds, and brandy. Cover the bowl and let sit in a cool place for 3 days.

3. Have ready several scalded bottles or jars (to scald, simply dip the bottles or jars and lids in boiling water). Strain the mixture through a jelly bag into a clean bowl; use a cheesecloth-lined strainer if you don't have a jelly bag. This will take some time—resist the temptation to squeeze the jelly bag to extract the juice, letting gravity do the work, otherwise your cordial will be cloudy. Add the sugar and stir until dissolved.

4. Pour into the bottles or jars and seal. The cordial keeps, refrigerated, for up to 3 months.

MAKES 6 TO 7 CUPS

INGREDIENT NOTE

The recipe originally called for bitter almonds, which are now prohibited in the United States because, when raw, they contain toxic hydrocyanic acid. However, bitter almonds are still used—after processing to remove the toxins—to make almond extract and almond liqueurs. I replaced them with regular almonds—perhaps a poor substitute, since the flavor is much different—but you could add a few drops of almond extract as well (in Step 3, along with the sugar). The almond flavor should be faint.

SERVING SUGGESTION

If serving with sparkling water or prosecco as a cocktail, Pork-and-Toasted-Rice-Powder Spring Rolls (p. 74)

SEPTEMBER 3, 1876: "THE HOUSEHOLD: RECEIPTS."

—1876

~ DELICIOUS MILK PUNCH

Mollie, a regular *Times* contributor in the late nineteenth century, must have realized that milk punch was a name in need of editing. "Delicious" does the trick, drawing your attention from the perverse-sounding collision of milk and booze. Savvy cocktailers know the benefits of milk: it quiets the bark of a coarse spirit and coats your stomach so the punch doesn't later punch you.

There is an alarming step in this recipe: when you combine the brandy and citrus, which you've been diligently macerating for half a week, with the hot milk, a thousand tiny milk curds float to the surface. Don't throw the whole thing out—that's what the straining in Step 3 is for (the final drink is actually clear). The first time I made the punch, I didn't realize this curdling was intentional, so I made it a second time, leaving out the juice but keeping the zest. The clarity and sharpness of the citrus was still there, but the character was lost.

Did I mention that you will love this drink and find it incredibly delicious?

———

2 oranges

I lemon

32 ounces (I quart) brandy

24 ounces (3 cups) rum

6 cups water

4 cups whole milk

½ nutmeg, grated

2¼ cups sugar

I. Using a vegetable peeler, pare the zest from the oranges and lemon in long thin strips. Juice the oranges and lemons; refrigerate the juice. Combine the zest and 1 cup brandy in a bowl or other container, cover, and let macerate in a cool place for 3 days.

2. Combine the brandy mixture with the orange and lemon juice, rum, remaining 3 cups brandy, and the water in a large bowl that fits in your refrigerator. Bring the milk to a boil with the nutmeg in a large saucepan, then gradually pour it into the brandy mixture, stirring rapidly. Add the sugar and stir until dissolved. Chill for 12 hours.

3. Strain the punch through a fine-mesh sieve into a punch bowl. Serve ladled over ice.

MAKES 12 TO 16 DRINKS

INGREDIENT NOTE
The punch is supposed to be cold, but you may like it served warm.

SERVING SUGGESTIONS
Fried Olives (p. 87), Nicole Kaplan's Gougères (p. 76)

JUNE 3, 1877: "THE HOUSEHOLD: RECEIPTS FOR THE TABLE." RECIPE SIGNED MOLLIE.

—1877

☞ BLACKBERRY BRANDY

Sometimes called a cordial, blackberry brandy—as well as brandy made with other fruits—was frequently found in the recipe pages of the *Times* in the nineteenth century. Most blackberry brandies are made by boiling the fruit with just enough sugar to create a syrup (and sometimes seasoning it with spices—here, nutmeg, cinnamon, allspice, and clove). Later, brandy is added to dilute and cure the syrup.

Drinking a fruit brandy is a totally different experience from drinking a distilled fruit eau-de-vie. This one is sturdy, viscous, and mischievous: as it charms you, it robs you of sobriety. Sip a little after dinner, when you're near a bed. Or add a little sparkling water and lime juice for an aperitif. Brush it on the layers of a vanilla cake before icing it. Pour it over lemon granita. Don't let it languish in your basement.

2¼ pounds blackberries
1 cup plus 3 tablespoons sugar
1 teaspoon freshly grated nutmeg
1 teaspoon ground cinnamon
½ teaspoon allspice berries
½ teaspoon whole cloves
10 ounces brandy

1. Have ready several scalded bottles (to scald, simply dip the bottles and lids into boiling water). Place the blackberries in a large saucepan and crush them with a potato masher. Bring the juices to a boil, then remove from the heat. Strain through a fine-mesh sieve into a bowl.

2. Combine 2 cups of the blackberry juice with the sugar, nutmeg, cinnamon, allspice, and cloves in a medium saucepan and bring to a boil, then reduce the heat and simmer for 15 minutes, skimming any foam. Remove the pan from the heat, pour in the brandy, and let cool completely.

3. Strain the brandy through a jelly bag or a sieve lined with several layers of cheesecloth; do not squeeze the bag or press on the solids. Using a funnel, pour the brandy into sterilized bottles and seal them. The brandy keeps, refrigerated, for up to 3 months.

MAKES ABOUT 4 CUPS

SERVING SUGGESTIONS
Classic Financiers (Buttery Almond Cakes; p. 697), Breton Butter Cake (p. 777)

AUGUST 12, 1877: "THE HOUSEHOLD: RECEIPTS FOR THE TABLE." RECIPE SIGNED MOLLIE.

—1877

☙ CLARET CUP

A claret cup is red wine handsomely tricked out as a cocktail. Brandy and sherry are enlisted for gravitas, lemon and sugar for diplomacy, and club soda for charisma. In my opinion, it's a summer drink to rival a Pimm's cup.

_____

3 ounces sherry

1 ounce brandy

3 tablespoons plus 1 teaspoon sugar

1 lemon

1 (750-ml) bottle red wine

2 to 4 cups chilled club soda or sparkling water

1. Combine the sherry, brandy, and sugar in a pitcher or other container. Using a vegetable peeler, pare the zest from the lemon in long strips. Add these to the liquor. Thinly slice the now-bald lemon and reserve for garnish. Pour in the wine and stir until the sugar is dissolved. Chill.

2. To serve, add club soda to taste (I liked it best with 3 cups). Fill tumblers with ice, pour over the claret cup, and garnish each with a lemon wheel.

MAKES 6 TO 8 DRINKS

INGREDIENT NOTE

The original recipe did not include a garnish. You can slice up the leftover lemon, as I do here, but you could also add a cherry or strawberry or a plum wedge.

SERVING SUGGESTIONS

Scotch Eggs (p. 62), Egg and Olive Canapés (p. 57), Goat's-Milk Cheese, Buttered Brown Bread, and Salted Onion (p. 75), Cucumber–Goat Cheese Dip with Radishes and Scallions (p. 70)

FEBRUARY 10, 1878: "THE HOUSEHOLD: USEFUL FAMILY HINTS." RECIPE SIGNED BEVERAGE.

—1878

☙ ROMAN PUNCH

There was a time—when turtle soup was a luxury dish and whiskey was an acceptable morning pick-me-up—when garnishing an icy-cold drink with a dollop of meringue seemed perfectly normal. And why not? The meringue floats on the surface like a regal, mysterious iceberg. As you mix it in, the sugar and whites add a touch of cream to what's otherwise a traditional sweet, boozy punch.

Although this one does not, many Roman punch recipes instruct you to freeze the mixture before serving, presumably so it gets nice and slushy before receiving its meringue cap. (Its kin would be Patsy's Bourbon Slush, p. 32.)

Roman punch was served as an intermezzo at society parties and at the White House during Rutherford B. Hayes's presidency. Hayes and his wife, who was known as "Lemonade Lucy," were temperance advocates, and to get around their strictures—the rumor was—someone in the kitchen devised the spiked sorbet, which was served to guests. By 1922, the drink was declared passé by Emily Post.

_____

2 cups lemonade

Juice of 2 oranges

8 ounces Champagne

8 ounces rum

2 large egg whites

2 cups confectioners' sugar

1. Stir together the lemonade, orange juice, Champagne, and rum in a punch bowl. Chill.

2. When ready to serve, make the meringue: whip the egg whites in a medium bowl until they hold soft peaks, then gradually beat in the confectioners' sugar. Pile into a serving bowl.

3. Fill punch cups with ice, ladle over the punch, and top each with a dollop of meringue. Serve with cocktail stirrers.

MAKES 6 TO 8 DRINKS

AUGUST 17, 1879: "THE HOUSEHOLD: USEFUL FAMILY HINTS." RECIPE SIGNED A.B.H.

—1879

CHERRY BOUNCE

Of all the nineteenth-century recipe contributors—and there were hundreds—Bob the Sea Cook was much the most memorable. A former galley cook (or so he claimed), he sent in recipes that were as much recollections of a life well traveled as instructions for how to get dinner on the table (see the Potted Salmon on p. 388 for another of his recipes).

"People kind of laugh at me because I jine yarns with receipts," Bob wrote, meandering his way toward the proportions for this drink, "but I can't think of a good thing to eat or drink without splicing it with something else. I never drink a glass of cherry bounce without thinking of my old granny, as lived at the jumping-off point of Long Island. There used to be a lot of straggling cherry trees that had a hard time to live, that bore a half-wild kind of fruit on them, which was grandmother's cherry-bounce trees—that is when I did not steal the cherries."

His grandmother's cherry bounce, made with whiskey, was apparently a local favorite, and if you make it, you will understand why. "Grandma used to say that cultivated cherries never was good for bounce," he added, "and that wild cherries made it better. Hifalutin people call this cherry cordial, but I say it's cherry bounce."

----

4 cups ripe sweet cherries
Whiskey to cover (about 16 ounces)
Sugar

1. Have ready a scalded 1-quart jar with a screw band and new lid. (To scald, simply dip the jars and rims in boiling water.) Fill jar with the cherries. Cover the cherries with whiskey, and seal the jar tightly. Let stand in a cool, dark place for 3 weeks.
2. Drain the cherries, reserving the liquid. Transfer the cherries to a bowl and, using a potato masher, mash them to extract as much juice as possible. Strain this juice into the cherry liquid.
3. For every 2 cups of liquid, measure out ½ cup sugar and 2 tablespoons water. Combine the sugar and water and heat over medium heat, stirring, until the sugar is dissolved and the liquid is beginning to boil. Remove from the heat and let cool for a few minutes.

4. Stir the sugar syrup into the cherry juice. Pour the bounce into a scalded bottle and seal. It will keep in the fridge for up to 3 months.

MAKES ABOUT 3 CUPS

SERVING SUGGESTIONS
You can serve the bounce in cordial glasses with a cherry or two. Or use it as a base for other drinks. For instance, add a bay leaf and strip of orange peel to a cup of the bounce, let it sit for a couple of hours, and then top with a little ice and a splash of club soda.
  Serve with Filbert Torte (p. 742), Coconut Loaf Cake (p. 774).

JUNE 20, 1880: "THE HOUSEHOLD: RECEIPTS FOR THE TABLE." RECIPE SIGNED BOB THE SEA COOK.

—1880

BRANDY (OR SHERRY) AND MILK

½ ounce brandy or 4 ounces dry sherry
½ to 1 teaspoon sugar
Freshly grated nutmeg
¾ cup whole milk, hot or steamed

Stir together the brandy and sugar in a latte bowl or mug. Add some grated nutmeg. Pour in the milk. Taste, adding more sugar if desired.

SERVES 1

SERVING SUGGESTION
Serve after dinner with Mary Ann's Fruitcake (p. 660) and a roaring fire.

MAY 1, 1881: "THE HOUSEHOLD: RECEIPTS." RECIPE SIGNED RINGER-HANDBOOK OF THERAPEUTICS.

—1881

RASPBERRY VINEGAR

In the early twentieth century, the food stories were often shoehorned awkwardly into a kind of rudimentary lifestyle section. The section was clearly aimed at women, but treated them as a mysterious species, whose needs were bothersome and whose motives difficult to ascertain.

The column in which this raspberry vinegar, a flavoring syrup for drinks, appeared—as well as a number of other terrific recipes, like coffee ice cream and cherry bounce (p. 13)—also contained discourses on whether or not women were more vain than men, the charm of "little white curly Porto Rican dogs," and a mother who, in order to keep her son from leaving the house to play with his friends, dressed him up in girls' clothing (a highly unsuccessful parenting strategy, with predictable results).

Buried in this lifestyle morass was a fascinating record of contemporary foodways. The same column offered tips for picnicking: Keep a list of things to bring to a picnic so you don't have to remember each time. Pack butter in a jelly jar, and set it on ice in a tin bucket to keep it cool and dry. Whip the cream for coffee in advance, because it will stay fresh longer. Orange marmalade is better than regular jam, because it won't soak into the bread. If you make a custard for dessert, make it with more eggs, because it will travel better. Deviled eggs may be breaded and deep-fried. And "candied ginger, and the little candied oranges that come from the Oriental shops, are dainties which go well with a picnic luncheon."

This raspberry vinegar (also known as shrub) is pure genius. The acidity threads though the drink, elevating the fruit and burying the sweetness. And it makes a knockout spritzer—just add sparkling water (or prosecco and a fresh raspberry!). For a classic shrub, top it off with rum or brandy. (If you don't have a bounty of raspberries, you can halve or quarter the recipe.)

———

1 cup red wine vinegar

1½ quarts raspberries

Sugar (approximately 2 to 3 cups)

1. Combine the vinegar and raspberries in a bowl. Cover and let macerate in the fridge for 3 days.
2. Mash the raspberries in the bowl, then strain the liquid through a fine-mesh sieve lined with cheesecloth. For every 1 cup juice, measure 3 cups of sugar. Combine the juice and sugar in a saucepan, bring to a boil, then lower the heat and simmer for 5 to 10 minutes, until it forms a thin syrup. Skim off any scum that rises to the surface.
3. Remove from the heat and let cool, then pour into sterilized bottles. The vinegar keeps, refrigerated, for up to 3 months.
4. To serve, add 1 to 2 teaspoons raspberry vinegar to a tumbler filled with ice. Add chilled sparkling water (or sparkling wine) to fill the glass.

MAKES ABOUT 4 CUPS

AUGUST 5, 1900: "WOMEN HERE AND THERE—THEIR FRILLS AND FANCIES."

—1900

CHAMPAGNE CUP

A journalist from the *London Telegraph* shared recipes for summer drinks as well as some tips, such as: "A liquid set on ice and slowly chilled is far more to be recommended than the drink in which the ice floats, but it is not everyone who will admit this truth." He's right: ice cubes dilute the magic.

———

3 ounces brandy

3 ounces maraschino liqueur

1 tablespoon sugar

1 (750-ml) bottle Champagne or prosecco, chilled

12 ounces chilled sparkling water

8 thin slices cucumber

A few sprigs of borage (optional)

Combine all of the ingredients in a bowl; stir to dissolve the sugar. Set the bowl in a bowl of ice. Ladle into tumblers or short stemmed glasses.

MAKES 7 CUPS

SERVING SUGGESTIONS

Cucumber Sandwiches (p. 56), Stuffed Hard-Cooked Eggs (p. 56), Shrimp Canapés à la Suede (p. 57), Pickled Shrimp (p. 95), Onion Rings (p. 61)

JULY 29, 1901: "SUMMER DRINKS AND FOODS: HINTS ON THEIR PREPARATION AND USE—THE SIMPLEST ARE THE BEST—SOME RECIPES." RECIPE ADAPTED FROM THE *LONDON TELEGRAPH*.

—1901

VERMOUTH CUP

As the recipe didn't specify sweet or dry, I was unsure which vermouth to use, so I tried both. Each version had its merits, but I preferred the sweet. The one made with dry vermouth is spare to the point of omission; you taste the bitters and fruit concisely, but the drink itself is a little soulless. With sweet vermouth, it's closer in spirit to a Pimm's cup, but with a stronger point of view, a weight. It's sweet and aromatic, refreshing even. I garnished the drink with a sliver of plum, but any berry, or even a little cucumber, would be flattering.

---

4 ounces sweet vermouth

6 drops Angostura bitters

½ cup seltzer or sparkling water

Ripe sweet raspberries, strawberries, or plums for garnish

Fill a tumbler with ice cubes. Pour in the vermouth and bitters and top with the seltzer. Garnish with a berry or two, or a sliver of plum.

SERVES 1

SERVING SUGGESTIONS
Seasoned Olives (p. 90), Pickled Shrimp (p. 95), Cheese Straws (p. 79)

JULY 29, 1901: "SUMMER DRINKS AND FOODS: HINTS ON THEIR PREPARATION AND USE—THE SIMPLEST ARE THE BEST—SOME RECIPES." RECIPE ADAPTED FROM THE *LONDON TELEGRAPH*.

—1901

RAMOS GIN FIZZ

Nowadays, when a politician wants to make a point to the "folks," he goes to a diner to meet and greet and empathize while scarfing down pancakes. For all of its hokeyness, it seems to work: people irrationally trust a politician who appears to eat the same foods they do.

So I had to laugh—and feel a little wistful, too—when I came across an article in the *Times* from 1935 in which Huey Long, the colorful Louisiana senator known as the Kingfish, chose not a diner in Peoria but the Hotel New Yorker in New York City as his venue for attacking President Roosevelt's New Deal. In the photo op (see p. 3), Long stood surrounded by journalists and friends, waving a cocktail shaker.

The senator had arranged for the head bartender from the Hotel Roosevelt in New Orleans to fly to New York to make the drink (a good use of taxpayers' money) while Long talked shop. "Now this here chap knows how to mix a Ramos gin fizz," Long explained. And mix he did, while to a growing crowd Long expounded on the fine points of the fizz and the dull points of Roosevelt's plan, calling the president "no good" and a "faker." "Why don't they hold the Democratic convention and the Communist convention together and save money?" Long asked his audience.

The gin fizz, which the cocktail historian Dale DeGroff defines as "just a sparkling version of a sour," had been around since the mid-nineteenth century. Back then, before seltzer and club soda were widely available, bartenders created the fizz with baking soda. The Ramos gin fizz, which was invented in 1888 by Henry C. Ramos at the Imperial Cabinet Saloon in New Orleans, is embellished with cream, milk, and orange-flower water.

Long's crowd-pleasing recipe called for a "noggin" of gin, egg white, orange-flower water, vanilla, milk, cream, powdered sugar, seltzer, and ice and was to be shaken for ten minutes (although I find that implausibly, or anyway exhaustingly, long). His fizzes were passed around to the journalists, and the *Times* reporter observed, "After some more posing for photographers and the talkies—the whole performance consumed fully an hour—the Kingfish left the bar with a broad grin, leading a crowd of reporters to his apartment on the twenty-second floor of the hotel, where he spent two hours discoursing on the political situation."

The following week, however, Long's recipe was politely questioned by W. D. Rose, a reader from Schenectady. "While the writer does not feel equal to enter into a controversy with the versatile and able senator on any subject, much less on that of Ramos fizzes," Rose wrote, "and while not denying that the formula announced by Senator Long may be that of a perfect fizz, still the writer feels obliged to submit to the readers of the *Times* the only authentic and original formula for that famous and delectable decoction."

Rose's Ramos gin fizz does not contain egg white, vanilla, or seltzer, and it is shaken for just one minute before being strained into a glass. Long's version is similar to those found in any cocktail book (although Ramos's original contained lime juice, less milk, and no vanilla), so I chose to feature Rose's.

Rose promised that the drink would "conjure up visions . . . of wistaria [*sic*] blooming in old patios, of sights and smells associated only with the Vieux Carré." Those images did not leap to mind when I made his version, but I was certainly bewitched by this cocktail, which doesn't so much impress you as envelop you. Beneath a dense cap of froth and a misty overlay of orange-flower water is an oddly sweet, tart, cool, and creamy drink.

———

1 tablespoon Simple Syrup (see Ingredient Notes below)

1 teaspoon fresh lemon juice

1½ ounces gin

⅛ to ¼ teaspoon orange-flower water

½ cup plus 2 tablespoons whole milk

1 tablespoon heavy cream

Combine the ingredients with 5 ice cubes in a cocktail shaker and shake for 1 minute. Strain into a tumbler.

SERVES 1

INGREDIENT NOTES

The original recipe called for "rich milk," which I took to mean old-style unhomogenized milk with a layer of cream. I replicated it with a mixture of whole milk and a dash of heavy cream.

To make simple syrup, combine 1 part water with 1 part sugar (varying the size of the portions with the size of the recipe) in a saucepan. Bring to a boil and stir to dissolve the sugar. Remove from heat and let cool.

Orange-flower water is readily available online, as well as at Middle Eastern and specialty markets.

SERVING SUGGESTIONS
Parmesan Crackers (p. 84), Salted and Deviled Almonds (p. 51), Julia Harrison Adams's Pimento Cheese Spread (p. 64)

JULY 26, 1935: "LONG HERE IN MOOD TO BOLT ROOSEVELT." AUGUST 3, 1935: "LETTERS TO THE EDITOR." LETTER SIGNED W. D. ROSE.

—1935

◡ VERMOUTH CASSIS

During the early 1940s, the weekly food column was called "Victuals and Vitamins" and was divided into topics—during the week that this drink recipe ran, there were "Coolers," "Herbs," "Homemade," and "Tidbits," although, frankly, most of it reads like tidbits. Kiley Taylor, the columnist, was airy, confident, and vague. She explained how to make fruit ices and sherbets as follows: "Fruit juice simply diluted with water, and sugared if extra sweetness is desired, emerges from the freezing tray after about three hours as a refreshing ice, while sherbets have the whites of eggs added to the juice." Got that?

Occasionally you can eke out an actual recipe from "Victuals and Vitamins," as in the case of the simple French aperitif vermouth cassis.

———

1 teaspoon cassis syrup (not the liqueur)

2 ounces dry vermouth

¼ cup plus 2 tablespoons club soda or sparkling water

Pour the cassis and vermouth "over the ice cubes in a thin-stemmed goblet." Then fill the glass with the club soda.

SERVES 1

SERVING SUGGESTIONS
Brie with Herbs in Bread (p. 69), Nicole Kaplan's Gougères (p. 76), Sophie Grigson's Parmesan Cake (p. 69)

In the same article, Taylor mentioned two trends of the moment: taro chips and fiddlehead ferns.

JUNE 2, 1940: "VICTUALS AND VITAMINS: COOLERS" BY KILEY TAYLOR.

—1940

ICED COFFEE

"For a cool drink that can be so completely delicious, iced coffee sometimes manages to be vapid and perversely disappointing." This thought from a 1940 story still applies today. The only difference is that back then Americans consumed nearly twice as much coffee as they do today.

---

1 long shot espresso
1 teaspoon sugar
1/4 cup heavy cream, whipped to soft peaks

Fill a tumbler with ice. Pour in the espresso and sugar, then fill the glass with the whipped cream. The layers will remain distinct until stirred, and if you stir gently enough, you'll end up with a fluffy glassful of coffee-scented foam.

SERVES 1

SERVING SUGGESTIONS
Bill Granger's Scrambled Eggs (p. 640), Fresh Plum Kuchen (p. 625), Amazing Overnight Waffles (p. 642)

JULY 7, 1940: "VICTUALS AND VITAMINS: ICED COFFEE" BY KILEY TAYLOR.

—1940

SAZERAC

The Sazerac lives or dies by the amount of sugar you add. Better to be conservative—when you get it right, you hardly notice the sweetness because you are so smitten with the bitters, which hover over the rye like a citrusy mist. This recipe comes from a bartender at the Old Absinthe House in New Orleans, who said it's the rye that "brings the drink to life."

One 1/2-inch sugar cube or 1/2 teaspoon sugar
Peychaud bitters
Angostura bitters
1 tablespoon water
1 1/2 ounces rye
A lemon twist

Put the sugar cube (or sugar) in a sturdy tumbler and saturate it with the bitters. Muddle (crush with a muddler or the back of a spoon) with the water. Add the rye, then an ice cube and the lemon twist, and stir.

SERVES 1

INGREDIENT NOTE
Peychaud bitters are available at Keg Works, www.kegworks.com.

SERVING SUGGESTIONS
Pickled Shrimp (p. 95), Toasted Mushroom Rolls (p. 72), Onion Rings (p. 61)

AUGUST 25, 1940: "VICTUALS AND VITAMINS: DRINKS" BY KILEY TAYLOR. RECIPE ADAPTED FROM THE OLD ABSINTHE HOUSE IN NEW ORLEANS.

—1940

WINE LEMONADE

Brilliant and refreshing.

1/4 cup sugar
3/4 cup fresh lemon juice (from about 3 lemons)
24 ounces sweet dessert wine (port, muscatel, or Tokay)
1 to 2 cups chilled sparkling water
1 lemon, cut into thin slices

Dissolve the sugar in the lemon juice in a large container with a tight-fitting lid. Add the wine and a handful of ice cubes, cover, and shake until cold. Strain into small tumblers of ice, filling them half- to three-quarters full. Top off the glasses with sparkling water. Stir, and garnish each serving with a slice or two of lemon, squeezing some of the juice into the drink before dropping in the slice.

MAKES 8 DRINKS

SERVING SUGGESTIONS
Onion Rings (p. 61), Julia Harrison Adams's Pimento Cheese Spread (p. 64), Cheese Ball with Cumin, Mint, and Pistachios (p. 85), Fried Sage Leaves (p. 87)

JULY 4, 1946: "NEWS OF FOOD: PENCHANT OF AMERICANS FOR COLD DRINKS BRINGS SOME SUGGESTIONS FOR SUMMER TIME," BY JANE NICKERSON.

—1946

ICED COCOA

Iced cocoa is not the same as chocolate milk—it's smoother, with distinct waves of bitterness emanating from the cocoa.

———

½ cup unsweetened cocoa
¼ cup sugar
⅛ teaspoon salt
I cup light corn syrup
½ cup water
Whole milk

1. Mix the cocoa, sugar, salt, corn syrup, and water together in a small saucepan, bring to a simmer, and simmer, stirring often, for 5 minutes—be careful, it boils over easily. Pour into a heatproof jar, cover, and chill.
2. For every serving of iced cocoa, stir 3 tablespoons of the syrup into an 8-ounce glass of milk.

MAKES ABOUT 1½ CUPS, ENOUGH SYRUP FOR ABOUT 8 DRINKS

JULY 7, 1946: "COLD DISHES HOT OFF THE ICE," BY JANE NICKERSON.

—1946

ASTORIA COCKTAIL

A martini turned inside out and invigorated with orange.

———

I ounce gin
2 ounces dry vermouth, preferably French
2 dashes orange bitters

Fill a cocktail shaker with ice, add all the ingredients, and stir. Strain into a martini glass or similar glass.

SERVES I

INGREDIENT NOTE
Orange bitters are available at www.wallywine.com.

SERVING SUGGESTIONS
Onion Rings (p. 61), The Minimalist's Gravlax (p. 418), Smoked Mackerel on Toasts (p. 80), Roasted Feta with Thyme Honey (p. 92), Hot Cheese Olives (p. 83)

OCTOBER 23, 1946: "NEWS OF FOOD: CLUB AND HOTEL COCKTAIL RECIPES SHOW AMERICANS' PREDILECTION FOR MIXED DRINKS," BY JANE NICKERSON. RECIPE ADAPTED FROM THE WALDORF-ASTORIA HOTEL IN NEW YORK CITY.

—1946

EL CHICO

El Chico, a luminescent moss-green drink, was named after a nightclub in Greenwich Village where the cocktail was served.

———

½ ounce dry vermouth, preferably Italian
1½ ounces Bacardi Gold Label rum (or other good rum)
Dash of grenadine
Dash of Curaçao
I maraschino cherry
A lemon twist

Stir the vermouth, rum, grenadine, and Curaçao with ice in a bartender's glass and pour into a cocktail glass. Add the maraschino cherry and lemon twist.

SERVING SUGGESTIONS
The Spice Boys' Cheese Ball (p. 79), Salted and Deviled Almonds (p. 51)

OCTOBER 23, 1946: "NEWS OF FOOD: CLUB AND HOTEL
COCKTAIL RECIPES SHOW AMERICANS' PREDILECTION FOR
MIXED DRINKS," BY JANE NICKERSON. RECIPE ADAPTED
FROM EL CHICO IN NEW YORK CITY.

—1946

SERVING SUGGESTIONS
Pâté Watch Hill Farm (p. 53), Eggs Suffragette (p. 52),
Rillettes de Canard (Duck Rillettes; p. 65), Spiced
Pecans (p. 82)

OCTOBER 23, 1946: "NEWS OF FOOD: CLUB AND HOTEL
COCKTAIL RECIPES SHOW AMERICANS' PREDILECTION FOR
MIXED DRINKS," BY JANE NICKERSON. RECIPE ADAPTED
FROM NICKY QUATTROCIOCCHI, THE OWNER OF EL
BORRACHO ON EAST 55TH STREET IN NEW YORK CITY.

—1946

NICKY FINN

When I tasted this drink with Merrill, who assisted
me with this book, she noted that we'd liked every
drink we'd made so far, whereas about half of all the
other cooking recipes we'd tried went directly into the
"No" pile. "What does that say about us?" she asked.
Well, it does say something about cocktail recipes,
which is that they're incredibly precise. There's room
for style—how you garnish the drink, what glass you
serve it in—but otherwise little is left to chance.

The name of this cocktail comes from El Borracho,
a New York restaurant owned by Nicky Quattrociocchi, and is a play on Mickey Finn, the drug-laced drink
that a Chicago bartender supposedly used to incapaci-
tate customers and then rob them. The Nicky Finn
does not contain "knock-out drops," as they were
called, but it will definitely knock you flat if you drink
more than one.

It's an ideal cocktail because while it is strong, none
of the components shouts. You taste the sweetness of
the Cointreau and the acidity of the lemon juice and
then, just when you think you've distinguished one
from the other, you get a whisper of Pernod.

1½ ounces brandy
1½ ounces Cointreau
3 tablespoons fresh lemon juice
⅛ teaspoon Pernod

Combine all the ingredients in a cocktail shaker with
5 to 6 ice cubes. Shake vigorously for 30 seconds, then
pour the drink and ice into a tumbler.

SERVES I

PARK AVENUE COCKTAIL

It's a pretty safe bet that the average 1940s Park Avenue pad stocked all three ingredients: brandy, Grand
Marnier, and Champagne.

1 ounce brandy
½ ounce Grand Marnier
Chilled Champagne

Pour the brandy and Grand Marnier into a Champagne glass over a cube of ice. Fill the glass with
Champagne and serve.

SERVES I

INGREDIENT NOTES
I made this with good brandy and with cheap brandy,
and I enjoyed it better with the latter. But don't stint
on the Champagne. Bad Champagne is unforgivable.

Although the recipe called for just one ice cube, I
liked the drink better when at least three or four were
bobbing around in my glass.

SERVING SUGGESTIONS
Nicole Kaplan's Gougères (p. 76), Hot Cheese Olives
(p. 83), Florentine Dip (p. 58), Spiced Pecans (p. 82),
Fried Olives (p. 87), Caramelized Bacon (p. 93)

OCTOBER 23, 1946: "NEWS OF FOOD: CLUB AND HOTEL
COCKTAIL RECIPES SHOW AMERICANS' PREDILECTION FOR
MIXED DRINKS," BY JANE NICKERSON. RECIPE ADAPTED
FROM THE STORK CLUB IN NEW YORK CITY.

—1946

PEACH BOWL

This is essentially wine with the fragrance of peaches, a sangria with subtlety. "Bowls," according to David Wondrich, a cocktail historian, "were German answers to the English punches and cups." Before Prohibition, many saloonkeepers (often German immigrants) would serve the Maibowle, a mixture of Champagne, brandy, sugar, and fresh woodruff (an herb), in the summertime.

---

6 small ripe peaches

3 tablespoons sugar or more to taste

2 (750-ml) bottles sauvignon blanc, chilled

1. Bring a large pot of water to a boil. Using the tip of a paring knife, make a shallow X in the bottom of 4 of the peaches. Add the peaches one at a time to the boiling water and blanch until the skin starts peeling back from the X, about 1 minute. Remove the peaches from the water and plunge into a bowl of ice water. Peel the peaches, then prick them all over with a fork.
2. Place the peaches in a punch bowl large enough to hold the wine. Sprinkle the sugar over them and add 16 ounces (2 cups) of the wine. Let stand for 1 hour, stirring occasionally.
3. Add the remaining 32 ounces (4 cups) wine to the peaches, then taste and add more sugar if needed. Chill.
4. Pit and thinly slice the remaining peaches. Ladle the punch into glasses and garnish each with a peach slice.

MAKES ABOUT 16 DRINKS

SERVING SUGGESTIONS
Fried Sage Leaves (p. 87), Toasts with Walnut Sauce (p. 73), Aloo Kofta (p. 74), Ricotta Crostini with Fresh Thyme and Dried Oregano (p. 93)

APRIL 25, 1948: "FOOD: PUNCHES FOR HOME OCCASIONS," BY JANE NICKERSON. RECIPE ADAPTED FROM TOM MARVEL, CO-AUTHOR WITH FRANK SCHOONMAKER OF *AMERICAN WINES*.

—1948

MOSCOW MULE

"The French may complain that Americans know only one sauce, but they cannot say we have only one drink," Jane Nickerson, a columnist for the *Times*, wrote, introducing this cocktail recipe. "Yankee ingenuity and inventiveness seem nowhere better evidenced than at our bars."

The Moscow mule was popularized at the Cock 'n' Bull, a trendy Hollywood restaurant on Sunset Boulevard. John Martin, a Smirnoff salesman, claimed to have devised the recipe with the restaurant's bartender as way of promoting the fledgling vodka brand. The drink, a refreshing zinger made with vodka, lime juice, and ginger beer, was served in copper cups. Clementine Paddleford, Nickerson's rival across town at the *New York Herald Tribune*, ran a piece about the Moscow mule a week after Nickerson. "The nicest thing about the mule," Paddleford wrote, "is that it doesn't make you noisy and argumentative, or quiet and sullen, but congenial and in love with the world. One wag of its tail and life grows rosy."

1½ ounces vodka

4 teaspoons fresh lime juice

6 ounces ginger beer

Fill a tumbler with 4 or 5 ice cubes. Pour in the vodka and lime juice and fill up the glass with ginger beer.

SERVES 1

INGREDIENT NOTE
Nickerson, who got the recipe from the restaurant, didn't include a garnish—if you'd like one, a sliver of lime is the way to go.

SERVING SUGGESTIONS
Salted and Deviled Almonds (p. 51), Cheese Straws (p. 79), Fresh and Smoked Salmon Spread (p. 72), Guacamole Tostadas (p. 67), North Carolina–Style Pulled Pork (p. 550), Monte's Ham (p. 548), Nueces Canyon Cabrito (Goat Tacos; p. 576)

JULY 17, 1948: "NEWS OF FOOD: FLAT OBLONG PACKAGES WITH FROZEN EDIBLES FIT READILY INTO ICE CUBE COMPARTMENTS," BY JANE NICKERSON. RECIPE ADAPTED FROM THE COCK 'N' BULL RESTAURANT IN LOS ANGELES.

—1948

IRISH COFFEE

In case you've never known the proportions for this classic drink, here they are. Don't mess around with the sugar—the drink should be only faintly sweet.

———

1½ ounces Irish whiskey
One ½-inch sugar cube or ½ teaspoon sugar
About 1 cup strong black coffee
Lightly whipped cream

Heat a stemmed whiskey goblet by filling it with hot water, then pouring out the water. Pour in the whiskey and add the sugar. Fill the goblet with strong black coffee to within 1 inch of the brim. Stir to dissolve the sugar. Top to brim with lightly whipped cream so that the cream floats on top. Do not stir after adding cream.

SERVES 1

SERVING SUGGESTIONS
Spice Krinkles (p. 688), Pepper-Cumin Cookies (p. 695)

MARCH 13, 1958: "IRISH GOURMETS READY FOR FEAST OF ST. PATRICK," BY CRAIG CLAIBORNE. RECIPE ADAPTED FROM MRS. FREDERICK BOLAND, WIFE OF THE IRISH AMBASSADOR TO THE UNITED NATIONS.

—1958

BLOODY MARY

Many Bloody Marys are too much bloody and not enough Mary. This one gets it right with a good splash of lemon juice and a tingly heat. Craig Claiborne, who wrote this recipe, left out the traditional celery garnish. Feel free to add it, or whatever else inhabits your vegetable drawer—cucumber, fennel, and the like.

———

½ cup tomato juice
2 ounces vodka
1 teaspoon Worcestershire sauce
Juice of ½ lemon
A few drops of Tabasco sauce
Salt and freshly ground black pepper to taste

Combine all the ingredients in a cocktail shaker with some shaved ice or 3 ice cubes. Shake vigorously and pour into a chilled glass.

SERVES 1

SERVING SUGGESTIONS
A heaping plate of "Breakfast" Shrimp and Grits (p. 641), Bill Granger's Scrambled Eggs (p. 640), Buttery Polenta with Parmesan and Olive-Oil-Fried Eggs (p. 645), Soft Scrambled Eggs with Pesto and Fresh Ricotta (p. 646)

MARCH 30, 1958: "EASTER BRUNCH," BY CRAIG CLAIBORNE.

—1958

GIN RICKEY

This is gin tidied with lime, a little sugar, and fizz. Perfect after a day at the beach, or after any day really.

———

Juice of 1 small or ½ large lime
2 ounces gin, preferably chilled
1 teaspoon Simple Syrup (p. 16)
Chilled club soda or sparkling water

Combine the lime, gin, and simple syrup in an 8-ounce glass. Add 2 large ice cubes and fill the glass with chilled club soda. Stir and serve with a stirring rod or small bar spoon.

SERVES 1

SERVING SUGGESTIONS
Anchovy Canapés (p. 51), Shrimp Canapés à la Suede (p. 57), Blue Cheese Dip (p. 54), Avocado Sandowsky (p. 54), Seasoned Olives (p. 90), The Best Spinach Dip, with Chipotle and Lime (p. 90), Cucumber–Goat Cheese Dip with Radishes and Scallions (p. 70), Cheese Ball with Cumin, Mint, and Pistachios (p. 85)

JUNE 15, 1958: "TEN DRINKS (BESIDES MARTINIS)," BY
CRAIG CLAIBORNE. RECIPE ADAPTED FROM *THE FINE ART
OF MIXING DRINKS* BY DAVID A. EMBURY.

—1958

∽ EGGNOG

Eggnogs have long been a *Times* recipe staple (see the blender recipe on p. 44). An 1895 article on Christmas-food traditions noted that Americans ate more lightly than the English throughout the season. The only exception, the writer added, "is eggnog [*sic*], a mixture of eggs, milk, sugar, spices, rum, brandy, and—headache. This beverage, however, has lately fallen somewhat out of favor. Either our stomachs have grown weaker or our brains stronger, and we are not willing to sacrifice future well-being for the sake of a momentary gratification, even though sanctioned by the precept and example of our ancestors." Well, pooh-pooh!

By the late 1950s, eggnog had staged a comeback. If you already have a favorite eggnog recipe, throw it out, because the one that Craig Claiborne ran in 1958 sweeps the field. What makes Claiborne's Southern-style family recipe singular is that it doesn't pretend to be a drink. He suggests you eat his nog with a spoon, and so you should: it's the only way to get it out of the punch cup.

You beat the egg yolks and sugar until they're as thick as meringue, then loosen them up with bourbon and Cognac and, eventually, fold in both whipped cream and whipped egg whites, so you end up with a giant bowl of faintly boozy chiffon. Claiborne smartly adds salt to the egg whites to amplify and sharpen the flavors. The alcohol, which may seem like a staggering amount when you're pouring it in, actually isn't much—just 2 cups to 6 cups other liquid—and so it swims through the layers of egg and cream as an echo to the nog rather than as a belt of good cheer.

The richness of the ingredients hits you about halfway through your cup, and by the time you've reached the bottom, you've had your fill.

———

12 large eggs, separated

1 cup sugar

8 ounces bourbon

8 ounces Cognac

½ teaspoon salt

6 cups heavy cream

Freshly grated nutmeg

1 to 2 cups whole milk (optional)

1. Beat the egg yolks with the sugar in a large bowl with an electric mixer until thick and lemon-colored. Slowly add the bourbon and Cognac, beating at slow speed. Transfer to a large punch bowl. Chill for several hours.
2. Add the salt to the egg whites in a large bowl and beat until almost stiff, or until the beaten whites form a peak that bends slightly.
3. Whip the cream until stiff in another large bowl. Fold the whipped cream into the yolk mixture, then fold in the beaten egg whites. Chill for 1 hour. (If desired, add 1 to 2 cups milk to the yolk mixture for a thinner nog.)
4. When ready to serve, sprinkle the eggnog with freshly grated nutmeg. Serve in punch cups with spoons.

MAKES ABOUT 40 PUNCH-CUP SERVINGS

SERVING SUGGESTIONS

Claiborne, noting that eggnog was increasingly popular, wrote, "A recurrent question is what to serve with it." He suggested "salted almonds, fruitcake, Champagne biscuits available in most fine food shops, and finger sandwiches. Fillings for such sandwiches might include sweet butter and watercress sprigs, sliced cold chicken, or ham. Sandwiches with onion flavors should be avoided." For dessert, Mary Ann's Fruitcake (p. 660).

DECEMBER 29, 1959: "THREE DRINKS TO FILL
CUP O' KINDNESS," BY CRAIG CLAIBORNE.

—1959

∽ SWEDISH GLÖGG

Glögg, made with aquavit, a clear spirit, and cardamom and lemon, feels like a leaner, more streamlined mulled wine.

———

1 (750-ml) bottle claret (Bordeaux)
1 (750-ml) bottle aquavit
1 medium orange, halved
11 cloves, plus more for garnish
6 whole cardamom pods, bruised
6 lemon slices
1½ teaspoons sugar
Blanched whole almonds and raisins for garnish

1. Heat the claret and aquavit in separate saucepans just until they're hot to the touch.

2. Squeeze the orange halves into the claret; add the orange halves, 5 cloves, and the cardamom. Keep the claret hot, at just below a simmer, for 15 minutes. Keep the aquavit warm.

3. Stud the lemon slices with the remaining 6 cloves, and set aside.

4. Put the sugar in a heatproof punch bowl and pour in 1 cup of the hot aquavit. Standing back, ignite it with a long match. Once it burns off, pour in the remaining aquavit and claret.

5. Put a clove and a few almonds and raisins into each mug. Fill with glögg, top each with a lemon slice, and serve hot.

MAKES 6 CUPS

SERVING SUGGESTION
Fyrstekake (Royal Cake; p. 629)

DECEMBER 8, 1963: "CHRISTMAS SPICE," BY CRAIG CLAIBORNE.

—1963

⌒ SANGRIA

———

1 navel orange, unpeeled, center core discarded and remainder diced
¼ grapefruit, unpeeled, center core discarded and remainder cut into ¼-inch dice, seeds discarded
½ lime, unpeeled, cut into ¼-inch dice, seeds discarded
½ lemon, unpeeled, cut into ¼-inch dice, seeds discarded
1 cup fresh pineapple chunks, with their juice
1 cup seedless or seeded grapes
1 red apple, cored and cut into ¼-inch dice
1 cup small cantaloupe balls

½ cup sugar
1 cup fresh orange juice (from about 3 oranges)
¼ cup fresh lemon juice
4 ounces Spanish brandy
1 (750-ml) bottle red Rioja
Chilled club soda or sparkling water (optional)

Combine all the ingredients, including club soda to taste if desired, in a large pitcher and stir well. Add ice cubes to cool the sangria before serving.

MAKES ABOUT 6 DRINKS

SERVING SUGGESTIONS
Pan con Tomate (p. 91), Catalan Tortilla with Aioli (p. 86), Potato, Ham and Piquillo Pepper Croquetas (p. 94), Fried Chickpeas (p. 88), Catalan Vegetable Paella (p. 323), Paella (p. 309), Cocido (p. 578), Rabbit Soup with Garlic, Peppers, and Chorizo (p. 152)

MARCH 18, 1973: "HOW TO HAVE 16 FOR DINNER (WITHOUT GOING BANKRUPT)," BY JEAN HEWITT.

—1973

⌒ SINGAPORE SLING

You don't meet many slings today, but in the 1920s, slings and flips and smashes were stalwarts of the "violet hour." A sling was really just another name for a sweetened cocktail, often interchangeable with the toddy. But the Singapore sling, called a "delicious, slow-acting, insidious thing" by Charles H. Baker, an epicure and author of *The Gentleman's Companion*, stands out. It's still shaken by the hundreds at Raffles Hotel in Singapore, where it was invented by Ngiam Tong Boon, a bartender.

If you're a fan of nuanced cocktails circa 2004, this may not be your bag, but I felt I'd be remiss to leave it out. Save it for your next Singapore-themed party.

———

1 ounce gin
¾ ounce cherry brandy
A few drops of Cointreau
Truly a few drops of Bénédictine
Juice of ½ lemon
¼ cup fresh pineapple juice

I to 2 drops Angostura bitters

A dash of grenadine, for color

A wedge of pineapple and a maraschino cherry for garnish

Place 4 ice cubes in a cocktail shaker and add all the ingredients except the garnish. Cover and shake vigorously for about 10 seconds. Strain into a 10-ounce glass containing 2 ice cubes. Garnish with the pineapple wedge and maraschino cherry.

SERVES I

INGREDIENT NOTE

"As for the pineapple juice," Colin Campbell, the Bangkok bureau chief of the *Times*, wrote, "the pineapples should be sweet, pale, and not quite ripe: A really ripe, soft pineapple makes the sling too sweet."

SERVING SUGGESTIONS

Salted and Deviled Almonds (p. 51), Parmesan Crackers (p. 84), Anchovy Canapés (p. 51)

DECEMBER 12, 1982: "SINGAPORE SLING IS SPOKEN HERE," BY COLIN CAMPBELL. RECIPE ADAPTED FROM DERRICK LEE, A BARTENDER AT RAFFLES HOTEL IN SINGAPORE.

—1982

CLASSIC RUM PUNCH

Rum punch is nothing more than rum treated the same way you flavor tea for iced tea, with sugar and citrus.

———

2 ounces medium-dark rum

Juice of ½ small lime

I teaspoon raw sugar (such as Sugar in the Raw or Demerara)

Pour the rum, lime juice, and sugar over an ice cube in a tumbler. Stir to dissolve the sugar.

SERVES I

SERVING SUGGESTIONS

Ceviche with Mint and Mango (p. 417), Guacamole Tostadas (p. 67), Grilled Onion Guacamole (p. 71),

The Best Spinach Dip, with Chipotle and Lime (p. 90), Yucatán Fish with Crisp Garlic (p. 431)

OCTOBER 21, 1984: "SPIRITS: RUM FOR ALL SEASONS," BY FRANK J. PRIAL.

—1984

HOT BUTTERED RUM

A descendant of the centuries-old buttered ale, which began as a medicinal drink before making the leap to pleasure.

———

2 ounces dark rum

I½ teaspoons raw sugar (such as Sugar in the Raw or Demerara)

2 whole cloves

Pinch of freshly grated nutmeg

¾ cup boiling water

A thin pat of unsalted butter (⅓ tablespoon)

I cinnamon stick

Combine the rum, sugar, cloves, and nutmeg in a mug. Pour in the boiling water, then float the butter on top and add the cinnamon stick.

SERVES I

SERVING SUGGESTIONS

Fresh Ginger Cake (p. 775), Pear Upside-Down Cake (p. 772), Breton Butter Cake (p. 777), Apple Galette (p. 843)

OCTOBER 21, 1984: "SPIRITS: RUM FOR ALL SEASONS," BY FRANK J. PRIAL. RECIPE ADAPTED FROM *RUM YESTERDAY AND TODAY* BY HUGH BARTY-KING AND ANTON MASSEL.

—1984

MINT JULEP

This recipe, published in the *Times* in 1987, belongs in 1938, really. It originally came from a book published that year by Helen Bullock, *The Williamsburg Art of Cookery or, Accomplish'd Gentlewoman's Companion: Being a Collection of upwards of Five Hundred of the most*

Ancient & Approv'd Recipes in Virginia Cookery. Juleps began as medicinal elixirs and later became social elixirs, and the mint julep, according to David Wondrich, the author of *Imbibe!* was the most popular drink in America for most of the nineteenth century.

Many mint julep recipes appear to be the same, yet numerous debates rage within the julep community: whether or not the mint leaves should be muddled, the ice crushed, brandy or bourbon used. In *Straight Up or On the Rocks*, William Grimes wrote: "When tired of bickering over mint leaves, julep pedants can address another vexed issue: Should the drink be sipped from the glass or through a straw? This point of contention, perpetually on the simmer, boiled over on a slow news day, when the *[Louisville] Courier-Journal* decided to lay down the law. Straws are mandatory, it declared, to keep one's face out of the mint shrubbery."

---

24 mint leaves, plus 3 sprigs for garnish
$\frac{1}{2}$ tablespoon confectioners' sugar
Whiskey, preferably bourbon (about 2 to 3 ounces)

ORIGINAL RECIPE

"Take a long, thin, glass Tumbler or a Silver Goblet and place it on a Tray. In the Bottom, place the Leaves from a Sprig of Mint and add one Half Tablespoonful of powdered Sugar. Crush the Mint well with the Sugar, and dissolve in a Tablespoonful of Water. Pack the Glass full with very finely-crushed Ice, trying not to wet the Outside of the Glass. Pour into this a Glass of Whiskey (Whiskey distilled from Corn is traditional but that made from Rye or other Grain in permissible). Some Authorities, having packed the Glass well with Ice, pour in the Whiskey until the Glass is full. Stir gently until the Glass is well-frosted on the Outside. Decorate on Top with three Sprigs of Mint and serve."

SERVES 1

SERVING SUGGESTIONS
Eggs Suffragette (p. 52), Pickled Shrimp (p. 95), Parmesan Crackers (p. 84), Pan-Barbecued Shrimp (p. 402)

MAY 17, 1987: "SUMMER COOLERS: DRINKS WITH A PAST," BY HOWARD G. GOLDBERG. RECIPE FROM *THE WILLIAMSBURG ART OF COOKERY OR, ACCOMPLISH'D GENTLEWOMAN'S COMPANION: BEING A COLLECTION OF UPWARDS OF FIVE HUNDRED OF THE MOST ANCIENT & APPROV'D RECIPES IN VIRGINIA COOKERY*, BY HELEN BULLOCK.

—1987

⌇ COCONUT DAIQUIRI

One of New York City Mayor Ed Koch's two favorite drinks. The other is the Ramos Gin Fizz, a fondness shared by fellow politician Huey Long—see p. 15.

Of all the drinks in this chapter, this daiquiri was the greatest surprise. We've all had daiquiris, and mostly bad ones. When made well, it's a zippy number with acid and fruit and just a smattering of coconut.

$\frac{1}{2}$ ripe pineapple, peeled, cored, and cut into chunks
Juice of 1 lime
2 tablespoons cream of coconut, preferably Coco Lopez
$7\frac{1}{2}$ ounces Bacardi or other light rum
20 ice cubes

Combine all the ingredients in a blender and whiz until smooth. Serve immediately.

MAKES ABOUT 5 DRINKS

INGREDIENT NOTE
David Margolis, a friend of the mayor who came up with this drink, noted in the article, "How much lime you use depends on how sweet the pineapple is. You don't want it too sweet. The tartness of the limes should come out."

SERVING SUGGESTION
Salted and Deviled Almonds (p. 51)

SEPTEMBER 4, 1987: "WHEN KOCH CALLS FOR HIS BOWL," BY MARIAN BURROS. RECIPE ADAPTED FROM DAVID MARGOLIS.

—1987

⌇ SWEET (OR SAVORY) LASSI

The recipe that follows is for a sweet lassi. For a savory lassi, leave out the sugar, and add 12 mint leaves and a generous pinch of sea salt. Try both—the sweet one with breakfast and the savory one with a fiery curry. You'll love them.

_____

1½ cups plain yogurt
9 to 10 ice cubes
¼ cup sugar, or to taste

Put all the ingredients in a blender or food processor and blend until the ice is crushed and the liquid is frothy. Add up to 1 more tablespoon sugar, if desired. Serve immediately in tall glasses.

MAKES 2 DRINKS

INGREDIENT NOTE
The original recipe called for low-fat or nonfat yogurt, but low-fat yogurt is an abomination. I used full-fat Fage Greek yogurt, and you should too.

SERVING SUGGESTIONS
Aloo Kofta (p. 74), Crab and Coconut Curry (p. 389), A Moley (Curried Turkey Hash; p. 452), Hot Pepper Shrimp (p. 403), Bademiya's Justly Famous Bombay Chili-and-Cilantro Chicken (p. 471)

AUGUST 9, 1989: "AN INDIAN DRINK TO COOL SUMMER'S FIRE," BY SANJOY HAZARIKA. RECIPE ADAPTED FROM ARUN CHOPRA, THE EXECUTIVE CHEF OF THE TAJ MAHAL HOTEL IN NEW DELHI.

—1989

☞ GINGER LEMONADE

_____

One 2-inch piece fresh ginger, cut into 4 or 5 pieces
½ cup water
⅓ cup sugar
¾ cup fresh lemon juice (from about 3 lemons)
1¼ cups chilled sparkling water

1. Put the ginger and water in a small saucepan and bring to a boil. Remove from the heat, cover, and let steep for 30 minutes. Uncover and refrigerate until cold.
2. Combine the sugar and lemon juice in a medium bowl, stirring until the sugar is dissolved. Remove the ginger pieces from the water and discard; stir the gin-

ger water into the sugar mixture. Add the sparkling water, stir, and pour into ice-filled glasses.

MAKES 2 DRINKS

SERVING SUGGESTION
Pork Belly Tea Sandwiches (p. 88)

JULY 13, 1994: "GOOD OLD-FASHIONED LEMONADE IS COMING BACK," BY SUZANNE HAMLIN. RECIPE ADAPTED FROM MAURY RUBIN, THE OWNER OF CITY BAKERY IN NEW YORK CITY.

—1994

☞ KAFFIR LIME LEMONADE

The perfect summer drink: fragrant, but ephemerally so, and discreet. An aperitif shouldn't step on the rest of a meal, and this doesn't. Just don't try saying "kaffir lime lemonade" after you've added vodka to it and had a glass or two.

The lemonade is an assembled drink. You make a kaffir lime syrup, then combine it in a glass with lemon juice and sparkling water. The proportions are even, so it's easy to make in a larger amount—I tripled it for a party of eight—and it can also be mixed up in advance in a pitcher. Chill the pitcher, but don't add the ice to the lemonade—put the ice in the tumblers just before pouring.

If you like a drink that's tart, as I do, add 1½ table-spoons of lemon juice instead of just 1 tablespoon to each glass. Garnish either version with a thin half-slice of lemon and a tiny kaffir lime leaf.

_____

2 cups water
1 cup sugar
10 kaffir lime leaves
½ cup fresh lemon juice (from about 2 lemons)
2 cups chilled club soda or seltzer
Vodka (optional)

1. Combine the water, sugar, and lime leaves in a small saucepan, and bring to a boil over medium heat, then lower the heat and simmer for 10 minutes. Set aside to cool, then refrigerate until cold.

2. Fill each tumbler with ice and top with ¼ cup of the lime syrup, 1 tablespoon lemon juice, and ¼ cup club soda. Add a splash of vodka if you like, and stir.

MAKES 8 DRINKS

INGREDIENT NOTES
Boil down the leftover kaffir lime syrup until it's a bit more viscous, then use it for drizzling over vanilla ice cream.

Squeeze the lemons the day you want to use them. Lemon juice loses its sparkle quickly. Kaffir lime leaves are available at Asian grocery stores.

SERVING SUGGESTIONS
Beef Satay with Peanut Sauce (p. 66), Pork-and-Toasted-Rice-Powder Spring Rolls (p. 74), Pork Belly Tea Sandwiches (p. 88), Pork and Squash in Coconut Milk (p. 555), Laotian Catfish Soup (p. 154).

JULY 9, 1995: "LEMON SQUEEZE," BY MOLLY O'NEILL.
—1995

∽ MANGO LASSI

The problem with the American milk shake and smoothie is that there's no tang, just sweet, sweet, sweet. Taste this, a revelation.

———

1 cup whole-milk Greek yogurt
2½ teaspoons sugar, or to taste
¼ cup fresh or canned mango pulp
½ teaspoon ground cardamom, plus a little extra
    for garnish
¼ cup water
3 ice cubes

Combine all the ingredients in a blender and puree until smooth. Add sugar to taste. Pour into a tumbler and garnish with a pinch of ground cardamom. Add a few extra ice cubes if you like.

SERVES 1

INGREDIENT NOTE
This recipe comes from Madhur Jaffrey, the cookbook author, who claims that Ratnagiri Alphonso mango pulp, available in cans in Indian shops in New York City, is better than most fresh mangoes sold here.

SERVING SUGGESTIONS
Aloo Kofta (p. 74), Bademiya's Justly Famous Bombay Chili-and-Cilantro Chicken (p. 471)

JULY 4, 1996: "DRINKS AS SWEET AS THE SUMMER AIR," BY ELAINE LOUIE. RECIPE ADAPTED FROM MADHUR JAFFREY.
—1996

∽ JAY GRELEN'S SOUTHERN ICED TEA

Regretting the birth of canned iced tea and the slow, painful death of homemade sweet, Southern iced tea, Jay Grelen, a journalist in Mobile, Alabama, decided to create an annual iced tea contest. As Rick Bragg noted in his tale about the contest, the power of sweet iced tea in the South is that it "spanned race and class; it was one thing Southerners had in common besides mosquitos and creeping mildew."

Grelen's technique of dissolving the sugar separately is worth noting. "Some people insist on putting the sugar into a boiling tea mixture, then adding cold water," he says. "It makes it a little bitter."

———

4 quarts water
Enough tea bags (about 8) or loose black tea to infuse
    4 quarts water
2 cups sugar

1. Bring 8 cups water to a boil in a medium saucepan. Turn off the heat and add the tea bags (or pour in the loose tea). Let steep for 8 minutes.
2. Dissolve the sugar in the remaining 8 cups water in a large pitcher. Pour in the steeped tea (discard the tea bags, or strain if you use loose tea). Chill. The tea is better the second day.

MAKES ABOUT 4 QUARTS

Use any mild, smooth, good-quality black tea. Grelen used Hill & Brooks tea.

SERVING SUGGESTIONS
Salade Niçoise (p. 178), Pork Burgers (p. 566), A Loose Interpretation of Cobb Salad (p. 193), Chicken Betty's Fried Chicken and Gravy (p. 462), Beer-Can Chicken (p. 473), Roast Chicken Salad (p. 492)

JULY 4, 1997: "SAVORING A SWEET TASTE OF SOUTHERN SUMMERS," BY RICK BRAGG. RECIPE ADAPTED FROM JAY GRELEN, A COLUMNIST FOR THE *MOBILE REGISTER* IN ALABAMA.

—1997

KIR ROYALE 38

This was the house drink at La Caravelle, one of a handful of ambitious French restaurants that opened in New York in the 1960s. With its wall murals and pink banquettes, *La Caravelle* became a perch for the Kennedys and pretty much everyone with a 10021 zipcode. The restaurant closed in 2004 after forty-four years.

This drink breaks from the Kir Royale by replacing the crème de cassis with Grand Marnier and Cognac, which makes it closer in character, though perhaps racier in proportion, to the Park Avenue Cocktail on p. 19.

———

1 teaspoon Cognac
1 teaspoon Grand Marnier
6 to 8 ounces Champagne
1/2 orange slice

Pour the Cognac and Grand Marnier into a Champagne flute. Fill the glass with Champagne and garnish with the orange slice.

SERVES 1

SERVING SUGGESTIONS
Fresh and Smoked Salmon Spread (p. 72), Smoked Mackerel on Toasts (p. 80), Egg and Olive Canapés (p. 57), Salted and Deviled Almonds (p. 51), Nicole Kaplan's Gougères (p. 76)

JANUARY 20, 1999: "THE APÉRITIF MOMENT: SIP OR FLINCH," BY WILLIAM GRIMES. RECIPE ADAPTED FROM LA CARAVELLE.

—1999

JAMES BEARD'S CHAMPAGNE PUNCH

There's really no way to put a specific date on this recipe—punches like this have been made for more than a century, appearing at events from proms (illegally) to weddings (providentially), but James Beard must have come up with this version later in his career. Beard was quoted in the *Times* in 1946, saying, "The perfect apéritif is, of course, Champagne, and not Champagne cocktails, which corrupt a fine wine." Hmm. I'd change that last part to "corrupt your bank account." Good Champagne is great in punch, but I'd make this with more economical prosecco or cava. And don't leave out the cucumber, which quietly suffuses the punch.

———

1/2 cup sugar
1/2 cup fresh lemon juice (from about 2 lemons)
2 cups fresh orange juice (from about 6 oranges)
2 (750-ml) bottles Cognac
16 ounces Cointreau
4 (750-ml) bottles Champagne (or prosecco or cava), chilled
Grated zest of 4 lemons
20 thin cucumber slices

1. Gently stir together the sugar, lemon juice, orange juice, Cognac, Cointreau, Champagne, and lemon zest in a large punch bowl. Chill.
2. Garnish the punch with the cucumber slices, and set the bowl on a bed of cracked ice.

MAKES ABOUT 40 PUNCH-CUP SERVINGS

SERVING SUGGESTIONS
Onion Rings (p. 61), Rillettes de Canard (Duck Rillettes; p. 65)

DECEMBER 15, 1999: "DIP INTO THE PAST: REDISCOVERING THE PLEASURES OF PUNCH," BY AMANDA HESSER. RECIPE BY JAMES BEARD, EXCERPTED FROM *CHAMPAGNE*

COCKTAILS BY ANISTATIA MILLER, JARED BROWN, AND DON GATTERDAM.

—1999

HONEY-ORANGE SMOOTHIE

And then we discovered the smoothie, an artfully— and often deliciously—repackaged shake.

———————

½ cup whole milk
1 ripe banana
1 tablespoon honey
½ cup orange juice
½ cup crushed ice

Combine all the ingredients in a blender. Blend until—well—smooth.

SERVES 1

SERVING SUGGESTION
Jordan Marsh's Blueberry Muffins (p. 635)

DECEMBER 26, 1999: "FOOD: GET OVER IT: HANGOVER REMEDIES FOR THE MORNING AFTER," BY MOLLY O'NEILL.

—1999

HOT CHOCOLATE

Great hot chocolate is sweet and bitter, frothy and hot, and it slips over your palate like silk. It is a luxury but not dessert. And it takes no longer to make than a bad hot chocolate—just 10 minutes of your time and a little finesse.

Most hot chocolate falls into one of two groups. There is the thick more-pudding-than-drink variety you find in Europe, which acts like an espresso: it hits you rather than warms you. And there is American hot chocolate, which is more like a watered-down latte: it leaves you warmed but unsatisfied. The best hot chocolate falls somewhere in between.

One of the major differences between the two styles is that American hot chocolate is made with cocoa and most fine European hot chocolate is based on melted bar chocolate. With cocoa, which has about 25 percent fat, compared with about 40 percent in bittersweet chocolate, you get a grittier texture and need more sugar and cream to give it roundness on the tongue.

But bitterness is the key to hot chocolate. It's what leaves the palate feeling clean and hungry for more, rather than being quieted by too much sweetness. And so you need both cocoa and chocolate—cocoa for its bitterness, chocolate to round out the edges. To a mixture of chocolate, cocoa, and milk, I add a little raw sugar and salt, and then top the drink with cocoa-scented whipped cream. A tablespoon or so of tightly whipped cream dropped in the hot chocolate melts into it and foams lightly, so that in the first few sips you get both hot and cool sensations and heightened creaminess.

———————

½ cup heavy cream
¼ cup plus 1 teaspoon best-quality unsweetened cocoa powder
¼ cup plus ½ teaspoon raw sugar (such as Sugar in the Raw or Demerara)
2½ ounces bittersweet chocolate (70 to 75% cacao), broken into 1-inch squares or smaller, plus more for grating
Large pinch of kosher salt
5 cups whole milk

1. Whisk the cream with 1 teaspoon cocoa and ½ teaspoon sugar in a small bowl until it forms firm peaks. Set aside.
2. Using a fine grater, grate 1 square of chocolate. Set aside.
3. Combine the remaining chocolate, the remaining ¼ cup each cocoa and sugar, salt, and milk in a medium saucepan and whisk gently over medium heat. Once the chocolate melts and the cocoa dissolves into the milk, raise the heat to medium-high and whisk more vigorously to create froth on the surface. When the mixture bubbles around the edges and seems ready to boil, remove from the heat; do not let it boil. Ladle into 4 small cups, with some froth on each. Spoon a dollop of cocoa whipped cream on top of each, and sprinkle with grated chocolate.

MAKES 4 DRINKS

Sweet-and-Salty Popcorn with Orange Blossom Honey (p. 76), Dorie Greenspan's Sablés (p. 703), Lemon Sablés (p. 704)

FEBRUARY 2, 2000: "WINTER MELTDOWN: REAL HOT CHOCOLATE, SECRET NO MORE," BY AMANDA HESSER.

—2000

☞ RHUBARB BELLINI

You can go ahead and pour the prosecco into the rhubarb puree, and you'll have yourself a spectacular Bellini—but do just pause for a moment and taste the puree, which is a fine little concoction. Then get out some sparkling water, and while the adults enjoy Bellinis, make some rhubarb spritzers for the little ones.

———

2 cups rhubarb (about 4 slender stalks) cut in 1-inch
    pieces
$^1/_2$ cup sugar
Grated zest of 1 lemon
$^1/_4$ cup water
2 tablespoons fresh lemon juice
1 (750-ml) bottle prosecco or other sparkling wine, chilled

1. Place the rhubarb, sugar, lemon zest, water, and lemon juice in a medium saucepan, bring to a simmer, and cook for about 15 minutes.
2. Remove from the heat and place the saucepan in a bowl of ice and water to cool it quickly, about 10 minutes.
3. Place about $1^1/_2$ tablespoons puree in each of 8 Champagne flutes. Pour in prosecco to fill about one-third full. Stir well to blend in the rhubarb puree. Gradually top up each glass with more prosecco, stirring to prevent the sparkling wine from bubbling over, then serve.

MAKES 8 DRINKS

Seasoned Olives (p. 90), Ricotta Crostini with Fresh Thyme and Dried Oregano (p. 93), Heavenly Hots (p. 634), Hazelnut-Lemon-Ricotta Pancakes (p. 644)

APRIL 12, 2000: "OUT OF THE PIE PAN, INTO THE APERITIF," BY FLORENCE FABRICANT. RECIPE ADAPTED FROM ESCA IN NEW YORK CITY.

—2000

☞ BLOODY PARADISE

When you write about food, occasionally you come across a neglected ingredient or a dish that seems ripe for rediscovery, and if no one is around to talk you out of it, you go on a mission to enlighten the world, or anyway the handful of people who read your work.

In 2000, I became smitten with grains of paradise, obscure tiny brown seeds that taste of citrus, nuts, butter, and pepper. The spice showed promise during the Middle Ages, when peppercorns were expensive and grains of paradise were slotted in as a cheap substitute. But as soon as trade routes were improved, peppercorns sent them back to the minor leagues.

I was sure I could convince Americans that this was a spice you couldn't live without. Grains of paradise have so much more range and zip! They're pretty too. The spice would sweep the nation. Cookbooks would be revised. Pepper-grinder manufacturers would redesign their grinders to accommodate the softer, more fragrant seeds. So now, do you have grains of paradise in your pantry? Hello?

———

$^1/_4$ teaspoon kosher salt, or to taste
$^1/_2$ teaspoon coarsely ground grains of paradise,
    plus more for garnish
1 cup tomato juice
2 tablespoons fresh lime juice
1 tablespoon balsamic vinegar
$1^1/_2$ ounces citron vodka
2 basil leaves, fried in olive oil and sprinkled with salt,
    for garnish (optional)

Combine the salt, grains of paradise, tomato juice, lime juice, vinegar, and vodka in a shaker and shake well. Pour into a glass of ice, and grind more grains of paradise over the glass. Garnish with the basil leaves, if desired.

SERVES 1

You can substitute black peppercorns for the grains of paradise; I'll avert my eyes. If you want the real thing, try www.worldspice.com.

SERVING SUGGESTIONS

Omelet with Asparagus (p. 624), Poached Scrambled Eggs (p. 645)

PERIOD DETAIL

Unsurprisingly, I was late to "discover" grains of paradise—Jane Nickerson talked up the spice back in 1949.

MAY 3, 2000: "WHAT PEPPERCORNS ONLY DREAM OF BEING," BY AMANDA HESSER. RECIPE ADAPTED FROM JEAN-GEORGES VONGERICHTEN, THE CHEF AT JEAN GEORGES, JOJO, AND VONG IN NEW YORK CITY.

—2000

⌒ PEPPAR TOMATO

No drinks have been diminished as regularly by adaptation as the martini and the Bloody Mary. The Peppar Tomato, served at Wallsé in the West Village, may be the first (and only) exception, for it manages to be an interpretation that plays it straight. It is part martini and part Bloody Mary, with the best qualities of both. There is the crispness and chill of the vodka, quickly converted to a flash of alcoholic warmth on the tongue. Then the vodka is joined by the familiar tomato and salt, and, finally, a pinch of heat at the back of your throat. It is as startling as it is delightful. It is clean yet meaty. Savory yet sweet. A martini yet a Bloody Mary.

After a few sips—which you will surely take in quick succession—a sweetness sinks in. Not a cloying sweetness, but a round, fresh sweetness like that of a ripe plum.

The drink calls for two kinds of vodka, but its foundation is tomato water, made with ripe local beefsteak tomatoes. You puree the tomatoes with salt and drain the mixture for at least 2 hours, or overnight, in cheesecloth. In the morning, you'll be left with a pale yellow juice, thin as water but concentrated and saline as oyster liquor. To finish the drink, you mix the tomato water with the vodkas, letting in a drop of Tabasco and a dash of celery salt, and then shake the living daylights out of it.

––––––

2 pounds very ripe, fragrant tomatoes, cored and cut into chunks
½ teaspoon sea salt
1 tablespoon chopped lemon thyme or lemongrass
4 ounces Absolut peppar vodka, or other pepper vodka
4 ounces vodka
¼ teaspoon celery salt
4 drops Tabasco sauce
Yellow, red, and green cherry tomatoes for garnish

1. Combine the tomatoes, sea salt, and lemon thyme in a food processor. Puree the tomatoes for about 1 minute. Line a colander with cheesecloth, allowing the cloth to overhang the edges by several inches. Set the colander over a bowl and pour in the tomato mixture. Tie the edges of the cheesecloth together, and set aside to drain for at least 2 hours, or as long as overnight.
2. If necessary, twist the cheesecloth to extract any remaining juice.
3. Combine the vodkas, celery salt, Tabasco, and 2 cups tomato water in a shaker filled with ice. Shake well, and strain into 4 martini glasses. Garnish with cherry tomatoes.

MAKES 4 DRINKS

SERVING SUGGESTIONS

Blue Cheese Cheesecake (p. 61), Roasted Feta with Thyme Honey (p. 92), Caramelized Onion and Quark Dip (p. 84)

AUGUST 30, 2000: "SIPS: BLOODY MARTINI, ANYONE?" BY AMANDA HESSER. RECIPE ADAPTED FROM WALLSÉ IN NEW YORK CITY.

—2000

HOLIDAY PUNCH

¾ cup sugar

¾ cup water

1½ bottles (750-ml bottles) zweigelt or zinfandel

1½ bottles (750-ml bottles) blaufränkisch or syrah

½ (750-ml) bottle dry riesling

8 ounces brandy

¾ cup elderberry or raspberry syrup (available from
    specialty food markets)

2 pears, cored and diced

2 apples, cored and diced

2 blood oranges, peeled, segmented, and
    segments cut in half

Seeds of 2 pomegranates

3 cinnamon sticks

2 vanilla beans

6 whole cloves

1. Combine the sugar and water in a small saucepan and heat over low heat, stirring, until the sugar dissolved. Allow to cool completely.
2. Combine all the remaining ingredients in a large punch bowl. Stir in the sugar syrup. Serve at room temperature.

MAKES 20 OR SO PUNCH-CUP SERVINGS

SERVING SUGGESTIONS
Rillettes de Canard (Duck Rillettes; p. 65), Buckwheat Blini with Crème Fraîche and Caviar (p. 81), Parmesan Crackers (p. 84)

DECEMBER 27, 2000: "GROWN-UPS DON'T NOG EGGS," BY AMANDA HESSER. RECIPE ADAPTED FROM WALLSÉ IN NEW YORK CITY.

—2000

TOM AND JERRY

Although Jerry Thomas, the revered author of many a nineteenth-century cocktail, is often credited with inventing the Tom and Jerry, the drink is much older. Thomas, however, happily promoted both the drink and the myth.

Not for delicate flowers, the Tom and Jerry is like eggnog on fire. Sweeten with more sugar if you like.

1 large egg, separated

1½ teaspoons sugar

2 ounces white rum

1 ounce brandy

¾ cup hot whole milk, foamed if possible

Freshly grated nutmeg

1. Beat the egg white until stiff. Beat the yolk until thickened and a lemon-yellow color.
2. Combine white and yolk in a Collins glass or other tall glass. Add the sugar, rum, and brandy and give this a gentle stir. Pour the hot milk over the mixture, spooning the foam from the milk on top. Sprinkle nutmeg over the foam.

SERVES 1

DECEMBER 27, 2000: "GROWN-UPS DON'T NOG EGGS," BY AMANDA HESSER. RECIPE ADAPTED FROM THE KING COLE BAR IN NEW YORK CITY.

—2000

PATSY'S BOURBON SLUSH

Before you begin making this drink, make sure you have enough room in your freezer to hold several shallow containers on a level surface. Then start mixing and thinking about what you'll serve with your drinkable bourbon granita.

You may want to serve the slush in tumblers with small espresso spoons. If it's a hot day, spoons won't be necessary, because the slush will melt at a sipping pace.

2 cups hot strong black tea (4 tea bags steeped
    in 2 cups boiling water)

½ cup sugar

Two 6-ounce cans frozen lemonade

One 6-ounce can frozen orange juice

5 cups crushed ice

2 cups ice water

16 ounces best-quality bourbon
4 cups chilled ginger ale, or to taste
Mint sprigs

1. At least 6 hours before serving, combine the tea and sugar in a 1-gallon plastic or glass container and stir until dissolved. Add the lemonade and orange juice and stir until thawed. Add the ice and ice water. Stir in the bourbon.

2. Pour the mixture into several shallow plastic containers, cover tightly, and place them in the freezer. Break up the slush with a fork and stir about every 2 hours to freeze the mixture evenly. (The slush can be made 3 to 4 days ahead. Transfer to a larger container and cover tightly; stir every 6 to 8 hours to keep the slush loose and evenly frozen.)

3. To serve, give the slush one last shredding with a fork, then spoon it into tall or stemmed glasses and top off with ginger ale. Garnish each glass with a mint sprig.

MAKES ABOUT 16 DRINKS

INGREDIENT NOTES
Buy crushed ice if you can, it's much easier than doing it yourself. If you must, place the ice, in batches, in a heavy-duty plastic bag or kitchen towel and crush with a rolling pin.

SERVING SUGGESTIONS
Saucisson Soûl (p. 67), Cleo's Daddy's Barbecued Ribs (p. 529), Caramelized Bacon (p. 93), North Carolina–Style Pulled Pork (p. 550)

DECEMBER 31, 2000: "STYLE & ENTERTAINING: SLUSH FUN," BY WILLIAM NORWICH. RECIPE ADAPTED FROM PATSY TRUEX.

—2000

⌒ JENNIFER'S MOROCCAN TEA

Yes, it does help to have a recipe for this tea, to remind you just how minty and sweet it needs to be. When it's right, it should taste almost like a tisane, and almost viscous, but not quite. My friend and Times colleague Jennifer Steinhauer has lived in Morocco, where she honed her tea-making skills. She says it's best drunk in the afternoon.

10 cups water
2 tablespoons loose Ceylon tea
2 large bunches mint
¾ cup sugar

1. Combine the water, tea, mint, and sugar in a large saucepan or teapot. Bring to a boil, then remove from the heat and let steep for 5 minutes.

2. Strain the tea into sturdy juice glasses or teacups.

MAKES 3 QUARTS

SERVING SUGGESTIONS
Moroccan Carrot Salad (p. 187), Spicy Orange Salad Moroccan-Style (p. 181), Blood Orange, Date, and Parmesan Salad with Almond Oil (p. 199), Moroccan Chicken Smothered in Olives (p. 482), Moroccan Rice Pudding (p. 848)

MARCH 28, 2001: "HOME IS WHERE THE PARTY IS," BY AMANDA HESSER. RECIPE ADAPTED FROM JENNIFER STEINHAUER.

—2001

⌒ JUNIPERO GIBSON WITH PICKLED RED ONION

The Gibson is a gin martini garnished with a pickled onion. Here you flash-pickle the onion, which keeps it fresh and punchy, an ample match for the fragrant Junipero gin.

½ red onion, sliced into very thin ribbons
Kosher salt
¼ cup red wine vinegar
Dry vermouth
16 ounces Junipero gin (or any other gin you like)

1. Chill 4 martini glasses in the freezer. Place the onion in a bowl and sprinkle with salt. Let sit for 10 minutes. Sprinkle the vinegar on top of the onion and let sit for 10 minutes more.

2. Fill a spray bottle with ¼ inch of vermouth and spray the inside of each chilled glass with it. Or pour a little vermouth into each glass, swirl it, and then pour it out, so the glass is just lightly coated. Place 3 or 4 pieces of onion in each glass (reserve the remaining onion for drinks on another day).

3. Fill a large cocktail shaker with ice, pour the gin over it, and shake vigorously. Strain into the glasses.

MAKES 4 DRINKS

SERVING SUGGESTIONS
Goat's-Milk Cheese, Buttered Brown Bread, and Salted Onion (p. 75), Feta Spread (p. 71), Beet Tzatziki (p. 89), Blue Cheese Dip (p. 54), Squashed Tomatoes (p. 90)

MAY 16, 2001: "THE CHEF: GABRIELLE HAMILTON: WHETTING THE APPETITE," BY GABRIELLE HAMILTON, THE CHEF AND OWNER OF PRUNE IN NEW YORK CITY, WITH AMANDA HESSER.

—2001

ᕶ THE VESPER

Jane Nickerson, a *Times* food columnist in the 1940s, liked a good drink (turn back to the 1940s to review the evidence), but no one wrote reverentially about cocktail making and drinking until William L. Hamilton took over the "Shaken and Stirred" column in 2002. Over the next few years, Hamilton, a feature writer, made his way from bar to bar in Manhattan, occasionally venturing out to cocktail frontiers like Williamsburg, uncovering the best in late-night philosophers and their concoctions. As luck would have it, he was witnessing a cocktail renaissance fueled by a strong economy. Bartenders began treating their work as a profession rather than a way station. Spirits became conduits for complex fruit and herb infusions, and homemade bitters a sign of authenticity. The "spirit consultant"—and I'm not talking about mediums—became a niche specialty. And no serious restaurant opened without a signature drink.

The Vesper was not one of the newfangled cocktails, but rather was excavated from the James Bond series. Named for Vesper Lynd, a double agent who meets an unfortunate end, the original drink called for 3 parts gin to 1 part vodka. But, as this recipe came from Pravda, a Russian bar, the vodka takes the front seat. It's a great drink, and appropriately dangerous.

———

3 ounces Stolichnaya Gold vodka (or other vodka)
1 ounce Beefeater dry gin (or other gin)
¼ ounce white Lillet
A lemon twist

Pour the vodka, gin, and Lillet into a cocktail shaker. Fill with ice and shake vigorously. Strain into a chilled martini glass. Garnish with the twist.

SERVES 1

SERVING SUGGESTIONS
Toasted Mushroom Rolls (p. 72), Smoked Mackerel on Toasts (p. 80), Onion Rings (p. 61), Russ & Daughters' Chopped Chicken Liver (p. 82), Cromesquis d'Huitres à la Sauce Tartare (p. 405)

DECEMBER 15, 2002: "SHAKEN AND STIRRED: EAST MEETS WEST," BY WILLIAM L. HAMILTON. RECIPE ADAPTED FROM PRAVDA, A BAR IN NEW YORK CITY.

—2002

ᕶ THE BONE

The Bone, which headlined at the Chickenbone Café in Williamsburg, was accompanied, if you dared, by smoked beef with chiles. Subtle? No. And yet, as William L. Hamilton, the "Shaken and Stirred" columnist, noted, the lime and sugar tame the drink, which will "dance you affectionately around the ring before it knocks you out." Along the way, you'll enjoy its crispness and the spiky hits of Tabasco before you fade.

———

2 ounces Wild Turkey (or other rye)
1 teaspoon fresh lime juice
¾ teaspoon superfine sugar
2 dashes Tabasco sauce

Mix all the ingredients in a cocktail shaker filled with ice. Shake well. Serve straight up in a shot glass.

SERVES 1

SERVING SUGGESTIONS
Caramelized Bacon (p. 93), Saucisson Soûl (p. 67), Spiced Pecans (p. 82), Julia Harrison Adams's Pimento Cheese Spread (p. 64)

MAY 11, 2003: "SHAKEN AND STIRRED: GRUFF BUT LOVABLE," BY WILLIAM L. HAMILTON. RECIPE ADAPTED FROM THE CHICKENBONE CAFÉ IN WILLIAMSBURG, NEW YORK CITY.

—2003

➣ LA PALOMA

William L. Hamilton wrote affectionately of this drink, "La Paloma, which translates as 'the dove,' and also, similarly, as a meek or a mild person, is an aptly named cocktail. It acts like it's never held a gun before, and then it blows the tin can into the air."

The recipe came from Sue Torres, a Manhattan chef and restaurateur, who was served a similar version of the drink at a Mexico ranch. There they called it a Mexican margarita. It's a shame we became so attached to the other margarita.

---

1 1/2 ounces Herradura Hacienda del Cristero Blanco tequila (or other good white tequila)
1 1/2 tablespoons fresh lime juice
1/2 cup Mexican Squirt soda (or 2 tablespoons fresh grapefruit juice and 6 tablespoons 7UP)
A lime slice

Pour the tequila over ice in a tall highball or Collins glass. Add the lime juice and Squirt, stir, and garnish with the slice of lime.

SERVES 1

INGREDIENT NOTE
I couldn't find Squirt, so I made this with grapefruit juice and 7UP instead. If I missed out, I certainly didn't feel it.

SERVING SUGGESTIONS
Guacamole Tostadas (p. 67), Grilled Onion Guacamole (p. 71), The Best Spinach Dip, with Chipotle and Lime (p. 90), Yucatán Fish With Crisp Garlic (p. 431), Coloradito (p. 547), El Parian's Carne Asada (Grilled Beef; p. 581)

AUGUST 3, 2003: "SHAKEN AND STIRRED: A TOUCH OF EVIL," BY WILLIAM L. HAMILTON. RECIPE ADAPTED FROM SUEÑOS RESTAURANT IN NEW YORK CITY.

—2003

➣ MARTINI

The best description of martini making that I've read comes from John Conti, a postal worker in Upstate New York. William L. Hamilton, the *Times*'s "Shaken and Stirred" columnist, heard about Conti's bartending skill and tracked him down and took notes while he made the drink. Using a 6:1 ratio of gin to vermouth, Conti poured the spirits over ice in a bartender's glass, then stirred with a long-handled spoon, "bent slightly so that it would follow the sides of the glass."

"You slide the spoon down and twirl, as opposed to agitating," Conti said. "The whole idea of a martini is a smooth drink. Agitation introduces air." Even when he strained the cocktail into a martini glass, he did so in a circular motion to prevent splashing.

---

3 ounces gin
1/2 ounce dry vermouth
A green olive

1. Chill a 7-ounce martini glass by filling it with ice and water.
2. Fill a bartender's glass or a tall 16-ounce glass two-thirds full with ice. Add the gin and vermouth, and stir with a long-necked spoon, keeping the spoon close to the side of the glass as you swirl the ice. Stir until the glass frosts, about 20 seconds. Empty the martini glass, and strain the contents of the bartender's glass into it. Garnish with the olive.

SERVES 1

SERVING SUGGESTIONS
Hot Cheese Olives (p. 83), Seasoned Olives (p. 90), Salted and Deviled Almonds (p. 51), Cromesquis d'Huîtres à la Sauce Tartare (p. 405)

OCTOBER 26, 2003: "SHAKEN AND STIRRED: THE MARTINI PRINCIPLES," BY WILLIAM L HAMILTON. RECIPE ADAPTED FROM JOHN CONTI, A POSTAL WORKER IN UPSTATE NEW YORK.

—2003

◠ SIR FRANCIS DRAKE

Perfect when you have a hangover. Or when someone has just fried some oysters. Or after a long, treacherous circumnavigation of the globe.

½ cup Mott's Clamato juice
Dash each of celery salt, black pepper, and Tabasco sauce
Pinch of grated fresh horseradish
2 ounces Tío Pepe or other dry sherry
A lemon wedge

1. Mix the Clamato juice with the spices and seasoning in a liquid measuring cup.
2. Pour the sherry into an 8-ounce glass filled with ice. Top off with the spiced Clamato juice, and garnish with the lemon wedge.

SERVES I

SERVING SUGGESTIONS
Spiced Pecans (p. 82), Florentine Dip (p. 58), Fried Olives (p. 87), Catalan Tortilla with Aioli (p. 86), Cromesquis d'Huítres à la Sauce Tartare (p. 405)

FEBRUARY 15, 2004: "SHAKEN AND STIRRED: MASTER AND COMMINGLER," BY WILLIAM L. HAMILTON. RECIPE ADAPTED FROM HEARTH IN NEW YORK CITY.

—2004

◠ CRANBERRY LIQUEUR

---

2 cups cranberries
I cup plus 2 tablespoons sugar
½ cup water
12 ounces vodka
2 cinnamon sticks

1. Combine the cranberries, sugar, and water in a saucepan, bring to a boil, and boil until the cranberries are soft and start to pop, 5 to 10 minutes.
2. Transfer to a food processor and puree. Pour into a jar. Add the vodka and cinnamon sticks. Refrigerate for at least 3 days and up to several weeks. Strain

through a fine-mesh sieve lined with cheesecloth (or through a jelly bag) before serving. Ladle into chilled glasses.

MAKES ABOUT 2 CUPS

SERVING SUGGESTIONS
Cocoa Christmas Cookies (p. 695), Swedish Ginger Cookies (p. 708), Papa's Apple Pound Cake (p. 774), Evelyn Sharpe's French Chocolate Cake (p. 752)

APRIL 18, 2004: "FOOD: SEEING RED," BY JONATHAN REYNOLDS.

—2004

◠ GINGER DAIQUIRI

The daiquiri (see p. 25), retooled.

For the Ginger Simple Syrup
I cup sugar
I cup water
4 ounces fresh ginger, peeled and sliced

For the Daiquiri
An orange twist
2 ounces Haitian white rum (or other white rum)
½ ounce Cointreau
I tablespoon fresh Meyer lemon juice
I tablespoon Ginger Simple Syrup (above)
Raw sugar, for frosting the rim

1. To make the ginger simple syrup, combine the sugar and water in a saucepan and bring to a boil, stirring to dissolve the sugar. Add the ginger. Remove from the heat, cool, and let stand for 2 days.
2. To make the daiquiri, swipe the orange peel on the rim of a cocktail glass; set the peel aside. Press the wet rim down into a shallow dish of the raw sugar to "frost" the rim.
3. Combine the remaining ingredients in a shaker with ice, shake, and strain into the glass, filling it to the brim. Garnish with the orange peel.

SERVES I

You'll have leftover ginger simple syrup. Covered, it will keep in the fridge for 2 months. Add it to sparkling water or lemonade, and spoon it over ice cream or cake.

It's important to use Meyer lemon juice, which is floral and light; regular lemon juice is too harsh for this drink.

SERVING SUGGESTIONS
Cucumber–Goat Cheese Dip with Radishes and Scallions (p. 70), Shrimp Toast (p. 60)

MAY 23, 2004: "SHAKEN AND STIRRED: MEDITATE, A SIP AT A TIME," BY WILLIAM L. HAMILTON. RECIPE ADAPTED FROM MAS IN NEW YORK CITY.

—2004

❧ GRAPEFRUIT WINE (VIN DE PAMPLEMOUSSE)

Modeled after Lillet and far more delicious. This needs to sit for forty days and forty nights, like Noah on the Ark, so plan ahead! If you're looking for a good food gift, this is it: it makes plenty for friends and neighbors.

———

3 Ruby Red grapefruits, scrubbed

3 white grapefruits, scrubbed

4 lemons, scrubbed

1 vanilla bean, split

3 cups sugar

6¼ bottles (750-ml bottles) sauvignon blanc, preferably Sancerre

32 ounces (1 quart) vodka

1. Start with a sterile 2½-gallon or larger bucket or crock. Thinly slice the grapefruits and lemons—rind and all—and toss them into the bucket. Add the vanilla bean and sugar. Pour the sauvignon blanc over the citrus and sugar, add the vodka, and stir.
2. Cover the bucket tightly with plastic wrap and let stand in a cool, dark place for 40 days. A basement is ideal; a closet is fine. For the first week, stir the grapefruit wine once a day; this is the period when the sugar

dissolves and the citrus oils are drawn from the rinds. Then, after the first week, stir every few days.
3. After 40 days, strain the wine through a sieve lined with several layers of cheesecloth into another large sterile bucket. Discard the vanilla and citrus. Have ready 8 scalded wine bottles (or other glass containers with lids; scald by dipping bottles and lids, if using, in boiling water). Using a funnel, decant the wine into the bottles, leaving 1 to 2 inches of space at the top. Boil new corks (available at www.thegrape.net) for 2 minutes to soften them, then seal the bottles. The grapefruit wine can be drunk now, but it will improve if aged in the bottle for another month; keep chilled in the refrigerator.
4. When serving, pour the grapefruit wine over ice in small stemmed glasses.

MAKES EIGHT 750-MILLILITER BOTTLES

SERVING SUGGESTIONS
Fried Olives (p. 87), Seasoned Olives (p. 90), Brie with Herbs in Bread (p. 69), Rillettes de Canard (Duck Rillettes; p. 65)

NOVEMBER 7, 2004: "THE DISH: NIBBLES AND SIPS," BY MONA TALBOTT.

—2004

❧ SAKETINI

In David Wondrich's excellent cocktail history *Imbibe!* he says the saketini belongs to "that sickly and dismal tribe" of chocolate martinis, mango martinis, and appletinis. I disagree! But, mind you, I would never drink any of the others.

———

2 ounces gin

1 ounce sake

A thin slice of cucumber

Fill a cocktail shaker with ice. Add the gin and sake and shake furiously, then strain into a chilled martini glass. Drop in the slice of cucumber.

SERVES 1

SERVING SUGGESTIONS
Fresh and Smoked Salmon Spread (p. 72), Edamame with Nori Salt (p. 92), Alaskan Salmon (p. 423), Coconut Rice Pudding with Lime Syrup (p. 846)

APRIL 3, 2005: "FREE RANGING," BY AMANDA HESSER.

—2005

❧ REBUJITO

Hands down, this is the best summer drink ever. It's nutty, lemony, fizzy, cool, and, most important, not too sweet. *Rebujito* means tangled or mixed, and here, sherry, lemon, and Sprite are tangled in just the right way.

———————

2 ounces manzanilla or other fino sherry
¾ cup Sprite (not 7UP)
A lemon twist

Fill a tall glass with ice. Pour in the sherry and top off with the Sprite. Stir. Add the lemon twist.

SERVES 1

INGREDIENT NOTE
Manzanilla is a fino sherry made in Sanlúcar Barrameda, a small seaside town about half an hour south of the town of Jerez, which gave sherry its name. The locals say that the seawater in the air infuses the sherry with salinity. If you've never had manzanilla sherry before, you should sample it straight before mixing into a drink like this. Champagne is fine, but manzanilla is what you should drink as an everyday aperitif. It's dry, nutty, and spare. Relatively inexpensive too. Manzanilla prepares you for great things but doesn't unfairly raise your expectations.

SERVING SUGGESTIONS
Fried Chickpeas (p. 88), Catalan Tortilla with Aioli (p. 86), Potato, Ham, and Piquillo Pepper Croquetas (p. 94), Lightly Smoked Salt Cod Salad (p. 437), Paella (p. 309)

SEPTEMBER II, 2005: "RAISING THE TAPAS BAR," BY AMANDA HESSER. RECIPE ADAPTED FROM TÍA POL IN NEW YORK CITY.

—2005

❧ LIMONCELLO

Unlike many fruits, the flavor in lemon seems to magnify when it is bottled. It becomes more blissfully fragrant and clear with none of the sharpness. For limoncello, you infuse vodka with lemon zest and sweeten the whole with sugar syrup. With less than an hour's work, you'll have holiday gifts for all your friends.

———————

12 lemons, scrubbed
1 (750-ml) bottle good vodka
½ cup sugar
½ water

1. Finely grate the zest of the lemons (reserve the lemons for another use, such as the Ginger Lemonade on p. 26). Combine the zest and vodka in a large jar. Seal tightly and let stand in a cool, dark place for 2 weeks.
2. Dissolve the sugar in the water in a small saucepan over medium heat. Let cool.
3. Line a sieve with cheesecloth and set it over a bowl. Strain the vodka mixture into the bowl. Stir in the sugar syrup. Use a funnel to pour the limoncello into a sterilized 1-liter bottle and seal. Let stand in a cool, dark place for 1 week, then keep chilled in the freezer.

MAKES ABOUT 6 CUPS

SERVING SUGGESTIONS
Hazelnut Baklava (p. 706), Cornmeal Biscotti (p. 696), Campton Place Buttermilk Chocolate Cake (p. 765)

NOVEMBER 6, 2005: "THE WAY WE EAT: CITRUS MAXIMUS," BY AMANDA HESSER.

—2005

IMPROVED HOLLAND GIN COCKTAIL

This recipe ran as a celebratory nod to the two-hundredth birthday of the cocktail and to the opening of a branch of the Museum of the American Cocktail in New York. No one knows exactly when the cocktail was born, but in 1806, the editor of the *Balance and Columbian Repository*, a publication printed in Hudson, New York, described the cocktail as "a stimulating liquor composed of spirits of any kind, sugar, water, and bitters—it is vulgarly called a bittered sling and is supposed to be an excellent electioneering potion inasmuch as it renders the heart stout and bold, at the same time that it fuddles the head." The editor added, "It is said also to be of great use to a Democratic candidate: because, a person having swallowed a glass of it, is ready to swallow any thing else."

This particularly engaging and long-lived cocktail tastes like gin wearing a perfume of licorice and cherries.

————

2 dashes Angostura bitters
½ to ¾ teaspoon Simple Syrup (see Ingredient Notes)
½ teaspoon Luxardo maraschino or other maraschino
    liqueur
A dash of absinthe, or substitute Pernod or Absente
2 ounces Holland gin (also called genever gin; Zuidam
    is a good brand)
A thin lemon twist

Combine all the liquid ingredients in a cocktail shaker with ice. Shake well and strain into a chilled martini glass. Twist the swatch of lemon peel over the drink so the oils are released into the cocktail, rub the peel around the rim of the glass, and drop it in.

SERVES 1

INGREDIENT NOTES
Holland gin, distilled from malt wine and infused with juniper, was more popular in America in the nineteenth century than London dry gin. Having sprung for the Luxardo maraschino liqueur and Pernod, I felt justified in using the Bombay gin I already owned. By all means, go for Holland gin if you like.

David Wondrich, a cocktail historian who created this recipe, recommended a richer-tasting simple syrup made by dissolving 2 parts raw sugar in 1 part boiling water.

SERVING SUGGESTIONS
Cromesquis d'Huîtres à la Sauce Tartare (p. 405), Onion Rings (p. 61)

MAY 14, 2006: "SHAKEN AND STIRRED: COCKTAIL, THE BICENTENNIAL," BY JONATHAN MILES. RECIPE ADAPTED FROM DAVID WONDRICH.

—2006

THE CUKE

In 2006, the *Times* ran a contest for the best summer cocktail recipe, and after the editors waded through hundreds of submissions, The Cuke, a dangerously refreshing drink, prevailed. It smells of fresh cucumber and tastes of lime, and, together, what a joy they are to drink. I'd serve it on any warm night while grilling.

————

6 limes, scrubbed
1 cup packed mint leaves, plus 6 sprigs for garnish
3 unwaxed cucumbers
½ cup sugar
16 ounces vodka or gin, preferably Hendrick's gin
Sparkling water

1. Thinly slice 3 of the limes and place in a pitcher. Juice the rest and add the juice to the pitcher. Add the mint leaves.
2. Slice 2 of the cucumbers and add to the pitcher, then add the sugar and muddle the ingredients (crush with a muddler or the back of a spoon). Add the vodka. Place in the refrigerator to steep for at least 30 minutes.
3. Peel the remaining cucumber and cut lengthwise into 6 spears.
4. Fill 6 highball or other large glasses with ice. Strain the vodka mixture into the glasses. Top each glass with a splash of sparkling water, garnish with a sprig of mint and a cucumber spear, and serve.

MAKES 6 DRINKS

SERVING SUGGESTIONS
Tuna Tartare (p. 416), Onion Rings (p. 61), Eggs Louisiana (p. 53), Shrimp Toast (p. 60)

JUNE 21, 2006: "A CONTEST WHERE VICTORY GOES TO THE COOLEST," BY PETER MEEHAN. RECIPE ADAPTED FROM ADAM FRANK, A GALLERY DIRECTOR AT THE HOSFELT GALLERY IN NEW YORK CITY.

—2006

MARCH 4, 2007: "SHAKEN AND STIRRED: MOLECULAR THEORY," BY JONATHAN MILES. RECIPE ADAPTED FROM DUSHAN ZARIC, CO-OWNER OF EMPLOYEES ONLY IN THE WEST VILLAGE, NEW YORK CITY.

—2007

⌒ BILLIONAIRE COCKTAIL

This recipe demonstrates the difference between new and old cocktails. New ones tend to be concentrated and layered, with each component calibrated to be tasted, while the old guard are usually more unified and diluted with citrus juices and water.

———

2 ounces Baker's 107-proof bourbon or other good
    Kentucky bourbon
2 tablespoons fresh lemon juice
1½ tablespoons Simple Syrup (p. 16)
¼ ounce absinthe, or substitute Absente or Herbsaint
1 tablespoon homemade grenadine syrup (see Ingredient
    Note) or high-quality grenadine
A lemon slice

Combine all the liquid ingredients in a cocktail shaker with ice. Shake vigorously and strain into a chilled cocktail glass. Garnish with the lemon slice.

SERVES 1

INGREDIENT NOTE
To make homemade grenadine syrup, combine 1 cup of pomegranate juice, 1½ ounces aged Spanish brandy, and ¼ cup sugar in a saucepan, bring to a boil, stirring to dissolve the sugar, and reduce over medium heat until syrupy. Let cool. The syrup will keep, refrigerated, for up to 3 months.

SERVING SUGGESTIONS
Salted and Deviled Almonds (p. 51), Spiced Pecans (p. 82)

⌒ PEPPADEW MARTINI

"According to Peppadew lore," wrote Merrill Stubbs, "a man referred to only as J.S. discovered an unusual pepper plant a decade ago near his home in South Africa. Delighted by the fruit's sweet and spicy kick, he began a global marketing campaign."

If that account is even partially true, J.S. would join a long list of food missionaries, including John Mackey, Bill Niman, and Michael Pollan—he is why entranced followers are now buying Peppadew peppers at Whole Foods for cocktail parties. Peppadews are most commonly found pickled, which is how they're used here. You stuff the peppers with goat cheese and mascarpone and lots of other delicious bits, then skewer them and suspend them over a pepper-and-spice-infused martini: hors d'oeuvres and cocktail in one.

———

2 jalapeño peppers
10 black peppercorns
5 allspice berries
5 juniper berries
One (750-ml) bottle good vodka
5 ounces goat cheese
¼ cup mascarpone cheese
½ teaspoon sherry vinegar
1½ teaspoons olive oil
2 tablespoons heavy cream
1½ teaspoons finely chopped shallot
1½ teaspoons finely chopped chives
Kosher salt and freshly ground black pepper
One 14¾-ounce jar Peppadew peppers in brine
    (about 20 peppers)
2 large limes, cut into 8 wedges each
2 cups lemon-lime soda
2 cups club soda or sparkling water

1. Halve the jalapeños lengthwise. Set a sauté pan over medium heat, add the jalapeños, peppercorns,

and allspice and juniper berries, and cook, stirring frequently, until the jalapeños are lightly browned, about 3 minutes. Let cool.

2. Combine the jalapeños and spices with the vodka in a bowl. Cover and let infuse for 24 hours. Strain.

3. Combine the goat cheese, mascarpone, vinegar, olive oil, and cream in a large bowl and beat with an electric mixer (preferably with the paddle attachment) until smooth (or use a hand mixer). Blend in the shallot, chives, and salt and pepper to taste. Cover and refrigerate up to 3 days.

4. To stuff the peppers, drain the peppers, reserving the brine. Spoon the goat-cheese mixture into a pastry bag fitted with a medium star tip and pipe into the peppers. The filled peppers can be refrigerated for up to 4 hours; remove them from the refrigerator about 20 minutes before preparing the cocktails.

5. To make the cocktails, using a muddler or the back of a spoon, muddle (crush) 2 lime wedges with a pinch of salt in a cocktail shaker. Fill the shaker with ice and add 1½ ounces of the infused vodka and 2 tablespoons of the pepper brine. Shake well, then strain into a 6-ounce martini glass and top off with equal parts lemon-lime soda and club soda. Garnish with 2 or 3 of the stuffed peppers on a skewer. Repeat to make more cocktails. (Store leftover vodka in a cool place.)

MAKES 8 DRINKS

SERVING SUGGESTIONS
Caramelized Bacon (p. 93), Ricotta Crostini with Fresh Thyme and Dried Oregano (p. 93), Roasted Feta with Thyme Honey (p. 92)

MAY 6, 2007: "THE NEW STAPLES," BY MERRILL STUBBS. RECIPE ADAPTED FROM LITTLE GIANT IN NEW YORK CITY.

—2007

⌒ ZOMBIE PUNCH

If not for Jeff Berry, a tiki culture aficionado with a persistent streak, the original recipe for Zombie Punch might have died along with the generation of waiters who worked at Don the Beachcomber's, a tiki restaurant in Hollywood. The drink was born there in 1934, and the secret recipe was recorded in code in notebooks kept by the waitstaff. By chance, Berry was given one of the notebooks, and after a year of sleuthing, he cracked the code.

———

1½ tablespoons fresh lime juice
1 tablespoon fresh white grapefruit juice
1½ teaspoons cinnamon syrup (see Ingredient Note)
1 tablespoon falernum (see Ingredient Note)
1½ ounces dark Jamaican rum, such as
    Appleton Estate V/X
1½ ounces gold rum, such as Cruzan 5-year-old
1 ounce 151-proof Lemon Hart Demerara rum
Dash of Angostura bitters
⅛ teaspoon Herbsaint or Pernod
1 teaspoon grenadine
¾ cup crushed ice
Sliced fruit or berries for garnish
A mint sprig for garnish

Put everything (except the garnishes) into a blender and blend at high speed for 5 seconds. Pour into a highball glass and add ice cubes to fill. Decorate with sliced fruit or berries and the mint sprig.

SERVES 1

INGREDIENT NOTE
The *Times* Dining editors noted, "Cinnamon syrup from Sonoma Syrup Company is sold at Dean & DeLuca, Whole Foods, and other retailers. To make it, boil ½ cup water with ½ cup sugar and 2 cinnamon sticks pounded in a mortar or with the back of a knife; stir until sugar dissolves, remove from heat, let sit for 2 hours, then strain. Excess can be kept refrigerated for a month. Names of retailers selling falernum, a syrup tasting of lime juice, almonds, and ginger, are available from Fee Brothers at (800) 961-FEES."

SERVING SUGGESTION
Caramelized Bacon (p. 93)

NOVEMBER 28, 2007: "CRACKING THE CODE OF THE ZOMBIE," BY STEVEN KURUTZ. RECIPE ADAPTED FROM DON THE BEACHCOMBER'S IN LOS ANGELES VIA JEFF BERRY, A TIKI CULTURE EXPERT.

—2007

☙ KUMQUAT-CLEMENTINE CORDIAL

Cordials are almost always better when made at home, where you can preserve a robust infusion of fruit, herbs, and spices and keep the sugar lean. This one lands brilliantly between a limoncello and a scented aquavit.

¼ cup sugar, preferably superfine

1 tablespoon boiling water

3 tablespoons fresh clementine juice (from 1 to 2 clementines), plus 1 clementine, thinly sliced

6 kumquats, thinly sliced and seeded

14 ounces white rum

3 allspice berries

2 star anise

1. Have a scalded jar with a lid or a glass bottle with a cork ready (to scald, simply dip the jar and lid or bottle and cork in boiling water). Place the sugar in a large glass measuring cup or bowl, add the boiling water, and stir for 1 minute. Add the clementine juice and continue stirring until the sugar dissolves, about a minute longer.

2. If using a jar, place the clementine and kumquat slices inside; if using a bottle, you might have to curl the slices into cylinders to fit them through the neck. Add the sugar syrup and the remaining ingredients; break the star anise in half if necessary to fit into the bottle. Seal the jar or cork the bottle. Let stand at room temperature for 1 week, shaking the jar or bottle once a day, then refrigerate until ready to use.

3. You can serve the drink several ways: as is; over ice; with a splash of sparkling water; topped with chilled white wine or sparkling wine; as a hot toddy, topped off with boiling water; or drizzled over ice cream.

MAKES ABOUT 2 CUPS

VARIATIONS

To make a brandy version of the cordial, substitute brandy for the rum, and replace the spices with a cinnamon stick and a whole clove. For a gin version, substitute gin for the rum, and replace the spices with 3 peppercorns and 6 coriander seeds.

SERVING SUGGESTIONS

When served as a cocktail with sparkling water or wine: Fried Olives (p. 87), Seasoned Olives (p. 90), Sophie Grigson's Parmesan Cake (p. 69), Smoked Mackerel on Toasts (p. 80), Pickled Shrimp (p. 95), Ricotta Crostini with Fresh Thyme and Dried Oregano (p. 93)

DECEMBER 12, 2007: "A GOOD APPETITE: HASTE MAKES CORDIAL," BY MELISSA CLARK.

—2007

☙ SPICED COLADA

Pete Wells, the editor of the Dining section of the *Times*, wrote that this drink's combination of spiced rum and Angostura bitters was "just the sort of crisp slap in the face that was needed to bring the piña colada back to life." You will agree—the colada is light, creamy, and balanced, the dash of bitters a delicious touch.

For the Syrup

One 15-ounce can coconut cream, preferably Coco López

¾ cup pineapple juice

6 tablespoons fresh lemon juice (from about 2 lemons)

6 tablespoons fresh lime juice (from about 3 limes)

½ cup water

½ cup superfine sugar

9 dashes Angostura bitters

For the Coladas

8 ounces spiced rum

6 cups ice cubes

4 to 8 dashes Angostura bitters

1. To make the syrup, pour the coconut cream, pineapple juice, lemon juice, lime juice, water, sugar, and bitters into a blender and blend until smooth, about 1 minute. Transfer the syrup to a jar or other container. You will have enough syrup for about 4 coladas.

2. For each colada, pour ½ cup of the colada syrup and 2 ounces rum into a blender, add 1½ cups ice and puree until the colada is thick but can still be poured, a minute or more. Pour into an appropriate vessel, such as a ceramic coconut shell, and sprinkle with a dash or

two of bitters. Serve with a straw snipped to rise 2 to 3 inches above the lip of the vessel.

MAKES 4 DRINKS

JUNE 25, 2008: "THE PULSE OF SUMMER: BLENDER DRINKS ARE BACK," BY PETE WELLS. RECIPE ADAPTED FROM THE RUSTY KNOT IN GREENWICH VILLAGE, NEW YORK CITY.

—2008

DELFT BLUE COCKTAIL

Genever was created in Holland in the seventeenth century. Made with malted grains, it's a little sweeter and fuller flavored than English gin and has a lower proof.

If you're wondering what to do with the leftover gin, try the Improved Holland Gin Cocktail on p. 39.

————

For the Syrup
1 cup blueberries
2 tablespoons sugar
2 grinds black pepper

For the Cocktails
8 ounces genever (Holland gin), chilled
2 ounces limoncello
Angostura bitters
Fresh lemon juice, to taste
4 lemon twists

1. To make the syrup, combine the blueberries, sugar, and pepper in a small saucepan and cook, stirring, over medium heat until the berries collapse and release their juices, about 5 minutes. Force through a sieve into a metal bowl. Place the metal bowl in a bowl of ice and water to chill the mixture. This makes enough syrup for 4 drinks.
2. For each single drink, place 2 ounces genever in a cocktail shaker and add 2 tablespoons of the blueberry syrup, 1/2 ounce limoncello, a dash of bitters, and a few drops of lemon juice. Add ice, shake, and pour into a cocktail glass—serve straight up or on the rocks, with a twist.

MAKES 4 DRINKS

INGREDIENT NOTE
Limoncello is easier to find in liquor stores now, but if you'd like to make your own (homemade is often better and fresher tasting than what you can buy), there's a recipe on p. 38.

SERVING SUGGESTION
Salted and Deviled Almonds (p. 51)

SEPTEMBER 24, 2008: "MALTY AND COMPLEX, THE ORIGINAL GIN IS MAKING A COMEBACK," BY FLORENCE FABRICANT.

—2008

THE NORMANDY

Mulled cider and digestif in one. And it's seasonal without being overbearing about it.

————

9 cranberries
2 thin slices green apple
1 teaspoon dark brown sugar
1 tablespoon fresh lemon juice
1 tablespoon Simple Syrup (p. 16)
2 ounces Calvados or other good-quality apple brandy

Combine 6 cranberries, 1 apple slice, the brown sugar, and lemon juice in a cocktail shaker and muddle (crush with a muddler or the back of a wooden spoon). Add the simple syrup, Calvados, and a few ice cubes, cover, and shake well. Strain into a rocks glass filled with ice and garnish with the remaining 3 cranberries and apple slice.

SERVES 1

SERVING SUGGESTIONS
Toasts with Walnut Sauce (p. 73), Nicole Kaplan's Gougères (p. 76), Roasted Feta with Thyme Honey (p. 92)

NOVEMBER 23, 2008: "THE WAY WE EAT; BRANDY RECOGNITION," BY ALEKSANDRA CRAPANZANO. RECIPE ADAPTED FROM XAVIER HERIT AT RESTAURANT DANIEL IN NEW YORK CITY.

—2008

☙ BLENDER EGGNOG

Make Craig Claiborne's Eggnog on p. 22 when you want a showpiece, and this one when you just want a great nog.

————

4 large eggs
¾ cup sugar, or to taste
1 teaspoon freshly grated nutmeg,
    plus more for sprinkling
4 ounces brandy
4 ounces spiced rum
1½ cups whole milk
1 cup heavy cream

1. Crack the eggs into a blender and process for 1 minute on medium speed. Slowly add the sugar and blend for 1 minute. With the blender running, add the remaining ingredients until combined. Refrigerate for at least 1 hour, or up to overnight.
2. Serve the eggnog in chilled wineglasses, grating nutmeg on top.

MAKES 6 TO 8 DRINKS

INGREDIENT NOTE
This will not fit in a standard blender. Use a large blender if you have one, or make the nog in two batches.

SERVING SUGGESTIONS
Rum Balls (p. 687), Christmas Stollen (p. 657), Swedish Ginger Cookies (p. 708)

DECEMBER 24, 2008: "PUNCH: IT'S NOT JUST FOR THE HOLIDAYS ANYMORE," BY STEVEN STERN. RECIPE ADAPTED FROM JEFFREY MORGENTHALER, A COCKTAIL BLOGGER.

—2008

☙ COCONUT HOT CHOCOLATE

Super-smooth and creamy—you'll want it in thimblefuls. A nap will follow.

————

2 tablespoons unsweetened cocoa powder
⅓ cup boiling water
One 15-ounce can unsweetened coconut milk
¼ packed cup dark brown sugar
Pinch of kosher salt
1 ounce bittersweet chocolate, chopped (about ¼ cup)
1 teaspoon vanilla extract
Whole milk (optional)
Meringue Topping (recipe follows)

1. Whisk the cocoa into the boiling water.
2. Combine the coconut milk, sugar, and salt in a small saucepan and bring to a simmer, stirring until the sugar is dissolved. Whisk in the cocoa mixture and chocolate until smooth and hot. Stir in the vanilla. Thin with milk, if desired. Serve with the topping.

MAKES 2 DRINKS

MERINGUE TOPPING

1 large egg white
3 tablespoons superfine sugar

Beat the egg white in a small bowl with an electric mixer on medium speed for 1 minute. Beat in the sugar tablespoon by tablespoon. Continue to beat until the egg white holds soft peaks and is shiny, 5 minutes.

MAKES ABOUT 1 CUP

INGREDIENT NOTES
Melissa Clark added, "If you started with a whole egg [for the meringue topping] and you'd like an even richer hot chocolate, whisk the egg yolk into the mixture after you've taken it off the heat."

You may want to thin the mixture with a little milk, but whatever you do, don't skip the meringue topping!

FEBRUARY 11, 2009: "A GOOD APPETITE: THIRD TIME'S THE CHARM, VALENTINE," BY MELISSA CLARK.

—2009

- If people are making hors d'oeuvres at home, they aren't writing in to the *Times* to tell anyone about them.

—1870s—

- Salted and Deviled Almonds (p. 51).

—1897—

- Eggs are seasoned and stuffed, deviled and otherwise (see p. 52).

—1909—

- The few dips that ever appear in the *Times* appear now.

—1940s—

- The dark ages: pigs in a blanket and bacon-wrapped chestnuts.

—1950s—

- The canapé.

—1960s—

- Pimento Cheese Spread (p. 64) and Duck Rillettes (p. 65) bridge the gap between dips and pâté.

—1970s—

- Shrimp Toast (p. 60).

—1973—

- Scotch Eggs (p. 62).

—1978—

- Hors d'oeuvres go international: satay, guacamole, and hummus.

—1980s—

- Endive leaves become the quintessential hors d'oeuvres boat.

- Cocktail party mainstay: smoked salmon, in mousse, on toasts, in pastry cups.

—1990s—

- A dish of olives and a bowl of olive oil with bread becomes the default amuse-bouche at Mediterranean restaurants and on the coffee tables of Mediterranean-obsessed home cooks.

- Deviled eggs escape the picnic and wind up as bar food.

—1999—

- Diners shift their searchlight from Italy to Spain and illuminate tapas.

—2000s—

- The French gougère (p. 76) reclaims its place at top New York City restaurants.

- Marian Burros notes the popularity of small plates.

—2002—

- In homes, the crostini trumps the canapé.

- Marcona almonds become standard snack fare at dinner parties; their price soars.

—2006—

- Pork belly meets the tea sandwich (p. 88) at Fatty Crab in New York City and becomes an instant classic.

2

HORS D'OEUVRES, SNACKS, AND SMALL DISHES

RECIPES BY CATEGORY

TO SUGAR OR CRYSTALLIZE POP-CORN

Otherwise known as caramel corn. See p. 76 for a modern interpretation with nuts, orange blossom honey, and sea salt.

_____

Corn oil
½ cup popcorn
1 tablespoon unsalted butter
3 tablespoons water
¾ cup sugar
Salt (optional)

1. Cover the bottom of a large heavy pot with corn oil. Add the popcorn, stir to coat, cover, and place over medium-high heat. Cook, shaking frequently, until all the popcorn has popped. Remove from the heat and keep covered.
2. Combine the butter, water, and sugar in another large pot, bring to a boil, and cook, stirring occasionally, until the sugar dissolves and the mixture begins to caramelize, 2 to 3 minutes. Remove from the heat, pour in the popcorn, and stir quickly to coat the kernels with the caramel—some will stick to the pot. Season with salt if desired, and scrape into a serving bowl.

MAKES 4 QUARTS

COOKING NOTES
I added salt to the recipe to contrast with the sweetness, but feel free to keep to the original.

SERVING SUGGESTION
Ginger Lemonade (p. 26)

FEBRUARY 10, 1878: "THE HOUSEHOLD: USEFUL FAMILY HINTS." RECIPE SIGNED M.W.K.

—1878

ANCHOVY CANAPÉS

This is a recipe that I changed liberally. The original instructed you to make "a little hollow" in slices of stale bread, then fry them in lard—a sure way to kill a piece of bread. Yet toast, anchovy butter, and Roquefort were all flavors I'd happily combine, so I just cut out the fat, literally, and toasted the bread rather than frying it. Magically, you could taste the bright salinity of the anchovies and blue cheese, unmarred by lard. The toasts are meant to be served after dinner with coffee, but I think they'd make a fine snack or hors d'oeuvre—and besides, I don't have an "after dinner" chapter in the book, so here you go.

These toasts appeared as part of a Lenten dinner story, in which the writer, Juliet Corson, pointed out that otter is the ideal Lenten staple, but that in absence of "a tame otter running around" the home cook's backyard, he may instead dine on salmon, trout, eels, wild duck, and anchovies. I'll leave the main course up to you.

_____

4 slices day-old country bread
1 tablespoon anchovy paste
3 tablespoons unsalted butter, at room temperature
2 ounces Roquefort cheese, cut into thin slices

1. Toast the bread and let cool.
2. Mash together the anchovy paste and butter in a small bowl. Spread the butter on the toasts, and serve them with the cheese.

SERVES 4

SERVING SUGGESTIONS
Astoria Cocktail (p. 19), Gin Rickey (p. 21), and Singapore Sling (p. 23) have just enough oomph to stand up to these salty toasts. And to accompany: Onion Rings (p. 61), Salted and Deviled Almonds (p. 51).

MARCH 5, 1882: "HINTS FOR THE HOUSEHOLD: A BILL OF FARE FOR A LENTEN DINNER," BY JULIET CORSON.

—1882

SALTED AND DEVILED ALMONDS

In 1897, the _Times_ featured a review of two cookbooks, one by a well-known New York maître d', the other by a top chef—the equivalent of today's Sirio Maccioni and Eric Ripert. Oscar Tschirky, who first ran the dining room at Delmonico's and later the Waldorf Hotel, released *The Cook Book* (which contained this recipe) and Adolphe Gallier, the chef at the Majestic, published *The Majestic Family Cook Book*.

Neither became *Fannie Farmer*, but New York's center-of-the-universe attitude was already firmly in place—the food editor remarked, "There are no cooks, and there is no cooking anywhere in the world, so people of experience say, such as are to be found in New York." Paris may have disagreed, but no one in New York was listening.

————

2 tablespoons unsalted butter

1 cup whole almonds (skins on)

½ teaspoon cayenne pepper

½ teaspoon coarse and flaky sea salt

Heat the butter in a small saucepan until foamy. Add the almonds, then shake the pan and cook until the almonds are lightly toasted. Season with the cayenne and salt. Pour into a bowl.

MAKES 1 CUP, ENOUGH TO SERVE 4

VARIATIONS

I've also made these with olive oil in place of the butter, adding a large pinch of smoked paprika. Rather than cooking them on the stove, I toasted the nuts in a small casserole dish in a 350-degree oven.

SERVING SUGGESTIONS

Ramos Gin Fizz (p. 15), Singapore Sling (p. 23), Coconut Daiquiri (p. 25), Billionaire Cocktail (p. 40), Delft Blue Cocktail (p. 43), Sweet-and-Salty Popcorn with Orange Blossom Honey (p. 76), Cheese Straws (p. 79), Parmesan Crackers (p. 84), Anchovy Canapés (p. 51), Hot Cheese Olives (p. 83), Seasoned Olives (p. 90)

JANUARY 3, 1897: "WISDOM OF TWO CHEFS: OSCAR OF THE WALDORF AND GALLIER OF THE MAJESTIC TALK." RECIPE ADAPTED FROM OSCAR TSCHIRKY, THE MAÎTRE D'HÔTEL AT THE WALDORF-ASTORIA HOTEL IN NEW YORK CITY.

—1897

⌁ EGGS SUFFRAGETTE

Deviled eggs too tame for you? Eggs suffragette are the love child of deviled eggs and egg-and-anchovy canapés. A century ago, these eggs were considered "the novelty of the moment" at the Colony Club, the first New York social club created for women. But were the anchovy-laden eggs meant to be amusing or earnest?

Stuffed eggs are a cinch to make—you simmer the eggs, then mash the yolks with the seasonings and stuff the yolks back into the eggs. Keep in mind that egg yolks are more cooperative if mashed while warm, and that the recipe doesn't need any salt: the mayonnaise, mustard, and anchovy add plenty.

————

6 large eggs

3 tablespoons mayonnaise

2 tablespoons Dijon mustard

2 teaspoons anchovy paste

½ teaspoon sweet paprika, plus more for garnish

1. Set the eggs in a saucepan large enough to hold them in a single layer, cover with cold water, and place over high heat. Bring just to a boil, then reduce the heat and simmer for 8 minutes. Remove from the heat and run the eggs under cold water until cool enough to handle.

2. Peel and halve the eggs and remove the yolks. Mash the yolks in a wide shallow bowl with the back of a fork. Blend in the mayonnaise, mustard, anchovy paste, and paprika. Using the back of a spoon, press the mixture through a fine-mesh sieve into another bowl.

3. Spoon the yolk mixture into the whites—if you want them to have a peak, then use a pastry bag with a ¼-inch plain round tip to do this. Dust with additional paprika.

SERVES 6

SERVING SUGGESTIONS

Astoria Cocktail (p. 19), Nicky Finn (p. 19), Pâté Watch Hill Farm (p. 53), Parmesan Crackers (p. 84), Goat's-Milk Cheese, Buttered Brown Bread, and Salted Onion (p. 75)

APRIL 4, 1909: "WAYS OF COOKING EGGS: THE ART OF THE CHEF IS BENT ON INVENTING REAL NOVELTIES AT EASTER."

—1909

∽ PÂTÉ WATCH HILL FARM

This chicken liver and liverwurst pâté, served stuffed into celery stalks, with glasses of dry sherry, was the hors d'oeuvre for a press lunch hosted by the American Spice Trade Association at the Astor Hotel in New York City. Improbable as it seems, the trade association had already been around for forty-one years. The publicity push that year was to announce the return of spices that had been in short supply during World War II, such as black pepper, Hungarian paprika, poppy seeds, and cinnamon. The seasonings in this pâté—curry powder and paprika—are fairly mild. Taste as you go and add as much as you like.

———

2 tablespoons unsalted butter

½ pound chicken livers, trimmed and chopped

1 pound best-quality soft liver sausage, such as Braunschweiger liverwurst

1 cup heavy cream

9 ounces cream cheese

½ teaspoon curry powder

1 teaspoon paprika, plus more for garnish

3 tablespoons Worcestershire sauce

Salt and freshly ground black pepper

Celery stalks or rye bread for serving

1. Melt the butter in a medium sauté pan over medium heat. When it is bubbling, add the chicken livers and sauté until just cooked through. Puree in a food processor.

2. Skin the sausage, cut it into chunks, and add it to the livers in the food processor. Add the cream, cream cheese, curry powder, paprika, and Worcestershire and pulse until smooth. Season with salt and pepper.

3. Fill celery stalks with the pâté and add a dash of paprika to each for garnish. Or serve on rounds of toasted rye bread (or in sandwiches).

MAKES ABOUT 4 CUPS, ENOUGH TO SERVE 16

COOKING NOTES

If you like a coarser pâté, you can chop the livers and mash the rest of the ingredients into the livers by hand.

This makes a lot of pâté—you can halve the recipe.

SERVING SUGGESTIONS

Nicky Finn (p. 19), Eggs Suffragette (p. 52), Parmesan Crackers (p. 84)

MAY 7, 1947: "NEWS OF FOOD: LUNCHEON ENDS SPICE TRADE'S CONVENTION AND RESULTS IN SOME TIPS ON SEASONING," BY JANE NICKERSON. RECIPE ADAPTED FROM THE AMERICAN SPICE TRADE ASSOCIATION.

—1947

∽ EGGS LOUISIANA

If you crossed deviled eggs with croquettes, you'd get eggs Louisiana. To make them, you mash the yolks of hard-boiled eggs with blue cheese, grated onion, and parsley, then put the seasoned yolks back inside the whites, press the whites together, bread them, and send them for a dip in boiling oil. The frying gives the eggs a crisp, bubbled shell and warms the interior. They are meant to be served with tomato sauce and bread, but you can simply lift them from the oil and declare your work done. Pick up a napkin and an icy beer on your way to the porch.

———

6 large hard-boiled eggs, peeled

2 teaspoons grated onion

1 teaspoon chopped flat-leaf parsley

3 tablespoons crumbled blue cheese

Salt and freshly ground black pepper

1 large egg

1 tablespoon water

½ cup fine dry bread crumbs

Vegetable oil for deep-frying

3 cups warm tomato sauce, preferably homemade (p. 605)

Country bread for sopping up the sauce

1. Halve the hard-boiled eggs lengthwise and remove the yolks. Keep the pairs of whites together. Mash the yolks with the onion, parsley, and blue cheese. Season

with salt and pepper. Pile the mixture into the halved whites and press the halves firmly together. Chill.

2. Lightly beat the egg with the water in a small bowl. Spread the bread crumbs on a small plate. Roll the stuffed eggs in the beaten egg, then in the bread crumbs to coat. Set on a plate.

3. Heat 2 inches of vegetable oil in a medium deep saucepan over medium-high heat. When the oil is hot enough to brown a bread crumb in 30 seconds, it's ready. Carefully lower the eggs into the oil, one at a time, and fry, turning occasionally, until golden brown on all sides. Adjust the heat as needed.

4. Serve the eggs in a shallow pool of warm tomato sauce, with good country bread on the side.

SERVES 6

COOKING NOTE

As I made these eggs, I kept finding myself dreaming up other stuffings to add, like mustard and smoked paprika, or ricotta and thyme. Think of this recipe as a stepping stone to seasonings. And while you ponder the options, take a look at the recipe for Scotch Eggs on p. 62 for more fried eggs possibilities.

SERVING SUGGESTIONS

Vermouth Cup (p. 15), Vermouth Cassis (p. 16), Mint Julep (p. 24), The Cuke (p. 39), Pickled Shrimp (p. 95), Cheese Straws (p. 79)

JUNE 19, 1947: "NEWS OF FOOD: BOYS, 10 TO 14, LEARN COOKING AT THE RITZ: CITY OFFERS IDEAS ON BEATING MEAT PRICES," BY JANE NICKERSON. RECIPE ADAPTED FROM *90 TEMPTING WAYS TO PREPARE EGGS*, A COOKING PAMPHLET PUBLISHED BY THE CITY DEPARTMENT OF MARKETS.

—1947

⌒ AVOCADO SANDOWSKY

Jane Nickerson, a longtime food columnist for the *Times*, got the recipe for this pale, buttery avocado spread from Reah Sandowsky, a pianist with the New York Philharmonic. I was tempted to add lemon or lime juice to the spread, but it really doesn't need the acidity. We ate it on Triscuits, which I promise was a good choice.

1 ripe avocado, halved, pitted, and peeled
3 ounces cream cheese, at room temperature
1 teaspoon onion juice (see Cooking Notes)
1 tablespoon light cream
Salt
Salty wheat crackers or sturdy tortilla chips

Mash the avocado in a bowl with an electric mixer (preferably with a paddle attachment). Mix in the cheese, beating until smooth. Add the onion juice, cream, and salt, and mix until light. Serve with crackers or chips.

MAKES 1 TO 2 CUPS

COOKING NOTES

Midcentury cooks used onion juice the way we now use garlic. They added it to sauces, dressings, and dips to punch up the flavor. You make it by grating onion, putting the pulp into a sieve set over a bowl, and pressing on it with the back of a spoon to extract the juice.

Do not let this spread sit, or it will brown; serve within an hour. And let your guests put the spread on the crackers—if you do it in advance, the crackers will get soggy.

VARIATION

Top the spread with chopped cilantro or finely slivered preserved lemon (homemade, p. 610, or store-bought).

SERVING SUGGESTIONS

Vermouth Cup (p. 15), La Paloma (p. 35), Anchovy Canapés (p. 51), Egg and Olive Canapés (p. 57), Blue Cheese Dip (p. 54), Seasoned Olives (p. 90), The Best Spinach Dip, with Chipotle and Lime (p. 90), Smoked Mackerel on Toasts (p. 80)

APRIL 7, 1948: "NEWS OF FOOD: PIANIST SANDOWSKY'S CULINARY CAREER PROVES RESULT LARGELY OF NECESSITY," BY JANE NICKERSON. RECIPE ADAPTED FROM REAH SANDOWSKY.

—1948

⌒ BLUE CHEESE DIP

This is the quintessential dip, founded on cream cheese, enriched with a more flavorful cheese, splashed with booze, and seasoned with onion juice. What's not to love?

This recipe reminded me that dip is essentially a cheese ball with more liquid. See pp. 79 and 85 for this dip's extended family.

———

3 ounces cream cheese, at room temperature
1/4 pound blue cheese, at room temperature
I tablespoon unsalted butter, softened
Onion juice (see Cooking Notes, p. 54), to taste
Freshly ground black pepper
About 3 tablespoons heavy cream
About 3 tablespoons dry sherry
Crudités, such as sliced cucumbers, celery, carrots, and fennel, for serving

Beat together the cheeses and butter in a bowl with an electric mixer (preferably with a paddle attachment) until smooth and light. Season to taste with onion juice (1 to 2 teaspoons) and pepper, and thin with the cream and sherry. Serve with the sliced vegetables.

MAKES ABOUT I CUP

SERVING SUGGESTIONS
The Vesper (p. 34), Martini (p. 35), Junipero Gibson with Pickled Red Onion (p. 33), Seasoned Olives (p. 90), Hot Cheese Olives (p. 83), Onion Rings (p. 61)

PERIOD DETAIL
Jane Nickerson, a *Times* food editor, suggested serving the dip and crudités on a lazy Susan. For a mundane item, the lazy Susan has garnered plenty of lore. First advertised in 1917 in *Vanity Fair*, its invention has been attributed to everyone from Thomas Edison to Thomas Jefferson, and the name has been linked to Susan B. Anthony. And somehow, after a brief period of mainstream popularity in the mid-twentieth century, lazy Susans became a (revolving) fixture in Chinese restaurants.

MAY I, 1953: "FOOD NEWS: VEGETABLES FOR APPETIZERS," BY JANE NICKERSON.

—1953

CRAIG CLAIBORNE'S SWISS FONDUE

Before Craig Claiborne became the most famous food columnist in the history of the *Times*, he was a popular subject and source for other food writers at the paper. In a holiday story, Jane Nickerson—whom Claiborne would replace the following year—featured recipes from "four fine cooks" in New York, including Claiborne, whom she described as the "gentleman with the charming Mississippi accent." At the time, he worked for Seranne and Gaden, food consultants and photographers. (See Ann Seranne's Rib Roast of Beef on p. 519.)

"As you know," Claiborne explained, "the 'fondue procedure' is to let guests spear cubes of crusty bread on two-pronged forks, dip them into the melted cheese, and eat them while they are hot. This recipe is from a wonderful *carnozet* (fondue hideaway) near Lausanne."

———

I clove garlic
1 3/4 cups dry Swiss white wine, such as Fendant or Neuchâtel, or as needed
3/4 pound Gruyère cheese, grated
I tablespoon cornstarch
3 tablespoons kirsch
Freshly ground black pepper
6 cups cubed country bread

1. Rub the bottom and sides of a casserole or chafing dish with the garlic. Add the wine and heat just below the boiling point; do not let it boil. Add the cheese, stirring constantly with a wooden spoon. Blend the cornstarch and kirsch. When the fondue is creamy and barely simmering, add the cornstarch mixture and stir until it bubbles. Season with pepper.
2. Set the casserole over an alcohol burner with a slow flame. Keep the fondue hot but not simmering. If it becomes too thick, add a little more white wine.

SERVES 4

COOKING NOTES
Claiborne's fondue is quite a boozy affair; you can start with 1 1/4 cups wine and add more later if you want.

It's also thinner than most, which I liked because it drapes the bread with a wispy but pungent veil of cheese sauce.

If your mother didn't give you her old chafing dish or fondue pot simply bring the casserole hot to the table and set it on a trivet, then reheat the casserole when necessary.

SERVING SUGGESTIONS

To make a light meal of this, serve the fondue followed by Green Goddess Salad (p. 176) or Salade à la Romaine (p. 171). For a bigger meal, here are some ideas: Carbonnades à la Flamande (Flemish Beef and Onion Stew; p. 515), Boeuf Bourguignon I or II (p. 516), Dijon and Cognac Beef Stew (p. 560), or Arundel (Sausages in Ale; p. 511), with Poached Pears in Brandy and Red Wine (p. 832) or Toasts with Chocolate, Olive Oil, and Sea Salt (p. 844).

DECEMBER 16, 1956: "WHEN THE GUESTS LINGER ON," BY JANE NICKERSON. RECIPE ADAPTED FROM CRAIG CLAIBORNE.

—1956

⌒ STUFFED HARD-COOKED EGGS

Butter is the secret ingredient to great deviled eggs—it lightens up the yolks and tempers the anger of Tabasco (or cayenne, if that's what you prefer).

————

6 large eggs, at room temperature
2 tablespoons unsalted butter, softened
1 tablespoon mayonnaise
Salt and freshly ground black pepper
Tabasco sauce
6 anchovy fillets, drained and halved

1. Fill a small saucepan with water and bring to a boil. Reduce the water to a simmer and gently lower the eggs into the water. When the water returns to a boil, cook for 9 minutes. Immediately place the eggs under cold running water. This will cause a jacket of steam to form between the shells and hard-cooked whites and make the eggs easy to peel.
2. Crack the eggshells and remove, still under cold running water. Split the eggs lengthwise, in half then

into quarters if desired. Remove the yolks and reserve the whites.
3. Combine the yolks, butter, and mayonnaise in a bowl. Season with salt and pepper. Work with a fork to form a smooth, stiff paste. Add Tabasco sauce, making the yolks as spicy as you like, and blend well.
4. Using a spoon or fork, stuff the whites. Or, if desired, push the stuffing through a fluted pastry tube into the whites. Garnish with pieces of anchovy.

SERVES 4 TO 6

SERVING SUGGESTIONS

Beet Tzatziki (p. 89), Goat's-Milk Cheese, Buttered Brown Bread, and Salted Onion (p. 75), Hot Cheese Olives (p. 83)

NOVEMBER 25, 1957: "APPETIZERS TO PRECEDE THE THANKSGIVING FEAST," BY CRAIG CLAIBORNE.

—1957

⌒ CUCUMBER SANDWICHES

All you need for these sandwiches is a cucumber, a sweet onion, bread, and mayonnaise. This isn't a recipe, just an idea—one you shouldn't forget, especially when guests are arriving on short notice.

————

Trim the crusts from thin slices of sandwich bread and spread the bread with mayonnaise. Cover with wafer-thin slices of cucumber and Bermuda onion. Sprinkle with salt and freshly ground black pepper and cut into quarters. Or, using a small cookie cutter, cut into circles.

SERVES AS MANY AS YOU LIKE

SERVING SUGGESTIONS

Vermouth Cup (p. 15), Mint Julep (p. 24), Stuffed Hard-Cooked Eggs (p. 56), Pickled Shrimp (p. 95), Egg and Olive Canapés (p. 57), Seasoned Olives (p. 90)

MARCH 6, 1958: "MENUS FOR THE WEEK-END."

—1958

SHRIMP CANAPÉS À LA SUEDE

If you read the ingredient list, you won't think much of this hors d'oeuvre (and it is a quintessential 1950s hors d'oeuvre, so get out your doilies), but when all the components are right—the shrimp lightly cooked and at room temperature, the toasts crisp yet springy, the dill fragrant—the world is a happier place. Serve them for parties, of course, but a couple of these also make a respectable lunch.

———

18 medium shrimp, cooked, shelled, and deveined
12 toast rounds (about 2½ inches diameter)
Salted butter, softened
Mayonnaise
12 dill sprigs
Freshly ground black pepper
12 small lemon wedges

1. Slice the shrimp lengthwise in half.
2. Butter the toast rounds and arrange 3 shrimp halves in a spiral on each round.
3. Garnish the canapés with mayonnaise "stars" pressed from a pastry tube—or just dollop it on (a scant ½ teaspoon). Top with dill sprigs and season with pepper. Serve with the lemon wedges.

SERVES 4 TO 6

SERVING SUGGESTIONS
Park Avenue Cocktail (p. 19), The Vesper (p. 34), Martini (p. 35), Egg and Olive Canapés (p. 57), Seasoned Olives (p. 90), Salted and Deviled Almonds (p. 51), Blue Cheese Dip (p. 54), Olive Oil–Tuna Spread with Lemon and Oregano (p. 95)

JANUARY 8, 1959: "DINNER MENUS, RECIPES LISTED FOR THE WEEK-END."

—1959

EGG AND OLIVE CANAPÉS

Nothing says 1959 like a canapé. In French, a *canapé* is a couch, and in food, it's traditionally a thin and slightly stale piece of bread—a couch built to host salty and spicy foods. If you'd like to compare these

toasts—mounded with mashed egg salad and sliced olives—to a modern canapé, take a look at the Crostini with Eggplant and Pine Nut Puree on p. 78 and the Pan con Tomate on p. 91.

———

Salted butter
4 slices thinly sliced sandwich bread, such as
    Pepperidge Farm
2 large hard-boiled eggs, peeled
1 tablespoon mayonnaise, or more to taste
Salt
12 pimento-stuffed olives, cut crosswise into 3 slices each

1. Toast the bread, then butter and cut each into 4 rectangular pieces.
2. Mash the eggs with a fork and fold in the mayonnaise, adding more if desired. Season with salt. Spread a thin layer of the mashed egg on each toast, and top with 3 olive slices.

SERVES 4

SERVING SUGGESTIONS
If I had a lawn here in Brooklyn Heights, I'd whip these up and pass them around outside with glasses of Wine Lemonade (p. 17), Gin Rickey (p. 21), or Claret Cup (p. 12), and serve the Cheese Ball with Cumin, Mint, and Pistachios (p. 85) or Avocado Sandowsky (p. 54). But since I don't, I'd just have the party inside and screen *Mad Men*.

PERIOD DETAIL
In the column containing this recipe, Craig Claiborne featured more than two dozen canapés from the book *Buffet Catering* by Charles Finance, the chef at the Sheraton-Palace Hotel in San Francisco. At the end of the story, he suggested that anyone who wanted to buy the book simply send $12 to the publishing house. That doesn't work anymore.

JUNE 14, 1959: "GOOD TASTE ON TOAST," BY CRAIG CLAIBORNE. RECIPE ADAPTED FROM *BUFFET CATERING* BY CHARLES FINANCE.

—1959

FLORENTINE DIP

There is little, if anything, Florentine about this dip, but you will love it anyway.

———

3 ounces cream cheese, at room temperature

2 tablespoons anchovy paste

1 cup sour cream

¼ cup chopped flat-leaf parsley

3 tablespoons chopped chives

2 teaspoons chopped capers

1 tablespoon fresh lemon juice

½ clove garlic, minced

⅛ teaspoon salt

⅛ teaspoon freshly ground black pepper

Sliced vegetables and/or sturdy potato chips for serving

1. Using a wooden spoon, blend the cream cheese and anchovy paste in a medium bowl. Add the remaining ingredients and stir until well blended. Place in the refrigerator for several hours to season.

2. Spoon the dip into a bowl and serve with sliced vegetables or potato chips, or both.

MAKES ABOUT 1½ CUPS

SERVING SUGGESTIONS

Park Avenue Cocktail (p. 19), Sir Francis Drake (p. 36), Seasoned Olives (p. 90), Deep-Fried Soft-Shell Crabs (p. 398), Fresh Salmon and Lime Cakes (p. 420)

AUGUST 13, 1959: "SOUR CREAM CAN BE USED AS A BASE FOR EVERY COURSE," BY CRAIG CLAIBORNE.

—1959

BAGNA CAUDA

Nearly fifty years ago, just before Julia Child unleashed a torrent of whisk-intensive French dishes on a nation of canned-string-bean devotees and a decade before Marcella Hazan introduced us to northern Italian wonders like risotto and frittata, Craig Claiborne, the *Times*'s food editor, was ushering groundbreaking recipes into the paper at an astonishing rate. He wrote about lebkuchen, Chinese spareribs, navarin d'agneau, and even an obscure Piedmontese peasant staple called bagna cauda.

Bagna cauda, also spelled *bagna caôda*, means "hot bath." The bath—olive oil—is gently warmed with garlic cloves and anchovies until the oil is scented, the garlic is softened, the anchovies dissolved and tamed. Essentially it's Italian dip. The Piedmontese eat it with fennel, cardoons, peppers, and carrots. Claiborne suggested cauliflower, green pepper, and cucumber. You can use whatever you like.

Although the original dish was very simple—often thrown together, as Matt Kramer noted in his book *A Passion for Piedmont*, "as a morning snack for chilled-to-the-bone vineyard workers pruning the vines in midwinter"—it has since moved into the realm of the home and been spruced up. In Alba, you might find it with truffles. Sometimes it's made with milk or butter. Sometimes it's made with walnut oil. The sauce is sometimes served over a candle to keep it warm.

While many of the dishes that Claiborne championed have lived on for decades—David Eyre's pancake (p. 813), boeuf bourguignon (p. 516), and paella (p. 309), to name a few—his bagna cauda vanished into the archives. But so did Marcella Hazan's and Fred Plotkin's and Matt Kramer's. All of these wonderful writers, and none of them could get us to embrace this extraordinarily good, simple recipe? Some blame the longstanding dearth of quality anchovies, but because this is no longer an issue, it's time, no? My husband makes bagna cauda, and it has become a staple of our dinner parties because it's delicious, involves no anxiety, and encourages people to mingle around a bowl of warm, garlicky oil.

Get out your saucepan—or that little cazuela you bought in Europe that's been collecting dust. Assemble the olive oil, butter, garlic, and anchovies you already have in your kitchen. Then trim that overload of vegetables from your C.S.A., and make the dish.

You can play around with the butter-to-oil ratio. Claiborne, a Francophile at heart, made his more about butter than oil. Hazan, from Emilia-Romagna, includes butter but emphasizes the oil. Plotkin, a Liguria expert, favors all oil. (I prefer more oil to butter, because I find the butter conceals the flavors of the garlic and anchovy.) Kramer cares most about the anchovy. "If someone's going to make this dish and they're going to take any trouble at all," he wrote, "they should get salt-dried anchovies." These anchovies are broader, longer, and altogether a higher-quality fish.

---

8 tablespoons (1 stick) unsalted butter
¼ cup olive oil
6 cloves garlic, sliced tissue-thin
One 2-ounce can anchovy fillets, drained
Salt
Fresh vegetables, left whole or cut into small pieces
    or slices, for serving

1. Combine the butter and oil in a small saucepan and add the garlic. Cook over the lowest possible heat for about 15 minutes; do not let the mixture boil.
2. Chop the anchovies and add to the garlic-oil mixture. Stir until the anchovies dissolve; do not let the sauce boil or brown. Season with salt.
3. Meanwhile, prepare an assortment of raw vegetables, such as sliced cucumber, cauliflowerettes, strips of green pepper, celery, carrots, and leaves of endive.
4. Keep the sauce hot over a candle or spirit lamp. Serve the vegetables separately to dip into the sauce.

SERVES 10

COOKING NOTES
The sauce is timeless, but you may want to update the selection of vegetables you serve. I love bagna cauda with sliced fennel, radishes, roasted beets, and lightly blanched Romanesco broccoli.

If you stick to this ratio of butter to oil, you will need to add a fair amount of salt. Keep tasting.

SERVING SUGGESTIONS
Pork Braised in Milk and Cream (p. 557), Rigatoni with White Bolognese (p. 344), Chicken Canzanese (p. 458), Italian Beef Stew with Rosemary (p. 522), Coda alla Vaccinara (Oxtail Braised with Tomato and Celery; p. 562), Raspberry Granita (p. 719), Bolzano Apple Cake (p. 783)

PERIOD DETAIL
I left the line "Keep it hot over a candle or spirit lamp" in the recipe because it's a snapshot of a time when chafing dishes and double boilers were kitchen staples. If the recipe had been written in the 1970s, it might have called for a hot plate. Now, in the twenty-first century, I'd simply say, eat right away!

SEPTEMBER 4, 1960: "ANCHOVY COOKERY," BY CRAIG CLAIBORNE.

—1960

☞ CHINESE PORK BALLS

These are more "Chinese" pork balls than Chinese pork balls, but that doesn't mean they don't taste great.

Three 5- to 6-ounce cans water chestnuts, drained,
    rinsed, and finely chopped
1½ cups finely chopped scallions
3 pounds lean ground pork
2 teaspoons salt
1 tablespoon soy sauce
4 large eggs, lightly beaten
1½ cups fine dry bread crumbs
1 tablespoon finely chopped fresh ginger
Cornstarch for dusting
Oil for deep-frying

For the Sauce
1¾ cups unsweetened pineapple juice
1¼ cups cider vinegar
¼ cup soy sauce
⅔ cup sugar
1½ cups chicken broth
3 tablespoons finely chopped crystallized ginger
½ cup cornstarch
1 cup water

1. Place the water chestnuts, scallions, pork, salt, soy sauce, and eggs in a large bowl. Mix with your hands. Add the bread crumbs and ginger, with your hands, mix well. Chill the mixture for 1 hour.
2. Shape the pork mixture into ¾- to 1-inch balls. Roll the balls in cornstarch.
3. Heat 2 inches of oil to 370 degrees in a large pot or deep skillet. Carefully drop the balls into the oil one at a time, a dozen at one cooking, provided the oil does not foam up dangerously near the top of the pot (the

oil should not extend above the halfway mark). Fry the balls for about 1 to 2 minutes, or until they are golden brown and rise to the top of the oil. Break one open to make sure it is cooked though; there should be no pink color left. Drain on paper towels. Reheat the oil in between batches.

4. Meanwhile, to prepare the sauce, place the pineapple juice, vinegar, soy sauce, sugar, broth, and ginger in a saucepan and bring to a boil. Mix the cornstarch with the water and, using a wire whisk or a wooden spoon, stir into the boiling mixture. Cook, stirring, for 3 minutes. Then reduce the heat to very low or place over hot water to keep hot while you continue frying the meatballs.

5. Place the pork balls in a chafing dish and stir in enough sauce to coat them. (The balls, without the sauce, can be refrigerated overnight, covered with aluminum foil. To serve, heat the pork balls, covered, in a preheated oven for about 20 to 25 minutes. Reheat the sauce while stirring.)

MAKES ABOUT 12½ DOZEN PORK BALLS; SERVES 20 TO 25

SERVING SUGGESTIONS
Ginger Daiquiri (p. 36), Oriental Watercress Soup (p. 111), Takeout-Style Sesame Noodles (p. 355), Poached Pears with Asian Spices (p. 856)

PERIOD DETAIL
The original recipe called for "imported soy sauce."

JUNE 4, 1972: "TOPICAL MEATBALLS," BY JEAN HEWITT.
—1972

⌒ SHRIMP TOAST

No one seems to know for sure where shrimp toast—an oddball dish made by spreading Asian-flavored shrimp paste on Western sandwich bread and deep-frying it—came from. But according to Andrew Coe, a food scholar, it appears to be a cross between creamed chipped beef (see Delmonico Hash, p. 507), which is minced meat bound with cream or béchamel and spooned over toast, and Chinese fried shrimp balls. Coe deduced that the dish's likely birthplace was Shanghai, sometime between 1900 and 1945, when the city enjoyed a healthy population of Western businessmen. Shrimp toast didn't become popular here, however, until the 1960s, when American food writers grew enchanted with it.

Shrimp toast is typically made on white sandwich bread, but this version uses English muffins, an innovation that earned John J. McGuire, a New York City police officer, first prize in a Thomas' English muffin cooking contest. McGuire's tweaking of an otherwise classic shrimp toast is fantastic, and if you haven't had shrimp toast in, say, thirty years, it's time to revisit.

Don't make this recipe—or any requiring deep-frying—for a large party, or you'll spend the whole time over the stove.

––––––––

I large egg, lightly beaten
I tablespoon cornstarch
I teaspoon soy sauce
½ pound shrimp, shelled, deveined, and finely chopped
½ teaspoon sugar
4 Thomas' English muffins
Corn or canola oil for deep-frying
Salt if needed

1. Beat the egg with the cornstarch, soy sauce, and sugar in a medium bowl. Stir in the shrimp.

2. Split the muffins and toast only to lightly crisp; do not brown.

3. Heat 2 inches of oil to 360 degrees in a medium deep heavy saucepan. Meanwhile, spread the shrimp mixture on the rough side of the muffin halves. Cut each half into quarters.

4. Place the toasts a few at a time, shrimp side down, in the oil and fry until golden, about 1 minute. Turn and fry for about 30 seconds longer. Remove with a slotted spoon and drain on paper towels. Sprinkle with salt if desired. Serve immediately.

MAKES 32 TOASTS; SERVES 6 TO 8

COOKING NOTES
I tried some without toasting the muffins first, and preferred them this way, lightly toasted. They have a better mix of textures—crisp on the outside, tender inside—and for some reason, they taste more strongly of shrimp.

Some shrimp toasts of the period—they were a fixture of the 1960s and 1970s—contained scallion and ginger. If you like these flavors, add 1 tablespoon chopped scallion and 1 teaspoon grated ginger to the shrimp mixture.

SERVING SUGGESTIONS
Start with Ginger Daiquiri (p. 36) or The Cuke (p. 39), and follow with Chinese Barbecued Spareribs (p. 517), Takeout-Style Sesame Noodles (p. 355), Chinese Pork Balls (p. 59), Oriental Watercress Soup (p. 111), or Clams in Black Bean Sauce (p. 442).

FEBRUARY 17, 1973: "WHEN THE SERGEANT COOKS, LOCAL CHILDREN RUSH INTO HIS HOME," BY JEAN HEWITT. RECIPE ADAPTED FROM JOHN J. MCGUIRE, A POLICE OFFICER IN NEW YORK CITY.

—1973

ONION RINGS

These are not fried onions, but round onion tea sandwiches trimmed with parsley, a recipe popularized by James Beard. The recipe actually came from Bill Rhode, one of Beard's partners in a Manhattan catering business they opened in the 1930s. Rhode apparently first tasted the dainty onion sandwiches at a Paris bordello.

———

6 thin slices firm white bread, on the sweet side,
    or 12 slices challah
Approximately ½ cup mayonnaise
1 small yellow onion
Salt
Approximately ¾ cup very finely chopped flat-leaf parsley

1. With a 1½- or 2-inch cookie cutter, cut 4 rounds from each slice of white bread or 2 rounds from each challah slice. Arrange them in 12 pairs. Spread each round with mayonnaise.

2. Using a mandoline or a very sharp vegetable peeler, thinly slice the onion (you need 12 slices). Put 1 slice on a bread round, salt lightly, and top with a second round.

3. When all 12 are assembled, thinly spread some mayonnaise on a piece of wax paper, and have the chopped parsley ready in a bowl. Take each sandwich between thumb and forefinger and roll the edges first in the mayonnaise, then in the chopped parsley. Make sure there are no bare spots; if there are, dab a bit of mayonnaise on the spot and dip again in parsley. Place on a plate lined with wax paper and cover with wax paper. Chill well.

MAKES 12 FINGER SANDWICHES

COOKING NOTE
Craig Claiborne said, "If it is too hard to get very thin slices of onions perfectly round, part slices will do too; use two or more parts. The thinness is important." Pepperidge Farm very thin white works well.

SERVING SUGGESTIONS
Something gutsy like Ginger Lemonade (p. 26), James Beard's Champagne Punch (p. 28), Improved Holland Gin Cocktail (p. 39), The Vesper (p. 34), Astoria Cocktail (p. 19), or Sazerac (p. 17); a plain old Martini (p. 35) would also be swell. Then: Smoked Mackerel on Toasts (p. 80), Hot Cheese Olives (p. 83), Pickled Shrimp (p. 95), Russ & Daughters' Chopped Chicken Liver (p. 82), Anchovy Canapés (p. 51), Toasted Mushroom Rolls (p. 72).

JUNE 9, 1976: "ONION SANDWICHES: A MEMORABLE WHIMSY OF HUMBLE ORIGIN," BY CRAIG CLAIBORNE.

—1976

BLUE CHEESE CHEESECAKE

Somewhere between a cheese ball and quiche lives the humble but lovable blue cheese cheesecake. Make this for a large party and serve it with crackers or toasts and something pickled, like onions and radishes.

———

⅓ cup fine dry bread crumbs
¼ cup freshly grated Parmesan cheese
Three and a half 8-ounce packages (28 ounces)
    cream cheese, at room temperature
4 large eggs
⅓ cup heavy cream
½ pound bacon
1 medium onion, finely chopped

½ pound blue cheese, crumbled

Salt and freshly ground black pepper

4 to 6 drops Tabasco sauce

Crackers or toasts, for serving

1. Heat the oven to 300 degrees. Butter the inside of an 8-by-3-inch springform pan (if the pan does not close tightly, wrap the outside in foil). Sprinkle the inside with the combined bread crumbs and Parmesan cheese. Shake the crumbs around the bottom and sides until coated. Shake out the excess crumbs.

2. Place the cream cheese, eggs, and heavy cream in the bowl of an electric mixer and beat until thoroughly blended and quite smooth and fluffy.

3. Sauté the bacon until very crisp. Drain on paper towels; reserve the rendered fat. Finely chop the bacon and set aside.

4. Sauté the onion in 1 tablespoon of the bacon fat until wilted, 5 to 7 minutes.

5. Add the bacon, onion, crumbled blue cheese, and salt, pepper, and Tabasco sauce to taste to the basic mixture, blending thoroughly.

6. Pour the batter into the prepared pan and shake gently to level the mixture. Set the pan in a slightly larger pan and pour 2 inches of boiling water into the larger pan. Do not let the edges of the pans touch. Bake until the cheese cake springs back in the center when touched, about 1 hour and 25 minutes. Turn off the oven and let the cake sit in the oven for 15 minutes.

7. Lift the cake out of its water bath and place it on a rack to cool for at least 2 hours before unmolding.

8. Unlock the sides of the springform pan and remove. Place a round cake plate over the cake and carefully turn both upside down to unmold the cake. Or, take the easy way out and simply serve the cake on the springform pan base set on a platter.

SERVES 12 TO 20

SERVING SUGGESTIONS

Peppar Tomato (p. 31), Salade Niçoise (p. 178), Watercress Salad (p. 171)

DECEMBER 4, 1977: "FOOD: . . . SOMETHING COMPLETELY DIFFERENT," BY CRAIG CLAIBORNE WITH PIERRE FRANEY. RECIPE ADAPTED FROM LORA BRODY.

—1977

⌒ SCOTCH EGGS

Scotch eggs, a picnic snack of yore, are typically made by wrapping sausage meat around hard-boiled eggs, breading them, and deep-frying them. These Scotch eggs, a creation of Craig Claiborne and Pierre Franey, are made with ground pork seasoned with marjoram and parsley. Scotch eggs can be served warm or cold. As recipes from the British Isles go, most seeming to originate in the days of King Arthur, Scotch eggs are fairly modern; they didn't appear until the nineteenth century.

————

8 large eggs

I pound ground lean pork

¾ cup fine fresh bread crumbs, preferably made from English muffins

Salt and freshly ground black pepper

1½ teaspoons crushed dried marjoram

I tablespoon chopped flat-leaf parsley

2 tablespoons heavy cream

Flour for dredging

1½ cups fine fresh bread crumbs, made from trimmed day-old sandwich bread (about 8 slices)

Vegetable or canola oil for deep-frying (about 8 cups)

1. Place 6 of the eggs in a saucepan and add lukewarm water to cover. Bring to a boil and simmer for 8 minutes. Drain the eggs and immediately run them under cold water. Drain once more, peel, and set aside.

2. Lightly beat 1 of the remaining eggs. Combine the pork, English muffin bread crumbs, beaten egg, salt and pepper to taste, marjoram, parsley, and cream in a large bowl. Blend well with your hands.

3. Divide the pork mixture into 6 equal portions. Place one portion on a sheet of plastic wrap. Cover with another sheet of plastic wrap. Press down evenly and smooth the meat into a flat oval large enough to enclose 1 hard-cooked egg. Remove the top sheet of plastic wrap.

4. Dredge the hard-boiled eggs in flour, shaking off the excess. Place 1 egg in the center of the meat and bring up the edges of the plastic wrap to enclose the egg, pinching the seams together and pressing so that the egg is neatly and evenly enclosed in the meat. Remove the plastic wrap, and finish the shaping in your palms.

Continue until all the eggs are wrapped in the pork mixture.

5. Lightly beat the remaining egg in a rimmed dish. Dredge the wrapped eggs once more in flour and dip in the beaten egg, turning to coat evenly. Spread the bread crumbs made from sandwich bread on a plate. Dredge in the bread crumbs.

6. Heat 2 inches of oil in a deep skillet, it's ready when a bread crumb added to the oil browns in 30 seconds. Add the eggs (do in batches if needed) and cook for 4 to 5 minutes, turning often, until the meat is cooked though and the coating is golden brown—the bubbling will get louder and hollow-sounding as the eggs get closer to being done. Serve the eggs hot or lukewarm, sliced in half, with the mustard mayonnaise described in the Cooking Note below.

MAKES 6 SCOTCH EGGS, ENOUGH FOR 6 FOR LUNCH

COOKING NOTE

This recipe ran with a from-scratch mustard-mayonnaise accompaniment, but since you're already deep-frying, I thought having to also make mayonnaise might cause you to miss the point of the eggs themselves. They're the kind of thing you make instead of grilling burgers. So just get out your store-bought mayonnaise—Hellmann's or Miracle Whip, whichever camp you live in—and blend it with Dijon mustard and a little Worcestershire sauce and Tabasco. Start with a few tablespoonfuls of mayonnaise and add the condiments to taste, and you can't go wrong.

SERVING SUGGESTIONS

Claret Cup (p. 12), Wine Lemonade (p. 17), Olive Oil–Tuna Spread with Lemon and Oregano (p. 95), Brie with Herbs in Bread (p. 59), Mezzaluna Salad (p. 185), Sand Tarts (Pecan Sandies; p. 688)

PERIOD DETAIL

A recipe for Scotch eggs stuffed with pickled tongue ran in the *Times* in 1879.

JANUARY 22, 1978: "FOOD: A CANNY WAY WITH EGGS," BY CRAIG CLAIBORNE WITH PIERRE FRANEY.

—1978

⤚ MARINA ANAGNOSTOU'S SPANAKOPETES (SPINACH TRIANGLES)

Although many people recommended this recipe, it took me months to work up the enthusiasm to try it. Every spanakopete I'd ever had was a greasy, saggy, soggy blight on my respect for Greece. Clearly I hadn't been eating the right ones. In this spanakopete, which came from Marina Anagnostou, whose family owned the Poseidon Confectionery Company in Manhattan, the phyllo billows like a jib, protecting a bright dill and feta filling beneath.

---

1 pound fresh spinach in bulk or one 10-ounce package fresh spinach

1½ tablespoons olive oil

2 tablespoons unsalted butter

2 cups chopped onions

1 teaspoon finely chopped garlic

1 cup chopped scallions

1 cup crumbled or chopped feta cheese (about 4 ounces)

¼ cup freshly grated Parmesan cheese

¼ cup finely chopped dill

⅓ cup finely chopped flat-leaf parsley

1 large egg

1 large egg yolk

Salt and freshly ground black pepper

¼ cup pine nuts

12 sheets phyllo pastry

6 tablespoons unsalted butter, melted

1. Heat the oven to 350 degrees. If using spinach sold in bulk, discard any tough stems and blemished leaves, wash, and drain well. If using packaged, rinse once and drain. Coarsely chop the spinach.

2. Heat the oil in a large skillet over medium-high heat. Add the spinach and cook until wilted. Drain well in a colander (set the pan aside) and press with the back of a large spoon to push out excess moisture.

3. Melt the butter in the same skillet over medium heat and cook the onions, garlic, and scallions until wilted, stirring often. When the mixture starts to brown, transfer it to a mixing bowl. Let cool.

4. Add the spinach, feta, Parmesan cheese, dill, and parsley to the onion mixture. Beat the egg and yolk

together lightly and add to the spinach mixture. Add very little salt, and season with pepper. Stir in the pine nuts—be careful not to overmix, you want the ingredients to remain distinct.

5. Use 1 sheet of phyllo pastry for each 2 spinach triangles. Brush a smooth work surface (or sheet of plastic wrap) with melted butter. Spread out 1 sheet of phyllo and brush with butter. (Keep the rest of the phyllo covered with a slightly dampened cloth, or it will dry out.) Using a sharp knife, cut it lengthwise in half. Fold each rectangle lengthwise in half to make a smaller rectangle. Place 1½ tablespoons of the spinach mixture in the bottom of one of the rectangles. Fold one corner of the rectangle over the spinach filling to make a triangle. Fold this triangle over itself toward the top—as you would fold a flag—and continue folding up until triangle is produced. Brush this all over with butter and put on a baking sheet. Continue making triangles until all the spinach filling is used.

6. Bake the triangles for about 20 minutes, or until puffed and golden brown. Serve warm.

MAKES 16 TO 20 TRIANGLES

COOKING NOTE
You can also use baby spinach, in which case you don't need to chop it.

SERVING SUGGESTIONS
This is a great lead-up to Shrimp Baked with Feta Cheese, Greek-Style (p. 397), Salade à la Grecque (p. 179), Broiled Lamb Leg Chops on Eggplant Planks with Mint-Yogurt Sauce (p. 549), Lemon Lotus Ice Cream (p. 724), Hazelnut Baklava (p. 706).

MAY 17, 1978: "PHYLLO PASTRY: MIRACLE ON 9TH AVENUE," BY CRAIG CLAIBORNE. RECIPE ADAPTED FROM MARINA ANAGNOSTOU.

—1978

⌒ JULIA HARRISON ADAMS'S PIMENTO CHEESE SPREAD

To the untrained eye, pimento cheese spread looks woefully sloppy, like a hodgepodge of leftovers or a sterling example of WASP cuisine (perhaps the two are synonymous). But they eat pimento cheese by the bucketful in the South, and it's rare that Southerners go wrong with food.

The recipe calls for a meat grinder to mash the cheese, but the coarse side of a box grater works just fine and is easier to deal with. Make sure the cheeses are at room temperature so they mash up well, and don't skimp on the mayonnaise. If it's not slippery and goopy, it's not pimento cheese.

———

½ pound mild yellow cheddar or longhorn cheese
½ pound aged white sharp cheddar cheese, preferably Vermont or New York
One 7-ounce can pimentos, with their juice
1 cup chopped scallions
½ cup mayonnaise, preferably homemade (p. 465)
2 teaspoons fresh lemon juice
1 teaspoon minced garlic
1 tablespoon Worcestershire sauce, or more to taste
6 dashes Tabasco sauce, or more to taste
½ teaspoon freshly ground black pepper
Crackers or raw vegetables, for serving

1. Use a meat grinder or the coarse side of a box grater to grate the cheese; for a grinder, use the cutter with large holes. Put the ground or grated cheese in a mixing bowl and add half the juice from the canned pimentos. Dice the pimentos and add them. Add the chopped scallions.

2. Combine the mayonnaise, lemon juice, and garlic. Add this to the cheese mixture. Add the Worcestershire, Tabasco, and black pepper and blend well; taste and adjust the seasoning.

3. Serve at room temperature as a spread for crisp crackers and raw vegetables or use as a sandwich spread. (Pimento cheese can be tightly sealed and kept for several days in the refrigerator.)

MAKES ABOUT 6 CUPS; SERVES 8 TO 12

SERVING SUGGESTIONS
There's no better cracker than a Triscuit, and it's particularly apt here. To go with: The Bone (p. 34), Mint Julep (p. 24), Wine Lemonade (p. 17), Pan-Barbecued Shrimp (p. 402), Shrimp Creole (p. 397), Crab Cakes Baltimore-Style (p. 407), Paul Prudhomme's Cajun-Style Gumbo (p. 125).

"Recipes from the *Times* have been my cooking class for many years, no matter where I lived. Especially valuable to me were the recipes of the '70s & '80s because we had just purchased a weekend cottage upstate in Columbia County, and I did need HELP. . . . On July 4, 1974, another full-page article, enclosed, came to my rescue—picnic recipes. One from that article is still a family favorite: Julia Harrison Adams's Pimento Cheese Spread."

Jeanne Y. Miles, Santa Fe, NM, letter

JULY 4, 1979: "TANGLEWOOD: A PICNIC AMONG THE MAS-TERS: SOME PICNIC HAMPER FAVORITES FOR A BANQUET ALFRESCO," BY CRAIG CLAIBORNE. RECIPE ADAPTED FROM JULIA HARRISON ADAMS.

—1979

RILLETTES DE CANARD (DUCK RILLETTES)

Rillettes can be made with almost any kind of meat or fish. Although they are similar to pâté and to potted meat, an English standard containing nuggets and dabs of meat (see Potted Salmon, p. 388), rillettes differ in that you slow-cook the meat in fat and then rake it with a fork or spoon as it cools, breaking it down into fine, delicate threads until the mixture is so smooth it's spreadable. Serve with hard rolls or buttered toast.

_____

2 ducks (4 to 5 pounds each)
Salt
1 medium onion, cut into quarters
1 bay leaf
1 clove garlic
2 cups dry white wine
Freshly ground black pepper
Melted lard

1. Quarter the ducks: Cut out the backbones with poultry shears, then quarter. Save all the scraps of fat, the necks, gizzards, and backbones. Carefully trim all the peripheral fat from each quarter. Add this and the other scraps of fat to a large wide casserole or Dutch oven and cook over low heat, without browning, until the fat is rendered.

2. Season the duck pieces with salt. Add the pieces of duck, skin side down, to the pot, then add the backbones, gizzards, and necks, and raise the heat to medium-low. As the pieces brown, stir and turn them. When they are lightly browned, add the onion, bay leaf, garlic, and wine. Cover and cook over low heat until the duck is very tender, about 3 hours.

3. Remove the pot from the heat and transfer the duck to a plate. Strain the fat into a large bowl, preferably stainless steel; set aside. Remove the meat and skin from the bones. Shred the meat with your fingers. Chop the skin, if desired. Discard the bones.

4. Add the skin (if using) and meat to the duck fat. Add salt and pepper to taste. (Rillettes are improved with a considerable quantity of black pepper.) Stir briskly with a wooden spoon, then chill the rillettes in the freezer for about 30 minutes; do not let the dish freeze. Stir and rake the rillettes until very stiff. Repeat until the rillettes are finely shredded.

5. Spoon the rillettes into earthenware crocks. Cover with melted lard and refrigerate until ready to use; the lard keeps the air out. (Rillettes will keep, refrigerated, for up to 2 weeks.) Scrape off and discard the lard before serving.

MAKES ABOUT 10 CUPS

COOKING NOTES

If your pan isn't large enough, you may need to brown the duck in batches. You could also use a small roasting pan for browning the duck, as long as the burners on your stove are large enough to heat it evenly; then transfer the browned pieces to a Dutch oven or casserole.

Step 3 is the most fun, because you get to remove the meat from the duck bones and shred it with your fingers. This step also instructs you to chop up and add the skin. I didn't do this—my duck skin was rubbery and I thought it would take away from the silky meat.

Step 4 is the most crucial. It will seem strange to alternate freezing and stirring the duck mixture, but this technique is what creates the fine texture of the rillettes. As the duck chills, the fat hardens the mixture, and as you stir, this tension helps shred the meat more finely. You'll need to stir the mixture a few times over the course of 3 to 4 hours, then you can transfer the rillettes to the fridge.

Oh, and do be generous with the pepper. Rillettes are extremely rich, and you need the heat and spice of pepper to counteract the fat!

This is enough for a large party, and then some. You can easily halve or quarter the recipe for smaller get-togethers.

SERVING SUGGESTIONS

Nicky Finn (p. 19), James Beard's Champagne Punch (p. 28), Holiday Punch (p. 32), Grapefruit Wine (p. 37), Fennel, Orange, Watercress, and Walnut Salad (p. 186), Diana Vreeland's Salade Parisienne (p. 192), Steak au Poivre (p. 573), Filet de Boeuf Rôti (Roast Fillet of Beef) with Sauce Bordelaise (p. 528), Fricassee of Chicken with Tarragon (p. 456), Rabbit in Mustard Sauce (p. 466), Tarte aux Fruits (p. 829), Apple Galette (p. 843), Judson Grill's Berry Clafoutis with Crème Fraîche (p. 844), Chocolate Mousse (p. 820), Almond Cake (p. 777)

PERIOD DETAIL

This recipe was one of eight suggested by *Times* readers as good holiday gifts. When was the last time you received a pot of rillettes?

DECEMBER 12, 1979: "RECIPES FOR A CHRISTMAS FROM THE KITCHEN," BY CRAIG CLAIBORNE.

—1979

∽ BEEF SATAY WITH PEANUT SAUCE

The peanut sauce here is a beauty—smooth as lacquer, with a flavor that rambles from chiles to peanuts to ginger.

———

For the Peanut Sauce

1 tablespoon corn, peanut, or vegetable oil
1 teaspoon minced garlic
1 tablespoon finely chopped onion
½ teaspoon crushed red pepper flakes
1 tablespoon grated fresh ginger
¼ teaspoon shrimp paste

3 tablespoons tamarind syrup
1½ tablespoons sugar
1 cup crunchy or smooth peanut butter
2 tablespoons fresh lime or lemon juice
Salt
1¼ cups boiling water

For the Satay

1 pound flank steak
Three 2-inch pieces lemongrass, finely chopped, or one 2-inch strip lemon zest
½ cup finely chopped onion
2 tablespoons ketjap manis (see Cooking Notes)
2 tablespoons corn, peanut, or vegetable oil
½ teaspoon shrimp paste
¼ teaspoon ground cumin
½ teaspoon ground coriander
½ teaspoon turmeric
Salt
½ teaspoon sugar

8 wooden skewers

1. To make the peanut sauce, heat the oil in a medium saucepan over medium-low heat. Add the garlic and onion and cook, stirring, until wilted. Add the pepper flakes, ginger, shrimp paste, tamarind syrup, sugar, peanut butter, lime juice, and salt to taste, then add the boiling water, whisking rapidly. When blended, remove the sauce from the heat. If it starts to curdle, add a little more water.

2. To make the satay, cut the steak into 1-inch cubes and put them in a bowl.

3. Put the lemongrass, onion, ketjap manis, oil, shrimp paste, cumin, coriander, turmeric, salt to taste, and sugar in a food processor or a blender and puree to a fine paste. Pour this over the meat and blend well. Let stand for 1 hour.

4. Meanwhile, light a charcoal or gas grill. Soak the wooden skewers in water.

5. Thread equal portions of the meat onto each skewer. Place the meat on the grill and cook for about 2 minutes. Turn and cook for about 2 minutes on the second side, until browned on the tips. Serve with the peanut sauce (which you may need to re-emulsify by whisking).

SERVES 4

Craig Claiborne and Pierre Franey, who wrote about this satay, said that if you can't find ketjap manis, a thick, dark, sweet Indonesia condiment (often containing star anise, garlic, and palm sugar), you can substitute "a dark soy sauce, blended with an equal volume of sugar, a touch of water, and a couple of crushed garlic cloves."

The beef needs to be grilled because you want it to caramelize and char a bit. In this case, a broiler is not a good alternative—you won't get a good crust on the meat.

SERVING SUGGESTIONS

Kaffir Lime Lemonade (p. 26), Zombie Punch (p. 41), Malaysian-Inspired Pork Stew with Traditional Garnishes (p. 552), Pork-and-Toasted-Rice-Powder Spring Rolls (p. 74), Green Beans with Coriander-Coconut Crust (p. 246), Basmati Rice with Coconut Milk and Ginger (p. 339)

AUGUST 28, 1983: "FOOD: AN INDONESIAN TREAT," BY CRAIG CLAIBORNE WITH PIERRE FRANEY.

—1983

⌒ SAUCISSON SOÛL

This dish lives in the fiefdom of pigs-in-a-blanket—it's sliced kielbasa in a sweet mustardy glaze. The saucisson serves six at a civilized party with other hors d'oeuvres. At my house, a recipe testing factory, it lasted for six minutes.

———

½ kielbasa (about 12 ounces)
¾ cup dry white wine, or as needed
1 scant teaspoon sugar (optional)
1½ tablespoons Dijon mustard, more to taste
1 tablespoon chopped flat-leaf parsley

1. Cut the kielbasa into 1-inch-thick slices and then into quarters. Put in a heavy skillet large enough to hold all the pieces in one layer and add wine to cover. Bring to a boil and boil rapidly until the wine has almost evaporated and looks syrupy—a scant teaspoon of sugar added here makes a nice glaze. Add the mustard to taste.

2. Toss the kielbasa with the parsley and serve hot or at room temperature with toothpicks.

SERVES 6

COOKING NOTE

I needed 1½ cups wine to cover the kielbasa.

SERVING SUGGESTIONS

These are fine alone, but they can also be accompanied by Hot Cheese Olives (p. 83), Toasted Mushroom Rolls (p. 72), Onion Rings (p. 61), or Blue Cheese Dip (p. 54).

OCTOBER 23, 1983: "TAILGATE FEASTS," BY BRYAN MILLER.

—1983

⌒ GUACAMOLE TOSTADAS

Think of this as the Tex-Mex version of a layered terrine—a foundation of beans supports levels of avocado, cumin-scented sour cream, tomatoes, scallions, olives, cheddar, and coriander. Tortilla chips are the toast points. Happy excavating!

———

1 cup dried pinto beans, rinsed and picked over
½ cup chopped onion
1 large clove garlic, pressed or minced
1½ teaspoons ground cumin
Salt
2½ tablespoons mild pure chile powder
1 tablespoon white vinegar
4 tablespoons unsalted butter, softened
4½ tablespoons tomato paste
¼ teaspoon ground coriander
8 drops of hot pepper sauce
Freshly ground black pepper
2 ripe avocados
2 tablespoons fresh lemon juice
1 cup sour cream
2 large tomatoes, chopped
¾ cup chopped scallions
1 cup chopped pitted black olives
2 cups coarsely grated sharp white cheddar cheese
⅔ cup coarsely chopped cilantro
Good-quality tortilla chips

1. To prepare the beans, either cover with water in a bowl and soak overnight, or cover with water in a saucepan and bring to a boil; boil for 2 minutes, then allow to stand for 1 hour.

2. Drain the beans and transfer to a medium saucepan. Cover the beans with fresh water, cover the pan and bring to a boil. Add the onion, the garlic, ½ teaspoon cumin, and ¼ teaspoon salt. Cover, reduce the heat, and simmer until the beans are tender, about 1 hour. Drain.

3. Place the beans in a food processor with ¾ teaspoon salt and ¾ teaspoon cumin, 1½ tablespoons chile powder, the vinegar, butter, tomato paste, coriander, and hot pepper sauce. Process until smooth. Adjust the seasoning, adding salt and pepper if desired.

4. Peel and pit the avocados and coarsely mash with the lemon juice, and salt and pepper to taste.

5. Mix the sour cream with the remaining 1 tablespoon chile powder and ¼ teaspoon cumin.

6. To serve, spread the bean mixture in a shallow serving dish. Top with the mashed avocados, then with the sour cream mixture. Scatter the tomatoes evenly over the sour cream, sprinkle on the scallions, olives, and cheese, and top with the cilantro. Serve with tortilla chips.

SERVES 16

COOKING NOTES

For the hot pepper sauce, I began with Tabasco but, finding it too mild, switched to Sriracha (Thai hot sauce).

Marian Burros, the *Times* columnist who wrote this story, noted that "the beans may be cooked a day or two ahead and mixed with seasonings. Remaining ingredients, with the exception of the avocado, may be prepared early on the day of the party."

SERVING SUGGESTIONS

Moscow Mule (p. 20), Classic Rum Punch (p. 24), La Paloma (p. 35), Tortilla Soup (p. 131), Yucatán Fish with Crisp Garlic (p. 431), Moroccan Chicken Smothered in Olives (p. 482), El Parian's Carne Asada (Grilled Beef; p. 581), Black Bean Soup with Salsa and Jalapeño Corn-Bread Muffins (p. 129), Maida Heatter's Cuban Black Beans and Rice (p. 281), Nueces Canyon Cabrito (Goat Tacos; p. 576)

MAY 25, 1985: "MEXICAN TREAT FOR HOLIDAYS," BY MARIAN BURROS.

—1985

HUMMUS BI TAHINI

Hummus takes much more salt than you think—keep tasting it until it's right. And please, please, please use the very best olive oil you have. If you don't have great olive oil, go buy some. It's an essential counterpoint to the chickpea puree.

———

1¾ cups freshly cooked or canned chickpeas
5 tablespoons chicken broth (see Cooking Note)
¾ cup tahini (sesame paste)
½ to ¾ cup fresh lemon juice
Salt if needed
2 tablespoons minced garlic
2 tablespoons chopped flat-leaf parsley
1½ tablespoons olive oil
Pita for serving

1. Put the chickpeas in a food processor or blender, and add the broth, tahini, and lemon juice to taste. Blend until smooth. Add salt if needed. Add the garlic and pulse to mix.

2. Spoon the hummus into a wide shallow serving dish. Sprinkle with the parsley and drizzle with the olive oil. Serve with pita.

SERVES 6

COOKING NOTE

Claiborne and Franey wrote, "If the chickpeas are freshly cooked, use ¼ cup of the cooking liquid as a substitute for the chicken broth. To cook dried chickpeas, use ⅓ cup of dried peas to produce 1 cup of cooked. Soak the chickpeas overnight in cold water to cover. Drain and add fresh water to cover to a depth of 1 inch. Add salt to taste if desired. Bring to the boil and cook about 3 hours, or until tender, adding more boiling water as necessary."

SERVING SUGGESTIONS

I like hummus with other small dishes like Beet Tzatziki (p. 89) and Seasoned Olives (p. 90). To round out the meal, try: Iraqi Grape Leaves Stuffed with Lamb, Mint, and Cinnamon (p. 510), Arnaki Araka (Lamb with Peas; p. 550), Spicy Orange Salad Moroccan-Style (p. 181), Pepper-Cumin Cookies (p. 695), Honey Spice Cookies (p. 685), Pine Nut Cookies (p. 689).

PERIOD DETAIL

Craig Claiborne and Pierre Franey, the authors of the story, noted, "It is perhaps a commonplace to say that the American kitchen has become the most adventure-filled room in the house during the last decade." (Focused on the culinary revolution, they seem to have missed the sexual revolution.) "If you look in the pantry and refrigerator now," they explained, "you are apt to discover herbs, spices, and other flavors that were all but unheard of in most American homes ten years ago. These might include fresh or bottled jalapeño peppers; fresh coriander leaves; radicchio and arugula lettuces; a spate of oils, mustards, and vinegars in various flavors; an abundance of sophisticated cheeses; and so on."

JUNE 9, 1985: "FOOD: SESAME PASTE," BY CRAIG CLAIBORNE WITH PIERRE FRANEY.

—1985

☞ BRIE WITH HERBS IN BREAD

An abundantly filled pressed sandwich. I believe that the best sandwiches owe their success as much to design as to ingredients, and this one conveniently proves my theory: the pressing unifies the texture and flavors and the order of layering is designed to moisten the interior while leaving the exterior firm and crisp. It is meant to be served as an hors d'oeuvre, but you're welcome to eat it as a sandwich.

I baguette (about 10 ounces)

¼ cup olive oil

3 tablespoons dry white wine

I teaspoon coarsely ground black pepper

2 cloves garlic, finely chopped (about I teaspoon)

One 10-ounce piece ripe Brie cheese

3 tablespoons chopped chives

I cup coarsely shredded basil leaves

I½ cups loosely packed coarsely shredded sorrel (other herbs or greens can be used instead, such as watercress and arugula)

1. Halve the baguette lengthwise. Sprinkle the cut surface of each half with the oil, wine, pepper, and garlic, dividing the ingredients evenly.
2. Trim the Brie to remove any rind and cut into long ¼-inch-thick slices. Spread half the herbs on the bottom half of the loaf and arrange the cheese slices on top of the herbs. Spread the remaining herbs on top of the Brie and place the top half of the bread on top to re-form the loaf. Press firmly together. Cut the sandwich in half. Roll each half as tightly as possible in plastic wrap and then in aluminum foil. (Tightly wrapping the sandwich makes the bread absorb the juices better.)
3. Put the sandwich on a baking sheet, top with another baking sheet, and refrigerate with 3 to 5 pounds of weight (a couple of cans or jars, perhaps) on top for 4 to 5 hours.
4. Cut the sandwich into slices to serve. It can be eaten cold or lukewarm.

SERVES 6

SERVING SUGGESTIONS

Place a teaspoon (or so) of Limoncello (p. 38) in a Champagne glass and fill with prosecco; or think about Grapefruit Wine (p. 37). Also, Scotch Eggs (p. 62), Stuffed Hard-Cooked Eggs (p. 56), Tom's Chilled Cucumber Soup (p. 117), A Loose Interpretation of Cobb Salad (p. 193), Salade Niçoise (p. 178), Brownies (p. 684), Lemon Bars (p. 690), Flat-and-Chewy Chocolate Chip Cookies (p. 706).

SEPTEMBER 4, 1988: "FOOD: THE LAST PICNIC SHOW," BY JACQUES PÉPIN.

—1988

☞ SOPHIE GRIGSON'S PARMESAN CAKE

You will notice that many of the recipes in the book have someone's name in the title (see, for instance, Lucas Schoormans's Lemon Tart on p. 857, David Eyre's Pancake on p. 813, and Kathleen Claiborne's

Hot Cakes on p. 633). People's names usually become attached to a recipe in one of two ways—either the person who created the recipe knew it was great and wanted to be sure no one else took credit, or, more often, a beneficiary of the recipe added it as a gesture of affection. In either case, it's usually a signal of something good to come—as it is here.

Grigson suggests serving it with hors d'oeuvres, which would be lovely (think of it as a cheese straw in cake form). I used it to accompany Braised Stuffed Breast of Veal (p. 558), which is eaten cold. You could also treat it like Yorkshire pudding and serve it warm with roast beef, to soak up the juices.

---

1 cup all-purpose flour

1½ teaspoons baking powder

½ teaspoon salt

2 ounces Parmesan cheese, finely grated

¼ cup semolina flour

Freshly ground black pepper

6 tablespoons unsalted butter, melted and cooled

3 large eggs, separated

¾ cup whole milk

1. Heat the oven to 375 degrees. Grease an 8-inch round cake pan. Sift the all-purpose flour, baking powder, and salt into a bowl. Add the Parmesan cheese, semolina, and pepper to taste, mixing well.
2. Make a well in the center of the dry ingredients. Pour in the butter, egg yolks, and milk and mix vigorously.
3. Beat the egg whites until stiff, and fold them into the batter.
4. Spoon into the cake pan and bake for 25 to 30 minutes, until firm to the touch and browned. Serve cut into 4 to 6 pieces as an hors d'oeuvre, or as a bread with stews to mop up the sauce, or merely toasted.

SERVES 4 TO 6

COOKING NOTE

For the Parmesan, use a Microplane grater if you have one; it produces featherweight cheese strands, which melt completely in the cake batter so you don't end up with leaden pockets of cheese.

SERVING SUGGESTIONS

Eat this cut into thin slices as an accompaniment to cocktails, such as Kumquat-Clementine Cordial (p. 42) or Vermouth Cassis (p. 16), or make thicker slices and use them to soak up the gravy in Boeuf Bourguignon I (p. 516).

APRIL 30, 1989: "FOOD: ALL IN THE FAMILY: CHILDREN WHO FOLLOW IN THE CULINARY FOOTSTEPS OF THEIR FAMOUS PARENTS," BY JOAN NATHAN. RECIPE ADAPTED FROM SOPHIE GRIGSON.

—1989

CUCUMBER–GOAT CHEESE DIP WITH RADISHES AND SCALLIONS

While this recipe is called a dip, it can also be used as a salad dressing for a sturdy green like romaine. If making dip, add less cucumber juice (¼ cup); if making a dressing, add more. Either way, you'll probably have leftover juice—a perfect excuse to try the Cucumber Risotto with Yellow Peppers and Herbs on p. 331.

---

2 large cucumbers, peeled, plus 1 medium cucumber, peeled, halved lengthwise, seeded, and cut into small dice

6 ounces reduced-fat or regular goat cheese, at room temperature

8 radishes, trimmed and cut into small dice

2 scallions, green parts only, thinly sliced

1 tablespoon chopped mint

1 teaspoon salt

Freshly ground black pepper

Raw vegetables, for dipping

1. Pass the 2 large cucumbers through a juice extractor into a bowl, or coarsely chop, then puree in a food processor. Skim off the foam. (If using a food processor, strain through a fine-mesh sieve.)
2. Place the goat cheese in a medium bowl. Gradually whisk in ¼ cup cucumber juice until smooth; add more as desired. Stir in the diced cucumber, radishes, scallions, and mint. Season with the salt and pepper to taste. Cover and refrigerate until cold.

MAKES ABOUT 2 CUPS

SERVING SUGGESTIONS
Mint Julep (p. 24), Ginger Daiquiri (p. 36), Egg and Olive Canapés (p. 57), Stuffed Hard-Cooked Eggs (p. 56), Seasoned Olives (p. 90), Crostini with Eggplant and Pine Nut Puree (p. 78)

JUNE 20, 1993: "FOOD: ADD AND EXTRACT," BY MOLLY O'NEILL.

—1993

⌇ GRILLED ONION GUACAMOLE

I'm not a big fan of tarting up classic dishes, but chef Dean Fearing's guacamole is an exception. The grilled onions add sweetness and smoke, and there's just the right balance of heat, acid, and cilantro.

———

2 tablespoons vegetable oil

2 tablespoons fresh lemon juice

1 tablespoon red wine vinegar

1 teaspoon ground cumin

¾ teaspoon salt, plus more to taste

1 teaspoon cracked black pepper

1 large red onion, cut into ¼-inch-thick slices

3 avocados

1 large tomato

2 cloves garlic, minced

2 serrano chiles, chopped

3 tablespoons chopped cilantro

Fresh lime juice

Tortilla chips, for serving

1. Combine the oil, lemon juice, vinegar, cumin, salt, and pepper in a small bowl. Pour into a shallow dish, add the onion, and let marinate for 1 hour.

2. Heat a charcoal or gas grill until hot (or heat the broiler, with the rack 6 to 8 inches from the flame).

3. Drain the onion and place on the grill (or on the broiler pan, under the broiler). Grill for 3 minutes per side (4 minutes per side if broiling). Let cool slightly, then coarsely chop, discarding any bits that have charred.

4. Peel, halve, and pit the avocados, and cut into ½-inch dice. Dice the tomato.

5. Combine the grilled onion, avocado, tomato, garlic, chiles, and cilantro in a bowl, mashing the avocados slightly as you go. Season with salt and lime juice. Keep at room temperature, and serve within 30 minutes.

SERVES 4 TO 6

SERVING SUGGESTIONS
La Paloma (p. 35), Yucatán Fish with Crisp Garlic (p. 431), Moroccan Chicken Smothered in Olives (p. 482), Black Bean Soup with Salsa and Jalapeño Corn-Bread Muffins (p. 129), Maida Heatter's Cuban Black Beans and Rice (p. 281), Tortilla Soup (p. 131), Nueces Canyon Cabrito (Goat Tacos; p. 576), Rosa de la Garza's Dry Chili (p. 521)

JULY 4, 1993: "FOOD: THE TEXAS THREE-STEP," BY MOLLY O'NEILL. RECIPE ADAPTED FROM DEAN FEARING, THE CHEF AND OWNER OF THE MANSION ON TURTLE CREEK IN DALLAS.

—1993

⌇ FETA SPREAD

The Greek name for this fiery red pepper and feta spread is *htipiti*, which means "beaten," a possible reference to the way it is made, according to Aglaia Kremezi, the cookbook author whose recipe this is. Her version is done in a food processor, but if you own a mortar and pestle and are looking for a way to kill time, by all means have at it.

I used the red pepper flakes instead of a fresh chile, and the heat—which can make or break a dish like this—was palpable but not overbearing. I served the spread with a platter of zucchini and cucumber sliced just thick enough to hold it, about ⅛ inch.

———

2½ tablespoons olive oil

1 Thai chile, seeded and minced, or ½ teaspoon crushed red pepper flakes

1 clove garlic, minced

1½ cups crumbled soft feta cheese (about 6 ounces)

2 roasted red bell peppers, peeled, cored, seeded, and coarsely chopped

1. Heat the oil in a small skillet over medium heat. Add the chile and cook for 1 minute. Stir in the garlic and remove from the heat. Let cool for 3 minutes.

2. Place the feta and red peppers in a food processor and process until smooth. Add the chile-oil mixture and process until well combined. Scrape the spread into a bowl and serve.

MAKES ABOUT 1½ CUPS

COOKING NOTE

The darker you roast the peppers, the smokier you'll make the dip.

SERVING SUGGESTIONS

Moussaka (p. 518), Broiled Lamb Leg Chops on Eggplant Planks with Mint-Yogurt Sauce (p. 549), Shrimp Baked with Feta Cheese, Greek-Style (p. 397), Sea Scallops with Sweet Red Peppers and Zucchini (p. 409), Cantaloupe–Star Anise Sorbet (p. 728), Honey Spice Cookies (p. 685)

APRIL 3, 1994: "FOOD: GREEK REVIVALISM," BY MOLLY O'NEILL. RECIPE ADAPTED FROM *THE FOODS OF GREECE* BY AGLAIA KREMEZI.

—1994

∽ TOASTED MUSHROOM ROLLS

A friend of mine described these rolls as "stuffing you can hold." They are, essentially, old-school duxelles—minced and sautéed mushrooms—and béchamel rolled up in toast. I made them with plain old white mushrooms, but feel free to upgrade to more potent varieties like shiitake or morels.

4 tablespoons unsalted butter, plus melted butter for brushing the rolls
½ pound white mushrooms or more exotic mushrooms, like portobello, cremini, shiitake, or morels, or some combination, trimmed and finely chopped
3 tablespoons all-purpose flour
1 cup light cream or half-and-half
1 tablespoon minced chives
1 teaspoon fresh lemon juice

Salt and freshly ground black pepper
20 slices white sandwich bread (like Pepperidge Farm)

1. Melt the butter in a medium skillet over medium-high heat. Add the mushrooms and sauté them until softened, 3 to 4 minutes. Remove from the heat and blend in the flour. Stir in the cream, return to medium heat and cook, stirring, until the mixture thickens. Remove from the heat. Stir in the chives and lemon juice, season with salt and pepper and let cool.

2. Remove the crusts from the bread. Roll each slice with a rolling pin until flat and thin. Spread each slice with some of the mushroom mixture, roll up, and place seam side down on a baking sheet. Brush with additional melted butter. Refrigerate, or pack and freeze if desired (see Cooking Note).

3. To serve, heat the oven to 400 degrees, defrost the rolls if they have been frozen. Bake the rolls, turning occasionally, for about 15 minutes, until the rolls are golden on all sides. Cut each roll into 3 or 4 slices and serve warm, not hot.

MAKES 60 TO 80 ROLLS

COOKING NOTE

Marian Burros, whose recipe this is, said that you can freeze the rolls for up to 2 weeks before baking and serving them, but you can also bake them right away.

SERVING SUGGESTIONS

Sazerac (p. 17), The Vesper (p. 34), Florentine Dip (p. 58), Onion Rings (p. 61), Blue Cheese Dip (p. 54)

DECEMBER 11, 1996: "PREPARING A PARTY, WITH TIME TO GOSSIP," BY MARIAN BURROS.

—1996

∽ FRESH AND SMOKED SALMON SPREAD

This ordinary-seeming salmon spread epitomizes many of the changes that swept home cooking as we neared the twenty-first century. People had become so accustomed to dining out—and the quality of cooking at most restaurants had improved so markedly—that they wanted food of equal sophistication at home.

And they got it by embracing restaurant techniques and threading new subtleties of preparation into their cooking.

This salmon spread from Le Bernardin, a 4-star Manhattan landmark, vastly improves on the standard. It rounds out the smoked salmon with cubes of flash-poached fresh salmon, which are mashed into the spread. This odd-seeming touch is shrewdly conceived—by poaching the fish in cubes, you increase the surface area that's heated, and 40 seconds is just enough time to cook the outside but leave the center pink and delicately textured. Plain smoked salmon spread can land with a salty thud, but the fresh fish lightens the mix, both literally and sensually.

———

1 (750-ml) bottle dry white wine

2 tablespoons chopped shallots

1 teaspoon fine sea salt, plus more to taste

2 pounds skinless salmon fillet, fat trimmed and cut into 1-inch cubes

6 ounces sliced smoked salmon, fat trimmed and cut into tiny dice

2 tablespoons thinly sliced chives

1/4 cup fresh lemon juice

1 cup mayonnaise, homemade (p. 465) or store-bought

1/4 teaspoon freshly ground white pepper

Toasted baguette slices for serving

1. Place the wine, shallots, and salt in a large saucepan and bring to a boil. Add the fresh salmon and poach for 40 seconds. Drain in a sieve and run cold water over the fish to stop the cooking. Drain well and refrigerate until cold, at least 1 1/2 hours. (Discard the poaching liquid.)

2. Place the smoked salmon in a large bowl and stir in the chives. Add the poached salmon and use the side of a wooden spoon to shred the fish as you mix. Stir in the lemon juice, mayonnaise, and pepper. Season with sea salt.

3. Refrigerate the spread for up to 6 hours, then serve with toasts.

MAKES 4 CUPS; SERVES 8 TO 12

COOKING NOTES

I was skeptical about the large amount of mayonnaise that's folded into the fish mixture. At first, I added

just 1/2 cup. The spread was sublime. Then I mixed in the rest. It was still good, but quite wet. When I tasted it a few hours later, though, it was perfect. The fish had absorbed the mayonnaise, and had I skimped, the spread would have been dry. If there's anything this recipe needs, it's a few more drops of lemon juice, which can be added to taste.

SERVING SUGGESTIONS

Eric Ripert, the chef of Le Bernardin, says to serve the spread on toasted slices of baguette. For a casual dinner party, why not use potato chips? Also, Kir Royale 38 (p. 28), The Vesper (p. 34), Saketini (p. 37), Edamame with Nori Salt (p. 92), Salted and Deviled Almonds (p. 51).

SEPTEMBER 9, 1998: "BY THE BOOK: A TALE OUT OF BRITTANY," BY FLORENCE FABRICANT. RECIPE ADAPTED FROM *LE BERNARDIN COOKBOOK: FOUR-STAR SIMPLICITY*, BY MAGUY LE COZE AND ERIC RIPERT.

—1998

✎ TOASTS WITH WALNUT SAUCE

This tasty little sauce can also be used on pasta.

———

7 ounces (about 2 cups) walnuts, broken

2 tablespoons dry bread crumbs

1 clove garlic, peeled

Sea salt

2 tablespoons freshly grated Parmesan cheese

Pinch of dried marjoram leaves

3/4 cup fresh ricotta

2 to 3 teaspoons tepid water

1/4 cup extra virgin olive oil

Toasted slices of country bread for serving

1. Combine the walnuts, bread crumbs, garlic, and a large pinch of salt in a large mortar. Pound with the pestle to form a coarse-textured paste. Add the Parmesan and marjoram. Pound again to blend. Add the ricotta, along with the tepid water, stirring with the pestle to mix. Slowly drizzle in the olive oil, stirring to combine. Taste and adjust the seasonings.

2. Serve the spread on small slices of toasted country bread.

MAKES 1 CUP

SERVING SUGGESTIONS
Peach Bowl (p. 20), The Normandy (p. 43), or a glass of good rosé or prosecco

APRIL 21, 1999: "TEST KITCHEN: ONE MOVING PART, NO BATTERIES: WHO'D EVER BUY IT?" BY AMANDA HESSER. RECIPE ADAPTED FROM *RECIPES FROM PARADISE*, BY FRED PLOTKIN.

—1999

PORK-AND-TOASTED-RICE-POWDER SPRING ROLLS

These spring rolls come from Bao-Xuyen Le, a wonderful home cook in southern California who makes them for her family's Vietnamese-influenced Thanksgiving dinner. I'd eat them any day of the year.

For the Dipping Sauce
½ cup superfine sugar
½ cup fresh lime juice (from about 4 limes)
½ cup Asian fish sauce

For the Spring Rolls
1½ cups dried pork skins
1 teaspoon salt
1 teaspoon rice vinegar or white vinegar
½ pound roasted pork tenderloin, cut into julienne
    (about 2 cups)
3 tablespoons toasted rice powder
3 cloves garlic, finely chopped
2 to 3 tablespoons Asian fish sauce
Sixteen 8-inch round rice paper spring roll wrappers
8 red-leaf lettuce leaves, stems removed and cut in half
1 to 2 large bunches cilantro, trimmed
32 shiso leaves
16 sprigs mint

1. To prepare the dipping sauce, combine the sugar, lime juice, and fish sauce in a small bowl and mix well. Set aside.
2. To prepare the spring rolls, combine the pork skins with the salt, vinegar, and water to cover in a medium bowl. Soak until softened, about 30 minutes. Drain well.
3. Combine the pork skins, roasted pork, rice powder, and garlic in a large bowl and mix well. Add just enough fish sauce to moisten the mixture, mixing well.
4. Heat a large pot of water just until hot to the touch. Dip a rice paper wrapper into the water and place on a large clean surface. Repeat so you have 4 wrappers laid out. Lay ½ lettuce leaf on the half of a wrapper closest to you. Cover evenly with several sprigs of cilantro, 2 shiso leaves, and a sprig of mint. Spread with about ¼ cup of the pork mixture. Roll the bottom half of the wrapper partway over the filling, fold in the sides, and continue rolling to the other end of the wrapper to make a neat, tight log. Place the finished roll seam side down on a plate, and continue to make the spring rolls.
5. Serve with the dipping sauce.

SERVES 8

COOKING NOTE
Although many of the ingredients are probably not available at Safeway, you can find them at any decent Southeast Asian grocery store.

SERVING SUGGESTIONS
Kaffir Lime Lemonade (p. 26), Beef Satay with Peanut Sauce (p. 66), Chinese Pork Balls (p. 59), Roasted Brine-Cured Turkey with Shiitake and Lotus Seed Stuffing (p. 477), Sticky Rice with Mango (p. 861)

NOVEMBER 15, 2000: "ADD A LITTLE VIETNAM, FRANCE, AND CALIFORNIA, AND MIX," BY AMANDA HESSER. RECIPE ADAPTED FROM BAO-XUYEN LE, A HOME COOK IN SOUTHERN CALIFORNIA.

—2000

ALOO KOFTA

These fried potato croquettes were featured as an example of something you could cook in a *kadhai*, a flat-bottomed wok-like pan, but you can also use a cast-iron skillet, as I did. Whatever you choose, the pan should have a heavy bottom that disperses and holds heat evenly, to help develop the lacy potato shell that cloaks the croquettes. The garam masala (a spice blend available at Indian groceries and stores like

Whole Foods) that you mix into the potatoes defines the flavor of the croquettes, so make sure you like the blend before using it here!

———

I pound white potatoes (about 3 large)

I tablespoon cornstarch

I cup cooked peas

I teaspoon cumin seeds

I teaspoon garam masala

I tablespoon fresh lemon juice

Salt

Cayenne pepper

¼ cup finely chopped scallions

I tablespoon chopped cilantro

½ cup all-purpose flour

I cup ghee (clarified butter, available in Indian grocery stores) or vegetable oil

1. Bring a large pot of lightly salted water to a boil. Add the potatoes and cook until tender, 20 to 30 minutes. Drain, cool, and peel.

2. Mash the potatoes in a large bowl. Add the cornstarch, peas, cumin, garam masala, and lemon juice. Season with salt and cayenne and mix well. Fold in the scallions and cilantro.

3. Roll the mixture into 1½-inch balls, then roll in flour to coat lightly. Place a 5- to 6-inch kadhai or cast-iron skillet over medium-high heat. When the pan is hot, add the ghee and allow it to heat again. Working in batches, fry the kofta until golden brown. Drain on paper towels, season with salt, and serve hot.

SERVES 6

SERVING SUGGESTIONS

Sweet (or Savory) Lassi (p. 25), Mango Lassi (p. 27), Crab and Coconut Curry (p. 289), Tuna Curry (p. 435), Ceylon Curry of Oysters (p. 391)

JANUARY 24, 2001: "THE PAN THAT CAME FOR DINNER," BY DENISE LANDIS.

—2001

ᑐ GOAT'S-MILK CHEESE, BUTTERED BROWN BREAD, AND SALTED ONION

This is more of a sequence than a recipe, but I've included it because it's a delicious combination and the kind of dish that ambitious cooks sometimes forget about. When Prune opened on the Lower East Side in 1999, the hors d'oeuvre list was made up almost entirely of home-grown snacks—radishes with fresh butter and salt, Triscuits with sardines and mustard, and this brown bread with cheese and onion. Crowds soon flocked, and continue to.

———

I red onion, halved and thinly sliced into ribbons

Kosher salt

4 slices brown bread

Softened unsalted butter for spreading

4 thick slices (the dimensions of a playing card) Spanish Garrotxa or other aged goat's-milk cheese

Extra virgin olive oil for sprinkling

Coarsely ground black pepper

I sprig thyme

1. Place the onion in a bowl and season with salt. Let sit for 10 minutes.

2. Meanwhile, spread the bread with a generous layer of butter. Cut the bread into triangles and arrange on a plate. Lay the slices of cheese next to the bread.

3. Lift the onion from the bowl (letting the juices run off), and mound at the edge of the plate. Sprinkle the bread, cheese, and onion with olive oil and black pepper. Garnish with the thyme.

SERVES 2

SERVING SUGGESTION

The Junipero Gibson with Pickled Red Onion (p. 33), also from Prune

MAY 16, 2001: "THE CHEF: GABRIELLE HAMILTON," BY GABRIELLE HAMILTON AND AMANDA HESSER.

—2001

NICOLE KAPLAN'S GOUGÈRES

Jonathan Reynolds wrote of the gougères at Eleven Madison Park, "Imagine a gossamer of Gruyère so light that it can be brought to your table by a butterfly and evaporate on your tongue seconds after making contact—leaving behind only the sound and memory of a thin crunch, the nutty aroma of milk's leap toward immortality, and a child-like impatience for more." The crisp, salty poufs have since become a fixture at the restaurant, where they're served while you sip a cocktail and browse the menu.

Good gougères like these are the kind of food that provokes the question "Why don't I make these more often?" The answer: any recipe that requires piping from a pastry bag is never going to be one you turn to regularly. But when you're in the mood, these can be fun to make: you get to whack the dough around the mixer until it's smooth and supple.

Reynolds offered three prudent suggestions: "First, after piping out the dough, refrigerate it for a couple of hours or freeze it overnight—it will rise better in the oven. Second, eat these . . . balloons immediately—like topical plays, they lose value every couple of minutes. And third, if you're serving them to friends, make millions."

———

1 cup water

4 tablespoons unsalted butter, softened

About ½ teaspoon kosher salt

¼ teaspoon cayenne pepper

1 cup bread flour

4 large eggs, at room temperature

6 ounces Gruyère cheese, grated (about 1½ cups),
    plus extra for sprinkling

1. Heat the oven to 350 degrees if you will be baking the gougères right away. Line 2 large baking sheets with parchment paper.

2. Bring the water, butter, ½ teaspoon salt, and the cayenne to a boil in a small saucepan. Place the flour in the bowl of a stand mixer, preferably fitted with the paddle attachment, add the boiling water mixture, and blend well (or use a wooden spoon and a large bowl; don't use a whisk—the dough is too heavy). Beat in the eggs one at a time until the dough is smooth. Beat in the cheese and mix until the dough is thick and the cheese has mostly melted. Place the dough in a pastry bag fitted with a medium (¼-inch) plain tip.

3. Pipe the dough into small (¾-inch-diameter) mounds on the lined baking sheets. Sprinkle each with a pinch of grated cheese and salt. The gougères can be baked right away or refrigerated or frozen before baking.

4. Bake for 20 to 25 minutes, until golden brown and puffed about 3 times their original size. Don't open the oven door for at least the first 12 minutes, to keep them from deflating. Serve and eat IMMEDIATELY!

MAKES ABOUT 4½ DOZEN GOUGÈRES

COOKING NOTES

Forget about the French canvas pastry bag and being green: disposable clear plastic pastry bags are the way to go. You'll do less damage to the environment than you do with paper towels, and you'll be a lot happier. They're available at www.sugarcraft.com.

Nicole Kaplan, the restaurant's pastry chef, pipes the gougères, sprinkles them with cheese, and refrigerates them for a few hours or freezes them overnight. Let the frozen gougères thaw at room temperature while you preheat the oven. Then sprinkle them with cheese and salt and bake until puffed and golden.

SERVING SUGGESTION

Kir Royale 38 (p. 28) and cocktail napkins

SEPTEMBER 30, 2001: "FOOD: SAY CHEESE BALLS," BY JONATHAN REYNOLDS. RECIPE ADAPTED FROM NICOLE KAPLAN, THE PASTRY CHEF AT ELEVEN MADISON PARK IN NEW YORK CITY.

—2001

SWEET-AND-SALTY POPCORN WITH ORANGE BLOSSOM HONEY

Popcorn is so easy to season, so willing to take on new flavors, and so relieved when it's not sprayed with fake butter that you really can't fail with it.

———

6 cups popped popcorn
1 cup salted roasted nuts (one kind, or a mixture; optional)
½ cup sugar
⅓ cup orange blossom honey
1 teaspoon coarse salt

1. Heat the oven to 250 degrees. Place the popcorn and nuts in a large ovenproof bowl and keep warm in the oven.
2. Pour the sugar into a small heavy saucepan and place over medium-low heat. When the sugar is melted and a light caramel color, add the honey and stir until smooth and liquid. Remove from the heat.
3. Remove the popcorn from the oven, sprinkle it with salt, and pour the sugar syrup over it. Using a pot holder to steady the bowl with one hand, stir quickly with a large fork to fluff and coat the corn. Spread on a greased baking sheet and let cool.
4. Break into large pieces, and store in an airtight tin.

SERVES 6

SERVING SUGGESTION
Hot Buttered Rum (p. 24) and a good movie

OCTOBER 3, 2001: "NOW PLAYING IN THE HEARTLAND: THE GREAT POPCORN HARVEST," BY AMANDA HESSER

—2001

✒ CROSTINI ROMANI

I learned this recipe from Paola di Mauro, an owner of Colle Picchioni, a winery in the Castelli Romani in the hills outside Rome. Mauro, who often found herself feeding visiting wine buyers, eventually became more well known for her cooking than for her exceptional wines, and American chefs from Mario Batali to Piero Selvaggio began flocking to cook with her, hoping that some of her culinary charm would rub off on them.

I spent a day with her in her kitchen, where, shuffling from counter to stove, she whipped up one of the best meals I've ever had—a feast of bucatini alla Amatriciana, baked zucchini with herbs (p. 250), saltim-bocca (p. 561), and a peppery potato and calves' liver casserole.

We began the lunch with this Roman crostini, a small dish layered with slices of fresh mozzarella and bread. It had been baked until bubbly and then slathered with a warm, creamy anchovy sauce. The sauce ran in rivulets over the cheese, giving each bite a candid pungency.

———

About ten ¼-inch-thick slices country bread or baguette (sliced diagonally)
¾ pound fresh mozzarella, sliced ¼ inch thick (about 10 slices)
4 tablespoons unsalted butter
2 tablespoons anchovy paste
¼ cup whole milk

1. Heat the oven to 425 degrees. Generously butter a small casserole dish. Stand a slice of bread up against one end of the casserole. Follow it with a slice of mozzarella and continue until the entire casserole is filled loosely with bread and mozzarella. Dot with 1 tablespoon butter.
2. Bake until the bread is toasted and the mozzarella is bubbly on the edges, 10 to 12 minutes.
3. Meanwhile, stir together the remaining 3 tablespoons butter, anchovy paste, and milk in a small sauce pan. Heat until the mixture is warm, stirring so that it is smooth and loose.
4. When the casserole is done, remove it from the oven and spoon the sauce on top. Spoon onto plates, making sure to get a little sauce on each plate.

SERVES 6

SERVING SUGGESTIONS
Salade à la Romaine (p. 171), Fennel and Blood Orange Salad (p. 195), Fettuccine alla Romana (p. 310), Risotto with Radicchio and Sausage (p. 322), Limoncello (p. 38)

DECEMBER 5, 2001: "A ROMAN MUSE FOR AMERICA'S GREAT CHEFS," BY AMANDA HESSER. RECIPE ADAPTED FROM PAOLA DI MAURO.

—2001

FOIE GRAS AND JAM SANDWICHES

I served these sandwiches at a party and a friend's child, who thought they were PB&Js (as opposed to FG&Js) and took a large bite of one. It didn't end well. Save these for adults, who love them!

---

8 slices white sandwich bread (soft and buttery, not dry)

$\frac{1}{2}$ cup foie gras mousse, at room temperature

Coarse sea salt

$\frac{1}{4}$ cup berry jam (preferably tart berries, like cranberries, blackberries, or currants)

1. Lay the slices of bread on a bread board. Spread the foie gras mousse on 4 of the slices. Sprinkle with coarse sea salt. Spread the jam on the other 4 slices of bread. Join the jam slices with the foie gras slices to make 4 sandwiches.
2. Using a bread knife, cut off the crusts with gentle sawing motions, then cut the sandwiches diagonally into quarters, so you end up with triangles. Stack on a serving platter and march them out to the party.

SERVES 4 PEOPLE, AGE 12 AND OLDER,
AS AN HORS D'OEUVRE

SERVING SUGGESTION
The Vesper (p. 34)

MAY 12, 2002: "FOOD DIARY: PERSONAL BEST," BY AMANDA HESSER.

—2002

CROSTINI WITH EGGPLANT AND PINE NUT PUREE

The very first recipe for crostini—a toast with a savory topping—to show up in the *Times* was for toasts topped with chicken livers, anchovies, capers, and butter. It was published in 1960, before Mario Batali, today's king of crostini, was even in diapers (he was born nine months after it appeared).

Eggplants provide great material for spreads because their insides puree smoothly, hold together, and soak up flavor well. Deborah Madison, who evolved from a vegetarian cooking expert to a vegetable cooking expert, came up with this recipe for *Local Flavors*, one of the eight cookbooks she's written. You broil eggplant slices, then grind them up with toasted pine nuts, garlic, and lemon juice in a mortar and pestle. To finish, you mix in chopped mint, parsley, and basil, capping it with an array of vibrant flavors. But I also loved the spread without the herbs.

---

1 pound eggplant, trimmed, peeled, and sliced into rounds about $\frac{1}{2}$ inch thick

Olive oil

$\frac{1}{3}$ cup pine nuts

1 to 2 cloves garlic

Sea salt

Fresh lemon juice

Freshly ground black pepper

1 tablespoon chopped mint

2 tablespoons chopped flat-leaf parsley

2 tablespoons chopped basil, plus whole leaves for garnish

Toasted baguette slices or crackers

1. Heat the broiler. Lightly brush both sides of each eggplant slice with oil and arrange on a baking sheet. Broil about 6 inches from the heat until golden, 4 to 5 minutes. Turn and brown the second side. Remove from the broiler and stack the slices so they steam to finish cooking.
2. Toast the pine nuts in a small skillet over low heat, shaking often, until golden. Cool.
3. Using a large mortar and pestle (or a food processor), grind the pine nuts with the garlic and $\frac{1}{2}$ teaspoon salt until smooth. Coarsely chop the eggplant, add to the mixture, and work into a somewhat rough puree with the pestle (or food processor). Add a little lemon juice to sharpen the flavor. Taste for salt and add more if needed, and season with pepper. Stir in the herbs.
4. Spread on baguette slices or crackers, and garnish each with a basil leaf.

MAKES 12 TO 16 CROSTINI

Eggplant chars quickly under the broiler—keep a close eye on it.

Don't go too crazy with the garlic—use 1 large clove or 2 small—or the eggplant (and everything else) will be overwhelmed by it.

You can use a food processor to puree the eggplant but then you lose some of the texture and moistness.

If the puree seems dry, add a little oil or water to loosen it.

I used about 2 teaspoons lemon juice.

SERVING SUGGESTIONS

Toasts with Walnut Sauce (p. 73), Ricotta Crostini with Fresh Thyme and Dried Oregano (p. 93), Seasoned Olives (p. 90)

AUGUST 14, 2002: "BY THE BOOK: A CHEF BEATS THE DRUM, LOUDLY, FOR FARMERS' MARKETS," BY REGINA SCHRAMBLING. RECIPE ADAPTED FROM *LOCAL FLAVORS*, BY DEBORAH MADISON.

—2002

☞ THE SPICE BOYS' CHEESE BALL

I included this cheese ball for its kitsch value. Serve it to people who have a sense of humor, because it looks like a tropical sea creature with fuchsia skin and glowing green scales. I set it out at a dinner party, embarrassed by its electric appearance, but my guests, most of whom grew up in the 1970s, devoured it.

---

1 pound cheddar cheese, grated, at room temperature

1 pound cream cheese, at room temperature

¼ pound blue cheese, at room temperature

¼ pound smoked cheese, at room temperature

1 tablespoon Dijon mustard

1 tablespoon onion salt

¼ teaspoon garlic salt

Port

2 tablespoons bottled horseradish

½ cup pickled beets, finely chopped

Finely chopped flat-leaf parsley

Crackers or rye or pumpernickel toasts for serving

1. Combine all the cheeses except 8 ounces of the cream cheese with the mustard and onion and garlic salts in a bowl and mix with enough port to soften. Form into a ball or log (or 2 of each). Cover with a coating of the remaining 8 ounces cream cheese mixed with the horseradish and chopped beets. Refrigerate for several hours.

2. Dust the cheese ball with finely chopped parsley. Set out on a tray with an assortment of crackers, or rye or pumpernickel toasts.

MAKES 1 GIANT OR 2 MEDIUM CHEESE BALLS OR LOGS

COOKING NOTES

This makes an enormous cheese ball—I recommend forming the mixture into 2 balls.

Before coating the ball with the beet-stained cream cheese, chill both the cheese ball and the cream cheese mixture. This will make the latter easier to apply.

SERVING SUGGESTIONS

Go all-out low-brow and make the Caramelized Bacon on p. 93 too. Then North Carolina–Style Pulled Pork (p. 550) or Cleo's Daddy's Barbecued Ribs (p. 529).

NOVEMBER 10, 2002: "MEMBERS ONLY," BY DAVID FELD. RECIPE ADAPTED FROM THE SPICE BOYS, A SUPPER CLUB IN AUSTIN, TEXAS.

—2002

☞ CHEESE STRAWS

After years of making too many different dishes for dinner parties and pulling my hair out just before people arrived, I finally discovered that all you have to make for the cocktail hour is cheese straws. Everyone likes them, no one eats too many (they're rich and spicy), they go with practically everything, and as with any dish that requires making a dough, people are always amazed that you assembled them from scratch.

Don't tell them that the dough only takes 5 minutes to put together. With cooking, smoke and mirrors are part of the fun.

As frequent *Times* contributors Matt Lee and Ted Lee pointed out, cheese straws are typically coin-shaped. Their way of cutting the dough into strips makes the straws, paradoxically, both more rustic and more elegant. Try them and see.

¼ pound extra-sharp cheddar cheese, grated
4 tablespoons unsalted butter, cut into 4 pieces and softened
¾ cup all-purpose flour
½ teaspoon salt
¾ teaspoon crushed red pepper flakes
1 tablespoon half-and-half, or as necessary

1. Heat the oven to 350 degrees. Combine the cheese, butter, flour, salt, and red pepper in a food processor and pulse until the mixture resembles coarse crumbs. Add the half-and-half and pulse until the dough forms a ball. Add more half-and-half if needed.
2. On a lightly floured surface, using a lightly floured pin, roll the dough out to a rectangle 8 by 10 inches. With a sharp knife, cut the dough crosswise into thin strips, ¼ to ⅓ inch wide. Gently transfer the straws to an ungreased baking sheet, leaving a ¼ inch between them. (The dough is fragile, so use the knife to slide the straws from the work surface onto the baking sheet.)
3. Bake for 17 minutes, or until the ends of the straws are barely browned; check on them after 12 minutes to see if the pan needs to be rotated. Let cool.

MAKES ABOUT 30 STRAWS

COOKING NOTES
Orange cheddar gives the straws a pleasant golden color.

If you don't have a food processor, these can be made by hand. Use a pastry blender to mix the dough to coarse crumbs.

The recipe instructs you to slice the dough into strips ¼ to ⅓ inch wide, but I think the thinner, the better: they're more delicate and attractive when the straws are just less than ¼ inch wide. Keep in mind that they'll bake more quickly.

SERVING SUGGESTIONS
With these, you need a refreshing drink like the Claret Cup (p. 12), Vermouth Cup (p. 15), or Moscow Mule (p. 20). For a full meal: Caramelized Bacon (p. 93), Pickled Shrimp (p. 95), North Carolina–Style Pulled Pork (p. 550), Docks Coleslaw (p. 191), Light Potato Salad (p. 301), Chocolate Dump-It Cake (p. 781).

PERIOD DETAIL
The earliest cheese straws in the *Times* appeared in 1878. The dough was very similar to this one except that it included Parmesan cheese in addition to cheddar and used cayenne for heat rather than crushed red pepper. Curiously, the dough was cut into both strips and a ring. After baking, the strips—just ⅛ inch thick—were strung through the cheese straw ring, like a bundle of sticks. The same could be done with the Lee brothers' recipe.

NOVEMBER 27, 2002: "WHILE THE BIRD'S STILL STUFFED, BUT BEFORE THE GUESTS ARE," BY MATT LEE AND TED LEE.
—2002

⌐ SMOKED MACKEREL ON TOASTS

Here I've treated smoked mackerel as you do salt cod in brandade and whipped it together with potato, garlic, olive oil, chives, and a little crème fraîche. Then all you need is something to transport it to your mouth: toast points or slices of baguette do the trick.

---

1 medium white potato (about 7 ounces), peeled
1 clove garlic
Sea salt
½ pound smoked mackerel or trout fillets, skinned
¼ cup extra virgin olive oil
6 tablespoons crème fraîche
Freshly ground black pepper
1 tablespoon thinly sliced chives
20 thin slices baguette, toasted

1. Place the potato and garlic clove in a small saucepan, cover with water, season with salt, and bring to a boil. Reduce the heat and simmer until the potato is very soft, about 20 minutes. Drain, reserving 1 cup of liquid.
2. Mash the potato in a bowl with a potato masher while it is still warm. Add the mackerel and oil and

mix with the potato masher or a fork until smooth and loose enough to spread. Thin as needed with the reserved potato water. Add the crème fraîche and season with pepper. Taste, and adjust the seasoning if necessary. Stir in the chives. Spread on toasts and serve.

SERVES 6

SERVING SUGGESTIONS
Astoria Cocktail (p. 19), The Vesper (p. 34), Kumquat-Clementine Cordial (p. 42), Onion Rings (p. 61), Salted and Deviled Almonds (p. 51), Seasoned Olives (p. 90)

NOVEMBER 27, 2002: "PAIRINGS: SOMETHING SHARP FOR A WINE THAT DOESN'T BELIEVE IN UNDERSTATEMENT," BY AMANDA HESSER.

—2002

BUCKWHEAT BLINI WITH CRÈME FRAÎCHE AND CAVIAR

It's impossible to go wrong with tangy cream and sturgeon eggs on salty, tender buckwheat blini. But these buckwheat blini are so perfect they deserve to be unyoked from the caviar and allowed to run free with other fish and fowl. Serve them with the Smoked Mackerel on p. 80, or the Fresh and Smoked Salmon Spread on p. 72 or, if you're in a hurry, fresh ricotta and a dribble of good olive oil will do.

————

1½ cups whole milk
4 tablespoons unsalted butter, plus extra for frying and serving
1 teaspoon sugar
2 tablespoons warm water
2 teaspoons active dry yeast
3 large eggs, separated
1 cup all-purpose flour
1 cup buckwheat flour
1 teaspoon salt
One 8-ounce container crème fraîche or sour cream
3 ounces caviar, preferably osetra, and preferably sustainable

1. Heat the milk and 4 tablespoons of butter in a small saucepan over low heat until the butter is melted. Let cool to room temperature.

2. Meanwhile, combine the sugar and warm water in a large bowl and stir to dissolve the sugar. Sprinkle the yeast over the water and let stand in a warm place until the yeast is frothy, about 5 minutes.

3. Pour the milk mixture into the yeast mixture, add the egg yolks, and whisk to blend. Combine the flours and salt and gradually whisk into the yeast mixture until smooth. Cover the bowl tightly with plastic wrap and let the batter rise in a warm place until doubled in bulk, about 1 hour.

4. Preheat the oven to 200 degrees. Stir to deflate the batter. (The batter can be covered and refrigerated for up to 24 hours before proceeding.) Beat the egg whites until soft peaks form. Gently fold into the batter just until blended.

5. Set a large griddle or skillet over medium to medium-high heat and add enough butter to coat the pan. When the butter sizzles, drop tablespoons of batter onto the surface to make blini roughly 2 inches in diameter. Cook until bubbles appear on top and the bottom is golden brown, about 1 minute. Turn and cook until the bottom is lightly browned, 15 to 20 seconds. Place the blini, overlapping but not stacked (or they will get soggy), on a baking sheet and keep warm in the oven while you cook the remaining batter. Stop using the batter when bubbles no longer appear on the top of the blini (there may be up to 1 cup left), or the blini will be thin and tough.

6. To serve, brush the blini lightly with melted butter and top each with a dab of crème fraîche and a small dollop of caviar.

MAKES ABOUT 6 DOZEN

COOKING NOTES
The batter is strangely elastic—don't let this put you off. Use two spoons to drop your batter onto the griddle: one to scoop, one to scrape.

Julia Reed, whose recipe this is, offered this convenient tip: "Blini may be made ahead, wrapped well, and frozen. Thaw, place on a baking sheet, cover loosely with foil, and heat in a 350-degree oven until warm, about 10 minutes."

SERVING SUGGESTIONS
Holiday Punch (p. 32), The Vesper (p. 34), Martini (p. 35), Improved Holland Gin Cocktail (p. 39), Rillettes de Canard (Duck Rillettes; p. 65)

DECEMBER 29, 2002: "FOOD: PARTY OF ONE," BY JULIA REED

RUSS & DAUGHTERS' CHOPPED CHICKEN LIVER

Jason Epstein, a contributor to the *Times Magazine*, called the Lower East Side's Russ & Daughters "New York's most hallowed shrine to the miracle of caviar, smoked salmon, ethereal herring, and silken chopped liver. It is the mother church of those latter-day temples—Zabar's, Barney Greengrass, and Murray's Sturgeon Shop that dot the Upper West Side and serve the great-grandchildren of Joel Russ's original customers."

You will understand what he means when you taste this chopped chicken liver, into which you mix hard-cooked eggs and caramelized onions. As it turns out, the sulphur and sweetness are just what chicken livers need.

———

1 pound chicken livers (about 16 livers)
2 tablespoons vegetable oil (schmaltz, rendered chicken fat, is available from some butchers, and can be used as a substitute)
2 tablespoons vegetable shortening
2 large Spanish onions (1 pound each), coarsely chopped
3 large hard-boiled eggs, chilled
Kosher salt and freshly ground black pepper
Matzoh or crackers for serving

1. Rinse the chicken livers and pat dry. Remove any connective tissue. Heat the oil in a large skillet over medium-high heat and sauté the livers until they are firm and but still slightly pink in the center, about 5 minutes, do not overcook. Remove with a slotted spoon and place on a plate to cool.
2. Melt the shortening in a large clean skillet over medium heat. Add the onions and cook, stirring occasionally until caramelized, 35 to 45 minutes; reduce the heat to low as the onions soften. Remove from the heat.

3. Coarsely chop the livers in a food processor and place in a bowl (or chop the livers with a knife, or a mezzaluna).
4. Peel the eggs and mash with a fork in a bowl. Add to the livers. Add the onions and mix well, stirring in just enough of their cooking juices to moisten the mixture. Season with salt and pepper.
5. Cover the chopped liver and let mellow in the refrigerator for at least a few hours. Remove from the refrigerator 15 minutes before serving, with matzoh or crackers.

SERVES 8 TO 10

COOKING NOTES
In Step 3, you are given the option of using a food processor or chopping the liver by hand. The food processor is obviously tempting, and I succumbed to temptation, which I later regretted, because although the top of the mixture was nice and coarse, the livers down by the blade were far too smooth. Food processors are difficult to control, and with something as delicate as chicken livers, using the machine means toying with disaster. Better to get out your best knife or mezzaluna—it's called *chopped* chicken liver, after all.

SERVING SUGGESTIONS
The Vesper (p. 34), Onion Rings (p. 61), Eggs Suffragette (p. 52), Shrimp Canapés à la Suede (p. 57)

PERIOD DETAIL
In 2009, after 100 years in business, Russ & Daughters went online with both a blog—Lox Populi—and a Twitter stream.

JANUARY 12, 2003: "LOX, STOCK, AND BARRELS," BY JASON EPSTEIN. RECIPE ADAPTED FROM RUSS & DAUGHTERS IN NEW YORK CITY.

—2003

SPICED PECANS

The earthy sweetness of pecans is often overwhelmed by their buttery flavor, but here, bitter and fiery spices underscore the nuts' loaminess.

———

¼ teaspoon salt

½ teaspoon sugar

2 teaspoons ground cumin

⅛ to ¼ teaspoon cayenne pepper

4 teaspoons vegetable or canola oil

2 cups pecans

1. Heat the oven to 350 degrees. Mix together the salt, sugar, cumin, and cayenne in a medium bowl. Stir in the oil to make a smooth mixture.

2. Toss the pecans with the seasonings to coat. Spread on a baking sheet in a single layer. Toast for 8 to 10 minutes, until they take on a little color. Let cool. (The pecans will keep in an airtight container in a cool, dry place for a week.)

MAKES ABOUT 2 CUPS

SERVING SUGGESTIONS

Park Avenue Cocktail (p. 19), The Bone (p. 34), Sir Francis Drake (p. 36), Billionaire Cocktail (p. 40), Sweet-and-Salty Popcorn with Orange Blossom Honey (p. 76)

JANUARY 15, 2003: "EATING WELL: PASS THE NUTS, PASS UP THE GUILT," BY MARIAN BURROS.

—2003

☞ HOT CHEESE OLIVES

A friend of mine once complained to me, "If I see one more Julia Reed recipe with mayonnaise or cheese, I'm going to stop buying the paper." This is a common form of threat: if you substitute Meyer lemons and crème fraîche for the mayonnaise and cheese, I'm sure the same protest has been lodged with colleagues about my work. Writers fall into ruts, and readers get tired of writers. Now that I've cooked many of Reed's recipes, though, I couldn't disagree more with my friend. Reed, who was a columnist for the Sunday *Magazine*, and is a staff writer for *Vogue*, hails from the South and has done more to revive Southern foods at the paper than anyone since Craig Claiborne (he was from Mississippi; she's from Louisiana). It just so happens that many foods from the South contain cheese and mayonnaise (and even the occasional Ritz cracker). What I like about Reed's recipes is what I like about any great food writer's recipes: they take you

on a journey with memorable detours and eye-opening asides until you reach something delicious. These olives, which are swaddled in a thin, spicy dough, are dangerously addictive.

———

8 tablespoons (1 stick) unsalted butter, softened

2 cups grated extra-sharp cheddar cheese (8 ounces)

1½ cups all-purpose flour

⅛ teaspoon salt

¼ teaspoon cayenne pepper

Dash of Worcestershire sauce

1 large egg, beaten with 2 tablespoons cold water

50 small pimento-stuffed cocktail olives, drained and patted dry

1. Beat the butter until creamy in a large bowl with a wooden spoon. Add the cheese and mix well. Stir in the flour, salt, cayenne, and Worcestershire until smooth. Add the beaten egg and mix just until incorporated. Refrigerate for 1 hour.

2. Heat the oven to 350 degrees. Flatten out a piece of dough about the size of a hazelnut into a thin round. Place an olive on top and shape the dough around the olive, pinching to repair any breaks and rolling it between your palms to smooth the seams. Place on an ungreased cookie sheet. Repeat with the remaining dough and olives.

3. Bake until the dough sets, about 15 minutes. Serve hot.

MAKES 50 OLIVES

COOKING NOTES

Grate your own cheddar cheese. Don't buy the pre-shredded nonsense.

To make these for a party, you can roll the olives in the dough, place them on the baking sheet covered, and refrigerate for up to a day. Then pop them in the oven just before your guests start arriving.

SERVING SUGGESTIONS

Astoria Cocktail (p. 19), Park Avenue Cocktail (p. 19), Martini (p. 35), Salted and Deviled Almonds (p. 51), Onion Rings (p. 61), Caramelized Bacon (p. 93)

MARCH 30, 2003: "HOSTESS CUPCAKES," BY JULIA REED.

—2003

✎ PARMESAN CRACKERS

These are a more polite version of Cheese Straws (p. 79), a whisper to their shout.

----

8 tablespoons (1 stick) unsalted butter, cut into 8 pieces

1 cup all-purpose flour

1 cup freshly grated Parmesan cheese

1. Combine the ingredients in a food processor and pulse until the dough comes together. Turn the dough out onto a piece of plastic wrap and form it into a log 1½ inches in diameter. Chill until firm, at least 2 hours.

2. Heat the oven to 325 degrees. Grease 2 baking sheets. Cut the log of dough into ¼-inch-thick slices, and place them 1 inch apart on the baking sheets.

3. Bake until firm, about 12 to 13 minutes. Remove the baking sheets from the oven and raise the temperature to 500 degrees.

4. When the temperature has come up to the correct heat, return the sheets to the oven and bake for 3 minutes more, or until the crackers are deeply golden brown all over. Let cool on a wire rack.

MAKES 40 CRACKERS

SERVING SUGGESTIONS
Ramos Gin Fizz (p. 15), Moscow Mule (p. 20), Singapore Sling (p. 23), Salted and Deviled Almonds (p. 51), Puntarelle with Anchovies (p. 194), Italian Beef Stew with Rosemary (p. 522), Veal Chops with Sage (p. 564), Panna Cotta (p. 840), Figs in Whiskey (p. 859)

SEPTEMBER 10, 2003: "TEMPTATION: DELICIOUS DECEPTION TO GO WITH WINE," BY MELISSA CLARK. RECIPE ADAPTED FROM MARILY MUSTILLI.

—2003

✎ CARAMELIZED ONION AND QUARK DIP

Quark is like schmaltz: no matter how good it may be, the name is a buzz kill (and when conjoined to the word "dip," there's almost no salvaging it). I don't know anyone who actually cooks with quark, but there it always sits in the grocery store. And thankfully so, because when it came time to make this much-recommended recipe, the quark—made by Vermont Butter & Cheese Company—was right there waiting. Quark is like a less artery-clogging crème fraîche (it has 10 percent fat to crème fraîche's 30 percent), and it shares flavor genes with cottage cheese. Which makes it perfect for dip: tart and bright.

I had long thought of our love of dip as a bad habit we needed to break. But this dip by Melissa Clark is a great example of twenty-first-century cooking; an old idea, dip, is sliced and diced and reexamined, its flavors magnified and focused. In this case, the dip transcends its roots and becomes a perfect blend of creamy and sharp, amiable yet prickly. Unfortunately, this process of improvement usually entails more ingredients, more chopping, and more cooking time. But the preparation time here isn't unbearable, though you must caramelize onions, which involves hanging close to your stove for an hour. Then you blend them with the quark and sour cream (to underline the tartness of the quark) and raw onions (to contrast with the sweetened onions) and several other tasty ingredients. And then you're done, and your dip is an überdip and you can proudly set it out on your coffee table with good crackers and endive and celery.

----

2 medium onions, 2 tablespoons minced, the rest thinly sliced

2 tablespoons fresh lemon juice

3 tablespoons extra virgin olive oil

3 sprigs thyme

1 teaspoon salt

1 teaspoon sugar

1½ cups quark

½ cup sour cream

¼ cup chopped chives

½ teaspoon sweet paprika

Crackers, endive, or celery, for serving

1. Place the minced onion in a small bowl. Add the lemon juice and set aside.

2. Place a large heavy skillet over medium heat and add the olive oil. Toss in the sliced onions, thyme, salt, and sugar, reduce the heat to medium-low, and cook,

stirring occasionally, until the onions are caramelized, 40 to 50 minutes. Remove the thyme sprigs and cool to room temperature.

3. Coarsely chop the caramelized onions. Combine the quark and sour cream in a bowl. Stir in the caramelized onions, raw onion mixture, chives, and paprika. Taste and adjust the seasoning, then transfer to a serving bowl.

MAKES ABOUT 2¾ CUPS

SERVING SUGGESTIONS
Peppar Tomato (p. 31), Sir Francis Drake (p. 36), Janice Okun's Buffalo Chicken Wings (p. 464), Pork Burgers (p. 566)

NOVEMBER 12, 2003: "CHEESE FOR ROCKET SCIENTISTS, AND OTHERS," BY MELISSA CLARK.

—2003

⌒ CHEESE BALL WITH CUMIN, MINT, AND PISTACHIOS

Cheese balls were probably a step below the kind of cooking the *Times* advocated, so recipes for them didn't show up until they had moved out of the mainstream and into the realm of irony (see The Spice Boys' Cheese Ball on p. 79). Here I took the recipe my mother used throughout my 1970s childhood and restrung it with twenty-first-century flavors.

———

8 ounces cream cheese, at room temperature
4 ounces fresh goat cheese, at room temperature
Grated zest of 1 lemon
1 tablespoon fresh lemon juice
½ cup freshly grated Pecorino Romano cheese, preferably Fulvi
1 teaspoon toasted, ground coriander seeds
1 teaspoon toasted, ground cumin seeds
½ cup finely sliced celery heart with leaves
⅓ cup chopped mint
¼ teaspoon freshly ground black pepper
Sea salt
⅓ cup salted pistachios, coarsely ground
Very thin plain crackers, for serving

1. Beat the cream cheese and goat cheese in a large bowl with a wooden spoon until creamy and light. Beat in the lemon zest and lemon juice. Fold in the Pecorino Romano, coriander, cumin, celery, mint, and pepper. Season to taste with salt.

2. Lay a large piece of plastic wrap on the counter. Using a spatula, scrape the cheese mixture onto the center of the plastic. Pull up the edges of plastic wrap and form the cheese into a ball. Wrap tightly, place in a bowl to maintain the shape, and chill in the refrigerator for at least 2 hours.

3. Pour the ground pistachios into a shallow bowl. Unwrap the cheese ball and roll it in nuts until coated. Place the ball on a serving plate, cover with plastic wrap, and chill until ready to serve (or for up to 2 days).

4. Half an hour before serving, unwrap the cheese ball and let it come to room temperature. Serve with crackers.

SERVES 8

COOKING NOTE
To toast spices or seeds, spread them in a small sauté pan and place over medium-low heat; shake the pan occasionally. As soon as you can smell the spices (or see that the seeds have turned golden), remove from the heat and pour into a bowl to cool.

SERVING SUGGESTIONS
Classic Rum Punch (p. 24), Gin Rickey (p. 21), Wine Lemonade (p. 17), Egg and Olive Canapés (p. 57), Oliver Clark's Meat Loaf (p. 554), High-Temperature Roast Lamb (p. 526), Epigram of Lamb (p. 509)

DECEMBER 24, 2003: "IF YOU WANT IT DELICIOUS, MAKE IT YOURSELF," BY AMANDA HESSER

—2003

↪ CATALAN TORTILLA WITH AIOLI

This tradition-bound tortilla is served with an aioli that's anything but classic. The tortilla, as usual, is turned many times, sealing the eggs, potatoes, and onions in a crisp, rounded shell, so that by the time you're done, it's like a firm wheel of cheese. To make the aioli, however, you simmer the garlic cloves in sweet sherry and then, rather than using the garlic in its usual way to form the foundation of the mayonnaise, you add it at the very end, giving the aioli a beguiling sweetness.

Andy Nusser, the chef at Casa Mono in New York, who created this dish, also serves the aioli with *patatas bravas*, or Spanish fried potatoes. You could just as well serve it with the Saratoga Potatoes on p. 273.

———

12 garlic cloves, plus 1 tablespoon minced garlic

1 cup sweet Spanish sherry

3½ pounds baking potatoes (about 7 medium), peeled

2 cups extra virgin olive oil

Salt and freshly ground black pepper

1 large Spanish onion, diced

12 large eggs

3 tablespoons chopped flat-leaf parsley

2 large egg yolks

3 tablespoons sherry vinegar

1. Heat the oven to 375 degrees. Line a baking sheet with parchment paper. Combine the garlic cloves and sherry in a small saucepan and bring to a simmer over medium heat. Simmer until the sherry is reduced to a syrup and the garlic is soft, about 40 minutes. Cool to room temperature.

2. While the garlic is simmering, thinly slice the potatoes (¹⁄₁₆ to ⅛ inch thick), preferably with a mandoline. Toss the potatoes with about ¼ cup olive oil in a large bowl and season liberally with salt and pepper (this is the only seasoning, so be generous). Spread the potatoes on the baking sheet and bake for 18 minutes. Let cool.

3. Place a large skillet over medium heat, add the onion and 2 tablespoons olive oil, and sauté until translucent, about 5 to 7 minutes. Remove from the heat.

4. Coat a 12-inch nonstick frying pan with olive oil.

Beat the 12 eggs with the parsley and minced garlic in a large bowl. Add the potatoes and onions, stirring to combine, and transfer the mixture to the skillet, pressing down on the potatoes to create horizontal layers.

5. Place the pan over medium-low heat and cook, uncovered, until the eggs are set, about 40 minutes. Carefully loosen the tortilla from the sides and bottom of the pan with a rubber spatula. Hold a plate (or rimless baking sheet) over the pan with one hand, grasp the pan handle with the other, and then flip; the tortilla should easily fall onto the plate. (If it does not, use the spatula to remove it, then add more oil to the pan.) Slide the tortilla from the plate into the pan, and cook on the other side for 15 minutes. Continue to flip, cooking on each side 2 additional times for 5 minutes each, or until the center is firm and the edges are rounded. Transfer to a plate and let cool to room temperature.

6. Meanwhile, to make the aioli, combine the egg yolks, vinegar, and ¼ cup oil in a food processor. Process until the mixture has emulsified, then drizzle in the 1¼ cups more oil in a slow, steady stream. When the aioli has thickened, add the cooled garlic-sherry mixture and blend until smooth. Check for seasoning, and refrigerate.

7. Immediately before serving the tortilla, slather a thick layer of aioli over the top, like icing on a cake. (Refrigerate leftover aioli for sandwiches or grilled vegetables.)

SERVES 12

COOKING NOTE

The tortilla must be flipped several times, and it is large and heavy. I laid a rimless nonstick baking sheet atop the skillet, inverted the skillet and sheet, and then slid the tortilla from the baking sheet back into the skillet. You cannot do this process timidly—you must flip it quickly and confidently, like a juggler with flaming torches.

SERVING SUGGESTIONS

Sangria (p. 23), Sir Francis Drake (p. 36), Rebujito (p. 38), Pan con Tomate (p. 91), Potato, Ham, and Piquillo Pepper Croquetas (p. 94), Fried Chickpeas (p. 88), Paella (p. 309), Cocido (Chickpea, Sparerib, and Chorizo Stew; p. 578), Rabbit Soup with Garlic, Peppers, and Chorizo (p. 152), Caramel Custard (p. 836)

SEPTEMBER 29, 2004: "NEW YORK STORY: LOCAL GARLIC MAKES GOOD," BY DANA BOWEN. RECIPE ADAPTED FROM ANDY NUSSER, THE CHEF AT CASA MONO IN NEW YORK CITY.

—2004

FRIED OLIVES

If you've never had a fried olive, do not let another day pass without tasting one. Going the extra step of stuffing olives with an anchovy or a slip of tuna, or perhaps the two together, then breading and frying them, yields plentiful rewards: crunch, warm brine, and a taste of the sea, readying you for the sip of a crisp white. "With anchovy- or tuna-stuffed olives, I serve small wedges of lemon," Mona Talbott, a contributor to *T Living*, wrote. Fried Cerignola olives, "benefit from a dusting of Parmesan cheese. Put out a saucer of fennel slices or radishes and slow-roasted almonds." If you can't already tell from the ingredients, Talbott is an Alice Waters acolyte; she now runs the kitchen at the American Academy in Rome, which is overseen by Waters.

————

24 mild brined olives, preferably Nyons, pitted
Slivers of anchovy, nuggets of oil-packed tuna,
    strips of roasted peppers, or almonds
¾ cup all-purpose flour
2 large eggs
1 cup dry bread crumbs
Mild olive oil for deep-frying

1. Stuff the cavities of the olives with the anchovies, tuna, roasted peppers, or almonds—or some combination thereof.
2. Put the flour in a small bowl. Beat the eggs with a fork in a second bowl. Put the bread crumbs into a third bowl. Begin what is known professionally as "standard breading": one hand is reserved for dry ingredients, the other for wet. Dip an olive in the flour, rolling it around to coat evenly. Drop the olive in the beaten egg and, with your "wet" hand, swish the olive in the egg, then roll the sticky olive in the crumbs with the floured hand. Place on a plate and bread the remaining olives. Cover the breaded olives with plastic wrap and refrigerate until ready to fry (or fry them right away).
3. Heat 2 inches of olive oil in a medium saucepan or a small wok over medium-high heat. When the oil is hot (375 degrees), add a few olives at a time and fry until golden brown; don't crowd the pan, because you need room to roll the olives around with a fork. Using a slotted spoon, lift out the olives and drain them on a paper towel.

SERVES 4

COOKING NOTE
The olives can be prepared up to 8 hours in advance.

VARIATION
If you don't like any of the stuffings listed in the recipe, Talbott said, "Feel free to use whatever tasty bits you find in the fridge. In Italy, they're often stuffed with braised meat, prosciutto, and cooked lemon." Talbott noted that she also likes frying Cerignola olives, "but they are difficult to pit, so fry them without stuffing."

SERVING SUGGESTIONS
Park Avenue Cocktail (p. 19), Sir Francis Drake (p. 36), Grapefruit Wine (p. 37), Kumquat-Clementine Cordial (p. 42), Nicole Kaplan's Gougères (p. 76), Fried Sage Leaves (p. 87)

NOVEMBER 7, 2004: "THE DISH: NIBBLES AND SIPS," BY MONA TALBOTT.

—2004

FRIED SAGE LEAVES

This delightfully simple snack, which seems to have been designed to go with a glass of chilled albariño, comes from Kurt Andersen, the novelist and founder of *Spy* magazine.

————

Olive oil for frying
Sage leaves, rinsed and patted dry
All-purpose flour
Salt and freshly ground black pepper

Heat ¼ inch of oil in a medium skillet over medium-high heat until hot enough to toast a bread crumb in 30 seconds. Toss the sage leaves in flour, shake vigorously to remove as much flour as possible, and fry until golden brown, 15 to 20 seconds per side. Drain on paper towels, sprinkle with salt and pepper, and serve.

SERVING SUGGESTIONS

Peach Bowl (p. 20), Wine Lemonade (p. 17), Fried Olives (p. 87), Nicole Kaplan's Gougères (p. 76)

JULY 17, 2005: "KITCHEN VOYEUR: KITCHEN SAGE," BY JONATHAN REYNOLDS. RECIPE ADAPTED FROM KURT ANDERSEN.

—2005

FRIED CHICKPEAS

Keep a can of chickpeas and a jar of smoked paprika in your pantry, and you have the instant makings of an impressive hors d'oeuvre. When the chickpeas hit the oil, their skins fly out like wings, encasing their soft bellies in a delicate shell. You can season the chickpeas with either hot or sweet smoked paprika, but if you go for the hot, count on serving more drinks.

————

Canola oil for deep-frying
One 16-ounce can chickpeas, rinsed, drained, and patted dry
Maldon sea salt
Spanish smoked paprika (pimentón)

Pour 1 inch of canola oil into a deep saucepan and heat over medium-high heat. When the oil is hot enough to toast a bread crumb in 30 seconds, it's ready. Carefully add the chickpeas to the oil and fry until the outer skins form crisp shells but the peas are still creamy inside, about 1 minute. Drain on paper towels, and season with Maldon salt and smoked paprika.

SERVES 4

SERVING SUGGESTIONS

Sangria (p. 23), Rebujito (p. 38), Potato, Ham, and Piquillo Pepper Croquetas (p. 94), Seasoned Olives (p. 90), Pan con Tomate (p. 91), Catalan Tortilla with Aioli (p. 86), Paella (p. 309), Cocido (Chickpea, Sparerib, and Chorizo Stew; p. 578), Rabbit Soup with Garlic, Peppers, and Chorizo (p. 152)

SEPTEMBER 11, 2005: "THE WAY WE EAT: RAISING THE TAPAS BAR," BY AMANDA HESSER. RECIPE ADAPTED FROM TÍA POL IN NEW YORK CITY.

—2005

PORK BELLY TEA SANDWICHES

Cheers to the cheeky *Times* editor who ran a recipe for tea sandwiches as part of a story on food for the Super Bowl, the most testosterone-fueled event of the year!

These are probably the huskiest tea sandwiches you'll find: white bread fused with chile fish sauce, and one fatty piece of pork. It's like Slash lunching at the Colony Club.

————

1⅓ cup ketjap manis (a sweet soy-based sauce, available in Asian grocery stores)
¼ cup Chinese black vinegar
2 tablespoons dark soy sauce
2 tablespoons Asian fish sauce
Juice of 1 lime
One 2-pound piece fresh pork belly, with skin
2 bunches scallions
Salt
½ cup rice vinegar
1½ cups mayonnaise
1 clove garlic, put through a press or minced
2 teaspoons sambal oelek (Indonesian Malaysian chile paste) or Sriracha (Thai chile sauce)
24 thick slices white bread
24 large sprigs cilantro

1. Combine the ketjap manis, black vinegar, soy sauce, fish sauce, and lime juice in a bowl. Place the pork belly in a heavy 1 gallon freezer bag with a zip closure, pour in the soy sauce mixture, and seal the bag. Place it in another freezer bag or bowl in case of leaks, and refrigerate for at least 24 hours (and up to 48 hours), turning from time to time.

2. The next day, heat the oven to 225 degrees.

3. Place the pork skin side up in a roasting pan with a close fit, pour in the marinade, and add about ⅓ cup water (more if needed), so the liquid comes halfway up the sides of the pork. Cover with a sheet of parchment, then cover tightly with foil. Roast for about 3 hours, until a skewer inserted in the pork meets little or no resistance. Allow to cool in the pan for about 30 minutes.

4. While the pork cooks, trim the scallions, discarding all but about an inch of green, and slice very thin on an angle. Place in a bowl, toss with a little salt, and pour the rice vinegar over. Cover and allow to marinate for at least 2 hours.

5. Mix the mayonnaise with the garlic and sambal oelek in a small bowl; refrigerate.

6. When the pork has cooled, remove the skin. Cut the pork into 4-inch-long chunks and cut each into very thin slices. You should be able to get at least thirty-six slices.

7. Place the bread on a work surface and spread with the mayonnaise mixture. Drain the scallions and scatter them over half the bread slices. Top each of these with 3 slices of pork lined up side by side. Place 2 cilantro sprigs on the pork, then cover with the remaining bread, mayonnaise side down. Trim the crusts from each sandwich. Leave the sandwiches whole or cut into thirds, between the slices of pork, and serve.

MAKES 12 SANDWICHES OR 3 DOZEN PIECES

SERVING SUGGESTIONS
Moscow Mule (p. 20), Ginger Lemonade (p. 26), Kaffir Lime Lemonade (p. 26)

FEBRUARY 1, 2006: "TEMPTATION: REFINED BUT READY FOR THE BIG GAME," BY FLORENCE FABRICANT. RECIPE ADAPTED FROM ZAK PELACCIO, OWNER OF FATTY CRAB IN NEW YORK CITY.

—2006

BEET TZATZIKI

This tzatziki is made with beets rather than cucumber, so it's sweet, tangy, and very pink.

———

5 baby beets (about the size of a golf ball), or 1 full-sized beet, peeled and quartered
½ teaspoon minced garlic
2 teaspoons fresh lemon juice
Salt
1½ cups plain whole-milk yogurt, preferably Greek-style
1 tablespoon extra virgin olive oil
1 tablespoon chopped dill
Freshly ground black pepper

1. Boil the beets until tender, about 20 minutes, drain. When the beets are cool enough to handle, rub the skins off with a kitchen towel (one you don't care about) or a paper towel. Coarsely grate the beets.

2. Combine the garlic, lemon juice, and 1 teaspoon salt in a medium bowl. Stir in the yogurt and olive oil, then the beets and dill. Season with additional salt and pepper. Chill until cold.

SERVES 6 TO 8

COOKING NOTE
You can boil the beets as the recipe instructs, but for more concentrated flavor, I recommend roasting them. Lay the beets on a sheet of foil, sprinkle with a little olive oil, and season with salt. Fold up the foil to make a packet, rolling the edges to seal them. Lay the packet on a baking sheet and roast in a 350-degree oven until tender, about 30 minutes. Let cool, then peel the beets.

SERVING SUGGESTIONS
Hummus bi Tahini (p. 68), Iraqi Grape Leaves Stuffed with Lamb, Mint, and Cinnamon (p. 510), Arnaki Araka (Lamb with Peas; p. 550), Cumin-Mustard Carrots (p. 237)

JUNE 21, 2006: "THE CHEF: ANA SORTUN: A BAZAAR FROM THE HARD YANKEE SOIL," BY JULIA MOSKIN. RECIPE ADAPTED FROM SPICE: FLAVORS OF THE EASTERN MEDITERRANEAN, BY ANA SORTUN.

—2006

THE BEST SPINACH DIP, WITH CHIPOTLE AND LIME

Yes, I was skeptical too. But this dip avoids the goopy absurdity of most spinach dips—it's smoky and raspy with spice.

———

Two 10-ounce packages frozen spinach,
    thawed and drained
8 ounces cream cheese, at room temperature
$\frac{1}{2}$ cup mayonnaise
$\frac{1}{2}$ cup sour cream
$\frac{1}{2}$ cup sliced scallions
$\frac{1}{3}$ cup chopped cilantro
1 tablespoon chopped chipotles in adobo sauce
$1\frac{1}{2}$ tablespoons fresh lime juice
$\frac{3}{4}$ teaspoon kosher salt
Freshly ground black pepper to taste
Tortilla chips for serving

1. Bundle the spinach in a clean dish towel and squeeze very tightly to remove all excess moisture.
2. Blend together all the ingredients except the spinach (and tortilla chips) in a food processor until very smooth, about 90 seconds. Pulse in the spinach just until combined. Taste and adjust the seasoning. Serve with tortilla chips.

MAKES ABOUT 3 CUPS

SERVING SUGGESTIONS
Gin Rickey (p. 21), Classic Rum Punch (p. 24), La Paloma (p. 35), Caramelized Onion and Quark Dip (p. 84), Salted and Deviled Almonds (p. 51), Parmesan Crackers (p. 84), Cheese Straws (p. 79)

MAY 23, 2007: "A GOOD APPETITE: SUMMERY, SMOKY, AND SPICY: NUDGING SPINACH DIP UPWARD," BY MELISSA CLARK.

—2007

SEASONED OLIVES

Smashing firm green olives before marinating them allows the seasonings to permeate their flesh. Contrary to the forensic evidence in those grocery store olive bins—soggy bits of rosemary, dregs of unidentifiable spices—you don't need much to improve an olive. Just a little minced carrot and celery leaf, garlic, a slice of lemon or two. Within a few hours, the flavors integrate, and you have densely scented olives.

———

3 cups (about 12 ounces) firm whole green olives
    in brine (such as Lucques), drained
$\frac{1}{4}$ cup extra virgin olive oil
2 tablespoons chopped celery leaves
$\frac{1}{2}$ teaspoon minced garlic
3 tablespoons finely diced carrots
3 paper-thin slices lemon
Salt and freshly ground black pepper

1. Using a meat pounder, crack the olives one by one, leaving the pits intact.
2. Place the olives in a bowl. Stir in the oil, celery leaves, garlic, carrots, and lemon. Season with a dash of salt and pepper to taste. Let sit for at least an hour at room temperature, or 4 hours in the refrigerator. Serve at room temperature.

SERVES 6

SERVING SUGGESTIONS
Junipero Gibson with Pickled Red Onion (p. 33), Blue Cheese Dip (p. 54), Avocado Sandowsky (p. 54), Ricotta Crostini with Fresh Thyme and Dried Oregano (p. 93)

JULY 22, 2007: "THE WAY WE EAT: LOW FOOD," BY AMANDA HESSER. RECIPE ADAPTED FROM GABRIELLA BECCHINA, CO-OWNER OF OLIO VERDE OLIVE OIL.

—2007

SQUASHED TOMATOES

My friend Nancy Harmon Jenkins taught me to make these squashed tomatoes, which can work as a topping for toasts scraped with garlic, a simple room-temperature pasta sauce, or a side with grilled chicken. You take small tomatoes, no bigger than golf balls, place them on a baking sheet, and put them under the broiler or on the grill until the skins begin to blister and singe and the fruit starts to soften. Then comes the fun part, as you take a fork and do what you should never do with meat: squash the tomatoes to release their juices. Next you season them with salt and a crumbled red chile and douse them with good, buttery olive oil. Unexpectedly, they're actually better in this rumpled form: released of their juices, and soaking in oil, they taste ripe and luxurious.

————

2½ pounds large cherry tomatoes
¼ cup extra virgin olive oil
Sea salt and freshly ground black pepper
1 dried red chile, crumbled
6 slices country bread, toasted and rubbed
　　with a garlic clove

1. Heat a broiler or grill. Set the cooking rack 3 inches from the heat.
2. Place the tomatoes on a rimmed baking sheet and broil until they soften and the skins start to blister and split, about 2 minutes. Using tongs, flip the tomatoes and broil until blistered but not totally soft, 2 minutes more. Or put them on the grill rack and cook, turning once.
3. Transfer the tomatoes to a serving dish and lightly squash with a fork so some of the juices run out. (Be careful to avoid spattering.) Sprinkle with the oil, salt and pepper, and chile and fold gently to combine. Serve over the toasted country bread.

SERVES 6

SERVING SUGGESTIONS
Junipero Gibson with Pickled Red Onion (p. 33), Seasoned Olives (p. 90), Ricotta Crostini with Fresh Thyme and Dried Oregano (p. 93)

JULY 22, 2007: "THE WAY WE EAT: LOW FOOD," BY AMANDA HESSER. RECIPE ADAPTED FROM *FLAVORS OF PUGLIA*, BY NANCY HARMON JENKINS.

—2007

↬ PAN CON TOMATE

Spanish *pan con tomate*—bread with tomato—is usually not so much a dish as it is an accompaniment to other tapas like serrano ham and grilled octopus.

While it shares a kinship and an ingredient list with Italy's tomato bruschetta (and the Squashed Tomatoes on p. 90) it's an entirely different recipe. With bruschetta, the tomatoes function as a topping. Here the tomato functions as a flavoring and tool. You rub the belly of a halved tomato onto the surface of hot toasted and oiled bread, softening the coarse edges, soaking the juices into the bread, flavoring it without adding substance. The order in which you add the toppings makes all the difference. The oil moistens the bread, the salt seasons between the layers of oil and tomato, and the tomato goes on last, because you want the first taste to be of fresh sweet tomato, followed by a touch of acid, salt, and oil.

I'd skip one ingredient in this recipe, which comes from Melissa Clark, a columnist for the Dining section (and the author of many excellent recipes in this book). She offers the option of topping the bread with sliced tomatoes, which seems unnecessary in my view. But I thoroughly agree with her when she says she could eat this Catalan dish "every single day."

————

4 slices country-style bread, toasted and still hot
1 fat clove garlic, halved
Good-quality extra virgin olive oil
Coarse sea salt
1 large tomato, halved crosswise
Sliced tomatoes for serving (optional)

Rub the bread with the garlic halves. Drizzle the slices with oil and sprinkle with salt. Rub the tomato cut side down on the toasted bread, generously squeezing the insides out as you go. Sprinkle with salt, and top with slices of tomatoes if desired.

MAKES 4 TOASTS

COOKING NOTES
Don't use a dense, heavy bread. You need one that has a firm crust but an airy interior. Rub the garlic onto the bread gently and sparingly. The garlic should be submissive.

SERVING SUGGESTIONS
Sangria (p. 23), Rebujito (p. 38), Catalan Tortilla with Aioli (p. 86), Potato, Ham, and Piquillo Pepper Croquetas (p. 94), Fried Chickpeas (p. 88), Paella (p. 309), Cocido (Chickpea, Sparerib, and Chorizo Stew;

p. 578), Rabbit Soup with Garlic, Peppers, and Chorizo (p. 152), Caramel Custard (p. 836)

AUGUST 22, 2007: "A GOOD APPETITE: SO MANY TOMATOES TO STUFF IN A WEEK," BY MELISSA CLARK.

—2007

ROASTED FETA WITH THYME HONEY

This is not the most beautiful hors d'oeuvre—the feta emerges from the oven with a war-torn look, and your casserole strewn with singed oil and blackened burned bits. But the abuse of the dish is all in the service of the feta, whose honey-slicked exterior turns to savory candy and whose interior softens to custard. Plus, the recipe is a breeze—it's a great hors d'oeuvre to include when you have a more ambitious meal to follow.

_____

One 8-ounce slab Greek feta cheese, blotted dry
2 tablespoons extra virgin olive oil
1 tablespoon Greek thyme honey or other honey
Freshly ground black pepper
Greek-style pita bread, toasted and cut into wedges
Heirloom tomatoes, roasted beets, nuts, or pickled
    vegetables (optional)

1. Heat the oven to 400 degrees. Select a small oven-to-table earthenware dish or a small ovenproof sauté pan and line it with aluminum foil, to help transfer the cheese to a plate after roasting.
2. Place the feta in the dish and cover with the olive oil. Bake until the cheese is soft and springy to the touch but not melted, about 8 minutes. Remove from the oven and heat the broiler.
3. Heat the honey in the microwave or in a metal bowl over a pan of simmering water until it is fluid enough to be spread with a pastry brush, and paint the surface of the feta with it. Broil until the top of the cheese browns and just starts to bubble. Season with pepper. Serve immediately, with pita wedges and, if desired, sliced heirloom tomatoes, roasted beets, nuts, or pickled vegetables.

SERVES 4 TO 6

COOKING NOTES

If you can't find thyme honey—I couldn't—use a mild-flavored honey like acacia and warm it with a few sprigs of fresh thyme.

Use a dish that's just large enough to hold the cheese, or the oil will pool on the open surfaces and could catch fire under your broiler.

I'd serve the feta not with pita, as in the original recipe, but with a rustic cracker or toasted thinly sliced country bread.

SERVING SUGGESTIONS

Astoria Cocktail (p. 19), Peppar Tomato (p. 31), Peppadew Martini (p. 40), Billionaire Cocktail (p. 40), The Normandy (p. 43)

SEPTEMBER 9, 2007: "THE WAY WE EAT: OLYMPIC DINNERS," BY SARA DICKERMAN.

—2007

EDAMAME WITH NORI SALT

My three-year-olds devoured the whole batch of this edamame—who knew? It could become the go-to snack at kids' birthday parties: down with Veggie Bootie!

_____

Sea salt
20 sheets nori
1 pound edamame, fresh or frozen and defrosted

1. Combine 4 quarts water and 1 tablespoon salt in a large pot and bring to a boil over high heat.
2. Meanwhile, quickly pass the nori sheets over an open flame, one by one, to toast and dry them. Tear into small pieces. Using a spice/coffee grinder grind the nori to a fine powder.
3. When the water has reached a rapid boil, add the edamame and cook until just tender, about 2 minutes. Drain well (do not cool) and quickly transfer to a large bowl. Add a generous dusting of nori powder and sea salt—taste it, because you may need more than you think. Serve immediately.

SERVES 4

Saketini (p. 37), Fresh and Smoked Salmon Spread (p. 72), Alaskan Salmon (p. 423), Coconut Rice Pudding with Lime Syrup (p. 846)

JANUARY 9, 2008: "NORI STEPS AWAY FROM THE SUSHI," BY J. J. GOODE. RECIPE ADAPTED FROM EVAN RICH, THE CHEF AT SUMILE SUSHI IN NEW YORK CITY.

—2008

⌒ CARAMELIZED BACON

The craft of recipe writing isn't a hot topic, even in food circles. No one is going to hold forth at a dinner party about whose recipe writing is crisper, more layered, or more thoughtful, Julia Child's or Marcella Hazan's. (And if someone does, you should probably strike that person from your dinner party list.) That said, the current trend toward pared-down, robotic instructions is abominable. Recipes should be more like a letter from your mother—somewhere between an instruction manual and a personal note. A good recipe will guide you with specifics and help you understand what the results should be. Which is why I like this recipe by Patricia Marx, a novelist, so much.

————

1 pound bacon

One 1-pound box light brown sugar (about 2 ¼ cups)

¼ cup water

1. Go to a butcher and spend as much money as you have on very good bacon. Cut it into medium-thick slices, say, ³⁄₁₆ of an inch.
2. Heat the oven to 400 degrees. Line a large rimmed baking sheet with parchment paper. Dump a box of brown sugar into a big bowl. Light brown sugar is best, but if you want to use dark brown, I won't stop you. Add ¼ cup of water, so that the sugar becomes more than damp but less than soupy. Some bacon caramelizers add a dash of cayenne pepper, but I think this makes the dish too nutritious.
3. Dredge the bacon in the sugar, one slice at a time. If the sugar isn't sticking to the bacon, add some more water a teaspoon at a time until it sticks. (By the way, you won't use all of the sugar, but it's good to have

extra.) Place the bacon strips on the parchment paper. I then smear some sugar on top of the bacon, on the theory that if a little sweet is good, more is better.
4. Place the bacon in the oven. It's impossible for me to tell you how long to cook the bacon, because it depends on whether you like it chewy or crispy. Some recipes tell you to keep it in the oven for 8 to 13 minutes per side, depending on the thickness of the bacon. I keep it in on the longer side. You should take yours out when it resembles the kind of bacon you would like to eat. Cut it into roughly 1½-inch triangles. Serve at room temperature.

SERVES 8 TO 10

COOKING NOTE

Marx said, "You can make this up to 3 days in advance. Keep in a tightly sealed container at room temperature. This is a dish that can't be ruined. You can freeze the leftovers. But why are there leftovers?"

SERVING SUGGESTIONS

Patsy's Bourbon Slush (p. 32), The Bone (p. 34), Martini (p. 35), Zombie Punch (p. 41), Hot Cheese Olives (p. 83)

JANUARY 13, 2008: "EAT, MEMORY: A NOT-SO-SIMPLE PLAN," BY PATRICIA MARX.

—2008

⌒ RICOTTA CROSTINI WITH FRESH THYME AND DRIED OREGANO

Fresh ricotta is fresh in every sense. A fresh take on milk. A fresh cheese. And so fresh that if it's great, it will turn on you overnight. For this crostini, it really is worth seeking out a local producer, because with excellent ricotta, you'll want nothing more than to spread it on toasted bread dabbed with a little oil. You whip the ricotta with milk and season it with herbs and a flash of salt. That is all.

If you can't buy top-quality ricotta, you can make your own; see p. 614.

————

About 8 slices (¾-inch-thick) crusty bread, such as
ciabatta or levain, chewy and substantial
but not very sour

Extra virgin olive oil

Kosher or flaky sea salt (like Maldon)

2 cups fresh ricotta, at cool room temperature

2 tablespoons heavy cream

1 teaspoon coarse sea salt

1 teaspoon coarsely ground black pepper

1 teaspoon thyme leaves

1 teaspoon dried oregano

2 large cloves garlic, unpeeled, halved

1. Heat a charcoal or gas grill or broiler to very hot. If the bread slices are very large, cut them in half or thirds. Brush the slices on both sides with olive oil and sprinkle with kosher or flaky sea salt.

2. Beat the ricotta and cream together in a bowl with an electric mixer (preferably) with a paddle attachment until light and fluffy. Add 1 teaspoon kosher or flaky salt and mix well. Transfer to a shallow serving bowl and sprinkle with the coarse sea salt, pepper, thyme, and oregano. Drizzle olive oil on top, about 2 to 3 tablespoons.

3. Grill or broil the bread, turning once until toasted all over and lightly charred in places. Lightly rub one side of each slice with the cut side of a garlic clove. Serve hot, with the ricotta on the side.

SERVES 6 TO 8

VARIATIONS

Julia Moskin, the author of the article, offered two other ricotta crostini:

Lemon Zest and Hazelnut (adapted from Lunetta in New York City)—Whisk together the ricotta, ¼ cup olive oil, 1 teaspoon salt, and the grated zest of 1 lemon. Spread on the toasted, garlic-rubbed bread and sprinkle with ½ cup hazelnuts, toasted, skins rubbed off, and coarsely chopped or smashed with a heavy skillet.

Pine Nut and Honey Variation (adapted from dell'Anima in New York City)—Spread the ricotta over the toasted bread (do not rub with garlic), drizzle on ¾ cup honey, preferably a farmers' market–type with good flavor, and sprinkle on ½ cup toasted pine nuts.

SERVING SUGGESTIONS

Peach Bowl (p. 20), Peppadew Martini (p. 40), Rhubarb Bellini (p. 30), Kumquat-Clementine Cordial (p. 42)

MAY 28, 2008: "SUDDENLY, RICOTTA'S A BIG CHEESE," BY JULIA MOSKIN. RECIPE ADAPTED FROM ANDREW CARMELLINI, THE CHEF AT A VOCE IN NEW YORK CITY.

—2008

☞ POTATO, HAM, AND PIQUILLO PEPPER CROQUETAS

While architectural food and gold-leaf-speckled desserts have come and gone, dishes born of thrift tend to last. Among the many examples are panzanella (Italian bread and tomato salad), bread pudding, leek and potato soup, apple cake, and croquettes. All these dishes are simple but satisfying; they don't try too hard.

There are dozens of recipes for croquettes in the *Times* nineteenth-century recipe files, and I was surprised to see that in this recent version, little other than the seasonings have changed. These Spanish croquetas use fancier meat and seasonings—serrano ham, smoked paprika—and employ a neat trick: after forming the croquetas, you chill them so they crisp well and hold together when sautéed. But the soul of the dish is unchanged—you're still taking a leftover meat and stretching its bounty through the cunning use of bread and potatoes.

---

3 cups seasoned mashed potatoes, chilled

2¼ cups plain dry bread crumbs

2 ounces serrano ham cut into small dice (about ½ cup)

½ cup piquillo or roasted red peppers, cut into small dice

5 large eggs

1 large egg yolk

Kosher salt

1 teaspoon freshly ground black pepper

¾ teaspoon Spanish smoked paprika (pimentón)

1 cup all-purpose flour

Olive or vegetable oil for frying

1. Combine the potatoes, ¾ cup bread crumbs, the ham, pepper, 1 egg, the yolk, a pinch of salt, ½ tea-

spoon black pepper, and the paprika, in a large bowl. Mix well.

2. Lightly beat the remaining 4 eggs in a wide shallow bowl. Place the remaining 1½ cups bread crumbs in a second bowl, and the flour in a third. Season the bread crumbs with ½ teaspoon each salt and the remaining ½ teaspoon pepper.

3. Using about 2 tablespoons of the croqueta mixture for each, form it into 3-inch-long fingers. Dip each finger in the flour, tapping off the excess, then dip in the egg mixture, letting the excess drip off, and then in the bread crumbs. Transfer to a large baking sheet. When you have finished forming the croquetas, cover the tray with plastic wrap and refrigerate for at least 12 hours, or overnight.

4. When ready to fry, heat ¼ inch of oil in a large skillet over medium-high heat. Fry the croquetas in batches, turning once, until dark golden all over, 2 to 3 minutes a side. Transfer to a paper-towel-lined plate and sprinkle with salt if desired. Serve hot.

MAKES ABOUT 3 DOZEN CROQUETAS

SERVING SUGGESTIONS
Sangria (p. 23), Rebujito (p. 38), Pan con Tomate (p. 91), Catalan Tortilla with Aioli (p. 86), Fried Chickpeas (p. 88), Paella (p. 309), Cocido (Chickpea, Sparerib, and Chorizo Stew; p. 578), Rabbit Soup with Garlic, Peppers, and Chorizo (p. 152), Toasts with Chocolate, Olive Oil, and Sea Salt (p. 844)

NOVEMBER 19, 2008: "A GOOD APPETITE: ALMOST HEAVEN; LEFTOVER MASHED POTATOES, UPLIFTED," BY MELISSA CLARK.

—2008

OLIVE OIL–TUNA SPREAD WITH LEMON AND OREGANO

This is the hors d'oeuvre version of tonnato sauce (see Vitello Tonnato, p. 559). With some strong seasonings (lemon, dried oregano, garlic) and plenty of fat (butter and oil), canned tuna can truly surprise. Here the tuna acts as anchovy does, offering a baseline ocean flavor. The seasonings provide tang and heat and the fats transform the shredded fish into silk.

————

One 6½-ounce can tuna packed in olive oil (do not drain)
4 tablespoons unsalted butter, softened
Grated zest of 1 lemon
2½ tablespoons fresh lemon juice
2 tablespoons extra virgin olive oil
½ teaspoon dried oregano
Salt and freshly ground black pepper
1 plump clove garlic
Breadsticks, crackers, or toasted slices of baguette brushed with olive oil for serving

Place the tuna, including the oil, in a food processor, add the remaining ingredients (except for the bread or crackers), and process until smooth and creamy. Transfer to a bowl and serve with breadsticks, crackers, or toast. Or refrigerate for up to 3 days; remove from the refrigerator 1 hour before serving and stir well.

SERVES 10 TO 12; CAN BE DOUBLED EASILY

COOKING NOTE
Use the best oil-packed tuna you can find—preferably the imported variety in glass jars. It's a bit more expensive but worth it.

SERVING SUGGESTIONS
Rhubarb Bellini (p. 30), Parmesan Crackers (p. 84)

NOVEMBER 26, 2008: "JUST A NIBBLE BEFORE WE GORGE OURSELVES," BY JULIA MOSKIN. RECIPE ADAPTED FROM PATRICIA WELL'S TRATTORIA, BY PATRICIA WELLS.

—2008

PICKLED SHRIMP

This makes a huge amount, which you can easily halve, but the shrimp are so good you'll want to feed twenty. They're best with a full day to marinate, so plan ahead.

————

3 pounds shrimp, shelled, deveined, and boiled or steamed just until pink
2 medium onions, quartered and thinly sliced
1 teaspoon celery seeds
1 cup extra virgin olive oil

6 garlic cloves, thinly sliced

4 lemons, preferably organic, thinly sliced

14 bay leaves

1 teaspoon fennel seeds

1 teaspoon mustard seeds

4 dried hot chile peppers

1 teaspoon freshly ground white pepper

1 teaspoon coriander seeds

½ cup fresh lemon juice

¼ cup white wine vinegar

1. Combine all the ingredients in a large bowl and toss thoroughly. Transfer to a serving bowl or glass crock, cover, and refrigerate for at least 6 hours, or overnight.
2. One hour before serving, remove the shrimp from the refrigerator. Remove the bay leaves. Serve on small plates or with toothpicks.

SERVES 15 TO 20

SERVING SUGGESTIONS

Vermouth Cup (p. 15), Sazerac (p. 17), Mint Julep (p. 24), The Cuke (p. 39), Kumquat-Clementine Cordial (p. 42), Caramelized Bacon (p. 93), Eggs Louisiana (p. 53), Onion Rings (p. 61), North Carolina–Style Pulled Pork (p. 550), Cheese Straws (p. 79), Julia Harrison Adams's Pimento Cheese (p. 64)

NOVEMBER 26, 2008: "JUST A NIBBLE BEFORE WE GORGE OURSELVES," BY JULIA MOSKIN. RECIPE ADAPTED FROM *FRANK STITT'S SOUTHERN TABLE*, BY FRANK STITT.

—2008

- Oxtail soup.
- If you are a clam or a lobster, there is a strong chance you'll end up in chowder or bisque.
- Gumbo (p. 125).
- Louis Diat creates his vichyssoise; the *Times* will publish a version of it in 1957 (p. 111).
- Soups are thickened with flour and drowned in cream.
- Gazpacho is imported from Spain, leaving behind the rest of its family of cured ham and tapas, but manages to charm anyway; it soon replaces tomato soup in popularity.
- Andy Warhol paints Campbell's Soup cans.
- Chilled soups are catchy; autumn soups are served in carved-out pumpkins and loaves of bread.
- Lipton introduces Cup-a-Soup.
- Carl and Shirley Sontheimer, the founders of Cuisinart, debut the food processor.
- Craig Claiborne appears to have been on an all-soup diet.
- The Southwestern food trend briefly elevates black bean soup (though recipes for it can be found as far back as the nineteenth century).
- Craig Claiborne cooks zucchini to death in broth and yet it survives deliciously (p. 123).
- Paul Prudhomme's Cajun-Style Gumbo (p. 125) is a culinary marathon worth training for.
- Sophisticated stay-at-home dinner = rustic Mediterranean soup sprinkled with olive oil and served with country bread and salad.
- *Chicken Soup for the Soul* is published.
- *Seinfeld* immortalizes the Soup Nazi, based on Al Yeganeh, a Midtown Manhattan soup vendor who owned Soup Kitchen International.
- Gazpacho again (p. 146), but this time better.

—1870s—
—1880s—
—1890s—
—1911—
—1940s—
—1960s—
—1962—
—1970s—
—1970—
—1973—
—1974—
—1980s—
—1980—
—1984—
—1990s—
—1993—
—1995—
—2000s—

- Milk-and-baking-soda-based tomato soup recipes are sent to the *Times* by the dozen.

- Colonial soups such as Mulligatawny (p. 113) and Crème Senagalese (p. 124) are in vogue.

- High-powered blenders and immersion blenders make the leap from restaurant kitchen to home kitchen. Pureed soups go from thin to silky and frothy; see *Yellow Pepper Soup with Paprika Mousse* (p. 147).

- Cocktail party riff: soup served in shot glasses.

3

SOUPS

Of all the recipes in this book, soups have changed the most since the *New York Times* began running recipes in the mid nineteenth century. Soups used to be simmered until they begged for mercy, and they were almost always thickened with flour or eggs. By the time Craig Claiborne took the helm as food editor in the late 1950s, soups were being cooked for slightly less time but they were usually enriched with a bucketful of heavy cream. (In most of the recipes in this book, I offer the option of less cream, but feel free to go old school, if it's OK with your family doctor.)

What changed soups was the invention of the blender in the 1930s and then of the food processor in the 1970s. Purees were no longer solely the domain of restaurant kitchens where some sad soul had the tedious job of pushing soup through a fine-mesh sieve. They could now be prepared in a galley kitchen in a few minutes.

Eventually cooks began to shed their reliance on cream for a sense of smoothness and on long cooking times to soften firm ingredients—a food processor could whip up a soup's texture so that it felt creamy even if there wasn't any cream in it. People also figured out that simmering a soup for

ages usually did little for its flavor—indeed, that cooking soups as little as possible (and sometimes not at all, as in the Watermelon Gazpacho on p. 150), made for zippier, more fragrant broths. And that while it's fine to simmer bones and beans for hours, if you want to taste such aromatics as thyme, garlic, chile, and star anise, adding them toward the end of cooking keeps their flavors fresh.

The readers who wrote to tell me of their favorite *Times* recipe were particularly passionate about their soups, and I relied heavily on their recommendations when assembling this chapter. As a result, you'll see some recurrent themes—butternut squash and black beans figure prominently, as do tomato soups and gazpachos. There is also a preponderance of recipes from chefs (Thomas Keller, for instance) and from the writers Barbara Kafka and Mark Bittman, who may or may not realize they have a beloved niche in soup.

There was a split over cold curried zucchini soups. One by Jaques Pépin ran in 1975, another by Craig Claiborne in 1980. Both are nearly the same, and both came with enthusiastic endorsements. I prefer the latter (see p. 123), but I loved one note I got about the Pépin version, from a reader, Neal O'Donnell of Corning, New York:

[D]uring the week after the article appeared, I made that soup for a small dinner party to great acclaim. On the weekend, I was invited to another dinner and the hostess served the very same soup. On Sunday, the hosts of the Saturday party and I were invited to a large bash up on Keuka—one of our Finger Lakes and not far from the Dr. Frank winery. As our lakeside hosts ladled their chilled soup into bowls and sprinkled the top with the julienned zucchini strips, the three of us guests broke out in such boisterous laughter that I'm sure could have been heard across the lake and over the hill. You guessed it!

RECIPES BY CATEGORY

⤚ TOMATO SOUP I

This is a fantastic old recipe to which I've added just one modern innovation: the immersion blender. Readers in the nineteenth century had an insatiable hunger for tomato soup recipes—on the day this one ran, it was "Tomato Soup IV" (and since there are two tomato soups in the book, I've called it Tomato Soup I). Generally, there were two varieties: those made with beef bones and those made with milk. The latter were the precursor to the tomato soups you find in diners and school lunchrooms, served with a grilled cheese sandwich. But those recipes were later tweaked in unfortunate ways—thickened with cornstarch, throttled with cream.

The old-style milk-based tomato soup, exemplified here, is a happily uncluttered combination. Fresh tomatoes are cooked down to a pulp. Milk is scalded. Butter and salt are added for flavor, and cracker crumbs for thickening. Many recipes also called for baking soda (a base), which prevented the tomatoes (an acid) from curdling the milk; this recipe, which does not contain baking soda, curdles the instant the tomatoes and milk are combined. It doesn't taste bad this way, but it looks a little like stracciatella, the Italian egg-drop soup. An immersion blender fixes this: in seconds all of the curdling vanishes and the fat is re-emulsified, returning the soup to a silky pink pool.

If you don't have an immersion blender, the pureeing can be done in small batches in a blender. Hold the lid on tight with a dish towel (hot soup likes to explode from the top). Or maybe this is the time to go get an immersion blender.

For some other variations on tomato soup, see Tomato Soup II (p. 114) and Moroccan Tomato Soup (p. 134).

———

3 pounds ripe tomatoes, cored and cut into chunks

4½ cups whole milk

3 tablespoons unsalted butter

2 teaspoons kosher salt, or more to taste

Freshly ground black pepper

2 tablespoons finely ground saltines (about 5 crackers)

1. Place the tomatoes in a medium saucepan, cover, and bring to a simmer over medium heat. Cook, stirring from time to time, until the tomatoes are soft and

broken down, 10 to 20 minutes. Pass the tomatoes through the fine plate of a food mill. Measure 4 cups stewed tomatoes.

2. Meanwhile, scald the milk: Pour the milk into a medium saucepan and set over medium-high heat. When bubbles form around the edges of the pan and the milk steams a little, remove from the heat.

3. Put the butter and salt in a tureen. Grind in some pepper. Add the finely ground crackers. Pour in the hot milk, followed by the tomatoes. Stir and adjust seasoning. If using an immersion blender, emulsify the soup. (Or use a regular blender, but do it in small batches.)

SERVES 6 TO 8

COOKING NOTE
The original recipe calls for "a piece of butter the size of an egg," a common measurement then. I determined this to be 3 tablespoons.

SERVING SUGGESTIONS
Welsh Rarebit (p. 365), Salade à la Romaine (p. 171), Roasted Bone Marrow and Parsley Salad (p. 201), Diana Vreeland's Salade Parisienne (p. 192), Alice Waters's Baked Goat Cheese with Salad (p. 181), Cheese Crusts (p. 366), Croque-Monsieur (p. 372), Spoon Lamb (p. 546), Snow Pudding (p. 800), Huntington Pudding (p. 802)

SEPTEMBER 2, 1877: "THE HOUSEHOLD: RECEIPTS FOR THE TABLE." RECIPE SIGNED NETTIE.

—1877

⤚ PALESTINE SOUP

I'm embarrassed to admit that the first time I made this soup, I used globe artichokes rather than Jerusalems—somehow I failed to make the obvious connection between Palestine and Jerusalem. The soup was terrific with either kind, but you'd probably want to shoot yourself after trimming and slicing enough small green artichokes to make 5 cups.

———

2 pounds Jerusalem artichokes

1 tablespoon unsalted butter

2 slices smoked bacon

2 bay leaves

3 cups chicken broth

1½ cups whole milk

Salt and freshly ground black pepper

1. Trim and peel the artichokes, and cut into 1- to 2-inch chunks. You should have about 5 cups.

2. Combine the butter, bacon, bay leaves, and artichokes in a medium saucepan. Cover the artichokes with a round of parchment, place the pan over medium-low heat, and sweat (gently soften) for 10 minutes. Pour in the chicken broth, bring to a simmer, and simmer, uncovered, until the artichokes are tender, about 10 minutes.

3. Discard the bacon and bay leaves. Puree the soup in a food processor. Then, if you want it really smooth, pass it through a food mill fitted with the finest plate. Pour the soup into a clean pan and bring to a simmer. Stir in the milk and season with salt and pepper.

SERVES 4

SERVING SUGGESTIONS

Roman Lamb (p. 542), Chicken à la Marengo (p. 453), Roast Quail with Sage Dressing (p. 453), Roasted Squab with Chicken Liver Stuffing (p. 454), Apple Galette (p. 843), Olive Oil and Apple Cider Cake (p. 771)

SEPTEMBER 5, 1880: "HINTS FOR THE HOUSEHOLD: RECEIPTS." RECIPE SIGNED A NEW YEAR'S DINNERS [*SIC*].

—1880

⌇ SOUPE À LA BONNE FEMME

The most difficult part of making this soup is finding a pound of sorrel. Try a farmers' market. The original recipe contained the amusing but baffling instruction to cut the leaves into diamond shapes—sorrel wilts when heated and those diamonds turn into blobs in an otherwise simple and delicious soup.

8 tablespoons (1 stick) unsalted butter

1 pound sorrel, trimmed and roughly chopped

Salt

10 cups chicken broth

6 large egg yolks

½ cup heavy cream

Homemade croutons (see Cooking Note)

1. Melt the butter in a large saucepan over medium heat. Add the sorrel, season with salt, and cook, stirring, until the sorrel has wilted slightly. Add the chicken broth and bring to a simmer. Simmer for 30 minutes, then remove from the heat.

2. Whisk together the yolks and cream in a small bowl. Whisk a cup of the soup into the yolk mixture to temper it, then whisk this into the soup; reheat gently, but do not let it boil. Check the seasoning, and serve with croutons.

SERVES 8

COOKING NOTE

To make croutons, heat the oven to 350 degrees. Cut four ½-inch-thick slices of country bread into ½-inch cubes. Spread on a baking sheet and bake until golden and dry, 10 to 15 minutes.

SERVING SUGGESTIONS

Chicken Paprikash (p. 461), Veal Shanks with Garlic Mashed Potatoes (p. 540), Braised Stuffed Breast of Veal (p. 558)

FEBRUARY 13, 1881: "HINTS FOR THE HOUSEHOLD: RECEIPTS." RECIPE SIGNED AMERICAN GASTRONOMIST.

—1881

⌇ CLAM CHOWDER

Chowders, like most soups, are cooked in stages, with the ingredients added progressively. But this recipe combines many of the stages, freeing you from the stove. After layering the ingredients in a pot, you let them simmer away. The resulting chowder has the perfect consistency, with a creamy salinity and heaps of potato, pork, and onion.

25 littleneck clams, scrubbed

1 cup water

1 tablespoon vegetable oil

1 cup sliced onions

¼ pound salt pork or thickly sliced pancetta, cubed

2 cups peeled, thinly sliced white potatoes

½ cup peeled (see Cooking Note, p. 146), seeded, and sliced tomatoes

Salt and freshly ground black pepper

⅛ teaspoon powdered thyme (see Cooking Note)

⅛ teaspoon dried marjoram

1 tablespoon chopped flat-leaf parsley

About 5 Pilot crackers or other plain crackers (about 5 ounces)

1 cup whole milk

1. Place the clams and water in a large pot, cover, and place over high heat. Cook until the clams begin to open, about 7 minutes; transfer them to a bowl as they open. Set the pot aside.

2. Once the clams are cool enough to handle, remove the meat from the shells, reserving the juices. Cut the soft belly from the clams, and chop the hard parts, reserving soft and hard parts in a bowl. Pour any remaining juices back into the pot as you go, and when you're all finished, strain the clam juices through several layers of cheesecloth.

3. Heat the oil in a large saucepan over medium-high heat. Add the onions and salt pork and cook until golden brown, 8 to 10 minutes. Arrange a layer of the potatoes, and then the tomatoes, on top of the onions and salt pork. Season with salt and pepper. Add the thyme, marjoram, and parsley. Cover with the clams, then a single layer of Pilot crackers. Pour in the clam juices. Add enough boiling water to just cover the layers, bring to a simmer, and cook—without ever boiling—for 15 minutes, undisturbed.

4. Just before serving, add the milk and heat through. Adjust the seasoning.

SERVES 6

COOKING NOTE

If you can't find powdered thyme, you can make it by grinding dried thyme with a mortar and pestle or in a spice/coffee grinder—or just use dried thyme.

SERVING SUGGESTIONS

Astor House Rolls (p. 652), Parmesan Crackers (p. 84), Caesar Salad (p. 174), Green Goddess Salad (p. 176), Salade Niçoise (p. 178), Brown Butter Peach Bars (p. 710)

FEBRUARY 27, 1881: "HINTS FOR THE HOUSEHOLD: SUGGESTIONS AS TO THE COOKERY OF SHELLFISH," BY JULIET CORSON.

—1881

⌐ LOBSTER BISQUE I

If you are accustomed to today's restaurant-style lobster bisque made with a lobster reduction and finished with lobster foam—and if you are, can I have your expense account?—this bisque will be a shock. A gentle shock, as everything about the soup is subtle. The lobster flavor is pure but discreet. The sweetness of the Sauternes echoes that of the shellfish, and, save for a little zing of cayenne, all the flavors are elegant and restrained.

The recipe contained an unusual instruction—to pound the lobster tail meat. With today's meek, tender crustaceans, you can probably skip this step and chop the meat instead. But I pounded it; it's kind of fun, and the meat mashes to a delicate pulp.

———

2 small live lobsters

5 cups fish broth (see p. 122)

4 tablespoons unsalted butter

6 tablespoons all-purpose flour

3 cups whole milk

Salt and freshly ground black pepper

¼ teaspoon ground mace, or more to taste

⅛ teaspoon cayenne pepper, or more to taste

1 cup Sauternes

1. Slightly undercook the lobsters using your preferred method, steaming or boiling (or see p. 353 for instructions). Let cool, then crack and pull the meat from the shells, reserving the shells. Cut the claw meat into 1-inch pieces. Cut the remaining meat into bite-sized pieces, then use a meat mallet to pound and flatten it along with the coral (the orange roe), if there is any.

2. Combine the fish broth and lobster shells (as many as will fit in the pan) in a large saucepan, bring to a

boil, and boil until reduced to 3 cups. Remove from the heat.

3. Melt the butter in a large saucepan over medium heat. When it's foamy, whisk in the flour and cook, whisking, for 1 minute. Gradually whisk in the reduced fish broth and the milk. Bring to a simmer and cook for 3 minutes. Season with salt and pepper, the mace, and cayenne, adding more as desired. Stir in the Sauternes and cook for 1 minute. Add the lobster meat and warm through.

SERVES 4

VARIATIONS

A bisque this simple invites playful variations. Add some finely diced potatoes, simmered until tender in the broth. Infuse the broth with a few sprigs of tarragon, a vanilla bean, or star anise and ginger.

SERVING SUGGESTIONS

Astor House Rolls (p. 652), Watercress Salad (p. 171), Raspberry Bavarian Cream (p. 807)

MARCH 6, 1881: "HINTS FOR THE HOUSEHOLD: A CHAPTER UPON CRABS AND LOBSTERS," BY JULIET CORSON.

—1881

OKRA SOUP WITH BEEF (AND OYSTERS)

Gumbo, much as I love it, is no beauty queen. And gumbo is the slightly more refined cousin of this okra soup. But as foie gras and oysters have proved, looks are no measure of flavor.

The main differences between this delicious soup and a typical gumbo are its use of beef rather than chicken or shrimp, and its lack of smoked meat. Many recipes for okra soup appeared in the *Times* during the late nineteenth century. Some were made with a broth of ham and veal knuckle and finished with crabmeat. Others contained shrimp. All included okra, tomatoes, and green pepper. This one is made with beef bones, and near the end of cooking, you add corn, lima beans, and if you want—and you do want!—fresh oysters.

Bob the Sea Cook, a regular contributor to the food pages, described a similar beef and okra soup he'd had at a plantation outside New Orleans (his recipe ran in 1881). "It was very thick, though but a very little of

the meat had been allowed to remain in it," he wrote. "The shrimps had been withdrawn. It was the quintessence of a vegetable soup, without any greasiness, only that when you had eaten two platesful of it there was no room for anything else."

Once you gather the ingredients, all you need is time. It takes 4 hours of gentle simmering to break down the meat and concentrate the soup. You should accomplish this over the course of 2 or more days. Once the broth is mostly cooked (a 3½-hour process), chilling it solidifies the fat, and you can lift the fat from the surface before proceeding. (Also, the extra time gives you a chance to air out the smell of beef fat and regain a desire to eat the soup.) Buy the oysters and corn the day you're serving it.

———

2 tablespoons unsalted butter

2 onions, sliced

4 pounds beef bones, with some meat attached

1 pound okra, sliced

1 green bell pepper, cored, seeded, and chopped

Salt and freshly ground black pepper

1 pound tomatoes, cored and peeled

2 cups corn kernels (ideally fresh, frozen in a pinch)

1 cup lima beans (frozen are fine)

24 freshly shucked oysters, drained (optional)

1. Bring 4 quarts of water to a boil in a medium pot. Melt the butter in a large pot over medium heat. Add the onions and beef bones and cook, stirring occasionally, until both onions and bones are well browned; be careful not to burn them.

2. Add the okra and green pepper to the bones, followed by the boiling water. Season lightly with salt and pepper, keeping in mind that the soup will reduce a lot. Bring to a boil, skimming occasionally, then reduce to a simmer and cook gently for 2 hours.

3. Add the tomatoes and cook for 1½ hours more. Turn off the heat and let cool completely.

4. Remove the beef bones. Chop up what meat there is, discarding the fat, and return it to the soup; discard the bones. Refrigerate the soup until ready to serve.

5. Before serving, lift the solidified fat from the surface of the soup. Place the pot of soup over medium heat. When it comes to a simmer, add the corn and lima beans and simmer gently for 15 minutes. Taste and adjust the seasoning—the soup will benefit from

a generous amount of black pepper. If adding oysters, drop them in and cook until they begin to get ruffly, about 2 minutes. Ladle the soup into bowls.

SERVES 8

COOKING NOTES

Because the original recipe was vague about a number of details, I had to make some guesses and adjustments. I used beef shin. After simmering, you are supposed to remove the beef and bones, but since all the meat had fallen off the bones, this wasn't really possible. I removed the bones, then broke up the large lumps of beef, removing any pieces of fat, chopped up the rest, and added it back to the soup. This was probably untraditional, but I wasn't going to waste the meat.

The oysters are supposed to be fried before going into the soup. After I'd cooked the soup for 4 hours, frying the oysters seemed like an unnecessary hassle. Instead, I poached them in the soup, which—in candor—means they lack the textural element of a fried oyster. If you want to fry yours, my hat is off to you.

Lastly, the directions say to replenish the water that has cooked off before serving. This seemed pointless to me (why dilute that delicious broth?), and since no other okra soup recipe in the archives contained this direction, I chose to ignore it.

SERVING SUGGESTIONS
Fresh Corn Griddle Cakes with Parmesan and Chives (p. 294), Fresh Blueberry Buckle (p. 815), Peach Salad (p. 805), Raspberry Granita (p. 719), Sour Cream Ice Cream (p. 730)

MARCH 19, 1882: "HINTS FOR THE HOUSEHOLD: AN EARLY SPRING DINNER WITH OKRA," BY JULIET CORSON.

—1882

COLD NICARDE (YELLOW SQUASH SOUP)

Yellow squash and onions are treated here as they should be: minimally. You soften them in butter, just until they're limp at the edges, then cook them through in a little chicken broth. At this point, you could buzz them in a food processor or blender, but then you'd end up with something that's too smooth, too likely to slip across your palate and vanish from your mind. Pushing the mixture through a food mill leaves you with soft scant bits, a subtle but important texture.

Cold Nicarde was part of a summer lunch menu suggested by the chef at the Café Pierre, a restaurant in New York City, together with beef salad Provençal, a fresh fruit tart, and coffee. The soup is supposed to be served "icy cold," at which temperature it's refreshing. I preferred it warm, just a bit above room temperature, which brings out its full sweetness.

———

4 cups diced (¼-inch) yellow squash
    (from about 1½ pounds squash)
½ cup finely chopped onion
2 tablespoons unsalted butter
2 cups chicken broth
Salt
½ cup heavy cream
½ teaspoon sugar
Freshly grated nutmeg

1. Soften the squash and onions in the butter in a medium saucepan over medium heat, about 5 minutes. Pour in the broth, add a pinch of salt, and bring to a boil. Lower the heat and simmer until the squash is tender, 5 to 10 minutes.
2. While the soup is still hot, pass it through a food mill fitted with the medium plate. Add the cream and sugar, and season with salt and nutmeg. Serve just warm, or chill and serve cold.

SERVES 2 TO 4 (SMALL SERVINGS)

COOKING NOTES
Use whole nutmeg and grate it on a fine grater—the flavor is so much better than preground nutmeg.

SERVING SUGGESTIONS
Scotch Eggs (p. 62), Chicken and Lemon Terrine (p. 495), Pan-Roasted Chicken with End-of-Season Tomatoes (p. 482), Shrimp in Green Sauce (p. 430), Crab Cakes Baltimore-Style (p. 407), Cold Beef with Tarragon Vinaigrette (p. 534), Tarte aux Fruits (p. 829), Fruit Crostatas (p. 855)

AUGUST 4, 1940: "VICTUALS AND VITAMINS," BY KILEY TAYLOR.

—1940

ORIENTAL WATERCRESS SOUP

Pork liver, which barely touches the broth before they head to the table together, gives the soup its depth and character. If you can't find pork liver—try an Asian market—skip this recipe.

———

¼ pound pork liver, rinsed
1 tablespoon soy sauce
1½ teaspoons vegetable oil
1 pork loin chop
4 cups water
1 bunch watercress, trimmed (tough stems discarded), washed, and coarsely chopped
4 large eggs
Salt

1. Cut the liver into slivers. Combine the liver with the soy sauce and oil in a bowl and set aside to marinate.
2. Cut the meat from the pork chop (reserve the bone) and slice into 1-by-¼-inch thick strips. Combine the pork, pork bone, and water in a medium pot and bring to a simmer. Add the watercress and liver and return to a simmer.
3. Crack the eggs into the pan, reduce the temperature, and cook until the eggs are poached, about 2 minutes. Season with salt. Remove the pork bone and serve immediately.

SERVES 4

SERVING SUGGESTIONS
Ginger Daiquiri (p. 36), The Cuke (p. 39), Chinese Barbecued Spareribs (p. 517), Chinese Pork Balls (p. 59), Shrimp Toast (p. 60), Clams in Black Bean Sauce (p. 442), Takeout-Style Sesame Noodles (p. 355)

FEBRUARY 13, 1949: "ADDING THE CHINESE TOUCH," BY JANE NICKERSON. RECIPE ADAPTED FROM MARY CHU, THE MANAGER AT RATHSKELLER, A CHINESE RESTAURANT IN NEW YORK CITY.

—1949

VICHYSSOISE À LA RITZ

Published alongside a recipe for Jellied Beef à la Mode, vichyssoise à la Ritz is a more modern form of the soup created by Louis Diat at the Ritz-Carlton in 1911. It's a total pain in the neck to make—you must rub the potatoes and leeks through a sieve—but it's worth the trouble, I promise. You may be alarmed by the addition of tomato juice, which makes for an unusual vichyssoise, but the juice offsets the richness of the cream with some much-needed acidity. What I love most about the soup is that you can serve it at three different stages: after Step 2—at which point it will be like the vichyssoise you know; after you add the tomato juice; or after you add the additional cream.

———

4 leeks, white part only, sliced and well washed
1 medium onion, sliced
4 tablespoons unsalted butter
5 medium white potatoes (about 1¾ pounds), thinly sliced
4 cups chicken broth
Salt
3 cups whole milk
2 cups heavy cream
2 cups tomato juice
Chopped chives

1. Soften the leeks and onions very lightly in the butter in a large saucepan. Add the potatoes, broth, and a generous pinch of salt, bring to a boil, and cook for 35 minutes, or until the leeks and potatoes are very tender.
2. Crush the potatoes, then pass the soup through a fine sieve into a bowl. Return to the pan, add the milk and 1 cup cream, and bring to a boil. Cool, and rub the soup again through a very fine sieve. Chill until cold.
3. Add the tomato juice and the remaining 1 cup cream to the soup. Chill thoroughly.
4. Serve garnished with chives.

SERVES 8 TO 10

SERVING SUGGESTIONS
Epigram of Lamb (p. 509), Arnaki Araka (Lamb with Peas; p. 550), Veal Chops with Sage (p. 564), Veal Chops Beau Séjour (p. 520), Rib-Eye Steaks with Pep-

pered Cranberry Marmalade and Swiss Chard (p. 562), Green Bean Salad with Savory Topping (p. 177), Raw Spinach Salad (p. 175), Grapefruit Fluff (p. 809)

JUNE 9, 1957: "SERVE IT COLD—AND IN STYLE," BY RUTH P. CASA-EMELLOS. RECIPE ADAPTED FROM THE CARLTON HOUSE IN NEW YORK CITY.

—1957

POTAGE CRESSONIÈRE (WATERCRESS SOUP)

It was a tough call, but in the end I think I made the right choice by including this recipe rather than the watercress and avocado gelatin mold.

---

4 tablespoons unsalted butter
1 garlic clove, minced
2 cups chopped onions
4 cups thinly sliced peeled white potatoes
1 tablespoon salt
$\frac{1}{4}$ teaspoon freshly ground black pepper
$2\frac{1}{4}$ cups water
1 large bunch watercress, trimmed and washed
$1\frac{1}{2}$ cups whole milk
2 large egg yolks
$\frac{1}{2}$ cup light cream

1. Melt the butter in a large saucepan. Add the garlic and onions and sauté until tender, about 5 minutes. Add the potatoes, salt, pepper, and $\frac{3}{4}$ cup water, cover, and bring to a boil. Reduce the heat and simmer until the potatoes are almost tender, about 15 minutes.
2. Cut the watercress stems into $\frac{1}{8}$-inch lengths. Coarsely chop the leaves.
3. Add all the watercress stems, half the leaves, the milk, and the remaining $1\frac{1}{2}$ cups water to the potato mixture. Simmer for 15 minutes.
4. Pass the soup through the fine plate of a food mill. Return the soup to the saucepan and reheat. Adjust the seasoning.
5. Blend together the egg yolks and cream. Gradually stir this mixture into the soup and cook, stirring constantly without letting it boil, until slightly thickened. Garnish with the remaining watercress leaves.

SERVES 6

SERVING SUGGESTIONS
Fricassee of Chicken with Tarragon (p. 456), Cold Beef with Tarragon Vinaigrette (p. 534), Sautéed Asparagus with Fleur de Sel (p. 241), Rhubarb-Strawberry Mousse (p. 835), Lemon-Almond Butter Cake (p. 780)

MARCH 8, 1959: "A TOUCH OF WATER CRESS," BY CRAIG CLAIBORNE.

—1959

MÁLAGA GAZPACHO

Although gazpacho has been around since the eighth century in Spain, it took New Yorkers until the 1960s to catch on. And even then it took them a little while to get it right. One of the first gazpacho recipes the *Times* ran appeared in 1948 and was essentially chopped vegetables doused with garlic powder and served in a glass bowl. Another early specimen was called a "soup-salad."

In 1968, Craig Claiborne, then the *Times*'s food editor, published a recipe for a refreshing, straightforward version from a home cook named Manola Drozdoski that was made with tomatoes, cucumbers, green pepper, garlic, and the rest. Claiborne called it Málaga Gazpacho. The thought was a nice tribute to an obscure city in southern Spain, except that Málaga (and its region, Andalusia) doesn't have just one version of gazpacho but many—some made with egg, others with fish, potato, and mayonnaise. If anything, Málaga is associated with *ajo blanco*, a "white" gazpacho made with almonds and garlic.

No real harm done. Given America's record for tampering with pizza, croissants, and lattes, doctrinal purity is hardly to be expected. Besides, gazpacho is a survivor, a poor man's soup thickened with yesterday's bread and sharpened with vinegar, so you can't really wreck it (unless you add garlic powder). In its original form, it was more of a bread soup mashed with olive oil, garlic, vinegar, and water. Tomatoes came later, with the discovery of the New World and all the ingredient confusion that wrought.

Over the centuries, gazpacho took on regional refinements, sometimes being made with ground almonds or pine nuts, sometimes featuring peppers, even the occasional sliced grape. It also varied in texture, from a thick puree (referred to as *salmorejo*) to a chunky, chopped-salad-like consistency to a thin liquid drunk by the glass. Many Spaniards keep gazpacho in the fridge in a pitcher much the way we keep iced tea.

Take a look at some other versions and derivatives in the book: White Gazpacho with Almonds and Grapes (p. 137), Green Gazpacho (p. 160), Watermelon Gazpacho (p. 150), Gazpacho with Cucumber Granita (p. 161), Fried Eggplant with Salmorejo Sauce (p. 251).

———

3 cups coarsely chopped tomatoes

1½ cups peeled, coarsely chopped cucumber

1 green bell pepper, cored, seeded, and coarsely chopped

1 clove garlic, sliced

½ cup water

5 tablespoons olive or corn oil

¼ cup red or white wine vinegar, or more to taste

Salt to taste

2 slices white bread (with crusts), cubed

1. Combine all the ingredients in a blender and blend at high speed, pausing to scrape down the sides with a rubber spatula as necessary.

2. Pour the mixture through a large sieve into a bowl. Press and stir the solids with a wooden spoon to extract as much liquid as possible; discard the solids. Taste the soup for seasoning and add more salt and vinegar if desired. Chill thoroughly before serving.

SERVES 6

SERVING SUGGESTIONS

Rebujito (p. 38), a glass of cava, Potato, Ham, and Piquillo Pepper Croquetas (p. 94), Fried Olives (p. 87), Catalan Vegetable Paella (p. 323), Paella (p. 309), Spanish Cream (p. 802), Caramel Custard (p. 836)

FEBRUARY 22, 1968: "RAISINS IN A SPANISH GAZPACHO? NEVER!" BY CRAIG CLAIBORNE. RECIPE ADAPTED FROM MANOLA DROZDOSKI, A HOME COOK IN NEW YORK CITY.

—1968

⌇ MULLIGATAWNY SOUP

This mulligatawny, whose name comes from a Tamil word meaning "pepper water," is neither peppery nor watery, but it is a memorably fragrant soup. The recipe comes from Craig Claiborne, and it's a terrific example of British colonial cooking, which often involved subduing spicy tropical dishes with butter, flour, and cream. Claiborne's version is considerably more complex than earlier versions I found, none of which included chicken or this array of spices. If you're going to make a throwback dish like mulligatawny, why not go all out?

———

One 3-pound chicken, cut into 8 serving pieces

6 cups chicken broth or water

1 onion, stuck with 4 cloves

2 small stalks celery with leaves

1 carrot, peeled and quartered

1 bay leaf

2 sprigs parsley

Salt

14 black peppercorns

½ small coconut or 1 cup defrosted frozen grated coconut

1 cup freshly cooked or canned chickpeas, drained (rinsed if canned)

4 tablespoons unsalted butter

5 tablespoons all-purpose flour

3 tablespoons turmeric

1 teaspoon grated fresh ginger or ½ teaspoon ground ginger

1 teaspoon ground coriander

1 clove garlic, finely minced

Cayenne pepper

1 cup heavy cream

Freshly ground black pepper

Lemon wedges for serving

Cooked jasmine rice for serving

1. Place the chicken in a large pot and add the broth. Add the onion, celery, carrot, bay leaf, parsley, salt to taste, and peppercorns and bring to a boil. Reduce the heat and simmer for about 20 minutes, or until the chicken is cooked through. Transfer the chicken to a plate and cover to keep warm. Strain the broth and let it cool.

2. If using a fresh coconut, crack open the shell with a hammer, discard the liquid, and remove the meat from the shell. Pare away the dark coating and cut the meat into small cubes. Put the cubes (or store-bought grated coconut) in a blender, add 2 cups of the cooled broth,

and blend on high speed. Line a sieve with cheese-cloth (if your sieve is fine, skip the cheesecloth) and strain the coconut milk. Press on the solids to extract as much of the liquid as possible; discard the residue.

3. Rinse out the blender. Return the coconut milk to the blender, add the chickpeas, and blend until they are thoroughly pureed. Add enough of the reserved chicken broth to make 4 cups (save the rest for another use).

4. Melt the butter in a large saucepan. Add the flour, turmeric, ginger, coriander, garlic, and cayenne to taste. Stir to blend and cook for a minute—the mixture will get thick and pasty. Remove from the heat.

5. Gradually add the coconut milk mixture to the butter-flour mixture, stirring rapidly until very smooth. Add the cream a little at a time (stop whenever you like—the full amount makes a very rich soup), then add the chicken. Gently reheat the chicken. Season with salt and pepper—and feel free to add more cayenne if you like. Serve accompanied by lemon wedges and hot rice (to be added to the soup bowls).

SERVES 4 TO 6

COOKING NOTE

As a number of the recipes I tested called for grating a fresh coconut, I was motivated to find a reliable alternative. Indian food stores often carry grated fresh coconut in the frozen section. Pick up ten bags, and you'll be set for a few years, give or take a little freezer burn. Don't shell and grate your own coconut: you'll end up hating the recipe, me, Craig Claiborne, and cooking in general.

SERVING SUGGESTIONS

This soup can be a main course. If serving it as a first course, then roast a fish and accompany with any of the following: String Beans with Ginger and Garlic (p. 260), Cucumbers in Cream (p. 225), Chopped Salad with Lemon Zest Vinaigrette (p. 188), for dessert: Mango Ice Cream (p. 729).

DECEMBER I, 1968: "TUREEN SPECIALS," BY CRAIG CLAIBORNE.

—1968

⌒ TOMATO SOUP II

Other equally delightful tomato soups live on pages 114 and 134.

_____

12 tablespoons (1½ sticks) unsalted butter
2 tablespoons olive oil
I large onion, thinly sliced (about 2 cups)
2 sprigs fresh thyme or ½ teaspoon dried thyme
4 basil leaves, chopped
Salt and freshly ground black pepper
2½ pounds ripe tomatoes, cored and cut into chunks, or one 35-ounce can tomatoes, preferably imported Italian
3 tablespoons tomato paste
¼ cup all-purpose flour
3¾ cups chicken broth (brought to room temperature if cold)
I teaspoon sugar
I cup heavy cream
Croutons (recipe follows)

1. Melt 8 tablespoons butter in a large saucepan over medium heat and add the olive oil. Add the onion, thyme, basil, and salt and pepper to taste and cook, stirring occasionally, until the onion is wilted. Add the tomatoes and tomato paste and stir to blend. Bring to a simmer and simmer for 10 minutes.

2. Place the flour in a small bowl and add about 5 tablespoons of the broth, stirring to blend. Stir this into the tomato mixture, add the remaining chicken broth, and bring to a simmer. Simmer for 20 minutes, stirring frequently all over the bottom of the pan to make certain that the soup does not scorch.

3. Put the soup through a fine sieve or a food mill fitted with the fine plate into a clean saucepan. Return it to the heat, add the sugar and cream, and simmer, stirring occasionally, for 5 minutes. Add the remaining butter, swirling it around in the soup to melt it.

4. Ladle into shallow bowls and serve with the croutons.

SERVES 8

CROUTONS

8 small slices day-old crusty French or Italian bread
I large clove garlic, split
I tablespoon olive oil

1. Heat the oven to 400 degrees. Rub the bread slices on both sides with the garlic, then brush generously with the olive oil.
2. Place the bread directly on an oven rack or on a baking sheet and bake until golden, turning once if necessary.

SERVES 8

SERVING SUGGESTIONS
Welsh Rarebit (p. 365), Salade à la Romaine (p. 171), Roasted Bone Marrow and Parsley Salad (p. 201), Diana Vreeland's Salade Parisienne (p. 192), Alice Waters's Baked Goat Cheese with Salad (p. 181), Cheese Crusts (p. 366), Croque-Monsieur (p. 372)

READERS
"It has to be the most delicious tomato soup of all time, and why not? Made with my own dead-ripe garden tomatoes and all that butter and cream. It is so rich that I make it only once a season, but I have been doing so for some 35 years. With the croutons, it is a complete meal."

Mrs. Richard A. Joseph,
Croton-on-Hudson, NY, letter

JULY 6, 1969: "TOMATO SOUP FOREVER!" BY CRAIG CLAIBORNE.

—1969

⌁ WATERZOOI
(FLEMISH CHICKEN SOUP)

If we can eat grits, then why can't the Belgians eat a dish called waterzooi? This soup from eastern Flanders, whose name means "watery mess," is actually not a watery mess at all, because the broth is thickened with egg yolks. Although it's usually prepared with fish and vegetables, it is sometimes made, as in this recipe, with chicken.

The pieces of chicken are bathed in warm butter, then joined in the pot by leeks, carrots, celery, parsley, nutmeg, peppercorns, and broth. You simmer this until the chicken is just cooked, and then you strain out all the vegetables, sharpen the broth with lemon juice, and add egg yolks and cream. Served in shallow bowls, the soup is a beauty: the poached chicken is framed by pale yellow, creamy, lemon-flavored broth. Craig Claiborne, whose recipe this is, tells you to garnish the soup with thin slices of lemon.

I'd serve this soup for a dinner party, but it's also a great recipe to have on hand for a last-minute meal, as it takes all of 30 minutes to prepare. Serve with forks, knives, and spoons.

———

Two 2½-pound chickens, cut into serving pieces
Salt and freshly ground black pepper
8 tablespoons (I stick) unsalted butter
5 cups chicken broth
6 stalks celery, trimmed and halved crosswise
2 carrots, trimmed and peeled
4 medium leeks, white and pale green parts, split
    and rinsed well under cold running water
8 sprigs flat-leaf parsley
12 black peppercorns
I blade dried mace or ⅛ teaspoon ground mace
    or freshly grated nutmeg
Juice of I lemon
4 large egg yolks
½ cup heavy cream
4 thin lemon slices, seeds removed
Cooked rice for serving

1. Season the chicken pieces with salt and pepper. Melt the butter in a large casserole. Add the chicken, cover, and simmer over low heat, turning the chicken occasionally, for 10 minutes. The chicken should more or less stew in the butter without browning.
2. Meanwhile, bring the chicken broth to a boil.
3. Add the celery, carrots, leeks, parsley, peppercorns, mace, and boiling broth to the chicken, cover once more, and simmer over low heat until the chicken is just cooked, 10 to 15 minutes.
4. Remove the chicken to a dish. Strain the broth into saucepan, add the lemon juice, and heat over medium heat until hot; do not let it boil. Beat the yolks lightly in a small bowl and add the cream. Gradually add this

to the hot broth, stirring vigorously, and cook, without boiling, until the soup thickens slightly. (Keep stirring and tasting—the texture will turn from watery to creamy all of a sudden, and then it's done.) Do not overcook, or the soup may curdle. Return the chicken to the soup, taste, and adjust the seasoning. Serve in hot soup bowls garnished with the lemon; serve the rice separately.

SERVES 8 AS A FIRST COURSE, 4 AS A MAIN COURSE

COOKING NOTES

The recipe called for two 2½-pound chickens, which can be difficult to find. I used a 4½-pound chicken, cut into 8 pieces. Also, because chicken broth now often comes in 32-ounce boxes, I combined one box in a pan with the chicken's backbone and wings, added a cup of water to make 5 cups total, and simmered it a few minutes before adding the broth to the soup.

Mace is the golden web-like covering on nutmeg. Old recipes often called for a "blade" of mace, which meant a piece of this covering. You can find whole mace in good Indian and Asian grocery stores—it's worth seeking out. But if you can't find it, use ground mace or grated nutmeg.

As with many of the older poultry and meat recipes, the stated cooking times are much longer than is now necessary. This soup is supposed to simmer for 30 minutes, but the chicken was done in 12. I asked Harold McGee, the author of *On Food and Cooking*, about the discrepancy. He wrote me that he believes these timing changes "do reflect the more lean, tender industrial meats, but also a new attentiveness to the texture of long-cooked meats." McGee pointed out that our meat supply had long been industrialized by 1970 but that it took food writers, who relied on established cooking times, decades to adjust.

You will have to go against your instincts to strain out the vegetables, but do it for the sake of the soup: the clean broth, containing nothing other than chicken, is terrific. And there's no need to discard the vegetables. Since they're barely cooked in the soup, you can finely chop them and fold them into mashed potatoes or rice. Or use them, as I did, in food for my toddlers. I chopped them up and mixed them with chopped pork.

Before adding the lemon, egg yolks, and cream, you may want to let the broth settle and skim its surface. Between the butter and the chicken, this dish isn't short on fat.

SERVING SUGGESTIONS

Begin with a salad: Salade à la Romaine (p. 171), Mezzaluna Salad (p. 185), Wallace Seawell's Spinach Salad (p. 180), Lattich Salat, Warme (Warm Lettuce Salad; p. 171), Fennel, Orange, Watercress, and Walnut Salad (p. 186), Fennel and Apple Salad with Juniper (p. 189). Then have Cranberry Upside-Down Cake (p. 776) or Fresh Ginger Cake (p. 775) for dessert.

JANUARY 25, 1970: "THINK SOUP," BY CRAIG CLAIBORNE.

—1970

SCOTCH BROTH

Craig Claiborne lamented home cooks' increasing lack of interest in soup. (An innocent observation that produced this woeful headline: "Who Says Nuts to Soup?") So how did he whip up his readership and lead them back to their stoves, ladles in hand? With chicken giblet soup and the lamb and barley concoction called Scotch broth. Giblet soup wouldn't have been my first choice for such a campaign, but, to be fair to Claiborne, who had a knack for identifying the tastes of his day, Scotch broth is a delicious soup—rustic to the point of ugliness, but bounding with flavor.

The Scots, while not known for an enviable cuisine, have been very successful at branding their few winners. This broth, which is the Scottish equivalent of American's chicken noodle soup, is one. Shortbread is another, as are Scotch eggs, which are hard-boiled eggs wrapped in sausage meat and breaded and fried (a recipe can be found on p. 62). But the deep-fried pizza, yet another Scottish delight, has never run in the *Times* and probably never will.

———

½ cup barley or pearl barley

2 pounds lamb neck and/or shoulder

2 tablespoons unsalted butter

I cup finely chopped onion, plus I onion, peeled

I clove garlic, finely minced

8 cups lamb broth or water

2 stalks celery, quartered

2 carrots, peeled and quartered

1 medium turnip, peeled

1 bay leaf

4 sprigs parsley

2 sprigs fresh thyme or ½ teaspoon dried thyme

Salt and freshly ground black pepper

1. Place the barley in a bowl, add water to cover, and soak overnight (if using pearl barley, skip this step).
2. Rinse the lamb and drain. Melt the butter over medium-high heat in a soup pot. Add the lamb, chopped onion, and garlic and cook, stirring occasionally, until the onion starts to brown, 5 to 7 minutes. Add the lamb broth, whole onion, celery, carrots, turnip, bay leaf, parsley, and thyme. Bring to a boil, skimming the surface as necessary to remove the scum and foam. Partially cover and simmer for about 1 ½ hours until the lamb is tender.
3. Strain the broth through a sieve lined with cheesecloth; save the lamb, carrots, and turnip.
4. Skim the fat from the broth, pour into a pot, and return it to a boil. Drain the barley and add it to the broth. Season with salt and pepper and simmer, partially covered, for 30 to 40 minutes, until the barley is tender.
5. Meanwhile, pull the meat from the bones and discard the bones. Cut the lamb into small pieces. Cut the carrots and turnip into match-like strips.
6. When the barley is tender, add the meat, carrot, and turnip and reheat. Serve piping hot in hot bowls.

SERVES 4

COOKING NOTES

The recipe called for regular barley, but if you use pearl barley, as I did, it needs much less time to cook, 25 to 35 minutes. (Pearl barley is polished, which removes some of the tough hull.)

I used lamb shoulder chops because they're easier to find than lamb neck.

The recipe called for lamb broth or water. I used water, and the soup's foundation didn't suffer a bit. Claiborne said that to make lamb broth, "Simmer lamb bones in salted water to cover for about 1 hour."

With any soup or stew containing meat, I prefer to make the recipe across 2 days. If you prepare the soup up through Step 3 on the first day, and chill the broth overnight, the next day you can lift off the hardened fat, which is much easier and more effective than skimming the broth while it's hot.

SERVING SUGGESTIONS

Cornell Bread (p. 658), No-Knead Bread (p. 670), Brown Sugar Shortbread (p. 690)

READERS

"I make it with leftover leg of lamb, using the bone and clinging sinewy meat for the broth. I then cook the veg and the removed cubed lamb, etc., in the broth."

Karin B. Morese, letter

MARCH 1, 1970: "WHO SAYS NUTS TO SOUP?" BY CRAIG CLAIBORNE.

—1970

TOM'S CHILLED CUCUMBER SOUP

Everyone needs a cold soup that can be made on the fly: this is it. A good blender makes the soup's texture feel like mousse and the walnuts give it depth and earthiness, not something you expect in a cucumber recipe. Unfortunately, Jean Hewitt, who wrote the story, never tells us who the brilliant Tom is.

2 cucumbers, peeled, halved lengthwise, seeded, and roughly chopped

1 clove garlic, crushed

1 cup plain whole-milk yogurt, preferably Greek-style

⅔ cup full-fat sour cream

2 tablespoons plus 2 teaspoons snipped dill

Salt and freshly ground black pepper

5 tablespoons chopped walnuts

1. Place the cucumber, garlic, yogurt, and sour cream in a blender and puree until smooth. Add 2 tablespoons dill, season with salt and pepper, and mix. Chill.
2. Place 1 tablespoon walnuts in each of 4 chilled bowls, pour in the soup, and garnish with the remaining tablespoon of walnuts and 2 teaspoons dill.

SERVES 4

The best yogurt for this recipe is Fage Total yogurt, the full-fat variety, which has a beautiful texture and flavor. Low-fat yogurt or sour cream will result in a watery soup.

SERVING SUGGESTIONS
Grapefruit Wine (p. 37), Stuffed Hard-Cooked Eggs (p. 56), Brie with Herbs in Bread (p. 69), Open-Faced Tomato Sandwich (p. 367), Lobster Roll (p. 368), Judy Rodgers's Warm Bread Salad (p. 198), Green Bean Salad with Savory Topping (p. 177), Gigi Salad (Shrimp, Bacon, and Green Bean Salad; p. 184), Strawberry Shortcakes (p. 799), Chocolate Chip Cookies (p. 709)

READERS
"Every summer when cucumbers come in I make Tom's Chilled Cucumber Soup . . . I omit the walnuts. They seem to be a fussy detail that adds nothing. There are other *NY Times* recipes I like, but this is my indispensable favorite."

Irene H. Ross, letter

JULY 29, 1973: "ELEGANCE SANS EFFORT: SOUPS WITH A SHIVER," BY JEAN HEWITT.

—1973

ᐧ GARDEN MINESTRONE

Carefully constructed vegetable soups like this were relatively rare in the early 1970s. Nika Hazelton, whose recipe this is, instructed you not to put the pot on the stove until you had layered it with tomatoes, onions, garlic, zucchini, lettuce, peas, parsley, basil, broad beans, and olive oil. "Be sure to follow this order, and do not stir," she wrote. Then you cook it all gently, letting each vegetable release its liquid on its own. No water or broth is added—the vegetables cook in their own juices and a slick of olive oil.

———

2 large tomatoes, peeled (see Cooking Note, p. 146)
    and sliced
2 medium onions, thinly sliced
1 clove garlic, minced
2 large zucchini, sliced

1 medium head Romaine lettuce, shredded
2 pounds fresh peas, shelled, or one 10-ounce
    package frozen peas
2 tablespoons minced basil
1 cup minced flat-leaf parsley
2 pounds fresh broad beans or lima beans, shelled,
    or one 10-ounce package frozen lima beans
1/3 to 1/2 cup olive oil
Salt and freshly ground black pepper
Freshly grated Parmesan cheese

1. Put the sliced tomatoes in the bottom of a deep 3-quart casserole that can go to the table. Top with the sliced onions and garlic. Top with the zucchini. Add the shredded lettuce. Place the peas on top of lettuce. Sprinkle the basil and half the parsley over the peas and top with the beans. Sprinkle the remaining parsley and the olive oil over all. Be sure to follow this order, and do not stir or mix the vegetables.
2. Cover the pot and cook over medium heat for 10 minutes, or until the vegetables at the bottom of the casserole release their liquid. Season with salt and pepper.
3. Now stir the vegetables and mix well. Cook, covered, over low heat, stirring frequently, just until the beans are tender, 15 to 20 minutes. Do not add water, the vegetables have enough moisture of their own. Serve hot or lukewarm, with Parmesan cheese.

SERVES 6

COOKING NOTES
I tried this recipe with both frozen peas and lima beans; each worked well.

If you have a small piece of Parmesan rind, you can add it to the soup at the beginning of cooking for extra flavor. Either way, before serving, you should stir a small amount of the grated cheese into the soup, and then sprinkle a little more on top.

SERVING SUGGESTIONS
No-Knead Bread (p. 670), Cornell Bread (p. 658), Parmesan Crackers (p. 84), Classic Ciabatta (p. 665), Fresh Raspberry (or Blackberry or Blueberry) Flummery (p. 824), Strawberry Ice Cream (p. 722), Blueberry Ice Cream (p. 726), Fruit Crostatas (p. 855)

SEPTEMBER 23, 1973: "AN ITALIAN ART: NO-MEAT STEWS,"
BY NIKA HAZELTON.

—1973

CREAM OF CARROT SOUP

Two hallmarks of the Craig Claiborne–Pierre Franey partnership are displayed in this recipe. Tabasco and Worcestershire sauce were their favorite seasonings— Claiborne once went so far as to say, "Tabasco sauce is like mother's milk to me." And there's nothing they loved more than creating a sinkful of pots and pans. After the soup is cooked, it is first passed through a food mill and then whipped until smooth in a blender.

Their foibles are forgiven: you're rewarded here with a sweet, buttery soup, each bite ending with a snap of heat. It is meant to be served cold, but it can also be drunk warm.

---

2 tablespoons unsalted butter

$1/2$ cup coarsely chopped onion

I pound carrots (8 to 10), peeled and cut
　　into I-inch rounds

I pound white potatoes (3 to 5), peeled
　　and cut into I-inch cubes

6 cups chicken broth

2 sprigs fresh thyme or $1/2$ teaspoon dried thyme

I bay leaf

I cup heavy cream

$1/4$ teaspoon Tabasco sauce, or more to taste

$1/2$ teaspoon Worcestershire sauce, or more to taste

$1/2$ teaspoon sugar

Salt and freshly ground black pepper

I cup whole milk

1. Melt the butter in a large soup pot. Add the onion and cook briefly, stirring. Add the carrots, potatoes, and broth and bring to a boil. Add the thyme and bay leaf, reduce the heat, and simmer for 30 to 40 minutes, until the carrots and potatoes are tender.

2. Put the mixture through a food mill and let it cool.

3. Put the soup in a blender and blend until very smooth (hold the lid on firmly with a kitchen towel); this may have to be done in 2 stages. If the soup is to be served hot, pour it into a pot, bring it to a boil, and add the remaining ingredients. Return to a boil and serve piping hot. If it is to be served cold, add the remaining ingredients to the blended mixture, stir well, and adjust the seasoning. Pour the soup into a bowl and chill thoroughly. Serve very cold.

SERVES 6 TO 8

COOKING NOTES

Claiborne and Franey often instructed readers to serve soups "piping hot." As this usually results in a burnt tongue or two, I think it's better to serve a soup just hot, not nearly boiling. The flavors are more easily appreciated that way too.

SERVING SUGGESTIONS

Marinated Flank Steak with Asian Slaw (p. 552), Grilled Hanger Steak (p. 551), Sugar Snap Peas with Horseradish (p. 259), Lemon Lotus Ice Cream (p. 724), Clove Granita (p. 727), Amazon Cake (Cocoa Cake; p. 779)

JUNE 23, 1974: "FOOD: SUMMER SOUPS: SOME LIKE THEM
COLD," BY CRAIG CLAIBORNE WITH PIERRE FRANEY.

—1974

CUCUMBER, TOMATO, AND AVOCADO SOUP

The 1970s produced some unusual foods, many of which were misfires. Remember ham and pineapple pizza? Chicken à la king? This soup—a fusion of a French pureed vegetable soup and guacamole—sounds like one of them, but somehow it works beautifully. The tomato and cucumber base is as smooth as cream, even a little viscous, floating with dabs of avocado. The soup can be served hot or cold.

---

4 tablespoons unsalted butter

I cup chopped onion

$1/4$ cup all-purpose flour

4 cups peeled (see Cooking Note, p. 146) cubed
　　($1/2$-inch) tomatoes, preferably fresh, although
　　canned may be used

4 cups peeled, cubed ($1/2$-inch) cucumbers

Salt and freshly ground black pepper

4 cups chicken broth

I ripe avocado

$1/4$ to I cup heavy cream

1. Melt the butter in a deep saucepan or pot. Add the onion and cook, stirring, until wilted. Sprinkle with the flour and add the tomatoes, stirring rapidly with a whisk. Add the cucumbers and season with salt and pepper. Stir in the broth, bring to a simmer, and simmer for 25 minutes.

2. Pour the mixture, a few ladlefuls at a time, into a blender and blend well. If the soup is to be served cold, pour into a bowl and chill. If it is to be served hot, return it to the stove and heat thoroughly.

3. Peel and pit the avocado. Finely chop and add it to the soup, whisking rapidly. Stir in ¼ cup cream. Taste the soup, and add more cream if desired. Serve very cold or piping hot.

SERVES 8

COOKING NOTES

During the 1970s, adding a cup of heavy cream seemed to be the capstone of every recipe. In this soup, that much cream deadens the flavor, so I reduced it to ¼ cup. Add more as you like.

The soup was strained after pureeing, a step I found unnecessary.

SERVING SUGGESTIONS

La Paloma (p. 35), Coloradito (Red *Mole* with Pork; p. 547)

JUNE 23, 1974: "FOOD: SUMMER SOUPS: SOME LIKE THEM COLD," BY CRAIG CLAIBORNE WITH PIERRE FRANEY.

—1974

✐ SOUPE À L'OIGNON GRATINÉE

There are some recipes you can serve only to your spouse or close friends—either because they look too weird or taste odd (but good!). This onion soup is one of them. It is almost too strange and too delicious to describe: imagine a fusion of bread pudding, grilled cheese, and soufflé.

The soup comes from the French cookbook *Gastronomie Pratique*, which was written in 1907 by Henri Babinski, an engineer whose pen name was Ali-Bab. The *Times* published the recipe in 1974, when the book was first translated into English.

You spread baguette toasts with butter and layer them with grated cheese, sautéed onions, and tomato puree. Then, in what seems to be a nod to stone soup, you gently pour in salted water. Finally you bring it to a simmer and bake it. "The soup is ready," Babinski declared, "when the surface is baked and looks like a crusty, golden cake, and the inside is unctuous and so well blended that it is impossible to discern either cheese or onions."

Babinski wrote a fine recipe but needed some tips on the social aspect of eating: he insisted that his guests arrive on time and remain silent during the meal.

————

1 baguette, cut into ½-inch slices (25 to 30)

9 tablespoons unsalted butter, softened

9 ounces Emmental cheese, finely grated (about 2¼ cups)

8 medium yellow onions, thinly sliced (about 12 cups)

1 tablespoon kosher salt, plus more to taste

1 cup tomato puree

6 cups water

1. Toast the baguette slices and let them cool. Spread a generous layer of butter on each slice (you will need about 5 tablespoons), then lay the slices close together on a baking sheet and top with all but ½ cup of the cheese.

2. Melt the remaining butter in a large saucepan over medium heat. Add the onions, season with salt to taste, and sauté, stirring occasionally, until very soft and golden, about 15 minutes. Remove from the heat.

3. Arrange a layer of bread slices butter side up (about one-third of them) in a 5-quart casserole. Spread one-third of the onions on top, followed by one-third of the tomato puree. Repeat for 2 more layers. Sprinkle with the remaining ½ cup cheese. (To prevent boiling over, the casserole must not be more than two-thirds full.)

4. Bring the water to a boil in a medium saucepan and add 1 tablespoon salt. Very slowly pour the salted water into the casserole, near the edge, so that the liquid rises just to the top layer of cheese without covering it. (Depending on the size of your casserole, you may need more or less water.)

5. Put the casserole on the stove, bring to a simmer, and simmer uncovered for 30 minutes.

6. Heat the oven to 350 degrees. Transfer the pot to the oven and bake uncovered for about 1 hour. "The soup is ready when the surface looks like a crusty, golden cake, and the inside is unctuous and so well blended that it is impossible to discern either cheese or onions." Serve each person some of the baked crust and some of the inside, which should be thick but not completely without liquid.

SERVES 6

COOKING NOTES

Good broth doesn't have to be a rich, concentrated meat stock. This soup's broth is made with plain old water and salt. The original recipe instructs you to pour the salted water into the casserole through a glass funnel—a step, and piece of equipment, that bewilders me.

Notice there are just five ingredients: onions, cheese, butter, bread, and tomato puree. It's worth tracking down Emmental cheese and a decent baguette—but don't get sourdough, which has too strong a flavor.

SERVING SUGGESTIONS

A glass of good red wine and call it a night. Or for a feast: Sole Grenobloise (Sautéed Sole with Capers and Lemons; p. 399), Sautéed Potatoes with Parsley (p. 283), Chocolate Eclairs (p. 800).

JULY 25, 1974: "FINALLY, MONUMENTAL COOKBOOK IS TRANSLATED," BY CRAIG CLAIBORNE. RECIPE ADAPTED FROM *GASTRONOMIE PRATIQUE*, BY ALI-BAB.

—1974

FAKI (GREEK LENTIL SOUP)

This recipe was sent to Craig Claiborne by a reader as a way of complaining about another lentil soup recipe he had recently published (the soup recipe was meant to be in honor of Esau, a son of Abraham, but Claiborne had included peppers and tomatoes, two New World ingredients). The reader was Vilma Liacouras Chantiles, the author of *The Food of Greece*. I've never made Claiborne's heretical lentil soup, but Chantile's is a memorable, robust one. You cook it forever and

think you'll be left with gruel, but the soup magically coalesces. Chantiles suggested serving it with "feta, olives, salad, crusty bread, and wine."

———

I pound lentils
About 8 cups warm water
I large onion, chopped
2 to 3 cloves garlic, chopped
2 small or I large stalk celery, finely chopped
5 to 6 canned Italian-style plum tomatoes, and their juices
I large bay leaf
4 sprigs parsley
Chopped mint, basil, or oregano to taste
1/3 cup olive oil
Salt and freshly ground black pepper
Red wine vinegar

1. Wash and pick over the lentils, and place in a soup pot with warm water to cover. Let stand for 1 hour.
2. Bring the pot of lentils to a boil. Add the onion, garlic, celery, and tomatoes, cover, and simmer for 1 hour.
3. Stir the herbs and oil into the soup and season with salt and pepper. Continue to simmer, covered, for another 1 1/2 hours, or until the soup is very thick and the lentils are tender, stirring occasionally, adding 2 tablespoons vinegar toward the end.
4. Serve hot, with additional vinegar on the side.

SERVES 10

COOKING NOTES

Use regular green lentils, not the tiny French le Puy ones. Well, I suppose you *could* use them, but I haven't tried it.

After the first hour of cooking, the soup will seem very stodgy, but it loosens up once you add the oil.

I used 3 sprigs of mint, about 10 large leaves.

Be generous with the salt. Lentils really soak it up.

This makes a huge amount—you may want to freeze half the batch.

SERVING SUGGESTIONS

See Chantiles's thoughts in the headnote. Alternatively: Salade à la Grecque (p. 179), Broiled Lamb Leg Chops on Eggplant Planks with Mint-Yogurt Sauce (p. 549), Sautéed Potatoes with Parsley (p. 283), Hazelnut Baklava (p. 706).

FEBRUARY 7, 1977: "DE GUSTIBUS: AND, NOW, A GREEK
WORD ON MAKING LENTIL SOUP," BY CRAIG CLAIBORNE.
RECIPE ADAPTED FROM VILMA LIACOURAS CHANTILES,
AUTHOR OF *THE FOOD OF GREECE*.

—1977

SOUPE DE POISSON JARDINIÈRE (FISH SOUP WITH VEGETABLES)

Early in Pierre Franey's career, decades before he became a writer at the *Times* in the 1960s, he was a junior *poissonièr* at Le Pavillon, New York's first important modern French restaurant (after Delmonico's, which served old-fashioned French food). It was his great skill with fish that got him noticed by Henri Soulé, the owner of Le Pavillon, and Franey eventually became the restaurant's head chef.

I was well into my research before I learned this about Franey, and, as it happens, I'd already tried many of his fish recipes and chosen a number of them for the book (see for instance, Sole Grenobloise on p. 399). He knew how to add flavor to fish without overpowering it. This fish soup is one of his more elaborate creations: nineteen ingredients, four steps, plus recipes for fish broth and croutons. But I can think of much simpler recipes that are more cumbersome to prepare—sausage, for instance. Just make the soup when you have a friend around to help you chop.

The vegetables and fish are the core of the recipe, of course, but it's the cream that really pulls it together, harmonizing the heat, the saffron, the peppers, and the fish.

———

¼ cup olive oil

1 cup chopped onion

2 cups chopped green or red bell peppers (preferably 1 cup of each)

2 cloves garlic, finely minced

1½ cups chopped leeks (white and pale green parts; about 2 medium)

1 teaspoon loosely packed saffron threads

1 dried hot red chile

1 bay leaf

2 sprigs fresh thyme or ½ teaspoon dried thyme

Salt and freshly ground black pepper

2 cups cored, peeled, and cubed tomatoes

1 cup dry white wine

1 cup peeled potatoes cut into ½-inch cubes, held in a bowl of cold water

3 cups Fish Broth (recipe follows), or use water or a combination of half bottled clam juice and half water

1¾ pounds skinless, boneless fish fillets, such as striped bass or blackfish, cut into 1½-inch chunks

½ cup heavy cream

2 tablespoons anise-flavored liqueur, such as Ricard or Pernod

¼ cup finely chopped flat-leaf parsley

Fresh Bread Croutons (recipe follows; optional)

1. Pour the oil into a casserole set over medium heat, add the onion, and cook until wilted. Add the peppers, garlic, leeks and saffron, and cook, stirring, for 1 minute. Add the chile, bay leaf, thyme, and salt and pepper to taste and cook until the leeks begin to soften, 3 to 5 minutes.

2. Add the tomatoes and cook, stirring, for 1 minute. Add the wine and potatoes, cover and cook until the potatoes are almost tender, about 10 minutes.

3. Add the fish broth, or the water or clam broth mixed with water. Add the fish and cook for 5 minutes.

4. Add the cream and bring to a boil. Add the liqueur. Serve sprinkled with the chopped parsley and if desired, with 2 croutons (1 if serving as a first course) for each serving.

SERVES 4 AS A MAIN COURSE, 6 AS A FIRST COURSE

FISH BROTH

Combine about 1½ pounds fish bones (with the heads but with gills removed) and 3 cups of water in a large saucepan or a small pot and bring to a boil. Reduce the heat and simmer for about 15 minutes, turning the fish bones once. Strain the broth.

MAKES ABOUT 3 CUPS

FRESH BREAD CROUTONS

Rub the crust of a section of French bread large enough to make 8 slices with a peeled clove of garlic. Cut into 8 slices (6 if serving this as a first course). Brush each slice with ½ teaspoon olive oil. Place under the broiler, turning once, until crisp and golden.

MAKES 6 OR 8 CROUTONS

COOKING NOTES

I used red snapper; I bought them whole and had them filleted. Two fish, weighing a total of 3½ pounds, yielded 1¾ pounds fillets and 1¾ pounds bones (for the broth).

While I have come to adore the precision and strategy in Franey's cooking, we part ways on the tomato. Franey never met a tomato he didn't peel. The choice is up to you. I used yellow tomatoes, which were like rays of light in the soup.

Do make the fish broth and croutons—both are worth the effort. The croutons feature a great trick. Rather than rubbing garlic on slices of bread, Franey has you rub it on the crust of the baguette before slicing the bread, which is much easier to do.

SERVING SUGGESTIONS

Crisp white wine. Cheese Straws (p. 79), Crostini with Eggplant and Pine Nut Puree (p. 78), Seasoned Olives (p. 90), Cucumber–Goat Cheese Dip with Radishes and Scallions (p. 70), An Honest Loaf of French Bread (p. 662), No-Knead Bread (p. 670), Lucas Schoorman's Lemon Tart (p. 857), Lemon Lotus Ice Cream (p. 724)

PERIOD DETAIL

Franey wrote, "There are, on occasion, certain ingredients that add such special character to a dish, they are really worth going out of one's way to find. In the fish soup listed here, . . . that special ingredient is chopped leek."

JUNE 22, 1977: "60-MINUTE GOURMET," BY PIERRE FRANEY.
—1977

✐ CURRIED ZUCCHINI SOUP

This was one of the first recipes I made when I started working on this book. The instructions said to cook the zucchini, covered, for 45 minutes, and I was sure it would turn out like prison food. But Craig Claiborne is famous for a reason: no matter how puzzling they may

sound, his recipes work. Somehow during the zucchini's slow, necessary simmer, it intensifies and takes on a light roasted flavor, and while the zucchini does turn a putrid green, the yellow curry gives it a golden hue.

---

6 small zucchini, trimmed and cut into chunks
1 large onion, thinly sliced (about 1 cup)
1½ teaspoons curry powder
½ teaspoon ground ginger
½ teaspoon dry mustard
3 cups chicken broth
3 tablespoons raw rice
1½ cups whole milk or heavy cream
Salt and freshly ground black pepper
Minced chives for garnish

1. Combine the zucchini, onion, curry powder, ginger, and mustard in a saucepan, add the chicken broth and rice, and bring to a boil. Cover and simmer for about 45 minutes.
2. Puree the mixture in a blender or pass it through a food mill. Add the milk and season with salt and pepper. Chill thoroughly or serve hot. Garnish with chives.

SERVES 6

COOKING NOTE

If your curry powder or ground ginger is more than a year old, toss and buy new!

SERVING SUGGESTIONS

Roasted Salmon with Herb Vinaigrette (p. 430), Pan-Barbecued Shrimp (p. 402), Beer-Can Chicken (p. 473), Tomatoes Vinaigrette (p. 218), Cucumbers in Cream (p. 225), Strawberry Charlotte (p. 810), Almond and Buttermilk Sorbet (p. 733), Strawberry Shortcakes (p. 799)

JUNE 30, 1980: "DE GUSTIBUS: A 'COOKBOOKLET' INSPIRED BY ZUCCHINI," BY CRAIG CLAIBORNE. RECIPE ADAPTED FROM GAD ZUKES, BY THE ALLENTOWN, PENNSYLVANIA, BRANCH OF THE AMERICAN ASSOCIATION OF UNIVERSITY WOMEN.
—1980

CRÈME SENEGALESE (CURRIED CREAM OF CHICKEN SOUP)

Crème Senegalese, a faintly sweet, hearty chicken soup that few in Senegal would recognize, is served chilled.

---

2 tablespoons unsalted butter

½ cup chopped onion

1 tablespoon curry powder

1 cup chopped leeks (white and pale green parts)

1 clove garlic, minced

½ cup diced bananas

1½ cups peeled, cored, and diced apples

1 cup peeled, chopped tomatoes

1 cup peeled, cubed potatoes

Salt and freshly ground black pepper

4 to 6 drops Tabasco sauce, or more to taste

3½ cups chicken broth

1 cup well-chilled heavy cream

½ cup finely diced cooked chicken breast

1. Melt the butter in a heavy casserole over medium heat. Add the onion and cook, stirring, for about 2 minutes. Add the curry powder and stir to coat the onion. Add the leeks, garlic, bananas, apples, tomatoes, and potatoes. Season with salt, pepper, and the Tabasco, and stir well. Add the chicken broth, bring to a simmer, and simmer for 20 minutes.

2. Pour half of the mixture at a time into a food processor or blender and blend well. Pour the soup into a bowl and season with salt. Chill thoroughly.

3. When ready to serve, add the heavy cream and chicken and mix well.

SERVES 4 TO 8

SERVING SUGGESTIONS

Ginger Daiquiri (p. 36), Egg and Olive Canapés (p. 57), Beef Satay with Peanut Sauce (p. 66), Caramelized Bacon (p. 93), Salted and Deviled Almonds (p. 51), Salade à la Romaine (p. 171), Spanish Cream (p. 802), Coconut Rice Pudding with Lime Syrup (p. 846), Almond Granita (p. 731), Frozen Lemon Soufflé (p. 725)

JULY 5, 1981: "COLD SOUPS FOR SUMMER," BY CRAIG CLAIBORNE WITH PIERRE FRANEY.

—1981

PAUL STEINDLER'S CABBAGE SOUP

Paul Steindler was a chef, ex–Olympic wrestler, and good friend of Craig Claiborne and Pierre Franey. The soup's cabbage, bacon, and preponderance of caraway, all fundamental elements of Eastern European cooking, will make you want to drink vodka and eat plum cake. There, you've been warned.

The caraway defines the soup, but the dashes of sugar and vinegar give it flair.

---

6 cups finely sliced cabbage (about 1 pound)

1 cup finely diced bacon (about 6 ounces)

¾ cup finely chopped onion

¼ cup all-purpose flour

4 cups chicken broth

½ cup peeled, finely diced carrots

1⅓ cups finely diced potatoes

Salt and freshly ground black pepper

1 teaspoon caraway seeds, crushed or pulverized

1 tablespoon white wine vinegar

½ teaspoon sugar (optional)

1 cup of heavy cream

Whole milk, if needed

¼ cup finely chopped dill

1. Bring enough water to cover the cabbage when it is added to a boil in a large pot. Add the cabbage and cook for 1 minute. Drain.

2. Cook the bacon in a casserole or small pot over medium-low heat until rendered of fat. Add the onion and cook, stirring, until wilted. Sprinkle with the flour and stir. Add the broth, stirring rapidly with a wire whisk. When the mixture simmers, add the cabbage, carrots, potatoes, salt and pepper to taste, and the caraway seeds. Stir in the vinegar and sugar and cook, stirring often from the bottom up until the vegetables are just tender, 25 to 30 minutes.

3. Stir in the cream and simmer for 5 minutes. This is

a very rich, thick soup. If desired, you may thin it with a little milk.

4. Serve in hot soup bowls, each serving sprinkled with dill.

SERVES 6 TO 8

COOKING NOTE

The original recipe called for 1½ cups heavy cream— 1 cup was plenty.

SERVING SUGGESTIONS

Saucisson Soûl (p. 67), Chicken Paprikash (p. 461), Veal Goulash with Spaetzle (p. 525), Queen of Puddings (p. 866), Papa's Apple Pound Cake (p. 774), Teddie's Apple Cake (p. 752), Polish Jewish Plum Cake (p. 769), Purple Plum Torte (p. 763)

NOVEMBER 6, 1983: "HEARTY SOUPS," BY CRAIG CLAIBORNE WITH PIERRE FRANEY. RECIPE ADAPTED FROM PAUL STEINDLER.

—1983

✎ BILLI-BI AU SAFRAN (MUSSELS IN SAFFRON CREAM)

Named for William B. Leeds—Billi-Bi—a regular at Maxim's in Paris, who loved this soup.

———

2 tablespoons unsalted butter
3 tablespoons coarsely chopped shallots
3 tablespoons coarsely chopped onion
½ clove garlic, finely minced
1½ teaspoons saffron threads
1½ quarts mussels, well scrubbed and debearded
Tabasco sauce
¼ cup finely chopped flat-leaf parsley
1 cup dry white wine
2 cups heavy cream
Salt and freshly ground black pepper

1. Melt the butter in a deep saucepan or pot. Add the shallots, onion, garlic, and saffron and cook, stirring, for about 3 minutes. Add the mussels. Add Tabasco to

taste, the parsley, and wine, cover, and cook until the mussels just begin to open, about 4 minutes.

2. Add the cream and bring to a boil. Add salt and pepper to taste. The mussels may be left in the whole shell, but it is preferable if one half of the shell is removed from each and they are served in the soup on the half-shell.

3. Serve the soup piping hot with good bread or toasts brushed with olive oil.

SERVES 4

COOKING NOTES

When measuring the saffron threads, don't pack them into the measuring spoon, just drop them in.

Be careful not to overcook the mussels in Step 1, because they'll cook further in Step 2.

SERVING SUGGESTION

Corn Cakes with Caviar (p. 282)

NOVEMBER 30, 1983: "60-MINUTE GOURMET," BY PIERRE FRANEY.

—1983

✎ PAUL PRUDHOMME'S CAJUN-STYLE GUMBO

This book contains a bunch of what I call two-man dishes—recipes that you wouldn't want to make alone, such as the Turducken on p. 485 and the Gâteau de Crepes on p. 785. This is another one. There are mountains of vegetables to chop, potatoes to peel, and shrimp to clean. Such culinary expeditions, though increasingly rare, are important trials. When you've finished, you'll feel as if you'd climbed Everest, except that the reward is a feast, rather than frostbite.

Prudhomme's gumbo could burn your nose off— you may want to start with 1 teaspoon cayenne and add more to taste, or torment.

———

1 cup melted pork lard (or use peanut, corn, or vegetable oil)

¾ cup all-purpose flour

2 cups finely chopped onions

1½ cups finely chopped green bell peppers

1 cup finely chopped celery

10 small or 5 large bay leaves

1¾ teaspoons cayenne pepper

2 teaspoons freshly ground white pepper

2 teaspoons freshly ground black pepper

4 teaspoons minced garlic

6 cups (about 1½ pounds) fresh, tender young okra, cut into ¼-inch-thick rounds, or three 10-ounce packages frozen cut okra

3 cups smoked ham cut into "sticks" about 1 inch long and ½ inch thick

¾ teaspoon garlic powder

Salt if desired

4 cups peeled (see Cooking Note, p. 146), seeded, and coarsely chopped ripe tomatoes (about 2 pounds), or chopped imported canned tomatoes

6 cups Fish Stock (recipe follows), or fish broth

1 pound peeled blanched (parboiled) crayfish tails

Filé powder to be added as desired (optional)

1. Heat ½ cup of the melted lard (or oil) in a heavy 12-inch skillet over medium-high heat until it is barely smoking. Add the flour and stir vigorously and constantly with a wire whisk for about 3 minutes, or until the mixture is the color of dark chocolate. Take care that it does not burn.

2. Quickly add half of the onions, ½ cup green peppers, and ½ cup celery, reduce the heat, and cook, stirring, for about 3 minutes. Add 4 small bay leaves or 2 large bay leaves, 1 teaspoon cayenne pepper, 1 teaspoon white pepper, and ½ teaspoon black pepper and cook, stirring, for about 1 minute. Add 1 teaspoon minced garlic and cook briefly, stirring—the mixture will be very dry at this point. Scrape the mixture into a large deep casserole and set aside.

3. Wash out the skillet and return it to the stove. Heat the remaining ½ cup melted lard (or oil) in the skillet over very high heat. When it is hot and almost smoking, add the okra and cook until tender, stirring often, for 12 to 15 minutes. (Frozen okra may take less time.) Add the remaining onions, green peppers, celery, and minced garlic, 1 cup ham, and the remaining bay leaves. Continue cooking over high heat, stirring occasionally, for 5 minutes.

4. Add the remaining ¾ teaspoon cayenne pepper, 1 teaspoon white pepper, and 1½ teaspoons black pepper, and the garlic powder. Add salt if desired, and cook until the mixture is quite dry, 2 to 5 minutes. Add the tomatoes, stir, and cook, stirring often for 8 to 10 minutes: stir carefully and often all over the bottom of the pot to prevent sticking and burning.

5. Pour and scrape this mixture into the large casserole containing the browned flour. Add the fish stock and the remaining 2 cups ham, bring to a simmer, and simmer for about 45 minutes, stirring often all over the bottom. (The base of this gumbo, before the seafood is added, can be made several days in advance and refrigerated; it can also be frozen.)

6. Add the crayfish tails (or shrimp) and bring to a boil. Let simmer for about 5 minutes (less time if using crab or oysters). Remove the bay leaves.

7. Serve the filé powder separately to be added by each guest according to taste. Serve with plain boiled or steamed rice.

SERVES 10

FISH STOCK

2 pounds bones from white-fleshed, nonoily fish (including heads if possible, but with gills removed)

6 cups water

1 cup dry white wine

1 cup coarsely chopped celery

1 cup coarsely chopped onion

3 sprigs fresh thyme or 1 teaspoon dried thyme

1 bay leaf

10 black peppercorns

Salt if desired

Run the fish bones under cold running water. Place the bones in a pot or deep saucepan and add all of the remaining ingredients. Bring to a boil and simmer for 20 minutes. Strain; discard the solids. (Leftover stock can be frozen.)

MAKES ABOUT 6 CUPS

COOKING NOTES

If you can get lard from a local farmer or a good butcher, it's worth the effort, as it forms the flavor base of the gumbo. I used rendered leaf lard from Flying Pigs Farm, www.flyingpigsfarm.com.

I bought fresh fish stock, but I've included Prud-homme's recipe for fish stock above if you can't get fresh.

Filé powder is available from Penzeys Spices, www.penzeys.com.

Tasso, a New Orleans specialty, is best for this gumbo; or if you'd like to make a Creole-style gumbo, use a mild, store-bought smoked ham, not a heavily smoked ham.

I couldn't get crayfish, so I used shrimp—a fine sub-stitute. If you'd like to convert this gumbo into a Cre-ole creation, use an equal weight of small shrimp and/or crabmeat and/or oysters, or a 1-pound combination of them all.

Claiborne wrote, "A 12-inch heavy cast-iron skil-let is almost essential for the preparation of this dish. I strongly recommend that all the ingredients be chopped and assembled before starting to cook. Com-bine and assemble them in the order in which they will be used so they may be added without hesitation."

When cooking the flour in the lard, I took it to the color of dulce de leche. The pan was beginning to smoke, and I didn't want to burn the mixture. Choose your comfort zone.

SERVING SUGGESTIONS

Fresh Succotash (p. 275), Rice (p. 282), Key Lime Pie (p. 826), Jean Halberstam's Deep-Fried Peaches (p. 860)

READERS

". . . the foundation of my kitchen, a recipe I double and make twice a year."

Christopher Bromsey, New York, NY, letter

MAY 6, 1984: "REGIONAL COOKING: SOUTHERN CUISINES," BY CRAIG CLAIBORNE WITH PIERRE FRANEY. RECIPE ADAPTED FROM PAUL PRUDHOMME, THE CHEF OF K-PAUL'S IN NEW ORLEANS.

—1984

ZUPPA DI FUNGHI SICILIANA (SICILIAN MUSHROOM SOUP)

So-called "wild mushrooms" (many of which were actually cultivated) were so new to readers in 1985 that the *Times* included a pronunciation for "porcini."

This delicious rustic soup contains an element from the Italian egg drop soup *stracciatella*, which translates as "little rags." Just before serving, 2 eggs are beaten into the soup, and strands of egg twist their way through the broth. The only detail I'd change is the way it's served. The soup is ladled onto thick coun-try bread toast, which immediately relaxes, leaving you with a soup of soft textures. If you want a little crunch, as I did, put the toast on top of the soup. (I can already hear Nancy Harmon Jenkins, whose recipe this is, protesting: "That's what the French would do, not Italians!")

———

4 cups homemade beef or chicken broth
    (do not use canned broth)
1½ tablespoons unsalted butter
1½ tablespoons olive oil
1 clove garlic, crushed
1 medium onion, finely chopped
1 pound wild mushrooms (such as morels,
    hen of the woods, black trumpets, and oyster),
    trimmed and thinly sliced
One 16-ounce can Italian plum tomatoes, drained and
    finely chopped, or 2 very ripe medium tomatoes,
    peeled (see Cooking Notes, p. 146), cored, seeded,
    and finely chopped
Salt and freshly ground black pepper
1 tablespoon finely chopped flat-leaf parsley
2 large eggs
4 to 6 slices (½-inch-thick) Italian or French
    country-syle bread, toasted
¾ cup freshly grated Parmesan cheese,
    plus extra for serving

1. Place the stock in a heavy-bottomed soup pot and bring to a slow simmer over medium heat.

2. Meanwhile, melt the butter in the olive oil in a medium saucepan over medium-high heat. When the foam has subsided, add the garlic and onion and sauté, stirring occasionally, until the onion is translucent, about 1 minute. Add the mushrooms and sauté, stir-ring frequently, until the mushroom liquid has evapo-rated and the slices are beginning to brown.

3. Add the mushroom mixture to the simmering stock, along with the tomatoes and salt and pepper to taste. Simmer very gently, uncovered, until the flavors are well blended, about 30 minutes.

4. Just before serving, stir the parsley into the soup. Beat the eggs with a fork in a small bowl until blended.

Slowly add the beaten eggs to the simmering soup, beating constantly with a long-handled fork. The eggs will spin out in threads.

5. To serve, place a piece of toasted bread in each of 4 soup plates. Ladle the hot soup over the bread. Sprinkle with the grated Parmesan and serve immediately, accompanied by a bowl of extra grated cheese.

SERVES 4 TO 6

SERVING SUGGESTIONS
Braised Ligurian Chicken (p. 491), Steamed Spinach with Balsamic Butter (p. 226), Italian Roast Potatoes (p. 300), Apple Snow (p. 808), Pine Nut Cookies (p. 689), Tartelettes aux Pommes Lionel Poilâne (Individual Apple Tarts; p. 834)

OCTOBER 23, 1985: "GROWING U.S. TASTE FOR MUSHROOMS," BY NANCY HARMON JENKINS.

—1985

✒ PUMPKIN–BLACK BEAN SOUP

If you're like me and raise an eyebrow about most black bean soups, this one may allay your suspicions. For one thing, it doesn't contain jalapeño. It's rich and succulent but not at all sludgy. The soup owes its charm to sherry and sharp sherry vinegar, and its lightness in texture to the pumpkin, which disappears into the inky blackness, imperceptible to your guests.

———

1 pound dried black beans (about 2 cups), rinsed and picked over
2 teaspoons salt, or more to taste
3 tablespoons unsalted butter
1½ cups finely chopped onions
3 large cloves garlic, minced
¾ cup canned tomatoes, drained
1 cup fresh or canned pumpkin puree
6 ounces boiled ham, cut into ⅛-inch cubes
2½ to 3½ cups beef broth
1 tablespoon ground cumin
3 to 4 tablespoons sherry vinegar
Freshly ground black pepper
½ to 1 cup medium sherry

A sugar pumpkin (optional)
2 tablespoons vegetable oil (optional)

1. Place the beans in a large heavy saucepan and cover with boiling water by about 2 inches. Add 1 teaspoon salt and return to a boil, then reduce heat and simmer, partially covered, 2 to 3 hours, or until the beans are tender. Add more water if the beans become dry.

2. Meanwhile, melt the butter in a heavy skillet over medium heat. When it has foamed, stir in the onions and garlic and sauté for 8 to 10 minutes, until lightly colored and tender. Set aside.

3. When the beans are tender, stir in the tomatoes. Transfer to a food processor, in batches, and, with a few pulses, process until the beans have started to smooth out but are still somewhat chunky.

4. Return the beans and tomatoes to the saucepan and stir in the pumpkin, ham, and 2½ cups stock. Add the sautéed onions and garlic, cumin, 3 tablespoons sherry vinegar, the remaining 1 teaspoon salt, and pepper to taste and stir to mix well. Bring to a boil, then reduce the heat and continue cooking, uncovered, for another 20 to 25 minutes, stirring occasionally.

5. Meanwhile, if you like, prepare a pumpkin for serving: Use a handsome pumpkin—a so-called sugar pumpkin has fewer seeds and heavier meat. Cut off the lid in a scalloped or zigzag pattern. Remove the seeds and pull off the strings from them. Toss the seeds with the oil and toast on a baking sheet in a preheated 400-degree oven for 7 to 9 minutes, until they are well colored. Remove from the oven and sprinkle with salt.

6. Stir ½ cup sherry into the soup and taste for salt, vinegar, and other seasonings. If the soup is too thick, add more stock or sherry. If it is too thin, continue cooking until thicker.

7. Fill the pumpkin with the soup (or transfer it to a tureen) and use the toasted seeds as garnish.

SERVES 8

COOKING NOTES
For "medium sherry," use a fino (dry) sherry.

The recipe calls for just 1 cup of canned pumpkin puree, marginally less than a standard 15-ounce can. If you find this annoying, as I did, simply add the rest.

Serving the soup in a pumpkin is entirely optional, but the style is characteristic of the period, so I left it in.

As for the ingredients with variable amounts, I used 3½ cups broth and 3 tablespoons vinegar; ½ cup sherry was sufficient, but a little more wouldn't hurt.

SERVING SUGGESTIONS

North Carolina–Style Pulled Pork (p. 550), Brine-Cured Pork Chops (p. 569), Mezzaluna Salad (p. 185), Wilted Chard with Pickled Red Onion (p. 261), Roasted Cauliflower (p. 248), Mushrooms with Manzanilla Sherry (p. 249), Gratin of Yams and Chipotle Cream (p. 291), Mashed Potatoes Anna (p. 294), Potato "Tostones" (Flattened Potatoes; p. 301), Madeleine Kamman's Apple Mousse (p. 816), Marcella's Pear Cake (p. 769)

OCTOBER 19, 1986: "THE GHOSTS OF MANY LANDS," BY JOANNA PRUESS.

—1986

✐ BLACK BEAN SOUP WITH SALSA AND JALAPEÑO CORN-BREAD MUFFINS

At the end of cooking this soup, you add lime juice, cayenne, cilantro, and cumin, and it's like shooting a current through the pot. The soup's flavor electrifies. At the table, you then add salsa and sour cream. Don't stir them in, just dip into them every now and then to revive your palate.

———

½ pound smoked slab bacon with rind
1½ cups finely chopped onions
1½ cups finely chopped celery
1½ cups finely diced carrots
1 bay leaf
1 tablespoon minced garlic
¼ cup finely chopped fresh oregano, or 1 tablespoon dried oregano, crumbled
1¼ teaspoons dried thyme
¼ cup ground cumin
1 teaspoon freshly ground black pepper
3 tablespoons tomato paste
4 quarts chicken broth, preferably homemade and concentrated
1 pound dried black turtle beans or other black beans (about 2 cups), rinsed and picked over
6 tablespoons fresh lime juice (from about 2 limes)
¼ teaspoon cayenne pepper
Salt
½ cup finely chopped cilantro
Salsa (recipe follows)
Sour cream for garnish
Jalapeño Corn-Bread Muffins (optional; recipe follows)

1. Slice off the rind of the bacon; reserve. Cut the bacon into ¼-inch cubes. There should be about 1½ cups.
2. Put the bacon cubes and rind into a heavy soup pot or casserole and cook over medium-low heat, stirring often, until rendered of fat. The bacon cubes should be well browned and crisp.
3. Add the onions, celery, carrots, bay leaf, garlic, oregano, thyme, 3 tablespoons cumin, and the black pepper. Stir to blend, cover the pot tightly, and cook for about 5 minutes. Do not allow the mixture to burn.
4. Add the tomato paste and stir briefly. Add the chicken broth and bring to a boil. Add the beans and cook, uncovered, over medium-high heat for about 2½ hours, stirring occasionally and skimming the surface occasionally to remove foam, scum, and fat as it rises to the top. The soup is ready when the beans are soft and some of them have disintegrated because of the cooking heat and stirring.
5. Stir in the lime juice, cayenne pepper, salt to taste, cilantro, and remaining tablespoon of cumin. Remove and discard the bacon rind and bay leaf.
6. Ladle the soup into soup bowls. Serve the salsa and sour cream on the side, to be added at will, and, if desired, with the corn-bread muffins as an accompaniment.

SERVES 8 TO 12

SALSA

½ cup finely chopped white or Spanish onion
2 cups tomatoes cut into ¼-inch cubes
1½ teaspoons finely chopped, seeded jalapeño peppers, or more to taste
Salt if desired
¼ cup finely chopped cilantro
2 tablespoons fresh lime juice

Combine all the ingredients in a bowl and blend well. Refrigerate until ready to serve.

JALAPEÑO CORN-BREAD MUFFINS

Melted butter or bacon fat for greasing the muffin tin

1 cup sifted all-purpose flour

1 cup cornmeal, preferably stone-ground

1 tablespoon sifted baking powder

1 teaspoon crushed red pepper flakes

¾ teaspoon salt

1½ teaspoons ground cumin

⅔ cup sour cream

⅔ cup whole milk

2 tablespoons unsalted butter, melted

1 large egg

⅓ cup finely diced hot chiles, jalapeños or poblanos, or use canned jalapeños

⅓ cup finely diced scallions

⅓ cup drained canned corn kernels

1¾ cups finely grated sharp cheddar cheese

1. Heat the oven to 375 degrees. Grease eight ½-cup muffin cups. Combine the flour, cornmeal, baking powder, red pepper flakes, salt, and cumin in a bowl and blend well.

2. Combine the sour cream and milk in a small bowl and blend well with a whisk. Beat in the melted butter and egg. Add the liquid ingredients to the cornmeal mixture and blend well. Add the chiles, scallions, corn, and cheese. Blend thoroughly.

3. Spoon equal portions of the batter into the muffin cups. The batter may be a bit higher than the top of the tin. Bake until the centers spring back when touched and a toothpick inserted in the center comes out clean, 20 to 25 minutes. These muffins are best eaten hot, fresh from the oven.

MAKES 8 MUFFINS

COOKING NOTES

This soup is better made at least a day in advance.

Double the muffin recipe if serving 12.

SERVING SUGGESTIONS

Nueces Canyon Cabrito (Goat Tacos; p. 576), Brined and Roasted Pork Belly (p. 556), Fish Tacos (p. 444), Beets in Lime Cream (p. 230), Chopped Salad with Lemon Zest Vinaigrette (p. 188), Zucchini Carpaccio with Avocado (p. 261), Zucchini and Vermouth (p. 227), Stewed Corn (p. 271), Peach Salad (p. 805), Jean Halberstam's Deep-Fried Peaches (p. 860)

JANUARY 4, 1987: "FOOD: THE HOMECOMING," BY CRAIG CLAIBORNE WITH PIERRE FRANEY.

—1987

✎ SOUPE À L'AIL (GARLIC SOUP)

The spare ingredient list belies the rich fragrance of this soup. Unlike other garlic soups I've had, this one calls for egg yolks and vinegar, which are swirled in at the end to achieve opposite goals. The yolks soften the broth and the vinegar makes the flavor more pointed. I don't really get it, but it works. See for yourself!

The best time to make this soup is in the late spring, when you can get garlic that's fresh from the soil at a farmers' market.

———

1 tablespoon unsalted butter

2 teaspoons olive oil

2 large heads garlic (about 36 cloves), separated into cloves, peeled, and coarsely chopped

8 cups water

Salt and freshly ground black pepper

3 ounces vermicelli or angel hair pasta, broken into small pieces

6 large eggs, separated

3 tablespoons white wine vinegar

1. Melt the butter with the oil in a large saucepan or a small pot over medium-high heat. Add the garlic and cook, stirring, for about 1 minute; do not brown the garlic. Add the water and season with salt (about 1 teaspoon) and pepper. Bring to a boil, cover, reduce the heat, and simmer for 15 minutes.

2. Strain the cooking liquid and reserve the garlic. Put the garlic and ½ cup of the cooking liquid in a blender or food processor and blend to a fine puree.

3. Put the remaining cooking liquid in a saucepan, add the puree, and bring to a boil. Add the vermicelli, stir, and cook for about 3 minutes; do not overcook.

4. Meanwhile, blend the egg yolks and vinegar in a bowl.

5. Turn off the heat under the saucepan. Drop in the egg whites and cover the pan. Do not stir—they will form a cloud-like mixture. When the whites are fully cooked, add the egg yolk mixture and stir very slowly. Taste and adjust the seasoning.

SERVES 4 TO 6

SERVING SUGGESTIONS
Spoon Lamb (p. 546), Buttermilk Roast Chicken (p. 493), Mashed Potatoes Anna (p. 294), Breton Butter Cake (p. 777)

AUGUST 28, 1988: "FOOD: BISTRO BASICS," BY BRYAN MILLER AND PIERRE FRANEY.

—1988

☞ TORTILLA SOUP

As with most recipes by Regina Schrambling, a *Times* food writer—see pages 285 and 560—every detail is carefully considered. The sour cream and avocado aren't there for comfort's sake, they're there to cool the heat of the chiles. My only suggestion is to be generous with the cilantro.

———

4 poblano or jalapeño peppers

6 large ripe tomatoes, cored

¼ cup bacon drippings or olive oil

2 onions, thinly sliced

4 cloves garlic, thinly sliced

4 cups beef broth

2 teaspoons dried oregano

1½ teaspoons ground cumin

4 cups vegetable oil

18 corn tortillas

Salt and freshly ground black pepper

1 cup sour cream

2 ripe California avocados

Cilantro sprigs for garnish

1. Heat a gas or charcoal grill or the broiler. Grill or broil the poblanos, turning frequently, until they're black and blistered on all sides, 5 to 8 minutes. Transfer to a paper bag or wrap in foil and let stand until cool enough to handle. Grill or broil the tomatoes briefly, turning occasionally, until their skin blisters and loosens. Let cool.

2. Slide the skins off the peppers and tomatoes. Remove the seeds from the peppers and coarsely chop the flesh.

3. Heat the bacon drippings in a Dutch oven or other large pot over medium-low heat. Add the sliced onions and garlic and cook slowly, stirring frequently, until golden and very soft, about 15 minutes.

4. Using your fingers, crush the tomatoes into the pot. Add the peppers, broth, oregano, and cumin and bring to a simmer, then simmer over low heat for 30 minutes.

5. Meanwhile, heat the vegetable oil in a deep heavy skillet over medium-high heat. Slice the tortillas into strips about ¾ inch wide. When the oil reaches a temperature of 365 degrees, fry the tortilla strips, a handful at a time, until they are crisp but not browned. Drain on paper towels and keep warm on a baking sheet in a 175-degree oven.

6. When the soup is done, transfer it to a blender or food processor, in batches, and puree until almost smooth. The consistency should be smoother than salsa. Return the soup to the pot, season with salt and pepper, and reheat over low heat.

7. To serve, peel, pit, and thinly slice the avocados. Arrange the tortillas in shallow soup bowls so that the ends of the strips protrude over the rim. Ladle the warm soup over. Top each bowlful with a large spoonful of sour cream. Divide the avocado among the bowls, fanning out the slices over the sour cream. Garnish with cilantro sprigs.

SERVES 6 TO 8

SERVING SUGGESTIONS
La Paloma (p. 35), Grilled Onion Guacamole (p. 71), Guacamole Tostadas (p. 67), Maida Heatter's Cuban Black Beans and Rice (p. 281), Hot Pepper Shrimp (p. 403), Salted Caramel Ice Cream (p. 733), Key Lime Pie (p. 826)

JULY 23, 1989: "FOOD: HOT STUFF," BY REGINA SCHRAMBLING.

—1989

MARMITAKO (BASQUE TUNA SOUP)

This soup is a strange one, but beguilingly so. The first thing you taste is the shrill flavor of the green peppers, followed by the building warmth of the dried sweet chiles, and finally the musky tuna. As the recipe requires a lot of determination (chopping) and patience (scraping the flesh from the rehydrated peppers)—serve the soup as the main course for a dinner party.

————

3 dried sweet red chiles such as ancho or New Mexico

3 tablespoons extra virgin olive oil

1½ pounds tuna, cut into ¾-inch cubes

4 medium onions, finely chopped

4 cloves garlic, minced

4 small green bell peppers (about 1 pound), cored, seeded, and finely chopped

2 tablespoons minced flat-leaf parsley

4 teaspoons paprika, preferably sweet/smoked Spanish paprika (pimentón)

2 tablespoons brandy

1½ pounds new or red waxy potatoes, peeled and cut into ¾-inch cubes

1 pound plum tomatoes, peeled (see Cooking Note, p. 146) and chopped

6 cups water (or, preferably, a mixture of half chicken or fish broth and half water)

1 large carrot, peeled and cut into 4 pieces

1 medium leek, white and pale green parts, split and washed well

1 dried hot red chile, cut crosswise in half and seeded, or ½ teaspoon crushed red pepper flakes

Salt and freshly ground black pepper

12 slices (about ⅜-inch-thick) coarse country bread

1. Remove the stems from the dried sweet chiles and shake out the seeds. Cover the chiles with warm water in a small bowl and let sit at room temperature for 20 minutes. Drain.

2. Heat the oil in a large shallow casserole until very hot. Quickly sear the tuna for about 1 minute, just until it loses its pink color. Remove the tuna and reserve. Lower the heat, add the onions, garlic, green peppers, and parsley, and simmer for 5 minutes. Cover

tightly and cook very slowly for 30 minutes (the onions should not brown).

3. Heat the oven to 375 degrees. Uncover the casserole and stir in the paprika. Raise the heat, add the brandy, and, using a long fireplace match, flame the brandy. When the flame dies, stir in the potatoes and sauté for 1 minute. Add the tomatoes and cook for 2 minutes. Pour in the water, then add the carrot, leek, and hot chile.

4. Scrape the flesh from the softened chiles, discarding the skin, and add the flesh to the casserole. Add salt and pepper to taste and bring to a boil, then reduce the heat and simmer for about 20 minutes, or until the potatoes are almost tender.

5. Meanwhile, place the bread on a baking sheet and toast in the oven for 5 minutes. Turn and toast for 5 minutes more, or until slightly golden. Reserve.

6. Remove the leek, carrot, and hot chile pepper from the pot, if you used it, and discard. Add the tuna, taste again for salt, and bring to a boil, then reduce the heat and simmer for 3 minutes, or until the tuna is just barely done. Cover and let sit for 5 minutes.

7. Serve in soup bowls with the toasted bread on the side, to be dunked in the soup.

SERVES 6

COOKING NOTES

I couldn't find ancho peppers, so I used chiles negros, which are as large as anchos but much darker.

I used small red creamer potatoes, so I didn't peel them.

SERVING SUGGESTIONS

Start with Rebujitos (p. 38) and a bunch of tapas: Fried Chickpeas (p. 88), Fried Olives (p. 87), Pan con Tomate (p. 91), Potato, Ham, and Piquillo Pepper Croquetas (p. 94). If you want to begin with the soup and go to a middle course, have Chorizo Revueltos (p. 640) or Lightly Smoked Salt Cod Salad (p. 437). End with: Reuben's Apple Pancake (p. 831), Lucas Schoorman's Lemon Tart (p. 857), Moroccan Rice Pudding (p. 848), Delicate Bread Pudding (p. 798), Toasts with Chocolate, Olive Oil, and Sea Salt (p. 844).

OCTOBER 15, 1989: "FOOD: SPAIN IN A STEW," BY PENELOPE CASAS.

—1989

CHESTNUT SOUP

It was surprisingly difficult to find a good chestnut soup recipe. After two failures, I was about to give up, but in the final hour gave this one a try. This one doesn't go off course with flavors like celery or pumpkin. It sticks to what matters in chestnut soup: the chestnuts!

Many people have a misguided impression of chestnut soup as a leaden bomb, reserved for hunting trips. Chestnuts possess more flavor than starch, so as long as you emphasize the former and loosen the latter (here, by pureeing it), you have a treat in store.

_____

8 cups chicken broth

Two 8-ounce jars peeled roasted chestnuts

3 ounces lean smoked slab bacon, cut into 3 pieces

3 sprigs fennel, plus a few sprigs for garnish

Salt and freshly ground black pepper

I to 2 cups goat's milk or goat yogurt (like Yo-Goat)

1. Bring the chicken broth to a boil in a large saucepan over high heat. Add the chestnuts, bacon, fennel, and salt and pepper to taste, reduce the heat, and simmer gently for 40 minutes. Remove the saucepan from the heat; discard the bacon.

2. Using a slotted spoon, transfer the chestnuts to a food processor. Add 2 cups of the broth and process to a smooth puree.

3. Pour the puree into a clean saucepan and add about ½ cup of the the remaining broth to thin the puree. Add 1 cup goat's milk and stir well to combine; add up to 1 cup more if you like. Correct the seasoning, adding more salt and pepper if desired. Heat gently and serve garnished with fresh fennel sprigs.

SERVES 6

COOKING NOTES

If you can't find jarred chestnuts, roast your own! Heat the oven to 400 degrees. Cut an X in the rounded side of the chestnuts and set them on a baking sheet. Roast until the X begins to expand and the chestnuts are tender when pricked with the tip of a knife, about 15 minutes. Remove from the oven and cover with a tea towel. When cool enough to handle, remove the outer shells as well as the brown skin that clings to the nuts.

If you can't find or don't like goat's milk, you can use regular whole milk or, better yet, combine some milk with a little Greek yogurt, so you get both the richness and tang.

SERVING SUGGESTIONS

Slow-Roasted Duck (p. 475), Roast Quail with Sage Dressing (p. 453), Quail with Rosemary on Soft Polenta (p. 467), Collared Pork (p. 507), The Most Voluptous Cauliflower (p. 241), Shallot Pudding (p. 247), Stewed Fennel (p. 245), Anton Mosimann's Braised Brussels Sprouts in Cream (p. 232), Apple Galette (p. 843), Apple Snow (p. 808), Chocolate Cake with Bay Leaf Syrup (p. 768)

DECEMBER 9, 1990: "FOOD: A TASTE OF CORSICA," BY COLETTE ROSSANT.

—1990

SPEEDY FISH STEW WITH ORANGE AND FENNEL

_____

I tablespoon olive oil

I large onion, thinly sliced

I teaspoon minced garlic

¾ cup dry white wine

One 14-ounce can crushed tomatoes in puree, preferably with no added salt

3 tablespoons tomato paste

Grated zest of I orange

½ to I teaspoon fennel seeds

I tablespoon minced fresh thyme or I teaspoon dried thyme

I small bay leaf

Salt and freshly ground black pepper

¾ pound fish fillets or boneless steaks (such as grouper, snapper, sea bass, or swordfish), cut into 1½- to 2-inch chunks

Boiled potatoes for serving

1. Heat the olive oil in a large nonstick skillet or pot. Add the onion and garlic and sauté until the onion softens and begins to brown. Add the wine, tomatoes, tomato paste, orange zest, fennel, thyme, and bay leaf. Season with salt and pepper. Cover and cook for 10 minutes.

2. Add the fish and cook for 2 to 3 minutes, just until the fish is done. Serve over boiled potatoes.

SERVES 2

SERVING SUGGESTIONS
Watercress Salad (p. 171), Pan con Tomate (p. 91), Tarte aux Pommes (French Apple Tart; p. 825), Almond and Buttermilk Sorbet (p. 733), Bittersweet Chocolate Semifreddo (p. 727)

MARCH 3, 1991: "SUNDAY MENU: FRESH FISH STEW WITH ORANGE AND FENNEL," BY MARIAN BURROS.

—1991

⌒ MOROCCAN TOMATO SOUP

Newspaper food writing is an odd blend of journalism, trend spotting, and whim. While the food section in the *Times* has grown increasingly news-driven over the past two decades, the opinions and tastes of the section's writers have always guided the coverage.

Sometimes there is no real reason for a story. Sometimes it's just that it's hot out and people want to eat cold food, and that's that. Such was the case with a 1991 column by Barbara Kafka, the author of the bestselling *Microwave Gourmet*. Kafka recalled eating Louis Diat's vichyssoise at The Ritz-Carlton in New York as a young girl, which inspired her lasting love for chilled soups. "Spurred by laziness, a dislike of heat, and my own love of the genre," she wrote, "I set out to devise a group of cold soups that can be made virtually without heat, in a kind of international journey of reading and remembering." And off she went, ruminating on grape gazpacho, African peanut soup, Russian spinach soup, and this Moroccan tomato soup.

Kafka's tomato soup isn't merely conveniently cool, it's riveting, in part because it's not gazpacho, the ubiquitous, aggressively seasoned, and often disjointed soup. Her soup is by no means meek—heat needn't be caloric, but it can be aromatic—it thrives on a pulse of cumin, cayenne, garlic, cilantro, and lemon juice, which tames the spiciness and makes the sweet tomatoes sparkle.

You toast the spices and garlic in a pan and pass the fresh tomatoes through a food mill. Then you join the two, add some finely chopped celery, season, and chill the mixture. Kafka says that if you don't have a food mill, you should peel, seed, and chop the tomatoes, creating small bits, which are preferable to the uniform texture achieved by a food processor. The soup should be slightly lumpy.

_____

5 medium cloves garlic, minced
2½ teaspoons sweet paprika
1½ teaspoons ground cumin
Large pinch of cayenne pepper
4 teaspoons olive oil
2¼ pounds tomatoes, cored and cut into 1-inch pieces
¼ cup packed cilantro leaves, chopped, plus whole leaves for garnish
1 tablespoon white wine vinegar
2 tablespoons plus 2 teaspoons fresh lemon juice
2 tablespoons water
2 teaspoons kosher salt, or more to taste
4 stalks celery, finely diced

1. Stir together the garlic, paprika, cumin, cayenne, and olive oil in a small saucepan, place over medium-low heat, and cook, stirring constantly, for 5 minutes. Remove from the heat.
2. Pass the tomatoes through a food mill fitted with the coarse plate. Stir in the cooked spice mixture, the cilantro, vinegar, lemon juice, water, 2 teaspoons salt, and the celery. Add more salt as desired. Refrigerate until cold.
3. Serve garnished with cilantro leaves.

SERVES 4

COOKING NOTES
You can grate the tomatoes on a box grater, but that can get perilous. A food mill is easiest, because it pushes the tomato pulp and juices through, leaving the skins and seeds behind.

Feel free to cut back on the garlic—5 cloves will infuse the soup as well as your entire house with their scent.

Cooking the spices and garlic before adding them to the tomatoes draws out the aroma of the spices and softens the garlic's tomahawk blow.

This makes an excellent prelude to grilled lamb or chicken, and if you're outdoors, you can simplify matters by ladling the soup into cups and having people drink it like gazpacho. Here are some other ideas: Cinnamon-Scented Fried Chicken (p. 490), Moroccan Chicken Smothered in Olives (p. 482), Cumin-Mustard Carrots (p. 237), Mediterranean Lentil Salad with Lemon-Thyme Vinaigrette (p. 288), Flourless Apricot Honey Soufflé (p. 846), Lemon Sablés (p. 704), Fontainebleau (p. 829).

JULY 28, 1991: "FOOD: COOL SOUPS, COOL KITCHENS," BY BARBARA KAFKA.

—1991

✎ PISTOU SOUP

A straight-shooting version of *soupe au pistou* (a sort of French minestrone), and although the vegetables lose their brightness and vigor the day after, the soup tastes even better then as the flavors relax and integrate. The recipe comes from Le Périgord, one of the early offshoots of Le Pavillon (New York's first modern French restaurant), along with La Caravelle and La Côte Basque.

————

1 tablespoon vegetable oil

1 small onion, cut into small dice

1 large carrot, peeled and cut into small dice

1 turnip, peeled and cut into small dice

4 cups water

2 cups chicken broth

1 tablespoon salt, or more to taste

2 large white potatoes, peeled and cut into small dice

1 large leek, white and pale green parts only, cut into small dice and washed well

1 small zucchini, cut into small dice

2 small handfuls green beans, cut into 1-inch pieces (about ¾ cup)

2 tablespoons finely chopped flat-leaf parsley

2 tablespoons finely chopped basil

2 large cloves garlic, minced

2 large tomatoes, peeled (see Cooking Note, p. 146), cored, seeded, and chopped

1 tablespoon olive oil

½ cup undrained canned flageolets or other white beans

1 handful thin spaghetti (about 3 ounces), broken into thirds

Freshly ground white pepper

1. Heat the oil in a large saucepan over medium heat. Add the onion and cook for 3 minutes. Add the carrot and turnip and cook for 1 minute. Stir in the water and chicken broth and bring to a boil. Reduce to a simmer and cook for 10 minutes.

2. Add the salt, potatoes, leek, zucchini, and green beans. Simmer for 20 minutes, skimming the foam from the surface as necessary.

3. While the soup simmers, combine the parsley and basil in a medium bowl. Stir in the garlic, tomatoes, and olive oil. Set aside.

4. Stir the beans and spaghetti into the soup. Simmer for 8 minutes.

5. Stir the tomato mixture into the soup, season with salt, if needed, and pepper, and simmer for 2 minutes longer. Serve hot or at room temperature, not chilled.

SERVES 6 AS A MAIN COURSE, 8 AS A FIRST COURSE

SERVING SUGGESTIONS

No-Knead Bread (p. 670), Stuffed Tomatoes (p. 213), Vitello Tonnato (p. 559), Raspberry Granita (p. 719), Fresh Raspberry (or Blackberry or Blueberry) Flummery (p. 824), Summer Pudding (p. 847), Jellied Strawberry Pie (p. 811), Forget-It Meringue Torte (p. 823)

AUGUST 19, 1992: "CLASSIC RESTAURANT MEALS WORTH A TRY AT HOME," BY BRYAN MILLER. RECIPE ADAPTED FROM LE PÉRIGORD IN NEW YORK CITY.

—1992

⌇ MATZOH BALL SOUP

Turns out Wolfgang Puck makes a fantastic matzoh ball—bouncy, a little eggy, and fragrant with thyme.

———

6 large eggs

2½ tablespoons finely chopped flat-leaf parsley

1½ tablespoons finely chopped thyme

2 teaspoons kosher salt

½ teaspoon freshly ground white pepper

⅛ teaspoon cayenne pepper (optional)

½ cup melted clarified unsalted butter

1½ to 1¾ cups matzoh meal

¼ teaspoon baking powder

1 cup club soda

12 cups your best chicken soup

1. Whisk the eggs in a medium bowl. Whisk in the parsley, thyme, salt, pepper, and cayenne, if using. Whisk in the clarified butter, 1½ cups matzoh meal, and the baking powder. Whisk in the club soda until well combined. Cover with plastic wrap and refrigerate for 2 hours.

2. Place 10 cups chicken soup in a large wide pot and bring to a boil.

3. Meanwhile, whisk the matzoh ball mixture. With moistened hands, form the mixture into twenty 2-inch balls. Drop the balls into the soup, in batches, reduce the heat so the soup simmers, and cook for 30 minutes. With a slotted spoon, remove the matzoh balls to a clean dry towel to drain. Add the remaining soup to the pot and repeat.

4. Return the first batch to the soup to reheat, then drain them again. Ladle the soup into bowls and place 2 matzoh balls in each. Serve immediately.

SERVES 8

COOKING NOTES

To clarify butter, slowly melt it in a small saucepan on the stove or in a bowl in the microwave. Skim off any scum that rises to the surface, then pour the clear yellow butter into a clean bowl, leaving behind the milky whey at the bottom.

It's a good idea to shape and simmer 1 matzoh ball before preparing the rest, to make sure the ones you've made will hold together. Mine didn't, and I needed to add ¼ cup more matzoh meal.

Matzoh balls expand a lot as they cook—cook in batches, adding only enough to cover half the surface of the soup.

The wider the pan you use, the better—matzoh balls are less likely to fall apart in a shallow bath of broth.

SERVING SUGGESTIONS

Matt's Whole Brisket with Tomato Gravy (p. 572), James Beard's Chicken with 40 Cloves of Garlic (p. 469), Al Forno's Roasted Asparagus (p. 233), Puree of Peas and Watercress (p. 296), Latkes (p. 280), Polish Jewish Plum Cake (p. 769), Evelyn Sharpe's French Chocolate Cake (p. 752), Macaroons (p. 681)

MARCH 31, 1993: "PUCK'S SEDER AT SPAGO: AS TRADITIONAL AS GEFILTE FISH WITH CAYENNE," BY MARIAN BURROS. RECIPE ADAPTED FROM WOLFGANG PUCK, THE CHEF AND CO-OWNER OF SPAGO IN LOS ANGELES.

—1993

⌇ BUTTERNUT SQUASH AND CIDER SOUP

Although Thomas Keller's butternut squash soup on p. 156 is wonderful in every way, it's the kind of soup you make for a dinner party. This one is great to have in your everyday arsenal. It's sweet and pure flavored, and it can be made in a flash. The recipe came from Canyon Ranch, back when the Berkshires spa was little known but expensive. Now it is only the latter.

———

1 shallot, sliced

1 clove garlic, minced

¼ cup water

3 cups peeled, seeded, and cubed butternut squash

½ cup chicken broth

¾ cup apple cider

¼ cup light sour cream

½ teaspoon salt, or more to taste

½ Honeycrisp or Granny Smith apple, unpeeled, cored, and finely diced

Cracked black pepper

1. Heat a medium saucepan over low heat. Add the shallot, garlic, and water and cook until the shallot and garlic are softened, being careful not to let them burn, 3 to 5 minutes. Add the squash and chicken broth and bring to a boil. Reduce the heat, cover, and simmer until the squash is soft, about 20 minutes.

2. Carefully pour the mixture into a blender; you should do this in batches. Holding the top down with a towel, blend until smooth. Add the cider, sour cream, and salt and blend until well combined. (The soup can be made ahead up to this point. Reheat over low heat.) Season with additional salt if needed.

3. Ladle the soup into 4 bowls. Garnish with the diced apple and cracked black pepper.

SERVES 4

COOKING NOTES

The recipe called for a Red Rome or Delicious apple, neither of which I found tart enough. I changed it to Honeycrisp or Granny Smith.

SERVING SUGGESTIONS

Spicy New England Pot Roast (p. 523), Brined and Roasted Pork Belly (p. 556), High-Temperature Roast Lamb (p. 526), Slow-Roasted Duck (p. 475), Brussels Sprouts "Slaw" with Mustard Butter (p. 253), Sweet Potatoes Anna (p. 297), Wilted Red Cabbage Salad (p. 196), Poached Pears in Brandy and Red Wine (p. 832), Apple Tarte Tatin (p. 837), Purple Plum Torte (p. 763), Apple Dumplings (p. 807)

READERS

"I've given this recipe to so many people, who have told me that they've passed it to so many people, that I do believe that if you come to my Livingston neighborhood on Thanksgiving Day, you can smell all the pots of it simmering!"

Jodi Eisner, Livingston, NJ, e-mail

AUGUST 29, 1993: "FOOD: REMEDIAL EATING," BY MOLLY O'NEILL. RECIPE ADAPTED FROM BARRY CORREIA, THE CHEF AT CANYON RANCH IN UPSTATE NEW YORK.

—1993

∽ WHITE GAZPACHO WITH ALMONDS AND GRAPES

This is a fun recipe to make, as most of it comes together in stages in the food processor. As you whirl together the almonds, garlic, and bread, the mixture seizes. Then you slowly add oil, ice water, and vinegar, and with each sprinkling of liquid, the soup loosens and unifies. After letting the gazpacho chill for a few hours, it miraculously transforms once more, becoming creamier, almost foamy.

For some variations on gazpacho, see pages 146, 160, and 161.

3/4 cup blanched whole almonds
3 small cloves garlic
1/2 teaspoon salt, or to taste
4 slices stale white bread, crusts removed
4 cups ice water
7 tablespoons olive oil
2 to 3 tablespoons white wine vinegar
2 tablespoons sherry vinegar
1 tablespoon unsalted butter
6 slices white bread, crusts removed
   and cut into 1/2-inch cubes
1 1/2 cups seedless green grapes, halved

1. Grind the almonds, 2 garlic cloves, and salt to a fine consistency in a food processor or blender. Soak the stale bread in 1 cup ice water, then squeeze to extract excess moisture and add to the processor. With the processor running, slowly add 6 tablespoons oil and 1 cup ice water in a steady stream. Add the vinegars and puree for 2 minutes. Add 1 cup ice water and mix for 2 more minutes.

2. Transfer to a bowl, add the remaining cup of ice water, and mix well. Adjust the seasoning with salt and vinegar. Refrigerate until chilled, up to 6 hours.

3. Heat the butter and remaining 1 tablespoon olive oil in a large skillet. Crush the remaining garlic clove and add to the pan, along with the bread cubes, tossing to coat them with butter and oil. Cook over very low heat, stirring occasionally, for 20 to 30 minutes, or until the cubes are golden.

4. Serve the soup ice-cold, garnished with the croutons and grapes.

COOKING NOTES

For the stale bread, I used four-day-old Pullman bread (from a bakery) and it had just the right density and unobtrusive flavor. For the croutons, I used a commercial white bread, which you'll be shocked to hear was a mistake. Next time, I'd use the bakery Pullman for both.

When it comes time to toast the bread in the skillet, you will probably question the 20- to 30-minute cooking time. It's correct: the slow cooking causes the bread to not only toast but also dry out, so by the time the croutons are done, they're as light and fragile as autumn leaves.

The recipe calls for green grapes, but you should use the best-tasting grapes you can find, even if they're small and dark. Commercial green grapes lack fragrance and can be unpleasantly acidic.

SERVING SUGGESTIONS

Pork and Watermelon Salad (p. 574), Fried Eggplant with Salmorejo Sauce (p. 251), Sautéed Cod with Potatoes in Chorizo-Mussel Broth (p. 428), Stuffed Tomatoes (p. 213), Fresh Raspberry (or Blackberry or Blueberry) Flummery (p. 824), Peach Salad (p. 805)

AUGUST 31, 1994: "WHAT MAKES A TRUE GAZPACHO: OIL, VINEGAR, AND GARLIC," BY MARK BITTMAN. ADAPTED FROM *FROM TAPAS TO MEZE*, BY JOANNE WEIR.

—1994

ꗠ ISMAIL MERCHANT'S VERY HOT CHICKEN SOUP

While chicken soups are typically thought of as soothing, this one is invigorating, with chile and ginger setting off sparks on your palate. Add the red chile peppers to taste—start with 2 and see what you think.

One 3-pound chicken

About 6 cups water

8 whole cloves

One 1-inch piece fresh ginger, peeled and crushed
    or very finely chopped

2 to 4 dried hot red chiles or ½ to 1½ teaspoons
    crushed red pepper flakes (to taste)

2 tablespoons olive oil or unsalted butter

2 small ripe or canned tomatoes, peeled (see Cooking
    Note, p. 146), seeded, and chopped

¾ to 1 teaspoon salt

½ teaspoon coarsely ground black pepper, or to taste

Cilantro or flat-leaf parsley leaves for garnish

1. Put the chicken in a 3-quart pot and add just enough water to cover. It should not take more than 6 cups. If it does, cut the chicken into quarters so no more water will be needed. Add all the other ingredients except for the cilantro, using the minimum amounts of dried red chile and salt. Bring to a simmer and simmer gently, partly covered, for 15 minutes, adding water if necessary to maintain the original level. Skim the soup occasionally.

2. Taste for seasoning, and cautiously add more chile, salt, and/or black pepper. Cook for another 15 to 25 minutes, until the chicken is just about falling off the bones; keep adding water to maintain the original level.

3. Remove the chicken, cloves, and chile pepper stems, if any. Pick the chicken meat from the bones. Discard the skin and bones and return the small chunks of chicken to the soup; heat through. Garnish with cilantro or parsley.

SERVES 4

SERVING SUGGESTIONS

No-Knead Bread (p. 670), Sophie Grigson's Parmesan Cake (p. 69), Salade à la Romaine (p. 171), Chiffonade Salad (p. 173), Grapefruit Fluff (p. 809), Orange Ice (p. 717), Almond Granita (p. 731)

FEBRUARY 21, 1996: "THE PROBLEM IS WINTER, THE ANSWER IS SOUP," BY SUZANNE HAMLIN. ADAPTED FROM ISMAIL MERCHANT, WHOSE RECIPE APPEARED IN *THE WHOLE WORLD LOVES CHICKEN SOUP*, BY MIMI SHERATON.

—1996

FERN BERMAN'S GINGER AND LENTIL SOUP

2 tablespoons extra virgin olive oil

1 large onion, chopped (1½ to 2 cups)

3 to 6 cloves garlic, chopped

3 to 4 tablespoons diced or grated fresh ginger

3⅔ cups water

3 to 4 carrots, peeled and diced

1 pound brown lentils, rinsed and picked over

6 cups chicken or vegetable broth

Fine sea salt and freshly ground black pepper

Balsamic vinegar

1. Heat the olive oil in a 6- to 8-quart heavy pot over medium heat. Add the onion, garlic, and ginger, and sauté until translucent. Add ⅔ cup water and the diced carrots and simmer for a minute.

2. Stir in the lentils and add the broth and remaining 3 cups water. Bring to a simmer, partially cover, and simmer over low heat, stirring often, for 30 to 40 minutes, until the lentils are cooked and the soup has the consistency of porridge. Remove from the heat and let cool briefly.

3. Stir in salt, pepper, and dashes of balsamic vinegar to taste.

SERVES 8

COOKING NOTE

Many of the ingredients offer a range for amounts. You can't really go wrong here—it's all dependent on how feisty with the garlic and ginger you are willing to be.

SERVING SUGGESTIONS

Winter Slaw with Lemon-Orange Dressing (p. 185), Moroccan Carrot Salad (p. 187), Pepper-Cumin Cookies (p. 695)

FEBRUARY 21, 1996: "THE PROBLEM IS WINTER, THE ANSWER IS SOUP," BY SUZANNE HAMLIN. RECIPE ADAPTED FROM FERN BERMAN.

—1996

THAI SOLE CHOWDER WITH LIMA BEANS AND CORN

I wasn't going to include this recipe because it seemed so far afield from real Thai cooking, but the raves from my family were so loud I couldn't deny it a place as a lovable relic of so-called global cooking, which in the late 1980s and early 1990s gave cooks license to blend Asian flavors like coconut milk and ginger with Western lima beans and corn. (It also gave them license to wear chile-pepper chef pants, so you can understand the lasting skepticism.)

7 cups chicken broth (see Cooking Note)

3 cloves garlic, crushed

½ teaspoon crushed red pepper flakes

4 thin slices fresh ginger

6 small red potatoes, quartered

One 10-ounce package frozen lima beans

1 cup frozen corn

2 teaspoons grated lemon zest

2 teaspoons grated lime zest

2 cups unsweetened reduced-fat coconut milk

3 sole or fluke fillets (about 6 ounces each)
    cut into 1-inch cubes

1 teaspoon kosher salt

Freshly ground black pepper

2 scallions, finely chopped

¼ cup chopped basil

3 tablespoons chopped cilantro

2 tablespoons chopped mint

1. Combine the chicken broth, garlic, red pepper flakes, and ginger in a large pot and bring to a boil. Reduce the heat and simmer for 45 minutes.

2. Strain the broth. Wash the pot and return the broth to it. Bring to a boil. Add the potatoes and lima beans and simmer for 10 minutes. Add the corn and simmer until all the vegetables are tender, about 5 minutes longer.

3. Stir in the lemon and lime zest and coconut milk and bring to a simmer. Turn the heat to low and add the fish. Cook without boiling for 5 minutes.

4. Stir in the salt, pepper to taste, scallions, and herbs. Immediately ladle into bowls and serve.

The quality of the chicken broth is crucial: if using store-bought, make sure it's light, flavorful, and low in sodium; otherwise, dilute it by one-third with water.

SERVING SUGGESTIONS
Kaffir Lime Lemonade (p. 26), Rhubarb Bellini (p. 30), Beef Satay with Peanut Sauce (p. 66), Pork-and-Toasted-Rice-Powder Spring Rolls (p. 74), Jasmine Tea Rice (p. 354), Glazed Mango with Sour Cream Sorbet and Black Pepper (p. 850), Sticky Rice with Mango (p. 861), Pineapple Sherbet (p. 719)

APRIL 7, 1996: "FOOD: NO BONES ABOUT IT," BY MOLLY O'NEILL.

—1996

CHILLED MELON SOUP WITH TOASTED ALMONDS

As Molly O'Neill, a longtime food columnist at the *Times Magazine*, observed, "The French have a saying: Friends are like melons. To find a good one, you try a hundred." Do your best—the better the melon, the better this soup.

————

1 small ripe honeydew melon, peeled, seeded, and cut into ½-inch cubes (about 7 cups)
½ cup fresh lime juice
2 teaspoons seeded, minced jalapeño peppers
½ cup plain nonfat yogurt
2¼ teaspoons salt
Freshly ground black pepper
½ cup sliced almonds
¼ cup chopped mint

1. Preheat the oven to 325 degrees. Place the melon, lime juice, jalapeño, yogurt, 2 teaspoons salt, and pepper to taste in a blender and process until smooth. Refrigerate until cold.
2. Place the almonds in a bowl and toss with 2 teaspoons water and then with the remaining ¼ teaspoon salt. Spread on a baking sheet and bake until toasted, about 15 minutes. Let cool.

3. Divide the soup among 4 bowls and top with the almonds and mint.

SERVES 4

COOKING NOTE
I recommend doubling the toasted almonds so you can keep some around for snacking. If you don't, I guarantee your soup will get short shrift.

SERVING SUGGESTIONS
Hot Penne with Chilled Tomato Sauce and Charred Tuna (p. 322), Char-Grilled Tuna with Toasted Corn Vinaigrette and Avocado Salad (p. 410), Roasted Salmon with Herb Vinaigrette (p. 430), Sautéed Cod with Potatoes in Chorizo-Mussel Broth (p. 428), Zucchini with Crème Fraîche Pesto (p. 250), Peach Salad (p. 805), Jean Halberstam's Deep-Fried Peaches (p. 860)

JULY 7, 1996: "FOOD: RIPENESS IS ALL," BY MOLLY O'NEILL.

—1996

TURKISH SPLIT-PEA SOUP WITH MINT AND PAPRIKA

This is a split-pea soup without ham, and you will love it even more.

Although lentils, peas, grains, and beans began showing up in *Times* recipes in the 1970s, it wasn't until the 1990s that we started treating them as ingredients worth building a recipe around. Grains like farro appeared in risotto, cranberry beans in stews, toasted quinoa was blended into smartly constructed salads, Israeli couscous in fish stews, and red lentils in soups.

————

½ pound split peas, rinsed and picked over
2 tablespoons unsalted butter
1 onion, thinly sliced
1 carrot, peeled and thinly sliced
1 bay leaf
5 to 6 cups chicken broth
½ pound spinach trimmed, washed, and chopped
1 tablespoon Hungarian paprika
Whole milk (optional, for thinning)

1 teaspoon coarse sea salt
Freshly ground black pepper
3 tablespoons chopped mint
Plain Greek yogurt for serving

1. Cover the split peas with cold water in a bowl and soak for at least 8 hours, or overnight. Drain.

2. Melt the butter in a large saucepan over medium heat. Add the onion and cook until soft and translucent, about 10 minutes. Add the split peas, carrot, bay leaf, and broth to cover and bring to a boil. Reduce the heat and simmer gently, covered, until the peas are very soft, 20 to 30 minutes. If the mixture seems dry, add more broth or water as needed.

3. Remove the bay leaf. Add the chopped spinach and 2 teaspoons of paprika and simmer until the spinach begins to wilt. Remove from the heat.

4. When the soup has cooled slightly, puree it in a blender or food processor. If necessary, add a little milk, water, or broth to thin it. Season with the salt and pepper. Reheat, if needed, and sprinkle with the chopped mint and remaining teaspoon of paprika. Pass a bowl of yogurt at the table.

SERVES 4 TO 6

SERVING SUGGESTIONS

Moroccan Chicken Smothered in Olives (p. 482), Spicy Orange Salad Moroccan-Style (p. 181), Wilted Chard with Pickled Red Onion (p. 261), Steamed Fennel with Red Pepper Oil (p. 263), Huntington Pudding (p. 802), Hazelnut Baklava (p. 706), Queen of Puddings (p. 866)

JANUARY 26, 1997: "ADDING A TWIST TO WINTER SOUPS," BY MOIRA HODGSON. RECIPE ADAPTED FROM *KITCHEN CONVERSATIONS*, BY JOYCE GOLDSTEIN.

—1997

⌒ PROVENÇAL FISH SOUP

The extra-rich fish stock and Pernod act like thunder and lightning. The Pernod is shrill and electric, the fish a boom of ocean flavor. What may surprise your guests is that the soup doesn't contain any pieces of fish—all the fish flavor is distilled into the stock.

————

1 medium onion, cut into ¼-inch dice
½ cup olive oil
8 medium cloves garlic, smashed, and coarsely chopped
1 teaspoon chili powder
½ teaspoon cayenne pepper
2 teaspoons saffron threads, or more to taste
½ cup dry white wine, preferably Mâcon
    or sauvignon blanc
One 28-ounce can plus one 14-ounce can whole
    tomatoes in puree, drained and lightly crushed
5 cups extra-rich Fish Stock (recipe follows)
¼ teaspoon dried thyme
½ bay leaf
2 teaspoons kosher salt, or to taste
Freshly ground black pepper
½ cup anise liqueur, such as Pernod

1. Cook the onion in the oil in a medium pot over low heat, stirring occasionally, for 10 minutes, or until translucent. Stir in the garlic and cook for 7 minutes. Stir in the chili powder and cayenne and cook, stirring, for 1 minute.

2. Meanwhile, soak the saffron in ¼ cup white wine for a few minutes.

3. Stir the saffron-wine mixture, tomatoes, fish stock, thyme, and bay leaf into the onions. Bring to a boil, then lower the heat and simmer for 45 minutes.

4. Remove the bay leaf. Pass the soup through a food mill fitted with the medium plate. Return the soup to the pot and season with salt and pepper. (The soup can be made ahead up to this point and refrigerated.)

5. Heat the anise liqueur in a small saucepan. Using a long match, carefully set it on fire, and allow the alcohol to burn off. Pour the liqueur into the soup, stir in the remaining ¼ cup wine, and bring to a boil. Serve immediately.

SERVES 4

FISH STOCK

5 pounds heads and bones from white-fleshed fish,
    like snapper, bass, or cod
10 cups water

1. Wash the fish heads and bones well to eliminate all traces of blood. Cut out the blood-rich gills with scissors.

2. Put the fish heads and bones in a medium pot and cover with the water. Place over high heat, and bring to a boil, skimming off the scum that rises to top. Lower the heat and simmer the stock for 4 to 6 hours, or until approximately 7 cups of broth remain, skimming as necessary. For extra-rich stock, simmer for an additional hour.

3. Strain the stock through a sieve (ideally lined with a damp cloth). The stock can be used immediately or refrigerated or frozen.

MAKES ABOUT 7 CUPS (5 CUPS EXTRA-RICH STOCK)

SERVING SUGGESTIONS
Stuffed Tomatoes (p. 213), An Honest Loaf of French Bread (p. 662), Pan con Tomate (p. 91), Crostini with Eggplant and Pine Nut Puree (p. 78), Ricotta Crostini with Fresh Thyme and Dried Oregano (p. 93), Seasoned Olives (p. 90), Wallace Seawell's Spinach Salad (p. 180), Tourtière (Apple, Prune, and Armagnac Tart; p. 827), Figs in Whiskey (p. 859), Tartelettes aux Pommes Lionel Poilâne (Individual Apple Tarts; p. 834), Rhubarb-Strawberry Mousse (p. 835)

NOVEMBER 5, 1997: "FISH STOCK DEMYSTIFIED," BY BARBARA KAFKA.

—1997

⌒ WINTER BORSCHT

This is the best borscht you will ever eat, and one of my favorite recipes in the book. The long cooking concentrates the flavor in the broth, but its consistency remains light and fluid, like a beet-and-beef tea.

———

2 pounds beef shin

6 cups water

I small onion, unpeeled, cut in half

2 medium carrots, peeled, I quartered, I grated

3 medium red beets, scrubbed well

6 tablespoons tomato paste

4 medium cloves garlic, smashed

1/2 pound red cabbage, shredded

2 medium tomatoes, cored and coarsely chopped

I bay leaf

2 tablespoons red wine vinegar

2 tablespoons plus 2 teaspoons sugar

I pound firm potatoes, peeled, cut into 1/2-inch cubes, and cooked in boiling salted water until tender

2 teaspoons kosher salt

Freshly ground black pepper

1/3 cup chopped dill

For the Garnish
1/2 boiled firm potato per person (optional)

Sour cream

Chopped dill

1. Cover the beef with the water in a large saucepan. Stir in the onion and quartered carrot and bring to a boil, skimming off any foam and fat that rises to the surface. Lower the heat and simmer gently for 1 1/2 hours.

2. Strain the broth through a fine-mesh sieve; there should be about 5 cups. Reserve the meat.

3. Return the beef and liquid to the pan and bring to a boil. Add the beets and return to a boil. Lower the heat and simmer for 20 to 30 minutes, or until the tip of a knife easily pierces the beets.

4. Remove the beets and allow to cool slightly, then peel them and coarsely grate. Return the grated beets to the soup.

5. Dissolve the tomato paste in 1/2 cup of the soup, and stir back into the pan. Stir in the garlic, grated carrot, cabbage, tomatoes, bay leaf, vinegar, and sugar and bring to a boil. Lower the heat and simmer, stirring occasionally, for 1 1/2 hours.

6. Remove the meat from the pan. Discard the bones and slice the meat 1/2 inch thick then stir into the soup, along with the cubed potatoes, salt, pepper to taste, and the dill. Return to a boil for 2 minutes.

7. If desired, place a half potato in the bottom of each large soup bowl. Ladle in the soup. Top each with a dollop of sour cream and a sprinkling of dill.

SERVES 4 TO 6

COOKING NOTES
After removing the meat from the soup, I found it difficult to slice, so I shredded it into bite-sized pieces.

I didn't serve this with the potato garnish—if you do, use white or Yukon Gold potatoes. Baking potatoes would be mealy.

Salade à la Romaine (p. 171), Winter Fruit Salad (p. 850), Bosiljka Marich's Serbian Torte (p. 751), Lemon Cake (p. 781), Teddie's Apple Cake (p. 752)

JANUARY 28, 1998: "VERSATILE BORSCHT, HUMBLE NO MORE," BY BARBARA KAFKA.

—1998

⌒ CREAMY FARRO AND CHICKPEA SOUP

Paula Wolfert belongs to a group of women food writers I think of as the mistresses of the Mediterranean. In the 1980s and 1990s, they conquered a whole swath of Europe: Greece (Claudia Roden, Aglaia Kremezi, Diane Kochilas); Italy (Nancy Harmon Jenkins, Carol Field, Faith Willinger, Lynn Rosetto Kasper); and Spain (Penelope Casas). Together, they shook up the cookbook world with fascinating works on the everyday foods of the Olive Oil Belt.

People often credit Craig Claiborne, Julia Child, and James Beard with getting Americans to travel to Europe to eat. But it was the mistresses who documented Mediterranean cuisines with intimacy and a reportorial approach that was new to cookbook writing. They got readers who traveled there to dig deeper, to breeze by the starred restaurants and tuck into the cramped bistros, trattorias, tapas bars, and tavernas. And, back home, to break away from pasta and explore the world of bitter greens, haloumi, and chestnut flour.

This recipe comes from Wolfert's *Mediterranean Grains and Greens*, her sixth book. You build the soup on a foundation of prosciutto, onion, and celery, later adding nutmeg and marjoram to the farro, and just before serving, you puree some of the cooked chickpeas to thicken the broth and integrate the parts into a coherent whole.

¾ cup dried chickpeas, rinsed, picked over, and soaked overnight in water to cover
½ teaspoon sea salt
2 bay leaves
3 tablespoons extra virgin olive oil, plus more for garnish
½ cup chopped onion
1 tablespoon chopped prosciutto
1 tablespoon minced celery
¾ cup farro or hulled barley, rinsed and soaked overnight in water to cover
4 cups chicken broth
½ teaspoon dried marjoram
2 pinches freshly grated nutmeg
Kosher salt and freshly ground black pepper
Chopped flat-leaf parsley for garnish

1. Drain the chickpeas and place in a medium saucepan. Cover with plenty of cold water and bring to a boil. Add the sea salt and bay leaves, reduce the heat, and cook, covered, until the chickpeas are very soft, about 1½ hours.
2. Meanwhile, heat the olive oil in a medium saucepan. Add the onion, prosciutto, and celery and cook gently for 4 to 5 minutes, stirring occasionally, until soft but not brown. Drain the farro and add it to the onion mixture, along with the chicken broth, marjoram, and nutmeg. Cook, partially covered, for 1 hour.
3. Drain the chickpeas, reserving the cooking liquid; discard the bay leaves. Puree the chickpeas with 1 cup of the reserved liquid in a food processor. Add the pureed chickpeas to the farro mixture; if necessary, add more of the cooking liquid from the chickpeas to achieve the consistency of a creamy soup. Adjust the seasoning with salt and pepper. Wait for 10 minutes before serving.
4. Sprinkle each portion with chopped parsley and a drizzle of olive oil.

SERVES 4

SERVING SUGGESTIONS
Seasoned Olives (p. 90), Ricotta Crostini with Fresh Thyme and Dried Oregano (p. 93), Roast Chicken with Bread Salad (p. 467), Steamed Spinach with Balsamic Butter (p. 226), Madeleine Kamman's Apple Mousse (p. 816), Bolzano Apple Cake (p. 783)

SEPTEMBER 2, 1998: "BY THE BOOK: MEDITERRANEAN NIGHTS," BY AMANDA HESSER. RECIPE ADAPTED FROM *MEDITERRANEAN GRAINS AND GREENS*, BY PAULA WOLFERT.

—1998

⌐ PHO BO (HANOI BEEF SOUP)

Recipes for pho, the fragrant beef soup that's served for breakfast in Vietnam, tend to be lengthy affairs involving rice noodles, fish sauce, and all manner of herbs. But barely any of the ingredients need to be prepped; the real work in pho, and the most interesting part, is making the broth. As water and oxtail and shin bones are brought to a simmer, you char onions and ginger in a dry skillet. You may find yourself hesitating—it feels so unnatural to burn food—but the onions behave just as they should, turning black without starting a fire, and they really do lend a persuasive smokiness to the broth. The smokiness is later complemented by the dewy fragrance of star anise, cinnamon, bay leaf, and fennel.

---

1 pound rice vermicelli
8 cups Vietnamese-Style Beef Stock (recipe follows)
¾ pound lean beef, preferably beef round,
    sliced paper-thin
½ cup mung bean sprouts
½ cup cilantro leaves
½ cup small basil leaves, chopped
2 scallions, chopped
1 lime, cut into wedges
3 red Thai or serrano chiles, seeded and chopped
Asian Fish sauce for serving
Freshly ground black pepper

1. Place the vermicelli in a large bowl and cover with cold water. Soak until pliable, about 30 minutes. Drain.
2. Place the stock in a large saucepan and bring it to a boil. Have 4 very large or 6 smaller individual soup bowls ready. Put a handful of vermicelli into a strainer that will fit in the pan and dip the strainer into the hot stock. Swirl the vermicelli until tender but still a little chewy, about 20 seconds. Shake the vermicelli dry and place it in a soup bowl. Repeat with the remaining noodles.
3. Divide the beef, sprouts, cilantro, basil, and scallions among the bowls. Ladle the hot stock into the bowls and squeeze a lime wedge over each—don't be shy with the lime. Serve with the chiles, fish sauce, and black pepper on the side.

SERVES 4 TO 6

VIETNAMESE-STYLE BEEF STOCK

2 pounds oxtail pieces
3 pounds beef bones (shin or neck)
½ teaspoon salt
14 cups cold water
One 3-inch piece of fresh ginger, split lengthwise
1 medium onion, unpeeled, halved
8 star anise
2 cinnamon sticks
2 large bay leaves
5 whole cloves
1 tablespoon sugar
2 teaspoons fennel seeds

1. Place the oxtails, beef bones, salt, and cold water in a large stockpot and slowly bring to a boil over medium heat.
2. Meanwhile, heat a small cast-iron skillet over high heat. Place the ginger and onion cut side down into the skillet and cook until charred black, about 3 minutes. Turn the pieces and cook, turning occasionally, until they are charred on all sides. Add them to the stock.
3. When the stock boils, reduce the heat and simmer, uncovered, skimming off any foam, for 30 minutes.
4. Add the star anise, cinnamon, bay leaves, cloves, and sugar to the stock. Put the fennel seeds in a tea ball or tie them in cheesecloth and add them to the stock. Continue to simmer, skimming occasionally, for 3½ more hours.
5. Strain the stock through a fine-mesh sieve, and discard the solids. Refrigerate until the fat solidifies on top of the stock, 3 to 4 hours. Remove the fat with a spoon and discard. (The stock will keep refrigerated for up to 3 days.)

MAKES ABOUT 8 CUPS

COOKING NOTES
The beef shins that I used had some meat attached. After simmering, I removed it from the bones and fed it to my kids.

Do not settle for any old rice vermicelli—make that trip to Chinatown.

Have your butcher slice the beef; it needs to be paper-thin, and if you do it at home, it probably won't be.

SERVING SUGGESTIONS

Pork-and-Toasted-Rice-Powder Spring Rolls (p. 74), Sticky Rice with Mango (p. 861), Mango Ice Cream (p. 729)

JANUARY 17, 1999: "FOOD: GOOD MORNING, VIETNAM," BY MOLLY O'NEILL. RECIPE ADAPTED FROM *SIMPLE ART OF VIETNAMESE COOKING*, BY BINH DUONG AND MARCIA KIESEL.

—1999

☞ CREAMY CURRIED SWEET POTATO SOUP

1 1/2 tablespoons olive oil
1 cup coarsely chopped onion
1 large clove garlic, coarsely chopped
1 tablespoon coarsely grated fresh ginger
1 teaspoon ground cumin
1/2 teaspoon ground coriander
1/4 teaspoon ground cardamom
1/4 teaspoon turmeric
1/8 teaspoon crushed red pepper flakes (optional)
2 1/2 pounds sweet potatoes, peeled
    and sliced 1/4 inch thick
6 cups chicken broth, or as needed
Salt and freshly ground black pepper
6 to 8 teaspoons fresh goat cheese

1. Heat the oil in a pot large enough to hold all the ingredients. Add the onion and sauté over medium heat until it begins to brown, about 10 minutes. Add the garlic and sauté, stirring, for 30 seconds. Add the ginger, cumin, coriander, cardamom, turmeric, and red pepper flakes, if using, and stir well. Add the sweet potatoes and broth and bring to a boil. Reduce the heat and simmer until the sweet potatoes are soft, about 20 minutes.

2. Puree the soup in batches in a blender or food processor. Season to taste with salt and pepper. (The soup can be made ahead of time and refrigerated. Reheat slowly to serve.) If the soup is too thick, add a little more stock.

3. Ladle into mugs, top each serving with a teaspoon of cheese, and stir to melt a little.

SERVES 6 TO 8

SERVING SUGGESTIONS

A Loose Interpretation of Cobb Salad (p. 193), Iceberg Lettuce with Smoked Bacon and Buttermilk Dressing (p. 200), Cinnamon-Scented Fried Chicken (p. 490), Beer-Can Chicken (p. 473), Monte's Ham (p. 548), Meat and Spinach Loaf (p. 524), Wilted Chard with Pickled Red Onion (p. 261), Spinach with Sour Cream (p. 216), Apple Crumb Pie (p. 841), Sally Darr's Golden Delicious Apple Tart (p. 839).

MARCH 3, 1999: "EATING WELL: SWEET POTATO TO THE RESCUE," BY MARIAN BURROS.

—1999

☞ CLEAR STEAMED CHICKEN SOUP WITH GINGER

To make this soup, which comes from *A Spoonful of Ginger* by Nina Simonds, you combine all the ingredients in a pot, cover it tightly with foil and a lid, and cook in a water bath in the oven for 2 hours. The steaming produces a limpid, intense broth. You remove the aromatics—ginger and scallion—before serving, so all you are left with are the chicken pieces and an aromatic, rice wine–infused tonic.

One 3- to 3 1/2-pound chicken, excess fat removed,
    cut into 10 to 12 pieces
1 3/4 cups rice wine, preferably Shaoxing
10 scallions, trimmed and smashed lightly
    with the side of a knife
10 slices fresh ginger (the size of a quarter),
    smashed with the side of a knife
6 cups boiling water
1 teaspoon salt, or more to taste

1. Heat the oven to 425 degrees. Bring 8 cups of water to a boil in a large pot. Blanch the chicken pieces for 1 minute. Drain.

2. Combine the chicken, rice wine, scallions, ginger, and boiling water in a Dutch oven or casserole with a lid. Cover tightly with heavy-duty aluminum foil, then cover with the lid. Place the pot in a roasting pan

and fill the pan with 1½ inches of boiling water. Bake for 2 hours, replenishing the boiling water as needed.

3. Skim the top of the broth to remove any impurities and fat. Add the salt. Remove the ginger and scallions and ladle the soup and chicken into bowl.

SERVES 6 AS A FIRST COURSE

COOKING NOTES
Ask your butcher to cut the chicken into pieces—it'll save you a lot of time.

SERVING SUGGESTIONS
Chinese-Style Steamed Black Sea Bass (p. 432), Hunan Beef with Cumin (p. 575), Warm Eggplant Salad with Sesame and Shallots (p. 203), Yogurt Rice (p. 356), Tea Ice Cream (p. 717)

MAY 5, 1999: "BY THE BOOK: YIN AND YANG LITE," BY AMANDA HESSER. RECIPE ADAPTED FROM *A SPOONFUL OF GINGER*, BY NINA SIMONDS.

—1999

⌒ THOMAS KELLER'S GAZPACHO

Thomas Keller, the chef at The French Laundry in Yountville, California, has a remarkable way with soups. Three of them appear in this book—a butternut squash soup on p. 156, a yellow pepper soup with paprika mousse on p. 147, and this gazpacho.

In the accompanying story, Keller insisted that good vegetable soups rely on a single technique: "Separate the flavor and color from what contains it, the cellulose." Unfortunately, his tool of choice for doing the separating is the chinois, a cone-shaped fine-mesh strainer. Pushing soups, or anything, for that matter, through a chinois is about much as fun as having a tooth extracted. But the effect, I regret to say, is worth it. The sieving gives this gazpacho the richness and polish of a velouté.

We often think of chefs as rigid taskmasters, but the best ones are flexible thinkers, always examining a dish from different angles. Keller noted that for him the line between a sauce and a soup is often blurred. "Think of it as gazpacho sauce," he said of this soup. "It goes perfectly with grilled chicken or fish, and I serve it at the restaurant as the sauce for an artichoke

salad. (Put a little vodka in your gazpacho sauce, and it becomes the world's best Bloody Mary.)"

Earlier gazpacho recipes can be found on pages 112 and 137.

———

1 cup chopped peeled tomatoes (about 1 large)
1 cup chopped peeled red onion (about 1 small)
1 cup chopped green bell pepper (about 1)
1 cup chopped English (seedless) cucumber (about ½ medium)
1½ teaspoons chopped garlic
1½ teaspoons kosher salt
¼ teaspoon cayenne pepper
¼ cup tomato paste
1 tablespoon white wine vinegar
6 tablespoons extra virgin olive oil
1 tablespoon fresh lemon juice
3 cups tomato juice
1 sprig thyme

1. Combine all of the ingredients in a large bowl. Cover and refrigerate overnight.

2. The next day, remove the sprig of thyme. Puree the remaining ingredients in a blender until smooth. Strain the soup. Refrigerate the gazpacho until well chilled.

3. Ladle the soup into bowls and serve cold.

SERVES 8 TO 16 (16 TINY SERVINGS)

COOKING NOTE
To peel tomatoes, cut a shallow X in the bottom of each tomato. Submerge in boiling water for 5 to 10 seconds to loosen the skins. Remove and chill in cold water. The skins will slip off.

SERVING SUGGESTIONS
Jean-Georges Vongerichten's Crab Salad (p. 415), Wok-Seared Spicy Calamari Salad (p. 443), Seared Tuna in Black Pepper Crust (p. 409), Sautéed Cod with Potatoes in Chorizo-Mussel Broth (p. 428), Ventresca Tuna Salad (p. 426), Beer-Can Chicken (p. 473), Grilled Hanger Steak (p. 551), Light Potato Salad (p. 301), Saratoga Potatoes (p. 273), Brownies (p. 684), Summer Pudding (p. 847)

JUNE 23, 1999: "THE CHEF: THE SPIRIT OF SUMMER, CAPTURED IN A SOUP," BY THOMAS KELLER AND MICHAEL

RUHLMAN. RECIPE ADAPTED FROM THOMAS KELLER, THE CHEF AND OWNER OF THE FRENCH LAUNDRY IN YOUNTVILLE, CALIFORNIA.

—1999

⌐ YELLOW PEPPER SOUP WITH PAPRIKA MOUSSE

This soup, the color of French butter, is sweet and subtle with an appealingly frank bitterness. After cooking the peppers in a lake of cream, and pureeing and straining them, you finish the soup by swirling in whipped cream, which floods it with soft, delicate bubbles and makes it very, very rich. I ate it both with and without the cream—see which you prefer. I liked both, but I'd serve the version with cream in sake cups.

If the paprika in your spice rack has been there since 1987, don't use it in the mousse (or anything else intended for human consumption). You need fresh, pungent, pleasantly bitter paprika. Half a teaspoon is a lot, so you can start with a little less. Or, if you feel like fiddling around with the flavor substitute sweet smoked paprika (pimentón) for the regular paprika, but cut the amount to $1/8$ teaspoon.

———

3 large yellow (or red) bell peppers, cored, seeded, and cut into 1-inch pieces

$1^3/4$ cups heavy cream

Kosher salt

$1/4$ cup crème fraîche

$1/2$ teaspoon paprika, or to taste

1. To prepare the soup, combine the peppers and $1^1/2$ cups heavy cream in a medium pot and simmer gently over medium-low heat until the peppers are tender and cooked through, about 15 minutes.

2. Transfer the cream and peppers to a blender and puree for 2 to 3 minutes. Strain through a chinois (fine-mesh conical sieve), pressing on the solids to release all the liquid. Season with salt. (The soup can be refrigerated for up to 2 days.)

3. To prepare the mousse, whip the crème fraîche and paprika in small bowl until the paprika is blended and the cream is stiff. Season with salt. Refrigerate until ready to use, or up to 2 days.

4. To serve, whip the remaining $1/4$ cup cream until

it forms peaks. Bring the soup to a boil in a medium saucepan over medium-high heat. Remove from the heat and vigorously whisk in the whipped cream to create a frothy consistency. Pour the soup into hot soup cups and garnish with the paprika mousse.

SERVES 4 AS A FIRST COURSE

COOKING NOTE

If you're serving this for a party and want to whip the cream in advance, whip it two-thirds of the way, then finish it just before serving.

SERVING SUGGESTIONS

'ino's Tuna with Black Olive Pesto Panini (p. 373), Salade Niçoise (p. 178), Gently Cooked Salmon with Mashed Potatoes (p. 415), Steamed Fish with Thyme and Tomato Vinaigrette (p. 408), Tomatoes Stuffed with Crab (p. 393), Sole Grenobloise (Sautéed Sole with Capers and Lemons; p. 399), Fresh Succotash (p. 275), Zucchini and Vermouth (p. 227), Fried Zucchini Blossoms (p. 243), Strawberry Sorbet (p. 732)

JUNE 23, 1999: "THE CHEF: THE SPIRIT OF SUMMER, CAPTURED IN A SOUP," BY THOMAS KELLER AND MICHAEL RUHLMAN. RECIPE ADAPTED FROM THOMAS KELLER, THE CHEF AND OWNER OF THE FRENCH LAUNDRY IN YOUNT-VILLE, CALIFORNIA.

—1999

⌐ ROASTED SQUASH SOUP WITH CUMIN

So many butternut squash soups overdo the sweetness. This one trots it out but keeps it under tight rein with cumin, vinegar, and cayenne—and salty cumin-scented squash seeds for added emphasis.

Readers expressed nearly equal love for this soup and the Butternut Squash and Cider Soup on p. 136. Seven people wrote to recommend that soup, and eight to recommend this. After making both, I decided both merited inclusion.

———

1 large butternut squash (about 3 pounds)

1 tablespoon vegetable oil

Kosher salt and freshly ground black pepper

1 teaspoon ground cumin
4½ cups chicken broth
1 clove garlic, minced
½ teaspoon cider vinegar
½ teaspoon sugar
Pinch of cayenne pepper
½ cup heavy cream

1. Heat the oven to 400 degrees. Line 1 large and 1 small baking sheet with aluminum foil. With a large knife, split the squash in half lengthwise. Scoop out and reserve the seeds. Brush the cut sides of the squash with 2 teaspoons oil and sprinkle with salt and pepper. Place cut side down on the large baking sheet and roast until very tender, 35 to 45 minutes.

2. Meanwhile, remove any orange fibers from the seeds and rinse the seeds under cold running water. Drain and place on paper towels to dry.

3. Toss the seeds with the remaining teaspoon of oil and ½ teaspoon cumin, and season with salt. Spread on the small baking sheet and roast along with the squash, stirring occasionally, until well browned, about 10 minutes. Remove from the oven and set aside.

4. Scoop the flesh from the squash shells and place in a pot. Add the chicken broth, garlic, vinegar, sugar, cayenne, and remaining ½ teaspoon cumin. Bring to a boil, then lower the heat and simmer, uncovered, for 10 minutes.

5. Working in small batches, transfer the soup to a blender and blend until smooth. Return the soup to the pot, stir in the cream, and bring just to a simmer. Season with salt and pepper and serve garnished with the squash seeds.

SERVES 4 TO 6

SERVING SUGGESTIONS
Roast Quail with Sage Dressing (p. 453), Short Ribs with Coffee and Chiles (p. 579), Fresh Mushrooms Stewed with Madeira (p. 214), Cumin-Mustard Carrots (p. 237), Stewed Fennel (p. 245), Barley Risotto (p. 327), Poached Pears in Brandy and Red Wine (p. 832), Fresh Ginger Cake (p. 775), Molasses Cup Cakes with Lemon Icing (p. 745)

SEPTEMBER 26, 1999: "FOOD: BASIC INSTINCTS," BY MOLLY O'NEILL.

—1999

⌒ POTAGE PARISIEN WITH SORREL CREAM

This is Vichyssoise à la Ritz (p. 111) meets Soupe à la Bonne Femme (p. 107)—in a blender.

———

1½ tablespoons unsalted butter
3 medium leeks, white and pale green parts only, split lengthwise, thinly sliced, and washed well
6 cups homemade chicken or vegetable broth
3 medium Yukon Gold potatoes, peeled and cut into ¼-inch dice
Salt and freshly ground white pepper
3 ounces sorrel, stemmed and washed
⅓ cup heavy cream, whipped to firm peaks

1. Melt the butter in a stockpot over low heat. Add the leeks and cook, stirring, until tender but not brown, 8 to 10 minutes. Pour in the broth, increase the heat, and bring just to a boil. Add the potatoes, season with salt and pepper, lower the heat, and simmer for 8 to 10 minutes, or until cooked through. Adjust the seasoning, and keep warm.

2. Process the sorrel to a smooth puree in a blender. If it seems stiff, add a tablespoon of the whipped cream. Delicately fold the puree into the whipped cream and season with salt and pepper.

3. Ladle the soup into bowls and top each with a spoonful of sorrel cream.

SERVES 4

COOKING NOTE
Make this with your best homemade chicken broth—the store-bought kind has nowhere to hide in this revealing soup.

SERVING SUGGESTIONS
Baked Flounder (p. 401), Elizabeth Frink's Roast Lemon Chicken (p. 478), Sugar Snap Peas with Horseradish (p. 259), Watercress Salad (p. 171), Marcella's Pear Cake (p. 769)

MARCH 29, 2000: "THE SECRET LIFE OF SORREL," BY AMANDA HESSER. RECIPE ADAPTED FROM CAFÉ BOULUD COOKBOOK, BY DANIEL BOULUD AND DORIE GREENSPAN.

—2000

BASIC CORN CHOWDER

This recipe is a classic foundation for corn chowder. The corncobs help to make the broth, doubling the corn flavor in the finished soup. But you should definitely add the cream and bacon, as instructed in the first variation. Without them, the chowder is well balanced. With them, it's a dish you won't forget.

———

5 ears corn
1 tablespoon unsalted butter or neutral oil,
    like canola or grapeseed
1 medium onion, chopped
2 medium potatoes, peeled and diced
Salt and freshly ground black pepper
2 tomatoes, cored, seeded, and chopped (optional)
1 cup whole or low-fat milk
½ cup chopped flat-leaf parsley (optional)

1. Shuck the corn, and use a sharp knife to strip the kernels into a bowl. Put the cobs in a pot with 4 cups water, bring to a boil. Cover, reduce the heat, and simmer while you continue.

2. Put the butter or oil in a saucepan and turn the heat to medium-high. When the butter melts or the oil is hot, add the onion and potatoes, along with a sprinkling of salt and pepper. Cook, stirring occasionally, until the onion softens, about 5 minutes. Add the tomatoes and cook, stirring, for another minute or two.

3. After the corncobs have cooked for at least 10 minutes, strain the liquid into the onion-potato mixture. Bring to a boil, then lower the heat to a simmer.

4. When the potatoes are tender, add the corn kernels and milk and heat through. Taste and adjust the seasoning. Garnish with the parsley and serve.

SERVES 4

VARIATIONS

Corn Chowder with Bacon and Cream: In Step 2, substitute ½ cup chopped bacon for the butter or oil. Cook it over medium heat until it renders some of its fat, then add the onion. In Step 3, use heavy cream or half-and-half in place of the milk.

Curried Corn Chowder: In Step 2, use the oil, and add 1 tablespoon each curry powder and peeled,

minced ginger to the onions. In Step 3, use sour cream in place of the milk; garnish with cilantro in place of the parsley.

SERVING SUGGESTIONS
Tomatoes Vinaigrette (p. 218), Squashed Tomatoes (p. 90), Jonathan Waxman's Red Pepper Pancakes (p. 228), Deep-Fried Soft-Shell Crabs (p. 398), Sea Scallops with Sweet Red Peppers and Zucchini (p. 409), Apple City World-Champion Baby Back Ribs (p. 582), Pork Burgers (p. 566), Spoonbread's Potato Salad (p. 288), Baked Zucchini with Herbs and Tomatoes (p. 250), Summer Pudding (p. 847), Raspberry Granita (p. 719)

AUGUST 23, 2000: "THE MINIMALIST: DON'T TOSS OUT THE COBS," BY MARK BITTMAN.

—2000

CAULIFLOWER SOUP WITH CREMINI MUSHROOMS AND WALNUT OIL

———

1½ tablespoons extra virgin olive oil
½ pound cremini mushrooms, trimmed
    and cut into ½-inch pieces
Sea salt
1 clove garlic, smashed and chopped
1¼ pounds cauliflower, trimmed and cut into florets
5 cups water
¼ cup heavy cream, plus more if desired
Freshly ground black pepper
About 3 tablespoons walnut oil

1. Place a large casserole over medium-high heat. Add the olive oil and heat until it shimmers, then add the mushrooms. Season with salt and sauté until softened, about 5 minutes. Add the garlic and cook for 1 minute more.

2. Add the cauliflower and water and bring to a boil. Reduce the heat and simmer until the cauliflower is tender, 5 to 7 minutes. Working in batches, use a blender or food processor to puree the soup until it's very smooth. Return the soup to the pot and place over medium heat. Stir in the cream, adjust the salt, and season with pepper.

3. To serve, stir the soup, or use an immersion blender to blend and froth the top of the soup. Ladle into warmed bowls and drizzle about 1½ teaspoons walnut oil over each.

SERVES 6

SERVING SUGGESTIONS

Slow-Roasted Duck (p. 475), Ginger Duck (p. 480), Chicken Paprikash (p. 461), Veal Shanks with Garlic Mashed Potatoes (p. 540), Lamb Shoulder Chops with Anchovy and Mint Butter (p. 567), Puree of Peas and Watercress (p. 296), Shredded Brussels Sprouts with Bacon and Pine Nuts (p. 235), Mushrooms Stuffed with Duxelles and Sausage (p. 223), Whiskey Cake (p. 784), Campton Place Buttermilk Chocolate Cake (p. 765)

JANUARY 17, 2001: "THE CELESTIAL CAULIFLOWER: EARNING A SPOT IN THE SUN," BY AMANDA HESSER.

—2001

∽ WATERMELON GAZPACHO

This probably bears a closer relationship to the Watermelon and Tomato Salad on p. 197 than it does to any gazpacho. Sure, it has the zing of a gazpacho, but it lives more in the realm of the sweet and refreshing than the robust and cool.

———

3 very ripe medium tomatoes, cored and seeded

4 cups 2-inch chunks seedless watermelon

½ large Vidalia onion or other sweet onion, cut into 1-inch chunks

1 medium cucumber, peeled, halved lengthwise, seeded, and cut into large chunks

1 clove garlic, minced

¼ cup packed basil leaves

¼ cup extra virgin olive oil

1½ tablespoons fresh lemon juice, or more to taste

Coarse sea or kosher salt and coarsely ground black pepper

1. Combine the tomatoes and watermelon in a blender, and puree for about 30 seconds. Add the onion, cucumber, garlic, basil, olive oil, and lemon juice, season with salt and pepper, and puree until very smooth, about 2 minutes. Adjust the lemon juice, salt, and/or pepper if desired. If necessary, thin the gazpacho with water until loose enough to drink from a glass. Refrigerate until thoroughly chilled, about 2 hours.

2. Place 2 ice cubes in each of 6 tall glasses. Fill the glasses with gazpacho and serve.

SERVES 6

COOKING NOTE

To seed a halved cucumber, drag the edge of a teaspoon down the channel of seeds; they should lift out easily.

SERVING SUGGESTIONS

Pamela Sherrid's Summer Pasta (p. 329), Corn and Yellow Tomato Risotto with Shrimp (p. 328), Shrimp in Green Sauce (p. 430), Pork Burgers (p. 566), Potato Salad with Shaved Ricotta Salata and Green Sauce (p. 299), Zucchini Carpaccio with Avocado (p. 261), Fried Corn (p. 274), Green Bean Salad with Savory Topping (p. 177), Strawberry Sorbet (p. 732), Peach Salad (p. 805), Fresh Blueberry Buckle (p. 815)

JULY 18, 2001: "IN FROM THE FIELDS, AN ELEGANT PARTNER," BY AMANDA HESSER.

—2001

∽ BEET AND GINGER SOUP WITH CUCUMBER

I came up with this soup as an antidote to all the rich restaurant food I used to have to eat—poor me! The beet-roasting technique is one I learned from a book by Tom Colicchio. The beets roast and steam at once, so their sweetness concentrates and their skins slip off easily. Once you get past this step, the soup is a snap to make. You soften the aromatics, add the beets and broth, and then whirl it all in a food processor. Just before setting it out on the table, you sprinkle in some finely diced cucumber—for an occasional, rousing hit of crispness.

———

1½ pounds small beets, trimmed and scrubbed

3 tablespoons olive oil

Coarse sea salt or kosher salt

1 small leek, white and light green parts only, chopped

1 clove garlic, smashed

3 tablespoons chopped fresh ginger, or more to taste

3 cups chicken broth

3 cups water

Juice of 1 lemon, or to taste

½ (seedless) English cucumber, peeled, halved lengthwise, seeded, and chopped into ⅛-inch cubes

Crème fraîche, for serving (optional)

1. Heat the oven to 325 degrees. Place the beets in a bowl, sprinkle with 1 tablespoon oil, and season with salt. Toss to coat. Place the beets on half of a large sheet of aluminum foil and fold it over to make a pouch. Seal tightly. Put on a baking sheet, place in the oven, and roast until a fork easily pierces the beets, about 1¼ hours. Remove from the oven and let cool.

2. Peel off the skin and cut the beets in quarters.

3. Warm the remaining 2 tablespoons olive oil in a soup pot over medium heat. Add the leek and cook, stirring occasionally, until it begins to soften, about 5 minutes. Add the garlic and ginger and cook for 2 minutes more. Season lightly with salt. Add the beets, chicken broth, and water, bring to a simmer, and cook for 10 minutes.

4. Transfer the soup, in batches, to a food processor and process until smooth. Return the soup to the pot. Add lemon juice to taste. Then adjust the seasoning, adding more salt, lemon juice, and ginger if you wish.

5. Just before serving (the soup should not be too hot; it could even be served chilled or at room temperature), add the cucumber and stir. Then ladle into bowls and serve. You can serve this with a dollop of crème fraîche.

SERVES 4

SERVING SUGGESTIONS
Ricotta Crostini with Fresh Thyme and Dried Oregano (p. 93), Smoked Mackerel on Toasts (p. 80), Roast Chicken with Bread Salad (p. 467), Italian Roast Potatoes (p. 300), Couscous Salad (p. 321), Escarole with Pan-Roasted Garlic and Lemon (p. 248), Fish Steamed over Vegetables and Fresh Herbs (p. 434), Grapefruit Granita (p. 731), Maple Shortbread Bars (p. 701), Sand Tarts (Pecan Sandies; p. 688), David Eyre's Pancake (p. 813), Steamed Lemon Pudding (p. 849), Dorie Greenspan's Sablés (p. 703)

SEPTEMBER 2, 2001: "FOOD DIARY: THE REGAL GOURMET," BY AMANDA HESSER.

—2001

➥ CARROT AND FENNEL SOUP

———

2 tablespoons unsalted butter

1 medium fennel bulb, trimmed, fronds reserved, and thinly sliced

1½ pounds carrots, peeled and thickly sliced

1 large clove garlic, thinly sliced

6 cups water

1 teaspoon salt, or to taste

⅓ cup fresh orange juice

¼ cup sour cream

Freshly ground black pepper

1. Heat the butter in a 3-quart heavy saucepan over medium heat until foamy. Add the fennel slices and cook, stirring, until softened, 8 to 10 minutes. Add the carrots and garlic and cook for another minute. Pour in the water and season with the salt. Bring to a simmer and simmer, covered, until the carrots are very tender, about 20 minutes.

2. Remove the soup from the heat and stir in the orange juice, sour cream, and reserved fennel fronds. Use the back of a spoon to mash some of the carrots and fennel, but leave the soup chunky. Season with salt and pepper.

SERVES 6

SERVING SUGGESTIONS
Pasta with Tuscan Duck Sauce (p. 343), Epigram of Lamb (p. 509), Breaded Veal Milan-Style (p. 523), Almond Cake (p. 777), Orange Marmalade Pudding (p. 803), Sour-Milk Cake (p. 741)

DECEMBER 9, 2001: "FOOD DIARY: THE FOODIE NETWORK," BY AMANDA HESSER. RECIPE ADAPTED FROM EPICURIOUS.COM.

—2001

⌒ RABBIT SOUP WITH GARLIC, PEPPERS, AND CHORIZO

If you're at all intimidated by rabbit, this is the perfect starter recipe. The rabbit is browned whole before it is simmered in the soup, and it is then cooked until the meat shreds, so there's no cutting the rabbit into pieces or worrying about keeping those pieces intact. And if you're squeamish about eating rabbit, this soup's broth is vibrant with spices, booze, and tomatoes—as with the beef in chili, the rabbit is a contributor, not a star. If you're still concerned, feel free to substitute a small chicken—or just scrap the idea!

———

One 3-pound rabbit

Kosher salt and freshly ground black pepper

½ cup extra virgin olive oil

½ pound mild fresh chorizo, pricked with a fork, or dried Spanish chorizo, cut into ½-inch thick slices

3 medium onions, cut into ¼-inch dice

3 red bell peppers, cored, seeded, and cut into ½-inch-wide strips

25 cloves garlic

1 tablespoon paprika

4 bay leaves

1 tablespoon chopped thyme

½ teaspoon crushed red pepper flakes

8 cups chicken broth, plus more if needed

2 cups freshly cooked or canned chickpeas, rinsed well if canned

2 tablespoons dry sherry

One 15-ounce can diced tomatoes, not drained

½ cup chopped flat-leaf parsley

1. Season the rabbit all over with salt and pepper. Heat the olive oil over medium heat in a Dutch oven or soup pot large enough to hold the rabbit and sausage in one layer. Add the rabbit and sausage and brown on all sides, about 5 minutes per side (if using dried chorizo, there's no need to brown it. Set it aside until Step 3). Transfer to a plate.

2. Add the onions to the pot, season with salt and pepper, and cook, stirring, until lightly browned, about 10 minutes. Lower the heat if the onions are cooking too fast. Add the red peppers, season with salt and pepper, and cook until the peppers just begin to soften, about

3 minutes. Add the garlic, paprika, bay leaves, thyme, and red pepper flakes and cook for 1 minute.

3. Add the chicken broth and bring to a boil. Lower the heat to a simmer and return the rabbit and sausage to the pot. Cover and cook for 1 hour.

4. Flip the sausage and rabbit so they cook evenly, add the chickpeas, and cook for another 30 minutes or so, adding more broth if needed. When done, the rabbit should be just about falling off the bone. Remove the rabbit and sausage from the pot.

5. When the rabbit is cool enough to handle, shred the meat and discard the bones. Cut the sausage into ½-inch diagonal pieces.

6. Remove the bay leaves from the soup and discard. Season the soup with salt and pepper. Return the rabbit and sausage to the pot. Heat the soup to warm everything through. Add the sherry, tomatoes, and parsley and simmer for 5 minutes. Ladle into warm bowls and serve.

SERVES 6

SERVING SUGGESTIONS

Potato, Ham, and Piquillo Pepper Croquetas (p. 94), Seasoned Olives (p. 90), Caramelized Onion and Quark Dip (p. 84), Saffron Rice with Pine Nuts (p. 318), Mushrooms with Manzanilla Sherry (p. 249), Bittersweet Chocolate Semifreddo (p. 727), Lemon-Almond Butter Cake (p. 780)

MARCH 6, 2002: "TRULY SPANISH CHORIZO, IN AMERICA AT LAST," BY AMANDA HESSER. RECIPE ADAPTED FROM *IN THE HANDS OF A CHEF*, BY JODY ADAMS.

—2002

⌒ WATERCRESS AND BASIL SOUP

I must have been in a healthy mood in 2002, the year I got married—see the Beet and Ginger Soup with Cucumber on p. 150 and Watermelon Gazpacho, also on p. 150, as well as the recipe below. By 2005, I'd reverted to my usual indulgent ways with the Oyster Chowder on p. 159.

———

1 1/2 tablespoons excellent olive oil,
    plus additional for garnish

2 scallions, thinly sliced

1 medium potato, peeled and cut into 1/4-inch dice

3 cups chicken broth, plus more if desired

3 cups water

1 1/2 bunches watercress, stems trimmed to 1 inch
    (about 2 packed cups) and washed

1/4 cup basil leaves

Coarse sea salt and freshly ground black pepper

1. Place a soup pot over medium-high heat. Pour in 1 1/2 tablespoons oil, and when it shimmers, add the scallions and potato and sauté for 2 minutes. Add the broth and water and bring to a simmer. Simmer until the potato is very soft, about 10 minutes. Add the watercress and basil and cook until wilted, about 1 minute.

2. Transfer to a blender, or use an immersion blender, and puree the soup until smooth. (If using an immersion blender, begin pureeing at low speed to avoid spattering hot soup.) If the soup is too thick, add a little broth or water. Season with salt and pepper to taste.

3. To serve, ladle into bowls and garnish each bowl with a sprinkling of olive oil.

SERVES 4 TO 6

SERVING SUGGESTIONS

Goat's-Milk Cheese, Buttered Brown Bread, and Salted Onion (p. 75), Ricotta Crostini with Fresh Thyme and Dried Oregano (p. 93), Crostini with Eggplant and Pine Nut Puree (p. 78), Caramelized Onion and Quark Dip (p. 84), Scallops with Pea Puree (p. 429), Fish Poached in Buttermilk (p. 419), Chicken and Lemon Terrine (p. 495), Roast Chicken with Bread Salad (p. 467), Breaded Veal Milan-Style (p. 523), Steak au Poivre (p. 573), Devil's Food Cake (p. 744), Rhubarb-Strawberry Mousse (p. 835), Tapioca Flamingo (p. 810), Strawberry Sorbet (p. 732)

JULY 10, 2002: "PAIRINGS: NO MATTER WHAT YOU'RE SERVING, MAKE SURE THE WINE IS COLD," BY AMANDA HESSER.

—2002

CHILLED CORN SOUP WITH HONEYDEW POLKA DOTS

I have a love-hate relationship with Kay Rentschler, the author of this recipe. I often talk out loud to her in my kitchen: You want me to use another goddamn pan! You want me to dice the radish *how small?*

But when I sit down to eat with my family, all is forgiven. Her recipes (see also pages 257, 298, and 856) stand out—there are layers of thought and nuance, and there is always a surprise.

Rentschler, an occasional contributor to the *Times*, seems to have been raised in a restaurant kitchen at Thomas Keller's knee. In this soup, some of the corn is cut from the cobs, some is grated, and some of the cobs are split and added to the soup. The water you add to the soup must be filtered spring water. The soup is chilled over ice, and so are the melon balls—separately. But the finished soup—cool, sweet with a hint of tang from the buttermilk and the surprise, a little prick of cayenne—is superb. It looks pretty and people praise me. And I quietly feel great respect for Rentschler, while disliking her just the same.

———

10 medium to large ears corn, shucked

2 cups homemade chicken broth, or one 15-ounce can
    chicken broth plus 1/4 cup filtered water

2 cups filtered water (if using canned broth, substitute
    milk for the water)

1 teaspoon salt (3/4 teaspoon if using canned broth
    and milk), or more to taste

1/8 teaspoon cayenne pepper, or more to taste

1 ripe honeydew melon

1 to 1 1/2 cups buttermilk, or more

2 teaspoons minced chervil, or 1 teaspoon minced basil

1. Grate the kernels from 4 ears corn into a large bowl, using the coarse side of a box grater (there should be 1 cup grated corn, including juices); discard the cobs. Cut the kernels from the remaining 6 ears (there should be 3 cups), reserving 4 of the cobs; set the kernels aside.

2. Break the 4 cobs in half. Combine with the grated corn, chicken broth, and water in a 6-quart stockpot. Bring to a simmer and cook, covered, for 10 minutes, stirring occasionally. Remove the cobs from the broth with tongs and discard.

3. Working in batches, pour the mixture into a blender and, holding the lid on tight with a dish towel, puree until completely smooth. Return to the pot. Stir in the whole kernels, bring to a simmer, and cook until the corn is crisp-tender, about 2 minutes. Transfer the soup to a bowl (not plastic). Stir in the salt and cayenne. Cover and refrigerate, or stir over an ice water bath at room temperature until very cold (about 5 hours in the refrigerator, 1 hour over ice).

4. Halve and seed the melon. With a small (Parisienne) melon baller, make tiny balls (there should be about 1¼ cups); or cut the melon into ¼-inch dice. Cover the melon balls and chill over ice until ready to use (up to 1 hour before serving).

5. To serve, stir 1 cup buttermilk (or more to taste) into the soup. Taste and adjust the seasoning. Toss the melon balls with the chervil and sprinkle with salt (or skip this step and just add them separately to the bowls). Divide the melon balls among 6 chilled shallow bowls. Pour the cold soup around the melon.

SERVES 6

COOKING NOTES

Grating and cutting the corn yielded much more than the amounts Rentschler's recipe required, so I used only the amounts she notes in parentheses in the method: 1 cup grated and 3 cups cut kernels. Also, I used canned chicken broth, ¼ cup filtered water, and 2 cups milk—the milk was pleasant and I recommend using it even if you have homemade chicken broth.

If you taste the soup just before adding the buttermilk, you'll think it's terrific, that it doesn't need another thing. But do add the buttermilk, and taste again: the transformation is fascinating. She calls for 1 to 1½ cups buttermilk—I used just 1 cup and thought it was the perfect amount.

SERVING SUGGESTIONS

Fried Mussels with Almond-Garlic Sauce (p. 439), Deep-Fried Soft-Shell Crabs (p. 398), Jonathan Waxman's Red Pepper Pancakes (p. 228), Sweet-and-Spicy Pepper Stew (p. 247), Potato "Tostones" (Flattened Potatoes; p. 301), Fresh Blueberry Buckle (p. 815), Summer Pudding (p. 847), Strawberry Sorbet (p. 732)

AUGUST 21, 2002: "CHILLED SOUP THAT REALLY TINGLES," BY KAY RENTSCHLER.

—2002

⌁ LAOTIAN CATFISH SOUP

I love making this for dinner parties because you can get the base of the soup ready earlier in the day, then just add the fish shortly before serving.

———

1½ pounds catfish fillets
12 cloves garlic, finely chopped
3 to 4 Thai chiles, seeded and finely chopped
3 kaffir lime leaves, stems and main veins removed, finely chopped
One 14-inch stalk lemongrass, tough outer layers removed, thinly sliced
2 shallots, finely chopped
2 tablespoons peanut or vegetable oil
4 cups chicken broth or water
2 tablespoons fresh lime juice
Two ¼-inch-thick slices peeled galangal (fresh or frozen) or ginger
¼ cup smooth peanut butter
One 14-ounce can unsweetened coconut milk
6 tablespoons Asian fish sauce
2 tablespoons finely chopped basil
2 tablespoons finely chopped cilantro
Cooked jasmine rice for serving (optional)

1. Cut the catfish fillets into strips about 1 inch long by ½ inch wide. Place on a plate, cover with plastic wrap, and refrigerate.

2. Sauté the garlic, chiles, lime leaves, lemongrass, and shallots in the oil in a deep skillet over medium heat until very fragrant, about 5 minutes. Add the chicken broth, lime juice, and galangal (or ginger) and bring the mixture to a slow simmer.

3. Whisk the peanut butter and ¼ cup coconut milk in a small bowl until blended, then whisk into the garlic mixture. Stir in the fish and the remaining coconut milk and warm gently (do not let it boil, or the coconut milk will separate) until the fish layers separate when prodded with a fork, about 2 minutes. Stir in the fish sauce, basil, and cilantro and simmer for 2 minutes. Serve immediately, with rice if desired.

SERVES 4 TO 6

COOKING NOTES

If you can't find Thai chiles, use serranos; just 2 will be plenty.

I didn't have kaffir lime leaves when I made this the first time, so I used 4 lemon leaves and the zest from 1½ limes, which worked well.

I recommend using chicken broth, which will enrich the soup.

I've made this with both galangal and ginger—you can't go wrong.

SERVING SUGGESTIONS
Pork-and-Toasted-Rice-Powder Spring Rolls (p. 74), Pad Thai–Style Rice Salad (p. 357), Pineapple Carpaccio with Lime Sorbet (p. 842), Mango Ice Cream (p. 729), Lemon Lotus Ice Cream (p. 724), Glazed Mango with Sour Cream Sorbet and Black Pepper (p. 850), Sticky Rice with Mango (p. 861)

MAY 18, 2003: "FOOD: CAT FIGHT," BY JULIA REED.

—2003

⌒ MANJULA GOKAL'S GUJARATI MANGO SOUP

This viscous, arrestingly fragrant soup could cloy in large doses but is wonderful in small ones. The foundation of the soup, mango, is overlaid with peppery, assertive spices.

———

2 tablespoons chickpea flour

⅛ teaspoon turmeric

¾ teaspoon ground cumin

¾ teaspoon ground coriander

2½ cups water

½ cup plain whole-milk yogurt

3 cups canned Alphonso mango pulp (sweetened), preferably Ratna brand

1¼ to 1½ teaspoons salt

½ teaspoon sugar, or to taste

2 bird's-eye chiles, 2 slits cut in each

2 tablespoons corn or peanut oil

Generous pinch of ground asafetida

½ teaspoon brown mustard seeds

½ teaspoon cumin seeds

2 dried hot red chiles

⅛ teaspoon fenugreek seeds

10 to 15 fresh curry leaves (optional)

1. Put the chickpea flour, turmeric, cumin, and coriander in a bowl. Very slowly stir in ½ cup water until no lumps are left. Whisk in the yogurt, mango, and remaining 2 cups water. Add the salt, sugar, and bird's-eye chiles. Mix well.

2. Pour the oil into a medium heavy saucepan and set over medium-high heat. When the oil is very hot, add the asafetida and then, in quick succession, the mustard seeds, cumin seeds, dried chiles, fenugreek seeds, and curry leaves, if using. Remove from the heat and stir in the mango mixture, then place over medium heat and simmer for 5 minutes, stirring. Remove from the heat, cover, and let sit for at least 30 minutes.

3. Stir the soup and reheat it gently. Strain through a coarse strainer. Spoon out some of the smaller seeds from the strainer and stir them back into the soup.

SERVES 8 (SMALL SERVINGS)

COOKING NOTES

If possible, use Fage Total (or other thick Greek) whole-milk yogurt.

If you can't find Alphonso mango pulp—Indian grocery stores are your best bet—try it with very ripe fresh mangoes. In Madhur Jaffrey's book *From Curries to Kebabs*, she says: "Squeeze [the mangoes] with both hands, almost as if you were giving them a good massage. The flesh should turn to pulp. Now peel them. 'Milk' the stone, collecting all the juice in a bowl. Pour a little hot water on the stone and 'milk' it some more. Do the same to the skin, pouring a tablespoon or so of hot water on it to get at all the juice. Collect all the mango juice in a bowl. . . . Use this thin juice whenever water is called for, letting it cool first."

Asafetida is bitter and pungent when raw; once cooked, it produces an onion-and-garlic aroma. Many of the specialty ingredients listed here are available by mail-order from Kalustyan's, www.kalustyans.com.

SERVING SUGGESTIONS
Crab and Coconut Curry (p. 389), Malaysian-Inspired Pork Stew with Traditional Garnishes (p. 552), Green Beans with Coriander-Coconut Crust (p. 246), Minced Fish Salad (p. 436), Pad Thai–Style Rice Salad (p. 357), Saffron Panna Cotta (p. 845), Tapioca

Flamingo (p. 810), Cantaloupe–Star Anise Sorbet (p. 728), Lemon Lotus Ice Cream (p. 724)

OCTOBER 5, 2003: "FOOD: DARK VICTORY," BY JONATHAN REYNOLDS. RECIPE ADAPTED FROM MANJULA GOKAL'S RECIPE IN *FROM CURRIES TO KEBABS*, BY MADHUR JAFFREY.

—2003

PASTA AND BEAN SOUP

Tom Valenti, the owner of Ouest, in New York City, is most famous for his braised veal shanks, a dish that kept his fans jockeying for reservations through the first decade of the twenty-first century. But Valenti is really a master of anything hearty and succulent—like this pasta and bean soup. You won't believe it doesn't have any meat other than some diced prosciutto. Even the broth is vegetable.

———

2 tablespoons olive oil

¼ pound prosciutto, cut into medium dice
    (double-smoked bacon can be substituted)

I small carrot, peeled and cut into small dice

I small Spanish onion, cut into small dice

I stalk celery, cut into small dice

2 cloves garlic, smashed

Coarse salt and freshly ground black pepper

I heaping tablespoon tomato paste

4 cups vegetable broth

4 cups water

2 medium baking potatoes, peeled

I cup ditalini pasta

Two 14½-ounce cans cannelloni beans,
    rinsed and drained

I tablespoon chopped rosemary

Pinch of crushed red pepper flakes

¼ cup freshly grated Parmesan cheese,
    plus more for sprinkling

Extra virgin olive oil

1. Heat the olive oil in a large heavy pot over medium heat. Add the prosciutto and cook, stirring, until it begins to render its fat, about 4 minutes. Add the carrot, onion, celery, and garlic, season with salt and pepper, and cook, stirring, until the vegetables are softened but not browned, about 5 minutes. Add the tomato paste, stir to coat the other ingredients, and cook for 2 minutes. Add the broth, water, and potatoes, raise heat to high, and bring to a boil. Lower the heat and simmer until the potatoes are very soft, 30 to 35 minutes. Transfer the potatoes to a bowl and mash them.

2. Meanwhile, add the pasta to the soup. When it is nearly done, return the potatoes to the soup. (If not serving immediately, let cool, cover, and refrigerate for up to a few days or freeze for up to 1 month. Reheat before proceeding.)

3. Add the beans to the soup and cook over medium heat until warmed through, about 3 minutes. Stir in the rosemary, crushed red pepper, and Parmesan. Taste and adjust the seasoning.

4. Ladle the soup into 8 bowls. Top each with more cheese and a drizzle of extra virgin olive oil.

SERVES 8

SERVING SUGGESTIONS
No-Knead Bread (p. 670), Classic Ciabatta (p. 665), Diane Forley's Arugula Salad with Artichoke, Ricotta Salata, and Pumpkin Seeds (p. 188), Chiffonade Salad (p. 173), Balducci's Tiramisù (p. 830), Canestrelli (Shortbread from Ovada; p. 692), Cornmeal Biscotti (p. 696)

DECEMBER 10, 2003: "AT LUNCH WITH: TOM VALENTI," BY ALEX WITCHEL. RECIPE ADAPTED FROM *TOM VALENTI'S SOUPS, STEWS, AND ONE-POT MEALS*, BY TOM VALENTI.

—2003

BUTTERNUT SQUASH SOUP WITH BROWN BUTTER

There are other memorable butternut squash soups in this book, but this one, which comes from *Bouchon*, by Thomas Keller, is the best. Greatness comes at a price, however; preparing the soup will take up the better part of a day. Some of the squash is roasted, some of it simmered. Crème fraîche is whipped with nutmeg, and sage leaves are crisped. The most important step of all comes last, when butter is browned and swirled into the soup, the toasty bits streaming into every molecule of broth. By the time it's in the bowl, you have something worth honoring, and you (almost) understand why dinner at a Thomas Keller restaurant costs as much as it does.

———

One 3- to 3½-pound butternut squash
2 tablespoons canola oil
Kosher salt and freshly ground black pepper
2 sprigs sage
1 cup thinly sliced (⅛-inch-thick) leeks
    (white and pale green parts only)
½ cup thinly sliced (⅛-inch-thick) carrots
½ cup thinly sliced (⅛-inch-thick) shallots
½ cup thinly sliced (⅛-inch-thick) onion
6 garlic cloves, smashed
2 tablespoons honey
6 cups vegetable broth, plus more if needed
A bouquet garni made of 8 sprigs thyme, 2 sprigs
    flat-leaf parsley, 2 bay leaves, and ½ teaspoon
    black peppercorns, wrapped in 2 green leek
    leaves and tied with kitchen string
¼ cup crème fraîche
Freshly grated nutmeg
4 tablespoons unsalted butter
Canola oil
12 sage leaves
Extra virgin olive oil

1. Heat the oven to 350 degrees. Line a small baking sheet with aluminum foil. Cut the neck off the squash and set it aside. Cut the bulb in half and scoop out and discard the seeds. Brush each half inside and out with about 1½ teaspoons canola oil. Sprinkle the cavities with salt and pepper and tuck a sprig of sage into each. Place cut side down on the baking sheet and roast until completely tender, about 1 hour. Remove the squash from the oven and let cool, then scoop out and reserve the flesh (discard the sage).

2. Meanwhile, using a paring knife or sharp vegetable peeler, peel away the skin from the neck of the squash until you reach the bright orange flesh. Cut the flesh into ½-inch pieces.

3. Put the remaining 1 tablespoon canola oil in a stockpot set over medium-high heat, add the leeks, carrots, shallots, and onion, and cook, stirring often, for 6 minutes. Add the diced squash, garlic, 1½ teaspoons salt, and ½ teaspoon pepper and cook gently for 3 minutes, reducing the heat as necessary to keep

the garlic and squash from coloring. Stir in the honey and cook, stirring, for 2 to 3 minutes. Add the broth and bouquet garni, bring to a simmer, and cook for 10 to 15 minutes, or until the squash is tender.

4. Add the roasted squash and simmer gently for about 30 minutes for the flavors to blend. Remove from the heat and discard the bouquet garni.

5. Transfer the soup to a blender, in batches, and purée. Strain the soup through a fine sieve into a bowl or other container, tapping the side of the strainer so the soup passes through. Taste the soup and adjust the seasoning. Let the soup cool, then refrigerate until ready to serve.

6. To complete, place the crème fraîche in a chilled small metal bowl and stir in nutmeg to taste. Whisk until the crème fraîche holds a shape. Cover and refrigerate.

7. Gently reheat the soup until just hot. If it is too thick, add a little more vegetable broth.

8. Meanwhile, heat a medium skillet over high heat. When it is very hot, add the butter and rotate the skillet over the heat as necessary to brown the butter evenly, scraping up any bits that settle in the bottom. As soon as the foaming has subsided and the butter is a hazelnut brown, pour it into the pot of soup—keep a safe distance, the butter may sputter—and stir.

9. Heat ⅛ inch of canola oil in a small skillet. When the oil is very hot, add the sage and cook for 30 to 45 seconds, turning the leaves to crisp them on both sides. When the bubbling stops, the moisture in the leaves will have evaporated and the leaves will be crisp. Drain the sage on paper towels and sprinkle with salt.

10. Ladle the soup into 6 serving bowls. Top each with a dollop of crème fraîche. Grind some black pepper over the top and garnish each with 2 sage leaves. Drizzle a little olive oil over the top.

SERVES 6

COOKING NOTES
Keller says the squash gets sweeter after resting, so serve this the next day.

SERVING SUGGESTIONS
Breaded Chicken Breasts with Parmesan Cheese (p. 465), Veal Shanks with Garlic Mashed Potatoes (p. 540), Saltimbocca (p. 561), Madame Laracine's Gra-

tin Dauphinois (p. 284), Shredded Brussels Sprouts with Bacon and Pine Nuts (p. 235), Red Wine Ice Cream (p. 730), Gooey Chocolate Stack (p. 778), Pear Upside-Down Cake (p. 772), Gâteau de Crepes (p. 785)

DECEMBER 12, 2004: "THE WAY WE EAT: LABOR PARTY," BY AMANDA HESSER. RECIPE ADAPTED FROM *BOUCHON* BY THOMAS KELLER WITH JEFFREY CERCIELLO.

—2004

⌒ MANHATTAN CLAM CHOWDER WITH HAKE AND CHORIZO

Steam the clams just until they begin to open—you don't want to fully cook them, because they'll cook again when you assemble the soup in the last step.

1/2 cup dry white wine

1 1/2 cups water

10 pounds quahogs or other large clams, scrubbed

5 tablespoons olive oil

5 ounces slab bacon, diced (about 1 cup)

3 cloves garlic, chopped

1 large onion, diced

1/4 fennel bulb, diced

1 stalk celery, diced

1 green bell pepper, cored, seeded, and diced

1 medium carrot, peeled and diced

2 bay leaves

1 1/2 teaspoons dried oregano

2 small dried red chiles, crushed, or 1/2 teaspoon crushed red pepper flakes

1 tablespoon tomato paste

1 large Yukon Gold potato (about 12 ounces), peeled and cut into 1/2-inch dice

1 cup bottled clam juice

6 ripe tomatoes, cored and diced

Four to six 6-ounce skin-on hake fillets (or other fine-fleshed white fish, like snapper or sole)

Sea salt and freshly ground black pepper

1/4 pound Spanish chorizo, sliced into thin rounds

1 pound bay scallops (optional)

1. Combine the wine and water in a large heavy pot, place over high heat, and bring to a boil. Add the clams, cover, and cook until they open, about 5 minutes. Discard any unopened clams, and transfer the others to a bowl. Strain the clam broth through a fine-mesh strainer into a bowl; set aside.

2. When the clams are cool enough to handle, remove from the shells and chop into 1/4-inch pieces.

3. Heat 3 tablespoons olive oil in a large soup pot over medium heat. Add the bacon and sauté until golden brown, about 2 minutes. Add the garlic, onion, fennel, celery, bell pepper, carrot, bay leaves, oregano, and chiles and sauté until the vegetables are softened, about 10 minutes. Add the tomato paste and cook, stirring, for 2 minutes. Add the potato, reserved clam broth, and bottled clam juice and bring to a boil, then lower the heat and simmer until the potato is tender, 8 to 10 minutes. Add the tomatoes and cook for 2 minutes. Turn off the heat.

4. Place a large nonstick skillet over medium heat and add the remaining 2 tablespoons olive oil. Season the hake on both sides with salt and pepper. When the oil is hot, sear skin side down for 2 minutes, then flip and cook until the fish is opaque in the center, 3 to 4 minutes. Transfer to a plate and cover loosely to keep warm.

5. Add the chorizo to the pan and sauté until lightly browned, about 1 minute. Transfer to a plate. If using the scallops, add them to pan and sauté just until opaque, about 1 minute. Remove from the heat.

6. Add the clams to the chowder and heat through. Adjust the salt and pepper if necessary. Ladle the chowder into bowls and top with the hake, chorizo, and scallops.

SERVES 4 TO 6

SERVING SUGGESTIONS

Gigi Salad (Shrimp, Bacon, and Green Bean Salad; p. 184), Green Goddess Salad (p. 176), Salade à la Romaine (p. 171), Lemon Lotus Ice Cream (p. 724), Lemon Cake (p. 781), Cherry and Coconut Brown Betty (p. 806), Whiskey Cake (p. 784)

JANUARY 26, 2005: "THE CHEF: LAURENT TOURONDEL: CLAM CHOWDER, REIMAGINED IN FRENCH," BY DANA BOWEN. RECIPE ADAPTED FROM LAURENT TOURONDEL, THE CHEF AND OWNER OF BLT FISH IN NEW YORK CITY.

—2005

OYSTER CHOWDER

This is a recipe you could have found in the *Times* archives at any point from the 1850s until now. The oysters today will have traveled farther—New York's harbor was once carpeted with bivalves—but some of the chowder's other elements are likely to be better. The celery is probably more tender, the cayenne fresher. This version comes from my grandmother Helen Getz.

¼ pound bacon, cut crosswise into ¼-inch-wide strips

1 cup chopped onion

1 cup chopped celery hearts

3 white potatoes, peeled and cut into ½-inch cubes (about 4 cups)

About 3 cups water

14 to 16 large oysters, shucked, with their liquor

Salt

Cayenne pepper

⅔ to 1 cup whole milk

1 tablespoon chopped flat-leaf parsley

1. Spread the bacon in a soup pot, place over medium heat, and cook until it is browned and its fat has rendered. Drain the bacon on paper towels.
2. Discard all but 1 tablespoon of the fat and put the pot back on the heat. Scrape the onion and celery into the pot and sauté until softened. Drop in the potatoes, add enough water to cover, and bring to a boil, then reduce the heat and simmer until the potatoes are tender, 15 minutes.
3. Take the pot off the heat and, using a potato masher, lightly crush the potatoes to thicken the chowder. Add the oysters and oyster liquor and season with salt and cayenne pepper. Simmer until the oysters curl, 3 to 5 minutes. Pour in the milk (use ⅔ cup if you prefer it less rich) and bring to a boil, then shut off the heat. Crumble in the bacon and stir in the parsley.

SERVES 4

SERVING SUGGESTIONS

Pan-Roasted Chicken with End-of-Season Tomatoes (p. 482), '21' Club Hamburger (p. 536), Saratoga Potatoes (p. 273), French Fries (p. 292), Stewed Corn (p. 271), Fresh Succotash (p. 275), Red Velvet Cake (p. 757), Chocolate Pudding (p. 858), Banana Cream Pie (p. 863), Blueberry Ice Cream (p. 726)

JANUARY 30, 2005: "THE ARSENAL," BY AMANDA HESSER. RECIPE ADAPTED FROM HELEN GETZ, MY GRANDMOTHER.

—2005

LOBSTER BISQUE II

In 1940s Los Angeles, there were only two kinds of dining. There was Chasen's and the Brown Derby, and there was everything else. At restaurants like Chasen's, you needed money and connections. You were expected to dress in your finest and eat steaks cooked tableside in oceans of butter.

But then, in 1950, an unknown actor named Harry Lewis and his plucky girlfriend (and soon-wife), Marilyn, had an idea. They would open a restaurant that would serve a good hamburger but still be stylish enough that directors, writers, and even agents would come to dine with hoi polloi. There would be leather booths and Löwenbräu beer and ice cream from Wil Wright (the Van Leeuwen of the time). On the corner of Hilldale and Sunset Boulevard, Hamburger Hamlet was born. And so, too, was the lasting American style of democratic dining.

"Who would expect lobster bisque, cherries jubilee, and French onion soup brought down to the level where one could comfortably dine in blue jeans, no tie or black tie, sitting next to a favorite movie star and at half the price?" Marilyn wrote in her memoir, *Marilyn, Are You Sure You Can Cook?*

No one did. Almost miraculously (because Marilyn could barely boil water back then), Hamburger Hamlet struck a chord. Ronald Reagan, Sammy Davis Jr., Bobby Short, and Dorothy Malone were all regulars. Zachary Scott would show up late at night and order the "No. 7" (a hamburger topped with Russian dressing), medium-rare, with a glass of milk.

Probably the most revered dish on the menu was this lobster bisque. During the Depression, Marilyn had watched her grandmother make the bisque from lobster and shrimp shells and no meat. The Hamlet's version is more heavily fortified, and Marilyn's recipe for it is flawless: creamy and substantial, with a subtle sweetness and a flash of heat from the cayenne.

For an earlier lobster bisque, see p. 108.

---

8 cups water

1 tablespoon kosher salt

One 1½-pound live lobster

1 pound medium shrimp

12 white peppercorns

6 sprigs thyme

3 tablespoons unsalted butter

1 medium yellow onion, diced

½ cup sliced carrots

½ cup sliced celery

1½ teaspoons grated lemon zest

1 cup dry white wine

½ cup dry sherry

¼ cup tomato paste

1 cup heavy cream

1 cup chicken broth

6 tablespoons long-grain rice

¼ teaspoon cayenne pepper

6 slices baguette, toasted

1 clove garlic

1. Bring the water and 2 teaspoons salt to a boil in a large pot. Add the lobster, head first, cover, and cook for 11 minutes. Set the lobster on a rack above a plate to catch any juices and let cool. Pour the lobster water into a large Dutch oven.

2. Remove the tail and claw meat from the lobster and reserve, chilled. Reserve the shells.

3. Peel and devein the shrimp and save all the shells, reserve the shrimp. Add the shells to the lobster water, along with the peppercorns, 3 sprigs thyme, and the lobster shells. Bring to a boil, then reduce the heat and simmer, covered, for 30 minutes.

4. Strain the lobster broth through cheesecloth into a bowl. Discard the shells. Wipe out the Dutch oven, put it over medium heat and drop in 2 tablespoons butter. When it's frothy, add the shrimp and cook, turning, until pink. Scrape into a bowl.

5. Put the Dutch oven back over the heat and add the remaining tablespoon of butter, followed by the onion, carrots, celery, the remaining 3 sprigs thyme, and the lemon zest. Stir and cook for 8 minutes. Pour in the white wine and sherry, add the tomato paste, and boil

for 2 minutes. Scrape up any cooked bits on the bottom of the pot. Remove to a bowl.

6. Put the Dutch oven back on the heat and pour in the lobster broth, cream, chicken broth, and rice. Cover and simmer until the rice is tender, about 20 minutes.

7. Working in batches, puree the shrimp, vegetable-wine mixture, and lobster-rice broth in a blender. Strain, pressing out as much liquid as possible, into the top of a double boiler. Add the cayenne pepper and remaining teaspoon of salt. Reheat gently.

8. Meanwhile, chop the lobster meat. Rub the toasted baguette slices with the garlic clove.

9. Ladle the warm broth into 6 shallow bowls. Top each with a piece of toast and a small mound of lobster meat.

SERVES 6

SERVING SUGGESTIONS

Nancy Reagan's Monkey Bread (p. 669), Parmesan Crackers (p. 84), Astor House Rolls (p. 652), Chiffonade Salad (p. 173), Salade à la Romaine (p. 171), Iceberg Lettuce with Smoked Bacon and Buttermilk Dressing (p. 200), Chez Panisse Meyer Lemon Meringue Pie (p. 833), Steamed Lemon Pudding (p. 849), Almond-Lemon Macaroons (p. 707)

MAY 22, 2005: "THE WAY WE EAT: WHEN HARRY MET MARILYN," BY AMANDA HESSER.

—2005

☞ GREEN GAZPACHO

2½ pounds ripe plum or grape tomatoes, coarsely chopped

1 stalk lemongrass, tough outer layers removed, coarsely chopped

¼ cup vodka

2 cucumbers, peeled and chopped

2 green bell peppers, cored, seeded, and chopped

4 tomatillos, husked, rinsed, and chopped

2 tablespoons white wine vinegar, or to taste

1 tablespoon sherry vinegar, or to taste

1 tablespoon fresh lemon juice

1 tablespoon sugar

Salt and freshly ground black pepper
½ avocado
I small handful chives
I small handful cilantro leaves
I small handful flat-leaf parsley leaves
I bunch scallions, trimmed

1. The day before serving, combine the tomatoes, lemongrass, and vodka in a blender and puree until smooth. Line a sieve with cheesecloth or paper towels, set over a bowl, and pour in the tomato mixture. Refrigerate overnight—clear liquid will slowly drain through; discard the solids.

2. Meanwhile, combine the cucumbers, green peppers, tomatillos, vinegars, lemon juice, sugar, and a generous sprinkling of salt and pepper in a bowl. Refrigerate overnight.

3. In a blender, puree the marinated vegetables, avocado, chives, cilantro, parsley, scallions, and tomato liquid until smooth. Taste for salt, pepper, and vinegar, adding more as needed. Serve very cold.

SERVES 6 TO 8

SERVING SUGGESTIONS
Deep-Fried Soft-Shell Crabs (p. 398), Decadent Lobster Salad (p. 440), Salmon and Tomatoes in Foil (p. 422), Pan-Roasted Chicken with End-of-Season Tomatoes (p. 482), Beer-Can Chicken (p. 473), Thai Beef Salad (p. 543), Fruit Crostatas (p. 855)

JULY 12, 2006: "WHEN THE SOUR NOTE IS JUST RIGHT," BY JULIA MOSKIN. RECIPE ADAPTED FROM ALEX UREÑA, THE CHEF AT UREÑA IN NEW YORK CITY.

—2006

⌒ GAZPACHO WITH CUCUMBER GRANITA

In 2006, I started a new *Times Magazine* column called "Recipe Redux" that grew out of the research I was doing for this book. As I dug through the archives, it became clear that while the past century had brought enormous changes to the way we eat, we often circle back to old recipes as we find new techniques in the kitchen.

For "Recipe Redux," I thought it would be interest-

ing to capture this evolution by taking an old *Times* recipe—in this case, the Málaga Gazpacho from 1968, on p. 112—and asking a chef to use it as a jumping-off point for creating a modern dish.

Michael Tusk, the chef of Quince Restaurant in San Francisco, treated the original to a down-to-the-bones renovation. He stripped out all of the flavors from the 1968 soup and essentially gave each ingredient its own pedestal. He ran a variety of tomatoes through a food mill to get a dense base. In it he floated a simple cucumber granita, given a little zip with cucumber vinegar (Champagne vinegar also works).

He treated the rest of the gazpacho ingredients as garnishes, poising them on the lip of the soup bowl to mix in at your pleasure. He fried cubes of bread and slivers of garlic in olive oil, minced peppers and serrano chiles, and peeled cherry tomatoes (the only maddening part of the recipe, though worth the tedium).

The two soups share a shopping list but little else. One is a smooth, poignant expression of summer flavors (and is a snap to make). The other keeps your palate riveted, as each spoonful carries bursts of pepper, the crunch of bread, and the stinging chill of the granita.

———

For the Cucumber Granita
2 cups peeled, seeded, and coarsely chopped cucumber
    (I to 2 cucumbers)
I tablespoon cucumber vinegar or Champagne vinegar
Salt

For the Gazpacho
3 pounds ripe Persimmon, or Golden Jubilee,
    or other large red or yellow tomatoes, cored
    and roughly chopped (about 6 cups)
Salt
¼ cup extra virgin olive oil
2 cloves garlic, thinly sliced
2 slices country bread, crusts removed
    and cut into ½-inch cubes
¼ cup finely chopped shallots
¼ cup finely chopped green bell pepper
2 tablespoons minced serrano chile
I cup grape, cherry, or sweet 100 tomatoes, peeled

1. Chill 6 shallow rimmed soup bowls in the refrigerator. To make the granita, place the cucumber in a food

processor and pulse until smooth. Add the cucumber vinegar and salt to taste and blend well. Pour into a wide shallow pan and place in the freezer. Run a fork through the granita, scraping it up, every 20 minutes for approximately 2 hours. Freeze until completely frozen and icy. (This can be done the day before.)

2. To make the gazpacho, pass the tomatoes through a food mill using the finest plate. Strain the tomato juice through a fine-mesh sieve. Season with salt (about 6 pinches), and chill in the refrigerator.

3. Place a medium sauté pan over medium-high heat and add the olive oil. When it is warm, sauté the garlic until golden. Use a slotted spoon to transfer it to paper towels, and season with salt. Add the cubed bread to the oil and fry until golden. Remove with a slotted spoon, drain on paper towels, and season with salt.

4. Ladle the chilled tomato juice into the chilled bowls. Float a large tablespoonful of granita in the center of each bowl. Arrange the garnishes—garlic, bread cubes, shallots, green pepper, chile, and cherry tomatoes—around the rims, or serve them separately and pass around at the table.

SERVES 6

COOKING NOTE
Gegenbauer cucumber vinegar is available at www.dibruno.com.

SERVING SUGGESTIONS
Fresh Salmon and Lime Cakes (p. 420), Deep-Fried Soft-Shell Crabs (p. 398), Docks Coleslaw (p. 191), Zucchini Carpaccio with Avocado (p. 261), String Beans with Ginger and Garlic (p. 260), Sugar Snap Peas with Horseradish (p. 259), Blueberry Ice Cream (p. 726), Strawberry Sorbet (p. 732)

JULY 23, 2006: "RECIPE REDUX, 1968: MÁLAGA GAZPACHO," BY AMANDA HESSER. RECIPE ADAPTED FROM MICHAEL TUSK, THE CHEF AND CO-OWNER OF QUINCE IN SAN FRANCISCO.

—2006

⌒ CHILLED ENGLISH PEA-MINT SOUP

Most pea and mint soups rely on the happy bond of peas' sweetness and mint's freshness. Here buttermilk streaks through, throwing in a little vim.

———————

2 cups buttermilk, homemade (p. 613)
4 cups peas, plus more for garnish
Salt
12 to 14 mint leaves
Freshly ground black pepper

1. Bring the buttermilk to a simmer in a medium saucepan. Add the the peas and a teaspoon of salt and simmer for 1 to 2 minutes over medium heat, stirring often so that the buttermilk does not boil over. The peas should still have a slight bite to them.

2. Transfer the peas and liquid to a blender, along with the mint leaves, and, starting on low speed, carefully blend (holding the lid on firmly with a dish cloth), working up to high speed for 60 seconds.

3. To preserve the vibrant color and flavor of the peas, the soup must be cooled immediately. Pass through a fine-mesh sieve into a bowl, then set the bowl in a larger bowl of ice water. Stir constantly until cool; taste occasionally—you will notice that the soup becomes sweeter as it cools. Adjust the seasoning with salt and pepper. Refrigerate until cold.

4. Ladle the soup into bowls and garnish with peas and black pepper.

SERVES 4

COOKING NOTES
A recipe for butter, and its offspring, buttermilk, is on p. 613. You can also use store-bought buttermilk—if you can get it at a farmers' market, all the better.

Make sure you have lots of ice on hand for cooling the soup—this sets the color, and you want your pea soup to look fresh as a baby leaf if you're feeling ambitious.

SERVING SUGGESTIONS
Lamb Shoulder Chops with Anchovy and Mint Butter (p. 567), High-Temperature Roast Lamb (p. 526),

Al Forno's Roasted Asparagus (p. 233), Artichauts Vinaigrette (p. 225), Italian Roast Potatoes (p. 300), New Jersey Blancmange (p. 797), Rhubarb-Strawberry Mousse (p. 835), Panna Cotta (p. 840), Coeur à la Crème with Rhubarb Sauce (p. 864)

JULY 1, 2007: "THE WAY WE EAT: CURD MENTALITY," BY DANIEL PATTERSON.

—2007

RED LENTIL SOUP WITH LEMON

3 tablespoons olive oil, plus more for drizzling

1 large onion, chopped

2 cloves garlic, minced

1 tablespoon tomato paste

1 teaspoon ground cumin

¼ to ½ teaspoon kosher salt, or more to taste

¼ teaspoon freshly ground black pepper

Large pinch of ground chile powder or cayenne pepper, or more to taste

4 cups chicken or vegetable broth

2 cups water

1 cup red lentils, picked over and rinsed

1 large carrot, peeled and diced

Juice of ½ lemon, or more to taste

3 tablespoons chopped cilantro

1. Heat the oil in a large pot over high heat until hot and shimmering. Add the onion and garlic and sauté until golden, about 4 minutes. Stir in the tomato paste, cumin, salt, black pepper, and chile powder and sauté for 2 minutes. Add the broth, water, lentils, and carrot and bring to a simmer, then partially cover the pot and turn the heat to medium-low. Simmer until the lentils are soft, about 30 minutes. Taste and add salt if necessary.

2. Using an immersion or regular blender or a food processor, puree half the soup, then return it to the pot; don't over-puree it, the soup should be somewhat chunky. Reheat the soup if necessary, then stir in the lemon juice and cilantro. Serve drizzled with olive oil and dusted lightly with chile powder if desired.

SERVES 4

SERVING SUGGESTIONS

Cutlets à la Kiev (p. 455), Warm Cabbage Salad with Goat Cheese and Capers (p. 183), Roasted Cauliflower (p. 248), Spinach with Sour Cream (p. 216), Poppy Seed Torte (p. 786), Marcella's Pear Cake (p. 769), Orange Marmalade Pudding (p. 803)

JANUARY 9, 2008: "A GOOD APPETITE: A LENTIL SOUP TO MAKE YOU STOP, TASTE, AND SAVOR," BY MELISSA CLARK.

—2008

• Egg-thickened cooked salad dressings are common, as are German-style salads with warm dressings.

—1880s—

• Watercress Salad (p. 171).

—1882—

• Chiffonade Salad (p. 173).

—1898—

• Shaved artichoke salad is featured 100 years before it becomes a fixture on Italian restaurant menus in New York City.

—1902—

• Caesar (p. 174) and Green Goddess (p. 176) do battle.

—1940s—

• The *Times* breaks a shocking story: "Iceberg Called Tasteless"; the editors favor romaine and Boston lettuce.

—1947—

• The *Times* shuns (mostly) the Jell-O-based salad.

—1950s—

• Salade Niçoise (p. 178)—the chef's salad of the sixties.

—1960s—

• Spinach becomes the green of choice.

—1970s—

• Moroccan orange salad shows up in various forms (p. 181) and then sadly vanishes.

—1980s—

• Raspberry vinegar enjoys an undeserved moment; it is replaced by balsamic vinegar, which overpowers dressings for the next decade or two.

• Alice Waters introduces her much-copied Baked Goat Cheese with Salad (p. 181).

—1983—

• Dried cranberries invade the salad.

—1990s—

• The chopped salad, brief obsession. The composed salad, long obsession.

• Italians teach us to mix bitter greens such as endive and radicchio and peppery greens such as arugula with our sweet romaine and Boston lettuces.

• Panzanella, a rustic bread and tomato salad, is the salad of the moment. Judy Rodgers's bread salad (p. 198) is less famous but just as good.

• Pear and Gorgonzola salad becomes a standard restaurant offering.

• Birth of the microgreen.

• Blood oranges and Meyer lemons epitomize the lust for California cooking.

—1998—

• Timeless frisée salad with soft boiled egg and lardons appears, still timeless.

—2000s—

• Watermelon and feta epitomizes the new sweet and salty salad. (See Watermelon and Tomato Salad on p. 197.)

—2002—

• Bagged salad becomes a $2-billion industry.

• Roasted Bone Marrow and Parsley Salad (p. 201), the signature dish of Fergus Henderson, chef and owner of St. John Restaurant in London.

—2003—

• Beet and goat cheese salad vanquishes pear and Gorgonzola.

—2004—

4

~

SALADS

Most dishes, once conceived, remain fairly stable through the years. A modern-day roast chicken is pretty much the same as the one medieval cooks turned on a spit, give or take an herb or a sauce, and a cupcake is always a cupcake.

The salad has been around since the Romans, who ate their vegetables and conquered the world. But it continues to change its identity, forever finding new ways to insist that it is an adaptable composition of loosely related ingredients (not necessarily vegetables) unified by a dressing. A cookbook I have from the late 1940s divided the empire of salads into eleven kingdoms: chilled, frozen, hot, bowl, decorative, platter, individual, molded, whole meal, fruit, and chicken.

This is both the beauty and the burden of salads. By their very lack of rules or constraints, they allow cooks to express the fascinations and anxieties of the period. The collective unconscious has more room to play with a free-form arrangement of dressed vegetables than with a chicken drumstick.

After World War II, America went through a stage of wanting to put its stamp on everything, which worked beautifully with the Marshall Plan and convertibles but much less so with the era's foods, which included a phenomenal number of strange, bland, yet intricately designed salads. It seemed there wasn't an ingredient on earth that couldn't be suspended in Jell-O, like a prehistoric bug in amber. Cooks floated chopped vegetables in lemon gelatin; made tomato aspic (a great version of which is on p. 595); and jellied pineapple and cucumbers. The nadir was the ginger-ale salad of the 1950s: canned fruit and celery preserved in a mold of ginger-ale-flavored gelatin. I've tried it, and you shouldn't.

By the 1970s, this kind of high-concept, low-reward fussiness had run its course. Salads were pared down to concoctions like potatoes with eggs, celery seed, and crunchy pickles wrapped in mayonnaise. Salads meant beans from a can and tart dressings whisked together with anonymous oils, combinations designed for a long ride in the station wagon, followed quite possibly by a long recline in the sun. Seventies salads were not about false restraint. They didn't waste time on heirloom vegetables, luxury tidbits, and the gentle waft of almond oil. They went for the kill: the potluck version of long sideburns. (For some high points, see Salade à la Grecque on p. 179 and Wallace Seawell's Spinach Salad on p. 180.)

Boom periods are busts saladwise. In the 1980s, chefs built empires on the plate, with layers of seared tuna, islands of sliced beets, and clouds of raspberry dressing. All your scattered ambitions, and in fact your entire meal, could be found in your salad. Ingredients were piled as high as Tina Turner's hair. (You can relive this abundance today if you order the Cobb salad at Michael's in Manhattan, or you can try the Char-Grilled Tuna with Toasted Corn Vinaigrette and Avocado Salad on p. 410.)

There followed a short, dull period of enforced simplicity. Surely you remember the introduction of mesclun greens, which rendered us dispassionate salad makers, dumping greens from bag to bowl and trying to make ourselves feel better about the "recipe" by drizzling on some overpriced olive oil.

Then, in the late 1990s, the microgreen was introduced, and we micromanaged our salads as much as we did our lives. Salad became serious, and expensive, a means to reconnect with the earth we had so long been ignoring. A plate of freshly dug beets and wild watercress was suddenly a dinner course, a sociopolitical statement about the environment, an exercise in discipline. (See Shaved Artichoke Salad with Pine Nuts and Parmesan Cheese on p. 191, and Diane Forley's Arugula Salad with Artichoke, Ricotta Salata, and Pumpkin Seeds on p. 188.)

How should we read the leaves in this new century? It's hard to say. On a trip to Los Angeles, I came across a tuna macaroni salad, dotted with cubes of cheddar cheese. The place was Clementine, a small cafe in Westwood known for its stylish take on home-style cooking. The last time I'd seen a salad like it was probably 1978 in a deli, and it wasn't $8.75 for a pint. The salad hit the spot and was tasty (see p. 441). But it made me wonder: Are we getting introspective and reevaluating the strengths of our past? Is tuna macaroni salad a way of reassuring ourselves when America's place in the world seems increasingly marginalized? Or is it time to just shut up and eat?

RECIPES BY CATEGORY

SALADE À LA ROMAINE

An excellent salad: oniony, peppery, sweet, and crisp.
I used a mix of butter and red leaf lettuce, although
romaine would work just fine.

For the Vinaigrette
1 tablespoon fresh lemon juice
2 to 3 tablespoons onion juice (see Cooking Notes, p. 54)
Pinch of cayenne pepper
Salt and freshly ground white pepper
Pinch of confectioners' sugar
3 tablespoons olive or peanut oil

4 to 6 handfuls washed and torn lettuce (romaine butter,
    and/or red leaf)
2 hard-boiled eggs, cut into quarters

1. Whisk together the lemon juice, onion juice, cayenne, salt and pepper to taste, and sugar in a large
salad bowl. Gradually whisk in the oil until emulsified.
Taste and adjust the seasoning.
2. Add the lettuce, starting with 4 handfuls, tossing
to coat the leaves with the dressing, adding more lettuce if needed. Lay the eggs on top of the salad before
serving.

SERVES 4

SERVING SUGGESTIONS
Crostini Romani (p. 77), Fettuccine alla Romana (p.
310), Ismail Merchant's Very Hot Chicken Soup (p.
138), No-Knead Bread (p. 670), Soupe à l'Oignon
Gratinée (p. 120), Winter Borscht (p. 142), Winter
Fruit Salad (p. 850), Limoncello (p. 38)

JANUARY 28, 1877: "RECEIPTS FOR THE TABLE."

—1877

WATERCRESS SALAD

This salad appeared in the first of a series of articles
by Juliet Corson, the owner of a cooking school in
New York City. Each column presented a menu that

incorporated seasonal and local ingredients. Sound
familiar?

ORIGINAL RECIPE
"Carefully pick over, wash, and drain a quart of water-
cresses; dress them with a tablespoonful of vinegar,
three of salad-oil, a saltspoonful of salt, and quarter
saltspoonful of pepper."

SERVES 4

COOKING NOTE
A "saltspoonful" is ¼ teaspoon. I used aged sherry
vinegar and vegetable oil (the recipe didn't specify
either), and would do so again. Eat this salad right
away—watercress gets soggy quickly.

SERVING SUGGESTIONS
Blue Cheese Cheesecake (p. 61), Speedy Fish Stew
with Orange and Fennel (p. 133), Frozen Meringue
Velvet (p. 723), Potage Parisien with Sorrel Cream
(p. 148), Elizabeth Frink's Roast Lemon Chicken (p.
478), Marcella's Pear Cake (p. 769)

FEBRUARY 5, 1882: "HINTS FOR THE HOUSEHOLD: A SEA-
SONABLE BILL OF FARE FOR A FAMILY," BY JULIET CORSON.

—1882

LATTICH SALAT, WARME
(WARM LETTUCE SALAD)

One of the best salads in the world. Its foundation—
hot bacon fat, onion, and vinegar—have endured for
more than a century (see the Raw Spinach Salad on
p. 175).

----

2 small or 1½ medium heads butter lettuce, torn into
    pieces
2 ounces bacon, diced (about ⅓ cup)
1 small onion, finely chopped
½ cup cider vinegar or red wine vinegar
Salt and freshly ground black pepper

1. Place the lettuce in a serving bowl.
2. Cook the bacon in a small sauté pan over medium

heat to render its fat. Once it begins to brown, add the onion and cook, stirring, until translucent. Pour in the vinegar and boil until reduced by half. Season with salt and pepper, keeping in mind that the bacon will also contribute salt. Pour the dressing over the lettuce, toss to coat, and serve.

SERVES 4

COOKING NOTE
If you want the bacon to remain crisp, remove it from the pan with a slotted spoon before pouring in the vinegar, then add it back before serving.

SERVING SUGGESTIONS
Breaded Veal Milan-Style (p. 523), Lamb Shoulder Chops with Anchovy and Mint Butter (p. 567), Veal Goulash with Spaetzle (p. 525), Mashed Potatoes Anna (p. 294), Stewed Fennel (p. 245), The Most Voluptuous Cauliflower (p. 241), Cumin-Mustard Carrots (p. 237), Laggtarta (Pancakes Layered with Strawberries; p. 750), Walnut Cake with Chocolate Walnut Buttercream (p. 758)

JUNE 11, 1882: "HINTS FOR THE HOUSEHOLD," BY JULIET CORSON.

—1882

☞ GREEN PEPPER SALAD

This is the merest suggestion of a recipe, but I included it because the technique is a handy one. The way these peppers are prepared is no different from the way an Italian restaurant prepares the marinated peppers you'll find on its antipasto table. You char the peppers (on a grill or under the broiler), peel off their skins, and season them with oil, vinegar, and salt. Since this recipe appeared, our fondness for green peppers has waned with the availability of sweeter red and yellow peppers. I happen to like the sharp, vegetal edge of green peppers, and I encourage you to revisit them.

The recipe appeared in a regular feature called "Her Point of View," which was a hodgepodge of vignettes that offered advice, gave instructions on everything from flower arranging to sewing, and, very occasionally, delivered bits of journalism. The recipe was submitted by "an esteemed correspondent" (not esteemed

enough to name) who called it "a popular dish among the old French Creoles in New Orleans."

Following this was an essay on American cooking, which began, "It is not denied that the so-called American disease 'nervitis' is largely the result of 'what we eat,' 'how we eat it,' and 'how it is cooked.' It is also a fact that we eat too fast, too much at a time, and that our cooking is bad." The writer goes on to attribute most of Americans' problems to the coal-fed iron stoves they used at the time, which cooked food too quickly. Again, two evergreen topics: American eating disorders and the wonders of slow-cooking.

———

ORIGINAL RECIPE
"Have very fresh green peppers; roast on hot coals, turning constantly. Do not allow them to burn. When roasted, put under cold-water faucet; the outer skin should come off very easily. Shred the roasted parts, being careful to reject the core and seeds. Season with salt, salad oil, and a little vinegar. Serve in a small dish, as a pickle. It is a delicious relish with meats and fish, hot and cold."

4 green bell peppers
Sea salt
Olive or safflower oil
Sherry vinegar

1. Arrange an oven rack 6 inches from the broiler and heat the broiler. Place the peppers on a broiling pan or baking sheet. Broil the peppers, turning them as each side chars, until lightly charred all over. Transfer them to a paper bag or aluminum foil and wrap them up so they steam. Let cool enough to handle.
2. Peel off the skin from the peppers and discard the cores and seeds. Thinly slice and put them in a serving dish. Season to taste with salt, oil, and vinegar.

SERVES 4

COOKING NOTES
Green peppers are the younger form of red peppers, so they contain more juice and will release more as you turn them in the oven. Don't be alarmed.

The peppers absorb a lot of salt, so start with what seems a regular amount, then wait a few minutes and taste and adjust the seasoning. Do this a few more times before serving if needed.

Caramelized Onion and Quark Dip (p. 84), Sausage, Bean, and Corn Stew (p. 538), Grilled Hanger Steak (p. 551), Fried Corn (p. 274), Fried Green Tomatoes (p. 212), Peach Salad (p. 805)

AUGUST 25, 1895: "HER POINT OF VIEW."

—1895

CHIFFONADE SALAD

A superb chopped salad from Oscar Tschirky, the maître d' at the Waldorf-Astoria Hotel in New York and the man behind both Veal Oscar and Waldorf Salad. *Chiffonade* means cut into thin strips.

———

- 2 cups curly endive cut into thin strips
- 2 cups romaine cut into thin strips
- 2 small plum tomatoes, cored, seeded, and cut into slivers (about 1 cup)
- 1 stalk celery, cut into 1-inch-long matchsticks (about 1 cup)
- 2 small beets, roasted (see Cooking Notes, p. 192), peeled, and cut into 1-inch-long matchsticks
- 1 hard-boiled egg
- 2 pinches paprika
- Pinch of salt
- ½ teaspoon Dijon mustard
- 1 teaspoon thinly sliced chives
- 1 teaspoon chopped tarragon
- 3 tablespoons cider vinegar or red wine vinegar
- 2 tablespoons olive oil

1. Combine the curly endive, romaine, tomatoes, celery, and beets in a large bowl.
2. To make the dressing, using the back of a spoon, press the egg through a sieve into a small bowl. Add the paprika, salt, mustard, chives, and tarragon. Whisk in the vinegar, then whisk in the oil until the dressing emulsifies. Taste and adjust the seasoning.
3. Pour the dressing over the salad and toss to coat. Taste and adjust the seasoning.

SERVES 4

SERVING SUGGESTIONS

Tschirky recommended the following menu with the salad: cantaloupe, clam broth, crab ravigote, chicken or squab mousse, ice cream, and coffee. You may also like: Egg and Olive Canapés (p. 57), Fresh and Smoked Salmon Spread (p. 72), Oyster Chowder (p. 159), Cutlets à la Kiev (p. 455), String Beans with Ginger and Garlic (p. 260), Baked Zucchini with Herbs and Tomatoes (p. 250), Filbert Torte (p. 742), Tea Ice Cream (p. 717).

PERIOD DETAIL

In 1892, the *Times* reprinted a story on salad making from the *St. Louis Globe Democrat*. The story declared, "It requires art to make a good salad. Perhaps genius is necessary to the preparation of a perfect one. . . . But many a little housewife has the requisite qualities to enable her to make nice salads without any assistance save her own keen sense of taste, quick perception, and excellent judgment." Among the ideas given was a nasturtium salad served in a "delicate glass dish."

AUGUST 7, 1898: "WOMEN CAN ORDER DINNERS: THAT IS, CULINARY POEMS PERFECT IN THE ESTIMATION OF GOURMET AND BON VIVANT."

—1898

RAW ARTICHOKE SALAD WITH CUCUMBER

———

- 2 cups very thinly sliced trimmed raw baby artichokes (about 20 artichokes)
- 1 cup thinly sliced cucumber
- ¼ cup vinaigrette (p. 225)
- Salt and freshly ground black pepper to taste

Combine all the ingredients and toss well. Adjust the seasoning.

SERVES 2 TO 3

SERVING SUGGESTIONS

Fried Olives (p. 87), Chilled English Pea–Mint Soup (p. 162), Jean Yves Legarve's Spaghetti with Lemon and Asparagus Sauce (p. 319), Pan-Roasted Chicken with End-of-Season Tomatoes (p. 482), Plum Fritters (p. 865), Rhubarb Orange (p. 864)

MARCH 30, 1902: "ARTICHOKES AND HOW TO COOK THEM."

—1902

ARTICHOKE SALAD WITH ANCHOVY AND CAPERS

This salad reminds me of vitello tonnato—the sliced artichokes are battened down with a blanket of potent, silky sauce. It appeared in an article devoted to artichokes, in which the writer, noting that Mrs. Cornelius Vanderbilt served them when Prince Henry of Prussia came to dinner, claimed artichokes "deserve to be better known."

"If one should ask at the fashionable hotels and restaurants for the status of the artichoke," the writer continued, "the reply would probably be that they are well liked; can be so easily brought from France, where they are largely cultivated; that there is no difficulty in obtaining them; and that as French steamers bring them in weekly, they can be found in the markets at all times." Along with this recipe were ones for a raw artichoke and cucumber salad dressed with vinaigrette (see p. 173; and see p. 191 for a modern Italian spin on this idea), fried artichokes, and artichoke salad with endive and chicory.

————

4 large artichokes, trimmed

1 large egg yolk

¾ teaspoon Colman's prepared mustard, or more to taste

1 clove garlic, smashed

2 teaspoons fresh lemon juice, or more to taste

Salt

½ cup vegetable oil

1 rounded teaspoon anchovy paste

1 tablespoon chopped capers

1 hard-boiled egg, finely chopped

Freshly ground black pepper

1. Bring a large pot of salted water to a boil. Add the artichokes, lay a lid or heatproof plate on top of them to weight them down, and cook until tender, about 15 minutes.

2. Meanwhile, whisk the egg yolk, mustard, garlic, and lemon juice in a small bowl until smooth. Season with salt. Very slowly pour in the oil as you continue to whisk, beginning with a drop at a time and increasing to a thread. The sauce should emulsify. Thin it by whisking in 2 to 3 tablespoons of the artichoke cooking water. It should be a beautiful butter yellow, highly seasoned, and pourable. Taste and adjust the seasoning, adding more salt, mustard, and lemon juice as desired.

3. Drain the artichokes. Trim them down to the edible heart and stem. (Save the trimmed leaves to eat at your leisure.) Cut the hearts and stems into ⅛-inch-thick slices.

4. Lay the artichoke slices on a serving platter. Spread with the anchovy paste, then spread the mayonnaise sauce on top. Sprinkle with the capers and egg, and season with pepper.

SERVES 4

COOKING NOTE
To trim an artichoke, pull off the tough outer leaves. Cut the bottom of the stem and trim the base. Cut off the top half of the leaves. Scoop out the choke using a small sharp-edged spoon.

SERVING SUGGESTIONS
Olive Oil–Tuna Spread with Lemon and Oregano (p. 95), Sole Grenobloise (Sautéed Sole with Capers and Lemons; p. 399), White Veal Stew with Mushrooms, Corn, and Sherry (p. 553), '21' Club Hamburger (p. 536), Seared Loin Lamb Chops with Olives and Soft Polenta (p. 556), Roast Chicken with Bread Salad (p. 467), Saratoga Potatoes (p. 273), Asparagus alla Fontina (p. 222), Bittersweet Chocolate Semifreddo (p. 727), Rhubarb-Strawberry Mousse (p. 835)

MARCH 30, 1902: "ARTICHOKES AND HOW TO COOK THEM."

—1902

CAESAR SALAD

Although the specific origins of Caesar salad may never be known, many people believe it was created in the 1920s by Caesar Cardini, a chef with restaurants in San Diego and Tijuana. Gladwyn Hill, the Los Angeles bureau chief for the *Times* in the 1940s, wrote that the salad "draws more ooh's and ah's from Eastern visitors these days than anything in the travel ads."

"It is variously called the Caesar, Caliente, and Western Way salad," he continued, "and has been extolled by many consumers as possibly the greatest advance in salad fabrication in several centuries."

Endearingly, he added, "Bland lettuce is not permitted."

———

For the Garlic Croutons
1 clove garlic, crushed
2 tablespoons olive oil
1 cup cubes (¾-inch) country bread

1 clove garlic, peeled
1 head romaine lettuce, torn into bite-sized pieces
¼ teaspoon salt
⅛ teaspoon freshly ground black pepper
2 ounces Parmesan cheese, grated
¼ teaspoon Colman's prepared mustard
3 tablespoons olive oil
1 tablespoon fresh lemon juice
1 large egg, at room temperature

1. To make the croutons, heat the broiler (or a toaster oven). Combine the crushed garlic and oil in a small saucepan and set over low heat while you toast the bread. Spread the bread cubes on a small baking sheet and toast under the broiler (or in the toaster oven).
2. Toss the toasted bread with the oil; discard the garlic.
3. Use the peeled garlic clove to rub the inside of a wooden salad bowl. Add the romaine, salt, pepper, Parmesan, mustard, oil, and lemon juice—do not toss yet.
4. To coddle the egg, bring a small saucepan of water to a boil. Carefully lower the egg into the water and simmer for exactly 2 minutes.
5. Remove from the water and immediately break the egg into the salad. Toss enough to mix thoroughly but not so vigorously as to bruise the greens. The leaves should be marinated but not "waterlogged." Sample the greens, adding seasoning to suit. An instant before serving, add the croutons, tossing enough to mix them in without making them soggy.

SERVES 4 TO 6

VARIATION

Early versions of the salad were made with coddled (lightly boiled) eggs but didn't contain anchovies; now the reverse is true. I recommend incorporating both. The eggs thicken the dressing, and good anchovies add a robust character that no other ingredient can provide. Start with one anchovy, mashed and added to the dressing. Add more to taste.

SERVING SUGGESTIONS

Clam Chowder (p. 107), Grand Central Pan Roast (p. 393), Breaded Chicken Breasts with Parmesan Cheese (p. 465), '21' Club Hamburger (p. 536), Steak au Poivre (p. 573), Broiled Steak with Oysters (p. 511), Chocolate Chip Cookies (p. 709), Chocolate Silk Pie (p. 838), Dick Taeuber's Cordial Pie (p. 817), Banana Cream Pie (p. 863)

PERIOD DETAIL

The *Times* has run many recipes for Caesar salad, but in 1979 they published what the writer J.M.C. claimed was the original recipe from the 1920s. It differs from this one in that it called for vinegar (in addition to lemon juice), Worcestershire sauce, and a raw egg rather than a coddled one. Feel free to play around with this recipe. A dash of Worcestershire would probably be great. But, original or not, I prefer a coddled egg to a raw one.

JANUARY 29, 1947: "NEWS OF FOOD: SOME ADVICE ON THE MEAT THERMOMETER AND ANOTHER NEW RECIPE FOR CAESAR SALAD," BY JANE NICKERSON.

—1947

RAW SPINACH SALAD

Obviously, one of the problems with this recipe title is its utter lack of sex appeal. The other is that it's not even accurate. The hidden charm of this salad is that it's dressed with a mixture of hot vinegar and bacon fat, which lightly wilts the leaves and diminishes the chalky edge of raw spinach.

A note about the spinach: do not dare use ratty old spinach, which wouldn't wilt if boiled, and do not use the baby leaves that come packaged in bags (they're too fragile). This recipe needs bright, fresh leaves, just fully grown and no older.

Once the spinach is cleaned and trimmed, the rest of the recipe takes 5 minutes. Be sure to follow every instruction, including warming the bowl, which will prevent the sauce from cooling before you reach the table. Cold bacon fat = not fun to eat.

———

4 or 5 strips of bacon, diced

I small onion, minced

I pound spinach

⅓ cup wine vinegar

Salt and freshly ground black pepper

1. Sauté the bacon with the onion in a small skillet until bacon is crisp.

2. Meanwhile, remove the roots and, if desired, the coarse stems of the spinach. Wash thoroughly and dry. Tear coarsely into a warm bowl.

3. Add the vinegar to the bacon and bring to a simmer. Pour over the spinach. Season the salad with salt and pepper and toss together until all the leaves are well coated with the dressing.

SERVES 4

COOKING NOTE

I used Champagne vinegar.

SERVING SUGGESTIONS

Egg and Olive Canapés (p. 57), Seared Tuna in Black Pepper Crust (p. 409), Veal Chops with Sage (p. 564), Broiled Steak with Oysters (p. 511), New York Strip Steak with Horseradish-Mint Glaze (p. 566), Potato "Tostones" (Flattened Potatoes; p. 301), Madame Laracine's Gratin Dauphinois (p. 284), Sautéed Potatoes with Parsley (p. 283), Chocolate Pudding (p. 858), Tapioca Pudding (p. 798), Breton Butter Cake (p. 777), Chocolate Ice-Box "Cake" (p. 746)

AUGUST 10, 1947: "FOOD: SIMPLE FARE—FOR GOURMETS," BY JANE NICKERSON. RECIPE ADAPTED FROM DAVID COWLES, THE CHEF AND OWNER OF TOWN PENGUIN IN NEW YORK CITY.

—1947

∽ GREEN GODDESS SALAD

Nothing sounds more retro than the green goddess salad, which calls to mind the days of Singapore slings served in Tom Collins glasses, big bands, and simple, arrestingly flavored food. Yet if you take some of today's cooking staples—anchovies, fresh herbs, and salad greens—and add mayonnaise and vinegar to them, green goddess is exactly what you end up with.

The *Times*'s recipe for green goddess dressing, which originally ran in 1948, is a garlicky, demanding mash-up for which the romaine acts as a soothing counterpoint. You cannot eat the salad dispassionately, because it commands your attention with pungent lashings of chives, vinegar, anchovies, and cracked black pepper. It's not a salad to have for lunch at work.

The salad was made famous at the Palace Hotel in San Francisco in 1923 as a tribute to George Arliss, the star of the play *The Green Goddess*. Descendant recipes vary, although most, including James Beard's in *American Cookery*, rely on a foundation of tarragon, anchovies, and scallion. Some include garlic, parsley, and chives, some sour cream. In a recent version by Ina Garten, found on the Food Network website, she replaced the tarragon with basil. The salad remained green, so no harm done. The bottled Seven Seas version of the dressing, so popular in the 1970s, however, went the way of moon boots as ranch and balsamic dressings elbowed their way onto shelves.

This decades-old *Times* recipe, which came from *The California Cook Book*, by Genevieve Callahan, varies from tradition by tossing Worcestershire sauce into the mix and, oddly enough, omitting the tarragon. Jesse Llapitan, the current chef at the Palace Hotel, still serves more than fifty green goddess salads every day. His faintly modernized version is dense with tarragon and is served over Dungeness crab.

Incidentally, it was the Caesar Salad recipe on p. 174 that caused Jane Nickerson, the *Times*'s food columnist, to write about green goddess salad. A friend of hers wrote in to declare Nickerson's article celebrating the Caesar "just so much nonsense"—a recipe inferior in all ways, apparently, to green goddess.

———

1 clove garlic, minced

⅓ cup mayonnaise

1 tablespoon white wine vinegar

1 tablespoon Worcestershire sauce

2 teaspoons minced chives

6 anchovy fillets, drained and finely chopped

1 tablespoon oil from the anchovies

Cracked black pepper

1 tablespoon chopped flat-leaf parsley

1 large head romaine lettuce, leaves separated

1. Place the garlic in a salad bowl, and whisk in the mayonnaise, vinegar, Worcestershire sauce, chives, anchovies, and anchovy oil. Add cracked pepper to taste. Let stand at room temperature for an hour or longer.

2. Just before serving, add the parsley and break the romaine leaves into the bowl. Toss until the dressing is well distributed.

SERVES 4 TO 6

COOKING NOTES

The *Times*'s green goddess recipe differs from most by ratcheting up the dressing's assertive flavor with garlic and Worcestershire sauce.

You may want to start with just half the romaine, toss the salad, and then add more romaine as needed.

SERVING SUGGESTIONS

Green Goddess likes to take the stage. Serve it with unadorned standards: Grilled Hanger Steak (p. 551) and a potato dish such as Mashed Potatoes Anna (p. 294) or Potato "Tostones" (Flattened Potatoes; p. 301). If going all out, add on a Martini (p. 35), Classic Ciabatta (p. 665), Florentines with Ginger (p. 689), and Chocolate Pudding (p. 858).

PERIOD DETAIL

According to Nickerson's story, Americans ate an average of 22 pounds of lettuce in 1947, and just 7 pounds in 1918. In 2005, the USDA reported that Americans consumed 34½ pounds.

APRIL 29, 1948: "NEWS OF FOOD: A READER SWEARS BY GREEN GODDESS SALAD AND WRITER COMES UP WITH A RECIPE," BY JANE NICKERSON.

—1948

ITALIAN SALAD

Salt

1 clove garlic

¼ cup olive oil

1 tablespoon fresh lemon juice or wine vinegar (red or white)

1 tablespoon mayonnaise

1 teaspoon dry mustard

Freshly ground black pepper

1 head romaine or other lettuce, cut into bite-sized pieces

1 fennel bulb, trimmed and cut into julienne strips

⅓ cup walnuts, coarsely chopped, or 3 anchovy fillets, finely chopped

1 tablespoon capers

2 hard-boiled eggs, sliced

Freshly grated Parmesan cheese for serving

Sprinkle the bottom of a salad bowl with salt and rub with the garlic clove. Add the oil, lemon juice, mayonnaise, mustard, and pepper and stir with a wooden spoon until well blended. Add the remaining ingredients (except the cheese) and toss lightly with a fork and spoon. Sprinkle with grated Parmesan cheese.

SERVES 6

SERVING SUGGESTIONS

Ricotta Crostini with Fresh Thyme and Dried Oregano (p. 93), Crostini Romani (p. 77), Mrs. Sebastiani's Malfatti (p. 313), Lasagna (p. 342) Cornmeal Biscotti (p. 696), Balducci's Tiramisù (p. 830)

MARCH 2, 1958: "LENTEN MENU—ITALIAN STYLE," BY CRAIG CLAIBORNE.

—1958

GREEN BEAN SALAD WITH SAVORY TOPPING

If Barney Greengrass and Alice Waters teamed up to make a picnic salad, this would be it. Dollops of egg salad are spooned on top of a bed of green beans and scallions that have been dressed with vinaigrette. It's a peculiar look, but a great idea—you get the crisp, assertive snap of beans and lemon juice overlapping with creamy bites of egg and mayonnaise.

As with many recipes of this period, the author assumed that you knew how to blanch a vegetable, hard-boil an egg, and brown bacon. Most people still know how to handle the egg and bacon. For blanching a vegetable, however, here's a brief primer: bring a large pot of salted water to a rolling boil, add the vegetable, and cook until crisp-tender, then drain and plunge into an ice water bath to stop the cooking.

This salad's stylistic soul mate, Asparagus Mimosa, is on p. 258.

½ cup vegetable oil
¼ cup fresh lemon juice or vinegar
Salt and freshly ground black pepper
Pinch of ground allspice
1 pound green beans, trimmed and blanched
    until crisp-tender
½ cup coarsely chopped scallions
4 hard-boiled eggs
3 tablespoons mayonnaise
1 teaspoon Dijon mustard
4 slices bacon, cooked until crisp, drained, and crumbled

1. Thoroughly mix the oil with 3 tablespoons lemon juice in a small bowl. Season to taste with salt, pepper, and allspice.
2. Mix the cooked green beans with the scallions in a serving bowl. Pour the dressing over the top and toss gently. Refrigerate for several hours.
3. Just before serving, chop the hard-boiled eggs. Mix the mayonnaise thoroughly with the remaining tablespoon lemon juice and the mustard, and combine with the chopped eggs. Add the crumbled bacon. Correct the seasoning, then arrange on top of the green bean mixture.

SERVES 4 AS A FIRST COURSE, 2 AS A MAIN COURSE

COOKING NOTES
I used lemon juice. If using vinegar, try cider or white wine vinegar.

Make sure your beans are young and thin. If old, they'll be tough and will fight with the texture of the egg salad.

SERVING SUGGESTIONS
Watermelon Gazpacho (p. 150), Thomas Keller's Gazpacho (p. 146), Open-Faced Tomato Sandwich (p. 367), Pamela Sherrid's Summer Pasta (p. 329), Corn and Yellow Tomato Risotto with Shrimp (p. 328), Tuna Salad (p. 435), Summer Squash Casserole (p. 252), Summer Pudding (p. 847), Lemon Bars (p. 690), Caramelized Brown Butter Rice Krispies Treats (p. 708)

READERS
"Almost six decades ago, I started collecting recipes from the NY Times, the ones my mother did not want. At the time, the Times home economist was Ruth P. Casa-Emellos. Then, a few years after my marriage, The New York Times Cookbook, edited by Craig Claiborne, appeared in the college bookstore, in Wisconsin, where my husband was teaching. I thought I had died and gone to heaven—and I was able to purge my recipe boxes of the recipes, which now appeared in his first cookbook. I think I now have most of the Times cookbooks, which have appeared over the years—yet I still have three large wooden recipe boxes with recipes which are 'keepers,' mostly from the Times. (I also have a large stack of recipes to try . . .) Over the years, our children have grown up and left, so I no longer make a dozen new recipes a week, as I used to. . . . Cooking is therapy, and I certainly got a lot when I made Morton Thompson's Turkey Stuffing, with its 32 ingredients!"

I've left Thompson's lengthy recipe out of this book, but I did include this salad, one of Whitcomb's favorites.

Helga N. Whitcomb,
South Burlington, VT, letter

JULY 30, 1962: "FOOD NEWS: BEAN CROP IS PLENTIFUL," BY NAN ICKERINGILL.

—1962

↩ SALADE NIÇOISE

This makes enough to feed everyone in Yonkers. If you don't have a giant bowl, divide the ingredients among two bowls. Or simply halve the recipe! The best part of the recipe is Step 4, the instruction to present the salad to your guests, a notion firmly rooted in the 1960s.

---

2 teaspoons mustard, preferably Dijon or Düsseldorf

2 tablespoons wine vinegar (red or white)

1½ teaspoons salt

1 to 2 cloves garlic, minced

6 tablespoons peanut or vegetable oil

6 tablespoons olive oil

1 teaspoon chopped fresh thyme or

   ½ teaspoon dried thyme

Freshly ground black pepper

2 pounds green beans, trimmed and cut

   into 1½-inch lengths

2 green bell peppers, cored, seeded, and sliced

   into thin rounds

2 cups thinly sliced celery

1 pint cherry tomatoes, halved

5 medium red-skinned potatoes, peeled, cooked,

   and sliced

Three 7-ounce cans or jars tuna, preferably

   the imported variety, in oil

One 2-ounce can anchovy fillets

10 pimiento stuffed olives

10 black olives, preferably Greek or Italian

1 small red onion, thinly sliced

2 tablespoons chopped fresh basil or

   1 teaspoon dried basil

⅓ cup finely chopped flat-leaf parsley

¼ cup thinly sliced scallions

6 hard-boiled eggs, quartered

1. Combine the mustard, vinegar, salt, garlic, peanut oil, olive oil, thyme, and pepper to taste in a small bowl. Beat with a fork until well blended.

2. Fill a medium saucepan with water, season generously with salt, and bring to a boil. Add the beans and cook until crisp-tender. Drain in a colander and run under cold water; drain.

3. Make a more or less symmetrical pattern of the green beans, peppers, celery, tomatoes, and potatoes in a large salad bowl (or 2 bowls). Flake the tuna and add it to the bowl. Arrange the anchovies on top and scatter the olives and onion over all. Sprinkle with the basil, parsley, and scallions. Garnish with the eggs.

4. Toss the salad with the dressing after you've presented the garnished bowl to guests for their enjoyment. Serve with a crusty loaf of French or Italian bread.

SERVES 10 AS A FIRST COURSE, 6 AS A MAIN COURSE

SERVING SUGGESTIONS

Jay Grelen's Southern Iced Tea (p. 27), Grapefruit Wine (p. 37), Lemon Syrup (p. 9), Tom's Chilled Cucumber Soup (p. 117), Yellow Pepper Soup with Paprika Mousse (p. 147), Blue Cheese Cheesecake (p. 61), Brie with Herbs in Bread (p. 69), Lemon Bars (p. 690), Strawberry Soup (p. 816), Classic Financiers (Buttery Almond Cakes; p. 697)

JULY 2, 1967: "A TASTE OF THE RIVIERA," BY CRAIG CLAIBORNE.

—1967

⌒ SALADE À LA GRECQUE

Craig Claiborne, who wrote for the *Times* from the late 1950s through the early 1980s, was the first food columnist at the paper to act as a trend spotter. I'd love to know if he was aware that he also fueled trends. Craig's stories were widely talked about, his recipes voraciously clipped. (While I worked on this book, I received hundreds of original clippings from his devoted flock.) Among the many foods he introduced *Times* readers to were gravlax, phyllo, bollito misto, pesto, and—here—feta.

He described feta as "a cheese that is becoming increasingly popular in America." In fact, feta didn't become that common until the 1980s, but Claiborne brought it to people's attention, not just with this recipe but many others, including Shrimp Baked with Feta Cheese, Greek Style, which he published in 1976 (p. 397), and Marina Anagnostou's Spanakopetes, published in 1970 (p. 63).

4 cups salad greens (escarole, romaine, chicory, and/or

   other greens), cut or torn into bite-sized pieces

4 to 8 radishes, cut into "roses"

8 black olives, preferably imported, such as

   Calamata or Alfonso

1 red onion, cut into thin rings (use according to taste)

1 small green bell pepper, cored, seeded,

   and cut into thin rings or strips

4 to 8 tomato wedges

4 to 8 anchovy fillets

1/2 cup crumbled feta cheese

Coarse salt

1 clove garlic, split

Freshly ground black pepper

2 tablespoons fresh lemon juice or vinegar, or to taste

4 to 6 tablespoons olive oil, preferably Greek

1. Have ready the salad greens, radishes, olives, onion, green pepper, tomatoes, anchovies, and cheese.

2. Pour a little coarse salt into a salad bowl and rub the salt around the inside of the bowl with the garlic clove. Add the salad greens and other ingredients. Sprinkle with the lemon juice and toss lightly. Add 1/4 cup oil and toss again. Add more lemon juice or vinegar and/or oil to taste.

SERVES 4 TO 6

COOKING NOTES

Don't make this salad with bagged mixed greens. They don't have enough sturdiness or character.

Claiborne, who was typically precise, seems to have been unable to make up his mind about various amounts in the recipe. Here's what I did with the nonspecific ingredient amounts, with pleasant results: I used 6 radishes, half a red onion, 8 tomato wedges, 5 anchovy fillets, and 1/4 cup olive oil.

I used Calamata olives (pitted) and lemon juice.

If you can't be bothered to cut the radishes into roses, you can just cut them into wedges.

SERVING SUGGESTIONS

Faki (Greek Lentil Soup; p. 121), Marina Anagnostou's Spanakopetes (Spinach Triangles; p. 63), Broiled Lamb Leg Chops on Eggplant Planks with Mint-Yogurt Sauce (p. 549), Arnaki Araka (Lamb with Peas; p. 550), Shrimp Baked with Feta Cheese, Greek-Style (p. 397), Flourless Apricot Honey Soufflé (p. 846), Honey Spice Cookies (p. 685), Hazelnut Baklava (p. 706), Almond Granita (p. 731)

MARCH 21, 1971: "FEASTING WITH FETA," BY CRAIG CLAIBORNE

—1971

⌇ WALLACE SEAWELL'S SPINACH SALAD

How do you make a great spinach salad? By not letting the spinach dominate—it works better in tandem with bright acids, herbs, and chromatics. Here the spinach is paired with crumbled bacon, chopped hard-cooked eggs, scallions, and croutons.

Sadly, we may never know the connection between Wallace Seawell, a well-known photographer who took portraits of Bette Davis and Audrey Hepburn, and this salad. The recipe was included without explanation as a side dish to Rock Salt Roast (beef roasted with a salt crust).

————

8 cups washed and well-drained spinach leaves

1/2 pound lean bacon, fried until crisp and crumbled

2 hard-boiled eggs, roughly chopped

5 scallions, chopped

Garlic croutons (see Cooking Notes)

1/2 cup mayonnaise

2 teaspoons Düsseldorf or Dijon mustard

1/4 cup fresh lemon juice

1/2 cup extra virgin olive oil

1 tablespoon tarragon vinegar or white wine vinegar

1/8 teaspoon sugar

Salt and freshly ground black pepper

1. Tear the spinach leaves into bite-sized pieces and place in a salad bowl. Arrange the bacon bits, eggs, scallions, and croutons over the spinach.

2. Combine all the remaining ingredients in a small bowl and whisk to blend. Just before serving, or at the table, pour one-third of the dressing over the salad and toss lightly, then add more if needed, until the salad is lightly coated.

SERVES 4

COOKING NOTES

The only Düsseldorf mustard I could find had horseradish in it, and it worked out just fine.

To make garlic croutons, heat the oven to 350 degrees. Lightly rub 2 thick slices of country bread with a clove of garlic. Brush both sides of the bread with olive oil. Cut the bread into small cubes, spread on a baking sheet, and toast in the oven, turning once, for about 10 minutes. This will probably make more than ¾ cup—save the extra for snacking.

SERVING SUGGESTIONS

Blue Cheese Dip (p. 54), Saucisson Soûl (p. 67), Provençal Fish Soup (p. 141), Ann Seranne's Rib Roast of Beef (p. 519), Veal Shanks with Garlic Mashed Potatoes (p. 540), Cabbage and Potato Gratin with Mustard Bread Crumbs (p. 298), Italian Roast Potatoes (p. 300), An Honest Loaf of French Bread (p. 662), Tourtière (Apple, Prune, and Armagnac Tart; p. 827), Chocolate Caramels (p. 683), Chocolate Rum Mousse (p. 814)

OCTOBER 1, 1972: "BEEF WITH A CRUST," BY JEAN HEWITT.

—1972

SPICY ORANGE SALAD MOROCCAN-STYLE

I have never seen an orange salad on a menu or been served one at someone's house. And now that I have tasted one, I'm outraged. Moroccan orange salad is one of the best salads in the world—sweet citrus juices countered with pungent onion and dueling kicks of spices and acidity.

Some cooks add olives and paprika, as Craig Claiborne did here. He kept his accessible with a little garlic, cayenne, olive oil, vinegar, and parsley. It grabs you, shakes you, then lets you enjoy the sweet fruit.

In Paula Wolfert's *World of Food*, she seasons the orange slices with the spice mixture *ras el hanout*, orange-flower water, lime and lemon zest, dates, and mint. Wolfert devotes an entire section to orange salads in her book *Couscous and Other Good Food from Morocco*, one with radishes and cinnamon, another with grated carrots and orange-flower water, and one very much like Claiborne's with olives and paprika. She even wrote, "Olives and oranges are one of those miracle combinations, like lamb and garlic, before which I sometimes feel I should bow in gratitude."

3 large navel oranges
⅛ teaspoon cayenne pepper
1 teaspoon paprika
½ teaspoon minced garlic

3 tablespoons olive oil
1 tablespoon vinegar
Salt and freshly ground black pepper
⅓ cup chopped flat-leaf parsley
12 pitted black olives, preferably Greek or Italian

1. Peel the oranges, paring away all the white pith. Cut each orange into 8 wedges, and cut each wedge into 1-inch pieces. Set aside.
2. Place the cayenne, paprika, garlic, olive oil, and vinegar in a salad bowl, add salt and pepper to taste, and blend well with a wire whisk. Add the oranges, parsley, and olives and toss gently to mix. Serve chilled or at room temperature.

SERVES 4

COOKING NOTE

I would happily eat this salad every day, but it really is best in winter, when oranges are sweetest. Feel free to use other citrus, like blood oranges, tangerines, or mandarins.

SERVING SUGGESTIONS

Olive Oil–Tuna Spread with Lemon and Oregano (p. 95), Jennifer's Moroccan Tea (p. 33), Turkish Split-Pea Soup with Mint and Paprika (p. 140), Moroccan Rice Pudding (p. 848), Huntington Pudding (p. 802), Aztec Hot Chocolate Pudding (p. 855)

DECEMBER 17, 1980: "A CHRISTMAS FEAST IN AN ISLAND SETTING," BY CRAIG CLAIBORNE.

—1980

ALICE WATERS'S BAKED GOAT CHEESE WITH SALAD

You probably would never have guessed that Alice Waters and her "delicious revolution" crossed paths with Craig Claiborne and his butter counterreformation, but indeed they did. In 1981, Claiborne, who covered most of the twentieth century's best culinary stories, also covered the early stages of what would become its most important crusade.

"Where American gastronomy is concerned," Claiborne wrote, "there is one commodity that is rarer than locally grown black truffles or homemade foie gras. That is a chef of international repute who was born in the United States. Even rarer is such a celebrated chef who is a woman."

Claiborne described Waters, whose name, he added, "may not be a household word," as "a modest, diminutive, gamine-like figure with fingers that are astonishingly small, considering her métier." As we now know, she wasn't really destined for the kitchen anyway.

One of the dishes Claiborne ate the day he met Waters at Chez Panisse, which he called "a cunningly designed, somewhat raffish establishment," was baked goat cheese with salad, which later became one of the iconic dishes of the decade. He included the recipe in his story and, two years later when reporting with Pierre Franey on the growing popularity of goat cheese, offered a slightly different version from Waters's book *The Chez Panisse Menu Cookbook*. I made both, and while both are good, this one is marginally better (thyme in the bread crumbs, red wine vinegar rather than balsamic).

This dish can easily be mishandled, and it often is in mediocre restaurants, where the salad is soggy and the cheese a molten wad. This is not the occasion for bagged "mesclun." Take the time to find great baby greens from a local farm or sturdy bunches of arugula, red leaf lettuce, mizuna, and/or baby watercress.

——————

4 rounds fresh goat cheese, about 2½ inches
    in diameter and about ½ inch thick
½ cup olive oil
4 sprigs fresh thyme or 1 teaspoon dried thyme
    plus 1 teaspoon dried thyme for blending
    with the bread crumbs
1 cup fine fresh bread crumbs
2 tablespoons red wine vinegar
Salt and freshly ground black pepper
4 cups lettuce leaves cut into bite-sized pieces (use
    greens such as arugula, red leaf lettuce, and so on)
Garlic Toast Slices (recipe follows)

1. Place the rounds of goat cheese in a flat dish and add ¼ cup oil. Add the thyme sprigs or sprinkle with 1 teaspoon dried thyme. Let stand for 8 hours, or longer refrigerated.
2. Blend the remaining teaspoon of dried thyme with the bread crumbs; set aside.
3. Heat the oven to 400 degrees. Remove the cheese rounds from the oil and coat them all over with the bread-crumb-and-thyme mixture. Put them in an oiled

baking dish and place in the oven. Bake for 6 to 10 minutes, or until the cheese is lightly bubbling and golden.
4. Meanwhile, blend the remaining ¼ cup oil with the vinegar and salt and pepper to taste. Pour this over the salad greens and toss.
5. Serve the cheese on warm plates, surrounded by the garlic toast, with the salad.

SERVES 4 AS A FIRST COURSE OR LIGHT MAIN COURSE

GARLIC TOAST SLICES

12 thin slices crusty French bread, preferably
    cut from a small round loaf
4 tablespoons unsalted butter, melted
1 clove garlic, cut in half

1. Heat the oven to 350 degrees.
2. Brush each slice of bread on both sides with melted butter. Arrange the slices on a baking sheet and place in the oven. Bake for 5 to 7 minutes, or until the bread is crisp and lightly browned. Rub each slice with a cut clove of garlic and serve warm.

MAKES 12 TOASTS

COOKING NOTES
You probably won't need a full cup of bread crumbs—save the leftovers for another use, such as on top of a cauliflower or potato gratin.

A thin flexible spatula comes in handy when transferring the warm cheese from the baking dish to plates.

SERVING SUGGESTIONS
Seasoned Olives (p. 90), Oven-Roasted Branzino with Hazelnut Picada (p. 441), Braised Duck Legs with Pinot Noir Sauce (p. 481), Cold Beef with Tarragon Vinaigrette (p. 534), Pots de Crème (p. 815), Chez Panisse Meyer Lemon Meringue Pie (p. 833)

JUNE 12, 1983: "FOOD: MATTERS OF CHANGING TASTE," BY CRAIG CLAIBORNE AND PIERRE FRANEY. RECIPE ADAPTED FROM *THE CHEZ PANISSE MENU COOKBOOK*, BY ALICE WATERS.

—1983

⌒ SPICY CUCUMBER SALAD

Not quite a pickle and not quite a salad, but quite addictive.

———

2 large cucumbers
3 tablespoons soy sauce
¼ teaspoon crushed red pepper flakes
1 teaspoon Asian sesame oil
1 tablespoon white vinegar

1. Pound the cucumbers lightly all over with a kitchen mallet to bruise them. Trim off the ends. Peel the cucumbers and cut lengthwise into quarters. Cut or scrape away the seeds.
2. Cut each cucumber strip into 1½-inch lengths. Trim the corners of each piece to round them and make them neater. Put the pieces in a bowl and add the remaining ingredients, tossing well. Chill before serving.

SERVES 4

SERVING SUGGESTIONS
Edamame with Nori Salt (p. 92), Chinese-Style Steamed Black Sea Bass (p. 432), Alaskan Salmon (p. 423), Clams in Black Bean Sauce (p. 442), Spicy, Supercrunchy Fried Chicken (p. 490), Stir-Fried Collards (p. 254), Asparagus with Miso Butter (p. 259), Grapefruit Granita (p. 731), Coconut Rice Pudding with Lime Syrup (p. 846)

SEPTEMBER 14, 1988: "60-MINUTE GOURMET," BY PIERRE FRANEY.

—1988

⌒ WARM CABBAGE SALAD WITH GOAT CHEESE AND CAPERS

The problem we long had with cabbage was the same problem we long had with lettuce. There was one kind, and it was a bad kind. Green cabbage is such an ornery variety, as we're discovering now that we've tasted the preposessing likes of Savoy cabbage and cavolo nero. Red cabbage, which emerged in the 1980s, served as the gateway cabbage to such delights; here it's in a pretty dish of its lightly cooked leaves festooned with toasted pine nuts, capers, and goat cheese.

———

¼ cup pine nuts
1 medium head red cabbage (about 2 pounds)
¼ cup extra virgin olive oil
2 small shallots, thinly sliced
Juice of 1 lemon
2 tablespoons balsamic vinegar
1 tablespoon capers
Salt and freshly ground black pepper
2 ounces soft goat cheese
2 tablespoons chopped flat-leaf parsley

1. Heat the oven to 300 degrees. Spread the pine nuts on a baking sheet and toast them until they start to brown, 5 to 7 minutes. Let cool.
2. Cut the cabbage into quarters and remove the tough core. Cut the leaves crosswise into very thin strips (julienne), discarding the ribs.
3. Heat the olive oil in a large skillet over medium-high heat. Add the shallots and cabbage strips and toss quickly, just until the strips start to wilt but are still crunchy, about 2 minutes. Add the lemon juice, balsamic vinegar, and capers, tossing until mixed. Remove from the heat and season with salt and pepper to taste.
4. Transfer the salad to a serving bowl. Sprinkle with the toasted pine nuts, then crumble the goat cheese over the top. Garnish with the parsley and serve warm.

SERVES 4

SERVING SUGGESTIONS
Spiced Pecans (p. 82), Red Lentil Soup with Lemon (p. 163), Butternut Squash Soup with Brown Butter (p. 156), Slow-Roasted Duck (p. 475), Quail with Rosemary on Soft Polenta (p. 467), Meat and Spinach Loaf (p. 524), Orange Marmalade Pudding (p. 803), Maria Tillman Jackson Rogers's Carrot Cake (p. 761)

MARCH 18, 1990: "FOOD: WHAT COMES NATURALLY," BY REGINA SCHRAMBLING.

—1990

✑ GIGI SALAD (SHRIMP, BACON, AND GREEN BEAN SALAD)

Jason Epstein, the longtime editorial director at Random House, who contributed food stories to the *Times* for more than two decades, wrote that he "appropriated" this terrific green bean, shrimp, and bacon chopped salad from the Palm Too, a steakhouse in New York City.

Like anyone who makes a good salad, Epstein treated the recipe as if he were a surgeon explaining how to do a transplant. "The beans and onion should be chilled, the tomato left at room temperature, and the shrimp and crumbled bacon kept slightly warm." He added, "It's nothing more than common sense applied to experience. You don't have to be Wolfgang Puck to know that cooked shrimp stored in the refrigerator become tough and lose their flavor, whereas shrimp cooked and left at room temperature actually taste the way shrimp should taste, assuming they're fresh to begin with."

———

I pound green beans, trimmed and cut into I-inch pieces
I large Spanish onion
¾ pound lean bacon
½ lemon
I pound shrimp
I large ripe tomato or 2 medium tomatoes, cored, seeded, and diced
3 tablespoons olive oil
I tablespoon red wine vinegar
Salt and freshly ground black pepper

1. Bring a large pot of generously salted water to a boil. Add the beans and boil until crisp-tender, about 5 minutes. Using a slotted spoon, transfer the beans to a colander, refresh them under cold running water, and then dry them in a salad spinner. Reserve the pot of water.

2. Chop the onion medium-fine, so that it retains some texture. Place the beans and onion in a large bowl, cover with plastic wrap, and chill for about 1 hour.

3. Cut the bacon slices into 1-inch-wide pieces and fry in a skillet until crisp. Remove them from the pan, drain on paper towels, and let cool. Crumble slightly and set aside.

4. Bring the water in the pot back to a boil. Add the lemon half (squeeze it into the water as you drop it in) and shrimp (in the shell). When the water returns to a boil, remove the shrimp and let them cool, then peel them and cut into ¾-inch dice.

5. Remove the onions and beans from the refrigerator. Add the crumbled bacon, chopped shrimp, tomato, and olive oil and mix thoroughly. Add the vinegar and season with salt and pepper.

SERVES 8 AS A FIRST COURSE, 4 AS A MAIN COURSE

COOKING NOTES
Remember that the recipe comes from a steakhouse: if you add the entire Spanish onion, you will live with the smell of this salad for days. I recommend you use half the onion; once you've chopped it, soak the pieces in a bowl of cold water for 20 minutes to lessen their bite, then drain and pat dry before adding to the beans.

VARIATION
Epstein wrote, "To vary the dressing, use 2 tablespoons olive oil and 1 tablespoon hot pepper oil. Hot pepper oil can be bought at most gourmet grocery stores or in any Chinese or Vietnamese market. To make it yourself, add a few dried chiles to a bottle of oil (olive, peanut, or other cooking oil) and refrigerate for a week or so."

SERVING SUGGESTIONS
Ricotta Crostini with Fresh Thyme and Dried Oregano (p. 93), Gently Cooked Salmon with Mashed Potatoes (p. 415), Oliver Clark's Meat Loaf (p. 554), Center-Ring Strip Steak Marinated in Scotch Whiskey (p. 536), New York Strip Steak with Horseradish-Mint Glaze (p. 566), Saratoga Potatoes (p. 273), Sautéed Potatoes with Parsley (p. 283), Chocolate Mousse (p. 820), Brownies (p. 684), Baked Alaska (p. 721), Frozen Lemon Soufflé (p. 725)

NOVEMBER 25, 1990: "IT TAKES A THIEF," BY JASON EPSTEIN. RECIPE ADAPTED FROM GIGI DELMAESTRO, THE GENERAL MANAGER AT THE PALM TOO IN NEW YORK CITY.

—1990

MEZZALUNA SALAD

This salad epitomizes the cooking of the easygoing Italian restaurants that you find on the Upper East Side of Manhattan. Regionally agnostic, with an emphasis on pasta and fresh vegetables, each restaurant seems to have a variation on this snappy, bright salad, after which you eat ravioli with butter and sage or veal Milanese (and then panna cotta, which everyone says they don't want but happily plunge spoons into anyway).

The artichoke and fennel mixture would be a good sauce for fish or base for a sandwich.

_____

6 marinated artichoke hearts, drained and thinly sliced

1/2 small fennel bulb, chopped medium-fine

1 stalk celery, chopped medium-fine

5 tablespoons olive oil

1 bunch arugula, torn into bite-sized pieces

1 small head of radicchio, torn into bite-sized pieces

2 ounces Parmesan cheese, thinly shaved

2 tablespoons balsamic vinegar

Salt and freshly ground black pepper

1. Mix the sliced artichoke hearts with the chopped fennel, celery, and 1 tablespoon olive oil in a medium bowl. Divide this mixture among 4 individual salad bowls. Divide the shredded arugula and radicchio among the bowls. Top each with shaved Parmesan cheese.
2. Pour the remaining 1/4 cup oil over the salads, about 1 tablespoon for each bowl. Pour the balsamic vinegar over the salads, about 1/2 tablespoon for each bowl. (The oil-to-vinegar ratio should be approximately 2 to 1.) Season with salt and pepper.

SERVES 4

SERVING SUGGESTIONS
Claret Cup (p. 12), Rhubarb Bellini (p. 30), Scotch Eggs (p. 62), Brie with Herbs in Bread (p. 69), Soupe à l'Ail (Garlic Soup; p. 130), Spicy, Lemony Clams with Pasta (p. 336), Pasta with Fast Sausage Ragu (p. 343), Breaded Veal Milan-Style (p. 523), Vitello Tonnato (p. 559), Sand Tarts (Pecan Sandies; p. 688), Cornmeal Biscotti (p. 696), Saffron Panna Cotta (p. 845), Ricotta Kisses (p. 852)

NOVEMBER 25, 1990: "IT TAKES A THIEF," BY JASON EPSTEIN. RECIPE ADAPTED FROM MEZZALUNA IN NEW YORK CITY.

—1990

WINTER SLAW WITH LEMON-AND-ORANGE DRESSING

Remember that low-fat diet that swept the nation in the early 1990s, producing dubious foods like low-fat coffee cake and, like all diets (except for the one where you eat less), caused no one to lose weight? There were exactly two good low-fat recipes that came out of that period: this pleasantly spicy slaw and the Moroccan Carrot Salad on p. 187.

_____

1/2 teaspoon grated lemon zest

1/2 teaspoon grated orange zest

1 1/2 tablespoons fresh lemon juice

1 tablespoon orange juice

2 1/2 teaspoons olive oil

1 tablespoon water

1/8 teaspoon cracked black pepper

1/8 teaspoon crushed red pepper flakes

1/8 teaspoon salt, or more to taste

1 tablespoon thinly sliced scallion greens

4 cups shredded Napa cabbage (about 1/2 large head)

1 cup thinly sliced red bell pepper

Whisk together all the ingredients except the cabbage and bell pepper in a small bowl. Toss the cabbage and bell pepper together in a medium bowl, then toss with the dressing.

SERVES 4

SERVING SUGGESTIONS
Hot Cheese Olives (p. 83), Fern Berman's Ginger and Lentil Soup (p. 139), Epigram of Lamb (p. 509), '21' Club Hamburger (p. 536), Moroccan Chicken Smothered in Olives (p. 482), Moroccan Carrot Salad (p. 187), Pepper-Cumin Cookies (p. 695), Lemon Cheese Pie (p. 812), Maple Shortbread Bars (p. 701)

MARCH 7, 1993: "FOOD: SORCERY ON THE SIDE," BY MOLLY O'NEILL. RECIPE ADAPTED FROM JOACHIM SPLICHAL, THE CHEF AND CO-OWNER OF PATINA IN LOS ANGELES AND A CONSULTANT FOR CANYON RANCH SPA IN TUSCON, ARIZONA.

—1993

⌒ ROSEMARY-FETA SALAD

This is a strange and lovable little salad. If you don't like feta, try farmers' cheese, firm ricotta, or a semi-aged sheep's-milk cheese. And when blueberries are out of season, make the salad with dried blueberries or tiny sweet grapes.

————

One 3-inch-long sprig rosemary
¼ cup extra virgin olive oil
½ pound feta cheese, preferably sheep's-milk
1 cup blueberries, or ½ pound seedless
    black grapes, halved
Freshly ground black pepper
3 handfuls torn romaine leaves
1 to 2 handfuls arugula
2 tablespoons raspberry vinegar

1. Combine the rosemary and olive oil in a small saucepan, set over low heat, and warm for 3 minutes. Remove from the heat and let cool.
2. Cut or crumble the feta cheese into ½-inch cubes and place in a bowl. Toss gently with the blueberries and 2 tablespoons rosemary-scented oil. Season liberally with black pepper.
3. Toss the romaine and arugula with the vinegar in a separate bowl, and divide among 4 salad plates. Spoon the feta cheese mixture onto the greens.

SERVES 4

SERVING SUGGESTIONS
Squashed Tomatoes (p. 90), Tom's Chilled Cucumber Soup (p. 117), Basic Corn Chowder (p. 149), Chilled Melon Soup with Toasted Almonds (p. 140), Roast Chicken with Bread Salad (p. 467), Wilted Chard with Pickled Red Onion (p. 261), Potato "Tostones" (Flattened Potatoes; p. 301), Almond-Lemon Macaroons (p. 707)

AUGUST 3, 1994: "A SALAD UNDAUNTED BY AUGUST," BY FLORENCE FABRICANT.

—1994

⌒ FENNEL, ORANGE, WATERCRESS, AND WALNUT SALAD

————

1 bunch watercress
1 large fennel bulb
2 navel oranges
1 tablespoon extra virgin olive oil
Juice of 1 orange, or more to taste
Salt
Freshly ground black pepper
⅓ cup walnuts, toasted and roughly chopped

1. Wash the watercress, cut off the tough stems, and put the leaves in a wide shallow bowl.
2. Cut off and discard the fennel stalks, reserving the fronds. Mince the fronds, and reserve. Cut a thin slice off the bottom of the bulb, then cut it lengthwise in half. Cut the halves crosswise into half-moons, discarding the core. Mix with the watercress.
3. Remove the orange peels by slicing off the top and bottom of the orange. Cut around the oranges with a serrated knife, using a sawing motion to cut off the white pith as well as the peel. Slice the oranges into thin rounds and add to the salad.
4. Mix the olive oil and ⅓ cup orange juice; season with salt. Mix with the salad, adding more orange juice if needed. Add pepper to taste and sprinkle with the minced fennel leaves and walnuts.

SERVES 4

SERVING SUGGESTIONS
James Beard's Champagne Punch (p. 28), Grapefruit Wine (p. 37), Rillettes de Canard (Duck Rillettes; p. 65), Steak au Poivre (p. 573), Filet de Boeuf Rôti (Roast Fillet of Beef) with Sauce Bordelaise (p. 528), Fricassee of Chicken with Tarragon (p. 456), Rabbit in Mustard Sauce (p. 466), Tarte aux Fruits (Fruit or Berry Tart; p. 829), Apple Galette (p. 843), Judson Grill's Berry Clafoutis with Crème Fraîche (p. 844), Chocolate Mousse (p. 820), Almond Cake (p. 777)

SEPTEMBER 28, 1994: "THE WALNUT: GOOD TASTE, GOOD SALES, GOOD FAT," BY SUZANNE HAMLIN.

—1994

☙ MOROCCAN CARROT SALAD

The secret to this salad is the dash of sugar, which acts like a keystone, holding the wayward flavors of cumin, lemon, and coriander in place.

————

I pound carrots, peeled and sliced ½ inch thick
I ½ tablespoons fresh lemon juice
I teaspoon ground cumin
¼ teaspoon ground coriander
½ teaspoon sugar
¼ teaspoon salt
Freshly ground black pepper
2 teaspoons extra virgin olive oil
I tablespoon chopped cilantro

1. Put the carrots in a saucepan with water to cover and bring to a boil, then reduce the heat and simmer for 8 to 12 minutes, until the carrots are tender but slightly firm.
2. Drain the carrots and put in a bowl. Add the lemon juice and mix well. Combine the cumin, coriander, sugar, and salt in a small dish, mix, and then add to the carrots. Toss well. Season with pepper, and fold in the olive oil and cilantro. Cover and allow to marinate for at least 6 hours before serving.

SERVES 4

COOKING NOTE
Florence Fabricant said, "This salad can be made with grated raw carrots instead of cooked carrots. The dressing is the same."

SERVING SUGGESTIONS
Jennifer's Moroccan Tea (p. 33), Seasoned Olives (p. 90), Roasted Feta with Thyme Honey (p. 92), Fern Berman's Ginger and Lentil Soup (p. 139), Moroccan Chicken Smothered in Olives (p. 482), Winter Slaw with Lemon-and-Orange Dressing (p. 185), Pepper-Cumin Cookies (p. 695), Moroccan Rice Pudding (p. 848)

JANUARY 8, 1995: "FOOD: FOR ROOT VEGETABLES, ADD IMAGINATION," BY FLORENCE FABRICANT.

—1995

☙ ARUGULA, PEAR, AND GORGONZOLA SALAD

Next time you're at a restaurant, take a look at the salad menu. Most of the selections will combine some kind of fruit, fresh or dried, with nuts and cheese. These fortified salads started showing up in the 1970s, the era of increasingly layered health food. But it wasn't until the rise of bistro food, around the time of this recipe, that the salads took on a more elegant construction. Arugula, pear, and Gorgonzola is a perfect extraction of 1996. By 2006, this salad would have been roasted beets (not a fruit, but still sweet), goat cheese, and lamb's-quarters. I'd happily eat both in 2016.

————

I large bunch arugula
4 teaspoons white wine vinegar
4 teaspoons olive oil
½ teaspoon sugar
2 tablespoons Gorgonzola dolce (crumble it
   if necessary to measure)
¼ cup pine nuts, toasted
I ripe pear

1. Wash the arugula and remove the tough stems; dry.
2. Whisk together the vinegar, oil, and sugar in a serving bowl. Whisk or crumble (depending on its texture) in the Gorgonzola. Stir in the pine nuts.
3. Peel the pear and cut into bite-sized pieces. Add the pear and arugula to the bowl and toss to dress well.

SERVES 4

COOKING NOTE
Gorgonzola dolce can be very runny, and it may be easier to whisk the cheese than crumble it into the dressing.

SERVING SUGGESTIONS
Smoked Mackerel on Toasts (p. 80), Fried Sage Leaves (p. 87), Fried Olives (p. 87), Ginger Duck (p. 480), Carbonnades à la Flamande (Flemish Beef and Onion Stew; p. 515), Bosiljka Marich's Serbian Torte (p. 751)

APRIL 10, 1996: "PLAIN AND SIMPLE: TUNA TAKES TO ARUGULA," BY MARIAN BURROS.

—1996

DIANE FORLEY'S ARUGULA SALAD WITH ARTICHOKE, RICOTTA SALATA, AND PUMPKIN SEEDS

While this isn't a dish you can whip together, it's a wonderful example of the composed salad—the quilt equivalent of salads, with multiple parts contributing to an ornate and pleasing whole. It is built around the complementary flavors of artichoke and tarragon, with pumpkin-seed oil adding a rich, moss-green veil and shavings of ricotta salata interjecting an eager tang.

———

For the Artichokes
4 large artichokes
1 lemon, halved
2 tablespoons olive oil
2 heads garlic, loose papery skin removed
    and halved horizontally
1½ cups dry white wine
½ cup Champagne vinegar
8 large sprigs tarragon
1 bay leaf
1 sprig thyme
10 black peppercorns
4 cups chicken broth
2 cups water

For the Vinaigrette
¼ cup grapeseed oil
¼ cup extra virgin olive oil
Salt and freshly ground black pepper

For the Salad
1 bunch arugula, tough stems removed
1 head frisée, tough stems removed
¼ pound ricotta salata cheese, thinly sliced or shaved
¼ cup toasted green pumpkin seeds (pepitas)
¼ cup pumpkin-seed oil

1. To prepare the artichokes, slice the top one-third off each one. Remove the outer leaves and rub the artichokes with the lemon.
2. Heat the oil in a pot; add the garlic and sauté for 5 minutes, or until golden. Add the wine and vinegar, bring to a low boil, and boil for 10 minutes, or until reduced by half. Add the herbs, peppercorns, broth,

and water, then add the artichokes and bring to a boil. Reduce the heat and simmer until tender, about 30 minutes.
3. Remove the artichokes and set aside to cool. Strain the braising liquid, discarding the garlic and herbs, and measure 2 cups. Pour the liquid into a small saucepan and simmer until reduced to ½ cup, about 15 minutes. Set aside to cool.
4. Remove the artichoke leaves (save to nibble on) scoop out the chokes, and slice each heart into 8 wedges.
5. To make the vinaigrette, put the reduced braising liquid in a blender and, with the machine on low, drizzle in the oils. Season to taste with salt and pepper.
6. To serve, toss the arugula, frisée, and artichoke hearts with the vinaigrette in a large bowl. Divide among 6 plates. Arrange the cheese on top and sprinkle with the pumpkin seeds. Drizzle the pumpkin-seed oil around the perimeter.

SERVES 6 AS A FIRST COURSE, 4 AS A LIGHT MAIN COURSE

SERVING SUGGESTIONS
Parmesan Crackers (p. 84), Chilled English Pea-Mint Soup (p. 162), Cold Nicarde (Yellow Squash Soup; p. 110), Fish Poached in Buttermilk (p. 419), Breaded Veal Milan-Style (p. 523), Seared Loin Lamb Chops with Olives and Soft Polenta (p. 556), Balducci's Tiramisù (p. 830), Macaroons (p. 681), Lemon Bars (p. 690)

OCTOBER 19, 1997: "FOOD: THE DAY THE CHEFS ATE LUNCH," BY MOLLY O'NEILL. RECIPE ADAPTED FROM DIANE FORLEY, THE CHEF AND OWNER OF VERBENA IN NEW YORK CITY.

—1997

CHOPPED SALAD WITH LEMON ZEST VINAIGRETTE

Molly O'Neill, the *Times Magazine* food columnist who created this recipe, found unexpected drama in zesting lemons. "The rind is packed with an aromatic oil so powerful as to change the odor of a large room (not to mention adding a clean edge to savory dishes and a subtle perfume to bread and cake)," she wrote. "The pith, or albedo, on the other hand, is dense with pectin, a soluble fiber bitter enough to wreak havoc on almost any dish. The cook must therefore tease apart this nearly inextricable mesh of pleasure and pain." Don't get her started on refilling the pepper grinder.

This recipe was published a year before the Microplane zester hit the mainstream and sapped zesting of all its excitement. The pith can really ruin a dish, so if you haven't yet sprung for a Microplane zester—a rasp grater—it's time. Its precision and efficiency make a big difference in this salad. The zest, and the garlic, lend fragrance first to the oil and later to the salad as a whole.

––––––

3 tablespoons olive oil

I tablespoon grated lemon zest

2 teaspoons fresh lemon juice

I clove garlic, minced

$1/2$ teaspoon salt

Freshly ground black pepper

2 tomatoes, cored, seeded, and chopped

2 Kirby cucumbers, peeled, halved, and thinly sliced

I bunch watercress, trimmed and washed

$1/2$ small red onion, thinly sliced

$1/4$ pound ricotta salata cheese, crumbled

2 tablespoons chopped dill

Whisk together the olive oil, lemon zest, lemon juice, garlic, salt, and a few grinds of pepper in a large bowl. Add the tomatoes, cucumbers, watercress, and onion and toss. Add the cheese and dill and toss until well combined.

SERVES 6

SERVING SUGGESTIONS

Salmon and Beet Tartare (p. 420), Asparagus alla Fontina (p. 222), New York Strip Steak with Horseradish-Mint Glaze (p. 566), Rhubarb-Strawberry Mousse (p. 835)

PERIOD DETAIL

Ricotta salata was first mentioned in the *Times* in 1980, in a story by Mimi Sheraton, the restaurant reviewer and reporter. She referred to it as "Easter cheese," a Sardinian specialty made from ewes' early-spring milk.

MAY 24, 1998: "FOOD: DR. PEEL GOOD," BY MOLLY O'NEILL.

—1998

⌖ FENNEL AND APPLE SALAD WITH JUNIPER

Fennel needs either acid or sweetness, or preferably both, to bridle its licorice scent. Here just a few simple ingredients—apple, lemon, and juniper—target the slivers of fennel, underlining the herbal aroma and subduing the medicinal one.

The accompanying story, which I wrote, was about the mandoline, a slide-shaped slicing tool unfamiliar at the time to most home cooks. A few companies made mandolines, but they were uniformly expensive. In the ensuing years, chefs and then home cooks discovered a Japanese company called Benriner that produces a cheap plastic version that works nearly as well as the pricey models. Other mandoline manufacturers have caught on, and now you can get a sturdy and pleasantly small mandoline for less than $20.

Why should you buy one? Certainly not just to make this salad. But mandolines not only make slicing go faster, they can slice ingredients thinner and more consistently than most home cooks can by hand. Extremely thin slices change the way a food feels and tastes, and they allow you to eat foods raw that would otherwise be too dense—Brussels sprouts, for instance. Fennel, which is normally crunchy and solid, becomes ribbony and translucent under a mandoline blade. Apple slices are so delicate you feel as if you're biting into one juicy cell at a time. A mandoline also comes in very handy for recipes such as Crisp Potato Crowns (p. 284), Apple Galette (p. 843), and Sweet Potatoes Anna (p. 297).

––––––

I fennel bulb

I Granny Smith apple

Juice of I lemon

2 tablespoons extra virgin olive oil

Salt and freshly ground black pepper

15 juniper berries

1. Trim the fennel, keeping some of the top feathery fronds to mince for garnish, then cut it in half through the core. Cut the apple into quarters and core it, but do not peel it.

2. Using a mandoline, slice the fennel against the grain as thin as possible. Also on the mandoline, cut the apple into the thinnest-possible slices. Toss together

the fennel, apple, lemon juice, and olive oil in a bowl. Season to taste with salt and pepper.

3. Crush the juniper berries with the side of a knife, then mince. Stir them into the salad, toss, and let sit for 5 minutes.

4. Just before serving, garnish the salad with the minced feathery fennel tops.

SERVES 4

SERVING SUGGESTIONS
Caramelized Onion and Quark Dip (p. 84), Toasts with Walnut Sauce (p. 73), Risotto with Radicchio and Sausage (p. 322), Braised Duck Legs with Pinot Noir Sauce (p. 481), Sand Tarts (Pecan Sandies; p. 688), Walnut Cake with Chocolate Walnut Buttercream (p. 758), Purple Plum Torte (p. 763)

JANUARY 27, 1999: "THE TOOL THAT CHEFS LOVE, AND HOME COOKS BARELY KNOW," BY AMANDA HESSER. RECIPE ADAPTED FROM JEAN-GEORGES VONGERICHTEN, THE CHEF AT JEAN GEORGES IN NEW YORK CITY.

—1999

☞ ASPARAGUS AND BULGUR WITH PRESERVED-LEMON DRESSING

You will taste this and wonder why you (and everyone else, myself included) fail to keep preserved lemons in your fridge, yet always have plenty of ketchup.

————

For the Dressing
1 small preserved lemon (see Cooking Notes)
7 tablespoons olive oil
¼ teaspoons ground cumin
¼ teaspoon freshly ground black pepper
Kosher salt if needed

For the Asparagus and Bulgur
1 pound asparagus
2 tablespoons olive oil
½ red onion, chopped
1 cup bulgur
½ teaspoon kosher salt

2 tablespoons chopped toasted pine nuts for garnish

1. To make the dressing, cut the preserved lemon in half. Chop one half and place it in a blender. Use a spoon to remove the pulp from the remaining half and add only the pulp to the blender. Discard the rind or save it for another use. Add the remaining dressing ingredients except salt to the blender and process until smooth. Season with salt if needed. Set aside.

2. To make the asparagus and bulgur, bring a large pot of salted water to a boil. Add the asparagus and cook until tender, 3 to 4 minutes. Drain and immediately plunge the asparagus into cold water to cool. Drain, then slice the asparagus on a diagonal into ½-inch pieces. Set aside.

3. Place a large skillet over medium-high heat and add the olive oil. Add the onion and cook, stirring, for 1 minute. Add the bulgur and cook, stirring, until lightly toasted, 4 to 5 minutes. Add 2 cups water and the salt and bring to a boil. Cover the skillet, reduce the heat to a simmer, and cook until the water has evaporated and the bulgur is tender, 12 to 15 minutes. Let cool.

4. Place the bulgur in a large serving bowl or on a platter. Toss the asparagus with the dressing and pour it over the bulgur. Sprinkle with the pine nuts.

SERVES 4 TO 6

COOKING NOTES
I changed the way the asparagus is sliced. The 2-inch lengths in the original recipe didn't blend well into the bulgur. I cut the asparagus into ½-inch lengths. If you do this on the bias, it creates a handsome pointed shape.

You can buy preserved lemons or make your own—see p. 610. And feel free to leave out the cardamom.

SERVING SUGGESTIONS
Rhubarb Bellini (p. 30), Heirloom Pea Pancakes (p. 295), The Minimalist's Gravlax (p. 418), Hearth's Fava Bean Salad (p. 202), Spring Lamb Salad with Pea Shoots and Sugar Snap Peas (p. 580), Rhubarb-Ginger Compote (p. 607)

MARCH 7, 1999: "FOOD: CURIOUS YELLOW," BY MOLLY O'NEILL.

—1999

⌐ SHAVED ARTICHOKE SALAD WITH PINE NUTS AND PARMESAN CHEESE

This recipe comes from Judy Rodgers, the owner of Zuni Café—one of San Francisco's most beloved restaurants—and the author of *The Zuni Café Cookbook*, one of the most beloved cookbooks of the early twenty-first century.

For another shaved artichoke salad—one from 1902—see p. 173.

————

10 small artichokes

½ lemon

¼ cup flat-leaf parsley leaves, coarsely chopped

¼ cup pine nuts

½ head radicchio, thinly sliced

¼ cup extra virgin olive oil

Fine sea salt and freshly ground black pepper

¼ cup thin shavings Parmesan cheese

1. Peel away the outer leaves of 1 artichoke until you get down to the tender pale green leaves. Cut off the stem and the spiny tops of the leaves. Cut the artichoke lengthwise in half and remove the fibrous choke. Slice the artichoke as thin as possible and place in a bowl. Squeeze a few drops of lemon juice over it and toss well. Repeat with the remaining artichokes.
2. Add the parsley, pine nuts, and radicchio to the bowl. Pour the olive oil over the salad and sprinkle with a little salt and pepper. Toss to coat. Add the cheese and toss gently. Taste for seasoning.

SERVES 4

SERVING SUGGESTIONS

For a mostly Rodgers meal, start with this salad and follow it with Roast Chicken with Bread Salad (p. 467). Punctuate the dinner with a dessert by one of Rodgers's San Francisco neighbors: Chez Panisse Meyer Lemon Meringue Pie (p. 833) or Daniel Patterson's Chamomile and Almond Cake (p. 786).

MARCH 10, 1999: "SO TOUGH IN THE FIELD, SUCH A BREEZE IN THE KITCHEN," BY AMANDA HESSER. RECIPE ADAPTED FROM JUDY RODGERS, THE CHEF AND OWNER OF ZUNI CAFÉ IN SAN FRANCISCO.

—1999

⌐ DOCKS COLESLAW

Coleslaw is an ancient salad whose name comes from the Dutch words *kool*—or cabbage—and *sla*—or salad. Molly O'Neill, a columnist for the Sunday *Magazine*, who included this recipe in a piece on coleslaw, wrote that the addition of mayonnaise is an American innovation, one facilitated by Richard Hellmann, a New York deli owner. In 1912, Hellmann started selling the bottled form of mayonnaise we all know and love. But in addition to mayonnaise, there are other distinguishing characteristics of American coleslaw, all present here: cider vinegar, sugar, and buttermilk (or sometimes sour cream).

————

½ green apple, peeled and cored

½ green bell pepper, seeded

1 stalk celery, coarsely chopped

¼ cup cider vinegar

1½ tablespoons sugar

1 teaspoon celery seeds

1 teaspoon caraway seeds

½ teaspoon garlic powder

½ teaspoon onion powder

1½ teaspoons kosher salt

½ teaspoon freshly ground black pepper

1¾ cups mayonnaise, preferably homemade (p. 465)

½ cup buttermilk

1 medium green cabbage (about 2½ pounds), quartered, cored, and very finely sliced

1½ cups shredded red cabbage

1 carrot, peeled and shredded

1. Combine the apple, bell pepper, and celery in a food processor and pulse until very finely chopped. Transfer to a bowl and add the vinegar, sugar, celery seeds, caraway seeds, garlic powder, onion powder, salt, and pepper. Stir to combine, and let stand for 10 minutes.
2. Stir in the mayonnaise and buttermilk, and refrigerate for 1 hour.
3. Combine the cabbages and carrot in a bowl, add half the dressing, and toss. Add more dressing to taste. (The slaw is best if refrigerated for at least 1 hour before serving.)

SERVES 12

This slaw holds up well for 3 days.

If you're not cooking for 12, you can halve the recipe.

SERVING SUGGESTIONS

Crab Cakes Baltimore-Style (p. 407), Lobster Roll (p. 368), '21' Club Hamburger (p. 536), French Fries (p. 292), North Carolina–Style Pulled Pork (p. 550), Gratin of Chipotle Cream and Yams (p. 291), Boston Baked Beans (p. 274), Ice Cream Pie (p. 726), Jellied Strawberry Pie (p. 811)

AUGUST 22, 1999: "FOOD: SLAW AND ORDER," BY MOLLY O'NEILL. RECIPE ADAPTED FROM STEVE GREENFIELD, CHEF AT DOCKS OYSTER BAR AND SEAFOOD GRILL IN NEW YORK CITY.

—1999

DIANA VREELAND'S SALADE PARISIENNE

Not all salads are sanctimonious. This one is a hedonist's delight—a messy, densely composed gathering of vegetables, bound with oil, anchovy, eggs, and pickles, loads of each. An unusual detail is the tuna, which is added to the dressing for seasoning, just as you might toss in a few capers. Elsa Maxwell, the legendary hostess who was friends with everyone from the Duchess of Windsor to C. Z. Guest, published this recipe by Diana Vreeland in her 1957 book *How to Do It, or the Lively Art of Entertaining.*

———

For the Vegetables

1½ cups each of the following: thinly sliced beets, new potatoes, and celery root, cooked

3 tablespoons white wine vinegar

½ cup olive oil

Salt and freshly ground black pepper

For the Vinaigrette

5 hard-boiled eggs, white and yolks separated

2 tablespoons anchovy paste

¼ cup olive oil

1 teaspoon Dijon mustard

2 tablespoons tarragon vinegar

¼ cup water-packed canned tuna, drained and pulled into bite-sized pieces

2 tablespoons cornichons or other sour pickles cut into tiny dice

1½ teaspoons chopped tarragon

1. Toss the vegetables with the vinegar and olive oil, season with salt and pepper, and let sit for 1 hour.
2. To make the vinaigrette, mash the egg yolks through a fine sieve into a bowl. Blend in the anchovy paste and whisk in the olive oil, stirring until smooth. Finely chop the egg whites. Add the mustard, tarragon vinegar, tuna, pickles, egg whites, and tarragon to the yolk mixture.
3. Drain the vegetables, place in a bowl, dress with the vinaigrette, and mix lightly.

SERVES 6

COOKING NOTES

I boiled the potatoes whole and the celery root peeled and quartered.

The beets I tossed with olive oil and salt and roasted, wrapped in foil, for an hour at 350 degrees.

SERVING SUGGESTIONS

Maxwell suggested serving this with sautéed sweetbreads (a recipe for fried sweetbreads lies on p. 506). You could also have the salad as a first course, or alongside a grilled porterhouse steak. Some other ideas: Grapefruit Wine (p. 37), James Beard's Champagne Punch (p. 28), Kir Royale 38 (p. 28), Park Avenue Cocktail (p. 19), Rillettes de Canard (Duck Rillettes; p. 65), Steak au Poivre (p. 573), Filet de Boeuf Rôti (Roast Fillet of Beef) with Sauce Bordelaise (p. 528), Fricassee of Chicken with Tarragon (p. 456), Rabbit in Mustard Sauce (p. 466), Tarte aux Fruits (Fruit or Berry Tart; p. 829), Apple Galette (p. 843), Judson Grill's Berry Clafoutis with Crème Fraîche (p. 844), Chocolate Mousse (p. 820), Almond Cake (p. 777).

JANUARY 30, 2000: "ENTERTAINING: ELSA ON MY MIND," BY WILLIAM NORWICH. RECIPE ADAPTED FROM *HOW TO DO IT* BY ELSA MAXWELL.

—2000

AVOCADO AND BEET SALAD WITH CITRUS VINAIGRETTE

The turn of the century was the time when sweet Chiogga and golden yellow beets became a mainstay in farmers' markets, and chefs began larding their menus with beets. Marian Burros, a longtime food reporter at the *Times* who wrote the accompanying story, asked Alice Waters, the owner of Chez Panisse, how her customers were warming to the vegetable. "They never send beets back," Waters responded, "and if they did, I would go out there and tell them to eat them."

6 medium red or golden beets
Salt and freshly ground black pepper
1 tablespoon red wine vinegar
¾ cup plus 1 tablespoon extra virgin olive oil
1 large shallot, finely diced
2 tablespoons white wine vinegar
1 tablespoon fresh lemon juice (zest the lemon first)
1 tablespoon fresh orange juice
1 tablespoon chopped chervil, plus sprigs for garnish
¼ teaspoon grated lemon zest
¼ teaspoon grated orange zest
2 small or 1 large firm but ripe avocados

1. Heat the oven to 400 degrees. Trim and wash the beets, and put them in a baking dish. Add a splash of water, cover tightly, and roast for 45 to 60 minutes, until tender. Let cool.
2. Peel the beets and cut into wedges. Place in a bowl and season with salt and pepper. Add the red wine vinegar and 1 tablespoon olive oil and toss gently.
3. Combine the shallot with the white wine vinegar, lemon and orange juices, and a pinch of salt in a bowl. Macerate for 15 minutes.
4. Whisk the ¾ cup olive oil into the shallots, and stir in the chervil and zest. Adjust the seasoning.
5. Cut the avocados lengthwise in half and remove the pits. Leaving the skin intact, cut the flesh of the avocados lengthwise into ¼-inch-thick slices. Scoop out the slices with a large spoon and arrange on a platter or individual dishes. Season with salt and pepper. Arrange the beets on top and drizzle with the shallot mixture. Garnish with chervil sprigs.

SERVES 4

SERVING SUGGESTIONS

Fried Olives (p. 87), Olive Oil–Tuna Spread with Lemon and Oregano (p. 95), Halibut with Parsley-Shellfish Sauce (p. 425), T-Bone Steak with 6666 Soppin' Sauce (p. 539), Lamb Shoulder Chops with Anchovy and Mint Butter (p. 567), Pineapple Carpaccio with Lime Sorbet (p. 842), David Eyre's Pancake (p. 813), Chocolate Quakes (p. 702)

MAY 31, 2000: "WHO PUT THE BEET IN THE MOUSSELINE?" BY MARIAN BURROS. RECIPE ADAPTED FROM *THE CHEZ PANISSE CAFÉ COOKBOOK*, BY ALICE WATERS, ET AL.

—2000

A LOOSE INTERPRETATION OF COBB SALAD

1 teaspoon peanut oil
3 slices prosciutto
2 teaspoons fresh lemon juice
½ teaspoon Dijon mustard
Sea salt and freshly ground black pepper
3 tablespoons extra virgin olive oil
½ ripe avocado
1 cup roughly chopped frisée
1 cup roughly chopped curly green-leaf lettuce
1 cup roughly chopped watercress
1 thin scallion, very thinly sliced
1 large hard-boiled egg

1. Place a medium sauté pan over medium-high heat. Add the peanut oil, then the slices of prosciutto, and sauté until crisped and browned on both sides, about 2 minutes. Remove to a dish lined with a paper towel. Set aside.
2. Whisk together the lemon juice, mustard, and a large pinch each of salt and pepper in a bowl. Slowly whisk in the olive oil until emulsified. Taste and adjust the seasoning; it should be intense.
3. Slice the avocado half lengthwise into ¼-inch wedges, then cut crosswise into ¼-inch triangular pieces. Chop the prosciutto into ¼-inch squares.
4. Combine the lettuces, watercress, scallion, avocado, and prosciutto in a large serving bowl. Pour half the dressing on top and toss to coat, adding more if necessary. Taste and adjust the seasoning. Using the back of

a spoon, press the egg, in halves, through a fine sieve over the salad, letting it fall evenly to cover the salad. Let sit for 15 minutes before serving.

SERVES 4

SERVING SUGGESTIONS
Jay Grelen's Southern Iced Tea (p. 27), Tom's Chilled Cucumber Soup (p. 117), Brie with Herbs in Bread (p. 69), Flat-and-Chewy Chocolate Chip Cookies (p. 706)

JUNE 14, 2000: "CRITIC'S NOTEBOOK: THE CHOPPED SALAD, REFINED," BY AMANDA HESSER.

—2000

CABBAGE SALAD WITH TOASTED CORIANDER AND CUMIN MAYONNAISE

This really is better with homemade mayonnaise, which is eggier than store-bought. But I'll look the other way if you cheat and add the spices to store-bought mayo. Rereading this recipe, I thought I might even add a little sour cream to sharpen up the flavors next time.

I teaspoon coriander seeds

I teaspoon cumin seeds

3 cups thinly shredded Savoy cabbage

2 cups thinly shredded red cabbage

I large egg yolk

2 tablespoons cider vinegar, or more to taste

I shallot, minced

I tablespoon thinly sliced chives

Sea salt and freshly ground black pepper

1¼ cups vegetable oil

1. Toast the coriander seeds and cumin seeds in a small skillet over high heat (or in a microwave oven at full power) just until fragrant. Grind them together using a mortar and pestle or a spice/coffee grinder, and set aside.

2. Combine the savoy cabbage and red cabbage in a large bowl, and set aside.

3. To prepare the mayonnaise, whisk together the egg yolk, vinegar, shallot, chives, coriander and cumin, and a large pinch each of salt and pepper in a small bowl. Beginning a drop at a time, whisk in the oil; as it emulsifies, begin to add the oil a little faster, in a slow steady stream. When the mixture is thick, whisk in more vinegar to taste; the mayonnaise should be highly seasoned.

4. Fold ⅓ cup mayonnaise into the cabbage. There should be enough to coat the cabbage generously; add more if necessary. Cover and refrigerate for at least an hour.

5. Before serving, adjust the seasoning, adding more salt and/or vinegar as needed.

SERVES 4

SERVING SUGGESTIONS
Squashed Tomatoes (p. 90), Pan con Tomate (p. 91), Fried Olives (p. 87), Lamb Shoulder Chops with Anchovy and Mint Butter (p. 567), Fruit Crostatas (p. 855), Maida's Blueberry Crumb Cake (p. 632), Coeur à la Crème with Rhubarb Sauce (p. 864), Pear Upside-Down Cake (p. 772)

AUGUST 2, 2000: "NOT YOUR MOTHER'S MAYONNAISE: A GREAT FRENCH SAUCE FOR SUMMER," BY AMANDA HESSER.

—2000

PUNTARELLE WITH ANCHOVIES

Puntarelle, a pleasantly bitter, faintly peppery Italian green is sadly not yet common here. Until it is, we have chicory as a substitute, and it works commendably in this dish, in a combination reminiscent of Caesar salad, only gutsier. If you are ever in Rome during the fall, puntarelle salads will be on practically every menu, and if you go to the market at the Campo dei Fiori, you can find farmers trimming and bunching the jagged, curly leaves.

I head puntarelle (about I pound)

3 anchovy fillets

I clove garlic

1½ tablespoons red wine vinegar

Salt and freshly ground black pepper
¼ cup extra virgin olive oil

1. Clean the puntarelle, removing the tough outer leaves. Cut off the tough base and separate the stalks. Wash and dry well, then cut lengthwise into thin strips. Soak in cold water for 2 to 3 hours to keep the leaves crisp.

2. Drain the puntarelle, dry, and place in a large salad bowl.

3. Place the anchovies and garlic in a mortar and use the pestle to mash until creamy and smooth. Pour in the vinegar to loosen the mixture, then transfer to a bowl and add salt and pepper to taste. Whisk in the oil until emulsified.

4. Pour the dressing over the puntarelle and toss well.

SERVES 4

COOKING NOTE
If you can't get puntarelle, use the leaves of half a large head of chicory, and cut them into 1½-inch pieces.

SERVING SUGGESTIONS
Parmesan Crackers (p. 84), Toasts with Walnut Sauce (p. 73), Ricotta Crostini with Fresh Thyme and Dried Oregano (p. 93), Veal Chops with Sage (p. 564), Coda alla Vaccinara (Oxtail Braised with Tomato and Celery; p. 562), Panna Cotta (p. 840), Canestrelli (Shortbread from Ovada; p. 692), Limoncello (p. 38)

FEBRUARY 14, 2001: "THE HOT NEW GREEN ON NEW YORK'S PLATE," BY PAULA DISBROWE. RECIPE ADAPTED FROM SANDRO'S IN NEW YORK CITY.

—2001

☞ CHOPPED SALAD OF ROMAINE, ARUGULA, DILL, AND LEMON

———

4 cups thinly sliced (¼-inch-wide) romaine leaves
2 cups packed arugula, chopped into ½-inch pieces
1½ tablespoons chopped dill
⅓ cup thinly sliced scallions
Coarse sea or kosher salt and freshly ground black pepper

1 tablespoon grated lemon zest
1 tablespoon fresh lemon juice
¼ cup extra virgin olive oil

Mix together the romaine, arugula, dill, and scallions in a salad bowl. Sprinkle with salt and grind pepper on top. Sprinkle the lemon zest and juice over the leaves. Pour on the olive oil. Using a salad fork and spoon, mix the leaves together until all the strips of lettuce are coated and the flavors are blended. Taste a leaf, and season again with salt, pepper, lemon juice, and/or more oil, whatever is needed.

SERVES 4

SERVING SUGGESTIONS
Serve with Niçoise olives, country bread, and slices of feta or aged goat cheese, sprinkled with olive oil and black pepper. Or: Feta Spread (p. 71), Marina Anagnostou's Spanakopetes (Spinach Triangles; p. 63), Shrimp Baked with Feta Cheese, Greek-Style (p. 397), Shrimp in Green Sauce (p. 430), Hazelnut Baklava (p. 706), Peach Balls (p. 804).

SEPTEMBER 2, 2001: "FOOD DIARY: THE REGAL GOURMET," BY AMANDA HESSER.

—2001

☞ FENNEL AND BLOOD ORANGE SALAD

One of the things that good chefs do—one that separates them from us—is put time and thought into emphasizing specific flavors in a dish. Not just their showstoppers, but every dish on their menu, including salads, like this one by Kurt Gutenbrunner, the chef at Wallsé in Manhattan. When you taste a dozen-ingredient dish like this, you experience flavors at both a global and granular level. To create the spectrum of flavors here, you toast walnuts to draw out their loamy oils and then toss them with walnut oil to redouble it. You slice fennel and blend it with Pernod and lemon juice to sharpen and reinforce the blow of licorice. And at the very end, once you've mixed the walnuts and fennel with the orange, shallots, and mint, you add a little lime zest to underline the dish's citric foundation. When you taste the salad, you may be surprised by the intensity and tautness of the flavors—but now you'll know how they were achieved.

———————

¼ cup very coarsely chopped walnuts

I teaspoon walnut oil

I medium-to-large fennel bulb, stems trimmed

Salt and freshly ground black pepper

Juice of I lemon

I tablespoon Pernod

2 large blood oranges

I tablespoon paper-thin slices shallot

10 mint leaves

2 tablespoons extra virgin olive oil

I teaspoon grated lime zest

1. Place the walnuts in a dry skillet and toast over medium heat, stirring until fragrant. Toss with the walnut oil, and set aside.

2. Slice about ½ inch from the bottom of the fennel and discard. Slice the fennel very fine on a mandoline, starting with the flat bottom. Put in a bowl, season with salt and pepper, and add the lemon juice and Pernod.

3. Slice off the tops and bottoms of the oranges. Cut around the oranges to remove all the peel and white pith. Holding the peeled fruit over the bowl of fennel, use a sharp knife to cut the sections from the membranes, letting them drop into the bowl. Discard the membranes.

4. Add the shallots, mint leaves, olive oil, and walnuts and toss gently. Sprinkle on the lime zest.

SERVES 3

COOKING NOTES

This needs to be served right away, or the fennel gets limp and the rest of the salad gets soggy.

Yes, it's annoying that this serves 3—make it when your fourth cancels! (Or double it for a party of 6.)

SERVING SUGGESTIONS

Crostini Romani (p. 77), Risotto with Radicchio and Sausage (p. 322), Oven-Roasted Branzino with Hazelnut Picada (p. 441), Roast Chicken with Bread Salad (p. 467), Slow-Roasted Duck (p. 475), Sautéed Potatoes with Parsley (p. 283), Tortoni (p. 720), Filbert Torte (p. 742), De Luxe Cheesecake (p. 748), Zabaglione (p. 813), Cornmeal Biscotti (p. 696)

JANUARY 23, 2002: "THE CHEF," BY FLORENCE FABRICANT AND KURT GUTENBRUNNER, THE CHEF AND OWNER OF WALLSÉ IN NEW YORK CITY.

—2002

WILTED RED CABBAGE SALAD

Cabbage can be wilted with either heat or acid, and in this case it's the latter, a sprinkling of red wine vinegar that softens the leaves. Slivers of fried bacon are added, but that's where the similarities between this and most red cabbage salads stop. The leaves, slackened from the vinegar but still a bit crunchy, are then slicked with lingonberry preserves and olive and hazelnut oils. On top of the salad goes a tuft of mâche, a beacon of urbanity on a country dish.

———————

I small head red cabbage (about 1½ pounds), outer leaves discarded, quartered, cored, and sliced paper-thin

5 tablespoons red wine vinegar

I teaspoon sugar

Salt and freshly ground black pepper

4 medium-thick slices country bacon, diced

2 tablespoons lingonberry or red currant preserves

I tablespoon extra virgin olive oil

I tablespoon hazelnut oil

I bunch mâche, leaves plucked from stems

1. Place the cabbage in a bowl and toss with the vinegar, sugar, 2 teaspoons salt, and pepper to taste. Set aside for 30 minutes to wilt.

2. Fry the bacon in a large skillet over medium heat until very lightly browned. Drain on paper towels.

3. Fold the lingonberry preserves into the wilted cabbage. Fold in the olive oil and hazelnut oil. Add additional salt and pepper if needed.

4. Divide the cabbage among 6 salad plates, leaving about ¼ cup of the liquid in the bowl. Toss the mâche with the liquid, and top the cabbage with the bacon and mâche.

SERVES 6

Kurt Gutenbrunner, the chef and owner of Wallsé in Manhattan, who came up with this salad, suggested serving it with a slice of foie gras terrine, which surely you have hanging around in your fridge. Or, if you prefer to accompany it with something like marinated herring, he said, you can add a little diced cooked beets and "a pinch of caraway." Here are some other ideas: Smoked Mackerel on Toasts (p. 80), Roasted Squash Soup with Cumin (p. 147), Veal Goulash with Spaetzle (p. 525), Boeuf Bourguignon I (p. 516), Poached Pears in Brandy and Red Wine (p. 832), Figs in Whiskey (p. 859), Olive Oil and Apple Cider Cake (p. 771).

JANUARY 23, 2002: "THE CHEF," BY FLORENCE FABRICANT AND KURT GUTENBRUNNER, THE CHEF AND OWNER OF WALLSÉ IN NEW YORK CITY.

—2002

✐ AIRPLANE SALAD

Not one to tolerate the "food" served on airplanes, I like to pack my own. This salad travels well at 30,000 feet.

————

I head Bibb lettuce, leaves torn into several pieces each
One 16-ounce can white beans, drained and rinsed
2 cups cherry tomatoes, halved
¼ pound smoked mackerel or smoked trout,
    pulled into shreds (½ cup)
I tablespoon aged sherry vinegar
I teaspoon Dijon mustard
Sea salt and freshly ground black pepper
¼ cup excellent olive oil

1. Combine the lettuce, white beans, tomatoes, and shredded mackerel in a large bowl.
2. Whisk together the vinegar, mustard, and a little salt and pepper in a small bowl. Add the oil a little at a time, whisking constantly so that the dressing emulsifies and thickens. Season to taste. Pour the dressing over the salad and toss to coat. Add more black pepper if desired. (If flying, pack into a plastic container.)

SERVES 4 AS A FIRST COURSE, 2 AS A MAIN COURSE

Salted and Deviled Almonds (p. 51), Brie with Herbs in Bread (p. 69), Cold Nicarde (Yellow Squash Soup; p. 110), Brownies (p. 684), Flat-and-Chewy Chocolate Chip Cookies (p. 706)

JUNE 16, 2002: "FOOD DIARY: THE SHELTERING SKY," BY AMANDA HESSER.

—2002

✐ WATERMELON AND TOMATO SALAD

Watermelon and tomato aren't an intuitive pairing until you taste them together, and then they seem like siblings, separated at birth. As Mark Bittman wrote of them, "Their distinctions become a little blurry and each masquerades as the other. The tomato's acidity becomes tamed, as does the melon's sweetness; their juices mingle, and even their flesh seems to meld."

There are two secrets to this recipe and they aren't the watermelon and the tomato. One is the crude bite of cayenne, added at your discretion (don't be shy), and the other is the showering of cilantro, enough that it becomes both a leafy green and an herb, not a mere garnish. Parsley is offered as an alternative to the cilantro; don't even consider it.

————

2½ cups seedless watermelon cut into I-inch cubes
    or balls (cut it over a bowl to catch the juice
    and reserve it)
1½ cups cherry or grape tomatoes, cut in half
½ cup finely diced or crumbled Stilton, Gorgonzola,
    Roquefort, or Maytag Blue cheese
½ cup minced scallions
Salt
2 tablespoons extra virgin olive oil
2 tablespoons sherry vinegar
Pinch of cayenne pepper
½ cup roughly chopped cilantro or parsley

1. Combine the watermelon, tomato, cheese, scallions, and salt to taste in a bowl.
2. Whisk or blend together about 2 tablespoons of the watermelon juice, the oil, vinegar, and cayenne. Dress

the salad with this mixture and garnish with cilantro. Do not refrigerate, and serve within 30 minutes.

SERVES 4

SERVING SUGGESTIONS
Cucumber–Goat Cheese Dip with Radishes and Scallions (p. 70), Feta Spread (p. 71), Roasted Salmon with Herb Vinaigrette (p. 430), Pork Burgers (p. 566), Grilled Hanger Steak (p. 551), Italian Roast Potatoes (p. 300), Strawberry Sorbet (p. 732)

PERIOD DETAIL
The combination of watermelon and tomato was first popularized by Geoffrey Zakarian, a chef in Manhattan, a few years before this recipe appeared.

JULY 24, 2002: "THE MINIMALIST: GROUNDS FOR MARRIAGE," BY MARK BITTMAN.

—2002

✎ JUDY RODGERS'S WARM BREAD SALAD

Panzanella, an Italian peasant tomato salad bulked up with bread to make it go further, became briefly, wildly popular in the late 1990s. In a search of the archives for a great version of the recipe to run in this book, I came up nearly empty-handed, but I did find this nifty bread salad seasoned with currants, pine nuts, scallions, and arugula—a combination more interesting than panzanella.

———

1 tablespoon dried currants
1 tablespoon red wine vinegar
2 tablespoons pine nuts
8 to 10 ounces slightly stale ciabatta or
     other open-textured white bread
½ cup extra virgin olive oil
About 1½ tablespoons Champagne vinegar
     or white wine vinegar
Salt and coarsely ground black pepper
3 cloves garlic, slivered
¼ cup thinly sliced scallions
¼ cup chicken broth or lightly salted water
4 cups arugula or mustard greens, rinsed and dried

1. Place the currants in a small dish, add the red wine vinegar and 1 tablespoon warm water, and set aside to plump.
2. Heat the broiler. Place the pine nuts in a small baking dish and toast under the broiler until very lightly colored. Set aside. (Leave the broiler on.)
3. Cut the bread into 3 or 4 large chunks. Closely trim off most of the crust (reserve, if desired, to toast and use for bread crumbs or to float in a soup). Brush the bread all over with 2 tablespoons olive oil. Briefly broil the bread chunks, turning occasionally, until crisp and golden on the surface. Trim off any charred tips, and tear the chunks into irregular pieces, from 2-inch wads to large crumbs. (You should have 4 cups.) Place in a wide metal, glass, or ceramic salad bowl.
4. Whisk ¼ cup olive oil with 1½ tablespoons Champagne vinegar. Season with salt and pepper. Drizzle 1½ tablespoons of this dressing over the bread and toss.
5. Place 1 tablespoon olive oil in a small skillet. Add the garlic and scallions and cook, stirring constantly, over low heat until softened but not colored. Add to the bread and fold in. Drain the currants and fold in. Add the pine nuts and fold in. Drizzle the salad with the broth and fold in. Taste a couple of pieces of bread, and add a little more vinegar, salt, and/or pepper if necessary. Toss well, and transfer to a 1-quart baking dish. (Do not wash the salad bowl.)
6. Heat the oven to 450 degrees. Place the bread salad in the oven, turn off the heat, and leave for 15 minutes. Return the salad to the bowl. Add the greens, the remaining vinaigrette, and enough of the remaining tablespoon of olive oil so bread is not dry. Toss again.

SERVES 4

SERVING SUGGESTIONS
Grapefruit Wine (p. 37), Roasted Feta with Thyme Honey (p. 92), Cream of Carrot Soup (p. 119), Ventresca Tuna Salad (p. 426), Buttermilk Roast Chicken (p. 493), Roasted Cauliflower (p. 248), Bolzano Apple Cake (p. 783)

AUGUST 14, 2002: "THE CHEF: JUDY RODGERS: EVERY BLESSED CRUMB," BY FLORENCE FABRICANT. RECIPE ADAPTED FROM JUDY RODGERS, THE CHEF AND OWNER OF ZUNI CAFÉ IN SAN FRANCISCO.

—2002

TOMATO, FIG, GOAT CHEESE, BASIL, AND OLIVE SALAD WITH BALSAMIC VINAIGRETTE

AUGUST 28, 2002: "EATING WELL: LOCAL HEROES," BY MARIAN BURROS. RECIPE ADAPTED FROM ANNE ROSEN-ZWEIG, THE CHEF AND OWNER OF INSIDE IN NEW YORK CITY.

—2002

2 tablespoons balsamic vinegar

¼ cup olive oil

4 cups frisée, broken into pieces

2 cups arugula, tough stems removed,
    torn into bite-sized pieces

Salt and freshly ground black pepper

4 large tomatoes, cored and cut into thin wedges

⅓ cup Calamata olives, pitted and sliced

A handful of basil leaves, torn

6 figs (still a little firm, not overripe), cut into quarters

3 ounces fresh goat cheese, crumbled

1. Put the balsamic vinegar in a bowl and whisk in the oil.

2. Combine the frisee and arugula in a large salad bowl. Season with salt and pepper and dress with half the vinaigrette; adjust the seasoning as needed. Spread the greens on a large platter.

3. Toss the tomatoes, olives, and basil in the salad bowl, season with salt and pepper, and dress with the remaining vinaigrette. Taste and adjust the seasoning. Top the greens with this mixture and scatter the figs and crumbled goat cheese on top.

SERVES 8 AS A FIRST COURSE, 4 TO 6 AS A MAIN COURSE

COOKING NOTES

This is a giant salad, and if you mix all of the ingredients together at once, as the original recipe instructed, the delicate ones get trampled. So I reconstructed the order of assembly—dressing the greens first, followed by the tomatoes and olives, and topping the salad with the fragile figs and goat cheese.

SERVING SUGGESTIONS

Chilled Corn Soup with Honeydew Polka Dots (p. 153), Jonathan Waxman's Red Pepper Pancakes (p. 228), Brined and Roasted Pork Belly (p. 556), Beer-Can Chicken (p. 473), Spicy, Supercrunchy Fried Chicken (p. 490), Roasted Potato Salad (p. 285), Fresh Blueberry Buckle (p. 815), Peach Balls (p. 804)

BLOOD ORANGE, DATE, AND PARMESAN SALAD WITH ALMOND OIL

This was the first of several recipes Suzanne Goin, the chef and co-owner of A.O.C. and Lucques in Los Angeles, created for a series I wrote in the *Times* (see Pork Burgers on p. 566 and Caramelized Chocolate Bread Pudding on p. 852 for others). Her blood orange, date, and Parmesan salad is a combination of sweet and salty in the extreme, and a marvelous interplay of textures.

"I love food where you get all different senses," she told me. "There is a little richness from the dates, spice from the arugula, sweetness from the orange, salt from the cheese. It's sweet, then chewy."

It's become a cliché to say that you must use the best-quality ingredients, but for this dish in particular, a handful of raw ingredients is all you have. None are changed by cooking, and none can be concealed. If the arugula is limp, the salad will be lifeless. If the dates are dry, they will be a chewy distraction. If the almond oil is not a pure extraction, it will fall flat.

Goin uses almond oil from France and locally grown arugula. She orders her Deglet Noor dates from the Coachella Valley, southeast of Los Angeles. Most supermarket Deglet Noors are dry and stringy, so it's worth seeking out a Middle Eastern market. Rich, pillowy Medjool dates can be substituted, but it's best to cut them into smaller slivers so you don't get a mouthful of date.

The trick of this dish is in the layering. Goin does it piece by piece, beginning with the arugula. She lays a few leaves down on a plate, using them to map out the area of the plate she wants the salad to take up. Then she places a few date halves on top and clusters the slices of blood orange near the center. She lays the pieces of cheese on top, a bit more sparsely, as the flavor of one slice goes a long way. Then she slips a few almonds in before beginning the layering process all over.

It is a low-lying salad. At the very end, she sprinkles freshly ground black pepper around the edges and dresses it with almond oil so that it glistens.

Goin worked at Al Forno in Providence, RI, while she attended Brown University. She said George Germon and Johanne Killeen, the chefs, "used to say that the food should look like it was born on the plate, and I've always kept that idea with me." When this dish is done right, that's exactly the way it appears.

———

3 blood oranges

30 small arugula leaves

8 moist fresh Deglet Noor dates (preferably from a Middle Eastern market), pitted and cut in two, or 4 Medjool dates (from a Middle Eastern market), quartered

12 to 16 large paper-thin slices Parmesan cheese

20 toasted almonds

3 tablespoons pure almond or hazelnut oil

Freshly ground black pepper

1. Slice the stem and flower ends from the oranges. Using a sharp paring knife and working from top to bottom, slice off the peel and white pith. Thinly slice each orange crosswise: you should get 8 to 10 slices from each orange.

2. Scatter one-third of the arugula leaves on a platter. Then layer the rest of the ingredients, placing one-third of the dates on top of and around the arugula, then the slices of orange and a few slices of cheese, and the almonds. Continue layering until all the ingredients mingle but are not piled up. Sprinkle with the oil and season lightly with pepper.

SERVES 4

SERVING SUGGESTIONS

Jennifer's Moroccan Tea (p. 33), Fried Olives (p. 87), Seasoned Olives (p. 90), Moroccan Carrot Salad (p. 187), Moroccan Chicken Smothered in Olives (p. 482), Pepper-Cumin Cookies (p. 695), Banana Meringue Steamed Custard (p. 812), Saffron Panna Cotta (p. 845)

MAY 7, 2003: "THE CHEF: SUZANNE GOIN: A SALAD THAT'S BORN ON THE PLATE," BY AMANDA HESSER. RECIPE ADAPTED FROM SUZANNE GOIN, THE CHEF AND CO-OWNER OF LUCQUES AND A.O.C. IN LOS ANGELES.

—2003

ICEBERG LETTUCE WITH SMOKED BACON AND BUTTERMILK DRESSING

Iceberg lettuce, which took a brutal bashing in the higher culinary spheres in the late twentieth century, bounced back in restaurants in the twenty-first. We came to accept that iceberg lettuce tastes like nothing, and we still adore it. We like its splintery crispness and watery bursts, and we especially like the way it slices as cleanly as bread. And what is so wrong with a sensible, unobtrusive conduit for a creamy dressing? Taste this and tell me.

———

2 heads iceberg lettuce

8 ripe plum tomatoes, thinly sliced

2 cups Buttermilk Herb dressing (recipe follows)

12 slices smoked bacon, cut into ½-inch dice (about 2 cups) and fried

1. Remove the loose outer leaves from the heads of iceberg, and cut each head into 4 wedges. Place in the freezer for 10 minutes, along with 4 serving plates.

2. Remove the chilled plates and arrange a circle of sliced tomatoes on each one. Set a lettuce wedge in the center of each plate. Nap with ¼ cup dressing. Sprinkle some of the bacon over each wedge.

SERVES 8

BUTTERMILK HERB DRESSING

1½ cups sour cream

1 cup buttermilk

½ cup Hellmann's (Best Foods) mayonnaise

½ cup freshly grated Asiago or Parmesan cheese

2 tablespoons chopped basil

2 tablespoons chopped chives

4 teaspoons finely chopped flat-leaf parsley

4 teaspoons cider vinegar

2 teaspoons sugar

2 teaspoons minced garlic

2 teaspoons Worcestershire sauce

A healthy pinch of salt

A healthy pinch of freshly ground white pepper

Combine all the ingredients in a bowl and mix well. Chill overnight to allow the flavors to develop.

MAKES ABOUT 3 CUPS

COOKING NOTES
This makes a huge amount—invite a crowd.

Oddly enough, the tomatoes are vital, a much-needed sweet element.

It's best to make the dressing a day ahead. Save leftover dressing for another salad, or for spreading on a tomato sandwich.

SERVING SUGGESTIONS
Hot Cheese Olives (p. 83), Pickled Shrimp (p. 95), Egg and Olive Canapés (p. 57), Steak au Poivre (p. 573), Mashed Potatoes Anna (p. 294), Spinach with Sour Cream (p. 216), Raw Spinach Salad (p. 175), Lattich Salat, Warme (Warm Lettuce Salad; p. 171), Al Forno's Roasted Asparagus (p. 233), Mrs. Hovis's Hot Upside-Down Apple Pie (p. 828), Junior's Cheesecake (p. 771), Caramelized Chocolate Bread Pudding (p. 852)

AUGUST 24, 2003: "FOOD: TIP OF THE ICEBERG," BY JULIA REED. RECIPE ADAPTED FROM ROBERT CARTER, THE CHEF AT THE PENINSULA GRILL IN CHARLESTON, SOUTH CAROLINA.

—2003

ROASTED BONE MARROW AND PARSLEY SALAD

Like the Caesar salad, this one will be remembered forever. It was made famous by Fergus Henderson, a chef of unmatched style and vision. With his restaurant St. John, in the Smithfield district of London, he sought to lend dignity to the esoteric and overlooked—dishes like game liver toast, deviled lamb's kidneys, and Bakewell tarts.

The space that St. John occupies was once a smokehouse. In its other former lives, it was used as a nursery for sprouts and later was a favored underground spot for raves. "By the time we got here," Henderson said when I interviewed him for a story, "there was this strange mixture of smoke, pork fat, dampness, and weird paintings. I thought, this one is for us."

He turned the space into a spare refectory where the only color is the diners' clothing or the food itself. There is no garnish shrouding the kidneys, just the kidneys. "It's all about enjoying limitation rather than wanting everything," he told me.

Henderson captured the aesthetic neatly in his first book, *Nose to Tail Eating: A Kind of British Cooking*, published in England in 1999 by Macmillan. (The American version is called *The Whole Beast*.) *Nose to Tail Eating* is a perfect cookbook much the way that St. John is a perfect restaurant. It is beautiful to look at, with bird's-eye-view photos of Henderson's dining-room table by Jason Lowe. Each dish is served to a group of friends and family. There are no faces, just hands reaching for a spoon, bringing food to the mouth.

Henderson has a lovely writing voice, so the text, which is largely recipes, has a rare lyrical charm. An ingredient might be "a large knob of butter" or "a good supply of toast." Instructions for this parsley salad read: "Meanwhile, lightly chop your parsley; just enough to discipline it." In another, for kidneys, he writes, "Add a hearty splash of Worcestershire sauce and the chicken stock, and let all the ingredients get to know each other."

If you haven't yet gotten to know Henderson, here is your chance.

———

Twelve 2-inch pieces beef or veal marrowbone
1½ cups tightly packed flat-leaf parsley leaves
1 shallot, thinly sliced
¼ cup extra-fine capers, drained
Juice of ½ lemon
1½ tablespoons extra virgin olive oil
Fine sea salt and freshly ground black pepper
8 slices country bread, toasted
Coarse sea salt

1. Heat the oven to 400 degrees. Put the marrowbones in a wide baking pan and roast until the marrow becomes loose and giving but has not melted away, about 15 to 20 minutes.
2. Meanwhile, chop the parsley and place it in a bowl with the shallot and capers. Mix. Dress with the lemon juice, olive oil, and salt and pepper to taste. Taste and adjust the seasoning, and place the salad in a serving bowl.

3. Place the marrowbones on a platter. Diners should scrape the marrow from the bones onto the toasts and season it with sea salt, then lay a pinch of parsley salad on top of this and eat.

SERVES 4

COOKING NOTE

Butchers and many supermarkets carry beef marrowbones, but veal marrowbones have to be ordered in advance from a butcher.

SERVING SUGGESTIONS

Claret Cup (p. 12), Vermouth Cup (p. 15), Scotch Eggs (p. 62), Roast Quail with Sage Dressing (p. 453), Roast Chicken with Bread Salad (p. 467), Collared Pork (p. 507), Brined and Roasted Pork Belly (p. 556), Epigram of Lamb (p. 509), Puree of Peas and Watercress (p. 296), Green Pea Fritters (p. 270), Fried Radishes (p. 215), Stewed Fennel (p. 245), Rice Croquettes (p. 799), Apple Snow (p. 808), Huntington Pudding (p. 802)

OCTOBER 15, 2003: "FOR A GENIUS OF THE OFF-CUT, LUNCH TIME IS THE RIGHT TIME," BY AMANDA HESSER. RECIPE ADAPTED FROM FERGUS HENDERSON, THE OWNER OF ST. JOHN IN LONDON.

—2003

⌒ HEARTH'S FAVA BEAN SALAD

For two months every spring, Marco Canora, the chef at Hearth in the East Village, serves a remarkably good fava bean and Pecorino salad. Tiny cubes of the soft cheese and barely cooked favas swim in a pool of olive oil flecked with parsley, oregano, and dried chiles. The sweet-bitter beans snap under your teeth, the sheep's-milk cheese slips a little tang into the mix, and then you soak up the fragrant oil with a piece of sesame-crusted bread from Sullivan Street Bakery—a delicious aggregate of flavors.

Canora's salad is specifically designed to celebrate the fava, the small, well-protected bean that's compact, kidney-shaped, and greener than a blade of grass. But it's a hard-won prize. Unlike standard peas, fava beans, once plucked from their pods, must also be extracted from their tough outer casings.

The beans grow in a fat, spongy pods about six to eight inches long. When buying favas, look for pods that are as clean, lightly fuzzy, and bright green as possible; they should not be limp or blackened on the ends, and you should be able to feel the beans inside. (It is not uncommon to come across a pod that looks nice and plump and contains one lonely bean.) The first order of business is to shuck the beans, which is done by snapping the stem end of the pod and using it to pull the tough strings down the seam of the pod. This makes it easier to crack the pod open, and then you can use your thumb to sweep out the beans inside. It's a mindless task, and this is why multitasking was invented: at Chez Panisse, everyone from the dishwasher to the executive chef must shuck favas during staff meetings.

If they are harvested young and the beans are very small—the size of a pea, a stage called *fevettes* in Provençal cooking—you can get off easy and eat them without peeling them. These smaller ones may also be braised whole. Generally, though, you want to get to the bean inside the pod. And you still want them small. Once the beans exceed three-quarters of an inch or the pod begins to yellow, it is too mature and will be starchy and bitter.

Methods for removing the inner shells vary. The most common way is to bring a pot of salted water to a boil, add the beans, and blanch for 30 seconds, then drain and plunge into ice water to halt the cooking. This softens the outer shell and allows you to slit it open and force out the bean.

Here, at last, is where the labor ends. You can simply douse the beans with good olive oil and sea salt and call it a day. With each tiny bean that passes your lips, you will forget, as a mother forgets the pain of childbirth, the efforts that led to this pleasure.

Fava beans, which are sometimes referred to as broad beans, were the primary bean in Europe before the discovery of the New World. Unsurprisingly, then, most fava recipes originated in Europe. Marco Canora's fava bean salad exemplifies the classic fava and Pecorino salads found all over Tuscany in the spring.

———

Salt
4 pounds fava beans
2 spring onions or scallions, finely chopped
Freshly ground black pepper

Extra virgin olive oil (Canora uses Laudemio)
2 cups diced (¼-inch) Pecorino Toscano
    (a sheep's milk cheese that's firm enough
    to dice but not so firm that it crumbles)
1 tablespoon crushed oregano, preferably
    imported from Greece
Small pinch of crushed red pepper flakes
⅓ cup finely chopped flat-leaf parsley
1 tablespoon dry white wine
1 tablespoon white wine vinegar

1. To prepare the fava beans, bring a pot of salted water to a boil. Shuck the beans and blanch for 30 to 40 seconds. Plunge the favas into a bowl of ice water to stop the cooking. Drain, and pop each bean out of its outer skin by pinching it with thumb and forefinger; you may have to slit the outer skin with a knife if the beans are mature. (You should have about 4 cups.)
2. Combine the favas with the onions in a bowl. Season lightly with salt and generously with pepper. Douse with olive oil. If serving immediately, fold in the cheese, oregano, red pepper flakes, parsley, white wine, and vinegar. If serving this later, add the remaining ingredients just before serving. Adjust the seasoning to taste. Serve with crusty bread, and be sure to spoon on extra oil for soaking up with the bread.

SERVES 6

SERVING SUGGESTIONS
Wine Lemonade (p. 17), Rhubarb Bellini (p. 30), Heirloom Pea Pancakes (p. 295), The Minimalist's Gravlax (p. 418), Asparagus and Bulgur with Preserved-Lemon Dressing (p. 190), Ventresca Tuna Salad (p. 426), Fricassee of Chicken with Tarragon (p. 456), Spring Lamb Salad with Pea Shoots and Sugar Snap Peas (p. 580), Lemon Cake (p. 781), Rhubarb-Ginger Compote (p. 607), Strawberry Short cakes (p. 799), Coeur à la Crème with Rhubarb Sauce (p. 864)

JUNE 12, 2005: "THE WAY WE EAT: BURIED TREASURE," BY AMANDA HESSER. RECIPE ADAPTED FROM MARCO CANORA, THE CHEF AT HEARTH IN NEW YORK CITY.

—2005

❧ WARM EGGPLANT SALAD WITH SESAME AND SHALLOTS

A delicious salad, showered with all manner of seasoning, condiments, and herbs.

———

1 pound Italian eggplants
2½ tablespoons superfine sugar
2 tablespoons soy sauce
1 tablespoon sake or very dry sherry
1 tablespoon rice vinegar
2 tablespoons coarsely ground sesame seeds
    (ground in a spice/coffee grinder or a mortar)
2 tablespoons Japanese sesame paste or
    unsweetened peanut butter
¼ cup very thinly sliced shallots
5 shiso leaves or a mix of mint and basil leaves,
    cut into strips

1. Cut off the stems of the eggplants, and cut lengthwise in half. Soak in cold water for 5 minutes, then drain and pat dry.
2. Arrange the eggplant on a microwave-safe plate, cover with plastic wrap, and microwave until softened and tender (3 to 6 minutes, depending on your microwave). Let stand for a few minutes to finish the cooking. (If you do not have a microwave, steam the eggplant for 5 to 7 minutes, until limp and tender.)
3. Combine the sugar, soy sauce, sake, vinegar, sesame seeds, and sesame paste in a bowl. Stir to dissolve the sugar, and thin the sauce with a little water, if needed. Cut the eggplant into strips about ½ inch wide and 3 inches long. Lay the strips between 3 layers of paper towels and press down on it with your palms to get rid of excess water. Mound on a serving plate. Drizzle the sauce over the eggplant, and scatter the shallots and shiso or herbs on top. Serve warm or at room temperature.

SERVES 4 TO 6

SERVING SUGGESTIONS
Edamame with Nori Salt (p. 92), Wok-Seared Spicy Calamari Salad (p. 443), Ginger Duck (p. 480), Broccoli Rabe Oshitashi (p. 262), Coconut Rice Pudding with Lime Syrup (p. 846), Gâteau de Crepes (p. 785),

Grapefruit Granita (p. 731), Cantaloupe–Star Anise Sorbet (p. 728)

APRIL 19, 2006: "EMPRESS OF DOMESTICITY DROPS IN," BY JULIA MOSKIN. RECIPE ADAPTED FROM HARUMI KURIHARA, A COOKBOOK WRITER AND FOOD SHOW HOST IN JAPAN.

—2006

ALMOND-CARROT SALAD

For the Almonds

¾ cup blanched whole almonds

2 teaspoons sugar

1 teaspoon ground cumin

1 teaspoon olive oil

Juice of ½ lemon

Salt and freshly ground white pepper

For the Salad

½ cup golden raisins

6 tablespoons white balsamic vinegar

1 pound carrots, peeled

2 teaspoons fresh lemon juice

1 tablespoon almond oil

1 tablespoon extra virgin olive oil

2 teaspoons minced shallot

Salt and freshly ground white pepper

1 packed cup mixed herb leaves, including flat-leaf
    parsley, chervil, dill, and mint

1. To prepare the almonds, heat the oven to 375 degrees. Toss together the almonds, sugar, cumin, olive oil, lemon juice, and a pinch each of salt and pepper in a small bowl. Spread the almonds on a baking sheet and toast until light brown, 10 to 12 minutes. Let cool.

2. To make the salad, bring the raisins and 4 tablespoons white balsamic vinegar to a boil in a small saucepan. Remove from the heat and let cool, then drain the raisins.

3. Using a mandoline or sharp vegetable peeler, slice the carrots lengthwise into ribbons (applying pressure on the peeler so the ribbons aren't too thin). Place the carrots, the remaining 2 tablespoons vinegar, lemon juice, oils, shallots, almonds, and raisins in a large bowl. Season with salt and pepper, mix to combine, and let marinate for 10 minutes.

4. Gently toss in the herbs and serve.

SERVES 4

SERVING SUGGESTIONS

Nicole Kaplan's Gougères (p. 76), Sole Grenobloise (Sautéed Sole with Capers and Lemons; p. 399), Gently Cooked Salmon and Mashed Potatoes (p. 415), Fish Poached in Buttermilk (p. 419), Veal Chops with Sage (p. 564), High-Temperature Roast Lamb (p. 526), Broccoli Puree with Ginger (p. 253), Roasted Cauliflower (p. 248), Huguenot Torte (Apple and Pecan Torte; p. 750), Marcella's Pear Cake (p. 769), Apple Galette (p. 843)

FEBRUARY 25, 2007: "EAT, MEMORY: THE GREAT CARROT CAPER," BY DAN BARBER, THE CHEF AND CO-OWNER OF BLUE HILL AT STONE BARNS IN POCANTICO HILLS, NEW YORK.

—2007

- Thomas De Voe writes *The Market Assistant*, detailing foods sold in New York City, Philadelphia, and Boston.

—1867—

- Asparagus Rolls (p. 365), Asparagus Salad (p. 214).

—1870s—

- Fried Green Tomatoes (p. 212).

—1878—

- Fried eggplant is a staple.

—1880s—

- Salsify is popular.

- The *Times* features a story on cooking artichokes: boiled, fried, and shaved.

—1902—

- "I say it's spinach, and I say the hell with it!" a *New Yorker* cartoon runs.

—1928—

- The first frozen vegetables are sold to the public under the Birds Eye Frosted Foods brand.

—1930—

- The decade of spinach.

—1940s—

- Nothing good is happening in veggie-land.

—1950s—

- Tomatoes Vinaigrette (p. 218), Leeks Vinaigrette (p. 217).

—1960s—

- Ratatouille (p. 219).

- Stuffed peppers (p. 223), stuffed tomatoes (p. 224), stuffed cabbage.

—1970s—

- Mollie Katzen writes *The Moosewood Cookbook*.

—1977—

- Vegetables meet balsamic vinegar.

—1980s—

- Marian Burros suggests sun-dried tomatoes as an exotic holiday gift.

—1981—

- Morels and fiddleheads come to symbolize spring. An expensive spring.

—Late— 1980s

- First mention of heirloom tomatoes in the *Times*.

- Deborah Madison writes *The Greens Cookbook*.

—1987—

- Al Forno roasts asparagus (p. 233); soon many other vegetables are roasted.

—1989—

- Macrobiotic diets become fashionable again, particularly for starlets.

- The "wild" mushroom pushes aside the button.
- Savory vegetable bread puddings (p. 242).

—1990s—

- The march of vegetable purees.

—1990—

- *Chez Panisse Vegetables* by Alice Waters is published.

—1996—

- Thomas Keller offers a nine-course vegetable tasting menu at Per Se.

—2004—

- The year of the Brussels sprout, which is served deep-fried, shredded, even raw.

—2008—

5

VEGETABLES

One chapter could never do justice to the spate of vegetable recipes that have appeared in the *Times*, nor to the variety of vegetables, so I had to draw some boundary lines. There was a very good, very simple recipe for sautéed salsify, but the five people who have access to salsify would love it, and the rest would be mystified. And I cut the only vegetable quiche recipe (made with leeks). I found it uninspiring. You can write me about all the phenomenal vegetable quiche recipes I missed, and I'll try them and get them into the next edition. In the meantime, quiche lovers, turn to Asparagus alla Fontina on p. 222 for what is, essentially, a quiche without a crust.

Our interest in vegetables has came in waves. In the second half of the nineteenth century, the *Times* published weekly reports on which produce was in the markets and ran recipes for vegetables ranging from artichokes to okra. But the instructions usually went something like this:

1. Boil to death.
2. Drench in butter, or in a buttery béchamel (optional).
3. Eat.
4. Die.

The memorable recipes from this period were straightforward braises and roasts that draw out the vegetable's primary flavors (see, for example, Baked Mushrooms on p. 212).

Strangely, the first half of the twentieth century was a black hole: vegetables got sucked in and vanished. After Craig Claiborne was hired in the late 1950s, he began talking up leeks and asparagus and an exotic item called eggplant. And suddenly, with the 1958 introduction of asparagus Polonaise (asparagus topped with toasted bread crumbs and sieved egg), we were hooked. For the last sixty years, we've been in a vegetable boom, eager to find new ways to combine, puree, season, slice, dice, pickle, infuse, and savor what comes from the garden. We don't just boil Brussels sprouts, we shave them and blend them with bacon and pine nuts (see p. 235), we toss them with mustard butter (p. 253), and we braise them with cream (p. 232). We mix broccoli with ginger (see p. 253) and carrots with cumin (pages 244 and 237). And we confidently pour saffron custard atop the now-familiar eggplant. These recipes reinvigorate that dreary old injunction, "Eat your vegetables."

RECIPES BY CATEGORY

➳ BAKED MUSHROOMS

This recipe is so simple and modern that if you didn't look at the date, you might think it was Tom Colicchio's. It extols mushrooms by doing very little to them, using heat to soften their flesh and distill the flavors. You sprinkle on a little butter, parsley, and lemon juice as the dish goes to the table.

————

I pound medium white mushrooms, trimmed
Salt and freshly ground black pepper
I tablespoon unsalted butter
4 tablespoons unsalted butter, melted
4 teaspoons fresh lemon juice
2 teaspoons chopped flat-leaf parsley

1. Heat the oven to 375 degrees. Set the mushrooms stem side up in a baking dish large enough to hold them in a single layer. Season them with salt and pepper and use the 1 tablespoon butter to dot each one.
2. Bake the mushrooms, basting occasionally with the melted butter, until they're wilted on the edges and just cooked through, 20 to 30 minutes. Remove from the oven and sprinkle with the lemon juice, parsley, salt and pepper, and any remaining melted butter.

SERVES 4 TO 6

SERVING SUGGESTIONS
Stuffed Clams (p. 400), Butternut Squash and Cider Soup (p. 136), Slow-Roasted Duck (p. 475), Center-Ring Strip Steak Marinated in Scotch Whiskey (p. 536), Grapefruit Fluff (p. 809)

JULY 8, 1877: "RECEIPTS FOR THE TABLE." RECIPE SIGNED MOLLIE.

—1877

➳ FRIED GREEN TOMATOES

The strange thing about fried green tomatoes is that if you close your eyes, you might think you were eating fried lemons—good jammy lemons, tart but not painfully so. Two details you want to pay attention to when

making fried green tomatoes: merely dust the tomatoes with flour (tap off any excess) and season with plenty of salt, to counteract the tartness.

————

2 firm medium green tomatoes, cored and
    cut into ½-inch-thick slices
Sea salt and freshly ground black pepper
½ cup all-purpose flour
Canola oil (or pork fat, if you like)

1. Season the tomatoes with salt and pepper. Spread the flour in a wide shallow bowl. Press the tomato slices into the flour on both sides, then tap off the excess flour.
2. Place a large cast-iron pan over medium-high heat and pour in ⅛ inch of oil. When it's hot, start adding the tomato slices (you'll need to do this in batches and fry until browned on the first side, about 2 minutes, then turn and brown on the other side. Drain on a plate lined with paper towels. Season with additional salt before serving.

SERVES 4

SERVING SUGGESTIONS
Sauce Rémoulade (for Shrimp; p. 601), Sweet-and-Spicy Pepper Stew (p. 247), Okra Soup with Beef (and Oysters; p. 109), Paul Prudhomme's Cajun-Style Gumbo (p. 125), Sausage, Bean, and Corn Stew (p. 538), Peach Salad (p. 805), Brown Sugar Ice Cream (p. 721)

ORIGINAL RECIPE
"Take fine large green tomatoes and wipe them perfectly clean, cut them in slices about half an inch thick, sprinkle with salt, pepper, and flour, and fry them in boiling fat."

SEPTEMBER 29, 1878: "RECEIPTS FOR THE TABLE." RECIPE SIGNED AUNT ADDIE.

—1878

➳ POINTE D'ASPERGE

This dish brings to mind silver salvers and Edith Wharton. Though fancy, it's easy enough to make: you fold blanched asparagus tips into a thin glaze made with butter, onions, egg yolks, salt, and, oddly enough, sugar. When done correctly—that is, swiftly—the sauce is sheer and buttery, a gloss for the asparagus. The sauce is also evanescent, so serve it right away.

———

1 pound asparagus
1 tablespoon unsalted butter
¼ cup thinly sliced onion
1 tablespoon water
1 large egg yolk
Salt
1 teaspoon confectioners' sugar

1. Bring a large pot of generously salted water to a boil. Trim the tips—3 inches long—from the asparagus: reserve the bottoms for another use. Blanch the tips until just tender, then transfer to a bowl of ice water. Drain and pat dry.
2. Melt the butter in a medium saucepan over medium-low heat. Add the onion and cook until tender, 6 to 8 minutes. Remove the pan from the heat and whisk in the water and egg yolk. The residual heat should thicken the sauce and make it glossy. Season with salt and the sugar. Fold in the asparagus tips, and serve immediately.

SERVES 2 TO 4

VARIATION
Sprinkle some chopped tarragon or thyme on top just before serving.

SERVING SUGGESTIONS
Veal Chops with Sage (p. 564), Fish Poached in Buttermilk (p. 419), Gently Cooked Salmon with Mashed Potatoes (p. 415), Roast Lobster with Vanilla Sauce (p. 411), Cecily Brownstone's Chiffon Roll (p. 747), Rhubarb-Strawberry Mousse (p. 835)

MAY 18, 1879: "RECEIPTS FOR THE TABLE." RECIPE BY "CHEF OF THE B___ CLUB."

—1879

⌒ STUFFED TOMATOES

This recipe, contributed by L.D.V., provided just the bare framework for stuffed tomatoes, which is just as well for something so timeless. After halving and hollowing out the tomatoes, L.D.V. said, "Take whatever cold meat you have, chop with onion, some herbs, crumbs of bread, and add to it two yolks of eggs." The tomatoes are then stuffed with this mixture, put in a buttered casserole dish, and slowly baked.

———

4 tennis-ball-sized tomatoes
Salt
1 tablespoon unsalted butter, softened
1¼ cups chopped cooked meat
    (pebble-sized pieces)
⅓ cup finely chopped onion
1 teaspoon chopped thyme
2 teaspoons thinly sliced chives
⅓ cup coarse fresh bread crumbs
2 large egg yolks
Freshly ground black pepper

1. Heat the oven to 325 degrees. Core the tomatoes and halve through the core. Using a melon baller or sharp spoon, scrape out the seeds and pulp. Season the insides of the tomatoes with salt. Generously butter a baking dish large enough to comfortably hold the tomato halves.
2. Stir together the meat, onion, thyme, chives, and bread crumbs in a bowl. Add the egg yolks, season with salt and pepper, and stir again. If the mixture seems dry, add a tablespoon of water to moisten it—it should just cling together. Fill the tomatoes with the mixture, mounding it at the top.
3. Set the tomatoes in the baking dish. Bake until the stuffing is cooked through and the top is crisp but not dry, 30 to 40 minutes.

SERVES 8 AS A SIDE DISH, 4 AS A FIRST COURSE, OR 2 AS A MAIN COURSE

COOKING NOTE
A fatty meat, something in the pork family, say, works best because it retains its moisture in the oven. I used a blend of sweet and hot Italian sausages, and my

bread crumbs were made from brioche crusts, a pretty fail-safe combination. But this is an infinitely flexible formula—next time I might try smoked ham and rye bread crumbs.

SERVING SUGGESTIONS
Tom's Chilled Cucumber Soup (p. 117), Cold Nicarde (Yellow Squash Soup; p. 110), Watercress Salad (p. 171), Roasted Potato Salad (p. 285), Deviled Crabs (p. 387), Fricassee of Chicken with Tarragon (p. 456), Broiled Steak with Oysters (p. 511), Summer Pudding (p. 847), Fresh Blueberry Buckle (p. 815)

AUGUST 3, 1879: "RECEIPTS FOR THE TABLE." RECIPE SIGNED L.D.V.

—1879

ASPARAGUS SALAD

I didn't put this in the salad chapter, because we wouldn't think of it as a salad—it's blanched asparagus with a homemade mayonnaise for dressing (or dipping, the way I like to serve it). Make this dish when you can get your hands on beautiful fat asparagus spears. Whisking the mayonnaise by hand is a real workout (and why shouldn't cooking be?). It takes two people to do, one pouring and one whisking, switching off every few minutes. (If alone and feeling lethargic, you can do it in your mixer.)

———

2 pounds large asparagus, trimmed

1 large egg yolk

1 teaspoon Colman's prepared mustard

1 teaspoon salt

Pinch of freshly ground white pepper

Pinch of cayenne pepper, or more to taste

1½ cups vegetable oil

1 tablespoon fresh lemon juice

2 to 4 tablespoons white wine vinegar

1. Bring a large pot of generously salted water to a boil. Add the asparagus and cook until just tender, 3 to 5 minutes. Drain and plunge into a bowl of ice water to cool, then drain and dry on a towel.

2. Arrange the asparagus with the tips in one direction on a serving platter.

3. Whisk together the egg yolk, mustard, salt, pepper, and cayenne in a medium bowl until smooth. Begin whisking in—a few drops at a time—the oil, lemon juice, and vinegar, alternating them as you go, so that the mixture is thickening when the oil goes in and thinning when the acids are added. Taste as you go, adding more pepper, salt, and cayenne as desired.

4. You can either pour enough mayonnaise over the asparagus to dress it, or pass it at the table for dipping.

SERVES 6

COOKING NOTES
The recipe called for 4 tablespoons vinegar, but I thought 2 was plenty. Taste it at 2 and decide for yourself. Also, feel free to vary the vinegar—sherry vinegar would be swell.

SERVING SUGGESTIONS
Filet de Boeuf Rôti (Roast Fillet of Beef) with Sauce Bordelaise (p. 528), Roman Lamb (p. 542), Saratoga Potatoes (p. 273), Fried Radishes (p. 215), Sugar Snap Peas with Horseradish (p. 259), Chocolate Rum Mousse (p. 814)

APRIL 2, 1882: "HINTS FOR THE HOUSEHOLD: A LITTLE DINNER AFTER ONE'S OWN STOMACH," BY JULIET CORSON.

—1882

FRESH MUSHROOMS STEWED WITH MADEIRA

In 1897, two New York restaurant figures published competing cookbooks. Adolphe Gallier, the chef at the Majestic Hotel, came out with *The Majestic Family Cook Book*, and Oscar Tschirky, the maître d' at the Waldorf-Astoria and formerly at Delmonico's, wrote *The Cook Book*. The *Times* featured recipes from both books, including this one from Gallier.

As is typical of nineteenth-century dishes, the sauce is thickened with flour, which encases the mushrooms in a slick of Madeira and butter. If you prefer a cleaner, more modern sauce, skip the flour and reduce the Madeira and broth by more than half, until they become a glaze.

---

4 tablespoons unsalted butter
I pound small cremini or white button mushrooms, trimmed
Salt and freshly ground black pepper
¾ cup Madeira
I cup chicken broth
I tablespoon all-purpose flour
2 tablespoons water

1. Put the butter in a large sauté pan and set over medium-high heat. When the butter begins to brown at the edges, add the mushrooms, season with salt and pepper and cook until lightly browned on the edges, about 3 minutes. Pour in the Madeira and bring to a boil, then add the broth and bring to a boil. Cook at a healthy boil until the liquid is reduced by half.
2. Dissolve the flour in the water, then stir it into the pan juices and cook, stirring, until the sauce has thickened and the raw taste of flour is gone, about 1 minute. Taste and adjust the seasoning.

SERVES 4

SERVING SUGGESTIONS
Roasted Squash Soup with Cumin (p. 147), Barley Risotto (p. 327), Roast Quail with Sage Dressing (p. 453), Grilled Hanger Steak (p. 551), Stewed Fennel (p. 245), Poached Pears in Brandy and Red Wine (p. 832)

JANUARY 3, 1897: "WISDOM OF TWO CHEFS: OSCAR OF THE WALDORF AND GALLIER OF THE MAJESTIC TALK."

—1897

✐ FRIED RADISHES

According to the story in the *Times*, these fried radishes were a good substitute for sautéed mushrooms. The anonymous writer noted, "When brown and tender, add to the steak [they were served with steak] and the similarity of the flavor will be a surprise. If the guests are not apprised of the substitution, the differense [*sic*] will often go unnoticed."

If your guests don't notice the difference between mushrooms and radishes, they have no taste buds. When you fry radishes, they become a little sweet—which makes them not like mushrooms but like turnips. The real revelation here is that cooked radishes are delicious and we shouldn't live without them.

Here's the catch: you have to use little farmers' market radishes and you have to peel them. By the fifth radish, you will hate me, but I had to peel mine too! Actually, I only peeled half of them because I wanted to see if you could get away with not peeling them, and then I suffered for you, because the unskinned radishes were bitter.

I tablespoon unsalted butter
I½ cups small radishes (no bigger than a cherry), peeled
Salt

Melt the butter in a small sauté pan over medium-high heat. When the foam begins to subside, add the radishes and cook, shaking the pan now and then, until they brown lightly and are soft on the edges. Season with salt as you go.

SERVES 2

COOKING NOTES
The original recipe gave no amounts, so I wrote the recipe to serve 2 people. The recipe can easily be doubled or tripled—just remember you have to peel all those little radishes.

I hate to sound like a produce snob, but this recipe is pointless if not made with those snappy baby radishes that you only seem to find at farmers' markets.

SERVING SUGGESTIONS
Caesar Salad (p. 174), Grilled Hanger Steak (p. 551), Broiled Steak with Oysters (p. 511), Mashed Potatoes Anna (p. 294), Potato "Tostones" (Flattened Potatoes; p. 301), Butterscotch Pudding (p. 851)

JUNE 26, 1910: "NEW DISHES FOR SUMMER."

—1910

FLORIDA BEETS

This recipe from 1946 was lauded as an "inexpensive dish." It still is. The beets simmer in a bath of orange juice, orange zest, butter, and salt, and by the time they come out of the oven, the juices are cooked down to a syrup that you could very well drizzle over ice cream. Jane Nickerson, who wrote the column the recipe appeared in, suggested serving the beets with poultry or pork, but you might also consider using them as the base for a warm salad, with a tuft of young arugula on top and a dollop of sheep's-milk ricotta.

2½ cups sliced raw beets
1 teaspoon grated orange zest
1 cup orange juice (from about 3 oranges)
1 tablespoon unsalted butter
1 teaspoon salt

Heat the oven to 350 degrees. Peel and thinly slice the beets. Arrange the beet slices in a greased casserole. Add the remaining ingredients. Cover and bake until the beets are just tender, about 1 hour.

SERVES 6

COOKING NOTES
I sliced the beets on a mandoline so they were thin enough to curl. Yet even after an hour of cooking, they retained a pleasant firmness.

The original recipe called for margarine, if you want to be a purist, but I don't recommend it. Margarine has a flatter flavor.

SERVING SUGGESTIONS
Cauliflower Soup with Cremini Mushrooms and Walnut Oil (p. 149), Collared Pork (p. 507), Brined and Roasted Pork Belly (p. 556), Veal Chops Beau Séjour (p. 520), Latkes (p. 280), Mashed Potatoes Anna (p. 294), Lee's Marlborough Tart (p. 816)

FEBRUARY 21, 1946: "NEWS OF FOOD: RESTAURANT SERVING FINANCIAL DISTRICT SINCE 1800 IS NOTED FOR ITS SPECIALTIES," BY JANE NICKERSON.

—1946

SPINACH WITH SOUR CREAM

Serve this dish right away so the cool cream seeps into the warm spinach as you devour it.

1¾ pounds young (not baby, not old) spinach, trimmed and washed
1 teaspoon salt, or to taste
1 teaspoon sugar or honey
Pinch of freshly ground black pepper, or to taste
½ cup sour cream
1 teaspoon grated onion

1. Place the spinach in a pot with the salt, sugar, and pepper and cook over medium-high heat, covered, until just tender, tossing with tongs now and then. Drain, chop if desired, and place in a serving dish. 2. Mix the sour cream with the onion and season to taste with salt and pepper if desired. Pile on top of the hot spinach and serve at once.

SERVES 4

SERVING SUGGESTIONS
Broiled Steak with Oysters (p. 511), Steak au Poivre (p. 573), Mashed Potatoes Anna (p. 294), Mrs. Hovis's Hot Upside-Down Apple Pie (p. 828), Marcella's Pear Cake (p. 769), Coupe Lena Horne (Coffee Ice Cream Sundae; p. 722)

APRIL 29, 1946: "NEWS OF FOOD: RECIPES SUGGESTED TO TAKE ADVANTAGE OF PLENITUDE OF VEGETABLES ON MARKET," BY JANE NICKERSON.

—1946

PUREE OF CELERY ROOT

---

4 large celery roots
2 medium potatoes
About 2 cups chicken broth
Salt and freshly ground black pepper
1 cup heavy cream, whipped to soft peaks

1. Peel the celery root and potatoes and cut into quarters. Boil the celery and potatoes separately in

salted water until tender, about 20 minutes. Do not overcook.

2. Place the celery in the blender and puree at low speed until smooth, adding enough chicken broth to aid the blending. (Alternatively, the celery may be put through a potato ricer.)

3. Mash the potatoes. (Or, the potatoes may be put through a ricer.) Mix with the pureed celery and season to taste with salt and pepper. Fold in enough whipped cream to ensure a smooth consistency.

SERVES 4 TO 6

COOKING NOTE

1950s cooks were not big on aromatics—so simmer a garlic clove, some thyme, and a bay leaf in the chicken broth before adding it to the celery root.

SERVING SUGGESTIONS

Wilted Red Cabbage Salad (p. 196), James Beard's Chicken with 40 Cloves of Garlic (p. 469), Slow-Roasted Duck (p. 475), Pork Arrosto with Prunes and Grappa (p. 577), Cumin-Mustard Carrots (p. 237), Madeleine Kamman's Apple Mousse (p. 816), Chocolate Mousse (p. 820)

APRIL 2, 1959: "DISHES OF DISTINCTION DO NOT REQUIRE LONG HOURS OF TOIL," BY CRAIG CLAIBORNE.

—1959

ꜱ LEEKS VINAIGRETTE

Recipes for this dish have made at least half a dozen appearances in the *Times*. Most recently, in 2007, Melissa Clark came up with a spicy version, in which she replaced the regular Dijon with extra-hot Dijon. You can do the same here.

---

12 thin leeks (6 if they're thick)

¹/₂ cup olive oil

¹/₂ cup vegetable or peanut oil

3 to 4 tablespoons red wine vinegar

2 teaspoons French or German mustard

2 tablespoons finely chopped shallots

2 tablespoons finely chopped flat-leaf parsley

1 teaspoon finely chopped tarragon

1 tablespoon chopped chives

2 hard-boiled eggs, finely chopped

Salt and freshly ground black pepper to taste

1. Bring a large saucepan of generously salted water to a boil. Trim the root ends of the leeks and split down the center, but do not cut through the root end. Tie the leeks with kitchen string to keep them together during cooking. Add to the boiling water and cook until tender when prodded with a fork. The cooking time will depend on size; 3 to 5 minutes, for 1-inch-thick leeks. Drain and let cool.

2. Combine the oils, vinegar, and mustard in a small bowl, and beat with a fork until well blended. Add the remaining ingredients and stir gently until well blended.

3. Remove the strings from the leeks and arrange in a single layer on a rimmed plate. Pour the sauce over the leeks and marinate in the refrigerator overnight before serving.

SERVES 6

COOKING NOTE

Once cooked, the leeks need a day to marinate, so plan ahead!

SERVING SUGGESTIONS

Braised Stuffed Breast of Veal (p. 458), Boeuf Bourguignon I (p. 516), Madame Leracine's Gratin Dauphinois (p. 284), Tourtière (p. 827), Apple Tarte Tatin (p. 837)

NOVEMBER 14, 1960: "FOOD NEWS: RICH MAN'S ASPARAGUS," BY CRAIG CLAIBORNE.

—1960

ꜱ CREAMED ONIONS

You know what's missing from twenty-first-century cooking? Sherry. It is what makes dishes like the White Veal Stew on p. 553, Pumpkin–Black Bean Soup on p. 128, and Sweet Potato Cecelia on p. 276. Sherry gives a sauce legs and keeps the flavors reverberating over your palate. I made these creamed onions with a fino sherry.

---

2 pounds small white onions, unpeeled,
    or frozen pearl onions (with no sauce)
4 tablespoons unsalted butter
¼ cup all-purpose flour
½ teaspoon salt
¼ teaspoon freshly ground black pepper
2 cups whole milk
¾ teaspoon chopped fresh marjoram
    or ¼ teaspoon dried marjoram
2 tablespoons sherry

1. If using fresh onions, steam the unpeeled onions over boiling water for 30 minutes, or until tender. Cool and peel. If using frozen onions, bring a pot of salted water to a boil, add the onions, and simmer just until tender. Drain.

2. Melt the butter in a medium saucepan. Remove from the heat and blend in the flour, salt, and pepper. Slowly add the milk, whisking constantly. Return to the heat and bring to a boil, whisking constantly. Add the onions and simmer for 2 minutes. Whisk in the marjoram and sherry. Taste and adjust the seasoning.

SERVES 6 TO 8

COOKING NOTES

I couldn't bring myself to peel two pounds of small white onions, so the first time I made this, I used frozen white onions, and—somewhat to my surprise—the dish was still great. The frozen onions plump up when simmered, and if drained well, they fuse with the sauce just as well as fresh onions do.

VARIATION

Try this with a mix of onions, like cipolline and baby red onions.

SERVING SUGGESTIONS

Ann Seranne's Rib Roast of Beef (p. 519) and Puree of Peas and Watercress (p. 296). This is also a fitting side dish for Thanksgiving: Roasted Brine-Cured Turkey (p. 474), Porcini Bread Stuffing (p. 350), Candied Sweet Potatoes (p. 276), Holiday Cranberry Chutney (p. 608), Mississippi Pecan Pie (p. 820), Rum Pumpkin Cream Pie (p. 823).

NOVEMBER 21, 1961: "TURKEY, OF COURSE, BUT WITH SUBTLY VARIED COMPANIONS," BY CRAIG CLAIBORNE.

—1961

⌒ TOMATOES VINAIGRETTE

An indispensable recipe oddly modern for its time—and yet introduced out of season, as it ran in June; an almost exact copy had run the previous April. April! The tomatoes are peeled and sliced, then doused with vinaigrette, so the supple, glistening swatches of tomato swim in a fruity tomato juice.

Craig Claiborne, the longtime food columnist for the *Times*, favored vinaigrettes that were heavier on the oil than the usual 3 parts oil to 1 part vinegar proportion. He used the following vinaigrette recipe to make that point (it's more like 4:1), and to emphasize the versatility of the French dressing. In his story, the vinaigrette served as the foundation for seven recipes, among them shrimp vinaigrette, asparagus vinaigrette, and boiled tongue vinaigrette, as well as this classic tomatoes vinaigrette.

Claiborne noted that you could also add chopped shallots, hard-cooked eggs, and dry mustard to the vinaigrette. I didn't try this, but I would if I were serving the tomatoes atop steamed asparagus. And the next time I make the dish, I might vary it by using red and yellow cherry tomatoes instead of just large reds.

A modern variation, Squashed Tomatoes, is on p. 90.

———

2 or 3 large ripe tomatoes

For the Vinaigrette`
3 tablespoons wine vinegar
¾ cup olive oil
I tablespoon chopped capers
½ teaspoon finely chopped onion
I teaspoon finely chopped cornichons or sour pickle
Salt and freshly ground black pepper
½ cup chopped flat-leaf parsley
I tablespoon finely chopped chives

I loaf French or Italian bread

1. Spear the stem end of each tomato with a 2-pronged fork and dip, one at a time, into rapidly boiling water for exactly 10 seconds. Remove the tomatoes and peel with a small paring knife. (After the hot water bath, the skins slips off easily.) Cut out the cores.

2. Slice the tomatoes and arrange on a serving dish. Chill.

3. To prepare the vinaigrette, combine all the ingredients except the parsley and chives in a bowl and beat with a fork until well blended. (Chill the sauce if it is to be used with the tomatoes or other chilled vegetables or shrimp. Heat the sauce to lukewarm if it is to be used with hot boiled beef, fish or chicken, pigs' feet, or calves' head.)

4. Just before serving, fold the parsley and chives into the vinaigrette. Serve separately or spooned over the tomatoes (you will only need about ¾ cup of the vinaigrette; reserve the rest for another use) with the loaf of bread.

SERVES 4

COOKING NOTES

I used red wine vinegar. You want something with a touch of sweetness, so sherry vinegar would also be fine.

Do not be tempted to skip peeling the tomatoes. The soft peeled texture is vital to the dish.

VARIATIONS

The day after I served this, I broke up some goat cheese and added it to the tomatoes, then spooned it over toasted country bread. The tomatoes and their juices can also be used as a salad dressing, over delicate arugula leaves, or as a room-temperature sauce for grilled (or roasted) fish or lamb.

SERVING SUGGESTIONS

Basic Corn Chowder (p. 149), Deep-Fried Soft-Shell Crabs (p. 398), New York Strip Steak with Horseradish-Mint Glaze (p. 566), Steak au Poivre (p. 573), Saratoga Potatoes (p. 273), Cucumbers in Cream (p. 225), Fruit Crostatas (p. 855)

JUNE 2, 1963: "A SAUCE THAT'S SAUCIER," BY CRAIG CLAIBORNE.

—1963

RATATOUILLE NIÇOISE

This is a slightly unorthodox ratatouille because it doesn't contain peppers or zucchini, but it's still great, a member of the braised and pleasantly oily school of ratatouille (as opposed to the roasted and dry school).

The recipe comes from Mrs. Jacques Kayaloff, the owner of Vieux Paris, an antiques store on East 55th Street. Kayaloff, according to Craig Claiborne, was an esteemed hostess, although the recipe may actually be the work of her cook, Lee Faith. The article never makes it clear.

———

1 large eggplant
Salt
½ cup olive oil
1 large onion, sliced wafer-thin
2 cloves garlic, finely minced
½ teaspoon ground coriander
1 sprig fresh thyme, chopped, or ½ teaspoon dried thyme
Freshly ground black pepper
1 bay leaf
2 ripe tomatoes, peeled (see Cooking Note, p. 146) and cored
6 basil leaves or 12 tarragon leaves, finely chopped
6 imported black olives (French, Greek, or Italian), pitted and sliced (optional)

1. Trim off the ends of the eggplant but do not peel it. Cut into ½-inch slices and cut each slice into large cubes. Generously sprinkle the eggplant with salt and place it in a colander. Weight it down with a plate and let stand for 1 hour to drain.

2. Place a heavy skillet over medium heat and add the oil. When it is hot, add the onion and garlic and cook, stirring, until the onion is wilted, 3 to 4 minutes. Add the eggplant and sprinkle with the coriander, thyme, and pepper. Add the bay leaf, cover, and simmer over low heat for 20 minutes.

3. Chop the tomatoes and add them to the eggplant, along with the basil. Simmer for 20 minutes, or until the ratatouille is thickened. Taste and adjust the seasoning. Add the olives, if desired, and serve hot or cold. (This dish is excellent the day after it is made.)

SERVES 6

COOKING NOTES

If you need instructions for peeling the tomatoes, turn to p. 146.

Originally the recipe had you simmer the eggplant and tomatoes with a cover on, and if the resulting mixture was too wet, you were supposed to pour off the excess liquid and cook it down separately. These extra steps can be eliminated by simply simmering the eggplant and tomatoes uncovered.

VARIATION

A ratatouille made with butternut squash can be found on p. 258. And caponata, a relative of ratatouille, is on p. 226.

SERVING SUGGESTIONS

Ricotta Crostini with Fresh Thyme and Dried Oregano (p. 93), Steamed Fish with Thyme and Tomato Vinaigrette (p. 408), Fish Poached in Buttermilk (p. 419), Veal Chops Beau Séjour (p. 520), Gigot à la Provençal et Gratin de Pommes de Terre (p. 537), Saffron Panna Cotta (p. 845)

JUNE 3, 1965: "A FLAIR FOR LANGUAGES CAN ADD FLAVOR TO MENUS," BY CRAIG CLAIBORNE. RECIPE ADAPTED FROM MRS. JACQUES KAYALOFF.

—1965

☙ YETTE'S GARDEN PLATTER

This dish has superb design. The foundation is a nod to the French *tian*, a shallow casserole of baked vegetables, but its reconstruction and fine-tuning are distinctly American. Potatoes, zucchini, and tomatoes are combined and layered in such a way that they all cook to the perfect, concentrated consistency.

You slice the potatoes into large slabs and spread them on the bottom of the baking dish, then top them with 1/2-inch-thick slices of zucchini and peeled, seeded, and chopped tomatoes seasoned with onion, garlic, and lots of olive oil. The tomatoes, having been drained of much of their juice before being added to the casserole, moisten the vegetables without making them soggy, and at the very bottom of the casserole, you get a beautiful tomato-scented oil. Make sure you spoon it over every serving.

———

3 medium potatoes, sliced 1/4 inch thick
3 medium zucchini, sliced 1/2 inch thick
4 tomatoes, peeled, (see Cooking Note, p. 146), cored, seeded, and chopped
1/4 cup chopped flat-leaf parsley
1 clove garlic, finely chopped
3/4 cup olive oil
2 medium onions, finely chopped
Salt and freshly ground black pepper

1. Heat the oven to 350 degrees. Layer the potatoes and then the zucchini in a shallow baking dish. Combine the remaining ingredients, and add to the dish.
2. Bake uncovered until the vegetables are tender and well-browned on the edges, about 1 1/2 hours.

**SERVES 3 AS A MAIN COURSE,
6 AS A FIRST COURSE**

COOKING NOTES

Sandra Capsis and Mrs. Charles Burke, the home cooks who devised this recipe, note that you can add peeled, sliced eggplant to the platter, which sounds promising, but I haven't tried it.

SERVING SUGGESTIONS

Salmon and Tomatoes in Foil (leave out the tomatoes; p. 422), Saltimbocca (p. 561), Grilled Leg of Lamb with Mustard Seeds (p. 544), Fresh Blueberry Buckle (p. 815), Sour Cream Ice Cream (p. 730)

JULY 24, 1969: "IT ALL BEGAN WHEN HER HUSBAND GAVE HER A PASTA MACHINE," BY JEAN HEWITT. RECIPE ADAPTED FROM SANDRA CAPSIS AND MRS. CHARLES BURKE.

—1969

☙ ARTICHOKES CROISETTE

Wonderful and utterly impractical, these artichoke hearts topped with poached eggs and rouille are the kind of dish that you'll serve and be compelled to tell everyone how much time—2 hours or so—it took you to make!

———

For the Artichokes

8 large artichokes

2 lemons, halved

4 teaspoons all-purpose flour

Salt

For the Rouille

I medium potato, peeled

3 cups chicken broth

1/4 cup chopped red bell pepper

2 small red chiles, stemmed

4 cloves garlic, mashed

4 to 6 tablespoons olive oil

Salt and freshly ground black pepper

For the Poached Eggs

2 tablespoons vinegar

8 large eggs

4 sprigs flat-leaf parsley, chopped

1. To prepare the artichokes, trim off the tough outer leaves of each one. Using a sharp knife, slice off the stems, and rub the cut surfaces with the lemon halves. Neatly slice through each artichoke, parallel to the base, leaving intact an artichoke bottom less than 1 inch thick. Again rub the cut surfaces with lemon. Place the bottoms in a large skillet.

2. Juice the lemon halves and combine the juice with the flour and enough water to make a smooth paste. Whisk in enough water to cover the artichoke bottoms, add salt to taste, and pour over the artichokes. Bring to a boil, then cover, reduce the heat, and simmer until tender, about 25 minutes. Drain, and when cool enough to handle, remove the fuzzy chokes.

3. Meanwhile, make the rouille: Place the potato in a small saucepan, cover with the chicken broth (adding water to cover, if needed), and bring to a boil. Reduce the heat and simmer until tender, about 20 minutes. Drain. Meanwhile, simmer the chopped peppers in salted water for 5 minutes, adding the chiles during the last 2 minutes; drain well.

4. Mash the peppers, potato, and garlic in a mortar with a pestle, or puree in a blender. Dribble in the olive oil as if for mayonnaise, beating or blending until you achieve a smooth, but not loose, consistency. Add salt and pepper.

5. To poach the eggs, heat enough boiling salted water to just cover 4 eggs in each of 2 small skillets. Add 1

tablespoon vinegar to each. Carefully drop 4 eggs into each pan (see Cooking Notes). Lower the heat and let the eggs poach in water just below the boiling point, about 4 minutes. Remove with a slotted spoon, and trim the edges with a cookie cutter.

6. Place a warm artichoke bottom on each plate, top with a poached egg, and spoon the warm rouille over. Garnish with the parsley.

SERVES 4 AS A MAIN COURSE, 8 AS A FIRST COURSE

COOKING NOTES

When poaching more than 1 egg, I think it helps to crack them one at a time into a small heatproof bowl that you can lower into the water and tip to the side, to gently pour the egg into the water. Doing this one at a time also helps when you fish out the eggs: remove them in the same order, so they all cook equally.

SERVING SUGGESTIONS

Sole Grenobloise (p. 399), Chicken à la Marengo (p. 453), Breaded Chicken Breasts with Parmesan Cheese (p. 465), Broiled Lamb Chops (p. 514), Rice Pilan (p. 309), Sautéed Potatoes with Parsley (p. 283), Pistachio Cream (p. 806), Strawberry Charlotte (p. 810)

FEBRUARY 6, 1972: "ARTICHOKE PLUS," BY RAYMOND SOKOLOV.

—1972

✐ BRAISED RED CABBAGE WITH CHESTNUTS

———

I large red cabbage (about 3 pounds)

12 chestnuts

1/4 pound salt pork or thickly sliced bacon or pancetta, cut into small cubes

1/4 cup finely chopped onion

3 cooking apples such as Granny Smith, Golden Delicious, or Honeycrisp (about 1 pound)

I cup dry white wine

Salt and freshly ground black pepper

2 tablespoons brown sugar

2 tablespoons unsalted butter

I tablespoon red wine vinegar

1. Heat the oven to 450 degrees. Pull off and discard any blemished outer leaves from the cabbage. Quarter the cabbage and finely shred it. Set aside.

2. Using a sharp paring knife, make an incision around the perimeter of each chestnut, starting and ending on either side of the "topknot," or stem end. Spread the chestnuts in a baking dish just large enough to hold them, place in the oven, and bake for about 10 minutes, or until they split open. Let the chestnuts cool just until they can be handled, then peel them while they are hot.

3. Cook the salt pork in a heavy ovenproof saucepan large enough to hold the cabbage. When the salt pork is rendered of its fat, add the onion and cook briefly to soften it.

4. Meanwhile, peel and core the apples and cut them into quarters. Thinly slice the apple quarters. (There should be about 4 cups.)

5. Add the apples to the saucepan, add the wine, and bring to a boil. Add the cabbage, salt and pepper to taste, brown sugar, and chestnuts. Cover, reduce the heat, and simmer for 10 minutes, stirring occasionally. Make sure that the bottom does not stick and burn.

6. Place the saucepan in the oven and bake for 30 minutes.

7. Reduce the oven heat to 375 degrees and bake for about 1 hour, or until the cabbage is thoroughly tender; stir occasionally as it cooks. Stir in the butter and vinegar and blend well.

SERVES 8 TO 12

COOKING NOTE

When you peel the chestnuts, some may split into pieces, which is just fine. If the skins start to stick, just pop the nuts back in the oven for a few minutes.

SERVING SUGGESTIONS

Cream of Carrot Soup (p. 119), Pork Chops with Rye Bread Stuffing (p. 514), Braised Duck Legs with Pinot Noir Sauce (p. 481), Black Forest Cake (p. 754), Breton Butter Cake (p. 777)

NOVEMBER 17, 1974: "FOOD: TRADITIONAL (WITH A FOREIGN ACCENT)," BY CRAIG CLAIBORNE WITH PIERRE FRANEY.

—1974

⮌ ASPARAGUS ALLA FONTINA

Mimi Sheraton described this dish as "much like a quiche without a crust." That's about right, and without a crust to bother with, it's much easier to make than a quiche.

———

Salt and freshly ground black pepper
1½ pounds thin asparagus, trimmed
4 tablespoons unsalted butter
Freshly grated nutmeg
⅓ cup grated Gruyère or fontina cheese
¾ cup finely minced or slivered prosciutto (about 4 ounces)
2 tablespoons minced flat-leaf parsley
3 large eggs, beaten
3 to 4 tablespoons freshly grated Parmesan cheese

1. Heat the oven to 350 degrees. Bring a large pot of generously salted water to a boil. Add the asparagus and cook until crisp-tender, 3 to 4 minutes. Drain.

2. Cut the asparagus into 1- to 1½-inch lengths. Return the asparagus to the pot, add the butter, and season with salt, pepper, and nutmeg. Set over low heat and stir to melt the butter.

3. Turn the asparagus and butter into a 9- or 10-inch pie plate, and arrange in an even layer. Sprinkle with the Gruyère, prosciutto, and parsley. Pour the beaten eggs on top, gently shaking the pan to distribute. Top with the Parmesan.

4. Bake until the eggs are set into a custard and a golden brown crust forms on top, about 35 minutes. Serve hot or warm.

SERVES 2 TO 3 AS A LIGHT MAIN COURSE, 4 TO 6 AS A FIRST COURSE

SERVING SUGGESTIONS

Spicy, Lemony Clams with Pasta (p. 336), Rhubarb Bellini (p. 30), Caesar Salad (p. 174), Roast Chicken with Bread Salad (p. 467), Sautéed Trout with Brown Butter, Lemon, and Macadamia Nuts (p. 392), Rhubarb Orange (p. 864)

MARCH 9, 1977: "ASPARAGUS: IT'S A RITE OF SPRING," BY MIMI SHERATON.

—1977

MUSHROOMS STUFFED WITH DUXELLES AND SAUSAGE

Stuffed mushrooms, an old-time dish, were revived in the 1970s, when mushroom production, well, mushroomed. (Sorry, couldn't resist.)

_____

For the Duxelles

1 pound large white mushrooms, trimmed
1½ teaspoons unsalted butter
1 teaspoon vegetable or olive oil
1 tablespoon finely chopped onion
1 tablespoon finely chopped shallot
Juice of ½ lemon
Salt and freshly ground black pepper

For the Stuffing

¼ pound sweet Italian sausage (casings removed if necessary)
1 tablespoon finely chopped flat-leaf parsley
Salt and freshly ground black pepper
2 tablespoons fresh bread crumbs
2 tablespoons freshly grated Parmesan cheese
1 tablespoon unsalted butter

1. Heat the oven to 400 degrees. To prepare the duxelles, remove the stems from the mushrooms. Reserve the 12 largest caps. Finely chop the stems and remaining caps. Measure out 1 cup.

2. Heat the butter and oil in a large skillet. Add the onion and shallot and cook until wilted. Add the chopped mushroom stems and stir. Sprinkle with the lemon juice and salt and pepper to taste. Cook, stirring, until all of the moisture has evaporated. Let cool briefly.

3. To make the stuffing, add the sausage and parsley to the duxelles and blend well. Season with salt and pepper.

4. Stuff the reserved mushroom caps with the sausage mixture, mounding it a bit. Sprinkle with a blend of the crumbs and cheese. Dot with the butter.

5. Grease a baking dish and arrange the caps stuffed side up in the dish. Bake for about 20 minutes, basting occasionally if there are any cooking juices (if not, don't worry), or until heated through and browned. Serve hot or cold.

SERVES 4

SERVING SUGGESTIONS
Fennel and Apple Salad with Juniper (p. 189), Almond-Carrot Salad (p. 204), Watercress Salad (p. 171), Roasted Squab with Chicken Liver Stuffing (p. 454), Mashed Potatoes Anna (p. 294), Lemon Bars (p. 690), Apple Crumb Pie (p. 841), Fresh Ginger Cake (p. 775)

APRIL 10, 1977: "FOOD: DELECTABLE CHAMPIGNONS," BY CRAIG CLAIBORNE WITH PIERRE FRANEY.

—1977

POIVRONS VERTS FARCIS (STUFFED GREEN PEPPERS)

The forgotten dinner of the 1970s. These stuffed peppers have a generously flavored filling that's brothy, rich, even a little crisp on top.

_____

4 green bell peppers (1¼ to 1½ pounds)
8 sweet and/or hot Italian sausages
1 cup finely chopped onion
1 clove garlic, finely minced
1 tablespoon curry powder
Salt and freshly ground black pepper
1½ cups slightly undercooked rice
1 large egg, lightly beaten
¼ cup chicken broth
2 tablespoons fresh bread crumbs
2 tablespoons freshly grated Parmesan cheese
2 tablespoons olive oil

1. Heat the oven to 400 degrees. Bring a large saucepan of water to a boil. Cut off the stem of each pepper and cut the pepper lengthwise in half. Clean out the seeds. Drop the peppers into the boiling water and cook for 1 minute. Drain.

2. Remove the meat from the sausage skins. Add the meat to a large skillet, set over medium heat, and cook, stirring to break up any lumps. Add the onion, garlic, curry powder, and salt and pepper to taste and cook, stirring often, for 8 minutes. Let cool briefly.

3. Scrape the sausage mixture into a bowl and add the rice, egg, and broth. Stir to blend. Stuff the pepper

halves with equal portions of the mixture. Arrange the halves in a baking dish. Blend the bread crumbs and cheese and sprinkle over the stuffed peppers. Sprinkle with the oil.

4. Bake for 20 minutes. Reduce the oven temperature to 375 degrees and continue baking until the stuffing is cooked through, 15 to 25 more minutes.

SERVES 4 AS A LIGHT MAIN COURSE OR AS A FIRST COURSE

COOKING NOTES

I had about 1½ cups leftover stuffing, so you might want to buy an extra pepper.

If the curry powder in your pantry is old, buy some fresh before you make these.

I used all sweet sausages, which were great, but next time I'd probably mix sweet and hot.

SERVING SUGGESTIONS

Tomato Soup II (p. 114), Manicotti with Ricotta Cheese (p. 314), Malfatti (p. 345), Orzo with Pine Nuts and Basil (p. 325), Malcolm and Kelly McDowell's Pink Rigatoni (p. 338), Chocolate Rum Mousse (p. 814), Apple Galette (p. 843), Plum Fritters (p. 865)

MAY 1, 1977: "STUFFED QUARTET," BY CRAIG CLAIBORNE WITH PIERRE FRANEY.

—1977

⌒ TOMATES FARCIES (STUFFED TOMATOES)

This recipe seems like a play on meatballs in tomato sauce, except in this case it's meatballs in tomatoes, on sauce.

A different, equally pleasing, take on stuffed tomatoes is on p. 213.

———

6 ripe but firm tomatoes (2¼ to 2½ pounds), cored
Salt and freshly ground black pepper
2 tablespoons unsalted butter
I cup finely chopped onion
I clove garlic
I bay leaf

½ teaspoon thyme
2 teaspoons chopped fresh basil or
    I teaspoon dried basil
¾ pound ground pork or pork and veal
3 tablespoons pine nuts (optional)
3 tablespoons freshly grated Parmesan cheese
2 tablespoons finely chopped flat-leaf parsley
½ cup plus I tablespoon bread crumbs
2 tablespoons peanut or corn oil

1. Heat the oven to 400 degrees. Using a sharp knife, cut off a thin slice from the bottom of each tomato; reserve. Using a melon ball cutter, starting at the bottom, scoop out the center pulp of each tomato, leaving the outside layer intact; reserve the pulp. Sprinkle the insides with salt and pepper and set aside.

2. Melt the butter in a large skillet and add the onion. Finely chop the garlic with the bay leaf, and add to the skillet. Add the tomato pulp and cook for about 10 minutes.

3. Spoon half the resulting tomato sauce over the bottom of a baking dish just large enough to hold the tomatoes in one layer. Add the thyme, basil, ground meat, pine nuts, if using, 2 tablespoons cheese, the parsley, and ½ cup bread crumbs to the remaining sauce. Mix gently with your hands or a fork.

4. Loosely stuff the tomatoes with the filling. (There may be leftover stuffing, in which case, quickly hollow out another tomato.) Arrange the tomatoes in the sauce in the baking dish. Place the reserved sliced bottoms on top.

5. Sprinkle with the remaining tablespoon of cheese blended with the remaining tablespoon of crumbs. Sprinkle with the oil and bake for 30 to 35 minutes, basting occasionally with the pan juices.

SERVES 2 TO 3 AS A LIGHT MAIN COURSE, 6 AS A FIRST COURSE

COOKING NOTES

It's important not to overwork the stuffing—you want to keep it light and tender, like a good bread pudding.

The filling will expand in the oven, so don't pack the tomatoes too snugly.

SERVING SUGGESTIONS

Pistou Soup (p. 135), Green Gazpacho (p. 160), Vitello Tonnato (p. 559), Raspberry Granita (p. 719)

MAY 1, 1977: "STUFFED QUARTET," BY CRAIG CLAIBORNE
WITH PIERRE FRANEY.

—1977

AUGUST 28, 1977: "FOOD: WHEN CUCUMBERS ARE BEST,"
BY FLORENCE FABRICANT.

—1977

∼ CUCUMBERS IN CREAM

This chilled cucumber salad comes from Florence Fabricant, a long-time reporter at the *Times* who is both feared and cherished for her dogged coverage of new products and restaurant news, and who is known around town as Flo Fab. Cucumber salad is the kind of dish that you can't avoid, as it lurks in delis, at picnics, and on buffets. But once you taste this one, you'll realize how often it's poorly made and sorely lacking lemon. The sour cream and lemon electrify each other's best traits: the floral aroma in the lemon zest and the richness in the sour cream. This salad is one of my favorite recipes in the book—thanks Flo Fab!

———

3 cups peeled, thinly sliced cucumbers (about 3
    regular cucumbers) or thinly sliced (peeled if
    desired) English (seedless) cucumbers
1 tablespoon kosher salt
1 cup sour cream
Grated zest and juice of 1 lemon
1 tablespoon minced chives
Freshly ground black pepper

1. Dust the cucumbers with the salt and let stand for at least 30 minutes. Rinse thoroughly and drain.
2. Combine the sour cream, lemon zest, and juice in a bowl. Toss the cucumbers in the dressing and dust with the chives and a generous sprinkling of pepper.

SERVES 6

SERVING SUGGESTIONS
Roast Chicken Salad (p. 492), Buttermilk Roast Chicken (p. 493), New York Strip Steak with Horseradish-Mint Glaze (p. 566), Eisenhower's Steak in the Fire (p. 512—or just a grilled steak!), Tomatoes Vinaigrette (p. 218), Saratoga Potatoes (p. 273), Lora Brody's Bête Noire (Intense Chocolate Cake; p. 763), Salted Caramel Ice Cream (p. 733), Fresh Raspberry (or Blackberry or Blueberry) Flummery (p. 824)

∼ ARTICHAUTS VINAIGRETTE

Eating these artichokes was an epiphany. As I formed most of my cooking habits during the Mediterranean cooking wave of the 1980s and 1990s, olive oil was my default dressing medium. But here the vinaigrette is based on peanut, vegetable, or corn oil, all of which are comparatively flavorless. The resulting vinaigrette is much cleaner and less assertive, allowing the artichokes' flavor, brightened by the vinegar, to dominate as it should.

Artichokes with vinaigrette may be served at any temperature, but I think they're best a little warm.

———

4 large artichokes (about 12 ounces each)
Salt
1 tablespoon Dijon mustard
2 tablespoons red wine vinegar
Freshly ground black pepper
¾ cup peanut, vegetable, or corn oil
Finely chopped flat-leaf parsley (about 1 tablespoon)

1. Place the artichokes one at a time on their sides and, using a sharp knife, cut off the upper leaves about 1 inch from the top. Slice off the stem, leaving a neat flat base. Using a pair of kitchen scissors, cut off the spiky tops of the artichoke leaves about 1 inch from the tip of each.
2. Put the artichokes in a pot or large saucepan with cold water to cover. Add salt to taste. Reduce the heat and cover the artichokes with a clean cloth or a plate to keep them submerged, and bring to a boil. Simmer for 30 to 45 minutes, until tender; do not overcook. Drain well and let stand until ready to serve.
3. Put the mustard, vinegar, and salt and pepper to taste in a small bowl and beat vigorously with a wire whisk. Gradually add the oil, beating constantly. Add the parsley.
4. Serve the artichokes with small bowls of the sauce on the side.

SERVES 4

After cooking the artichokes, place them stem side up on a baking rack, and once they're cool enough to handle, gently squeeze them to release any excess moisture. No one wants a soggy artichoke.

SERVING SUGGESTIONS

Jean Yves Legarve's Spaghetti with Lemon and Asparagus Sauce (p. 319), Sea Scallops with Sweet Red Peppers and Zucchini (p. 409), Steamed Fish with Thyme and Tomato Vinaigrette (p. 408), Crepes Suzette (p. 821), Strawberry Soup (p. 816), Strawberry Sorbet (p. 732), Dorie Greenspan's Sablés (p. 703)

FEBRUARY 25, 1981: "60-MINUTE GOURMET," BY PIERRE FRANEY

—1981

✎ CAPONATA

Caponata, a bright eggplant relish textured with olives, capers, garlic, and herbs, is a great dish to serve with rich, fatty meat, like lamb and steak.

———

- 1 large eggplant, peeled if desired and cut into ¾-inch cubes
- ¼ cup olive oil
- 2 onions, coarsely chopped
- 2 large stalks celery, coarsely chopped
- 3 cloves garlic, minced
- 6 large canned tomatoes, drained
- 36 Sicilian olives, pitted and cut into large pieces
- One 3-ounce jar capers, with its brine
- ½ teaspoon dried thyme or oregano
- Salt and freshly ground black pepper to taste

1. Soak the eggplant in cold salted water for 20 minutes. Drain.
2. Heat the olive oil in a heavy pot. Add the onions, celery, and garlic and simmer, covered, until the onions are translucent.
3. Add the remaining ingredients, breaking up the tomatoes with the side of a spoon, and simmer until the eggplant is quite tender, 30 to 40 minutes. Correct the seasoning, adding more vinegar and/or salt as desired. Serve warm or cool.

SERVES 6

COOKING NOTES

Craig Claiborne said, "This is better the second or third day, and it makes an excellent recipe for home canning. Simply increase all quantities as needed."

To make cold salted water for Step 1, dissolve 3 tablespoons salt in ½ cup warm water, then add 3½ cups cold water.

When you soak the eggplant, it will float to the surface; you may want to keep it submerged by laying a plate on top of it.

In Step 3, I cooked the caponata partly with the lid on, partly with it off, so that as the eggplant softened, the juices also cooked down, thickening slightly. You want caponata to be neither dry nor sloppy. The water content of eggplant varies, so adjust the heat as needed.

SERVING SUGGESTIONS

Chopped Salad of Romaine, Arugula, Dill, and Lemon (p. 195), Shrimp Baked with Feta Cheese, Greek-Style (p. 397), Grilled Leg of Lamb with Mustard Seeds (p. 544), Potato "Tostones" (Flattened Potatoes; p. 301), Moussaka (p. 518), Iraqi Grape Leaves Stuffed with Lamb, Mint, and Cinnamon (p. 510), Broiled Lamb Leg Chops on Eggplant Planks with Mint-Yogurt Sauce (p. 549), Grilled Hanger Steak (p. 551), Honey Spice Cookies (p. 685), Vanilla Plum Ice (p. 734)

APRIL 15, 1981: "RECIPES FROM CHILDHOOD SEDERS IN THE MIDDLE EAST," BY ROBERT FARRAR CAPON.

—1981

✎ STEAMED SPINACH WITH BALSAMIC BUTTER

Succulence and austerity don't often meet at the table, but they pair nicely in this easy little recipe.

I suppose I could say about every ingredient in the book that it's important to use the very best quality—it's always vital with chocolate and oils—but in this recipe, the balsamic vinegar is a deal breaker. You need a balanced, concentrated vinegar that's syrupy enough to emulsify the butter and good enough not to turn bitter when boiled. (Try www.formaggiokitchen.com.)

The recipe makes far more balsamic butter than you'll need for the spinach, so save the rest for another use, such as spreading on roasted salmon or braised endive.

———

¼ cup balsamic vinegar

2 tablespoons red wine

6 tablespoons cold unsalted butter

Salt and freshly ground black pepper

3 bunches spinach, washed and trimmed

1. Combine the vinegar and wine in a saucepan, bring to a boil, and reduce by half. Remove from the heat and add the butter 1 tablespoon at a time, whisking until all the butter is incorporated. Season with salt and pepper.

2. Steam the spinach for 2 to 3 minutes, or until wilted; use tongs to toss the leaves so they wilt evenly. Transfer to a serving bowl.

3. Spoon one-third of the balsamic butter over the spinach and toss to mix. Taste, adding more butter if needed (reserve the rest for another use).

SERVES 6

SERVING SUGGESTIONS

Zuppa di Funghi Siciliana (Sicilian Mushroom Soup; p. 127), Creamy Farro and Chickpea Soup (p. 143), Braised Ligurian Chicken (p. 491), Italian Roast Potatoes (p. 300), Apple Galette (p. 843), Lemon Mousse for a Crowd (p. 861)

PERIOD DETAIL

"Balsamic" and "vinegar" were first mentioned together in the *Times* in an 1852 perfumery advertisement touting "balsamic toilet vinegar" among other products such as cologne and pomades. According to Mandy Aftel, a perfume maker in Berkeley, California, it was likely made with "Mecca balsam" and was used as a restorative. Chandler Burr, also a perfume expert, said these vinegars "were drunk as often as they were put on the body." Balsamic vinegar as we know it didn't appear in the *Times* until 1980.

OCTOBER 23, 1983: "THE HUNTER'S BOUNTY," BY ROBERT FARRAR CAPON.

—1983

ZUCCHINI AND VERMOUTH

Any embellishment upon zucchini sautéed in olive oil is likely to be a mistake, but vermouth is appropriately subtle, its low, gentle aroma stirring and murmuring in the background.

———

1 tablespoon olive oil

3 medium zucchini, coarsely grated

1 to 2 splashes (2 tablespoons) dry vermouth

Salt and freshly ground black pepper

1. Heat the oil in a large skillet over medium-high heat, add the zucchini and cook until it begins to soften and the liquid evaporates, 3 to 5 minutes; stir occasionally.

2. Add the vermouth and continue cooking until the liquid has evaporated, 2 to 3 minutes. Season with salt and pepper.

SERVES 3

COOKING NOTE

You want to use a skillet that's large enough to spread the shredded zucchini out in a thin layer so it cooks without stewing. The pan should be dry enough when the vermouth is added that the liquid is a shock to the hot pan.

SERVING SUGGESTIONS

Sole Grenobloise (Sautéed Sole with Capers and Lemons; p. 399), Halibut with Parsley-Shellfish Sauce (p. 425), Breaded Chicken Breasts with Parmesan Cheese (p. 465), Stir-Fried Chicken with Creamed Corn (p. 483), Fresh Raspberry (or Blackberry or Blueberry) Flummery (p. 824), Blueberry Pie with a Lattice Top (p. 853)

JANUARY 8, 1984: "HEALTH/FOOD: EATING SENSIBLY," BY MARIAN BURROS.

—1984

⌐ JONATHAN WAXMAN'S RED PEPPER PANCAKES

As I explain in the book's introduction, many of the post-1960s recipes included here are ones that readers suggested to me. I cooked every recipe that was recommended by three or more people (and hundreds of others as well), and was struck by the groupings that became clear. Two excellent black bean soup recipes emerged from 1986 and 1987, and two red lentil soups from the 1990s; tomatoes vinaigrette recipes ran months apart in 1963; and these red pepper pancakes from Jonathan Waxman, then the chef at Jams in New York, appeared just a few months earlier than a corn-cake recipe by his nearby rival, Anne Rosenzweig, the chef at Arcadia. In some cases, I chose one recipe from such pairs, but occasionally both deserved admission; see p. 282 for the corn cakes.

Rosenzweig and Waxman played with the same trope—reimagining blini with crème fraîche and caviar—but went in completely different directions. Rosenzweig used corn as the medium for her neat, taut cakes and emphasized its sweetness and crunch against the tart cream and salty fish eggs. Waxman's feather-weight corn and red pepper pancakes are typical of 1980s restaurant cooking, a panoply of flavors. The pancakes are perched on top of a creamy red pepper and corn sauce and adorned with two kinds of caviar, chopped cilantro, and chives.

———

2 large red bell peppers

2 tablespoons unsalted butter

1 tablespoon olive oil

1 ear corn, shucked and kernels cut off

1 shallot, finely chopped

Salt and freshly ground black pepper

1 cup heavy cream

1½ cups all-purpose flour

1 tablespoon baking powder

1 cup whole milk

3 large eggs, separated

Olive oil for greasing the griddle

1 tablespoon osetra caviar

1 tablespoon red caviar

⅓ cup sliced chives

¼ cup chopped cilantro

1. Grill the peppers over an open flame or under the broiler, turning occasionally, until charred all over. Place in a paper bag or wrap in aluminum foil and allow them to steam and cool a bit.

2. Peel the peppers and remove the cores and seeds. Cut 1 pepper into very small dice. Cut the second pepper in half. Cut one half into very fine strips. Mince the other half, almost to the point of a puree. Set aside.

3. Heat the butter and oil in a large skillet over medium heat. Add the corn, pepper dice and strips, and shallot and sauté for 2 minutes. Season with salt and pepper, add the cream, reduce the heat to medium-low, and simmer until the pepper and corn are just tender, about 15 minutes. Remove from the heat and cover to keep warm.

4. Meanwhile, sift the flour, baking powder, and 1 teaspoon salt into a bowl. Stir in the milk, egg yolks, and pepper to taste. Beat the egg whites in a large bowl until they form soft peaks, and fold into the egg yolk mixture. Fold in the minced peppers.

5. Grease a griddle or nonstick sauté pan with olive oil and heat over medium-high heat. Working in batches, spoon the batter onto the griddle to make 3-inch pancakes. Cook until lightly browned on the bottom, about 2 minutes, then flip and cook on the other side, about 1 minute longer. Stack on a plate and cover to keep warm while you continue making pancakes. You will need 16 pancakes.

6. Spoon some warm pepper and corn sauce onto each plate and top with 2 pancakes. Garnish with the caviars, chives, and cilantro.

SERVES 4 AS A MAIN COURSE, 8 AS A FIRST COURSE

COOKING NOTE
As much as I'd love to say you can skip the caviar, you shouldn't. Choosing one kind rather than two is fine, and there's nothing wrong with a domestic farm-raised variety, as long as you like the flavor.

SERVING SUGGESTIONS
Thomas Keller's Gazpacho (p. 146), Deep-Fried Soft-Shell Crabs (p. 398), Zucchini and Vermouth (p. 227), Fresh Blueberry Buckle (p. 815)

JUNE 2, 1985: "FOOD: A TRIBUTE TO AMERICAN COOKING," BY MARIAN BURROS. RECIPE ADAPTED FROM JONATHAN WAXMAN, THE CHEF AT JAMS IN NEW YORK CITY.

—1985

⤙ FRIED ARTICHOKES AZZURRO

Rather than blanching and then frying, as you normally do when frying artichokes, this Sicilian recipe melds the two steps. You combine the artichoke wedges in a pan with olive oil, water, and seasonings and then blast them with heat, so as the water boils off, the artichokes steam, and by the time the water is all gone, they're glistening with oil.

————

1¾ pounds tender artichokes
    (4 to 6 artichokes)
1 lemon, halved
2½ tablespoons extra virgin olive oil
⅓ cup water
½ teaspoon salt
2 tablespoons chopped flat-leaf parsley
1¼ teaspoons mashed garlic

1. Slice off 1 inch from the tops of the artichokes. Remove the outer layers of leaves from each one until you reach the tender pale yellow-green leaves. Trim off all hard green parts around the base and the stem. Rub with the lemon juice; then squeeze the juice into a bowl of water. Add the artichokes and soak for 1 hour; drain.

2. Spread the inner leaves of each artichoke open and use a melon baller (or a sharp spoon) to remove the choke from the center of the artichoke. Cut the artichokes lengthwise in half and cut each half into ¼-inch-thick wedges.

3. Place the artichokes and remaining ingredients in a 9- or 10-inch heavy skillet and cook over high heat, tossing, until all the water has evaporated, 2 to 3 minutes. Do not allow them to fry, or the garlic will turn bitter. The artichokes will be slightly crunchy. Pour into a serving dish and serve warm.

SERVES 4

COOKING NOTES

I used small artichokes, weighing 4 ounces each, but it doesn't matter what size you use—you just need a total of 1¾ pounds. Also make sure your wedges are no more than ¼ inch thick, or they won't cook through.

Paula Wolfert, whose recipe this is, noted: "Soaking softens the leaves so they will spread easily. Arti-chokes can be cleaned 1 to 2 hours before cooking. Keep submerged in acidulated water (4 cups water to 2 tablespoons vinegar) in the refrigerator." I used lemon juice instead of vinegar.

SERVING SUGGESTIONS
Spaghettini with Vegetables and Pepper Vodka Sauce (p. 320), Saltimbocca (p. 561), Risotto with Lemon and Crème Fraîche (p. 345), Pork Braised in Milk and Cream (p. 557), Balducci's Tiramisù (p. 830), Rhubarb-Strawberry Mousse (p. 835), Saffron Panna Cotta (p. 845)

DECEMBER 15, 1985: "FOOD: A DISH OF SICILIAN HISTORY," BY PAULA WOLFERT.

—1985

⤙ ISMAIL MERCHANT'S SPINACH PUREE (PALAK BHARTA)

Ismail Merchant, who with his partner James Ivory made more than thirty films, was also a talented cook. He published a number of cookbooks, including *Ismail Merchants's Indian Cuisine* and *Ismail Merchant's Passionate Meals*.

Merchant's cooking resided somewhere between India and the West, as you can see in this spinach puree. A heady foundation of steamed spinach, scallions, and garlic is blended with butter and Dijon mustard. It's an outrageously pungent dish: not exactly a condiment and not really a side dish, but an addictive little mixture that your fork keeps searching for more of. Serve this with other forthright food—a good tuna curry (p. 435), for instance—and do not leave the house afterward, or you'll be trailed by an onion cloud.

————

1½ pounds spinach, tough stems and blemished
    leaves removed and rinsed well
2 large spring onions (or 7 scallions),
    trimmed and coarsely chopped
    (about 1 cup loosely packed)
2 cloves garlic
1 tablespoon unsalted butter
Salt and freshly ground black pepper
1 tablespoon Dijon mustard

1. It is preferable that the spinach be steamed rather than boiled. Bring water to a boil in the bottom of a

metal steamer. Place the rack over the boiling water, cover, and steam the spinach until it is wilted, 2 to 3 minutes.

2. Put the hot spinach into the container of a food processor and add the green onions, garlic, butter, salt and pepper, and mustard. Blend thoroughly.

MAKES ABOUT 2 CUPS; SERVES 4 TO 6

COOKING NOTE

Merchant called for "green onions" which is the British name for scallions. But since 2 scallions will not yield a cup chopped, I suspect that he may have meant young, or spring, onions, the kind that have not yet developed a dry skin. They are often sold in bunches at farmers' markets in the summer. I made this in the winter, so I used scallions, and it took 7 to make 1 cup chopped.

SERVING SUGGESTIONS

Gigi Salad (Shrimp, Bacon, and Green Bean Salad; p. 184), Madame Laracine's Gratin Dauphinois (p. 284), Steak au Poivre (p. 573), Junior's Cheesecake (p. 771)

AUGUST 31, 1986: "FOOD: CURRYING FAVOR," BY CRAIG CLAIBORNE. RECIPE ADAPTED FROM ISMAIL MERCHANT.

—1986

✑ BEETS IN LIME CREAM

An excellent dish in every way.

Beets went through a significant culinary transformation in the mid-twentieth century, when cooks finally realized that boiling the hell out of them wasn't doing anyone any good. The title of the article says it all: "Sweet Praise for Lowly Beets."

---

1 bunch beets with greens (1¼ to 1½ pounds)

2 tablespoons unsalted butter

1 cup minced onion

Finely shredded zest of 1 large lime

1 cup heavy cream

Fresh lime juice to taste

Salt

1 lime, cut into wedges, for garnish

1. Cut off the beet greens and reserve. Peel the beets with a vegetable peeler, and cut them into large strips the size of French fries. (There should be about 3 cups.) Coarsely chop the greens. Reserve.

2. Melt the butter in a medium skillet over medium-high heat. Sauté the onion for 15 minutes, or until it turns golden and browns around the edges. Lower the heat to medium, stir in the lime zest, and cook, stirring, for about 2 minutes more, just until the zest toasts. (The pan will be very dry at this point, but don't worry—the beets will add moisture.) Add the beets, and cook, stirring occasionally, until they turn translucent, about 10 minutes.

3. Stir in the cream, lower the heat slightly, and cook for 15 to 20 minutes more, until the beets are tender and the cream has gently bubbled away to a thick sauce; stir only often enough to prevent sticking and scorching. Do not overcook.

4. While the beets cook, steam the greens for about 15 minutes, or until tender. (Plan to have them ready when beets are.)

5. As soon as the beets are tender, add lime juice in teaspoons and salt in pinches until seasoned to taste.

6. To serve, arrange the greens on a warm serving platter and, using the back of a spoon, form 6 little nests. Remove the beets from the sauce with a slotted spoon and put into nests. Garnish the platter with lime wedges, and pass the sauce separately.

SERVES 6

COOKING NOTES

I used 4 teaspoons of lime juice.

The serving style is very 1980s—if you'd prefer a more modern approach, do away with the nests. Spread the greens on a serving platter, and spoon the beets and sauce on top.

SERVING SUGGESTIONS

Black Bean Soup with Salsa and Jalapeño Corn-Bread Muffins (p. 129), Staff Meal Chicken with Salsa Verde (p. 484), Buttermilk Roast Chicken (p. 493), Salted Caramel Ice Cream (p. 733), Aztec Hot Chocolate Pudding (p. 855)

FEBRUARY 11, 1987: "SWEET PRAISE FOR LOWLY BEETS," BY LESLIE LAND.

—1987

CASSOLETTE OF MORELS, FIDDLEHEADS, AND ASPARAGUS

Fiddlehead ferns were like the Jon Bon Jovi haircut. They seemed cool at the time, but you look back and cringe. However, it's not that fiddlehead ferns were undeserving of interest, it's that we put them through so many culinary indignities during their brief popularity. Fiddlehead fern spaghettini—no, no, no! This recipe is an exception: tender fiddleheads and asparagus are nestled in individual casserole dishes under a layer of morels and cream and a crisp cheese-and-bread-crumb topping.

---

4 cups small fresh morels or 2 ounces dried morels

1 tablespoon unsalted butter

3 tablespoons chopped shallots

1 teaspoon minced garlic

1 cup heavy cream

1/3 cup dry Madeira

Salt and freshly ground black pepper

6 ounces thin asparagus, cut into 1-inch pieces (about 1 1/2 cups)

6 ounces fiddlehead ferns, cleaned of brown leaves (about 1 1/2 cups)

1/2 cup fresh bread crumbs

1/3 cup freshly grated Parmesan cheese

1/3 cup grated Swiss cheese

1 tablespoon chopped basil

1 teaspoon chopped thyme

1. If using dried morels, put the mushrooms into a small saucepan with 3 cups of water and bring to a boil. Turn off the heat and let the mushrooms steep for 1 hour. Drain the mushrooms, reserving the soaking liquid, and rinse under running water to remove all residual sand and dirt. Strain the reserved liquid through cheesecloth or a coffee filter.

2. Remove the stems from the mushrooms (reserve for another recipe that calls for chopped mushrooms). Melt the butter in a large skillet over medium heat. Add the mushrooms and shallots, stir, and sauté until tender, about 8 minutes. Add the garlic and sauté for 2 minutes. Add the cream, Madeira (and 1/2 cup of the mushroom soaking liquid if using dried morels), and

salt and pepper to taste, bring to a simmer, and simmer over medium-low heat for 5 minutes. If using fresh morels, remove the mushrooms from the sauce and reduce the liquid, for about 10 minutes, stirring occasionally, until it coats the back of a spoon, then stir the mushrooms back into the sauce. If using dried morels, reduce the liquid without removing the mushrooms.

3. Meanwhile, blanch the asparagus and fiddleheads in a pot of boiling salted water for 1 1/2 to 2 minutes. Drain and rinse under cold running water to stop the cooking; drain well.

4. Combine the bread crumbs, Parmesan, Swiss cheese, basil, and thyme and mix thoroughly.

5. Heat the oven to 375 degrees. Divide the blanched asparagus and fiddleheads among 6 small heatproof casseroles. Spoon the morel cream over the asparagus and fiddleheads and top with the seasoned crumbs.

6. Bake for 10 minutes. If desired, place under the broiler until the tops are light brown.

SERVES 6 AS A SIDE DISH OR FIRST COURSE

COOKING NOTE

I used dried morels, because who can afford 4 cups of fresh ones?

SERVING SUGGESTIONS

Nicole Kaplan's Gougères (p. 76), Chilled English Pea–Mint Soup (p. 162), Gently Cooked Salmon with Mashed Potatoes (p. 415), Fricassee of Chicken with Tarragon (p. 456), Rhubarb-Strawberry Mousse (p. 835), Strawberry Soup (p. 816)

MAY 24, 1987: "FOOD: MOREL CONQUESTS," BY JENIFER LANG. RECIPE ADAPTED FROM HARLAN PETERSON, THE CHEF AND OWNER OF TAPAWINGO IN ELLSWORTH, MICHIGAN.

—1987

HARICOTS VERTS WITH BALSAMIC VINAIGRETTE

There's a great lesson in this recipe: if you want to make a delicious balsamic vinaigrette, balsamic vinegar cannot be the only acid. It's too strong to go on a salad alone, unless you happen to own the kind they sell by the dropper, in which case you shouldn't be mixing it into vinaigrette. But if you're using the average junk we all buy at the supermarket, you need to cut it, as this recipe demonstrates, with something like red wine vinegar.

It's a lovely accompaniment to the haricots verts with dill and scallions, but the vinaigrette could go on almost anything you like. If you can't find haricots verts, feel free to use regular green beans, or even wax beans.

For the Vinaigrette
1 ½ teaspoons salt
2 tablespoons balsamic vinegar
2 tablespoons red wine vinegar
2 teaspoons Dijon mustard
Freshly ground black pepper (30 turns of the mill)
¾ cup olive oil

For the Haricots Verts
¼ pound haricots verts or green beans
¼ cup scallions cut into ⅛-inch-thick rounds
1 tablespoon chopped dill

Lettuce greens of your choice

1. To make the vinaigrette, dissolve the salt in the vinegars in a glass jar. Add the mustard, pepper, and olive oil. Secure the lid and shake vigorously. (The vinaigrette can be refrigerated for up to 5 days. The yield is 1 cup; you need 2 tablespoons for this recipe.)
2. Steam the haricots verts for 3 to 4 minutes, then plunge them into ice water to stop the cooking and hold the color. Drain well. Remove the stem ends only.
3. Place the beans in a serving bowl. Add the scallions, dill, and 2 tablespoons vinaigrette and toss until well combined. Serve immediately, or within a few hours, on a bed of lettuce greens.

SERVES 2

SERVING SUGGESTIONS
Pan-Roasted Chicken with End-of-Season Tomatoes (p. 482), Grilled Leg of Lamb with Mustard Seeds (p. 544), Mashed Potatoes Anna (p. 294), Bolzano Apple Cake (p. 783), Peach Salad (p. 805)

OCTOBER 18, 1987: "FOOD: STOCKING UP," BY KAREN LEE AND ALEXANDRA BRANYON.

—1987

ANTON MOSIMANN'S BRAISED BRUSSELS SPROUTS IN CREAM

2 cups heavy cream
1 ½ pounds Brussels sprouts
1 teaspoon finely minced fresh ginger
1 teaspoon finely minced garlic
Freshly grated nutmeg
Salt and freshly ground white pepper

1. Put the cream in a heavy saucepan, bring to a boil over medium-low heat, and cook at a slow but steady boil until the cream is reduced by one-third and is thick and yellow.
2. Meanwhile, rinse and trim the Brussels sprouts. Cut each into quarters and grate on a box grater or process in a food processor until the sprouts are the texture of homemade coleslaw. (In the food processor, this is best done in 2 batches, using the pulse mechanism.)
3. When the cream is reduced, add the ginger and garlic and mix well. Grate 8 to 10 scrapings of nutmeg into the cream, or more if you wish. Add the shredded sprouts and turn in the cream to coat well. Season with salt and pepper. Turn the heat to medium and braise the sprouts, uncovered, stirring and turning frequently, for 5 to 6 minutes. They should be al dente, that is, cooked through but with a crisp bite to them. Check for seasoning, adding salt and pepper if necessary.

SERVES 6

SERVING SUGGESTIONS
Elizabeth Frink's Roast Lemon Chicken (p. 478), Brine-Cured Pork Chops (p. 569), Pork Arrosto with Prunes and Grappa (p. 577), Filet de Boeuf Rôti with Sauce Bordelaise (p. 528), Sweet Potato Cecilia (p. 276), Italian Roast Potatoes (p. 300), Bordeaux Jelly (p. 593), Queen of Puddings (p. 866), Polish Jewish Plum Cake (p. 769)

DECEMBER 13, 1987: "FOOD: A CHRISTMAS FEAST," BY NANCY HARMON JENKINS. RECIPE ADAPTED FROM ANTON MOSIMANN, THE CHEF AT THE DORCHESTER IN LONDON.

—1987

✑ AL FORNO'S ROASTED ASPARAGUS

You'll love the strategy in this recipe. By placing your oven rack on the highest shelf and roasting the asparagus on it with the oven cranked to 500 degrees, you get perfectly roasted spears—shocked with heat on the outside, moist as morning grass inside.

————

1 ½ pounds asparagus
2 to 3 tablespoons olive oil
Kosher salt

1. Move an oven rack to the highest shelf and heat the oven to 500 degrees. Wash the asparagus under cold running water. Cut away about 1 inch from the bottom of each spear. Place the asparagus in a single layer in a roasting pan and brush with the olive oil. Sprinkle with salt to taste, and shake the pan or roll the asparagus so the salt disperses.
2. Roast the asparagus until the spears are tender when pierced with the tip of a knife, 10 to 12 minutes, depending on the thickness. Transfer to a serving platter.

SERVES 6

COOKING NOTES
Thick spears work best.

Judith Barrett, who wrote about this recipe, said, "This technique can be applied to onions, peppers, eggplant, tomatoes, broccoli, leeks, and potatoes. Cooking times may vary."

SERVING SUGGESTIONS
Oven-Roasted Branzino with Hazelnut Picada (p. 441), Roast Chicken with Bread Salad (p. 467), Mashed Potatoes Anna (p. 294), Coeur à la Creme with Rhubarb Sauce (p. 864)

JUNE 4, 1989: "FOOD: VEGETATING," BY JUDITH BARRETT. RECIPE ADAPTED FROM AL FORNO RESTAURANT IN PROVIDENCE, RHODE ISLAND.

—1989

✑ SPINACH ROMAN-STYLE

Sometimes I think we don't feel enough shame for the abominations we ate in the 1980s—the mosaics of tuna sprouting chives, the squiggles of mayonnaise. But in the decade's defense, it did usher in the love-fest for Italian cooking. The *Times* published a spate of stories about Italian dishes like risotto, polenta, and biscotti. In an article on antipasti in the Sunday *Magazine*, there was this terrific recipe for spinach "Roman style," sautéed spinach with raisins and pine nuts.

The original recipe came from *The Food of Southern Italy*, by Carlo Middione. In unskilled hands, the dish can be a real dud—the spinach soggy from too much oil, the nuts bland, the raisins hard. But Middione examined every ingredient and cooked each so as to amplify its presence: the garlic is browned, the pine nuts are toasted, and the raisins are first soaked in water, because American raisins, he wrote, "tend to be very sweet and do not have much depth of flavor." Soaking drains them of some of this excess sweetness and plumps them. At the very end, the raisins are nipped with heat, caramelizing them ever so lightly.

The recipe says to serve the spinach hot, but it's great at room temperature as well.

————

3 tablespoons smallest-available raisins (black or golden)
4 medium bunches spinach (about 2 ½ pounds), trimmed and washed at least twice but not dried
⅓ cup olive oil, or as needed
5 medium cloves garlic, well crushed
¼ cup pine nuts
Big pinch of salt
6 or 7 grinds of black pepper

1. Put the raisins in a small bowl with enough warm water to cover and soak for about 15 minutes.
2. Put the wet spinach in a skillet large enough to hold it all (or do in batches) and cook over high heat, stirring constantly, until the spinach collapses and turns dark green. Transfer the spinach to a colander and set aside. If the pan is wet, dry it with a paper towel.
3. Pour the olive oil into the pan and heat over medium-high heat. Add the garlic and brown, being careful it doesn't burn, then remove and discard it. Take the raisins from the water, squeeze them as dry

as possible, and add them to the oil, along with the pine nuts. Turn the heat to medium and cook until the nuts turn a golden color. Be careful, because they can burn easily.

4. Off the heat, return the spinach to the pan, stir it with a fork, and add salt and pepper to taste. Mix all the ingredients, place back on the heat, and cook for about a minute. You can add additional olive oil if you think the spinach looks dry.

SERVES 4

COOKING NOTES
The recipe calls for peeling and then crushing the garlic. I like to use the side of a large chef's knife or a meat pounder: the cloves should be flattened like a pressed flower, so they cook into crisp fans.

Middione instructs you to discard the caramelized garlic after you flavor the oil, but don't! Save it and either eat it as is, sprinkled with salt, or serve it as a garnish.

SERVING SUGGESTIONS
Ann Seranne's Rib Roast of Beef (p. 519), Veal Chops with Sage (p. 564), Italian Roast Potatoes (p. 300), Zabaglione (p. 813), Grapefruit Granita (p. 731)

JUNE 4, 1989: "FOOD: VEGETATING," BY JUDITH BARRETT. RECIPE ADAPTED FROM *THE FOOD OF SOUTHERN ITALY*, BY CARLO MIDDIONE.

—1989

⌐ ICE-COLD TOMATOES WITH BASIL

Years before he built his Manhattan restaurant empire, Daniel Boulud ran the kitchen at Le Cirque, where he served this chilled tomato salad. This dish goes against the current fashion for lush, sun-warmed tomatoes. Serve it on a hot day if you're in the mood for something candid and bracing.

---

4 very ripe tomatoes (about 6 ounces each)
Salt and freshly ground black pepper
2 tablespoons sherry vinegar

3 tablespoons extra virgin olive oil
1 tablespoon minced shallot
2 tablespoons minced chives
8 to 10 large basil leaves
1 bunch arugula, stems removed, rinsed, and dried

1. Cut the tomatoes into thin slices and array the slices in a single layer in a large shallow pan (two, if needed); to help re-form the tomatoes when you serve them, keep the slices in the order in which they were cut. Sprinkle with salt and pepper, the vinegar, olive oil, shallots, and three-quarters of the chives. Mince half the basil and sprinkle over the tomatoes.

2. Place the pan of tomatoes in the refrigerator for about an hour, until thoroughly chilled, or put in the freezer for 10 to 15 minutes. Chill individual plates or a serving platter as well.

3. Arrange the arugula leaves in a circle on each plate or on the platter. Re-form tomatoes and place on the arugula. Sprinkle with the remaining chives, decorate with the remaining basil leaves, and spoon any dressing left in the pan over the top. Serve at once.

SERVES 4

COOKING NOTES
Select tomatoes that are no larger than a tennis ball.

Unless your refrigerator is set very cold, you should put the tomatoes in the freezer so they chill and begin to firm up.

Serve with either very sharp or serrated knives—otherwise, the tomato layers will skid all over people's plates.

SERVING SUGGESTIONS
Zucchini with Crème Fraîche Pesto (p. 250), Fresh Succotash (p. 275), Cold Beef with Tarragon Vinaigrette (p. 534), Lemon Bars (p. 690)

JUNE 13, 1990: "A LITTLE WARMTH IS SAID TO DO WONDERS FOR THE FLORIDA TOMATO," BY FLORENCE FABRICANT. RECIPE ADAPTED FROM DANIEL BOULUD, THE CHEF AT LE CIRQUE.

—1990

☙ GOLDEN WINTER PUREE

Bright and yellow, like a buttercup.

———

Salt
1 pound carrots, peeled and cut into 1-inch chunks
1 pound rutabaga (yellow turnips), peeled and cut into
    1-inch chunks
1 large firm but ripe pear, peeled, cored, and cut into
    1-inch cubes
6 tablespoons unsalted butter, softened
¾ cup heavy cream
½ teaspoon ground ginger
Freshly ground black pepper
1 teaspoon freshly grated nutmeg

1. Bring 4 quarts of salted water to a boil in a large
heavy pot. Add the vegetables and pear and simmer
until they are tender enough to be pierced easily with
a fork, about 25 minutes. Drain.
2. Puree the vegetables and pear in a food processor
and transfer to a bowl; or mash with a potato ricer or
in a food mill. Add the butter in small pieces. Stir in
the cream and ginger. Season to taste with salt and
pepper. Transfer to a saucepan and reheat briefly, then
transfer to a serving dish, smooth the top, and sprinkle
with the nutmeg. (Or, refrigerate the puree. An hour
before serving, allow it to come to room temperature,
then reheat it on top of the stove or transfer to a baking dish and bake at 350 degrees for 20 minutes. Sprinkle with nutmeg before serving.)

SERVES 10

SERVING SUGGESTIONS
Crisp-Braised Duck Legs with Aromatic Vegetables (p.
487), Braised Duck Legs with Pinot Noir Sauce (p.
481), Roasted Brine-Cured Turkey with Wild Mushroom Stuffing (p. 274), Short Ribs with Coffee and
Chiles (p. 579), Wilted Red Cabbage Salad (p. 196),
Figs in Whiskey (p. 859)

NOVEMBER 18, 1990: "INSPIRATION FOR THANKSGIVING'S
COOKS," BY FLORENCE FABRICANT. RECIPE ADAPTED
FROM *THANKSGIVING DINNER*, BY ANTHONY DIAS BLUE
AND KATHRYN K. BLUE.

—1990

☙ SHREDDED BRUSSELS SPROUTS WITH BACON AND PINE NUTS

Like crushing ice cubes into shards, shredding Brussels
sprouts alters the way you experience them. It sub-
dues their cabbage flavor and allows you to cook them
without blanching them first—a step so maddening
it's amazing people continued to eat them for so many
years. Here, in Aimee Lee Ball's recipe—published in
an article on Christmas dinner—the sprouts are tossed
into a food processor and a few pulses later, the shredding is complete.

The sprouts are then wilted in bacon fat and
blended with fried bacon, scallions, nutmeg, and
toasted pine nuts. If that combination isn't good, then
what is?

———

4 pints Brussels sprouts
½ pound bacon, diced
½ cup pine nuts
3 scallions, finely minced
¼ teaspoon freshly grated nutmeg
Salt and freshly ground black pepper

1. Trim and core the sprouts. Put them in a food processor (in 3 to 4 batches) and coarsely shred.
2. Fry the bacon in a large skillet until it is crisp.
Remove and drain on paper towels.
3. Add the pine nuts to the fat remaining in the pan
and stir over medium heat until lightly browned, 2
to 3 minutes. Add the sprouts, scallions, and nutmeg.
Cook, stirring, until the sprouts are cooked through
but still crisp, 6 to 8 minutes. Stir in the bacon and
season generously with salt and pepper.

SERVES 8 TO 10

COOKING NOTES
Ball instructs you to core each Brussels sprout, a step
I had no interest in following. I aggressively trimmed
the sprouts and cut off the stems with a small paring
knife.

This dish reheats well in a sauté pan coated with a
film of olive oil.

Around 2002, chefs in a couple of New York City restaurants began serving a dish of shredded raw Brussels sprouts, sprinkled with olive oil, salt, pepper, and shavings of Pecorino Romano cheese. In this case, shredding the sprouts in the food processor won't work because you need the slices to be even—so you'll want to use a mandoline. Dress the shreds with the olive oil, salt, and pepper, then spread a small mound of the sprouts on each plate. Finish with the shavings of cheese.

SERVING SUGGESTIONS

Butternut Squash Soup with Brown Butter (p. 156), Veal Shanks with Garlic Mashed Potatoes (p. 540), Red Wine Ice Cream (p. 730); also, Thanksgiving dinner

READERS

"We will be having this tonight—for about the millionth time (I skip the pine nuts)."

Mitzi Maxwell, Orlando, Fl, e-mail

"I learned the trick of cutting up and sautéing Brussels sprouts in this recipe, which is the very best way to treat them. I now use that technique when I cook them plain or with onions and lemon."

Laura E. Perry, e-mail

DECEMBER 16, 1990: "COMING HOME," BY AIMEE LEE BALL.
—1990

⌒ RED CABBAGE GLAZED WITH MAPLE SYRUP

———

5 slices bacon, minced

1 onion, minced

1 medium firm, tart apple, peeled, cored, and sliced

1 pound red cabbage (about ½ head), cored, outer leaves removed, remainder shredded

1 bay leaf

½ cup maple syrup

Salt and freshly ground black pepper

1. Heat the oven to 350 degrees. In an ovenproof saucepan or a casserole large enough to hold all the ingredients, sauté the bacon until crisp. Add the onion and sauté until translucent.

2. Add the remaining ingredients, cover, and transfer to the oven. Bake for 30 minutes.

SERVES 4 TO 6

SERVING SUGGESTIONS

Slow-Roasted Duck (p. 475), Turducken (p. 485), Brine-Cured Pork Chops (p. 569), Corn Bread Stuffing (p. 312), Mashed Potatoes Anna (p. 294), Stewed Fennel (p. 245), Creamed Onions (p. 217), Apple Crumb Pie (p. 841), Sour Cream Ice Cream (p. 730)

APRIL 21, 1991: "FOOD: THE SWEET SEASON," BY MARIALISA CALTA. RECIPE ADAPTED FROM YVES LABBE, THE CHEF AT LE CHEVAL D'OR, JEFFERSONVILLE, VERMONT.
—1991

⌒ JAMES BEARD'S PUREED PARSNIPS

We should all think of such good easy recipes, but only James Beard did so consistently. A version of this dish appeared in his book *The James Beard Cookbook* (this one contains cream as well as butter; in the book, it's just butter). I've made it several times, but the first time I had no Madeira and substituted Marsala. I actually preferred my (cheap) Marsala and its nutty, oaky aroma to the Madeira, but you won't go wrong with either.

Beard leaves the topping to you. I've used chopped pecans, which I've tossed in olive oil and salt and toasted before sprinkling on the snowy puree. Moira Hodgson, a writer for the *Times* noted in the article, "The puree is also good formed into small patties, rolled in flour, and browned in butter."

Eat this dish fresh. Its flavor fades with time.

———

3 pounds parsnips, cooked

1 teaspoon salt, or to taste

1 teaspoon sugar

8 to 12 tablespoons (1 to 1½ sticks) unsalted butter, melted, plus more (unmelted) for dotting the top

3 to 4 tablespoons heavy cream

¼ cup Madeira, or to taste

2 tablespoons coarse dry bread crumbs or finely chopped nuts

1. Heat the oven to 350 degrees. Puree the parsnips in a food processor or by putting them through a food mill. If using a processor, don't overpuree them, or they'll get gluey.

2. Combine the puree with the salt, sugar, melted butter, cream, and Madeira in a bowl, and whip together well with a rubber spatula or a whisk. Taste and adjust the seasoning.

3. Spoon the puree into a 1-quart baking dish. Dot with butter and sprinkle with the crumbs (or chopped nuts). Bake for 20 to 30 minutes.

SERVES 6

COOKING NOTE

Beard assumes you know how to cook parsnips. If you don't, here's how: peel them, cut them into 1½-inch pieces, place them in a pan, cover them with water, salt the water generously, and bring to a boil, then simmer until tender, 10 to 15 minutes.

SERVING SUGGESTIONS

Roast Lemon Pepper Duck with Honey Lemon Sauce (p. 470), Steamed and Crisped Duck (p. 476), Roasted Brine-Cured Turkey with Wild Mushroom Stuffing (p. 474), Boeuf Bourguignon I (p. 516), Shredded Brussels Sprouts with Bacon and Pine Nuts (p. 235), Marcella's Pear Cake (p. 769), Bolzano Apple Cake (p. 783)

NOVEMBER 22, 1992: "FOOD: MOVING THE VEGETABLES OUT OF THE SHADOW OF THE TURKEY," BY MOIRA HODGSON. RECIPE ADAPTED FROM *THE JAMES BEARD COOKBOOK*, BY JAMES BEARD.

—1992

3 tablespoons fresh lemon juice
3 tablespoons unsalted butter

1. Thinly slice the carrots in a food processor fitted with the slicing attachment. Steam over boiling water until they are tender but still firm.

2. Mix the cumin, mustard, and lemon juice in a serving dish. Add the butter, cutting it into small pieces.

3. When the carrots are cooked, drain and stir into the serving bowl.

SERVES 8

COOKING NOTES

The term "baby carrots" has changed its meaning over the years. It once meant small young carrots, but it has also come to refer to carrots that have been shaved down into short nubs—"baby" carrots rather than "baby carrots." You can use either here: the point is simply to use slender carrots so you can slice them and have even-sized circles.

The recipe said to slice the carrots in a food processor, but since I couldn't find my slicing attachment, I sliced them by hand, which takes less time than you might think.

SERVING SUGGESTIONS

Moroccan Tomato Soup (p. 134), Buttermilk Roast Chicken (p. 493), Mediterranean Lentil Salad with Lemon-Thyme Vinaigrette (p. 288), Flourless Apricot Honey Soufflé (p. 846)

NOVEMBER 17, 1993: "EATING WELL," BY MARIAN BURROS.

—1993

⌇ CUMIN-MUSTARD CARROTS

The cumin and carrot idiom seems to have been born of the Moroccan carrot salads that became popular in the 1970s (and remained popular in the 1990s: see p. 187). This is a warm version—the sweet root, a tart dressing, both polished with butter.

———

2 pounds baby carrots, peeled if necessary
1½ teaspoons ground cumin
3 tablespoons whole-grain mustard

⌇ CURRIED ROOT VEGETABLE STEW WITH DUMPLINGS

You are reminded as you eat this of how sweet root vegetables can be. And you realize that pairing the sweet stew with the dumplings (which are much like currant scones with more salt) is a stroke of genius—one of many by *Sunday Magazine* columnist Molly O'Neill.

———

For the Stew

1½ teaspoons unsalted butter

1 small onion, chopped

3 cloves garlic, minced

1½ teaspoons curry powder

4 cups vegetable broth

2 medium carrots, peeled, halved lengthwise,
    and cut into ½-inch lengths

2 large parsnips, peeled, thick ends halved lengthwise,
    and cut into ⅛-inch-thick slices

1 small celery root, trimmed, peeled,
    and cut into ¼-inch cubes

1 medium sweet potato, peeled
    and cut into ½-inch cubes

3 tablespoons all-purpose flour

2 teaspoons salt

Freshly ground black pepper

1 tablespoon chopped flat-leaf parsley

For the Dumplings

1 cup all-purpose flour

1½ teaspoons baking powder

¾ teaspoon salt

½ teaspoon ground mace

2 tablespoons cold unsalted butter

¼ cup dried currants

6 tablespoons whole milk

1. To make the stew, melt the butter in a large pot over medium heat. Add the onion and cook for 3 minutes. Stir in the garlic and curry powder and cook for 30 seconds. Stir in the broth, carrots, and parsnips and bring to a boil, then reduce to a simmer, cover, and cook for 15 minutes. Stir in the celery root and sweet potato and cook for 10 minutes.

2. Meanwhile, make the dumplings: Combine the flour, baking powder, salt, and mace in a bowl. Rub in the butter until the mixture resembles coarse meal. Mix in the currants. Stir in the milk just to combine.

3. On a lightly floured surface, with floured hands, shape the dough into 1-inch balls.

4. Form a smooth paste by stirring ¼ cup of the simmering broth into the 3 tablespoons flour, then stir it into the stew. Season with the salt and pepper to taste. Place the dumplings on top of the simmering stew, cover, and cook for 15 minutes.

5. Divide the stew and dumplings among 4 bowls. Garnish with the parsley.

SERVES 2 AS A MAIN COURSE, 4 AS A FIRST COURSE

COOKING NOTE

I was nervous about adding flour to thicken the stew, but it worked well—the flour makes the broth viscous enough to coat the dumplings. If you don't like flour-based sauces, you can skip this, or halve the amount of flour.

SERVING SUGGESTIONS

Cheese Ball with Cumin, Mint, and Pistachios (p. 85), Apple Snow (p. 808), Olive Oil and Apple Cider Cake (p. 771)

JANUARY 30, 1994: "A SIMMER OF HOPE," BY MOLLY O'NEILL.

—1994

⌒ CARAMELIZED ENDIVE

In the classic version of this dish, the bitterness of the endive must single-handedly overthrow the muffling quality of the butter. But here the endive is aided by both sugar and lime juice in a clever update by Alfred Portale—the chef and owner of Gotham Bar & Grill and the headmaster of the school of towering restaurant food that flourished in the 1990s. It's an important flavor lesson, one I wish I had learned much earlier—good cooks will pull and tug the sensual components of a dish in many directions. To emphasize bitterness, you don't just add bitterness, you add bitterness's converse, sweetness (here, sugar). And you ratchet up the bitterness even more with its complementary flavor component: sourness (here, lime juice).

———

2 tablespoons unsalted butter

3 Belgian endives, halved lengthwise

¼ teaspoon kosher salt

Freshly ground black pepper

1 tablespoon sugar

1 tablespoon fresh lime juice

1. Melt the butter in a large nonstick skillet over medium-low heat. Season the endive with the salt and pepper to taste and place cut side down in the skillet.

Cook until lightly browned on the bottom, about 8 minutes.

2. Sprinkle the sugar and lime juice over the endive and cook, turning occasionally, until the endive is caramelized and tender when pierced with a knife, about 15 minutes longer.

SERVES 3 TO 4

COOKING NOTES

When the endive is cooking, make sure the heat is high enough—the endive should be caramelizing, not stewing.

SERVING SUGGESTIONS

Wilted Red Cabbage Salad (p. 196), Sautéed Potatoes with Parsley (p. 283), Frozen Lemon Soufflé (p. 725)

MARCH 12, 1995: "AN EDIBLE COMPLEX," BY MOLLY O'NEILL.

—1995

⌒ CHILLED SESAME SPINACH

John Willoughby and Chris Schlesinger, who often share a byline in the *Times*, came up with this recipe using spinach as a substitute for kangkong, a water spinach grown in Southeast Asia. You now commonly see water spinach at Asian markets. It has a smaller, firmer leaf than regular spinach, and a bright, stronger mineral flavor that, like spinach, balances astringency with sweetness. (If you can find it, feel free to use it here.)

Serve the spinach on its own or with a strongly flavored fish like tuna, bluefish, or mackerel. The dressing, which contains a ton of fresh ginger, is pungent, and addictively so. Use the leftovers as smelling salts.

2 pounds crinkly leaf spinach or 2 bunches flat-leaf spinach, stemmed and well washed
¼ cup soy sauce
¼ cup white vinegar
3 tablespoons Asian sesame oil
2 tablespoons sugar
2 tablespoons minced fresh ginger

1 tablespoon freshly ground white or black pepper
¼ cup sesame seeds, toasted

1. Bring a large pot of salted water to a boil over high heat. Fill a sink or a large stockpot with ice and cold water. Add the spinach to the boiling water (in 2 batches if necessary) and leave for 5 seconds, then remove using a slotted spoon, tongs, or a skimmer and immediately plunge into the cold water to stop the cooking.

2. Drain the spinach, gently squeezing it between your hands, and roughly chop. Place in a medium bowl, cover, and refrigerate until well chilled, about 15 minutes.

3. Combine the soy sauce, vinegar, sesame oil, sugar, ginger, and pepper, in a small bowl and mix well.

4. Pour half the dressing over the spinach and mix well with a fork, fluffing it to make sure it is coated with dressing. Add more if needed (save the rest for another use). Stir in the toasted sesame seeds.

SERVES 4

COOKING NOTES

I increased the amount of spinach from the 1¼ pounds in the original recipe to 2 pounds (before trimming).

Don't use bagged baby spinach here—it doesn't have enough texture.

Don't attempt to wash spinach in a salad spinner or by running water through the bunch—you need to fill a sink or a very large bowl or pot with water and really swish the leaves around. Grit in food is one of my bugaboos, so I like to do this twice.

To toast the sesame seeds, spread them in a small pan and set over medium heat. Shake frequently. They're done when the seeds turn golden brown.

SERVING SUGGESTIONS

Edamame with Nori Salt (p. 92), Alaskan Salmon (p. 423), Nina Simonds's Broiled Halibut with Miso Glaze (p. 413), Ginger Duck (p. 480), Tea Ice Cream (p. 717), Grapefruit Granita (p. 731)

APRIL 2, 1997: "SPINACH FINDS IT CONVERSES WELL IN THE TROPICAL-GREEN SET," BY JOHN WILLOUGHBY AND CHRIS SCHLESINGER.

—1997

⌒ BEET TARTARE

In the early twentieth century, *Times* reporters turned to chefs like Hippolyte Bonnefoux at the Plaza and maître d's like Oscar Tschirky at the Waldorf for recipes. But the cult of the chef took decades to form, and the food world didn't become fully chef-obsessed until the early 1990s. In 1997, the *Times* started "The Chef," a column that gave talked-about chefs a four- to eight-week platform in which to demonstrate their cooking philosophy and style. The column lasted until 2008 and featured the likes of Alain Ducasse, David Chang, Deborah Madison, Marcus Samuelsson, and Gabrielle Hamilton. A number of excellent recipes in this book are drawn from this column: Thomas Keller's Gazpacho (p. 146), Madison's Eggplant Gratin with Saffron Custard (p. 242), Tom Colicchio's Potato Gnocchi (p. 340), and Eric Ripert's Sautéed Cod with Potatoes and Chorizo-Mussel Broth (p. 428). This beet tartare is from Jean-Georges Vongerichten, who at the time was the chef at Jean Georges, JoJo, and Vong, all in Manhattan. He has since gone on to open about a dozen more restaurants.

One of the goals of "The Chef" was to adapt the complexities of restaurant cooking to the home kitchen, so each column had a collaborator, usually a reporter, who served as the translator and editor, streamlining the recipes for the home cook who shops at Trader Joe's. (In this case it was Mark Bittman, who did his job well.) Vongerichten's beet tartare was his attempt to fiddle with the country club beef tartare of yore, using roughly the same seasonings. Every step works seamlessly. When you put the beets in a food processor, there's just enough liquid to help chop the beets fine without pureeing but not so much that they slide around. The mayonnaise is the perfect amount for binding the beets, acting like the egg does in beef tartare, and the mix of acidity, heat, and sweetness is such that all the flavors miraculously remain distinct. Vongerichten treated the resulting tartare as something between a condiment and a vegetable, serving a mound of it, Bittman wrote, "in the center of a plate surrounded by scallops." The recipe says to serve it with steamed fish. The choice is yours.

6 medium beets (about 1¼ pounds), trimmed
1 shallot, chopped

1 teaspoon Worcestershire sauce, or to taste
1 teaspoon sherry vinegar, or to taste
Few drops Tabasco or other hot sauce
6 cornichons, roughly chopped
⅓ cup capers, drained
1 tablespoon mayonnaise
2 tablespoons chopped flat-leaf parsley,
    plus more for garnish
Salt and freshly ground black pepper

1. Heat the oven to 350 degrees. Wash the beets, leave them wet, and wrap them individually in aluminum foil. Place them on a baking sheet and bake for about 1½ hours, or until they are tender (to test, poke a thin-bladed knife through the foil). Let cool in the foil. (To cook in water, drop the beets into a saucepan of salted water to cover, bring to a boil, and cook over medium heat until tender, 45 minutes to an hour.)

2. When the beets are cool enough to handle, peel them and cut them into eighths. Transfer to a food processor and add the shallot, Worcestershire, vinegar, Tabasco, cornichons, and capers. Pulse until the mixture is minced but not pureed. (You may have to scrape the mixture down between pulses.)

3. Spoon the beets into a bowl and stir in the mayonnaise and parsley. Taste and adjust the seasonings; you may need to add salt and pepper and more vinegar, Worcestershire and/or Tabasco. (This dish keeps well for as long as 2 days; refrigerate, well wrapped or in a covered container, and bring to room temperature before serving.) Garnish with parsley and serve with steamed fish.

SERVES 4

COOKING NOTE

Step 1 offers you the option of baking or boiling the beets. I boiled them, but I'd bake them next time, because baking concentrates the sweetness of the root.

SERVING SUGGESTIONS

Salmon Mousse (p. 394), Fish Steamed over Vegetables and Fresh Herbs (p. 434), Steamed Fish with Thyme and Tomato Vinaigrette (p. 408), Fish Poached in Buttermilk (p. 419), Scallops with Pea Puree (p. 429), Taillevent Pear Soufflé (p. 835)

DECEMBER 10, 1997: "THE CHEF," BY JEAN-GEORGES VONGERICHTEN AND MARK BITTMAN.

—1997

THE MOST VOLUPTUOUS CAULIFLOWER

Any recipe that contains butter, cream, Gruyère, mascarpone, and Parmesan had *better* be voluptuous! This one really is.

_____

1 head cauliflower, cored and cut into florets
2 tablespoons unsalted butter
1¼ cups heavy cream
1½ cups grated Gruyère cheese (about 6 ounces)
Salt and freshly ground black pepper
¼ cup mascarpone cheese
½ cup freshly grated Parmesan cheese

1. Heat the oven to 450 degrees. Pour about ½ inch of water into a pot fitted with a steaming basket and bring to a boil over high heat. Add the cauliflower, cover, and steam until crisp-tender, 3 to 5 minutes.
2. Heat the butter, cream, and 1 cup Gruyère in a medium heavy saucepan over low heat until bubbling. Season to taste with salt and pepper. Add the cauliflower and cook for 2 minutes.
3. Spread the cauliflower in a shallow 2-quart baking dish, and sprinkle with the remaining ½ cup Gruyère, salt, and pepper. Dot with the mascarpone and sprinkle with the Parmesan.
4. Bake for 1 minute. Turn the oven to broil (or transfer to a separate broiler, about 6 inches from heating element). Broil until the surface is golden brown, 1 to 2 minutes.

SERVES 4

SERVING SUGGESTIONS
Sweet-and-Sour Salmon in Almond Prune Sauce (p. 431), James Beard's Chicken with 40 Cloves of Garlic (p. 469), Rib-Eye Steaks with Peppered Cranberry Marmalade and Swiss Chard (p. 462), Lattich Salat, Warme (Warm Lettuce Salad; p. 171), Chocolate Cake with Bay Leaf Syrup (p. 768)

MARCH 4, 1998: "CRITIC'S NOTEBOOK: CAULIFLOWER: FROM DOWAGER TO DEBUTANTE," BY RUTH REICHL. RECIPE ADAPTED FROM ANNE ROSENZWEIG, THE CHEF AT THE LOBSTER CLUB IN NEW YORK.

—1998

SAUTÉED ASPARAGUS WITH FLEUR DE SEL

It doesn't take much to make asparagus great—just great asparagus. But a little butter, fleur de sel, and truffle oil don't hurt.

_____

1½ tablespoons unsalted butter, or as needed
1½ pounds thin asparagus, trimmed and stalks peeled
Fleur de sel
White truffle oil (optional)

1. Melt the butter in a large sauté pan over medium heat. When it is bubbling, add the asparagus spears, placing them in a single layer (alternate tips to bottoms so they fit snugly), immediately cover with a piece of parchment paper cut to the size of the pan, and lower the heat to low so the asparagus will sweat without browning. (You may need to do this in batches. For the second batch, wipe out the pan and add 1½ tablespoons fresh butter; keep the first batch warm in a low oven.) Turn the asparagus from time to time, and cook until just tender, 10 to 12 minutes.
2. Transfer the asparagus to 4 plates and sprinkle with fleur de sel. Drizzle a little white truffle oil, if you like, around the asparagus.

SERVES 4

SERVING SUGGESTIONS
Hearth's Fava Bean Salad (p. 202), Sautéed Cod with Potatoes in Chorizo-Mussel Broth (p. 428), Shad and Roe Grenobloise (p. 400), Sautéed Potatoes with Parsley (p. 283), A Perfect Batch of Rice (p. 316), Lemon Mousse for a Crowd (p. 861), Rhubarb Orange (p. 864)

MAY 6, 1998: "EN ROUTE: FRANCE: FROM THE FRENCH MARSHES, A SALTY TREASURE," BY AMANDA HESSER. RECIPE ADAPTED FROM ALAIN PASSARD, THE CHEF AT ARPÈGE IN PARIS.

—1998

EGGPLANT GRATIN WITH SAFFRON CUSTARD

The gratin contains not just eggplant, but also a jammy stew of peppers, tomatoes, garlic, and anise seeds. The two parts are delicious together, but it's the saffron custard's succinct, punctuated flavor that draws out the sultriness of the vegetables. The recipe was created by Deborah Madison, the former chef at Greens in San Francisco and now the doyenne of vegetable cookbooks.

———

About ½ cup olive oil

3 cups diced onions

Salt

2 large bell peppers, preferably I yellow and I red, cored, seeded, and chopped

I tablespoon minced garlic

½ teaspoon anise seeds, crushed with the side of a knife

3 large tomatoes, peeled (see Cooking Note, p. 146), cored, seeded, and diced

2 tablespoons tomato paste

Freshly ground pepper, preferably white

3½ pounds eggplants, cut into slices just under ½ inch thick

⅛ to ¼ teaspoon saffron threads

¼ cup hot water

1½ cups ricotta cheese

3 large eggs

¾ cup freshly grated Parmesan cheese

I cup plus 2 tablespoons whole milk or heavy cream

½ cup torn basil leaves

1. Heat the oven to 425 degrees. Place 3 tablespoons oil in a large deep skillet or saucepan and turn the heat to medium. Add the onions with a healthy pinch of salt and cook, stirring, until translucent, 5 to 10 minutes. Add the peppers, garlic, and anise seeds and cook, stirring occasionally, until the peppers are very tender, about 15 minutes.

2. Add the tomatoes and tomato paste, adjust the heat so the mixture simmers steadily, and cook, stirring occasionally, until thick and jammy, about 30 minutes. Taste and add salt and pepper as needed.

3. Meanwhile, lightly brush each slice of eggplant with olive oil and place the slices in one layer on one or

more baking sheets. Bake, turning after about 15 minutes, until the eggplant is lightly brown and slightly shriveled, 25 to 30 minutes. Remove the eggplant, and turn the heat to 375 degrees.

4. Dissolve the saffron in the hot water. Mix together the ricotta, eggs, Parmesan, milk, and salt and pepper to taste; add the saffron and its liquid. Stir the basil into the tomato sauce.

5. Brush a large gratin dish or baking pan with oil. Make a layer of half the eggplant, then one of half the tomato sauce; repeat. Top with the custard. Bake for 30 to 35 minutes or until nicely browned. Serve hot, warm, or at room temperature.

SERVES 8 AS A SIDE DISH, 4 AS A MAIN COURSE

COOKING NOTE

I used a 3-quart oval Le Creuset casserole, and the eggplant and custard filled it.

SERVING SUGGESTIONS

Crème Senegalese (p. 124), Shrimp in Green Sauce (p. 430), Seared Loin Lamb Chops with Olives and Soft Polenta (p. 556), Confit of Carrot and Cumin (p. 244), Cantaloupe–Star Anise Sorbet (p. 728), Hazelnut Baklava (p. 706)

AUGUST 5, 1998: "THE CHEF," BY DEBORAH MADISON AND MARK BITTMAN.

—1998

SAVORY BREAD PUDDING

Some recipes are like messy closets. You know what needs to be done—folding, sorting, stacking, weeding out. And you know the result: virtuous triumph. But it requires fortitude to tackle the job. This, I'm afraid, is one of those recipes. There is cheese to be grated, spinach and Swiss chard to be trimmed and chopped, and leeks to be sliced—as thin as filaments—and then each vegetable needs to be cooked separately. There is also an unusual and unnerving technique: the pudding is baked, then inverted onto a baking sheet and broiled.

But the result is a wildly fragrant bread pudding with an interior that is part custard, part greens, and part bread, and a roof woven with crisp bits of sourdough bread and cheese. Much more gratifying than a clean closet.

½ pound sourdough bread, cut into 1-inch cubes
¼ pound Swiss cheese, grated
2 ounces Parmesan cheese, grated
3 tablespoons unsalted butter
¼ pound mixed wild mushrooms (shiitake, oyster, black trumpet, and/or others), trimmed and sliced
2 cups roughly chopped spinach
1 cup chopped Swiss chard leaves plus ⅓ cup diced Swiss chard stems
1 leek, white and light green parts only, very thinly sliced and washed well
1 large egg
¾ cup whole milk
¾ cup heavy cream
Salt and freshly ground black pepper

1. Combine the bread, Swiss cheese, and half of the Parmesan cheese in a large bowl.
2. Melt 1 tablespoon butter in a large skillet over medium heat. Add the mushrooms and sauté until tender, 3 to 5 minutes. Transfer the mushrooms to the bowl. Add 1 more tablespoon butter to the skillet, then add the spinach and Swiss chard and sauté until wilted, about 1 minute. Transfer to the bowl.
3. Bring a small pan of water to a boil. Add the leeks and Swiss chard stems and blanch for 1 minute, then drain well. Add to the bread mixture.
4. Heat the oven to 400 degrees. Grease an 8-inch square baking pan with the remaining 1 tablespoon butter. Beat the egg in a medium bowl just until blended.
5. Combine the milk and heavy cream in a small saucepan and bring to a boil over medium-low heat; remove from the heat. Whisking vigorously, add about ½ cup of the hot milk mixture to the egg, then return the mixture to the pan and whisk until blended. Add the milk mixture to the bread mixture and stir well. Season with salt and pepper to taste.
6. Transfer the mixture to the baking pan, pressing gently on the surface. Bake the pudding until set, about 15 minutes. Remove from the oven.
7. Heat the broiler with the rack about 6 inches from the heat. Unmold the pudding onto a baking sheet, sprinkle with the remaining Parmesan cheese, and place under the broiler until golden brown, 1 to 3 minutes.

SERVES 8

COOKING NOTES
I liked the pieces of bread that contained crust best, so err on the crusty side with your cubes.

Because the last step is done on a baking sheet, there's no serving dish for the pudding. Either plate it or cut it into pieces and arrange on a platter.

SERVING SUGGESTIONS
Rillettes de Canard (p. 65), Dijon and Cognac Beef Stew (p. 560), Salade à la Romaine (p. 171), Breton Butter Cake (p. 777), Evelyn Sharpe's French Chocolate Cake (p. 752), Chocolate Mousse (p. 820)

NOVEMBER 18, 1998: "STUFFING BOREDOM? A BOLD ANTIDOTE," BY WILLIAM GRIMES. RECIPE ADAPTED FROM JEAN-GEORGES VONGERICHTEN, THE OWNER OF NOUGATINE AT JEAN GEORGES.

—1998

❧ FRIED ZUCCHINI BLOSSOMS

With zucchini blossoms, I think simple is best. Chickpea flour adds a very faint and sweet nuttiness to the blossoms.

⅔ cup Indian chickpea flour
Chilled seltzer water or ice water
Kosher salt
Cayenne pepper
4 cups olive or canola oil
20 zucchini blossoms

1. Place the chickpea flour in a medium bowl. Whisk in cold water a little at a time until a smooth batter forms. Season with salt and cayenne.
2. Heat the oil to 375 degrees in a deep-fryer or deep heavy pot. Frying in batches so you don't crowd the pot or lower the oil temperature, dip each blossom into the batter, coating it, shake off the excess batter, and fry until crisp and golden brown, about 30 seconds

a side. Drain the blossoms on a plate lined with paper towels. Season with salt and serve immediately.

SERVES 4

SERVING SUGGESTIONS
Spicy, Lemony Clams with Pasta (p. 336), Scallops with Pea Puree (p. 429), Epigram of Lamb (p. 509), Green Pea Fritters (p. 270), Asparagus alla Fontina (p. 222), Strawberry Soup (p. 816), Fresh Raspberry (or Blackberry or Blueberry) Flummery (p. 824)

JUNE 16, 1999: "ZUCCHINI BURSTS INTO BLOOM, AND SO DOES A COOK'S IMAGINATION," BY AMANDA HESSER.

—1999

CONFIT OF CARROT AND CUMIN

A long warm bath in orange juice and oil concentrates the flavor of the carrots and allows them to absorb the cumin, garlic, and cayenne. Don't be shy with the cayenne!

This is a dinner-party standby for a number of my friends, who love the dish because you can toss it together in five minutes and get it in the oven while you worry about the rest of the meal.

For more carrot and cumin recipes, see pages 187 and 237.

———

1½ pounds carrots (about 16 thin carrots) preferably organic, peeled
Large pinch of cumin seeds
¼ cup extra virgin olive oil
1 small clove garlic, minced
Grated zest of 1 orange
Juice of 3 oranges
Kosher salt
Cayenne pepper
2 tablespoons thinly sliced cilantro leaves

1. Heat the oven to 275 degrees. Combine the carrots, cumin seeds, olive oil, garlic, orange zest and juice in a large casserole. Season with salt and cayenne. Cover tightly with a lid or aluminum foil and bring to a boil on the stovetop.

2. Transfer the casserole to the oven and bake until a knife can easily be inserted into the carrots, at least 2 hours. Just before serving, add the cilantro.

SERVES 4

SERVING SUGGESTIONS
Crème Senegalese (p. 124), Eggplant Gratin with Saffron Custard (p. 242), Broiled Lamb Leg Chops on Eggplant Planks with Mint-Yogurt Sauce (p. 549), Moussaka (p. 518), Cantaloupe–Star Anise Sorbet (p. 728), Coconut Loaf Cake (p. 774)

PERIOD DETAIL
By 1999, confit had become a major menu buzzword, and foie gras and salmon tartare were also peaking.

AUGUST 4, 1999: "THE WORD CHEFS CAN'T RESIST: CONFIT," BY AMANDA HESSER. RECIPE ADAPTED FROM JOJO IN NEW YORK CITY.

—1999

LEEK AND SHIITAKE BREAD PUDDING

———

4 medium leeks, white and pale green parts, halved lengthwise and washed well
4 tablespoons unsalted butter
Kosher salt and freshly ground black pepper
7 ounces shiitake mushrooms, brushed, stems trimmed, and halved, quartered if large
3 cups whole milk
1 clove garlic, crushed
Eight ½-inch-thick slices day-old semolina bread
3 large eggs
½ cup heavy cream
Pinch of ground coriander

1. Heat the oven to 350 degrees. Cut the leeks diagonally into 2-inch sections. Melt the butter in a large sauté pan over medium-low heat. Add the leeks, season with salt and pepper, cover, and simmer over low heat until the leeks are just tender but not mushy, about 10 minutes.

2. Add the mushrooms, toss to coat, and cook until

tender, about 5 minutes. Uncover and boil off all but 2 tablespoons of the liquid. Check the seasoning and add salt and/or pepper; set aside.

3. Heat the milk in a small saucepan over medium-high heat until bubbles form around the edges; while it heats, season to taste with salt and pepper. Remove from the heat and add the garlic. Place the bread in a bowl, and pour the milk over it. Let it soak for 10 minutes.

4. Whisk the eggs and cream in a small bowl. Season with salt, pepper, and the coriander.

5. Bring a medium pot of water to a boil. Place a roasting pan large enough to hold a 5-quart oval casserole in the oven. Butter the casserole. Using a slotted spatula, lift a slice of bread from the milk, letting it drain well, and press the bread up against one end of the casserole so that it comes up the side. Spoon some leek mixture over it. Place a second bread slice atop the first, covering two-thirds of it. Repeat with all the bread and the leek mixture. The layers should be snug, with the slices looking like fallen dominoes. Discard the milk and garlic.

6. Whisk the cream and eggs again, and pour evenly over the bread and leeks. Place the casserole in the roasting pan and pour enough boiling water around the casserole to come halfway up the sides. Bake for 40 minutes, or until the pudding is set at the edges but still a little wet in the middle. Increase the oven setting to 375 degrees and bake for 10 minutes more to set the middle and crisp the top.

SERVES 6

COOKING NOTES

To trim and wash a leek, cut off the root end at the point where it meets the white base. Be careful not to slice into the layers. Cut off the green tops about 2 inches above where the green begins. Cut the leek lengthwise in half.

Wash one half at a time. Hold the leek with the root upward under a running faucet and spread the leaves with your thumbs, starting in the center and working to the outside—they should fan out like a deck of cards. This lets water pass between the leaves to rinse out the dirt.

SERVING SUGGESTIONS

Breaded Chicken Breasts with Parmesan Cheese (p. 465), Winter Slaw with Lemon-and-Orange Dressing (p. 185), Lemon Cheese Pie (p. 812)

OCTOBER 6, 1999: "THE ONION THAT WON'T MAKE YOU CRY," BY AMANDA HESSER.

—1999

⌒ STEWED FENNEL

Sometimes a food story takes on a life of its own, as was the case with Mark Bittman's piece on Jim Lahey's "no-knead" bread, which ran in the newspaper in 2006. The story was reprinted around the world, and it remained at the top of the "most-e-mailed" list for weeks. A book based on the technique came out in 2009, and the original recipe is on p. 670.

The piece from which this stewed fennel recipe derives was another one of these stories, except that it appeared in the paper a few years before readers were able to e-mail stories, and before there was a digital trail for tracking a piece's success. The story's construction was a typical "reporter-visits-chef, finds-good-Thanksgiving-recipes." But the reporter in this case was R. W. "Johnny" Apple Jr., a bon vivant with a lion's appetite, and the chef was Alice Waters, the missionary of seasonal and local foods.

I heard about the story the old-fashioned way, through the mail. When I started working on this book, readers from around the world praised all four recipes in the story: the fennel, Roasted Brine-Cured Turkey (p. 474), Wild Mushroom Stuffing (p. 337), and Cranberry Upside-Down Cake (p. 776). Each was recommended by at least three readers. And each deservedly so.

My only reservation about this dish is its name, which is not only misleading but glosses over the most interesting part of the process. Rather than being stewed, which suggests slow cooking, the fennel is hyperbraised. You cut the bulb into wedges; douse it with olive oil; season it with fennel fronds, fennel seeds, and red pepper flakes; and then blast it with heat until the liquid is cooked off and the fennel is just tender. The texture of the bulb ends up, somewhat miraculously, like confit—it holds together but is like a concentrated fennel pudding inside. And the fennel seeds infuse the vegetable with the anise perfume you wish for in cooked fennel and so rarely get.

––––––––––

4 large fennel bulbs, including stalks with feathery fronds
(or substitute ¼ cup chervil leaves for the fronds)
½ cup extra virgin olive oil
1½ cups water
2 tablespoons fennel seeds, finely ground in a
spice/coffee grinder or with a mortar and pestle
2 pinches of crushed red pepper flakes
1 teaspoon kosher salt
2 tablespoons fresh lemon juice

1. Trim the fennel bulbs, cutting off the stalks and reserving the fronds. Finely chop the fronds; set aside. Cut the bulbs into eighths.

2. Place the sliced fennel in a medium saucepan, add the olive oil and water, cover, and bring to a boil over high heat. Immediately reduce the heat to medium, stir the fennel, cover, and let stew for 5 minutes.

3. Add the chopped fennel fronds, ground fennel seeds, red pepper flakes, and salt. Stir, raise the heat to medium-high, and cook, covered, until the liquid has nearly evaporated and the fennel is thoroughly cooked and soft, about 10 more minutes. (If necessary, simmer uncovered for a few minutes to reduce the liquid.) Remove the pan from the heat and add the lemon juice. Add more salt if needed, and toss to mix well.

SERVES 4 TO 6

COOKING NOTES
The fennel I used yielded ½ cup chopped fronds, and I only used the soft small fronds between the stalks.

You need a heavy saucepan for the fennel to cook properly. If you have an enameled cast-iron saucepan or casserole, use it.

VARIATION
I once made the fennel and then tossed it with fusilli, sautéed sweet Italian sausage, olive oil, Parmesan, and lots of freshly ground black pepper.

SERVING SUGGESTIONS
Monkfish Encrusted with Pistachios (p. 403), Pork Arrosto with Prunes and Grappa (p. 577), Roasted

Brine-Cured Turkey with Wild Mushroom Stuffing (p. 474), Couscous Salad (p. 321), Barley Risotto (p. 327), Apple Crumb Pie (p. 841), Cranberry Upside-Down Cake (p. 776), Winter Fruit Salad (p. 850)

NOVEMBER 17, 1999: "NEW AMERICAN TRADITIONS: IN A BERKELEY KITCHEN, A CELEBRATION OF SIMPLICITY," BY R. W. APPLE JR. RECIPE ADAPTED FROM ALICE WATERS, THE OWNER OF CHEZ PANISSE IN BERKELEY, CALIFORNIA.

—1999

GREEN BEANS WITH CORIANDER-COCONUT CRUST

Playing off the fresh bean flavor is a complex spice mixture of chana dal, coriander, cinnamon, and a healthy smack of cumin. The coconut coats the beans, mellows the spices, and thoroughly enriches the dish.

––––––––––

¼ cup chana dal (yellow split peas)
3 tablespoons dhana dal (roasted coriander seeds)
½ teaspoon cayenne pepper
¼ teaspoon cumin seeds
4 whole cloves
One 2-inch piece cinnamon stick
Coarse salt
6 tablespoons ghee or clarified butter
1 pound green beans, trimmed
1 cup coconut puree (puree fresh coconut
in a blender with enough water to bind it)

1. Combine the chana dal, dhana dal, cayenne, cumin, cloves, and cinnamon in a small sauté pan and toast over medium heat, stirring constantly, until the spices are golden brown and very aromatic, about 3 minutes. Stir in the salt, along with 1 tablespoon ghee, and remove from the heat.

2. Heat the remaining 5 tablespoons ghee in a large sauté pan over medium heat. Add the beans, coconut puree, and spice mixture and cook, stirring occasionally, for 15 minutes, or until the beans are tender and the sauce has thickened.

SERVES 6

Chana dal, dhana dal, and ghee can be found in Indian grocery stores; try www.kalustyans.com.

For the coconut puree, remove the coconut meat from a coconut by cracking its shell open with a hammer. Pull out the coconut meat (you may need to cut it out with a small sharp knife). Cut the meat into small pieces. Puree the coconut in a blender, adding just enough water to bind it. Of course, this whole process is easier if you can buy coconut out of the shell!—many Indian markets carry frozen grated coconut.

SERVING SUGGESTIONS
Ceylon Curry of Oysters (p. 391), Spicy, Garlicky Cashew Chicken (p. 494), Bademiya's Justly Famous Bombay Chile-and-Cilantro Chicken (p. 471), A Moley (Curried Turkey Hash; p. 452), Yogurt Rice (p. 356), Mango Ice Cream (p. 729)

FEBRUARY 9, 2000: "BY THE BOOK: FRENCH AND INDIAN, IN HARMONY," BY AMANDA HESSER. RECIPE ADAPTED FROM "RAJI CUISINE: INDIAN FLAVORS, FRENCH PASSION," BY RAJI JALLEPALLI.

—2000

❧ SHALLOT PUDDING

This silky pouf of egg and shallot lies somewhere between a frittata and a soufflé and is a companion, in spirit if not in technique, to the Cheese Pudding Soufflés on p. 643. Both are terrific, but this is the recipe to make when you're pressed for time, or if you're having a dinner party and need an easy but impressive first course. Prepare the shallots in advance and the eggs just before baking. March it directly from the oven to the table to dish out—it's a beauty, and you'll want your guests to admire it while it's still pillowy.

---

4 tablespoons unsalted butter
2 cups sliced shallots
3 large eggs
1 teaspoon salt
1 teaspoon baking powder
1 cup heavy cream
1/2 cup shredded Gruyère cheese
Freshly ground black pepper

1. Heat the oven to 350 degrees. Butter a shallow 1-quart baking dish, such as a ceramic quiche pan. Melt the butter in a large heavy skillet over medium-high heat. Add the shallots and sauté over medium heat, stirring frequently until richly browned, about 10 minutes. Let cool slightly.
2. Lightly beat the eggs with the salt and baking powder in a medium bowl. Stir in the cream and cheese, season with pepper, and fold in the shallots. Pour into the baking dish and bake for 25 to 35 minutes, until the pudding is browned and firm to the touch.

SERVES 6 AS A SIDE DISH OR FIRST COURSE

COOKING NOTES
I used a 9-inch round ceramic quiche pan.

SERVING SUGGESTIONS
Chestnut Soup (p. 133), Ann Seranne's Rib Roast of Beef (p. 519), Spinach Roman-Style (p. 233), Sugar Snap Peas with Horseradish (p. 259), Bolzano Apple Cake (p. 783), Reuben's Apple Pancake (p. 831)

MARCH 15, 2000: "THE SHALLOT CONQUERS THE KITCHEN, AND NOT A TEAR IS SHED," BY FLORENCE FABRICANT. RECIPE ADAPTED FROM ELI'S RESTAURANT IN NEW YORK CITY.

—2000

❧ SWEET-AND-SPICY PEPPER STEW

I would like to have a container of this pepper stew in my refrigerator all summer long. Eberhard Müller, the former chef and owner of Lutèce in New York City, whose work of genius this recipe is, figured out a way to avoid the dreariness of roasting and peeling peppers while making one of the world's best vegetable stews. He did this by coring and slicing raw peppers, then stewing them, covered, in a sea of cipollini-scented olive oil. The covered pot keeps the peppers moist as they soften. The pepper juices vaporize, rising up to the lid and then falling back into the cooking juices, so you're left with slivers of silky pepper and a concentrated pepper oil. I served this in tiny bowls because I knew no one would want to miss even a drop of the cooking juices.

2/3 cup extra virgin olive oil

8 to 12 small cipollini onions, trimmed, peeled and thinly sliced (generous 1 cup)

Salt and freshly ground white pepper

2 medium cloves garlic, minced

4 pounds large orange, yellow, and red bell peppers (about 9 total), cored, seeded, and thinly sliced

2 Hungarian wax peppers, cored, seeded, and thinly sliced

1 red jalapeño pepper, halved, seeded and thinly sliced

1. Place the oil and onions in a large braising pan or casserole, turn the heat to medium, and season the onions generously with salt and pepper. Cover and cook until softened, about 4 minutes. Stir in the garlic, cover, and cook until softened, about 1 minute.

2. Add the bell peppers (they will mound high in the pan) and 2 tablespoons water, cover, and cook, stirring once or twice, until the peppers begin to release their liquid, about 6 minutes. Stir in the wax peppers and jalapeño, cover, and cook, stirring several times, until the peppers are tender but not mushy, about 10 minutes longer. Adjust the seasonings, and serve hot, warm, or at room temperature.

SERVES 8

SERVING SUGGESTIONS

Steamed Fish with Thyme and Tomato Vinaigrette (p. 408), Sautéed Cod with Potatoes in Chorizo-Mussel Broth (p. 428), Border Town Hunter's Stew with Antelope (or Venison) Poblanos, Pumpkin, and Hominy (p. 571), Gigot à la Provençal et Gratin de Pommes de Terre (p. 537), Steamed Lemon Pudding (p. 849), Plum Fritters (p. 865)

SEPTEMBER 13, 2000: "THE CHEF," BY EBERHARD MULLER AND JACK BISHOP.

—2000

⌇ ROASTED CAULIFLOWER

These cross-sections of cauliflower look like cross-sections of a miniature fir tree, caramelized at the tips of their needles and trunk, the sweet periphery of a silky center. This is a technique popularized by Jean-Georges Vongerichten, who a few years earlier

had begun serving paper-thin slips of caramelized cauliflower with scallops and a caper-and-raisin emulsion. You can head in that refined direction, or do as I tend to and roast up a bunch to go with steak. I sometimes sprinkle the roasted cauliflower with a very good aged vinegar. Or cut the florets into smaller pieces and add to a salad.

———

1 pound cauliflower (1/2 medium cauliflower), cored and cut into 1/4-inch-thick slices

Extra virgin olive oil

Sea salt and coarsely ground black pepper

1. Heat the oven to 375 degrees. Place the cauliflower in a large bowl. Pour on enough olive oil to coat (a few tablespoons), season generously with salt and pepper, and toss gently until evenly coated.

2. Lay the cauliflower pieces out on a baking sheet. Drizzle any remaining oil from the bowl on top. Bake, turning once, until caramelized on the edges and tender, 25 to 30 minutes. Serve warm or at room temperature.

SERVES 4

SERVING SUGGESTIONS

Manjula Gokal's Gujarati Mango Soup (p. 155), Crab and Coconut Curry (p. 389), Slow-Roasted Duck (p. 475), Steak au Poivre (p. 573), String Beans with Ginger and Garlic (p. 260), Saffron Panna Cotta (p. 845), Moroccan Rice Pudding (p. 848)

JANUARY 17, 2001: "THE CELESTIAL CAULIFLOWER: EARNING A SPOT IN THE SUN," BY AMANDA HESSER.

—2001

⌇ ESCAROLE WITH PAN-ROASTED GARLIC AND LEMON

How do you cook escarole? By barely cooking it. The best way to handle it is to nip it with heat, which wilts the outer portion of the leaves and preserves the crunch of the spines. Here Denise Landis, a longtime recipe tester for the Dining section (and its unsung savior), wilts the escarole in the oil that has been used to slowly soften the garlic cloves. The garlic is like candy, and the oil like a warm tonic that wraps the leaves before a showering of lemon juice and salt sharpens them up.

———

1 large head escarole
8 to 10 cloves garlic
⅓ cup extra virgin olive oil
Juice of ½ lemon, or to taste
Salt
½ lemon, cut into 6 wedges and seeded

1. Slice the escarole crosswise into ribbons about 1½ inches wide. Rinse well, drain, and pat dry with paper towels. Set aside.
2. Halve any large cloves of garlic lengthwise; the cloves should be of uniform size. Set aside.
3. Place a 12-inch or bigger sauté pan over medium-low heat and add the olive oil. When the oil is warmed, reduce the heat to as low as possible, add the garlic, and toss to coat well with oil. Cook partly covered, stirring occasionally, until the garlic is translucent and very tender, about 25 minutes; do not allow the garlic to brown, or it will be bitter.
4. Raise the heat to medium-high and immediately add the escarole, then turn off the heat and toss the escarole until it is well coated with oil and just beginning to wilt, about 1 minute. Add the lemon juice and salt to taste and toss again. Add the lemon wedges and toss until the escarole is barely tender and still green. Serve immediately.

SERVES 4 TO 6

COOKING NOTES
The lemon wedges are tossed into the salad, which means you (and your guests) will need to pick them out if you want to squeeze the juice over the escarole. If you don't like getting your fingers greasy, don't add the lemon wedges in the last step. Instead, serve them on the side, for squeezing over the dish at the table.

This is delicious at room temperature as well.

SERVING SUGGESTIONS
Fish Poached in Buttermilk (p. 419), Gently Cooked Salmon with Mashed Potatoes (p. 415), Grilled Hanger Steak (p. 551), Roman Lamb (p. 542), Potato "Tostones" (Flattened Potatoes; p. 301), The Most Voluptuous Cauliflower (p. 241), Evelyn Sharpe's

French Chocolate Cake (p. 752), Chocolate Pudding (p. 858), Panna Cotta (p. 840)

JANUARY 31, 2001: "BRIDGING SEASONS WITH ESCAROLE," BY DENISE LANDIS.

—2001

⌒ MUSHROOMS WITH MANZANILLA SHERRY

This is a tapa you find everywhere in Spain. You could pick up some serrano ham and olives, and with the manzanilla left in the bottle, you could be happy, indeed. Or be American about it and reframe it as a side dish. Either way, you'll be pleased to have this as part of your repertory.

———

2 tablespoons extra virgin olive oil
1½ pounds mixed mushrooms (like cremini, oyster, and white button), trimmed and thinly sliced
A sliver of garlic
3 tablespoons manzanilla or fino sherry
Sea salt

Place a large sauté pan over medium heat and add the olive oil. When the oil is hot, add the mushrooms and garlic, season lightly with salt, and sauté until the mushrooms soften and release their liquid. Continue to sauté until most of the liquid evaporates, then add the sherry and sauté for 1 more minute. Season with salt to taste.

SERVES 4 AS A SIDE DISH OR TAPA

SERVING SUGGESTIONS
Rabbit Soup with Garlic, Peppers, and Chorizo (p. 152), Cocido (Chickpea, Sparerib, and Chorizo Stew; p. 578), Veal Chops with Sage (p. 564), Saffron Rice with Pine Nuts (p. 318), Potato "Tostones" (Flattened Potatoes; p. 301), Bittersweet Chocolate Semifreddo (p. 727), Toasts with Chocolate, Olive Oil, and Sea Salt (p. 844)

MARCH 28, 2001: "AN OVERNIGHT SENSATION, 200 YEARS IN THE MAKING," BY AMANDA HESSER.

—2001

ZUCCHINI WITH CRÈME FRAÎCHE PESTO

AUGUST 15, 2001: "SPOONING UP A CLOUD," BY AMANDA HESSER. RECIPE ADAPTED FROM *THE CRÈME FRAÎCHE COOKBOOK* BY SADIE KENDALL.

—2001

Save any leftover pesto for tossing with angel hair pasta or spreading on toasted country bread.

———

½ cup packed basil leaves

1½ teaspoons toasted pine nuts

½ clove garlic, smashed

About 3 tablespoons extra virgin olive oil

Coarse sea or kosher salt

1½ tablespoons crème fraîche

2 tablespoons freshly grated Parmesan cheese

1½ pounds small zucchini, cut into ½-inch dice (or blanched fresh beans, like green beans, lima beans, or cranberry beans)

Freshly ground black pepper

1. Combine the basil, pine nuts, garlic, a scant tablespoon olive oil, and a pinch of salt in a blender or food processor and puree, scraping down the sides once or twice with a spatula, until a coarse mixture develops. Add the crème fraîche and puree until the mixture is a smooth paste the color of a fresh pea. Add the Parmesan and pulse until combined. Adjust the seasoning if necessary, transfer to a jar or other container, and refrigerate.

2. Heat the remaining 2 tablespoons olive oil in a large sauté pan over medium heat. When it shimmers, add the zucchini and stir to coat with oil. Season generously with salt and pepper and sauté until the zucchini brightens and turns soft on the edges but is still fairly firm. Add 2 heaping tablespoons of pesto and stir to coat the zucchini, then add more pesto if needed. Adjust the seasonings if necessary.

SERVES 4

SERVING SUGGESTIONS

Basic Corn Chowder (p. 149), Crab Cakes Baltimore-Style (p. 407), Baked Flounder (p. 401), Roman Lamb (p. 542), Butterscotch Pudding (p. 851), Fresh Raspberry (or Blackberry or Blueberry) Flummery (p. 824), Strawberry Shortcakes (p. 799)

BAKED ZUCCHINI WITH HERBS AND TOMATOES

Every ingredient in this dish is used judiciously to flatter the flavor of zucchini. And the vegetables are cooked at the confident temperature of 425 degrees, so they roast quickly, rather than stewing.

———

10 firm baby zucchini (or 5 small zucchini), trimmed and sliced lengthwise into ¼-inch-thick sticks

1 small onion, chopped

2 scallions, white part only, thinly sliced

Leaves from 3 inner stalks celery

6 leaves basil

About ¼ cup all-purpose flour

2 ripe plum tomatoes, cored, and coarsely chopped

Sea salt

⅓ cup extra virgin olive oil

Freshly ground black pepper

1. Heat the oven to 425 degrees. Combine the zucchini, onion, and scallions in a colander. Tear celery and basil leaves into small pieces and sprinkle on top. Sprinkle the flour over all. Using one hand, press and toss the ingredients together until well mixed and coated (it will get a little moist but not gooey). Add the tomatoes, season with salt, and toss once more.

2. Pour half the olive oil into a medium baking dish or ceramic pie plate. Fill with the zucchini mixture, then grind pepper over top. Sprinkle the remaining oil on top, and bake for about 20 minutes, or until the vegetables are just cooked but still firm.

SERVES 6

SERVING SUGGESTIONS

Crostini Romani (p. 77), Open-Faced Tomato Sandwich (p. 367), Pork Burgers (p. 566), Saltimbocca (p. 561), Flat-and-Chewy Chocolate Chip Cookies (p. 706), Panna Cotta (p. 840)

DECEMBER 5, 2001: "A ROMAN MUSE FOR AMERICA'S
GREAT CHEFS," BY AMANDA HESSER. RECIPE ADAPTED
FROM PAOLA DI MAURO, AN OWNER OF COLLE PICCHIONI
IN MARINO, ITALY.

—2001

RACHEL'S GREEN BEANS
WITH DILL

These beans come from my friend Rachel Urquhart, who was raised on food from Craig Claiborne's *New York Times Cookbook* and became an elegant cook herself. Rachel served the beans with poached salmon.

———

Sea salt
4 large handfuls haricots verts or green beans, trimmed
2 tablespoons unsalted butter
2 to 3 tablespoons chopped dill
Coarsely ground black pepper

1. Fill a pot with water, season with salt so that you can taste it, and bring to a boil. Plunge the beans into the water and cook for 2 to 3 minutes, or until just tender but still quite firm. (If you're using green beans, it will take a minute or so longer.)
2. Drain, then return the beans to the pot. Add the butter, stir in 2 tablespoons dill, season with pepper and stir and toss the beans over low heat until the butter is melted. Taste a bean and season with salt and more pepper and/or dill if desired.

SERVES 4

SERVING SUGGESTIONS
Scotch Eggs (p. 62), Thomas Keller's Gazpacho (p. 146), Salmon and Tomatoes in Foil (p. 422), Elizabeth Frink's Roast Lemon Chicken (p. 478), Docks Coleslaw (p. 191), Spoonbread's Potato Salad (p. 288), Fresh Raspberry (or Blackberry or Blueberry) Flummery (p. 824), Fontainebleau (p. 829), Junior's Cheesecake (p. 771), Chocolate Chip Cookies (p. 709)

APRIL 14, 2002: "FOOD DIARY: BASIC INSTINCT," BY
AMANDA HESSER. RECIPE ADAPTED FROM RACHEL
URQUHART.

—2002

FRIED EGGPLANT WITH
SALMOREJO SAUCE

In Spain, the lines between sauce and soup are pleasantly blurred. Salmorejo, the bread-thickened, vinegar-tinged tomato soup from Córdoba, can also double as a viscous sauce; and here it becomes a topping for thin disks of fried cornmeal-dusted eggplant. This iteration of the dish comes from *¡Delicioso!: The Regional Cooking of Spain* by Penelope Casas.

The sauce should be served in a wide shallow dish so you have plenty of surface area for the chopped egg and serrano ham. The eggplant can be served hot, if you like the stress of frying in batches and keeping everything warm. If you don't mind it at room temperature, then cool the eggplant on baking racks as you fry it, taking care not to overlap the pieces, so they don't steam and stick together.

If you have leftover sauce, serve it as a soup in small bowls, topped with the egg and ham, or spoon it on top of roasted chicken.

———

For the Eggplant
1 large eggplant (about 1½ pounds)
4 to 5 cups whole milk
¼ teaspoon salt
1 cup fine yellow cornmeal
1 cup all-purpose flour
Vegetable oil for frying

For the Sauce
Three ½- to ¾-inch-thick slices country bread, crusts
    removed and torn into pieces (about 1½ cups)
1 pound ripe tomatoes, peeled (see Cooking Note,
    p. 146), cored, and seeded
1 clove garlic, minced
¾ teaspoon salt, plus more to taste
¼ cup fruity extra virgin olive oil
1 teaspoon sherry vinegar or red wine vinegar
1 hard-boiled egg, chopped
¼ cup chopped thinly sliced serrano ham or prosciutto

1. To prepare the eggplant, peel it and slice into ⅛-inch-thick slices. Combine 4 cups milk and the salt in a large shallow baking dish and add the eggplant. If necessary, add more milk to cover the eggplant. Let soak for at least 30 minutes before cooking.

(You can do this several hours ahead and refrigerate the eggplant.)

2. Meanwhile, make the sauce: Soak the bread briefly in water and squeeze dry. Place the tomatoes, garlic, and salt in a food processor and puree. With the processor running, gradually add the bread, processing until smooth, then drizzle in the olive oil. Add the vinegar and taste for salt. Transfer to a serving bowl and top with the egg and ham. Set aside.

3. Heat the oven to 200 degrees. Mix the cornmeal and flour in a pie plate. Pour 1 inch of vegetable oil into a large skillet and heat until the oil quickly browns a cube of bread. Remove the eggplant from the milk, but do not dry. Quickly coat the slices with the cornmeal and flour mixture, patting to make sure it adheres well. Slide a few of the slices into the oil, without crowding, and fry until golden, turning once (a few minutes). Drain on paper towels and keep warm in the oven on a rack on a baking sheet while you fry the remaining slices. Serve accompanied by the sauce.

SERVES 4 TO 6 AS A LIGHT LUNCH OR FIRST COURSE

COOKING NOTES

Casas gives you the option of sherry vinegar or red wine vinegar. I believe there is no option: sherry vinegar is the only way to go. And if you can find an aged version, all the better.

With almost any other recipe that said to slice something $\frac{1}{8}$ inch thick, I'd be insistent that you not go thicker, but here I'd say slices that are somewhere between $\frac{1}{8}$ and $\frac{1}{4}$ inch thick are ideal, because you want the eggplant to retain some inner pulp after frying.

The slices are soaked in a mixture of salt and milk. The salt draws out the eggplant's bitterness and the milk keeps it from absorbing too much oil when fried.

SERVING SUGGESTIONS

White Gazpacho with Almonds and Grapes (p. 137), Catalan Tortilla with Aioli (p. 86), Fried Chickpeas (p. 88), Pan con Tomate (p. 91), Rabbit Soup with Garlic, Peppers, and Chorizo (p. 152), Paella (p. 309), Cocido (p. 578) Caramel Custard (p. 836)

JULY 28, 2002: "FOOD: PURPLE PASSION," BY JULIA REED. RECIPE ADAPTED FROM ¡DELICIOSO!: THE REGIONAL COOKING OF SPAIN, BY PENELOPE CASAS.

—2002

⌒ SUMMER SQUASH CASSEROLE

Warning to food snobs: the following recipe contains Ritz crackers.

As much as the *Times* food writers and editors (myself included) like to think we're covering the nation's foodways, it's a bit of a lie. We are and have been preponderantly New Yorkers, smitten with the new and the best on our little island, and we have sometimes ignored—or even turned up our noses at—the way most Americans are cooking.

Julia Reed, who wrote regularly for the *Magazine* in the early 2000s, was one of the few who had the guts to run recipes involving jarred mayonnaise and iceberg lettuce (see p. 200). In this casserole—and I mean casserole in the American, pile-in-the-ingredients sense, not the French—a moist squash puree is held together with grated cheddar and Ritz cracker crumbs. It's the kind of dish that probably won a cooking contest or two, and it will win you plenty of compliments. Whether or not you reveal the secret ingredient is up to you.

———

2 pounds yellow squash

7 tablespoons unsalted butter

1 large onion, chopped

1 large clove garlic, chopped

$\frac{1}{2}$ red bell pepper, chopped

$\frac{1}{2}$ green bell pepper, chopped

1 jalapeño pepper, seeded and chopped (optional)

4 slices white bread, toasted

24 Ritz crackers, crumbed in the food processor

$\frac{1}{2}$ pound sharp cheddar cheese, grated

4 large eggs, beaten

$\frac{1}{2}$ cup heavy cream

1 teaspoon sugar

1 teaspoon salt

$\frac{1}{4}$ teaspoon cayenne pepper

1. Heat the oven to 350 degrees. Butter a $2\frac{1}{2}$-quart baking dish. Cut the squash into $\frac{1}{2}$-inch-thick slices. Cook in boiling salted water until tender, about 10 minutes; drain. Puree in a food processor.

2. Melt 6 tablespoons butter in a large skillet over medium heat. Add the onion, garlic, and peppers and cook until just tender.

3. Meanwhile, crumb the toast in a food processor.

Melt the remaining tablespoon of butter and toss together with the toast crumbs.

4. Mix the squash puree, cracker crumbs, and cheese in a bowl. Stir in the eggs, cream, sugar, and seasonings. Blend well. Pour into the baking dish. Top with the bread crumbs and bake until browned, about 40 minutes.

SERVES 8 TO 10

SERVING SUGGESTIONS
Pickled Shrimp (p. 95), Cheese Straws (p. 79), Spicy, Supercrunchy Fried Chicken (p. 490), Chicken Betty's Fried Chicken and Gravy (p. 462), Oliver Clark's Meat Loaf (p. 554), Summer Pudding (p. 847)

SEPTEMBER 8, 2002: "FOOD: APPLAUSE, APPLAUSE," BY JULIA REED. RECIPE BY NANCY PETERKIN, A FRIEND OF REED'S FROM HOUSTON, TEXAS.

—2002

✒ BROCCOLI PUREE WITH GINGER

A rival to one of my other favorite side dishes, the Puree of Peas and Watercress on p. 296. And the winner of the best baby-food dish in the book. My twins ate it as if it were their last meal.

One 2-inch piece fresh ginger, peeled
1½ teaspoons olive oil
1 cup thinly sliced onion
1 large clove garlic, finely chopped
½ cup heavy cream
2 pounds broccoli, cut into florets with 1 inch of stem
Salt
Cayenne pepper

1. Cut off a ¼-inch-thick slice of ginger and reserve. Grate the remainder and add it to a fine sieve set over a bowl. Press on the ginger to extract the juice. Reserve the juice and discard the grated ginger.

2. Heat the oil in a medium saucepan over medium heat. Add the ginger slice, onion, and garlic, cover, and sweat until the onions are soft but not browned,

5 to 8 minutes. Add the cream and bring to a boil, then reduce the heat and simmer until slightly thickened, about 4 minutes. Discard the ginger slice and keep the cream warm.

3. Bring a large pot of salted water to a boil. Add the broccoli and cook until very tender, 8 to 10 minutes. Drain, reserving some of the cooking water.

4. Put the broccoli in a food processor, add half the cream mixture and a pinch each of salt and cayenne, and process until smooth; if the puree seems dry, add a little of the reserved cooking water. Add the remaining cream mixture and ½ teaspoon ginger juice; blend well. Adjust the seasoning, adding more ginger juice if desired.

SERVES 4 TO 6

SERVING SUGGESTIONS
Creamy Curried Sweet Potato Soup (p. 145), Slow-Roasted Duck (p. 475), Bademiya's Justly Famous Bombay Chile-and-Cilantro Chicken (p. 471), Ann Seranne's Rib Roast of Beef (p. 519), Lamb in Mustard-Mascarpone Sauce (p. 564), Potato "Tostones" (Flattened Potatoes; p. 301), Jasmine Tea Rice (p. 354), Aztec Hot Chocolate Pudding (p. 855), Almond Granita (p. 731), Coffee Caramel Custard (p. 849)

OCTOBER 13, 2002: "TURNING GREEN," BY JULIA REED. RECIPE ADAPTED FROM COOKING WITH DANIEL BOULUD, BY DANIEL BOULUD.

—2002

✒ BRUSSELS SPROUTS "SLAW" WITH MUSTARD BUTTER

Julia Reed, a writer for Vogue who was for several years a food columnist for the Times Magazine, has an unmistakable cooking style—Southern ease meets East Coast poise. She'd present casseroles seasoned with Ritz crackers (see p. 252) one week and steaks cooked in Champagne the next.

This warm, sharply tangy slaw is a hybrid of her tastes—a sophisticated ingredient wrapped in an everyman cloak. Reed makes a point of telling you not to shred the sprouts in a food processor because the shreds would be too fine. She's probably right, but I leave it to you: deal with shreds that are marginally too fine or deal with your mood after trimming, halving, and head-shredding a pound of Brussels sprouts.

I've made this recipe many times, in both KitchenAid and Cuisinart food processors. The KitchenAid left a few errant chunks that wouldn't shred. I tossed them in with the rest, and they cooked just fine. The Cuisinart pulverized the sprouts. You can avoid that by pulsing them in small batches.

This dish should be eaten instantly—it unfortunately loses its vigor when reheated.

---

8 tablespoons (1 stick) unsalted butter, softened
1 large clove garlic, mashed
2 to 3 tablespoons Dijon or whole-grain Meaux
    mustard (I usually use half Dijon, half Meaux
    or other whole-grain mustard)
3 tablespoons minced scallions
2 tablespoons chopped flat-leaf parsley
Salt and freshly ground black pepper
1 pound Brussels sprouts
1 teaspoon caraway seeds or celery seeds,
    bruised in a mortar
Lemon wedges

1. Place the butter in a medium bowl and add the garlic, 2 tablespoons mustard, the scallions, and parsley. Mix well. Add more mustard if necessary and salt and pepper to taste; set aside.
2. Trim the root ends of the sprouts and remove any loose or discolored leaves. Cut the sprouts in half and then shred them in a food processor or with a knife. Melt ¼ cup of the mustard butter in a large skillet over medium heat. Sauté the sprouts until tender but still a little crisp, about 5 minutes. Lower the heat and stir in the caraway seeds, more mustard butter as desired, and salt and pepper to taste. Serve with lemon wedges.

SERVES 4 TO 6

COOKING NOTES
I love butter, but I couldn't bring myself to sauté the shredded sprouts in half a cup of it, as the original recipe instructs you to do. You want the sprouts crisp, tender, and gently dressed in the mustard butter. Start with 4 tablespoons and fold in a tablespoon or two more at the end.

For Thanksgiving, I quadrupled the recipe and it worked just fine, but if increasing the recipe, cook it in batches.

The leftover mustard butter shouldn't last long: I used it to top some broiled skirt steaks; shaved Parmesan cheese onto rye bread spread with the butter, then slipped the open-faced sandwich under the broiler; and made another sandwich using the butter, toasted whole wheat bread, smoked ham, and sheep's-milk cheese.

SERVING SUGGESTIONS
Butternut Squash and Cider Soup (p. 136), Roast Quail with Sage Dressing (p. 453), Roasted Brine-Cured Turkey with Wild Mushroom Stuffing (p. 474), Spoon Lamb (p. 546), Mashed Potatoes Anna (p. 294), Madame Laracine's Gratin Dauphinois (p. 284), Apple Galette (p. 843)

OCTOBER 13, 2002: "TURNING GREEN," BY JULIA REED.
—2002

⟿ STIR-FRIED COLLARDS

This is a brilliant work of adaptation and ingenuity— a recipe from the Chow family in Clarksdale, Mississippi, descendents of Chinese immigrants who settled in the Mississippi Delta more than a century ago. The heat of a wok unleashes a refreshing mineral flavor in the collard greens. To balance this purity, you finish them with a little oyster sauce and sugar.

---

3 bunches tender collard greens (2½ to 3 pounds total)
Pinch of salt, or to taste
2 tablespoons peanut or canola oil
6 cloves garlic, chopped
A few grinds of black pepper
2 to 3 tablespoons oyster sauce
½ teaspoon sugar

1. Bring a large pot of water to a boil. Have a bowl of ice water ready. Wash and trim the greens, and cut into 2-by-3-inch pieces. Blanch in batches in the boiling water for 1 minute (begin counting after the water returns to a boil), then immediately transfer to the bowl of ice water. Drain well. Lift the greens up by

handfuls and squeeze out the excess water, then spread out on a kitchen towel and pat dry.

2. Heat a wok over high heat (medium-high if you have a powerful stove), then add the salt and let it brown lightly. Add the oil. When the oil is hot, add the garlic and stir until lightly browned. Add the greens and pepper and stir-fry for about 1 minute. Stir in 2 tablespoons oyster sauce and the sugar, then taste and adjust the seasoning. Serve immediately.

SERVES 6 TO 8

COOKING NOTE
I blanched the collards in 3 batches.

SERVING SUGGESTIONS
Spicy, Supercrunchy Fried Chicken (p. 490), Light Potato Salad (p. 301), Pickled Watermelon Rind (p. 598), Red Velvet Cake (p. 757), Key Lime Pie (p. 826), Pralines (p. 684)

JUNE 4, 2003: "EAST MEETS SOUTH AT A DELTA TABLE," BY JOAN NATHAN. RECIPE ADAPTED FROM YUNG CHOW.

—2003

SPINACH AND ARTICHOKE CASSEROLE

This recipe may have been published in the *Times* in 2003, but it certainly wasn't created that recently. I cringed when I first read the ingredient list—both cream cheese and Ritz crackers?—but was won over by the result, which is indeed a surprisingly pleasant and rich gratin. It was contributed by Julia Reed, a columnist for the Sunday *Magazine*, and is her mother's recipe, one her mother served at countless parties, without irony.

"I first remember my mother making it for Pat and Bill Buckley," Reed wrote in an e-mail, "when they came to our house for dinner [in Greenville, Mississippi], and it subsequently became part of what she called her 'vd dinner' repertoire (as in 'visiting dignitary'). I have only ever seen it scribbled in her handwriting on a piece of notepaper." Reed doesn't know where the recipe came from, but she is pretty sure the Ritz cracker crumbs that get spread on top of the

casserole are her mother's addition. She added, "At Thanksgiving, she tops so many casseroles with them she has to buy the boxes by the case.

"Once in my twenties, I decided to update the vd dinner and I slaved for hours doing real braised artichoke bottoms filled with Julia Child's gratinéed spinach (made from fresh spinach, of course) and real buttered bread crumbs, the whole thing, and I swear you can't beat that frozen spinach with the cream cheese and lemon juice."

———

1 tablespoon unsalted butter for the baking dish
Two 10-ounce packages frozen chopped spinach
8 tablespoons (1 stick) unsalted butter, melted, plus 1 tablespoon for drizzling
One 8-ounce package cream cheese, at room temperature
1 teaspoon fresh lemon juice
One 14-ounce can artichoke hearts, drained and quartered
1/2 cup Ritz cracker crumbs (about 10 crackers)

1. Put a rack in the middle of the oven and heat the oven to 350 degrees. Generously butter a shallow 2-quart casserole. Cook the spinach according to the package directions; drain well and place in a bowl.

2. Add the 8 tablespoons melted butter, cream cheese, and lemon juice to the spinach and blend well with a fork.

3. Scatter the artichoke quarters evenly over the bottom of the greased casserole. Cover with the spinach mixture and smooth the top. Cover the top with the Ritz crumbs and drizzle with the remaining 1 tablespoon melted butter.

4. Bake until bubbly in the center and lightly browned on the top, about 25 minutes. Let stand for about 5 minutes before serving.

SERVES 6 TO 8

SERVING SUGGESTIONS
Reed's mother served this with Ann Seranne's Rib-Roast of Beef (p. 519) or roast tenderloin. "I know scalloped oysters were part of the menu too," Reed wrote, "and I swear I think in the earliest days she also included Uncle Ben's wild rice with sautéed mushrooms, and maybe almonds, without embarrassment." Some other ideas: Iceberg Lettuce with Smoked Bacon and Buttermilk Dressing (p. 200), Oliver Clark's Meat

Loaf (p. 554), Italian Roast Potatoes (p. 300), Mashed Potatoes Anna (p. 294), Sally Darr's Golden Delicious Apple Tart (p. 839), Buttermilk Pie (p. 859).

OCTOBER 26, 2003: "FOOD: PANNING OUT," BY JULIA REED.

—2003

EGGPLANT INVOLTINI

Involtini are small stuffed and rolled pouches, often composed of thin slices of beef with a bread crumb stuffing, or sometimes swordfish, or, as in this recipe, eggplant. These involtini capture the technique's best qualities—a thin wrapping around a light and delicate filling, much like good ravioli. You take long pliable strips of sautéed eggplant and fill them with a mixture of feta, pine nuts, plumped raisins, mint, lemon zest, and parsley. Then you tuck them into a baking dish, top them with crushed tomatoes and thin sheets of mozzarella, and bake until bubbly and inviting.

———

3 eggplants (about 1 pound each), trimmed and cut lengthwise into ¼-inch-thick slices (about 18 slices total)

About ¾ cup olive oil

½ pound feta cheese, crumbled

½ cup pine nuts

⅓ cup raisins, plumped in hot water for 10 minutes and drained

¼ cup extra virgin olive oil, plus more for drizzling

2 tablespoons bread crumbs

1 clove garlic, minced

Finely grated zest of 1 lemon

1½ teaspoons dried mint

2 tablespoons chopped flat-leaf parsley

1 large egg, beaten

Salt and freshly ground black pepper

2½ cups drained canned crushed tomatoes

1 ball (no more than 1 pound) fresh mozzarella, cut into ⅛-inch-thick slices

1. Heat the oven to 375 degrees. Place a cast-iron skillet, preferably a ridged one, or other heavy skillet over medium-high heat. Working in batches, brush the eggplant slices on both sides with olive oil and cook, turning, until soft and, if using a ridged pan, crisscrossed with grid marks. Set aside to cool.

2. Combine the feta, pine nuts, raisins, extra virgin olive oil, bread crumbs, garlic, lemon zest, mint, and parsley in a large bowl. Mix in the egg and season to taste with salt and pepper.

3. Lay the eggplant slices out on a work surface. Divide the stuffing evenly among them, placing 1 to 2 tablespoons at one end of each slice. Roll up the slices tightly and place seam side down in a 9-by-13-inch baking dish (or other shallow baking pan in which the rolls fit snugly in a single layer).

4. Pour the crushed tomatoes over the eggplant rolls. Arrange the mozzarella slices in a line down the center of pan. Drizzle a tablespoon or two of extra virgin olive oil evenly over the pan, and sprinkle with salt and pepper.

5. Bake until the cheese has melted and the sauce is bubbling and fragrant, 25 to 30 minutes. Allow to stand for 5 to 10 minutes before serving.

SERVES 3 AS A LIGHT MAIN COURSE, 6 AS A FIRST COURSE

COOKING NOTE

I don't have a ridged cast-iron skillet, so I just used my regular one, with its flat bottom, and the eggplant cooked fine.

SERVING SUGGESTIONS

Caesar Salad (p. 174), Ed Giobbi's Sweet Red Pepper Sauce for Pasta (p. 318), Corn and Yellow Tomato Risotto with Shrimp (p. 328), Pine Nut Cookies (p. 689), Ricotta Kisses (p. 852)

DECEMBER 10, 2003: "AT MY TABLE: A SIGNPOST OF GREECE, A CLOAK OF ITALY," BY NIGELLA LAWSON.

—2003

SFORMATA DI RICOTTA (RICOTTA CUSTARD)

Imagine a ricotta–crème fraîche custard crust and pockets of sweet tomatoes that are like resting stations between rapturous bites of the pudding, and you have this sformata. It is the work of two of London's best-known chefs, Ruth Rogers and Rose Gray, the owners of the River Café (until Gray's death in early 2010). In opening their restaurant in Hammersmith on the Thames in 1987, Rogers and Gray came up with a new and lasting model: they took rustic Old World Italian dishes, sharpened their flavors, and served them in a spare modern space designed by Rogers's husband, Richard. The two styles should have fought like dogs under a blanket, but Rogers and Gray found ways for each to influence the other. Much of their food employs the use of a wood oven, which they installed like a secret window in the middle of a vast, empty white wall in the dining room. And they took uncomplicated dishes like broad beans and pancetta, 12-hour beef shank, and lemon apple cake and framed them with glistening white plates.

———

2 tablespoons unsalted butter, softened

2 ounces Parmesan cheese, grated

10 ounces (about 1 pint) cherry tomatoes

1 large clove garlic, halved lengthwise

1 tablespoon extra virgin olive oil, plus extra for drizzling

Salt and freshly ground black pepper

6 large eggs

2 ¼ cups fresh ricotta cheese

1 cup crème fraîche

2 tablespoons thyme leaves (no stems)

1. Heat the oven to 400 degrees. Grease the bottom of a 2-quart baking dish with 1 tablespoon butter and sprinkle with 2 tablespoons Parmesan. Add the tomatoes and garlic; drizzle with the 1 tablespoon olive oil and season with salt and pepper. Shake the dish to coat the tomatoes with the cheese.

2. Bake for 15 minutes, or until the tomatoes are hot and starting to split, shaking the dish occasionally. Remove from the oven and let cool in the dish. (Leave the oven on.)

3. Spoon the tomatoes and their juices into a bowl; set the baking dish aside.

4. When the baking dish is cool enough to touch, grease the bottom and sides with the remaining tablespoon of butter. Blend the eggs and ricotta in a food processor until smooth. Add the crème fraîche and half the thyme and process until mixed. Season with salt and pepper.

5. Spread the ricotta mixture in the baking dish. Scatter the tomatoes, with their juices, and the remaining thyme on top. Sprinkle with the remaining Parmesan

and drizzle with olive oil. Bake until a knife inserted in the center comes out clean but the center still jiggles a little, 25 to 35 minutes. Let stand for 10 minutes before serving.

SERVES 6 TO 8

SERVING SUGGESTIONS
Classic Ciabatta (p. 665), Salade à la Romaine (p. 171), Green Goddess Salad (p. 176), Steak au Poivre (p. 573), Broiled Lamb Chops (p. 514), Sour Cream Ice Cream (p. 730), Fresh Raspberry (or Blackberry or Blueberry) Flummery (p. 824), Canestrelli (Shortbread from Ovada; p. 692), Spice Krinkles (p. 688)

JULY 18, 2004: "ITALIAN FOR BEGINNERS," BY JULIA REED. RECIPE ADAPTED FROM *ITALIAN EASY: RECIPES FROM THE LONDON RIVER CAFÉ*, BY RUTH ROGERS AND ROSE GRAY.

—2004

⌒ BLACK-SKILLET OKRA

———

⅓ cup all-purpose flour

⅓ cup fine yellow cornmeal

1 pound tender young okra, washed

½ teaspoon coarse sea salt

½ teaspoon freshly ground black pepper

¼ cup vegetable oil, preferably peanut or grapeseed

1. Heat the oven to 200 degrees. Stir the flour and cornmeal together in a small bowl; set aside. Heat a well-seasoned 9- or 10-inch cast-iron skillet over medium heat for 5 minutes.

2. Trim the stems and pointed ends from the okra, and slice the pods into ½-inch-thick rounds, dropping them into a fine-screen footed colander. Spray lightly with water, shake to remove excess drops, and toss the okra well with salt and pepper. Sprinkle the coating mixture over the okra in the colander, and toss to coat evenly. Shake the colander to remove excess coating.

3. Increase the skillet heat to high. Add half the oil to the skillet. Drop half the okra into the skillet in a single layer. Wait 5 seconds, and stir. Continue to fry and stir until the okra is deep brown and crisp with spotty char marks, about 5 minutes. Transfer to a baking sheet and keep warm in the oven. Using mitts,

remove the hot skillet from the stove, and wipe clean with paper towels. Return the hot skillet to the burner over high heat, add the remaining oil, and fry the remaining okra.

SERVES 4 TO 6

SERVING SUGGESTIONS

The original recipe said to "serve the okra hot, with sliced tomatoes, cucumbers, fluffy rice, and fried chicken or pork chops, or as croutons in a green salad." I'd pair it with Jay Grelen's Southern Iced Tea (p. 27), Summer Squash Casserole (p. 252), Brine-Cured Pork Chops (p. 569), Pan-Roasted Chicken with End-of-Season Tomatoes (p. 482), and Buttermilk Pie (p. 859).

JULY 28, 2004: "IT'S NOT FAIR WHAT THEY SAY ABOUT OKRA," BY KAY RENTSCHLER.

—2004

RATATOUILLE WITH BUTTERNUT SQUASH

I thought the butternut squash might feel like an interloper in such a codified and familiar classic, but squash is a good chameleon, happy to provide sweetness where the tomatoes do not, and also content to be the heft that makes the dish more of a main course. This recipe appeared in a column by Nigella Lawson, the British food writer and television host known for her love of old-fashioned British foods, her sensible working-mother recipes, and a sensuousness that makes American food writers feel nervous.

———

$^1/_3$ cup olive oil

2 medium onions, halved and thinly sliced (2$^1/_2$ cups)

1 teaspoon cumin seeds

1 teaspoon ground coriander

2 teaspoons sea salt, or more to taste

1 clove garlic, minced

1 medium eggplant, quartered lengthwise
  and thinly sliced (6$^1/_2$ cups)

1 small butternut squash, peeled, seeded, quartered
  lengthwise, and thinly sliced (5 cups)

2 medium zucchini, trimmed and sliced
  into $^1/_4$-inch-thick rounds (2 cups)

1 yellow bell pepper, cored, seeded,
  and sliced into strips (1$^1/_2$ cups)

One 28-ounce can diced tomatoes

1. Place a large deep skillet or a Dutch oven over medium heat and add the oil. When it's hot, add the onions, cumin, coriander, and salt and sauté until the onions are tender, about 3 minutes. Add the garlic and sauté for 1 minute.

2. Add the eggplant and butternut squash and cook, stirring occasionally, until they begin to soften, 3 to 4 minutes. Add the zucchini, bell pepper, and tomatoes, stir well, and bring to a simmer. Reduce the heat to medium-low and simmer, partially covered, stirring occasionally, for 1 hour.

3. Remove from the heat, and add salt to taste. Allow to cool to room temperature before serving. (Or cover and refrigerate; reheat gently before serving.)

SERVES 6

COOKING NOTE

Lawson suggests serving this the day after it is made. I second this opinion.

SERVING SUGGESTIONS

Watercress Salad (p. 171), Roast Quail with Sage Dressing (p. 453), Buttermilk Roast Chicken (p. 493), Italian Roast Potatoes (p. 300), Walnut Cake with Chocolate Walnut Buttercream (p. 758), Olive Oil and Apple Cider Cake (p. 771), Lucas Schoormans's Lemon Tart (p. 857)

SEPTEMBER 15, 2004: "AT MY TABLE: AN INHERITANCE OF FLAVORS AND COLORS," BY NIGELLA LAWSON.

—2004

ASPARAGUS MIMOSA

I love going to the farmers' market in the spring and buying asparagus and eggs to make this dish—asparagus topped with sieved egg, a little lemon, and coarse salt and pepper. The fluffy yellow-and-white sieved egg resembles mimosa flowers—hence the name.

———

1½ pounds asparagus, trimmed

1 large egg

Extra virgin olive oil

½ lemon

Maldon or other flaky sea salt and
 freshly ground black pepper

1. Fill a large pot with water, season with salt, and bring to a boil. Fill a large bowl with ice water. Drop the asparagus into the boiling water and cook until just tender, about 4 minutes. Lift out the spears and plunge them into the ice water. Once cool, drain and dry the asparagus on tea towels.

2. Bring the water to a boil again and drop in the egg. Cook for 9 minutes; let it cool before peeling it.

3. Arrange the asparagus on a platter. Sprinkle with olive oil, and squeeze over a little lemon juice. Place the egg in a sieve and use the back of a spoon to mash it through the sieve and over the asparagus. Finish the dish with a dash of salt and a coarse grind of pepper.

SERVES 4

SERVING SUGGESTIONS
Potage Parisien with Sorrel Cream (p. 148), Chilled English Pea–Mint Soup (p. 162), Roasted Salmon with Herb Vinaigrette (p. 430), Italian Roast Potatoes (p. 300), Grapefruit Granita (p. 731), Even-Greater American Pound Cake (p. 788), Straight-Up Rhubarb Pie (p. 862)

MARCH 27, 2005: "THE ARSENAL," BY AMANDA HESSER.
—2005

🍃 SUGAR SNAP PEAS WITH HORSERADISH

The peas are neither blanched nor sautéed, but something in between. David Chang, the wunderkind behind Momofuku (Noodle, Ssäm and Milk Bars, and Ko) glaze-steams them in a small amount of reduced stock (preferably some kind of pork broth) and soy sauce. He then wraps them in butter, padding the sweet green peas before they're blitzed with horseradish.

From now on, I will have a hard time cooking them any other way.

———

1½ cups good broth, preferably pork

2 tablespoons soy sauce

1 pound sugar snap peas, trimmed

2 to 3 tablespoons unsalted butter

Salt and freshly ground black pepper

6 tablespoons freshly grated horseradish

1. Combine the broth and soy sauce in a deep skillet over high heat, bring to a boil, and reduce to a glaze, about 10 minutes. Add the peas and stir frequently until they are bright green and tender, about 5 minutes.

2. Turn the heat to medium and stir in the butter and salt (easy at first, because of the soy sauce) and pepper to taste. Put in a warmed bowl and top with the horseradish.

SERVES 4

SERVING SUGGESTIONS
Cream of Carrot Soup (p. 119), Marinated Flank Steak with Asian Slaw (p. 552), Poached Pears with Asian Spices (p. 856), Tangerine Sherbet (p. 734)

APRIL 12, 2006: "THE CHEF: DAVID CHANG: FISH AND VEGETABLES, COZYING UP TO MEAT," BY MARK BITTMAN. RECIPE ADAPTED FROM DAVID CHANG, THE CHEF AND CO-OWNER OF MOMOFUKU SSÄM BAR (AND OTHERS) IN NEW YORK CITY.
—2006

🍃 ASPARAGUS WITH MISO BUTTER

In a dish containing asparagus and miso, a lot can go wrong. If the emphasis is too much on the asparagus, you could end up with something that's thin on flavor; if it's on the miso, you could end up with a salt lick. The peripheral ingredients do the vital balancing work here. The pork fat and butter give the asparagus roundness. The vinegar balances the salt in the miso. The eggs blanket the dish, tempering any conflicts. And you end up with a dish that transforms asparagus into a lush, hearty, and entirely addictive dish.

———

¼ cup rendered pork or bacon fat or vegetable oil

1 pound asparagus, trimmed, stalks peeled if thick

Salt and freshly ground black pepper

¼ cup not-too-salty miso, preferably white

4 tablespoons unsalted butter

1½ teaspoons sherry vinegar

2 poached (or warm-bath-cooked) eggs

1. Put the fat or oil in a large skillet and turn the heat to medium-high. Add as much asparagus as will fit in one layer, season with salt and pepper to taste, and toss and stir until browned and shriveled, about 10 minutes. Transfer to a platter and keep warm while you cook the remaining asparagus.

2. Meanwhile, whisk together the miso and butter in a small saucepan over low heat so they combine and the butter softens but does not melt. Whisk in the vinegar, remove from the heat, and keep warm.

3. When the asparagus is done, spread a generous spoonful of the miso butter on the bottom of a warm serving plate. Blot the excess fat from the asparagus if you like, put it on top of the miso butter, and top with the poached eggs.

SERVES 2 AS A MAIN COURSE, 4 AS A FIRST COURSE

SERVING SUGGESTIONS
Shrimp Toast (p. 60), Warm Eggplant Salad with Sesame and Shallots (p. 203), Jasmine Tea Rice (p. 354), Sautéed Fluke with Grapefruit Vinaigrette (p. 437), Chinese-Style Steamed Black Sea Bass (p. 432), Rhubarb-Soy-Marinated Duck with Rhubarb-Ginger Compote (p. 468), Grilled Hanger Steak (p. 551), Lemon Lotus Ice Cream (p. 724)

APRIL 19, 2006: "THE CHEF: DAVID CHANG: WHEN IN DOUBT, ADD AN EGG, JAPANESE-STYLE," BY MARK BITTMAN. RECIPE ADAPTED FROM DAVID CHANG, THE CHEF AND CO-OWNER OF MOMOFUKU SSÄM BAR IN NEW YORK CITY.

—2006

✐ STRING BEANS WITH GINGER AND GARLIC

What every Thanksgiving table needs—definitively gingery green beans to snap you out of your turkey slumber.

———

2½ pounds green beans (haricots verts work especially well), trimmed

¼ cup vegetable oil

¼ cup minced fresh ginger (about a 6-inch piece of ginger)

4 medium cloves garlic, minced

1. Bring a large pot of salted water to a boil. Fill a large bowl with ice water. Working in 2 batches, boil the beans until just tender but still crisp and bright green; start testing after 4 minutes or so, being careful not to overcook them. When done, plunge the beans into the ice water to stop the cooking; lift out immediately when cool and drain on towels.

2. Heat 2 tablespoons oil in a wide skillet over high heat. Add half the beans, half the ginger, and half the garlic, and cook, stirring and tossing constantly, until the beans are heated through and the ginger and garlic are softened and aromatic. Sprinkle with salt and transfer to a serving dish. Repeat with the remaining oil, beans, ginger, and garlic.

SERVES 10

SERVING SUGGESTIONS
Mulligatawny Soup (p. 113), Bademiya's Justly Famous Bombay Chile-and-Cilantro Chicken (p. 471), Tibs (p. 545), Yogurt Rice (p. 356), Mango Ice Cream (p. 729). Or Roasted Brine-Cured Turkey (p. 474) and the rest of your Thanksgiving menu.

NOVEMBER 15, 2006: "A LITTLE SNAP, TO TAKE THE TABLE BEYOND TAN," BY JULIA MOSKIN.

—2006

WILTED CHARD WITH PICKLED RED ONION

You will love the dimension that pickled onion adds to the chard. I could eat the whole batch in one sitting. I mean it—this dish is my pint of cookie dough ice cream.

_____

For the Onions
2 large red onions, sliced into thick rings, rings separated
1½ cups white wine vinegar
2 bay leaves
4 sprigs thyme
½ teaspoon crushed red pepper flakes
1 tablespoon sugar
2 teaspoons black or mixed peppercorns, bruised, plus more for garnish

For the Chard
4 pounds red or green Swiss chard
¼ cup olive oil
2 cloves garlic, crushed
Salt and freshly ground black pepper

1. To make the onion, bring a kettle of water to a boil. Place the onion slices in a colander, set in the sink, and pour the boiling water over them.
2. Combine the remaining ingredients in a bowl, stirring to dissolve the sugar. Add the onions, submerging them by placing a plate on top; if more liquid is needed, add equal amounts of vinegar and hot tap water. After about 15 minutes, the onions will turn bright pink. (The onions can be made ahead and refrigerated for up to 3 days.)
3. To make the chard, bring a large pot of salted water to a boil. Cut the stems off the chard and set aside; slice the leaves across into wide ribbons. Working in batches if necessary, boil the leaves until tender but not mushy, 3 to 7 minutes. Boil the stems separately until tender; drain in a colander. Cut the stems into ½-inch-thick slices.
4. Heat the oil in a wide skillet over medium heat. Add the garlic and chard, and heat through, turning to coat evenly with the oil. Season to taste with salt and pepper. Transfer the chard to a serving dish, top with some pickled onions, and garnish them with peppercorns. Pass the remaining onions at the table.

SERVES 10

COOKING NOTES
I needed an extra ½ cup water and ½ cup vinegar to submerge the onions.

You can halve the recipe if you're not cooking for an army.

SERVING SUGGESTIONS
Seared Tuna in Black Pepper Crust (p. 409), Beer-Can Chicken (p. 473), Veal Shanks with Garlic Mashed Potatoes (p. 540), Stewed Lamb Shanks with White Beans and Rosemary (p. 542)

NOVEMBER 15, 2006: "A LITTLE SNAP, TO TAKE THE TABLE BEYOND TAN," BY JULIA MOSKIN. RECIPE ADAPTED FROM _VEGETARIAN COOKING FOR EVERYONE_, BY DEBORAH MADISON.

2006

ZUCCHINI CARPACCIO WITH AVOCADO

For decades, Patricia Wells has maintained an army of devoted followers who have looked to her for restaurant recommendations (on her blog, and in _Food Lover's Guide to Paris_) and counted on her to find the best recipes from Paris chefs and translate them for the home (_Bistro Cooking_ and _The Paris Cookbook_).

Appreciated mostly for her work as a journalist and tastemaker, she then surprised her fans with _Vegetable Harvest_, a book that proved she is also an excellent and inventive cook. And that not every recipe needs to be fueled with butter and cream. Wells attempted to redefine our notions about the role vegetables play in a meal. Lesser cooks would do this by replacing meats with grains and legumes; Wells focused on flavor. So in a crab "ravioli" recipe (given to her by Pascal Barbot, the chef at the Paris restaurant Astrance), avocado is used in place of pasta, the small amount of crab is blended with lots of chives and orange and lime zest, and the dish is finished with another distinct flavor, almond oil. Here vivid lemon juice and pistachio oil both sharpen and enrich strips of zucchini and avocado. This makes an elegant lunch, first course, or side dish.

_____

4 teaspoons fresh lemon juice

½ teaspoon fine sea salt, plus more to taste

¼ cup best-quality pistachio oil, almond oil,
   or extra virgin olive oil

4 small zucchini (about 4 ounces each), trimmed

I ripe avocado, pitted, peeled, and very thinly sliced

¼ cup salted pistachios

4 sprigs lemon thyme or regular thyme,
   preferably with flowers

1. Stir together the lemon juice and salt in a small jar. Add the oil, cover, and shake to blend.

2. Slice the zucchini lengthwise as thin as possible, using a mandoline or very sharp knife. Spread the slices on a platter and drizzle with the lemon mixture. Tilt the platter to coat the slices evenly. Cover with plastic wrap and marinate at room temperature for 30 minutes to an hour.

3. Alternate the zucchini and avocado slices on individual salad plates, slightly overlapping the slices. Sprinkle with the pistachios. Season with salt, garnish with the lemon thyme, and serve.

SERVES 4 AS A SIDE DISH, FIRST COURSE,
OR LIGHT LUNCH

SERVING SUGGESTIONS
Salt-Roasted Striped Bass with Salsa de la Boca (p. 427), Fresh Salmon and Lime Cakes (p. 420), Buttermilk Roast Chicken (p. 493), Yogurt Rice (p. 356), Light Potato Salad (p. 301), Tangerine Sherbet (p. 734), Brown Sugar Shortbread (p. 690), Fontainebleau (p. 829)

JUNE 6, 2007: "THE MINIMALIST: IN PARIS, BRINGING VEGETABLES OUT TO PLAY," BY MARK BITTMAN. RECIPE ADAPTED FROM *VEGETABLE HARVEST*, BY PATRICIA WELLS.

—2007

☞ BROCCOLI RABE OSHITASHI

―――

I large bunch broccoli rabe (about I pound)

½ cup white sesame seeds

8 teaspoons best-quality soy sauce, or to taste

2 teaspoons mirin (sweet rice wine) or
   ½ teaspoon raw sugar or to taste

1. Bring a large pot of salted water to a boil. Prepare an ice water bath. Trim off the bottoms and any tough leaves from the broccoli rabe and cut into 2-inch lengths. Boil just until crisp-tender, about 2 minutes. Drain and plunge into the ice water to stop the cooking and set the color. When cool, remove from the water and drain on a kitchen towel.

2. Pour the sesame seeds into a heavy skillet, set over medium-low heat, and toast, stirring often, just until fragrant and golden brown. Immediately transfer to a plate. While the seeds are still warm but not hot, use a mortar and pestle or mini food processor to crush them to a paste.

3. Add the soy sauce and mirin to the crushed seeds, stir, and taste. Adjust the seasonings with soy and/or mirin if necessary. If the paste is too thick, thin with a little warm water.

4. To serve, put the drained broccoli rabe in a bowl, add half the sesame sauce, and toss to coat. Pass the rest of the sauce at the table.

SERVES 6

SERVING SUGGESTIONS
Edamame with Nori Salt (p. 92), Alaskan Salmon (p. 423), Coconut Rice Pudding with Lime Syrup (p. 846)

DECEMBER 26, 2007: "A CELEBRATION OF THE NEW YEAR USHERS IN A BIT OF JAPAN," BY JULIA MOSKIN. RECIPE ADAPTED FROM MARIKO HASHIMOTO.

—2007

☞ BUTTER-BRAISED ASPARAGUS AND OYSTER MUSHROOMS WITH PEAS AND TARRAGON

This terrific recipe by Melissa Clark, a columnist for the Dining section of the *Times*, is entirely modern, but her reassuringly precise instructions echo those of Pierre Franey. Knowing that each vegetable must be cooked for the proper amount of time, Clark has you add them in stages, so nothing is overcooked. Franey measured every chopped ingredient in cups and tablespoons so there would be no debate about what a medium onion is, and, like Clark, he was an expert on recipe order. (See his Spaghettini with Vegetables and Pepper Vodka Sauce on p. 320, and Steamed Fish with Thyme and Tomato Vinaigrette on p. 408.)

---

3 tablespoons unsalted butter

7 ounces oyster mushrooms, trimmed and cut into ¾-inch-wide fan-shaped pieces (about 2 cups)

Kosher salt and freshly ground black pepper

1 pound asparagus, trimmed and cut into 1¼-inch lengths

3 scallions, thinly sliced (about ¼ cup)

½ cup frozen peas

1 tablespoon chopped tarragon

1. Melt 2 tablespoons butter in a large skillet over medium heat. Add the mushrooms and a pinch each of salt and pepper, stir to coat the mushrooms with butter, cover, and cook for 5 minutes.

2. Stir in the asparagus, scallions, and remaining 1 tablespoon butter. Season with salt and pepper. Cover and cook for about 2 minutes if using pencil-thin asparagus, up to 7 minutes for jumbos, until the asparagus is al dente.

3. Stir in the peas and tarragon; cover and cook for about 2 minutes longer, until the peas are heated through and the asparagus is tender. Taste and adjust the seasoning.

SERVES 4 TO 6

SERVING SUGGESTIONS

Ricotta Crostini with Fresh Thyme and Dried Oregano (p. 93), Rabbit in Mustard Sauce (p. 466), A Perfect Batch of Rice (p. 316), Breton Butter Cake (p. 777), Lemon-Almond Butter Cake (p. 780)

MAY 7, 2008: "AN IMPROVISED ASPARAGUS DISH IS A HAPPY ACCIDENT," BY MELISSA CLARK.

—2008

STEAMED FENNEL WITH RED PEPPER OIL

This simple recipe is the work of David Tanis, a chef with a brilliant and enviable arrangement: he spends half of each year as the chef at Chez Panisse in Berkeley and half in Paris, where he runs an underground restaurant out of his apartment.

The recipe has all the markings of a Chez Panisse dish: a focus on a single ingredient, not much prep work, lots of lemon and olive oil. Enjoy the simplicity. The fennel is lightly steamed to tease out its silky underlayer, then arranged on a platter shrouded with lemon wedges. A spicy oil is passed at the table and guests are invited to dress their own with lemon, oil, and salt. The recipe comes from Tanis's first book, *A Platter of Figs and Other Recipes*.

½ cup olive oil

½ to 1 teaspoon crushed red pepper flakes

6 to 8 fennel bulbs

Salt and freshly ground black pepper

Lemon wedges

1. Heat the oil in a small saucepan until warm. Turn off the heat and stir in the red pepper flakes. Let cool, and transfer to a serving bowl.

2. Trim the fennel bulbs, reserving a few fronds. Cut the bulbs into ½-inch-thick slices. (Cut out and discard the fibrous core at the bottom of each bulb.) Put the fennel into the perforated top of a steamer and sprinkle with salt and pepper. Set over boiling water and steam, tightly covered, until the fennel is silky but slightly crisp, 3 to 5 minutes.

3. Arrange the fennel on a platter, sprinkle with the reserved fronds, and surround with lemon wedges. Pass the red pepper oil and salt at table.

SERVES 6 TO 8

SERVING SUGGESTIONS

Salmon and Tomatoes in Foil (p. 422), Mashed Potatoes Anna (p. 294), Bulgur Salad with Pomegranate Dressing and Toasted Nuts (p. 354), Vanilla Plum Ice (p. 734), Steamed Lemon Pudding (p. 849)

OCTOBER 22, 2008: "SOME HEAVY READING, RECIPES INCLUDED," BY JULIA MOSKIN. RECIPE ADAPTED FROM *A PLATTER OF FIGS AND OTHER RECIPES*, BY DAVID TANIS.

—2008

- Several recipes for *pommes de terre à la maître d'hôtel* show up in the recipe pages (see p. 272).

- Potato croquettes and potato salads are big.

- Saratoga (potato) chips were invented at the Moon's Lake House in 1853; recipes for them show up every couple of years in the *Times* (p. 273).

- Boston baked beans are ubiquitous.

- Succotash (p. 275).

- Jane Nickerson publishes a photo how-to on Candied Sweet Potatoes (p. 276).

- The double-stuffed baked potato is born; it lives on in steak houses.

- Tater Tots hit the supermarket.

- Americans adventure beyond baked navy beans to pintos, lentils, and black-eyed peas.

- Janson's Temptation (p. 278), a gratin of potatoes and anchovies, is an oddball hit.

- Three- and four-bean salad enter the picnic pantheon (see p. 278).

- French chef Joël Robuchon beats together 1 part butter to 2 parts mashed potatoes—the recipe becomes famous and keeps cardiologists in business.
- The decade of corn, tuna, and the black beans.

- Yukon Golds take on whites and russets.

- Smashed potatoes are the new mashed potatoes.

- Smoked Mashed Potatoes (p. 300).

- Potato "Tostones" (p. 301).

—1870s—
—1880s—
—1904—

—1937—
—1940s—
—1948—

—1950s—

—1954—
—1960s—

—1960—

—1970s—

—1980s—

—1984—
—1990s—
—2004—
—2007—

- Stewed Corn (p. 271), more pudding than stew.

- Baked hominy and hominy fritters.

- Super-sweet corn is developed by botanist John Laughnan at the University of Illinois.

- Green lentils pass the baton to black beans.

- Corn cakes are the first course of the moment, sometimes topped with caviar (see p. 282).
- If you aren't baking a potato gratin, you are probably trying out the nifty new recipe for roasted potato salad (p. 285).

- Red lentils pass the baton to chickpeas.

6

⁓

POTATOES, CORN, AND LEGUMES

People who have written about food for the *Times* have shared a love for potatoes, corn, and fresh peas, and a general lack of interest in the rest of the legume family—lentils, chickpeas, and such. But legumes are in fact kindred spirits with potatoes and corn: they're substantive, faintly sweet, and receptive to just about any flavor. There are a few such gems here—the Green Lentils with Roasted Beets and Preserved Lemon on p. 289 and the Roasted Carrot and Red Lentil Ragout, also on p. 289. Isn't it time to embrace them too?

RECIPES BY CATEGORY

GREEN PEA FRITTERS

I thought these fritters were going to be a complete failure when I dropped the first spoonful of batter into the pan—it was so thin all looked hopeless. But then the batter seized and behaved like a cross between a crepe and a pancake, resulting in thin, delicate, even lacy cakes flecked with green peas—a fresh take on blini. Serve the fritters with a dab of crème fraîche topped with a pickled ramp or a nugget of smoked fish blended with chives and tarragon, or wrap them around crab dressed with lemon and coriander (admittedly, not how they ate them in 1876).

***

2 cups fresh or frozen peas
Salt and freshly ground black pepper
2 large eggs
I cup whole milk
½ cup all-purpose flour
¼ teaspoon baking soda
½ teaspoon cream of tartar
Unsalted butter for greasing the pan

1. Cook the peas in ½ inch of boiling salted water just until tender, about 2 minutes for frozen peas, longer for fresh. Drain. Coarsely mash the peas and season with salt and pepper.

2. Whisk together the eggs and milk in a medium bowl. Mix together the flour, baking soda, and cream of tartar. Gradually whisk the dry ingredients into the egg mixture, and whisk until smooth. Add the peas and season the batter. Let rest for at least 30 minutes.

3. Heat the oven to 175 degrees. Place a nonstick crepe pan or skillet over medium-high heat and butter the pan. Drop the batter in in 2-tablespoonful-dollops—they should spread to 2- to 2½-inch pancakes. Cook until lightly browned on the bottom, about 1 minute, then flip and cook on the other side, 20 to 30 seconds. Place in a single layer on a baking sheet, and keep warm in the oven while you cook the remaining fritters.

MAKES ABOUT 30 FRITTERS; SERVES 6

COOKING NOTE

I cooked the fritters in a nonstick crepe pan because the pan's low sides made maneuvering a spatula and flipping much easier.

SERVING SUGGESTIONS

Fresh and Smoked Salmon Spread (p. 72), Roasted Salmon with Herb Vinaigrette (p. 430), Fricassee of Chicken with Tarragon (p. 456), Sugar Snap Peas with Horseradish (p. 259), Strawberry Ice Cream (p. 722)

SEPTEMBER 24, 1876: "RECEIPTS."

—1876

POTATO SALAD WITH BEETS

This recipe appeared as part of a menu called "Lunch Bill of Fare" sent in by a reader, who wrote, "The midday meal should be light, as several hours of active employment follow it. We always have tea at lunch, hot at this season, iced in summer, with a slice of lemon in lieu of milk; bread, biscuits, cake of some kind; cold meat, if any to spare, if not, stewed oysters; ham and eggs; potato or lobster salad; preserves, cheese, and any fruit in season."

What's interesting about this salad is that you marinate the beets in vinegar for 30 to 60 minutes before adding the potatoes and mayonnaise. This flash pickling gives the beets a sharpness that contrasts well with the bluntness of potatoes.

***

4 medium Yukon Gold potatoes
4 medium beets, trimmed and scrubbed
3 tablespoons red wine vinegar
¾ cup chopped onion
I tablespoon capers
16 olives, such as Cerignola, Picholine, or Sicilian, pitted and chopped
Salt
Cayenne pepper
½ cup mayonnaise

1. Place the potatoes in a medium saucepan, cover with salted water, and bring to a boil. Lower the heat and simmer until tender. Meanwhile, do the same

with the beets. Drain the potatoes and beets, then peel them. Cut the potatoes into $\frac{1}{8}$-inch-thick slices; set aside. Finely chop the beets—you need 2 cups.

2. Combine the beets and 2 tablespoons vinegar in a bowl and let marinate for 30 to 60 minutes. Drain.

3. Combine the potatoes, beets, onion, capers, and olives in a large bowl. Season with salt and cayenne. Add the mayonnaise and remaining 1 tablespoon vinegar. Mix until well blended. Adjust the seasoning.

SERVES 4

SERVING SUGGESTIONS
Stuffed Hard-Cooked Eggs (p. 56), Cucumber Sandwiches (p. 56), Brine-Cured Pork Chops (p. 569), Docks Coleslaw (p. 191), Strawberry Shortcakes (p. 799), Blueberry Ice Cream (p. 726), Buttermilk Pie (p. 859)

MARCH 10, 1878: "RECEIPTS FOR THE TABLE." RECIPE SIGNED SOUTH CAROLINA.

—1878

LARDED POTATOES À LA *NEW YORK TIMES*

I was drawn to this recipe because I'd recently had a delicious potato dish by the cookbook author and celebrity chef Jamie Oliver that involved boring holes in potatoes and stuffing them with bacon, sage, anchovies, garlic, and lemon zest, then baking them. The flavors of the stuffing seeped through the core of the potatoes as they softened, perfuming the whole.

Was the *Times* 130 years ahead of its time with its larded potatoes? Well, sort of. Sort of not. The concept is there: infusing a potato's interior is a smart idea. Using a larding needle to do so is not. Oliver's apple-corer technique can and should be used instead. What follows is my slightly modernized version: I larded each of my potatoes with chopped smoked bacon, sprinkled them with olive oil, coarse salt, and a lot of coarsely ground black pepper, and roasted them. The recipe is a bit of a stunt, as there are easier ways to combine bacon and potatoes, but it's fun nonetheless to slice into a potato and discover a steamy sliver of cured pork.

1 pound baby white potatoes, scrubbed
4 slices bacon, chopped
Olive oil
Chicken broth
Salt and freshly ground black pepper

1. Heat the oven to 350 degrees. Use an apple corer to make holes—end to end—through the potatoes. Stuff the bacon into the cavities. Place the potatoes in a roasting dish just large enough to hold them. Sprinkle with olive oil and a few tablespoons of chicken broth. Season with salt and pepper.

2. Cover the dish with foil. Roast the potatoes until tender, 40 to 60 minutes; remove the foil after 30 minutes.

SERVES 4

SERVING SUGGESTIONS
Iceberg Lettuce with Smoked Bacon and Buttermilk Dressing (p. 200), Broiled Steak with Oysters (p. 511), Tomatoes Vinaigrette (p. 218), Evelyn Sharpe's French Chocolate Cake (p. 752)

APRIL 13, 1879: "RECEIPTS FOR THE TABLE." RECIPE SIGNED MELANIE.

—1879

STEWED CORN

"Stewed," a word that suggests misery in a pan, should be removed from the food lexicon, or at least from this terrific recipe. To make the dish, you scrape the corn and its sappy juices from the cob, gather them all up, and simmer them with tiny bits of cream, butter, salt, white pepper, and a corn water made from the cobs. What you end up with is nothing like creamed corn, but more like a silky corn pudding.

There are two things to remember about stewed corn. It will change every time you make it (I've had it three times), because its sweetness and texture depend on the variety of corn you use and how the corn matures throughout the season. A version prepared in August with white corn was loose and sweet; in October, one made with yellow corn was thick and creamy like porridge. Both were remarkably good.

And to get the right balance of corn pulp to kernel, you need a $3 tool called a corn slitter. Cutting the kernels from the cob, then scraping out the excess juices with a regular knife will produce a different (though not terrible) outcome. A corn slitter scores the kernels and pushes out the creamy pulp, leaving behind the kernels' chewy pods. One can be found at www.lehmans.com. You'll pay more for the shipping than the slitter itself, but take the long view: you'll get to have stewed corn every summer for the rest of your life.

----

16 ears corn, shucked
1 tablespoon unsalted butter
1 tablespoon heavy cream
Salt and freshly ground white pepper

1. Using a corn slitter, score the kernels and scrape the pulp from the cobs. Reserve the pulp and juices. Put the cobs in a pan, barely cover with water, and bring to a boil. Boil for 30 minutes, then discard the cobs.
2. Measure out 4 cups of corn pulp and juices and place in a saucepan. Pour in ¼ cup corn water and bring to a simmer. Stir in the butter and cream, season with salt and pepper, and cook until slightly thickened, 1 to 2 minutes.

SERVES 6

COOKING NOTES
In this recipe, as in many old recipes, corn is referred to as "a rather indigestible vegetable." It seems to have been drier and less sweet than the corn we know today. This may be why D.D.L., the author of this recipe, instructed you to add a lot of corn water to the corn pulp. I reduced the amount so that the finished dish remains a stew rather than a soup.

Corn water is incredibly delicious—you'll have extra, so freeze it and use it for soups and risottos in the winter.

I reduced the original recipe, which called for 24 ears of corn. If you're planning a feast, though, the recipe can easily be doubled or tripled.

VARIATIONS
Make a corn risotto by using the leftover corn water to cook the rice and stirring in some stewed corn at the end. Leftover stewed corn can also be stirred into chowders (a trick I learned from my sister, Rhonda, who has also made this recipe).

SERVING SUGGESTIONS
Beer-Can Chicken (p. 473), Fried Green Tomatoes (p. 212), Summer Pudding (p. 847), Fresh Raspberry (or Blackberry or Blueberry) Flummery (p. 824)

PERIOD DETAIL
This dish evolved from the rustic corn stews of Native Americans and over time was shined up into something closer to a pudding. In *The Story of Corn*, Betty Fussell writes about a corn custard from Eliza Leslie, in 1837, in which the corn was blended with milk, sugar, eggs, and butter and served with a sweetened nutmeg-scented butter.

AUGUST 10, 1879: "RECEIPTS FOR THE TABLE." RECIPE SIGNED D.D.L.

—1879

⟿ MAÎTRE D'HÔTEL POTATOES

This recipe—potato balls suspended in a béchamel with lemon and parsley butter—was part of a menu that included broiled shad, but you can serve it with anything that you usually eat with potatoes, such as duck, beef tenderloin, or salmon. Just be sure to invite friends who will appreciate your potato-carving ability.

----

5 large white potatoes, peeled
2½ tablespoons unsalted butter, 1 tablespoon softened
1½ teaspoons chopped flat-leaf parsley
Juice of ¼ lemon
Salt and freshly ground black pepper
1½ tablespoons all-purpose flour
2 cups whole milk, heated to just under a simmer

1. Using a melon baller, cut the potatoes into little balls. You should have 3 cups of marble-sized potatoes; reserve the trimmings for another use.
2. Bring a large saucepan of salted water to a boil. Add the potatoes and cook until tender. Drain.
3. Meanwhile, mash together the 1 tablespoon soft-

ened butter with the parsley and lemon juice. Season with salt and pepper. Chill.

4. Melt the remaining 1½ tablespoons butter in a large saucepan. When it is foamy, whisk in the flour and cook, whisking, for 1 minute. Gradually whisk in the hot milk, bring to a boil, whisking, and cook until thickened, 2 to 3 minutes. Season with salt and pepper. Fold in the lemon butter and potato balls. Taste and adjust the seasoning.

SERVES 4

COOKING NOTE

After carving the potatoes, you'll have plenty of trimmings ready for mashed potatoes. Just boil them in salted water and mash with warm milk and butter.

SERVING SUGGESTIONS

Shad and Roe Grenobloise (p. 400), Filet de Boeuf Rôti with Sauce Bordelaise (p. 528), Roasted Salmon with Herb Vinaigrette (p. 430), Slow-Roasted Duck (p. 475), Spinach with Sour Cream (p. 216), Frozen Lemon Soufflé (p. 725)

FEBRUARY 26, 1882: "HINTS FOR THE HOUSEHOLD: A SPRING DINNER FOR A SMALL FAMILY," BY JULIET CORSON.

—1882

⌒ SARATOGA POTATOES

In *America Cooks*, published by Cora, Rose, and Bob Brown in 1940, the authors wrote, "A century ago, when Saratoga Springs was in its heyday as a fashionable resort, specialties from there swept the country; and one of them, Saratoga Chips, will endure as long as there are spuds left to slice." They were partially right. The recipe has endured, but "Saratoga" vanished from the name. We now call them potato chips. In the nineteenth century, there were many recipes for potato chips in the *Times*—this one from the turn of the century seemed to me the best of the lot—and you can find plenty of recipes elsewhere in cookbooks of the era. (They are most often attributed to George Crum, the chef at Moon's Lake Lodge in Saratoga.)

To make Saratoga chips, you slice the potatoes, as the Browns instructed in their book, "to fairy-like thinness" and fry them in lard. The *Times* recipe is unusual in calling for olive oil, a smart modification that gives the potatoes a cleaner flavor. If you can't achieve fairy-like thinness, then aim for a plumper hobbit-like thickness. They'll be chewier but just as great.

———

3 large white potatoes, peeled
Olive oil for frying
Salt

1. Slice the potatoes ⅛ inch thick; use a mandoline if you have one. Soak the potato slices in cold water until ready to fry, then drain and dry them thoroughly on a towel.

2. Heat the oven to 175 degrees. Fill a large sauté pan with ½ inch of olive oil. Heat over medium-high heat—the oil is ready when it browns a bread crumb in 30 seconds. Drop a handful of potato slices at a time into the oil and fry until the edges begin to brown, 3 to 4 minutes, then turn the slices and brown the other side, 1 to 2 minutes. Drain on a baking sheet lined with paper towels. Keep warm in the oven while you fry the rest of the potatoes.

3. Pile the potatoes into a bowl and season with salt, tossing to disperse the seasoning.

SERVES 4 TO 6 AS A SIDE DISH, 8 AS AN HORS D'OEUVRE

COOKING NOTE

I used fleur de sel for seasoning, because why not?

SERVING SUGGESTIONS

Asparagus Salad (p. 214), New York Strip Steak with Horseradish-Mint Glaze (p. 566), Tomatoes Vinaigrette (p. 218), Cucumbers in Cream (p. 225), Chocolate Rum Mousse (p. 814)

PERIOD DETAIL

Olive oil, it turns out, had been covered extensively in the *Times* long before Rachael Ray began touting "EVOO." In 1897, William Drysdale wrote in detail about olive oil being pressed at J. E. Blanc in Velaux, Provence. In 1904, another feature cited producers in France, Italy, and even California. "In the kitchen it has come to supersede, where its cost is not regarded, all fats for frying," the reporter wrote. That seems to have been an exaggeration, but olive oil was indeed a common ingredient in *Times* recipes then.

Another recipe in this article was for sliced apples fried in olive oil, dusted with cinnamon sugar, and served with buttered brown bread.

JUNE 26, 1904: "SOMETHING ABOUT OLIVE OIL: ITS EDIBLE MERITS AND KITCHEN USES—THE GARDEN PRODUCE AND FISH MARKETS."

—1904

✎ BOSTON BAKED BEANS

I'm including this recipe not because it's so amazing—although it is pretty great—but because it's so different from baked beans as we know them. The texture is creamy, like refried beans, and the sauce isn't nearly as sweet and syrupy.

Florence Brobeck, who wrote the story, noted that baked beans were once treated as a main course. With "brown bread, the inevitable pickles or piccalilli, and hot tea or chocolate," you'd have a meal—which would be impossible with cloying modern baked beans. These have an actual balance of sweet and savory.

———

2 cups dried white pea beans, rinsed, picked over, and soaked overnight in water to cover

¾ pound salt pork, blanched in boiling water and rind scored, or pancetta, sliced ¼ inch thick

1 small onion

2 teaspoons Colman's prepared mustard

1 heaping teaspoon salt

1 cup boiling water

3 tablespoons molasses

1. Drain the beans, cover them with fresh water in a large saucepan, and heat slowly to a simmer. Cook until the skins burst, about 40 minutes. (The original recipe noted, "Any old-fashioned cook knows that the only way to tell when that stage is reached is to lift out a spoonful of the beans and blow on them. If they're done, the pale shells blow off.") Drain the beans and put them in a large heavy braising pan.

2. Heat the oven to 250 degrees. Nestle the salt pork and onion in the beans, leaving the rind exposed.

Blend together the mustard, salt, boiling water, and molasses, then pour the mixture into the pan of beans. Cover and bake until the beans are very tender and most of the liquid has boiled off, 3 to 4 hours.

3. Remove the lid and bake for another hour.

SERVES 8

COOKING NOTES

As with many of the recipes in the book that originally called for dry mustard, I used Colman's prepared mustard instead because I've found the dry to lack flavor—as in any flavor at all.

I used pancetta in place of the salt pork.

SERVING SUGGESTIONS

North Carolina–Style Pulled Pork (p. 550), Docks Coleslaw (p. 191), Fresh Succotash (p. 275), Jellied Strawberry Pie (p. 811), Strawberry Shortcakes (p. 799)

JANUARY 10, 1937: "YANKEE COOKS IMMORTALIZED IN OUR MENUS," BY FLORENCE BROBECK.

—1937

✎ FRIED CORN

Fried corn (like its friend, Stewed Corn, p. 271) won't seal your reputation as a great cook, but it's an excellent, uncomplicated recipe and a staple of a solid repertoire.

In the story accompanying the recipe, Jane Nickerson, a longtime *Times* columnist, delivered a brief diatribe on how long to boil fresh corn on the cob, a debate that strangely lingers on today. "It being agreed, then, that corn is good, how shall we prepare it?" she wrote. "By boiling it 2 minutes, and no more. That quick, direct statement is an attempt to destroy the wicked precedent that says that the ears must boil and bubble 7 to 12 minutes. All wrong." Got that?

———

4 slices bacon or 3 tablespoons unsalted butter

2 cups corn kernels (from 3 to 4 ears)

1 small onion, minced

½ teaspoon salt

Freshly ground black pepper

3 tablespoons heavy cream

1. Pan-broil the bacon till crisp; drain and set aside.

2. Pour off all but 3 tablespoons of fat from the pan; or if bacon was not used, add the butter to the pan and melt it. Add the onion, salt, and pepper and sauté, stirring occasionally, until the corn has browned very lightly, about 15 minutes.

3. Add the cream and heat thoroughly. Serve garnished with the reserved bacon, if you used it, crumbled.

SERVES 4

COOKING NOTES

When cutting corn from the cob, always run the back of the knife down the stripped cob to scrape out any leftover pulp and juices.

Don't use a bacon that's been injected with liquid "wood smoke." That false flavor will really come through in a dish like this.

During this period, the *Times* test kitchen had an unfortunate habit of making the key aromatics in a dish optional. For instance, in this recipe, the onion and cream were optional. Onion and cream are a cook's best friends, so I removed "optional." Also, the recipe calls for a small onion. Since it was 1947, a small onion was likely to be very small by today's standards. Adjust accordingly.

SERVING SUGGESTIONS

Beer-Can Chicken (p. 473), Brine-Cured Pork Chops (p. 569), Wilted Chard with Pickled Red Onion (p. 261), French Potato Salad (p. 277), Jean Halberstam's Deep-Fried Peaches (p. 860)

AUGUST 3, 1947: "WAYS TO PREPARE CORN," BY JANE NICKERSON. RECIPE BY THE *NEW YORK TIMES* TEST KITCHEN STAFF.

—1947

✑ FRESH SUCCOTASH

Remember how we used to cook? Before we extracted flavors and reduced sauces? We would put the ingredients in a pan and turn on the heat. And if we had other stuff to do, we'd put the pan on the back of the stove until we were ready to eat. At the table, we wouldn't talk about the texture of the corn or the salinity of the butter. We'd just eat it. And sometimes, as with this succotash, it was really good.

———

1½ cups cooked fresh lima beans (about 2½ pounds in the shell) or frozen lima beans
1¾ cups corn kernels (from 3 to 4 ears)
⅓ cup whole milk
⅓ cup heavy cream
2 to 3 tablespoons unsalted butter
Salt and freshly ground black pepper

Combine the beans and corn in a medium saucepan. Add the milk, cream, and butter and season to taste with salt and pepper. Bring to a simmer and simmer until the corn is cooked but still a little crisp, about 5 minutes.

SERVES 6

COOKING NOTES

The original recipe called for ⅔ cup milk or cream. I used ⅓ cup of each, and it worked well. Use whole milk—not just in this recipe, but in any recipe that calls for milk.

When cutting corn from the cob, always run the back of the knife down the stripped cob to scrape out any leftover pulp and juices.

SERVING SUGGESTIONS

North Carolina–Style Pulled Pork (p. 550), Cleo's Daddy's Barbecued Ribs (p. 529), Fried Green Tomatoes (p. 212), Black-Skillet Okra (p. 257), Docks Coleslaw (p. 191), Boston Baked Beans (p. 274), Peach Salad (p. 805), Blueberry Ice Cream (p. 726), Fresh Blueberry Buckle (p. 815)

AUGUST 26, 1947: "NEWS OF FOOD: TO PRESERVE VITAMIN C IN LIMA BEANS, BUY THEM IN THE SHELL AND COOK THEM SOON," BY JANE NICKERSON.

—1947

SWEET POTATO CECELIA

I like to call the 1940s through the 1960s the "Just Add Sherry" era. People turned to sherry as if it were salt and pepper, to flavor sweet potatoes, vegetables (See Creamed Onions, p. 217), sauces (Foamy Sauce, p. 603), stews, and any dessert they could get their hands on. The wine does add a smidgen of acid, but, more important, it gives a sense of depth to simple dishes.

――――――

3 pounds sweet potatoes or yams
8 tablespoons (1 stick) unsalted butter, softened
1/2 cup sherry (optional)
1/4 teaspoon freshly grated nutmeg
1/4 teaspoon ground cinnamon, plus more for sprinkling
About 1/4 cup whole milk
Salt and freshly ground black pepper to taste

1. Boil the potatoes in their jackets till tender, 30 to 45 minutes.
2. Heat the oven to 450 degrees. Drain the potatoes, peel, and rice into a bowl. Add 6 tablespoons butter and the remaining ingredients, beating in enough milk to moisten the mixture. Spread the potatoes in a greased casserole, dot with the remaining 2 tablespoons butter, and sprinkle a little extra cinnamon on top. Bake until browned, 10 to 20 minutes.

SERVES 6

COOKING NOTE
I used yams, butter, and fino sherry.

SERVING SUGGESTIONS
Anton Mosimann's Braised Brussels Sprouts in Cream (p. 232), Ginger Duck (without the rice; p. 480), A Moley (Curried Turkey Hash; p. 452), Huguenot Torte (Apple and Pecan Torte; p. 750), Queen of Puddings (p. 866)

OCTOBER 18, 1947: "NEWS OF FOOD: EXPERT AT CORNELL PUBLISHES RESULTS OF A TWO-YEAR STUDY ON CHEAP FOODS," BY JANE NICKERSON.

—1947

CANDIED SWEET POTATOES

I am not a fan, but about 250,000,000 Americans are, so here is my faint nod to their mystifying tastes.

――――――

6 medium sweet potatoes
1 cup packed light brown sugar
1 teaspoon salt
1/2 teaspoon freshly grated nutmeg
Approximately 1/3 cup (5 1/3 tablespoons) unsalted butter

1. Boil the sweet potatoes in water to cover until tender, 25 to 35 minutes.
2. Heat the oven to 375 degrees. Drain the potatoes, peel, and cut into 1/2-inch-thick slices. Arrange the slices in 2 layers in a large greased casserole, sprinkling each layer with half the brown sugar, salt, nutmeg, and bits of butter. Bake for 30 minutes, basting frequently with the syrup in the casserole.

SERVES 6 TO 8

SERVING SUGGESTIONS
Creamed Onions (p. 217), Roasted Brine-Cured Turkey (p. 474), Wild Mushroom Stuffing (p. 337), Holiday Cranberry Chutney (p. 606), Mississippi Pecan Pie (p. 820)

NOVEMBER 22, 1948: "NEWS OF FOOD: THANKSGIVING'S CANDIED SWEET POTATO ALMOST AS ESSENTIAL AS TURKEY ITSELF," BY JANE NICKERSON.

—1948

BACON POTATO PUFFS

Recipes for baked stuffed potatoes appear in the *Times* archive going back to at least 1878, so these are a fairly polished model, the filling loosened with milk and scented with bacon. As you scoop the bellies of the baked potatoes from their skins, you'll feel empathy for the countless unsung cooks in steakhouses around the country who made these by the hundred.

Making this pedestrian but lovable dish requires some skill and delicacy. As you scoop out the potato flesh, you want to attempt to keep the skin, which is as thin as tissue paper, in one piece. As you progress, heavy patches of shell sometimes begin caving and tearing. Go slowly and scrape gingerly. Try to get the sides as thin as ⅛ inch. If the skin breaks, the filling can later be used as glue.

————

4 large baking potatoes
¼ cup melted bacon drippings
I cup hot whole milk, or as needed
4 slices bacon, cooked and crumbled
Salt and freshly ground black pepper

1. Bake the potatoes. When they are done, cut a slice from the top of each, scoop the contents into a bowl, and mash as for mashed potatoes, adding the bacon fat instead of butter and enough hot milk to whip them into a snowy, fluffy mass. Fold in the crumbled bacon. Season to taste with salt and pepper.
2. Refill the potato shells, heaping them high. Set under a preheated broiler (or the oven set to 400 degrees) long enough to brown the edges of the potatoes.

SERVES 4

COOKING NOTES
To bake potatoes, heat the oven to 350 degrees. Wrap each potato in aluminum foil, place directly on the center oven rack, and bake until soft when pierced with a fork, 40 to 60 minutes.

The recipe calls for ¼ cup bacon drippings and 4 slices of cooked bacon. The problem is that it takes 8 slices of bacon to yield ¼ cup drippings. So you can either cook 8 slices and reserve the 4 extra slices for another use, or cook 4 slices, measure the rendered drippings, and supplement with butter.

SERVING SUGGESTIONS
Raw Spinach Salad (p. 175), Ann Seranne's Rib Roast of Beef (p. 519), '21' Club Hamburger (p. 536), Orange Ice (p. 717)

MAY 16, 1949: "NEWS OF FOOD: BACON, PLENTIFUL AND CHEAPER, IS FOUND TASTY FOR OTHER MEALS THAN JUST BREAKFAST," BY JANE NICKERSON.

—1949

⌒ FRENCH POTATO SALAD

Jane Nickerson, a food editor and writer for the *Times*, offered three salient pointers on potato salad: use old potatoes, because they'll soak up the dressing best; dress the salad while the potatoes are still warm; and never serve it cold.

————

4 to 5 medium potatoes (2 pounds)
I teaspoon salt
Freshly ground black pepper
I to 3 tablespoons vinegar (use the smaller amount with wine, the larger amount with water)
⅓ to ½ cup vegetable oil
¼ cup dry white wine or water
I tablespoon minced onion
Chopped chives, flat-leaf parsley, chervil, or tarragon

1. Boil the potatoes in their skins until just tender. Drain, peel, and slice. Put in a bowl.
2. Mix the salt, pepper to taste, vinegar, oil, wine, onion, and herbs. Pour two-thirds of the dressing over the potatoes; toss lightly with a fork to coat with dressing. Add more if needed. Serve warm or at room temperature.

SERVES 4

COOKING NOTES
I used red-skinned potatoes. White would also work, but I'd avoid Yukon Golds or Idahos, which don't have the right smooth, light texture.

I used 2½ tablespoons vinegar, the wine, and a scant tablespoon of sliced chives.

SERVING SUGGESTIONS
Fried Sweetbreads with Maître d'Hôtel Sauce (p. 506), Epigram of Lamb (p. 509), Broiled Lamb Chops (p. 514), Meat and Spinach Loaf (p. 524), Watercress Salad (p. 171), Coconut Loaf Cake (p. 774), Lee's Marlborough Tart (p. 816)

PERIOD DETAIL
The price of potatoes, a topic of no concern now, was actually considered a news item in the 1950s. From 1952 to 1953, the price of potatoes plummeted from

13 cents a pound to 3. At the price height in 1952, Nickerson wrote about potato substitutes (pasta, rice, and cornmeal) and the following year, with potatoes back in favor, she ran this story, chockablock with potato recipes.

MAY 8, 1953: "FOOD NEWS: POTATO SALAD CAN HAVE MANY GUISES," BY JANE NICKERSON. RECIPE BY MRS. RUTH P. CASA-EMELIOS, A HOME ECONOMIST FOR THE *TIMES*.

—1953

↩ JANSON'S TEMPTATION

In researching who Janson was, I came across plenty of interesting details about the dish, none of them convincingly accurate. I read that the name came from an opera singer, a movie, or, possibly, a religious zealot. Some believe that earlier forms of the dish—a gratin of potatoes, anchovies, onions, and cream that comes from Sweden—included sprats rather than anchovies. And one person who wrote me about the dish's history added her own delicious-sounding variation: she substitutes Greek yogurt for the cream.

———

2 onions, sliced

3 tablespoons unsalted butter

2 cups raw potatoes cut into match-like strips

Two 2-ounce tins anchovy fillets, chopped,
    oil reserved

1 1/2 cups heavy cream

About 1/2 cups fresh bread crumbs

Chopped flat-leaf parsley for garnish

1. Heat the oven to 400 degrees. Cook the onions in 2 tablespoons butter until they are wilted.
2. Sprinkle half the potatoes over the bottom of a buttered 8- or 9-inch baking dish. Sprinkle with the onion and then with the anchovies. Cover with the remaining potatoes and pour a tablespoon of the liquid from the anchovy over all. Pour half the cream over the layers and sprinkle with bread crumbs. Dot with the remaining 1 tablespoon butter.
3. Bake for 10 minutes. Pour over the remaining cream and bake for 10 minutes longer.
4. Reduce the heat to 300 degrees and bake for 20 to 25 minutes longer, or until the potatoes are soft. Serve sprinkled with chopped parsley.

SERVES 6 TO 8

COOKING NOTE
Don't be tempted to add salt—the dish doesn't need it.

SERVING SUGGESTION
Roasted Squash Soup with Cumin (p. 147), Florida Beets (p. 216), Königsberger Klopse (Meatballs in Creamy Caper Sauce; p. 526), Arnaki Araka (Lamb with Peas; p. 550), Swedish Nut Balls (p. 694), Fresh Ginger Cake (p. 775)

SEPTEMBER 4, 1960: "ANCHOVY COOKERY," BY CRAIG CLAIBORNE.

—1960

↩ FOUR-BEAN SALAD

An excellent version of the quintessential picnic salad. The article, from 1976, was titled: "Ethnic Delights Are Hiding on Supermarket Shelves."

———

1 cup canned red kidney beans

1 cup canned white beans, such as cannellini,
    Great Northern, or white kidney

1 cup canned chickpeas

1 cup canned black beans

1 cup finely chopped scallions or finely minced red onion

1 small clove garlic, crushed to a paste with
    1/2 teaspoon salt, or more to taste

1/2 teaspoon dry mustard

2 to 4 tablespoons fresh lemon juice

3 tablespoons olive oil

Salt if necessary

Freshly ground black pepper

2 tablespoons minced dill

Thin onion rings and lemon wedges for garnish (optional)

1. All beans should be rinsed of their canning liquid: place them in a strainer or colander and let cold water run through them until they are clear and shiny. Drain thoroughly.
2. Place the beans in a large bowl, along with the scal-

lions, crushed garlic, mustard, 2 tablespoons lemon juice, and the olive oil. Toss gently with a wooden spoon until all the beans are well coated with dressing. Add salt, pepper, garlic, oil, and/or lemon juice if needed. Gently fold in the dill.

3. Let stand in the refrigerator for at least 1 hour before serving, tossing gently once or twice to distribute the dressing. (If refrigerated for more than 1 hour, let stand at room temperature for about 15 minutes before serving.)

4. Put the beans in a serving dish and garnish with onion rings and lemon wedges, if desired.

SERVES 8 TO 10

COOKING NOTE

The quality of the canned beans is obviously important. Look for brands with smaller, firmer beans.

SERVING SUGGESTIONS

Scotch Eggs (p. 62), Elizabeth Frink's Roast Lemon Chicken (p. 478), Tomatoes Vinaigrette (p. 218), Spoonbread's Potato Salad (p. 288), Strawberry Sorbet (p. 732), Brownies (p. 684)

MARCH 10, 1976: "ETHNIC DELIGHTS ARE HIDING ON SUPERMARKET SHELVES," BY MIMI SHERATON.

—1976

MUSSEL AND POTATO MAYONNAISE

———

1 pound baby red potatoes
2 cups shucked Steamed Mussels (recipe follows)
1 cup mayonnaise
2 teaspoons Dijon or Düsseldorf mustard
1 teaspoon white wine vinegar
1/2 cup finely chopped onion
3 tablespoons chopped chives

1. Place the potatoes in a large saucepan, cover with salted water, and bring to a boil. Cook until tender, about 20 minutes. Drain them and let cool. Cut the potatoes into 1-inch cubes or slightly smaller.

2. Put the mussels in a bowl and add the potatoes.

3. Blend the remaining ingredients, and add half the

mayonnaise mixture to the mussels and potatoes. Mix thoroughly, adding more mayonnaise as needed. Cover and chill until ready to serve.

SERVES 8

STEAMED MUSSELS

3 1/4 pounds mussels, scrubbed well and debearded
1/4 cup white wine vinegar
1 bay leaf
Salt
12 black peppercorns
2 sprigs fresh thyme or 1/2 teaspoon dried thyme

1. Put the mussels in a large pot. Add the remaining ingredients. Cover closely and cook until the mussels have opened, 3 to 5 minutes.

2. Transfer the mussels to a bowl and let cool, then shuck them.

MAKES 2 CUPS SHUCKED MUSSELS

SERVING SUGGESTIONS

Tom's Chilled Cucumber Soup (p. 117), Gigi Salad (p. 184), Green Pepper Salad (p. 172), Stuffed Hard-Cooked Eggs (p. 56), Key Lime Pie (p. 826)

JULY 20, 1977: "THE PICNIC: FOR ROMANTICS AND REVELERS," BY CRAIG CLAIBORNE.

—1977

BLENDER CORN PUDDING

———

3 large eggs
3 tablespoons unsalted butter, melted
1 tablespoon sugar
1 tablespoon all-purpose flour
1 1/2 teaspoons salt
1 1/3 cups whole milk, heated to just under a simmer
1 small onion, chopped
1 1/2 cup corn kernels (fresh or frozen)

1. Heat the oven to 350 degrees. Butter a 1-quart casserole. Put the eggs into a blender and blend at low speed until beaten. Add the remaining ingredients

except for the corn and process until smooth. Add the corn and process very briefly to mix it in.

2. Pour into the prepared casserole. Bake until puffed and just cooked through, about 1 hour.

SERVES 4

SERVING SUGGESTIONS

Green Gazpacho (p. 160), Oliver Clark's Meat Loaf (p. 554), Zucchini with Crème Fraîche Pesto (p. 250), Jean Halberstam's Deep-Fried Peaches (p. 860), Summer Pudding (p. 847)

JULY 29, 1979: "LOCAL CORN LENDS AN EAR TO SWEET TALK," BY FLORENCE FABRICANT. ADAPTED FROM *ALE-WIVES TO ZUCCHINI*, A COOKBOOK PUBLISHED BY THE SOUTHAMPTON HISTORICAL SOCIETY (1976)

—1979

LATKES

Trying to track down the very best latke recipe, like trying to pinpoint the best apple pie recipe, is a fraught exercise. Everyone believes his or her own is superior to all others. So I won't claim that this latke recipe is the best, but it must be close. These potato pancakes, which look like fried soft-shell crabs when they come out of the pan, are lavishly crisp and sting with white pepper.

For the uninitiated, the interesting part of making latkes is handling the potatoes. After grating them, you squeeze out as much liquid as possible from the potato shreds and save it. After letting it settle for a few minutes, you pour off the watery part and are left with a layer of thick, spackle-like potato starch. This goes back into the potato shreds, along with seasonings and the other binding ingredients, egg yolks and matzoh meal. Finally, you aerate this well-bound mixture with whipped egg whites before slipping spoonfuls into a hot pan.

This version is from Mimi Sheraton, a once-feared restaurant reviewer and terrific columnist for the *Times*, who wrote that the pancakes should be "prepared and fried as close to serving time as possible." Serving them with applesauce is fine, according to Sheraton, but, "The less said about sour cream with potato pancakes, the better, even if the final topping is caviar." I thought them so good even the applesauce was superfluous.

2½ pounds old baking potatoes (about 5 large)
1 large onion
2 extra-large eggs, separated
2 tablespoon potato flour or matzoh meal
Scant 1 tablespoon salt
1 teaspoon freshly ground white pepper
1 tablespoon minced flat-leaf parsley (optional)
Corn oil for frying
Applesauce for serving (optional)

1. Peel the potatoes. (If working ahead, cover them with cold water until you are ready to make the pancakes.)

2. Grate the potatoes and onion into a strainer suspended over a bowl, to catch the juices; grate them alternately, as the onion juice will help prevent the potatoes from darkening. (If this is hard to manage, grate the potatoes and onion into a bowl, then turn into a strainer suspended over another bowl.)

3. Picking up handfuls of the grated potato mixture, firmly squeeze out as much liquid as possible back into the bowl, and put the squeezed potato and onion mixture in a clean bowl. Let the liquid settle in the bowl for 2 or 3 minutes.

4. Carefully pour off the watery part of the potato liquid, leaving the thick, starchy paste at the bottom of the bowl. Scrape that into the potato mixture. Add the egg yolks, potato flour, salt, pepper, and parsley, if using it. Mix thoroughly, preferably using your hands.

5. Beat the egg whites into stiff, shiny peaks and gently fold them into the potato mixture, again using your hands.

6. Heat ⅜ inch of oil in a heavy skillet, preferably cast iron. Drop the potato mixture into the hot oil, about 2 tablespoons per pancake, flatten slightly, and fry, turning once, until the pancakes are a deep golden brown on both sides; total frying time for each batch of pancakes should be about 5 minutes. Drain on paper towels. Keep the fried pancakes warm while you fry the rest. Put the drained pancakes on a rack on a baking sheet and place in a low oven (about 250 degrees). Do not hold for more than 15 minutes before serving, or they will become soggy.

7. Serve with applesauce if desired.

SERVES 8

I used matzoh meal.

Sheraton called for "old" potatoes, which contain more sugar and brown better.

When squeezing the liquid from the potatoes, do so as firmly as you can. This will lighten the texture of the pancakes.

In Step 4, it's best to mix the potatoes using your hands so you can feel whether or not the starch is well distributed.

If you have someone to help you, fry the pancakes using 2 pans. It will save a lot of time.

SERVING SUGGESTIONS

Joyce Goldstein's Pickled Salmon (p. 404), Matt's Whole Brisket with Tomato Gravy (p. 572), Fried Artichokes Azzurro (p. 229), Olive Oil and Apple Cider Cake (p. 771), Purple Plum Torte (p. 763)

DECEMBER 19, 1981: "DE GUSTIBUS: LATKES: FOOD FIT FOR A HOLIDAY," BY MIMI SHERATON.

—1981

MAIDA HEATTER'S CUBAN BLACK BEANS AND RICE

I never would have tried this dish had not so many people written to me about it. Just look at how long the recipe is—would you? But I've joined the chorus: you've never had beans and rice like this. You think it's going to be a two-component dish, and it ends up colorful, varied, and phenomenally good.

Find someone to help you shop and chop. After that, it's not at all difficult to prepare and, as with so many Maida Heatter recipes, it's filled with interesting techniques—such as steaming the cooked rice with a towel laid on top of it to keep it fluffy and light—and meaningful detail, like adding a little sugar, oil, and vinegar to the chopped sweet onions, which coats them in a light glaze.

Heatter, who is known for her baking (see pages 632 and 657), lives in Miami—hence the Cuban recipe.

1 pound dried black beans, preferably turtle beans

6 cups cold water

2 small ham hocks (about 1¼ pounds total)

½ cup olive oil

3½ cups finely chopped onions

1½ cups chopped green bell peppers

2 tablespoons finely minced garlic

2 bay leaves

¼ teaspoon crushed red pepper flakes

3 tablespoons red wine vinegar

Salt and freshly ground black pepper

¼ teaspoon cayenne pepper

¼ teaspoon Tabasco sauce

3 tablespoons dark rum

Rice for Black Beans (recipe follows)

Onions for Black Beans (recipe follows)

1. Pick over the beans carefully to remove any foreign particles. Rinse well in several changes of cold water. Put the beans in a bowl with the 6 cups cold water. Cover and let stand overnight.

2. Drain the beans, reserving the water in which they soaked. Measure the water and add enough water to make 8 cups. Combine the beans, water, and ham hocks in a small pot and bring to a boil. Reduce the heat and cook slowly, uncovered, skimming the surface as necessary to remove any foam, until the beans are tender, 4 to 6 hours (see Cooking Notes).

3. Meanwhile, heat the oil in a large skillet. Add the onions and green peppers and cook, stirring, until the mixture is wilted. Add the garlic and cook briefly, stirring. Remove from the heat.

4. After the beans have cooked for about 2 hours, add the onion mixture, bay leaves, pepper flakes, vinegar, and salt and pepper to taste. Continue cooking until the beans are tender, for 30 minutes.

5. Remove the pot from the heat and remove the ham hocks. When they are cool enough to handle, remove and discard the skin, fat, bone, and gristle. Shred the meat and return it to the beans. Remove the bay leaves, and add the cayenne pepper and Tabasco. This dish improves if cooked one day in advance.

6. When ready to serve, heat the bean mixture thoroughly. Just before serving, stir in the rum. Serve with rice on the side or spoon a portion of the bean mixture over individual servings of rice. Add the onions according to taste.

SERVES 8

RICE FOR BLACK BEANS

> 2 cups long-grain white rice
> Salt
> 1 tablespoon fresh lemon juice
> 2 tablespoons unsalted butter

1. Rinse the rice in several changes of cold water until the water remains clear.
2. Bring 4 quarts of water to a boil in a large saucepan. Add salt to taste and the lemon juice. Add the rice a handful at a time. Stir the rice until the water returns to a boil. Cook, uncovered, for about 17 minutes, or until the rice is tender. Drain immediately in a sieve.
3. Melt the butter in the pan in which the rice cooked. Add the rice, and cover with a towel. Cover the towel with the pot's lid, place the rice over the lowest heat possible, and let steam for about 20 minutes. Carefully stir the rice occasionally to keep the grains separate.

SERVES 8

ONIONS FOR BLACK BEANS

> 3 cups finely chopped sweet white onions
> Salt
> 1 teaspoon sugar
> 1 tablespoon olive or corn oil
> 1 tablespoon white wine vinegar

Combine the ingredients in a bowl and let stand until ready to serve.

MAKES ABOUT 3 CUPS

COOKING NOTES
Heatter's recipe said the beans would take 4 to 6 hours to cook; mine were done in 1 hour and 50 minutes. Keep an eye on yours, and add the onion mixture accordingly.

Make sure the towel you use for the rice doesn't smell of detergent, or your rice will too.

SERVING SUGGESTIONS
This is the ideal dish for a family get-together or Sunday dinner. Start with Guacamole Tostadas (p. 67) and La Paloma (p. 35), and finish with Spanish Cream (p. 802) or Caramel Custard (p. 836) for dessert. For a more ambitious menu, add Yucatán Fish with Crisp Garlic (p. 431), Nueces Canyon Cabrito (Goat Tacos; p. 576), or Hot Pepper Shrimp (p. 403).

JANUARY 27, 1985: "FOOD: THE CUBAN CONNECTION," BY CRAIG CLAIBORNE WITH PIERRE FRANEY. RECIPE ADAPTED FROM MAIDA HEATTER.

—1985

⌒ CORN CAKES WITH CAVIAR

Don't let the caviar prevent you from making these corn cakes. You'll be just as happy eating the cakes plain (as a side dish, like hushpuppies), or topped with dollops of crème fraîche and chives. The cakes—from a recipe by Anne Rosenzweig, when she was the chef at Arcadia in New York—are unlike any I've had. They're crisp, pebbly with bits of corn, and lacy on the edges.

A more recent corn cake recipe can be found on p. 294.

————

> 8 small ears corn, shucked, or 3 cups frozen
>   corn kernels, defrosted
> 1/3 cup whole milk
> 1/3 cup all-purpose flour
> 4 tablespoons unsalted butter, melted
> 1/3 cup cornmeal
> 2 large eggs
> 1 large egg yolk
> 3 tablespoons finely chopped chives
> Salt and freshly ground black pepper
> 1/4 cup melted clarified unsalted butter
> 1 cup crème fraîche
> 6 tablespoons golden whitefish caviar, preferably fresh
> 2 tablespoons black caviar, preferably fresh

1. If using fresh corn, cut the corn kernels from the cobs; you need 3 cups. Put the corn (fresh or frozen) in a food processor, add 2 tablespoons milk, and blend to a coarse puree.
2. Put the corn in a medium bowl and add the remaining milk, the flour, 4 tablespoons melted butter, and cornmeal, stirring to blend well. Add the eggs, egg

yolk, 2 tablespoons chopped chives, and salt and pepper to taste and blend thoroughly.

3. Heat the clarified butter in a nonstick skillet over medium heat. Spoon about 1½ tablespoons of the batter per cake into the skillet, without letting the cakes touch, and cook for about 1½ minutes, until golden brown on the bottom. Turn the cakes and cook on the other side for about a minute, or until golden brown and cooked through. Transfer to a baking sheet and keep warm in a 175-degree oven while you cook the rest of the cakes.

4. Arrange slightly overlapping corn cakes on each of 6 salad plates. Add a mound of crème fraîche to the center of each plate. Spoon 1 tablespoon golden caviar on top of each mound of crème fraîche and 1 teaspoon black caviar on top of the golden caviar. Sprinkle with the remaining tablespoon of chopped chives and serve.

SERVES 6 AS A SIDE DISH (WITHOUT THE CRÈME FRAÎCHE AND CAVIAR) OR A FIRST COURSE

COOKING NOTES

It's worth clarifying the butter, because it will burn otherwise. To clarify butter, melt it in a pan over low heat; then skim the top and carefully pour the clear yellow butter into a bowl, leaving behind the solids.

The batter spits a lot when frying: be careful. Also, it's best to work with 2 spatulas when flipping the corn cakes—the half-cooked cakes can be unwieldy, and the second spatula is handy for saving flipping disasters.

SERVING SUGGESTIONS

These are designed to be served as a first course, but if you're skipping the caviar, you can use them as a side dish for fried chicken, burgers, or chili. For a fancier meal: Billi-Bi au Safran (Mussels in Saffron Cream; p. 125), Mezzaluna Salad (p. 185), and Purple Plum Torte (p. 763).

OCTOBER 2, 1985: "FROM ANTHROPOLOGY TO HAUTE CUISINE," BY CRAIG CLAIBORNE. RECIPE ADAPTED FROM ANNE ROSENZWEIG, THE CHEF AT ARCADIA IN NEW YORK CITY.

—1985

SAUTÉED POTATOES WITH PARSLEY

There is a similar recipe in Julia Child's *Mastering the Art of French Cooking*, except that Child has you cook the potatoes in a single stretch in one pool of butter. The result can be magnificent, the potatoes having soaked up the nutty perfume of butter and crisped all around. But you must remain ceaselessly vigilant lest the butter burn, the potatoes stick, and the dinner be ruined. This recipe by Pierre Franey cuts out all the worry with a slightly more labor-intensive but foolproof method. You boil the potatoes, ensuring their tenderness, then you slice them and crisp them in oil in a nonstick pan. And finally you bathe them in butter. This way, you get the caramelized edge, the pillowy centers, and the sweet taste of fresh butter.

———————

5 medium white potatoes (1½ pounds or slightly less)
Salt and freshly ground black pepper
About ¼ cup corn, peanut, or vegetable oil
1 tablespoon unsalted butter
1 tablespoon finely chopped flat-leaf parsley

1. Put the potatoes in a saucepan and add cold water to cover. Add salt to taste and bring to a boil. Cook for about 20 minutes, or until the potatoes are tender.

2. Drain the potatoes, and when they are cool enough to handle, peel them. Cut them into slices about 1 inch thick. Sprinkle with salt and pepper.

3. Heat about 2 tablespoons oil in a large skillet, preferably nonstick over high heat. When it is quite hot, add half the potato slices and cook for 2 to 3 minutes, until crisp and brown on one side. Turn the slices and cook on the other side until crisp and brown, 2 to 3 minutes. Drain on paper towels. Add more oil to the skillet if necessary, and cook the remaining potato slices as before.

4. Pour off any remaining oil from the pan. Wipe the skillet clean and add the butter. Return the potatoes to the skillet and stir gently to coat. Sprinkle with the parsley.

SERVES 4

The number of batches and the amount of oil you need will depend on the size of your potatoes and the size of your pan. I have a 12-inch nonstick skillet, so I got them all into a single batch and used just 2 tablespoons of oil.

SERVING SUGGESTIONS

Carbonnades à la Flamande (Flemish Beef and Onion Stew; p. 515), Sole Grenobloise (Sautéed Sole with Capers and Lemons; p. 399), Pork Arrosto with Prunes and Grappa (p. 577), Salade à la Romaine (p. 171), Chocolate Eclairs (p. 800)

FEBRUARY 26, 1986: "60-MINUTE GOURMET," BY PIERRE FRANEY.

—1986

flexible spatula or knife, loosen the potatoes from the baking dishes, and very carefully turn out each potato crown.

SERVES 4

COOKING NOTE

You really do need a mandoline to slice the potatoes, because the slices must be wafer-thin.

SERVING SUGGESTIONS

Tomato, Fig, Goat Cheese, Basil, and Olive Salad with Balsamic Vinaigrette (p. 199), Oolong-Crusted Scallops (p. 441), Macaroons (p. 681)

AUGUST 10, 1986: "FOOD: FRENCH SALAD DAYS," BY PATRICIA WELLS. RECIPE ADAPTED FROM JEAN-PAUL LACOMBE, THE OWNER OF LÉON DE LYON IN LYONS, FRANCE.

—1986

CRISP POTATO CROWNS

The original recipe came with a forgettable salad, so I've forgotten it. But the crown, which is actually a thin, crisp potato cake, is a great little recipe and something that you can use in countless ways: top it with a poached egg and herb butter, serve it with spinach and hot bacon dressing or Caesar Salad (p. 174), or use it as a bed for chicken stew. Employ it anywhere that a crisp potato disk seems apt.

———

3 tablespoons unsalted butter
4 small evenly shaped oval potatoes
    (about 4 ounces each)
Salt and freshly ground black pepper

1. Melt the butter. Using half of it, brush a circle over the bottom of each of four 6-inch round baking dishes, such as porcelain gratin dishes. Chill until the butter is hardened, about 10 minutes.
2. Peel the potatoes and cut into paper-thin slices. Arrange one-quarter of the slices, overlapping, on each circle of hardened butter, pressing down firmly. If necessary, make double layers to use up all the potatoes. Brush the slices with the remaining melted butter and chill for 30 minutes.
3. Heat the oven to 425 degrees. Bake the potato disks until crisp and brown, 20 to 25 minutes. Using a

MADAME LARACINE'S GRATIN DAUPHINOIS

A potato gratin from the Savoy in southeast France. The sliced potatoes are first simmered in milk with garlic, then baked in a bath of crème fraîche and grated Gruyère.

———

3 pounds medium baking potatoes,
    peeled and very thinly sliced
2 cups whole milk
2 cups water
3 cloves garlic, minced
Sea salt
3 bay leaves
Freshly grated nutmeg
Freshly ground black pepper
1 cup crème fraîche or heavy cream
10 ounces Gruyère cheese, grated

1. Heat the oven to 375 degrees. Place the potatoes in a large saucepan and cover with the milk and water. Add the garlic, a generous amount of salt, and the bay leaves, partially cover the pan, and bring to a boil over medium-high heat, stirring occasionally so that the potatoes do not stick to the bottom of the pan.

Reduce the heat to medium and cook, stirring from time to time, until the potatoes are tender but not falling apart, about 10 minutes.

2. Using a large slotted spatula or spider, transfer half the potatoes to a 2-quart gratin dish. Taste a potato—if it needs salt, season the potatoes. Sprinkle with nutmeg, and pepper, and dot with half the crème fraîche and half the cheese. Cover with the remaining potatoes, sprinkle again with pepper and nutmeg, and dot with the remaining cream and cheese. (Discard the milk in which the potatoes were cooked.)

3. Bake until the gratin is crisp and golden on top, 40 to 60 minutes.

SERVES 6 TO 8

COOKING NOTE
Use whole nutmeg and grate it generously.

SERVING SUGGESTIONS
Boeuf Bourguignon I and II (p. 516), Watercress Salad (p. 171), Steak au Poivre (p. 573), Broccoli Puree with Ginger (p. 253), Junior's Cheesecake (p. 771), Apple Tarte Tatin (p. 837)

MARCH 13, 1988: "FOOD: THE FARMER'S BANQUET," BY PATRICIA WELLS. RECIPE ADAPTED FROM MICHÈLE LARACINE, A FARMER AND AUBERGE OWNER IN SAVOY, FRANCE.

—1988

5 tablespoons olive oil
Salt and freshly ground black pepper
1½ tablespoons red wine vinegar
1 tablespoon whole-grain mustard
2 teaspoons minced chives
1 teaspoon minced rosemary

1. Heat the oven to 425 degrees. Cut the potatoes into quarters or, if they are more than 2 inches in diameter, into eighths. Place them in a single layer in a baking dish. Scatter the garlic, 3 tablespoons olive oil, and salt and pepper to taste over the potatoes, and toss.

2. Roast for 30 to 40 minutes, tossing gently every 10 minutes so the potatoes cook evenly.

3. Beat the vinegar and mustard in a large bowl. Whisk in the remaining 2 tablespoons olive oil until smooth. Add the roasted potatoes and mix gently. Season, if desired, with additional salt and pepper, and cool to room temperature.

4. Just before serving, fold in the chives and rosemary.

SERVES 6

SERVING SUGGESTIONS
Cold Beef with Tarragon Vinaigrette (p. 534), Haricots Verts with Balsamic Vinaigrette (p. 231), Brownies (p. 684)

MAY 21, 1989: "OLD FAVORITES, NEW TASTES," BY FLORENCE FABRICANT.

—1989

ROASTED POTATO SALAD

You may not remember 1989 as the Potato Renaissance, but that was the year that we began roasting them with olive oil, producing sweeter, caramelized potatoes with more depth to them. It was also when thin-skinned baby potatoes and waxier varieties like Yukon Golds started making inroads on the Idaho.

After browning the potatoes in a roasting pan, you toss them with vinegar and mustard. Then, just before serving, shower them with chives and rosemary.

———

2½ pounds baby Red Bliss or Yukon Gold potatoes, scrubbed
1 clove garlic, chopped

POTATO, SHIITAKE, AND BRIE GRATIN

With Humboldt Fog and Garrotxa cheese now at our fingertips, it's hard to remember why we were all once so smitten with Brie. In France, you can find handsome specimens of Brie de Meaux with downy rinds and buttery centers. But here the cow's-milk Brie tends to resemble silicone grouting. Which may explain why in the 1980s we were so eager to wrap it in puff pastry and bake it. Everything goes down easier melted and warm, chased by a river of wine.

Still, Brie was an important gateway food. It let us know that cheese could be soft and gooey, that there was such a thing as a rind, and that cheese was not a means to an end (a layer in a sandwich, a topping on a burger) but an end in itself. Without Brie, we might never have been ready for robiola, Epoisses, and the like. And because of its creamy texture, commercial Brie retains some charm as a cooking ingredient.

In the late 1980s, Regina Schrambling, a writer for the *Times*, used the cheese in a delicious potato and mushroom gratin. The dish is a happy mash-up of 1980s fads: French bistro food was catching on, so potatoes *au gratin* (oh-GROT-in) was becoming potato gratin (gra-TAN)—a leaner, meaner iteration with less cheese sauce and more attitude. Brie was entering the mainstream, and shiitakes had become the urbane antidote to pedestrian white mushrooms, paving the way for the "wild mushroom" deluge of the 1990s.

To make the gratin, you layer sliced potatoes with slivers of shiitakes and cubes of Brie and then batten them down with cream, garlic, and thyme (followed later by a covering of bread crumbs and Parmesan cheese). Into the oven you send them, assured of a tasty outcome. Schrambling has you bake the gratin for an hour or more, far longer than necessary to cook the potatoes through, but the extra time in the oven gives the top a chance to brown and crisp.

---

6 good-sized new red potatoes, scrubbed

1 teaspoon unsalted butter

1/2 pound shiitake mushrooms, stems removed

1/2 pound fairly firm Brie, rind removed

Salt and freshly ground black pepper

1 cup heavy cream

1 clove garlic, minced

1 teaspoon chopped thyme

2 tablespoons freshly grated Parmesan cheese

1/4 cup fine dry bread crumbs

1. Using a mandoline or sharp knife, cut the potatoes into slices about 1/8 inch thick. Place them in a large bowl of cold water and soak for 30 minutes, changing the water twice. Drain and pat the slices dry.

2. Set one rack on the middle shelf and one in the bottom third of the oven (with enough room between them for the gratin dish) and heat the oven to 425 degrees. Butter a shallow gratin dish or glass baking dish about 10 inches across. Thinly slice the shiitake caps.

3. Using your fingers, pinch the Brie into gumdrop-sized pieces. Layer a third of the potato slices in the dish. Lay half the shiitakes and half the cheese evenly over the top. Season liberally with salt and pepper. Add another third of the potatoes and top with the remaining shiitakes and Brie. Season with salt and pepper. Arrange the remaining potato slices on top. Combine the cream, garlic, and thyme and pour over the potatoes, pressing down on them so that all the liquid is absorbed. Cover the pan tightly with foil and bake on the center oven rack for 30 minutes.

4. Combine the Parmesan cheese and bread crumbs and season with salt and pepper. Remove the foil from the pan and sprinkle the crumbs over the potatoes. Place the pan on the bottom oven rack and bake for 30 to 40 minutes longer, until the potatoes are very tender and the top is crusty and dark brown.

SERVES 6 TO 8

COOKING NOTES

The potatoes are soaked and drained twice before cooking to remove excess starch.

I used my 3-quart oval Le Creuset casserole dish, and it worked perfectly.

Before pouring the cream over the gratin, make sure you disperse the garlic, because it tends to pour out all at once.

SERVING SUGGESTIONS

Roman Lamb (p. 542), Lattich Salat, Warme (Warm Lettuce Salad; p. 171), Almond-Carrot Salad (p. 204), Apple Galette (p. 843)

PERIOD DETAIL

Raymond Sokolov first wrote about the mandoline in the *Times* in 1971; mentions of Brie go back to 1906.

OCTOBER 1, 1989: "CAMPFIRE CACHET," BY REGINA SCHRAMBLING.

—1989

❧ SWEET POTATO CASSEROLE

I've never understood why many people see cooking sweet potatoes as an opportunity to subordinate their natural flavor. We joyfully eat regular potatoes plain—roasted, fried, or sautéed with little more than salt—so why do we need to smother sweet potatoes with molasses and marshmallows?

Jimmy Sneed, the chef and co-owner of The Frog and The Redneck in Richmond, Virginia, found a subtler way to underline sweet potatoes' natural sugars. After roasting, you mash them up with a little sugar, orange juice, vanilla, butter, and eggs (which lighten them). As a top layer, you make a crumble that's heavy on pecans and light on sugar. The result is a downy casserole that tastes like a savory Creamsicle.

------

6 large sweet potatoes
6 tablespoons brown sugar
2 large eggs, beaten
¼ cup orange juice
2 tablespoons unsalted butter, melted
1 teaspoon vanilla extract
½ teaspoon salt

For the Topping

3 tablespoons unsalted butter, slightly softened
½ cup packed brown sugar
¾ cup chopped pecans

1. Heat the oven to 375 degrees. Bake the sweet potatoes on a baking sheet until very tender, about 1 hour and 20 minutes. Remove and let cool slightly. Reduce the heat to 350 degrees.

2. When the potatoes are cool enough to handle, cut them in half, scoop the flesh into a bowl, and mash until smooth. (You should have 4 to 5 cups.) Stir in the brown sugar, eggs, orange juice, butter, vanilla, and salt. Place in a casserole dish.

3. To make the topping, combine the butter, brown sugar, and pecans. Sprinkle over the sweet potato mixture. Bake until the nuts are toasted and the casserole has puffed, about 30 minutes.

SERVES 8

COOKING NOTES

The recipe did not specify light or dark brown sugar; I used a combination.

An 8-inch square baking dish worked well.

SERVING SUGGESTIONS

Cleo's Daddy's Barbecued Ribs (p. 529), Spinach and

Artichoke Casserole (p. 255), Old South Buttermilk Biscuits (p. 655), Cashew Butterscotch Bars (p. 697)

NOVEMBER 18, 1992: "ON THANKSGIVING, WHAT'S A CHEF TO DO?" BY MARIAN BURROS. RECIPE ADAPTED FROM JIMMY SNEED.

—1992

DRUNKEN BEANS

------

2 slices bacon, diced
1 onion, diced
2 cloves garlic, minced
2 cups dried pinto beans, picked over, soaked
    overnight in water to cover, and drained
4 cups chicken broth, or water
2 cups beer
2 to 4 jalapeño peppers, thinly sliced
Salt and freshly ground black pepper
2 tablespoons chopped cilantro

1. Place the bacon in a large pot and cook over medium heat until the fat is rendered. Remove the bacon with a slotted spoon and discard (or enjoy as a cook's treat). Add the onion and garlic and cook until soft, about 5 minutes. Add the beans, broth, and beer and bring to a boil, then reduce the heat to a simmer and cook for 30 minutes.

2. Stir in the jalapeños. Cook until the beans are tender, about 30 minutes, adding water if necessary to keep the beans covered. Season with salt and pepper to taste and stir in the cilantro.

SERVES 6 TO 8

SERVING SUGGESTIONS

La Paloma (p. 35), Grilled Onion Guacamole (p. 71), Staff Meal Chicken with Salsa Verde (p. 484), Border Town Hunter's Stew with Antelope (or Venison), Poblanos, Pumpkin, and Hominy (p. 571), Grapefruit Granita (p. 731), Churros with Chocolate Sauce (p. 866)

JULY 4, 1993: "THE TEXAS THREE-STEP," BY MOLLY O'NEILL. RECIPE ADAPTED FROM THE NEW TEXAS CUISINE, BY STEPHAN PYLES.

—1993

☙ MEDITERRANEAN LENTIL SALAD WITH LEMON-THYME VINAIGRETTE

I made this with the minuscule French le Puy lentils: You should too. They're light, snappy, and low on starch. And I recommend cutting everything up nice and small to mirror the lentils.

———

1 cup le Puy lentils (available at specialty markets)

1 tomato, cored and chopped

½ cup oil-cured black olives, pitted and coarsely chopped

½ cup crumbled feta cheese

2 stalks celery, peeled and thinly sliced

¼ cup fresh lemon juice

2 large cloves garlic, minced

2 teaspoons minced thyme

2 tablespoons plus 2 teaspoons olive oil

½ teaspoon salt, or more to taste

Freshly ground black pepper

1 tablespoon chopped flat-leaf parsley

1. Combine the lentils and 5 cups water in a large saucepan and bring to a boil. Reduce the heat and simmer until the lentils are tender but not mushy, 15 to 20 minutes. Drain, place in a large bowl, and let cool completely.

2. Toss the lentils with the tomato, olives, feta, and celery.

3. Whisk together the lemon juice, garlic, and thyme in a medium bowl. Slowly whisk in the olive oil. Whisk in the salt and pepper to taste. Toss the salad with the vinaigrette and season to taste.

4. Divide among 4 plates and garnish with the chopped parsley.

SERVES 4

SERVING SUGGESTIONS

Moroccan Tomato Soup (p. 134), Cinnamon-Scented Fried Chicken (p. 490), Moroccan Chicken Smothered in Olives (p. 482), Lamb Shoulder Chops with Anchovy and Mint Butter (p. 567), Cumin-Mustard Carrots (p. 237), Flourless Apricot Honey Soufflé (p. 846), Fresh Blueberry Buckle (p. 815)

☙ SPOONBREAD'S POTATO SALAD

A perfectly calibrated American potato salad: creamy, sweet, tart, and pungent. Mixing the oil, vinegar, salt, and paprika with the still-warm potatoes is a crucial step. The potatoes absorb the flavors and mellow out the sharp notes in the dressing, and then, when later mixed with the mayonnaise, some potato gets mashed into the dressing, which binds the salad.

Spoonbread is the name of the Manhattan catering company that made this salad.

———

2 pounds white potatoes, scrubbed

5 tablespoons vegetable oil

2 tablespoons cider vinegar

1 teaspoon salt

¼ teaspoon paprika

1 small onion, minced

½ cup diced celery

2 hard-boiled eggs, chopped

½ cup mayonnaise

1 tablespoon Colman's prepared mustard

1 teaspoon celery salt or to taste

Optional garnish (olives, green pepper rings, and sliced grilled red peppers

1. Cut the potatoes in half if large. Put them in a pot and add enough lightly salted water to cover them by 2 inches. Bring to a boil, uncovered, and boil gently for 15 to 25 minutes, until just tender. Drain.

2. When the potatoes are cool enough to handle, peel and cut into coarse chunks. Place in a large bowl.

3. Whisk together the oil, vinegar, salt, and paprika in a small bowl. Mix with the still-warm potatoes. Cover and chill for several hours.

4. Right before serving, add the minced onion, celery, and chopped eggs to the potatoes. Mix together the mayonnaise and mustard, stir into the salad, and season with the celery salt. If desired, garnish with olives and red and green peppers.

COOKING NOTE

The original recipe instructed you to add 1/4 teaspoon dry mustard to the oil and vinegar mixture; I used Colman's prepared mustard instead.

SERVING SUGGESTIONS

Lobster Roll (p. 368), Pork Burgers (p. 566), Docks Coleslaw (p. 191), Summer Pudding (p. 847)

JULY 2, 1997: "CULINARY FIREWORKS, CLASSIC AND COOL," BY SUZANNE HAMLIN. RECIPE ADAPTED FROM NORMA JEAN DARDEN AND CAROLE DARDEN, THE OWNERS OF SPOONBREAD INC., A CATERING COMPANY IN NEW YORK CITY.

—1997

ROASTED CARROT AND RED LENTIL RAGOUT

This is a hot one—you get a splash of sweetness from the carrots and then a stampede of burning heat. It's terrific served over basmati or jasmine rice, which tames the spice a little. If you're not into hot food, reduce the chile powders to 1/2 teaspoon each.

Red lentils cook very quickly and, together with the carrots, turn this ragout the color of embers. It's soft and porridge-like, with a toasted, spicy warmth. Serve with rice, or as a thick stew.

———

1 1/2 pounds carrots, peeled

5 tablespoons olive oil

2 1/2 teaspoons kosher salt

Freshly ground black pepper

1 medium onion, thinly sliced

3/4 teaspoon ancho chile powder

3/4 teaspoon chipotle chile powder

1/8 teaspoon cayenne pepper

1 cup red lentils, rinsed and picked over

5 cups chicken broth

1. Heat the oven to 450 degrees. Lay the carrots in a roasting pan or a baking sheet and toss with 3 tablespoons oil. Season with 1 1/2 teaspoons salt and a few grinds of pepper. Roast for 20 minutes.

2. Turn the carrots, add the onion, and roast for 15 minutes, or until the carrots are brown and tender. Remove from the oven.

3. When the carrots are cool enough, cut them into 1/4-inch dice.

4. Heat the remaining 2 tablespoons oil in a large saucepan. Add the carrots and onions, chile powder, and cayenne pepper, and cook, stirring, for 1 minute. Stir in the lentils, add the broth, and bring to a simmer. Simmer, stirring occasionally, for 20 to 25 minutes, until the lentils are falling apart. Season with the remaining 1 teaspoon salt and pepper to taste.

SERVES 6

COOKING NOTE

When roasting the carrots and onions, I put the onions on top of the carrots so the onions wouldn't burn.

SERVING SUGGESTIONS

Yogurt Rice (p. 356), Moroccan Chicken Smothered in Olives (p. 482), Cucumbers in Cream (p. 225), Pepper-Cumin Cookies (p. 695)

JANUARY 11, 1998: "FOOD: SIMMER DOWN," BY MOLLY O'NEILL.

—1998

GREEN LENTILS WITH ROASTED BEETS AND PRESERVED LEMON

Sharpen your chef's knife for this one; much chopping awaits. When it says "finely" chopped and diced, do your very best, because the tinier those pieces are, the prettier and more delicate this dish will be. When you pull it all together with its dices and cubes, shreds, mashed pulp and zest, you get a salad that you'll make for a lifetime.

The recipe comes from Deborah Madison, a pioneer of vegetarian cooking. She lifted vegetarian food out of its heavy brown slump and made it into a colorful, desirable, and often elegant way of cooking.

———

For the Salad

5 small beets (about 1 pound), peeled

1 teaspoon olive oil

Salt and freshly ground black pepper

1 cup French green (le Puy) lentils, rinsed and picked over

1 carrot, peeled and finely diced

½ small onion, finely diced

1 bay leaf

4 sprigs flat-leaf parsley, plus ⅓ cup chopped parsley

2 sprigs thyme

1 preserved lemon (see Cooking Notes) or 2 teaspoons grated lemon zest

2 tablespoons chopped mint

For the Vinaigrette

1 teaspoon grated lemon zest

2 tablespoons fresh lemon juice

1 shallot, finely chopped

¼ teaspoon salt, or more to taste

5 tablespoons extra virgin olive oil

Freshly ground black pepper

Mint sprigs for garnish

1. Heat the oven to 350 degrees. Reserve 1 beet for garnish and cut the remaining 4 into ½-inch cubes. Toss with the oil, season with salt and pepper, and spread on a small baking sheet. Roast until tender, 30 to 35 minutes, stirring occasionally. Remove from the oven.

2. Meanwhile, place the lentils, carrot, onion, bay leaf, parsley and thyme sprigs, and ½ teaspoon salt in a small pot and add water to cover by about ¾ inch. Bring to a boil, then reduce the heat and simmer, covered, until the lentils are tender, 15 to 20 minutes. Drain well, discard the herbs, and transfer to a large bowl.

3. To make the vinaigrette, combine the lemon zest, juice, shallot, and salt in a small bowl and let stand for 15 minutes. Whisk in the olive oil and season to taste with pepper and more salt if necessary.

4. Quarter the lemon and scrape out the soft pulp. Finely chop enough of the pulp to make 2 teaspoons and stir into the vinaigrette (or add the lemon zest). Finely chop the lemon peel and add it to the lentils, along with the vinaigrette, roasted beets, and chopped parsley and mint. Toss well and transfer to a platter. Grate the reserved beet and use it for garnish, along with mint sprigs.

SERVES 4 TO 6

COOKING NOTES

This is best made with tiny French le Puy lentils.

Preserved lemons are available in Mediterranean markets or specialty shops, or see p. 610 for a recipe.

Don't overcook the lentils: they'll continue cooking and softening even after they're drained. You want them to retain some snap—15 to 17 minutes of simmering is plenty.

SERVING SUGGESTIONS

Buttermilk Roast Chicken (p. 493), Wilted Chard with Pickled Red Onion (p. 261), Steamed Lemon Pudding (p. 849)

FEBRUARY 15, 1998: "FOOD: DEBBIE DOES CABBAGE," BY MOLLY O'NEILL. RECIPE ADAPTED FROM *VEGETARIAN COOKING FOR EVERYONE*, BY DEBORAH MADISON.

—1998

⌒ YOGURT WITH PLANTAIN AND MANGO

Some might call this a side dish, others a condiment, but both parties will agree that it's fragrant, tangy, and delicious. Serve the yogurt at room temperature or cold, with steamed basmati rice.

———

1 medium yellow plantain, peeled and cut into ¾-inch dice

1½ cups plain yogurt, preferably Greek-style

1 cup water

½ teaspoon salt

1 tablespoon vegetable oil

1 teaspoon chana dal (yellow split peas)

1 teaspoon brown mustard seeds

2 dried hot red chiles, halved

15 fresh curry leaves or basil leaves

1 medium shallot, cut into fine slivers

3 thin slices fresh ginger, cut into fine shreds

1 cup diced (¾-inch) mango

1. Place the plantain in a small pan, cover with water, and bring to a boil. Cover, reduce the heat to low, and

cook until the plantain is tender, 10 to 15 minutes. Drain and set aside.

2. Beat the yogurt with a fork in a small bowl until smooth and creamy. Slowly add the water and salt. Set aside.

3. Put the oil in a small deep frying pan over medium heat. When the oil is hot, add the dal and stir until it just starts to turn reddish. Add the mustard seeds. As soon as the seeds begin to pop, a matter of seconds, add the chiles. Stir once and add the curry leaves. Stir again and add the shallot and ginger. Reduce the heat to medium-low and stir and fry until golden, about 2 minutes.

4. Add the spice mixture to the yogurt and stir to combine. Fold in the diced plantain and mango and serve at room temperature or cold.

SERVES 4

COOKING NOTES

Use a good thick Greek yogurt, like Fage. Not low-fat.

Brown mustard seeds, chana dal and curry leaves are available at Indian food markets, like Kalustyan's (www.kalustyans.com).

SERVING SUGGESTIONS

Creamy Curried Sweet Potato Soup (p. 145), Country Captain (p. 455), Spicy, Garlicky Cashew Chicken (p. 494), Bademiya's Justly Famous Bombay Chile-and-Cilantro Chicken (p. 471), Cucumbers in Cream (p. 225), Green Beans with Coriander-Coconut Crust (p. 246), Almond Cake (p. 777)

JULY 29, 1998: "TRICK TO PLANTAINS IS IN THE PEEL," BY AMANDA HESSER. RECIPE ADAPTED FROM *MADHUR JAFFREY'S WORLD VEGETARIAN*, BY MADHUR JAFFREY.

—1998

⌒ GRATIN OF YAMS AND CHIPOTLE CREAM

This appears to be a simple gratin, a tall stack of yams, browned on top and sagging on the edges. As you sink your fork into it, though, it reveals layer upon fine layer, like a piece of puff pastry. And when you bite into it, the layers, separated by a smoky chipotle-scented cream, collapse in your mouth.

What makes this gratin so exceptional is the precise slicing of the yams, which is done using a mandoline, the slicing tool that made the leap to the home kitchen around the time this article ran. If you don't have a mandoline yet, the good news is that the best one available today is a plastic Japanese model that costs less than $20. (You can find one at most good cookware stores.)

———

I cup heavy cream
I teaspoon chipotle sauce from canned chipotles
I ½ pounds yams, peeled and cut into
    ⅟₁₆-inch-thick slices
Kosher salt and freshly ground black pepper

1. Heat the oven to 375 degrees. Whisk together the cream and chipotle sauce in a bowl until smooth.

2. Arrange a thin layer of the yams in an 8½-inch-by-4½-inch-by-2¾-inch-deep terrine or loaf pan. Season with a little salt and pepper and spoon over a little of the cream mixture. Repeat, layering the remaining yams and cream mixture, seasoning every other layer. Press firmly on the gratin to compact the layers.

3. Cover the terrine with aluminum foil and bake for 30 minutes. Remove the foil and continue baking for 35 to 40 minutes, or until most of the cream has been absorbed and the yams are tender and browned. Remove from the oven and let rest for 10 minutes.

4. Cut the gratin into 4 rectangular pieces and carefully transfer to serving plates, using a spatula and a fork.

SERVES 4

SERVING SUGGESTIONS

Slow-Roasted Duck (p. 475), North Carolina–Style Pulled Pork (p. 550), Docks Coleslaw (p. 191), Roasted Cauliflower (p. 248), Boston Baked Beans (p. 274), Tapioca Flamingo (p. 810), Summer Pudding (p. 847), Caramelized Chocolate Bread Pudding (p. 852)

JANUARY 27, 1999: "THE TOOL THAT CHEFS LOVE, AND HOME COOKS BARELY KNOW," BY AMANDA HESSER. RECIPE ADAPTED FROM BOBBY FLAY, THE CHEF AT MESA GRILL IN NEW YORK CITY.

—1999

✎ FRENCH FRIES

In the late 1990s, I made the mistake of doing a few stories that involved finding the best way to prepare an ingredient or dish. When you write a story like that, you end up cooking dozens of variations, and those variations tend to be your sustenance for that week. By the time you're done, you never want to see that ingredient or dish ever again. It took me years to eat duck again after roasting, steaming, and braising ducks to come up with a few great methods (one is on p. 475.) And I've made maybe one or two batches of fries since writing this recipe a decade ago. But I can promise you this: if you make French fries, this is the recipe to use.

Getting that perfect fry—long, thin as a chopstick, speckled with salt crystals large enough to feel on your tongue, brown as toast, nutty but not too greasy, and, like a ficelle, crisp on the outside and tender on the inside—requires great synergy. In this recipe, the hand-cut potatoes are soaked twice, fried once in peanut oil at a low temperature to cook them through, and then fried again at a higher temperature to brown them.

————

4 large long Idaho potatoes
Peanut oil
Kosher or coarse sea salt

1. Peel the potatoes. Place in a bowl, cover with water, and refrigerate for 8 hours.
2. Slice the potatoes lengthwise into ¼-inch-thick sticks. Place in a bowl, cover with water, and refrigerate for 8 hours more.
3. Drain the potato sticks and lay out on dish towels to dry. Be sure they are completely dry before frying.
4. Heat 2 inches of oil to 300 degrees in a large deep pot with a frying basket and a deep-frying thermometer clipped to the side. Add just enough potatoes to cover the bottom of the frying basket and cook until slightly limp, 1½ to 2 minutes; do not brown. Lift the basket and drain the fries, then transfer the potatoes to a wire rack set over a baking sheet and separate the sticks. Repeat with the remaining potatoes.
5. Increase the heat to 375 degrees. Again add the potatoes in batches to the oil and fry until chestnut brown on the edges and crisp. Drain and transfer to a bowl lined with paper towels. Immediately season with salt, tossing to coat.

SERVES 4

COOKING NOTES

I had always considered the Idaho potato—properly called the Russet Burbank—a plebeian tuber, something that large growers foisted on the American public because it was cheap to grow and high in yield. Baked, it has the appeal of ground-up chalk. But almost every chef I spoke with used it to make fries. And I discovered that it does have redeeming qualities when fried in oil. Its interior expands like a soufflé and turns creamy; its exterior becomes crisp before absorbing too much oil. And browning the outside, which means caramelizing the potato's sugars, gives it just the right bitterness. French fries need a touch of bitterness and loam, smoothed out with fat.

Soaking the potato slices beforehand draws out the starch, making them more rigid and less likely to stick together.

VARIATIONS

For a light pork flavor, add a 3-inch-long slice of bacon or prosciutto to every 2 quarts of oil. For duck flavor, add 7 ounces of duck fat to every 2 quarts of oil.

For herbed fries, toss a handful of fresh leaves (any combination of rosemary, parsley, basil, sage, savory, oregano, and/or tarragon) into the oil a minute before the fries have finished browning during the second frying. (Serve the fries with the crisped herbs.)

SERVING SUGGESTIONS

'21' Club Hamburger (p. 536), Docks Coleslaw (p. 191), Kosher Pickles the Right Way (p. 608), Brownies (p. 684), Brown Butter Peach Bars (p. 710)

MAY 5, 1999: "DEEP SECRETS: MAKING THE PERFECT FRY," BY AMANDA HESSER.

—1999

✐ BAKED CHICKPEAS

½ cup olive oil

2 medium onions, thinly sliced

6 cloves garlic, finely sliced

I dried chile, mild or spicy

I tablespoon coriander seeds

2 bay leaves

3 cups chickpeas (garbanzo beans), rinsed, picked
    over, and soaked in cold water for 24 hours
    at room temperature

5 to 6 cups vegetable broth

10 saffron threads

I tablespoon kosher salt, or more to taste

¼ teaspoon freshly ground white pepper, or more to taste

1. Heat the oven to 450 degrees. Warm the olive oil in a large casserole over medium-high heat. Add the onions, garlic, chile, coriander, and bay leaves and sauté for 5 minutes.

2. Drain the chickpeas and add them to the pot, along with the broth, saffron, salt, and pepper. Cover and bring to a boil. Transfer to the oven and bake until the beans are soft and cooked through, 45 to 50 minutes. Season with salt and pepper if necessary.

SERVES 6

SERVING SUGGESTIONS

Matt's Whole Brisket with Tomato Gravy (p. 572), Arnaki Araka (Lamb with Peas; p. 550), Warm Cabbage Salad with Goat Cheese and Capers (p. 183), Ratatouille with Butternut Squash (p. 258), Moroccan Rice Pudding (p. 848), Revani Verrias (Semolina Cake; p. 788)

READERS

"After the prepared recipe comes to a boil, I stick the pot in the oven with whatever else I am baking that day, at whatever temperature those recipes need—usually 350 degrees—so the dish takes a while to bake. I check the pot every now and then and have never found it overdone. After transferring the chickpeas to a smaller pot or glass bowl (depending on the presentation of the day), my treat is the leftover caramelized gunk on the bottom of the pan, which tastes delicious! The dish is always a hit."

Ruth Leah Kahan, Brooklin, MA, letter

JUNE 9, 1999: "BY THE BOOK: AUTHENTICALLY BASQUE," BY AMANDA HESSER. RECIPE ADAPTED FROM *THE BASQUE KITCHEN*, BY GERALD HIRIGOYEN.

—1999

✐ CHICKPEAS IN GINGER SAUCE

¼ cup canola oil

2 cups chopped onions

2 tablespoons minced fresh ginger

2 teaspoons minced garlic

2 teaspoons ground coriander

½ teaspoon ground cardamom

½ teaspoon mango powder or I ½ teaspoons
    fresh lemon juice

¼ teaspoon cayenne pepper

¼ teaspoon freshly ground black pepper

I medium tomato, cored and chopped

4 cups cooked or canned chickpeas,
    with I cup of their liquid

½ cup water

Salt

I medium onion, thinly sliced

I green chile, seeded, and shredded

1. Put the oil in a large skillet and turn the heat to medium-high. Add the chopped onions; cook, stirring occasionally, until they turn light brown, about 5 minutes. Add the ginger and garlic, reduce the heat to medium, and cook for 2 minutes, stirring.

2. Add the coriander, cardamom, mango powder (not the lemon juice if using), cayenne, and black pepper; stir. Add the tomato and cook until the tomato becomes saucy and begins to separate from the oil, about 5 minutes.

3. Add the reserved chickpea liquid, water, the lemon juice if you are using it, and salt to taste. Cover, turn the heat to low and simmer for about 10 minutes, or until the mixture is thickened. Add the chickpeas, cover, and cook for 10 minutes longer. Taste and adjust the seasoning. Serve, passing the sliced onion and chile at the table.

SERVING SUGGESTIONS
Spicy, Garlicky Cashew Chicken (p. 494), Ismail Merchant's Spinach Puree (p. 229)

OCTOBER 13, 1999: "A SHELF OF TREASURES, ALWAYS FRESH," BY MARK BITTMAN. RECIPE ADAPTED FROM JULIE SAHNI, A COOKBOOK AUTHOR AND COOKING TEACHER.

—1999

SERVING SUGGESTIONS
Bouillabaisse (p. 390), Sea Scallops with Sweet Red Peppers and Zucchini (p. 409), Roast Lobster with Vanilla Sauce (p. 411), The Most Voluptuous Cauliflower (p. 241), Haricots Verts with Balsamic Vinaigrette (p. 231), Cherry and Coconut Brown Betty (p. 806)

AUGUST 11, 1999: "IF CORN'S OFF THE COB, USE YOUR IMAGINATION," BY JACK BISHOP.

—1999

◢ FRESH CORN GRIDDLE CAKES WITH PARMESAN AND CHIVES

Another stellar corn cake recipe lives on p. 282.

———

4 medium ears corn, shucked
I large egg
¼ cup all-purpose flour
¼ cup freshly grated Parmesan cheese
I tablespoon snipped chives
½ teaspoon salt
Freshly ground black pepper
I tablespoon unsalted butter

1. Working over a large bowl, grate the corn on the large holes of a box grater until the cobs are clean; discard the cobs. Add the egg, flour, cheese, chives, salt, and pepper to taste to the corn, stirring until the batter is smooth.
2. Melt the butter in a large nonstick skillet over medium heat. Scoop up ¼ cup batter and scrape it (the batter will be thick) into the pan to form a round cake. Repeat with all the remaining batter; you should get 6 cakes. Cook, turning once, until the griddle cakes are a rich golden brown on both sides, about 9 minutes. Serve immediately.

SERVES 4 TO 6

COOKING NOTE
This makes large cakes—I'd make them half the size next time, because they'd be easier to handle.

◢ MASHED POTATOES ANNA

I included this recipe not because it had anything particularly interesting to say about the period (the return of comfort food—y-a-w-n!), but because it's a great mashed potato recipe, and if you don't already have a great one, now you do. No bells and whistles. Just the same sound technique that has worked for generations. You rice the potatoes before gradually whisking in the milk, butter, and cream to emulsify them; that is how you get the mash to fluff. But fluffiness doesn't last, so ignore what everyone tells you about mashed potatoes and their resiliency. Serve these right away.

The original recipe came from an impoverished Parisian cook named Anna, whose recipes were collected and published—*Le Carnet d'Anna*—by Edouard de Pomiane, a French doctor and beloved food writer.

———

2 pounds baking or Yukon Gold potatoes, peeled and cut into cubes
I cup whole milk
4 tablespoons unsalted butter
⅓ cup heavy cream
1½ teaspoons salt
Freshly ground black pepper

1. Place the potatoes in a saucepan, add enough cold salted water to cover, and bring to a boil. Partially cover the pan, lower the heat, and simmer for 20 minutes, or until the potatoes are tender.
2. Meanwhile, place the milk in a saucepan over medium-low heat and heat until bubbles just form

around the edges of the pan. Remove from the heat, cover, and set aside.

3. Drain the potatoes and put them through a ricer or mash with a potato masher. Return them to the pan and place over low heat. Gradually whisk in the hot milk, butter, cream, salt, and a few grinds of pepper.

SERVES 4

COOKING NOTE
I cut the potatoes into 1-inch cubes.

SERVING SUGGESTIONS
Iceberg Lettuce with Smoked Bacon and Buttermilk Dressing (p. 200), Steak au Poivre (p. 573), Spinach with Sour Cream (p. 216), Al Forno's Roasted Asparagus (p. 233), Mrs. Hovis's Hot Upside-Down Apple Pie (p. 828), Coconut Pie (p. 801)

DECEMBER 5, 1999: "FOOD: GOOD AND PLENTY," BY MOLLY O'NEILL. RECIPE ADAPTED FROM *A PASSION FOR POTATOES*, BY LYDIE MARSHALL.

—1999

✍ HEIRLOOM PEA PANCAKES

¼ pound sugar snap peas, trimmed
½ cup freshly shelled green peas
2 tablespoons whole milk
1 tablespoon heavy cream
1 large egg, lightly beaten
¼ cup all-purpose flour
½ teaspoon baking powder
⅛ teaspoon sugar
⅛ teaspoon salt
2 tablespoons unsalted butter, or as needed
Salt and freshly ground black pepper

1. Heat the oven to 450 degrees. Bring a pot of lightly salted water to a boil. Fill a bowl with ice water. Add the snap peas to the boiling water and blanch for 2 minutes. Remove with a wire skimmer or a slotted spoon and immediately plunge into the ice bath. Remove the snap peas from the ice water and set aside.

Repeat the procedure for the fresh peas, blanching them for 3 minutes, or until tender. Set aside.

2. Puree the sugar snap peas with the milk and cream in a blender or food processor. Pour into a large bowl and whisk in the egg. Sift the flour, baking powder, sugar, and salt into the mixture, and whisk to combine. Coarsely puree the blanched peas in a food processor, then fold into the batter.

3. Melt ½ tablespoon butter in a large ovenproof skillet over medium-high heat. Drop tablespoonfuls of the batter into the pan. When the edges are lightly browned, place the pan in the oven and bake for 1½ minutes. Flip the pancakes over gently with a spatula and cook over medium-high heat until the bottoms are lightly browned, then return to the oven for another minute. Transfer to a plate lined with paper towels; sprinkle with salt and pepper. Repeat the process until all the batter is used.

MAKES ABOUT 14 PANCAKES; SERVES 4 TO 6 AS A SIDE DISH OR HORS D'OEUVRES

SERVING SUGGESTIONS
Wine Lemonade (p. 17), James Beard's Champagne Punch (p. 28), Rhubarb Bellini (p. 30), Kir Royale 38 (p. 28), The Minimalist's Gravlax (p. 418), Hearth's Fava Bean Salad (p. 202), Asparagus and Bulgur with Preserved-Lemon Dressing (p. 190), Spring Lamb Salad with Pea Shoots and Sugar Snap Peas (p. 580), Fontainebleau (p. 829)

JULY 12, 2000: "MY, THOSE ARE LOVELY PEAS YOU HAVE," BY MELISSA CLARK. RECIPE ADAPTED FROM JUDSON GRILL IN NEW YORK CITY.

—2000

✍ RALPH VETTER'S SWEET POTATOES WITH LEMON

Ralph Vetters, a quiet and methodical cook, was a student at Harvard Medical School when I met him. I watched him make this family recipe, a brilliant spin on candied sweet potatoes (p. 276), for a story I was doing for a Thanksgiving issue. Traditional sweet potato recipes are loved for one's memory of the flood of sugar, but in practice they tend to cloy, which is why people only make them once a year. In this variation, the acid in lemon juice and the fragrance of its zest sharpens every bite.

---

6 medium sweet potatoes, scrubbed
2 cups sugar
1/2 cup water
1 teaspoon freshly grated nutmeg
Two 3-inch-long strips lemon zest
1/2 teaspoon salt
6 tablespoons unsalted butter
6 tablespoons fresh lemon juice (from about 2 lemons)

1. Place the potatoes in a large pot and cover with water. Bring to a boil, then reduce the heat to medium-low and simmer until the potatoes are just tender, about 25 minutes. Drain and allow to cool completely.
2. Heat the oven to 425 degrees. Combine the sugar, water, nutmeg, lemon zest, and salt in a small saucepan, bring to a simmer over medium-low heat, and simmer for 10 minutes. Add 5 tablespoons butter and the lemon juice and stir well. Remove from the heat.
3. Peel the sweet potatoes and slice them into 1/2-inch disks. Grease a shallow 9-by-12-inch baking dish with the remaining tablespoon of butter. Lay the sweet potatoes into the pan in overlapping rows so that they cover the pan evenly. Pour the lemon syrup over the potatoes.
4. Bake until bubbling and very lightly browned, about 30 minutes. Serve hot.

SERVES 6 TO 8

SERVING SUGGESTIONS
Roasted Brine-Cured Turkey (p. 474), Slow-Roasted Duck (p. 475), String Beans with Ginger and Garlic (p. 260), Baked Mushrooms (p. 212), Caramelized Endive (p. 238), Marcella's Pear Cake (p. 769), Evelyn Sharpe's French Chocolate Cake (p. 752)

NOVEMBER 15, 2000: "AMERICA CELEBRATES: SOMERVILLE, MASS: A BLEND OF TOWN AND COUNTRY," BY AMANDA HESSER. RECIPE ADAPTED FROM RALPH VETTERS, A MEDICAL STUDENT IN SOMERVILLE, MASSACHUSETTS.

—2000

⮒ PUREE OF PEAS AND WATERCRESS

I have probably made this recipe more often than any other in the book. I learned it from my husband, who got it from *The Loaves and Fishes Cookbook*, by Anna Pump. You simmer frozen peas—yes, frozen, which work better than fresh here—in water and toss in some watercress during the last minute of cooking, then ladle the vegetables into a food processor, and buzz away, working some butter, salt, and pepper into the green-on-green puree. It couldn't be simpler or more lovely to eat—the epitome of an indispensable recipe.

---

4 cups frozen peas
Two 1-pound bunches watercress, trimmed
    to 2 to 3 inches and washed well
4 tablespoons unsalted butter, cut into small pieces
3/4 teaspoon sea salt, or more to taste
1/2 teaspoon freshly ground black pepper, or more to taste

1. Fill a large saucepan with water and bring to a boil. Add the peas and return to a boil. Turn off the heat, add the watercress to the peas, and cover the saucepan. Let sit for 5 minutes so that the watercress wilts.
2. Drain the peas and watercress and transfer to a food processor. Add the butter, salt and pepper, and process until smooth. Taste and adjust the seasoning.

SERVES 4

SERVING SUGGESTIONS
Sautéed Red Snapper with Rhubarb Sauce (p. 421), Ginger Duck (p. 480), High-Temperature Roast Lamb (p. 526), Al Forno's Roasted Asparagus (p. 233), Mushrooms with Manzanilla Sherry (p. 249), Forget-It Meringue Torte (p. 823), Almond Cake (p. 777), Coeur à la Crème with Rhubarb Sauce (p. 864)

READERS
"Some twenty years ago, we couldn't get the Sunday *NYT* in Lincoln. So a small group of enterprising people, lusting for news, talked the local newspaper distributor into bringing the *Times* to Lincoln. We became the 'paper boys and girls' and delivered them to our friends. . . . Suffice to say we're 'out here' in Lin-

coln with sophisticated tastes but often lacking many of the ingredients for recipes available on both coasts, no Whole Foods, blank stares when asking for watercress (a local farmer grows curly cress for your recipe), a wonderful seasonal farmers' market, entrepreneurial farmers, GREAT cooks, and, in my case, piles of slick pages torn from the Food section of Sunday's *Times*."

Natalie Olson, Lincoln, NE, e-mail

JULY 15, 2001: "FOOD DIARY: LOVIN' SPOONFULS," BY AMANDA HESSER. RECIPE ADAPTED FROM *THE LOAVES AND FISHES COOKBOOK*, BY ANNA PUMP.

—2001

SWEET POTATOES ANNA

According to *Larousse Gastronomique*, potatoes done "Anna style" are thinly sliced, layered with butter, and cooked in a covered baking dish. Slicing potatoes is an old trick for lightening a heavy ingredient and blunting the starch: you layer the potatoes with another flavor like butter or cheese. The only odd part of this recipe is when you are told to toss the sliced sweet potatoes with the melted butter and seasonings. The melted butter seizes up as soon as it touches the room-temperature potatoes, so it's more like spreading spackle than dressing them. Stick with it—the finished layered potato cake with its toasted top layer is worth the minor inconvenience.

6 medium sweet potatoes, peeled
10 tablespoons (1¼ sticks) unsalted butter, melted
1 tablespoon fresh thyme leaves or 1 teaspoon
    dried thyme
Coarse sea salt and freshly ground black pepper

1. Heat the oven to 425 degrees. Using a mandoline or sharp knife, slice the potatoes about ⅛ inch thick. Place in a very large bowl and add the butter, thyme, and salt and pepper to taste. Toss until all the slices are well coated with butter and seasonings.
2. Reserve about a dozen of the best-looking slices for the top layer. Arrange a layer of slightly overlapping slices in a 10-inch round gratin dish, ovenproof skillet, or other shallow ovenproof pan. Layer the potatoes

until all are used, topping the gratin with the reserved slices.
3. Place a sheet of parchment or heavy-duty foil directly on top of the potatoes. Place the pan in the oven and place a heavy pan slightly smaller in diameter than the first pan directly on the foil. Bake for 30 minutes.
4. Remove the top pan and carefully peel away the parchment. (If necessary, use a spatula to help separate the parchment from the potatoes.) Continue baking until the potatoes are soft and the top is almost caramelized, 20 to 30 minutes longer.
5. If the potatoes haven't browned to your liking, place the dish under the broiler for a few seconds to crisp the top layer. Cut into wedges and serve.

SERVES 6 TO 8

COOKING NOTES

A mandoline makes your life easier (you can slice the potatoes in half before sliding them crosswise down the mandoline if it makes them easier to control).

After layering the potatoes in the baking dish, use a rubber spatula to scrape the excess butter and seasonings from the mixing bowl onto the gratin—it would be sad to waste such good flavors!

For covering the potatoes, parchment is preferable to foil.

To get a little extra crispness on top, I broiled the dish for a minute before serving.

SERVING SUGGESTIONS

A Moley (Curried Turkey Hash; p. 452), Pork Arrosto with Prunes and Grappa (p. 577), Brussels Sprouts "Slaw" with Mustard Butter (p. 253), Banana Meringue Steamed Custard (p. 812)

NOVEMBER 14, 2001: "SWEET POTATOES WITH NARY A MARSHMALLOW IN SIGHT," BY REGINA SCHRAMBLING.

—2001

✎ HOPPIN' JOHN

Hoppin' John, wrote Matt Lee and Ted Lee, isn't a singular recipe but one of a family of rice and peas recipes found all over the world. The earliest record appears to be a thirteenth-century manuscript from Baghdad, which described a chickpea and rice stew "seasoned with sheep fat, cinnamon, dill, coriander, and ginger." Hoppin' John, a dish associated with Southern cooking, is made with either the black-eyed pea or the field pea, which, the Lees explained, "produces a ruddy broth as it boils, and tastes beefier, more nutty and less earthy than the black-eyed pea."

"The muted depth of the dish," the Lees wrote, "the felty, soothing, starch-on-starch texture of it, begs for at least a little richness—a little fat. Which is where the pork comes in." Here they add smoked pork jowl, and to make sure you're not lulled to sleep by the starch and fat, they also impose a wallop of red pepper flakes and the acid tang of tomatoes.

---

1 cup dried black-eyed peas or field peas, rinsed and picked over

2 tablespoons olive oil (if using the hog jowl)

1 smoked hog jowl or ¼ pound (3 strips) thick-cut smoked bacon

1 medium onion, coarsely chopped

6 cups water

1 teaspoon salt

½ teaspoon freshly ground black pepper

½ to ¾ teaspoon crushed red pepper flakes

5 or 6 tomatoes, peeled (see Cooking Note, p. 146), or half a 28-ounce can, drained (optional)

1½ cups long-grain white rice

1. Soak the peas for 4 hours in ample fresh water.
2. When ready to cook, heat the olive oil in a 4-quart pot over medium-high heat and brown the hog jowl on both sides. (If using bacon, omit the olive oil, and simply render its fat in the pot for 5 minutes before adding the next ingredients.) Add the onion and cook until softened, about 5 minutes.
3. Add the water, salt, black pepper, and red pepper, and bring to a boil. Let the mixture boil for 10 minutes, then add the peas. Maintain a low boil, uncov-

ered, until the peas are nearly tender (25 minutes for black-eyed peas, 30 minutes for field peas).
4. Lightly crush the tomatoes if using, in a bowl and add to the pot. Add the rice, reduce the heat to low, and simmer, covered, for 20 minutes.
5. Turn off the flame and allow the hoppin' John to steam in the pot, lid on, for 5 minutes. If using hog jowl, remove it from the pot and shred the meat. Fluff the hoppin' John with a fork, and add the shredded jowl if you have it.

SERVES 6

SERVING SUGGESTIONS
North Carolina–Style Pulled Pork (p. 550), Stewed Corn (p. 271), Brandied Peaches (p. 599), Sour Cream Ice Cream (p. 730)

JANUARY 1, 2003: "HOPPIN' JOHN SMILES ON THE NEW YEAR," BY MATT LEE AND TED LEE.

—2003

✎ CABBAGE AND POTATO GRATIN WITH MUSTARD BREAD CRUMBS

Kay Rentschler, an occasional contributor to the *Times*, said a Hungarian chef once told her that no cabbage deserves to be boiled. And when you taste what Rentschler does with cabbage here, and see how splendid and sophisticated the vegetable can be, you understand exactly what the chef meant.

⅓ cup diced (¼-inch) slab bacon

¾ cup diced (¼-inch) onion

1½ cups diced (½-inch) Yukon Gold potatoes

1 small bay leaf

1¼ teaspoon salt

½ teaspoon freshly ground black pepper

8 cups sliced (1-inch squares) green cabbage

½ cup heavy cream

For the Bread Crumbs

2 tablespoons unsalted butter

1¼ cups fresh bread crumbs

1 clove garlic, minced

Pinch of salt

Pinch of cayenne pepper

2 teaspoons Dijon mustard

2 teaspoons chopped flat-leaf parsley

¾ cup grated Comté or Gruyère cheese

1. Heat the oven to 425 degrees. Place the bacon in a 12-inch sauté pan, set over medium heat, and cook for about 2 minutes to render some fat. Add the onion and sauté, stirring frequently, until the bacon is crisp and the onion is golden, about 5 minutes. Add the potatoes, bay leaf, salt, and pepper and sauté for 2 minutes. Add the cabbage and sauté, stirring frequently, until it wilts a bit, 5 to 7 minutes.

2. Turn the cabbage mixture into a large bowl. Pour the cream into a saucepan and boil over high heat, stirring constantly with a wooden spoon, until reduced by half, about 2 minutes. Pour the cream over the cabbage and stir to mix.

3. Slide the cabbage mixture into a shallow 1½- or 2-quart casserole dish. Cover the casserole with foil. Bake for 10 minutes.

4. Meanwhile, make the bread crumbs: Melt the butter in a 10-inch skillet over low heat. When it's foamy, add the bread crumbs and sauté, stirring constantly with a wooden spoon, until crisp and golden, 5 to 7 minutes. Remove from the heat and add the garlic, salt, cayenne pepper, mustard, and parsley, stirring well to combine.

5. Sprinkle the casserole with the cheese, then with the bread crumbs, and return to the oven, uncovered. Bake until fragrant and bubbling slightly around the edges, about 5 minutes.

SERVES 4 TO 6

SERVING SUGGESTIONS

Spicy New England Pot Roast (p. 523), Elizabeth Frink's Roast Lemon Chicken (p. 478), Spoon Lamb (p. 546), Broiled Lamb Chops (p. 514), Ismail Merchant's Spinach Puree (p. 229), Raw Spinach Salad (p. 175), Frozen Lemon Soufflé (p. 725), Tourtière (Apple, Prune, and Armagnac Tart; p. 827)

JANUARY 22, 2003: "GIVING CABBAGE THE ROYAL TREATMENT," BY KAY RENTSCHLER.

—2003

POTATO SALAD WITH SHAVED RICOTTA SALATA AND GREEN SAUCE

2 pounds medium Yukon Gold potatoes or fingerlings

Sea salt or kosher salt

½ cup packed mint leaves

¼ cup packed basil leaves

3 tablespoons sliced chives

6 tablespoons extra virgin olive oil

Freshly ground black pepper

Approximately ¼ pound ricotta salata

1. Peel the potatoes, rinse, and spread in a large pot. Cover with water and season the water generously with salt. Bring to a simmer and cook gently until the potatoes are just cooked through but not mushy, about 20 minutes. Drain and transfer to a bowl. Let cool.

2. Meanwhile, drop the mint, basil, and chives into a food processor with a pinch of salt. With the motor running, begin pouring the olive oil through the feed tube and process for about 1 minute, to a bright green puree.

3. Slice the potatoes into 1-inch cubes and put on a serving platter. Pour over the green herb oil and season with a few grinds of pepper. Gently fold together to dress the potatoes. Peel wide thin shavings of ricotta over the potatoes, about ½ cup—a light covering, the amount you would add to pasta, is good. Serve at room temperature.

SERVES 4

SERVING SUGGESTIONS

Fresh Salmon and Lime Cakes (p. 420), Elizabeth Frink's Roast Lemon Chicken (p. 478), Salade à la Romaine (p. 171), Pots de Crème (p. 815)

JUNE 4, 2003: "THE 3 THAT MAKE A KITCHEN COMPLETE," BY AMANDA HESSER.

—2003

ITALIAN ROAST POTATOES

You may think, as I did, "I know how to roast potatoes!" But if you let Nigella Lawson guide you through her simple but nuanced method, you'll end up feeling enlightened and with a deeper understanding of the technique. By cutting the potatoes into cubes and roasting them in a pan in which they are not crowded, they gain a crust on their cut sides while remaining pillowy in the center. And because the potatoes are not seasoned until you can move them to a serving dish, they retain their French-fry crispness.

2½ pounds waxy potatoes (about 6 medium),
    scrubbed and cut into 1-inch cubes
12 cloves garlic
2 teaspoons dried oregano
½ cup olive oil
Salt

1. Heat the oven to 425 degrees. Combine the potatoes, garlic, oregano, and oil in a large roasting pan. Stir until the potatoes are well coated, and spread them evenly in the pan.
2. Place in the oven and roast until the potatoes are golden brown and crisp, 1 to 1¼ hours. (If the potatoes are crowded in the pan, they will take longer to crisp.)
3. Remove the potatoes and garlic from the oven and transfer to a serving dish. Sprinkle with salt to taste and serve immediately.

SERVES 4

COOKING NOTES
The first time I made these potatoes, I misread the recipe and used chopped fresh oregano. I tried it again with dried oregano. Both are lovely.

The recipe simply called for "salt"—since you're sprinkling it on at the end, use a coarse salt, whose crystals will not melt but will add their own crunch. Maldon sea salt, kosher salt, or, if you're feeling lavish, fleur de sel, all work well.

SERVING SUGGESTIONS
Zuppa di Funghi Siciliana (Sicilian Mushroom Soup; p. 127), Braised Ligurian Chicken (p. 491), Steamed Spinach with Balsamic Butter (p. 226), Panna Cotta (p. 840), Ricotta Kisses (p. 852), Bolzano Apple Cake (p. 783)

SEPTEMBER 17, 2003: "AT MY TABLE: IT ISN'T LA DOLCE VITA, BUT IT'S PRETTY CLOSE," BY NIGELLA LAWSON.

—2003

SMOKED MASHED POTATOES

Matt Lee and Ted Lee, who wrote about these mashed potatoes, described them best—as having "a suave smokiness" and "a sweet vanilla-like edge." They're a lot of effort for making mashed potatoes—in fact, I e-mailed the Lees before tackling the recipe to ask if they were *sure* it was worth it—but the rewards are plentiful.

---

4 teaspoons kosher salt, or to taste
2 pounds baking potatoes, peeled and quartered
2 pounds Yukon Gold potatoes, peeled and quartered
3 tablespoons unsalted butter, cut into pieces
½ cup heavy cream, half-and-half, or whole milk
Freshly ground black pepper

1. Pour 4 quarts of water into a 6-quart stockpot, add 3 teaspoons salt, and bring to a boil over high heat. Add the potatoes and cook until fork-tender, about 25 minutes. Drain, reserving 1 cup of the cooking water.
2. Smoke the potatoes to taste in a smoker according to the manufacturer's instructions. If you do not have a smoker, set a 13-by-16-inch aluminum roasting pan with a rack on the stovetop so that it spans 2 burners. Scatter 2 tablespoons ground hickory, apple, or cherry wood chips (for stovetop smokers) evenly in the pan. Lay a double thickness of foil over the rack and crimp any overhanging foil around the edges. Arrange the potatoes in a single layer on the foil. Cover the pan tightly with foil—use 2 sheets of foil laid side by side if necessary. Turn both burners to medium-low and smoke the potatoes for 15 minutes.
3. Transfer the potatoes to a large bowl and mash them with a fork, or pass them through a ricer or food mill. Add the remaining 1 teaspoon salt, the butter, cream, and ½ cup of the potato cooking water and whip until thoroughly combined. Add more cooking

water 2 tablespoons at a time until the potatoes reach a smooth, fluffy consistency. Season with salt if necessary and pepper to taste.

SERVES 6

SERVING SUGGESTIONS
Monte's Ham (p. 548), Stir-Fried Collards (p. 254), Bourbon Pecan Pie (p. 842)

APRIL 28, 2004: "NEW WAVE COOKING: DO TRY THIS AT HOME," BY MATT LEE AND TED LEE. ADAPTED FROM WYLIE DUFRESNE, THE CHEF AT RESTAURANT WD-50 IN NEW YORK CITY.

—2004

☞ LIGHT POTATO SALAD

I liked how this salad takes the best elements of German potato salad—bacon and vinegar—and blends them with the best elements of French potato salad—garlic and oil. Maybe it should be called Potatoes Luxembourg.

————

Salt
5 pounds new potatoes, creamers, or other small (1 to 1½-inch-diameter) potatoes, scrubbed
6 scallions, thinly sliced
2 tablespoons garlic oil
10 slices (½ pound) bacon
2 tablespoons yellow mustard seeds
¼ cup good quality white wine vinegar
Freshly ground black pepper

1. Put the potatoes in a large wide pot of salted water, bring to a boil, and cook until tender, about 20 minutes.
2. Drain the potatoes, cut in two, and place in a large bowl. Add the scallions and toss gently to mix.
3. Return the dry potato pot to medium heat and add the garlic oil and bacon. Cook the bacon until it's very crisp; transfer to paper towels.
4. Add the mustard seeds to the bacon fat in the pot. After a few moments, they will begin to pop. Immediately turn off the heat and add the vinegar. Scrape this over the potato mixture and toss together. Season with salt and pepper. Cover the salad with plas-

tic wrap and allow to stand at room temperature for about an hour.
5. To serve, transfer the potato salad to a serving bowl and crumble the crisp bacon on top.

SERVES 8 TO 10

COOKING NOTE
If you don't have garlic oil, warm 2 tablespoons of olive oil and a smashed garlic clove in a small pan over medium-low heat; remove the garlic from the pan before it begins to brown.

SERVING SUGGESTIONS
Spicy, Supercrunchy Fried Chicken (p. 490), Stir-Fried Collards (p. 254), Pickled Watermelon Rind (p. 598), Key Lime Pie (p. 826)

MAY 26, 2004: "AT MY TABLE: AN UNLIKELY GUEST SIMPLIFIES THE FEAST," BY NIGELLA LAWSON.

—2004

☞ POTATO "TOSTONES" (FLATTENED POTATOES)

Many foods benefit from a good pounding and leveling—see the Seasoned Olives on p. 90 and the Squashed Tomatoes, also on p. 90. Flattened foods give you more surface area to work with and allow the aromatics to better penetrate the ingredient.

As enjoyable as pounding the living daylights out of an innocent garlic clove or olive may be, probably the most satisfying flat food of all to prepare is Susan Spungen's potato "tostones." You steam baby potatoes until they're just tender, let them cool enough so they can be handled, and then press them between your palms until they flatten a bit and you hear their skins begin to snap. Next you heat up some oil in a skillet and fry the potatoes until they're nice and brown on their flat sides. Each potato is crisp and caramelized but still moist inside.

————

2 pounds (about 20) small potatoes, like Yukon Gold
1 teaspoon kosher salt
Olive oil
Coarse sea salt

1. Place a steamer basket in a large pot filled with an inch of water and add the potatoes and salt. Cover and bring to a boil over medium heat. Steam until the potatoes are just tender when pierced with a paring knife, about 25 minutes. (Don't overcook, or they won't hold together when flattened.) Remove the basket and let the potatoes cool enough so they can be handled.

2. Gently squeeze the potatoes, one at a time, between your palms so that they flatten slightly but remain in one piece (some will break, but they can still be used). Pour 1/4 inch of oil into a medium skillet set over medium-high heat. Add the potatoes, in batches to avoid crowding, and fry on both sides until crisp and browned, 2 to 3 minutes per side. Drain on a plate lined with paper towels.

3. Arrange the potatoes on a platter and sprinkle with sea salt.

SERVES 6

COOKING NOTE
When you sauté the potatoes, you want them to get a thick, golden crust. For this, a well-seasoned cast-iron skillet works best.

SERVING SUGGESTIONS
Pan-Roasted Chicken with End-of-Season Tomatoes (p. 482), Stewed Corn (p. 271), Fresh Blueberry Buckle (p. 815), Raspberry Granita (p. 719), Summer Pudding (p. 847)

JULY 22, 2007: "THE WAY WE EAT: LOW FOOD," BY AMANDA HESSER. RECIPE ADAPTED FROM *RECIPES*, BY SUSAN SPUNGEN.

—2007

⌒ CRISPY TOFU WITH SHIITAKES AND CHORIZO

———

1 pound extra-firm tofu, drained and sliced crosswise into 3/4-inch-thick slabs
2 tablespoons peanut oil
1 1/2 cups thinly sliced shiitake mushroom caps (4 ounces)
3 ounces cured chorizo (1 1/2 small links), diced (or cured Chinese sausage)
2 scallions, thinly sliced, dark green parts reserved for garnish
1/4 cup chicken broth
3 to 4 teaspoons soy sauce
2 teaspoons mirin (sweet rice wine) or dry sherry

1. Using paper towels, pat the tofu dry. Heat the oil in a large nonstick skillet over medium-high heat. Add the tofu slabs and cook, peeking as little as possible, until golden on the bottom, about 3 minutes. Turn and cook the other side, 2 to 3 minutes more. Drain on a paper-towel-lined plate.

2. Increase the heat to high, add the mushrooms, chorizo, and scallions (white and light green parts), and cook, tossing occasionally, until the mushrooms are softened and light golden, about 3 minutes. Stir in the broth, soy sauce, and mirin and cook until the sauce reduces and thickens slightly, about 1 minute.

3. If the tofu is no longer hot, push the vegetables in the pan to one side, add the tofu, and cook until heated through. Transfer the tofu to serving plates and top with the mushroom mixture and pan sauce. Sprinkle with the scallion greens.

SERVES 2

SERVING SUGGESTIONS
Clear Steamed Chicken Soup with Ginger (p. 145), Almond and Buttermilk Sorbet (p. 733)

APRIL 9, 2008: "TOFU MEETS ITS MATCH IN A DISH FIT FOR CARNIVORES," BY MELISSA CLARK.

—2008

• Bob the Sea Cook contributes a recipe for polenta with a ragout of small birds; Molly O'Neill will run a similar recipe (p. 467) in 1993.

—1870s—

• Potato croquettes, rice croquettes.

• An 1879 macaroni recipe takes a crucial beginning step toward al dente: "The great mistake in preparing macaroni is to overcook it; macaroni should not be soft, so as to drop to pieces."

—1880s—

• Italian immigration is at its peak; risotto is mentioned in the *Times* for the first time.

—1885—

• Curried turkey and rice.

—1887—

• Craig Claiborne publishes the first of half a dozen paella recipes (see p. 309).

—1957—

• An early pesto recipe made with butter and oil (p. 311).

—1969—

• Noodles Romanoff (p. 311), part macaroni and cheese and part noodles with sour cream.

—1970s—

• Cold Sesame Noodles (p. 355).

• Craig Claiborne writes about Marcella Hazan. She publishes *The Classic Italian Cook Book* three years later.

—1970—

• Le Cirque's Spaghetti Primavera (p. 314).

—1977—

• A Perfect Batch of Rice (p. 316)—recommended for inclusion in this book by thirteen readers.

—1978—

• Florence Fabricant publishes a recipe for pasta with chilled tomato sauce, a revelation that will spawn a handful of similar recipes over the next two decades.

—1979—

• Pasta with Vodka (p. 317) is born.
• Athletes carbo-load.
• We get excited about couscous.

—1980s—

• Stuffing leaves turkey for health reasons and is creatively reborn.

• Macaroni with Ham and Cheese (p. 319) puts its hat in the ring; many competing recipes appear over the years.

—1988—

• The Atkins diet sweeps the nation. Babbo, Mario Batali's flagship restaurant in New York City, introduces a pasta tasting menu; the restaurant becomes known for mint love letters and beef cheek ravioli.

—1990s—

• We get much more excited about risotto.

• Exhausted with risotto, *Times* writers publish recipes for stuck-pot rice, pittu, hoppers, yogurt rice, and pad Thai–style rice salad.

—2000s—

• Revival of Bolognese.

7

❧

PASTA, RICE, GRAINS, AND STUFFINGS

RECIPES BY CATEGORY

⌒ RICE PILAN

Even in the nineteenth century, food editors felt compelled to run recipes for leftover Thanksgiving turkey. I thought this leftovers solution was particularly appealing. Start with 3 cups cooked rice.

ORIGINAL RECIPE

"Cook rice; put it aside till wanted; then place a stewpan on fire, add one large spoon of butter, two large onions sliced, and fry the onions till brown. Then add one teaspoon of yellow curry powder or saffron powder, and add the rice which you cooked beforehand. Stir the whole and add a quarter of a pound of raisins (sun raisins without stones) to it, and keep over a hot oven; then fry a few mutton chops or roast a fowl. When serving, dish up the mutton chops or roast fowl (why not our Thanksgiving turkey in convenient pieces?) and cover it with the Pilan rice and sprinkle it over with some fried parsley, mint, and onions."

SERVES 4 AS A LIGHT MAIN COURSE

SERVING SUGGESTIONS

The leftovers from the Roasted Brine-Cured Turkey (p. 474), Watercress Salad (p. 171), Rum Pumpkin Cream Pie (p. 823)

NOVEMBER 25, 1887: "CURRY FOR THE TURKEY."
RECIPE ADAPTED FROM AN UNNAMED BOOK BY DANIEL SAUTIAGOE.

—1887

⌒ PAELLA

For most people, this recipe, which calls for lobster, clams, mussels, shrimp, chorizo, and salt pork, will require a deep dive into grocery-shopping hell. I hate to turn anyone away from an excellent recipe—and this one really is excellent—but unless you live in Maine, or near a great fish store, move on. I waited to make the dish until we were on vacation on Long Island, about a mile from the storied Seafood Shop on Route 27 in Wainscott. The shrimp came cleaned, the lobsters steamed, the mussels and clams firmly shut and sparkling—and because it was the Hamptons, it cost about half my book advance. However, the dinner was worth it.

Craig Claiborne, whose recipe this is, published about half a dozen paellas during his career at the *Times*. Several of them appeared again in his annual round-ups of "Favorite Recipes" and many readers wrote to tell me which of these they liked most. This paella is the last "favorite" that Claiborne ran, and I chose to make it because it appears to be his perfected version. It's extraordinarily good, so I hope the fans of his other paellas will reconsider.

----

2 cloves garlic
½ teaspoon dried thyme
1 teaspoon salt
1 tablespoon sherry vinegar or red wine vinegar
¼ cup olive oil
½ teaspoon ground coriander
One 2½-pound chicken, cut into pieces
¼ pound salt pork or pancetta, diced
1 pound medium shrimp, shelled and deveined
2 links chorizo or hot Italian sausage
¾ cup chopped onion
1 teaspoon saffron threads
2 tablespoons capers
⅓ cup chopped tomatoes
½ cup dry white wine
2½ cups short-grain rice (Valencia or Arborio)
3½ to 4 cups chicken broth
Salt and freshly ground black pepper
One 9-ounce package frozen artichoke hearts, partially thawed
½ cup freshly cooked or frozen peas
One 4-ounce jar pimentos, drained
20 mussels, well scrubbed and debearded
20 clams, well rinsed
One 2-pound live lobster, cooked (see p. 353) and cut into serving pieces
1 teaspoon anise liqueur

1. Chop the garlic with the thyme and salt. Scrape into a large bowl and add the vinegar, oil, and coriander. Add the chicken pieces and stir to coat with the mixture; allow to stand for 30 minutes.
2. Sauté the pork in a paella pan or very large casserole until the fat is rendered and the pork bits are brown. Remove the pork with a slotted spoon and reserve.
3. Sauté the shrimp in the pork fat remaining in the

pan until it's just turning pink, less than 1 minute; remove and reserve.

4. Fry the chorizo in the same pan until almost cooked through. Slice and reserve.

5. Brown the coated chicken pieces in the fat remaining in the pan. Sprinkle with the onion, saffron, capers, and tomatoes. Return the pork pieces to the pan and add the wine, rice, and 3½ cups chicken broth. Season with salt and pepper to taste. Cover and simmer gently for about 10 minutes.

6. Add the artichoke hearts and peas to the chicken and rice. Cook, covered, for 5 minutes. Add the shrimp, chorizo, and pimentos and continue cooking for a few minutes more.

7. Meanwhile, steam the mussels and clams separately in ¼ cup of water each until they open, about 2 minutes for the mussels and 5 minutes for the clams. Remove and reserve.

8. Check on the rice: If all the liquid has been absorbed, add the liquid from the clams or more chicken broth. The rice should be moist but without excess liquid. The shrimp should be just cooked through.

9. Add the lobster and liqueur to the rice. Check and adjust the seasoning. Garnish with the mussels and clams. Serve directly from the pan or casserole.

SERVES 8 TO 10 AS A MAIN COURSE

COOKING NOTES

Paella is all about timing—adding each component at just the right moment so none of them overcook. I made some changes to the original recipe to make it easier to get the sequence right, and also to reduce some of the cooking times, because we tend to cook seafood for less time than we used to (so that it's just cooked through, as opposed to cooked until rubbery).

If you use dried chorizo, thinly slice it before frying.

According to Colman Andrews in *Catalan Cuisine*, paella is meant to be eaten warm, not hot, so there's no need to stress about getting everyone to the table on time. Finish the dish, then start the round-up.

SERVING SUGGESTIONS

Sangria (p. 28), Rebujito (p. 38), Chorizo Revueltos (Scrambled Eggs with Chorizo; p. 640), Catalan Tortilla with Aioli (p. 86), Fried Chickpeas (p. 88), Pan con Tomate (p. 91), Potato, Ham, and Piquillo Pepper Croquetas (p. 94), Toasts with Chocolate, Olive Oil, and Sea Salt (p. 844), Caramel Custard (p. 836), Strawberry Sorbet (p. 732)

JANUARY 2, 1966: "READERS' TASTES—EXOTIC," BY CRAIG CLAIBORNE.

—1966

⌖ FETTUCCINE ALLA ROMANA

The instructions to this recipe are noteworthy because they're all about timing and sequence, about having every step thought through in advance so you can seamlessly assemble the dish and get it to the table before the cream sauce begins to stiffen.

_____

½ pound fresh fettuccine (store-bought or homemade)
Salt
4 tablespoons unsalted butter, cut into 8 pieces, softened
½ cup freshly grated Parmesan cheese
¼ cup hot heavy cream
½ cup freshly cooked peas, preferably freshly shelled
⅓ cup finely shredded imported or domestic prosciutto
Freshly ground black pepper

1. With this recipe, you must have all the ingredients ready. The fettuccine must be tossed with the other ingredients and served within seconds after they are cooked. Heat a serving dish for the fettuccine and have a colander in the sink.

2. Place the fettuccine in boiling salted water to cover and cook until al dente, as preferred by Italians. Test the fettuccine for doneness a strand at a time. Remove the strand with a fork, let cool briefly, and then bite into it.

3. When the pasta is nearly done, add the butter to the hot serving dish.

4. When the fettuccine is done, pour it into the colander. Drain quickly and not too thoroughly. Pour the moist pasta into the serving dish and toss quickly. Add the cheese, cream, peas, and prosciutto and continue tossing. Serve quickly on hot plates. Let each guest season it himself with a pepper mill.

SERVES 2 AS A MAIN COURSE,
4 AS A FIRST COURSE

To save yourself a pan, heat the cream in the same pot you use to cook the peas (after you've removed the peas).

SERVING SUGGESTIONS
Limoncello (p. 38), Crostini Romani (p. 77), Fennel and Blood Orange Salad (p. 195), Hazelnut Baklava (p. 706)

PERIOD DETAIL
Craig Claiborne included notes about where to find fettuccine, instructions for thinly slicing the prosciutto (almost all of which was domestic at the time), and using fresh Parmesan rather than the faux commercial kind. He also called for "water to cover" the pasta, an instruction that's now dated. Water to cover means just enough water to cover the pasta once it's added to the pot. But you should really cook pasta in much more water so that when you add the pasta, the water doesn't cool enough to stop boiling.

MAY 5, 1968: "EATING LIKE A ROMAN," BY CRAIG CLAIBORNE.

—1968

1. Put the basil, garlic, nuts, butter, oil, Parmesan cheese, and salt to taste in a blender and blend until pureed, stirring down with a rubber spatula. Blend for 2 or 3 minutes, until the pesto has the consistency of a thick puree.

2. Cook the spaghetti in generously salted boiling water until al dente. Ladle out some cooking water and reserve; drain the pasta quickly in a colander and empty it immediately into a hot serving dish. Add half the pesto and toss quickly, adding more as desired. Also, you may want to sprinkle in a little pasta water to loosen the sauce. Serve with additional Parmesan cheese.

SERVES 6 AS A MAIN COURSE,
8 AS A FIRST COURSE

SERVING SUGGESTIONS
Tomatoes Vinaigrette (p. 218), Breaded Veal Milan-Style (p. 523), Lemon Cake (p. 781), Fruit Crostatas (p. 855)

JUNE 15, 1969: "PRESTO, PESTO," BY CRAIG CLAIBORNE. RECIPE BY LORANE SCHIFF, A READER FROM GENOA.

—1969

✍ LORANE SCHIFF'S PESTO GENOVESE

I'd become so accustomed to bright, feathery pestos made with olive oil and basil that the slab of butter and blizzard of cheese in this pesto—the first to appear in the *Times*—took me by surprise. Its fragrance is matched by its burliness. (The pesto in Marcella Hazen's *The Classic Italian Cookbook* contains butter too.)

―――――

3 cups packed basil leaves (from about 3 bunches)
1 clove garlic
¼ cup pine nuts
4 tablespoons unsalted butter, softened
¼ cup olive oil
½ cup freshly grated Parmesan cheese, plus more for serving
Salt
1½ pounds spaghetti

✍ NOODLES ROMANOFF

Noodles Romanoff was a satisfying and popular side dish through the 1960s, and it established the model for decades of pasta and cheese eating. It was sometimes made with chopped pimento, grated onion, or cheddar rather than Parmesan (the Parmesan is an early attempt to refine the dish). Next time I make the noodles, I'll be more aggressive with the Worcestershire and Tabasco, and I might put the noodles under the broiler at the end to get some crisp bits, but these are tiny refinements.

―――――

½ pound broad egg noodles
2 cups sour cream
1 cup cottage cheese
2 to 4 tablespoons grated onion
1 small clove garlic, finely minced
¼ cup finely chopped flat-leaf parsley

¼ cup finely chopped chives (optional)

I teaspoon Worcestershire sauce

Tabasco sauce

Salt and freshly ground black pepper

½ cup freshly grated Parmesan cheese

1. Heat the oven to 350 degrees. Cook the noodles in boiling salted water until nearly tender, 3 to 4 minutes; do not overcook. Drain.

2. Combine the sour cream, cottage cheese, onion, garlic, parsley, chives, Worcestershire sauce, Tabasco, and salt and pepper to taste. Toss with the noodles and pour the mixture into a buttered 8-inch square baking dish. Sprinkle with the Parmesan cheese.

3. Bake for 25 to 30 minutes, or until bubbling and hot.

SERVES 6 AS A SIDE DISH

COOKING NOTE

Use low-fat sour cream and cottage cheese at your peril; I don't recommend them. And if you want to take the matter up with me, first read *Real Food* by Nina Planck, which explains the value of butterfat—it not only contains a full dose of flavor and vitamins but is also the means to help your body digest the protein.

SERVING SUGGESTIONS

Köenigsberger Klopse (Meatballs in Creamy Caper Sauce; p. 526), Choresh Qormeh Sabzi (Green Herb Stew; p. 533), Haricots Verts with Balsamic Vinaigrette (p. 231), Bosiljka Marich's Serbian Torte (p. 751)

JANUARY 16, 1970: "MENUS AND RECIPES FOR THE WEEKEND."

—1970

CORN BREAD STUFFING

No frills here, just a great corn bread stuffing.

3 cups crumbled day-old corn bread

3 cups cubed white bread

Liver, gizzard, and heart of a 12- to 15-pound turkey

½ pound (2 sticks) unsalted butter, plus extra for the top of the stuffing

2 cups chopped onions

2 cups chopped celery

I cup chopped green bell pepper

3 cloves garlic, finely minced

I teaspoon chopped fresh thyme or
    ½ teaspoon dried thyme

⅓ cup finely chopped flat-leaf parsley

I tablespoon chopped fresh basil or
    1½ teaspoons dried basil

Salt

¾ teaspoon freshly ground black pepper, or more to taste
    (black pepper is a vital flavor in this stuffing)

I bay leaf, very finely chopped

Tabasco sauce

1. Heat the broiler. Crumble the corn bread into a large bowl.

2. Toast the white bread under the broiler, tossing occasionally to redistribute the cubes and let them brown evenly. Add to the corn bread.

3. Put the liver, gizzard, and heart through the fine blade of a meat grinder.

4. Heat the oven to 350 degrees. Heat half the butter in a large skillet and add the liver mixture, onions, celery, green pepper, garlic, thyme, parsley, basil, salt and pepper to taste, bay leaf, and Tabasco (about 1 teaspoon). Cook, stirring, over medium to low heat for about 20 minutes.

5. Add the remaining butter. When it melts, add the contents of the skillet to the bread. Stir to blend well.

6. Spoon the stuffing into an 8-inch square baking dish. Dot with butter and bake for 30 minutes. To brown the top, place under the broiler for about 1 minute.

MAKES ENOUGH STUFFING TO GO WITH A 12- TO 15-POUND TURKEY; SERVES 8

SERVING SUGGESTIONS

Red Cabbage Glazed with Maple Syrup (p. 236), Turducken (p. 485), Mashed Potatoes Anna (p. 294), Stewed Fennel (p. 245), Creamed Onions (p. 217), Apple Crumb Pie (p. 841), Sour Cream Ice Cream (p. 730)

NOVEMBER 15, 1970: "TURKEY TALK," BY CRAIG CLAIBORNE.

—1970

MRS. SEBASTIANI'S MALFATTI

Italians don't make excuses for what they cook; they just joke about it. Which is why there are almond cookies named *brutti ma buoni* ("ugly but good"), a potato dish referred to as *patati con agnello scappato* ("potatoes with escaped lamb," which contains no lamb) and both a pasta shape and dumplings referred to as *malfatti* ("poorly made"). The beauty of such derogatory nicknaming is that the pressure is off. You can slap the cookies together and no one's going to complain. No need to explain where the lamb went or to shape your malfatti to look like hens' eggs.

In America, the dumpling form of malfatti has come to mean a spinach-and-ricotta ravioli filling without the pasta—sometimes called "gnudi" (or nude). But this malfatti recipe relies on bread rather than ricotta for substance; it is flecked with spinach and bound with Parmesan. It's a more direct descendent of the *cucina povera* from which the dish originates, when cooks would make a meal of bread and what few other ingredients they had.

The recipe came from Sylvia Sebastiani, then an owner of Sebastiani Vineyards in Sonoma, California. After shaping the dumplings, she instructed readers to give them a dip in boiling water before nestling them in a baking dish, covering them with tomato sauce and cheese, and broiling them. The tomato sauce was a New World touch.

For a modern, more Italian and less Italian-American spin on malfatti, see p. 345.

---

3 pounds spinach (you'll need 2 pounds after trimming) or two 10-ounce packages frozen spinach

6 ounces crusty Italian bread (about half a loaf)

1 onion, finely chopped

1 clove garlic, finely chopped

2 tablespoons olive oil

1/2 to 1 cup dry bread crumbs

1 cup freshly grated Parmesan cheese, plus more for serving

1/2 cup chopped flat-leaf parsley

1 teaspoon salt

1/4 teaspoon freshly ground black pepper

1 teaspoon dried basil

4 large eggs, lightly beaten

Flour

3 cups tomato sauce, preferably homemade (see p. 605), heated until hot

1. Cook the fresh spinach, if using, in the water clinging to the leaves after washing, or cook the frozen spinach according to package instructions. Drain, squeezing out as much water as possible—do this in small handfuls so you can press out the most water, and do it over a bowl to reserve the water—and chop.

2. Soak the bread briefly in the reserved spinach water plus more hot water as needed, and squeeze dry.

3. Sauté the onion and garlic in the olive oil in a large skillet until tender, 3 to 5 minutes.

4. Mix the spinach, bread, and onion and garlic and put through the finest blade of a meat grinder, or pulse in a food processor until chopped, then scrape into a bowl. Add 1/2 cup bread crumbs, the cheese, parsley, salt, pepper, and basil. Stir in the eggs. With lightly floured hands, gently shape the mixture into sausage-like links, 1 inch thick by 3 inches long. If they do not hold together, add more bread crumbs. Lay on a baking sheet.

5. Heat the broiler. Drop the malfatti, one at a time, into a pot of boiling salted water. Reduce the heat to a bare simmer and cook until the malfatti float to the surface, 1 to 2 minutes. Remove with a slotted spoon, drain on paper towels, and place in a greased baking dish, large enough to hold the malfatti in a single layer.

6. Spoon the tomato sauce over the malfatti, sprinkle with lots of cheese, and reheat under the broiler.

SERVES 10 TO 12 AS A FIRST COURSE

COOKING NOTES

Squeeze every last drop of water from the spinach, or your malfatti will not only be "poorly made" but watery.

If you happen to have homemade tomato sauce in the freezer, this is the moment to use it. I resorted to store-bought, which, thanks to brands like Rao's, is no longer a disappointment.

VARIATION

Skip the tomato sauce and, after poaching the dumplings, dot with butter, sprinkle with Parmesan and nutmeg, and broil.

Green Goddess Salad (p. 176), Panna Cotta (p. 840), Bittersweet Chocolate Semifreddo (p. 727)

JULY 18, 1971: "TUSCAN DUMPLING," BY JEAN HEWITT. ADAPTED FROM SYLVIA SEBASTIANI.

—1971

✒ MANICOTTI WITH RICOTTA CHEESE

This is not what you think it is: the manicotti are actually Parmesan-flecked crepes, airy veils that encase the ricotta filling without burdening it with the weight of pasta.

———

2 cups ricotta cheese, drained

2 large egg yolks

2 tablespoons finely chopped flat-leaf parsley

Salt

1/8 teaspoon freshly grated nutmeg

1 cup plus 2 tablespoons freshly grated Parmesan cheese

Freshly ground black pepper

Parmesan Cheese Crepes (recipe follows)

2 cups tomato sauce, preferably homemade

2 tablespoons unsalted butter, melted

1. Heat the oven to 400 degrees. Combine the ricotta cheese, egg yolks, parsley, salt to taste, nutmeg, 1 cup Parmesan cheese, and pepper to taste and blend well. Spoon equal portions of the filling down the center of each crepe and roll it up.

2. Spoon about 3 tablespoons tomato sauce over the bottom of a baking dish (a rectangular dish measuring about 8 by 14 inches would be appropriate). Place the rolled crepes seam side down in the dish. Spoon the remaining sauce over the crepes and sprinkle with the remaining 2 tablespoons cheese. Pour the melted butter over all.

3. Bake until heated through, about 20 minutes.

SERVES 4 AS A MAIN COURSE

PARMESAN CHEESE CREPES

3/4 cup all-purpose flour

1 large egg

Salt

1 cup whole milk

2 tablespoons unsalted butter, melted

1/4 cup freshly grated Parmesan cheese

Unsalted butter for the crepe pan

1. Scoop the flour into a bowl and add the egg and salt to taste. Add the milk while stirring with a wire whisk. Add the melted butter and cheese. Let stand for at least 30 minutes.

2. Heat an 8-inch crepe pan over medium heat. Butter the cooking surface. Pour a scant 1/4 cup batter into the pan and spread over the base. Cook until browned on the bottom. Turn and brown the other side. Transfer to a baking sheet. Repeat with the remaining batter, buttering the pan as needed. Do not stack the crepes.

MAKES ABOUT 8 CREPES

COOKING NOTES

It's important to drain the ricotta well before adding it to the filling—a small but crucial step that prevents the filling from becoming watery.

I used Rao's Homemade Marinara Sauce, a good store-bought option.

SERVING SUGGESTIONS

Garden Minestrone (p. 118), Poivrons Verts Farcis (Stuffed Green Peppers; p. 223), Salade à la Romaine (p. 171), Tortoni (p. 720)

JUNE 12, 1977: "FOOD: THE CREPE CULT," BY CRAIG CLAIBORNE AND PIERRE FRANEY.

—1977

✒ LE CIRQUE'S SPAGHETTI PRIMAVERA

I see you rolling your eyes at the thought of spaghetti primavera. The dish, rarely seen now, became a cliché of 1980s "seasonal cooking," the raspberry coulis of its day. Meant to be an expression of spring, the mad jumble of vegetables over pasta was mostly an expression of the death match between French and Italian cuisine (cream versus olive oil, lots of sauce versus scant sauce).

But in the late 1970s, when New York's Le Cirque popularized spaghetti primavera, Craig Claiborne and Pierre Franey called it "by far, the most talked-about dish in Manhattan." It was also the most controversial, with at least three people laying claim to its creation. According to David Kamp, who attempted to get to the bottom of the issue in his excellent book *The United States of Arugula*, spaghetti primavera was the brainchild of either Ed Giobbi, an artist and cook, who prepared it for Sirio Maccioni, the owner of Le Cirque, and Jean Vergnes, the chef; Maccioni's wife, as Maccioni claimed in his memoir; or Vergnes, who doctored up Giobbi's version with French touches like cream and more vegetables. (Despite his claim to have invented it, Vergnes apparently hated the dish so much that he forced his cooks to prepare it in a hall outside the kitchen.)

It is probably the brainchild of all three cooks, as no recipe evolves in a vacuum. In Giobbi's book *Eat Right, Eat Well, the Italian Way*, he described his version: when Maccioni and Vergnes came to visit him before they opened Le Cirque, he served them what he called pasta primavera, but it was a dish much like Pamela Sherrid's Summer Pasta (p. 329): a union of ripe tomatoes, basil, parsley, garlic, and oil. He claims that that recipe, along with one additional ingredient—pine nuts—became part of Le Cirque's original menu. Over time, cream and other vegetables crept into the mix.

Regardless, the dish flourished, infiltrating the menu of every mediocre Italian restaurant in North America, until the pasta, as Giobbi put it, "looked as though it had been dragged through the vegetable garden." I encourage you to make the Le Cirque version—all twelve pain-in-the-neck steps of it—because, despite its tempestuous origins, it's wonderful.

———

1 bunch broccoli

2 small zucchini

4 asparagus spears, trimmed to 5 inches

1½ cups green beans, cut into 1-inch lengths

Salt

½ cup fresh or frozen peas

¾ cup snow peas

1 tablespoon peanut, vegetable, or corn oil

2 cups thinly sliced mushrooms

Freshly ground black pepper

1 teaspoon finely chopped hot red or green chile or about ½ teaspoon crushed red pepper flakes

¼ cup finely chopped flat-leaf parsley

6 tablespoons olive oil

1 teaspoon finely chopped garlic

3 cups ripe tomatoes cut into 1-inch cubes

6 fresh basil leaves, chopped (about ¼ cup), or about 1 teaspoon dried basil

1 pound spaghetti or spaghettini

4 tablespoons unsalted butter

2 tablespoons chicken broth

Approximately ½ cup heavy cream

⅔ cup freshly grated Parmesan cheese

⅓ cup toasted pine nuts

1. Trim the broccoli and break it into bite-sized florets.
2. Trim off the ends of the zucchini. Cut the zucchini into quarters. Cut each quarter into 1-inch or slightly longer lengths. There should be about 1½ cups, no more.
3. Cut each asparagus spear into thirds.
4. Cook each of the green vegetables separately in boiling salted water: the essential thing is to cook each so that it remains crisp but tender. The broccoli, zucchini, asparagus, and green beans should take about 2 to 3 minutes. Drain well in a colander, then run under cold water to chill, and drain again thoroughly. Combine the cooked vegetables in a bowl.
5. Then cook the peas and snow peas: about 1 minute if fresh, 30 seconds if frozen. Drain, chill under cold water, and drain again. Combine with the rest of the vegetables in the bowl.
6. Heat the peanut oil in a large skillet over medium-high heat and add the mushrooms. Add salt and pepper to taste, shaking the skillet and stirring, and cook for about 2 minutes. Add the mushrooms to the other vegetables. Add the chopped chile and parsley.
7. Heat 3 tablespoons olive oil in a saucepan. Add half the garlic, the tomatoes, and salt and pepper to taste and cook for about 4 minutes, stirring gently so as not to break up the tomatoes any more than necessary. Add the basil, stir, and set aside.
8. Add the remaining 3 tablespoons olive oil to a large skillet, along with the remaining garlic and the veg-

etable mixture. Cook, stirring gently, just long enough to heat through and soften the garlic.

9. Drop the spaghetti into boiling salted water and cook until almost but not quite tender; that is to say, al dente. The spaghetti must retain just a slight resilience in the center. Drain well. Return the spaghetti to the pot.

10. Select a pot large enough to hold the spaghetti and all the vegetables. To this, add the butter and melt over medium-low heat. Then add the chicken broth, ½ cup cream, and the cheese, stirring constantly. Cook gently, moving the pot on and off the heat, until smooth. Add the spaghetti and toss quickly to blend. Add half the vegetables and pour in the liquid from the tomatoes, tossing and stirring over very low heat.

11. Add the remaining vegetables and, if the sauce seems too dry, add 3 to 4 tablespoons more cream. The sauce should not be soupy. Add the pine nuts and give the mixture one final tossing.

12. Serve equal portions of the spaghetti in warmed bowls. Spoon equal amounts of the tomatoes over each serving.

SERVES 4 AS A MAIN COURSE,
8 AS A FIRST COURSE

COOKING NOTES
While this recipe uses broccoli, zucchini, asparagus, beans, and peas, you could mix in any spring vegetables you like—artichokes and ramps, for instance.

Don't settle for a mundane supermarket pasta. The spaghetti's flavor and texture are crucial to the dish— and after chopping all those vegetables, why cheap out on a primary ingredient? Try Rustichella d'Abruzzo, for instance.

Pasta is done when biting into it feels like biting into a fresh stick of gum—when it's firm but pliable.

SERVING SUGGESTIONS
Rhubarb Bellini (p. 30), Fried Olives (p. 87), Toasts with Walnut Sauce (p. 73), Hearth's Fava Bean Salad (p. 202), Puntarelle with Anchovies (p. 194), Angel Food Cake (p. 742), Strawberry Ice Cream (p. 722), Le Cirque's Crème Brûlée (p. 844)

READERS
". . . we still eagerly await the ripening of our home-grown tomatoes and fresh basil for the dish."

Judith Thomas, Nashville, TN, letter

OCTOBER 2, 1977: "SPAGHETTI WITH A FRENCH ACCENT," BY CRAIG CLAIBORNE WITH PIERRE FRANEY. RECIPE ADAPTED FROM LE CIRQUE IN NEW YORK CITY.

—1977

⌒ A PERFECT BATCH OF RICE

One part rice, one and a half parts liquid, cooked for 17 minutes in the oven. I've been using this formula for fifteen years and it has never failed.

———

3 tablespoons unsalted butter
½ cup finely chopped onion
2 cups long-grain white rice
Salt
Cayenne pepper or Tabasco sauce
3 cups chicken broth
A few parsley sprigs
1 bay leaf
1 sprig fresh thyme or ½ teaspoon dried thyme

1. Heat the oven to 400 degrees. Heat 2 tablespoons of the butter in an ovenproof saucepan. When it melts, add the finely chopped onion. Stir and cook until the onion wilts. Add the rice and stir until the grains are coated. Add salt to taste and a pinch of cayenne pepper (or a dash or two of Tabasco sauce).

2. Add the chicken broth. Make a bouquet garni with the parsley sprigs, bay leaf, and thyme; tie the bouquet garni with a string. Add to the rice and let the broth come to a boil.

3. Cover the pan and place it in the oven. Set a kitchen timer for 17 minutes.

4. Remove the pan from the oven and remove and discard the bouquet garni. Add the remaining 1 tablespoon butter and toss to blend.

SERVES 8 AS A SIDE DISH

COOKING NOTE
Craig Claiborne and Pierre Franey said this recipe can easily be halved, adding that, "The basic formula is 1 cup of rice for each 1½ cups of liquid."

For Saffron Rice, use 1 teaspoon loosely packed saffron threads. Crumble it, add it to the saucepan, and stir just before adding the rice.

For Cumin Rice, use 1 clove finely minced garlic and 1 teaspoon ground cumin. Add it to the saucepan and stir just before adding the rice.

SERVING SUGGESTIONS
Paul Prudhomme's Cajun-Style Gumbo (p. 125), James Beard's Chicken with 40 Cloves of Garlic (p. 469), Chicken à la Marengo (p. 453), Fricassee of Chicken with Tarragon (p. 456), Ed Giobbi's Rabbit Cacciatora (p. 461), Spicy, Garlicky Cashew Chicken (p. 494) Blanquette of Veal (p. 508), Choresh Qormeh Sabzi (Green Herb Stew; p. 533), White Veal Stew with Mushrooms, Corn, and Sherry (p. 553)

PERIOD DETAIL
Claiborne and Franey suggested serving the rice with "creamed dishes such as chicken, crab, shrimp, scallops, and so on."

MAY 28, 1978: "FOOD: PRECISE RICE," BY CRAIG CLAIBORNE WITH PIERRE FRANEY.

—1978

✐ PASTA WITH VODKA

You've probably never had a vodka pasta like this. Most are overwrought, jammed up with too much tomato and cream and lacking any indication of why they're called vodka pasta. This version realigns the components in a simple ratio of essentially equal parts vodka, tomatoes, cream, and cheese. Also, unconventionally, the recipe has you add the vodka at the beginning rather than the end.

Vodka pasta was born in Italy, according to Arthur Schwartz, the author of *Naples at Table* (and of the Spaghetti with Fried Eggs and Roasted Peppers on p. 339), where it was dreamed up as part of a vodka marketing campaign. But it only became a hit here. What Italians dismissed as gimmicky and expensive, Americans embraced as sophisticated.

The Italian version was made with hot pepper vodka, unavailable here at the time, so American recipes separated the alcohol and heat, calling for plain vodka and red pepper flakes. Which is just as well, because the spiciness is in your hands.

A slightly more complex version can be found on p. 320.

———

Salt
1½ pounds pasta, such as penne or ziti
7 tablespoons unsalted butter
½ teaspoon crushed red pepper flakes
¾ cup plus 2 tablespoons Polish or Russian vodka
1 cup canned Italian plum tomatoes
1 cup heavy cream
1 cup freshly grated Parmesan cheese

1. Bring a large pot of generously salted water to a boil. Add the pasta and cook until al dente.
2. Meanwhile, melt the butter in a casserole or saucepan large enough to hold the cooked pasta. Add the pepper flakes and vodka and bring to a boil. Reduce the heat and let simmer for 2 minutes.
3. Add the tomatoes and cream and bring to a boil. Let simmer for 5 minutes. Season with salt.
4. When the pasta is cooked, drain it and add it to the hot sauce. With the heat on low, add the cheese and mix thoroughly.

SERVES 6 AS A MAIN COURSE

COOKING NOTE
It's particularly important in a recipe this subtle to add enough salt to the pasta water (the water should taste salty) and to cook it to truly al dente.

SERVING SUGGESTIONS
Fried Olives (p. 87), Puntarelle with Anchovies (p. 194), Veal Chops with Sage (p. 564), Escarole with Pan-Roasted Garlic and Lemon (p. 248), Filbert Torte (p. 742), Balducci's Tiramisù (p. 830), Tortoni (p. 720)

DECEMBER 5, 1982: "FOOD: GOING BY THE BOOK," BY CRAIG CLAIBORNE WITH PIERRE FRANEY. RECIPE ADAPTED FROM *ITALIAN COOKING IN THE GRAND TRADITION*, BY JO BETTOJA AND ANNA MARIA CORNETTO.

—1982

❧ ED GIOBBI'S SWEET RED PEPPER SAUCE FOR PASTA

In 1984, with nouvelle cuisine in full career, red peppers, the riper version of green peppers, were *the* ingredient—there wasn't a salad or a coulis to be found without them in it. Nor, according to Craig Claiborne, could you avoid them at stores and markets. He might be surprised to know that red peppers have returned to the land of passé, replaced by Peppadews, piquillos, and pimientos de Padrón. But this sweet, quite spicy red pepper sauce deserves to live on.

---

3 very red unblemished sweet red peppers
    (about 1 pound or slightly more)
1 or 2 onions (about 1 pound)
¼ cup olive oil
1 tablespoon finely chopped garlic
¼ to ½ teaspoon crushed red pepper flakes
2 cups chicken broth
Salt and freshly ground black pepper
¼ cup finely chopped basil

1. Cut the peppers in half. Cut away and discard the cores, veins, and seeds. Coarsely chop the peppers. There should be about 4 cups. Coarsely chop the onion. There should be about 1 cup.
2. Heat the oil in a fairly large deep skillet or casserole and add the peppers. Cook, stirring, for about 5 minutes. Add the onions, garlic, and ¼ teaspoon red pepper flakes and cook, stirring often, for about 2 minutes. Add the broth and salt and pepper to taste. Cover, and cook for 15 minutes. (After 5 minutes, taste and see if you like the amount of heat—if you want more, add more red pepper flakes.)
3. Pour the mixture into the container of a food processor or blender, in batches if necessary, and blend thoroughly.
4. Pour the sauce into a saucepan and bring to a boil. Let reduce, if needed, to cook off the water and tighten the sauce a little. Stir in the basil.

MAKES 5 CUPS

COOKING NOTE
I served this sauce on angel hair pasta, which was superb. There's enough sauce for at least a pound of pasta, if not 2.

SERVING SUGGESTIONS
Crostini Romani (p. 77), Yettes Garden Platter (p. 220), Eggplant Involtini (p. 256), Cornmeal Biscotti (p. 696), Almond Granita (p. 731)

JUNE 17, 1984: "FOOD: A GROWING TASTE FOR SWEET RED PEPPERS," BY CRAIG CLAIBORNE WITH PIERRE FRANEY. ADAPTED FROM ED GIOBBI, A COOKBOOK AUTHOR AND ARTIST.

—1984

❧ SAFFRON RICE WITH PINE NUTS

⅓ cup pine nuts
2 tablespoons unsalted butter
⅓ cup finely chopped onion
½ teaspoon finely minced garlic
1 teaspoon loosely packed saffron threads
1 cup basmati rice
1½ cups chicken broth
Salt and freshly ground black pepper
2 tablespoons finely chopped flat-leaf parsley

1. Put the pine nuts in a skillet and cook them over medium-low heat, shaking the skillet and stirring so that the nuts cook evenly, until they are golden brown or slightly darker, about 2 minutes, depending on the intensity of the heat; do not overcook. Pour the nuts onto a cool surface.
2. Melt 1 tablespoon butter in a saucepan and add the onions. Cook briefly, then add the garlic and saffron. Stir and add the rice. Add the broth and salt and pepper to taste. Bring to a boil. Cover closely and let simmer for exactly 17 minutes.
3. Stir in the remaining tablespoon of butter and the parsley. Stir in the pine nuts.

SERVES 4 AS A SIDE DISH

SERVING SUGGESTIONS
Crab and Coconut Curry (p. 389), Bombay Curry (p. 452), Rabbit Soup with Garlic, Peppers, and Chorizo (p. 152), Madeleine Kamman's Apple Mousse (p.

816), Coconut Loaf Cake (p. 774), Revani Verrias (Semolina Cake; p. 788)

AUGUST 11, 1985: "FOOD; SPICING UP VERSATILE RICE," BY CRAIG CLAIBORNE WITH PIERRE FRANEY.

—1985

JEAN YVES LEGARVE'S SPAGHETTI WITH LEMON AND ASPARAGUS SAUCE

Like a lemon carbonara, the sauce on this pasta is delicate and creamy with a penetrating citrus fragrance. When you first combine the pasta and sauce, it will seem too loose; heating the sauce thickens it visibly. But take the sauce off the heat before it gets too tight, and don't be tempted to add more cheese, cream, or lemon. The proportions here are just right.

———

6 tablespoons unsalted butter

8 thick asparagus spears, stalks peeled and cut into 1-inch lengths

Grated zest and juice of 1 lemon

2 large eggs

¾ cup heavy cream

2 tablespoons freshly grated Parmesan cheese

4 gratings of nutmeg

3 tablespoons chopped flat-leaf parsley

Salt

½ pound spaghetti

Freshly ground black pepper

1. Melt the butter in a medium skillet over medium heat. Add the asparagus and cook until just tender, about 6 minutes.

2. Meanwhile, combine the lemon zest, half of the lemon juice, the eggs, cream, Parmesan cheese, nutmeg, and parsley in a bowl and blend well. Taste the sauce. The lemon flavor should be subtle, but not overpowering. Add more lemon juice if needed.

3. Bring a large pot of water to a rolling boil. Stir in enough salt that the water tastes salty. Add the spaghetti, stir, and cook, stirring often, until al dente, 5 to 7 minutes.

4. Drain the spaghetti well. Immediately return it to the pot, and add the asparagus, with the butter, and lemon sauce. Toss well.

5. Turn the heat to low and gently toss the pasta over the heat for about 30 seconds, until the sauce thickens slightly and adheres to the pasta. Season to taste with salt and pepper.

SERVES 2 AS A MAIN COURSE,
4 AS A FIRST COURSE

SERVING SUGGESTIONS
Hearth's Fava Bean Salad (p. 202), Roasted Salmon with Herb Vinaigrette (p. 430), Fried Radishes (p. 215), Rhubarb-Strawberry Mousse (p. 835), Macaroons (p. 681), Rhubarb Orange (p. 864)

NOVEMBER 9, 1986: "FOOD; GETTING AWAY FROM IT ALL," BY MICHELE EVANS. RECIPE ADAPTED FROM FASHION DESIGNER JEAN YVES LEGARVE.

—1986

MACARONI WITH HAM AND CHEESE

Entire cookbooks could be made of the macaroni and cheese recipes in the *New York Times* archives. They are numberless, going back to "Macaroni au Gratin" in 1904 and many claim to be the best. In the article accompanying this recipe, Pierre Franey admitted that the ham and mushrooms are unusual touches. But he was French, and we can cut him a little slack, particularly as his recipe is fantastic. I won't dare say it's *the* best, but it's certainly going to stay in my rotation.

———

Salt

½ pound macaroni (about 2 cups)

¾ pound sliced cooked ham (½-inch-thick)

⅓ pound mushrooms

½ pound sharp cheddar cheese

3 tablespoons unsalted butter

1 tablespoon all-purpose flour

2 cups whole milk

⅜ teaspoon freshly grated nutmeg

Freshly ground black pepper

½ cup finely chopped onion

⅛ teaspoon cayenne pepper, or more to taste

1 cup heavy cream

3 tablespoons freshly grated Parmesan cheese

1. Heat the oven to 425 degrees. Bring 3 quarts of water to a boil in a large pot. Add salt to taste. Add the macaroni and cook for 10 to 12 minutes, or until tender. Drain and return to the pot.

2. Meanwhile, cut the ham into ½-inch cubes. There should be about 2 cups. Set aside.

3. Slice the mushrooms. There should be about 2 cups. Set aside.

4. Cut the cheddar into slices about ¼ inch thick. Stack the slices and cut them into ¼-inch-wide strips. Cut the strips into ¼-inch cubes. There should be about 2 cups.

5. Melt 2 tablespoons butter in a medium saucepan over medium heat. Add the flour, stirring with a wire whisk, and cook for about a minute, then add the milk, whisking rapidly. Let simmer for about 1 minute, and add the nutmeg, cheddar cheese, and salt and black pepper to taste, whisking until smooth. Remove from the heat.

6. Melt the remaining tablespoon of butter in a skillet. Add the onion and mushrooms and cook, stirring, until the mushrooms are wilted, 5 to 7 minutes. Add the ham and cook, stirring, for about 1 minute. Add the cheese sauce, cayenne, and cream and cook, stirring, for about 1 minute. Taste, adding more cayenne if needed.

7. Add the macaroni to the sauce and mix well. Transfer to a buttered 3-quart baking dish. Sprinkle the top with the Parmesan cheese, and bake for 10 minutes.

8. Turn the broiler to high. Brown the macaroni and cheese under the broiler until the top is nicely browned, 2 to 3 minutes.

SERVES 6 AS A MAIN COURSE

SERVING SUGGESTIONS
Mezzaluna Salad (p. 185), Tangerine Sherbet (p. 734), Brownies (p. 684)

JANUARY 6, 1988: "60-MINUTE GOURMET," BY PIERRE FRANEY.

—1988

SPAGHETTINI WITH VEGETABLES AND PEPPER VODKA SAUCE

I've learned a lot about recipe writing from Pierre Franey, who collaborated with Craig Claiborne on a cooking column from 1974 to 1988 and then had his own column, "The 60-Minute Gourmet," from 1976 to 1993. Almost every one of his recipes that I've tried has been a hit. One reason is that Franey never left anything to chance. He didn't call for "a small bunch" of parsley or two "large" tomatoes; he gave you a weight and an additional measurement once the vegetable or fruit was chopped.

We tend to think of precise cooks as uninspired, but I believe Franey understood that by giving readers the means to re-create his dishes exactly, he could encourage them to later take his recipes in further interesting directions. Which you may want to do with this pasta dish, a cross between pasta primavera and penne alla vodka. You could replace the broccoli and snow peas with zucchini and young green beans, add ramps instead of garlic, etc.

Franey could have been a cook on a ship, because he assembled his recipes as if he had a foot of counter space and one burner. "I always reserve the poaching liquid from the vegetables and cook the pasta in it, which adds extra flavor," he wrote, noting, "A bit of the vegetable poaching liquid is set aside after the pasta goes in, to be used at the very end to bind the finished sauce." The flavors are layered and the whole thing is performed in a pot and a skillet. The sauce is light and brothy, rimmed with the perfume of basil and vodka.

———

1 bunch broccoli (about 1¼ pounds)

¼ pound snow peas

5 ripe plum tomatoes (about 1 pound)

Salt

¾ pound spaghettini

2 tablespoons olive oil

1 tablespoon finely chopped garlic

¼ pound sliced prosciutto, cut into ¼-inch-wide strips

⅛ teaspoon crushed red pepper flakes

⅓ cup Absolut pepper vodka

½ cup heavy cream

Freshly ground black pepper
½ cup freshly grated Pecorino Romano cheese
12 basil leaves, coarsely chopped
⅓ cup chopped chives

1. Cut the broccoli florets off the stem and cut them into bite-sized pieces. Peel away the stem's outer skin. Cut the stem into 1¼-inch lengths, then lengthwise into ½-inch-thick slices. There should be about 6 cups of stems and florets.
2. Trim the snow peas.
3. Core the tomatoes. To peel, drop the tomatoes into boiling water for 10 to 12 seconds; do not overcook. Drain immediately and peel. The skin should come off easily if you use a paring knife. Cut the tomatoes into ½-inch cubes. There should be about 2 cups.
4. Bring 3 quarts salted water to a boil in a large pot. Add the broccoli, bring to a simmer, and cook for 1 minute. Add the snow peas and bring to a boil. Cook for 2 minutes. Do not overcook; the vegetables must remain crisp. Drain, reserving the cooking liquid.
5. Bring the reserved cooking liquid to a boil in the same pot and add the spaghettini. Stir and cook until al dente. Drain, reserving ½ cup of the cooking liquid.
6. Heat the oil in a large skillet. Add the garlic and prosciutto and cook, stirring, briefly without browning. Add the tomatoes and red pepper flakes and cook, stirring, for 1 minute. Add the vodka, cream, and salt and pepper to taste, bring to a simmer, and cook for 1 minute.
7. Add the pasta to the skillet. Add the broccoli, snow peas, cheese, basil, chives, and reserved ½ cup cooking liquid, bring to a simmer, and toss well for 1 minute.

SERVES 4 AS A MAIN COURSE

COOKING NOTE
If you like spicy food, add a dash more red pepper flakes. Taste first before deciding.

SERVING SUGGESTIONS
Fried Artichokes Azzurro (p. 229), Fried Zucchini Blossoms (p. 243), Balducci's Tiramisù (p. 830)

JUNE 29, 1988: "60-MINUTE GOURMET," BY PIERRE FRANEY.

—1988

⌒ COUSCOUS SALAD

This well-crafted recipe is simple on the surface, intricate beneath. The cinnamon melds with the ginger and saffron to give the salad an unaccountable yet inviting boozy aroma. Use the best cinnamon you can find—I had some Saigon cinnamon, which I'd recommend for this and any other recipe that calls for the spice.

———

6 cups chicken broth
½ cup plus 1 tablespoon olive oil
½ teaspoon ground ginger
¼ teaspoon saffron threads
3 cups couscous
¾ cup currants
¾ cup dates, pitted and chopped
2¼ cups finely diced celery
1½ cups finely diced carrots
1 cup minced scallions
½ cup minced flat-leaf parsley
2 tablespoons plus 1 teaspoon fresh lemon juice
¾ teaspoon salt
½ teaspoon ground cinnamon
¾ cup toasted pine nuts

1. Bring the broth, 6 tablespoons oil, the ginger, and saffron to a boil in a large saucepan. Add the couscous and boil until the liquid begins to be absorbed. Remove from the heat and fold in the currants and dates. Cover and let stand for 15 minutes.
2. Add the celery, carrots, and scallions to the couscous. Mix well.
3. Combine the parsley, lemon juice, salt, cinnamon, and remaining 3 tablespoons olive oil in a small bowl. Toss well with the couscous, breaking up any clumps. Cover and refrigerate overnight.
4. Bring the couscous to room temperature. Adjust the seasoning and sprinkle with the pine nuts.

SERVES 16 AS A SIDE DISH

COOKING NOTES
Use Medjool dates if possible.
When it says to finely dice the celery and carrots, this really does mean fine, about ⅛ inch. That way,

the exterior of the vegetables will be softened by the steam but the interior will retain a little crunch.

This makes an enormous amount. You can easily halve the recipe.

SERVING SUGGESTIONS
Beet and Ginger Soup with Cucumber (p. 150), Steamed Fennel with Red Pepper Oil (p. 263), Veal Chops Beau Séjour (p. 520), Buttermilk Roast Chicken (p. 493), Lemon Bars (p. 690), Moroccan Rice Pudding (p. 848)

MAY 15, 1988: "SUMMER PASTIMES: AN AFTERNOON BY THE POOL," BY NANCY HARMON JENKINS.

—1988

HOT PENNE WITH CHILLED TOMATO SAUCE AND CHARRED TUNA

This recipe belongs to the family of uncooked tomato sauces that were wildly popular during the 1980s. Charred tuna was another popular dish of the time. I'd never seen the two combined, but this recipe came recommended by three readers, so I had to at least try it. I'm so glad I did: the addition of capers, olives, and balsamic vinegar give it the appealing punch of a salade Niçoise, and more complexity than the equally delicious Summer Pasta on p. 329.

———

4 large ripe tomatoes (about 3 ½ pounds), cored and quartered

3 cloves garlic

½ cup basil leaves

1 tablespoon capers, rinsed and patted dry

16 black Niçoise olives, pitted

½ cup plus 1 tablespoon extra virgin olive oil

3 tablespoons balsamic vinegar

3 strips lemon zest

Kosher salt and freshly ground black pepper

1 pound penne

One 12-ounce to 16-ounce fresh tuna steak

1. Place the tomatoes, garlic, basil, capers, olives, ½ cup olive oil, balsamic vinegar, lemon zest, and salt and pepper to taste in a food processor. Pulse on and off until roughly chopped. Pour the sauce into a bowl, cover, and refrigerate until ready to use.

2. Bring 4 quarts of water to a boil in a large pot and add 1 tablespoon salt, or to taste. Add the penne, stirring with a fork, and cook until al dente.

3. Meanwhile, place a cast-iron skillet over high heat and sprinkle the pan with 1 tablespoon salt. When the salt begins to sputter, add the tuna steak, sprinkle the top of the steak with more salt, and cook, turning once, until lightly charred, about 3 minutes per side. Transfer the tuna to a cutting board.

4. Drain the pasta and toss with the remaining tablespoon of olive oil. Divide the pasta among 4 shallow bowls. Slice the tuna into ¼-inch-thick slices and place over the pasta. Serve immediately.

SERVES 4 AS A MAIN COURSE

SERVING SUGGESTIONS
Ricotta Crostini with Fresh Thyme and Dried Oregano (p. 93), Fried Zucchini Blossoms (p. 243), Basic Corn Chowder (p. 149), Peach Salad (p. 805), Jean Halberstam's Deep-Fried Peaches (p. 860)

AUGUST 7, 1988: "FOOD: HOT TOMATOES," BY CHRISTOPHER IDONE.

—1988

RISOTTO WITH RADICCHIO AND SAUSAGE

Although risotto recipes have appeared regularly in the *Times* since 1942, no one seemed to notice them until the 1980s, when Americans suddenly became smitten with all things Italian. Bryan Miller, then the restaurant critic of the *Times*, declared that there was a "risotto craze" in New York restaurants that was beginning to spread across the country. Food crazes often lead to unfortunate dishes, and this craze was no exception. The River Café even served up a risotto with oysters and horseradish.

Risotto with radicchio and sausage, a recipe from the popular Manhattan restaurant Arqua, proved more lasting. Like most traditional Italian cooking, it's economical. With a cheap, filling ingredient like rice, a modest amount of meat—eight ounces—is stretched to serve eight. You mince the sausage and add it to the aromatics at the beginning of cooking, so its fat and flavor permeate the entire dish. Next you combine this rich, rib-sticking foundation with a wash of bitterness from the radicchio and endive: you add half of the radicchio in the beginning, letting it melt into the flavor base, and the rest at the end, allowing it to merely wilt.

Many people overcook risotto. You should take it off the heat just before the rice is cooked through. Like pasta, risotto is done when biting into it feels like biting into a stick of gum. Five minutes before the end of cooking, invite your family or guests to the table. If you wait until the risotto is finished to call them, it will be mush when you sit down.

---

6 tablespoons unsalted butter

¼ cup olive oil

2 sweet Italian sausages, preferably without fennel seeds (about 8 ounces), casings removed and minced

½ medium onion, chopped

Pinch of ground cloves

Pinch of freshly grated nutmeg

½ cup dry white wine

I large head endive, shredded

2 large heads radicchio, shredded

3 cups Arborio or Vialone Nano rice

8 to 10 cups chicken broth, heated until hot

Salt and freshly ground black pepper

¾ cup freshly grated Parmesan cheese

1. Melt 2 tablespoons butter with the olive oil in a large heavy saucepan over high heat. Add the sausage, onion, cloves, and nutmeg and cook for about 2 minutes, stirring constantly, until the onion wilts. Add the white wine and cook until the alcohol evaporates, about 2 minutes. Add the endive, stir well, and add half of the shredded radicchio. Stir well until the radicchio wilts.

2. Add the rice and stir to coat it thoroughly with the oil. Lower the heat to medium-low and start adding the chicken broth 1 cup at a time. Add the next cup only when the previous cup has been absorbed by the rice. It should take about 3 to 4 minutes for each cup to be absorbed, and this process should take 20 to 25 minutes. When the last cup of broth is absorbed, taste to see if the rice is cooked yet al dente. Add salt and pepper to taste.

3. Remove the pan from the heat. Add the remaining 4 tablespoons butter and remaining radicchio.

Blend well. Add the Parmesan and blend well. Serve immediately.

SERVES 8 AS A MAIN COURSE

COOKING NOTES

The recipe calls for sweet sausages without fennel seeds, but those can be hard to find, and I don't think the fennel makes a big difference.

Miller noted that many chefs prefer Vialone Nano rice over Arborio, for its more even cooking, but in the two decades since this article appeared, Arborio has won out. (I prefer Carnaroli, which maintains its texture best.)

The original recipe called for 8 cups of broth. I found mine needed 10 cups. This may vary, so be flexible on the amount of liquid.

SERVING SUGGESTIONS

Crostini Romani (p. 77), Fennel and Blood Orange Salad (p. 195), Tortoni (p. 720), Canestrelli (Shortbread from Ovada; p. 692)

JANUARY 11, 1989: "CHEFS SEARCH FOR THE PERFECT VERSION," BY BRYAN MILLER. RECIPE ADAPTED FROM LEONARDO PULITO, THE CHEF AT ARQUA IN NEW YORK CITY.

—1989

CATALAN VEGETABLE PAELLA

I have no idea what makes this Catalan ("imported" paprika?), but it's so good I'll take Perla Meyers's word for it. Meyers, who wrote about this paella for the Sunday *Magazine*, suggested serving it at room temperature, sprinkled with lemon juice and olive oil. That should be an instruction rather than a suggestion.

¼ cup olive oil, plus (optional) more for drizzling

I small green chile pepper, finely minced

I large Bermuda onion, quartered and thinly sliced

I large red bell pepper, cored, seeded, and thinly sliced

I large green bell pepper, cored, seeded, and thinly sliced

2 large cloves garlic, finely minced

I½ teaspoons Spanish paprika

I tablespoon thyme leaves

4 large ripe tomatoes, peeled (see Cooking Note, p. 146), cored, seeded, and chopped

Salt and freshly ground black pepper

1 medium zucchini, cut into ½-inch cubes

1¼ cups Arborio rice

2 cups low-sodium chicken broth

Finely minced flat-leaf parsley for garnish

Fresh lemon juice for serving (optional)

1. Heat the olive oil in a large deep cast-iron skillet over medium-high heat. Add the chile pepper, onion, and bell peppers, reduce the heat to medium-low, and cook for 20 minutes, or until the vegetables are tender and the onion is lightly browned.

2. Add the garlic, paprika, thyme, and tomatoes. Season generously with salt and pepper. Cover the skillet and simmer for 5 minutes.

3. Add the zucchini and simmer for 10 minutes more.

4. Stir in the rice and chicken broth and bring to a boil. Reduce the heat to medium-low, cover, and simmer for 20 to 25 minutes, or until the rice is tender. Taste and correct the seasoning. Garnish with minced parsley. Serve the paella hot, directly from the skillet, at room temperature, doused with lemon juice and a drizzle of olive oil.

SERVES 6 TO 8 AS A MAIN COURSE

SERVING SUGGESTIONS
Málaga Gazpacho (p. 112), Deep-Fried Soft-Shell Crabs (p. 398), Coffee Caramel Custard (p. 849), Almond Granita (p. 731)

JULY 30, 1989: "FOOD: SKILLET SKILLS," BY PERLA MEYERS.
—1989

⌒ ELDORADO PETIT'S FRIED NOODLES WITH GARLIC MAYONNAISE

This sublime noodle dish, which is made by toasting noodles in oil, braising them in fish broth, and then tossing with a garlic mayonnaise, appeared in an article on Catalan food by Patricia Wells. She appealed to readers to give Catalan cooking a chance, arguing that although the cuisine "is made up of just a dozen or so ingredients," she never felt bored. Spanish cuisine was just stepping onto the world stage: Colman Andrews

had published his groundbreaking book *Catalan Cuisine: Europe's Last Great Culinary Secret* in 1988, and the year this recipe appeared in the *Times* was the year El Bulli, under the direction of Ferran Adriá, gained its second Michelin star.

————

3 large fresh cloves garlic

¼ teaspoon salt

1 large egg yolk, at room temperature

½ cup plus 2 tablespoons extra virgin olive oil

½ pound fideos (or angel hair pasta, capellini, or vermicelli) broken into 2-inch lengths

2 cups fish or chicken broth

1. Peel the garlic and halve lengthwise, then remove and discard the green sprout-like germ.

2. Pour hot tap water into a mortar to warm it. Discard the water and dry the mortar. Place the garlic and salt in the mortar and mash together evenly with a pestle to form a very smooth paste. (At this point, you can transfer the mixture to a bowl and whisk in the remaining ingredients.) Add the egg yolk. Stir, pressing slowly and evenly with the pestle, to thoroughly blend the garlic and yolk. Very slowly work about 2 tablespoons oil into the yolk, drop by drop, until the mixture is thick and smooth. Gradually whisk in 6 more tablespoons oil in a slow, thin stream until the sauce is thickened to a mayonnaise consistency.

3. Position a rack in the center of the oven and heat the oven to 350 degrees. Toss the pasta with the remaining 2 tablespoons oil in a large bowl. Spread evenly on a nonstick baking sheet. Bake, shaking the pan from time to time, until golden brown, 5 to 7 minutes; do not allow the pasta to burn. Remove from the oven.

4. Bring the broth to a boil in a large saucepan over high heat. Add the browned noodles, stir well, and cook over medium heat until most of the liquid is absorbed, about 10 minutes.

5. Stir in several tablespoons of the garlic mayonnaise. Serve immediately, passing the remaining mayonnaise.

SERVES 4 AS A SIDE DISH

COOKING NOTE
Garlic mayonnaise (aioli) is easy to make and easy to ruin. Garlic, if not fresh, can add a bitter edge to the

sauce, as can cheap olive oil. If you don't have great olive oil, hedge your bets by using half olive oil, half canola or vegetable oil. And if your garlic isn't fresh and juicy, use less of it.

SERVING SUGGESTIONS

Patricia Wells noted that the noodles should be served with fish or steamed clams. So, how about Sautéed Cod with Potatoes in Chorizo-Mussel Broth (skip the potatoes; p. 428)? Begin with Potato, Ham, and Piquillo Pepper Croquetas (p. 94) or Raw Artichoke Salad with Cucumber (p. 173), and end with Chocolate Caramel Tart (p. 847).

PERIOD DETAIL

A 1949 headline read: "New Vermicelli: Cooks in 2 minutes; 'Hair of an Angel,' Italians call it."

MAY 13, 1990: "SPAIN: A CATALAN OLÉ," BY PATRICIA WELLS. RECIPE ADAPTED FROM JEAN-LUC FIGUERAS, THE CHEF AT ELDORADO PETIT IN BARCELONA.

—1990

∽ ORZO WITH PINE NUTS AND BASIL

This can be served warm or at room temperature. Either way, don't add the basil until just before you carry it to the table.

———

1½ cups orzo
1 cup pine nuts
Salt and freshly ground black pepper
2 tablespoons olive oil
⅔ cup tightly packed basil leaves

1. Bring 3 quarts of salted water to a boil in a large pot. Add the orzo and cook until it is just tender, 6 to 8 minutes. Drain thoroughly.
2. Meanwhile, place the pine nuts in a large dry skillet and cook, stirring, over medium heat for about 5 minutes, until lightly browned. Remove from the heat.
3. Mix the toasted pine nuts with the orzo in a bowl, season with salt and pepper, and toss with the olive oil.
4. Just before serving, finely chop the basil and fold it into the orzo.

SERVES 6 TO 8 AS A SIDE DISH

SERVING SUGGESTIONS

Poivrons Verts Farcis (Stuffed Green Peppers; p. 223), Baked Zucchini with Herbs and Tomatoes (p. 250), Crab Cakes Baltimore-Style (p. 407), Lobster Roll (p. 368), Butterscotch Pudding (p. 851), Fresh Raspberry (or Blackberry or Blueberry) Flummery (p. 824)

PERIOD DETAIL

The recipe included this note, invoking that staple of late 1980s cooking, the dreaded timbale: "For more formal service, the finished orzo can be packed tightly in 4-ounce cups or ramekins and unmolded onto each plate."

JUNE 3, 1990: "THE GREAT OUTDOORS: SETTINGS FOR AN ALL-OCCASION MENU," BY FLORENCE FABRICANT.

—1990

∽ CONCHIGLIE AL FORNO WITH MUSHROOMS AND RADICCHIO

George Germon and Johanne Killeen, the owners of Al Forno in Providence, Rhode Island, are often credited with introducing Americans to pasta as it's prepared in Italy. Not that there's anything wrong with Italian-American dishes like spaghetti and meatballs or lasagna (see p. 342), but before 1980, when Al Forno opened, "Italian" pastas were dishes created and popularized by immigrants who lacked the raw materials of their homeland. They made do with inferior tomatoes, ground meats, and a dearth of vegetables.

At Al Forno, they did things differently. Pastas contained just enough sauce to coat the noodles, cheese was used judiciously, unfamiliar shapes like pappardelle and penne rigate were added to a landscape of ziti and linguine. This is not to say that Al Forno claimed to be authentic. As with most imported cuisines, the food at the restaurant was (and still is) interpretive, and it bears the stamp of Germon and Killeen, who loved their wood-fired oven and created a menu around it.

Carol Kramer and Lori Longbotham, who wrote about this recipe, pointed out that baked pastas go back at least to the days of Pope Pius V, who relished his favorite *timpano*, a mammoth layered and baked pasta dish that contained pasta, prosciutto, mozzarella, the "meat of a young heifer," and white truffle. Even until relatively recently in Italy, baked pastas were reserved for the rich, the only ones who had ovens in their home kitchens.

In America, by contrast, baked pastas were often just a way to repurpose leftovers. So Germon and Killeen's highly calibrated technique marked a genuine departure. Here the pasta is half cooked in heavily salted water, then blended with sliced radicchio, sautéed mushrooms, cheeses, and a shocking amount of cream. Don't skimp on the cream; they've calculated its measurement precisely. The pasta is then baked at 450 degrees, and the cream and cheese form a loose sauce that's pungent with cheese and yet not gooey. The mushrooms contribute nuttiness to the dish and the radicchio a note of bitterness. But the key detail is in the top layer. The high heat of the oven browns and toasts the tips of the pasta, giving it the flavor of a gratin and the crunch of a perfect potato chip.

———

Salt

6 ounces shiitake mushrooms (about 18 medium), cleaned

8 tablespoons (1 stick) unsalted butter

1 pound imported conchiglie rigate (ridged pasta shells)

1 tablespoon olive oil (optional)

2½ cups heavy cream

2 small heads radicchio, cored and finely shredded (about ½ inch wide)

½ cup freshly grated Parmesan cheese

½ cup shredded Bel Paese cheese

½ cup crumbled Gorgonzola

Coarse salt

6 sage leaves (optional)

1. Heat the oven to 450 degrees. Bring a large pot of generously salted water to a boil.

2. Remove the stems from the mushrooms and discard. Slice the mushroom caps ¼ inch thick. Melt 6 tablespoons butter in a medium skillet over medium heat. Add the mushrooms and cook, stirring frequently, for 3 to 4 minutes, until they are softened. Remove from the heat.

3. Add the pasta to the boiling water and cook for 5 minutes. Add the olive oil, if desired, to keep the pasta from sticking together. Drain the pasta. Run cold water over it to stop the cooking process, then drain again.

4. Combine the cream, shredded radicchio, Parmesan, Bel Paese, Gorgonzola, and mushrooms in a large bowl. Add the pasta and toss. Stir in salt to taste and the sage leaves, if desired.

5. Butter a glass or earthenware baking dish, about 13 by 9 by 2 inches. Transfer the pasta mixture to the dish. Dot with the remaining 2 tablespoons butter.

6. Bake for 30 to 35 minutes, until the pasta is bubbly and crusty brown on top. Let stand for 5 minutes before serving.

SERVES 6 AS A MAIN COURSE,
10 AS A FIRST COURSE

COOKING NOTE

Of the optional ingredients, I would not add the oil to the water. This is an old cooking myth: the oil does not prevent the pasta from sticking—it just makes a mess of your pot. But don't skip the sage, which adds dimension and a musky aroma to the dish.

SERVING SUGGESTIONS

Bagna Cauda (p. 58), Diane Forley's Arugula Salad with Artichoke, Ricotta Salata, and Pumpkin Seeds (p. 188), Mezzaluna Salad (p. 185), Pine Nut Cookies (p. 689), Zabaglione (p. 813), Olive Oil and Apple Cider Cake (p. 771), Bolzano Apple Cake (p. 783)

PERIOD DETAIL

The first appearance of Parmesan cheese in the *Times* was in 1866; the first for Parmigiano-Reggiano was in 1985 in a recipe for pumpkin risotto by Nancy Harmon Jenkins. Al Forno wasn't mentioned until 1987.

SEPTEMBER 16, 1990: "PASTA'S PAST," BY CAROL KRAMER AND LORI LONGBOTHAM. RECIPE ADAPTED FROM GEORGE GERMON AND JOHANNE KILLEEN, THE OWNERS OF AL FORNO IN PROVIDENCE, RHODE ISLAND.

—1990

BARLEY RISOTTO

In 1990, America was on the brink of recession and home cooking was on the upswing. Molly O'Neill claimed that the 1990s would be "*the Epoque de la Maison.*" And home cooking wasn't the meat and potatoes of yore, but something more "organic" and "politically correct." She even used the emergent term "whole foods." Nearly twenty years later, the terms have evolved a bit—"politically correct" is now "sustainable," "organic" is more legal and detailed in meaning, and Whole Foods has become a household brand name. And we're still at it, still searching for the perfect feel-good way to feed ourselves. This barley risotto feels *and* tastes good.

I carrot, cut into 4 pieces, plus 3 tablespoons minced carrots

I stalk celery, cut into 4 pieces, plus 3 tablespoons minced celery

I onion, halved, plus 3 tablespoons minced onions

I clove garlic, mashed

5 sprigs parsley

I teaspoon peppercorns

5½ cups water

½ cup barley

I teaspoon canola oil

I small sprig rosemary

I bay leaf

I teaspoon salt

¼ teaspoon freshly ground black pepper

1. Combine the carrot and celery pieces, halved onion, garlic, parsley sprigs, peppercorns, and water in a medium saucepan, bring to a simmer, and simmer, uncovered, for 1 hour. Strain the broth and set aside.
2. Toast the barley in a heavy skillet over low heat, shaking the pan frequently and adjusting the heat as necessary, for 20 minutes, or until the barley turns light brown and smells nutty. Remove from the heat and set aside.
3. Heat the oil in a large heavy skillet over medium-low heat. Add the minced carrots, onions, and celery and cook, stirring, for 3 minutes, or until the onions are soft and translucent. Add the barley and stir to coat the grains. Add the rosemary, bay leaf, 1½ cups

of the reserved vegetable broth, the salt and pepper, bring to a simmer, and simmer, covered, until the barley is tender and the liquid is absorbed, about 35 minutes; add more broth if the risotto is too dry (reserve any remaining broth for another use).

SERVES 2 AS A MAIN COURSE, 6 AS A FIRST COURSE

SERVING SUGGESTIONS
Roast Quail with Sage Dressing (p. 453), Spoon Lamb (p. 546), Stewed Fennel (p. 245), Fresh Mushrooms Stewed with Madeira (p. 214), Cumin-Mustard Carrots (p. 237), Poached Pears in Brandy and Red Wine (p. 832)

DECEMBER 30, 1990: "FOOD: WHAT'S COMING UP," BY MOLLY O'NEILL. RECIPE ADAPTED FROM LUMA IN NEW YORK CITY.

—1990

FRESH MOREL, ASPARAGUS, AND SWEET PEA RISOTTO

This year was the peak moment for vegetable risottos, and this recipe is the consummate example: creamy rice inflected with spring.

---

6 thick asparagus spears

4 tablespoons unsalted butter

6 ounces morel or cremini mushrooms, trimmed and cut into bite-sized pieces

2¼ teaspoons kosher salt

Freshly ground black pepper

6 to 8 cups chicken broth

2 tablespoons extra virgin olive oil

4 shallots, minced

2 cloves garlic, minced

I pound Arborio rice

½ cup dry white wine

¼ cup cooked tiny peas

3 tablespoons minced chives

¼ cup chervil leaves

1. Cook the asparagus in boiling salted water until tender, about 4 minutes. Drain and refresh under cold

running water to stop the cooking. Cut diagonally into ¼-inch-thick slices and set aside.

2. Melt 1 tablespoon butter in a medium skillet over medium heat. Add the mushrooms and sauté until soft, about 10 minutes. Season with ⅛ teaspoon salt and pepper to taste, and set aside.

3. Bring the broth to a boil in a medium saucepan; reduce the heat and keep at a low simmer.

4. Meanwhile, melt 2 tablespoons butter with the olive oil in a large saucepan over medium-low heat. Add the shallots and garlic and sauté until soft, about 5 minutes. Stir in the rice with a wooden spoon, turning to coat well. Cook, stirring constantly, for 4 minutes. Stir in the wine, raise the heat to medium, and cook until the wine is absorbed, about 1 minute.

5. Begin adding the broth ½ cup at a time, stirring constantly and adding more broth as it is absorbed by the rice. Adjust the heat so the rice and broth cook at a steady simmer. After about 15 minutes, the rice should be somewhat tender, and there should be some broth left. Cook for another few minutes, adding more broth as needed, until the rice is al dente.

6. Stir in the asparagus, mushrooms, peas, chives, and the remaining tablespoon of butter. Season with salt and pepper if needed.

7. Divide among 6 shallow bowls and garnish with the chervil.

**SERVES 6 AS A MAIN COURSE,
8 AS A FIRST COURSE**

COOKING NOTES
My fresh peas were uncommonly large and plump, so I used ⅓ cup rather than ¼ cup.

I couldn't find chervil, but the dish was still delicious. You can substitute tarragon for chervil, but use half the amount, and chop it.

If fresh morels are difficult to come by, you may also use ¾ ounce dried. Soak them in warm water for 20 minutes, then drain well and roughly chop.

SERVING SUGGESTIONS
Rhubarb Bellini (p. 30), Fish Poached in Buttermilk (p. 419), Elizabeth Frink's Roast Lemon Chicken (p. 478), Chiffonade Salad (p. 173), Marjolaine (Multilayered Chocolate and Praline Cake; p. 766), Fontainebleau (p. 829), Rhubarb Orange (p. 864)

MARCH 12, 1995: "AN EDIBLE COMPLEX," BY MOLLY O'NEILL. RECIPE ADAPTED FROM ALFRED PORTALE, THE CHEF AND OWNER OF GOTHAM BAR AND GRILL IN NEW YORK CITY.

—1995

⌣ CORN AND YELLOW TOMATO RISOTTO WITH SHRIMP

5 to 6 cups vegetable or chicken broth
2 teaspoons olive oil
½ cup chopped onion
1 cup Arborio rice
½ cup dry vermouth
Salt
½ pound ripe tomatoes, preferably yellow
10 ounces cooked shrimp, cut in half
2 cups corn (from 3 ears)
¼ cup chopped basil
½ cup plus 2 tablespoons coarsely grated Parmesan cheese, plus more for serving
Freshly ground black pepper

1. Bring the broth to a simmer in a medium saucepan; keep at a low simmer.

2. Heat the oil in a nonstick pot. Add the onion and sauté until it takes on a little color. Add the rice, stirring until it is well coated and lightly toasted. Stir in the vermouth and cook until it has evaporated, a couple of minutes.

3. Add about a cup of the broth and cook over medium-high heat, stirring often, until the liquid has been absorbed (if it becomes difficult to manage, turn the heat down to medium). Repeat until the rice is tender but firm, seasoning with salt as you go.

4. While the rice simmers, core and coarsely chop the tomatoes. About 2 minutes before the rice is done, add the shrimp, corn kernels, tomatoes, and basil and stir well. (You may not need to add all of the broth.)

5. Stir the cheese into the risotto. Season with salt and pepper. Serve, passing more cheese at the table.

SERVES 3

COOKING NOTE
It's better to buy raw shrimp and half-cook it yourself in the simmering broth (it will finish cooking later in

the risotto). This way, you can control exactly how long it's cooked, and the shrimp infuses extra flavor in the broth.

SERVING SUGGESTIONS
Fried Zucchini Blossoms (p. 243), Jean-Georges Vongerichten's Crab Salad (p. 415), Baked Zucchini with Herbs and Tomatoes (p. 250), Cold Nicarde (Yellow Squash Soup; p. 110), Fresh Raspberry (or Blackberry or Blueberry) Flummery (p. 824), Raspberry Granita (p. 719), Summer Pudding (p. 847)

SEPTEMBER 13, 1995: "PLAIN AND SIMPLE; A RISOTTO DISH GAINS BRIGHT ACCENTS WITH YELLOW TOMATOES," BY MARIAN BURROS.

—1995

FARFALLE AI PORRI E SALSICCE (FARFALLE WITH LEEKS AND SAUSAGES SAUCE)

This is one of two recipes recommended by readers that come from product ads within the paper (the Allegretti Chiffon Cake on p. 746 is the other). The recipe is from Lidia Bastianich, an owner of Felidia in Manhattan and the author of many cookbooks.

Many of the best pasta dishes are scraped together from a few forlorn ingredients. Here a small lump of sausage fattens up shallots, leeks, and peas. Chicken broth stretches the meager sauce. Add a little farfalle, and you have a perfectly tempered dish.

———

2 large leeks
2 tablespoons olive oil
2 sweet Italian sausages, casings removed
1 teaspoon minced shallot
1 tablespoon unsalted butter
1 cup young peas, blanched in boiling water
    until just tender, 2 to 3 minutes
1 cup chicken broth
Salt and freshly ground black pepper
1 pound farfalle (bow-tie pasta)
½ cup freshly grated Parmesan cheese,
    plus more for serving

1. Bring a large pot of salted water to a boil. Meanwhile, trim the leeks, discarding the top one-third of the rough green portion, and slice into ½-inch rounds. Rinse in several changes of cold water to remove all soil and grit; drain well.

2. Heat the olive oil in a large skillet over medium-high heat. Add the leeks and sausages and sauté for about 5 minutes. Add the shallot and cook, stirring, for 1 minute. Add the butter, peas, and broth and simmer gently for 5 minutes. Season to taste with salt and pepper, and keep warm over low heat.

3. Add the farfalle to boiling water and cook, stirring occasionally, until al dente. Drain well and return to the pot.

4. Add the sauce to the pasta and toss well to coat. Add the cheese and toss well. Serve with additional cheese on the side.

SERVES 4 AS A MAIN COURSE

SERVING SUGGESTIONS
Fried Olives (p. 87), Bagna Cauda (p. 58), Toasts with Walnut Sauce (p. 73), Wallace Seawell's Spinach Salad (p. 180), Pistachio Cream (p. 806), Apple Galette (p. 843)

FEBRUARY 25, 1996: "PASTA FOR PRIMAVERA"—A DISPLAY AD.

—1996

PAMELA SHERRID'S SUMMER PASTA

It took us a long time to arrive at cacio e pepe and spaghetti with crab and sea urchin. In the Dark Ages of pasta, we understood it to be a small and inconsequential category, containing only lasagna and spaghetti and meatballs. Then came the false spring of pasta salads. Remember those? Those efficient '70s dishes that combined pasta—cooked ahead of time! served cold!—and exotica like broccoli, pine nuts, and sun-dried tomatoes? Eaten straight from the fridge, you got both that chilled gumminess and the wan crunch of broccoli.

Then, when we were discovering Italy in the '80s and early '90s—just before Mario Batali thoroughly reprogrammed the Italian section of our brains around 1998—the *Times* published a number of recipes for pasta with room-temperature tomato sauce. (Hot Penne with Chilled Tomato Sauce and Charred Tuna, an early example, can be found on p. 322.) They were a revelation akin to the discovery by women in the 1930s that they could wear pants. After years of thinking that all pasta sauces were long-simmered affairs, cooks were relieved to learn that they could simply chop a few tomatoes, add some seasonings and hot pasta, and—voilà!—dinner.

Pamela Sherrid's summer pasta is a quintessential crossover dish: part tomatoes and warm pasta, part pasta salad. It includes ripe summer tomatoes, garlic, olive oil, basil, and cubes of fresh mozzarella. Her recipe relies on prudent technique and a slacker's sense of pace. First you combine the garlic, basil, and oil and let the mixture marinate. Many hours later, you add tomatoes and let it sit some more. Next, you pour the cooked rigatoni over the tomatoes, scatter the cubes of mozzarella over the rigatoni, and gently mix the cheese into the pasta, coating it with a buttery veil of fat, before tossing it with the tomatoes at the bottom. If you have great tomatoes and mozzarella and you don't overcook the pasta, it is a remarkably good dish. A puddle of sweet and salty tomato broth will form at the bottom of your bowl, so be sure to have some bread on hand to soak it up.

———

5 large cloves garlic

½ to ¾ cup olive oil

12 or more basil leaves

6 to 8 large ripe tomatoes

Salt

1 pound rigatoni

1 pound mozzarella, packaged or fresh

Country bread for serving

1. Take out your largest bowl. Cut into the bottom of it 5 cloves of nice, fat, juicy garlic. Pour over that ½ to ¾ of a cup of your favorite olive oil. (Start with half a cup and add the rest later if you think you need it.) With scissors, snip a dozen or more basil leaves into shreds over the bowl. Let this sit all day. The aroma in your kitchen will be as tantalizing as it is when you're grilling steaks.

2. About 2 hours before dinner, chop 6 to 8 large ripe tomatoes into the bowl.

3. When you're ready to eat, boil enough salted water to cook a pound of rigatoni. Add the pasta. While it is cooking (and you'll naturally want it to be al dente),

cut 1 pound of mozzarella into cubes. In this instance, I actually prefer packaged to fresh, but if you use fresh, add salt (maybe a teaspoon) to the mixture of oil, basil, and garlic.

4. Now, here's where you must follow directions: Drain the pasta. Pour it on top of the tomato, garlic, basil, and oil mixture. Do not stir. Toss the cubed cheese onto the hot pasta and toss only the pasta and cheese, so the hot pasta melts the cheese. When all the cheese is melted, stir up from the bottom.

5. Serve with bread to mop up the olive oil. This pasta is delicious when you make it and even better the next day, when the ingredients have had longer to marinate.

SERVES 4 AS A MAIN COURSE,
6 AS A FIRST COURSE

COOKING NOTES

Set out the mozzarella in advance so it can warm to room temperature.

Tear the basil rather than cut it; chop the tomatoes however you want; and use any stubby tube-shaped pasta you like.

You should eat this as soon as the rigatoni is cooked.

Supermarket tomatoes don't have enough flavor or juice to make the dish sparkle, so unless you can get great local tomatoes, skip this one.

Cook the rigatoni in water that contains enough sea salt to taste salty. The pasta is done when it feels like biting into a piece of gum—you want some resistance when you eat it.

SERVING SUGGESTIONS

Fried Zucchini Blossoms (p. 243), Eggplant Involtini (p. 256), Roasted Salmon with Herb Vinaigrette (p. 430), Brine-Cured Pork Chops (p. 569), Zucchini with Crème Fraîche Pesto (p. 250), Italian Roast Potatoes (p. 300), Summer Pudding (p. 847)

MAY 26, 1996: "FEASTS ALFRESCO," BY FRAN SCHUMER. RECIPE BY PAMELA SHERRID.

—1996

TRENETTE, FAGIOLINI, E PATATE AL PESTO (PASTA, GREEN BEANS, AND POTATOES WITH PESTO)

On the September day in 1997 when this recipe appeared, the *Times*'s food coverage had gone through a major transformation. Until then, food stories had been sprinkled throughout the Living section, which also featured fashion and home stories. Those sections were now divided into stand-alone sections. Dining In/Dining Out was essentially a weekly food magazine containing everything from short briefs about restaurant openings and new products to long features and restaurant reviews. The paper also switched to color that week, illuminating pages that for more than 130 years had been in dim black and white. An apple turnover looks luscious in color; in black and white, it is easily mistaken for an old baseball mitt.

The story that featured this recipe was the cover story in the Dining section's debut and was itself groundbreaking, because it once and for all demystified the cooking of pasta.

"We all know what pasta al dente means, or think we do," Nancy Harmon Jenkins wrote. "It's pasta that is tender through and through but that still retains a pleasant, slightly chewy texture." You can see when it's cooked correctly by cutting into a piece of the pasta, she said. Jenkins added, "It will appear cooked through, except for a white ghost, a tiny spot of not-quite-rawness, at the center of the strand," what is called by some "the anima, the soul of the pasta."

Jenkins also noted, "The point of the dish is not the sauce but the pasta. Like butter on bread, the sauce is there simply as a counterpoint. There should be sufficient sauce to lightly coat each strand of pasta and no more—no puddles of sauce congealing in the bottom of the dish, no oily emulsions from the corkscrews of pasta. In Italian, the word for sauce, *salsa*, is rarely used with pasta. Instead, Italians speak of the *condimento*, the condiment, that dresses the dish."

---

2 cups packed tender young basil leaves
¼ cup pine nuts
1 teaspoon salt
2 plump cloves garlic, crushed
½ cup extra virgin olive oil, or more to taste
½ cup freshly grated Parmesan cheese, or more to taste
Salt
½ pound small potatoes, peeled and sliced about ¼ inch thick
¼ pound tender young green beans, cut into 1-inch lengths
1 pound trenette or other long thin pasta

1. Add the basil, pine nuts, salt, and garlic to a food processor and pulse until the mixture is coarse and grainy. With the motor running, add the oil in a slow, steady stream. Add the cheese; process just enough to mix well. If the sauce is too dry, add a little more oil. Taste and add more cheese and or salt, if desired.
2. Bring 6 quarts of water to a rolling boil. Add at least 2 tablespoons salt and the potato slices. Cook for about 3 minutes, or until the potatoes have started to soften but are not cooked through. Add the green beans and continue boiling for another 2 minutes.
3. Add the pasta, and stir. Start testing the pasta at 8 minutes. When it's done, and the potatoes and beans are tender, drain (reserve about ¾ cup pasta water and then add as needed) and immediately turn the pasta and vegetables into a heated bowl. Add the pesto and mix thoroughly. Add cheese as needed.

SERVES 8 AS A FIRST COURSE

SERVING SUGGESTIONS
Vitello Tonnato (p. 559), Squashed Tomatoes (p. 90), Panna Cotta (p. 840), Fruit Crostatas (p. 855)

SEPTEMBER 17, 1997: "FROM ITALY, THE TRUTH ABOUT PASTA," BY NANCY HARMON JENKINS.

—1997

CUCUMBER RISOTTO WITH YELLOW PEPPERS AND HERBS

Other than the rice and the slow addition of liquid, this lean and not-so-mean risotto isn't very Italian. In place of broth, you use cucumber juice to cook the rice, which keeps the dish disarmingly light. And the dish is seasoned with shallots, yellow pepper, jalapeño, lime, and coriander.

---

3 yellow bell peppers

10 large cucumbers, peeled and cut into 1-inch chunks

4 to 6 jalapeño peppers

2 tablespoons extra virgin olive oil

1 tablespoon minced shallot

1 teaspoon kosher salt

1/8 teaspoon freshly ground black pepper

1 3/4 cups Arborio rice

1 cup dry white wine

2 tablespoons unsalted butter

3/4 cup chopped cilantro

1 tablespoon fresh lime juice

1. Heat the broiler. Place the bell peppers on the broiler rack, 2 to 3 inches from the heating element, and roast, turning occasionally, until the skin bubbles and blackens. Let cool, then peel, core, and seed the peppers. Cut into 1/2-inch dice. Reserve.

2. Using a food processor or blender, process the cucumbers to a smooth puree, about 3 minutes. Do this in batches if necessary. Strain the puree through a fine-mesh strainer into a large bowl, stirring and pressing on the puree to extract as much juice as possible. Measure 6 cups cucumber juice; supplement with water if needed.

3. Place the juice in a medium saucepan and bring to a boil, then remove from the heat and reserve.

4. Halve, seed, and mince the jalapeños. Heat the olive oil in a 3-quart saucepan over medium-high heat. Add the jalapeños and sauté for 2 minutes. Remove the peppers with a slotted spoon and reserve. Add the shallots, salt, and pepper to the saucepan and sauté for 2 minutes, or until the shallots are soft.

5. Add the rice and stir for about 2 minutes. Lower the heat to medium, add the wine, and stir until the wine is absorbed. Begin adding the cucumber juice 1/2 cup at a time, stirring constantly. Allow each addition of juice to be absorbed before adding more. Continue until the risotto is creamy and the rice grains are al dente, 25 to 30 minutes.

6. Stir in the jalapeños, bell peppers, and butter. Season to taste with salt and pepper, and stir in the cilantro and lime juice, and serve immediately.

SERVES 6 AS A FIRST COURSE

COOKING NOTE

When mincing the chiles, wear rubber or latex gloves, if possible, to avoid burning your fingers—burns from peppers are no more fun than burns from the oven.

SERVING SUGGESTIONS

Spicy, Garlicky Cashew Chicken (p. 494), Seared Tuna in Black Pepper Crust (p. 409), Ice-Cold Tomatoes with Basil (p. 234), Peach Salad (p. 805)

SEPTEMBER 24, 1997: "THE CHEF: MICHAEL ROMANO," BY AMANDA HESSER. RECIPE ADAPTED FROM MICHAEL ROMANO, THE CHEF AT UNION SQUARE CAFE IN NEW YORK CITY.

—1997

⌐ PASTA WITH BONES

This is a great reminder of how little effort it takes to prepare a succulent and concentrated meat sauce—even with only a scrap of meat. It can be difficult to track down a veal shank, but do make the effort. Veal shanks have just the right fat content and the teaspoon or so of marrow that you scoop out and stir into the sauce at the end makes itself felt.

I was skeptical about Mark Bittman's insistence that a sauce like this doesn't need cheese. He's right, though. Cheese would make the dish too fatty and would take away from the sweet-tart quality of the cooked-down tomatoes.

———

1 piece meaty veal shank (1/2 to 1 pound)

1/4 cup olive oil

2 small dried hot red chiles (optional)

3 cloves garlic, roughly chopped

Salt and freshly ground black pepper

One 28-ounce can plum tomatoes, with their juice

1 pound ziti, penne, or other cut pasta

1/2 cup or more roughly chopped flat-leaf parsley or basil

1. Place 2 tablespoons olive oil in a small heavy sauté pan over medium-high heat. Add the veal shank and cook, turning as necessary, until the meat is nicely browned, 10 minutes or more. Remove the meat to a plate.

2. Heat the remaining 2 tablespoons olive oil in a medium saucepan. After a minute, add the chiles, if using, and cook for about 30 seconds. Add the veal,

garlic, and salt and pepper to taste. When the garlic has softened a bit, crush the tomatoes and add them, with their juice. Turn the heat to medium-low to maintain a steady simmer. If you are using a broad pan, partially cover it. Cook, stirring occasionally, until the meat is tender and just about falling off the bone, at least 1 hour.

3. Bring a large pot of water to a boil and salt it. Cook the pasta until it is tender but firm. Meanwhile, remove the veal shank, coarsely chop the meat, scoop out any marrow from the bones and return it and the meat to the sauce (discard the bone). Remove and discard the chiles, if you used them.

4. Drain and sauce the pasta. Sprinkle it with the herb and toss.

SERVES 4 AS A MAIN COURSE

COOKING NOTES

I recorded the first steps of this recipe so that you brown the shank in a sauté pan and then transfer it to a saucepan for the rest of the cooking. When I made it, following the original recipe, which had you browning and cooking all in one pan, the oil and chile burned before the shank was browned. Since I used a small Le Creuset pot—one of the heaviest and most evenly heating pots around—I figured this could be a problem for others as well. Not to worry, Mark, my tweaks don't change the fundamental flavor or character of the dish.

I partially covered the pot, as instructed, and the veal took 1 hour and 15 minutes to become tender.

VARIATION

Six years after Bittman published this recipe, he ran a variation made with ribs that called for 6 to 8 spareribs (about 1½ to 2 pounds), penne rather than ziti, and no olive oil (ribs have plenty of fat). The rest of the ingredients are nearly identical. You pile all the ingredients except the pasta and parsley into a Dutch oven and put it in a 250-degree oven for an hour or two, until the rib meat is fork-tender. Boil the pasta, then spoon over some ribs and sauce (removing the bones). I've made this at least a dozen times, each time marveling at its ratio of ease to pleasure.

SERVING SUGGESTIONS

Puntarelle with Anchovies (p. 194), Steamed Lemon Pudding (p. 849), Tortoni (p. 720)

OCTOBER 8, 1997: "THE MINIMALIST: TOMATO SAUCE WITH A LITTLE MEAT TO IT," BY MARK BITTMAN.

—1997

⤎ THE MINIMALIST'S PAELLA

In technique, this recipe bears a strong relationship to the Conchiglie Al Forno with Mushrooms and Radicchio on p. 325. Both use the power of an extremely hot oven—in this case, 500 degrees—to quickly reduce the cooking liquid, finish the rice (pasta in the other recipe), and add a vital crunch to the edges of the dish, all without overcooking the most delicate ingredients (here, shrimp; there, radicchio). This is a brilliant cheat on paella and a multi-textured alternative to risotto.

———

4 cups chicken broth
Pinch of saffron threads
3 tablespoons olive oil
1 medium onion, minced
2 cups Arborio rice
Salt and freshly ground black pepper
2 cups peeled shrimp cut into ½-inch chunks
Minced flat-leaf parsley for garnish

1. Heat the oven to 500 degrees. Warm the broth in a saucepan with the saffron.

2. Place a 10- or 12-inch skillet over medium-high heat and add the oil. One minute later, add the onion and cook, stirring occasionally, until translucent, about 5 minutes. Add the rice and cook, stirring occasionally, until glossy—just a minute or two. Season liberally with salt and pepper, and add the warmed broth, taking care to avoid the rising steam. Stir in the shrimp, and transfer the pan to the oven.

3. Bake for 20 to 25 minutes, until all the liquid is absorbed and the rice is dry on top. Garnish with the parsley and serve.

SERVES 4 AS A MAIN COURSE

COOKING NOTES

Use the best chicken broth you can get your hands on. Ask your fishmonger to give you the shrimp shells, and simmer them in the broth with the saffron before straining out the shells and adding the broth to the rice.

If you have a baking stone, put it in the oven to preheat, and place the cast-iron skillet on top of the stone when you bake the paella.

Mark Bittman's original recipe called for just shrimp, and he suggested alternatives in the accompanying story. Next time, I'd add ½ pound fresh chorizo, sliced ½ inch thick.

SERVING SUGGESTIONS

Rebujito (p. 38), Sangria (p. 23), Fried Chickpeas (p. 88), Lightly Smoked Salt Cod Salad (p. 437), Rabbit Soup with Garlic, Peppers, and Chorizo (p. 152), Catalan Tortilla with Aioli (p. 86), Caramel Custard (p. 836), Toasts with Chocolate, Olive Oil, and Sea Salt (p. 844), Grapefruit Granita (p. 731)

JANUARY 6, 1999: "THE MINIMALIST: THE HOMEY JOYS OF SIMPLE PAELLA," BY MARK BITTMAN

—1999

✐ CREMINI MUSHROOM PASTA WITH WILTED ARUGULA, GOAT CHEESE, AND EXTRA VIRGIN OLIVE OIL

If the cooking of the 1990s had to be summed up in a single dish, this would be it. And if it had to be summed up by a single person, Alfred Portale, the chef and owner of Gotham Bar & Grill, who came up with this recipe, would be a pretty good choice.

The trick to the dish is to not overcook the pasta—a point that sounds dumb, because you should never overcook pasta. But some sauces—Bolognese, for instance—are more forgiving of soft noodles. This one will punish you to the last sticky bite. Goat cheese can be clingy, especially when warmed, and once it goes into the dish, the cheese begins melting and melding the strands of pasta. The recipe calls for adding some of the pasta water, which loosens up the sauce but which also gets absorbed by the pasta, so if you overcook the pasta, you end up with mush.

If you get it right, though, you'll be rewarded with a creamy, tangy sauce interwoven with bits of mushroom and pieces of arugula that are as delicate as tis-

sue paper—all flavors that epitomized 1990s cooking. Portale suggested some alternatives for the dish: he said you could use another pasta shape, like penne or farfalle (I'd try penne rigate next time), grated aged goat cheese (half the amount) instead of fresh, and radicchio or watercress if you couldn't find arugula—which,—thanks to the 1990s, is now in every supermarket.

―――――

Salt
1 pound spaghetti
½ cup plus 2 tablespoons extra virgin olive oil
2 pounds cremini mushrooms, trimmed and very thinly sliced
Freshly ground white pepper
2 tablespoons finely minced garlic
3 cups tightly packed arugula, cut into thin strands
¾ pound soft fresh goat cheese, crumbled, at room temperature
¼ cup chopped flat-leaf parsley

1. Bring a large pot of salted water to a boil over high heat. Add the spaghetti, and cook until it is al dente, about 10 minutes.

2. Meanwhile, warm 1 tablespoon olive oil in a large nonstick sauté pan over high heat. Add half the mushrooms, season to taste with salt and white pepper, and cook, stirring often, for about 3 minutes. Add half the garlic and cook, stirring, until the garlic is fragrant and the mushrooms have softened, another 2 to 3 minutes. Transfer the mushrooms and garlic to a bowl, cover to keep warm, and cook the remaining mushrooms and garlic in another tablespoon of oil.

3. When the spaghetti is cooked, reserve about ½ cup of the cooking water and drain the pasta. Return the pasta to the pot and add the sautéed mushrooms, arugula, goat cheese, remaining ½ cup olive oil, the reserved pasta water, and parsley. Toss gently until the arugula wilts and the goat cheese melts into a creamy sauce. Season to taste with salt and pepper and serve immediately.

SERVES 4 AS A MAIN COURSE

COOKING NOTES

Your instincts will tell you not to cook the mushrooms over high heat, but do. It prevents them from stewing and later making the pasta sauce soggy—just keep them moving in the pan, and they won't burn.

I'd save 1 cup of the pasta water, and after adding ½ cup to the sauce, I'd put the rest of the water on the table to be added as desired. The sauce tightens up as it sits.

SERVING SUGGESTIONS
Fresh and Smoked Salmon Spread (p. 72), Gazpacho with Cucumber Granita (p. 161), Chilled Corn Soup with Honeydew Polka Dots (p. 153), Coffee Caramel Custard (p. 849), Warm Soft Chocolate Cake (p. 773)

JANUARY 13, 1999: "THE CHEF," BY ALFRED PORTALE AND DORIE GREENSPAN.

—1999

⤚ SWISS CHARD CASSEROLE WITH FARFALLE AND CHEESES

Eating this, you realize that pasta with cheese really benefits from the astringency of a green like chard.

———

1 pound Swiss chard
¼ cup extra virgin olive oil
1 medium onion, chopped
3 cloves garlic, minced
¼ cup chopped scallions
1 cup finely chopped well-drained canned plum tomatoes
Salt
½ pound farfalle (bow-tie pasta)
½ cup crumbled goat cheese
¼ cup freshly grated Parmesan, plus more if desired
Freshly ground black pepper

1. Rinse the chard, drain it, and chop it fine.
2. Heat 2 tablespoons oil in a large heavy skillet over medium heat. Add the onion and sauté until tender but not brown. Stir in the garlic, add the scallions and tomatoes, and then add the chard. Cook for about 8 minutes, until the chard has wilted.
3. Meanwhile, heat the oven to 350 degrees. Bring a large pot of salted water to a boil. Cook the farfalle until al dente. Drain it and toss with the remaining 2 tablespoons oil.

4. Remove the chard mixture from the heat and stir in the goat cheese and half the Parmesan. Fold in the farfalle and season to taste with salt and pepper.
5. Spoon the chard and farfalle mixture into a 1½-quart casserole. Sprinkle the remaining Parmesan on top, adding more if you like. Bake until heated through, about 15 minutes.

SERVES 4 AS A MAIN COURSE,
6 AS A FIRST COURSE

COOKING NOTE
Chopping the chard is an onerous task, but keep at it because the little bits will integrate well with the farfalle.

SERVING SUGGESTIONS
Bagna Cauda (p. 58), Fennel, Orange, Watercress, and Walnut Salad (p. 186), Shaved Artichoke Salad with Pine Nuts and Parmesan Cheese (p. 191), Fried Artichokes Azzurro (p. 229), Chocolate Cake with Bay Leaf Syrup (p. 768), Lemon Cheese Pie (p. 812)

JANUARY 31, 1999: "ADDING MEATY FLAVOR FROM SWISS CHARD TO PASTAS AND FRITTATAS," BY FLORENCE FABRICANT.

—1999

⤚ FETTUCCINE WITH PRESERVED LEMON AND ROASTED GARLIC

This is Molly O'Neill at her best. She's an ingredient fanatic who loves to take a plain-Jane recipe like pasta with lemon and garlic and electrify it with an unusual flavor. Here that flavor is preserved lemon.

———

2 heads garlic
1 tablespoon plus 2 teaspoons olive oil
Salt
1 pound fettuccine
2 tablespoons unsalted butter
1 preserved lemon, pulp and rind finely chopped
½ cup freshly grated Parmesan cheese, plus more for serving
3 tablespoons chopped flat-leaf parsley
Freshly ground black pepper

1. Heat the oven to 400 degrees. Chop the top third off each head of garlic and discard. Drizzle the heads with a teaspoon each of olive oil, wrap in foil, and roast until the garlic is very soft and golden brown, 50 to 70 minutes. Remove from the oven and let cool slightly.

2. Squeeze the garlic out of the skins. Set aside.

3. Bring a large pot of salted water to a boil. Cook the fettuccine until al dente. Toward the end of cooking, scoop out about ½ cup of the pasta cooking water and reserve. Drain the pasta and place in a serving bowl.

4. Meanwhile, combine the remaining tablespoon of olive oil and the butter in a small pan over medium-low heat. When the butter melts, add the roasted garlic and preserved lemon and cook for 1 minute.

5. Toss the fettuccine with the preserved lemon mixture. Toss again with the Parmesan and parsley, and season generously with salt and pepper. Add a little of the reserved pasta water if needed.

SERVES 4 AS A LIGHT MAIN COURSE,
6 AS A FIRST COURSE

COOKING NOTES
For a preserved lemon recipe, see p. 00.

You can leave out the cardamom if you wish, but I really liked it with this pasta.

SERVING SUGGESTIONS
Breaded Chicken Breasts with Parmesan Cheese (p. 465), Watercress Salad (p. 171), Roasted Cauliflower (p. 248), Almond and Buttermilk Sorbet (p. 733)

MARCH 7, 1999: "FOOD: CURIOUS YELLOW," BY MOLLY O'NEILL.

—1999

☙ SPICY, LEMONY CLAMS WITH PASTA

This recipe had me at spicy, lemony clams. And it did not disappoint.

———

Salt
1 pound spaghetti, linguine, or other long pasta
½ cup extra virgin olive oil
8 cloves garlic, thinly sliced
36 littleneck clams, well scrubbed
¾ cup dry white wine
½ to 1 tablespoon crushed red pepper flakes
Finely grated zest of 2 lemons
Juice of 1 lemon, or to taste
½ cup chopped flat-leaf parsley
Fresh ground black pepper

1. Fill a large pot with water, add 1 tablespoon salt, and bring to a boil over high heat. Add the pasta and boil until the pasta is al dente, 7 to 8 minutes; drain well.

2. Meanwhile, heat the olive oil in a large skillet over medium-low heat. Add the garlic and sauté just until translucent, about 2 minutes. Add the clams and wine, cover immediately, and raise the heat to medium-high. Shake the pan often, and check the clams after 4 minutes. If any have opened, transfer them to a bowl so they do not overcook. Simmer the remaining clams until all have opened.

3. Combine the clams and the broth from the pan in a large serving bowl. Add 1½ teaspoons pepper flakes, the lemon zest, lemon juice, parsley, and salt and pepper to taste. Mix well. Add the pasta and, using tongs, toss well. Add more red pepper flakes and lemon juice, if desired. Serve in soup bowls.

SERVES 4 AS A MAIN COURSE

COOKING NOTE
One problem with spaghetti and clams is that long strands and small round bits don't like to mix evenly. You can accomplish the task in a large bowl with tongs in each hand, but it's like trying to mix beads into a pile of yarn. As an alternative, mix the spaghetti with the sauce, then scatter the clams on top.

Fried Olives (p. 87), Ricotta Crostini with Fresh Thyme and Dried Oregano (p. 93), Artichoke Salad with Anchovy and Capers (p. 174), Watermelon and Tomato Salad (p. 197), Chopped Salad with Lemon Zest Vinaigrette (p. 188), Strawberry Sorbet (p. 732), Fontainebleau (p. 829), Rhubarb Orange (p. 864)

AUGUST 11, 1999: "WHY DIG FOR GOLD, IF THERE ARE CLAMS?" BY ELAINE LOUIE. RECIPE ADAPTED FROM THE LOBSTER CLUB IN NEW YORK CITY.

—1999

WILD MUSHROOM STUFFING

This stuffing ran with the recipe for Roasted Brine-Cured Turkey on p. 474. See that recipe for the turkey cooking instructions and serving suggestions.

———

4 tablespoons unsalted butter

2 shallots, finely diced

4 cloves garlic, minced

1 pound chanterelles, trimmed and cut crosswise in half

Salt and freshly ground black pepper

1 cup finely chopped onion

¼ pound smoked bacon

1 turkey or chicken liver, diced

1 day-old baguette, crust removed and cut into 1-inch cubes (you need 4 cups)

3 cups whole milk, or as needed

1 teaspoon finely chopped thyme

2 tablespoons chopped flat-leaf parsley

1 large egg, lightly beaten, if desired

1. Melt 2 tablespoons butter in a large skillet over medium heat. Add the shallots and one-quarter of the garlic and sauté until soft, about 2 minutes. Add the mushrooms, season with salt and pepper to taste, and sauté until soft, about 8 minutes. Transfer to a plate and let cool slightly, then coarsely chop and place in large bowl.

2. Melt the remaining 2 tablespoons butter in the same skillet. Add the onion and the remaining garlic and sauté until softened, about 3 minutes. Season with salt and pepper to taste, and add to the bowl of mushrooms.

3. Return the skillet to medium heat and add the bacon. Cook until crisp, then remove the bacon (save for another purpose), leaving the fat in the pan. Add the diced liver and sauté until browned, about 2 minutes. Drain well, season with salt and pepper to taste, and add to the mushrooms.

4. Combine the bread cubes and enough milk to saturate them in a large bowl. Drain the bread, squeezing it gently; add to the mushrooms, and mix gently. Add the herbs and mix again. If desired, add the egg to bind the stuffing.

MAKES ENOUGH FOR A 12- TO 14-POUND TURKEY

NOVEMBER 17, 1999: "NEW AMERICAN TRADITIONS: IN A BERKELEY KITCHEN, A CELEBRATION OF SIMPLICITY," BY R. W. APPLE JR. RECIPE ADAPTED FROM ALICE WATERS, THE OWNER OF CHEZ PANISSE IN BERKELEY, CALIFORNIA.

—1999

SPAGHETTI WITH CAVIAR, SCALLIONS, AND CHOPPED EGG

I served this on New Year's Eve 2000, and it was a good way to end the millennium—pasta and caviar had reached their peak of popularity and together they clearly summed up Americans' penchant for both high brow and low at the table.

———

Coarse sea salt

4 large eggs

1 pound spaghetti

5 tablespoons unsalted butter

Freshly ground black pepper

6 scallions, thinly sliced

1½ ounces osetra caviar, or more to taste

1. Fill a large pot with water, season generously with sea salt, and bring to a boil. Meanwhile, fill a small pan with water and bring to a boil. Add the eggs to the small pan, reduce the heat to an active simmer, and

cook for 9½ minutes. Drain. When the eggs are cool to the touch, peel and finely chop. Set aside.

2. When the large pot of water boils, add the spaghetti and cook until al dente. Drain, reserving ½ cup of the cooking liquid. Add the butter and a few tablespoons of the cooking water to the pot and place over medium-high heat. When the butter is melted and bubbling, add the spaghetti and toss to coat. Season with salt and a generous amount of pepper.

3. Divide the spaghetti among 4 plates. Sprinkle the chopped egg and scallions on top. Spoon the caviar in the center. Serve immediately; guests will mix the spaghetti as they eat.

SERVES 4 AS A LIGHT MAIN COURSE

COOKING NOTE

If possible, try to buy sustainable caviar from farm-raised white sturgeon or paddlefish. Both are available from U.S. producers such as California Caviar and The Little Pearl.

SERVING SUGGESTIONS

Nicole Kaplan's Gougères (p. 76), Caesar Salad (p. 174), Lora Brody's Bête Noire (p. 763)

DECEMBER 29, 1999: "THE ULTIMATE NIGHT, AT HOME," BY AMANDA HESSER.

—1999

✑ MALCOLM AND KELLEY McDOWELL'S PINK RIGATONI

A tomato sauce, whose rough acidic edges are planed with salted butter and a dash of sugar.

———

10 cloves garlic, roughly chopped

6 tablespoons olive oil

10 ripe plum tomatoes, quartered (canned may be used off-season)

½ teaspoon salt

½ teaspoon freshly ground black pepper

½ cup dry red wine

1 pound rigatoni

6 tablespoons salted butter, cut into pieces

½ cup freshly grated Parmesan cheese

½ teaspoon sugar

1. Sauté the garlic in the oil in a large skillet over medium heat until it begins to brown. Add the tomatoes, salt, and pepper and cook, stirring occasionally, for 30 minutes, or until the tomatoes break down and the sauce thickens.

2. Pour in the wine and cook for 20 to 30 minutes, until the sauce is thickened. Remove from the heat and let stand for 10 minutes.

3. Meanwhile, cook the rigatoni in boiling salted water until al dente; drain.

4. Fold the butter, Parmesan, and sugar into the sauce until it turns the famous pink. Dump in the rigatoni, mix, and serve.

SERVES 4

SERVING SUGGESTIONS

Poivrons Verts Farcis (Stuffed Green Peppers; p. 223), Veal Chops with Sage (p. 564), Spinach Roman-Style (p. 233), Ricotta Kisses (p. 852), Cornmeal Biscotti (p. 696), Balducci's Tiramisù (p. 830)

OCTOBER 22, 2000: "FOOD: MEAT LOAF: THE MUSICAL," BY JONATHAN REYNOLDS. RECIPE ADAPTED FROM MALCOLM AND KELLEY McDOWELL.

—2000

✑ SHIITAKE AND LOTUS SEED STUFFING

This stuffing ran with the recipe for Roasted Brine-Cured Turkey on p. 477. See that recipe for the turkey cooking instructions and serving suggestions.

———

¾ cup dried lotus seeds

½ cup sliced dried shiitake mushrooms

3½ cups ground chicken (breast and thigh)

Giblets from 1 turkey or chicken, chopped

1 cup chopped shallots

1 cup chopped onion

¾ cup chopped canned water chestnuts

1 cup dried sweet rice flakes, preferably green

1 tablespoon mushroom powder

1½ tablespoons Asian fish sauce

Freshly ground black pepper

1. Place the lotus seeds in a bowl with water to cover. Soak for 2 hours.

2. Drain the seeds and transfer to a saucepan. Cover with water and bring to a boil, then reduce the heat to low and simmer until the seeds are slightly firmer than cooked chickpeas, about 1 hour. Drain well, and allow to cool.

3. Split the seeds in half, discarding any bitter green shoots in the centers. Set aside.

4. Meanwhile, cover the mushrooms with hot water and allow to soak until softened, about 15 minutes. Lift the mushrooms from the water, leaving any grit behind.

5. Combine the lotus seeds, mushrooms, chicken, giblets, shallots, onion, water chestnuts, rice flakes, and mushroom powder in a large bowl. Mix well with a wooden spoon. Season with the fish sauce and black pepper to taste.

MAKES ENOUGH FOR A 12- TO 14-POUND TURKEY

COOKING NOTE

Lotus seeds, dried sweet rice flakes, and mushroom powder can be found in Southeast Asian grocery stores.

NOVEMBER 15, 2000: "AMERICA CELEBRATES: HUNTING-TON BEACH, CALIF: ADD A LITTLE VIETNAM, FRANCE AND CALIFORNIA, AND MIX," BY AMANDA HESSER. RECIPE ADAPTED FROM ALICE WATERS AND BAO-XUYEN LE.

—2000

☙ BASMATI RICE WITH COCONUT MILK AND GINGER

———

2 cups basmati rice

1 1/2 cups unsweetened coconut milk, or as needed

1 cup chicken broth

1 cup water

1 teaspoon kosher salt, or more to taste

3 scallions, thinly sliced

2 tablespoons finely chopped fresh ginger

1. Place the rice in a fine-mesh strainer, and rinse with cold water until the water runs clear. Transfer to a medium saucepan. Add the coconut milk, chicken broth, water, and salt, cover, and place over medium-high heat. Bring to a boil, then reduce the heat and simmer until the liquid has been absorbed and the rice is tender, about 15 minutes.

2. Remove from the heat and stir in the scallions and ginger. Add a little more coconut milk if the rice is too dry. Season to taste with salt.

SERVES 4 AS A SIDE DISH

FEBRUARY 7, 2001: "GINGER, IN FULL FLOWER," BY AMANDA HESSER.

—2001

☙ SPAGHETTI WITH FRIED EGGS AND ROASTED PEPPERS

One of my favorite home-alone dinners. You could also skip the roasted peppers and capers, paring the recipe down to the essentials: pasta with eggs and a little seasoning.

———

2 red bell peppers

1 tablespoon salt-packed capers, thoroughly rinsed, coarsely chopped if large

1 large clove garlic, finely chopped

1/4 cup finely chopped flat-leaf parsley

Sea salt and freshly ground black pepper

3 rounded tablespoons coarse dry bread crumbs

5 tablespoons extra virgin olive oil

3/4 pound spaghetti

2 large eggs

Freshly grated Parmesan and Pecorino Romano cheese for serving

1. Roast the peppers under a broiler or on a gas burner with the flame on low. Turn them regularly so that they char all over. When they are fully blistered, place them in a paper or plastic bag and let cool.

2. Peel the peppers. When you cut them open, catch any pepper liquid in a small bowl. Trim off the stem end, scrape out the seeds, and cut out the ribs. Slice the peppers lengthwise into 1/4-inch-wide strips.

3. Combine the peppers, capers, garlic, and parsley in a small baking dish. Season with salt and pepper. Sprinkle the bread crumbs on top. Set aside.

4. Heat the oven to 350 degrees. Bring a large pot of salted water to a boil. Just before it boils, sprinkle 2

tablespoons olive oil over the red peppers and place in the oven for 10 minutes.

5. Add the pasta to the boiling water and cook until al dente.

6. Meanwhile, heat the remaining 3 tablespoons olive oil in a medium sauté pan over medium heat. When it shimmers, crack in the eggs and fry, sunny side up, until the whites are set and the yolks are still runny. Remove from the burner.

7. Scoop out a cup of the pasta water and drain the pasta. Pour it into a large warm serving bowl. Using 2 forks, toss in the baked peppers and fried eggs, adding some of the egg-cooking olive oil. As you toss, break the whites into pieces and let the yolks act as sauce; they will spread over the pasta and cook further from the heat. Add a little reserved pasta water if it gets too thick. Season to taste with salt and pepper and serve, passing the cheese on the side.

SERVES 4 AS A MAIN COURSE

SERVING SUGGESTIONS
Puntarelle with Anchovies (p. 194), Licorice Ice Cream (p. 728), Grapefruit Granita (p. 731), Marcella's Pear Cake (p. 769)

READERS
"I love this because of its simplicity and richness at the same time . . . I also love watching the egg yolk flow over the spaghetti . . . it's pretty cool that an egg yolk can act as spaghetti sauce."

Andrea Wallach, New York, NY, e-mail

FEBRUARY 14, 2001: "A MARRIAGE OF CONVENIENCE," BY AMANDA HESSER. RECIPE ADAPTED FROM *NAPLES AT TABLE* BY ARTHUR SCHWARTZ.

—2001

∽ POTATO GNOCCHI

If you want to understand the difference between recipes a hundred years ago and now, this one provides a handy primer. Potato gnocchi, a simple country dish, becomes, in Tom Colicchio's hands, an obsessively detailed project. The owner of Craft and its many satellites laid out even more pointers in the accompany-

ing story. He noted that standard potato ricers do not shred the potato fine enough; that you should not add salt to the gnocchi, or it will trap moisture and weigh them down; and that you should add as little flour as possible, because you want to taste the potatoes and only the potatoes.

If you follow the instructions to the letter, you will be amply rewarded. These gnocchi taste only of potato, delicious potato, and are as weightless as down.

———

Kosher salt
5 pounds baking potatoes (10 to 12, uniform size), scrubbed
3 large egg yolks, lightly beaten
Freshly ground white pepper
Approximately 1¼ cups all-purpose flour
8 cups ice cubes
½ pound (2 sticks) unsalted butter
1 cup water
¼ pound Parmesan cheese, grated

1. Heat the oven to 350 degrees. Cover a jelly-roll pan with a 1-inch layer of kosher salt. Place the potatoes on the salt and bake for 1½ hours.

2. Remove the potatoes and cut lengthwise in half. Deeply score the flesh in a crisscross pattern. Place the halves on racks; let cool to room temperature, at least 30 minutes.

3. Scoop the potato flesh into a large bowl. Force the potato flesh through a fine ricer or sieve. Weigh it! you need 2¼ pounds.

4. Spread the riced potatoes on a work surface and shape loosely into a flat mound. Drizzle with the egg yolks. Sprinkle with pepper to taste. Cut into the potato mound at 1-inch intervals with a pastry scraper, spatula, or cleaver to incorporate the egg yolks; sprinkle with the flour as you go. Work the mound by cutting and folding, not kneading; sprinkle on the flour in handfuls until the potato mixture feels fairly dry and is no longer sticky and a small piece can be rolled easily into a ball.

5. Line 2 baking sheets with parchment. Lightly dust with flour. Clean the work surface with a scraper and lightly dust with flour. Shape the potato mixture into a loaf about 1½ inches high, 4 inches wide, and 12 inches long. Cut a 1½-inch-wide slice from the loaf

with the scraper or a knife. Roll it into a rope about ½ inch thick and 30 inches long. Cut at 1-inch intervals. Smooth the ends of each piece lightly with your fingertips, and place the gnocchi on a paper-lined pan. Repeat with the remaining dough.

6. Bring a large pot of water, with 1 heaping tablespoon salt for each quart of water, to a boil. Place the ice cubes in a large bowl, add 4 quarts cold water, and put a large colander in the bowl so that it fills with ice water.

7. Slide the gnocchi from 1 baking sheet into the boiling water. After about 1½ minutes the gnocchi will begin floating to the surface. Remove to the colander with a slotted spoon or skimmer. Repeat with the second batch.

8. Line the baking sheets with fresh parchment. With a skimmer, transfer the gnocchi to the baking sheets. The gnocchi can be served at once, set aside for several hours, or frozen for future use; frozen gnocchi can be heated in butter without thawing.

9. To serve, melt the butter in a small saucepan. Whisk in the water until emulsified. (If not using the entire batch of gnocchi, make proportionately less butter sauce.) Transfer the sauce to 1 or 2 skillets large enough to hold the gnocchi in a single layer. Add the gnocchi and heat over medium heat until the butter starts to bubble and the gnocchi are warmed through. Dust with the cheese and serve.

SERVES 8 AS A MAIN COURSE,
16 AS A FIRST COURSE

COOKING NOTE
You need a scale for this recipe. If you don't yet own one, this recipe is a great excuse to indulge.

SERVING SUGGESTIONS
Italian Beef Stew with Rosemary (p. 522), Coda alla Vaccinara (Oxtail Braised with Tomato and Celery; p. 562), Roman Lamb (p. 542), Osso Buco alla Milanese (p. 535), Steamed Spinach with Balsamic Butter (p. 226), Panna Cotta (p. 840), Tortoni (p. 720)

JULY 18, 2001: "THE CHEF: TOM COLICCHIO," BY TOM COLICCHIO AND FLORENCE FABRICANT. RECIPE ADAPTED FROM LAURA SBRANA (THE MOTHER OF MARCO CANORA; SEE P. 202).

—2001

⌒ PASTA WITH YOGURT AND CARAMELIZED ONIONS, FROM KASSOS

Since I wrote about this surprising and delightful dish from Kassos in Greece, many of my friends have cooked it and raved about it to me (for the record, I have nothing to do with its greatness—that is all due to Diane Kochilas, whose recipe it is). So this comes to you with multiple recommendations.

———

2 cups sheep's-milk yogurt
5 tablespoons extra virgin olive oil
6 cups coarsely chopped onions
Sea salt
1 pound tagliatelle
1 cup coarsely grated kefalotyri or
   Pecorino Romano cheese

1. Line a colander with cheesecloth and set over a bowl or in the sink. Add the yogurt and let drain for 2 hours.
2. Heat the olive oil in a large nonstick skillet over medium-high heat. Add the onions, reduce the heat to medium-low, and cook, stirring frequently, until the onions are soft and golden brown, 20 to 30 minutes.
3. Meanwhile, fill a large pot with water and bring to a boil. Season with enough salt so that you can taste it. Add the pasta and cook until soft (not al dente).
4. Combine the drained yogurt with ½ cup of the pasta cooking water in a large bowl and mix well.
5. Drain the pasta and toss with the yogurt mixture. Divide among 4 bowls. Sprinkle generously with the cheese, and top with the caramelized onions and their juices.

SERVES 4 AS A MAIN COURSE

SERVING SUGGESTIONS
Fried Artichokes Azzurro (p. 229), Hearth's Fava Bean Salad (p. 202), Lemon-Almond Butter Cake (p. 780), Tangerine Sherbet (p. 734), Hazelnut Baklava (p. 706)

SEPTEMBER 26, 2001: "BY THE BOOK: AN OLD-WORLD EXPLORER," BY AMANDA HESSER. RECIPE ADAPTED FROM *THE GLORIOUS FOODS OF GREECE*, BY DIANE KOCHILAS.

—2001

◡ LASAGNA

There are no surprises in this lasagna—just a traditional recipe that produces a perfect baked dish. Some of you may be disappointed that I didn't include Ed Giobbi's Lasagna from 1973, but I tried it and decided that this one edged Giobbi's out. I hope you'll make it and judge for yourself. If you don't agree, tell all your friends I don't know what I'm talking about.

———

For the Sauce
1 cup extra virgin olive oil
2 medium red onions, finely diced
4 large cloves garlic, 2 minced, 2 left whole
½ pound sliced (¼-inch-thick) pancetta, diced (¼-inch cubes)
Salt and freshly ground black pepper
1½ cups dry red wine, preferably Italian
Two 28-ounce cans Italian plum tomatoes
3 tablespoons tomato paste
2 cups lukewarm water
¾ pound ground sirloin
¼ cup freshly grated Pecorino Romano cheese
2 large eggs
10 sprigs flat-leaf parsley, leaves only, washed and dried
Approximately ½ cup all-purpose flour
1 pound Italian sausage—a mix of hot and sweet

For the Lasagna
One 15-ounce container ricotta cheese
2 extra-large eggs
2 cups freshly grated Pecorino Romano cheese
½ cup chopped flat-leaf parsley
1 pound mozzarella, grated
Salt and freshly ground black pepper
16 fresh lasagna noodles

1. To make the sauce, heat ½ cup oil in a large Dutch oven or other heavy pot over low heat. Add the onions, minced garlic, and pancetta and cook, stirring, for 10 minutes, or until the onions are wilted. Season liberally with salt and pepper. Raise the heat slightly, add the wine, and cook until it has mostly evaporated, about 20 minutes.

2. Crush the tomatoes into the pan, and add their juice. Add the tomato paste and lukewarm water and simmer for 1 hour.

3. Combine the sirloin, cheese, and eggs in a large bowl. Chop the parsley with the whole garlic cloves until fine, then stir into the beef mixture. Season lavishly with salt and pepper. Using your hands, mix until all the ingredients are well blended. Shape into meatballs and set aside.

4. About 20 minutes before the sauce is done, heat the remaining ½ cup oil in a large skillet over medium-high heat. Dust the meatballs lightly with the flour, shaking off excess, and lay in the hot oil. Brown the meatballs on all sides (do not cook through) and transfer to the sauce.

5. Brown the sausages in a clean skillet over medium-high heat. Transfer to the sauce. Simmer for 1½ hours. Remove from the heat.

6. To make the lasagna, heat the oven to 350 degrees. Combine the ricotta, eggs, Pecorino Romano, parsley, and all but 1 cup of the mozzarella in a large bowl. Season well with salt and pepper. Mix thoroughly.

7. Remove the meatballs and sausage from the sauce and let cool slightly, then coarsely chop. Spoon a thick layer of sauce into the bottom of a 9-by-12-inch baking pan. Cover with a layer of 4 noodles. Spoon more sauce on top, then add a third of the meat and a third of the cheese mixture. Repeat for 2 more layers, using all the meat and cheese. Top with a layer of noodles and cover with the remaining sauce. Sprinkle the remaining mozzarella evenly over the top.

8. Bake until heated through and bubbling, about 30 minutes. Let stand for 10 minutes before serving.

SERVES 8 TO 10 AS A MAIN COURSE

SERVING SUGGESTIONS
Caesar Salad (p. 174), Brown Sugar Ice Cream (p. 721), Balducci's Tiramisù (p. 830), Chocolate Rum Mousse (p. 814)

OCTOBER 31, 2001: "THE NOODLE AND I: A FACE-OFF AT THE OVEN," BY REGINA SCHRAMBLING. RECIPE ADAPTED FROM GIULIANO BUGIALLI.

—2001

PASTA WITH FAST SAUSAGE RAGU

This is a brilliant recipe, the kind of dish that every single beginner cook should learn. There are infinite variations too. You could add hot red pepper flakes, vodka, roasted mushrooms . . .

———

1 tablespoon extra virgin olive oil
1 medium onion, chopped
1/2 pound sweet Italian sausage, removed from casings if necessary
1 cup whole milk, or as needed
1/4 cup tomato paste
Salt and freshly ground black pepper
1 pound pasta
At least 1/2 cup freshly grated Parmesan cheese

1. Set a large pot of water on to boil for the pasta. Put the oil in a 10-inch skillet and turn the heat to medium. A minute later, add the onion and cook, stirring occasionally, until it softens, about 5 minutes. Add the sausage in bits, turn the heat to medium-high, and cook, stirring occasionally, until the sausage is nicely browned, 5 to 10 minutes.

2. Add the milk and tomato paste, along with some salt and pepper; stir to blend and simmer until thickened but not dry, a minute or two. Keep the sauce warm if necessary; if it becomes too thick, add a little more milk or water.

3. Meanwhile, salt the water and cook the pasta. When the pasta is tender but not mushy, drain it. Toss with the sauce and Parmesan; taste, adjust the seasoning, and serve.

SERVES 4 AS A MAIN COURSE

COOKING NOTES
I made this with orecchiette, and it turned out great.

Pasta is done when you bite into it and it feels like biting into a new stick of gum.

SERVING SUGGESTIONS
Salade à la Romaine (p. 171), Papa's Apple Pound Cake (p. 774), Ricotta Kisses (p. 852), Coupe Lena Horne (Coffee Ice Cream Sundae; p. 722)

NOVEMBER 28, 2001: "THE MINIMALIST: BONDING, TENDERLY," BY MARK BITTMAN.

—2001

PASTA WITH TUSCAN DUCK SAUCE

Mark Bittman's "Minimalist" column requires that his recipes use a handful or fewer of ingredients, be short and succinct, not require a trip to Chinatown (at least not every week), and must be easily cooked up on a weeknight. Creating fifty-two such recipes every year is no enviable task.

So when Bittman comes up with a great recipe—and he has come up with many since he began the column in 1997—it's like someone inventing pound cake.

While writing this book, I cooked more than 100 of Bittman's recipes. I planned to offer a healthy sample of his work, yet not so many that it would leave other writers feeling neglected. But there were so many winners I started to refer to him as "Goddamn-Bittman." Bittman's brilliance lies in his attention to technique; he has taken many classic dishes and reengineered them in ways that make cooking them easier and result in better flavor. This is the reason people around the world count his paella (p. 333—baked at high heat in a cast-iron skillet), no-knead bread (p. 670—Jim Lahey's recipe, which Bittman codified), and steamed fish (p. 434—the fish is steamed directly on top of the vegetables) among their favorite recipes.

This duck sauce doesn't have the mass appeal of the aforementioned recipes, but it has the ingenuity. Bittman, in attempting to replicate the dark, rich pasta sauces you find in Tuscany, came up with a method of cooking the duck in its own fat, then building the sauce on this fat and a red wine reduction. Using a small amount of meat—just two duck legs—and a single pan, he produced a robust, succulent sauce, like something from the Old Country.

———

2 duck legs
Salt
1 medium onion, chopped
1 1/2 cups dry red wine
One 28-ounce can plum tomatoes, drained and chopped

Freshly ground black pepper

I pound pasta, like penne

Freshly grated Pecorino Romano or Parmesan cheese
for serving

1. Trim any visible fat from the duck legs, then lay them skin side down in a 10-inch skillet. Turn the heat to medium; when the duck begins to sizzle, turn the heat to low and cover. Cook undisturbed for about an hour (check once to be sure the legs aren't burning); the skin should be golden brown.

2. Turn and cook until the duck is very tender, at least 30 minutes more.

3. Set a large pot of salted water on to boil for the pasta. Remove the duck from the pan and set aside. Add the onion to the skillet and turn the heat to medium-high. Cook, stirring occasionally, until the onion is soft, about 5 minutes.

4. Add the wine to the skillet and raise the heat to high; cook until the liquid is reduced by about half. Add the tomatoes and some salt and pepper and cook over medium-high heat, stirring occasionally, until the mixture is saucy, about 15 minutes. Taste and adjust the seasoning.

5. Meanwhile, shred the duck from the bones and add it to the simmering sauce. A few minutes after adding the tomatoes to the sauce, start to cook the pasta.

6. When the pasta is tender but not mushy, drain it and serve it with the sauce, along with some cheese.

SERVES 3 AS A MAIN COURSE,
4 AS A FIRST COURSE

COOKING NOTE
I suggest cutting the pasta from 1 pound to ¾ pound.

SERVING SUGGESTIONS
Carrot and Fennel Soup (p. 151), Butternut Squash and Cider Soup (p. 136), Chestnut Soup (p. 133), Almond Cake (p. 777), Huguenot Torte (Apple and Pecan Torte; p. 750)

FEBRUARY 13, 2002: "THE MINIMALIST," BY MARK BITTMAN.
—2002

⌐ RIGATONI WITH WHITE BOLOGNESE

I learned this recipe from my friend Giuliano da Empoli's mother, Heidi. She is sylph-like—and Swiss—so you don't expect her to cook such rich and succulent food. Yet she served this hearty Bolognese as a prelude to veal cutlets.

It's called white Bolognese because it lacks tomatoes. In their place are dried porcini, which you reconstitute in warm water, and then use that water as a broth, infusing the sauce with a lovely earthiness. My husband asks me to make this for him every year on his birthday.

————

Extra virgin olive oil

½ sweet white onion, finely chopped

2 medium carrots, peeled and finely chopped

I stalk celery, finely chopped

Sea salt and freshly ground black pepper

I pound mild Italian pork sausages, removed from casings

I pound ground beef (not lean)

1½ cups dry white wine, preferably Italian

I beef bouillon cube, dissolved in 2 cups simmering water

1½ ounces dried porcini mushrooms, rehydrated in
3 cups lukewarm water

⅓ cup heavy cream

I pound rigatoni

¾ cup freshly grated Parmesan cheese

1. Add enough oil to a large deep sauté pan to coat the base and place over medium-high heat. When the oil shimmers, add the onion, carrots, and celery and sauté until glassy and just tender, about 5 minutes. Season lightly with salt and pepper. Add the sausage and beef to the pan, breaking it into walnut-sized pieces, and brown well.

2. Pour in the wine and keep at a rapid simmer until the pan is almost dry. Then pour in 1½ cups beef bouillon and lower the heat to medium (reserve the remaining bouillon for another use). Simmer gently, uncovered, until the bouillon is nearly gone, stirring now and then. Meanwhile, chop the rehydrated porcini into small pieces; reserve the liquid.

3. Bring a large pot of salted water to a boil. Meanwhile, add enough of the mushroom liquid to the sauce to cover the meat halfway (about 1 cup), along

with the porcini, and continue simmering until the sauce is loose but not soupy, about 10 minutes. Taste and adjust the salt and pepper; the sauce should be highly seasoned. When the consistency is right, fold in the cream. Remove from the heat and cover.

4. When the pasta water is at a full boil, add the rigatoni and cook until still just firm but not hard in the center. Scoop out 1 cup of the water and reserve. Drain the pasta and return it to the pot. Pour the pasta sauce on top and fold in with a wooden spoon. The pasta should not be dry. Add a little pasta water or mushroom liquid to loosen it if necessary. (It will continue to soak up sauce on the way to the table.) Serve in one large bowl or in individual bowls, passing the cheese at the table.

SERVES 4 AS A MAIN COURSE

SERVING SUGGESTIONS
Fried Olives (p. 87), Fried Artichokes Azzurro (p. 229), Bagna Cauda (p. 58), Almond Cake (p. 777), Cherry Spumoni (p. 732), Transparent Pudding (p. 805)

FEBRUARY 17, 2002: "FOOD DIARY: LOCAL HERO," BY AMANDA HESSER. RECIPE ADAPTED FROM HEIDI DA EMPOLI.

—2002

RISOTTO WITH LEMON AND CRÈME FRAÎCHE

Italians, avert your eyes—I'm about to put crème fraîche into risotto. The rest of you: get out a saucepan, you're in for a treat!

————

I tablespoon unsalted butter
I tablespoon olive oil
I pound Arborio rice
5 cups chicken broth, brought to a simmer
Grated zest of I lemon
$1/3$ to $1/2$ cup crème fraîche
$1/4$ cup freshly grated Parmesan cheese
Sea salt

1. Melt the butter in the oil in a large deep skillet and heat until foamy. Add the rice and stir well until all the grains are coated. Cook for a few minutes, until glassy, then begin adding the hot chicken broth a little at a time, just enough to loosen the rice without making it sloshy. Continue stirring and adding more broth as it's absorbed. When you've added half the broth, stir in half the lemon zest. You may run out of broth before the rice is done; if so, add ladles of hot water, one at a time, cooking until the liquid has been absorbed before adding more. The rice should be al dente, not at all mushy.

2. Stir in the crème fraîche, Parmesan cheese, and the remaining lemon zest. The risotto should be loose and creamy. Season with salt if needed.

SERVES 4

SERVING SUGGESTIONS
Asparagus Mimosa (p. 258), Veal Chops with Sage (p. 564), Rhubarb Orange (p. 864)

SEPTEMBER 22, 2002: "FOOD DIARY; STOVE-TOP SEMINAR," BY AMANDA HESSER.

—2002

MALFATTI

The first time I ate malfatti at Al Di La Trattoria in Park Slope, I got very worried. The tender egg-shaped gnocchi transcended all my impressions of what a good pasta dish should be. They were robust but light, and as you ate them, you could pick out the many flavors inside: fresh ricotta, chard, grated nutmeg, nutty browned butter, and sage. I worried that I might not get back for more before the menu changed.

Others worried too, apparently, because Anna Klinger, the chef, has never been able to take them off the menu. Not a bad response to a dish whose name actually means "misshapen." (They are also sometimes called *gnocchi gnudi* or *ravioli gnudi*, "nude gnocchi" or "nude ravioli," respectively.)

While most versions call for spinach, Klinger favors Swiss chard, which yields more volume and sweetness. She blanches the chard, squeezes—really squeezes—it dry in towels, chops it—and dries it again. Wet chard makes for sodden malfatti. The other crucial element is the ricotta, and Polly-O won't cut it. (Klinger prefers A & S brand or Calabro.)

Then comes the fun part: shaping the malfatti. You drop a spoonful of the chard mixture into a floured wineglass and swirl it like a 1982 Bordeaux. A quenelle forms before your eyes. (If you have kids around, they'll love doing this, plus you'll simultaneously be prepping them for 4-star dining.)

Klinger freezes them by the dozen, then drops them into boiling water when an order rolls in. (You can do the same when friends come to dinner.) Then she slices sage and tosses it into a pan of bubbling butter. The best nonpasta pasta you have ever tasted is only seconds away.

For an earlier malfatti, see Mrs. Sebastiani's on p. 313. Hers are heartier and are nestled in a warm tomato sauce.

———

1 pound ricotta

Kosher salt

4 bunches Swiss chard (about 4 pounds)

½ pound (2 sticks) unsalted butter

¼ cup all-purpose flour, plus more for shaping

½ teaspoon freshly grated nutmeg

1 large egg

4 large egg yolks

Freshly ground black pepper

24 sage leaves

A chunk of Parmesan cheese for serving

1. Drain the ricotta overnight in a sieve lined with cheesecloth in the refrigerator.
2. Measure out 1¼ cups ricotta; reserve the rest for another use.
3. Bring a large pot of water, heavily seasoned with salt, to a boil. Trim the chard, removing all stems and large ribs. Add half the chard to the boiling water and cook until soft, about 3 minutes. Fish out with tongs and plunge into a bowl of ice water. Repeat with the remaining chard.
4. Squeeze out the chard with your hands. Spread the chard in a circle the size of a pie on a dish towel. Roll up the towel and have someone help you twist the ends to squeeze out as much moisture as possible. Pulse the dried chard in a food processor until finely chopped. Squeeze out in a dish towel once more, until very dry.
5. Melt half the butter. Mix the chard and ricotta in a bowl. Add the melted butter, flour, 1 heaping teaspoon

salt, and the nutmeg and mix again. Drop in the egg and egg yolks; season with pepper, and stir again.
6. Sprinkle a cutting board with flour. Shape the ricotta mixture into 1-ounce balls, about 1 tablespoon each, dropping them onto the board; you should have about 24. Put a teaspoon of flour into a narrow wineglass. Drop in a ball and swirl until it forms an oval. Repeat (you may need to change the glass). You can freeze the malfatti at this point.
7. Bring a pot of salted water to a boil. Drop in the malfatti and cook until they float, about 8 minutes (10 minutes if frozen).
8. Meanwhile, put the remaining butter in a small sauté pan and heat until bubbling, shaking the pan. When it smells nutty, add the sage and cook for 30 seconds. Season with salt.
9. Drain the malfatti and arrange on plates. Spoon on the butter and sage. Grate Parmesan over each plate.

SERVES 4 TO 6 AS A LIGHT MAIN COURSE, 6 TO 8 AS A FIRST COURSE

SERVING SUGGESTIONS
Ricotta Crostini with Fresh Thyme and Dried Oregano (p. 93), Artichoke Salad with Anchovy and Capers (p. 174), Sea Bass in Grappa (p. 443), Canestrelli (Shortbread from Ovada; p. 692), Chicken Canzanese (p. 458), Panna Cotta (p. 840), Pruneaux du Pichet (Prunes in a Pitcher; p. 822)

NOVEMBER 17, 2002: "FOOD: NAKED CAME THE PASTA," BY AMANDA HESSER. RECIPE ADAPTED FROM ANNA KLINGER, THE CHEF AND CO-OWNER OF AL DI LA IN BROOKLYN.

—2002

✐ RED WINE RISOTTO

This is a great recipe to turn to when you need a rice dish to round out a winter menu.

———

2½ cups chicken broth

2 tablespoons unsalted butter

1 tablespoon olive oil

1 medium yellow onion, chopped

2 cloves garlic, smashed

1 cup Arborio rice

2 cups dry red wine

Kosher salt

I cup grated Parmesan cheese

2 tablespoons thinly sliced chives

I teaspoon thyme leaves

1. Bring the broth to a simmer in a small saucepan. Melt 1 tablespoon butter in the oil in a medium saucepan over medium-low heat. When it foams, add the onion and garlic; cook until softened. Pour in the rice and stir to coat. Cook, stirring slowly, until the rice is lightly toasted, about 3 minutes.

2. Pour in 1 cup wine and reduce over medium-high heat until almost gone. Add the second cup and reduce once more. When the pan liquid is syrupy, begin ladling in the hot broth ½ cup at a time, stirring the rice and adjusting the heat so that the broth is just bubbling at the edges. Continue stirring and adding broth as needed. Season with salt as you go. The rice is done when it is tender but still firm to the bite in the center. (If you run out of broth before the rice is cooked, add hot water.) The mixture should be creamy and loose, not soupy. Taste and adjust the seasoning.

3. Stir in ½ cup cheese and the remaining tablespoon of butter. Fold in the chives and thyme. Serve, passing the remaining cheese at the table.

SERVES 4 AS A FIRST COURSE

SERVING SUGGESTIONS

Raw Spinach Salad (p. 175), Crisp-Braised Duck Legs with Aromatic Vegetables (p. 487), Pierre Hermé's Chocolate Sablés (p. 704)

MAY 28, 2003: "PAIRINGS: COOKING RISOTTO WITH AN INEX-PENSIVE AND DECENT RED WINE," BY AMANDA HESSER.

—2003

🖎 PIERRE FRANEY'S PASTA WITH CLAMS

Sam Sifton, my former boss and the man behind "The Cheat" food column in the *Magazine*, insisted I include this recipe. Yes, he conceded, it does contain an ocean of cream. Yes, it does contain just a lot of everything. But, he promised, it's fantastic. And it is.

I tablespoon olive oil

2 medium cloves garlic, finely chopped

2 teaspoons thyme leaves

I cup fresh clam juice

¼ cup dry white wine

I cup heavy cream, or more as needed

I cup tightly packed basil leaves, plus more to taste

I pint shucked chowder or cherrystone clams, coarsely chopped

Salt and freshly ground black pepper

I pound fresh fettuccine

½ cup freshly grated Parmesan cheese, or to taste

1. Heat the olive oil in a 10- or 12-inch skillet over medium heat and sauté the garlic until fragrant, taking care not to burn it. Add the thyme and clam juice and simmer until reduced by half, about 4 minutes. Add the wine and reduce, by half, about 2 minutes. Add the cream and simmer until the mixture thickens slightly, about 5 minutes. Remove from the heat.

2. Combine 1 cup basil leaves and the clams and add to the sauce. Season with salt and pepper. Set aside, loosely covered to keep warm.

3. Cook the fettuccine in boiling salted water until al dente. Reserve 1 cup of the cooking water, then drain. Add the pasta to the sauce and stir to coat. Add Parmesan to taste. Correct the seasoning. If the sauce is too thick, add some of the reserved pasta water or additional cream, sparingly. Simmer the pasta, stirring until the sauce is the desired thickness. Add more basil to taste.

SERVES 4 AS A MAIN COURSE

COOKING NOTES

I added ¼ cup of the reserved pasta water in Step 3, but I could have added a bit more.

A little freshly grated lemon zest over each plate would be a great touch.

SERVING SUGGESTIONS

Caesar Salad (p. 174), Strawberry Sorbet (p. 732), Coupe Lena Horne (Coffee Ice Cream Sundae; p. 722)

JULY 13, 2003: "FOOD: CLAM DIGGER," BY JASON EPSTEIN. RECIPE ADAPTED FROM PIERRE FRANEY.

—2003

⌒ PUMPKIN, SAGE, CHESTNUT, AND BACON RISOTTO

Jamie Oliver, the British celebrity chef, doesn't stint on ingredients. So when he made this autumnal risotto for a column I was writing about him, he threw in just about every emblem of fall except dry leaves.

You can use butternut squash if you can't find pumpkin, and you can roast it and the bacon ahead of time. (A little advance planning helps with this recipe.) And, like Oliver, you can buy vacuum-packed chestnuts. Plan for a 2-minute pause before serving the risotto. "The real key," Oliver told me, "is to take it off the heat, stir in your butter, seasonings. Then you put the lid on and let it sit 2 minutes. That's what I learned from the old Italian birds. Lid on top, 2 minutes, let it relax."

If you've achieved the right texture, the risotto, once plated, will spread like melting ice cream.

For some recipes by Oliver's mentors, Ruth Rogers and Rose Gray, see the Strawberry Sorbet on p. 732, Sformata di Ricotta on p. 256, and Rhubarb Orange on p. 864.

————

I small sweet cooking pumpkin or large
   butternut squash (about 2½ pounds)
Olive oil
I tablespoon coriander seeds
Sea salt and freshly ground black pepper
12 slices bacon or pancetta
2 ounces peeled chestnuts (vacuum-packed are fine),
   about ⅓ cup
15 sage leaves
4 cups chicken broth
3 shallots, finely chopped
5 small stalks celery, finely chopped
I cup Arborio rice
½ cup dry white wine or dry vermouth
4 tablespoons unsalted butter
¾ cup freshly grated Parmesan cheese,
   plus more for serving
About I cup mascarpone cheese (optional)

1. Heat the oven to 375 degrees. Halve the pumpkin lengthwise and peel it. Remove the seeds, rinse and drain them, and reserve. Cut the pumpkin lengthwise into thick slices and spread in a layer across a large baking sheet. (If using squash, cut it into quarters.) Sprinkle the pumpkin with olive oil.

2. Using a mortar and pestle, pound the coriander seeds until crushed. Sprinkle over the pumpkin, along with salt and pepper. Bake until soft, about 40 minutes.

3. Remove the pumpkin from the oven (leave the oven on) and lay the bacon over it. Combine the reserved pumpkin seeds, chestnuts, sage, and salt and pepper to taste in a small bowl. Add 1 tablespoon olive oil and mix well. Sprinkle over the pumpkin and bacon. Bake until the bacon is crisp, 10 to 15 minutes.

4. Remove the pumpkin from the oven. Scrape the bacon, chestnuts, sage, and pumpkin seeds onto a plate; reserve. Finely chop about half the pumpkin. Chop the other half so that it is slightly chunky; reserve.

5. Bring the chicken broth to a simmer in a small pan over medium-low heat, then reduce the heat to very low to keep warm.

6. Place a large saucepan over medium heat and add 1 tablespoon olive oil, the shallots, celery, and a pinch of salt. Stir, cover, and cook for 3 minutes. Increase the heat to medium-high, add the rice, and stir constantly until the rice is translucent, 2 to 3 minutes. Stir in the wine until it is absorbed, 1 to 2 minutes.

7. Begin adding the broth to the rice a ladleful at a time, stirring constantly. Allow each ladleful to be absorbed before adding the next; this process will take about 20 minutes. When ready, the rice will be soft with a slight bite. Season with salt and pepper to taste.

8. Remove the rice from the heat, add the finely chopped pumpkin, and stir vigorously until mixed. Fold in the pumpkin chunks. Mix in the butter and Parmesan. Place a lid over the saucepan and let sit for 2 minutes.

9. Place a portion of risotto on each of 6 serving plates. Top each portion with crumbled bacon, and sprinkle with the mixture of chestnuts, sage, and pumpkin seeds. Add a dash more Parmesan cheese. Garnish each plate with a dollop of mascarpone, if desired, and serve immediately.

SERVES 4 AS A MAIN COURSE,
6 AS A FIRST COURSE

COOKING NOTE
When eating risotto, you're supposed to start at the outer perimeter of the rice and work your way toward the center. This way you eat the coolest parts first.

SERVING SUGGESTIONS
Fennel, Orange, Watercress, and Walnut Salad (p. 186), Saffron Panna Cotta (p. 845), Apple Galette (p. 843), Marcella's Pear Cake (p. 769)

OCTOBER 22, 2003: "THE CHEF: JAMIE OLIVER: EVER MADE RISOTTO, MATE?" BY AMANDA HESSER. RECIPE ADAPTED FROM JAMIE OLIVER.

—2003

HOPPERS (COCONUT CREPES)

Stands selling "hoppers" abound in Sri Lanka, and I fell in love with them on a trip there. Called *appa* in Sinhalese, these bowl-shaped crepes are crisp on the edges and have a gentle whiff of coconut. Roadside cooks mix a batter of rice flour and coconut milk fermented with toddy, a spirit from the kitul palm, and cook the batter in small woks swabbed with coconut oil. Hoppers come plain or with an egg cracked into the center and are sometimes sweetened with honey. They were once a fixture of Sri Lankan breakfasts, served with curries. Now they're eaten any time of day. I would happily eat one right now.

———

1 1/2 cups rice flour
1/4 teaspoon active dry yeast
1 teaspoon sugar
1/2 teaspoon salt
1 cup unsweetened coconut milk
6 tablespoons tepid water
Coconut or vegetable oil for frying
12 large eggs, at room temperature (optional)

1. Stir the rice flour, yeast, sugar, salt, coconut milk, and water together in a large bowl. Cover and refrigerate for at least 8 hours.
2. Stir the batter. It should have the consistency of paint; if necessary, add water to thin it. Place an 8-inch wok or a crepe pan over medium-high heat. Using paper towels or a brush, lightly swab the surface of the pan with oil; there should be a very thin film. Using a ladle, pour about 3 tablespoons of batter into the center of the pan, then quickly tilt and turn the pan so the batter spreads across the surface and up the sides. The hopper should be as thin as paper at the edges and no thicker than cardboard in the center.
3. Crack an egg in the center (hoppers may also be made without the eggs), cover the pan, and cook until the white of the egg is just cooked through and the hopper is crisp and browned on the bottom, about 4 minutes. Loosen the hopper using a knife and slide onto a platter. Repeat with the remaining batter (and eggs).

SERVES 6 AS A SIDE DISH

SERVING SUGGESTIONS
Ceylon Curry of Oysters (p. 391), Tuna Curry (p. 435), Katta Sambol (p. 611), Country Captain (p. 455), Bombay Curry (p. 452), Pineapple Carpaccio with Lime Sorbet (p. 842), Cantaloupe–Star Anise Sorbet (p. 728), Sticky Rice with Mango (p. 861)

NOVEMBER 7, 2004: "THE SPICE ROUTE," BY AMANDA HESSER.

—2004

MI QUANG (RICE NOODLES WITH SHRIMP, HERBS, AND FRIED PORK RINDS)

On a trip to Vietnam, I spent most of my time eating street foods. In Hoi An, I became smitten with *mi quang*, a rice noodle soup prepared by a shy, rather round woman named Sao. She had reduced her kitchen to two bamboo baskets carried over her shoulders on a wooden yoke. One basket was lined with metal and topped with a box of burning charcoal. On this she warmed the broth. The other basket brimmed with fresh ingredients. When customers stopped her, she set down her portable kitchen and began warming noodles in the broth, arranging them atop lettuce and basil, spooning tiny cooked shrimp and eggs over them, and then scattering the top with scallions, ground peanuts, and fried pork rinds. Sliced green chile and half a kumquat were served on the side.

———

1 1/2 teaspoons turmeric
1 pound rice noodles (as thick as spaghetti)
2 tablespoons peanut oil

1 tablespoon Asian fish sauce

1 teaspoon tamarind paste

1 tablespoon sugar

½ teaspoon chili powder

Sea salt

½ pound small shrimp

6 quail eggs, hard-boiled for 5 minutes and peeled

A handful of small watercress leaves

A handful of Thai basil leaves, or Italian basil

½ cup bean sprouts

1 scallion, thinly sliced

2 tablespoons chopped cilantro

2 tablespoons coarsely ground peanuts

4 handfuls fried pork rinds, crushed into pieces
the size of a quarter

4 kumquats, each halved like a grapefruit

2 teaspoons finely sliced green chile

1. Fill a large pot with 3 quarts water, add the turmeric, and bring to a boil. Add the rice noodles and cook until tender, about 12 minutes. Drain, and return the cooking water to the pot.

2. Meanwhile, combine the oil, fish sauce, tamarind paste, sugar, chili powder, and a pinch of salt in a small sauté pan and place over medium-high heat. When the oil bubbles, add the shrimp and cook for 2 minutes on each side. Remove from the heat and stir in the quail eggs.

3. Divide the watercress, basil, and bean sprouts among 4 large rice bowls. Quickly dip the rice noodles into the hot cooking water and then divide among the bowls, so they are slicked with some of the cooking water. Spoon over the shrimp and quail eggs with their cooking oil. Then sprinkle with the scallion, cilantro, peanuts, a pinch of salt each, and the pork rinds. Serve, passing the kumquats and chile at the table.

SERVES 4 AS A MAIN COURSE

SERVING SUGGESTIONS
Pork Belly Tea Sandwiches (p. 88), Mango Ice Cream (p. 729)

NOVEMBER 7, 2004: "THE SPICE ROUTE," BY AMANDA HESSER.

—2004

⌒ PORCINI BREAD STUFFING

I'd hate for people to associate this stuffing only with Thanksgiving. It's an excellent cold-weather side dish, like a savory bread pudding without the pudding. Serve it with any kind of game, and especially with pork.

———

1 cup dried porcini or morel mushrooms

2 cups warm water

1 cup Calvados or Cognac

5 tablespoons unsalted butter

3 onions, thinly sliced

Salt

10 to 12 cups torn sourdough or regular
country bread (1 large loaf)

¼ cup finely chopped flat-leaf parsley

2 tablespoons finely chopped rosemary

2 tablespoons finely chopped sage

1 cup applesauce

¾ cup raisins or dried cherries

½ cup coarsely chopped walnuts or pecans

1 to 2 cups chicken or vegetable broth

Freshly ground black pepper

1. Soak the mushrooms in the warm water for about 30 minutes. Drain, reserving the liquid, and thickly slice the mushrooms.

2. Meanwhile, simmer the Calvados in a saucepan until reduced to about ⅓ cup.

3. Heat the oven to 375 degrees. Butter a 9-by-13-inch baking dish with a teaspoon or two of the butter. (The oven can be anywhere from 350 to 400 degrees, if you need to cook both the stuffing and the turkey in it.)

4. Melt the remaining butter in a large deep pot. Add the onions and sauté until translucent, about 5 minutes; sprinkle with salt if the onions are browning too fast. Add the sliced mushrooms and sauté for 2 minutes. Add the bread, reserved mushroom liquid, parsley, rosemary, and sage. Stir in the reduced Calvados, applesauce, raisins, nuts, and enough stock so the mixture is moist but not wet. Season to taste with salt and pepper.

5. Turn into the buttered baking dish. Bake for 45 minutes to 1 hour, until firm and crusty.

COOKING NOTES

I used a regular loaf of country bread, not sourdough—I worried that the flavor of sourdough would overpower the mushrooms and Calvados.

If the onions are browning, too fast in Step 4, add some salt, which releases their juices and slows their cooking.

I only needed ½ cup of stock—play it by ear.

I used large Flame raisins, which soaked up the Calvados and puffed up like cold birds.

SERVING SUGGESTIONS

Roast Lemon Pepper Duck with Honey Lemon Sauce (p. 470), Slow-Roasted Duck (p. 475), Pork Arrosto with Prunes and Grappa (p. 577), Roasted Brine-Cured Turkey (p. 474), Ralph Vetter's Sweet Potatoes with Lemon (p. 295), The Most Voluptuous Cauliflower (p. 241), Molasses Cup Cakes with Lemon Icing (p. 745), Apple Crumb Pie (p. 841)

NOVEMBER 17, 2004: "THERE'S ONLY ONE STUFFING: ASK ANY COOK," BY JULIA MOSKIN. RECIPE ADAPTED FROM JULIAN M. COHEN.

—2004

↩ STUCK-POT RICE WITH YOGURT AND SPICES

"Those of us who learned how to cook in the '60s and '70s heard as many lies about rice as we did about sex," Mark Bittman, "The Minimalist" columnist, wrote. "While prudence forbids me from elaborating on the second, I have plenty to say about the first." And indeed he did, debunking the notion that cooking rice requires skill or constant vigilance. "Most of all," he concluded, "rice is not 'ruined' when it sticks to the bottom of the pot."

The crisp grains that stick to the base of a rice pan are beloved in many parts of the world, just as the crusty bits that form on the bottom of a pan when roasting potatoes are relished here.

Making stuck-pot rice is a two-step process. First you boil the rice, then you fold it together with season-ings—here, yogurt, curry powder, and lime juice—and cook it once more. The best part is that you can throw this together, then blithely retreat from the stove.

And when you return to the stove, you'll have a spectacular treat, with chunks of crunchy, caramelized rice strewn through the tangy, moist grains.

———

Salt
1½ cups basmati rice, well rinsed
Freshly ground black pepper
¼ cup peanut oil or neutral oil, like grapeseed or corn oil
¼ cup plain yogurt, preferably whole-milk
1 tablespoon fresh lime juice
1 tablespoon good curry powder

1. Fill a medium pot with lightly salted water and bring to a boil. Stir in the rice and return to a boil, then lower the heat so the water is at a lively simmer and cook undisturbed for 5 minutes; drain. The rice will be only partly done. Season to taste with salt and pepper.

2. Whisk together 2 tablespoons oil, the yogurt, lime juice, and curry powder in a large bowl. Season to taste with salt and pepper and whisk until smooth. Add the rice and toss gently to coat with the yogurt mixture.

3. Put the 2 remaining tablespoons oil in a large heavy pot with a tight-fitting lid and turn the heat to medium-high. Add the rice mixture, pressing it down in the pot with a fork. Wrap a clean kitchen towel around the pot lid so it completely covers the inside of the lid; gather the corners on top so they do not fall anywhere near the heat, and place the lid on the pot, sealing it tightly. The mixture will sizzle immediately. When the rice and spices are fragrant—3 to 5 minutes—turn the heat down very low. Cook undisturbed for about 30 minutes; the rice should smell toasty but not burned. Remove from the heat and let sit for 5 minutes.

4. Carefully remove the lid and cloth, and turn the pot upside down over a platter. If the rice comes out in a single crust, terrific. If not, use a spatula to scrape the crisp pieces out of the pot and onto the remaining rice. Season to taste with salt and pepper and serve.

SERVES 4 TO 6 AS A SIDE DISH

For extra flavor, lightly toast the curry powder in a small pan over low heat, before beginning the recipe.

The first time you make this, you're bound to have some scorched rice. Don't give up—you'll eventually figure out the right pot and temperature, and then you'll be very happy indeed.

SERVING SUGGESTIONS

Tibs (p. 545), Broiled Lamb Leg Chops on Eggplant Planks with Mint-Yogurt Sauce (p. 549), Almond-Carrot Salad (p. 204), Baked Mushrooms (p. 212), Hazelnut Baklava (p. 706), Tapioca Pudding (p. 798)

JANUARY 11, 2006: "THE MINIMALIST: RICE, LIES, AND VIDEOTAPE: A CELEBRATION OF DARKNESS," BY MARK BITTMAN.

—2006

RABBIT RAGU WITH PAPPARDELLE

———

1 rabbit (2½ to 3½ pounds), cut into 8 pieces
Kosher salt and freshly ground black pepper
¼ cup olive oil
1 anchovy fillet (optional)
1 medium onion, diced
1 carrot, peeled and diced
1 stalk celery, diced
Pinch of crushed red pepper flakes
1 tablespoon minced garlic
1 teaspoon tomato paste
1 cup dry red wine
1 cup seeded, chopped canned San Marzano tomatoes
1 cup chicken broth
2 bay leaves
2 sprigs thyme
2 tablespoons unsalted butter, cut into pieces
¾ pound pappardelle
Freshly grated Pecorino Romano cheese for serving

1. Pat the rabbit pieces dry and season with salt and pepper. Heat the oil in a Dutch oven over medium-high heat and brown the pieces, working in batches if needed to avoid crowding. Transfer to a plate.

2. Reduce the heat to medium. Add the anchovy, if you choose, and mash it until it dissolves into the oil. Add the onion, carrot, and celery and cook, stirring, until soft, about 5 minutes. Add the red pepper flakes, garlic, and tomato paste and stir for another minute. Deglaze the pan with the wine, scraping up the browned bits, turn the heat to high, and boil to burn off the alcohol, about 4 minutes. Add the tomatoes, broth, bay leaves, and thyme. Return the rabbit pieces to the pot, spacing them evenly so they are partly covered by the liquid. Bring to a boil, then reduce the heat and simmer, covered, until the rabbit is falling off the bone, about 1½ hours; turn the pieces at least once.

3. Turn off the heat and discard the thyme and bay leaves. Remove the rabbit from the sauce and let cool.

4. Pull the meat from the bones. Shred some pieces and leave others large. Simmer the sauce until thickened, 10 to 15 minutes, then return the meat to the pot. Stir in the butter piece by piece. Season to taste with salt and pepper.

5. Meanwhile, bring a large pot of salted water to a boil. Add the pappardelle and cook until al dente. Before draining, save a cup of the pasta water.

6. Toss the pappardelle with the sauce over low heat, adding pasta water as necessary if the sauce is too thick. Divide among pasta bowls and top with the grated cheese.

SERVES 6 AS A MAIN COURSE

SERVING SUGGESTIONS

Leeks Vinaigrette (p. 217), Crostini with Eggplant and Pine Nut Puree (p. 78), Fennel and Blood Orange Salad (p. 195), Almond Cake (p. 777), Figs in Whiskey (p. 859), Lucas Schoormans's Lemon Tart (p. 857)

MARCH 12, 2006: "THE WAY WE EAT: RABBIT IS RICH," BY RANDY KENNEDY, A *TIMES* REPORTER.

—2006

⌒ THE WAY LIFE SHOULD BE (FETTUCCINE WITH LOBSTER AND HERBS)

"Since the invention of license plates, the humble state of Maine has been burdened with two fairly onerous slogans," Heidi Julavits, a novelist and part-time Maine resident, wrote in the *Magazine*. "During the '90s, 'Vacationland' was followed by 'The Way Life Should Be,' a motto that has been interpreted by former Vacationlanders not as an exhortation to be poor, addicted to coffee liqueur, or permanently swaddled in thermals, but as a God-given right to be served boiled lobster for dinner every single night of their holidays.

"These slogan believers, also known as my friends, spend a night or two at my house en route to Acadia, arriving at my doorstep demanding The Way Life Should Be," Julavits continued. "I accommodate the first guests of the summer with a weary smile. By the fourth, fifth, ninth visitor who specifies boiled lobster, my husband starts to become inhospitable." To preserve their sanity, she and her husband came up with this pasta dish (as well as a lobster salad, see p. 440), which allows you to cook and shell the lobsters ahead of time, and marinate them in oil and herbs. All there is to do at dinnertime is boil up some fettuccine.

The marination is a little like that in Pamela Sherrid's Summer Pasta on p. 329, in which tomatoes soak in oil and aromatics before you add the hot pasta. Here the marination is particularly potent. The lobster and herbs scent the oil and, later, the whole dish. I was smitten.

————

Six 1¼-pound live lobsters

⅓ cup fresh lemon juice (from about 2 lemons)

½ cup extra virgin olive oil

2 cloves garlic, minced

2 dried red chiles, crumbled

A small handful of mint leaves, chopped (optional, but really good)

A small handful of flat-leaf parsley leaves, chopped (optional, but also really good)

A small handful of basil leaves, chopped (optional)

2 large pinches salt

1 pound fettuccine or spaghetti

2 garlic scapes or garlic chives (optional)

1. Boil the lobsters according to the recipe that follows. Let cool.

2. Remove the meat from the shells and cut into large chunks.

3. To make the marinade, combine the lemon juice, olive oil, garlic, chiles, and mint, parsley, and basil, if using, in a large bowl. Season with the salt. Add the lobster meat. Let sit at room temperature for 30 to 60 minutes; do not refrigerate.

4. Bring a large pot of salted water to a boil. Add the pasta and cook until al dente. Drain and return to the pot.

5. Pour the entire bowl of lobster and marinade onto the pasta, toss, and serve garnished with snipped garlic scapes.

SERVES 6 AS A MAIN COURSE

FAILPROOF WAY TO BOIL LOBSTER

Julavits wrote, "This recipe comes from Paul Brayton, a priest at the Universal Life Church, who helped to develop the small Maine Bouchot mussel (and who also performed my wedding ceremony).

"Bring a very large pot of salted water (or, ideally, ocean water) to a boil. Add the lobsters to the pot—in batches if necessary—and wait until the water returns to a rolling boil. Watch the lobsters: when they turn bright red, tug on one of the feelers. If it comes loose with very little resistance, the lobsters are done. Drain and let cool."

COOKING NOTE
I took a "small handful" of each herb to mean ½ cup loosely packed (of each).

SERVING SUGGESTIONS
Thomas Keller's Gazpacho (p. 146), Eggplant Involtini (p. 256), Strawberry Sorbet (p. 732)

JULY 2, 2006: "THE WAY WE EAT: BOILING POINT," BY HEIDI JULAVITS.

—2006

BULGUR SALAD WITH POMEGRANATE DRESSING AND TOASTED NUTS

2¾ cups quick-cooking bulgur, preferably coarse-ground

Salt

¾ cup olive oil

7 tablespoons pomegranate molasses (available at Middle Eastern markets), or more to taste

Juice of 4 lemons, or more to taste

6 tablespoons tomato paste

2 teaspoons ground cumin

2 teaspoons ground coriander

1 teaspoon ground allspice

½ teaspoon cayenne pepper, or more to taste

Freshly ground black pepper

2 cups walnuts, toasted and coarsely chopped

¼ cup pine nuts, lightly toasted

1 bunch flat-leaf parsley leaves, finely chopped (about 1 cup)

1. Put the bulgur in a large bowl and cover with lightly salted cold water. Let soak until tender, for 2 hours, depending on the coarseness of the bulgur.

2. Drain the bulgur in a sieve, firmly pressing out excess water, and transfer to a serving bowl.

3. Whisk the olive oil with the pomegranate molasses, lemon juice, tomato paste, and spices in a bowl. Add salt and pepper and taste; the mixture should be pleasingly tangy. Add more pomegranate molasses and lemon juice if needed. It will taste as if it has too much tomato paste at first, but this mellows once it's mixed with the bulgur. Pour half the dressing over the bulgur and mix well. Set aside for about 10 minutes to let the bulgur absorb the dressing.

4. Taste the bulgur for salt, adding more if needed. Add half the remaining dressing and all the nuts and parsley and mix well. Taste again and add more dressing as needed.

SERVES 8 TO 10 AS A SIDE DISH

SERVING SUGGESTIONS
Epigram of Lamb (p. 509), Steamed Fennel with Red Pepper Oil (p. 263), Roasted Cauliflower (p. 248), Huntington Pudding (p. 802), Plum Fritters (p. 865)

JULY 12, 2006: "WHEN THE SOUR NOTE IS JUST RIGHT," BY JULIA MOSKIN. RECIPE ADAPTED FROM CLAUDIA RODEN, A COOKBOOK AUTHOR.

—2006

JASMINE TEA RICE

Daniel Patterson, the chef and owner of Coi in San Francisco, writes occasional pieces for the *Magazine* in which he translates for the home a technique or idea that he's pursuing in his restaurant kitchen. In a piece on teas, he showed how to use brewed tea "like a quick, flavorful stock"—in this case, jasmine tea as the stock for cooking rice. Once you've tried it, it seems a natural technique. We probably once had the same hesitation about combining salt and chocolate.

2½ tablespoons jasmine-tea pearls

1½ cups jasmine rice

1 teaspoon kosher salt

1. Bring 2 cups water to a boil in a medium saucepan. Place the tea in a heatproof bowl. Cover with the hot water and let steep for 5 minutes. Strain through a sieve set back into the saucepan and let cool.

2. Rinse the rice with cold water in a large bowl until the water runs clear. Drain and add to the cooled tea. Stir in the salt and let sit for 30 minutes.

3. Cover the saucepan and bring to a boil over medium-high heat, then reduce the heat and simmer for 17 minutes. Let stand for 5 minutes.

SERVES 6 AS A SIDE DISH

COOKING NOTE
Jasmine tea pearls can be found in Asian markets and at specialty tea stores. If you can't get your hands on the pearls, you can use jasmine-scented tea leaves.

SERVING SUGGESTIONS
Warm Eggplant Salad with Sesame and Shallots (p. 203), Rhubarb-Soy-Marinated Duck with Rhubarb-Ginger Compote (p. 468), Lemon Lotus Ice Cream (p. 724)

DECEMBER 17, 2006: "THE WAY WE EAT: STEEP INCREASE," BY DANIEL PATTERSON.

—2006

TAKEOUT-STYLE SESAME NOODLES

It took me forever to decide which sesame noodle recipe to include in the book. There was Emily Tom's Cold Noodles in Sesame Sauce from 1978 (simple, light, and not too oily), Marian Burros's Chinese Carryout Noodles from 1994 (textured with chicken and bok choy), and a whole constellation of others sprinkled across the archives. But then Sam Sifton, then the culture editor and a food columnist at the *Times* (now the restaurant critic), did the work for me. He pored over these old recipes, talked to Chinese food experts in New York, and also got to work in the kitchen, developing a recipe that borrows ideas from other sesame noodle recipes as well as from his own childhood memory of the dish.

Sesame noodles first showed up in the 1970s. "Bright with flavor, slippery against the plastic chopsticks," Sifton wrote, "they represented one of the great steps forward for Chinese food in the United States in the post–chop-suey era: away from bland monotony and toward real complexity of flavor." The dish is often attributed to Shorty Tang, a Chinese immigrant who cooked his way around Manhattan. Sifton offered a Twitter-like history of the dish's path to America: "The Communists took over China in 1949. Tang and other great chefs began to slip and slide toward the United States soon after, riding to Taiwan with banquet crews loyal to Chiang Kai-shek—and from there to Hong Kong, India, Brazil, East Broadway, and the Upper West Side."

In Sifton's perfected recipe, he left out the chicken and broccoli, an addition considered blasphemous by some. He minimized the sugar to keep the flavors clean, and while he added ginger, he omitted the scallions. What you get is a full-court press of flavors: sweetness, spice, ginger, sesame, garlic, peanuts, and the occasional cooling flash of cucumber.

---

1 pound Chinese lo mein egg noodles (1/8 inch thick), frozen or, preferably, fresh (available in Asian markets)
2 tablespoons Asian sesame oil, plus a splash
3 1/2 tablespoons soy sauce
2 tablespoons Chinese rice vinegar, or other unseasoned rice vinegar
2 tablespoons Chinese sesame paste or tahini
1 tablespoon smooth peanut butter
1 tablespoon sugar
1 tablespoon finely grated fresh ginger
2 teaspoons minced garlic
2 teaspoons chile-garlic paste (sambal oelek) or to taste
1/2 cucumber, peeled, halved lengthwise, seeded, and cut into 1/8-by-1/8-by-2-inch sticks
1/4 cup chopped roasted peanuts

1. Bring a large pot of water to a boil. Add the noodles and cook until barely tender, about 5 minutes; they should retain a hint of chewiness. Drain, rinse with cold water, drain again, and toss with a splash of sesame oil.

2. Whisk together the remaining 2 tablespoons sesame oil, the soy sauce, rice vinegar, sesame paste, peanut butter, sugar, ginger, garlic, and chile-garlic paste in a medium bowl.

3. Pour half the sauce over the noodles and toss. Add more sauce as desired. Transfer to a serving bowl, and garnish with the cucumber and peanuts.

SERVES 4 AS A MAIN COURSE

COOKING NOTES
Sifton observed:

"The 'Chinese sesame paste' . . . is made of toasted sesame seeds; it is not the same as tahini, the Middle Eastern paste made of plain untoasted sesame. But you could use tahini in a pinch. You need only add a little toasted sesame oil to compensate for flavor, and perhaps some peanut butter to keep the sauce emulsified.

"On which subject, the whole point of cold sesame noodles is what's called in the food trade its 'mouth feel,' the velvety-smooth feeling of perfectly combined ingredients. That's why you find so much peanut butter in preparations of cold sesame noodles. Peanut butter emulsifies better than sesame paste.

"Hey, where are the Szechuan peppercorns? Szechuan food depends on their tingly numbing power! Perhaps, but the little fruits were banned from the United States from 1968 until 2005 by the Food and Drug Administration because they were feared to carry citrus canker, a bacterial disease. And while you could always find them in Chinatowns somewhere (sitting, dry and baleful, in a pile), there are few in the true cult of sesame noodles who use them in their recipes.

By all means, add some if you like: toast a tablespoon's worth in a dry pan, crush lightly, and whisk the resulting mess into your sauce."

SERVING SUGGESTIONS
Shrimp Toast (p. 60), Oriental Watercress Soup (p. 111), Chinese Barbecued Spareribs (p. 517), Chinese Pork Balls (p. 59), Hunan Beef with Cumin (p. 575), Clams in Black Bean Sauce (p. 442), Chinese-Style Steamed Black Sea Bass (p. 432), Sugar Snap Peas with Horseradish (p. 259), Lemon Lotus Ice Cream (p. 724), Tea Ice Cream (p. 717), Poached Pears with Asian Spices (p. 856)

APRIL 1, 2007: "THE WAY WE EAT; NEW YORK NOODLE-TOWN," BY SAM SIFTON. RECIPE ADAPTED FROM MARTIN YAN, MARIAN BURROS, AND MEMORY.

—2007

Cover the dish with foil and place it in a roasting pan. Add enough tepid water to come halfway up the sides of the baking dish. Bake until the custard is just set, about 1½ hours.

SERVES 8 AS A SIDE DISH

SERVING SUGGESTIONS
Roast Chicken with Bread Salad (p. 467), Zucchini and Vermouth (p. 227), Lamb Shoulder Chops with Anchovy and Mint Butter (p. 567), Grilled Hanger Steak (p. 551), Raspberry Granita (p. 719), Pine Nut Cookies (p. 689)

MAY 13, 2007: "THE WAY WE EAT: THE CHEESE STANDS ALONE," BY AMANDA HESSER. RECIPE ADAPTED FROM SUNDAY SUPPERS AT LUCQUES, BY SUZANNE GOIN.

—2007

⌒ SAVORY RICOTTA PUDDING

Yes, I know, it's strange to put this recipe in this chapter, but where else should it go? It's an orphan pudding, and even orphan pudding deserves a loving home. Plus this sublime ricotta version—somewhere between a savory custard and a soufflé—is a boon companion to the chapter's other hearty side dishes.

———

2 extra-large eggs
1 extra-large egg yolk
2 cups whole-milk ricotta, drained overnight in a refrigerator in a strainer set over a bowl
1 cup heavy cream
1 cup whole milk
1½ teaspoons thyme leaves
2 teaspoons kosher salt
¼ teaspoon freshly ground black pepper
1 dried chile de árbol, thinly sliced on the diagonal

1. Heat the oven to 350 degrees. Butter a 9-inch square baking dish. Whisk together the eggs, egg yolk, and ricotta in a bowl. Whisk in the cream, milk, 1 teaspoon thyme, the salt, and pepper. The batter will be a little lumpy.
2. Pour the batter into the baking dish. Sprinkle the top with the chile and remaining ½ teaspoon thyme.

⌒ YOGURT RICE

The real name of this dish, which comes from India, is Thayir Choru, but I have a feeling you'll end up calling it yogurt rice. I love this dish as much as I love my children and my husband.

———

4 cups cooked long-grain white rice, at room temperature
1½ cups plain whole-milk yogurt, drained overnight in the refrigerator in a cheesecloth-lined strainer set over a bowl
Salt
2 tablespoons vegetable oil
1 teaspoon brown or black mustard seeds
1½ teaspoons urad dal (split hulled black lentils)
1½ teaspoons chana dal (split hulled yellow peas)
2 tablespoons coarsely chopped raw cashews
3 fresh green Thai or serrano chiles (or 1 jalapeño pepper), thinly sliced
1 tablespoon grated fresh ginger
15 to 20 fresh curry leaves
Pappadums for serving (optional)
Indian pickles for serving (optional)

1. Combine the rice and yogurt in a bowl, mixing well, and season with salt to taste.
2. Heat the oil in a small skillet. Add the mustard

seeds. When they sputter, add the urad dal, chana dal, and cashews. When the dal and cashews turn golden brown, turn the heat to low, add the chiles, ginger, and curry leaves and stir-fry for 1 to 2 minutes.

3. Remove the spice blend from the heat and pour over the rice mixture. Mix well and adjust the seasoning if needed. Serve at room temperature with, if desired, pappadums and/or Indian pickles.

SERVES 4 TO 5 AS A SIDE DISH

COOKING NOTE
The dals, curry leaves, pappadums, and pickles are available at Indian markets, or on line at www.kalustyans.com.

SERVING SUGGESTIONS
Curried Zucchini Soup (p. 123), Bademiya's Justly Famous Bombay Chile-and-Cilantro Chicken (p. 471), String Beans with Ginger and Garlic (p. 260), Tapioca Pudding (p. 798), Mango Ice Cream (p. 729)

JULY 18, 2007: "TRANSLATING INDIA, SOMETIMES FLUENTLY," BY ANNE MENDELSON. RECIPE ADAPTED FROM *GRAINS, GREENS, AND GRATED COCONUTS*, BY AMMINI RAMACHANDRAN.

—2007

1. Heat the oil in a heavy saucepan with a tight-fitting lid over medium heat. Add the garlic and scallion and cook, stirring, just until softened, about 3 minutes; reduce the heat if necessary to prevent browning. Add the rice, coconut milk, water, thyme, Scotch bonnet, if using, beans, and the salt. Bring to a boil over high heat, then stir well, reduce the heat to very low, cover tightly, and cook without disturbing for 25 to 30 minutes, until the liquid has been absorbed and the rice is very tender.

2. Add the black pepper and, if desired, more salt. Fluff before serving.

SERVES 8 AS A SIDE DISH

SERVING SUGGESTIONS
North Carolina–Style Pulled Pork (p. 550), Beer-Can Chicken (p. 473), Brined and Roasted Pork Belly (p. 556), Fennel and Apple Salad with Juniper (p. 189), Cucumbers in Cream (p. 225), Molasses Cup Cakes with Lemon Icing (p. 745), Fresh Ginger Cake (p. 775), Clove Granita (p. 727)

JULY 2, 2008: "SWEET HEAT: FOR JAMAICANS, IT'S ABOUT JERK," BY JULIA MOSKIN. RECIPE ADAPTED FROM *JERK BARBECUE FROM JAMAICA*, BY HELEN WILLINSKY.

—2008

～ RICE AND PEAS (JAMAICAN RICE WITH COCONUT AND RED BEANS)

2 teaspoons vegetable oil
1 clove garlic, minced
1 scallion, thinly sliced
2 cups jasmine rice
One 14-ounce can unsweetened coconut milk, well shaken
1 1/2 cups water
1 sprig thyme
1 Scotch bonnet or other hot chile (optional)
About 3 cups cooked small red beans or pinto beans (start with 1 1/2 cups dried beans or use two 15-ounce cans, drained and rinsed)
1 teaspoon salt, or more to taste
Freshly ground black pepper

～ PAD THAI–STYLE RICE SALAD

I'd like to have this in my refrigerator at all times—the perfect working-at-home lunch.

1 1/2 to 2 cups long-grain white rice, preferably jasmine
Salt
5 tablespoons peanut or neutral oil, like grapeseed or corn
2 large eggs, lightly beaten
4 cloves garlic, minced
1/4 pound shrimp (about 5 large), peeled and chopped
1/4 pound chicken meat (about 1 small boneless, skinless thigh), chopped
4 scallions, cut into 1-inch lengths
1 cup bean sprouts, rinsed and trimmed (optional)
2 tablespoons Asian fish sauce, or more to taste
2 chiles, preferably Thai, seeded and sliced (optional)
1 tablespoon plus 1 1/2 teaspoons tamarind paste or ketchup

2 teaspoons sugar (if you use tamarind)

2 tablespoons fresh lime juice

¼ cup chopped peanuts

¼ cup chopped cilantro

I lime, cut into wedges

1. Cook the rice in abundant salted water, as you would pasta, until it's just done, 12 to 15 minutes. Drain, spread in a thin layer on a baking sheet, and refrigerate to cool. When cool, transfer to a large bowl.

2. Heat 2 tablespoons oil in a wok or a large skillet, preferably nonstick, over medium heat. Add the eggs and scramble quickly for the first minute or so with a fork almost flat against the bottom of the pan; you're aiming for a thin egg crepe of sorts, one with the smallest curd you can achieve. Cook just until set, and remove the crepe to a cutting board. Cut into ¼-inch-wide strips and add to the bowl.

3. Raise the heat to high and add the remaining 3 tablespoons oil. When the oil is hot, add the garlic and shrimp and cook, stirring occasionally, until the shrimp lose their raw gray color; transfer to the bowl with a slotted spoon. Add the chicken to the wok and sauté until just done. Transfer with the slotted spoon. Add the scallions and half the bean sprouts to the wok and cook, stirring occasionally, for 3 minutes. Transfer with the slotted spoon.

4. Add the fish sauce, chiles, tamarind, and sugar (or ketchup), lime juice, and a little water (start with ¼ cup) to the wok. Stir just to combine and deglaze the pan (add a little more water if necessary), then drizzle the warm dressing over the salad. Toss, taste, and adjust the seasoning, then top with the peanuts, cilantro, and remaining bean sprouts. Serve with lime wedges on the side.

SERVES 8 AS A SIDE DISH, 4 AS A LIGHT LUNCH

SERVING SUGGESTIONS

Pork and Watermelon Salad (p. 574), Laotian Catfish Soup (p. 154), Thai Beef Salad (p. 543), Mango Ice Cream (p. 729), Tapioca Flamingo (p. 810), Sticky Rice with Mango (p. 861)

JULY 30, 2008: "THE MINIMALIST: A WHITE, OR BROWN, CANVAS," BY MARK BITTMAN.

—2008

⌒ COCONUT BARLEY PILAF WITH CORN, CHICKEN, AND CASHEWS

I large boneless, skinless chicken breast (about 10 ounces), patted dry

I teaspoon salt, plus more to taste

Freshly ground black pepper

2 tablespoons extra virgin olive oil

½ cup salted roasted cashews, roughly chopped

½ medium onion, cut into small dice (about I cup)

I jalapeño pepper, diced

2 cups pearl barley

One 15-ounce can unsweetened coconut milk

2 ears corn, shucked and kernels sliced off the cobs (about 1½ cups)

2 tablespoons chopped mint, cilantro, or parsley

1. Cut the chicken into 1-inch chunks; season with ½ teaspoon salt and pepper to taste.

2. Heat 1 tablespoon oil in a medium pot over medium-high heat. Add the chicken and cook, stirring occasionally, until light golden and almost cooked through, about 4 minutes. Stir in the cashews and cook for 1 minute more. Transfer to a plate.

3. Add the remaining tablespoon of oil to the pot. Stir in the onion, jalapeño, and a pinch of salt. Cook, stirring, until the onion is slightly softened, 2 to 3 minutes. Stir in the barley and ½ teaspoon salt; cook for 1 minute. Add enough water to the coconut milk to yield 2 cups liquid and add to the pot. Bring to a simmer, then reduce the heat to low and cook, covered, until the barley is almost tender, about 40 minutes.

4. Stir in the corn. If the mixture looks dry, stir in 1¼ cups more water; cover and cook until the barley and corn are tender, 10 to 15 minutes more.

5. Return the chicken mixture to the pot and stir well. Fold in the herbs and add more salt to taste.

SERVES 4 AS A MAIN COURSE

SERVING SUGGESTIONS

Watercress and Basil Soup (p. 152), Lemon Bars (p. 690)

SEPTEMBER 23, 2009: "A GOOD APPETITE: THE COMFORT OF COCONUT," BY MELISSA CLARK.

—2009

• Welsh Rarebit (p. 365) and its bedfellows, Scotch Woodcock (p. 366), Scotch Rarebit, and Golden Buck.

• Open-faced creamed mushroom sandwiches: delicious.

• Lombardi's, the first pizzeria in America, opens in New York City.

• Tea sandwiches.

• The comic strip *Blondie* debuts; Dagwood is always making giant sandwiches.

• Jane Holt explains what pizza is: "a pie made from a yeast dough and filled with any number of different centers, each one containing tomatoes. Cheese, mushrooms, anchovies, capers, onions, and so on may be used."

• A story on how to make pizza appears.

• Open-Faced Tomato Sandwich (p. 367).

• The lobster roll on p. 368 is from 1970, but Craig Claiborne had also published a recipe six years earlier.

• There is no quiche in this book, but this was the decade for it.

• George Germon and Johanne Killeen grill a pizza; the world changes.

• Tarte Flambée (p. 370) tries for fame but comes up short.

• Jason and Jennifer Denton open 'ino, the first serious paninoteca in New York City.

• *Nancy Silverton's Sandwich Book* comes out.

• Franny's Clam Pizza (p. 374).

• Banh mi is the new pho.

• The *New York Times* and *New York* magazine rate New York City's pizza joints. Kesté and Una Pizza Napoletana are on top.

—1870s—
—1902—
—1905—
—1910s—
—1930—
—1944—
—1945—
—1962—
—1964—
—1970s—
—1980—
—1990s—
—1998—
—2002—
—2005—
—2008—
—2009—

• Croque-Monsieur (p. 372) rides the bistro wave.

• The breakfast pizza (p. 646) catches on.

8

SANDWICHES, PIZZA, AND SAVORY PIES

I decided to have a chapter that blended sandwiches with pizzas and other savory tarts because foods that depend heavily on a dough—no matter what its form—share a common goal. Doughs, whether bread or pastry, are there to contain the rest of the ingredients. Often they provide texture (crispness in the Franny's Clam Pizza on p. 374, delicacy in the Foie Gras and Jam Sandwiches on p. 78) and substance (heft in the Welsh Rarebit on p. 365, lightness in the Lobster Roll on p. 368). In the very best examples, the bread itself provides important flavor, like the rye-scented dough used in the Chez Panisse Calzone, p. 369.

Sandwiches and pizzas don't need to have great ambitions. They're something you make when you aren't in the mood to assemble a multidish meal. The most memorable are often so easy they don't even require a written recipe—for instance, this tomato sandwich from Craig Claiborne, who merely described the recipe to Harold Faber, his *Times* colleague. Faber wrote to me:

Centuries ago when I worked on 43rd Street, I remember Craig telling me that one of his favorite summer meals was a simple tomato sandwich, made with slices of a vine-ripened tomato, with Hellmann's mayonnaise on untoasted bread—no salt, no pepper, no lettuce, nothing else. I don't know if he ever put this in one of his cookbooks. I do know, however, that it is a magnificent sandwich that I enjoy repeatedly during the summer.

RECIPES BY CATEGORY

☙ WELSH RAREBIT

Welsh rarebit, surprisingly underappreciated here in the land of grilled cheese, is warm toasted bread smothered with a seasoned—and sometimes spiked—cheese sauce.

Although I included this 1875 recipe because it offers precise measurements, a story that ran in 1892 contained much more conviction about the dish (sometimes called Welsh rabbit). Its author declared, "The merits of the Welsh rarebit lie in its hasty making and hot serving." You melt cheese—"any domestic full-cream cheese that is well ripened is best for the purpose, and the dried layer next to the rind is quite excellent"—with butter until smooth and emulsified, then season the sauce with mustard, salt, and black pepper or cayenne and quickly pour it over hot toasts.

"There are recipes and individuals that call for a small quantity of ale, beer, or port wine," the writer continued, "but, according to an accepted English authority, when such ingredients are added the mixture is no longer a Welsh but a Scotch rarebit, a great national distinction based on a very little difference." So perhaps this recipe, which contains ale or port, is Scotch rarebit. (There is also Golden Buck, a rarebit seasoned with Worcestershire and Tabasco and crowned with a poached egg; Yorkshire Buck, rarebit served on Yorkshire pudding with a poached egg; and English Monkey, made with bread crumbs and Worcestershire.)

Nowhere near finished, the writer waxed on about the details of the toast making: "If the room in which the cooking takes place has an open fireplace, with a great deal of trouble and much scorching of face and hands, the bread toasting can be accomplished there with the assistance of a long toasting fork. But it is far better to have the cook below stairs toast and butter the slices of bread and send them up in a covered metal hot-water dish." Yes, infinitely preferable to have your servant scorch her face and hands.

---

4 tablespoons unsalted butter
½ pound medium-aged cheddar cheese, grated
2 ounces Gruyère cheese, grated
½ teaspoon Colman's prepared mustard
¼ cup dark English ale or port
Salt
Cayenne pepper
8 slices country bread, toasted

Melt the butter in a double boiler. Add the cheeses and whisk until thoroughly melted and blended. Stir in the mustard and ale and season with salt and cayenne. Spoon the sauce over the warm pieces of toast.

SERVES 4 FOR LUNCH, 8 AS A FIRST COURSE

COOKING NOTE
I added cayenne to the recipe.

SERVING SUGGESTIONS
Tomato Soup I (p. 106), Tomato Soup II (p. 114), Salade à la Romaine (p. 171), Apple Dumplings (p. 807), Teddie's Apple Cake (p. 752)

DECEMBER 19, 1875: "THE HOUSEHOLD." RECIPE SIGNED OLIVIA.

—1875

☙ ASPARAGUS ROLLS

This is like a vegetarian sloppy Joe, and it's a recipe that cropped up a few times in the nineteenth-century archive. You fold blanched asparagus into a creamy béchamel scented with mace and spoon it onto toasted buns.

Salt
1 pound thick asparagus, trimmed
3 tablespoons unsalted butter
3 tablespoons all-purpose flour
2 cups whole milk, plus more if needed
2 large egg yolks
Freshly ground black pepper
Freshly grated nutmeg
A pinch of ground mace
4 small soft rolls or toast points

1. Bring a large pot of generously salted water to a boil. Add the asparagus and cook until just tender. Transfer to a bowl of ice water to stop the cooking, then drain

and pat dry. Cut the spears diagonally into ¾-inch-long pieces.

2. Melt the butter in a medium saucepan over medium heat. When it's foamy, whisk in the flour and cook for 1 minute. Gradually add the milk, whisking until smooth. Bring to a boil and cook, whisking, for 1 minute. Off the heat, whisk in the egg yolks and season with salt, pepper, nutmeg, and mace. Thin with milk if needed. Fold in the asparagus and warm through.

3. If using rolls, halve them and scoop out the centers. Arrange the rolls or toast points on 4 plates. Spoon the asparagus and sauce on top.

SERVES 4 AS A FIRST COURSE OR PART OF LUNCH

SERVING SUGGESTIONS
Chilled English Pea–Mint Soup (p. 162), Vichyssoise à la Ritz (p. 111), Deviled Crabs (p. 387), Scallops with Pea Puree (p. 429), Baked Flounder (p. 401), Sugar Snap Peas with Horseradish (p. 259), Almond Custard Cake (p. 741)

MAY 13, 1877: "RECEIPTS FOR THE TABLE." RECIPE SIGNED AUNT ADDIE.

—1877

⌐ SCOTCH WOODCOCK

"Cool evenings, the chafing dish and the amateur cook unite forces with wonderful results," wrote an unidentified columnist in the *Times* about Scotch woodcock—toast with anchovies and cream sauce, a relative of the open-faced sandwich Welsh rarebit (p. 365). "Men particularly love this dainty style of cooking, and they employ their talents with pleasure on Welsh rarebits, oysters, terrapin, and even candy." Although there weren't a whole lot of anecdotes backing up this claim—in fact, there were none—it's probably not coincidental that the modern-day equivalent of a chafing dish, the grill, is also a tool that encourages macho showmanship. The writer continued, "Illustrious men have been proud to acknowledge a creation in gastrinomia [*sic*]. After Hume left off writing history, he created a soup that he valued more highly than his books." The soup was sheep's-head broth—and history gives the nod to Hume's books.

Because you'd kill me if I called for a chafing dish—or because I'm a woman—I've adapted the recipe to toasters and saucepans.

————

4 anchovy fillets, drained
4 small slices country bread
Softened unsalted butter
3 large egg yolks
½ cup heavy cream
Salt

1. Mash the anchovies in a mortar and pestle. Toast the bread, and spread it generously with butter, then the anchovy paste. Keep warm.

2. Whisk together the yolks and cream in a small heavy saucepan over medium-low heat. The mixture will get foamy, then thicken enough to coat the back of a spoon. Remove from the heat and season lightly with salt.

3. Arrange the toasts on 2 plates. Spoon the cream sauce on top.

SERVES 2 AS A LIGHT LUNCH, 4 AS A FIRST COURSE

SERVING SUGGESTIONS
Park Avenue Cocktail (p. 19), Al Forno's Roasted Asparagus (p. 233), Chiffonade Salad (p. 173), Steamed Lemon Pudding (p. 849)

NOVEMBER 8, 1892: "THE USEFUL CHAFING DISH: NO WELL-ORDERED FAMILY SHOULD BE WITHOUT ONE."

—1892

⌐ CHEESE CRUSTS

Cheese crusts are what we now call cheese toasts. This recipe—it's actually more of a technique—appeared in an article titled "What Shall We Eat Today? Wherewith Shall Our Hunger Be Stayed?" and was part of a menu for "noonday breakfast, or for the children's dinner" that included cream of tomato soup—still the traditional accompaniment—as well as some dishes that didn't make the modern-day kids' menu: sweet omelet with jelly, ragout of small birds with polenta, and cod's head with pickle sauce.

————

"These are small slices of bread trimmed free from crusts, buttered a little, seasoned with salt and pepper, and covered with a little heap of grated cheese; a bit of butter on the top of the cheese makes it brown quicker. Care must be taken lightly to brown the crusts without burning them. They make a most appetizing accompaniment for any green salad which is plentiful at this season."

SERVING SUGGESTIONS
Tomato Soup I (p. 106), Tomato Soup II (p. 114), Green Goddess Salad (p. 176), Chocolate Pudding (p. 858)

FEBRUARY 16, 1896: "WHAT SHALL WE EAT TODAY? WHEREWITH SHALL OUR HUNGER BE STAYED?" BY JULIET CORSON.

—1896

⌇ CLUB SANDWICH

ORIGINAL RECIPE
Go to the club.
Drink six toasts.
Eat a slice of meat.
Drink six more toasts.

JANUARY 13, 1907: "A FEW RECIPES."

—1907

⌇ OPEN-FACED TOMATO SANDWICH

This sandwich is too simple to screw up, but if you want it to be extra good, then thick, juicy slices of tomato and top-quality anchovies are key. It's essentially a double cheese melt, with slices of mozzarella and gratings of Parmesan encasing a layer of tomatoes, oregano, and anchovy.

If you want to reengineer the sandwich as an hors d'oeuvre, simply layer the toppings on slices of baguette.

6 slices firm-textured sandwich bread
Unsalted butter, softened, for spreading
1 ball fresh mozzarella cheese (about 1 pound), thinly sliced
2 large firm but ripe tomatoes
1/2 teaspoon crumbled dried oregano
1/8 teaspoon freshly ground black pepper
1 tablespoon unsalted butter, melted
Salt
18 anchovy fillets
Freshly grated Parmesan cheese (about 1 1/2 cups)
Chopped flat-leaf parsley for garnish (optional)

1. Heat the broiler. Spread one side of each slice of bread with softened butter. Cover each with the sliced mozzarella cheese (3 to 4 slices for each piece of bread).
2. Cut the tomatoes into 1/2-inch-thick slices. Place 1 of the largest slices on each sandwich. (Sprinkle the leftover tomato slices with salt and pepper and eat while you finish the sandwiches.)
3. Combine the oregano, black pepper, and butter. Brush over the tomato slices. Sprinkle with salt and drape 3 anchovies on each sandwich. Cover with grated Parmesan cheese (about 3 to 4 tablespoons for each sandwich).
4. Place under the broiler, about 6 inches from the heating element, until the cheese has melted and is bubbly, 3 to 5 minutes. Serve hot, garnished with parsley, if desired.

SERVES 6

SERVING SUGGESTIONS
Grapefruit Wine (p. 37), Tom's Chilled Cucumber Soup (p. 117), Oyster Chowder (p. 159), Basic Corn Chowder (p. 149), Ventresca Tuna Salad (p. 426), Petit Beurre Cookies (p. 699)

AUGUST 9, 1964: "PRIME TIME FOR TOMATOES," BY CRAIG CLAIBORNE.

—1964

❧ LOBSTER ROLL

An unnamed *Times* columnist wrote in 1892, "The raison d'être for the lobster, no matter what opinion the gawky thing may hold on its cause for existence, is to gratify and please the human palate, no matter how much it may displease the human stomach."

This lobster roll pleases the human palate very much. As a general life rule, buttering and toasting the buns makes all the difference.

————

8 hot dog buns
4 tablespoons unsalted butter, melted
3 cups (1 to 1½ pounds) cooked lobster meat
    cut into bite-sized pieces
¾ to 1 cup mayonnaise
½ cup minced heart of celery
1 small clove garlic, minced
2 tablespoons chopped fresh basil or
    ½ teaspoon dried basil
1 tablespoon chopped flat-leaf parsley
¼ cup finely chopped scallions
Tabasco sauce
Fresh lemon juice
Salt and freshly ground black pepper

1. Heat the oven to 400 degrees. Split the buns and arrange them split side up in a baking dish. Brush them with the butter and bake until lightly brown, about 5 minutes. Remove from the oven and set aside.
2. Combine the lobster, mayonnaise, celery, garlic, basil, parsley, scallions, Tabasco sauce to taste, lemon juice to taste, and salt and pepper to taste. Blend well.
3. Spoon equal parts of the filling onto the split buns.

SERVES 8

SERVING SUGGESTIONS
Tom's Chilled Cucumber Soup (p. 117), Thomas Keller's Gazpacho (p. 146), Docks Coleslaw (p. 191), Saratoga Potatoes (p. 273), Summer Pudding (p. 847), Flat-and-Chewy Chocolate Chip Cookies (p. 706)

JUNE 21, 1970: "PATRIOTS' SNACK," BY CRAIG CLAIBORNE.
—1970

❧ ANITA SHELDON'S TORTA DI SPINACI

This is a great Sunday dinner dish. Elegant it's not, but not everything needs to be. There is one detail that will make or break the recipe: you must squeeze every last drop of liquid from the cooked spinach before chopping it, or you'll end up with a soggy torta. So, just when you think you've extracted the last molecule of water, squeeze it some more.

————

For the Pastry
3 cups all-purpose flour
¾ teaspoon salt
½ pound (2 sticks) unsalted butter, cut into pieces
1 large egg yolk
Approximately 3 tablespoons water

For the Filling
3 tablespoons olive oil
2 large onions, finely chopped
1¾ pounds fresh spinach, trimmed and washed well,
    or two 10-ounce packages frozen chopped spinach
Three 1-inch-thick smoked pork chops or pork loin
    (about 1 pound), any fat and bones removed
    and meat diced, or ½ pound bacon, diced
1½ cups freshly grated Parmesan cheese
    (about 5 ounces)
1 cup (8 ounces) ricotta cheese
Salt and freshly ground black pepper
4 large eggs, lightly beaten
1 large egg white, lightly beaten

1. To make the pastry, place the flour, salt, and butter in a bowl. With a pastry blender, 2 knives, or your fingertips, work the butter into the flour until the mixture resembles coarse oatmeal.
2. Mix the egg yolk with 3 tablespoons water and sprinkle over the mixture. Stir with a fork, adding only enough extra water to make a dough that just clings together. Divide the dough in half and form into 2 disks. Wrap each one in wax paper and chill briefly.
3. Meanwhile, prepare the filling: Heat the oil in a large skillet and sauté the onions until tender but not browned. Set aside.
4. If using fresh spinach, place the washed spinach

leaves, with just the water that clings, in a large saucepan, cover tightly, and cook until the leaves wilt. Drain well and let cool enough to touch. In batches, gather the leaves in your palm and press out all the liquid by squeezing as firmly as possible. Chop the spinach. Or, if using frozen spinach, cook according to the package directions; drain well, cool, and squeeze dry.

5. Combine the chopped spinach and onions in a bowl and let cool completely, then add the diced smoked pork, Parmesan cheese, ricotta, salt and pepper to taste, and lightly beaten eggs.

6. Heat the oven to 425 degrees. Roll out half the pastry on a lightly floured work surface into 12-inch circle and line a 10-inch pie plate with it. Brush the bottom and sides of the shell with the lightly beaten egg white. Pour in the filling.

7. Roll out the remaining pastry and cover the filling. Trim, seal, and crimp the edges. Make a steam hole and if you're up for it place leaves, cut from the pastry scraps, around the hole (not over it).

8. Bake for 40 to 50 minutes, or until the pastry is golden and done. Let stand for 10 to 15 minutes before cutting.

SERVES 8 TO 10

COOKING NOTES

The torta can be baked early in the day and reheated in a 375-degree oven. Cover loosely with foil to prevent overbrowning.

After the torta has cooled, if you wrap it well in aluminum foil, it will keep in the freezer for up to 2 months. Allow to thaw at room temperature for 3 hours and then let it finish thawing and reheat in a 375-degree oven for about 1 hour.

SERVING SUGGESTIONS

Palestine Soup (p. 106), Carrot and Fennel Soup (p. 151), Caponata (p. 226), Zabaglione (p. 813), Chocolate Quakes (p. 702), Madeleine Kamman's Apple Mousse (p. 816)

MARCH 19, 1972: "AN ELEGANT EASTER PIE," BY JEAN HEWITT.

—1972

↶ CHEZ PANISSE CALZONE

Once you taste this calzone, all the soggy calzones of your past will be wiped from memory. This is the perfect version. The rye flour infuses the dough with a pleasantly stony, austere aroma. And, unlike most calzones, it contains not a wad of cheese, but a carefully arranged matrix of ham and herbs and cheeses.

¼ pound goat cheese

7 ounces mozzarella cheese

2 thin slices prosciutto (about 2 ounces)

2 tablespoons finely chopped chives

2 tablespoons finely chopped flat-leaf parsley

1 teaspoon finely chopped fresh thyme
    or ½ teaspoon dried thyme

½ teaspoon finely chopped fresh marjoram
    or ¼ teaspoon dried marjoram

1 teaspoon minced garlic

Freshly ground black pepper

Calzone Dough (recipe follows)

1 tablespoon olive oil

1. Crumble the goat cheese into a bowl.

2. Grate the mozzarella and add it to the goat cheese.

3. Stack the prosciutto slices and cut into very thin strips. Add to the cheese. Add the chives, parsley, thyme, marjoram, garlic, and pepper to taste. Blend thoroughly.

4. Heat the oven to 475 degrees. The calzones can be baked in a pizza pan, but it is best to use a baking stone placed on or near the bottom of the oven. Divide the calzone dough in half and roll into loose balls. Using a rolling pin and very little flour, roll out the dough, one half at a time, into circles about 8 inches in diameter. Spoon half the filling onto the bottom half of each circle, leaving a bottom margin of about 1 inch. Fold the other half of each circle of dough over to enclose the filling. Twist the edges of the dough over neatly to seal.

5. Place the calzones in the oven and bake for 15 to 18 minutes, or until quite brown and crisp. Remove from the oven and brush the tops with the olive oil. Cut into serving portions with a serrated knife.

MAKES 2 CALZONES; SERVES 4

CALZONE (OR PIZZA) DOUGH

¾ cup lukewarm water

2 teaspoons active dry yeast (not rapid-rise)

¼ cup rye flour

I tablespoon whole milk

2 tablespoons olive oil, plus oil for greasing the bowl
and dough

½ teaspoon salt, if desired

Approximately 1¾ cups unbleached all-purpose flour

1. Put ¼ cup lukewarm water in a small bowl. Add the yeast and rye flour. Stir to blend. Let stand in a warm place for 20 to 30 minutes. (This mixture is called a sponge.)

2. Put the milk, olive oil, and salt, if desired, in a larger bowl and add the remaining ½ cup lukewarm water and the sponge. Using a wooden spoon, stir in 1¾ cups all-purpose flour. Turn the dough out onto a lightly floured board. Knead for 10 to 15 minutes. The dough will be soft and slightly sticky. Work it with quick, light motions. Add as little flour as possible, but work the dough until it does not stick. A soft, slightly moist dough will make for a crispier crust.

3. Lightly brush the inside of a large bowl with olive oil and add the ball of dough. Lightly oil the surface of the dough. Cover with a towel and set in a warm place (approximately 90 to 110 degrees). An oven heated by a pilot light can be used, but it must not be too warm. Let the dough rise until almost doubled, about 2 hours.

4. Punch down the dough. Shape it into a ball, return it to the bowl, and let rise once more, about 40 minutes. It is now ready to use.

MAKES ENOUGH FOR 2 MEDIUM CALZONES OR ONE 12- TO 14-INCH PIZZA

COOKING NOTES

Yeast doughs are incredibly patient as long as you treat them well. Lots of old recipes insist that you let the dough rise in a warm place, but dough will also rise happily in a cold place—it just takes longer. Sometimes this delay is helpful: for instance, I made this dough the night before I wanted to serve the calzones. After kneading the dough, I covered the bowl tightly and put it in the fridge overnight. The next day, after its slow-motion rise, I punched down the dough and proceeded with the recipe.

Claiborne and Franey, who wrote the accompanying story, noted, "At Chez Panisse, a blend of half California Sonoma goat cheese and half French goat cheese (such as Bûcheron or Lezay, available in this country in fine cheese shops) is used."

SERVING SUGGESTIONS
Salade à la Grecque (p. 179), Green Goddess Salad (p. 176), Tortoni (p. 720)

JULY 8, 1984: "FOOD: GETTING TO KNOW CALZONE," BY CRAIG CLAIBORNE WITH PIERRE FRANEY. RECIPE ADAPTED FROM CHEZ PANISSE IN BERKELEY, CALIFORNIA.

—1984

⌒ TARTE FLAMBÉE

Two details will help make your tarte flambée triumphant: rolling the dough as thin as possible (tarte flambée is about the toppings, not the dough) and seasoning the tarte with lots of coarsely ground black pepper.

———

Tarte Flambée Dough (recipe follows)

Flour for sprinkling

I cup fromage blanc or crème fraîche, or ¾ cup
sour cream thinned with ⅓ cup whole milk

⅓ to ½ cup minced onion

⅓ to ½ cup minced bacon

Salt and freshly ground black pepper

1. Knead the dough lightly and place it on a lightly floured surface. Sprinkle it with a little more flour and cover with plastic wrap or towel. Let it rest while the oven heats.

2. Pat or roll out the dough as thin as possible to a diameter of 12 inches, using more flour as necessary. The process will be easier if you allow the dough to rest occasionally between rollings. If you are using a pizza stone, transfer the rolled-out dough to the floured peel or long-handled board; if you do not, lay the dough on a baking sheet lightly brushed with olive oil. Let the dough rest for 15 to 30 minutes, or until it begins to puff ever so slightly.

3. Heat the oven to at least 500 degrees (600 is bet-

ter, if your oven goes that high); if you have a pizza stone set it on a rack in the lower third of the oven. Spread the fromage blanc (or alternatives) on the dough. Sprinkle with the onion, bacon, a little salt, and plenty of pepper. Slide it onto the pizza stone, or slide the baking sheet into the oven, and bake until nicely crisp, about 10 minutes; if the tart is browning unevenly, rotate it back to front about halfway through the cooking time. Serve hot.

SERVES 4

TARTE FLAMBÉE DOUGH

> 1 teaspoon instant or rapid-rise yeast
> 3 cups (about 14 ounces) all-purpose or bread flour,
>   plus more if needed
> 2 teaspoons salt
> 1 cup water
> 2 tablespoons plus 1 teaspoon olive oil

1. Combine the yeast, flour, and salt in a food processor. Turn the machine on and add the water and 2 tablespoons oil through the feed tube. Process for about 30 seconds, adding more water through the feed tube a little at a time until the mixture forms a ball and is slightly sticky to the touch. If it is dry, add another tablespoon or two of water, and process for another 10 seconds. (In the unlikely event that the mixture is too sticky, add more flour a tablespoon at a time.)

2. Turn the dough out onto a floured work surface and knead for a few seconds to form a smooth, round ball. Grease a bowl with the remaining 1 teaspoon olive oil and place the dough in it. Cover with plastic wrap or a damp cloth and let rise in a warm, draft-free area until the dough just about doubles in size, at least 1 hour. (You can also let the dough rise more slowly in the refrigerator, for as long as 6 to 8 hours.)

MAKES ENOUGH FOR TWO 12-INCH PIZZAS

SERVING SUGGESTIONS

James Beard's Champagne Punch (p. 28), Boeuf Bourguignon I (p. 516), Braised Duck Legs with Pinot Noir Sauce (p. 481), Caramelized Endive (p. 238), The Most Voluptuous Cauliflower (p. 241), Dorie Greenspan's Sablés (p. 703)

SEPTEMBER 23, 1998: "VIVE LA PIZZA: SIMPLE, RUSTIC, AND, YES, FRENCH," BY MARK BITTMAN.

—1998

GREEN TOMATO PIZZA

This pizza is surprisingly bright and lemony. I'd serve it as a snack or first course, or as part of a larger meal.

> 1 medium and 2 large green tomatoes
> Coarse salt
> Pizza Dough, divided into balls, allowed to rest,
>   and patted out (recipe follows)
> 1 cup freshly grated Parmesan cheese
> 1/2 cup coarsely chopped or torn basil
> Olive oil

1. Heat the oven to 500 degrees. Thinly slice the tomatoes, salt lightly, and let sit for at least 20 minutes, then drain off any accumulated liquid.

2. Top the pizza rounds with the tomato slices and Parmesan. Bake for about 10 minutes, or until nearly done.

3. Sprinkle the pizzas with the basil and cook until done, about 1 minute more. After removing them from the oven, sprinkle the pizzas with more salt and a splash of olive oil.

MAKES 2 MEDIUM OR MORE SMALLER PIZZAS

MARK BITTMAN'S PIZZA DOUGH

> 3 cups all-purpose or bread flour, plus more as needed
> 2 teaspoons active dry yeast
> 2 teaspoons coarse sea or kosher salt, plus extra for
>   sprinkling
> 1 cup water
> 2 tablespoons olive oil

1. To make the dough using a food processor, combine the flour, yeast, and salt in the work bowl. Turn the machine on and add the water and oil through the feed tube. Process for 30 seconds, adding up to 1/4 cup more water a little at a time until the mixture forms a

ball and is slightly sticky to the touch. (In the unlikely event that the mixture is too sticky, add more flour a tablespoon at a time.) To make the dough by hand, combine half the flour with the yeast and salt in a bowl and stir to blend. Add the water and olive oil; stir with a wooden spoon until smooth. Add the remaining flour a bit at a time; when the mixture becomes too stiff to stir with a spoon, begin kneading it in the bowl, adding as little of the flour as possible—just enough to keep the dough from being a sticky mess. Knead for 5 to 10 minutes.

2. Turn the dough out onto a floured work surface and knead for a few seconds to form a smooth, round ball. Transfer to a bowl and cover with plastic wrap; let rise until doubled in size, 1 to 2 hours. (You can cut the rising time if you are in a hurry, or—preferably—you can let the dough rise more slowly in the refrigerator, for 6 to 8 hours. The dough can then be used immediately or wrapped tightly in plastic wrap and frozen for up to a month. Defrost in a covered bowl in the refrigerator or at room temperature.)

3. Form the dough into a ball and divide into 2 or more pieces; roll each piece into a ball. Place on a lightly floured surface, sprinkle with a little flour, and cover with plastic wrap or a towel. Let rest until slightly puffed, about 20 minutes.

4. Oil one or more baking sheets, as needed, then press each dough ball into a flat round directly on the sheet. Pat out the dough as thin as you like, using oiled hands if necessary.

5. Proceed with the pizza recipe.

MAKES ENOUGH FOR 2 MEDIUM OR MORE SMALLER PIZZAS

SERVING SUGGESTIONS
Stuffed Clams (p. 400), Chiffonade Salad (p. 173), Flat-and-Chewy Chocolate Chip Cookies (p. 706)

JULY 26, 2000: "THE MINIMALIST; ON A ROLL: ENDLESS COMBINATIONS IN ELEGANT SIMPLICITY," BY MARK BITTMAN.

—2000

↪ CROQUE-MONSIEUR

The French grilled cheese, or croque-monsieur—literally, "crunch-sir"—is a surprisingly tricky sandwich to get right. Great croque-monsieurs have a few elements in common: a single layer each of ham and Gruyère squeezed between two thin slices of bread. (Some are also filled with béchamel, or white sauce, which makes the whole thing creamier. Others have broiled cheese and béchamel on top.) The bread is brushed with butter, and the sandwich is cooked on a griddle or toasted under a broiler so that the cheese almost liquefies and the dangling bits of ham and cheese caramelize. It is rich, substantial, and salty, so you reach for a glass of wine or beer between bites.

As there are very few ingredients, they must all be good. You need French ham, which is similar to American ham but a little drier, fattier, and saltier. The Gruyère should be bought in a large piece and sliced at home. You'll need good butter too. You can mess around and substitute other cheeses and hams, but then you won't have a croque-monsieur, and you'll have to live with that. OK?

The correct bread is the most difficult element. In no event should sourdough or whole wheat be used—health has no place here. White sandwich bread is good, because it's often made with shortening or butter, which gives the sandwich an added roundness of flavor, but white bread can turn mushy when toasted in a griddle. I had the most success with a sturdy thick-crusted country bread, which had enough moisture to blend with the cheese and meat and the bonus of a distinctive tang.

I sliced the bread $1/4$ inch thick and the cheese paper-thin; I bought ham sliced as thin as prosciutto. I spread one side of a bread slice with a thick layer of béchamel. On it I laid two slices of ham and a single slice of cheese, making sure a little bit of each hung over the sides—like a tablecloth over a table. I brushed both sides of the sandwich with butter, letting it soak in, then pressed it in a sandwich maker that had been heating on medium-high for about 20 minutes. When the sandwich was browned and compressed, and the cheese was leaking out and boiling on the metal, bliss was within reach. The bread was toasted dark and the weight of the griddle had flattened it. The exterior had become a thin crackly shell, like a potato chip, with cooked bits of cheese and ham at the edges. The center of the sandwich, with the béchamel and the melted cheese, was like a warm, thick custard. My inner perfectionist chortled.

OCTOBER 4, 2000: "BORN IN A FRENCH CAFÉ, GROWING UP IN NEW YORK," BY AMANDA HESSER.

—2000

5 tablespoons salted butter

I tablespoon all-purpose flour

²/₃ cup whole milk

Sea salt

Freshly grated nutmeg

Four ¹/₃-inch-thick slices country bread

4 thin slices French ham

2 thin slices Gruyère cheese

1. Heat a two-sided electric griddle or sandwich press on medium-high to high for about 20 minutes, or heat the oven to 300 degrees and heat a cast-iron skillet on top of the stove for about 5 minutes. To prepare the béchamel sauce, melt 1 tablespoon butter in a small saucepan over medium heat. When the bubbles have subsided, add the flour and whisk vigorously for 1 minute. Slowly whisk in the milk until smooth. Bring to a boil and cook, whisking, until thick. Remove from the heat and season to taste with salt and nutmeg.

2. Spread 2 slices of bread generously with the sauce. Lay 2 slices of ham on top of each, and top each with a slice of cheese; the ham and cheese should slightly overlap the edges of the bread. Top each with a second slice of bread.

3. Melt the remaining 4 tablespoons butter in a small saucepan. Brush the sandwiches on both sides with the butter, making sure that the edges are well covered. If you're using a griddle, place the sandwiches cheese side down on it, close the griddle, and cook until the bread is toasted dark and the cheese is leaking out and bubbling. If you're using a skillet, place the sandwiches cheese side down on the pan and cook on the stovetop until well browned, then turn and brown again. Transfer the skillet to the oven and bake until the cheese is bubbling. Serve hot.

SERVES 2

SERVING SUGGESTIONS

Tomato Soup I (p. 106), Tomato Soup II (p. 114), Watercress Salad (p. 171), Sally Darr's Golden Delicious Apple Tart (p. 839), Coffee Caramel Custard (p. 849)

⌒ 'INO'S TUNA WITH BLACK OLIVE PESTO PANINI

Food trends are rarely subtle. Jonathan Reynolds, a columnist for the *Magazine*, captured one exactly as it was. "Man," he wrote, "you can't swing a dead endangered species in this town without hitting a panini sign, and you can't swing two without hitting a panino itself."

But the panino deserved its turn in the spotlight. Panini aren't just grilled sandwiches. As Reynolds explained, "What gives them their unique appeal is the contrast in textures—the serious snap of their grilled sheath with the soft, gooey insides. (Cheese is ubiquitous.)" I'd add that the heavy grill also compresses the layers, fusing them and making for an uncommonly unified sandwich—one that can be paired with a glass of wine and called dinner.

This version comes from the West Village's 'ino, a panini restaurant the size of a panino.

For the Pesto

I cup Gaeta or other pungent black olives, pitted

10 caper berries, stems removed

Grated zest and juice of I lemon

I cup olive oil

For the Sandwiches

One 6- to 8-ounce can Italian tuna in olive oil, drained

6 caper berries, stems discarded, sliced into thin disks

2 tablespoons olive oil

I teaspoon Champagne vinegar

I tablespoon fresh lemon juice

Pinch of crushed red pepper flakes

Ciabatta rolls

1. To make the pesto, combine all the ingredients in a blender or food processor and blend until just a bit chunky.

2. To make the sandwiches, combine the tuna, caper berries, olive oil, vinegar, lemon juice, and pepper

flakes in a bowl and toss. Slice off the top third of the ciabatta rolls and discard. Split the remainder of each roll and spread 1 tablespoon pesto on each half. Place ⅓ cup of the tuna mixture inside each.

3. Grill in a preheated sandwich press or a George Foreman grill until nicely browned, 3 to 6 minutes. Serve warm or at room temperature.

SERVES 4

SERVING SUGGESTIONS
Rhubarb Bellini (p. 30), Lemon Syrup (p. 9), Hearth's Fava Bean Salad (p. 202), Asparagus alla Fontina (p. 222), Pistachio Gelato (p. 730)

JUNE 15, 2003: "FOOD: CONSTRUCTION PROJECTS," BY JONATHAN REYNOLDS. RECIPE ADAPTED FROM 'INO IN NEW YORK CITY.

—2003

✌ FRANNY'S CLAM PIZZA

I'm not going to lie—this pizza is a project. But it's easy to do in stages: the pizza dough and clam sauce can be assembled in the morning, the baking of the pizza at night. And by the time it's done, it's like childbirth: you won't regret the effort. The pizza emerges from the oven hot, crisp, tasting of the ocean and oil, and radiating the warmth of chiles.

———

¼ cup extra virgin olive oil, plus more for drizzling

½ Spanish onion, cut into chunks

4 garlic cloves, smashed

1 bay leaf

Crushed red pepper flakes

1¼ cups dry white wine

4½ dozen littleneck clams (about 6 pounds), scrubbed well

1½ cups heavy cream

Flour for dusting

Pizza Dough (recipe follows)

Chopped flat-leaf parsley for garnish

1. Place a pizza stone on the top rack of the oven. Heat the oven to 550 degrees for 45 minutes to 1 hour.
2. While the oven heats, place the oil in a large pot over medium heat. Add the onion and sauté until it is limp, about 5 minutes. Add the garlic, bay leaf, and a pinch of red pepper flakes and sauté for 7 minutes longer. Add the wine and bring to a simmer. Add the clams, cover the pot, and cook until they start to open, about 10 minutes. As they open, use tongs to transfer them to a large bowl. When all the clams are cooked, 15 to 20 minutes and (set the pot aside) cooled, pluck out the meat and discard the shells.
3. Simmer the liquid left in the pot until it reduces to a thick, syrupy glaze, about 20 minutes. Add the cream and continue simmering until the mixture is reduced by a quarter, 10 to 15 minutes longer. Strain the sauce through a fine-mesh sieve, and set aside.
4. Flour a pizza peel or rimless cookie sheet. Stretch one dough ball into a 12-inch round and lay it on the peel. Paint the entire surface with ¼ cup clam glaze, and scatter a dozen or so clams over the pizza. Add a sprinkle of crushed red pepper flakes (be conservative on the first one; adjust as necessary for the second).
5. Slide the pie onto the heated stone and bake until the crust is browned on the bottom (use tongs to check), about 4 minutes. If your broiler is part of the oven, turn it to high and broil the pizza until the top is nicely browned, 30 seconds to 1 minute. If your broiler unit is separate, use tongs to transfer the pizza to a cookie sheet, and slide it under the broiler for 30 seconds or so. Continue with the remaining pizzas. Drizzle the pies with olive oil and sprinkle with parsley before serving.

MAKES FOUR 12-INCH PIZZAS; SERVES 4 TO 6

FRANNY'S PIZZA DOUGH

1¾ cups warm water

1½ teaspoons active dry yeast

2 tablespoons extra virgin olive oil, plus more for coating the dough

1½ tablespoons salt

1 tablespoon sugar

5 cups bread flour

1. Put the warm water in a mixer bowl or other large bowl, add the yeast, and stir until it dissolves. Add the oil, salt, and sugar and mix well. Stir in the flour. Knead in the mixer, preferably using a dough hook, or by hand on a floured surface, until the dough comes together. Cover and let rest for 20 minutes.

2. Knead the dough until it's springy, about 5 minutes in a mixer or 10 minutes by hand. Form into a ball, coat with oil, and place in a large bowl. Cover with plastic and refrigerate overnight.

3. Remove the dough from the refrigerator and let it come to room temperature (2 to 4 hours) before proceeding.

4. Press the dough down and knead it briefly. Divide it into 4 pieces and roll each piece into a loose ball; let rest for 10 minutes.

5. Flatten the dough into disks and cover with cloth towels until ready to use.

MAKES ENOUGH DOUGH FOR FOUR
12-INCH PIZZAS

COOKING NOTES

I made the pizza dough in a mixer fitted with the dough hook, kneading it for 5 minutes on medium-low speed. If you have one, put it to work.

The key step comes right before serving the pie, when you sprinkle it with olive oil. This polishes the flavors and gives the texture a providential slickness, which it needs.

SERVING SUGGESTIONS

Artichoke Salad with Anchovy and Capers (p. 174), Bittersweet Chocolate Semifreddo (p. 727), Raspberry Granita (p. 719)

APRIL 20, 2005: "THE CHEF; ANDREW FEINBERG: A STU-DENT OF THE PIZZA DOES A LITTLE HOMEWORK," BY MELISSA CLARK. RECIPE ADAPTED FROM ANDREW FEIN-BERG, THE CHEF AT FRANNY'S IN BROOKLYN, NEW YORK.

—2005

⌒ WILD MUSHROOM QUESADILLAS

¼ cup vegetable oil

1 pound chanterelles, black trumpets, or other wild mushrooms (or substitute oyster, cremini, or clamshell mushrooms; do not use shiitake), trimmed and roughly chopped

Salt

½ cup minced onion

¼ pound Oaxaca or domestic Muenster cheese, grated

¼ pound panela or fresh or smoked mozzarella cheese, grated

¼ pound cotija or Parmesan cheese, grated

⅓ cup finely chopped cilantro

½ teaspoon dried oregano

Pinch of ground coriander

Freshly ground black pepper

Eight 8-inch flour or corn tortillas

1. Place a medium sauté pan over medium-high heat and add 2 tablespoons vegetable oil. When the oil shimmers, add the mushrooms and a generous pinch of salt and sauté until the mushrooms release their liquid, the liquid evaporates, and the mushrooms begin to brown, 7 to 10 minutes.

2. Add the onion and sauté, adjusting the heat as necessary, until the onion is soft and the entire mixture is golden brown, about 5 minutes. Remove from the heat and allow to cool slightly.

3. Using a food processor or a knife, finely chop the mushroom-onion mixture, then transfer to a large bowl. Add the grated cheeses, cilantro, oregano, and coriander. Season to taste with salt and pepper.

4. Place a large nonstick or well-seasoned cast-iron skillet over medium heat and add the remaining 2 tablespoons vegetable oil. While the pan heats, place a large spoonful of the mushroom-cheese mixture into the center of a tortilla and fold the tortilla in half to make a half-moon. Place the filled tortilla in the hot skillet and cook, turning once, until the tortilla is nicely browned on both sides and the cheese is melted. Transfer to a platter. Repeat to make a total of 8 filled tortillas. Serve immediately.

SERVES 8

SERVING SUGGESTIONS

La Paloma (p. 35), Guacamole Tostadas (p. 67), Tortilla Soup (p. 131), Yucatán Fish with Crisp Garlic (p. 431), Nueces Canyon Cabrito (Goat Tacos; p. 576), Salted Caramel Ice Cream (p. 733), Grapefruit Granita (p. 731)

MAY 25, 2005: "THE CHEF: TRACI DES JARDINS: TORTILLAS LET A COOK COME HOME AGAIN," BY KIM SEVERSON. RECIPE ADAPTED FROM TRACI DES JARDINS, THE CHEF AT JARDINIÈRE IN SAN FRANCISCO, CALIFORNIA.

—2005

⌇ PAN BAGNAT

Once you've had a pan bagnat, there's no going back to the tuna fish sandwich, which suddenly seems stingy and uncouth. The pan bagnat is like a salade Niçoise tucked between halves of a loaf country bread. You layer tuna with cucumbers, tomato, red onion, olives, and egg, all napped with an anchovy vinaigrette. The sandwich is then pressed with weights before eating, which compacts the filling and disperses the dressing evenly. Sandwich engineering 2.0.

———

2 anchovy fillets, minced (optional)

1 very small clove garlic, minced

1 teaspoon red wine vinegar

½ teaspoon Dijon mustard

Pinch of salt

Freshly ground black pepper

2 tablespoons extra virgin olive oil

One 8-inch round crusty country loaf or
    small ciabatta, split

1 Kirby cucumber or ½ regular cucumber

1 medium ripe tomato, sliced

½ small red onion, sliced

One (5- to 6-ounce) jar imported tuna packed
    in olive oil, drained

8 large basil leaves

2 tablespoons sliced pitted olives, preferably
    a mix of black and green

1 hard-boiled egg, thinly sliced

1. Whisk together the anchovies, if using, the garlic, vinegar, mustard, salt, to taste and pepper in a small bowl. Slowly drizzle in the oil, whisking constantly.
2. If using a country loaf, pull out some of the soft interior crumb to form a cavity. If using a ciabatta, you won't need to eliminate anything.
3. If using a Kirby cucumber, thinly slice it. If using a regular cucumber, peel, halve lengthwise, and scoop out the seeds from one half. Thinly slice the seedless half (reserve the remaining half for another use). Add the sliced cucumber to the vinaigrette and toss well.
4. Spread half the cucumbers on the bottom of the bread. Top with the tomato and onion slices, then with the tuna, basil, olives, and egg slices. Top with the remaining cucumbers and vinaigrette. Cover with

the second bread half and firmly press the sandwich together.
5. Wrap the sandwich tightly in foil, wax paper, or plastic wrap, then place in a plastic bag. Put the sandwich under a weight such as a cast-iron skillet topped with a filled kettle (or have a child about seven years old sit on it). Weight the sandwich for 7 to 10 minutes, then flip and weight it for another 7 to 10 minutes (or as long as you can get the child to sit still).
6. Unwrap, slice, and serve immediately, or keep it wrapped for up to 8 hours before serving.

SERVES 2 TO 3

SERVING SUGGESTIONS
Claret Cup (p. 12), Stuffed Tomatoes (p. 213), Tarte aux Fruits (p. 829), Blueberry Pie with a Lattice Top (p. 853), Plum Fritters (p. 865), Peach Salad (p. 805)

AUGUST 8, 2007: "A GOOD APPETITE: LUNCH RECIPE: TAKE ONE 7-YEAR-OLD . . . ," BY MELISSA CLARK.

—2007

⌇ PIZZA WITH CARAMELIZED ONIONS, FIGS, BACON, AND BLUE CHEESE

Elaine McCool, a reader from Bainbridge Island, Washington, sent me the following e-mail: "Before we were married, in September 1945, my husband had briefly visited friends in Philadelphia, where he was introduced to a new Italian thing called pizza, which he fell in love with. . . . He very much wanted me to start making pizza, but at the time I was doing well to boil an egg.

"However, we bought the Sunday edition of the NY Times every Wednesday, which is when it arrived at our local newsstand in Norman, Oklahoma. I don't know the date, but it must have been in the winter of '45-'46, or the spring of '46, that a full-page article about pizza appeared. It gave complete instructions for making the dough, the sauce, and the toppings, putting it all together and baking it, and the writer predicted that if pizza caught on in the U.S., it would someday compete with hamburgers and hot dogs as the national favorite food. I have been making pizza regularly ever since, and have never been satisfied with any ready-made version. For years, I had the torn-out page, then as it crumbled, typed out a copy, which has now also disappeared. I wish I could remember the writer's name, but I cannot."

The article came out in 1947 and the writer's name was Jane Nickerson. And, indeed, she wrote, "The pizza could be as popular a snack as the hamburger if Americans only knew more about it." They do now. In the first half of 2009, pizza leapt from cheap take-out food to high art. *New York* magazine featured a section on the top twenty pizzerias in the city. Alan Richman, *GQ*'s food writer, ranked the twenty-five best pizzas in the country. Frank Bruni, the *Times*'s restaurant critic, did an extensive review of New York pizza. And Sam Sifton, then the *Times*'s culture editor and closet food maven (now the restaurant reviewer), made a persuasive case for baking pizza at home.

Sifton insisted: "[You] should never listen to the deadbeats who tell you that it's hard, that it can't be done at home, that if you are baking pizza at home, then what you are making is somehow not pizza because you don't have a professional pizza oven that burns at 800 degrees." No, he said, all you really need is a baking stone and a peel for transporting the pizza to and from your conventional oven. And if you don't have them, buy them. "Use the things five times over the year," Sifton wrote, "and they'll pay for themselves in what you'll save by not calling Ray's or Tony's or the Albanian joint for a large."

Make the dough the day before, keep the toppings simple, and apply them softly, "as if you were placing flower petals on a cloud." So don't be a deadbeat—delicious homemade pies await!

———

2 tablespoons unsalted butter

1 large Spanish onion

2 teaspoons thyme leaves

2 bay leaves

Kosher salt and freshly ground black pepper

4 thick slices bacon, cut into ¼-inch-wide batons

1 ball Pizza Dough (recipe follows)

Flour for dusting

12 dried Black Mission figs, stems removed and cut into quarters or small pieces

¾ cup crumbled Gorgonzola cheese

Extra virgin olive oil for drizzling

Coarsely cracked black pepper

1. At least 45 minutes before cooking, heat the oven and a pizza stone, set on the lowest rack, to 550 degrees.

2. Meanwhile, melt the butter in a large sauté pan over high heat. Add the onion, thyme, and bay leaves and cook for 5 minutes, stirring often, until the onion begins to wilt; season with salt and pepper. Reduce the heat to medium-low and cook, stirring occasionally, until the onions have softened and turned a deep golden brown, about 25 minutes. Season to taste with salt and pepper. Remove the bay leaves and transfer the onions to a small bowl.

3. Add the bacon to the pan, set over high heat, and cook, stirring occasionally, until brown and crispy. Using a slotted spoon, transfer the bacon to a small bowl.

4. Place the pizza dough on a heavily floured surface and stretch and pull it, using your hands or a rolling pin, into about a 14-inch round. Place on a lightly floured pizza peel or rimless baking sheet. Cover with the toppings, being careful not to press on the dough and weigh it down: the caramelized onions first, then the figs and bacon, and finally the Gorgonzola, leaving roughly a ½-inch border.

5. Shake the pizza peel slightly to make sure the dough is not sticking. Carefully slide the pizza onto the baking stone in one quick forward-and-back motion. Cook until the crust has browned on the bottom and the top is bubbling and browning in spots, about 7 minutes. Drizzle with a little olive oil and some cracked black pepper. Serve hot.

MAKES 1 PIZZA; SERVES 2

SAM SIFTON'S PIZZA DOUGH

1½ cups unbleached all-purpose flour

1½ cups unbleached bread flour, plus more for dusting

¾ teaspoon active dry yeast

2¼ teaspoons Diamond Crystal kosher salt

1½ cups cold water

3 tablespoons extra virgin olive oil

1. The morning or, ideally, the day before cooking, prepare the dough: Using a whisk, combine the flours, yeast, and salt in the bowl of a stand electric mixer. Switch to a wooden spoon and stir in the water and

olive oil until a rough dough forms. Set the bowl on the mixer stand and, using the paddle attachment, mix on low speed for 1 minute. Increase the speed to high and beat for 4 to 6 minutes, until it becomes a wet and vaguely menacing mass. (If it forms into a ball, lower the mixer speed to medium-high; if not, stop the mixer to scrape down the sides once.)

2. Scrape and pour the dough onto a heavily floured work surface. Keeping your fingers, the countertop, and the dough well floured, fold one dough end over the other so that half the floured underside covers the rest of the dough. Let rest for 10 minutes.

3. Cut the dough into 2 equal pieces. Shape each piece into a smooth ball. Place each ball on a well-oiled plate, dust generously with flour, and cover loosely with plastic wrap. Let the dough rise until it is at least doubled in size, about 3 hours.

4. Punch the dough balls down, shape into rounds, and place each in a quart-size freezer bag. Refrigerate the dough for at least 1 hour, or up to 4 hours.

MAKES ENOUGH FOR TWO 14-INCH PIZZAS

SERVING SUGGESTIONS
Watercress Salad (p. 171), Salade à la Romaine (p. 171), Strawberry Sorbet (p. 732)

APRIL 19, 2009: "THE CHEAT: CRUST FUND," BY SAM SIFTON. PIZZA DOUGH RECIPE ADAPTED FROM JEFFREY STEINGARTEN, THE FOOD CRITIC AT *VOGUE* AND AUTHOR OF *THE MAN WHO ATE EVERYTHING*.

—2009

- Deviled Crabs (p. 387).

—1870s—

- Instructions on how to clean and fry soft-shell crabs appear in the food pages.

—1877—

- Shrimp, salmon, and lobster are potted with butter.

—1880s—

- Cooking teacher Juliet Corson gives courses on cooking skate.

—1880—

- Curries, including Crab and Coconut Curry (p. 389), are surprisingly common.

—1881—

- Oysters are abundant in New York harbor; the city's inhabitants gorge.

—1890s—

- Oysters Rockefeller is created at Antoine's in New Orleans.

—1899—

- Unconventional yet delicious Bouillabaisse (p. 390).

—1904—

- The Oyster Bar opens in Grand Central Terminal.

—1913—

- Zabar's, specializing in smoked fish, opens on Manhattan's Upper West Side.

—1934—

- Pierre Franey moves from France to New York and is hired as the fish cook at Le Pavillon.

—1939—

- Tomatoes Stuffed with Crab (p. 393) find their audience at hotels and then country clubs.

—1940s—

- Lobster Thermidor: shellfish meet cream sauce.

—1946—

- Maryland Crab Cakes (p. 407)— a love that lasts for decades.

—1947—

- Craig Claiborne runs a recipe for Grand Central Pan Roast (p. 393), one of the world's best dishes, and it can be made in five minutes.

—1958—

- Does any dish say 1960s more than Coquilles St.-Jacques (p. 396)?

—1960s—

- There is a time for Salmon Mousse (p. 394) and it is this decade.

—1961—

- Greek food is in: shrimp meets feta, with delicious consequences (see p. 397).

—1970s—

- Soft-shell crabs move beyond a regional specialty.

—1980s—

- Craig Claiborne writes about making gravlax at home.

—1983—

- Alfred Portale creates a tower of lobster, making his dish—Lobster Salad Max—and his plating style famous.

—1986—

- Monkfish and skate, former trash fish, become popular.
- Broiled cod with a miso glaze, a specialty of Nobu in New York, is copied everywhere.
- Chilean sea bass, aka Patagonian toothfish, becomes a hit.

—1990s—

- Meunière and Grenobloise (p. 399).

- Tuna is seared, sometimes with black peppercorns, sometimes not.
- Ubiquitous wedding hors d'oeuvre: mini crab cakes.
- Tuna tartare (p. 416) and ceviche (p. 417).

• Mark Bittman writes *Fish*.	—1994—
• Slow-cooked salmon (see p. 415) foreshadows the days of *sous-vide*.	—1997—
• "Line-caught" and "day boat" become catch phrases for higher-quality fish caught in a humane fashion and brought to shore fresh rather than frozen.	—1998—
• Thomas Keller publishes his butter-poached lobster recipe in *The French Laundry Cookbook*.	—1999—
• Sushi. Sushi. And more sushi.	—2000s—
• Julia Moskin explains that there are really only four kinds of oysters, they just live in different waters, which impart different flavors.	—2002—
• Masa, a sushi bar, opens in New York City and earns 4 stars from the *Times*. Its tasting menu runs from $300 to $500.	—2004—
• Fulton Fish Market, open since 1822, moves from near the Brooklyn Bridge to the Bronx.	—2005—
• Tartare is replaced by crudo; same thing, larger pieces of fish.	—2006—
• The United Nations reports that overfishing is a global issue.	—2008—

• Chilean sea bass is overfished, and is removed from many menus.

9

⤳

FISH AND SHELLFISH

The *Times*'s food pages' particular area of expertise, as it happens, has been fish and shellfish. Among its most well-known writers have been fish experts such as Bob the Sea Cook from the nineteenth century; Pierre Franey, who was hired as the fish chef at Le Pavillon in 1939; and Mark Bittman, who wrote a book called *Fish* before beginning his column "The Minimalist." And the feeding ground for *Times* food writers is New York City, which has some of the best fish and shellfish chefs in the world. You will meet some of them—Eric Ripert, David Pasternack, and Jean-Georges Vongerichten—on the following pages.

Over the decades, the ways we cook fish and shellfish have become increasingly varied and nuanced. In addition to French-style sautés and sauces, and American fish chowders, we now make Chinese Clams in Black Bean Sauce (p. 442), Yucatán Fish with Crisp Garlic (p. 431), Broiled Halibut with Miso Glaze (p. 413), and Laotian Minced Fish Salad (p. 436).

But this chapter is one of a few in which the basic recipes haven't really changed all that much in 150 years. The instructions given in 1882 for serving oysters on the half-shell are exactly what they would be today: "Have half a dozen oysters on the half-shell ready for each guest. Be careful, in ordering them, to state that they must be small. Half a lemon should be served with each plate." In 1881, Juliet Corson, a cooking school teacher who was a frequent *Times* contributor, published a recipe for poached trout with peas that's not all that different from Nigella Lawson's Scallops with Pea Puree (p. 429). And the Deviled Crab (p. 387) from 1878 is nearly the same as a deviled crab casserole from 1992 that was recommended by readers (but not included here because the old one was better).

The only real change with fish is that the world's fish supply has been devastated in recent decades. As buying can be fraught, it's always a good idea to check sources like www.sustainablefish.org and www.edf.org, which post updates on which fish are best to buy.

A few cooking tips before you get started. In 2009, Sam Sifton, then a *Times* editor and now the paper's restaurant critic, buttonholed David

Pasternak, the chef at Esca, for his fish sautéing technique and extracted three rules that Sifton set down as follows:

1. Get over the fear. You're going to make fish at home, it's going to be easy, and it's not going to take up your day or destroy your kitchen. The recipe is going to work. Trust the process.

2. Buying fish is half the battle. Pasternack said, "The first thing you want to do is you want to find a thick fillet of fish. You want a nice thick fillet so you can develop the color and the crust." Pasternack speaks in a soft Long Island growl that turns any conversation into an intimacy, a prelude to something possibly criminal and certainly fun. "Ask for the large," he continued. "They have large in the back. They always do."

3. Crust is crucial. Pasternack's method: "You want to make sure the bottom of your pan is completely covered in fat. It's on a medium flame. You add a pat of butter for flavor, and you put the fillet in the pan. You turn it to medium-high, and you watch it cook until it turns a deep golden brown on the bottom. That's like 3, 4 minutes. Then you turn it. A minute later, you take it out, put it on paper towels, season it with a little salt."

RECIPES BY CATEGORY

POISSON À L'HUILE (SALMON WITH SAUTERNES AND OLIVE OIL)

I was taken by the addition of Sauternes in the cooking broth and the specification of olive oil from Lucca in the vinaigrette—long before the age of competitive ingredient fetishes. In the recipe's defense, it is such a simple dish that you really do need the character of a great olive oil. But, of course, it's fine if yours comes from Liguria or Catalonia or even California, as long as its flavor pleases you.

The writer of this recipe had come across this dish at a party. Having sought out the hostess who ushered him to the buffet, he described how "she showed me a superb salmon, stretched at length on a silver platter, where in quiet repose it seemed as real as if it were a live fish on an argent wave. Just then, I might have been on the eve of declaring my love, either for the lady or for the salmon, but it was the fish which fascinated me."

Soon enough he was in the kitchen, asking the chef how to prepare the fish. "Believe me, sir," the chef is quoted as saying, "this method is the best, the simplest; and at a ball, after dancing, there is nothing so recuperating."

————

For the Poaching Liquid

4 cups water

2 bottles (375-ml) Sauternes or I (750-ml) bottle
    ice wine or Riesling

6 sprigs flat-leaf parsley

3 sprigs thyme

I bay leaf

I sage leaf

I small onion, halved

2 teaspoons salt

I ½ tablespoons black peppercorns

One 3-pound skinless salmon fillet, any pin bones
    removed (see Cooking Note, p. 418)

2 slices hearty white sandwich bread

I clove garlic, peeled

For the Vinaigrette

6 tablespoons fresh lemon juice

¾ cup your best extra virgin olive oil

¼ cup finely chopped tarragon

2 tablespoon finely chopped flat-leaf parsley

Salt

1. To make the poaching liquid, combine the water and wine in a saucepan large enough to hold the salmon. Add the parsley, thyme, bay leaf, sage, onion, salt, and peppercorns and bring to a boil.

2. Lower the heat to medium so the poaching liquid simmers gently and lower the salmon into the pan. If the salmon is not covered, add more water until it is. Simmer until the salmon is just cooked through (test with the tip of a knife). Remove the fish to a plate to cool.

3. Meanwhile, lightly toast the bread, and rub it with garlic while it is still warm. Set aside to cool.

4. To make the vinaigrette, beat together the lemon juice, olive oil, tarragon, parsley, and salt to taste.

5. Crumb the cooled toast in the food processor.

6. To serve, lay the fish on a platter and spoon the dressing over it. Sprinkle with the garlic bread crumbs.

SERVES 6 TO 8

COOKING NOTE

This recipe can easily be doubled or tripled—and if you can find a whole salmon, by all means, buy it! It will take longer to cook, so build in a few extra minutes when poaching.

SERVING SUGGESTIONS

Asparagus Salad (p. 214), Yette's Garden Platter (p. 220), Artichoke Salad with Anchovy and Capers (p. 174), Asparagus and Bulgur with Preserved-Lemon Dressing (p. 190), Rhubarb Orange (p. 864)

OCTOBER II, 1874: "HOW TO DRESS FISH: LEAVES FROM A SENTIMENTAL COOKBOOK."

—1874

DEVILED CRABS

Warm sweet crab with a zing of cayenne and Worcestershire. I like this fiery—if you're not a fan of spicy food, begin with a small pinch of cayenne.

Deviled crab is an ancestor of deviled eggs, which—much as we love them—are a neutered form of deviling. Deviled crab and deviled kidneys were meant to be spicy and bracing, the kind of food you had after a long night of drinking. Deviling grew out of a dish called "a devil," Anne Mendelson, a food historian, wrote in an e-mail, which you made "by taking odd bits of meat, fish, poultry, game, feathered game, offal—anything from turkey legs to fish bones—and broiling them with plenty of hot condiments and/or serving them with some strong-flavored relish."

In *David Copperfield*, Mr. Micawber saves a dinner party by turning undercooked mutton into a devil. Dickens wrote:

"Traddles cut the mutton into slices; Mr. Micawber (who could do anything of this sort to perfection) covered them with pepper, mustard, salt, and cayenne; I put them on the gridiron, turned them with a fork, and took them off, under Mr. Micawber's direction; and Mrs. Micawber heated, and continually stirred, some mushroom ketchup in a little saucepan. . . . With the novelty of this cookery, the excellence of it, the bustle of it, the frequent starting up to look after it, the frequent sitting down to dispose of it as the crisp slices came off the gridiron hot and hot, the being so busy, so flushed with fire, so amused, and in the midst of such a tempting noise and savour, we reduced the leg of mutton to the bone."

———

¼ cup mayonnaise

1½ teaspoons Dijon mustard

Large pinch of cayenne pepper

1 teaspoon cider vinegar

½ pound crabmeat, picked over for shells and cartilage

2 tablespoons minced onion

½ teaspoon chopped thyme

½ teaspoon Worcestershire sauce

About 2 tablespoons fine fresh bread crumbs

1 tablespoon unsalted butter, cut into 4 thin slices

1. Heat the oven to 350 degrees. Blend the mayonnaise, mustard, cayenne, and vinegar in a bowl. Add the crab and fold together. Add the onion, thyme, and Worcestershire and fold once more. Taste and adjust the seasoning.

2. Spoon the mixture into four 6-ounce ramekins (or the cleaned crab shells if you have them). Sprinkle with the bread crumbs and top each with a slice of butter. (At this point, the ramekins can be covered and refrigerated for up to 8 hours.)

3. Place the ramekins on a baking sheet and bake until heated through, about 20 minutes. Then place under the broiler until golden brown on top, 30 to 60 seconds, depending on the distance between the heating element and the ramekins.

SERVES 4 AS A FIRST COURSE

SERVING SUGGESTIONS

Gin Rickey (p. 21), Sea Scallops with Sweet Red Peppers and Zucchini (p. 409), Baked Flounder (p. 401), '21' Club Hamburger (p. 536), Saratoga Potatoes (p. 273), Delicate Bread Pudding (p. 798), Peach Balls (p. 804), Tapioca Pudding (p. 798)

FEBRUARY 24, 1878: "THE HOUSEHOLD." RECIPE SIGNED BOSTON COOK.

—1878

⌒ POTTED SALMON

Bob the Sea Cook, who fancied himself a man of culinary prowess, submitted dozens of recipes to the *Times* during the late nineteenth century. He wrote cannily and conversationally, was a consummate food enthusiast, and showed more know-how than most of the contributors of his time—although he could be alarmingly sexist. In giving the instructions for a lobster and chicken curry, made on a ship, he wrote, "Take a big chicken, cut him in bits, and put the pieces in salt and water; boil about a five-pound lobster and pick it. If there are any ladies on board, make them do it."

Of this salmon, he noted, "An old man, as I knowed [*sic*], as good a sailor as ever sailed, was mighty fussy over his eating, and he first showed me how to make potted salmon out of the fish in cans. It is a tip-top relish spread on a bit of bread."

After testing this recipe and deciding to add it to the book, I came across a strikingly similar potted salmon that was published in Craig Claiborne and Pierre Franey's column in 1981. Turns out, Claiborne and Franey were also featuring Bob the Sea Cook's dish—as part of a brief dip into the archives—only they halved the recipe (which you may also do) and increased the amount of vinegar to 1 tablespoon.

One 1-pound skinless salmon fillet, any pin bones
  removed, poached (see Cooking Notes, p. 418
  and below)
4 tablespoons unsalted butter
2 anchovy fillets, mashed
Pinch of cayenne pepper, or more to taste
1/8 teaspoon ground mace, or more to taste
3 black peppercorns
1/2 teaspoon tarragon vinegar, or more to taste
Salt
Toast points, for serving

1. Using your hands, finely shred the salmon into a double boiler. Set over medium heat and cook, stirring, until the salmon is hot to the touch. Beat in the butter and then the anchovies, cayenne, mace, peppercorns, vinegar, and salt to taste. Remove from the heat and beat for another minute. Let cool for 10 minutes. Taste and adjust the seasoning, adding more vinegar, cayenne, mace, and salt as desired.

2. Beat the salmon for another minute, then pack it into a small crock or dish. Press a sheet of plastic wrap directly on the surface of the salmon. Chill (the salmon can be refrigerated for up to 5 days).

MAKES 1½ CUPS; SERVES 4 AS AN HORS D'OEUVRE
OR, WITH A SALAD AND TOASTS,
AS A FIRST COURSE

COOKING NOTE

To poach the salmon, fill a saucepan large enough to hold the fish with water. Season the water with salt and some aromatics, such as a quartered onion, a few sprigs of parsley and thyme, and 5 peppercorns. Bring the water to a simmer and lower in the salmon. Simmer until the salmon is lightly cooked but still pink in the center. Shut off the heat and let cool in the water.

SERVING SUGGESTIONS

Park Avenue Cocktail (p. 19), Onion Rings (p. 61), Salade Niçoise (p. 178), Pots de Crème (p. 815)

JANUARY 4, 1880: "RECEIPTS FOR THE TABLE." RECIPE
SIGNED BOB THE SEA COOK.

—1880

⌒ CRAB AND COCONUT CURRY

This simple little curry appeared in an article filled with crab and lobster recipes. The writer also suggested mixing crabmeat with vinegar, mustard, cayenne, salt, and pepper and serving it in its shell.

For a party, I'd serve this as an hors d'oeuvre on thin rice crackers or rice pancakes (p. 357; made into individual pancakes) or on Green Pea Fritters (p. 270), topped with diced tomato. For dinner, I'd serve it warm, with steamed rice and a sambol or other condiment.

1/2 pound crabmeat, picked over for shells and cartilage
1¾ cups unsweetened grated coconut
¾ teaspoon curry powder
1/2 teaspoon Worcestershire sauce, plus more to taste
Salt
1/2 teaspoon coconut oil or canola oil (optional)

Mix together the crabmeat, coconut, curry powder, Worcestershire, salt to taste, and oil if using, in a bowl. Taste and adjust the seasoning.

SERVES 6 TO 8 AS AN HORS D'OEUVRE,
4 AS A FIRST COURSE OR LIGHT MAIN COURSE
(WITH RICE AND CONDIMENTS)

SERVING SUGGESTIONS

Sweet (or Savory) Lassi (p. 25), Manjula Gokal's Gujarati Mango Soup (p. 155), Aloo Kofta (p. 74), Bademiya's Justly Famous Bombay Chile-and-Cilantro Chicken (p. 471), Mango Ice Cream (p. 729)

MARCH 6, 1881: "HINTS FOR THE HOUSEHOLD: A CHAPTER
UPON CRABS AND LOBSTERS" BY JULIET CORSON.

—1881

⌒ SALMON SALAD

This would be a great salad to make with the leftovers from Poisson à l'Huile on p. 387.

One 10-ounce skinless salmon fillet, any pin bones
    removed, poached (see Cooking Notes, pp. 418
    and 389)

2 hard-boiled eggs

1 teaspoon Colman's prepared mustard

2 tablespoons olive oil

Salt

6 tablespoons red wine vinegar

½ cup celery, thinly sliced on a bias

3 heaping tablespoons prepared horseradish

Chopped flat-leaf parsley for garnish

1. Put the salmon in a small saucepan and place over low heat until just warmed through.

2. Meanwhile, remove the yolks from the eggs and mash the yolks with a fork in a small bowl. Work in the mustard and olive oil. Season with salt. Whisk in the vinegar.

3. Finely chop the egg whites.

4. Combine the salmon, celery, and horseradish in a bowl. Mix well, pour in the dressing, and mix again. Adjust the seasoning if necessary. Spoon the salad into a nice bowl and top with the chopped egg whites and parsley.

SERVES 4 AS PART OF A LUNCH WITH
OTHER SALADS

SERVING SUGGESTIONS
Rachel's Green Beans with Dill (p. 251), Potato Salad with Beets (p. 270), Frozen Lemon Soufflé (p. 725)

APRIL 3, 1881: "OTHER RECEIPTS." RECIPE SIGNED MARY B., BROOKLYN.

—1881

⌒ BOUILLABAISSE

In 2002, R. W. Apple Jr., the *Times* reporter and noted bon vivant, wrote that "controversy clings to bouillabaisse like barnacles to a ship. Is it a soup? Perhaps not, because the broth and the solids are eaten separately. Is it a stew? Surely not, because a stew by definition is cooked very slowly, and bouillabaisse must be boiled furiously to achieve an amalgamation of olive oil with water and wine. It is best described as a fish boil, which is what its name seems to imply." Alan Davidson, in *The Oxford Companion to Food*, points out that a nineteenth-century dictionary by Littré interprets it as *bouillon abaissé*, or "broth lowered," meaning the broth is boiled down.

Whatever you want to call it—broth lowered or fish boil, soup or stew—bouillabaisse is meant to contain a bunch of fish, olive oil, and water, and is not supposed to take three days to make. A century ago, it was much simpler. It was an ideal dish for home cooks: there was no doting over perfect slices of fish, no high-octane fish stock, and no mention of garlicky rouille. It began with water, olive oil, and sometimes wine, an onion or two, tomatoes, saffron, some herbs, and fish. Then you gave the mix a blast of heat so the oil and broth would come to an excited boil and engulf the aromatics.

This 1904 recipe I settled on contained equal parts water and oil and half the amount of white wine. The saffron- and herb-scented oil insulates the fish and dresses it as the fish breaks down, making for a rich and rustic oily broth. It completely changed my sense of what bouillabaisse could be.

If you'd prefer to take on the more complex, modern form of bouillabaisse, the challenge (and reward) is all yours on p. 406.

---

1 cup olive oil

2 medium tomatoes, peeled (see Cooking Note, p. 146),
    cored, seeded, and sliced

1 small onion, thinly sliced

1 carrot, peeled and very thinly sliced

2 pinches saffron threads, or to taste

1 bay leaf

4 sprigs parsley

2 cloves garlic

1 pound each skinless cod, halibut, and bluefish fillets
    (fluke or sea bass may be substituted for two of
    these), cut into 2-inch pieces

2 cups peeled, deveined medium shrimp (about 1 pound)

Juice of ½ lemon, or to taste

Salt and freshly ground black pepper

1 cup fish broth

½ cup dry white wine

6 slices country bread, toasted

1. Heat the oil in a large saucepan over medium-high heat. Add the tomatoes, onion, carrot, saffron, bay leaf, and parsley. Crush 1 garlic clove and add it to the pan. Cook for 2 minutes. Add the fish, shrimp, and lemon juice, season with salt and pepper, and boil for 10 minutes.

2. Add the fish broth and wine, bring to a rapid simmer, and simmer until the fish is just cooked through. Adjust the seasoning, adding more saffron, lemon juice, salt, and/or pepper as desired.

3. Rub the toasts with the remaining garlic clove. Set a toast in the bottom of each of 6 bowls and ladle the bouillabaisse on top.

SERVES 6

COOKING NOTES

Set out your fish for 20 minutes beforehand.

You can halve the amount of oil if you find it alarming.

VARIATION

Spice up the soup by adding a little smoked paprika, red pepper flakes, lemon juice, and more garlic.

SERVING SUGGESTIONS

Squashed Tomatoes (p. 90), Nicole Kaplan's Gougères (p. 76), Hot Cheese Olives (p. 83), Salade à la Romaine (p. 171), Classic Financiers (Buttery Almond Cakes; p. 697)

JULY 3, 1904: "BOUILLABAISSE AND CHOWDERS: AN EEL SOUP DIGRESSION—WHO NOW GET THE BEST VEGETABLES AND FRUITS—A DEAR FISH MARKET."

—1904

❧ CEYLON CURRY OF OYSTERS

Just as Germany was preparing to invade Poland and America was wondering whether it would have to go to war, New Yorkers, according to the *Times*, were dabbling in Indian cuisine, with new restaurants opening and hotels putting Indian dishes on their menus. Charlotte Hughes, then a reporter for the paper, none-

too-definitively declared, "Everybody in India, apparently, eats curry." And she noted that although curries were complicated to prepare, "nevertheless, American cooks with a pioneering spirit can master curry dishes."

Yet seventy years later, we have not. But there is still time. A Ceylonese curry of oysters—one of several vaguely composed recipes included in Hughes's article—would be a fine place to start.

First, a few disclaimers: Oyster curry, according to Andrew F. Smith, the author of *The Oxford Companion to American Food and Drink*, was a popular dish in the nineteenth century, particularly in England—so popular that mixes for it were sold. By the time Hughes revisited it, the recipe was well established and westernized. Back then, food writers didn't often travel in order to better understand foreign cuisines, so some of the ingredients in Hughes's recipes were adaptations or innocent misunderstandings. In place of chiles, for instance, she called for a green pepper, which would make for a meek variation of a typically fiery Ceylonese curry. Bay leaves seem to have been substituted for either curry leaves or pandanus leaf, both common in Ceylonese cooking; butter stands in for coconut oil; and curry powder is a Western convenience for cooks who don't want to measure out each spice individually. Otherwise, it's totally authentic!

But even Hughes knew where to draw a line. Using good curry powder is imperative, she wrote, adding, "One cannot just make a white sauce and stir in a little curry powder."

She got her recipe for the oyster curry from someone named Darmadasa at the East India Curry Shop on East 57th Street. You begin by sautéing shallots, garlic, and green pepper. Next you season them with turmeric, curry powder, cinnamon, cloves, and bay leaves and simmer it all in coconut milk. At the end, you slip in the oysters and their liquor and season the curry with lemon juice. The whole process takes about 10 minutes, and the payoff lasts for years, because you'll want to make it again and again.

Hughes suggested serving the curry with rice. "Dry, fluffy rice, each particle as separate from the next as a grain of sand on a sunbaked dune, is important to the excellence of a curry dish," she wrote. Everybody in India, apparently, also eats rice.

2 tablespoons unsalted butter or coconut oil

4 small shallots, finely chopped

I clove garlic, minced

½ serrano or Thai chile, seeded and minced

I tablespoon curry powder

Large pinch of turmeric

I cinnamon stick

3 cloves

I bay leaf

I cup unsweetened coconut milk

½ teaspoon salt, plus more to taste

12 oysters, shucked, liquor reserved

Juice of ½ lemon

1. Melt the butter in a medium saucepan over medium heat. Add the shallots, garlic, and chile and sauté until softened and starting to brown, 2 to 3 minutes. Stir in the curry powder, turmeric, cinnamon stick, cloves, and bay leaf and cook for 1 minute. Reduce the heat to low and add the coconut milk and salt. Simmer for 3 minutes.

2. Add the oysters and their liquor; simmer until the oysters are just firm, 3 to 4 minutes. Take the pan off the heat and add lemon juice and salt to taste.

SERVES 2

COOKING NOTES

This recipe won't win any beauty contests. When oysters are cooked, they shrivel up and warp. You can always sprinkle some chopped cilantro on top.

Hughes's recipe called for 3 bay leaves; I used only one. Since chiles are now commonly available, I used a serrano rather than the sweet green pepper Hughes suggested.

SERVING SUGGESTIONS

A cold lager or, as the article suggested, a cup of Darjeeling tea, Kaffir Lime Lemonade (p. 26), Sweet (or Savory) Lassi (p. 25), Yogurt Rice (p. 356), Stuck-Pot Rice with Yogurt and Spices (p. 351), Jasmine Tea Rice (p. 354), Hoppers (Coconut Crepes; p. 349), Aloo Kofta (p. 74), Saffron Panna Cotta (p. 845)

MARCH 12, 1939: "FOR GOURMETS AND OTHERS: CURRY COMES TO THE TABLE," BY CHARLOTTE HUGHES. RECIPE ADAPTED FROM DARMADASA AT THE EAST INDIA CURRY SHOP ON EAST 57TH STREET, NEW YORK CITY.

—1939

∽ SAUTÉED TROUT WITH BROWN BUTTER, LEMON, AND MACADAMIA NUTS

Tart lemons and fatty macadamia nuts mix well, as if you'd crossed a chatty person with a laconic one and come up with the perfect conversationalist.

———

¼ cup whole milk

½ cup all-purpose flour

2 whole trout, filleted (you can have the fish market do this)

Salt and freshly ground black pepper

4 tablespoons unsalted butter, or as needed

2 tablespoons fresh lemon juice

3 tablespoons chopped macadamia nuts

I tablespoon chopped flat-leaf parsley

Chopped candied pineapple for garnish (optional)

1. Set 2 wide shallow bowls near the stove. Fill one with the milk, the other with the flour. Season the trout fillets with salt and pepper.

2. Place a large nonstick sauté pan over medium-high heat. Add 1 tablespoon butter, and, while it melts, dip a trout fillet first in the milk, and then the flour, shaking off any excess. Lay the fillet flesh side down in the foaming butter. Repeat with remaining fillets. (If you can't fit all the trout in the pan, do it in batches, adding more butter as needed.) When lightly browned, turn the fillets and brown until just cooked through, 3 to 5 minutes total. Remove to a serving plate and keep loosely covered.

3. Melt 3 tablespoons butter in a small saucepan over medium heat. Let it foam and boil, and when it begins to brown, swirl in the lemon juice, macadamia nuts, and parsley. Let the mixture cook for a few seconds to coalesce. Spoon the sauce over the trout, and garnish with candied pineapple (or not).

SERVES 4

SERVING SUGGESTIONS

Yellow Pepper Soup with Paprika Mousse (p. 147), Asparagus Salad (p. 214), Junior's Cheesecake (p. 771), Lemon Mousse for a Crowd (p.861), Sally Darr's Golden Delicious Apple Tart (p. 839)

APRIL 7, 1940: "VICTUALS AND VITAMINS," BY KILEY TAYLOR. RECIPE ADAPTED FROM THE LOMBARDY IN NEW YORK CITY.

—1940

TOMATOES STUFFED WITH CRAB

In 1948, André Simon, the founder of the Wine and Food Society, came from England to America to promote a new edition of *André Simon's French Cook Book*, which advocated seasonal cooking. He also seemed determined to assess the state of American cuisine. "In England," he told Jane Nickerson, a *Times* columnist, "there's enough food, but not enough variety. Here there is enough food, but too much variety.

"Your markets," he continued, "simultaneously offer endive, which is a winter vegetable, and melon, which is a summer fruit. You eat strawberries in January as well as in June. You enjoy so much variety the year round that your meals must end by becoming the same month in and month out. Perhaps that is good. But I think not. Do we not look forward to the new leaves of spring, to the hot sunshine of summer, to the bright foliage of autumn, to the briskness of winter? Isn't it kindness to our palates to preserve in our diets, too, this varied rhythm of the seasons?"

After that trenchant and moving statement, Simon offered this recipe for stuffed tomatoes from the "spring" menu in his book! Sigh. Make them in August, you'll adore them.

———

1 tablespoon unsalted butter
¼ pound white mushrooms, trimmed and sliced
1 cup (about ½ pound) crabmeat, picked over
    for shells and cartilage
¼ cup heavy cream
Salt and freshly ground black pepper
2 tablespoons dry sherry
6 small tomatoes
Chopped flat-leaf parsley

1. Heat the oven to 375 degrees. Bring a large pot of water to boil.
2. Melt the butter in a small sauté pan over medium-

low heat. Add the mushrooms and cook until softened. Remove from the heat.
3. Heat the crabmeat in the cream. Season with salt, pepper, and sherry; add the mushrooms.
4. Blanch the tomatoes in the boiling water (briefly!) to loosen their skins, and plunge them into ice water to stop the cooking. Peel the tomatoes. Cut a hole about the size of a quarter in the top of each, where the stem was attached, and using a melon baller, hollow out a space in the center, making sure not to cut through the sides.
5. Fill the centers of the tomatoes with the hot crabmeat and sprinkle with chopped parsley. Arrange the tomatoes in a baking dish. Warm in the oven for 10 minutes.
6. Place each tomato in a shallow bowl, garnish with more parsley, and spoon over any juices left in the baking dish.

SERVES 6 AS A FIRST COURSE

COOKING NOTE
The tomatoes must be small and ripe but not mushy, or they'll fall apart. I used firm yellow tomatoes, which were both delicious and beautiful.

SERVING SUGGESTIONS
Wine Lemonade (p. 17), Salmon and Tomatoes in Foil (p. 422), Zucchini and Vermouth (p. 227), Fresh Blueberry Buckle (p. 815), Pavlova (p. 826)

MAY 29, 1948: "NEWS OF FOOD; BRITISH FOOD LEADER, HERE FOR TOUR, SEES TOO MUCH VARIETY IN OUR MEALS," BY JANE NICKERSON. RECIPE ADAPTED FROM *ANDRÉ SIMON'S FRENCH COOK BOOK*, BY ANDRÉ SIMON, FOUNDER OF THE WINE AND FOOD SOCIETY.

—1948

GRAND CENTRAL PAN ROAST

Pan roasts have been around forever: the best version is this one, which the Grand Central Oyster Bar still serves (for $10.45 on this day in 2009). It's ugly as hell but sensationally good, with plump, sweet oysters set against a spicy, tangy sauce.

———

16 freshly shucked oysters, with their liquor

1 tablespoon unsalted butter

1 tablespoon hot pepper sauce

2 teaspoons Worcestershire sauce

A few drops of fresh lemon juice

Pinch of celery salt

Pinch of paprika

1/2 cup heavy cream, plus more if desired

2 pieces dry toast

1. Combine the oysters, in their liquor, with the butter, hot pepper sauce, Worcestershire, lemon juice, celery salt, and paprika in a medium saucepan. Bring to a boil and simmer, stirring constantly, just until the oysters plump and ruffle. Taste and adjust the seasonings.

2. Add the cream and heat until bubbles form around the perimeter of the pan, then pour over the toasts set in shallow bowls. Sprinkle with additional paprika.

SERVES 2

COOKING NOTES

I used Frank's Hot Sauce.

Make sure you get oysters with their liquor (the oyster's natural juices), because it adds to the volume and consistency of the sauce. Be flexible with the amount of cream you use—you want just enough sauce to soak into the bread and pool around it a little.

SERVING SUGGESTIONS

Crab Cakes Baltimore-Style (p. 407), Docks Coleslaw (p. 191), Blueberry Pie with a Lattice Top (p. 853), Banana Cream Pie (p. 863)

JANUARY 2, 1958: "VARIED WAYS WITH OYSTERS, NOW AT THEIR JUICY PEAK," BY CRAIG CLAIBORNE.

—1958

SALMON MOUSSE

Salmon mousse appeared regularly along with paella and cheesecake as part of Craig Claiborne's annual round-up of most frequently requested recipes. Of the three, only the mousse seems to have been 86'd over time. A mistake, in my view.

The mousse may seem a little strange, because we tend not to combine fish and gelatin in a blender these days, but it's delicious, and it has an amazing firm consistency, neither bouncy nor stiff. The salmon flavor, which can easily overpower, is contained and flattered by lemon, cream, and dill.

And you will love how easy the mousse is to prepare—it's a fun dish to make with kids because it involves a lot of pouring of ingredients into a blender and then watching them whirl around.

The only vexing question is how to serve it. Claiborne suggested it as a first course or "luncheon specialty." You could plate up thin slices topped with a tuft of young greens, dressed with a sherry and shallot vinaigrette. I think it's best in small doses, say, as an hors d'oeuvre. Serve it on toasts sprinkled with olive oil, or with a coarse wheat or Swedish rye cracker. A smooth cracker won't provide enough contrast to the mousse.

———

1 envelope (1/4 ounce) powdered gelatin

2 tablespoons fresh lemon juice

1 small slice onion

1/2 cup boiling water

1/2 cup mayonnaise

1/4 teaspoon paprika

1 teaspoon dried dill

One 1-pound can salmon, drained and
    picked over for bones

1 cup heavy cream

Salt (optional)

1. Empty the envelope of gelatin into a blender. Add the lemon juice, onion slice, and boiling water. Place the blender cover on the container, turn the motor to high speed, and blend the ingredients for 40 seconds. Turn the motor off. Add the mayonnaise, paprika, dill, and salmon, cover, and blend briefly at high speed.

2. Remove the cover and add the cream, 1/3 cup at a time, blending for a few seconds after each addition. Then blend for 30 seconds or longer. Season with salt if needed. Pour into a 4-cup mold; chill until set.

SERVES 8 AS A FIRST COURSE OR HORS D'OEUVRE

COOKING NOTE

I used canned wild salmon—buy the best you can find.

Beet Tartare (p. 240), Raw Spinach Salad (p. 175), Steak au Poivre (p. 573), Taillevent Pear Soufflé (p. 835)

JANUARY 1, 1961: "WIN, PLACE, AND SHOW IN '60," BY CRAIG CLAIBORNE.

—1961

MRS. REARDY'S SHRIMP AND ARTICHOKE CASSEROLE

Viola Reardy was Adlai E. Stevenson's housekeeper and cook. This casserole, which she served for lunch to President Kennedy and UN Acting Secretary General U Thant, greatly intrigued readers, who sent a rush of letters requesting the recipe. When Craig Claiborne tracked down Reardy at Stevenson's well-equipped suite in the Waldorf-Astoria Hotel to extract the sought-after details, she asked him, confidingly, "Was there ever so much to-do over a recipe?" It is pretty darn good. When I made it, I thought I'd happily eat just the sherried béchamel.

Stevenson was apparently a decent cook himself, and the enterprising Claiborne also managed to pry from him his recipe for lamb curry.

————

1 pound small shrimp, shelled and deveined
6½ tablespoons unsalted butter
4½ tablespoons all-purpose flour
¾ cup whole milk
¾ cup heavy cream
Salt and freshly ground black pepper
One 14-ounce can artichoke hearts, drained,
    or one 9-ounce package frozen artichoke hearts,
    cooked according to the package directions
¼ pound mushrooms, trimmed and sliced
¼ cup dry sherry
1 tablespoon Worcestershire sauce
¼ cup freshly grated Parmesan cheese
Paprika

1. Heat the oven to 375 degrees. Bring 8 cups of water to a boil in a saucepan. Add the shrimp and cook for 15 seconds. Use a slotted spoon to remove the shrimp. Reserve both the shrimp and broth.

2. Melt 4½ tablespoons butter in a saucepan and stir in the flour; cook, stirring, for 30 seconds. When blended, gradually add the milk and cream, stirring constantly with a wire whisk. Bring to a simmer and cook, whisking, until thickened and smooth. Season well with salt and pepper; remove from the heat.

3. Arrange the artichokes over the bottom of a buttered 8-inch square baking dish. Scatter the shrimp over the artichokes.

4. Melt the remaining 2 tablespoons butter in a medium saucepan over medium heat. Add the sliced mushrooms and cook until they begin to brown on the edges, 5 to 8 minutes. Spoon the mushrooms over the shrimp and artichokes.

5. Add the sherry and Worcestershire to the cream sauce. If the sauce is too thick, you can thin it with a little reserved shrimp broth and milk. Pour it over the contents of the baking dish.

6. Sprinkle with the Parmesan cheese and paprika and bake for 20 minutes.

SERVES 4 TO 6

COOKING NOTES
If you use frozen artichoke hearts, undercook them slightly.

Also slightly undercook the shrimp when you boil them.

SERVING SUGGESTIONS
Asparagus Mimosa (p. 258), A Perfect Batch of Rice (p. 316), Chiffonade Salad (p. 173), Mrs. Foster's Frosty Lime Pie (p. 724), Lee's Marlborough Tart (p. 816)

PERIOD DETAIL
Paprika was still living in the jail cell of pointless garnish. Here it adds nothing but color to the casserole's dubious muted shades of white and green. If you want to update the recipe ever so slightly, use smoked paprika, which will contribute not only color, but—whoa!—flavor.

READERS
"My mother always claimed credit for getting [this recipe] published. A news article about the Democratic nominee mentioned that Kennedy had been a guest of Adlai Stevenson's for a Friday lunch. Stevenson served a shrimp and artichoke casserole because Kennedy

could not eat meat on Friday. My mother wrote or called the *Times* asking for the recipe and shortly afterwards it appeared in the paper. She always assumed that it was her request that had been answered."

Linda S. Kaufman, Cambridge, MA, e-mail

JANUARY 29, 1962: "FOOD NEWS: STEVENSON'S RECIPE FOR A PRESIDENT," BY CRAIG CLAIBORNE. ADAPTED FROM VIOLA REARDY, HOUSEKEEPER TO ADLAI E. STEVENSON.

—1962

∽ COQUILLES ST.-JACQUES

In the article featuring this recipe, Craig Claiborne complained that most coquilles St.-Jacques recipes are burdened by cream, whereas his version, thickened with flour, egg yolks, and butter, was lighter—the contents without all the baggage. Anyone born after 1969 will not think of this dish—scallops in a buttery sauce topped with toasted bits of Parmesan—as light! But it is really delicious. The tulip-yellow sauce covers the scallops like an airy layer of silk, allowing their salinity to shine.

———

1 1/2 pounds scallops, preferably bay scallops

2 sprigs fresh thyme or 1/2 teaspoon dried thyme

1 sprig parsley

1 bay leaf

8 black peppercorns

Salt

1/2 cup dry white wine

1/2 cup water

7 tablespoons unsalted butter

3 tablespoons all-purpose flour

2 large egg yolks

1 teaspoon fresh lemon juice

Cayenne pepper

Freshly grated Parmesan cheese

1. Heat the oven to 400 degrees. Combine the scallops, thyme, parsley, bay leaf, peppercorns, salt to taste, wine, and water in a small saucepan and bring to a boil. Cover and simmer for exactly 2 minutes. Remove the parsley, thyme, and bay leaf, and drain the scallops; reserve the cooking liquid. Let the scallops cool.

2. If using bay scallops, cut them in half and set them aside. If using sea scallops, remove the tough side muscle, and cut them into thin slices (so the slices are circular; set aside.

3. Melt 2 tablespoons butter in a saucepan and stir in the flour with a wire whisk; cook for 30 seconds, whisking. When blended, add the scallop liquid, stirring vigorously with the whisk; simmer for 1 minute.

4. Remove the sauce from the heat and, beating vigorously by hand or with an electric beater, add the remaining 5 tablespoons butter a little at a time. It must be added very gradually. Beat in the egg yolks and continue beating until the sauce is cool. Add the lemon juice and cayenne to taste—and you should be able to taste them! Season with salt.

5. Spoon a little of the sauce into 12 small scallop shells or 6 large scallop shells or ramekins. Top with equal amounts of scallops. Cover with the remaining sauce and sprinkle with Parmesan cheese.

6. Bake for 5 to 10 minutes, or until bubbling and golden brown.

SERVES 6 AS A FIRST COURSE

COOKING NOTE

You can prepare the recipe up through Step 5 ahead, spooning the scallops and sauce into ramekins, then refrigerate the ramekins until you're ready for dinner. Take them out of the fridge 15 minutes before you are ready to finish them, then proceed with the cheese and baking.

SERVING SUGGESTIONS

Gigi Salad (Shrimp, Bacon, and Green Bean Salad; p. 184), Crisp Potato Crowns (made to fit over the ramekins; p. 284), Filet de Boeuf Rôti (Roast Fillet of Beef) with Sauce Bordelaise (p. 528), Macaroons (p. 681), Strawberry Charlotte (p. 810)

READERS

Reader Betty Hartik noted that this was one of her enduring favorites. "I am eighty years old—still cook and bake and still turn to the food page of the *Times* first and will have to live to be at least 200 to cook and bake everything that interests me."

Betty Hartik, Pikesville, MD, letter

MAY 11, 1969: "THE GENUINE ARTICLE," BY CRAIG CLAIBORNE.

—1969

∽ SHRIMP CREOLE

I might not serve this unprepossessing dish for a dinner party, but I'd definitely make it for a Sunday dinner with family. What it does possess is flavor and rib-sticking goodness. The trick is to season the rice with enough Tabasco so the sweet Creole sauce works as a relief.

_____

6 tablespoons unsalted butter

2 cups chopped onions

I cup chopped green bell pepper

I cup chopped celery

2 cloves garlic, finely minced

One 35-ounce can Italian plum tomatoes

½ cup plus I tablespoon tomato paste
    (three-quarters of a 6-ounce can)

Salt and freshly ground black pepper

I teaspoon Worcestershire sauce, or to taste

3 small slices lemon peel

2 whole cloves

½ teaspoon sugar

2 sprigs fresh thyme or ½ teaspoon dried thyme

I bay leaf

¼ cup olive oil

I small eggplant, diced (skin left on)

I½ pounds (about 45 medium) shrimp,
    peeled and deveined

I tablespoon capers

3 tablespoons finely chopped flat-leaf parsley

Rice (recipe follows)

1. Melt 4 tablespoons butter in a large skillet or casserole. Add the onions, green pepper, and celery and cook, stirring occasionally, until the onions are translucent. Add the garlic and tomatoes, with the liquid from the can. Break up the tomatoes with a large kitchen spoon. Add the tomato paste, salt and pepper to taste, Worcestershire sauce, lemon peel, cloves, sugar, thyme, and bay leaf. Simmer for about 10 minutes, stirring frequently.

2. Meanwhile, heat the olive oil in a large skillet and sauté the eggplant until lightly browned.

3. Add the eggplant to the tomatoes and cook for 5 minutes. Add the shrimp and cook for 5 to 7 minutes longer. Discard the lemon peel and bay leaf. Stir in the remaining 2 tablespoons butter and the capers.

4. Transfer the dish to a hot serving platter and sprinkle with the chopped parsley. Serve very hot with the freshly cooked hot rice.

SERVES 4 TO 6

RICE

2 tablespoons unsalted butter

I tablespoon minced onion

½ teaspoon finely minced garlic

I cup long-grain white rice

Tabasco sauce

2¼ cups chicken broth

1. Melt the butter in a small saucepan and cook the onion and garlic in it without browning. Add the rice and Tabasco sauce to taste and cook, stirring, for about 2 minutes.

2. Meanwhile, bring the chicken broth to a boil.

3. Add the broth to the rice. Cover and simmer for exactly 20 minutes. Taste and adjust the seasoning.

SERVES 4 TO 6

SERVING SUGGESTIONS
Mint Julep (p. 24), Julia Harrison Adams's Pimento Cheese Spread (p. 64), Key Lime Pie (p. 826)

JUNE 14, 1970: "CREOLE CAPERS," BY CRAIG CLAIBORNE.
—1970

∽ SHRIMP BAKED WITH FETA CHEESE, GREEK-STYLE

A relentless and delicious assault of fire, shrimp, herbs, garlic, tangy feta, and an anise-scented spirit. You can't eat this dish slowly, because there's so much going on you keep going back to it, back to it.

_____

¼ cup olive oil

I teaspoon finely chopped garlic

3 cups canned Italian plum tomatoes

¼ cup fish broth or bottled clam juice

I teaspoon crushed dried oregano

1 teaspoon crushed red pepper flakes

2 tablespoons capers

Salt and freshly ground black pepper

3 tablespoons unsalted butter

1 pound large shrimp (about 24), shelled and deveined

1/4 pound feta cheese

1/4 cup ouzo (Greek anise-flavored liqueur)

1. Heat the oven to 350 degrees. Heat the olive oil in a medium saucepan or deep skillet and add the garlic, stirring. Add the tomatoes and cook until broken down and reduced to about 2 cups. Stir often to prevent burning and sticking. Add the fish broth, oregano, pepper flakes, capers, and salt and pepper to taste.

2. Meanwhile, heat the butter in a large heavy saucepan or skillet. Add the shrimp and cook briefly, less than 1 minute, stirring and turning the shrimp until they turn pink.

3. Spoon equal portions of half the sauce into 4 shallow baking dishes. Arrange 6 shrimp plus equal amounts of the butter in which they cooked into each dish. Spoon the remaining sauce over the shrimp. Crumble the cheese and scatter it over all.

4. Place the dishes in the oven and bake for 10 to 15 minutes, or until bubbling hot. Remove the dishes from the oven and sprinkle each one with 1 tablespoon ouzo; if desired, ignite it. Serve immediately.

SERVES 4 AS A FIRST COURSE

COOKING NOTE

Tell your guests to mix in the ouzo before eating.

SERVING SUGGESTIONS

Marina Anagnostou's Spanakopetes (Spinach Triangles; p. 63), Salade à la Grecque (p. 179), Flourless Apricot Honey Soufflé (p. 846), Hazelnut Baklava (p. 706)

MAY 30, 1976: "FOOD: FROM THE GREEK," BY CRAIG CLAIBORNE WITH PIERRE FRANEY.

—1976

⌔ DEEP-FRIED SOFT-SHELL CRABS

4 soft-shell crabs

Salt and freshly ground black pepper

1 large egg

3 tablespoons water

1/2 cup all-purpose flour

Vegetable oil for deep-frying

Lemon wedges

Tartar Sauce (recipe follows)

1. To prepare the soft-shell crabs for cooking, lift up and pull back the apron or flap attached to the base of each crab. Cut it off with scissors or pull it off. Lift up the pointed left and right tips of each crab. As each side is lifted, use your fingers to pull away and discard the soft porous "lungs" beneath the shell. Using a pair of kitchen scissors, cut off the "mouth" and eyes of the crabs. If the crabs are large, pull off the parchment-like covering on the upper surface; if the crabs are quite small, this is not necessary. Rinse the crabs if dirty; pat completely dry. Sprinkle the crabs on all sides with salt and pepper.

2. Break the egg into a flat dish and add the water and salt and pepper to taste. Beat to blend well. Place the flour in a separate flat dish and add salt and pepper. Blend.

3. Dip the crabs first in egg, then in flour.

4. Heat the oil in a deep cast-iron skillet, if possible, or other deep pan and add the crabs. Cook, turning as necessary, until crisp and golden brown, 3 to 4 minutes total (keep a grease shield on the pan, if you have one). Drain on paper towels. Serve hot with lemon wedges and tartar sauce.

SERVES 4

TARTAR SAUCE

1 cup mayonnaise

1/4 cup chopped sour pickles, preferably cornichons

1 tablespoon chopped capers

1 tablespoon finely chopped onion

1 tablespoon chopped flat-leaf parsley

Combine all the ingredients in a bowl.

MAKES 1¼ CUPS

COOKING NOTES

If you're going to go to the trouble of buying and deep-frying the crabs, why not make a party of it and double the recipe?

The original recipe included a third coating of bread crumbs, but I thought it intruded on the crab flavor and omitted it.

Use a grease shield on your pan when frying the crabs. They will spit oil all over your kitchen.

If you don't want to clean the crabs yourself, have your fishmonger prepare them for cooking.

SERVING SUGGESTIONS

Ginger Lemonade (p. 26), The Bone (p. 34), Málaga Gazpacho (p. 112), Catalan Vegetable Paella (p. 323), Fresh Morel, Asparagus, and Sweet Pea Risotto (p. 327), Sauce Rémoulade (p. 601), Italian Roast Potatoes (p. 300), Docks Coleslaw (p. 191), Coffee Caramel Custard (p. 849), Blueberry Pie with a Lattice Top (p. 853)

PERIOD DETAIL

Soft-shell crabs, which were to become a mainstay of Manhattan restaurants, have been sold in the city's markets since as early as 1876.

AUGUST 24, 1977: "RECIPES TO PUT CRAB ON THE TABLE," BY CRAIG CLAIBORNE.

—1977

╭⌒ SOLE GRENOBLOISE (SAUTÉED SOLE WITH CAPERS AND LEMONS)

Grenobloise sauce is like meunière (butter, lemon, and parsley), except that it includes capers—and is less popular. But it shouldn't be: the capers' little explosions of brine provide a bracing counterpoint to the lemon and butter.

————

4 small sole fillets (about 1¼ pounds total)
¼ cup whole milk
Salt and freshly ground black pepper
1 small lemon
½ cup all-purpose flour
½ cup peanut, vegetable, or corn oil
4 tablespoons unsalted butter
1 tablespoon drained capers
Coarse salt
1 tablespoon finely chopped flat-leaf parsley

1. Place the fillets in a dish large enough to hold them in one layer. Pour the milk over them and add salt and pepper to taste. Turn the fillets in the milk so that they are coated on all sides.

2. While they stand, peel the lemon with a paring knife, cutting away and discarding all the white pith as well as the yellow skin. Cut the lemon into thin slices and discard the seeds. Cut the slices into small cubes. Set aside.

3. Scatter the flour over a large plate and add salt and pepper to taste. Blend well.

4. Heat the oil with 1 tablespoon butter in a large skillet. As the oil heats, remove the fillets from the milk, but do not drain, and coat the fish on all sides in the seasoned flour, shaking to rid the fillets of excess flour.

5. When the oil is quite hot but not smoking, add the fillets (this might have to be done in 2 steps) and cook until nicely browned on one side. Turn and brown on the other side. The total cooking time for each fillet should be from 2 to 5 minutes. As the fillets are cooked, transfer them to a warm platter.

6. Melt the remaining 3 tablespoons butter in a small skillet and cook, shaking the skillet, until the butter foams up and takes on an appetizing hazelnut-brown color. Remove from the heat. Add the cubed lemon and capers.

7. Pour the sauce evenly over the fillets. Sprinkle with coarse salt and the chopped parsley.

SERVES 4

SERVING SUGGESTIONS

Vichyssoise à la Ritz (p. 111), Zucchini and Vermouth (p. 227), Sautéed Potatoes with Parsley (p. 283), Chocolate Eclairs (p. 800), Pots de Crème (p. 815)

SEPTEMBER 7, 1977: "60-MINUTE GOURMET," BY PIERRE FRANEY.

—1977

⤚ SHAD AND ROE GRENOBLOISE

Seasonal shad and its roe don't need to be coddled. Fatty and rich, they need ingredients that clean up their flavor. This sauce, with caramelized lemon sections and snappy capers, is just the thing. (And I'd happily pair this sauce with any succulent fish.)

———

I small lemon
I shad fillet (about I pound)
½ pair shad roe
Salt and freshly ground black pepper
¼ cup whole milk
Flour for dredging
½ cup peanut, vegetable, or corn oil
3 tablespoons unsalted butter
3 tablespoons drained capers
Chopped flat-leaf parsley

1. To prepare the lemon, slice around it to remove the rind, including the white pith; discard the rind. Cut between the membranes to remove the lemon sections. Set aside on a plate.
2. The fillet may be cut in half crosswise or left whole; it will be easier to handle if cut in half. Place the fillet and roe in a shallow dish and sprinkle with salt and pepper. Add the milk and turn to coat the fish and roe with it.
3. Place the flour in a flat dish and season it with salt and pepper. Dredge the fish and roe with the flour.
4. Heat the oil in a heavy skillet large enough to hold the fillet and roe in one layer. The fish and roe should be cooked over relatively high heat. Add the fillet and roe and cook for about 3 minutes, until crisp and golden brown on one side. Turn and cook the fish and roe, basting occasionally with the oil, until crisp and brown on the other side, about 3 minutes. Transfer to a warm platter.
5. Heat the butter in a skillet, and when it is starting to brown, add the capers.
6. Sprinkle the juice that has accumulated around the lemon sections over the fish. Add the lemon sections to the capers and butter. Cook until piping hot, bubbling, and starting to brown. Pour this over the fish. Sprinkle with chopped parsley and serve.

SERVES 2 AS A MAIN COURSE, 4 AS A FIRST COURSE

SERVING SUGGESTIONS
Sautéed Asparagus with Fleur de Sel (p. 241), Hearth's Fava Bean Salad (p. 202), Maître d'Hôtel Potatoes (p. 272)

MARCH 15, 1978: "THE SHAD ARE RUNNING," BY CRAIG CLAIBORNE.

—1978

⤚ STUFFED CLAMS

There were loads of stuffed clam recipes in the archives; the nineteenth century was particularly stocked with them. But none were as detailed in flavor as these.

———

18 to 24 cherrystone clams, scrubbed
½ cup water
8 tablespoons unsalted butter (I stick), softened
3 tablespoons finely chopped shallots
I teaspoon minced garlic
¼ cup finely chopped flat-leaf parsley
I tablespoon chopped fresh basil or
    I½ teaspoons dried basil
I cup fresh bread crumbs
½ cup freshly grated Parmesan cheese
2 tablespoons dry white wine
¼ cup thinly sliced prosciutto or other cured ham,
    finely chopped
⅛ teaspoon crushed red pepper flakes
Salt and freshly ground black pepper
2 tablespoons olive oil

1. Heat the oven to 425 degrees. Place the clams in a large pot with the water. Cover and cook over high heat until the clams open, about 10 minutes. Remove the clams from their shells; there should be about 1 cup. Reserve 24 shells for stuffing (you may not need all 24). Reserve the broth in the pot for another use, if desired.
2. Process the clams briefly in a food processor. Do not overprocess, or the clams will become liquid.
3. Combine the clams, butter, shallots, garlic, parsley,

basil, bread crumbs, 6 tablespoons cheese, the wine, prosciutto, pepper flakes, and salt and pepper to taste in a bowl. Stuff the reserved clam shells with the mixture, smoothing over the tops.

4. Sprinkle the remaining 2 tablespoons cheese over the top of the clams. Arrange the clams in a shallow baking dish. Sprinkle with the olive oil.

5. Place in the oven and bake for 15 minutes. Run the clams briefly under the broiler for a final glaze.

SERVES 4 TO 6 AS A FIRST COURSE

COOKING NOTES

The leftover clam broth can be frozen for up to 6 months.

You can finely chop the clams by hand, but if you have a food processor, using it is a nifty shortcut.

If your clams are large, they may have tough parts. After steaming the clams, trim off and discard any chewy sections.

SERVING SUGGESTIONS

Pamela Sherrid's Summer Pasta (p. 329), Green Tomato Pizza (p. 371), Grilled Hanger Steak (p. 551), Chiffonade Salad (p. 173), Maida's Blueberry Crumb Cake (p. 632), Sour Cream Ice Cream (p. 730)

JUNE 15, 1980: "FOOD: A CLAM BY ANY NAME CAN TASTE AS SWEET," BY CRAIG CLAIBORNE WITH PIERRE FRANEY.

—1980

⌒ BAKED FLOUNDER

I dismissed this cooking school–style recipe until I made it: you spread the fillets with dill, stack them in pairs, and top with mustard and bread crumbs. Then you broil the fish surrounded by a moat of soy sauce and lemon juice. Turns out I was totally wrong: the light and deliberate seasoning adds definition without overpowering the delicate flavor of flounder. I look forward to making it again, this time for a dinner party.

———

1½ pounds small flounder fillets (try for
    even numbers: 4, 8, or, ideally, 12)
Salt and freshly ground black pepper

4 tablespoons unsalted butter, melted
1 tablespoon finely chopped dill
2 teaspoons Dijon mustard
1½ tablespoons fine fresh bread crumbs
3 tablespoons fresh lemon juice
1 teaspoon light soy sauce
3 tablespoons chopped scallions

1. Heat the broiler. Sprinkle each fillet with salt and pepper to taste.

2. Select a baking dish large enough to hold 4 fillets in one layer (see Cooking Note). Brush the bottom of the dish with some of the melted butter. Arrange 4 fillets skinned side down over the bottom of the baking dish. Divide the chopped dill into 2 portions. Sprinkle the tops of the fillets with 1 portion of the chopped dill. Cover each fillet with another fillet and sprinkle the tops with the remaining dill. Place the remaining 4 fillets on top of the others, so that there are 4 stacks of 3 fillets each. Brush the top of each stack with an equal portion of the mustard. Sprinkle each stack with an equal amount of the bread crumbs. Pour an equal portion of the remaining melted butter on each stack.

3. Blend the lemon juice and soy sauce. Pour this around and between the stacks.

4. Place the fish under the broiler about 6 inches from the source of heat. Watch the dish carefully, and cook for 5 minutes, taking care that the bread crumbs on top of the fish do not burn.

5. Sprinkle the fish with the scallions and reduce the oven heat to 450 degrees. Place the dish on the bottom rack of the oven. Close the oven door and bake for 10 to 15 minutes. Remove the dish from the oven and baste the fish with the cooking liquid.

SERVES 4

COOKING NOTE

Hopefully you'll have 12 small fillets. But if you have just 4 large ones, season the fillets and then roll them from the tail end toward the head (or where the head was). If you have 8, stack them in pairs; divide the seasoning accordingly.

SERVING SUGGESTIONS

Potage Parisien with Sorrel Cream (p. 148), String Beans with Ginger and Garlic (p. 260), Jasmine Tea Rice (p. 354), Watercress Salad (p. 171), Queen of

Puddings (p. 866), Poached Pears in Brandy and Red Wine (p. 832)

READERS
"Over the years I have changed it somewhat. I now use 2 larger fillets per portion and stuff them with chopped spinach, feta cheese, a little butter, and white pepper. Everything else more or less the same. . . . The dish can be assembled in advance, just add lemon juice, soy sauce and cook. It's done in 10 minutes."

Melvin D. Wolf, New York, NY, letter

FEBRUARY 22, 1984: "60-MINUTE GOURMET," BY PIERRE FRANEY.

—1984

☞ PAN-BARBECUED SHRIMP

Make these shrimp when you're in the mood for something fiery and sloppy. Get a cold beer, roll up your sleeves, and dig in, peeling the shrimp as you go. Then sop up the sauce with some ciabatta or country bread.

———

8 tablespoons (1 stick) unsalted butter

1 tablespoon minced garlic

½ teaspoon rosemary leaves, crushed

½ teaspoon dried oregano

1 bay leaf, crumbled

3 to 5 fresh sprigs thyme, chopped, or
    ½ teaspoon dried thyme

Salt

½ to ¾ teaspoon cayenne pepper

½ teaspoon freshly ground black pepper

2 pounds large shrimp (approximately 20 to 24),
    rinsed briefly in cold water (not shelled)

½ cup bottled clam juice

¼ cup dry white wine

1. Melt 4 tablespoons butter in a large sauté pan over high heat. Add the garlic, rosemary, oregano, bay leaf, thyme, salt to taste, cayenne, and black pepper. Stir well and add the shrimp. Cook for about 3 minutes, stirring and shaking the pan. Add the remaining 4 tablespoons butter, the clam juice, and wine. Cook, stirring and shaking the pan, for 3 more minutes.

2. Serve immediately, with the hot butter from the pan and country bread.

SERVES 4

COOKING NOTES
This recipe is crazy hot if you use the original amount of cayenne, which was 1 teaspoon. I cut it back to ½ to ¾ teaspoon.

You can shell the shrimp first, if you like; they'll be much easier to eat (they'll also cook more quickly).

SERVING SUGGESTIONS
Mint Julep (p. 24), Cheese Straws (p. 79), Julia Harrison Adams's Pimento Cheese Spread (p. 64), French Potato Salad (p. 277), Fried Green Tomatoes (p. 212), Peach Salad (p. 805)

PERIOD DETAIL
Bryan Miller and Pierre Franey wrote, "Five years ago, if a restaurant served grilled tuna steak that was so pink and rare in the center that it resembled warm sushi, chances were that a diner would send back the dish in a huff. Something as pristine as tartare of raw salmon also would be greeted with astonishment, except perhaps in a sushi bar. Today, these two creations are among the most popular dishes in contemporary French and American restaurants. It is no exaggeration to say that there has been a revolution in seafood cooking in recent years."

SEPTEMBER 14, 1986: "SEAFOOD COMES OF AGE," BY BRYAN MILLER WITH PIERRE FRANEY. RECIPE ADAPTED FROM PAUL PRUDHOMME, A CHEF IN NEW ORLEANS.

—1986

☞ CALAMARI RIPIENI (STUFFED SQUID)

———

6 medium calamari

2 ounces bacon, sliced

1 head radicchio, cored and cut into ¼-inch-thick slices

Salt and freshly ground black pepper

½ cup fresh bread crumbs, moistened in water
    and squeezed dry

1 large egg
3 tablespoons extra virgin olive oil
¼ cup dry white wine

1. To clean the calamari, remove the ink sacs, if any, and the intestinal matter and discard. Cut off the tentacles and set the bodies and tentacles aside.
2. Sauté the bacon in a large skillet until slightly brown. Add the radicchio, tentacles, and salt and pepper to taste, cover, and cook over low heat until the radicchio goes limp, about 4 minutes, adding water if needed.
3. Remove the ingredients to a chopping board or food processor and finely chop. Place the mixture in a medium bowl, add the bread crumbs and egg, and mix thoroughly.
4. Stuff the calamari bodies with the mixture. Place the squid and olive oil in a large skillet and cook over medium heat for about 20 minutes, basting with the wine.

SERVES 3 AS A LIGHT MAIN COURSE, 6 AS A FIRST COURSE

SERVING SUGGESTIONS
Braised Ligurian Chicken (p. 491), Mezzaluna Salad (p. 185), Pine Nut Cookies (p. 689)

JUNE 17, 1987: "A MODERN LIFE IN THE HOUSE OF MEDICI," BY NANCY HARMON JENKINS, A COOKBOOK AUTHOR AND COOKING TEACHER.

—1987

⌐ MONKFISH ENCRUSTED WITH PISTACHIOS

½ cup shelled pistachios
1¼-pound monkfish fillet, trimmed
¼ cup clarified unsalted butter
Salt and freshly ground black pepper
1 large egg, beaten in a shallow bowl

1. Heat the oven to 350 degrees. Grind the pistachios in a food processor until very fine but not a paste. Transfer to a plate and set aside.

2. Slice the monkfish into 4 servings of approximately equal size. Flatten each slightly between 2 sheets of wax paper or plastic wrap using a meat mallet.
3. Heat the clarified butter over medium-high heat in a large ovenproof skillet. Meanwhile, season the monkfish with salt and pepper. Dip each piece in the beaten egg and then dredge, on one side only, in the pistachios.
4. Add the fish, pistachio side down, to the butter and cook for 10 seconds. Turn over carefully and cook for 10 seconds more. Place the skillet in the oven and bake for 10 minutes.

SERVES 4

SERVING SUGGESTIONS
Stewed Fennel (p. 245), Steamed Spinach with Balsamic Butter (p. 226), The Most Voluptuous Cauliflower (p. 241), Barley Risotto (p. 327), Apple Crumb Pie (p. 841), Moroccan Rice Pudding (p. 848)

SEPTEMBER 23, 1987: "IN NEW ENGLAND, CHEFS CULTIVATE THE LOCAL BOUNTY," BY MARIAN BURROS. RECIPE ADAPTED FROM WHEATLEIGH IN LENOX, MASSACHUSETTS.

—1987

⌐ HOT PEPPER SHRIMP

If you've never made a wok dish like this, you're in for a surprise. When you add the vinegar mixture to the pan, the effect is like flipping a switch. The sauce instantly clears and seizes, tightening up as if all the liquid were extracted.

I used jalapeños and seeded them to avoid too much heat, but that ended up removing all of it—so don't seed yours! Turns out, though, you don't need much chile for this dish to be great: there's acid, sweetness, richness, and a pleasant muskiness from the fermented black beans.

1 pound large shrimp, peeled, deveined, and rinsed
1 large egg white, lightly beaten
2 tablespoons cornstarch
3 tablespoons rice vinegar
2 tablespoons soy sauce

1 tablespoon sugar

2 tablespoons rice wine

4 cloves garlic, finely minced

¼ cup chopped scallions (white part only)

⅓ cup hot green chiles, thinly sliced
(or 12 dried red chiles)

1 tablespoon fermented (Chinese) black beans,
rinsed and drained

3 cups corn oil for deep-frying

White rice for serving

1. Place the shrimp in a bowl, add the egg white, and stir to coat all the shrimp. Sprinkle with half the cornstarch and mix well again.

2. Combine the vinegar, soy sauce, sugar, rice wine, and the remaining cornstarch in a small bowl and, in another, the garlic, scallions, chiles, and black beans.

3. Heat the oil in a wok. When it is hot, add the shrimp and deep-fry, stirring, until they are pink, about 1½ minutes. Drain, saving the oil. Return 3 tablespoons of the oil to the wok, turn the heat to the maximum, add the black bean mixture, and cook, stirring, for 1 minute. Add the shrimp and then the vinegar mixture and cook until the shrimp are well coated with the sauce.

4. Transfer the shrimp and sauce to a heated serving platter. Serve with plain white rice.

SERVES 4

COOKING NOTES

Have all your ingredients ready by the stove. Additionally, place nearby a bowl for the spent oil, a paper-towel-lined plate for draining the shrimp, and a serving bowl.

The recipe uses a painfully large amount of oil that cannot be reused (unless you are frying shrimp again the next day), but the payoff is worth it.

SERVING SUGGESTIONS

Oriental Watercress Soup (p. 111), Takeout-Style Sesame Noodles (p. 355), String Beans with Ginger and Garlic (p. 260), Sugar Snap Peas with Horseradish (p. 259), Pepper-Cumin Cookies (p. 695), Pine Nut Cookies (p. 689)

JANUARY 3, 1988: "FOOD: HEAT WAVE," BY JULIE SAHNI. RECIPE ADAPTED FROM SHUN LEE PALACE IN NEW YORK CITY.

—1988

⌒ JOYCE GOLDSTEIN'S PICKLED SALMON

Joyce Goldstein, the San Francisco restaurateur, said that the technique she used in this recipe was an improvement on her mother-in-law's, which required soaking smoked salmon for days to draw out the salt before pickling it. Goldstein circumvented this step by using fresh salmon.

Although Goldstein makes this dish for Passover, to be served with matzoh, butter, and sliced cucumbers dressed with sour cream, it should really be enjoyed all year round. The fish is cut into small pieces and cold-cured, which leaves the salmon fresh, springy, and delicate. On non-Passover occasions, I recommend serving it with buttered pumpernickel, blending it into a creamy potato salad, or making sandwiches of it with mayonnaise, sliced red onion, dill, and butter lettuce.

———

2 cups white vinegar

1½ cups water

6 tablespoons sugar

2 tablespoons kosher salt

2 pounds skinless salmon fillet, any pin bones removed
(see Cooking Note, p. 418)

2 tablespoons pickling spices

6 bay leaves

2 white or yellow onions, sliced ¼ inch thick

1. Bring the vinegar, water, sugar, and salt to a boil in a saucepan. Let cool completely.

2. Cut the salmon into pieces that are approximately 1 by 2 inches.

3. Place a layer of salmon pieces in a ceramic crock, glass bowl, or plastic container, then add a sprinkling of pickling spices and bay leaves and a layer of onions, then salmon, spices, and onions—continue until you have used all. Pour the cooled marinade over the fish. Cover the container and refrigerate for 3 to 4 days.

4. Serve the salmon with its marinated onions.

SERVES 10 TO 12 AS A FIRST COURSE

COOKING NOTE

Pickling spices can be found in the spice section of the supermarket. The pickled salmon will keep for 3 to 4 days.

For Passover, serve with matzoh, butter, and sliced cucumbers dressed with sour cream. The rest of the year: Latkes (p. 280), Fried Artichokes Azzurro (p. 229), Matt's Whole Brisket with Tomato Gravy (p. 572), Raw Spinach Salad (p. 175), Olive Oil and Apple Cider Cake (p. 771).

MARCH 27, 1988: "COMFORTING TRADITIONS," BY JOAN NATHAN. RECIPE ADAPTED FROM JOYCE GOLDSTEIN, A RESTAURATEUR IN SAN FRANCISCO.

—1988

⌒ CROMESQUIS D'HUÎTRES À LA SAUCE TARTARE (FRIED OYSTERS WITH CREAMY TARTAR SAUCE)

Leave it to the 3-star Parisian restaurant L'Ambroisie to take bar food to new heights. You begin by plumping the oysters in their own liquor, so when they're later dipped in bread crumbs, the coating spreads out thinly across the belly of the oysters. After frying, you pair the oysters with a super-pungent tartar sauce and fried leek filaments. The leeks, which spray a cloud of nutty, sweet onion aroma over the dish, underline the oysters' brininess.

You shouldn't see this as a stand-alone recipe, but rather as three recipes that can be used in lots of different ways. I'd make the tartar sauce to pair with smoked salmon and crab cakes. And the leeks, which I assumed would be nothing but a pain in the neck to prepare, were sweet and smoky, something I'd cook to serve with roasted fish.

———

For the Oysters
Peanut oil for deep frying
1 leek, white part only, well washed
12 large oysters, scrubbed
1/2 cup all-purpose flour
2 large eggs
2 large egg yolks
1 cup fresh bread crumbs

For the Tartar Sauce
2 tablespoons very finely chopped cornichons or dill pickle
2 tablespoons capers, very finely chopped
1 teaspoon Dijon mustard
1/2 teaspoon paprika
1/2 cup very finely minced flat-leaf parsley
1/2 cup well chilled crème fraîche or heavy cream

1. To prepare the oysters, heat 1 inch oil to 280 degrees in a deep skillet. Cut the leek into matchsticks about 3 inches long and as thin as possible. In several batches, drop the leeks into the oil and fry until golden brown, 3 to 4 minutes. The oil should not be too hot, or the leeks will burn. Drain on paper towels. (This can be done up to 2 hours in advance.) Set the pan of oil aside.
2. Open the oysters, reserving the oyster liquor; strain it to remove any portions of shell or sand. Place the liquor in a small saucepan and bring to a boil over high heat. Add the oysters and poach them for just 30 seconds, then drain, again reserving the liquor. When the oysters and the liquor have cooled, combine them again, to keep the oysters moist and plump. (This can be done up to 2 hours in advance.)
3. To prepare the tartar sauce, combine the cornichons, capers, mustard, paprika, and parsley. Whip the crème fraîche until stiff. Carefully fold in the cornichon mixture. Adjust the seasoning if necessary.
4. Heat the oil to 375 degrees, or until a bread cube dropped into the olive oil browns in 30 seconds. Prepare 3 shallow bowls for coating the oysters: one with the flour, one with the eggs and egg yolks whisked together, and a third with the fresh bread crumbs.
5. Drain the oysters and dredge them, one at a time, in the flour. Dip them into the egg mixture, then dredge them in the bread crumbs. Fry the oysters, 3 or 4 at a time, until nicely browned, about 45 seconds. Between batches, check that the oil temperature remains steady.
6. To serve, place the oysters on a platter, top with a nest of fried leeks, and place a spoonful of tartar sauce alongside.

SERVES 4 AS A FIRST COURSE

COOKING NOTES
I used Wellfleet oysters.

I used coarse bread crumbs, which gave the oysters an appealing shaggy-dog quality with lots of crunch. Panko would also work.

Four bits of strategy will make this recipe more manageable:

Have the fish shop shuck the oysters—and save the liquor—for you.

Double or triple the recipe—if you're going to fry oysters, you might as well do it for a crowd.

Make the tartar sauce ahead of time (no need to double this if doubling the oysters).

Fry the leeks in the same oil you use to fry the oysters; do the leeks first, and make sure you fish all of them out of the oil before adding the oysters.

SERVING SUGGESTIONS

The Vesper (p. 34), Martini (p. 35), Improved Holland Gin Cocktail (p. 39), Fried Olives (p. 87), Onion Rings (p. 61)

JULY 31, 1988: "PARISIAN STAR," BY PATRICIA WELLS. RECIPE ADAPTED FROM L'AMBROISIE IN PARIS.

—1988

⌇ GILBERT LE COZE'S BOUILLABAISSE

Looking for a weekend challenge? Here you go! The cooking isn't so bad, but the shopping may vex you. Stay strong.

———

For the Fish Broth

5 pounds scraps and bones from white-fleshed fish, such as halibut, red snapper, cod, or monkfish

2 medium-to-large cooked blue crabs, chopped

$\frac{1}{2}$ cup extra virgin olive oil

$\frac{1}{2}$ cup thinly sliced fennel

2 leeks, white part only, thinly sliced and washed well

1 large onion, thinly sliced

3 shallots, finely chopped

1 head garlic, cloves separated, peeled, and finely chopped

1 small conger eel, skinned and filleted, bones reserved

2 to 3 medium sea robins, skinned and filleted, bones reserved

1 cup dry white wine

A bouquet garni—1 bay leaf and 2 to 3 sprigs each parsley and thyme, tied in cheesecloth

3 ripe tomatoes, cored and chopped

3 tablespoons tomato paste

About 3 quarts water

Kosher salt

Pinch of cayenne pepper

Large pinch of saffron threads

For the Bouillabaisse

7 cups Fish Broth (above)

4 medium-to-large new red potatoes (about 1 pound), peeled and sliced $\frac{1}{4}$ inch thick

12 small mussels, scrubbed and debearded

12 littleneck clams, scrubbed

4 large sea scallops, cut horizontally in half

One 10- to 12-ounce red snapper, filleted (you can have the fishmonger do this) and cut into 4 pieces

10 to 12 ounces monkfish fillet, cut into medallions

Rouille (see p. 221)

8 slices French bread, toasted and rubbed with garlic and olive oil

1. To make the fish broth, place all the fish bones and scraps, along with the crabs, in a large piece of cheesecloth and tie securely.

2. Heat the oil in a 10- to 12-quart stockpot. Add the fennel, leeks, onion, shallots, garlic, eel, and sea robin fillets and cook slowly until the vegetables are tender.

3. Add the wine. Place the bag of fish bones and the bouquet garni in the pot and add the tomatoes, tomato paste, and enough water to completely cover the fish bones. Season lightly with salt and cayenne. Bring to a simmer and cook very slowly for $2\frac{1}{2}$ hours.

4. Remove the bag of fish bones and the bouquet garni. Pass the broth mixture through a food mill into a large saucepan. Add the saffron, bring to a simmer, and simmer for 25 minutes to reduce it further. Adjust the seasoning. Strain the broth through several thicknesses of cheesecloth. There should be between $2\frac{1}{2}$ and 3 quarts. (The broth can be prepared in advance and frozen.)

5. To make the bouillabaise, bring 2 cups of the fish soup broth to a boil in a saucepan and cook the potatoes in it until they are tender. Drain the potatoes, reserving the liquid, and wrap in foil to keep warm.

6. Transfer the fish broth used for the potatoes to a 3-quart saucepan and place the mussels and clams in

it. Cover and steam the mussels and clams, until they just open. Remove from the heat and keep covered.

7. Place the remaining 5 cups fish broth in a saucepan just large enough to hold all the rest of the seafood. Heat to just barely simmering, add the remaining seafood, and cook until just done; remove each type of seafood to a warm dish as it is cooked.

8. To serve, divide the potato rounds among 4 warmed shallow soup plates. Arrange the cooked fish over the potatoes, then divide the mussels and clams, with the top shells removed, among the plates. Stir some of the broth used to poach the seafood into the rouille, then whisk the rouille back into the broth. Bring to a bare simmer, then pour over the seafood in the plates and serve with the toasted bread.

SERVES 4

COOKING NOTES

If conger eel and sea robin are unavailable—and there's a 99.9 percent chance they will be—add 1 pound of monkfish or other fish fillets and 2 or 3 fish heads to the fish scraps.

If you want a slightly coarser soup, skip the straining in Step 4.

The original rouille that went with the bouillabaisse had some flavor issues, so you should make the one on p. 221.

SERVING SUGGESTIONS

Kir Royale 38 (p. 28), Nicole Kaplan's Gougères (p. 76), Pistachio Cream (p. 806), Campton Place Buttermilk Chocolate Cake (p. 765), Lucas Schoormans's Lemon Tart (p. 857)

SEPTEMBER 11, 1988: "FOOD: NO PLACE LIKE HOME," BY FLORENCE FABRICANT.

—1988

⌁ CRAB CAKES BALTIMORE-STYLE

I tried several crab cake recipes and these were the best for one reason: every other ingredient is included to complement but in no way distract you from the crab.

————————

2 large eggs, well beaten
½ cup chopped celery
1 cup crushed saltines
1 tablespoon Dijon mustard
1 teaspoon Old Bay seasoning
¼ teaspoon crushed red pepper flakes
2 teaspoons Worcestershire sauce
2 tablespoons finely chopped flat-leaf parsley
½ cup finely chopped scallions
Salt and freshly ground black pepper
1 pound crabmeat, preferably lump,
    picked over for shells and cartilage
½ cup fresh bread crumbs
¼ cup vegetable oil
Rémoulade Sauce (recipe follows)

1. Combine the eggs, celery, saltines, mustard, Old Bay seasoning, pepper flakes, Worcestershire sauce, parsley, scallions, and salt and pepper to taste in a large bowl and blend well. Add the crabmeat, folding it in lightly without breaking it up.

2. Divide the mixture into 12 equal portions. Shape them into hamburger-like patties. Dredge them lightly in the bread crumbs.

3. Heat approximately 2 tablespoons oil in a large nonstick skillet over medium heat. Cook the crab cakes for 2 to 3 minutes on each side, or until golden brown, using the remaining 2 tablespoons oil if necessary. Drain on paper towels, and serve with the rémoulade sauce.

SERVES 4

RÉMOULADE SAUCE

1 large egg yolk

3 tablespoons Dijon or Creole-style mustard

¼ cup white wine vinegar

1 tablespoon paprika

1 cup vegetable oil

2 tablespoons grated horseradish (fresh or prepared)

1 teaspoon finely chopped garlic

⅓ cup finely chopped scallions

⅓ cup finely chopped celery

2 tablespoons finely chopped flat-leaf parsley

2 tablespoons ketchup

Salt and freshly ground black pepper to taste

Put the egg yolk, mustard, vinegar, and paprika in a medium bowl. Blend with a wire whisk. Add the oil gradually, beating briskly, then add the remaining ingredients and blend well.

MAKES 2 CUPS

SERVING SUGGESTIONS

The Cuke (p. 39), Julia Harrison Adams's Pimento Cheese Spread (p. 64), Basic Corn Chowder (p. 149) Zucchini with Crème Fraîche Pesto (p. 250), Stewed Corn (p. 271), Fresh Raspberry (or Blackberry or Blueberry) Flummery (p. 824), Peach Balls (p. 804)

JANUARY 25, 1989: "60-MINUTE GOURMET," BY PIERRE FRANEY.

—1989

⌒ STEAMED FISH WITH THYME AND TOMATO VINAIGRETTE

Fresh, bright, and healthy, without tasting as if it's meant to be good for you. This recipe made me wonder why I don't steam fish more often—it's a technique that's easy to control and keeps the fish moist and delicate.

————

1 tablespoon Dijon mustard

3 tablespoons rice vinegar

⅓ cup olive oil

½ cup peeled (see Cooking Note, p. 146), seeded, and diced tomatoes

2 tablespoons finely chopped scallions

2 tablespoons grated fresh ginger

2 tablespoons chopped coriander

1 tablespoon light soy sauce

Pinch of crushed red pepper flakes

Salt and freshly ground black pepper

4 skinless fish fillets, such as weakfish, red snapper, sea bass, or salmon (about 6 ounces each)

4 sprigs fresh thyme or 1 teaspoon dried thyme

1. Put the mustard and vinegar into a bowl and add the oil, whisking in vigorously. Stir in the remaining ingredients except the thyme and fish, seasoning with salt only if needed and with pepper. Keep the sauce at room temperature.

2. Pour water into a steamer. Place the fillets on the steamer rack. Sprinkle with salt and pepper to taste. Place 1 sprig of thyme on each fillet (or sprinkle with the dried), and cover the steamer. When the water begins to boil, reduce the heat to medium and steam for 3 to 4 minutes; do not overcook. Remove the thyme sprigs. Serve immediately, with the sauce spooned over the fillets.

SERVES 4

COOKING NOTE

I don't own a steamer, so I improvised by using a 12-inch round braising pan with a round baking rack set inside.

SERVING SUGGESTIONS

Cold Nicarde (Yellow Squash Soup; p. 110), Zucchini Carpaccio with Avocado (p. 261), Artichauts Vinaigrette (p. 225), Ratatouille Niçoise (p. 219), Risotto with Lemon and Crème Fraîche (p. 345), Marjolaine (Multilayered Chocolate and Praline Cake; p. 766), Fontainebleau (p. 829)

JULY 26, 1989: "60-MINUTE GOURMET," BY PIERRE FRANEY.

—1989

SEA SCALLOPS WITH SWEET RED PEPPERS AND ZUCCHINI

Ho-hum, right? But if great cooking is what you can do with the most mundane of ingredients, this dish really is great. Think about all those nights after work when you succumb to sautéed chicken breasts. In less than twenty minutes, you could whip this up instead (and use up some of that Ricard that's been languishing in your cabinet).

If you don't like scallops but have nonetheless read this far, you can substitute any firm-fleshed white fish fillets, skinned and cut into small pieces.

___

2 tablespoons olive oil

2 tablespoons unsalted butter

2 red bell peppers, cored, seeded, and cut into ½-inch cubes

1½ cups sliced zucchini (⅛-inch-thick slices)

¼ teaspoon Tabasco

Salt and freshly ground black pepper

1¼ pounds sea scallops, tough side muscles removed; if large, cut them into slices

1 teaspoon finely chopped garlic

2 sprigs fresh thyme, leaves only, or ½ teaspoon dried thyme

2 tablespoons Ricard or Pernod liquor

2 tablespoons fresh lemon juice

¼ cup coarsely chopped basil or flat-leaf parsley

1. Heat 1 tablespoon olive oil and 1 tablespoon butter in a large nonstick skillet or wok over medium heat. Add the red peppers and zucchini and cook, tossing, for about 3 minutes. Add the Tabasco and salt and pepper to taste.

2. When the red peppers and the zucchini are nearly cooked, add the remaining tablespoon each of butter and olive oil. Increase the heat to high and add the scallops, garlic, thyme, Ricard, lemon juice, and basil. Check the seasoning. Cook and stir for about 2 to 3 minutes, until the scallops are just cooked through; do not overcook.

SERVES 4

SERVING SUGGESTIONS

Roasted Feta with Thyme Honey (p. 92), Blender Corn Pudding (p. 279), Fried Corn (p. 274), Sautéed Potatoes with Parsley (p. 283), Fried Potatoes (p. 417), Almond Granita (p. 731), Honey Spice Cookies (p. 685)

OCTOBER 16, 1991: "60-MINUTE GOURMET," BY PIERRE FRANEY.

—1991

SEARED TUNA IN BLACK PEPPER CRUST

Having had my fill of seared tuna in the 1990s, I was prepared to find this recipe dated and pointless. But, no, it turns out I'm just a trend drone, slavishly, hungrily traveling from one new dish to the next, never looking back for perspective. It wasn't that I had stopped liking seared tuna or that there was anything wrong with it, I had simply moved on to the next thing (tuna tartare!—see p. 416). After my forced revisit, I can report that seared tuna, when done well, is a fantastic little dish.

___

1 tablespoon fresh lime juice

1 tablespoon chopped fresh marjoram or oregano or 1 teaspoon dried

¼ cup olive oil

1½ pounds tuna in one thick piece

1 tablespoon cracked black pepper

2 tablespoons canola oil

1 pound spinach, trimmed, washed, and dried

1 cup freshly cooked cannellini beans

Salt and freshly ground black pepper

1. Beat the lime juice, marjoram, and 2 tablespoons olive oil together. Set this vinaigrette aside.

2. Trim any dark areas from the tuna, then cut it into 4 equal pieces, trimming them a little if necessary to make 4 rectangular logs. Press the cracked black pepper all over the sides of the fish.

3. Heat all but a teaspoon of the remaining olive oil with the canola oil in a large heavy skillet. When the oil is very hot, carefully place the fish in the skillet (to

avoid splattering) and sear for barely a minute, then turn and continue to sear the fish briefly on each of the remaining 3 sides. The fish should still be rare in the middle. Remove the fish to a warm plate.

4. Wipe out the skillet and add the remaining olive oil. Add the spinach and sauté for a few minutes, until barely wilted. Add the beans, season with salt and pepper, and continue to sauté until the spinach is wilted but is still a bright green and the beans are completely heated through.

5. Divide the spinach among 4 dinner plates. Cut the blocks of seared tuna into ½-inch-thick slices and array the slices on top of the spinach. Briefly beat the vinaigrette, then drizzle it around the tuna and spinach.

SERVES 4

COOKING NOTES

The only pain-in-the-neck part of this recipe is the beans—canned beans really won't cut it here. Make a batch the night before, saving some for a white bean soup, or perhaps the Four-Bean Salad on p. 278.

Cutting the tuna into logs is tricky because most tuna steaks are triangular. I cut each triangle into thick rectangular logs, which left me with a few tiny cubes. The shapes don't really matter, because you later slice the cooked tuna; just pay attention to the cooking times if you're sautéing variously sized pieces.

SERVING SUGGESTIONS

Fresh Corn Griddle Cakes with Parmesan and Chives (p. 294), Zucchini Carpaccio with Avocado (p. 261), Catalan Vegetable Paella (p. 323), Cucumber Risotto with Yellow Peppers and Herbs (p. 331), Avocado and Beet Salad with Citrus Vinaigrette (p. 193), Strawberry Soup (p. 816), Lemon Cake (p. 781)

JANUARY 24, 1993: "USING NUTS OR SPICES TO COAT THE FISH," BY FLORENCE FABRICANT. RECIPE ADAPTED FROM ALAN HARDING, THE CHEF AT NOSMO KING IN NEW YORK CITY.

—1993

⌇ CHAR-GRILLED TUNA WITH TOASTED CORN VINAIGRETTE AND AVOCADO SALAD

Tuna, corn, avocado, and cilantro, the pillars of 1990s cooking, convene here with a delicious outcome.

———————

For the Tuna
2 teaspoons grated lemon zest
1 tablespoon chopped rosemary
2 tablespoons chopped basil
2 cloves garlic, minced
1 teaspoon finely chopped fresh ginger
Four 3-by-3-by-2-inch cubes fresh tuna (6 ounces each)
½ teaspoon salt
Freshly ground black pepper
2 tablespoons olive oil

For the Vinaigrette
½ cup olive oil
½ cup fresh corn kernels
⅓ cup minced red onion
⅓ cup chopped scallions
¾ teaspoon finely chopped fresh ginger
1 small clove garlic, minced
2 tablespoons balsamic vinegar
2 tablespoons fresh orange juice
¾ teaspoon chopped thyme
1½ teaspoons chopped basil
¾ teaspoon chopped cilantro, plus a few whole leaves for garnish
Salt and freshly ground black pepper

For the Salad
4 cups mixed salad greens
2 avocados, halved, pitted, peeled, and each half sliced lengthwise in half

1. To make the tuna, combine the lemon zest, rosemary, basil, garlic, and ginger in a large bowl. Toss with the tuna and let marinate, covered, in the fridge for at least 1 hour or up to 8 hours.

2. To make the vinaigrette, heat 2 tablespoons olive oil in a medium cast-iron skillet over medium heat. Add the corn and cook until browned, 3 to 5 minutes. Add the red onion and scallions and cook until

translucent. Add the ginger and garlic and cook for 3 minutes. Stir in the vinegar and orange juice and remove from the heat.

3. Slowly stir in the remaining 6 tablespoons olive oil and the herbs. Season with salt and pepper. Let stand at room temperature.

4. Heat a grill, preferably using hardwood. When the grill is hot, season the tuna on both sides with the salt and pepper and brush with the olive oil. Place on the grill and cook until tuna is charred on the outside and medium in the center, about 3 to 4 minutes per side. Remove from heat and cut each piece into 4 slices.

5. Divide the greens among 4 plates. Cut each avocado lengthwise into thirds, but leave the narrow ends intact. Fanning out the slices, lean 2 pieces against the outside of each portion of greens. Drape 4 slices of tuna across the top of each salad. Spoon the vinaigrette over the top and garnish with cilantro leaves.

SERVES 4

COOKING NOTE

The tuna is cut into 3-by-3-by-2-inch cubes; so you may want to special-order the fish cut this way to save time/angst.

SERVING SUGGESTIONS

Ice-Cold Tomatoes with Basil (p. 234), Raspberry Granita (p. 719)

JULY 11, 1993: "FOOD: HOT TUNA," BY MOLLY O'NEILL. RECIPE ADAPTED FROM OLIVES IN BOSTON.

—1993

ROAST LOBSTER WITH VANILLA SAUCE

In the article where this recipe appeared, Camilla Nielsen, the president of Nielsen-Massey, a top producer of vanilla beans, offered a handy tip for judging vanilla beans. "A good vanilla bean," she said, "should be moist enough that you can tie it in a knot."

Lobster and vanilla met in nouvelle cuisine, and have largely remained a restaurant pairing. Other than the expense, though, there's no reason you can't cook it at home. Think of it as two dishes in one: the roasted lobster and the lobster chowder you make with the leftover lobster shells (make sure you save them!).

————

Two 1¼- to 1½-pound lobsters
1 tablespoon olive oil
7 tablespoons plus 2 teaspoons unsalted butter
3 shallots, finely chopped
¼ cup dry white wine
1½ tablespoons white wine vinegar
½ vanilla bean, split
½ teaspoon kosher salt
Freshly ground black pepper
1 pound watercress, trimmed and washed
¾ pound spinach, trimmed and washed

1. Place a roasting pan large enough to hold the lobsters in the oven and heat the oven to 450 degrees. With the tip of a sharp knife, pierce each lobster between the eyes to sever the spinal cord and kill it instantly. Crack the claws using the back of a cleaver or a hammer.

2. Place the lobsters in the hot roasting pan, drizzle with the oil, and roast until red, about 15 minutes. Remove from the oven and set aside.

3. Melt 2 teaspoons butter in a small saucepan. Add the shallots and sauté over low heat until soft and translucent, about 3 minutes. Add the wine and vinegar, raise the heat, and cook at a moderate boil until the liquid is reduced to 1 tablespoon, about 5 minutes.

4. Remove the pan from the heat and whisk in 6 tablespoons butter, about 1 tablespoon at a time, until all is incorporated. Scrape the seeds from the vanilla bean into the sauce and stir to combine; strain into a clean saucepan. Season with ¼ teaspoon salt and pepper to taste, and set aside.

5. When the lobsters are cool enough to handle, remove the meat from the claws. Detach the tails (discard the bodies). With a pair of scissors, cut down through the shell on the underside of each tail; remove the meat and cut it into ¼-inch-thick slices. Cover the meat loosely with aluminum foil and keep warm.

6. Melt the remaining tablespoon of butter in a large pot. Add the watercress and spinach and stir until the greens have melted down, then continue to cook, stirring occasionally, until they are tender, about 5 minutes. Season with the remaining ¼ teaspoon salt and pepper to taste.

7. Reheat the sauce over low heat until warm, whisking constantly. Place a bed of greens on each plate, arrange the lobster meat on top, and spoon the sauce over the lobster.

SERVES 2

COOKING NOTES

You don't really need this much watercress. If you want to cook it all, just use what you need for the dish, saving the rest for later.

You can prepare the recipe up through Step 5 up to a day in advance—chill the lobster and sauce separately in the fridge, and reheat the lobster by adding it to the gently rewarmed sauce.

SERVING SUGGESTIONS

Pointe d'Asperge (p. 212), Fresh Corn Griddle Cakes with Parmesan and Chives (p. 294), Evelyn Sharpe's French Chocolate Cake (p. 752), Tangerine Sherbet (p. 734), Strawberry Soup (p. 816)

MAY 31, 1995: "VANILLA: THE DEFINITION OF PLAIN IS GETTING SOPHISTICATED" BY KAREN KOCHEVAR. RECIPE ADAPTED FROM ALAIN SENDERENS, LUCAS-CARTON RESTAURANT, PARIS.

—1995

⌇ LOBSTER SHEPHERD'S PIE

———

Five 1½-pound live lobsters

6 large baking potatoes

7½ tablespoons unsalted butter

4 large shallots, minced

4 large leeks, white and pale green parts only, julienned and washed well

1½ cups finely diced carrots

8 cups shiitake mushrooms, stemmed and cut into large dice

Kosher salt and freshly ground black pepper

1 cup dry white wine

1 cup heavy cream

1 cup frozen baby peas, defrosted

1 cup half-and-half

¼ cup chopped chives

1. Steam the lobsters until slightly underdone, about 9 minutes. Let cool.

2. Meanwhile, peel the potatoes and cut them into 1-inch pieces. Boil them until they're soft; drain and pass through a ricer. Set aside.

3. Shell the cooled lobster meat. Cut into large chunks and set aside.

4. Melt 1½ tablespoons butter in a large skillet over medium heat. Add the shallots and sauté for 1 minute. Add the leeks and carrots and cook over medium-low heat for 10 minutes. Add the mushrooms, season with salt and pepper to taste, and cook for 10 minutes.

5. Add the wine, bring to a simmer, and simmer for 3 minutes. Stir in the cream and peas and simmer for 2 minutes. Season to taste with salt and pepper, and set aside.

6. Heat the oven to 350 degrees. Place the potatoes in a large saucepan over medium heat, add the remaining 6 tablespoons butter and the half-and-half, and stir until the butter is melted and the mixture is smooth. Season with salt and pepper to taste. Stir the lobster into the vegetable mixture.

7. Spoon the lobster mixture into a large shallow oval casserole (or a lasagna pan). Spread the potatoes over the top. Bake until heated through, about 25 minutes. Garnish with the chives.

SERVES 10

SERVING SUGGESTIONS

Stuffed Tomatoes (p. 213), Salade à la Romaine (p. 171), Basic Corn Chowder (p. 149), Cashew Butterscotch Bars (p. 697), Whiskey Cake (p. 784)

DECEMBER 24, 1995: "BEEN THERE, ATE THAT," BY MOLLY O'NEILL.

—1995

⌇ SWORDFISH IN GREEN CURRY–BASIL SAUCE

———

One 15-ounce can unsweetened coconut milk

2 tablespoons Thai green curry paste

1 tablespoon fish sauce, preferably Asian nuoc mam

4 swordfish steaks (about 6 ounces each)

1 teaspoon grated lemon zest

1 jalapeño pepper, seeded and minced

1 teaspoon kosher salt

¾ cup torn basil leaves

2 teaspoons fresh lemon juice

White rice for serving

1. Whisk together the coconut milk, green curry paste, and fish sauce in a large skillet and bring to a boil over medium-high heat. Lower the heat so the liquid simmers, add the swordfish, and simmer until just cooked through, about 6 minutes.

2. Remove the swordfish from the sauce and keep warm. Stir in the lemon zest, jalapeño, and salt and simmer slowly for 2 minutes. Remove from the heat and stir in the basil and lemon juice.

3. Divide the swordfish among 4 plates, spoon the sauce over, and serve with rice.

SERVES 4

SERVING SUGGESTIONS

Yogurt Rice (p. 356), String Beans with Ginger and Garlic (p. 260), Mango Ice Cream (p. 729)

AUGUST 11, 1996: "BRINGING UP BASIL," BY MOLLY O'NEILL.

—1996

➤ NINA SIMONDS'S BROILED HALIBUT WITH MISO GLAZE

Although many people wrote about Nobu Matsuhisa's black cod with miso—perhaps the iconic New York dish of the 1990s—no one at the *Times* published his recipe. In a story on miso (my first story for the paper), I included this excellent variation by Nina Simonds, a cookbook author, made with more accessible halibut.

———

1 teaspoon grated fresh ginger

2 tablespoons mirin (sweet rice wine)

3 tablespoons mellow white miso

One ¾-pound skin-on halibut fillet, cut into 4 pieces

1. Combine the ginger, mirin, and miso in a small bowl and mix until smooth. Rub on the flesh side of the halibut pieces. Marinate for 30 minutes.

2. Heat the broiler. Brush the broiler pan with oil. Lay the fish skin side down in the pan and broil for 7 to 9 minutes, until the flesh flakes and the glaze bubbles and browns.

SERVES 4

SERVING SUGGESTIONS

Simonds said to serve the halibut with steamed sticky rice and sautéed greens. Or, try Edamame with Nori Salt (p. 92), Pork and Watermelon Salad (p. 574), Jasmine Tea Rice (p. 354), String Beans with Ginger and Garlic (p. 260), Warm Eggplant Salad with Sesame and Shallots (p. 203), Coconut Rice Pudding with Lime Syrup (p. 846).

SEPTEMBER 3, 1997: "MISO GOES BEYOND JAPANESE COOKING," BY AMANDA HESSER. RECIPE ADAPTED FROM *A SPOONFUL OF GINGER*, BY NINA SIMONDS.

—1997

➤ SALMON CAKES WITH YOGURT CHIPOTLE SAUCE

When I asked Denise Landis, a longtime recipe tester and contributor for the *Times*, for her favorite recipes, this was among them. Landis has cooked everything from sea urchin to long beans, and yet she chose this very plain-seeming salmon dish. Once I tried it, I understood exactly why she picked it: it's the kind of recipe that you'll go back to again and again. The ingredients are easy to find, yet not too ordinary; it's simple to cook, yet not mindless; and it's versatile, so you can make larger cakes for a dinner at home or smaller cakes for a cocktail party.

———

For the Yogurt Chipotle Sauce

1 cup plain yogurt

1 or 2 canned chipotle chiles, depending on the heat desired, seeded

¼ cup water

Salt

For the Salmon Cakes

One 1-pound skinless salmon fillet, any pin bones removed (see Cooking Note, p. 418)

1 tablespoon safflower oil

½ large onion, chopped

I teaspoon thyme leaves

½ red bell pepper, chopped

4 large eggs

I cup mayonnaise

I teaspoon salt

I teaspoon freshly ground black pepper

I cup fresh bread crumbs, plus ½ cup crumbs for coating

Vegetable oil spray

1. To make the sauce, place the yogurt in a small strainer lined with cheesecloth or paper towels set over a bowl, cover with plastic wrap, and drain in the refrigerator for 6 to 24 hours.

2. Puree the chiles in a blender with the water. Mix with the yogurt and add salt to taste. Refrigerate until ready to use.

3. To make the salmon cakes, bring a large pot of water to a simmer. Add the salmon and simmer for 3 to 4 minutes, until cooked. Drain and cool, then break into chunks.

4. Combine the safflower oil, onion, and thyme in a large skillet and sauté over low heat until the onion is translucent, about 5 minutes. Add the red pepper and cook for 1 more minute. Cool.

5. Heat the oven to 450 degrees. Combine the salmon, onion mixture, and remaining ingredients except the bread crumbs for coating in a large bowl. Spray a baking sheet with vegetable spray. Shape the patties: 1 ounce for hors d'oeuvres (about 40 cakes), 3 ounces for first-course servings (12 cakes), 6 ounces for main-course servings (6 cakes). Coat the patties with the remaining bread crumbs and place on a baking sheet.

6. Bake 3-ounce patties for about 5 minutes. Turn over, and bake for 2 more minutes, or until lightly browned. Adjust the baking time for other sizes as needed. Serve with the yogurt chipotle sauce.

MAKES 40 HORS D'OEUVRES; SERVES 6 AS A
MAIN COURSE, 12 AS A FIRST COURSE

COOKING NOTES

I used Fage Total yogurt, and I recommend that you do too. It has the ideal balance of tang and creaminess, and the texture is like a tightly knit cream.

These cakes are baked, but they can be sautéed in a mixture of butter and oil if you want crisper edges.

SERVING SUGGESTIONS

Smoked Mashed Potatoes (p. 300), Beets in Lime Cream (p. 230), String Beans with Ginger and Garlic (p. 260), Lime Sherbet (p. 722)

JANUARY 1, 1997: "CASTING FOR SILVER SALMON, RENEWING A LIFE," BY CAROL LAWSON.

—1997

⌒ GRANDMA TEDESCO'S MUSSELS AND GRAVY

The gravy here is a concentrated herb-and-shellfish broth enriched with butter. And yes, I'd slather it on mashed potatoes, so gravy it is!

_____

3 cloves garlic, chopped

2 tablespoons olive oil

2 tablespoons chopped basil

2 tablespoons chopped flat-leaf parsley

4 pounds mussels, scrubbed and debearded

I cup bottled clam juice

2 tablespoons unsalted butter

1. Sauté the garlic in the olive oil in a 6-quart pot over medium-high heat until browned on the edges, about 2 minutes. Add the basil, parsley, and mussels and stir gently for 30 seconds. Add the clam juice. Cover the pot, increase the heat to high, and steam until the mussels open, about 5 minutes. Remove the mussels to serving plates.

2. Boil until the sauce is concentrated, about 2 to 3 minutes. Whisk the butter 1 tablespoon at a time into the sauce. Spoon over the mussels.

SERVES 4

COOKING NOTE

To remove the beards from mussels, locate the stringy attachment in the seam of the mussel's shell and pull it off.

SERVING SUGGESTIONS

Diana Vreeland's Salade Parisienne (p. 192), Crisp Potato Crowns (p. 284), Reuben's Apple Pancake (p. 831)

OCTOBER 8, 1997: "BELLE OF THE BIVALVES: THE NEW MUSSEL," BY AMANDA HESSER. RECIPE ADAPTED FROM STEVEN TEDESCO, A HOME COOK IN THE BRONX.

—1997

JEAN-GEORGES VONGERICHTEN'S CRAB SALAD

One Sunday afternoon in 1997, Molly O'Neill, the *Times*'s Sunday food columnist, gathered four of New York City's top chefs in her loft to cook lunch and talk about their work. "New Yorkers want their food to have the intellectual flair of an artist and the solace of an earth mother," she wrote. "They want their food to be both a reflection of their life and an antidote to it. They want it all, and they want it fast."Jean-Georges Vongerichten, who at that point had what now seems a modest grouping of four restaurants (one of which, Jean-Georges, had already earned 4 stars), prepared this salad, one of his signature dishes. The dish hasn't aged a bit. While Vongerichten may be best remembered for showing chefs how to turn their talents into global brands—he now has nineteen restaurants—he began simply as an inventive cook with a gifted palate. That Sunday afternoon, he told O'Neill, "There is no new fish coming out of the ocean. We must make something different from the same things."

_____

For the Cumin Crisps

¾ cup plus 2 tablespoons all-purpose flour

1½ tablespoons sugar

1½ tablespoons cumin seeds

⅔ cup white wine vinegar

3 tablespoons water

1½ tablespoons unsalted butter, melted

For the Crab Salad

1½ pounds crabmeat

2 small ripe tomatoes, cored and quartered

1½ shallots, coarsely chopped

1 large clove garlic, chopped

1½ tablespoons fresh lemon juice

3 tablespoons olive oil

1½ tablespoons sherry vinegar

3 basil leaves

Kosher salt and freshly ground black pepper

2 bunches mâche (about 2 cups)

1½ mangoes, peeled, pitted, and cut into ¼-inch dice

1. To make the crisps, heat the oven to 425 degrees. Mix together the flour, sugar, and cumin seeds in a small bowl. Add the vinegar, water, and butter, and mix thoroughly, but do not overmix.

2. Working in batches, using a pastry brush, dab very thin 2-inch disks of batter onto 2 nonstick baking sheets. Bake until golden, 3 to 5 minutes. Cool on wire racks.

3. To make the crab salad, break up the lumps of crab with your fingers to remove any shell or cartilage, leaving the crab as intact as possible. Transfer to a bowl and refrigerate.

4. Combine the tomatoes, shallots, garlic, lemon juice, oil, vinegar, and basil in a blender and blend until smooth. Season to taste with salt and pepper.

5. Slowly stir the tomato sauce into the crabmeat. Coat the crab, but do not soak it.

6. Place 3 scoops of crab salad in a row on each of 6 plates, then place 2 cumin crisps between the scoops. Garnish with the mâche and the mangoes.

SERVES 6

SERVING SUGGESTIONS

Moroccan Tomato Soup (p. 134), Baked Alaska (p. 721), Strawberry Soup (p. 816), Dorie Greenspan's Sablés (p. 703)

OCTOBER 19, 1997: "FOOD: THE DAY THE CHEFS ATE LUNCH," BY MOLLY O'NEILL. RECIPE ADAPTED FROM JEAN-GEORGES VONGERICHTEN, THE CHEF AT JEAN-GEORGES IN NEW YORK CITY.

—1997

GENTLY COOKED SALMON WITH MASHED POTATOES

Good, rich salmon, a glistening hill of mashed potatoes, and a river of chive oil.

You should commit this salmon technique to memory—it's stress-free, makes the salmon silky, and is something you can do anywhere as long as you have a pan and an oven. I have a similar slow-cooking method that I use for any kind of fish and shellfish: I place the fish in a casserole dish just large enough to hold it and then, rather than employing butter, I douse the fish in olive oil and cook it at 300 degrees, basting it now and then. It's a technique I use for dinner parties, so I can serve fish without worrying about overcooking it.

———

2 pounds Yukon Gold or white potatoes (5 or 6), peeled and cut into quarters

Salt

3 tablespoons plus ¼ teaspoon unsalted butter

Four 6-ounce skin-on center-cut salmon fillets, about 1¼ inches thick at the thickest point, any pin bones removed (see Cooking Note, p. 418)

½ ounce chives (a small handful; about 40 to 60)

¼ cup neutral oil, like grapeseed or canola

¾ cup whole milk, gently warmed

Freshly ground black pepper

Coarse salt and cracked black pepper

1. Boil the potatoes in a pot of salted water to cover until soft; this will take about 30 minutes.

2. Meanwhile, smear a baking dish with the ¼ teaspoon butter and place the salmon skin side up on the butter. Let sit while you heat the oven to 250 degrees.

3. Mince a tablespoon or so of the chives for garnish. Tear the rest of the chives into 2-inch lengths, and place in the container of a blender with the oil and a little salt. Blend, stopping the machine to push the mixture down once or twice, until the oil has a cream-like consistency.

4. When the potatoes are done, put the salmon in the oven and set a timer for 10 minutes.

5. Drain the potatoes, then mash them well or put them through a food mill. Return them to the pot over very low heat and stir in the remaining 3 tablespoons butter and, gradually, the milk, beating with a wooden spoon until smooth and creamy. Season with salt and pepper to taste. Keep warm.

6. Check the salmon after 10 minutes; the skin should peel off easily, the meat should flake, and an instant-read thermometer should display about 120 degrees. It may look undercooked, but if it meets these criteria, it is done. (If it is not finished, or you prefer it more

well done, return it to the oven, checking every 5 minutes.) If you like, scrape off the gray fatty matter on the skin side (or just turn the fish over). Sprinkle with coarse salt and cracked black pepper.

7. To serve, place a quarter of the mashed potatoes on each plate and top with a piece of salmon. Drizzle chive oil all around the plates and garnish with the minced chives.

SERVES 4

SERVING SUGGESTIONS

Airplane Salad (p. 197), Paul Steindler's Cabbage Soup (p. 124), Escarole with Pan-Roasted Garlic and Lemon (p. 248), Caramelized Chocolate Bread Pudding (p. 852), Teddie's Apple Cake (p. 752), David Eyre's Pancake (p. 813)

NOVEMBER 26, 1997: "THE CHEF," BY JEAN-GEORGES VONGERICHTEN WITH MARK BITTMAN. RECIPE ADAPTED FROM JEAN-GEORGES VONGERICHTEN, WITH CHEF DIDIER VIROT.

—1997

◜ TUNA TARTARE

Although fish tartares had become trendy restaurant fare by the 1980s, it took more than a decade for home cooks to get up the nerve to serve raw fish to their friends.

When the tuna is chopped finely enough, it feels like cool little droplets on your palate. What makes this recipe noteworthy is that while each seasoning offers a flicker of flavor, none calls too much attention to itself.

———

½ pound sushi-quality tuna

2 tablespoons minced cilantro

1 tablespoon minced shallot

½ teaspoon finely grated fresh ginger

1 teaspoon safflower oil

½ teaspoon kosher salt

6 grinds black pepper

1 teaspoon fresh lime juice

½ small red onion, sliced paper-thin

1 medium cucumber, sliced paper-thin

20 large caper berries or 2 tablespoons capers

16 toast points (without crusts)

1. Dice the tuna as fine as possible, or put it through a meat grinder using the largest plate. Transfer to a small bowl and add the cilantro, shallot, ginger, oil, salt, and pepper. Mix until the ingredients are thoroughly combined. Cover and refrigerate until chilled, or for up to 2 hours.

2. When ready to serve, mix the lime juice into the tuna. Divide the tuna among 4 small plates, mounding it in the center of the plates. Divide the onion, cucumbers, caper berries, and toast points among the plates and serve immediately.

SERVES 4 AS A FIRST COURSE

COOKING NOTE

If you're not in the mood to make toast points, you could serve the tartare with pappadums or good, puffy rice crackers.

SERVING SUGGESTIONS

The Cuke (p. 39), Jonathan Waxman's Red Pepper Pancakes (p. 228), Fish Poached in Buttermilk (p. 419), Zucchini and Vermouth (p. 227), Sour Cream Ice Cream (p. 730)

JULY 19, 1998: "NAME THAT TUNA," BY MOLLY O'NEILL.

—1998

CEVICHE WITH MINT AND MANGO

Good ceviche, like this one, should be exciting, with flashes of acid, sweetness, brightness, heat, and brine in every bite.

_____

1 pound small bay scallops

1 cup fresh lime juice (7 to 8 limes)

1 mango, peeled, pitted, and cut into ⅓-inch dice

½ red onion, finely diced

1 clove garlic, minced

2 tablespoons vegetable oil

1 red chile, or to taste, seeded and minced

⅓ cup chopped mint

1. Combine the scallops and lime juice in a small bowl and stir to coat the scallops. Cover and refrigerate for 6 to 8 hours.

2. Drain the scallops, discarding the lime juice. Transfer to a medium bowl, add the mango, onion, garlic, oil, and half the chile, and toss. Add the mint; toss. Taste and adjust the seasoning.

SERVES 6 AS A FIRST COURSE

COOKING NOTE

If the scallops are larger than a hazelnut, halve them.

SERVING SUGGESTIONS

La Paloma (p. 35), The Best Spinach Dip, with Chipotle and Lime (p. 90), Yucatán Fish with Crisp Garlic (p. 431), Coloradito (Red _Mole_ with Pork; p. 547), Caramel Custard (p. 836)

AUGUST 9, 1998: "FOOD: WORTH A MINT," BY MOLLY O'NEILL.

—1998

SKATE WITH SAUTÉED SPINACH AND FRIED POTATOES

_____

1 cup vegetable oil

2 large baking potatoes, peeled, cut into ½-inch cubes, and held in a bowl of cold water

4 large skinless skate wing fillets (5 to 7 ounces each)

2 cups whole milk

1½ pounds spinach

2 tablespoons unsalted butter

Salt and freshly ground black pepper

¾ cup all-purpose flour

⅔ cup cracker meal or panko

3 tablespoons clarified unsalted butter (homemade, or ghee from an Indian market), or vegetable oil

2 tablespoons finely sliced chives

2 lemons, cut into wedges

Flat-leaf parsley sprigs for garnish

1. Place a large sauté pan over medium-high heat and add the oil. Drain the potatoes and dry thoroughly on paper towels. Add a single cube to the oil. If the cube begins sizzling immediately, add the rest of the potatoes. Fry until barely golden, about 1½ minutes. Transfer to a plate lined with paper towels, and set aside. Reserve the pan with the oil.

2. Combine the skate wings and milk in a wide shallow bowl and soak for 15 minutes.

3. Meanwhile, remove the stems and wilted leaves from the spinach, wash it thoroughly, and drain well. Melt the 2 tablespoons butter in a large sauté pan over medium heat. Add the spinach and toss until wilted. Season to taste with salt and pepper. Drain well, return to the pan, and cover to keep warm.

4. Return the pan of oil to medium-high heat. When the oil is hot, return the potatoes to the pan and fry until golden brown and crispy. Drain on paper towels, and season with salt to taste.

5. Combine the flour and cracker meal in a large bowl. Remove the skate wings from the milk and season on both sides with salt and pepper to taste. Dredge the wings in the flour mixture, pat off the excess, and set aside on a plate. Heat the clarified butter in a large sauté pan over medium-high heat until sizzling. Add the skate wings, smoother sides down, and sauté until golden brown, about 2 minutes. Turn the wings and cook for an additional 2 minutes.

6. To serve, mound one-quarter of the spinach at the top of each plate. Place a skate wing like an inverted fan beneath the spinach. Scatter the potatoes over the spinach and sprinkle the sliced chives over the skate wings. Garnish the plates with the lemon wedges and parsley sprigs.

SERVES 4

SERVING SUGGESTIONS

Palestine Soup (p. 106), Beet and Ginger Soup with Cucumber (p. 150), Stuffed Clams (p. 400), Grapefruit Fluff (p. 809), Lee's Marlborough Tart (p. 816)

PERIOD DETAIL

In 1880, a writer, reporting on the scarcity of some fish species, documented a cooking class in which the instructor, Juliet Corson, introduced an unfamiliar fish: "It was not a salamander, a phoenix, a barnacle goose, or some strange phenomenal creature which she was cooking to the amazement of the world, but only an ordinary fish—a skate . . . !"

AUGUST 28, 1998: "MILD IN TASTE, ELEGANT IN LOOK, SKATE JOINS THE A-LIST," BY ELAINE LOUIE. RECIPE ADAPTED FROM REBECCA CHARLES, THE CHEF AT PEARL OYSTER BAR IN NEW YORK CITY.

—1998

⌒ THE MINIMALIST'S GRAVLAX

When you rinse off the salt and sugar cure, after a day or so in the fridge, the salmon is dark and firm like a block of quince paste. You will think all is lost. Get out your sharpest knife and start shaving off paper-thin slices. You will be astounded that you've recreated Zabar's at home with almost no effort. Mark Bittman—aka The Minimalist—says to serve the gravlax "plain or with lemon wedges, crème fraîche, sour cream, or a light vinaigrette."

———

1 cup salt
2 cups sugar
1 bunch dill, stems and all, chopped
One 2- to 3-pound skin-on salmon fillet, any pin bones removed (see Cooking Note)

1. Mix together the salt, sugar, and dill. Place the salmon skin side down on a large sheet of plastic wrap. Cover the flesh side of the salmon with the salt mixture, making sure to coat it completely. (There will be lots of salt mix; just pile it on.)

2. Wrap the fish well. If the temperature is below 70 degrees, and it is not too inconvenient, let it rest outside the refrigerator for about 6 hours, then refrigerate for 18 to 24 hours. Otherwise, refrigerate immediately, for about 36 hours.

3. Unwrap the salmon and rinse off the cure. Pat dry, then slice on the bias.

SERVES 12 AS A FIRST COURSE

COOKING NOTE

To remove the pin bones, run your fingers down the center of the fillet to feel for the bones, and use tweezers to pull them out.

SERVING SUGGESTIONS
James Beard's Champagne Punch (p. 28), Onion
Rings (p. 61), Heirloom Pea Pancakes (p. 295), Salade
Niçoise (p. 178), Papa's Apple Pound Cake (p. 774)

NOVEMBER II, 1998: "THE MINIMALIST: GRAVLAX WITHOUT
FEAR, A STUNNING DISH JUST LOOKS HARD," BY MARK
BITTMAN.

—1998

FISH POACHED IN BUTTERMILK

Jean-Georges Vongerichten, the well-known New
York chef, based this dish on the French technique
of poaching fish in milk. By swapping out the milk
for buttermilk, he added another dimension of flavor:
acidity. Then he threw in a bunch of seemingly inconsequential and disparate flavor notes, all of which
magically coalesce on the plate: a little cayenne, spinach, dill, and a bit of rye bread and mushroom stuffing.
There's also a finishing touch: the buttermilk poaching
liquid, now sharpened with lemon and whizzed in the
blender, spooned over all.

8 tablespoons (1 stick) unsalted butter
½ shallot, finely chopped
1½ cups cubed white mushrooms
1½ teaspoons thyme leaves
½ clove garlic, finely chopped
1½ cups cubed dry rye bread crusts
¾ cup chicken broth
Kosher salt and freshly ground black pepper
1 tablespoon chopped chives
1 tablespoon olive oil
1 pound spinach, trimmed and washed
Pinch of sugar
Four 6-ounce turbot, cod, halibut, or black sea bass fillets
Cayenne pepper
3 cups buttermilk
6 sprigs dill, leaves stripped from stems
Juice of 1 lemon, or to taste

1. Melt 3 tablespoons butter in a medium sauté pan
over medium-low heat. Add the shallot and cook until
soft, about 3 minutes. Add the mushrooms, thyme, and
garlic and cook until the mushrooms are soft, about 5
minutes. Add the bread and stir to combine. Add the
broth, bring to a simmer, and simmer until the bread
has soaked up the liquid. Season with salt and pepper
and stir in the chives. Cover and keep warm.
2. Place the olive oil and 1 tablespoon butter in a large
sauté pan over medium-high heat. When the butter is
melted and foaming, add the spinach and toss, using
tongs, to wilt the leaves. Add the sugar and season to
taste with salt and pepper. Set aside and keep warm.
3. Season both sides of the fish with salt and cayenne
pepper. Combine the fish, buttermilk, and dill in a
sauté pan large enough to hold the fish in a single
layer, cover, and place over medium heat. When the
buttermilk begins to simmer, cook for 2 minutes. Turn
the fish and cook for about another minute. The fish
is done when firm to the touch.
4. Remove the fish from the pan and keep warm. With
an immersion blender or in a regular blender, whirl the
buttermilk with the remaining 4 tablespoons butter.
When it is emulsified, season to taste with salt, pepper,
and lemon juice.
5. Arrange the spinach in 4 shallow bowls. Place the
fish on top and pour the buttermilk sauce over each,
topping it off with a spoonful of stuffing.

SERVES 4

COOKING NOTE
When you poach the fish, the buttermilk broth will
separate. Not to worry. When you add a little butter
at the end and blend the broth, it turns into a creamy
and clean sauce.

SERVING SUGGESTIONS
Escarole with Pan-Roasted Garlic and Lemon (p. 248),
Mashed Potatoes Anna (p. 294), Rice Croquettes (p.
799), Warm Soft Chocolate Cake (p. 773), Fresh Ginger Cake (p. 775)

SEPTEMBER 29, 1999: "TEMPTATION: THERE'S A FISH IN MY
BUTTERMILK," BY AMANDA HESSER. RECIPE ADAPTED FROM
JOJO IN NEW YORK CITY.

—1999

SALMON AND BEET TARTARE

In the 1990s, we began eating beets as a treat rather than an obligation. Farmers had begun growing sweeter varieties and harvesting them younger, and cooks had learned to roast them rather than boil them: it was as simple as that. Boiled beets inspired generations of beet haters; the process bleeds them of their vigor. Roasting them, on the other hand, concentrates their sweetness and produces a buttery root. By the turn of the century, roasted beet and goat cheese salad had replaced pear and Gorgonzola as the first-course standby, and beet tartare was a close second (also see the Beet Tartare on p. 240).

———

4 medium beets, trimmed and scrubbed

1½ teaspoons finely chopped chives

1½ teaspoons minced tarragon

1 teaspoon Dijon mustard

1 tablespoon finely chopped shallot

2 tablespoons fresh lemon juice

3 drops Tabasco sauce

2½ tablespoons extra virgin olive oil

Salt and freshly ground black pepper

One ½-pound skinless salmon fillet, any pin bones removed (see Cooking Note, p. 418), cut into very small dice

1½ teaspoons finely chopped flat-leaf parsley

Pea shoots for garnish (optional)

1. Heat the oven to 400 degrees. Place the beets in small roasting pan with ½ cup water. Cover and cook until tender when pierced with a fork, about 1 hour. Cool.

2. Peel the beets and cut into very fine dice. Transfer to a bowl and add ¾ teaspoon chives, ¾ teaspoon tarragon, ½ teaspoon mustard, and 1½ teaspoons shallot. Add 1½ tablespoons lemon juice, the Tabasco, and 1½ tablespoons olive oil, mix well, and season with salt and pepper to taste. Cover and refrigerate.

3. Combine the salmon and the remaining ¾ teaspoon each chives and tarragon and 1½ teaspoons shallots in a medium bowl. Add the parsley, the remaining ½ teaspoon mustard, ½ tablespoon lemon juice, and 1 tablespoon oil, and season to taste. Mix well, cover, and chill.

4. To serve; place one-quarter of the beet tartare in the bottom of a 3-inch ring mold on each of 4 serving plates. Top each with an even layer of one-quarter of the salmon tartare. Pat gently to compress. Remove the ring molds, and garnish with pea shoots, if desired.

SERVES 4

COOKING NOTES

If you don't have ring molds you can use ramekins to shape the tartare.

You'll want some kind of toast or cracker to eat with the tartare—crisp and airy rice crackers would be my first choice.

SERVING SUGGESTIONS

Raw Artichoke Salad with Cucumber (p. 173), Sole Grenobloise (Sautéed Sole with Capers and Lemons; p. 399), Leek and Shiitake Bread Pudding (p. 244), Steamed Lemon Pudding (p. 849)

MAY 31, 2000: "WHO PUT THE BEET IN THE MOUSSELINE?" BY MARIAN BURROS. RECIPE ADAPTED FROM ESCA IN NEW YORK CITY.

—2000

FRESH SALMON AND LIME CAKES

This recipe really wowed me. The kaffir lime leaves infuse the salmon cakes with an irresistible herbal aroma that's difficult to describe. You must make them.

The recipe comes from *Flavours*, one of Australian food writer Donna Hay's dozen or so books. Like Martha Stewart, Hay built a lifestyle empire on an aesthetic, the viewfinder through which she presents her recipes. For the photographs in her large-format cookbooks, the food is often shot on white plates on a white background, a clean frame for her vivid, unembellished cooking. Although I've been a fan of her books, it wasn't until I made these cakes that I realized there was more to her cooking than the look of the food.

———

One 1-pound skinless salmon fillet, any pin bones removed (see Cooking Note, p. 418), chopped into ¼-inch dice

I large egg white, lightly beaten

3 tablespoons rice flour

2 kaffir lime leaves, chopped, or 6 thin strips
   lime zest, chopped

I tablespoon minced fresh ginger

I teaspoon wasabi paste

3 tablespoons chopped chervil or flat-leaf parsley

¼ cup fresh lime juice (from about 2 limes)

¼ cup soy sauce

2 tablespoons brown sugar

Oil for frying (something neutral, like corn,
   canola, or vegetable)

1. Combine the salmon, egg white, rice flour, lime leaves, ginger, wasabi paste, and chopped chervil in a medium bowl.

2. Combine the lime juice, soy sauce, and brown sugar in a small bowl and mix well.

3. Heat the oven to 200 degrees. Heat ½ inch of oil in a large skillet over medium heat. For each cake, place 2 tablespoons of the salmon mixture into the hot oil, and cook for 35 to 45 seconds on each side, or until lightly golden; do not overcook. Drain on paper towels, and keep warm in the oven while you cook the remaining salmon. Serve with the lime juice dipping sauce.

MAKES 15 TO 18 SMALL CAKES; SERVES 4 TO 6

COOKING NOTES

Kaffir lime leaves can be found in specialty markets and in Southeast Asian grocery stores.

SERVING SUGGESTIONS

Gazpacho with Cucumber Granita (p. 16), Zucchini Carpaccio with Avocado (p. 261), Yogurt Rice (p. 356), Raspberry Granita (p. 719)

DECEMBER 20, 2000: "BY THE BOOK: FROM AUSTRALIA, THE BEAUTY OF SIMPLICITY," BY REGINA SCHRAMBLING. RECIPE ADAPTED FROM *FLAVOURS*, BY DONNA HAY.

—2000

⌒ SAUTÉED RED SNAPPER WITH RHUBARB SAUCE

If you haven't already discovered the combination of rhubarb and fatty fish, start here. Mark Bittman adds an interesting twist with a pinch of saffron that, while barely perceptible, works to soften rhubarb's sharpness.

———————

I pound rhubarb, trimmed and cut into
   ¾-inch-long pieces

⅓ cup sugar, or more to taste

Pinch of saffron threads

Salt and freshly ground black pepper

2 tablespoons olive oil

2 tablespoons unsalted butter (or a little more oil)

Four 6-ounce skin-on red snapper fillets

Chopped mint or flat-leaf parsley for garnish (optional)

1. Combine the rhubarb, sugar, and saffron in a small saucepan, cover, and turn the heat to low. Cook, stirring only occasionally, for about 20 minutes, or until the rhubarb becomes saucy. Add salt to taste and a little more sugar if necessary. If the mixture is very soupy, continue to cook a little longer to make it thicker.

2. Meanwhile, when you judge the rhubarb to be nearly done, put a large skillet, preferably nonstick, over medium-high heat. A minute later, add the oil and butter. When the butter foam subsides, add the fillets skin side down and cook for 4 to 5 minutes, or until the fish is nearly done. Turn carefully; and lightly brown the flesh side, seasoning it with salt and pepper as it cooks. Transfer the fish to a plate lined with paper towels to absorb excess oil.

3. Serve the fish napped with a bit of the sauce and garnished, if you like, with the herb.

SERVES 4

VARIATION

I haven't tried this option, but Bittman said, "You can also use this sauce as the base for a fool, a simple summer dessert that's little more than fruit and whipped cream. Just blend the rhubarb sauce with an equal amount of sweetened whipped cream—or yogurt, sour cream, or crème fraîche."

SERVING SUGGESTIONS

Puree of Peas and Watercress (p. 296), Al Forno's
Roasted Asparagus (p. 233), Forget-It Meringue Torte
(p. 823)

MAY 30, 2001: "THE MINIMALIST: RHUBARB IN A SAVORY
MOOD," BY MARK BITTMAN.

—2001

⌐ SALMON AND TOMATOES IN FOIL

More than any other chapter in the book, this one
is filled with simple recipes in which one ingredient
or technique gives the finished dish its memorable
character. In the Fresh Salmon and Lime Cakes on
p. 420, kaffir lime leaves add extraordinary aroma; in
the Bouillabaisse on p. 390, olive oil helps the fish
maintain its delicate texture. In this case, it's the
basil: when steamed with the fish in a foil packet, the
leaf softens and attaches itself to the salmon. When
you open the packet, you are met with a beautiful fragrance and sight: the basil leaves glisten with oil and
look like decoupage on the salmon.

———

¼ cup extra virgin olive oil
One 1½- to 2-pound skinless salmon fillet,
    any pin bones removed (see Cooking Note,
    p. 418), cut into 4 pieces
12 cherry tomatoes, sliced in half
Salt and freshly ground black pepper
16 leaves basil

1. For each of the 4 packages, place one 12-inch-long
sheet of aluminum foil on top of another. Smear the
top sheet with ½ tablespoon olive oil and layer a fillet
of salmon, 6 tomato halves, salt and pepper to taste,
4 basil leaves, and another ½ tablespoon of oil on it.
Seal the package by folding the foil over itself and
crimping the edges tightly. Refrigerate until ready to
cook, no more than 24 hours later.

2. When you are ready to cook, heat the oven to 500
degrees. Place the packages in a roasting pan. (They
can also be cooked on top of the stove in 2 skillets
over medium-high heat.) Cook for 5 minutes, for
medium-rare, to 8 minutes from the time the oil starts
to sizzle, roughly 10 to 12 minutes total.

3. Let the packages rest for a minute, then cut a slit
along the top of each with a knife. Use a knife and fork
to open the package, and spoon the salmon, garnish,
and juices onto a plate.

SERVES 4

SERVING SUGGESTIONS

Zucchini Carpaccio with Avocado (p. 261), Fresh
Corn Griddle Cakes with Parmesan and Chives (p.
294), Fried Corn (p. 274), Smoked Mashed Potatoes
(p. 340), Yogurt Rice (p. 356), Plum Fritters (p. 865)

JULY 25, 2001: "THE MINIMALIST ENTERTAINS: MIDWEEK,
AND THE COOK'S COOL," BY MARK BITTMAN. RECIPE
ADAPTED FROM JEAN-GEORGES VONGERICHTEN.

—2001

⌐ CLAMBAKE IN A POT

A clambake without sand in your food.

———

½ to 1 pound kielbasa (optional)
½ to 1 pound good slab bacon, in one piece (optional)
3 to 4 pounds hard-shell clams, scrubbed
    (more if you omit the meat)
3 to 4 pounds mussels, scrubbed and debearded
    (more if you omit the meat)
Approximately 1 pound tiny new potatoes,
    or waxy potatoes cut into small chunks
Two 1¼- to 1½-pound live lobsters
4 ears corn, shucked
½ cup water
Melted butter for serving (optional)

1. Put the kielbasa and bacon, if using, in a large deep
pot. Add the clams and mussels, then the potatoes.
Top with the lobsters and corn. Add the water, cover,
and turn the heat to high. Cook, shaking the pot every
few minutes, for about 20 minutes. Remove the lid
carefully, and check a potato to see if it is done. If
not, cover again and cook for 10 minutes more. The
lobsters should be red.

2. Put the corn, meat, and lobsters on a platter. Put
the clams and mussels in a large bowl, and ladle some
cooking juices over them. Serve, if you like, with
melted butter.

SERVES 4

COOKING NOTE
You need a *really* big pot for this recipe. If you don't have one, divide everything evenly between 2 pots.

SERVING SUGGESTIONS
Málaga Gazpacho (p. 107), Flat-and-Chewy Chocolate Chip Cookies (p. 706), Blueberry Pie with a Lattice Top (p. 853), Lemon Lotus Ice Cream (p. 724)

AUGUST 29, 2001: "THE MINIMALIST ENTERTAINS: THE CLAMBAKE, MINUS THE BEACH," BY MARK BITTMAN.

—2001

↶ ALASKAN SALMON

Tetsuya Wakuda, the owner of Tetsuya's in Sydney, is famous for this dish. He leaves his fish very pink—cook it longer if you like.

———

One ¾-pound skinless wild Alaskan salmon fillet,
    any pin bones removed (see Cooking Note, p. 418)
⅓ cup grapeseed oil
¼ cup olive oil
10 basil leaves
1½ teaspoons ground coriander
1 teaspoon thyme leaves
¼ teaspoon finely chopped garlic
½ teaspoon freshly ground white pepper
2 stalks celery, finely chopped
2 small carrots, peeled and finely chopped

For the Parsley Oil
⅓ cup olive oil
½ cup flat-leaf parsley leaves
1½ teaspoons salt-packed capers, rinsed and drained,
    or capers in brine, drained

For the Fennel Salad
¼ large fennel bulb
⅓ teaspoon grated lemon zest
1 teaspoon fresh lemon juice
Salt and freshly ground white pepper
3 tablespoons finely chopped chives
¼ cup shredded kombu (kelp; available in
    Asian grocery stores—optional)

½ teaspoon sea salt
2 tablespoons ocean trout (or salmon) caviar

1. Cut the fish into 4 pieces. Combine the oils, basil, coriander, thyme, garlic, and pepper in a bowl. Add the salmon, turning to coat, and marinate in the refrigerator for 2 hours, turning the pieces frequently.
2. Remove the salmon from the refrigerator and let sit at room temperature for 30 minutes before cooking.
3. Heat the oven to 175 degrees (or its lowest temperature). Spread out the celery and carrots on a baking tray and place the fish on top. Bake with the oven door propped open with a wooden spoon until the fish is just lukewarm, about 10 minutes. Remove and let cool to room temperature.
4. Meanwhile, to make the parsley oil, combine the oil and parsley in a blender and puree. Add the capers and pulse until finely chopped.
5. To make the salad, slice the fennel as thin as possible using a mandoline or a very sharp knife. Place in a bowl, add the lemon zest and juice, and season with salt and pepper.
6. To serve, arrange a mound of salad on each of 4 plates. Mix the chives and kombu and pat onto the top of the salmon. Set the salmon on the salads and sprinkle with the sea salt. Drizzle with the parsley oil and dot the caviar around each plate.

SERVES 4

COOKING NOTES
I didn't love the kombu (kelp), because it was very chewy. If you leave it out, I won't tell anyone.

My fish took 15 minutes longer to cook than the recipe says. Tetsuya uses ocean trout, but since that's not available here, the recipe calls for Alaskan salmon.

SERVING SUGGESTIONS
Saketini (p. 37), Edamame with Nori Salt (p. 92), Asparagus with Miso Butter (p. 259), Jasmine Tea Rice (p. 354), Chilled Sesame Spinach (p. 239), Coconut Rice Pudding with Lime Syrup (p. 846)

NOVEMBER 4, 2001: FOOD; GENIUS DOWN UNDER," BY JONATHAN REYNOLDS. RECIPE ADAPTED FROM TETSUYA WAKUDA OF TETSUYA'S IN SYDNEY, AUSTRALIA.

—2001

GRILLED MOROCCAN SARDINES

2 pounds sardines, cleaned and scaled

3 cloves garlic, mashed to a paste

Finely grated zest and juice of 1 lemon

3 tablespoons olive oil

1½ tablespoons chopped cilantro

1½ tablespoons chopped flat-leaf parsley

2 teaspoons paprika

1 teaspoon ground coriander

Pinch of saffron threads

Pinch of crushed red pepper flakes

1 teaspoon kosher salt

1. Place the sardines in a single layer in a baking dish. Mix the remaining ingredients in a bowl. Then pour over the sardines and turn the sardines to coat. Cover and marinate for 1 hour.

2. Heat a grill or heat the broiler. Remove the sardines from the marinade and grill or broil until cooked through, about 2 minutes on each side.

SERVES 4 TO 6 AS A FIRST COURSE

SERVING SUGGESTIONS
Spicy Orange Salad Moroccan-Style (p. 181), Sautéed Cod with Potatoes in Chorizo-Mussel Broth (p. 428), Brown Butter Peach Bars (p. 710)

FEBRUARY 24, 2002: "FOOD: DINNER AND A MOVIE," BY JONATHAN REYNOLDS. RECIPE ADAPTED FROM THE MOROCCAN COLLECTION, BY HILAIRE WALDEN.

—2002

CLAM STEW WITH POTATOES AND PARSLEY PUREE

This is more of a steamed clam dish with sauce than a stew. No matter: the idea is brilliant, and while it may not be the world's most refined dish, it's a recipe you can make on the fly. You steam the potatoes and clams together and then stir in a fresh parsley, garlic, and olive oil puree. Buy a baguette when you shop!

4 pounds small clams, like littlenecks, cockles, or butter clams

¾ pound waxy potatoes, peeled and cut into ¼-inch dice

1 cup dry white wine

1 bunch flat-leaf parsley, thickest stems tied in a small bundle, leaves and thin stems reserved

1 small clove garlic

⅓ cup extra virgin olive oil

About ½ cup water

Salt

1. Wash the clams well in several changes of water until the water contains no traces of sand. Put in a wide deep skillet or a saucepan, along with the potatoes, wine, and parsley stems, cover, and turn the heat to high. Cook until the potatoes are tender, about 15 minutes.

2. While the clams and potatoes cook, combine the parsley leaves and thin stems with the garlic and oil in a blender. Blend, adding water as necessary to make a smooth puree; it will take ½ cup or more. Add salt to taste, and transfer to a bowl.

3. Remove and discard the thick parsley stems from the clam-potato mixture. Stir half the puree into the clams and serve, passing the rest at the table.

SERVES 4

COOKING NOTE
You need to cut the potatoes into true ¼-inch dice, or they won't cook through in time.

SERVING SUGGESTIONS
Blood Orange, Date, and Parmesan Salad with Almond Oil (p. 199), Mezzaluna Salad (p. 185), Rice Croquettes (p. 799), Straight-Up Rhubarb Pie (p. 862), Winter Fruit Salad (p. 850)

MARCH 27, 2002: "THE MINIMALIST: SAVE THE LAST SLURP FOR ME," BY MARK BITTMAN.

—2002

∼ HALIBUT WITH PARSLEY-SHELLFISH SAUCE

Food writing often contains an element of salesmanship. I'm guilty, too: I often want to tell you just how great a dish is, hoping to inspire you to put the paper down and get in the kitchen. A caption that ran with this recipe said, "Halibut in parchment: Presto! It's done." In truth, this was a big fat lie. This recipe, which I will now sell to you by telling you that it's fantastically delicious—it is, it really is!—is by Alain Ducasse, the most famous chef in France. I can assure you that there's no presto anywhere in this recipe; it's undoubtedly a chef-style dish.

Invite your three best friends for dinner and no one else. I doubled this recipe when I made it and almost died prematurely from exhaustion (well, isn't every death premature?). However, all your toiling, your cutting squares of parchment, your whisking of the parsley butter, your arranging of the cooked fish in a square on the plates will be worth it.

And the cooking technique that Ducasse uses for the fish is very cool. You arrange strips of halibut between sheets of parchment and cook them in a hot dry pan, which preserves the purity of the fish and makes it easier to flip.

———

One 1⅓-pound skinless center-cut halibut fillet

1½ tablespoons extra virgin olive oil

¼ cup packed flat-leaf parsley leaves, plus 4 sprigs

8 tablespoons (1 stick) unsalted butter, softened

1 cup dry white wine

1 bay leaf

¼ cup minced fennel

2 tablespoons minced shallots

1 clove garlic, sliced

36 cockles (1½ to 2 pounds), scrubbed

1 teaspoon fresh lemon juice

Freshly ground white pepper

¼ pound lump crabmeat, picked over
    for shells and cartilage

Fleur de sel

1. Cut the halibut in half at the central "seam," then cut each half in 8 slices about ¼ inch thick. Brush the slices on both sides with the olive oil. Place 4 slices side by side on a 6-inch-square of parchment paper. Top with another square of parchment. Repeat with the remaining halibut. Set the packages aside.

2. With the food processor running, drop the parsley leaves through the feed tube. Process until minced. Add the butter and process until well blended. Remove to a dish.

3. Place the wine, bay leaf, fennel, shallots, and garlic in a saucepan with a tight-fitting lid and cook over medium-high heat until the wine is reduced to about ½ cup. Add the cockles, cover, lower the heat, and simmer until they open, about 5 minutes. Remove the cockles, shuck into a small bowl, and cover with plastic wrap. Set aside.

4. Strain the cooking liquid, pressing on the solids, into a clean saucepan. Simmer until reduced to ¼ cup. Reduce the heat to very low, and whisk in the parsley butter about a tablespoon at a time. Add the lemon juice. Taste for seasoning, adding white pepper. Fold in the cockles and crabmeat, remove from the heat, and cover to keep warm.

5. Place a 12-inch nonstick skillet over medium heat. Place 1 package of halibut in the pan and cook for 30 to 60 seconds on each side (the fish should be just cooked through); remove from the pan with a spatula. Repeat with the remaining fish. Peel off the paper and arrange 4 slices of fish on each of 4 warm plates, making a square. Season lightly with fleur de sel and pepper.

6. Spoon some of the warmed seafood butter sauce into the center of each square, then spoon a little more around the outside. Garnish with the parsley sprigs.

SERVES 4

COOKING NOTES
One half of the fish fillet will yield smaller pieces.

The fish slices may stick together when cooking, and you may need a thin spatula to separate them.

Cockles are saltier than clams—keep this in mind when seasoning. I added more lemon juice to the sauce.

SERVING SUGGESTIONS
Nicole Kaplan's Gougères (p. 76), Chilled English Pea–Mint Soup (p. 162), Cream of Carrot Soup (p. 119), Zucchini and Vermouth (p. 227), Sugar Snap Peas with Horseradish (p. 259), Queen of Puddings (p. 866)

APRIL 17, 2002: "THE CHEF: ALAIN DUCASSE," BY ALAIN DUCASSE WITH FLORENCE FABRICANT.

—2002

❧ VENTRESCA TUNA SALAD

There are three very different tuna salads in this book, all excellent. This one comes from David Pasternack, the amiable and unpretentious chef who cooked his way around New York's better French kitchens before finding his sweet spot—Italian fish cookery—at Esca in the Theatre District, not far from the *Times* and Condé Nast. Back when people still had expense accounts, if you went to lunch at Esca, every table was filled with editors. It's the most consistently great restaurant I know in the city.

I think of this recipe from Pasternack as a gift, a perfect salad with all the right elements and proportions. You poach the fish in oil and aromatics that perfume the succulent tuna belly, then mix it with vegetables and an assertive ratio of 2 parts oil to 1 part vinegar. Fold the ingredients, then fold them a few more times, and get ready for a tuna salad unlike those on pages 433 and 435, and indeed unlike any other—with precise acidity, buttery slices of potato, and slivers of fragrant tuna that do not shred.

———

1½ pounds fresh tuna in 1 thick piece, preferably
　yellow fin or albacore belly cut

Sea salt and freshly ground black pepper

2 large cloves garlic, smashed

About 2 cups extra virgin olive oil

3 sprigs lemon thyme, or regular thyme plus
　1 teaspoon grated lemon zest

2 bay leaves

4 large salt-packed anchovies, preferably Recca brand,
　or 8 anchovy fillets in oil

¾ pound fingerling potatoes

1 pound flat (romano) green beans or
　regular green beans, trimmed

1 small red onion, sliced paper-thin

½ cup flat-leaf parsley leaves

¼ cup lovage leaves or inner celery leaves

¼ cup red wine vinegar, preferably Italian

1. Cut the tuna into 1½-inch chunks. Season well with salt and pepper. Place in a saucepan with the garlic and enough olive oil so the tuna is just covered. Bring to a gentle simmer and cook over low heat for about 10 minutes, taking care that the oil does not boil. Remove from the heat, add the lemon thyme (or thyme and lemon zest) and bay leaves, and set aside to cool. (The tuna can be used at this point but is better if allowed to marinate overnight.)

2. Transfer the contents of the pan to a bowl, cover, and refrigerate overnight. Bring to room temperature at least an hour before serving.

3. If using salt-packed anchovies, soak in water for 2 hours, drain, remove the bones, cut into ½-inch pieces, and toss with a little olive oil. Or drain anchovies packed in oil and cut into pieces.

4. Place the potatoes in a pot of salted water, bring to a boil, and cook until tender, about 20 minutes. Drain, peel when cool enough to handle, and halve lengthwise. Place in a large bowl.

5. Bring 6 quarts salted water to a boil in a medium pot. Add the beans and cook until tender, 5 to 7 minutes. Drain and place in a bowl of ice water. When cool, drain well, pat dry on paper towels, and add to the bowl with the potatoes.

6. Add the anchovies, onion, parsley, and lovage to the potatoes and beans. Drain the tuna, reserving the oil, and scrape off the excess fat and gelatin. Break into bite-sized pieces and add to the bowl.

7. Beat the vinegar with 2 tablespoons olive oil and ¼ cup oil from the tuna. Season with salt and pepper. Pour the dressing over the tuna and fold together. Season with salt and pepper.

SERVES 4

COOKING NOTES

This recipe reveals a gap between what's available to chefs and to a regular shopper, even one living in New York City. I couldn't find lemon thyme, romano beans, fingerling potatoes, or lovage. The good news is the salad did not suffer.

I used baby Yukon Golds in place of the fingerlings. And I did not peel them after boiling—couldn't be bothered.

SERVING SUGGESTIONS

Grapefruit Wine (p. 37), Open-Faced Tomato Sandwich (p. 367), Squashed Tomatoes (p. 90), Chilled

English Pea–Mint Soup (p. 162), Garden Minestrone (p. 118), Petit Beurre Cookies (p. 699), Panna Cotta (p. 840)

JUNE 19, 2002: "THE CHEF: DAVID PASTERNACK," BY DAVID PASTERNACK WITH FLORENCE FABRICANT.

—2002

SEAFOOD SALAD

½ pound cleaned calamari

½ pound sea scallops

¾ pound cooked scungilli (sold in some fish markets)

3 large cloves garlic, sliced paper-thin

About ¾ cup extra virgin olive oil

3 dried red chiles

3 large strands fresh seaweed

Zest of 2 lemons—removed with a vegetable peeler and finely slivered

Sea salt

1 pound large shrimp, peeled and deveined

1 pound mussels, scrubbed and debearded

12 littleneck clams, scrubbed and shucked, juices reserved

½ cup fresh lemon juice (from 2 lemons)

¼ cup red wine vinegar

1 small red onion, finely chopped

⅓ cup minced flat-leaf parsley

⅓ cup minced mint

1 teaspoon crushed red pepper flakes, or to taste

Freshly ground black pepper

Leaves from 6 sprigs parsley and 6 sprigs mint for garnish

1. Remove the tentacles from the calamari and reserve. Slice the calamari bodies into thin rings. Remove and discard the hard nugget of muscle on the side of each scallop. Slice the scallops horizontally in half. Cut the scungilli in half and, with the point of a knife, pry out the sac in the middle of each half. Cut off any narrow dark rubbery protrusions.

2. Combine the garlic and 2 tablespoons olive oil in a small dish.

3. Place the chiles, seaweed, and half the lemon zest in a 6-quart pot, add 4 quarts water, and bring to a boil, then reduce the heat and simmer for 20 minutes. Stir about 2 tablespoons sea salt into the poaching liquid, add the scungilli, and simmer for 5 minutes. Remove

with a slotted spoon, drain, and set aside. Add the calamari rings and tentacles to the pot and simmer for 1 minute, then remove with a slotted spoon, drain, and set aside. Add the scallops and cook for about 2 minutes; remove, drain, and set aside. Add the shrimp and cook for about 2 minutes; remove, drain, and set aside. Bring the liquid to a boil, add the mussels, and cook just until they open; remove and drain. (Discard the poaching liquid.)

4. Cook the garlic in the 2 tablespoons oil in a small skillet until softened. Transfer the garlic and oil to a large bowl. Add the clams, and juice, calamari, shrimp, and scallops. Thinly slice the scungilli and add it. Add the remaining lemon zest, lemon juice, vinegar, onion, minced herbs, and ½ cup olive oil. Fold together. Add the mussels, in their shells, and more oil to taste, the red pepper flakes, and black pepper to taste. Let stand, covered, for about 1 hour.

5. Toss the ingredients. Add more oil and seasonings if needed. Spoon into a serving dish. Bruise the mint and parsley leaves between your fingers, and scatter on top.

SERVES 4 AS A FIRST COURSE

SERVING SUGGESTIONS
Crostini with Eggplant and Pine Nut Puree (p. 78), Ed Giobbi's Sweet Red Pepper Sauce for Pasta (p. 318), Saffron Panna Cotta (p. 845), Almond Granita (p. 731)

JULY 3, 2002: "THE CHEF: DAVID PASTERNACK," BY DAVID PASTERNACK WITH FLORENCE FABRICANT.

—2002

SALT-ROASTED STRIPED BASS WITH SALSA DE LA BOCA

If you've never salt-roasted a fish, give it a try—the fish, unearthed from its salt crust, is fabulously succulent and moist. You pack the whole fish in a mound of damp salt until it's fully covered. When it is baked in a hot oven, the top layer of salt hardens like dried mud, and you have to break it off in pieces to uncover the steamy fish. You can also do this with a chicken. Either is fun to make with kids, who can apply their sandbox expertise.

For the Salsa

2 cups extra virgin olive oil

I cup chopped flat-leaf parsley

½ cup finely chopped garlic

½ cup oregano leaves

Finely diced zest of 2 lemons (zest removed
    with a vegetable peeler)

Fleur de sel

Cracked black pepper

For the Fish

Five 3-pound boxes kosher salt

4 to 5 cups water

One 8-pound striped bass, cleaned but not scaled,
    head and tail removed

1. To make the salsa, combine all the ingredients in a small bowl. Cover and set aside.

2. Position a rack in the lower third of the oven and heat the oven to 500 degrees. Pour all the salt into a very large bowl or a clean plugged sink. Add 4 cups water and toss the salt to incorporate it evenly. The consistency should be like spring snow, slightly wet and lightly clumping. If necessary, add up to 1 cup more water.

3. Tamp down a 1-inch layer of the damp salt in a large roasting pan (about 16 inches long). Place the bass diagonally on top of the salt. Insert a meat thermometer (not instant-read) into the thickest part of the fish and leave it there. Pour the rest of the damp salt into the pan, spreading it to make a 1-inch-thick layer over the fish. Tamp down the salt to compact it.

4. Bake the fish until the thermometer reaches 150 degrees, about 55 minutes. Remove from the heat and allow to rest for 20 minutes.

5. Tap the salt crust with a hammer or mallet until it cracks. Remove and discard the crust. Brush any remaining salt from the fish, and lift off and discard the skin from the top fillet.

6. To serve, use 2 large spoons to lift the fish from the backbone and transfer to plates, then remove the bottom fillet. Garnish with the salsa.

SERVES 8

COOKING NOTES

Leaving the scales on the fish protects it—they'll come off when you remove the salt after baking. The origi-nal recipe called for an unscaled fish, but don't sweat it if you can't find one.

Boca is the name of a Buenos Aires neighborhood.

SERVING SUGGESTIONS
Palestine Soup (p. 106), Roasted Squash Soup with Cumin (p. 147), Sweet-and-Spicy Pepper Stew (p. 247), Wilted Chard with Pickled Red Onion (p. 261), Smoked Mashed Potatoes (p. 300), Baked Chickpeas (p. 293), Potato "Tostones" (Flattened Potatoes; p. 301), Buttermilk Pie (p. 859), Olive Oil and Apple Cider Cake (p. 771)

OCTOBER 23, 2002: "LOOK WHAT'S FOR DINNER," BY PETER KAMINSKY. RECIPE ADAPTED FROM FRANCIS MELLMEN, THE CHEF AT PATAGONIA WEST IN WESTHAMPTON BEACH, NEW YORK.

—2002

SAUTÉED COD WITH POTATOES IN CHORIZO-MUSSEL BROTH

A beautifully composed dish from Eric Ripert, the chef at Le Bernardin, a 4-star restaurant in New York. The chorizo does a lot of work in the broth, adding dimension, color, and aroma. Don't forget the lemon, which brightens the whole dish.

———

9 large cloves garlic, 4 left unpeeled, 2 thinly sliced,
    and 3 finely minced

I0 tablespoons plus I teaspoon extra virgin olive oil

1½ pounds medium Yukon Gold potatoes, peeled

Salt

3 large shallots, thinly sliced, plus ¼ cup minced shallots

½ cup dry white wine

I pound mussels, scrubbed and debearded

2 ounces dried chorizo, preferably Spanish,
    peeled and thinly sliced

I cup bottled clam juice

I sprig thyme, plus 4 small sprigs for garnish

I sprig rosemary, plus 4 small sprigs for garnish

4 tablespoons unsalted butter

5 tablespoons minced flat-leaf parsley

1½ tablespoons fresh lemon juice

Four 5- to 6-ounce skinless cod fillets

Freshly ground white pepper

1. Heat the oven to 350 degrees. Brush the unpeeled garlic with 1 teaspoon olive oil, wrap in foil, and bake for 40 minutes.

2. Meanwhile, place the potatoes in a pot of salted water to cover, bring to a boil, and cook over medium heat until very tender, about 30 minutes.

3. Heat 1 tablespoon olive oil in a 3-quart saucepan. Add the sliced shallots and sliced garlic and cook over low heat until soft but not colored. Add the wine, bring to a simmer, and add the mussels. Cover and cook until the mussels open, about 3 minutes. Drain in a fine sieve, reserving the cooking liquid. Shuck the mussels and reserve, covered. Clean the pan.

4. Place 2 tablespoons oil in the mussel pan. Add the minced shallots and minced garlic and sauté until soft. Add the chorizo and sauté until starting to brown. Add the clam juice and mussel cooking liquid and bring to a simmer. Add 1 sprig each thyme and rosemary, remove from the heat, add the shucked mussels, and set aside, covered.

5. When the roasted garlic is done, remove it from the foil and peel the cloves.

6. When the potatoes are done, drain them and return them to the cooking pot. Mash with a fork, adding the roasted garlic, butter, and ¼ cup olive oil. Place over low heat, fold in 4 tablespoons parsley, add 2 teaspoons lemon juice, and season to taste with salt. Keep warm over very low heat.

7. Pat the fish dry and season with salt and pepper on both sides. Add the remaining 3 tablespoons oil to a heavy skillet large enough to hold the fish without crowding and place over high heat. When the oil is hot, cook the fish, turning once, until golden brown, 4 to 5 minutes.

8. Meanwhile, reheat the chorizo-mussel broth over low heat, and add the remaining 2½ teaspoons lemon juice. Remove the thyme and rosemary, and add the remaining tablespoon of parsley.

9. To serve, place a portion of potatoes in the center of each of 4 shallow soup plates. Place the fish on the potatoes. Spoon the broth, chorizo, and mussels around the potatoes, and garnish with thyme and rosemary.

SERVES 4

SERVING SUGGESTIONS
Rebujito (p. 38), Pan con Tomate (p. 91), Fried Chickpeas (p. 88), Catalan Tortilla with Aioli (p. 86), Chocolate Caramel Tart (p. 847), Caramel Custard (p. 836)

NOVEMBER 6, 2002: "THE CHEF; ERIC RIPERT: UPSTAIRS AT LE BERNARDIN, A WHIFF OF THE SPANISH BORDER," BY FLORENCE FABRICANT. RECIPE ADAPTED FROM ERIC RIPERT.

—2002

SCALLOPS WITH PEA PUREE

A terrific pairing, but the pea puree, emulsified with fresh rosemary oil, is so good it could go with almost anything.

———

1 clove garlic
One 6-inch sprig rosemary
⅓ cup olive oil
4 cups frozen peas (about two 10-ounce packages)
Salt
1 tablespoon cornstarch
Freshly ground black pepper
6 to 8 large sea scallops, tough side muscle removed, each scallop halved to make 2 slim disks

1. Combine the garlic, rosemary, and oil in a small saucepan and place over medium-low heat until the oil starts to bubble. Turn off the heat and leave the mixture to infuse.

2. Place the peas in a large saucepan of lightly salted water and bring to a boil. Reduce the heat to low and simmer until the peas are tender but still bright green, about 30 seconds. Drain and transfer to a food processor. Add ¼ cup of the infused oil (discard the garlic and rosemary) and process until pureed, then return to the pan, cover, and keep warm.

3. Season the cornstarch with salt and pepper to taste. Lightly dust the scallop halves with the seasoned cornstarch. Place a heavy nonstick skillet or well-seasoned cast-iron skillet over medium heat and add the remaining infused oil. When the oil is hot, add the scallops to the pan. Cook until browned, about 2 minutes on each side.

4. Divide the pea puree between 2 plates, and add the scallops.

SERVES 2

Avocado and Beet Salad with Citrus Vinaigrette (p. 193), Potage Parisien with Sorrel Cream (p. 148), Butter-Braised Asparagus and Oyster Mushrooms with Peas and Tarragon (p. 262), Rhubarb-Strawberry Mousse (p. 835)

FEBRUARY 19, 2003: "AT MY TABLE: QUICK AND HEART-WARMING FOR EVERYDAY," BY NIGELLA LAWSON.

—2003

ROASTED SALMON WITH HERB VINAIGRETTE

The salmon is perched atop a bed of thinly sliced potatoes; then roasted. You can use this clever method with any fish. For a similar method with lamb and potatoes, see p. 537.

———

About ½ cup olive oil
1½ medium baking potatoes, peeled and cut into ¼-inch-thick slices
Kosher salt and freshly ground black pepper
¼ cup red wine vinegar
1 teaspoon Dijon mustard
1 small clove garlic, finely chopped
½ teaspoon finely chopped rosemary
½ teaspoon finely chopped sage
½ teaspoon finely chopped thyme
1 tablespoon finely chopped flat-leaf parsley
Two 6-ounce skinless salmon fillets, any pin bones removed (see Cooking Note, p. 418)

1. Heat the oven to 400 degrees. Brush two 8-inch terra-cotta cazuelas or other shallow baking dishes with olive oil. Arrange the potato slices in a single layer in the bottom of each. Brush the potatoes with olive oil and season with salt and pepper. Bake for 12 to 15 minutes.
2. While the potatoes bake, whisk together the vinegar, mustard, garlic, and herbs in a medium bowl. Slowly whisk in 6 tablespoons olive oil until emulsified. Season with salt and pepper to taste, and set aside.
3. Brush the salmon fillets with olive oil and season with salt and pepper.

4. When the potatoes are done, remove the cazuelas and reduce the oven temperature to 250 degrees. Place the fillets on top of the potatoes, skinned side down, and return to the oven. Roast until the salmon is medium-rare, about 12 minutes, or longer if you like your salmon cooked through. Remove the salmon from the oven and drizzle each fillet with the vinaigrette.

SERVES 2

SERVING SUGGESTIONS
Fresh Morel, Asparagus, and Sweet Pea Risotto (p. 327), Chiffonade Salad (p. 173), Almond-Carrot Salad (p. 204), Al Forno's Roasted Asparagus (p. 233), Sugared Puffs (p. 867), Rhubarb Orange (p. 864), Sour Cream Ice Cream (p. 730)

FEBRUARY 26, 2003: "THE CHEF: BOBBY FLAY: SALMON HOT FROM THE OVEN, AND NO SLAVING AT THE SINK," BY MATT LEE AND TED LEE.

—2003

SHRIMP IN GREEN SAUCE

I love this technique: masking the shrimp in a paste-like sauce and blasting them in a 500-degree oven. I love the gutsy garlic-and-scallion-soaked sauce. And I love the resulting dish, which needs nothing but a loaf of good bread and an icy beer to constitute a perfect low-key dinner.

———

6 cloves garlic
⅓ cup extra virgin olive oil
6 scallions, chopped
1 cup flat-leaf parsley leaves and thin stems
2 pounds medium shrimp, peeled, deveined if desired
Salt and freshly ground black pepper
4 dried chiles, crushed, or a few pinches of crushed red pepper flakes, or to taste
⅓ cup broth (shrimp, fish, or chicken), dry white wine, or water

1. Heat the oven to 500 degrees. Combine the garlic and oil in a small food processor and blend until smooth, scraping down the sides as necessary. Add the

scallions and parsley and pulse until minced. Toss with the shrimp, salt and pepper, and chiles.

2. Put the shrimp in a large roasting pan. Add the broth and place the pan in the oven. Roast, stirring once, until the mixture is bubbly and hot and the shrimp are all pink, 10 to 15 minutes.

SERVES 4

SERVING SUGGESTIONS
See headnote.

MARCH 5, 2003: "THE MINIMALIST: TOO MUCH GARLIC? IMPOSSIBLE," BY MARK BITTMAN.

—2003

SWEET-AND-SOUR SALMON IN ALMOND PRUNE SAUCE

Vegetable oil or nonstick vegetable spray
Four 6-ounce skinless salmon fillets, any pin bones
  removed (see Cooking Note, p. 418)
Salt and freshly ground black pepper
1/4 cup honey
1 tablespoon Dijon mustard
1/4 cup cider vinegar
2 to 3 sprigs fresh thyme or 1/2 teaspoon
  dried thyme leaves
1/2 teaspoon ground ginger
1/4 cup whole almonds, toasted and finely ground
1/2 cup chopped scallions
12 pitted prunes, whole or halved
1/4 teaspoon crushed red pepper flakes
1 tablespoon pomegranate molasses (available in Middle
  Eastern markets and specialty food stores)

1. Heat the broiler with the rack 6 to 8 inches below the heat source. Lightly oil a large cast-iron skillet or other shallow pan suitable for both broiler and stovetop use. Arrange the fillets in the pan skinned side down and sprinkle with salt and pepper to taste.
2. Combine the honey and mustard in a small saucepan. Brush the fish with about half the mixture, and set aside. Add the vinegar, thyme, ginger, 1/2 teaspoon salt, the almonds, scallions, prunes, red pepper flakes, and pomegranate syrup to the saucepan and mix well.

3. Place the pan of fish under the broiler and cook until the surface is golden brown, 4 to 6 minutes.
4. While the fish cooks, place the saucepan over medium-low heat, bring to a simmer, and cook for 2 to 3 minutes.
5. Spread the sauce on and around the fillets in the pan. Transfer the pan to the top of the stove, over medium heat, cover, and allow the sauce to simmer until it is thickened and the fish is flaky when probed with a fork, 5 to 7 minutes.

SERVES 4

SERVING SUGGESTIONS
Blood Orange, Date, and Parmesan Salad with Almond Oil (p. 199), Couscous Salad (p. 321), Judy Rodgers's Warm Bread Salad (p. 198), Roasted Cauliflower (p. 248), Apple Dumplings (p. 807), Delicate Bread Pudding (p. 798), De Luxe Cheesecake (p. 748)

APRIL 2, 2003: "TAKING COMFORT FROM AN UNEXPECTED SOURCE," BY RALPH BLUMENTHAL. RECIPE ADAPTED FROM DELIGHTS FROM THE GARDEN OF EDEN, BY NAWAL NASRALLAH.

—2003

YUCATÁN FISH WITH CRISP GARLIC

1/4 cup neutral oil, like corn or canola
5 cloves garlic, thinly sliced
Salt and freshly ground black pepper
4 large or 8 small flounder fillets or
  1 1/2 pounds other flatfish fillets
3 small dried hot red chiles, or to taste
1/2 cup fresh lime juice (from about 4 limes)
1 cup cherry or grape tomatoes (optional)
1/2 cup chopped cilantro

1. Combine 2 tablespoons oil with the garlic in a small heavy saucepan over medium heat, shaking the pan occasionally, until the garlic browns, 2 to 3 minutes. Season with a little salt and pepper and turn off the heat.
2. Meanwhile, put the remaining 2 tablespoons oil in a large nonstick skillet over medium heat. A minute

later, add the fish and chiles and cook undisturbed for about 2 minutes. Reduce the heat to medium-low and add all but a tablespoon or two of the lime juice, along with the tomatoes, if desired. Cook for another 2 minutes or so, until the fish is cooked through; do not turn the fish.

3. Carefully remove the fish to a platter. Stir the cilantro into the pan juices and spoon, with the tomatoes, over the fish, along with the garlic, its oil, and the remaining lime juice.

SERVES 4

COOKING NOTES
I couldn't fit all the fish in one skillet, so I used two.

It's a good idea to heat the oven to 350 degrees before starting the fish. If the fish doesn't cook through on the stove, you can transfer the skillet to the oven to finish cooking.

You might want to break the fish into pieces and fold it with the garlic, tomatoes, and cilantro into corn tortillas.

SERVING SUGGESTIONS
Classic Rum Punch (p. 24), The Best Spinach Dip, with Chipotle and Lime (p. 90), Ceviche with Mint and Mango (p. 417), Caramel Custard (p. 836)

JULY 16, 2003: "THE MINIMALIST: LOTS OF LIME, CHILES TOO," BY MARK BITTMAN.

—2003

⌒ CHINESE-STYLE STEAMED BLACK SEA BASS

This is the kind of recipe you make once and then never again have to look up the amounts. It's impossible to screw up. The main issue you have to figure out is which cooking vessel to use. I used a wide soup pot. If you've been smart enough to buy a steamer, this is the moment to dig it out from behind the juicer.

One 1¾-pound black sea bass, cleaned, scaled, and fins removed
2 tablespoons peanut oil
1 teaspoon salt
½ teaspoon freshly ground black pepper
1 teaspoon sugar
3 tablespoons julienned fresh ginger
¼ cup thinly sliced (on the bias) scallions, white parts only (about 2 bunches), plus tops of 1 bunch
8 sprigs cilantro
¼ cup soy sauce

1. Lay the fish on a cutting board. Make 2 diagonal bone-deep cuts perpendicular to the backbone (they should be 2 inches apart at the thickest part of the body). Turn the fish over and repeat the cuts. Transfer the fish to a pie plate and brush both sides of the fish and the cavity with the oil. Season with the salt, pepper, and sugar. Press the ginger and sliced scallions onto the skin on both sides of the fish, into the incisions, and into the cavity. Stuff the cavity with half the scallion tops. Lay the remaining tops and the cilantro over the fish. Pour the soy sauce in a thin stream over the fish.

2. Pour an inch of water into a steamer or a pot large enough to accommodate the plate with the fish on it. Place a rack or a ring of crumpled aluminum foil in the pot and place the plate of fish on top; the plate should sit just above the water. Cover the pot, bring the water to a boil, and steam the fish for 8 to 15 minutes, or until the flesh nearest the bones is opaque.

3. Carefully remove the fish with 2 spatulas. Spoon the liquid from the plate over the fish.

SERVES 2

SERVING SUGGESTIONS
Clear Steamed Chicken Soup with Ginger (p. 145), String Beans with Ginger and Garlic (p. 260), Warm Eggplant Salad with Sesame and Shallots (p. 203), Tea Ice Cream (p. 717)

JANUARY 21, 2004: "WHEN THE WHOLE IS GREATER THAN ITS PARTS," BY MATT LEE AND TED LEE. RECIPE ADAPTED FROM ANITA LO, THE CHEF AT ANNISA IN NEW YORK CITY.

—2004

BRANDADE
(SALT COD MOUSSE)

Creamy and light, just as a mousse should be.

————————

1 pound boneless salt cod, soaked for 2 days
   (change the water 3 to 4 times a day), and drained
2 cloves garlic, or to taste
²⁄₃ cup extra virgin olive oil
²⁄₃ cup heavy cream or whole milk
Freshly ground black pepper
Juice of 1 lemon, or to taste
⅛ teaspoon freshly grated nutmeg
Salt if necessary
Bread, toasts, or crackers for serving

1. Bring a medium pot of water to a simmer. Add the salt cod and simmer for 15 minutes, then drain and cool.
2. Place half the cod in a food processor with the garlic and 2 tablespoons olive oil. Process, stopping the machine to scrape down the sides once or twice, until as smooth as possible. Add the remaining cod and repeat.
3. Add small amounts of olive oil alternating with small amounts of cream through the feed tube, continuing until the mixture becomes smooth, creamy, and light. (You may not need all the oil and cream.) Add pepper to taste, some lemon juice, and the nutmeg. Blend, and taste; the mixture may need salt and more lemon juice. (You can prepare the dish several hours or even a day ahead to this point; cover and refrigerate.)
4. Just before serving, heat the brandade very gently in a nonstick saucepan or in a 300-degree oven, covered. Serve with bread, toast, or crackers.

SERVES 6 TO 8 AS AN HORS D'OEUVRE
OR FIRST COURSE

SERVING SUGGESTIONS
Puntarelle with Anchovies (p. 194), Chiffonade Salad (p. 173), Cocido (Chickpea, Sparerib, and Chorizo Stew; p. 578), Roman Lamb (p. 542), Pork Braised in Milk and Cream (p. 557), Churros with Chocolate Sauce (p. 866)

FEBRUARY 4, 2004: "THE MINIMALIST: THE COD TRANSFORMED: FIRST BY SALT, THEN BY FIRE," BY MARK BITTMAN.

—2004

MY MOTHER'S TUNA SALAD

An American classic, in detail, from Julia Reed's mom. If you didn't already have a recipe for it, now you do.

————————

One 12-ounce can StarKist solid white
   albacore tuna in water
½ cup Hellmann's mayonnaise
4 large stalks celery, peeled and finely chopped
3 hard-boiled eggs, chopped
3 tablespoons chopped sweet pickles, with their juice
1 tablespoon minced onion
1 teaspoon celery salt, or more to taste
1 teaspoon McCormick Season-All, or more to taste
6 dashes Tabasco sauce
Salt and cracked black pepper to taste

Drain the tuna, place it in a bowl, and break it up with a fork. Add ¼ cup mayonnaise and blend well. Mix in the remaining ingredients and add the rest of the mayonnaise. Check for celery salt, Season-All, and salt and pepper. This is better if it sits for at least 1 hour before serving.

MAKES ABOUT 3 CUPS

COOKING NOTES
I liked the bites with pickle and might add more next time I make it.
   I tripled the Tabasco, whose flavor surfaced after the salad sat for a bit.

SERVING SUGGESTIONS
Spoon between slices of good white sandwich bread, and mix some Lemon Syrup (p. 9) into a glass of sparkling water (or make a batch of Ginger Lemonade, p. 26, or Jay Grelen's Southern Iced Tea, p. 27).

FEBRUARY 22, 2004: "FOOD: CLASSIC FROM A CAN," BY JULIA REED.

—2004

SHRIMP BURGERS

This is what happens when an Asian fish cake gets in the hands of an American with a grill.

I large clove garlic

I dried or fresh chile, stemmed, seeded, and deveined, or more to taste

One I-inch piece fresh ginger, peeled and roughly chopped

1½ pounds shrimp, peeled, and deveined if you like

¼ cup roughly chopped shallots, scallions, or red onion

¼ cup roughly chopped red or yellow bell pepper (optional)

Salt and freshly ground black pepper

½ cup cilantro leaves, or to taste

Neutral oil, like corn or canola, as needed

4 toasted buns (optional)

Lime wedges or ketchup for serving

1. Start a charcoal or gas grill; the fire should be moderately hot and the rack about 4 inches from the heat source. Combine the garlic, chile, ginger, and one-third of the shrimp in a food processor and puree, stopping the machine to scrape down the sides of the container as necessary. Add the remaining shrimp, along with the shallots, bell pepper, if using, salt and pepper to taste, and cilantro and pulse as many times as necessary to chop the shrimp, but not too finely. Shape the mixture into 4 patties.

2. Brush the grill or patties lightly with oil and place the patties on the grill. Cook undisturbed until a dark crust appears on the bottom and they release fairly easily with a spatula, about 5 minutes. Turn and cook an additional 3 to 4 minutes on the other side. Serve on buns or not, as you like, with lime juice or ketchup as a condiment.

SERVES 4

COOKING NOTE
The burgers can also be cooked on the stove. Heat a grill pan or skillet over medium-high heat. Brush lightly with oil, then place the shrimp patties in the pan. Cook undisturbed for 5 minutes on each side, to form a nice dark crust. Lower the heat to medium and

cook for about 5 minutes, turning occasionally, until the burgers are cooked through.

SERVING SUGGESTIONS
Pad Thai–Style Rice Salad (p. 357), French Fries (p. 292), Chilled Sesame Spinach (p. 239), Tapioca Flamingo (p. 810), Coconut Pie (p. 801)

MAY 26, 2004: "THE MINIMALIST: NEW PARTNER FOR A BUN," BY MARK BITTMAN.

—2004

FISH STEAMED OVER VEGETABLES AND FRESH HERBS

Efficiency fiends, listen up: you can make ratatouille and steam fish in one swoop. Mark Bittman tells you how.

---

3 tablespoons olive oil

I tablespoon minced garlic

I large onion, chopped

I red bell pepper, cored, seeded, and sliced

2 medium zucchini, cut into thin half-moons

2 small eggplants, cut into I-inch chunks

Salt and freshly ground black pepper

2 medium tomatoes, cored and roughly chopped, with their juices

I teaspoon thyme or marjoram leaves

½ cup good black olives, pitted (optional)

1½ pounds skinned red snapper, striped bass, or other firm-fleshed white fish fillets

½ cup roughly chopped basil

1. Put 2 tablespoons olive oil in a large skillet and turn the heat to medium-high. Add the garlic and, when it sizzles, the onions and red bell pepper. Cook, stirring occasionally, for about 5 minutes.

2. Add the zucchini, eggplant, and salt and pepper to taste and cook, stirring occasionally, until the eggplant is fairly soft, 10 to 15 minutes. Add the tomatoes, thyme, and olives, if you are using them, and cook, stirring occasionally, until the tomatoes begin to break up, about 5 minutes. Taste and adjust the seasoning.

3. Sprinkle the fish with salt and pepper and lay it on top of the vegetables. Adjust the heat so the mixture simmers, cover, and cook for 8 to 12 minutes, or until a thin-bladed knife inserted into the fish at its thickest point meets little resistance. Remove the fish to a plate.

4. If the vegetables aren't yet done to your liking, cook them a little longer, then stir the basil into the vegetables and spoon them around the fish; drizzle with the remaining tablespoon of oil (use a little more if you like).

SERVES 4

SERVING SUGGESTIONS
Potato "Tostones" (Flattened Potatoes; p. 301), Forget-It Meringue Torte (p. 823)

JULY 21, 2004: "THE MINIMALIST: GRILL-LESS IN PROVENCE," BY MARK BITTMAN.

—2004

☞ TUNA SALAD

Writing about the salade composée, France's impeccable layered main-course salad, Toby Cecchini, an occasional contributor to the *Times*, claimed that it was salade Niçoise that inspired him to rework his own tuna salad, shunning mayonnaise and courting oil and zeroing in on "lemon, mustard, dill, and the mild, crunchy burn of Greek peppers to temper the pungency of the fish." He forgot to mention the brilliant and delicious addition of smoked almonds.

So delicious, I ate the salad as is, with bread. Cecchini had intended it as part of a composed salad, which I thought too tedious (you can look it up online if you really want it). But it would be a shame not to include his depiction of the composing process which may strike a chord with your own tendencies (it did with me): "Like any fanny-packed tourist, I will often shuffle right over the French mandate of elegant restraint and inadvertently chuck the whole larder into my delicate constructions," he confessed. "Beginning with the lightest touch, I'll lay on a feather's worth at a time—some sautéed zucchini here, those roasted red peppers; oh, and don't leave out the artichoke hearts, and absolutely those caper berries, and

the ricotta salata—until the creaking colossus threatens to bury whichever wide-eyed guests have been lured to my table."

I'm happy to stick with just the tuna part, which is a god in the salad universe.

---

10 to 12 ounces good-quality solid tuna
    packed in olive oil, well drained
2 scallions, finely chopped
6 pepperoncini, stemmed and julienned
3 tablespoons chopped dill
¼ cup roasted or smoked almonds, roughly chopped,
    or a small handful of toasted pine nuts
¼ cup good-quality olive oil (or the oil
    the tuna was packed in)
1 tablespoon Dijon mustard
1 tablespoon whole-grain mustard
1 teaspoon balsamic vinegar
1 teaspoon fresh lemon juice, or more to taste
¼ freshly ground black pepper, or more to taste

Mix all the ingredients well with a fork in a medium bowl. Taste and adjust the lemon juice and pepper if necessary. (The salad can be made up to 3 days in advance and refrigerated.)

MAKES ABOUT 2 CUPS; SERVES 2 TO 4

SERVING SUGGESTIONS
Limoncello (p. 38), Seasoned Olives (p. 90), White Gazpacho with Almonds and Grapes (p. 137), Squashed Tomatoes (p. 90), Watercress Salad (p. 171), Mezzaluna Salad (p. 185), Cornmeal Biscotti (p. 696), Pine Nut Cookies (p. 689)

SEPTEMBER 5, 2004: "FOOD: ASSEMBLY REQUIRED," BY TOBY CECCHINI.

—2004

☞ TUNA CURRY

Sri Lankan cooking is utterly unknown in America. If we had any clue how delicious the cuisine is—a cross between southern India and Thai cooking—it wouldn't be. Begin your adventure here.

---

1 teaspoon turmeric

1 cup water

1 pound fresh tuna, cut into 2-inch cubes

Sea salt

1 tablespoon coconut oil or vegetable oil

3 cloves garlic, chopped

2 teaspoons chopped fresh ginger

1 teaspoon black mustard seeds

2 small tomatoes, cored and sliced

2 shallots, thinly sliced

2 long green chiles, sliced in half and seeded

1 cup unsweetened coconut milk

2 teaspoons tamarind concentrate, or more to taste

Cooked rice

Katta Sambol (p. 611)

1. Mix the turmeric and water in a medium saucepan. Add the tuna and season with salt. Place over medium-low heat, bring to a simmer, and cook for 2 minutes, turning the tuna cubes once. Remove from the heat.

2. Place a large sauté pan over medium heat and add the oil. When it shimmers, add the garlic, ginger, and mustard seeds and cook for 2 minutes. Add the tomatoes, shallots, and chiles; cook for 1 minute. Add the tuna, about ⅓ cup of its cooking water, the coconut milk, tamarind, and salt to taste. Stir to dissolve the tamarind. Bring to a simmer and cook, covered, until the sauce has blended and thickened slightly, 8 to 10 minutes.

3. Serve over rice, with the katta sambol as a condiment.

SERVES 4

COOKING NOTE

Tamarind concentrate and black mustard seeds are sold in Middle Eastern and Indian markets.

SERVING SUGGESTIONS

Kaffir Lime Lemonade (p. 26), Sweet (or Savory) Lassi (p. 25), Hoppers (Coconut Crepes; p. 349), Katta Sambol (p. 611), Mango Ice Cream (p. 729)

OCTOBER 13, 2004: "JUST OFF INDIA, KISSED BY EUROPE," BY AMANDA HESSER. RECIPE ADAPTED FROM GEETHA ILLANGASARIYA, A HOME COOK IN SRI LANKA.

—2004

◇ MINCED FISH SALAD (KOY PA)

This Laotian dish is the perfect lunch on a hot summer day.

———

¾ pound skinless red snapper, yellowtail snapper, or other white-fleshed fish fillets, minced

2 tablespoons fresh lime juice, or more to taste

1 tablespoon Asian fish sauce, or more as needed

1 tablespoon toasted rice powder (available in Asian food markets), or 1 tablespoon raw sticky rice, toasted and ground to a powder

¾ cup green beans, trimmed and thinly sliced

1 red chile, thinly sliced

2 tablespoons finely chopped tender inner parts of lemongrass stalks (2 stalks)

2 cloves garlic, thinly sliced, plus ½ teaspoon minced garlic

8 sprigs cilantro, leaves only, half the leaves chopped and half left whole

8 sprigs mint, leaves only, half the leaves chopped and half left whole

1 scallion, green top only, sliced

Sliced cucumber, watercress, and additional cilantro, mint, and green beans for serving

1. Combine the fish, lime juice, and fish sauce in a small bowl. Mix well. Cover and refrigerate for 2 hours.

2. If necessary, drain the fish. Combine the fish, rice powder, sliced green beans, chile, lemongrass, sliced and minced garlic, cilantro, mint, and scallion in a bowl. Toss to mix well. Taste and adjust the seasoning, adding more fish sauce if desired.

3. Transfer the fish salad to a serving bowl. Serve with the cucumber, watercress, and additional cilantro, mint, and green beans offered separately.

SERVES 4

SERVING SUGGESTIONS

Kaffir Lime Lemonade (p. 26), Laotian Catfish Soup (p. 154), Mi Quang (p. 349), Pad Thai–Style Rice Salad (p. 357), Strawberry Soup (p. 816), Mango Ice Cream (p. 729), Tapioca Flamingo (p. 810)

JULY 13, 2005: "TO EAT IN LAOS," BY AMANDA HESSER. RECIPE ADAPTED FROM 3 NAGAS IN LUANG PRABANG, LAOS.

—2005

LIGHTLY SMOKED SALT COD SALAD

This variation on a salt cod salad that you see all over Spain is superb and, with its brightness and fragrance, unlike any I've had. You smoke the salt cod over a mixture of rice, sugar, cinnamon, peppercorns, and tea leaves (your kitchen will smell great for days), then pull it into pieces and rest it on top of grated tomato, onion, herbs, olives, and a thick pool of olive oil.

One 5-ounce cod fillet, from the tail end
Kosher salt
½ cup sugar
½ cup packed dark brown sugar
2 cinnamon sticks
2 teaspoons Sichuan peppercorns
¼ cup white rice
2 black tea bags, moistened with water
3 small plum tomatoes, halved
¼ cup olive oil, plus more for sprinkling
3 thin slices red onion
⅔ cup halved cherry tomatoes
1 tablespoon finely chopped flat-leaf parsley
1 teaspoon chopped oregano
12 Empeltre or Niçoise olives, pitted

1. Place the cod in a baking dish and generously coat on all sides with salt. Cover with plastic wrap and weight down with a 5-pound weight. Let cure in the refrigerator for 1 hour.
2. Rinse the cod and pat it dry with paper towels. Fold it in half, wrap in plastic wrap, and freeze overnight.
3. The next day, defrost the cod for 20 minutes. Line a wok or other deep heavy pan with foil. Add the sugars, cinnamon sticks, peppercorns, rice, and tea (emptied from the bags). Set a rack in the pan at least 1 inch above the seasonings.
4. Lay the partially frozen cod on the rack. Place the pan over high heat. When the seasonings begin to smoke, cover the pan with a lid or foil, reduce the heat to medium, and smoke for 4 minutes. Move the pan off the heat and let rest, covered, for 15 minutes.
5. Meanwhile, grate the tomatoes on a coarse grater (with the cut sides facing the grater); discard the skin. Pour into a wide shallow serving dish. Season with salt. Add the olive oil and stir together.
6. Mix the onion, cherry tomatoes, parsley, and oregano in a small bowl. Season lightly with salt.
7. Using your fingers, pull the cod into shreds, like pulled pork. Blend with the cherry tomato salad and a sprinkling of olive oil. Spoon the salt cod mixture on top of the grated tomato. Scatter the olives over the salad.

SERVES 4

SERVING SUGGESTIONS
Fried Chickpeas (p. 88), Pan con Tomate (p. 91), Potato, Ham, and Piquillo Pepper Croquetas (p. 94), Catalan Tortilla with Aioli (p. 86), Málaga Gazpacho (p. 112), Eldorado Petit's Fried Noodles with Garlic Mayonnaise (with roasted fish; p. 324), Cocido (Chickpea, Sparerib, and Chorizo Stew; p. 578), Caramel Custard (p. 836), Churros with Chocolate Sauce (p. 866)

SEPTEMBER 11, 2005: "THE WAY WE EAT: RAISING THE TAPAS BAR," BY AMANDA HESSER. RECIPE ADAPTED FROM TÍA POL IN NEW YORK CITY.

—2005

SAUTÉED FLUKE WITH GRAPEFRUIT VINAIGRETTE

This recipe comes from Cyril Renaud, a New York chef who is one of the finest—and most underappreciated—fish cooks in the city. Before owning his own restaurants, Fleur de Sel and Bar Breton, he was the chef at La Caravelle, where he transformed the house classic—fish quenelles—into feathery clouds.

2 tablespoons olive oil
2 tablespoons soy sauce
2 tablespoons balsamic vinegar
¼ teaspoon harissa

One ¼-inch piece fresh ginger, peeled and grated

½ clove garlic, finely chopped

1 red or pink grapefruit

Four 6-ounce fluke fillets

Salt and freshly ground black pepper

2 tablespoons canola oil

1 teaspoon thinly sliced mint leaves

¼ teaspoon chopped rosemary

¼ pound frisée, trimmed (about 3 cups)

1. Heat the oven to 450 degrees. Whisk together the olive oil, soy sauce, vinegar, harissa, ginger, and garlic in a small saucepan; set aside.

2. Peel the grapefruit and trim away all the white pith. Working over a bowl to catch the juices, cut the grapefruit segments free from the membranes. Set the segments aside and squeeze the remaining juice from the membranes into the bowl. Whisk 3 tablespoons grapefruit juice into the olive oil mixture.

3. Lightly season the fluke on both sides with salt and pepper. Heat 1 tablespoon canola oil in a large oven-proof nonstick skillet. When the oil shimmers, add 2 fluke fillets and cook for about 1 minute. Flip and cook for 30 more seconds. Transfer the skillet to the oven and cook for about 2 minutes. Keep the fish warm, and repeat with the remaining tablespoon of canola oil and 2 fillets.

4. To serve, warm the vinaigrette over medium-low heat. Add the mint, rosemary, and grapefruit segments and warm for about 1 minute, or until the segments are heated through.

5. Lay a handful of frisée on each plate, followed by a piece of fish. Top the fish and frisée with some grapefruit segments and a few spoonfuls of vinaigrette.

SERVES 4

COOKING NOTE

If you're holding the dish before serving, don't add the grapefruit segments until you're ready to sit down. They disintegrate quickly in the pan.

SERVING SUGGESTIONS

Beet and Ginger Soup with Cucumber (p. 150), Tuna Tartare (p. 416), Sugar Snap Peas with Horseradish (p. 259), Gâteau de Crepes (p. 785), Tea Ice Cream (p. 717), Coconut Loaf Cake (p. 774)

NOVEMBER 27, 2005: "EAT, MEMORY: THE IDEOLOGY OF TASTE," BY ROY BLOUNT JR. RECIPE ADAPTED FROM CYRIL RENAUD, THE CHEF AT FLEUR DE SEL IN NEW YORK CITY.

—2005

⌒ BAKED GOAN FISH WITH FRESH GREEN CHILE CHUTNEY

For the Chutney

2 cups cilantro leaves and stems

6 green cayenne or other hot chiles, coarsely chopped (use 4 or 5 chiles to reduce the heat)

8 cloves garlic, chopped

2 teaspoons minced fresh ginger

1 cup fresh or frozen grated coconut

1 teaspoon cumin seeds

3 tablespoons fresh lime juice (from about 2 limes)

1 teaspoon sugar

1 teaspoon kosher salt, plus more to taste

For the Fish

One 2-pound firm-fleshed fish, like pickerel, trout, or red snapper, cleaned and scaled

¼ cup vegetable oil

2 tablespoons fresh lime juice

1 tablespoon fine sea salt

1. To make the chutney, place the cilantro, chiles, garlic, and ginger in a food processor and process to a paste. Add the coconut and blend. Transfer to a bowl.

2. Lightly crush the cumin seeds with a mortar and pestle or a spice/coffee grinder and add to the chile mixture. Stir in the lime juice, sugar, and salt. Add more salt if desired.

3. Place a rack in the center of the oven and heat the oven to 400 degrees. Wash and dry the fish. Cut a deep slit down the length of the fish on each side of the backbone. Line a rimmed baking sheet or roasting pan with foil and spread with 3 tablespoons oil. Rub the fish with the lime juice and salt. Using ½ cup of chutney, stuff some of it into the slits and put the remainder in the fish's cavity. Lay the fish on the foil. Pour the remaining tablespoon of oil over the top of the fish. Cover the fish with foil and crimp together the top and bottom pieces to make a packet.

4. Bake for about 30 minutes, depending on the size and thickness of the fish. The fish is done when the thickest part yields a little to the touch or the flesh flakes with a fork.

5. To serve, lift sections of the top fillet off the bone; when the first side is finished, flip over the fish to serve the second fillet. Serve warm or at room temperature, with the pan juices and additional chutney.

SERVES 4

SERVING SUGGESTIONS
Sweet (or Savory) Lassi (p. 25), Yogurt Rice (p. 356), Hoppers (Coconut Crepes; p. 349), Mango Ice Cream (p. 729), Coconut Rice Pudding with Lime Syrup (p. 846)

JANUARY 29, 2006: "IT TAKES A VILLAGE," BY AMANDA HESSER. RECIPE ADAPTED FROM *MANGOES AND CURRY LEAVES*, BY JEFFREY ALFORD AND NAOMI DUGUID.

—2006

⌁ SCANDINAVIAN SEAFOOD SALAD

6 fingerling or 2 Yukon Gold potatoes

2 cups (about 10 ounces) cooked peeled small shrimp, cut into small pieces

1½ cups (about 10 ounces) chopped smoked salmon

1½ cups (about 10 ounces) crabmeat, picked over for shells and cartilage

4 hard-boiled eggs, finely chopped

2 shallots, finely chopped

2 anchovy fillets, chopped

1 tablespoon chopped cilantro

1 tablespoon sliced chives

½ cup fresh lime juice (from about 4 limes)

3 tablespoons mayonnaise

2 tablespoons sour cream

Kosher salt and freshly ground black pepper

2 small heads iceberg lettuce, separated into leaves

1. Heat the oven to 400 degrees. Roast the potatoes in a small baking dish for 30 to 40 minutes, until fork-tender. Let cool completely, then peel and cut into ½-inch dice.

2. Combine the potatoes, shrimp, salmon, crabmeat, eggs, shallots, anchovies, cilantro, and chives in a large bowl. Whisk together the lime juice, mayonnaise, and sour cream in a small bowl. Fold into the salad and season to taste with salt and pepper.

3. Arrange the lettuce leaves on a platter and serve alongside the salad. To eat, roll a lettuce leaf around a dollop of salad, like a spring roll.

SERVES 6

SERVING SUGGESTIONS
Onion Rings (p. 61), Cucumber Sandwiches (p. 56), Chilled Corn Soup with Honeydew Polka Dots (p. 153), Lemon Bars (p. 690), Fresh Raspberry (or Blackberry or Blueberry) Flummery (p. 824)

MAY 14, 2006: "THE ARSENAL," BY AMANDA HESSER. RECIPE ADAPTED FROM *AQUAVIT*, BY MARCUS SAMUELSSON.

—2006

⌁ FRIED MUSSELS WITH ALMOND-GARLIC SAUCE

Inspired by fried mussels on a stick—a street food found in Turkey—Ana Sortun, the chef at Oleana in Boston, paired these stickless fried mussels with another Turkish specialty: tarator, an almond and garlic sauce. I can't think of a better way to combine mussels, almonds, and garlic. I ate the leftover sauce with poached lobster and blanched peas. Although here the sauce is made with some of the mussel broth, you could use any kind of stock, freeing you up to pair it with chicken, shrimp, or, better yet, artichokes.

1½ pounds mussels, scrubbed and debearded

1 cup dry white wine

1 clove garlic, smashed, plus 2 teaspoons minced garlic

¼ cup extra virgin olive oil

½ cup blanched whole almonds

1 teaspoon fresh lemon juice

Salt and freshly ground black pepper

Vegetable or canola oil for deep-frying

¾ cup all-purpose flour

¾ cup cornstarch

1¼ cups beer (not dark)

2 teaspoons chopped flat-leaf parsley

Small romaine lettuce leaves for serving

I lemon, cut into wedges

1. Put the mussels, wine, and smashed garlic clove in a large pot with a tight-fitting lid, bring to a boil, cover, and steam for 3 to 5 minutes, until the mussels open. Uncover and drain in a fine strainer set over a bowl; reserve the liquid. Pull the mussels out of their shells and set aside.

2. To make the sauce, pour ½ cup of the cooking liquid into a blender and add the oil, minced garlic, almonds, and lemon juice. Puree until thick and completely smooth, at least 3 minutes. Season to taste with salt and pepper.

3. Heat 2 inches of oil in a small heavy pot. Combine the flour and cornstarch in a medium bowl and whisk in the beer, parsley, ½ teaspoon salt, and ¼ teaspoon pepper. When the oil is hot (drop in a bit of batter; it should bubble vigorously), stir a handful of mussels into the batter and drop them one at a time into the oil. Fry until golden brown, about 2 minutes. Drain on paper towels and sprinkle with salt. Repeat with the remaining mussels.

4. Serve immediately on whole romaine leaves, drizzled with plenty of sauce; serve the remainder on the side. Squeeze the lemon wedges over the top.

SERVES 6 TO 8 AS A FIRST COURSE

COOKING NOTE

This makes a huge greasy mess—use a spatter guard when frying.

SERVING SUGGESTIONS

Rebujito (p. 38), Fried Chickpeas (p. 88), Sautéed Cod with Potatoes in Chorizo-Mussel Broth (p. 428), Pork Burgers (p. 566), Almond-Lemon Macaroons (p. 707), Toasts with Chocolate, Olive Oil, and Sea Salt (p. 844)

JUNE 7, 2006: "THE CHEF: ANA SORTUN: A MEDITERRA-NEAN STYLE ALL HER OWN," BY JULIA MOSKIN. RECIPE ADAPTED FROM *SPICE: FLAVORS OF THE EASTERN MEDITERRANEAN*, BY ANA SORTUN.

—2006

ᔡ DECADENT LOBSTER SALAD

4 large handfuls arugula

I tablespoon fresh lemon juice

I tablespoon Champagne vinegar

¼ cup extra virgin olive oil

Salt and freshly ground black pepper

Six 1¼-pound live lobsters, cooked, shelled, and marinated as in The Way Life Should Be (p. 353)

2 garlic scapes or garlic chives, snipped (optional)

2 tablespoons unsalted butter

6 slices white bread

1. Lightly toss the arugula with the lemon juice, vinegar, and oil in a large bowl. Season to taste with salt and pepper. Divide the salad among 6 plates.

2. Remove the lobster from the marinade and arrange on top of the arugula. Garnish with snipped garlic scapes. If you have a panini maker, serve with buttered and pressed white bread—it will recall the buttery hotdog bun that is the crux of every good lobster roll. If you don't have a panini maker, butter the bread and toast it in a nonstick pan over medium heat. Sprinkle the toasts with salt.

SERVES 6

COOKING NOTE

When making the toasts, don't be stingy: use good white bread and plenty of butter, and sprinkle the buttered toasts with salt while they are still warm.

SERVING SUGGESTIONS

Vermouth Cup (p. 15), Ricotta Crostini with Fresh Thyme and Dried Oregano (p. 93), Thomas Keller's Gazpacho (p. 146), Basic Corn Chowder (p. 149), Saratoga Potatoes (p. 273), Strawberry Sorbet (p. 732), Judson Grill's Berry Clafoutis with Crème Fraîche (p. 844), Strawberry Charlotte (p. 810)

JULY 2, 2006: "THE WAY WE EAT: THE BOILING POINT," BY HEIDI JULAVITS.

—2006

CLEMENTINE'S TUNA MACARONI SALAD

Salt
1/2 pound elbow macaroni
1/2 cup diced (1/4-inch) celery
2 ounces sharp cheddar, cut into 1/4-inch cubes
1/4 cup thinly sliced scallions
1/4 cup sliced cornichons
2 tablespoons mild Tennessee chow-chow (optional)
1 cup mayonnaise
Two 6-ounce cans chunk light tuna in water, drained
Freshly ground black pepper to taste

1. Bring a large pot of salted water to a boil. Add the macaroni and cook until al dente. Drain and cool completely.
2. Fold together the macaroni with the remaining ingredients in a large bowl. Season with salt, if needed.

SERVES 6

COOKING NOTE
Chow-chow is a vegetable relish. A recipe for it from 1880 can be found on p. 00. It can also be purchased in grocery stores and online.

SERVING SUGGESTIONS
Scotch Eggs (p. 62), Onion Rings (p. 61), Spoonbread's Potato Salad (p. 288), Rachel's Green Beans with Dill (p. 251), Chocolate Chip Cookies (p. 709), Caramelized Brown Butter Rice Krispies Treats (p. 708)

JULY 9, 2006: "THE WAY WE EAT: SALAD DAZE," BY AMANDA HESSER. RECIPE ADAPTED FROM CLEMENTINE IN LOS ANGELES.

—2006

OOLONG-CRUSTED SCALLOPS

Juice of 1/2 orange
Juice of 1/2 lemon
Juice of 1/2 lime
8 tablespoons (1 stick) unsalted butter, cut into small pieces
Salt
4 teaspoons oolong tea leaves, finely ground in a spice/coffee grinder
12 sea scallops, tough muscle removed and patted dry
Freshly ground black pepper
2 tablespoons olive oil

1. Heat the citrus juices in a saucepan to just below a simmer, then whisk in the butter a few pieces at a time. Season with salt and keep warm.
2. Place the ground tea on a plate. Season the scallops with salt and pepper, then press both sides into the ground tea.
3. Heat the oil in a large cast-iron skillet or sauté pan over medium heat. Sear the scallops until just warmed through but not fully opaque, 1 to 2 minutes per side. Place 3 scallops in each of 4 shallow bowls and spoon the sauce around them.

SERVES 4 AS A FIRST COURSE OR
AS PART OF A LARGER MAIN COURSE

SERVING SUGGESTIONS
Asparagus with Miso Butter (p. 259), Broccoli Rabe Oshitashi (p. 262), The Most Voluptuous Cauliflower (p. 241), Marinated Flank Steak with Asian Slaw (p. 552), Pineapple Carpaccio with Lime Sorbet (p. 842), Plum Fritters (p. 865)

DECEMBER 17, 2006: "THE WAY WE EAT: STEEP INCREASE," BY DANIEL PATTERSON, THE CHEF AND OWNER OF COI IN SAN FRANCISCO.

—2006

OVEN-ROASTED BRANZINO WITH HAZELNUT PICADA

I never expected a seasoned hazelnut and bread-crumb "crumble" to deliver so much flavor—you sprinkle it on as the fish emerges from the oven, then leave it to your guests to further garnish each bite as they carve their way through the fish.

About 3 tablespoons olive oil

2 slices hearty white bread (about 2 ounces)

20 hazelnuts, roasted, peeled, and chopped

I clove garlic, minced

I teaspoon chopped mint

I teaspoon grated orange zest

4 whole branzino (about 1⅓ pounds each),
    cleaned and scaled

Salt and freshly ground black pepper

I lemon, cut into eight ¼-inch-thick slices

1. Heat 3 tablespoons olive oil in small sauté pan and fry the bread until golden. Remove the bread and let cool, then crush into crumbs.

2. Place the bread crumbs, hazelnuts, garlic, mint, orange zest, and ½ teaspoon olive oil in a medium bowl and mix thoroughly. Taste and adjust the seasoning, then let sit for at least 30 minutes to let the flavors develop.

3. Heat the oven to 400 degrees. Season the fish with salt and pepper. Stuff the cavities of each fish with 2 slices of lemon. Coat the fish with olive oil and arrange in an oiled baking pan.

4. Roast the fish, turning once, for 7 minutes on each side, or until done. Scatter the hazelnut picada on top of the fish to serve.

SERVES 4

COOKING NOTES

If you can't get all the skins off the hazelnuts, it's no big deal.

I liked the fish with a little olive oil sprinkled on at the table.

SERVING SUGGESTIONS

Almond-Carrot Salad (p. 204), Judy Rodgers's Warm Bread Salad (p. 198), Couscous Salad (p. 321), Mushrooms with Manzanilla Sherry (p. 249), Potato "Tostones" (Flattened Potatoes; p. 301), Apple Galette (p. 843), Madeleine Kamman's Apple Mousse (p. 816), Purple Plum Torte (p. 763)

JANUARY 10, 2007: "FLAVORED WITH FLAME AND STONE," BY OLIVER SCHWENER-ALBRIGHT. RECIPE ADAPTED FROM *THE ZUNI CAFÉ COOKBOOK*, BY JUDY RODGERS.

—2007

✐ CLAMS IN BLACK BEAN SAUCE

Fermented black beans, like anchovies and Worcestershire sauce, seem to possess special powers, an ability to transform a dish, define a sauce, leave you wanting more. Here, they underline the fire and brine, like a shadow underscoring sunlight.

———

2 tablespoons fermented (Chinese) black beans

2 tablespoons peanut oil

3 cloves garlic, minced

2 scallions, finely chopped

2 tablespoons minced fresh ginger

I teaspoon crushed red pepper flakes

2 pounds Manila or littleneck clams, scrubbed and dried

3 tablespoons Shaoxing wine or dry sherry

¾ cup chicken broth

I teaspoon cornstarch, dissolved in
    I tablespoon warm water

2 tablespoons chopped cilantro

1. Soak the fermented beans in ½ cup warm water for 10 minutes. Drain and coarsely mash with a fork.

2. Set a wok over high heat and pour in the oil. Add the garlic, scallions, and ginger and stir-fry for 30 seconds. Add the beans and red pepper flakes and cook for 30 seconds. Drop in the clams and stir-fry for 30 seconds, then pour in the wine and broth. Reduce the heat to medium and cook, covered, until most of the clams have opened, about 2 to 4 minutes.

3. Add the cornstarch mixture and raise the heat to high. Stir and cook, uncovered, until the sauce adheres to the clams, about 2 minutes. Sprinkle in the cilantro.

SERVES 4

SERVING SUGGESTIONS

Shrimp Toast (p. 60), Oriental Watercress Soup (p. 111), String Beans with Ginger and Garlic (p. 260), Warm Eggplant Salad with Sesame and Shallots (p. 203), Chilled Sesame Spinach (p. 239), Grapefruit Granita (p. 731)

AUGUST 5, 2007: "THE WAY WE EAT: DOUBLE HAPPINESS," BY NICOLE MONES. RECIPE ADAPTED FROM PAUL MONES, THE AUTHOR'S HUSBAND.

—2007

∼ WOK-SEARED SPICY CALAMARI SALAD

After tasting this, you may feel remorseful about all the mediocre fried calamari you've had. Don't. See this as an opportunity for personal growth.

———

I pound cleaned calamari, the smaller the better,
    sliced into thin rings, tentacles included
20 roasted salted cashews, chopped
I tablespoon minced cilantro
I tablespoon mint leaves
2 to 4 teaspoons Sriracha sauce
Salt and freshly ground black pepper
4 cups tatsoi, baby arugula, or other spicy greens
I endive, cored and slivered
2 tablespoons extra virgin olive oil
¼ cup fresh lime juice (from about 2 limes)

1. Place the calamari in a bowl, add the cashews, cilantro, mint, and Sriracha to taste, and toss. Season with ½ teaspoon salt and pepper to taste. Set aside.
2. Mix the greens and endive and divide among 4 shallow bowls.
3. Place a wok or large skillet over high heat and add the oil. When it is smoking hot, add the calamari and seasonings and stir-fry for about 20 seconds, until the calamari rings start to turn opaque. Add the lime juice, toss, and remove from the heat. Taste the sauce and adjust the salt and Sriracha if necessary. Pour the mixture over the greens.

SERVES 4 AS A FIRST COURSE

SERVING SUGGESTIONS
Mi Quang (Rice Noodles with Shrimp, Herbs, and Fried Pork Rinds; p. 349), Southeast Asian Chicken Two Ways (p. 489), Malaysian-Inspired Pork Stew with Traditional Garnishes (p. 552), Laotian Catfish Soup (p. 154), Pho Bo (Hanoi Beef Soup; p. 144), Mango Ice Cream (p. 729), Vanilla Plum Ice (p. 734)

JANUARY 9, 2008: "PAIRINGS," BY FLORENCE FABRICANT. RECIPE ADAPTED FROM TENPENH IN WASHINGTON, D.C.
—2008

∼ SEA BASS IN GRAPPA

Once I learned about *New Yorker* writer Jane Kramer's excellent sea bass recipe, it became my no-stress dinner party standby. I serve it with M'hamsa hand rolled couscous (easily found online).

———

2 large cloves garlic, minced
¼ cup extra virgin olive oil
One 14-ounce can Italian plum tomatoes, chopped,
    with their juices
Salt and freshly ground black pepper
½ teaspoon saffron threads
1¼ cups water
One 2-pound sea bass, cleaned and scaled,
    or one I-pound tail-end striped bass fillet
¼ cup grappa
Finely chopped flat-leaf parsley for garnish

1. Heat the garlic in the oil in a deep skillet until fragrant. Add the tomatoes and their juices and a pinch each of salt and pepper and cook for 5 to 10 minutes to reduce. Add the saffron and water, mix well, and cook for 5 minutes more.
2. Slip the fish into the pan and simmer, covered, until opaque throughout, 5 to 8 minutes. Add the grappa and let the alcohol burn off. Sprinkle in the parsley.

SERVES 2

COOKING NOTES
This recipe can be doubled or tripled easily.

Make sure the sauce reduces enough to thicken slightly in Step 1. And season the sauce generously, because you don't season the fish.

SERVING SUGGESTIONS
Puntarelle with Anchovies (p. 194), Italian Roast Potatoes (p. 300), Mashed Potatoes Anna (p. 294), Panna Cotta (p. 840), Marcella's Pear Cake (p. 769), Chamomile and Almond Cake (p. 786), Coffee Caramel Custard (p. 849)

JANUARY 6, 2008: "THE WAY WE EAT: THE GRAPES OF WRATH," BY ALEKSANDRA CRAPANZANO. RECIPE ADAPTED FROM JANE KRAMER, THE AUTHOR'S MOTHER.
—2008

➣ ARCTIC CHAR WITH ANCHO-SHALLOT BUTTER

Ancho chiles were to the aughts what jalapeño peppers were to the nineties.

———

For the Ancho-Shallot Butter

2 teaspoons vegetable oil

I small shallot, finely minced

¼ cup dry white wine

½ pound (2 sticks) unsalted butter, softened

4 teaspoons ancho chile powder

I teaspoon ground coriander (optional)

I teaspoon honey

¼ teaspoon salt

Four 5- to 6-ounce skinless Arctic char fillets

1. To make the ancho-shallot butter, heat the oil in a small skillet over medium heat. Add the shallot and sauté until softened, about 5 minutes. Add the wine and simmer until evaporated, about 5 minutes. Remove from the heat and allow to cool.

2. Combine the butter, ancho chile, coriander, if using, honey, salt, and shallot in a bowl and mix until blended and smooth. (The butter can be used immediately, covered and refrigerated for up to 3 days, or well wrapped and frozen for up to 3 months; bring to room temperature before using.)

3. Heat the oven to 250 degrees. Lightly oil a shallow baking pan and arrange the fillets in it in a single layer. Spread each with 1 tablespoon of the ancho-shallot butter.

4. Bake until barely cooked through, 10 to 12 minutes, depending on the thickness of the fillets.

SERVES 4

COOKING NOTES

You will have leftover butter, which shouldn't go to waste. Spread it on grilled steak, whip it into mashed potatoes, or slather it on boiled corn.

This is a great weeknight recipe, especially if you make the butter ahead of time.

SERVING SUGGESTIONS

La Paloma (p. 35), Broccoli Puree with Ginger (p. 253), Barley Risotto (p. 327), Amazon Cake (Cocoa Cake; p. 779), Lemon Mousse for a Crowd (p. 861)

JANUARY 30, 2008: "FEED ME: A CELEBRATION UNTO ITSELF," BY ALEX WITCHEL. RECIPE ADAPTED FROM NORTH POND IN CHICAGO.

—2008

➣ FISH TACOS

The fish taco is a West Coast delight that we East Coast food writers continuously celebrate as the next hamburger—our attempts to galvanize the locals haven't worked all that well so far, but maybe this time will be the charm.

———

2 medium tomatoes, cored, seeded, and finely chopped

I small red onion, finely chopped

I clove garlic, minced

½ cup roughly chopped cilantro

I jalapeño pepper, halved lengthwise, seeded, and cut crosswise into half-moons (optional)

¼ cup mayonnaise

½ cup sour cream

2 limes, I halved, I cut into wedges

Kosher salt and freshly ground black pepper

I tablespoon finely chopped canned chipotle pepper in adobo, or to taste (optional)

½ cup flour, preferably Wondra or other fine-milled flour

1½ teaspoons ch ili powder

½ cup whole milk

One I-pound flounder or any firm white-fleshed fish fillet, cut across the grain into strips about ½ inch wide by 3 inches long

¼ cup peanut oil, plus a splash more for greasing the pan

A pat of butter

Twelve 6-inch fresh corn tortillas

2 cups shredded green cabbage

A saucy hot sauce, like Tapatio or Frank's

1. Combine the tomatoes, onion, garlic, cilantro, and jalapeño, if using, in a medium bowl.

2. Whisk the mayonnaise and sour cream in a small bowl until combined. Season to taste with the juice of the halved lime, salt and pepper, and the chipotle, if using.

3. Mix together the flour, chili powder, and 1½ teaspoons each salt and black pepper in a medium bowl. Pour the milk into another medium bowl, and place the fish in it.

4. Pour the peanut oil into a 12-inch skillet and heat over medium-high heat until it shimmers and is about to smoke. Remove the fish strips from the milk bath and dredge them lightly in the flour mixture, shaking to remove excess. Add the butter to the pan. Place some fish strips in the oil, without crowding them, and cook until deep golden brown on one side, 3 to 4 minutes. Turn carefully and cook for 1 minute more. Remove to a paper-towel-lined plate and sprinkle with salt. Repeat with the remaining fish.

5. Meanwhile, lightly grease a skillet with a drizzle of oil and set over medium heat. Heat the tortillas, 1 or 2 at a time, until soft and hot. Keep them warm, wrapped in a dish towel.

6. Fill each tortilla with 3 pieces of fish, browned side up, followed by some tomato salsa and a pinch of cabbage. Drizzle with the sour cream sauce. Serve with the lime wedges and hot sauce on the side.

SERVES 4 TO 6

SERVING SUGGESTIONS
La Paloma (p. 35), Guacamole Tostadas (p. 67), Strawberry Sorbet (p. 732)

MARCH 22, 2009: "THE CHEAT: BAJA REFRESHER," BY SAM SIFTON.

—2009

- Pigeon and quail are common: they're broiled, glazed, jugged, potted, roasted, stewed, and made into pie. Chicken, not so much.

—1870s—

- Curried Turkey Hash (p. 452).

—1887—

- Chicken à la Marengo (p. 453) shows up in the *Times*, but no one notices until Craig Claiborne popularizes it in the 1960s.

—1908—

- Cutlets à la Kiev (p. 455).

—1946—

- The recipe for Chicken with 40 Cloves of Garlic (p. 469) is first printed in the *Times*; it lives on for decades.

—1961—

- Birth of Buffalo chicken wings; the *Times* recipe is from 1981 (p. 464).

—1964—

- Eugene Beals invents the pop-up timer for turkeys.

—1960s—

- Lee Lum's Lemon Chicken (p. 459) is one of the first Chinese dishes to really strike a chord with readers.

—1969—

- Turducken (p. 485) begins seeping into Thanksgiving culture.

—1980s—

- Chicken Paprikash (p. 461).

—1980—

- Florence Fabricant refers to "free-range chickens"—a first in the *Times*.

- *The Silver Palate Cookbook* is published, and every cook in America serves chicken Marbella at dinner parties until everyone is sick of it.

—1982—

- Judy Rodgers is hired as chef at Zuni Café in San Francisco; the restaurant will become known for her roast chicken with bread salad (p. 467).

—1987—

- Duck breast becomes standard fare on high-end restaurant menus.

—1990s—

- If you aren't deep-frying turkey in a pot of boiling peanut oil for Thanksgiving you are brining the bird (see p. 474).

- Beer-Can Chicken (p. 473) is all the rage on the barbecue circuit—chicken loses its remaining dignity, but it tastes good.

—1999—

- For reasons that cannot be explained rationally, Americans stop eating chicken skin altogether. Commercial chicken continues its downward spiral toward flavorlessness.

—2000s—

- Proportionately fewer chicken recipes are printed in the *Times*.

- "Pastured" and "pasture-raised" chickens one-up free-range chickens—the birds forage in fields, not open pens.

—2003—

- Jamie Oliver's Braised Ligurian Chicken (p. 491) becomes a favorite of *Times* readers.

- Both the *Los Angeles Times* and the *New York Times* write about dry-brining the Thanksgiving turkey. Trend meters go berserk.

—2009—

10

⌇

POULTRY AND GAME

A little more than a hundred years ago, we cooked quail with bacon, turkey with curry, squab with marjoram, and chicken with leeks and prunes, each bird a frequent inhabitant of the Dutch oven. You'll notice that as this chapter progresses, the kitchen aviary gets much, much smaller. As hunting diminished and farmers discovered that chicken could be raised efficiently (its feed-to-flesh ratio is lower than even beef), the use of seasonal game and turkey declined, and chicken swept the field.

Luckily, chicken also happens to be a delicious bird that easily feeds a family of four. And it's flattered by seasonings as varied as jerk (p. 496) and buttermilk (p. 493). The recipes I loved most are ones in which familiar combinations are improved through technique. In Elizabeth Frink's Roast Lemon Chicken (p. 478), she has you add lemon zest and juice in so many ways that the bird tastes as if it had been raised on lemons alone. Steve Raichlen teaches you how to grill a whole chicken propped on top of a beer can (don't ask, just do; p. 473). And Mark Bittman makes frying chicken a snap by using much less oil.

But don't forget about turkey, duck, quail, and squab (pigeon). Small game birds are easy to cook (they're tiny little things—you just season them and toss them in the oven) and there are techniques here for duck and turkey that will change the way you cook them forever. Now I always roast duck partially at high heat and partially at low heat (see p. 475), and brine my turkeys à la Alice Waters before roasting them (see p. 474), which keeps the meat moist and the skin as crisp as a dry leaf.

RECIPES BY CATEGORY

BOMBAY CURRY

If you can get grated fresh (or frozen) coconut—usually available at Asian and Indian markets—this is a great, easy dish for a weeknight dinner. While you're at the store, pick up some fresh curry powder, too.

One 4-pound chicken, cut into 6 pieces
Salt and freshly ground black pepper
2 tablespoons unsalted butter
½ medium onion, thinly sliced
2 tablespoons curry powder
Grated zest and juice of 1 lemon
1 cup grated fresh or frozen coconut
½ cup light unsweetened coconut milk
¼ cup water

1. Season the chicken all over with salt and pepper. Melt the butter in a large sauté pan over medium-high heat. When the foam subsides, add the chicken skin side down and cook, turning occasionally until browned on all sides. Remove the chicken to a plate.
2. Lower the heat to medium, add the onion to the pan, and cook until softened, 3 to 5 minutes. Stir in the curry and cook for 30 seconds. Stir in the lemon zest and juice. Add the coconut, coconut milk, and water, return the chicken to the pan, and cover with a lid. Simmer for 15 minutes. Baste the chicken with the pan juices, and check the breast meat. If it's done, remove the breasts from the pan. Otherwise, put the lid back on and continue cooking, removing the breasts as they finish cooking. Then remove the lid and finish cooking the legs with the lid off.
3. Arrange the chicken on a platter. Taste and adjust the seasoning of the sauce. Spoon it over the chicken.

SERVES 4

SERVING SUGGESTIONS
Kaffir Lime Lemonade (p. 26), Sweet (or Savory) Lassi (p. 25), Beet and Ginger Soup with Cucumber (p. 150), Hoppers (p. 349), Yogurt Rice (p. 356), Jasmine Tea Rice (p. 354), Tangerine Sherbet (p. 734)

APRIL 25, 1880: "RECEIPTS FOR THE TABLE" RECIPE SIGNED A.D.V.

—1880

A MOLEY (CURRIED TURKEY HASH)

To make the case that Americans should make curry rather than hash with their leftover Thanksgiving turkey, the writer of the story adapted a bunch of curry recipes, including this *moley*, from a cookbook by Daniel Sautiagoe, a Tamil from Ceylon (now Sri Lanka).

The distinction between a curry—a vegetable, fish, or meat dish seasoned with a blend of spices—and a moley mystifies me. This moley sure seems like a curry (note the meat and the spices). It is heavily skewed for the American kitchen, calling for butter rather than coconut oil, curry powder in place of a homemade curry mixture, and milk and cream instead of coconut milk.

---

2 cups sliced onions
1 tablespoon unsalted butter
1 teaspoon curry powder
⅛ teaspoon ground cinnamon
⅛ teaspoon ground cloves
Pinch of cayenne pepper
Salt
2 cups whole milk
4 cups diced cooked turkey
1 tablespoon heavy cream
¼ teaspoon cider vinegar

1. Soften the onion in the butter, with the curry powder, cinnamon, cloves, and cayenne, in a medium saucepan over medium heat. Season with salt, add the milk, and bring to a simmer. Cook until reduced by half and thickened a little.
2. Add the turkey and heat through, then stir in the cream and vinegar. Adjust the seasoning if necessary.

SERVES 4

SERVING SUGGESTIONS
Sweet (or Savory) Lassi (p. 25), Crab and Coconut Curry (p. 389), Hot Pepper Shrimp (p. 403), Green Beans with Coriander-Coconut Crust (p. 246), Basmati Rice with Coconut Milk and Ginger (p. 339), Tapioca Pudding (p. 798)

NOVEMBER 25, 1887: "CURRY FOR THE TURKEY." RECIPE
ADAPTED FROM A COOKBOOK BY DANIEL SAUTIAGOE.

—1887

3. Turn the quail and roast for 6 more minutes for medium-rare, 8 more minutes for medium well.

4. Serve the birds on a bed of the bread crumbs.

SERVES 2 AS A MAIN COURSE, 4 AS A FIRST COURSE

SERVING SUGGESTIONS

Bagna Cauda (p. 58), Nicole Kaplan's Gougères (p. 76), Ratatouille with Butternut Squash (p. 258), Fresh Mushrooms Stewed with Madeira (p. 214), Barley Risotto (p. 327), Stewed Fennel (p. 245), The Most Voluptuous Cauliflower (p. 241), Cumin-Mustard Carrots (p. 237), Poached Pears in Brandy and Red Wine (p. 832), Lemon Mousse for a Crowd (p. 861), Snow Pudding (p. 800)

ROAST QUAIL WITH SAGE DRESSING

This article appeared in late October, in anticipation of quail season, which at the time began and ended in November. With so little time to enjoy the birds, there was no room for a mistake in the kitchen. As the author noted, "Those who eat quail for the sake of the real flavor of the flesh will advocate the plainest methods of cookery and such simple seasonings as butter, pepper, and salt, or, at the most, the fat of salted bacon." Beyond that, readers were offered instructions for quail roasted at high heat and served over toasts spread with giblet butter; stuffed quail; roasted quail wrapped in grape leaves; and this carefully constructed bacon-cloaked roasted quail poised on a bed of seasoned and toasted bread crumbs. I can think of no better way to enjoy the birds.

If you've never cooked quail before (I hadn't), jump in and try it. You'll have dinner on the table in less than 30 minutes.

———

2 tablespoons unsalted butter

2½ cups fresh bread crumbs

Salt and freshly ground black pepper

1½ teaspoons dried sage

1 tablespoon onion juice (see Cooking Notes, p. 54)

4 quail (about 5 ounces each)

8 slices bacon

Flour for dusting

1 tablespoon butter, melted

1. Heat the oven to 450 degrees. Melt the 2 tablespoons butter in a medium skillet over medium heat. Add the bread crumbs and toast them to the color of a hazelnut. Season with salt and pepper. Off the heat, stir in the sage and onion juice. Keep warm.

2. Wrap each quail in 2 slices of bacon, securing it with toothpicks. Dust the birds with flour and place on their sides in a roasting pan. Roast for 6 minutes, basting with the remaining tablespoon of butter.

CHICKEN À LA MARENGO

Some people may be disappointed that I didn't include Craig Claiborne's chicken Marengo, which I'd heard was *the* dish to serve in the 1960s. I made two of his versions and liked them, but then I tried this much older recipe and thought it blew Craig's away. His were uniform, polite, their sauces thickened with flour; this one reminded me of the kinds of country home cooking you find in Italy. You get crisp pieces of chicken, a whiff of garlic, some mushrooms, and a concentrated oil-slicked wash of tomato.

According to *Larousse Gastronomique*, the original dish was created by Napoleon's chef after the battle of Marengo (although *The Oxford Companion to Food* points out that tomatoes were not used in this way at the time). It is said to have been garnished with crawfish and fried eggs—hardly what we think of as battlefield fare.

———

One 14-ounce can whole tomatoes

⅓ cup chopped carrot

⅓ cup chopped celery

⅔ cup chopped onion

2 tablespoons chopped flat-leaf parsley

Salt

2 tablespoons unsalted butter

3 tablespoons olive oil

1 clove garlic, crushed

One 4½-pound chicken, cut into 4 pieces

Freshly ground black pepper

½ pound white mushrooms, trimmed and quartered

1. Pour the can of tomatoes into a small saucepan. Crush the tomatoes using a potato masher or fork. Add the carrot, celery, onion, and parsley. Bring to a boil, then reduce the heat and simmer until thickened and reduced to about 1 cup, about 40 minutes. Season with salt about halfway through.

2. Press the tomatoes through the fine disk of a food mill into a bowl, then stir in 1 tablespoon butter and check the seasoning.

3. Melt the remaining 1 tablespoon butter with the oil in a 12-inch sauté pan or casserole over medium-high heat. Add the garlic. Season the chicken pieces with salt and pepper. Add the dark meat pieces to the pan. Once they begin to get crisp on the edges, reduce the heat to medium. After 5 minutes, add the breast pieces. Turn the chicken as it browns and remove the pieces to a platter as they finish cooking, 15 to 18 minutes total time. After 15 minutes, add the mushrooms to the pan, season them, and cook until lightly browned and cooked through—they may need to cook for a few minutes after the chicken has been removed.

4. Remove the pan from the heat and spoon off all but 1 to 2 tablespoons of fat. Add 1 cup tomato puree to the mushrooms and stir up any bits stuck to the bottom of the pan. Simmer until the sauce thickens and forms a glaze with the fat in the pan. Taste and adjust the seasoning.

5. Spoon the sauce over the chicken.

SERVES 4

SERVING SUGGESTIONS

Artichokes Croisette (p. 220), Italian Roast Potatoes (p. 300), Pistachio Cream (p. 806), Queen of Puddings (p. 866)

MAY 17, 1908: "HOW TO COOK CHICKENS: THERE ARE NUMEROUS DEVIATIONS FROM THE UNIMAGINATIVE ROAST OR BOIL—HERE ARE SOME OF THEM."

—1908

ROASTED SQUAB WITH CHICKEN LIVER STUFFING

Squab is the kind of bird—it's gamy, but delicately so—that you need to eat with your hands if you want to enjoy it properly, so let the birds cool for ten minutes before serving. Give your guests large napkins and small sharp knives for carving away at the tiny specimens. This recipe came from Louis Diat, the French chef best known for vichyssoise.

————

4 squab (about 1 pound each)

3 tablespoons unsalted butter, 2 tablespoons softened

½ finely chopped onion

Salt and freshly ground black pepper

1½ tablespoons chopped flat-leaf parsley

¼ teaspoon ground ginger

¾ cup coarse dry bread crumbs

2 tablespoons whole milk

1. Heat the oven to 425 degrees. Remove the hearts and livers from the squab. Melt 1 tablespoon butter in a medium skillet over medium heat. Add the onion, hearts, and livers, season with salt and pepper, and cook until the onion has softened and the giblets are cooked through. Remove from the heat and cool slightly.

2. Chop the hearts and livers and return to the onions. Stir in the parsley, ginger, and bread crumbs. Pour in the milk and toss to moisten.

3. Fill the cavities of the birds with the stuffing, then truss them. Rub ½ tablespoon of the remaining butter over each and season with salt and pepper. Place in a roasting pan and bake until an instant-read thermometer inserted into the thickest part of the legs reads 160 degrees, 30 to 40 minutes.

SERVES 4

SERVING SUGGESTIONS

Mushrooms Stuffed with Duxelles and Sausage (p. 223), Sautéed Potatoes with Parsley (p. 283), Watercress Salad (p. 171), Creamy Salad Dressing (p. 605), Fresh Ginger Cake (p. 775), Spanish Cream (p. 802)

In the introduction to this recipe, Kiley Taylor, the reporter, wrote excitedly of the plump new squab created with "scientific raising" and "special feeding"—which seems sinister now that we know the ills that factory farming has wrought.

SEPTEMBER 1, 1940: "VICTUALS AND VITAMINS," BY KILEY TAYLOR. RECIPE ADAPTED FROM LOUIS DIAT, THE CHEF AT THE RITZ IN NEW YORK CITY.

—1940

✐ CUTLETS À LA KIEV

A photo caption accompanying this story and recipe read: "The chef at the Casino Russe rolls a whole chicken breast around an elongated lump of butter, dips the bundle into flour, egg, and crumbs, and fries it in deep fat. Cutlet à la Kiev, as this is called, is as exotic as vodka." As you cut into the chicken, the butter in the center is supposed to spurt out, like the jelly in a doughnut. Spoiler: it does. It also has the perfect culinary yin-yang of crunch and moisture.

––––––––––

6 small skin-on, boneless chicken breasts (5 to 7 ounces each)
12 tablespoons (1 $\frac{1}{2}$ sticks) unsalted butter
3 large eggs
$\frac{1}{2}$ cup all-purpose flour
1 $\frac{1}{2}$ cups fine dry bread crumbs
Salt
Canola oil for frying

1. Lay the chicken breasts skin side down on a cutting board. With the tip of a sharp knife, make 2 tiny lengthwise slits in each breast. Flatten the breasts with a meat mallet until they're $\frac{1}{3}$ inch thick.
2. Cut the butter into 2-tablespoon portions and roll each portion into log shape. Lay 1 log at the bottom edge of each chicken breast, then roll the chicken breast, "making a bundle that looks roughly like a chicken leg."
3. Beat the eggs in a shallow bowl. Put the flour in another shallow bowl and the bread crumbs in a third bowl. Season each rolled breast with salt, then dip first

in the flour, then in egg, and then in bread crumbs. Dip it in the egg and bread crumbs once more.
4. Heat $\frac{1}{2}$ inch of oil in a deep 12-inch skillet until it's hot enough to toast a bread crumb in 30 seconds. Add the chicken bundles skin side down and fry until nut brown, regulating the heat as needed (the fat should be bubbling but the bread crumbs should not be burning), then turn and brown the other side, 10 to 12 minutes total. Drain on paper towel and serve immediately.

SERVES 6

COOKING NOTE
The recipe calls for fine dry breadcrumbs, which work well, but why not try Panko (Japanese bread crumbs) for an extra-crunchy effect?

SERVING SUGGESTIONS
Garden Minestrone (p. 118), Tomato Soup I or II (pp. 106 and 114), Risotto with Lemon and Crème Fraîche (p. 345), Steamed Spinach with Balsamic Butter (p. 226), String Beans with Ginger and Garlic (p. 260), Purple Plum Torte (p. 763)

AUGUST 6, 1946: "NEWS OF FOOD: CHEF CHALLENGES HOUSEWIVES, SAYS FEW KNOW HOW TO DO KIEV CHICKEN CUTLETS," BY JANE NICKERSON. RECIPE ADAPTED FROM GABRIEL SIDORENKO, THE CHEF AT CASINO RUSSE, A RESTAURANT IN NEW YORK CITY.

—1946

✐ COUNTRY CAPTAIN

Country captain is the Lowcountry's version of chicken cacciatore, an unpretentious dish you put on the stove and let bubble away until it's done. Sam Sifton, who wrote about it in 2009, called it "a meal you could cook for company and probably ought to, an elegant dinner of no great complication, what the food historian and raconteur John T. Edge calls in the very best sense a Southern woman's dish, devoid of macho chef-man technique and frippery."

You brown some chicken, sprinkle in chopped green pepper, garlic, and curry (Charleston and Savannah were ports for the spice trade), fill in the gaps with tomatoes, and leave it to simmer. When it's almost all cooked down, you put some rice on the stove, then open up a jar of chutney, sprinkle the chicken with almonds (remember to leave out the frippery), and call everyone to the table. Franklin D. Roosevelt was a fan of country captain. So, too, was General Patton. But it was Cecily Brownstone, the Associated Press food writer, who kept the recipe alive for decades. Brownstone got James Beard to teach the recipe at his school and Irma Rombauer to publish it in *The Joy of Cooking*.

¼ cup all-purpose flour

I teaspoon salt

¼ teaspoon freshly ground black pepper

One 2½-pound chicken, cut into serving pieces

4 to 5 tablespoons unsalted butter

⅓ cup finely diced onion

⅓ cup finely diced green bell pepper

I clove garlic, crushed

1½ teaspoons curry powder

½ teaspoon dried thyme

One 14-ounce can stewed tomatoes, with their liquid

Toasted blanched almonds

Bottled chutney, such as Major Grey's

1. Season the flour with the salt and pepper, and dredge the chicken in the flour. Melt 4 tablespoons butter in a large skillet and brown the chicken on all sides; if necessary, add more butter.

2. Remove the chicken from the skillet and add the onion, green pepper, garlic, curry powder, and thyme. Cook briefly, stirring, until the onion wilts, about 3 minutes. Add the tomatoes, with their liquid, return the chicken to the skillet, skin side up, and bring to a simmer. Cover the skillet, lower the heat, and cook until the chicken is tender, about 20 minutes.

3. Sprinkle with toasted almonds and serve with chutney.

SERVES 4

SERVING SUGGESTIONS
Pork Belly Tea Sandwiches (p. 88), Sweet Potatoes Anna (p. 297), Stuck-Pot Rice with Yogurt and Spices (p. 351), A Perfect Batch of Rice (p. 316), Sugar Snap Peas with Horseradish (p. 259), Almond Cake (p. 777), Coconut Pie (p. 801)

AUGUST 15, 1963: "NEW MENUS ARE OFFERED HOME COOK."
—1963

⌒ FRICASSEE OF CHICKEN WITH TARRAGON

Fricassee, a technique now usually called braising, involves a quick browning of meat with aromatics, then filling the pan with wine and broth and shuttling it to the oven, where the textures relax and the flavors intensify. Fricassee of chicken with tarragon is to a French person what fried chicken is to an American Southerner. Not all chicken with tarragon is created equal—this one's magic lies in the addition of fresh nutmeg and thyme and an elegant sauce lavished with cream, lemon, and egg yolks.

---

4 tablespoons unsalted butter

2 cups finely chopped onions

Two 3-pound chickens, cut into serving pieces

Salt and freshly ground black pepper

I clove garlic, finely chopped

I bay leaf

I teaspoon chopped fresh thyme
    or ½ teaspoon dried thyme

½ teaspoon freshly grated nutmeg

3 tablespoons chopped fresh tarragon
    or 2 teaspoons dried tarragon

I bundle tarragon stems, tied with kitchen string
    (optional)

Cayenne pepper

½ cup all-purpose flour

I cup chicken broth

I cup dry white wine

2 cups heavy cream

2 large egg yolks

Juice of ½ lemon, or to taste

Chopped flat-leaf parsley or tarragon

1. Heat the oven to 400 degrees. Melt the butter in a large casserole and add the onion, chicken, salt and pepper to taste, garlic, bay leaf, thyme, nutmeg, tarragon, tarragon stems, if using, and cayenne. Cook, stirring occasionally, for about 5 minutes. Do not brown the chicken.

2. Sprinkle the chicken with the flour and stir until all the pieces are well coated. Add the chicken broth and wine and stir well. Bring to a boil, cover, put in the oven, and bake for 45 to 55 minutes, or until the chicken is fork-tender.

3. Place the casserole on top of the stove again. Skim off excess fat. Add half the cream and bring to a boil. Blend the remaining cream with the egg yolks and stir this into the sauce. Cook for 30 seconds—do not let it boil—then remove from the heat. Season with lemon juice, salt, and pepper. Sprinkle with parsley.

SERVES 6

COOKING NOTES

Use a very large braising pan so you have enough room to move the chicken and other ingredients around—otherwise, it's impossible to disperse the flour in Step 3.

Keep adding lemon until the acid in the sauce and the cream taste good to you.

I'd make a big batch of rice to serve with the chicken—it will soak up the sauce and clean up the somewhat messy-looking dish.

SERVING SUGGESTIONS

Rillettes de Canard (Duck Rillettes; p. 65), Fennel, Orange, Watercress, and Walnut Salad (p. 186), Diana Vreeland's Salade Parisienne (p. 192), Cassolette of Morels, Fiddleheads, and Asparagus (p. 231), A Perfect Batch of Rice (p. 316), Tarte aux Fruits (p. 829), Apple Galette (p. 843), Judson Grill's Berry Clafoutis with Crème Fraîche (p. 844), Chocolate Mousse (p. 820), Almond Cake (p. 777)

FEBRUARY 4, 1968: "STEW À LA FRANÇAISE," BY CRAIG CLAIBORNE.

—1968

⟶ TURKEY WITH NOODLES FLORENTINE

This giant turkey casserole—it serves 24, so get out your lasagna pans—was included in Craig Claiborne's annual roundup of the year's most popular recipes.

———

One 12-pound whole turkey breast or two 5- to 6-pound
    half-breasts, or one 15- to 16-pound whole bird, cut
    into 6 to 8 large pieces
Salt
¼ cup black peppercorns

4 carrots, scraped and trimmed
6 stalks celery
3 to 4 pounds spinach
8 tablespoons (1 stick) plus 5 tablespoons butter
Freshly ground black pepper
¼ teaspoon freshly grated nutmeg
¾ cup all-purpose flour
8 cups strained turkey broth (from Step 1)
    or chicken broth
2 cups heavy cream
One 16-ounce package egg noodles
2 large egg yolks, lightly beaten
1 cup freshly grated Parmesan cheese

1. Place the turkey in a large pot and add cold water to cover, salt to taste, the peppercorns, carrots, and celery. Bring to a boil, reduce the heat, and simmer until the turkey is tender, 2 hours for a 12-pound breast (two 5-pound breasts, cooked in separate pots, should be simmered for 1 hour; a 16-pound bird in pieces will take 1½ hours for breasts, 3½ hours for legs). Do not overcook. Transfer the turkey to a platter.

2. While the turkey is cooking, rinse the spinach and place in a covered saucepan. Cook over medium heat just until wilted. Drain, run under cold water, and press between your hands to remove the moisture. Toss the spinach in 2 tablespoons butter. Season with salt, pepper, and nutmeg.

3. Remove the turkey from the bones. Cut meat into bite-sized cubes.

4. Melt 8 tablespoons butter in a large saucepan and add the flour, stirring with a whisk. When blended, add the stock, stirring rapidly with the whisk. Simmer gently, stirring frequently, until the sauce has concentrated but isn't thick, about 45 minutes. Stir in the cream and continue cooking, stirring, for about 10 minutes.

5. Meanwhile, cook the noodles in boiling salted water until al dente. Do not overcook, since they will be reheated in the sauce. Drain the noodles and run under cold running water. Drain well.

6. Heat the oven to 400 degrees. Using a large casserole or 2 smaller ones, total capacity about 10 quarts, make layers of the noodles, spinach, and turkey until all the ingredients are used. Pour half the sauce over the layers and stir with a two-pronged fork.

7. Combine the yolks with the remaining sauce and pour over all. Sprinkle with the grated cheese and dot with the remaining 3 tablespoons butter.

8. Bake the casserole until heated through. Run the casserole under the broiler just until the cheese is golden brown.

SERVES 24

COOKING NOTE

Use the turkey broth from cooking the turkey parts—no need to buy or make more separately.

SERVING SUGGESTIONS

Green Goddess Salad (p. 176), Fennel, Orange, Watercress, and Walnut Salad (p. 186), Teddie's Apple Cake (p. 752)

JULY 7, 1968: "CROWD PLEASER," BY CRAIG CLAIBORNE.

—1968

CHICKEN CANZANESE

Any food historian will tell you that trying to track down the origin of a recipe is like chasing tadpoles. There are so many, and they all look alike. Even when you find what seems to be the original source, you can't necessarily believe it because adapting recipes is an age-old industry. Nonetheless, I thought I'd give the hunt a try with chicken Canzanese, an unusual recipe that ran in the *Times* in 1969.

A Google search for "chicken Canzanese" yielded many results, a number of them facsimiles, or slight variations of the chicken dish that appeared in the *Times*. There's one on Cooks.com that's a close adaptation of the *Times*'s recipe, another by Mario Batali on the Food Network's website and one by Anna Teresa Callen, the cookbook author and teacher, on her own website. Batali's and Callen's, which vary only slightly from the *Times*'s recipe, are nearly word for word the same. Only one recipe that I found sourced the *Times*'s recipe, which itself came from Ed Giobbi, a cookbook author, and was written about by Craig Claiborne.

You can also find plenty of turkey recipes done in the style of Canzanese (Canzano is in the Abruzzo region in Italy), which refers to braised turkey, served cold with chopped turkey aspic. But chicken Canzanese, which is not mentioned in important Italian cookbooks like *Le Ricette Regionali Italiane* (*Italian Regional Cooking*), is completely different. When you make it, you

understand why it's still kicking around after all these decades. After flash-brining the chicken, you throw everything into the pan at the same time—chicken, cubed prosciutto, sage, bay leaves, rosemary, garlic, chile, cloves, peppercorns, and wine—and end up with a dish that has the fragrance of Chinese steamed duck and the succulence of a Bolognese sauce.

I sensed that it would be impossible to come to a conclusion about where chicken Canzanese originated (Giobbi's recipe was the earliest I could find), and this was confirmed as soon as I started calling people. Callen said she grew up in Abruzzo eating chicken Canzanese. Batali, who regularly credits people from whom he adapts recipes, said that he must have gotten his from Callen, and was apologetic about the borrowing. Giobbi, whose recipe came from a family friend in Abruzzo, suggested that perhaps Callen was influenced by him. When I asked Callen if there was any chance she referred to Giobbi's recipe when writing about her family's dish, she said, "Could be, very well." I didn't intend this to be an investigation—recipes are adapted all the time, it's one of the primary ways cuisines evolve—so I did not chase down the dozens of sites that appear to have copied Callen or Batali. One thing is clear, though: a good recipe has a thousand fathers, but a bad one is an orphan.

———

Kosher or coarse sea salt
One 3-pound chicken, cut into serving pieces
2 sage leaves
2 bay leaves
1 clove garlic, sliced lengthwise
6 whole cloves
2 sprigs fresh rosemary or ½ teaspoon dried rosemary
12 black peppercorns, crushed
1 dried hot red chile, broken and seeded
One ⅛-inch-thick slice prosciutto (about 4 ounces)
½ cup dry white wine
¼ cup water

1. Add 3 tablespoons kosher salt or coarse sea salt to a large bowl. Dissolve in about ½ cup warm water. Lay the chicken pieces in the bowl and cover with cold water (about 4 cups). Let stand for about 1 hour. Drain and pat dry.
2. Arrange the chicken pieces in one layer in a skillet and add the sage, bay leaves, garlic, cloves, rosemary,

peppercorns, and red pepper. Cut the prosciutto into small cubes and sprinkle it over the chicken. Add the wine and water. Do not add salt, since the prosciutto will season the dish. Cover and simmer until the chicken is just cooked through, 30 to 35 minutes.

3. Remove the chicken to a plate and reduce the cooking juices until concentrated and a little syrupy—taste it to see. Serve the chicken in shallow bowls with the juices (and slivered garlic and prosciutto) spooned on top. Mop up juices with country bread.

SERVES 2, OR 4 IF THERE ARE LOTS OF
OTHER DISHES

COOKING NOTES

A great chicken dish deserves (and depends on) a great chicken—buy the highest-quality bird you can find. The best place to look is a farmers' market.

The chicken never browns, so if presentation is your thing, avert your eyes—or simply pull the meat from the bones and make a warm salad with escarole, the broth, and prosciutto. Or use the meat and sauce to make a very simple pasta dish. Whatever you do, be careful not to overcook the chicken. And serve it right after cooking, when its aromatics are most intense.

The original recipe said it serves 4, but when I made the dish for my mother and me, we polished off the whole thing. Only count on it serving 4 if you're making a bunch of side dishes.

It may seem strange to buy expensive prosciutto and cut it into cubes, but don't skimp on the quality of prosciutto. I did once and was punished with a salty sauce. If you can only get indifferent prosciutto, add less of it.

SERVING SUGGESTIONS

Ricotta Crostini with Lemon Zest and Hazelnut (p. 94), Zuppa di Funghi Siciliana (p. 127), Fried Artichokes Azzurro (p. 229), Italian Roast Potatoes (p. 300), Balducci's Tiramisù (p. 830)

READERS

"I remember that I used the recipe the first time because chicken was affordable for a crowd and the ingredients then seemed different but not weird. This recipe as I read and reread it over the years pushed me to learn more about cooking. Why not brown the chicken pieces? (Giobbi does not.) What about put-ting it all together and sticking it in the oven? What if I chopped the seasonings and put them in the cavity and under the skin of a roasting chicken and then, well, roasted it? The recipe with its time-proven flavors (back to the Renaissance at least?) has never failed.

"For me, this is one of those recipes that permutes endlessly as the seasons, the occasion, or the cook's mood changes. Sometimes (often) I do brown the chicken, sometimes use pancetta instead of prosciutto, sometimes add a little chopped tomato, sometimes introduce porcini mushrooms. If the company at dinner have dietary restrictions, oil-cured black olives can stand in for the pork. I have tried it with boneless chicken breasts only—satisfactory—and with guinea hen—excellent."

From Jonatha Ceely, e-mail

MAY 18, 1969: "CHICKEN BIG," BY CRAIG CLAIBORNE. RECIPE BY ED GIOBBI, WHO ADAPTED IT FROM A FAMILY FRIEND IN ITALY.

—1969

⌒ LEE LUM'S LEMON CHICKEN

Lee Lum was the chef at Pearl's Chinese Restaurant in Manhattan. Don't balk at his ingredient list, just make the recipe—a strange and sublime dinner awaits you. I took out the teaspoon of MSG; I have the feeling you'll forgive me.

8 small or 6 large boneless, skinless chicken breasts
2 tablespoons light soy sauce
¼ teaspoon Asian sesame oil
1 teaspoon salt
1 tablespoon gin or vodka
3 large egg whites
1 cup water-chestnut flour or powder
    (available at Asian markets)
Peanut or salad oil for frying
¾ cup sugar
½ cup white vinegar
1 cup chicken broth
1 tablespoon cornstarch, dissolved in 2 tablespoons water
Finely chopped zest and juice of 1 lemon

¼ head iceberg lettuce, finely chopped

3 small carrots, peeled and cut into julienne

½ large green bell pepper, cut into julienne

3 scallions, cut into julienne

½ cup shredded canned pineapple

One 1-ounce bottle lemon extract

1. Place the chicken in a shallow earthenware dish or bowl. Combine the soy sauce, sesame oil, salt, and gin and pour over the chicken. Toss to coat and let sit for 30 minutes.

2. Drain the chicken and discard the marinade. Beat the egg whites until frothy in a bowl. Add chicken pieces and toss to coat. Place the water chestnut flour on a plate and coat the chicken pieces with the flour.

3. Add ½ inch of peanut oil to a large skillet and heat to about 350 degrees. Carefully add the chicken pieces, a few at a time if necessary, and brown one side, then turn and brown the other, about 10 minutes total. Drain on paper towels.

4. Meanwhile, place the sugar, vinegar, broth, cornstarch mixture, and lemon zest and juice in a small pan and bring to a boil, stirring until the mixture thickens.

5. Cut the chicken into 1-inch crosswise slices and place it on top of the shredded lettuce on a serving platter. (If necessary, keep it warm in a 200-degree oven.)

6. Add the vegetables and pineapple to the sauce and return to a simmer, just to reheat. Remove from the heat, stir in the extract, and pour over the chicken.

SERVES 4

COOKING NOTE

Wisely anticipating people's doubt about the large amount of lemon extract he called for, Craig Claiborne attached this note to the recipe: "This amount of lemon extract is accurate. It should be added at the very last moment."

SERVING SUGGESTIONS

Oriental Watercress Soup (p. 111), Jasmine Tea Rice (p. 354), Chinese Barbecued Spareribs (p. 517), Tea Ice Cream (p. 717)

SEPTEMBER 14, 1969: "ORIENTAL TANG," BY CRAIG CLAIBORNE. RECIPE ADAPTED FROM LEE LUM, THE CHEF AT PEARL'S CHINESE RESTAURANT IN NEW YORK CITY.

—1969

CHICKEN WINGS WITH OYSTER SAUCE

This recipe comes from the period when we were just dipping our toes in Asian cooking—when any recipe containing scallions, ginger, and soy sauce connoted the Far East. Although this dish may now seem comically Westernized, it's still fragrant and succulent and simple in its Asian-esque way.

————

8 chicken wings

1 tablespoon cornstarch

3 tablespoons peanut, vegetable, or corn oil

1 tablespoon dark soy sauce

1 teaspoon sugar

¼ cup chicken broth

1 teaspoon minced garlic

1 tablespoon finely chopped fresh ginger

½ cup chopped scallions

2 tablespoons oyster sauce

3 tablespoons water

1 tablespoon Shaoxing wine or dry sherry

1. Cut off and discard the small tips of the wings. Cut the main wing bone from the second joint and reserve both.

2. Put the pieces in a bowl and add 2 teaspoons cornstarch and 1 tablespoon oil, the dark soy sauce, and the sugar. Blend well.

3. Heat the remaining 2 tablespoons of oil in a wok or skillet. Add the chicken mixture and cook, stirring, for about 5 minutes, taking care that the sauce does not burn. Add the chicken broth, cover, and cook for 5 to 10 minutes or until chicken pieces are cooked through. Remove the chicken and set aside.

4. Reduce the liquid in the wok to a glaze. Add the garlic, ginger, and scallion and cook, stirring, until softened. Add the oyster sauce and 2 tablespoons water.

5. Blend the remaining cornstarch with the remaining tablespoon of water and stir this in. Add the wine. Return the chicken wings to the pan and stir over high heat to coat with the sauce.

SERVES 4 AS A FIRST COURSE

SERVING SUGGESTIONS

Chinese Barbecued Spareribs (p. 517), Jasmine Tea Rice (p. 354), Stir-Fried Collards (p. 254), Chilled Sesame Spinach (p. 239), Warm Eggplant Salad with Sesame and Shallots (p. 203), Lemon Lotus Ice Cream (p. 724)

JANUARY 21, 1979: "WINGING IT," BY CRAIG CLAIBORNE WITH PIERRE FRANEY.

—1979

✎ CHICKEN PAPRIKASH

This classic is incomplete without buttered noodles.

————

One 3-pound chicken, cut into serving pieces
Salt and freshly ground black pepper
2 tablespoons unsalted butter
1 cup thinly sliced onions
1 tablespoon finely minced garlic
1 tablespoon sweet paprika
$\frac{1}{2}$ cup chicken broth
1 cup sour cream
1 tablespoon all-purpose flour

1. Sprinkle the chicken with salt and pepper to taste. Melt the butter in a large heavy skillet. Add the chicken pieces skin side down and cook over moderately high heat until browned, 5 to 10 minutes. Turn the pieces and continue cooking for about 5 minutes, until brown on the second side.
2. Scatter the onions and garlic around the chicken pieces. Sprinkle with paprika and stir. Add the chicken broth, cover, and let simmer for 10 minutes or longer until chicken is done. Remove the chicken to a warm serving dish. Pour off excess fat.
3. Blend the sour cream and flour and stir it into the sauce. Simmer, stirring, for about 1 minute. Pour the sauce over the chicken.

SERVES 4

VARIATION
Try this with smoked paprika (pimentón), either the sweet or the spicy.

SERVING SUGGESTIONS

Smoked Mackerel on Toasts (p. 80), Vichyssoise à la Ritz (p. 111), Cucumbers in Cream (p. 225), Confit of Carrot and Cumin (p. 244), Gingersnaps (p. 679), Delicate Bread Pudding (p. 798), Apple Galette (p. 843)

JANUARY 6, 1980: "FOOD: THERE'S MORE TO PAPRIKA THAN COLOR," BY CRAIG CLAIBORNE WITH PIERRE FRANEY.

—1980

✎ ED GIOBBI'S RABBIT CACCIATORA

Ed Giobbi, an artist and accomplished cook who lives in Katonah, New York, was one of a handful of Craig Claiborne's recipe pinch hitters. Every few years, he'd give Craig a stellar recipe that Claiborne's readers would then remain loyal to for decades. (See Chicken Canzanese on p. 458, Ed Giobbi's Sweet Red Pepper Sauce for Pasta on p. 318, and, though his claim to its authorship is controversial, the Spaghetti Primavera on p. 314.) This rabbit cacciatore is another one of them—and it exemplifies what makes Giobbi such a fine cook. His cacciatore hews closely to any classic version: you brown the rabbit, braise it with tomatoes and mushrooms, and add red pepper flakes to give the sauce a pulse of heat. But Giobbi slips an extra step into the recipe: he has you soak dried mushrooms and layer them and the rehydrating broth into the sauce. The dried mushrooms act something like a dye, saturating the sauce with a warm earthy aroma, making the heat of the red pepper flakes all the more integral. Giobbi also has you cook the regular mushrooms separately, ridding them of moisture that might otherwise dilute the sauce.

————

8 dried mushrooms, preferably porcini
1 rabbit (3$\frac{1}{2}$ to 4 pounds), cut into serving pieces, liver reserved (see Cooking Notes)
Salt and freshly ground black pepper
$\frac{1}{4}$ cup olive oil
4 tablespoons unsalted butter
$\frac{1}{2}$ teaspoon crushed red pepper flakes (optional)
1 tablespoon finely chopped garlic

1 cup dry white wine

1 tablespoon chopped fresh rosemary or
    1 1/2 teaspoon dried rosemary

1/4 pound mushrooms, trimmed and thinly sliced
    (about 2 cups)

2 cups canned Italian tomatoes

1. Place the dried mushrooms in a bowl and add hot water to cover. Let stand for about 20 minutes, or until softened.

2. Sprinkle the rabbit pieces with salt and pepper to taste. Heat half the oil and half the butter in a large heavy skillet. Add the rabbit pieces and cook, turning occasionally, until golden brown on all sides, about 10 minutes.

3. Sprinkle the rabbit with the red pepper flakes, if using, and garlic. Add the wine, bring to a boil, and cook until reduced by half. Sprinkle the rabbit with the rosemary. Drain the dried mushrooms, reserving about 2 tablespoons of soaking liquid. Squeeze the mushrooms to extract most of the moisture and add them to the rabbit. Add the reserved 2 tablespoons soaking liquid, cover, and cook for 10 minutes.

4. Meanwhile, melt the remaining butter in a large skillet and add the fresh mushrooms. Cook until wilted, then continue cooking until most of the mushroom liquid evaporates.

5. Add the mushrooms to the rabbit. Add the tomatoes and salt and pepper to taste, cover, and cook for about 30 minutes. Ten minutes before the rabbit is done, add the liver to the pan. Once the liver is cooked through, remove it from the pan, thinly slice it, and then return it to the finished dish.

6. Sprinkle the dish with the remaining olive oil and serve, preferably, with polenta.

SERVES 4

COOKING NOTES

If your rabbit is small, as mine was, use 2. If it comes without the liver, chicken liver may be used in its place.

And if the rabbit is frozen, let it defrost overnight in the refrigerator.

SERVING SUGGESTIONS

Fried Olives (p. 87), Italian Salad (p. 177), Artichoke Salad with Anchovy and Capers (p. 174), Fennel and Apple Salad with Juniper (p. 189), Soft Polenta (p. 556), Bolzano Apple Cake (p. 783), Cornmeal Biscotti (p. 696)

JANUARY 23, 1980: "SIX RECIPES FROM ACROSS THE ATLANTIC FOR PREPARING RABBIT," BY CRAIG CLAIBORNE. RECIPE ADAPTED FROM ED GIOBBI.

—1980

☞ CHICKEN BETTY'S FRIED CHICKEN AND GRAVY

The chicken fries to a deep nut brown, and if you season it well, you get that salty, sticky skin that's the hallmark of excellent fried chicken. Don't be turned off by the nine steps in the recipe—think of it as one small peak to climb in your effort to conquer the kitchen.

———

For the Chicken

One 3- to 3 1/4-pound chicken

1 large egg

2/3 cup whole milk

About 1 1/2 cups all-purpose flour

3/4 to 1 cup lard

3/4 to 1 cup vegetable shortening

1 1/2 tablespoons salt

2 tablespoons freshly ground black pepper

For the Gravy

2 scant tablespoons all-purpose flour

2 to 3 cups whole milk

Salt and freshly ground black pepper

1. The chicken should be cut into 9 pieces that include the backbone, 2 thighs, 2 breasts, 2 drumsticks, and 2 wings. Pat each piece thoroughly dry. To be thoroughly cooked in the time indicated here, the chicken should be close to room temperature; remove it from the refrigerator 20 to 30 minutes before it is to be prepared for frying.

2. Beat the egg with the milk in a wide bowl. Have on hand a plate or a sheet of wax paper on which to season the chicken. Place the flour in a baking pan that is roughly 9 by 13 inches.

3. Combine 3/4 cup lard and 3/4 cup vegetable shorten-

ing in a 12-inch skillet, preferably made of black cast iron, set over medium-high heat. You want the melted fat to reach a depth of $\frac{1}{2}$ to 1 inch. This will vary with the size of the pan you use, so adjust the amount of fats if necessary, keeping the half-and-half proportion of lard and vegetable shortening.

4. Dip each piece of chicken into the egg-and-milk liquid, covering both sides of each piece. Let the excess drip off slightly, then place the chicken on the plate or wax paper and season liberally on both sides with salt and pepper. Place the pieces of seasoned chicken in the pan of flour.

5. Turn the chicken, a few pieces at a time, in the flour until thoroughly coated on all sides. Press and thump the chicken into the flour as you turn it so the flour adheres to all sides. Tap the floured pieces of chicken against each other gently to shake off excess flour, and place in the hot fat. Chicken pieces should not be crammed in the pan, but they can be fairly close.

6. Fry the chicken until golden brown on one side, then turn and brown the second side. It should take 6 to 7 minutes to brown each side, so adjust the heat accordingly. The chicken will brown further as it cooks and the final result should be a deep copper color without any hint of blackness. When the chicken is golden brown on both sides, place a splatter screen on top if you have one. Reduce the heat so the frying continues steadily but gently. Allow 5 to 10 minutes frying time after you cover the pan. Turn the pieces several times during that period and lower the heat if the chicken browns too quickly. Add fat, if necessary, to keep the chicken "swimming."

7. Drain the chicken on paper towels. Continue frying until all pieces are done. If you must fry the chicken in more than one batch, keep the fried pieces hot by placing them on a rack on a baking sheet in a preheated 250-degree oven.

8. To make the gravy, pour off all but 2 tablespoons of the fat, leaving the browned flour in the pan. (If you have used 2 frying pans, pour off the fat from both and combine the browned particles in one pan.) Place the pan over low heat until the fat is simmering. Stir in the flour and cook, stirring constantly, for 7 to 8 minutes, or until the flour browns and the mixture is a thick paste. Pour in about $1\frac{1}{2}$ cups milk. Stir with a whisk and simmer until the gravy is smooth and fairly thick. Add salt and pepper to taste. The gravy should

simmer for 7 or 8 minutes more, so additional milk will be necessary to achieve the consistency of very heavy cream. Adjust the seasonings; the gravy should be very peppery and a creamy cocoa brown in color.

9. Serve the chicken in a basket lined with paper napkins or towels. Serve the gravy in a heated gravy boat. The sauce should be spooned over homemade baking powder biscuits and/or stiff, buttery mashed potatoes, not over the chicken. Coleslaw provides a refreshing contrast in flavor and texture.

SERVES 2 TO 3

COOKING NOTES

The original recipe called for MSG. I took it out.

Mimi Sheraton said, "If you fry 2 chickens, use 1 jumbo egg and 1 cup of milk, plus an extra cup of flour for dredging. All the other ingredients can be doubled. If you use 2 pans for frying, keep the breasts in one and thighs and drumsticks in another. Giblets, wings, and backbones can be fried when other pieces are done, as they will cook thoroughly in about 10 minutes after they have browned."

I used kosher salt and crushed a variety of peppercorns (red, green, white, and black—because I didn't have enough black in the house) in a mortar and pestle, which worked very well.

You will want more than this recipe makes. I'd suggest doubling it—2 chickens, 2 pans.

To save time, have your butcher cut up the chicken.

When frying the chicken, adjust the heat so the fat creates a foamy bubble, not a rapid one. If you can't fit all the chicken pieces in the pan, set aside the wings; once the other pieces cook and shrink a little, you can add them, and they cook faster because they're smaller.

After you fry the chicken, the fat in the pan will be very hot. You can either serve the chicken without gravy or keep the chicken warm in a 250-degree oven while you let the fat cool down a little and then make the gravy.

The backbone is worth frying—great for picking!

SERVING SUGGESTIONS

Mimi Sheraton, who wrote about this fried chicken, said the gravy is to be served over biscuits—try the Old South Buttermilk Biscuits (p. 655). For a menu:

Jay Grelen's Southern Iced Tea (p. 27), Mint Julep (p. 24), Julia Harrison Adams's Pimento Cheese Spread (p. 64), Málaga Gazpacho (p. 112), Iceberg Lettuce with Smoked Bacon and Buttermilk Dressing (p. 200), Ice-Cold Tomatoes with Basil (p. 234), French Potato Salad (p. 277), Red Velvet Cake (p. 757).

READERS

"'You made this with LARD???' People cannot believe they are being fed something so politically incorrect. But they love it. (Nowadays Mario Batali serves lardo pizza, a welcome swing of the pendulum.) Not much to say about this recipe. It is perfection, and impossible to ruin because of its depth of detail."

Reynold Weidenaar, New York, NY, e-mail

MAY 18, 1980: "KANSAS CITY'S PIED PIPER OF CHICKEN-DOM," BY MIMI SHERATON. RECIPE ADAPTED FROM CHICKEN BETTY LUCAS OF KANSAS CITY, MISSOURI.

—1980

JANICE OKUN'S BUFFALO CHICKEN WINGS

The precise origin of the Buffalo chicken wing—the tasty morsel that spawned a national franchise with scantily clad servers—has eluded food writers for decades. It has been repeated so often that these wings were invented at the Anchor Bar on Main Street in Buffalo that pretty much everyone accepted it as the truth. There has been less consensus, however, about whether the wings were created when a mistaken delivery of wings arrived at the bar and Frank Bellissimo asked his wife, Teressa, to do something with them. Or when Dom, their son, asked his mother to concoct a late-night snack for regulars at the bar. Either way, it was Teressa who in 1964 came up with the idea of combining spicy wings with crisp celery and blue cheese dressing.

In 1980, however, Calvin Trillin, a writer for *The New Yorker*, came across John Young, a man who claimed to have invented the spicy sauce (but not the celery and blue cheese part). His wings were blanketed with what he called "mambo sauce" and his restaurant, John Young's Wings 'n Things, was open in Buffalo around the time the dish became famous.

Buffalo itself has wisely avoided taking sides in the debate. The city simply declared July 29 "Chicken Wing Day" and left it at that.

———

24 chicken wings (about 4 pounds)
Salt and freshly ground pepper
4 cups peanut, vegetable, or corn oil for deep-frying
4 tablespoons unsalted butter
2 to 5 tablespoons (one 2½-ounce bottle)
    Frank's Louisiana Red Hot Sauce
1 tablespoon white vinegar
Blue Cheese Dressing (recipe follows)
Celery sticks

1. Set the chicken wings out on the counter 30 minutes before cooking. Cut off and discard the small tip of each wing. Cut the main wing bone and second wing bone apart at the joint. Sprinkle the wings with salt and pepper.
2. Heat the oil in a deep-fat fryer or large casserole. When it is quite hot, add half the wings and cook for 7 to 9 minutes, stirring occasionally. When the chicken wings are golden brown and crisp, remove them and drain well on paper towels. Repeat with the remaining wings.
3. Melt the butter in a small saucepan and add hot sauce to taste and the vinegar. Put the chicken wings on a warm serving platter and pour the butter mixture over them. Serve with the blue cheese dressing and celery sticks.

SERVES 4 TO 6

BLUE CHEESE DRESSING

1 cup homemade mayonnaise (recipe follows)
    or store-bought mayonnaise
2 tablespoons finely chopped onion
1 teaspoon minced garlic
¼ cup finely chopped flat-leaf parsley
1 cup sour cream
1 tablespoon fresh lemon juice
1 tablespoon white vinegar
¼ cup crumbled blue cheese, or more to taste
Salt and freshly ground black pepper to taste
Cayenne pepper to taste

Combine all of the ingredients in a bowl. Add more blue cheese if desired. Chill for an hour or longer.

MAKES ABOUT 2½ CUPS

MAYONNAISE

I large egg yolk
Salt and freshly ground black pepper
I teaspoon imported mustard, such as Dijon or Düsseldorf
I teaspoon cider vinegar or fresh lemon juice
I cup peanut, vegetable, or olive oil

Place the yolk in a bowl and add salt and pepper to taste, the mustard, and vinegar. Beat vigorously for a second or two with a wire whisk or electric beater. Start adding the oil gradually, beating continuously with the whisk or electric beater. Continue beating and adding the oil until all of it is used.

MAKES ABOUT I CUP

COOKING NOTE
The recipe called for 2 to 5 tablespoons hot sauce; I added 3 tablespoons.

SERVING SUGGESTIONS
The Bone (p. 34), Sir Francis Drake (p. 36), Spoonbread's Potato Salad (p. 288), Green Goddess Salad (p. 176), Macaroni with Ham and Cheese (p. 319), Chocolate Pudding (p. 858)

AUGUST 30, 1981: "WINGING IT IN BUFFALO," BY CRAIG CLAIBORNE WITH PIERRE FRANEY. RECIPE ADAPTED FROM JANICE OKUN, FOOD EDITOR OF THE *BUFFALO EVENING NEWS*.

—1981

⌒ BREADED CHICKEN BREASTS WITH PARMESAN CHEESE

You can also make this dish with pork or veal cutlets. They'll cook more quickly.

————

4 small skinless, boneless chicken breast halves (about 1¼ pounds total)
Salt and freshly-ground black pepper
2 tablespoons all-purpose flour
I large egg
2 tablespoons water
I cup coarse fresh bread crumbs
¼ cup freshly grated Parmesan cheese
2 tablespoons corn, peanut, or vegetable oil
4 tablespoons unsalted butter
I tablespoon finely chopped tarragon
2 tablespoons fresh lemon juice

1. Cut away and discard any white membranes or traces of fat from the breast halves. Sprinkle each with salt and pepper. Put the flour in a shallow dish. Dip the breasts in the flour. Coat well, and shake off the excess.
2. Combine the egg with the water and salt and pepper to taste in another shallow dish and beat to blend. Combine the bread crumbs with the Parmesan cheese in a third dish and blend.
3. Dip the breast halves in the egg mixture, coating thoroughly. Drain off excess. Dip the pieces in the bread crumb mixture, also coating thoroughly. Pat the pieces lightly with the side of a large knife to make the crumbs adhere.
4. Heat the oil in a large skillet, preferably nonstick, over medium-high heat. Add the breasts (do this in 2 batches, if necessary) and cook until golden brown on one side, 3 to 4 minutes. Turn and cook for 2 to 3 minutes, or until golden brown on the second side.
5. Transfer the chicken to a warm platter; pour off the fat, if there is any, from the skillet. Add the butter and cook until bubbling. Add the tarragon and lemon juice; blend. Pour the sauce over the chicken.

SERVES 4

If the chicken breasts are large, slice them crosswise in half.

I like the technique in Step 3 of seasoning the egg, rather than the flour, because it ensures more evenly seasoned chicken, and is a tip that can be applied to all breading recipes.

SERVING SUGGESTIONS
Artichauts Vinaigrette (p. 225), Fettuccine with Preserved Lemon and Roasted Garlic (p. 335), Zucchini and Vermouth (p. 227), Orzo with Pine Nuts and Basil (p. 325), Italian Roast Potatoes (p. 300), Zabaglione (p. 813), Ricotta Kisses (p. 852)

AUGUST 12, 1987: "60-MINUTE GOURMET," BY PIERRE FRANEY.

—1987

∕ RABBIT IN MUSTARD SAUCE

The mustard is wiped off the rabbit before cooking, a step I was sure would spell doom but the mustard flavor really comes through in the finished dish. I'd happily eat the succulent sauce over pasta. Alternatively, serve the whole dish with pasta: I spooned it over angel hair egg noodles tossed with olive oil and a little of the pasta water.

½ cup Dijon mustard

1 rabbit (about 3½ pounds), cut into 6 or 7 pieces

2 slices bacon, diced

1 onion, minced

½ cup all-purpose flour

2 tablespoons unsalted butter

2 cups dry white wine

3 cups chicken broth

½ teaspoon dried thyme

½ teaspoon dried rosemary

1 bay leaf

¼ cup heavy cream

Salt if needed

Freshly ground black pepper

2 tablespoons minced flat-leaf parsley

1. Rub the mustard all over the rabbit. Let rest in the refrigerator for 3 hours.

2. About 15 minutes before the rabbit is ready, sauté the bacon in a large deep skillet until crisp. Remove the bacon with a slotted spoon. Add the onion and cook until translucent, about 5 minutes. Scrape into a bowl and reserve. Set the skillet aside.

3. Wipe the mustard off the rabbit. Toss the rabbit with the flour. Add half the butter to the skillet and set over medium heat. Working in 2 batches, and adding the remaining butter for the second batch, sauté the rabbit pieces until golden on both sides, about 8 minutes for each batch. Remove the rabbit from pan and set aside.

4. Pour the wine into the pan and bring to a simmer over medium-high heat while scraping up the browned bits from the bottom of the pan. Add the chicken broth, thyme, rosemary, and bay leaf. Add the rabbit and onions and bring to a simmer, then reduce the heat so the liquid barely simmers. Cook until the rabbit is tender, about 1 hour, skimming the surface as necessary.

5. Remove the rabbit from the pan. Increase the heat and simmer the sauce until thickened, about 10 minutes. Stir in the cream and simmer for 2 minutes. Stir in salt if needed and pepper. Remove the bay leaf.

6. Return the rabbit and bacon to the pan and stir in the parsley. Serve with noodles.

SERVES 4

COOKING NOTE
To make your guests happier, you may want to take the rabbit meat off the bones in Step 5 before returning the meat to the sauce.

SERVING SUGGESTIONS
Claret Cup (p. 12), Ricotta Crostini with Fresh Thyme and Dried Oregano (p. 93), Butter-Braised Asparagus and Oyster Mushrooms with Peas and Tarragon (p. 262), Breton Butter Cake (p. 777), Lemon-Almond Butter Cake (p. 780)

FEBRUARY 7, 1993: "FOOD: RABBIT IS RICH," BY MOLLY O'NEILL.

—1993

QUAIL WITH ROSEMARY ON SOFT POLENTA

People see game in the title of a recipe and immediately think: project. Not here. These quail take 5 minutes to prep and 10 minutes to cook.

For the Quail

8 quail, wing tips removed
12 sprigs rosemary
Salt and freshly ground black pepper
16 thin slices pancetta

For the Polenta

3¾ cups water
¾ teaspoon salt
¾ cup yellow cornmeal

1. To prepare the quail, preheat the oven to 425 degrees. Place 1 sprig of rosemary in the cavity of each quail, cutting the sprigs as needed to fit. Put the quail in a roasting pan and drape 2 slices of pancetta atop each quail. Set aside.
2. To prepare the polenta, combine the water and salt in a medium saucepan and bring to a boil over medium heat. Whisking constantly, add the cornmeal very gradually, pouring it in a light, steady stream. Change from the whisk to a wooden spoon, reduce the heat so that the mixture is at a slow simmer, and stir constantly until the polenta thickens, about 10 minutes. Remove from the heat and cover to keep warm.
3. Meanwhile, when the polenta is almost done, place the quail in the oven and roast for 12 minutes, then brown under the broiler (at least 5 inches from the flame) for 1 to 3 minutes, depending on how rare you want it.
4. Divide the polenta among 4 plates, top each serving with 2 quail, and garnish with a sprig of rosemary.

SERVES 4

COOKING NOTE

After roasting the quail, I crisped the skin for 3 minutes under the broiler (about 6 inches from the flame).

SERVING SUGGESTIONS

Puntarelle with Anchovies (p. 194), Panna Cotta (p. 840)

PERIOD DETAIL

Polenta is a staple of the *Times* recipe archives. In the nineteenth century, the paper ran a recipe similar to this one for a "ragout of small birds" served with squares of fried polenta. Bob the Sea Cook, a frequent receipe contributor of the period, wrote, "There used to be in my time, in Milan, in the poorer quarters, people going around in the market places with great big pots of mush—that was all it was—which was yellow as gold." This mush, of course, was polenta. Bob offered a recipe for sausages served with a heap of soft polenta. I tried it, but it was so simple—even simpler than this quail one—that I felt no recipe was required.

DECEMBER 12, 1993: "FOOD: RUFFLING SOME FEATHERS," BY MOLLY O'NEILL.

—1993

ROAST CHICKEN WITH BREAD SALAD

I joked at one point that this book should be called *Chicken and Dessert*, because the thousands of recipes that readers suggested were so dominated by these two categories. I reached a point where I vowed not to add a single more chicken dish to the book. But what vow, other than marriage, is ever really kept? I broke my promise for this dish, and I have no regrets. This chicken, which comes from Judy Rodgers, the owner of Zuni Café in San Francisco, is legendary. The night before cooking the chicken, you slip garlic and thyme under the skin and generously season the bird. The following day it comes out of the oven in a fragrant cloud, with skin as crisp as parchment.

The bread salad is also delicious, a smart flavor grid of warm toasted bread cubes, sautéed scallions and garlic, bitter greens, and dried currants. I won't say it's an easy salad to make—it'll fill your sink with bowls, measuring spoons, and baking vessels. But if you want your chicken to turn out the way Rodgers's does, then suck it up.

For the Chicken

One 2½-pound chicken
1½ teaspoons salt
Freshly ground black pepper
4 sprigs thyme
4 cloves garlic, lightly crushed

For the Salad

1 teaspoon red wine vinegar
1 tablespoon warm water
1 tablespoon currants
6 cups stale Tuscan-style bread cut into 1-inch cubes
    (most of the crust removed)
1½ tablespoons olive oil
2 teaspoons Dijon mustard
¼ cup Champagne vinegar
½ teaspoon salt
Freshly ground black pepper
3 cloves garlic, slivered
4 scallions, thinly sliced
3 cups mixed young bitter greens,
    like arugula, chicory, and/or frisée

1. To prepare the chicken, the day before serving, sprinkle the chicken with the salt and pepper. Run your fingers between the skin and flesh over the breasts and legs to make 4 small pockets. Place a sprig of thyme and a garlic clove in each pocket. Wrap the chicken in plastic and refrigerate overnight.

2. About 2 hours before serving, start the salad: Heat the broiler. Combine the red wine vinegar and warm water in a small bowl. Add the currants and let stand for 1 hour.

3. Meanwhile, place the bread in a large bowl and toss with 2 teaspoons olive oil. Spread on a baking sheet and toast the bread under the broiler for about 2 minutes; set aside.

4. Heat the oven to 425 degrees. Place the chicken breast side up in a shallow roasting pan. Roast for 30 minutes.

5. Turn the chicken over and roast until the juices run clear when the chicken is pricked in the thickest part of the thigh, about 15 to 20 minutes longer. Let stand for 10 minutes. (Leave the oven on.)

6. Meanwhile, whisk together the mustard, Champagne vinegar, salt and pepper in a large bowl. Slowly whisk in 2 teaspoons olive oil. Add the bread and toss to coat. Set aside.

7. Heat the remaining ½ teaspoon of olive oil in a small nonstick saucepan over medium heat. Add the garlic and scallions and cook for 2 minutes. Drain the currants and toss them in the bread mixture, along with the scallions and garlic. Place the salad in a baking dish.

8. When the chicken is done, place the salad in the oven and bake for 5 minutes. Turn off the oven and leave the salad in for 10 minutes.

9. Meanwhile, carve the chicken into 8 pieces, reserving the pan juices.

10. Toss the salad with 2 tablespoons of the pan juices and the greens. Divide the salad among 4 plates and top with 2 pieces of chicken.

SERVES 4

COOKING NOTE

For the salad, you may want to use less dressing and more chicken juices—play around with it and see what proportions you like.

SERVING SUGGESTIONS

Claret Cup (p. 12), Seasoned Olives (p. 90), Garden Minestrone (p. 118), Sformata di Ricotta (Ricotta Custard; p. 256), Plum Fritters (p. 865), Dorie Greenspan's Sablés (p. 703), Kumquat-Clementine Cordial (p. 42)

MAY 8, 1994: "THE PRUDENT GOURMET," BY MOLLY O'NEILL. RECIPE ADAPTED FROM JUDY RODGERS, THE CHEF AND CO-OWNER OF ZUNI CAFÉ IN SAN FRANCISCO.

—1994

☙ RHUBARB-SOY-MARINATED DUCK WITH RHUBARB-GINGER COMPOTE

A burble of sweetness, succulence, and zing, tied together with an undercurrent of salt.

———

1 cup thinly sliced rhubarb
½ cup low-sodium soy sauce
1 tablespoon grated fresh ginger
2 small whole skinless, boneless duck breasts, split
1 teaspoon olive oil
1¼ cups Rhubarb-Ginger Compote (p. 607)

1. Place the rhubarb, soy sauce, and ginger in a small saucepan and bring to a boil over medium-high heat. Reduce heat and simmer for 8 minutes. Strain.

2. Place half of the soy mixture in a shallow glass or ceramic dish. Add the duck breasts and marinate for 1 hour, turning the breasts from time to time.

3. Heat the oil in a medium cast-iron or nonstick skillet over medium-high heat. Add the duck and sear for 4 minutes. Turn the duck and keep the heat at medium-high for 1½ minutes, then turn it down to medium to finish the cooking. The duck is done when it's well browned but still medium-rare in the center. Remove the from skillet and let rest for 10 minutes.

4. Add the remaining soy mixture and marinade to the skillet and deglaze the pan—this happens really quickly. Remove from the heat.

5. Cut the breasts on the diagonal into thin slices. Fan the slices out on 4 plates and spoon the sauce over them. Divide the compote among the plates.

SERVES 4

SERVING SUGGESTIONS

Asparagus with Miso Butter (p. 259), Jasmine Tea Rice (p. 354), Warm Eggplant Salad with Sesame and Shallots (p. 203), Stir-Fried Collards (p. 254), Lemon Lotus Ice Cream (p. 724), Transparent Pudding (p. 805), Huntington Pudding (p. 802)

MAY 15, 1994: "RHUBARB BITES," BY MOLLY O'NEILL.

—1994

JAMES BEARD'S CHICKEN WITH 40 CLOVES OF GARLIC

This is one of those recipes that begins with one writer and as it succeeds and is passed along from friend to friend, leaves behind its original source. My husband, Tad, makes this stew for dinner parties because it's prepared in a single pot, requires no potatoes or rice on the side, and can be made ahead of time and rewarmed for the party, eliminating any unwelcome last-minute performance anxiety. He had been making a version of this recipe for a few years before this original was brought to my attention. His recipe called for a cup of celery leaves, rather than ribs, and it had a touch of broth in addition to the wine.

Both braised dishes are excellent, but it turns out that James Beard's recipe also appeared in the *Times* with two variations. In addition to this version, one from 1961 called for Cognac rather than vermouth, no onions, and for sealing the pot with a flour-and-water paste before sending it on its fateful journey in the oven. Clearly, that last step had no chance of surviving to the current day.

———

4 stalks celery, cut into long strips
2 medium onions, coarsely chopped
40 cloves garlic, unpeeled
6 sprigs parsley
1 tablespoon chopped tarragon
⅔ cup olive or vegetable oil
16 chicken legs—any mix of drumsticks and thighs
2½ teaspoons salt
¼ teaspoon freshly ground black pepper
Freshly grated nutmeg
½ cup dry vermouth
Sliced French bread, warmed

1. Heat the oven to 375 degrees. Cover the bottom of a heavy 8-quart casserole with one-third of the celery, onions, garlic, parsley, and tarragon. Place the oil in a shallow dish. Dip one-third of the chicken pieces into the oil, coating all sides evenly, and place in the casserole. Sprinkle with one third of the salt and pepper and a few gratings of nutmeg. Repeat to make 2 more layers. Pour the vermouth over the chicken.

2. Cover the casserole tightly with aluminum foil (or parchment paper) and fit the lid over the foil to create an airtight seal. Bake for 1½ hours, without removing the cover. Check the chicken for doneness; return the casserole to the oven if the chicken seems underdone.

3. Serve the chicken along with the pan juices, the garlic, and thin slices of heated French bread to be spread with garlic squeezed from the root ends of the cloves.

SERVES 8

COOKING NOTE

I made a few adjustments to the recipe. The original called for vegetable oil, which is fine but tasteless. There is enough oil that I suggest using a buttery olive oil, which weaves its own flavor into the mix and forms a delicious dipping pool for the bread. The recipe instructed you to put the vegetables on the bottom and the chicken on top, but layering them together allows the flavors to mingle and lets you more easily serve bits of both chicken and vegetables.

SERVING SUGGESTIONS

Crostini with Eggplant and Pine Nut Puree (p. 78), Asparagus Salad (p. 214), Puree of Peas and Watercress (p. 296), Polish Jewish Plum Cake (p. 769), Tartelettes aux Pommes Lionel Poilâne (Individual Apple Tarts; p. 834), Tourtière (Apple, Prune, and Armagnac Tart; p. 827), Raspberry Bavarian Cream (p. 807)

OCTOBER 26, 1997: "THREE HEADS ARE BETTER THAN ONE," BY MOLLY O'NEILL.

—1997

ROAST LEMON PEPPER DUCK WITH HONEY LEMON SAUCE

For the Duck

2 tablespoons minced lemon zest

I teaspoon minced thyme

I teaspoon kosher salt

I teaspoon coarsely ground black pepper

Two 5-pound ducks, necks, giblets, and livers removed

For the Sauce

2 tablespoons unsalted butter

2 shallots, sliced

I clove garlic, sliced

½ jalapeño pepper, finely chopped

2 tablespoons chopped thyme

2 tablespoons chopped sage

2 tablespoons chopped rosemary

¼ cup honey

⅓ cup fresh lemon juice (from about 2 lemons)

3 tablespoons all-purpose flour

I tablespoon water

2 cups veal or chicken broth

1. Heat the oven to 425 degrees. Combine the lemon zest, thyme, salt, and pepper in a small bowl. Using your fingers, loosen the skins of the ducks over the breastbones, legs, and thighs. Tuck the lemon-pepper mixture evenly beneath the skin, covering each breast,

leg, and thigh. Tie the legs together with kitchen twine.

2. Heat a roasting pan in the oven for 10 minutes. Place the ducks on a rack in the roasting pan and cook for 1 hour and 10 minutes. Remove the ducks from the pan and cool to room temperature. Set the roasting pan aside.

3. Quarter the ducks, trimming off any excess fat.

4. To prepare the sauce, place the roasting pan over medium-high heat and add the butter, shallots, garlic, and jalapeño. Sauté until softened, about 2 minutes. Add the thyme, sage, and rosemary and sauté for 1 minute more. Add the honey and lemon juice. Make a paste of the flour and water and add to the pan. Add the stock, bring to a simmer and reduce until the sauce lightly coats the back of a spoon, about 5 minutes. The sauce may be cooled and refrigerated for up to 24 hours.

5. To serve, heat the oven to 450 degrees. Heat an ovenproof skillet over high heat. Add the duck pieces skin side down and cook until the skin begins to sizzle, about 1 minute. Reduce the heat to low and crisp the duck skin, 5 to 7 minutes. Cover with a lid or foil and reheat in the oven for 10 minutes.

6. Meanwhile, reheat the sauce in a small pan over medium heat.

7. Transfer the duck to a warm platter and serve with the sauce.

SERVES 4

SERVING SUGGESTIONS

James Beard's Pureed Parsnips (p. 236), Porcini Bread Stuffing (p. 350), Sweet Potatoes Anna (p. 297), Raw Spinach Salad (p. 175), Pear Upside-Down Cake (p. 772)

DECEMBER 3, 1997: "THE PRECOOKED MASTERPIECE: HOW CHEFS CREATE GRAND ILLUSIONS," BY AMANDA HESSER. RECIPE ADAPTED FROM MICHAEL ROMANO, THE CHEF AT UNION SQUARE CAFÉ IN NEW YORK CITY.

—1997

⌒ BADEMIYA'S JUSTLY FAMOUS BOMBAY CHILE-AND-CILANTRO CHICKEN

Oh, how I love this dish! The chile-and-cilantro coating is lightweight but powerful, and it reminds me of the bright, fragrant cooking of Kerala. You sweat as you eat it, but it's hard to stop eating.

The sauce would also be great with fish.

1½ tablespoons coriander seeds

2 teaspoons black peppercorns

1 teaspoon cumin seeds

6 cloves garlic, roughly chopped

One 2-inch piece fresh ginger, peeled and thinly sliced

3 tablespoons vegetable oil

¼ cup water, or as needed

1 tablespoon cayenne pepper or hot paprika

2 tablespoons fresh lemon juice

1½ teaspoons kosher salt

½ cup cilantro leaves, chopped

4 whole chicken legs (2¼ pounds), skinned, or one
    4-pound chicken, cut into 8 pieces and skinned

For Serving

Sliced red onion

Thinly sliced limes and lemons

Cilantro Sauce (recipe follows) for dipping

Tamarind concentrate for dipping

Naan bread for serving

1. Toast the coriander seeds, peppercorns, and cumin seeds in a small skillet over medium heat until fragrant, 1 to 2 minutes. Transfer to a coffee or spice mill or mortar and pestle and grind to a fine powder.

2. Combine the ground spices, garlic, ginger, oil, water, cayenne, lemon juice, and salt in a blender and puree to a paste. Transfer to a bowl and stir in the cilantro. Add the chicken and thoroughly coat with the spice paste. Marinate in the refrigerator for 4 to 6 hours.

3. When ready to cook, prepare a charcoal fire (or use a gas grill set to medium). Grill the chicken, turning once, until done, 10 to 15 minutes per side. Serve with the onions, limes and lemons, cilantro sauce, tamarind concentrate, and naan bread.

SERVES 2 TO 4

CILANTRO SAUCE

1 cup chopped cilantro

3 cloves garlic

1 jalapeño pepper/halved and seeded or not

½ cup walnuts

⅓ cup fresh lemon juice (from about 2 lemons),
    or to taste

¼ teaspoon ground cumin

1 teaspoon kosher salt, or to taste

½ teaspoon freshly ground black pepper

¼ cup water

Combine the cilantro, garlic, jalapeño, walnuts, lemon juice, cumin, salt, and pepper in a blender or food processor and blend to a puree. Add the water, and pour into a serving container. Add salt or lemon juice to taste.

MAKES 1 CUP

COOKING NOTES
Those who don't possess a grill can broil the chicken (about 5 inches from the flame): 8 minutes on one side, 4 minutes on the other. Finish cooking in a 350-degree oven for 10 to 15 minutes.

You can leave the chicken skin on.

SERVING SUGGESTIONS
Mango Lassi (p. 27), Aloo Kofta (p. 74), String Beans with Ginger and Garlic (p. 260), Stuck-Pot Rice with Yogurt and Spices (p. 351), Yogurt Rice (p. 356), Coconut Pie (p. 801), Vanilla Plum Ice (p. 734)

JUNE 28, 1998: "FOOD: PIT STOPS," BY MOLLY O'NEILL. RECIPE ADAPTED FROM *THE BARBECUE! BIBLE*, BY STEVEN RAICHLEN.

—1998

⌐ LUXURY CHICKEN POTPIES

In the early 1990s, Molly O'Neill took over the most desired position in all food writing, the Sunday *Magazine* food column. Unfortunately for her, she had to fill the shoes of Craig Claiborne, who had stepped down in the late 1980s. (In between, a random mix of columnists filled the spot.)

But Molly didn't flinch. Unlike Craig, Molly had worked in restaurants in addition to attending LaVarenne, and having grown up in a generation of cooks influenced by Claiborne, she took to food in an utterly liberated way. She embraced fusion cooking (see p. 139), the French bistro movement (p. 837), New York's sacred haunts (if you don't have it already, you should buy her *New York Cookbook*), and trendy ingredients (p. 26), and was a genius at spotting new chef talent (p. 540). She flourished in the Sunday *Magazine* for a decade and her work at the *Times* was twice nominated for the Pulitzer Prize.

This recipe captures her crossover interests in six neat little potpies. They're highbrow and low. Satisfying yet amusing. And just the kind of thing you wish you'd thought up yourself.

1½ pounds boneless, skinless chicken breasts

2 cups chicken broth

4 tablespoons unsalted butter

1 medium onion, chopped

½ pound red potatoes (about 3 small),
    cut into ⅓-inch dice

8 baby carrots, peeled and halved lengthwise

½ cup fresh or frozen peas

¼ pound baby pattypan or yellow squash, halved

¼ pound baby zucchini

Kosher salt and freshly ground black pepper

6 tablespoons all-purpose flour

1¼ cups whole milk

¾ cup heavy cream or another ¾ cup milk

4 drops Tabasco sauce

2 tablespoons dry sherry

2 tablespoons chopped mixed herbs
    (flat-leaf parsley, chives, thyme)

1 pound (or one 17.3-ounce package)
    frozen puff pastry, thawed

1 egg, lightly beaten

1. Place the chicken and broth in a large saucepan and bring to a boil, then lower the heat and simmer until the chicken is cooked through, 15 to 20 minutes. Remove from the heat and strain, reserving the stock; set the meat aside to cool.

2. Melt 1 tablespoon butter in a large skillet over medium heat. Add the onion and potatoes and cook, stirring frequently, for 10 minutes. (Do not let them brown.) Add the carrots, peas, squash, and zucchini and cook until the vegetables just become tender, 6 to 7 more minutes. Season with salt and pepper and set aside.

3. Melt the remaining 3 tablespoons butter in a large saucepan over low heat. Add the flour and cook, stirring, for 1 minute. Slowly whisk in the reserved chicken broth. Whisk in the milk and cream. Raise the heat to medium and continue whisking until the mixture boils. Remove from the heat and stir in the Tabasco, sherry, and herbs. Season to taste with salt and pepper.

4. Cut the chicken into bite-sized pieces. Combine the chicken, cooked vegetables, and cream sauce in a bowl, and divide the mixture among 6 ovenproof bowls with a capacity of at least 2 cups each. (The potpies can be prepared to this point ahead and refrigerated for up to 24 hours.)

5. Heat the oven to 400 degrees. On a lightly floured surface, roll the pastry dough out to a thickness of ⅛ inch. Cut out 6 circles of pastry just slightly bigger than the diameter of your bowls. Fit the pastry over the tops of the bowls, brush them lightly with the beaten egg, and use the tip of a knife to poke a few holes in the pastry. Bake until the tops have browned and the filling bubbles, about 25 minutes.

SERVES 6

SERVING SUGGESTIONS
Iceberg Lettuce with Smoked Bacon and Buttermilk Dressing (p. 200), Mississippi Mud Cake (p. 762), Chocolate Pudding (p. 858)

SEPTEMBER 20, 1998: "FOOD: A SMOKE SCREEN," BY MOLLY O'NEILL.

—1998

GEORGIA PECAN TURKEY SALAD

2½ cups very finely minced cooked turkey
½ cup chopped pecans
¼ cup sweet pickle relish
½ teaspoon celery salt
⅔ cup mayonnaise
Salt and freshly ground black pepper

Mix the turkey, pecans, relish, and salt together. Fold in the mayonnaise. Season to taste with salt and pepper, and serve.

SERVES 4

COOKING NOTE

If you don't have leftover turkey, buy a turkey leg (or two). Place it in a small roasting pan and sprinkle with olive oil, salt, and pepper. Scatter some thyme leaves on top and tuck 2 smashed garlic cloves underneath. Cover the pan with foil and bake in a 375-degree oven until cooked through, about 30 minutes.

SERVING SUGGESTIONS

Old South Buttermilk Biscuits (p. 655), Fennel and Apple Salad with Juniper (p. 189), Winter Slaw with Lemon-and-Orange Dressing (p. 185), String Beans with Ginger and Garlic (p. 260), Spinach with Sour Cream (p. 216), Bourbon Pecan Pie (p. 842)

NOVEMBER 25, 1998: "PECANS FROM HEAVEN: THE GEORGIA HARVEST," BY FLORENCE FABRICANT. RECIPE ADAPTED FROM MARY PEARSON OF PEARSON FARMS IN PERRY, GEORGIA.

—1998

BEER-CAN CHICKEN

You are not a true American until you've taken our beloved chicken, placed it in an undignified position atop an open can of beer, and set it on a grill. The beer nestled in the cavity of the bird steams, keeping the bird moist on the inside and infusing the meat with a hoppy fragrance without dampening the skin.

The classic version of the recipe (classic being a relative term, as the dish first showed up on the barbecue circuit around 1994) is chicken on Budweiser, but aficionados have expanded the repertory to include seasoning the bird (and beer) with Cajun spices, garlic, onion juice, apples, and even crab boil. Steven Raichlen, whose recipe this is, invites you to use whatever barbecue rub you like for the exterior of the bird. There's a good one by John Berwald on p. 607, and one in the North Carolina–Style Pulled Pork recipe on p. 551.

2 cups hickory or oak chips
Two 12-ounce cans beer
½ cup of your favorite barbecue rub
Two 3½- to 4-pound chickens

1. Place the wood chips in a bowl. Pop the tab of each beer can and make 2 additional holes in each top, using a church-key opener. Pour half the beer from each can over the chips. Add additional beer or water to cover chips and soak them for 1 hour; drain.
2. Set up the grill for indirect grilling (see Raichlen's Grill Instructions, below). Sprinkle 1 teaspoon barbecue rub in the neck cavity and 2 teaspoons in the main cavity of each chicken. Add 1 tablespoon rub to each half-full open can of beer. (Don't worry if it foams up.) Season the outside of each bird with 2 tablespoons rub.
3. Stand the beer cans on a work surface. Holding each chicken upright, lower it over a can so that the can goes into the main cavity. Pull the chicken legs forward to form a sort of tripod: the chicken should sit upright over the can. Carefully transfer the chickens to the grill in this position, placing them in the center over the drip pan, away from the heat.
4. If using charcoal, toss half the wood chips on each mound of coals. If using gas, place the chips in a smoker box. Barbecue the chickens until nicely browned and cooked through, about 1 to 1½ hours, keeping the temperature about 350 degrees. (If using charcoal, replenish the coals as needed.) The internal temperature of the birds, taken in the thickest part of the thigh, should be at least 165 degrees.
5. Carefully transfer the birds to a platter, in the same position. To carve, lift the birds off the cans, and discard the cans.

SERVES 4

COOKING NOTES

I used the rub from the North Carolina–Style Pulled Pork recipe on p. 551.

The seasoning instructions in Step 2 are somewhat tedious—once you get the hang of it, there's no need to measure.

RAICHLEN'S GRILL INSTRUCTIONS

"On a backyard grill, you need to use the indirect method. This means that you configure your fire so that it is hottest away from the food.

"On a charcoal kettle grill, light the charcoal or Charwood in a chimney starter. When it glows red, dump it in two piles at opposite sides of the grill. (Some grills come with side baskets for this purpose.) Place a foil drip pan in the center of the grill, between the mounds of embers. Place the grate on the grill, and cook the chicken in the center over the drip pan. Toss soaked wood chips on the coals to generate smoke. Keep the grill covered, adjusting the vents to keep the temperature at 350 degrees. After cooking the chicken for an hour, add 10 fresh briquettes or an equal amount of Charwood. Leave the grill uncovered for a few minutes, until the coals ignite.

"On a gas grill, if it has two burners, light one side on high, and cook the chicken on the other. On a three-burner grill, light the front and rear or outside burners, and cook the chicken in the center. On a four-burner grill, light the outside burners, and cook in the center. Many gas grills come with smoker boxes, in which you can put the wood chips. If you don't have a smoker box, loosely wrap the chips in heavy-duty foil, make a few holes on top, and place the foil package under the grate over one of the burners."

SERVING SUGGESTIONS

Jay Grelen's Southern Iced Tea (p. 27), Pickled Shrimp (p. 95), Julia Harrison Adams's Pimento Cheese Spread (p. 64), Fried Corn (p. 274), Salade Niçoise (p. 178), Tomatoes Vinaigrette (p. 218), Jean Halberstam's Deep-Fried Peaches (p. 860)

READERS

"We have made this dozens of times! We serve the thighs and drumsticks warm and save the breast pieces for salad or soup, including the skin. We particularly like that so much of the fat ends up in the drip pan. We use our old faithful Weber cooker."

Karen Dooley Bower, Glenside, PA, letter

JULY 7, 1999: "KEEPING THE EMBERS AT BAY," BY STEVEN RAICHLEN.

—1999

ROASTED BRINE-CURED TURKEY WITH WILD MUSHROOM STUFFING

You'll need steak knives to get through the lacquered skin and rosy meat, and to fend off anyone who attempts to steal your turkey skin. The cure is well calibrated so that the turkey is succulent and the herbal brine glides over your palate without tasting salty.

This recipe ran twice in the newspaper, once with its original Wild Mushroom Stuffing and once with a Shiitake and Lotus Seed Stuffing (p. 477) created by a Vietnamese immigrant for her family's Thanksgiving dinner. Both are superb. I didn't include any other Thanksgiving turkey recipes (well, except Turducken on p. 485, but that's its own category of weird and wonderful), and after you make this one, you'll understand why.

---

8 quarts water

¾ cup plus 2 tablespoons kosher salt

¾ cup sugar

1 carrot, peeled and diced

1 large onion, diced

¼ cup diced (½-inch) celery

1 leek, white and pale green parts only, diced (½-inch) and washed well

2 bay leaves

1 tablespoon black peppercorns

1 tablespoon coriander seeds

¼ teaspoon crushed red pepper flakes

¼ teaspoon fennel seeds

2 star anise

2 or 3 sprigs thyme

One 12- to 14-pound naturally fed, free-range turkey

Wild Mushroom Stuffing (p. 337)

¼ cup olive oil or 4 tablespoons unsalted butter

Rosemary branches (optional)

1. Bring the water to a boil in a 16-quart or larger stockpot. Add the salt and sugar, and stir until completely dissolved. Turn off the heat and add the carrot,

onion, celery, leek, bay leaves, peppercorns, coriander, red pepper, fennel seeds, star anise, and thyme. Refrigerate until cold.

2. Remove the giblets from the turkey. Cover and refrigerate the liver if using it in the stuffing. Discard the remaining giblets or reserve for another use. Add the turkey to the stockpot. If necessary, weight it with a plate so that it stays below the brine's surface. Refrigerate for 72 hours.

3. Remove the turkey from the brine (discard the brine) and allow to come to room temperature.

4. Heat the oven to 425 degrees. Loosely fill the turkey at both ends with the stuffing, and truss. (You can, of course, bake the stuffing separately in a buttered baking dish.)

5. Place the turkey in a large roasting pan and roast until it starts to brown, about 25 minutes. Reduce the oven to 350 degrees and roast for 12 minutes more per pound, or until the internal temperature at the thickest part of the leg reaches 130 degrees on an instant-read thermometer. (Total roasting time will be about 3 hours.) Baste frequently with the olive oil and pan juices, using rosemary branches as a brush if desired. If the bird begins to darken too much, cover it loosely with a piece of foil.

6. Remove the turkey from oven, cover loosely with foil if you have not already done so, and allow it to rest for 20 minutes before carving the bird and spooning the stuffing into a serving dish.

SERVES 12 TO 15

COOKING NOTES
I basted with olive oil.

If you don't have a 16-quart pot, make and cool the brine, then brine the turkey in a clean bucket, or similar food-safe vessel.

If you don't stuff the turkey—I didn't—it will take an hour less to cook.

SERVING SUGGESTIONS
Creamed Onions (p. 217), Sweet Potatoes Anna (p. 297), Candied Sweet Potatoes (p. 276), Stewed Fennel (p. 245), Holiday Cranberry Chutney (p. 608), Mississippi Pecan Pie (p. 820), Rum Pumpkin Cream Pie (p. 823)

PERIOD DETAIL
By Thanksgiving of 2009, brine-curing turkey was fast being replaced with dry-brining, which is appealing because it doesn't require moving your refrigerator shelves to accommodate a vat of sloshing brine. Judy Rodgers's Roast Chicken on p. 467 is dry-brined, which means it's simply rubbed with salt (and herbs) the day before roasting. As Kim Severson, a reporter for the Dining section, pointed out, you can apply the same method to turkey. Use 1 tablespoon kosher salt for every pound of turkey. Two days before roasting, rub the salt (and herbs and spices, if desired) all over the bird, wrap it in plastic wrap, and refrigerate it. The next day, turn the turkey over. A few hours before cooking, take the turkey out of the fridge, remove the plastic wrap, and pat it dry with paper towels. Then roast the turkey as you usually would.

NOVEMBER 17, 1999: "NEW AMERICAN TRADITIONS: IN A BERKELEY KITCHEN, A CELEBRATION OF SIMPLICITY," BY R. W. APPLE JR. RECIPE ADAPTED FROM ALICE WATERS.

—1999

ᕲ SLOW-ROASTED DUCK

I once did a deep-dive into duck cookery for the Dining section, and the duck aroma in my kitchen only subsided after about six months. But the revelations were worth it. I discovered that roasting duck as you do a chicken—at moderate, even temperature—is not the way to go. Duck has more fat and thicker skin. You need to find ways of rendering the fat so that it moistens the meat on its way out. I found two good ways of doing this.

Steaming followed by sautéing, it turns out, produces the consummate crisp and succulent duck. Steaming softens the meat while rendering the fat and also infuses the seasonings into the duck. You can do that part up to a day ahead, then crisp the duck in a pan before serving. You can find this technique in the next recipe, on p. 476. The other technique, given here, involves roasting. Starting at a high temperature—500 degrees—for the first few minutes of cooking, then lowering it to 300 degrees crisps the duck skin crisp and caramelized yet allows the meat to relax as it would in a braise.

One 5-pound duck
Kosher salt and freshly ground black pepper
10 sprigs thyme
10 cloves garlic, unpeeled
¾ pound thin carrots, peeled and cut into pieces
¾ pound turnips, peeled and cut into wedges
¾ pound golden beets, peeled and cut into wedges
4 shallots, unpeeled, halved

1. Heat the oven to 500 degrees. Season the duck generously inside and out with salt and pepper. Put 1 or 2 pieces each of thyme, garlic, carrots, turnips, beets, and shallots in the cavity. Truss the duck and set it in a large casserole or medium roasting pan. Scatter the rest of the ingredients and the neck around the duck; season with salt and pepper. Cover loosely with foil.

2. Roast the duck for 10 minutes, then lower the temperature to 300 degrees and roast for 3½ hours, basting the vegetables and duck with the pan juices and skimming off the fat occasionally.

3. Remove the foil. Take out the vegetables and neck and set aside. Roast the duck uncovered for 1 more hour (if the vegetables are not tender, continue roasting until they are, then remove them). The skin should be well browned and crisp; the meat, extremely tender.

4. Transfer the duck to a cutting board. Skim the fat off the pan juices, and add water to the pan if necessary to make ½ cup. Bring the juices to a boil, adjust the seasoning, and transfer to a serving bowl. Reheat the vegetables and neck in a baking dish in the oven.

5. Carefully carve the duck (the meat may fall off the bone), adding the vegetables from the cavity to the pan. Pull the meat from the neck and add it to the pan as well. Serve the duck with the pan juices and vegetables.

SERVES 3

VARIATION

In 1993, Florence Fabricant wrote about a technique she'd perfected for roasting duck breast. You score the fat on the breasts in a crisscross pattern and season (or marinate) the breasts however you like. Heat a large, heavy skillet, preferably nonstick, to very hot. Sear the duck breasts skin-side down until browned, about 2 minutes. Pour off the fat. Turn the duck breasts and brown the other side. Then transfer the duck breasts,

skin-side up, to a baking dish, and slow-roast them in a 175-degree oven for 1 hour. By this time the duck breasts will be uniformly pink throughout.

SERVING SUGGESTIONS

Hot Cheese Olives (p. 83), Cauliflower Soup with Cremini Mushrooms and Walnut Oil (p. 149), Mushrooms Stuffed with Duxelles and Sausage (p. 223), Cabbage and Potato Gratin with Mustard Bread Crumbs (p. 298), Whiskey Cake (p. 784), Chocolate Mousse (p. 820)

JANUARY 19, 2000: "DUCK, DEMYSTIFIED: MASTERING THE WHOLE BIRD," BY AMANDA HESSER. TECHNIQUE ADAPTED FROM GREG SONNIER, THE CHEF AT GABRIELLE IN NEW ORLEANS.

—2000

⌇ STEAMED AND CRISPED DUCK

Don't feel hemmed in by the Asian flavors: you can use any array of spices you like. For instance, try some Indian seasonings like turmeric, ginger, cardamom, and chiles.

For another technique that results in a duck with crisp skin and succulent meat, see p. 475.

———

5 scallions, smashed with the side of a cleaver
Six ⅛-inch-thick slices fresh ginger, smashed with the side of a cleaver
1 tablespoon rice wine
2 tablespoons salt
2 teaspoons Sichuan peppercorns
1 star anise, smashed with the side of a cleaver
One 5-pound duck

1. Mix all the seasoning ingredients in a small bowl. Rub the mixture over the duck, inside and out. Put the duck breast side down in a dish, cover with plastic wrap, and refrigerate overnight.

2. The next day, take the duck out of the refrigerator and let it warm to room temperature. Place the duck on a steamer rack small enough to fit into a wok. Fill the wok with water to come to the bottom of the rack and bring to a boil. Place the rack over the boiling

water, cover with a lid or foil, and steam the duck over high heat until extremely tender, about 1½ to 2 hours. Replenish the boiling water when necessary.

3. Transfer the duck to a cutting board and let cool slightly.

4. Quarter the duck. Heat a large ovenproof nonstick sauté pan over medium-high heat. When hot, add the duck pieces skin side down and sauté until the skin begins to sizzle and brown, about 1 minute. Reduce the heat to low and crisp the skin for 5 to 7 minutes. Turn and brown the other side, then lower the heat and cook until heated through. Transfer the pieces to a platter; serve.

SERVES 3

SERVING SUGGESTIONS
Oriental Watercress Soup (p. 111), James Beard's Pureed Parsnips (p. 236), Red Cabbage Glazed with Maple Syrup (p. 236), Stir-Fried Collards (p. 254), Sugar Snap Peas with Horseradish (p. 259), Steamed Fennel with Red Pepper Oil (p. 263), Marcella's Pear Cake (p. 769), Coconut Rice Pudding with Lime Syrup (p. 846)

JANUARY 19, 2000: "DUCK, DEMYSTIFIED: MASTERING THE WHOLE BIRD," BY AMANDA HESSER. RECIPE ADAPTED FROM *CLASSIC CHINESE CUISINE*, BY NINA SIMONDS.

—2000

◝ TIP FOR CRISP SKIN

The secret to producing a roasted chicken or duck with skin so crisp it crackles lies in how you treat the bird long before it goes in the oven. A decade back I visited Café Boulud, on Manhattan's Upper East Side, where the crisping process begins with the raw birds that are cleaned, trussed, and hung on meat hooks in the walk-in refrigerator for a few days. The uncovered skin dries out and firms up. When it hits a hot pan, it crisps like a potato chip, yet the meat stays moist. Andrew Carmellini, the restaurant's chef at the time, told me that the idea came from the preparation of suckling pigs, which are usually hung in the refrigerator to draw moisture out of the skin. With chickens,

hens, and squab, the cooks brown the birds in clarified butter and roast them at 450 degrees, spooning on butter and herbs in the last few minutes.

This technique can be adapted to the home kitchen. On a Thursday, I bought a quail, a guinea hen, and a chicken, rinsed them, dried them, and placed them on a baking rack on a baking sheet, then put them in the refrigerator, turning them once each day. On Sunday, I bought another set of the same birds and roasted the fresh and the dried together. The difference was marked. The dried birds started out with darkened, leathery skin and emerged from the oven brown like a hazelnut, with a thick crackly shell. The skin of the fresh birds was paler, thinner, and flabbier.

Next time, I would dry the birds for just 2 days. With the quail, 1 day would be sufficient: it's a skinny bird with very little fat, and the legs were dry. One last tip: when you're ready to cook, rub the bird with oil or butter before seasoning, or the salt won't cling to the dried skin.

SEPTEMBER 27, 2000: "TIDBIT: A DRY BIRD IS QUICK TO SIZZLE," BY AMANDA HESSER.

—2000

◝ ROASTED BRINE-CURED TURKEY WITH SHIITAKE AND LOTUS SEED STUFFING

The best Thanksgiving menus, in my view, come from immigrants who adapt the mainstays of the traditional American Thanksgiving to tastes they grew up with. This turkey is the creation of Bao-Xuyen Le, a Vietnamese woman who has spent time in France and now lives in Huntington Beach, California. The brined turkey—a recipe adapted from Alice Waters—is new American, the stuffing decidedly fusion. It's made of Vietnamese ingredients, and it evolved from a stuffing Le created for chicken in Vietnam. Instead of chestnuts, she buys lotus seeds. Rather than bread, she uses dried sweet rice flakes. In place of pork, there is ground chicken and giblets. What results is nothing like American stuffing. It is light and moist, with little tastes of shallot, giblets, bits of water chestnut and shiitake mushrooms, and a whisper of fish sauce.

Preceding the turkey, Le serves toasts spread with foie gras; spring rolls stuffed with pork (roasted French-style with bay leaves and garlic), toasted rice flour, cilantro, mint, and shiso leaves (p. 887); and dumplings. To go with the turkey, she makes mashed potatoes, a smooth puree, which she seasons with Asian mushroom powder ("the secret," she said), milk, butter, and sel de Guérande. For her "salade," she plucks greens and herbs from her garden.

Sometimes, someone brings a pie, but generally the Les stick to lighter sweets. A plate stacked high with persimmons is set on the table, along with a platter of petits fours and Vietnamese cakes—translucent blocks of rice, yam, and bean paste in bright-green-leaf colors and round, dense coconut cakes.

———

8 quarts water

¾ cup plus 2 tablespoons kosher salt

¾ cup sugar

I carrot, peeled and diced (½ inch)

I large onion, peeled and diced (½ inch)

¼ cup diced celery (½ inch)

I leek, white and pale green parts only,
    diced (½ inch) and well washed

2 bay leaves

I tablespoon black peppercorns

I tablespoon coriander seeds

¼ teaspoon crushed red pepper flakes

¼ teaspoon fennel seeds

2 star anise

2 or 3 sprigs thyme

One 12- to 14-pound naturally fed, free-range turkey

Shiitake and Lotus Seed Stuffing (p. 338)

¼ cup olive oil or 4 tablespoons unsalted butter

1. Bring the water to a boil in a 16-quart or larger stockpot. Add the salt and sugar, and stir until completely dissolved. Turn off the heat and add the carrot, onion, celery, leek, and herbs and spices. Refrigerate until cold.

2. Remove the giblets from the turkey, and cover and refrigerate if using in the stuffing. Add the turkey to the stockpot. If necessary, weight it with a plate so that it stays below the brine's surface. Refrigerate for 72 hours.

3. Remove the turkey from the brine (discard the brine) and allow to come to room temperature.

4. Heat the oven to 425 degrees. Loosely fill the turkey at both ends with the stuffing, and truss. (You can, of course, bake the stuffing separately in a buttered baking dish.)

5. Place the turkey in a large roasting pan and roast until it starts to brown, about 25 minutes. Reduce the oven to 350 degrees and roast for 12 minutes more per pound, or until the internal temperature at the thickest part of the thigh reaches 130 degrees on an instant-read thermometer. Baste frequently with the olive oil and pan juices. If the bird begins to darken too much, cover loosely with foil.

6. Remove the turkey from the oven, cover loosely with foil if you have not already done so, and allow to rest for 20 minutes before carving the bird and spooning the stuffing into serving dish.

SERVES 12 TO 15

COOKING NOTES
If you don't have a 16-quart pot, make and cool the brine, then brine the turkey in a clean bucket or similar food-safe vessel.

If you cook the stuffing on the side, the turkey will take an hour less to cook.

SERVING SUGGESTIONS
Pork-and-Toasted-Rice-Powder Spring Rolls (p. 74), Mashed Potatoes Anna (p. 294), Mississippi Pecan Pie (p. 820), sliced persimmons

NOVEMBER 15, 2000: "AMERICA CELEBRATES: HUNTING-TON BEACH, CALIF.: ADD A LITTLE VIETNAM, FRANCE, AND CALIFORNIA, AND MIX," BY AMANDA HESSER. RECIPE ADAPTED FROM ALICE WATERS AND BAO-XUYEN LE.

—2000

⌒ ELIZABETH FRINK'S ROAST LEMON CHICKEN

Julia Reed, a columnist for the *Times Magazine*, argued that this roasted chicken, which is delicious hot, is the ideal picnic dish served cold. The recipe came from Elizabeth Frink, a sculptor, who contributed it to *The Artists' and Writers' Cookbook*. Sometimes it's difficult to determine what makes one recipe better than another, but here it's the technique.

Frink carefully formulated every step with repetitions of lemon: you rub strips of lemon peel on the chicken skin, squeeze lemon juice over the inside and outside of the bird, stuff the lemon pieces into the cavity, and then, for good measure, squeeze the juice of a second lemon over the chicken 30 minutes before it's done roasting.

As Reed noted, "Not only is the chicken good cold, it makes the most delicious sandwiches (another picnic staple, best on thin-sliced brioche with butter or a little homemade mayonnaise, salt, and black pepper) because the meat is infused with the taste of lemon." Indeed, and the skin is downright tart.

One 3-pound chicken
½ teaspoon salt
¼ teaspoon freshly ground black pepper
2 lemons
6 cloves garlic
2 tablespoons unsalted butter
2 tablespoons olive oil
1 tablespoon coarsely chopped flat-leaf parsley,
    plus more for serving

1. Heat the oven to 325 degrees. Place the chicken in a large baking dish and season inside and out with salt and pepper. Remove the skin from 1 lemon in strips with a vegetable peeler, and rub the skin over the outside of the chicken. Then quarter the lemon and squeeze the juice over and into the chicken. Put the lemon pieces and garlic cloves inside the cavity.

2. Melt the butter with the olive oil in a small pan. Pour about one-third of the butter mixture inside the chicken. Tie the legs together with kitchen string. Pour the remaining butter and oil over the chicken. Reseason the top of the chicken.

3. Roast the chicken for 1½ hours, or until an instant-read thermometer inserted in the thickest part of the leg registers 165 degrees, basting it every 15 minutes with the pan juices. Half an hour before the chicken is done, pour the juice from the second lemon over the chicken and sprinkle with the parsley.

4. Transfer the chicken to a cutting board to sit for 15 minutes before carving. Meanwhile, pour ½ cup water (or broth, if you have some) into the roasting pan and place it over high heat. As it comes to a boil, scrape up the pan drippings with a wooden spoon. Reduce the pan juices to the desired consistency, and season to taste with salt and pepper.

5. Carve and serve the chicken, passing the sauce on the side.

SERVES 4

COOKING NOTES

In 1945, the *Times* ran its first chicken recipe containing instructions for measuring the internal temperature of the bird—measured at the thickest part of the leg—as a test for doneness. Since then, that has become a standard part of roasted chicken recipes. As most chefs will tell you, 165 degrees is as high as they will go. Once the chicken is removed from the oven, it will continue to cook and the temperature will rise, usually another 5 to 7 degrees. So a bird taken out of the oven at 165 degrees will have reached at least 170 degrees by the time it's served. You should cook poultry to whatever temperature you're comfortable with, but if you come for dinner at my house, the chicken will be 170 degrees.

The original recipe does not call for a sauce, but the pan juices were so delicious that I added one more step to deglaze the pan and capture the drippings and juices.

SERVING SUGGESTIONS

Vermouth Cup (p. 15), Potage Parisien with Sorrel Cream (p. 148), Salmon Mousse (p. 394), Artichauts Vinaigrette (p. 225), Roasted Potato Salad (p. 285), Watercress Salad (p. 171), Diana Vreeland's Salade Parisienne (p. 192), Marcella's Pear Cake (p. 769) Fruit Crostatas (p. 855)

PERIOD DETAIL

This lemon chicken recipe was by no means the first lemon chicken to appear in the *Times*—there are some eighteen others in the archives—and by no means the last. A recipe for Lee Lum's Lemon Chicken, a Chinese dish, is on p. 459.

JULY 8, 2001: "THE PICNIC PAPERS," BY JULIA REED. ELIZABETH FRINK'S RECIPE APPEARED IN *THE ARTISTS' AND WRITERS' COOKBOOK*.

—2001

CHICKEN ROASTED WITH SOUR CREAM, LEMON JUICE, AND MANGO CHUTNEY

My husband, Tad, served this dish the first time he cooked for me. To make it, you whisk together lemon juice, sour cream, Major Grey's chutney, curry powder, and, of all things, mayonnaise, pour it over chicken breasts, and bake them in a hot oven. The shiny yellow sauce sounds about as promising as green goddess dressing, but it's marvelous. And here's why: it has all the components of a good sauce: cream, egg yolks, lemon juice, and salt. (Turned out, he had all the components of a good husband; generosity, intelligence, a sense of humor, and a few good recipes under his belt.)

———

2 whole boneless, skinless chicken breasts
  (8 ounces each), cut in half
½ cup Hellmann's (or Best Foods) mayonnaise
½ cup sour cream
2 tablespoons Major Grey's mango chutney
1 teaspoon curry powder
Juice of 1 lemon, preferably a Meyer lemon
Freshly ground black pepper

1. Heat the oven to 450 degrees. Lay the chicken in a medium baking dish (either Pyrex or enameled cast iron).
2. Whisk together the mayonnaise and sour cream in a small bowl. Add the chutney and curry powder and whisk until smooth. Add the lemon juice a little at a time, tasting as you go. It should taste quite tangy. Stop when it is to your liking.
3. Spoon the sauce evenly over the chicken. Place in the oven and roast until the chicken is just cooked through, about 15 minutes. Season with pepper and serve.

SERVES 2

SERVING SUGGESTIONS
Soupe à l'Ail (Garlic Soup; p. 130), Puree of Peas and Watercress (p. 296), Sugar Snap Peas with Horseradish (p. 259), Sautéed Potatoes with Parsley (p. 283), Campton Place Buttermilk Chocolate Cake (p. 765)

READERS
"Never fails to be enjoyed, so easy, perfect."
  Mitzi Maxwell, Orlando, FL, e-mail

JULY 15, 2001: "FOOD DIARY: LOVIN' SPOONFULS," BY AMANDA HESSER. RECIPE ADAPTED FROM *FIFTEEN MINUTE MEALS*, BY EMALEE CHAPMAN.

—2001

GINGER DUCK

My late mother-in-law, Elizabeth Friend, made this for dinner on my first meet-the-parents weekend. She used the cooking broth to make the rice, and she tucked watercress under the duck when serving it—a snappy counterpoint to the rich bird. Alongside, we had Puree of Peas and Watercress (p. 296) and for dessert, Almond Cake (p. 777). All of which made me feel incredibly daunted by her culinary prowess.

Elizabeth, whose cooking style blossomed during the Julia Child years, tended toward bold, self-contained dishes, most of which could be made at least partially ahead, allowing her to be part of the cocktail hour (a great strategy for all cooks to heed). This recipe came to Elizabeth from Baba, her family's cook when she was young, and it is now sustaining a fourth generation.

———

1 duck, giblets removed
1 onion, cut in half, or 3 shallots
2 stalks celery, cut into 3-inch-long pieces
2 teaspoons ground ginger
½ cup sugar
½ cup soy sauce
1 teaspoon salt
½ cup dry sherry
1 small bunch watercress, trimmed and washed

1. The day before serving, stuff the duck with the onion and celery. Place the duck breast side up in a large pot with enough water to half-cover it. Add the ginger and bring to a boil. Cover and reduce the heat so that it simmers gently for an hour.
2. Turn the duck over. Add the sugar, soy sauce, and salt. Continue simmering for another hour.

3. Turn the duck once again and simmer until tender and almost falling apart, about another hour. Turn off the heat and, when it's cool enough, remove the duck from the pot and place in a roasting pan. Cover and refrigerate. Pour the broth into a container and refrigerate overnight. A layer of fat will form on top; scrape it off and discard. Reserve 1 cup for the duck; what remains is delicious in rice and soups and can be frozen for months.

4. Before roasting, bring the duck to room temperature in the roasting pan. Heat the oven to 350 degrees.

5. Add the sherry and 1 cup of the defatted duck broth to the roasting pan and place in the oven. Roast for 30 to 45 minutes, basting the duck occasionally with the juices from the pan. The duck is done when it is heated through and the skin is crisp and chestnut brown.

6. Transfer the duck to a serving platter and garnish with the watercress.

SERVES 3

COOKING NOTE

A whole duck serves 4, but barely. As with most of the whole duck recipes in the book, doubling this is best if your 4 have big appetites.

SERVING SUGGESTIONS

Some other ideas: Cream of Carrot Soup (p. 119), Butternut Squash and Cider Soup (p. 136), Chilled Sesame Spinach (p. 239), Sugar Snap Peas with Horseradish (p. 259), The Most Voluptuous Cauliflower (p. 241), Lemon Lotus Ice Cream (p. 724), Tea Ice Cream (p. 717), Apple Galette (p. 843).

AUGUST 12, 2001: "FOOD DIARY: AMATEUR NIGHT," BY AMANDA HESSER. RECIPE ADAPTED FROM ELIZABETH FRIEND.

—2001

✐ BRAISED DUCK LEGS WITH PINOT NOIR SAUCE

A friend aptly described this as "duck bourguignon"— a quick and dirty version.

————

8 duck legs
Salt and freshly ground black pepper
I tablespoon dried herbes de Provence
I tablespoon olive oil
I shallot, minced
I sprig thyme
I bay leaf
8 cups duck or chicken broth
About 3 cups pinot noir
Mixed sturdy greens, such as arugula, curly endive,
    tatsoi, and escarole, for serving (optional)

1. Heat the oven to 375 degrees. Season the duck legs well on both sides with salt and pepper. Crumble the herbes de Provence evenly over all sides. Lay the legs skin side up in a 3-inch-deep baking dish just large enough to hold them in a single layer.

2. Roast the duck for 1 hour.

3. Meanwhile, heat the olive oil in a small saucepan. Add the shallot and cook until lightly colored. Add the thyme, bay leaf, and 2 cups broth. Bring to a boil and cook until reduced by half, skimming frequently. Add 2 cups more stock and continue cooking, reducing, and skimming, and adding more stock 2 cups at a time, until all the stock has been added, about 30 minutes. Remove from the heat.

4. Pour off the duck fat from the baking dish and reserve for another use. Heat the pinot noir to a bare simmer in a small saucepan. Pour over the legs so that the meat is immersed but the skin is exposed. Roast for 20 to 30 minutes, or until the skin is golden red.

5. Remove the legs from the roasting pan and keep warm. Pour the braising liquid into a large measuring cup. Add 1 cup of the liquid to the saucepan of stock and cook until reduced enough to lightly coat the back of a spoon. Strain through a fine sieve. Season with salt and pepper.

6. Arrange the duck legs on serving plates (over mixed greens, if you like) and pour the sauce on top.

COOKING NOTE

COOKING NOTE

It's important to use a fresh jar of herbes de Provence.

SERVING SUGGESTIONS

Seasoned Olives (p. 90), Nicole Kaplan's Gougères (p. 76), Braised Red Cabbage with Chestnuts (p. 221), Golden Winter Puree (p. 235), Figs in Whiskey (p. 859), Black Forest Cake (p. 754)

JANUARY 9, 2002: "DUCK LEG CONFIDENTIAL," BY REGINA SCHRAMBLING. RECIPE ADAPTED FROM *BAY WOLF RESTAURANT COOKBOOK*, BY MICHAEL WILD AND LAUREN LYLE.

—2002

MOROCCAN CHICKEN SMOTHERED IN OLIVES

This Paula Wolfert dish is similar in technique to James Beard's Chicken with 40 Cloves of Garlic (p. 469) in that you layer the chicken pieces with aromatics, then cover it with broth and simmer it, but it's totally different in spirit. The chicken tastes exactly as you would expect a Wolfert recipe to taste—soulful and assertive.

———

¼ cup salt for brining (optional)

½ cup sugar for brining (optional)

8 chicken thighs, skin removed and discarded

2 onions, halved and sliced

1 teaspoon ground ginger

2 teaspoons turmeric

2 teaspoons ground cumin

1 tablespoon sweet Spanish smoked paprika (pimentón)

4 cloves garlic, chopped

¾ cup chopped cilantro

2 cups chicken broth

11 ounces (about 1½ cups) pitted green olives in brine, like Goya's, drained

Juice of 1 lemon

1. To brine the chicken (optional), combine the salt, sugar, and 1 cup hot water in a large bowl and stir until the sugar is dissolved. Add 3 cups cold water and

the chicken pieces. Cover and refrigerate for 2 hours. Drain, rinse, and drain again.

2. Arrange the onions in a large casserole and top with the chicken pieces. Sprinkle with the ginger, turmeric, cumin, paprika, garlic, and cilantro. Pour the chicken broth over all. Bring to a boil over high heat, then reduce the heat to medium-low, cover, and simmer for 30 minutes, turning once.

3. Meanwhile, combine the olives with several cups of water in a small saucepan and bring to a boil. Boil for 2 minutes, then drain well and set aside.

4. Add the olives and lemon juice to the chicken and simmer, uncovered, for 10 minutes. If desired, simmer longer to reduce and thicken the sauce. Serve.

SERVES 4

COOKING NOTE

Go ahead, brine the chicken. It's easy and worth it— brining lightly cures the meat and helps keep it moist.

SERVING SUGGESTIONS

Roasted Carrot and Red Lentil Ragout (p. 289), Moroccan Carrot Salad (p. 187), Spicy Orange Salad Moroccan-Style (p. 181), Blood Orange, Date, and Parmesan Salad with Almond Oil (p. 199), Winter Slaw with Lemon-and-Orange Dressing (p. 185), Pepper-Cumin Cookies (p. 695), Moroccan Rice Pudding (p. 848), Revani Verrias (Semolina Cake; p. 788), Sugared Puffs (p. 867)

JUNE 12, 2002, "FOR THE LITERARY SET, HOME COOKING, UNEDITED," BY ALEX WITCHEL. RECIPE ADAPTED FROM *MEDITERRANEAN COOKING*, BY PAULA WOLFERT.

—2002

PAN-ROASTED CHICKEN WITH END-OF-SEASON TOMATOES

Brining the chicken the morning you make this dish is a trick I learned from my mother. It keeps the chicken moist and helps the skin crisp in the oven.

———

1 tablespoon sea salt, plus more for seasoning

One 4-pound chicken, cut into 6 pieces

¾ cup all-purpose flour

Freshly ground black pepper

1 tablespoon olive oil

1 tablespoon unsalted butter

3 sprigs thyme

1 shallot, finely chopped

½ cup fino sherry

3 very ripe tomatoes (from a farm stand if possible), coarsely chopped

1 teaspoon aged sherry vinegar, plus more to taste

1. Pour the salt into a bowl large enough to hold the chicken. Add a cup of tepid water and dissolve the salt. Add the chicken pieces, then cover with more water. Refrigerate for 2 to 12 hours, until ready to cook.

2. Heat the oven to 375 degrees. Remove the chicken from the water and pat it dry. Place the flour and salt and pepper to taste in a plastic bag. Add the chicken pieces 2 at a time and shake to lightly coat them, then vigorously shake off excess flour.

3. Place a deep ovenproof sauté pan over medium-high heat and add the oil and butter. When the foam subsides, add the chicken pieces skin side down and brown well, adjusting the heat as needed, then turn and cook for 3 minutes.

4. Add the thyme sprigs and transfer the pan to the oven. Roast the chicken, basting every few minutes, until it is cooked 20 to 30 minutes.

5. Transfer the chicken to a platter and keep warm. Pour off all but 1 tablespoon fat from the pan and place the pan on the stove over medium heat. Add the shallot and sauté for 1 minute. Pour in the sherry and boil, scraping up any pan drippings, until the pan is almost dry. Add the tomatoes, increase heat to high and cook until the tomatoes have broken down and the juices have condensed, 10 minutes. The sauce should be pulpy, not drippy. Taste and adjust the seasoning, sprinkle with the vinegar, then spoon over the chicken.

SERVES 4

SERVING SUGGESTIONS

Watermelon Gazpacho (p. 150), Zucchini Carpaccio with Avocado (p. 261), Haricots Verts with Balsamic Vinaigrette (p. 231), Saratoga Potatoes (p. 273), Angel Food Cake (p. 742—with Brandied Peaches,

p. 599), Blueberry Ice Cream (p. 726), Forget-It Meringue Torte (p. 823)

SEPTEMBER 11, 2002: "A MEAL WITH LOVED ONES CLOSES THE CIRCLE OF LIFE," BY AMANDA HESSER.

—2002

STIR-FRIED CHICKEN WITH CREAMED CORN

Inspired by a fish and corn dish he'd had at Ocean Star, a Chinese restaurant in Monterey Park, California, Mark Bittman devised this brilliant variation made with chicken. He spiced it aggressively and included fresh corn in addition to the dubious-but-essential canned creamed corn. The dish is like pigs-in-a-blanket—its success cannot be explained. Just accept and enjoy.

1 pound boneless chicken (breasts or thighs), cut into ½-inch chunks

2 tablespoons soy sauce

1 teaspoon Asian sesame oil

1 tablespoon sherry, rice wine, sake, or dry white wine

2 tablespoons peanut or other neutral oil, like corn or grapeseed

1 tablespoon minced garlic

1 tablespoon minced fresh ginger

1 small chile, seeded and minced (or crushed red pepper flakes to taste)

One 15-ounce can creamed corn

1 cup corn kernels (fresh, frozen, or canned)

Chopped cilantro for garnish

1. Mix the chicken with the soy sauce, sesame oil, and wine in a small bowl. Put the peanut oil into a deep skillet or wok, preferably nonstick, and turn the heat to high.

2. Drain the chicken. When the oil is hot, add the chicken to the skillet and cook undisturbed until the bottom browns, about 2 minutes. Stir once or twice, and cook for 2 minutes longer.

3. Turn the heat down to medium-low. Add the garlic, ginger, and chile and stir; 15 seconds later, add the creamed corn and corn kernels. Cook, stirring occa-

sionally, until heated through, 3 to 4 minutes. Garnish with cilantro and serve over white rice.

SERVES 4

COOKING NOTES

Use chicken thighs, which have more flavor than breasts.

I used frozen corn (with no water added), it worked well.

Serve with jasmine or basmati rice if possible.

SERVING SUGGESTIONS

Zucchini and Vermouth (p. 227), String Beans with Ginger and Garlic (p. 260), Chilled Sesame Spinach (p. 239), Jasmine Tea Rice (p. 354), Summer Pudding (p. 847), Lemon Bars (p. 690), Vanilla Plum Ice (p. 734)

OCTOBER 2, 2002: "THE MINIMALIST; CREAMED CORN? REALLY?" BY MARK BITTMAN.

—2002

ꙅ STAFF MEAL CHICKEN WITH SALSA VERDE

Every once in a while, a crude and spicy dish sneaks into the pages of the *Times* (see Beer-Can Chicken on p. 473). Enjoy it!

——————

2 tablespoons fresh lemon juice
I heaping tablespoon granulated garlic
   (not garlic powder)
I heaping tablespoon granulated onion
   (not onion powder)
I tablespoon plus ¾ teaspoon freshly ground
   white pepper
3 tablespoons paprika
2 tablespoons kosher salt
I tablespoon to ¼ cup crushed red pepper flakes,
   depending on desired heat
½ cup olive oil
One 3- to 3½-pound chicken, cut into 8 pieces
Salsa Verde (recipe follows)

1. Combine the lemon juice, garlic, onion, pepper, paprika, salt, red pepper flakes, and olive oil in a large bowl and whisk to blend into a paste. Add the chicken pieces and turn until well coated on all sides. Marinate for at least 1 hour, or as long as overnight; if marinating more than 1 hour, cover the bowl and refrigerate. Turn pieces occasionally.

2. Heat the oven to 400 degrees. Arrange the chicken pieces in a single layer on a large foil-lined baking sheet, leaving ample space between the pieces. Roast for 30 minutes.

3. Reduce the oven heat to 300 degrees and continue cooking for 15 to 20 minutes, or until the skin is crisp and the meat is tender. Serve hot or at room temperature, with the salsa and, ideally, with rice.

SERVES 4

SALSA VERDE

¼ pound jalapeño peppers (3 to 4 large),
   stems removed (not seeded)
2 to 3 cups chicken broth
I¼ pounds tomatillos, husked and rinsed
I small bunch cilantro, leaves and stems
   chopped (½ cup)
I teaspoon salt

1. Place the jalapeños in a medium saucepan and add enough broth to cover. Bring to a boil, then reduce to a simmer and cook until the jalapeños are slightly tender, about 6 to 8 minutes.

2. Add the tomatillos and cook for about 5 minutes, until the tomatillos have lost their brightness and the vegetables are soft but not mushy.

3. Using a slotted spoon, transfer the vegetables to a blender or food processor, and process until chunky, adding cooking liquid as needed to make a thick but loose purée. Transfer to a bowl and stir in the cilantro and salt. Serve warm or at room temperature.

MAKES ABOUT 2 CUPS

SERVING SUGGESTIONS

Black Bean Soup with Salsa and Jalapeño Corn-Bread Muffins (p. 129), Beets in Lime Cream (p. 230), Rice (p. 282), Salted Caramel Ice Cream (p. 733), Aztec Hot Chocolate Pudding (p. 855)

Interest in the behind-the-scenes life of restaurants supported a wave of books from Anthony Bourdain's *Kitchen Confidential* to Bill Buford's *Heat*. Even the staff meal—traditionally, the grub served to those who later make your dinner—was dissected and celebrated. New York's Chanterelle made a book of it: *Staff Meals from Chanterelle*; Thomas Keller included his staff's lasagna recipe in *The French Laundry Cookbook*; and Regina Schrambling wrote in the *Times* about this chicken dish served in the basement kitchen of Artie's Delicatessen in New York.

OCTOBER 16, 2002: "UPSTAIRS, HOT PASTRAMI; DOWNSTAIRS, JALAPEÑOS," BY REGINA SCHRAMBLING. RECIPE ADAPTED FROM ANTONIO MARTINEZ OF ARTIE'S DELICATESSEN IN NEW YORK CITY.

—2002

⌒ TURDUCKEN

Once upon a time, possibly at a lodge in Wyoming, possibly at a butcher shop in Maurice, Louisiana, or maybe even at a plantation in South Carolina, an enterprising cook decided to take a boned chicken, a boned duck, and a boned turkey, stuff them one inside the other like Russian dolls, and roast the result. He called his masterpiece turducken.

In the years that followed its disputed birth, turducken has become a Southern specialty and holiday feast. A well-prepared turducken is a marvelous treat, a free-form poultry terrine layered with flavorful stuffing and moistened with duck fat. Once it's assembled, it looks like a turkey and it roasts like a turkey, but when you carve it, you can slice it like a loaf of bread. In each slice, you get a little bit of everything: white meat from the turkey breast, dark meat from the legs, duck, carrots, bits of sausage, bread, herbs, juices, and chicken too.

Although Louisiana chef Paul Prudhomme likes to claim credit for the turducken, the annals of culinary history are stuffed with birds stuffed into birds. There is a reference in the diaries of John B. Grimball from 1832 for a Charleston preserve of fowl. It consisted of a dove stuffed into a quail, the quail into a guinea hen, the hen into a duck, the duck into a capon, the capon into a goose, and the goose into a peacock or a turkey. The whole thing was then roasted and cut into "transverse sections." It makes turducken seem like the lazy way out.

Barbara Wheaton, a food historian, said that in the fourteenth century, peacocks were boned and roasted and restuffed into their still-feathered skin. In his *Encyclopedia of Practical Gastronomy*, published at the turn of the last century, Henri Babinski, who used the pseudonym Ali-Bab, gives instructions for stuffing boned ortolans into truffles (not a bad way to go, if you're an ortolan, I guess).

"In the Republic of Georgia," Darra Goldstein, a professor of Russian at Williams College and the editor of *Gastronomica*, a journal of food and culture, wrote in her book *The Georgian Feast*, "there's a very old feast dish that calls for a huge ox roasted on a spit, stuffed successively with a calf, a lamb, a turkey, a goose, a duck, and finally a young chicken, and seasoned throughout with spices. The art lay in ensuring that each type of meat was perfectly roasted."

Layering a bunch of birds (or beasts) is clearly a culinary stunt, but it also makes for a great-tasting dish. One problem with turkey is that eating it gets monotonous very quickly, but when each bite of turkey is alternated with chicken, duck, or possibly pork stuffing, you may end up eating too much, but you never get bored.

½ pound sliced pancetta (¼ inch thick), cut into ½-inch squares

¾ pound sweet Italian sausages with fennel

1 tablespoon olive oil

1 cup chopped onion, plus 4 onion halves for pan

1 cup chopped carrots, plus 4 carrot halves for pan

1½ cups chopped celery

2 cloves garlic, mashed

1 teaspoon anise seeds

One 3- to 3½-pound chicken, boned, wings and giblets reserved

One 4- to 5-pound duck, boned, wings and giblets reserved

Sea salt and freshly ground black pepper

¼ cup brandy

1 tablespoon chopped thyme

3 tablespoons chopped tarragon

2 cups ½-inch cubes stale baguette

One 10- to 12-pound turkey, boned

1. The day before serving, cook the pancetta in a large sauté pan over low heat until the fat is rendered and the pancetta is browned, 10 to 15 minutes. Drain on paper towels. Remove the sausage from the casings, break into small pieces, and add to the pan. Cook the sausage until it's no longer pink. Drain on paper towels.

2. Pour off the fat in the pan. Add the oil, along with the chopped onion, carrots, and celery, garlic, and anise seeds, and cook over medium heat for 2 minutes. Add the chicken and duck giblets, season with salt and pepper, and cook until the giblets are almost cooked through. Raise the heat to high and pour in the brandy. Reduce until almost gone, then shut off the heat and stir in the thyme and tarragon. Remove from the heat.

3. Remove the giblets from the pan and chop. Fold together the pancetta, sausage, vegetables, giblets, and bread cubes in a large bowl. Taste and adjust the seasoning. Let cool, then refrigerate overnight.

4. The next day, lay the turkey out on the counter, skin side down. Season with salt and pepper. Spread one-third of the stuffing over its surface, pressing some into each drumstick to make it plump again. Trim about two-thirds of the fat from the duck, leaving some fat on the breast. Butterfly the duck drumsticks. Lay the duck pieces on top of the turkey over their corresponding parts. Season with salt and pepper. Spread one-third of the stuffing over the duck. Lay the chicken on top, again skin side down, and corresponding *in arrangement* to the turkey. Season with salt and pepper, and spread with the remaining stuffing.

5. Heat the oven to 250 degrees. Thread a carpet or upholstery needle with 2 feet of butcher's twine. Beginning at the tail end, begin pulling the edges of the turkey together, re-forming its body, stitching every inch or so. Have someone hold the bird while you stitch. Do not sew the turducken together too tight, or it will split open when cooking.

6. Turn the bird over. With a 3-foot piece of twine, truss it, wrapping the twine around the tips of the drumsticks, then crisscrossing it and going down around base of the drumsticks. Crisscross the twine under the bird, then bring it up the sides and crisscross it on top, wrapping it down and around the wings, crisscrossing it on the back and up again, tying it over the breast.

7. Season the roasting pan with salt and pepper. Place the turducken in the pan breast side up and season it. Place the chicken and duck wings, along with the halved onions or carrots, in the pan.

8. Cover the pan with aluminum foil and bake. After 2 hours, begin checking the bird every 30 minutes or so and basting once the juices form. Turn the pan every now and then so the turducken cooks evenly. When an instant-read thermometer inserted in the center of the turducken reads 130 degrees (probably after about 4 or 5 hours), remove the aluminum foil and turn the heat up to 375 degrees. Baste every 15 minutes or so until the turducken reaches 165 degrees in the center. Remove from the oven and let cool for 10 minutes or so.

9. With sturdy spatulas, lift the turducken onto a platter. Cover with foil and let sit for another 15 to 20 minutes. Meanwhile, strain the pan juices and spoon off the fat.

10. Using a bread knife or carving knife, slice the turducken like a loaf of bread. Serve, passing the cooking juices.

SERVES 12

COOKING NOTES

Preserve your sanity; find a butcher who will bone the birds for you.

Making turducken, it turns out, is not unlike preparing a turkey with stuffing, and not unlike cooking a rolled and tied butterflied leg of lamb. You want the stuffing to be full flavored and sturdy; it should fill the dips and cavities where the bones once were, without making the bird bulky. If you fill the turkey too full, it will split open when cooking.

Assembling a turducken is simple. You lay the boned turkey skin side down (if your butcher hasn't butterflied the bird, slice through the skin where the backbone was and open up the bird so it lies flat), season it with salt and pepper, and spread it with some of the stuffing. Make sure to tuck some stuffing into the drumsticks. Lay the duck in the same manner on top of the turkey and repeat. The same goes for the chicken. Then you have a choice: you can sew up the bird using a carpet or upholstery needle and butcher's twine, or thread thin skewers through the edges of the bird and then lace the skewers with twine.

I recommend sewing—and enlisting someone to help. Begin at the tail end, folding up the tail skin and pulling the edges of the bird, close to the wings, back together. Stitch the bird from side to side about an inch from each edge, pulling the twine to tighten it. Continue sewing up to the neck end, then tie off the string. I recommend trussing the assemblage as you would a chicken, which will help outline the drumsticks and re-form the birds into one plump turducken.

You will need a thermometer, because that is the only way to know what's going on inside. When the center reaches 130 degrees, you remove the foil and increase the oven heat. The outside will get brown, and basting will allow the mix of juices to moisten the entire turducken.

When the turducken is done (165 degrees), you set it on a platter, use a gravy boat to collect the cooking juices—which are rich and concentrated, like a demiglace—and march both to the table. Give someone who's never encountered a turducken the honor of taking a long thin knife and slicing.

SERVING SUGGESTIONS

Corn Bread Stuffing (p. 312), Red Cabbage Glazed with Maple Syrup (p. 236), Brussels Sprouts "Slaw" with Mustard Butter (p. 253), Mashed Potatoes Anna (p. 294), Stewed Fennel (p. 245), Creamed Onions (p. 217), Broccoli Puree with Ginger (p. 253), Apple Crumb Pie (p. 841), Sour Cream Ice Cream (p. 730), Pear Upside-Down Cake (p. 772)

NOVEMBER 20, 2002: "TURKEY FINDS ITS INNER DUCK (AND CHICKEN)," BY AMANDA HESSER.

—2002

CRISP-BRAISED DUCK LEGS WITH AROMATIC VEGETABLES

One of the hallmarks of Mark Bittman's "The Minimalist" column has been his interest in technique. He often takes a classic recipe and plays around with the method to underline the characteristics that cooks would desire in the finished dish. Take, for instance, this recipe for braised duck legs. Two small revisions give the finished legs a crisp skin, a detail often lost in braising: Bittman first very slowly renders the fat from the duck legs and crisps the skin in a pan. Later the legs are braised, raised up on a levee of chopped

vegetables and covered in liquid just up to the level of the skin, in an uncovered pan. The legs braise fairly quickly, and maintain their crispness.

————

4 duck legs, trimmed of excess fat
Salt and freshly ground black pepper
1 large onion
½ pound carrots
3 stalks celery
6 cloves garlic, lightly crushed
8 sprigs thyme
2 cups chicken broth

1. Heat the oven to 400 degrees. Put the duck legs skin side down in an ovenproof skillet large enough to accommodate all the ingredients comfortably; turn the heat to medium. Brown the duck legs carefully and evenly, sprinkling them with salt and pepper as they cook.

2. Meanwhile, peel the onion and carrots and dice all the vegetables.

3. When the legs are nicely browned, turn them over and sear for just a minute or two. Remove to a plate; remove all but enough fat to moisten the vegetables from the pan. Add the vegetables to the skillet, along with some salt and pepper, and cook over medium-high heat, stirring occasionally, until they begin to brown, 10 to 15 minutes.

4. Return the duck legs to the pan, skin side up, and add the garlic, thyme, and stock; the stock should come about halfway up the duck legs but should not cover them. Turn the heat to high, bring to a boil, and transfer to the oven.

5. Cook for 30 minutes, then lower the heat to 350 degrees. Continue to cook, undisturbed, until the duck is tender and the liquid reduced, at least another half hour. The duck is done when a thin-bladed knife pierces the meat with little resistance. (When done, the duck will hold nicely in a warm oven for another hour.)

SERVES 4

COOKING NOTES

I used a Le Creuset braiser for this recipe, and some of the edges of the duck skin stuck to the pan. Use a nonstick pan if you have one.

The original recipe did not call for garlic and thyme; they were included as a variation in Bittman's text. But without them, the dish is too one-dimensional. He also recommended a habanero chile and a few slices of ginger as an alternative.

VARIATION

When spreading the vegetables in the roasting pan, add 1 cup green or black olives, and instead of just chicken stock, use half stock, half canned whole tomatoes.

SERVING SUGGESTIONS

Seasoned Olives (p. 90), Red Wine Risotto (p. 346), Raw Spinach Salad (p. 175), Shredded Brussels Sprouts with Bacon and Pine Nuts (p. 235), Pierre Hermé's Chocolate Sablés (p. 704)

PERIOD DETAIL

By 2000, *Times* food writers had begun writing more recipes for duck legs and chicken legs and thighs than for breast meat. American cooks—or *Times* readers, at least—had finally come to the conclusion that duck breasts and chicken breasts, praised in the past for their simplicity, are often tasteless, not to mention difficult to cook well.

DECEMBER 25, 2002: "THE MINIMALIST: DUCK LEGS, A.S.A.P.," BY MARK BITTMAN.

—2002

✑ CHICKEN BOUILLABAISSE

The best chicken bouillabaisse—a peasant stew coarsing with the mineral and garlic flavors of Marseilles—comes from a chef best known for cooking fish, Eric Ripert.

———

One 3- to 3½-pound chicken, cut into 10 pieces
Salt and freshly ground white pepper
¾ cup plus 2 tablespoons extra virgin olive oil
2 medium onions, thinly sliced
1 cup thinly sliced leeks (white and pale green parts only)
1 head garlic, separated into cloves and peeled, all but 2 cloves thinly sliced

½ fennel bulb, thinly sliced
3 pinches saffron threads
¼ teaspoon cayenne pepper, or to taste
⅔ cup diced ripe tomato or well-drained canned tomato
1 tablespoon tomato paste
1½ teaspoons all-purpose flour
3½ cups chicken broth
8 small Yukon Gold potatoes
1 tablespoon boiling water
One 6-inch piece baguette
1 large egg yolk
One 6-inch strip orange peel
2 tablespoons Pernod or Ricard
4 branches thyme

1. Pat the chicken dry and season with salt and pepper. Pour 2 tablespoons oil into a deep sauté pan or casserole large enough to hold the chicken in a single layer (or brown in batches if your pan isn't large enough) and place over high heat until starting to smoke. Add the chicken skin side down and cook until golden brown, turning to brown both sides. Remove the chicken to a platter and lower the heat to medium. Add the onions, leeks, sliced garlic, and fennel and cook, stirring, until starting to soften.

2. Sprinkle on 2 pinches saffron and the cayenne and cook for a few minutes longer, then add the tomato and tomato paste and cook for a minute more. Sprinkle with the flour, stir, and then return the chicken to the pan, along with any juices from the platter. Add the broth, bring to a simmer, and cook for 12 minutes. Remove the 4 breast pieces from the pan. Continue cooking the remaining chicken for 10 to 15 minutes longer, until done, then remove from the pan. Skim any foam from the surface of the sauce, and set the pan aside.

3. While the chicken cooks, place the potatoes in a saucepan, add salted water to cover, and boil until just tender, 15 to 20 minutes. Drain. Peel when cool enough to handle.

4. Place the remaining pinch of saffron in a small dish and pour the boiling water over it.

5. Slice the piece of baguette lengthwise into 4 slices, and toast. Rub with 1 garlic clove and brush with a little oil.

6. Place the egg yolk in a mixing bowl. Force the remaining garlic clove through a press—or just finely chop it—and add it to the yolk, beating with a whisk.

Strain in the water from steeping the saffron, whisking. Slowly drizzle in the remaining olive oil, whisking vigorously, until the mixture thickens to mayonnaise consistency. Season with salt and pepper and refrigerate until ready to serve.

7. Add the orange peel, Pernod, and thyme to the pan the chicken cooked in, and simmer for 5 minutes; then remove the orange peel and thyme. Season the sauce with salt and cayenne. Add the potatoes and chicken to the pan and reheat.

8. Serve the chicken and potatoes in warm soup plates with the sauce. Spread some of the garlic-saffron mayonnaise (aioli) on the toasted baguette slices (reserve the remaining aioli for another use), and place 1 alongside each serving.

SERVES 4

COOKING NOTE
The aioli takes a while to thicken—keep beating!

SERVING SUGGESTIONS
Seasoned Olives (p. 90), Artichauts Vinaigrette (p. 225), Salade à la Romaine (p. 171), No-Knead Bread (p. 670), Le Cirque's Crème Brûlée (p. 844), Lemon Mousse for a Crowd (p. 861), Frozen Meringue Velvet (p. 723)

JANUARY 1, 2003: "THE CHEF: ERIC RIPERT: BOUILLA-BAISSE, UNSTRICTLY SPEAKING," BY FLORENCE FABRICANT. RECIPE ADAPTED FROM ERIC RIPERT, THE CHEF AT LE BERNARDIN IN NEW YORK CITY.

—2003

✎ SOUTHEAST ASIAN CHICKEN TWO WAYS

Chicken is to Mark Bittman what the puppy is to Jeff Koons—a subject inspiring endless variations. Here, after using a soy, garlic, ginger, and chile marinade for the chicken, Bittman has you finish half the dish with lime wedges and cilantro (Thai-style) and half with more garlic and ginger and fish sauce (Vietnamese-style). The first is fragrant and moist. The second has a sticky, savory glaze. You can make the entire dish one way or the other, but I think it's fun to make it both ways.

One 3- to 4-pound chicken, cut into serving pieces and trimmed of excess fat
3 tablespoons soy sauce
1 to 2 tablespoons minced garlic
1 to 2 tablespoons minced fresh ginger
1 to 2 teaspoons crushed red pepper flakes
1 tablespoon corn oil
Lime wedges
Chopped cilantro
¼ cup sugar
2 tablespoons water
2 tablespoons Asian fish sauce, preferably Thai

1. Place the chicken in a large bowl with the soy sauce, 1 tablespoon each garlic and ginger, and 1 teaspoon red pepper flakes. Toss well to coat. (The chicken can be covered and refrigerated for up to a day.)

2. Heat the oil in a large deep nonstick skillet over medium-high heat. Remove the chicken from the marinade and add skin side down to the hot oil. Brown well on both sides, about 4 minutes per side, then lower the heat, and cook, turning once, until the chicken is cooked through, 20 to 25 minutes. At this point, half the chicken can be served with lime wedges and cilantro, if you wish.

3. For Vietnamese-style chicken, remove the chicken from the pan, then turn the heat to low, and add the sugar, another tablespoon each of garlic and ginger, and another teaspoon of red pepper flakes, along with the water. Raise the heat to high and cook, stirring occasionally, until the sugar melts and the sauce thickens and foams. Add the fish sauce and any juices accumulated around the chicken and cook for 1 minute more, then return the chicken to the pan and cook, turning the pieces occasionally, until they are nicely glazed and the chicken is hot.

4. Remove from the skillet, spoon the sauce on top and garnish with lime and cilantro.

SERVES 4

COOKING NOTES
Remove the chicken from the fridge 30 minutes before starting the recipe—it will cook more evenly.

I cut the breasts in half so the pieces of chicken were more evenly sized.

I used a splatter screen to keep the fat from flying everywhere as I sautéed the chicken. This had the added benefit of holding some of the heat in the pan, helping the chicken cook through more quickly.

Remove the chicken pieces from the pan as they finish cooking. Keep warm in a low oven.

The amount of red pepper flakes seems outrageous, but somehow it works. The dish is spicy but not intolerably so.

SERVING SUGGESTIONS

Kaffir Lime Lemonade (p. 26), Pork-and-Toasted-Rice-Powder Spring Rolls (p. 74), Pork Belly Tea Sandwiches (p. 88), Steamed Fennel with Red Pepper Oil (p. 263), Pad Thai–Style Rice Salad (p. 357), Glazed Mango with Sour Cream Sorbet and Black Pepper (p. 850), Sticky Rice with Mango (p. 861)

FEBRUARY 12, 2003: "THE MINIMALIST: A DUAL ROLE FOR CHICKEN," BY MARK BITTMAN.

—2003

⌒ SPICY, SUPERCRUNCHY FRIED CHICKEN

Ready for a tip that will change your life? You don't need to deep-fry chicken: you can shallow-fry it in half an inch of oil, which means less mess and wasted fat.

———

I good chicken, cut into serving pieces and trimmed
of excess fat, or 8 to 10 leg pieces (drumsticks
and thighs), trimmed of excess fat
2 teaspoons salt
I teaspoon freshly ground black pepper
I tablespoon curry powder
½ teaspoon ground allspice
2 tablespoons minced garlic
I Scotch bonnet or habanero, or other hot chile, seeded
and minced, or cayenne pepper to taste (optional)
I large egg
2 tablespoons water
I cup all-purpose flour, or as needed
Lard and unsalted butter combined or
vegetable oil for frying
½ cup cubed country ham
Lemon or lime wedges for garnish

1. Toss the chicken with the salt, pepper, curry, allspice, garlic, chile, egg, and water in a bowl. When thoroughly combined, blend in the flour, using your hands. Keep mixing until most of the flour is blended with the other ingredients and the chicken is coated (add more water or flour if the mixture is too thin or too dry; it should be dry but not powdery). Let sit while you heat the fat. (The chicken can marinate, refrigerated, for up to a day.)

2. Choose a skillet or casserole at least 12 inches in diameter that can be covered. Add enough fat to come to a depth of about ½ inch and turn the heat to medium-high. If you are using butter, skim any foam as it rises to the surface. When the oil is hot (a pinch of flour will sizzle), raise the heat to high. Add the cubed ham, then slowly add the chicken pieces (if you add them all at once, the temperature will plummet). Cover the skillet, reduce the heat to medium-high, and cook for 7 minutes.

3. Uncover the skillet, turn the chicken, and continue to cook, uncovered, for another 7 minutes. Turn the chicken again and cook for about 5 minutes more, turning as necessary to ensure that both sides are golden brown. Remove the chicken from the skillet and drain on paper towels.

4. Serve the chicken at any temperature, with lemon or lime wedges.

SERVES 4

COOKING NOTES

Use a deep cast-iron skillet if you have one—it holds heat most evenly.

Covering a pan of hot oil while frying can be dangerous. Do not leave the stove while you do it, and keep an eye on the pan, lifting the lid occasionally to make sure the temperature isn't too high.

Adding cubed ham to the fat before frying adds another layer of succulence to the chicken.

VARIATION

Cinnamon-Scented Fried Chicken: While the fat heats, mix together 2 cups all-purpose flour with 1 tablespoon coarse salt, 2 tablespoons ground cinnamon, and 1 teaspoon freshly ground black pepper in a plastic bag. Toss the chicken in the bag, 2 or 3 pieces at a time, until well coated. Put the pieces on a rack as you finish. Fry the chicken as instructed in the recipe.

SERVING SUGGESTIONS
Pickled Shrimp (p. 95), Cucumbers in Cream (p. 225), Wilted Chard with Pickled Red Onion (p. 261), Stewed Corn (p. 271), Light Potato Salad (p. 301), Pickled Watermelon Rind (p. 598), Red Velvet Cake (p. 757), Key Lime Pie (p. 826), Buttermilk Pie (p. 859)

MAY 21, 2003: "THE MINIMALIST ENTERTAINS; FOR PERFECT FRIED CHICKEN THIS SUMMER, BREAK THE RULES," BY MARK BITTMAN.

—2003

⌇ BRAISED LIGURIAN CHICKEN

Jamie Oliver, the tufted blond celebrity chef, prepared this for me in the cramped basement kitchen of Passione restaurant in London. It was a typically damp, sodden London day and yet the flavors of the Mediterranean sang in the pan. "It's quite delicately flavored," Oliver said to me. "It's perfumed with the wine and the rosemary. You get this kind of meaty kind of saltiness from the olives, and what's really interesting is if an English housewife got hold of the recipe, she'd probably stone the olives and have quite a lot of them. But in Italy, literally for eight people they put that much"—in his hand, he cradled about two dozen olives—"and they leave the pits in."

Oliver, who can as easily rattle on entertainingly about a floor board, continued, "When you cook olives whole like this, it's almost like an anchovy. The salt comes out of the olives, and the olive becomes more like a vegetable. And the salt from the olive flavors the chicken really wonderfully." Readers seemed to think so—nine people wrote in to recommend this recipe for the book.

2 heaping tablespoons all-purpose flour
Sea salt and freshly ground black pepper
One 4-pound chicken, cut into 8 pieces
¼ cup extra virgin olive oil
4 to 5 sprigs rosemary
6 cloves garlic, thinly sliced
1½ cups dry white wine
4 anchovy fillets
½ cup Calamata olives (not pitted)
3 ripe plum tomatoes, halved, seeded, and coarsely chopped

1. Combine the flour with salt and pepper to taste in a large bowl. Add the chicken pieces and toss until evenly coated.
2. Place a large casserole over medium-high heat and heat the olive oil. Add the chicken pieces and fry until golden underneath, about 5 minutes. Turn the chicken, add rosemary and garlic, and fry until the garlic is softened but not colored, about 3 minutes. Add the wine. When it comes to a boil, add the anchovies, olives, and tomatoes. Partially cover the pan and reduce the heat to medium-low. Simmer until the chicken is cooked and tender and the broth is reduced to a rich sauce, 15 to 20 minutes.
3. To serve, discard the rosemary sprigs, and season the sauce well with salt and pepper. Place a piece or two of chicken on each plate and top with a spoonful of sauce.

SERVES 4

SERVING SUGGESTIONS
Crostini Romani (p. 77), Zuppa di Funghi Siciliana (Sicilian Mushroom Soup; p. 127), Italian Roast Potatoes (p. 300), Steamed Spinach with Balsamic Butter (p. 226), Roasted Cauliflower (p. 248), Saffron Panna Cotta (p. 845), Frozen Lemon Soufflé (p. 725), Coffee Caramel Custard (p. 849)

NOVEMBER 19, 2003: "THE CHEF: JAMIE OLIVER: THE MEDITERRANEAN SUN WARMS RAINY LONDON," BY AMANDA HESSER. RECIPE ADAPTED FROM JAMIE OLIVER.

—2003

⌇ CAROLINA CHICKEN BOG

From the land of grits and gumbo, chitterlings, and chow-chow comes bog, a toasty chicken and pepper stew. Sam Sifton and Mark Bittman, who wrote about this recipe by Robert Stehling, a chef in Charleston, said the name "derives from the way in which the pieces of chicken sit in the pot, like hummocks in a bog."

3 tablespoons bacon fat or neutral oil, like corn or canola

6 ounces chicken gizzards and hearts, minced

Salt and freshly ground black pepper

2 medium green bell peppers, cored, seeded, and diced

2 medium red bell peppers, cored, seeded, and diced

4 medium-to-large white onions, diced

4 stalks celery, diced

2 tablespoons minced garlic

I cup dry red wine

One 35-ounce can tomatoes, chopped, with their liquid

6 tablespoons unsalted butter

¼ cup all-purpose flour

I pound mixed sausages and cured meats, like
    kielbasa, Italian sausage, breakfast links,
    chorizo, diced ham, and/or bacon

2 cups chicken broth

I branch thyme

¼ teaspoon crushed red pepper flakes, or to taste

2 bay leaves

1½ pounds boneless chicken, preferably thighs, chopped

8 chicken livers, trimmed and cut in half

I tablespoon cider vinegar

½ cup Dijon mustard

Cooked white rice for serving

1. Put the fat in a deep skillet or large casserole over medium-high heat. A minute later, add the gizzards and hearts and cook until quite brown and sticking to the pan, at least 3 minutes. Stir once, sprinkle with salt and pepper, and then brown the other side. Add the peppers, onions, celery, and garlic and cook, stirring occasionally, until the vegetables are soft, 8 to 10 minutes. Add the red wine and tomatoes and bring to a boil, then adjust the heat so the mixture simmers; cook for about 10 minutes.

2. Meanwhile, melt 4 tablespoons butter in a small skillet or saucepan over medium heat. Add the flour and stir until smooth. Cook, stirring occasionally, until the mixture turns quite brown, about 10 minutes. Add this roux to the simmering stew; cook 5 minutes.

3. Add the meats, broth, thyme, red pepper flakes, and bay leaves to the stew and cook at a lively simmer, stirring occasionally, for about 40 minutes. Add the chicken meat and cook for another 15 minutes or more (this dish can sit on the stove, simmering, for hours; add a little water or stock if it threatens to dry out).

4. Meanwhile, melt the remaining 2 tablespoons butter in an 8- or 10-inch nonstick skillet over medium-

high heat. When the foam subsides, add the livers and cook until quite brown on one side; sprinkle with salt and pepper as they cook. Turn and brown on the other side.

5. Stir the vinegar and mustard into the stew. Add the livers and stir. Serve over white rice.

SERVES 8

COOKING NOTE

If you can't find chicken gizzards and hearts, substitute chicken necks.

SERVING SUGGESTIONS

Cheese Straws (p. 79), Green Goddess Salad (p. 176), Iceberg Lettuce with Smoked Bacon and Buttermilk Dressing (p. 200), Bourbon Pecan Pie (p. 842)

JANUARY 28, 2004: "SUNDAY ON THE COUCH WITH CHICKEN AND BEANS," BY MARK BITTMAN AND SAM SIFTON. RECIPE ADAPTED FROM ROBERT STEHLING, CHEF AND THE OWNER OF HOMINY GRILL IN CHARLESTON, SOUTH CAROLINA.

—2004

ROAST CHICKEN SALAD

10 cups baby spinach

5½ cups roughly shredded roast chicken
    (from a 3-pound roast chicken; see p. 478)

4 scallions, thinly sliced

I cup chopped cilantro

2 ripe avocados

1½ teaspoons Maldon salt, or table salt to taste

Finely grated zest of I lime

¼ cup fresh lime juice

¼ cup extra virgin olive oil

Freshly ground black pepper

1. Combine the spinach, chicken, scallions, and about ¾ cup cilantro in a large mixing bowl.

2. Halve the avocados and discard the pits; scoop out curls with a spoon. Or peel the avocados and cut the fruit into chunks or slices. Add to the salad.

3. Stir together the salt, lime zest, and lime juice in a small bowl. Whisk in the oil and pepper to taste. Pour over the salad, tossing gently by hand to mix.

4. Arrange the salad on a large plate or in a salad bowl and sprinkle with the remaining chopped cilantro.

SERVES 4

SERVING SUGGESTIONS
Ginger Lemonade (p. 26), Watermelon and Tomato Salad (p. 197), Al Forno's Roasted Asparagus (p. 233), No-Knead Bread (p. 670), Blueberry Pie with a Lattice Top (p. 853), Brownies (p. 684)

READERS
"Eaten weekly if possible."
Carrie Harmon, Short Hills, NJ, e-mail

JUNE 9, 2004: "AT MY TABLE: A COLD LUNCH, EASY ON THE COOK," BY NIGELLA LAWSON.

—2004

✎ BUTTERMILK ROAST CHICKEN

A soak in seasoned buttermilk followed by some time in a hot oven work wonders for chicken—its skin crisps and turns bronze.

Because you can only buy buttermilk in quart-size containers—a racket!—and no recipe calls for more than 2 cups buttermilk you will have some left over. For some ideas on how to use it up, see Fish Poached in Buttermilk on p. 419, Chilled English Pea–Mint Soup on p. 162, Old South Buttermilk Biscuits on p. 655, or the Buttermilk Pie on p. 859.

One 4-pound chicken
2 cups buttermilk
6 tablespoons vegetable oil
2 cloves garlic, lightly crushed
1 tablespoon Maldon or other sea salt
1 tablespoon crushed black pepper
2 tablespoons roughly chopped rosemary
1 tablespoon honey

1. To butterfly the chicken, place it breast side down on a cutting board and use heavy-duty kitchen shears to cut down along both sides of backbone. Discard the backbone, turn the chicken over, and open it like a book. Press gently to flatten it.
2. Place the chicken in a large freezer bag. Add the buttermilk, ¼ cup oil, the garlic, salt, pepper, rosemary, and honey. Seal the bag securely and refrigerate overnight, or for up to 2 days.
3. Heat the oven to 400 degrees. Remove the chicken from the marinade and place it on a rack over a plate so the excess can drip off. Line a roasting pan with foil and place the chicken in the pan. Drizzle with the remaining 2 tablespoons oil. Roast for 45 minutes.
4. Reduce the heat to 325 degrees and continue roasting until the chicken is well browned and an instant-read thermometer inserted in the thickest part of the thigh reads 165 F, about another 20 minutes. Transfer chicken to a carving board and allow to rest for 10 minutes before cutting into serving pieces.
5. Place a portion of chicken on each of 4 plates, and drizzle with the pan juices.

SERVES 4

COOKING NOTE
To brown the bird evenly, halfway through cooking, rotate the roasting pan 180 degrees.

SERVING SUGGESTIONS
White Gazpacho with Almonds and Grapes (p. 137), Watercress Salad (p. 171), Blood Orange, Date, and Parmesan Salad with Almond Oil (p. 199), Saratoga Potatoes (p. 273), Potato "Tostones" (Flattened Potatoes; p. 301), Green Pea Fritters (p. 270), Summer Squash Casserole (p. 252), Fresh Succotash (p. 275), Light Potato Salad (p. 301), Summer Pudding (p. 847)

READERS
"Even if you don't have buttermilk on hand, the recipe provides a good technique for roasting a spatchcocked chicken, which is faster than a whole chicken and provides a simple solution to the white-meat/dark-meat cooking time problem. Not only is this a terrific recipe, but it also taught me the wonderful British word 'spatchcock,' a term that no self-respecting cook should be without. Alas, it's too long for Scrabble."
Cynthia J. Eiseman, e-mail

JULY 21, 2004: "AT MY TABLE: SPATCHCOCK THE CHICKEN, CUT THE CAKE. AH, SUMMER!" BY NIGELLA LAWSON.

—2004

FRIED SAMBAL WINGS WITH CUCUMBER CREAM

½ cup yuzu juice

½ cup kosher salt, plus more as needed

2 tablespoons sugar

8 cups water

18 chicken wings, about 3½ pounds, wing tips removed, each wing cut in half

6½ tablespoons unsalted butter

¼ cup sambal

¼ cup Sriracha sauce (Asian hot sauce)

1 tablespoon rice wine vinegar

½ English cucumber, quartered lengthwise and seeded

One 4-inch piece fresh ginger

1 cup sour cream

4 cups vegetable oil for shallow frying

1. To make the brine, combine the yuzu juice, salt, sugar, and water in a container large enough to hold the wings. Stir until the salt and sugar dissolve. Add the wings and refrigerate overnight.

2. Drain the wings, rinse well, and pat dry.

3. Combine the butter, sambal, hot sauce, and vinegar in a small saucepan, bring to a simmer over low heat, and simmer for a few minutes, stirring occasionally. Transfer to a blender and puree until smooth.

4. Cut the cucumber crosswise into ⅛-inch-thick pieces. Sprinkle them lightly with salt and let them sit for 10 minutes. Pat dry with a towel.

5. Grate the ginger over a towel or cheesecloth and squeeze out 2 tablespoons juice into a bowl. Add ½ teaspoon salt to the juice, then combine with the sour cream and cucumber. Season to taste.

6. Pour 2 inches of oil into a large deep pot and place over high heat. When the oil reaches 375 degrees, fry the chicken wings, in batches, for about 15 minutes, or until nicely browned. Transfer to a bowl. Toss the wings with the hot sauce and serve with the cucumber cream.

SERVES 6 AS A FIRST COURSE

COOKING NOTE

Yuzu is a type of citrus often used in Asian cooking. If yuzu juice is unavailable, use 6 tablespoons fresh lemon juice (from about 2 lemons) and 2 tablespoons fresh lime juice, plus the grated zest of 1 lemon and 1 lime.

SERVING SUGGESTIONS

Pork-and-Toasted-Rice-Powder Spring Rolls (p. 74), Beet and Ginger Soup with Cucumber (p. 150), Malaysian-Inspired Pork Stew with Traditional Garnishes (p. 552), Chicken with Lime, Chile, and Fresh Herbs (Larb Gai; p. 497), Mango Ice Cream (p. 729)

JULY 30, 2006: "THE ARSENAL," BY JILL SANTOPIETRO. RECIPE ADAPTED FROM TAKU RESTAURANT IN BROOKLYN, NEW YORK.

—2006

SPICY, GARLICKY CASHEW CHICKEN

Extraordinarily spicy, garlicky, and good.

---

1 cup salted roasted cashews

6 tablespoons chopped cilantro (with some stems)

¼ cup canola or safflower oil

4 cloves garlic, roughly chopped

2 tablespoons soy sauce

2 teaspoons brown sugar

1 to 2 jalapeño peppers, sliced (discard seeds or not, to taste)

Juice of 1 lime

2 tablespoons water

Kosher salt and freshly ground black pepper

3 pounds chicken thighs and/or drumsticks

Lime wedges for garnish

1. Combine the nuts, 2 tablespoons cilantro, the oil, garlic, soy sauce, brown sugar, jalapeño, lime juice, and water in a blender or food processor and blend until smooth, scraping down the sides as necessary. Taste and season with salt and pepper.

2. Season the chicken all over with salt and pepper. Set aside ⅓ of the cashew mixture. Smear on enough of the remaining mixture to thoroughly coat the chicken. Let marinate at room temperature while you heat a grill or broiler. (Or refrigerate for up to 12 hours before cooking.)

3. Grill or broil the chicken, turning frequently, until

it is crisp and golden on the outside and done on the inside (cut a small nick to check), 20 to 30 minutes.

4. Sprinkle the chicken with the remaining ¼ cup cilantro and serve with lime wedges and the reserved cashew mixture.

SERVES 4

SERVING SUGGESTIONS
Manjula Gokal's Gujarati Mango Soup (p. 155), Chinese Barbecued Spareribs (p. 517), Stuck-Pot Rice with Yogurt and Spices (p. 351), Jasmine Tea Rice (p. 354), Green Beans with Coriander-Coconut Crust (p. 246), Mango Ice Cream (p. 729), Macaroons (p. 681)

JULY 11, 2007: "A TRAIL THAT LEADS THROUGH MANY MEALS," BY MELISSA CLARK.

—2007

~ CHICKEN AND LEMON TERRINE

One of the most flavorful terrines I've ever tasted. Delicate pieces of brined and poached chicken and lemon confit are suspended in a Meyer lemon and herb gelatin. Serve with peppery baby arugula, tossed with olive oil and good salt, and a stellar lunch is yours.

———

13 ounces (about 1½ cups) fine sea salt,
    plus 2½ teaspoons, plus more as needed
4 quarts cold water
Two 3-pound chickens, halved
7 Meyer lemons
1 large leek, white and pale green parts only,
    cut into 3-inch pieces and washed well
2 onions, quartered
1 head garlic, halved like a grapefruit
1 bunch cilantro, leaves and stems chopped
3 sprigs thyme
2 bay leaves
15 black peppercorns
1 whole clove
1¼ cups dry white wine
1 cup sugar
About 2½ ounces (½ cup) powdered gelatin
¾ teaspoon freshly ground black pepper, or to taste

1. Two days before serving, whisk the salt and cold water together in a nonreactive 3-gallon container until the salt has dissolved. Submerge the chicken halves in the brine and refrigerate for at least 12 hours.

2. The day before serving, discard the brine and rinse the chickens well in cold water. Place the chickens in a large stockpot and cover with water by 1 inch. Bring to a boil slowly, then reduce the heat and skim the water of impurities.

3. Halve 4 of the lemons and add them to the pot, along with the leek, onions, garlic, half the cilantro, the thyme, bay leaves, peppercorns, clove, and white wine. Bring back to a boil, then gently simmer until the meat can be pulled from the bone, about 45 minutes. Let the chicken cool in the liquid (bouillon).

4. Meanwhile, to prepare the lemon confit, squeeze the juice from the remaining 3 lemons over a sieve, and chill the juice. Scoop the pulp from the rinds and discard it. Place the rinds in a medium pot, cover with water, and bring to a boil, then drain; repeat twice with fresh water. Then add the sugar and enough water to cover. Bring to a boil, then simmer until the rinds are tender, about 20 minutes. Drain and let cool. Cut the rinds into ¼-inch pieces.

5. Transfer the chicken to a bowl and, while they are still warm, separate the meat from the skin and bones, leaving the meat in large chunks. Discard the skin and bones. Strain the bouillon through a sieve lined with three layers of cheesecloth. Discard the vegetables.

6. Weigh the chicken (you should have about 2¼ pounds). Measure out the same weight of bouillon as chicken (about 1 quart; freeze any extra to use later as stock).

7. Bring the bouillon to a boil in a saucepan, and skim the top. Reduce to a simmer and whisk in 1 ounce of gelatin for every 14 ounces of liquid (about ¾ cup plus 1½ tablespoons gelatin for 2¼ pounds bouillon) until dissolved. Remove from the heat and fold in the chicken (do not stir, or the chicken will become stringy). Let cool slightly.

8. When the liquid is just warm, fold in the lemon confit and remaining cilantro. Season with the 2½ teaspoons salt and pepper. Season to taste with the remaining lemon juice and more salt and pepper as necessary. (Add a touch more salt than you think is needed, as the flavor becomes muted when chilled.) Transfer to a 2-quart or 4-by-11-by-3-inch terrine, cover with plastic, and refrigerate for 1 day.

9. Turn the terrine out, slice and serve at room temperature.

SERVES 16 AS A FIRST COURSE OR LIGHT LUNCH.

COOKING NOTE

To halve the chickens, use poultry shears to cut out the backbone, then use a chef's knife to split the breastbone.

Don't substitute regular lemons for the Meyer lemons—they're too bitter.

SERVING SUGGESTIONS

See headnote. For dessert: Raspberry Granita (p. 719).

APRIL 27, 2008: "THE WAY WE EAT: BLOCK PARTY," BY CHRISTINE MUHLKE. RECIPE ADAPTED FROM DANIEL BOULUD AND SYLVAIN GASDON AT BAR BOULUD IN NEW YORK CITY.

—2008

⌒ JERK CHICKEN

Julia Moskin was hired as a food reporter for the *Times* around the time I began working on this book, so by rights there shouldn't be many of her recipes here. But so many of her stories already seem timeless. Julia has written about Dorie Greenspan's and Pierre Hermé's sablés (pp. 703 and 704), her own Croq-Télé (p. 711), and Sugar Snap Peas with Horseradish (p. 259), among others. She also helpfully pointed me in the direction of some of her favorites, like the exceptional Tuna Salad (p. 435), Swedish Ginger Cookies (p. 708), and Sour Cream Ice Cream (p. 730).

Here, Moskin introduced readers to the art of making jerk chicken.

"Jerk is Jamaica to the bone, aromatic and smoky, sweet but insistently hot," wrote Moskin. "All of its traditional ingredients grow in the island's lush green interior: fresh ginger, thyme, and scallions; Scotch bonnet peppers; and the sweet wood of the allspice tree, which burns to a fragrant smoke.

"Its components are a thick brown paste flecked with chiles, meat (usually pork or chicken, occasionally goat or fish), and smoke, from a tightly covered charcoal grill, that slowly soaks into the food."

Jerk descends from the Maroons and the Tainos in Jamaica, who dug pits to smoke wild pigs with allspice wood.

————

Two 3½- to 4-pound chickens, quartered, or 8 whole chicken legs, or 5 to 6 pounds chicken thighs
1 large bunch scallions (about 8), trimmed
2 shallots, halved
4 to 6 Scotch bonnet or habanero peppers, stems removed
One 2-inch piece fresh ginger, peeled and coarsely chopped
6 garlic cloves
¼ cup fresh thyme leaves or 1 tablespoon dried thyme
2 tablespoons ground allspice, plus more for sprinkling
2 tablespoons soy sauce
2 tablespoons dark brown sugar
1 tablespoon salt, plus more for sprinkling
1 tablespoon freshly ground black pepper
½ cup vegetable oil
1 tablespoon white or apple cider vinegar
Juice of 2 limes
2 large handfuls pimento wood sticks and chips or other aromatic chips, or as needed, soaked in water for 30 minutes.

1. At least 1 day before cooking, pat the chicken dry with paper towels. Combine the remaining ingredients in a blender or food processor and grind to a coarse paste. Slather all over the chicken, including under the skin. Refrigerate for 12 to 36 hours.
2. Bring the chicken to room temperature before cooking, and lightly sprinkle with more salt and allspice.
3. Prepare a charcoal grill: Clean and oil grates and prepare a medium-hot fire, using one chimney of charcoal. The temperature can start as high as 300 degrees and go as low as 250. For best results, the coals should be at least 12 inches away from the chicken. If necessary, push the coals to one side of grill to create indirect heat. Add the soaked wood sticks and chips to the coals, then close the grill. When thick white smoke billows from the grill, place the chicken on the grate, skin side up, and cover. Let cook undisturbed for 30 to 35 minutes.
4. Uncover the grill. The chicken will be golden and even mahogany in places. Chicken thighs may already be cooked through. For other cuts, turn the chicken over and add more wood chips and charcoal if needed.

Cover and continue cooking, checking and turning every 10 minutes. The chicken is done when the skin is burnished brown and the juices run are completely clear, with no pink near the bone. For large pieces, this can take up to an hour.

SERVES 8

COOKING NOTE
Pimento (allspice) wood sticks and chips are available at www.pimentowood.com.

VARIATIONS
Moskin noted, "If you have no grill, the chicken can be baked in the oven at 375 degrees for about 45 minutes; the smokiness will be lost but seasoning will be intact. Jerk rub can also be used on a boneless leg of lamb or pork roast, to be cooked on a medium-hot grill or in the oven."

SERVING SUGGESTIONS
Ginger Lemonade (p. 26), Rice and Peas (p. 357), Mango Ice Cream (p. 729)

JULY 2, 2008: "SWEET HEAT: FOR JAMAICANS, IT'S ABOUT JERK," BY JULIA MOSKIN.

—2008

CHICKEN WITH LIME, CHILE, AND FRESH HERBS (LARB GAI)

I hope these Asian minced salads catch on, because they're wonderful to eat in the summer, the herbs and acidity much more spirited than the torpid mayonnaise-based chicken salads we're used to. There's also a Minced Fish Salad, a recipe from Laos, on p. 436. This recipe comes from Kwan Thai, an immigrant from Thailand who owns Kwan Bellhouse in Pearl River, New York.

———

¼ cup Thai or Lao sticky rice or 2 tablespoons roasted rice powder (available at Asian markets)
1 pound coarsely ground or finely chopped white- or dark-meat chicken (lean beef, such as sirloin, can be substituted)
½ teaspoon hot chile powder, preferably Thai or Lao

4 teaspoons Asian fish sauce, preferably Thai
5 teaspoons fresh lime juice, or more to taste
¼ cup slivered red onion
2 tablespoons chopped cilantro
2 tablespoons sliced scallions
10 mint leaves, plus more for serving
Salt
Lettuce leaves and cucumber spears for serving
4 cups cooked sticky or jasmine rice for serving

1. If using raw rice, to make roasted rice powder, heat a wok or skillet over high heat. Add the rice and cook, stirring often, until the rice is toasted and dark brown but not black, 3 to 5 minutes. Remove from the wok and let cool, then grind to a coarse powder in a mortar, blender, or spice/coffee grinder.
2. Heat a wok or skillet over medium-high heat. When it is very hot, add 2 tablespoons water, then add the chicken, stirring constantly to break up any lumps. Cook just until cooked through, about 2 minutes, then transfer to a bowl.
3. When the chicken is just warm, add the remaining ingredients and roasted rice powder. Mix gently but thoroughly. Taste and adjust the seasonings, adding salt if needed. The mixture should be tangy, salty, and lightly spicy.
4. Spoon onto a serving plate and surround with mint leaves, lettuce, and cucumber. Serve with rice. If serving with sticky rice, pinch some off, mold into a small ball, and dip into larb, scooping up a little of each ingredient. Or scoop the larb into lettuce leaves.

SERVES 4 TO 6

COOKING NOTE
Larb gai is traditionally served with long-grain Thai or Lao sticky rice, sometimes labeled "glutinous." It is not the same as Japanese short-grain rice.

SERVING SUGGESTIONS
Kaffir Lime Lemonade (p. 26), Pork-and-Toasted-Rice-Powder Spring Rolls (p. 74), Mango Ice Cream (p. 729), Sticky Rice with Mango (p. 861)

JUNE 17, 2009: "A TOUCH OF ASIA, TANGY AND HOT," BY JULIA MOSKIN. RECIPE ADAPTED FROM KWAN BELLHOUSE IN PEARL RIVER, NEW YORK.

—2009

- All manner of beef is cooked, from shin to tail to intestine. Pepperpot, tripe à la mode de Caen, and beef à la mode thrive.

—1870s—

- Delmonico Hash—hashed lamb spooned over cream-soaked bread (p. 507).

—1877—

- Early sighting of gulyas (goulash) in the *Times*.

—1880—

- Stuffed breast of veal (see p. 558 for a modern version).

—1882—

- Broiled Steak with Oysters (p. 511) and Eisenhower's Steak in the Fire (p. 512) revive old-timey concepts.

—1940s—

- Iraqi Grape Leaves Stuffed with Lamb, Mint, and Cinnamon (p. 510).

—1940—

- Chinese barbecued spareribs (see p. 517) are in vogue.

—1950s—

- International dishes rule: Carbonnades à la Flamande (p. 515).

—1959—

- Bring on the choucroute and bratwurst!

—1960s—

- Craig Claiborne publishes not one but two boeuf bourguignon recipes (p. 516).

—1960—

- Julia Child's *Mastering the Art of French Cooking* is published. More boeuf bourguignon.

—1961—

- In flat rejection of European braises and stews, Americans latch onto meat loaf.

—1970s—

- Roast leg of lamb or butterflied leg of lamb is the centerpiece of many a suburban dinner party.

- We eat too much pot roast and way too much filet mignon.

—1980s—

- Osso Buco alla Milanese (p. 535).

—1985—

- The '21' Club Hamburger (p. 536) marks the birth of the rarefied hamburger.

—1987—

- People become fanatical about cassoulet (p. 530) and braised lamb shanks (p. 564).

—1990s—

- Grilled steaks with Asian slaw (see p. 552).

- José Bové, a French farmer, destroys a McDonald's in France as a protest against the company's use of hormone-treated beef.

—1999—

- Fergus Henderson writes *Nose to Tail Eating* and rouses cooks' interest in trotters, kidney, and even spleen.

- DB Bistro Moderne causes a stir with the DB Burger, a behemoth that packs in truffles, foie gras, and short ribs.

—2001—

- Michael Pollan buys a steer. Things don't end well for the steer, or us.

—2002—

- Mad cow scare, well, scares us.

—2003—

- Mario Batali popularizes beef cheeks, but the cut doesn't make it into the home kitchen.

- Readily available short ribs replace beef cheeks. Short Ribs with Coffee and Chiles (p. 579).

—2005—

- Restaurants revive the art of charcuterie. Artisan producers like Fatted Calf in Napa and Fra'Mani in Berkeley (California) lead the way.

—2006—

- Americans treat bacon as if it were a new culinary beacon. Bacon Band-Aids and T-shirts are produced.

—2007—

- Consider the lamb belly (see p. 580).

—2008—

BEEF, VEAL, LAMB, AND PORK

One of the many wonderful aspects of the *Times* archive is that it contains the occasional accounting of daily life—the foods sold in the public markets, the menu from a men's-club lunch, and the following, a record of one family's meals and food costs over the course of a week in 1878.

How a Family of Four Persons with One Servant Lived for a Week, and What It Cost.

SUNDAY.—*Breakfast*—Waffles (made from the rice left from Saturday as per receipt in last Sunday's *Times*), fresh boiled eggs. French bread, butter, and café au lait. *Dinner*, 6 o'clock—Roast leg of mutton, currant jelly (home made), mashed potatoes, white turnips, boiled rice (see last Sunday's *Times* to cook it), pickles. Dessert—Custard, with preserved strawberries (home made), celery, Roquefort cheese, apples, café noir.

As coffee, bread, and butter form part of each breakfast, and celery, cheese, and coffee of the dinner, they will not be repeated; when we have salad, celery is left out.

MONDAY.—*Breakfast*—Hominy (fine), bacon cut very thin and fried crisp, &c. *Dinner*—Cold mutton from yesterday, have your chafing dish on the table, slice nicely sufficient mutton, put in the chafing dish with a lump of butter, a wine-glass or two of water, half wine-glass of sherry, a little salt, a dash of cayenne pepper, and currant jelly, light your spirit lamp and cook for a few moments; baked potatoes (in skin); maccaroni [sic] plain. Dessert—Sliced oranges, sugared, pour over half wine-glass of sherry, &c.

TUESDAY.—*Breakfast*—Pork tenderloins, fried potatoes from yesterday, &c. *Dinner*—Baked ham (see receipt in last Sunday's *Times*), mashed potatoes, rice, and tomatoes, boiled onions. Dessert—Baked apples with tapioca, &c.

WEDNESDAY.—*Breakfast*—Buckwheat cakes, sausage, &c. *Dinner*—Remains of cold mutton from Sunday, if sufficient; if not, buy one-half pound beef, cut in pieces about the size of a small marble; the beef should be cut up and stewed for three hours before required; add six white potatoes boiled; four sweet potatoes; two turnips; two small carrots, parsley, and six boiled onions, all cut up; curry powder to suit the taste—a delicious stew; cold sliced ham and lettuce. Dessert—Apples, oranges, &c.

THURSDAY.—*Breakfast*—Rice griddle-cakes, fried smelts, &c. *Dinner*—Roast turkey, cranberries (one pound of sugar to a quart, pour hot into a mold), roast white potatoes, sweet potatoes (boiled, cut in slices and fried in butter, and sprinkled thick with brown sugar), maccaroni au gratin. Dessert— Stewed peaches with custard, &c.

FRIDAY.—*Breakfast*—Hot biscuit, scrambled eggs, &c. *Dinner*—Boiled cod with oyster sauce, mashed potatoes, boiled onions. Dessert—Apple dumplings, &c.

SATURDAY.—*Breakfast*—Hominy, smelts, &c. *Dinner*—Remains of Thursday's cold turkey, sweet potatoes (cooked as above), rice and tomatoes, maccaroni. Dessert—Rice pudding with quince jelly (home made), &c.

Cost of above:

Fourteen loaves bread per week at 8c.	$1.12
Eight quarts milk at 10c.	$.80
One-half bushel white potatoes 50c., sweet do. 20c.	$.70
Turnips 15c., onions 20c., 2 cans tomatoes 25c.	$.60
Maccaroni 18c., eggs 60c., sausage $1\frac{1}{2}$ pounds 18c.	$.96
$3\frac{1}{2}$ pounds table butter at 40c., $1 40, 3 pounds cooking at 25c., 75c.	$2.15
Leg mutton, 13 pounds, at $12\frac{1}{2}$c.	$1.63
Turkey, 14 pounds, at 13c.	$1.82
Ham, 8 pounds, at 13c.	$1.04
Pork tenderloins, 2 pounds, at 14c.	$.28
For the week $3\frac{1}{2}$ pounds coffee at 35c., $1 23 4 pounds sugar at $10\frac{1}{2}$c., 42c.	$1.63
One-half pound Roquefort cheese at 28c., 4 pounds Neufchâtel at 25c.	$.53
Oranges 25c., lemons 10c., lettuce 10c.	$.45
Smelts, 3 pounds for 25c., cod 3 pounds 30c.	$.55
Oysters 25c., apples 40c., celery 30c.	$.95
Milk crackers and gingersnaps.	$.44
Seven days' lunch including small items.	$3.50

Twenty-one meals for $19.15, 91c. each; for 5 persons, 18c. each.

The above is the exact cost of a week's living. Lunch does not cost 50 cents. It generally consists of tea, with a slice of lemon in lieu of milk, preserves, apple-butter, orange marmalade, &c., and anything left from other meals. I have said nothing about soups; if the cook or the lady of the house understands her business, she will require no advice on this subject. If possible, do your marketing at Washington Market. If you reside below Fiftieth-Street it will be sent home free. I have paid during the past month $12\frac{1}{2}$ cents per pound for turkeys, ducks, and chickens, and $12\frac{1}{2}$ cents for a leg of mutton or saddle—the best in the market. By always going to the same parties, you will be well served. This is plain living, but if well cooked, the table-cloths and napkins clean, the knives and glasses bright, and the table nicely set, and the whole seasoned with cheerful conversation, it will be enjoyable. Eat slowly.—SOUTH CAROLINA.

FEBRUARY 24, 1878: "THE HOUSEHOLD; RECEIPTS FOR THE TABLE."

RECIPES BY CATEGORY

SPANISH FRICCO (BEEF, POTATO, AND ONION STEW)

Every cook needs a few esoteric recipes in her collection: make this stew one of yours. The layering of beef and vegetables is similar to that in the Boeuf Bourguignon I on p. 516, except that here there's almost no added liquid, just a few spoonfuls of cream. The beef, potatoes, and onions cook in their own juices, insulated by a water bath surrounding the pot. By the time the stew is finished, the cooking broth looks like a wreck with rivulets of cream streaming through the beef juices. Don't be discouraged, you've succeeded: you will soak up every last drop with bread.

In fact, the best way to serve the stew is to spoon it over toasted country bread that's been rubbed with garlic and brushed with olive oil. Follow it with a salad of bitter greens, like Puntarelle with Anchovies on p. 194.

––––––––––

2 pounds boneless beef shoulder

4 large white potatoes

1½ large yellow onions

Salt and freshly ground black pepper

3 tablespoons unsalted butter

4 bay leaves

¼ cup heavy cream or crème fraîche

1. Heat the oven to 350 degrees. Cut the beef into ½-inch-thick slices. Using a meat mallet, flatten each slice between sheets of wax paper to ¼ inch thick.
2. Peel the potatoes and cut into ¼-inch-thick slices. Cut the onions into ⅛-inch-thick slices.
3. Have ready 2 Dutch ovens or heavy pots, one that's large enough to hold all the ingredients and a larger one that will hold it comfortably. Cover the bottom of the smaller pot with one-quarter of the potatoes. Season with salt and pepper. Dot with 1 tablespoon butter. Add a bay leaf, and cover with one-third of the beef and one-third of the onions. Season again. Repeat this 2 more times. Cover with the remaining potatoes, season once more, and add the remaining bay leaf. Using your palms, press down on the ingredients to compress the mixture. Pour in the cream.
4. Cover the pot, set it inside the larger pot, and fill the larger pot with enough boiling water to come half-

way up the smaller pot. Transfer to the oven and bake until a knife inserted in the layers slips right through, 1½ to 2 hours. Lift the smaller pot from the larger pot, to make serving easier.

SERVES 6

SERVING SUGGESTIONS
See the headnote. For dessert: Ofenschlupfer (Almond Bread Pudding; p. 804) or Chocolate Mousse (p. 820).

APRIL 1, 1877: "RECEIPTS FOR THE TABLE." RECIPE SIGNED EMILIA.

—1877

FRIED SWEETBREADS WITH MAÎTRE D'HÔTEL SAUCE

If you're looking for a good, tart salad to accompany the sweetbreads, the Raw Spinach Salad on p. 175 is ideal.

––––––––––

2 large eggs

1 cup coarse dry bread crumbs

1 pound sweetbreads, cleaned and
    cut into ½-inch-thick slices

Salt and freshly ground black pepper

10 tablespoons (1¼ sticks) unsalted butter

2 tablespoons chopped flat-leaf parsley

1 tablespoon fresh lemon juice

4 lemon wedges

1. Beat the eggs in a shallow bowl. Spread the bread crumbs in another bowl. Lightly season the sweetbreads with salt. Dip them in the egg, then the bread crumbs. Season with salt and pepper.
2. Melt 6 tablespoons butter in a large nonstick skillet over medium heat. When the butter is foaming, add the sweetbreads and cook until the edges are nicely browned, then turn and brown the other side, 6 to 8 minutes total.
3. Meanwhile, melt the remaining 4 tablespoons of butter in a small saucepan. When it begins to foam, add the parsley and lemon juice.
4. Divide the sweetbreads among 4 plates. Spoon the

sauce over them and accompany each with a lemon wedge.

SERVES 4 AS A LIGHT MAIN COURSE, WITH
SALAD, AS A FIRST COURSE

COOKING NOTE
It's important to use coarse bread crumbs; fine, uniform crumbs won't provide enough crunch.

SERVING SUGGESTIONS
See headnote. Also: French Potato Salad (p. 277), Watercress Salad (p. 171), Apple Tarte Tatin (p. 837), Winter Fruit Salad (p. 850).

JUNE 10, 1877: "THE HOUSEHOLD: RECEIPTS FOR
THE TABLE."

—1877

3. Place a toast in each of 2 bowls. Spoon the lamb and cooking juices on top, and enjoy.

SERVES 2

VARIATION
Although there's really no need to vary this dish in any way, no one would complain if you topped it with a sprinkling of fresh herbs like chives, thyme, and tarragon.

SERVING SUGGESTIONS
Salade à la Romaine (p. 171), Plum Fritters (p. 865); if serving for brunch, pair it with Omelet with Asparagus (p. 624) or Eggs with Mushrooms and Caraway (p. 624).

JUNE 24, 1877: "RECEIPTS FOR THE TABLE." RECIPE
SIGNED STICKWELL.

—1877

DELMONICO HASH

This is lamb hash on toasts that have been buttered and toasted, then dipped in cream. Need I say more? Yes, I will: whatever you do, don't skip the cream. The toasts are ridiculously indulgent and so, so good.

This is a great way to use up leftovers from other lamb recipes in this chapter. You can double or triple the recipe.

½ tablespoon unsalted butter, plus more for the toasts
¾ cup finely diced cooked lamb
¼ cup water
Salt and freshly ground black pepper
Two ½-inch-thick slices country bread
¼ cup heavy cream

1. Melt the butter in a small skillet. Add the lamb, water, salt and pepper, bring to a simmer, and simmer to warm the lamb and emulsify the water, butter, and lamb juices. Add more water if needed; the liquid should act like a liaison, not a soup. Cover and keep warm.
2. Toast the bread, then butter both sides. Pour the cream into a wide shallow bowl. Dip the toasts in the cream, lightly coating both sides.

COLLARED PORK

The herbs and spices in the stuffing, dominated by mace and sage, are so hardy they're almost medicinal. I served this to my family over the Christmas holidays one year, and after the first bite, we all shot skeptical looks at one another. But soon everyone was having seconds.

One 6-pound pork shoulder, boned (by the butcher)
½ pound day-old country bread, cut into chunks
1 tablespoon dried sage
1 tablespoon dried marjoram
1 tablespoon freshly grated nutmeg
2 teaspoons ground cloves
1 teaspoon ground mace
3 teaspoons chopped fresh sage
3 teaspoons chopped fresh thyme
1½ teaspoons salt
Freshly ground black pepper
8 tablespoons (1 stick) unsalted butter, softened
1 large egg, lightly beaten

1. Remove the pork from the refrigerator at least 30 minutes before cooking. Heat the oven to 375 degrees.

Grind the bread to coarse crumbs in a food processor (you should have about 4 cups).

2. Combine the bread crumbs, dried sage, marjoram, nutmeg, cloves, mace, chopped sage, thyme, salt, pepper to taste, and butter in a large bowl. Rub together to spread the butter through the mixture. Fold in the egg and blend well.

3. Open out the pork on a work surface and season well inside and out. Spread the stuffing over the inside. Roll up the meat and tie with kitchen twine.

4. Lay the pork fat side up on a roasting rack set in a roasting pan. Add enough water to the pan to just cover the bottom and place in the oven. Roast, basting occasionally, until the internal temperature reaches 160 degrees, 1½ to 2 hours. Let rest for 15 minutes before slicing.

SERVES 8

COOKING NOTES

Make sure the butcher leaves a thick layer of fat on the shoulder when he bones and trims it. This insulates the meat, naturally bastes the pork as it cooks, and produces a beautiful crust on the roast.

If you'd like to make gravy, add some red wine to the roasting pan and cook over medium-high heat, scraping up the drippings, until reduced to a glaze. Then pour in 2 cups of chicken broth and reduce by half. You can also add a handful of golden raisins if you'd like a little sweetness.

SERVING SUGGESTIONS

Florida Beets (p. 216), Madame Laracine's Gratin Dauphinois (p. 284), Mashed Potatoes Anna (p. 294), Stewed Fennel (p. 245), De Luxe Cheesecake (p. 748), Teddie's Apple Cake (p. 752), Apple Galette (p. 843), Almond Granita (p. 731)

JANUARY 20, 1878: "RECEIPTS FOR THE TABLE." RECIPE SIGNED COUSIN JERUSHA.

—1878

⌒ BLANQUETTE OF VEAL

The nineteenth century was definitely a substance-over-style period when it came to meat dishes. Blan-quette de veau, a dish whose beauty has never matched its flavor, is particularly homely here. Although you can serve it to your spouse, for anyone else, you'll need to chop a thick covering of parsley—or dim the lights. But this version makes up for its unprepossessing looks with excellent flavor; it is more like a silky soup containing veal than a stew.

———

2 pounds veal stew meat, cut into 1½-inch pieces

1 tablespoon salt, plus more to taste

1 onion, stuck with 10 whole cloves

1 stalk celery, sliced

1 parsnip, peeled and sliced

1 small turnip, peeled and sliced

4 to 5 sprigs dill

1 leek, white and pale green parts only, chopped and washed well

1 tablespoon unsalted butter

2 tablespoons all-purpose flour

Chicken broth if needed

¼ teaspoon freshly ground white pepper

¼ teaspoon freshly grated nutmeg

2 large egg yolks

1 pound boiled small potatoes for serving

1. Place the veal in a large pot, cover with water, and add the salt. Bring to a simmer, adding the onion, celery, parsnip, turnip, dill, and leek as it heats. Simmer, skimming occasionally, until the veal is just tender, about 45 minutes.

2. Remove the meat to a plate and strain the cooking broth. You'll need 4 cups; if necessary, supplement with chicken broth; skim off excess fat. (At this point, you can stop and finish the dish the following day. Pour the broth over the meat before refrigerating.)

3. Clean out the pot and return it to the stove. Add the butter and melt over medium heat. Whisk in the flour and cook, stirring, for 1 minute—add a little of the veal broth if needed. Whisk in the (remaining) veal broth and bring to a simmer, whisking. Season with salt, pepper, and nutmeg.

4. Ladle out about 1 cup broth and gradually whisk it into the egg yolks to temper them, then whisk this mixture back into the pot; cook, stirring, until the sauce thickens—do not let it boil. Stir the meat into the sauce and adjust the seasoning. Serve over the boiled potatoes.

SERVING SUGGESTIONS

Improved Holland Gin Cocktail (p. 39), Green Pea Fritters (p. 270, with crème fraîche and chives), Fresh Morel, Asparagus, and Sweet Pea Risotto (p. 327), Butter-Braised Asparagus and Oyster Mushrooms with Peas and Tarragon (p. 262), A Perfect Batch of Rice (p. 316), Fennel, Orange, Watercress, and Walnut Salad (p. 186), Rosh Hashanah Plum Pie (p. 838), Snow Pudding (p. 800), Straight-Up Rhubarb Pie (p. 862)

AUGUST 8, 1878: "RECEIPTS FOR THE TABLE." RECIPE SIGNED TWENTY-FIVE CENT DINNERS.

—1878

⌇ EPIGRAM OF LAMB

Every once in a while, a dish becomes famous as much for its name as for its flavor. Take, for instance, Thomas Keller's "Oysters and Pearls," made with oysters, tapioca, and caviar. Another such dish was veal hocks *à l'epigramme*, or braised veal, which appeared in La Varenne's seventeenth-century cookbook *Le Cuisinier François*.

Over the years, cooks swapped lamb for the veal and changed the way it was prepared. Epigram of lamb came to mean a dish that overturned your expectation of a dense, fatty cut of lamb by transforming it into thin, breaded cutlets. "Epigram" may refer to the preparation or to the small cuts of meat, but the playful word has inevitably managed to irk some literal-minded chefs. One of La Varenne's contemporaries claimed the dish was emblematic of all that was wrong in cooking. And Ken Albala, a food historian at the University of the Pacific in Stockton, California, pointed me to *Apicius Redivivus, or the Cook's Oracle*, a nineteenth-century cookbook in which one critic is quoted as saying, "What can any person suppose to be the meaning of a shoulder of lamb in epigram, unless it were a poor dish, for a Penniless Poet?" Meow!

The epigram that ran in the *Times* in 1879 came from a publication called *Young Ladies' Magazine*. Although it takes two days to make, the actual work involved is brief. You braise lamb breast with some vegetables until its bones can be easily removed, then press it between two plates. The next day, you slice the meat on the bias to create cutlets, bread them, and fry them in butter. The braising makes for tender, fragrant cutlets, and the second cooking makes the fat in the lamb crisp and extra succulent.

For a modern take on this concept, see the lamb belly on p. 580.

———

One 2-pound boneless lamb breast, trimmed of excess fat
½ Spanish onion, chopped
1 large carrot, peeled and chopped
2 stalks celery, chopped
3 whole cloves
8 black peppercorns
3 sprigs parsley
4 sprigs thyme, or sage, or rosemary (or all 3)
Salt and freshly ground black pepper
2 large eggs
1 to 2 cups coarse dry bread crumbs
1 tablespoon unsalted butter, plus more if needed
1 tablespoon olive oil, plus more if needed
1 lemon, cut into wedges
Cooked fresh peas

1. Lay the lamb in a large heavy braising pot. Add the onion, carrot, celery, cloves, peppercorns, parsley, thyme, and salt to taste. Add just enough water to cover and bring to a boil over medium-high heat, then reduce the heat and simmer, covered, until the meat is falling off the bone, 1¼ to 2 hours. Let the meat cool in the liquid.

2. Lay the meat on a large plate or baking sheet. Cover with plastic wrap. Set with another plate or baking sheet on top, place a weight on top, and refrigerate overnight.

3. The next day, slice the lamb against the grain; the slices should be about ⅓ inch thick. Season with salt and pepper. Lightly beat the eggs in a shallow bowl, and spread bread crumbs in another bowl. Place a large nonstick sauté pan over medium heat and add the butter and olive oil. Dip the lamb cutlets first in the egg, then the bread crumbs, and fry until golden brown on both sides, 2 to 3 minutes per side; do this in batches, adding more butter and olive oil if needed.

4. Serve with lemon wedges and fresh green peas.

SERVES 4

VARIATIONS

Substitute pork shoulder for the lamb, and rub some chopped fresh thyme into the bread crumbs before coating the cutlets. For a slightly different texture, replace the bread crumbs with panko, sharp and crisp Japanese bread crumbs (available at Asian grocery stores and some supermarkets).

COOKING NOTES

The original recipe called for sautéing the lamb cutlets in lard. I changed this to butter and olive oil. If you want to be authentic and do it in lard, go for it.

I included lemon wedges for squeezing over the cutlets at the table, an Italian touch.

SERVING SUGGESTIONS

Rhubarb Bellini (p. 30), Spring Lamb Salad with Pea Shoots and Sugar Snap Peas (p. 580, the salad part), Asparagus and Bulgur with Preserved-Lemon Dressing (p. 190), Butter-Braised Asparagus and Oyster Mushrooms with Peas and Tarragon (p. 262), Puree of Peas and Watercress (p. 296), Pea Puree (from Scallops with Pea Puree, p. 429), Straight-Up Rhubarb Pie (p. 862), Fontainebleau (p. 829)

MAY 11, 1879: "RECEIPTS FOR THE TABLE." RECIPE ADAPTED FROM *YOUNG LADIES' MAGAZINE*.

—1879

SAUCE FOR VENISON STEAK

This sauce is a great cheat—a little boiling and stirring, and you have a compact jus that seems as if it must have taken hours to prepare. It comes out best if you start with a concentrated, viscous veal stock. If you can't get any, begin with 2 cups regular veal stock and reduce it by half. (You can do the same using chicken or beef stock as a substitute.) Then all you have to do is sauté a few venison steaks, and in less than 20 minutes, dinner is made.

The sauce would also be delicious with duck.

---

1 cup veal stock
Salt (if stock isn't seasoned)
½ teaspoon freshly ground black pepper
Cayenne pepper
2 whole cloves
3 allspice berries
2 tablespoons unsalted butter, softened
1 teaspoon all-purpose flour
1 teaspoon currant or blueberry jelly, plus more to taste
½ cup dry red wine
1½ tablespoons canola oil
Two ½-inch-thick venison steaks (4 if they're small)

1. Combine the veal stock, salt, if needed, black pepper, cayenne to taste, cloves, and allspice in a small saucepan, bring to a boil, and reduce by half.
2. Meanwhile, blend the butter and flour. Whisk into the stock. Add the jelly and wine and boil, whisking, until the sauce is thick enough to coat the back of a spoon. Taste, adding more jelly, salt, and/or cayenne as desired.
3. Heat the oil in a medium skillet over medium-high heat. Season the steaks, with salt and pepper and add to the skillet. Brown well on both sides, and cook to desired doneness (I like it to be a little pink inside). Serve, passing the sauce at the table.

SERVES 2

SERVING SUGGESTIONS

Roasted Cauliflower (p. 248), Mashed Potatoes Anna (p. 294), Red Wine Risotto (p. 346), Cream Dressing for Salad (p. 592), Reuben's Apple Pancake (p. 831), Apple Snow (p. 808)

NOVEMBER 7, 1880: "RECEIPTS." RECIPE FROM "HINTS TO HOUSEWIVES."

—1880

IRAQI GRAPE LEAVES STUFFED WITH LAMB, MINT, AND CINNAMON

"American housekeepers are generous in serving leg of lamb, lamb chops, shoulders, and stews," Kiley Taylor, a *Times* food columnist, wrote, "but beyond these few ideas, the imagination does not seem to extend." To remedy this situation, Taylor whipped out a few cookbooks for inspiration, and although she never named the source for this recipe, she chose well. The cinnamon-and-mint-scented filling and the tangy grape leaves make a fine pair.

_____

20 jarred or canned grape leaves
I pound ground lamb
½ cup cooked jasmine rice
2 tablespoons unsalted butter, softened
2 tablespoons chopped mint
½ teaspoon ground cinnamon
¾ teaspoon salt
½ teaspoon freshly ground black pepper

1. Soak the grape leaves in a bowl of water for at least 1 hour. Drain, rinse, and dry them.

2. Heat the oven to 350 degrees. Gently mix the lamb, rice, 1 tablespoon butter, the mint, cinnamon, salt, and pepper in a bowl. Lay 1½ tablespoons of this mixture at the stem end of a grape leaf. Form mixture into a log shape. Fold the sides of the leaf over the mixture, then roll up toward the tip of the leaf. Repeat with the remaining leaves and stuffing. Some of the leaves may tear; you should end up with about 18 rolls.

3. Arrange the rolls in an 8-inch square baking dish. Dot with the remaining tablespoon of butter. Sprinkle with 3 tablespoons water. Lay a piece of foil over the dish, then lay another casserole or plate on top of the foil to weigh down the rolls. Press the foil against the edges to seal the dish.

4. Bake until the lamb is just cooked through, 30 to 40 minutes.

SERVES 4

SERVING SUGGESTIONS
Hummus bi Tahini (p. 68), Beet Tzatziki (p. 89), Arnaki Araka (Lamb with Peas; p. 550), Cumin-Mustard Carrots (p. 237), Spicy Orange Salad Morrocan-Style (p. 181), Saffron Panna Cotta (p. 845)

SEPTEMBER I, 1940: "VICTUALS AND VITAMINS," BY KILEY TAYLOR.

—1940

ARUNDEL (SAUSAGES IN ALE)

German sausages such as weisswurst, bratwurst, or krainerwurst paired with a hefty ale work best. Serve the sausages with a variety of sharp, peppery, sweet, and grainy mustards.

_____

1½ pounds German sausages
2 tablespoons unsalted butter
I cup ale
Mustard for serving (sweet, spicy, grainy, whatever you like)

1. Prick the sausages with a fork. Heat the butter in a large saucepan over medium-high heat until foamy. Add the sausages and brown on all sides. Pour off the fat.

2. Pour in the ale and bring to a boil, then cover the pan, reduce the heat to low, and simmer for 15 minutes.

SERVES 4

SERVING SUGGESTIONS
Beer! Also, Peach Bowl (p. 20), Craig Claiborne's Swiss Fondue (p. 55), Raw Spinach Salad (p. 175), Light Potato Salad (p. 301), Lattich Salat, Warme (Warm Lettuce Salad; p. 171), Toasts with Chocolate, Olive Oil, and Sea Salt (p. 844), Black Forest Cake (p. 754), Springerle Cookies (p. 686)

MAY II, 1941: "FOR THE PICNIC SEASON," BY KILEY TAYLOR. RECIPE ADAPTED FROM *THE BROWNS' WINE COOK BOOK*, BY THE BROWNS.

—1941

BROILED STEAK WITH OYSTERS

This steak-and-oysters combination (also known as a carpetbagger steak) appeared as part of a "brush-up course" on cooking meat, which had become available again after the war. There's not much to the dish, but don't knock it—steak and oysters will change your mind about surf 'n' turf. Oysters are brinier than lobster. Poised atop the steak, their liquor, the wash of lemon-parsley butter, and the meat juices, create an irresistible sauce.

---

1 porterhouse steak, 1 inch thick (about 2 pounds)
Salt and freshly ground black pepper
20 shucked oysters, drained
4 tablespoons unsalted butter, melted
2 tablespoons chopped flat-leaf parsley
1½ tablespoons fresh lemon juice

1. Heat the broiler. Place the steak in a sturdy flameproof pan and place under the broiler so the top of the meat is 2 to 3 inches from the tip of the flame. Cook, turning once, sprinkling each side with salt and pepper after browning. The total broiling time will be about 10 minutes for rare, 12 for medium. Remove the pan from the broiler.

2. Toss the oysters in about half the fat that has accumulated in the pan and then distribute over the steak. Place under the broiler flame and cook until the oyster edges curl. Transfer the steak and oysters to a platter.

3. Skim off any excess fat from the pan, and mix the pan juices with the butter, parsley, and lemon juice. Pour over the oysters and steak.

SERVES 4 TO 5

COOKING NOTE
The original recipe called for "fortified margarine," which I changed to butter.

SERVING SUGGESTIONS
Tomatoes Vinaigrette (p. 218), Spinach with Sour Cream (p. 216), Mashed Potatoes Anna (p. 294), Mrs. Hovis's Hot Upside-Down Apple Pie (p. 828), Junior's Cheesecake (p. 771), Banana Cream Pie (p. 863)

DECEMBER 2, 1945: "FOOD; REFRESHER COURSE ON COOKING MEAT," BY JANE NICKERSON.

—1945

⌒ EISENHOWER'S STEAK IN THE FIRE

General Dwight D. Eisenhower's steak recipe, which he picked up on fishing trips in Wisconsin, first appeared in a letter to Ethel Wyman, the wife of the chief of staff of the First Army, who was stationed on Governors Island, New York. It later showed up in a cookbook, *What's Cooking on Governors Island*.

Here is the recipe in Eisenhower's words:

"(a) Get a sirloin tip four inches thick (as thick as it is wide).

(b) Make a dry mixture of salt, black pepper, and garlic powder. Put it in a flat wide bowl.

(c) Roll and rub the steak in the mixture until it will take up no more.

(d) Two hours before ready to start cooking, build, on the ground, a bonfire, on which dump a good-sized basketful of charcoal. Keep fire going well until charcoal has formed a good thick body of glowing coals.

(e) Forty minutes before time to eat, throw the steak into the fire (use no grates, grills, or anything of the kind).

(f) Nudge it over once or twice but let it lie in the fire about thirty-five minutes.

(g) Take out, slice slant-wise (about three-eighths-inch thick). Serve hot.

"If a sauce is desired: In a skillet (while steak is cooking), heat some beef juice and drippings with butter. Add some Worcester [*sic*] sauce and lemon juice to taste. (One steak will serve three persons generously.)"

SERVING SUGGESTIONS
Chiffonade Salad (p. 173), Saratoga Potatoes (p. 273), Cucumbers in Cream (p. 225), Lora Brody's Bête Noire (Intense Chocolate Cake; p. 763), Salted Caramel Ice Cream (p. 733)

DECEMBER 3, 1949: "NEWS OF FOOD: EISENHOWER GIVES RECIPE: GET 4-INCH STEAK, COOK IT RIGHT ON THE COALS FOR 35 MINUTES" BY JANE NICKERSON. RECIPE FROM *WHAT'S COOKING ON GOVERNORS ISLAND*.

—1949

ᘖ CHOUCROUTE
À L'ALSACIENNE

Choucroute, or sauerkraut with cured meats, sounds so darn intimidating, but as long as you can get your hands on good sauerkraut and sausages, you're in for the easiest dinner party dish in the world. All you do is pile the kraut and meats into a pot—this is the moment for that Le Creuset Dutch oven you got for your wedding—and let them slowly stew in the oven for a few hours while you make dessert and go to yoga. The recipe came from food writer James Beard, a friend of Craig Claiborne's.

---

8 cups sauerkraut (canned or in bulk)
Pork rind, salt pork, or sliced bacon
2 cloves garlic, chopped
Coarsely ground black pepper
About 4 cups dry white Alsatian wine
I onion, stuck with whole cloves
Frankfurters, other meats (see Cooking Note)

1. Heat the oven to 300 degrees. Wash the sauerkraut, then drain and squeeze dry.
2. Line a heavy pot with the pork rind, salt pork, or bacon. Add the sauerkraut, garlic, pepper, and wine to cover. Add the onion stuck with cloves. Cover tightly and cook in the oven (or simmer gently on top of the stove) for $3\frac{1}{2}$ hours (see Cooking Note). Add additional wine as necessary.

SERVES 6

COOKING NOTE
Claiborne, author of the piece in which this recipe appeared, wrote, "Many combinations of meats may be used in the preparation of this dish. Mr. Beard recommends the following:

Pig's knuckles; cook on sauerkraut for 4 hours.

Polish sausages or Italian cotechino; add for last 35 minutes of cooking.

Bauernwurst or knockwurst; add for last 15 or 20 minutes of cooking.

Salt pork cut in serving pieces; parboil, cook with sauerkraut for 1 hour.

Smoked pork loin; cook in a moderate oven (350 degrees) for 15 to 20 minutes per pound. Serve sliced.

Cooked ham slices; heat through in a little white wine.

Frankfurters; cook on sauerkraut for 5 minutes."

SERVING SUGGESTIONS
Cream of Carrot Soup (p. 119), Tarte Flambée (p. 370), Apple Tarte Tatin (p. 837), Apple Snow (p. 808), Pruneaux du Pichet (Prunes in a Pitcher; p. 822)

JANUARY 12, 1958: "SAUERKRAUT IN FANCY DRESS," BY CRAIG CLAIBORNE.

—1958

ᘖ CROWN ROAST OF LAMB

Crown roast of lamb (prepared by your butcher), at room temperature
Salt and freshly ground black pepper
Stuffing (see Puree of Peas and Watercress, p. 296)

1. Heat the oven to 325 degrees. Cover the tips of the roast's bones with aluminum foil to prevent them from charring when the roast cooks.
2. Salt and pepper the roast. Cook it until an instant-read thermometer inserted in the center of the chops reads 130 degrees (for rare), about 1 to $1\frac{1}{4}$ hours.
3. Remove the aluminum foil and replace with paper frills. Fill the center of the roast with the stuffing and serve.

SERVES 6

SERVING SUGGESTIONS
Artichauts Vinaigrette (p. 225), Vichyssoise à la Ritz (p. 111), Billi-Bi au Safran (Mussels in Saffron Cream; p. 125), Al Forno's Roasted Asparagus (p. 233), Rhubarb-Strawberry Mousse (p. 835)

MARCH 16, 1958: "WELCOME TO SPRING LAMB," BY CRAIG CLAIBORNE.

—1958

⌒ BROILED LAMB CHOPS

---

6 double lamb chops
Olive oil
1 clove garlic, sliced
Salt and freshly ground black pepper
Unsalted butter
Chopped dill (or other herbs)
Fresh lemon juice (optional)

1. Marinate the lamb chops in a little olive oil with the garlic for 30 to 60 minutes.
2. Heat the broiler. Set the chops on a rack about 2 inches from the source of heat and brown on both sides, cooking for a total of 8 minutes for rare.
3. Transfer the chops to a warm platter; season with salt and pepper, and place a pat of butter on each. Sprinkle with chopped dill. Sprinkle with lemon juice, if desired.

SERVES 6

VARIATION
Herb-Stuffed Lamb Chops: Before cooking, slit the chops in the thickest part. Cream a little butter with parsley, tarragon, or rosemary. Stuff the chops with the mixture and seal the openings with toothpicks. Broil, following the directions above.

SERVING SUGGESTIONS
Craig Claiborne said to serve the chops with "fried julienne potatoes and watercress," so how about trying the Sautéed Potatoes with Parsley (p. 283) or Saratoga Potatoes (p. 273) and the Watercress Salad (p. 171)? And an unassuming red wine.

MARCH 16, 1958: "WELCOME TO SPRING LAMB," BY CRAIG CLAIBORNE.

—1958

⌒ PORK CHOPS WITH RYE BREAD STUFFING

Thrift is often the catalyst for culinary invention. Penny-pinching dishes such as panzanella, poule au pot, and beef ragu were all devised in hard times. Like-wise, the recipe for these pork chops with rye bread stuffing, which the *Times* published in 1959, was billed as a dinner on the cheap. Pork chops were inexpensive (they were then 85 cents a pound), and bread stuffing was used, as it has been for hundreds of years, to stretch the portions.

When seasoned with sautéed onion, garlic, parsley, and caraway, the rye bread, with its strong grain flavor, gives the stuffing unexpected distinction. The technique is pure 1950s: the chops are browned in the oven, and a sauce is made with the brown but succulent drippings. The result is very . . . brown. But it's toothsome: like a better-dressed cousin of pastrami on rye. A similar recipe for stuffed and baked pork chops showed up in *America Cooks* (1940) by Cora, Rose, and Bob Brown. The chops were called "Little Turkeys" and came from Oklahoma. This version clearly comes from New York City.

I reworked the recipe a bit, cooking the meat covered in the oven to keep it moist, then finishing it under the broiler. Even so, if you use supermarket pork chops—which are invariably thin and industrially produced—the resulting dish will have the texture of particleboard. It's worth the effort to find a butcher who carries good fat-marbled chops and who can cut them thick—an inch is best. If you have the time, brine the chops first; a great recipe for brining pork chops is on p. 569.

Six 1-inch-thick pork loin chops
3 tablespoons unsalted butter
1 medium onion, finely chopped
1 large clove garlic, minced
3½ cups soft rye-bread crumbs (without caraway seeds, a mix of large and small pieces)
½ teaspoon caraway seeds
3 tablespoons finely chopped flat-leaf parsley
Salt and freshly ground black pepper
1 large egg, lightly beaten with 3 tablespoons water
1 tablespoon all-purpose flour
¾ cup chicken broth

1. If the butcher didn't do this for you, cut a generous pocket in each chop.
2. Heat the oven to 350 degrees. Melt 2 tablespoons butter in a sauté pan over medium heat. Add the onion and garlic and cook until softened, about 5 minutes. Scrape into a large bowl and add the bread

crumbs, caraway seeds, parsley, ¾ teaspoon salt, and ¼ teaspoon pepper. Add the beaten egg and mix with a fork until blended.

3. Fill the chops with the stuffing, then seal the pockets with toothpicks. Season on all sides with salt and pepper. Arrange in a braising pan or other shallow flameproof baking dish with a lid. Bake, covered, until an instant-read thermometer inserted into the thickest part of the meat, not the stuffing, reaches 155 degrees, 40 to 45 minutes.

4. Remove the lid and turn on the broiler. Place the pan under the broiler just until the chops are browned and the temperature in the thickest part of the meat is 160 degrees, 3 to 5 minutes. Transfer to a serving platter and keep warm.

5. Set the braising pan on the stove over medium heat and reduce the pan juices to a thick glaze. Add the remaining tablespoon of butter. Stir in the flour and cook for 1 minute. Add the broth and simmer, scraping up the pan drippings, until thick enough to coat the back of a spoon; strain. Season to taste.

6. Serve the sauce with the pork chops.

SERVES 6

COOKING NOTES

If you want to maximize the flavor of the stuffing, toast the caraway seeds in a dry pan over low heat, then lightly bruise them with a mortar and pestle.

Don't grind the bread crumbs too fine—large, coarse pieces give the stuffing a devil-may-care insouciance.

Have the butcher cut a generous pocket in each chop—or do it yourself!

SERVING SUGGESTIONS

Egg and Olive Canapés (p. 57), Turkish Split-Pea Soup with Mint and Paprika (p. 140), Paul Steindler's Cabbage Soup (p. 124), Braised Red Cabbage with Chestnuts (p. 221), Anton Mosimann's Braised Brussels Sprouts in Cream (p. 232), Black Forest Cake (p. 754), Madeleine Kamman's Apple Mousse (p. 816)

MAY 7, 1959: "LESS COSTLY MEAT CUTS CAN BE DELECTABLE," BY CRAIG CLAIBORNE.

—1959

⌘ CARBONNADES À LA FLAMANDE (FLEMISH BEEF AND ONION STEW)

This is an old Flemish stew that calls for beer rather than broth. Use a heavy beer, such as ale or stout. The 1950s seasonings are timid, so you may want to add another garlic clove, some fresh thyme, and more parsley.

———

⅓ cup all-purpose flour
2 teaspoons salt
¼ teaspoon freshly ground black pepper
2 pounds boneless beef chuck, cut into 1-inch cubes
¼ cup vegetable oil
6 medium onions, sliced
One 12-ounce bottle or can of beer
1 clove garlic
1 tablespoon chopped flat-leaf parsley
1 bay leaf
¼ teaspoon dried thyme

1. Combine the flour, salt, and pepper in a shallow bowl. Dredge the meat in the seasoned flour.

2. Heat the oil in a large skillet. Add the onions and cook until tender but not brown. Remove the onions. Add the meat and brown on all sides.

3. Return the onions to the pan. Add the beer, garlic, and remaining ingredients. Cover and cook over low heat until the meat is tender, about 1¼ hours. Remove the garlic clove.

SERVES 4 TO 6

SERVING SUGGESTIONS

Soupe à l'Oignon Gratinée (p. 120), Cauliflower Soup with Cremini Mushrooms and Walnut Oil (p. 149), Watercress and Basil Soup (p. 152), Sautéed Potatoes with Parsley (p. 283), Sautéed Asparagus with Fleur de Sel (p. 241), Chocolate Eclairs (p. 800)

JUNE 11, 1959: "BEER CONTRIBUTES AN INTERESTING FLAVOR TO MANY DISHES," BY CRAIG CLAIBORNE.

—1959

✍ BOEUF BOURGUIGNON I

Following the lead of Mapie de Toulouse-Lautrec, a well-known food writer for *Elle* in the 1960s, Craig Claiborne claimed that there were two accepted methods for making boeuf bourguignon, and he included both versions in his weekly column. The most popular method (Boeuf Bourguignon II, which can be found below) involves browning the meat before adding the vegetables and wine. The other version, which Toulouse-Lautrec called the "true" recipe—this one—is prepared by simply layering the meat and vegetables, pouring over the wine, and simmering it all on the stovetop. This housewife method is the same as that used in the daube de boeuf in Julia Child's *Mastering the Art of French Cooking*.

An unusual detail about this stew is that although its liquid is almost entirely red wine, once it's cooked, the wine turns pale, bleached of all its color.

After making both recipes, I favored this one, but when I served the Boeuf Bourguignon II to a crowd of guests, they lobbied me to include that version too. In addition to being easier to make, this one produces a brothier, boozier sauce. The other contains flour and acquires a thick, robust consistency. Both should be spooned onto a bed of buttered egg noodles.

One way to decide which to make: this easy one serves 6, the more complex one serves 12, better for a large party. Both should be made a day before serving—the first rule in stew making—because the meat relaxes and the flavors coalesce.

———

2 tablespoons vegetable oil

2 large slices salt pork or 6 slices bacon

1 1/2 cups diced carrots

One 2-pound boneless chuck or beef rump roast, cut into 1/4-inch-thick slices

Salt and freshly ground black pepper

2 medium onions, coarsely chopped

1 clove garlic, minced

2 shallots, finely chopped

1/2 pound mushrooms, trimmed and chopped

1/2 bottle (750-ml bottle) Burgundy or pinot noir

1/3 cup Cognac

1. Pour the oil into a large casserole and add 1 slice salt pork (or 3 slices bacon). Add the diced carrots and cover them with one-third of the sliced beef in a single layer. Sprinkle with salt and pepper. Sprinkle the meat with half the onions, garlic, shallots, and mushrooms. Cover with a layer of half the remaining beef and sprinkle with more salt and pepper. Add the remaining onions, garlic, shallots, and mushrooms and cover with a final layer of the remaining beef. Top with the second slice of salt pork (or remaining 3 slices of bacon). Pour the Burgundy and Cognac over all. Season with additional salt and pepper.

2. Place the casserole over high heat, and when it begins to simmer, cover and lower the heat. Cook for 2 to 2 1/2 hours, or until the meat is tender when tested with a fork.

SERVES 6

COOKING NOTES

If you make the stew a day ahead and put it in the fridge, the chilled fat will rise to the surface and solidify, so you can peel it off with a spoon before reheating the stew.

Beef must be more tender than it was fifty years ago, because both times I made this it took just over 2 hours. The original recipe said to cook it for 3 to 3 1/2 hours.

When the casserole is cooking, the liquid should barely bubble.

SERVING SUGGESTIONS

Madame Laracine's Gratin Dauphinois (p. 284), Haricots Verts with Balsamic Vinaigrette (p. 231), Chocolate Mousse (p. 820), Apple Tarte Tatin (p. 837)

SEPTEMBER 11, 1960: "WHEN BEEF BECOMES BOEUF," BY CRAIG CLAIBORNE.

—1960

✍ BOEUF BOURGUIGNON II

I love almost any kitchen task, but there are a few things for which I believe life is too short: peeling tomatoes, chopping parsley for a garnish, and peeling small white onions with their flinty, infuriating skins. This recipe called for peeling thirty-six of the evil little orbs. Since you can't really get away with unpeeled onions, I used frozen ones.

———

5 pounds boneless chuck beef, cut into 2-inch cubes

Flour

9 tablespoons unsalted butter

6 tablespoons olive oil

Salt and freshly ground black pepper

¼ cup Cognac, warmed

½ pound bacon, diced

3 cloves garlic, minced

2 carrots, peeled and coarsely chopped

2 leeks, white and pale green parts only,
    coarsely chopped and washed well

3 cups coarsely chopped onions

2 tablespoons chopped flat-leaf parsley,
    plus additional for garnish

1 bay leaf

1 teaspoon dried thyme

1 (750-ml) bottle Burgundy or pinot noir

36 small onions (you can use frozen small white onions)

Sugar

36 mushroom caps

Juice of ½ lemon

1. Heat the oven to 350 degrees. Roll the beef cubes in flour. Heat 4 tablespoons each butter and olive oil in a large skillet over high heat and brown the beef, in batches, on all sides.

2. Return all the meat to the skillet. Sprinkle the meat with salt and pepper, pour the Cognac over it, and carefully ignite. When the flame dies, put the meat in a casserole.

3. Add the bacon, garlic, carrots, leeks, onions, and parsley to the skillet. Cook, stirring, until the bacon is crisp and the vegetables are lightly browned.

4. Transfer the bacon and vegetables to the casserole with the meat and add the bay leaf, thyme, Burgundy, and enough water barely to cover the meat. Cover and bake for 1½ hours.

5. Prepare a beurre manié by blending 1 tablespoon each butter and flour. Stir into the casserole bit by bit. Return the casserole to the oven and continue cooking until the meat is very tender, 30 to 60 minutes longer.

6. Meanwhile, brown the small onions in 2 tablespoons butter with a dash of sugar in a large skillet. Add a little water, cover, and cook until the onions are almost tender. (If using frozen onions, follow the cooking directions on the package, then brown them in butter with a little sugar.) Set aside.

7. Sauté the mushrooms in the remaining 2 table-spoons each butter and oil in a large skillet until lightly browned on one side. Sprinkle them with lemon juice and turn to brown the other side.

8. To serve, add the onions to the casserole and garnish with the mushrooms and parsley.

SERVES 12

COOKING NOTES

Before making this recipe, read the headnote for Boeuf Bourguignon I on the previous page.

If you can't get your Cognac to ignite, don't fret. Just simmer the alcohol for a minute and move on.

SERVING SUGGESTIONS

Salade à la Romaine (p. 171), Cream Dressing for Salad (p. 592), Madame Laracine's Gratin Dauphinois (p. 284), Chocolate Mousse (p. 820), Apple Tarte Tatin (p. 837)

SEPTEMBER 11, 1960: "WHEN BEEF BECOMES BOEUF," BY CRAIG CLAIBORNE.

—1960

✑ CHINESE BARBECUED SPARERIBS

Back in the 1960s, when Chinese food meant chop suey and chicken chow mein and no one knew that the Chinese would have scoffed at maraschino cherries in sweet-and-sour pork, there was a brief passion for Chinese barbecued spareribs.

Compared with many "Chinese" imports, the spareribs, for which the *Times* printed at least four recipes during the '50s and '60s, were only mildly inauthentic. The marinades usually contained soy sauce and garlic, ingredients actually available in China (or, more specifically, Canton; most of the early Chinese cooking in America was based on Cantonese cuisine). The dishes also harbored a few dubious items such as ketchup, honey, and red wine. All the recipes aimed for a similar result: a sweet and salty, lightly lacquered pork rib—one that at least looked as if it might be found in Shanghai or Canton (now Guangzhou).

Nina Simonds, an authority on Chinese cooking, says these efforts amounted to "basically someone trying to duplicate Ah-So sauce." The Chinese condiment, which comes in a jar, contains corn syrup, fermented soybeans, and garlic.

In *The Pleasures of Chinese Cooking* (1962), a groundbreaking introduction to the cuisine, Grace Zia Chu defended such adaptation. She wrote, "A dish with ingredients that are not typically Chinese may still be a Chinese dish—if it is prepared in the Chinese way."

½ cup honey

½ cup soy sauce

2 cloves garlic, crushed

3 tablespoons ketchup

½ cup water

4 pounds spareribs, cut into serving pieces

1. Combine the honey, soy sauce, garlic, ketchup, and water in a pan large enough to hold the ribs. Marinate the spareribs in this mixture in the refrigerator for several hours, turning a few times.

2. Heat a gas or charcoal grill to low. Drain the spareribs, reserving the marinade, and arrange in a hinged grill basket (or place directly on the grill). Grill, basting occasionally with the reserved marinade, for 1½ hours, or until the ribs are shiny brown and fork-tender. As the meat cooks, turn the basket (or ribs) frequently so that neither side gets charred.

SERVES 4

COOKING NOTE

In an earlier version of this recipe, June Owen, who also wrote the piece about this one, recommended first roasting the ribs for 55 minutes in an oven set at 350 degrees. That way, when you finish them on the grill, they will be less likely to char and spoil the lacquered look. The choice is yours.

SERVING SUGGESTIONS

Shrimp Toast (p. 60), Oriental Watercress Soup (p. 111), Clams in Black Bean Sauce (p. 442), Sugar Snap Peas with Horseradish (p. 259), Lemon Lotus Ice Cream (p. 724)

JUNE 30, 1961: "NEWS OF FOOD: A BARBEQUE FAVORITE," BY JUNE OWEN.

—1961

✑ MOUSSAKA

Moussaka is a little bit like Shepherd's Pie with Curried Meat (p. 534) and also a little like Lasagna (p. 342), with layers of eggplant and lamb topped not with potatoes but with a fluffy custard. In this splendid version, the lamb is scented with coffee and cinnamon and the custard is enriched with ricotta.

---

4 medium eggplants (about 1 pound each)

Salt

2 pounds ground lamb

3 onions, chopped

8 tablespoons (1 stick) unsalted butter

2 tablespoons tomato paste

¼ cup dry red wine

¼ cup extra-strong coffee

¼ cup finely chopped flat-leaf parsley

¼ teaspoon freshly ground black pepper

⅛ teaspoon ground cinnamon

2 large eggs, lightly beaten

1 cup freshly grated Parmesan cheese

¾ cup fresh bread crumbs

Vegetable oil

4 medium tomatoes, sliced

6 tablespoons all-purpose flour

3 cups hot whole milk

⅛ teaspoon freshly grated nutmeg

4 large egg yolks, lightly beaten

2 cups ricotta cheese

1. Cut the eggplants into ¼-inch-thick slices. Sprinkle with salt and let stand for 15 minutes.

2. Meanwhile, brown the lamb and cook the onions in 2 tablespoons butter in a large skillet (you may need to do this in 2 pans—better than crowding one pan). Add the tomato paste, wine, coffee, parsley, 2 teaspoon salt, the pepper, and cinnamon. Simmer until the liquid is absorbed. Let cool.

3. Stir the eggs, ⅓ cup Parmesan cheese, and ¼ cup bread crumbs into the lamb mixture. Set aside.

4. Wipe off the excess salt from the eggplant and brown on both sides in oil in a large skillet. Drain on paper towels.

5. Heat the oven to 350 degrees. Create 2 layers each of the remaining ½ cup bread crumbs and ⅔ cup Parmesan cheese, the eggplant, lamb mixture, and tomato

slices, in a greased 4-quart casserole or lasagna pan, reserving enough eggplant to end with a layer of it.

6. Melt the remaining 6 tablespoons butter in a saucepan over medium heat. When bubbling, add the flour and cook, while whisking, for 1 minute. Gradually stir in the milk and bring to boil, stirring. Add the nutmeg. Pour a little of the hot mixture onto the beaten egg yolks, mixing well, then return all to the pan and cook for 2 minutes. Season with salt. Remove from the heat and cool slightly.

7. Stir the ricotta into the cream soup and pour over the top of the casserole. Bake for 1 hour, or until bubbling hot and browned on top. Cool for 20 to 30 minutes before serving.

SERVES 8

COOKING NOTES

Sautéing the eggplant takes forever. You can either do it in advance (it will hold for up to a day in the fridge) or change the method: Brush the eggplant with oil and roast on baking sheets in a 400-degree oven, turning once.

If you need to use 2 pans for Step 2, use one for the lamb and one for the onions.

You can make this a day ahead and refrigerate it overnight. Reheat in a 300-degree oven for 30 minutes to serve.

SERVING SUGGESTIONS

Roasted Feta with Thyme Honey (p. 92), Shrimp Baked with Feta Cheese, Greek-Style (p. 397), Salade à la Grecque (p. 179), Couscous Salad (p. 321), Hazelnut Baklava (p. 706)

JANUARY 3, 1966: "SIMPLE DISH TO SERVE 12," BY JEAN HEWITT.

—1966

⌒ ANN SERANNE'S RIB ROAST OF BEEF

Cooking beef—especially an expensive cut like rib roast—to the right doneness while also tending to guests is not what I call fun. But back in the 1960s, Ann Seranne, a food consultant and author of more than a dozen cookbooks, solved the problem. Craig Claiborne wrote that her technique "is so basic, so easily applied, and so eminently satisfactory in its results, the astonishing thing is it is not universally known." As it still isn't, I include it here once more.

The technique is as follows: you bring the meat to room temperature; pat it with a mixture of flour, salt, and pepper; put it in a 500-degree oven for an amount of time determined by the weight of the beef; and then turn off the heat and leave the meat in the oven for 2 hours—". . . long enough," Seranne told Claiborne, "for a game of golf or an appointment at the hairdresser."

What I also loved about this recipe is the excellent crust that develops from the flour cooking into the layer of fat rimming the beef.

A similar technique for lamb can be found on p. 526.

———

One 2- to 4-bone beef rib roast
  (4½ to 12 pounds)
Flour for dusting
Salt and freshly ground black pepper

1. Remove the roast from the refrigerator 2½ to 4 hours before cooking, depending on its size.

2. Heat the oven to 500 degrees. Place the roast in a shallow roasting pan, fat side up. Sprinkle with a little flour and rub the flour lightly into the fat. Season all over with salt and pepper.

3. Put the roast in the preheated oven and roast according to the roasting chart on the next page, timing the minutes exactly.

4. When the cooking time is finished, turn off the oven. Do not open the door at any time. Allow the roast to remain in the oven until the oven is lukewarm, about 2 hours. The roast will still have a crunchy brown outside, and an internal heat suitable for serving even after 4 hours.

Number of ribs	Weight (without short ribs)	Roasting Time at 500 degrees
2	4½ to 5 pounds	25 to 30 minutes
3	8 to 9 pounds	40 to 45 minutes
4	11 to 12 pounds	55 to 60 minutes

MAKES ABOUT 2 SERVINGS PER RIB

COOKING NOTE

Make sure your oven temperature is accurate before consulting the time chart.

VARIATION

If you have leftovers, which I doubt you will, thinly slice the meat and serve it cold with a sauce of mayonnaise, mustard, and horseradish (4:1:1).

SERVING SUGGESTIONS

Martini (p. 35), Fried Olives (p. 87), Toasts with Walnut Sauce (p. 73), Maida Heatter's Preheated-Oven Popovers (p. 657), Shallot Pudding (p. 247), Spinach Roman-Style (p. 233), Apple Tarte Tatin (p. 837), Coffee Caramel Custard (p. 849) Pruneaux du Pichet (Prunes in a Pitcher; p. 822)

JULY 28, 1966: "ANN SERANNE'S RECIPE FOR A PERFECT ROAST: PUT IT IN THE OVEN AND RELAX," BY CRAIG CLAIBORNE. RECIPE ADAPTED FROM ANN SERANNE.

—1966

✍ VEAL CHOPS BEAU SÉJOUR

Make sure you brown the veal well on every surface, even the edges, because that pays off in the end with a good crust on the chops and a rich, dense sauce. The garlic is the showman, the vinegar its sidekick.

---

6 veal chops, preferably cut from the rack, 1½ inches thick, Frenched (ask the butcher to do this)

Flour

¼ cup vegetable oil

4 tablespoons unsalted butter

6 cloves garlic

2 medium bay leaves

½ teaspoon dried thyme

Salt and freshly ground black pepper

2 tablespoons red wine vinegar

½ cup chicken broth

¼ cup water

1. Dredge the chops lightly on all sides in flour. Heat the oil and 3 tablespoons butter in a skillet large enough to hold all 6 chops. Brown the chops.

2. Scatter the garlic cloves around the chops. Cut the bay leaves into 3 pieces each and place 1 piece on each chop. Add the thyme and salt and pepper to taste. Cook the chops, tightly covered, over medium to low heat for about 20 minutes, or until they are cooked through and the natural sauce in the skillet is syrupy.

3. Transfer the chops to a hot serving dish, leaving the garlic and bay leaves in the skillet, and keep warm. Add the vinegar to the skillet and cook, stirring, until it has evaporated. Add the broth and water and cook, stirring until the sauce has reduced and concentrated to your liking, about 5 minutes. Check the seasoning. Turn off the heat and swirl in the remaining tablespoon of butter.

4. Pour the sauce over the chops and garnish each chop with a garlic clove.

SERVES 6

COOKING NOTE

Don't use a cast-iron skillet, or the vinegar will make your sauce muddy.

SERVING SUGGESTIONS

Ratatouille Niçoise (p. 219), Yette's Garden Platter (p. 220), Mushrooms with Manzanilla Sherry (p. 249), Mashed Potatoes Anna (p. 294), Pots de Crème (p. 815)

READERS

"I'm still using the original copy from the paper, now deep yellow with age, fragile, held together with Scotch tape. We were married 13 years when I first found it and tried it. It's been 50 years now, and this favorite dinner, I think, has contributed to the longevity of our marriage. It's so easy, so quick. I couldn't do without it."

Lotti Morris, Bennington, VT, letter

NOVEMBER 19, 1967: "BEAU REPAST," BY CRAIG CLAIBORNE.

—1967

✑ ROSA DE LA GARZA'S DRY CHILI

I'm assuming that most people already have a good chili recipe, so I'm introducing an esoteric one for chili fanatics (a "dry" chili, which means it's intensely spiced and not brothy). The recipe comes from Rosa de la Garza, a daughter of Mexican immigrants, who cooked for a wealthy Texas family. (Craig Claiborne often stumbled upon great recipes by writing about the upper crust and the cooks who fed them.)

De la Garza's recipe reappeared in the *Times* in 1977, when, in response to another story about chili, John C. Schenck, then the publisher of *Sports Illustrated*, reminded Claiborne of de la Garza's recipe, noting, "It remains to this day the single most ambrosial substance which is possible for a human being to digest, and any discussion of chili, food in general, the quality of life, immortality, Democratic administrations, or the choral movement of Beethoven's Ninth Symphony is incomplete without including it." (I learned of the recipe from Schenck, a friend, who invited me to his annual chili party.)

It's a very simple recipe with cumin, garlic, bay leaf, and chili powder the only seasonings, but the shopping is a killer. You must track down beef suet (look at ethnic or specialty butchers), and you must find a patient butcher or family member who is willing to cut 5 pounds of beef into ¼-inch cubes. Don't do it yourself, or you'll end up firebombing my house.

---

1 pound beef suet, cut into chunks
    (see headnote)
5 pounds boneless lean beef, cut into very small
    (¼-inch) cubes—do not grind
1½ tablespoons very finely chopped bay leaf
1½ tablespoons chopped garlic
5 tablespoons ground toasted cumin seeds
¾ cup all-purpose flour
1 cup plus 2 tablespoons chili powder
2 tablespoons salt
Water to reconstitute, or as needed

1. Place the suet in a large deep casserole and cook over medium-low heat, stirring, until rendered of its fat and lightly browned. Remove any solid bits.
2. Add the beef and cook, stirring, over relatively high heat until the liquid that accumulates evaporates. Take care to stir well.
3. Add the remaining ingredients plus 2 tablespoons water and cook, stirring with a wooden spoon, until all the ingredients are thoroughly blended. Be sure to stir the bottom to scrape up any browned bits; do not let it burn.
4. If you wish to serve the chili without freezing, add water to cover the meat plus an extra 4 cups and simmer until the meat is tender, about 45 minutes. Or, to prepare the dry chili for freezing, line 3 small baking pans with a generous length of plastic wrap. Spoon one-third (about 1 pound) of the hot chili into each pan, filling it full. Fold over the plastic wrap to seal well. Let cool. Unmold, if desired, and freeze.
5. To reconstitute the chili, add 6 to 8 cups water to each pound of dry chili, and slowly bring to a simmer.

MAKES ABOUT 3 POUNDS OF DRY CHILI;
SERVES 10 TO 12

COOKING NOTES
I used beef chuck.

I served it over jasmine rice with sliced limes, chopped cilantro, salted chopped onions, and chopped tomatoes as condiments.

If possible, use fresh bay leaves, and chop them in a spice/coffee grinder. And use the very best chili powder and cumin you can buy—poor-quality spices have a tendency to smell musty, and the spices are so prominent in this dish that they could easily ruin it.

SERVING SUGGESTIONS
La Paloma (p. 35), Guacamole Tostadas (p. 67), Raw Spinach Salad (p. 175), Bacon Potato Puffs (p. 276), Maida Heatter's Cuban Black Beans and Rice (p. 281), Tangerine Sherbet (p. 734), Strawberry Soup (p. 816), Caramel Custard (p. 836), Mango Ice Cream (p. 729)

DECEMBER 4, 1969: "TAMALE COOK PAR EXCELLENCE," BY CRAIG CLAIBORNE. ALSO, JANUARY 17, 1977: "DEGUSTIBUS: SOME GOOD NEWS FOR SOUTHPAW CHEFS," BY CRAIG CLAIBORNE.

—1969

ITALIAN BEEF STEW WITH ROSEMARY

I would happily make this recipe once a week. It's smartly conceived, with everything done in a single pot. You trim the meat first and let it come to room temperature while the vegetables cook. After simmering the vegetables, you run them through a food mill, which gives the resulting tomato sauce an appealing pebbly texture. Next you brown the meat, deglaze the pan with white wine, and add the tomato sauce. The tomatoes help break down the meat while it stews, and because the sauce is prepared in advance, there's no transferring of the meat and reducing the sauce before serving. You spoon the stew right from the pot onto rafts of garlic-rubbed toast. The sauce soaks into the bread, and by the time you reach it with your fork, the toast will have attained a fluffy succulence.

The recipe says it serves 4, and it does, as long as there are other courses. In this sense it is a true Mediterranean recipe: a small amount of meat stretched with a sauce and a slab of bread.

————

- 1½ pounds boneless lean beef, such as top or bottom round or chuck
- 3 cups chopped ripe tomatoes or canned tomatoes with basil
- ¾ cup chopped celery
- ½ cup loosely packed chopped flat-leaf parsley
- ¼ teaspoon dried oregano
- ¼ teaspoon dried thyme
- 2 tablespoons olive oil
- Salt and freshly ground black pepper
- 4 tablespoons unsalted butter, plus softened butter for the bread
- 1 teaspoon finely chopped garlic, plus 1 clove garlic
- ½ cup dry white wine
- 1 sprig fresh rosemary or 1 teaspoon dried rosemary
- 8 thin slices French or Italian bread

1. Trim the meat if necessary, and cut it into 1-inch cubes. Set aside.
2. Combine the tomatoes, celery, parsley, oregano, thyme, oil, and salt and pepper to taste in a wide casserole, cover, and bring to a boil. Reduce the heat and simmer for 30 to 40 minutes, until the vegetables are just tender. Put the sauce through a food mill and set aside; clean the casserole.
3. Melt butter in the casserole over medium-high heat. Add the beef and cook, stirring, until the meat browns. Lower the heat to medium, add the chopped garlic, and stir. Transfer the meat to dish.
4. Add the wine to the casserole and cook over high heat until it is reduced by half. Add the meat, rosemary, tomato sauce, and, if necessary, salt and pepper to taste. Cover and simmer until the meat is very tender, 1½ to 2 hours. Taste and adjust the seasoning.
5. Meanwhile, heat the broiler. Spread the bread with butter, and toast on both sides under the broiler. Rub on both sides with the garlic clove and place 2 slices in each of 4 hot soup bowls.
6. Spoon the meat and sauce over the toasts.

SERVES 4

COOKING NOTES

If your food mill has various sizes of plates, use the one with largest holes. If you don't have a food mill, a potato masher or a food processor (pulse just a few times) will do the trick.

The recipe called for oregano and thyme, and I used dried herbs, which were more common at the time than fresh. If you'd like to use fresh herbs, double the amounts and measure the chopped leaves.

Almost any white wine will work for the cooking liquid—actually, I used fino sherry, which leant the stew a nutty scent.

SERVING SUGGESTIONS

Ricotta Crostini with Fresh Thyme and Dried Oregano (p. 93), Parmesan Crackers (p. 84), Puntarelle with Anchovies (p. 194), Panna Cotta (p. 840)

PERIOD DETAIL

I thought this might be the first instance of a recipe calling for "freshly ground black pepper" (as opposed to simply "pepper"), an instruction I associate with Marcella Hazan, but in fact, it debuted in an article on cold dishes for Thanksgiving in 1907.

AUGUST 15, 1971: "ROSEMARY STEW."

—1971

⌇ SPICY NEW ENGLAND POT ROAST

I wouldn't call this spicy—the horseradish mellows—but it's certainly flush with candid warming flavors like bacon, cinnamon, and cranberries.

———

3 tablespoons all-purpose flour

2 teaspoons salt

$\frac{1}{4}$ teaspoon freshly ground black pepper

One 4-pound boned and tied beef arm, blade, or bottom round roast

3 tablespoons bacon drippings or vegetable oil

$\frac{1}{2}$ cup freshly grated horseradish or drained prepared horseradish (4-ounce jar)

1 cup whole-berry cranberry sauce

1 cinnamon stick, broken in two

4 whole cloves

1 cup beef broth

16 small white onions

1 bunch carrots, peeled and cut into 3-inch lengths

1. Mix the flour with the salt and pepper. Dredge the meat in the flour, rubbing the mixture into all the surfaces.
2. Heat the drippings in a Dutch oven or other heavy casserole and brown the meat very well on all sides over high heat. Pour off the drippings into a skillet and reserve.
3. Mix together the horseradish, cranberry sauce, cinnamon, cloves, and broth and add to the meat. Bring the mixture to a boil, cover tightly, and simmer gently for about 2 hours, or until the meat is barely tender.
4. Meanwhile, brown the onions in the reserved drippings in the skillet. Add the carrots and cook for 2 minutes longer. Remove from the heat.
5. When the meat is barely tender, using a slotted spoon, add the onions and carrots. Cover cook for about 15 minutes longer, or until the vegetables and meat are tender.

SERVES 8

COOKING NOTE

Why not use one of the cranberry sauces on pp. 606 and 608?

SERVING SUGGESTIONS

Butternut Squash and Cider Soup (p. 136), Cabbage and Potato Gratin with Mustard Bread Crumbs (p. 298), Ismail Merchant's Spinach Puree (p. 229), Frozen Lemon Soufflé (p. 725), Madeleine Kamman's Apple Mousse (p. 816)

SEPTEMBER 3, 1972: "POT ROAST WILL NEVER BE THE SAME," BY JEAN HEWITT.

—1972

⌇ BREADED VEAL MILAN-STYLE

Scaloppine, the butcher's go-to cut of the 1970s.

———

$\frac{1}{2}$ pound veal scaloppini

Flour for dredging

Salt and freshly ground black pepper

1 large egg

1 teaspoon water

2 tablespoons plus $\frac{1}{2}$ teaspoon peanut, vegetable, or olive oil

$\frac{1}{4}$ teaspoon freshly grated nutmeg

$1\frac{1}{2}$ cups coarse fresh bread crumbs

$\frac{1}{2}$ cup freshly grated Parmesan cheese

2 tablespoons unsalted butter

2 to 4 lemon slices

1. Unless the scaloppine are very small, cut them into pieces measuring about 3 inches by 3 inches or slightly larger. Place the scaloppine between sheets of wax paper and pound lightly to flatten, using the bottom of a heavy skillet or a flat mallet.
2. Generously season the flour with salt and pepper. Beat the egg with the water, $\frac{1}{2}$ teaspoon oil, and the nutmeg in a shallow bowl. Blend the bread crumbs with the Parmesan.
3. Dip the scaloppine on both sides first in the flour, then in egg, and finally in the bread crumb mixture. As the scaloppine are breaded, place them on a flat surface and tap lightly to help the bread crumbs adhere.
4. Heat half the butter and 1 tablespoon oil in a heavy skillet over medium-high heat. Add half the scaloppine and cook until golden brown on one side, 2 to 4 minutes. Cook until golden brown on the other side.

Transfer to a plate. Repeat with the remaining butter, oil, and scaloppini. Serve with sliced lemon.

SERVES 2

COOKING NOTE

It's important to use homemade bread crumbs, which tend to be coarser—in a good way!

SERVING SUGGESTIONS

Diane Forley's Arugula Salad with Artichoke, Ricotta Salata, and Pumpkin Seeds (p. 188), Spinach Roman-Style (p. 233), Sautéed Potatoes with Parsley (p. 283), Balducci's Tiramisù (p. 830), Ricotta Kisses (p. 852)

JULY 28, 1974: "FOOD: THREE WAYS WITH VEAL SCALOP-PINE: WHEN IT'S DINNER FOR TWO," BY CRAIG CLAIBORNE.

—1974

‹€ MEAT AND SPINACH LOAF

I learned about this recipe from my *Times* colleague Nathan Lump, who wears pocket squares, permits not a scrap of paper on his desk, and is the last person you'd expect to like meat loaf. Indeed, he told me, "It's the only meat loaf I would serve to guests."

By then I'd already tested at least six other recipes, and was loathe to make another. I'm glad I sucked it up, because this awfully named "meat and spinach" loaf did not disappoint. It's finely textured, carefully spiced, as tailored as you will find. Which, come to think of it, may explain Nathan's enthusiasm.

———

1 pound loose fresh spinach or one
     10-ounce package spinach
1¼ pounds ground veal, pork, or beef
     or a combination of all three
½ cup fresh bread crumbs
Salt
1½ teaspoons freshly ground pepper
¼ teaspoon freshly grated nutmeg
½ cup coarsely chopped celery
½ cup loosely packed flat-leaf parsley leaves
¼ cup whole milk
1 clove garlic, finely minced
1 tablespoon unsalted butter

½ cup finely chopped onion
2 large eggs, lightly beaten
3 slices bacon
Tomato sauce for serving (optional)

1. Heat the oven to 350 degrees. Pick over the spinach to remove any tough stems or slimy leaves. Rinse the spinach well in cold water, drain, place in a saucepan, and cover. It is not necessary to add liquid; the spinach will cook in the water clinging to the leaves. Cook for about 2 minutes, stirring once or twice, until wilted.
2. Transfer the spinach to a colander and douse with cold water to chill. Drain and press with your hands to extract most of the moisture. Chop the spinach.
3. Put the meat in a bowl and add the chopped spinach, bread crumbs, salt to taste, the pepper, and nutmeg.
4. Put the celery, parsley, and milk in a blender. Blend well, and add to the meat mixture. Add the garlic.
5. Heat the butter in a small skillet. Add the onion and cook until wilted. Add to the meat mixture. Add the eggs and blend well with your hands. Shape and fit into an oval or round baking dish, or place in a loaf pan. Cover with the bacon.
6. Bake until just cooked through, 1 to 1¼ hours, turning the pan 180 degrees halfway through. Pour off the fat and let the loaf stand for 20 minutes before slicing. Serve, if desired, with tomato sauce.

SERVES 4

COOKING NOTES

Use a combination of meats and make sure they're not lean.

Nathan tweaked the recipe slightly: he makes a homemade tomato jam (tomatoes, red onion, and a little sugar) and spreads it on top of the loaf with the bacon. If you want try this with tomato preserves, there's a recipe on p. 602.

SERVING SUGGESTIONS

Hot Cheese Olives (p. 83), Mashed Potatoes Anna (p. 294), String Beans with Ginger and Garlic (p. 260), Reuben's Apple Pancake (p. 831), Banana Cream Pie (p. 863), Lemon Mousse for a Crowd (p. 861)

SEPTEMBER 29, 1974: "SUBLIME . . . MEAT LOAVES," BY CRAIG CLAIBORNE WITH PIERRE FRANEY.

—1974

VEAL GOULASH WITH SPAETZLE

Meat cooked with onions and spices has been around forever in Hungary. Infusing the stews with paprika is a relatively new idea that originated in the nineteenth century.

_____

3 tablespoons lard, vegetable oil, or unsalted butter

4 pounds boneless veal or pork, cut into 2-inch cubes

4 cups halved and sliced onions (about 1 pound)

1 to 3 tablespoons paprika

2 tablespoons finely chopped garlic

Salt and freshly ground black pepper

2 tablespoons all-purpose flour

2½ cups chicken broth

1½ cups green bell peppers cut into 1-inch-wide strips

½ cup sour cream, at room temperature (optional)

Spaetzle (optional; recipe follows)

1. Heat the oven to 350 degrees. Heat half the lard in a Dutch oven or other heavy casserole over medium-high heat. Add half the veal and cook until browned, then remove from the pot. Add the remaining veal. Once it's browned, remove the veal, and add the onions. Cook until lightly browned.

2. Return the veal to the pot. Reduce the heat to medium, sprinkle in the paprika, stir, and cook for 5 minutes. Sprinkle with the garlic and salt and pepper to taste. Stir briefly, and sprinkle with the flour, stirring to coat the pieces of meat. Add the chicken broth and bring to a boil. Cover with a round of wax paper and put the lid on.

3. Place in the oven and bake for 1½ to 2 hours. Cooking time will depend on the quality of the meat; best-quality veal cooks more rapidly than that of a lesser quality. Pork cooks more quickly.

4. About 30 minutes before the stew is cooked, sprinkle with the pepper strips. Continue cooking for 30 minutes, or until the meat is tender.

5. Lightly beat the sour cream. Whisk a ladleful of broth into the sour cream, then slowly stir this into the goulash. Serve the stew with the spaetzle, if desired.

SERVES 8

SPAETZLE

4 cups sifted all-purpose flour

6 large eggs

1⅓ cups whole milk

Salt

¼ teaspoon freshly grated nutmeg

4 tablespoons unsalted butter

Freshly ground black pepper

1. Place the flour in a bowl. Beat the eggs and add them to the flour, stirring with a wire whisk or beating with a hand mixer. Gradually add the milk, beating or stirring constantly. Add salt to taste and the nutmeg.

2. Bring a large pot of water to a boil and add salt. Pour the spaetzle mixture into a colander set over the boiling water and press the mixture through the holes of the colander with a rubber spatula or large spoon. The spaetzle are done when they float. Drain and spoon them onto a clean towel or paper towels to dry briefly.

3. Melt the butter in a large nonstick skillet. When it is hot, add the spaetzle and cook, tossing and stirring until it's golden brown and crisp on the edges for 3 to 5 minutes. Season with salt and pepper.

SERVES 8 TO 10

COOKING NOTES

Splitting the difference, I used 2 tablespoons paprika, but I wouldn't have minded more. To ramp up the flavor of the dish, use 1 tablespoon Spanish smoked paprika (pimentón) and 1 tablespoon regular paprika

Use shoulder cuts of pork and veal, if possible.

If you don't feel like making the spaetzle, serve the goulash over buttered noodles.

SERVING SUGGESTIONS

Cucumbers in Cream (p. 225), Braised Red Cabbage with Chestnuts (p. 221), Sautéed Potatoes with Parsley (p. 283), Caramelized Chocolate Bread Pudding (p. 852), Dick Taeuber's Cordial Pie (p. 817), Baumkuchentorte (Crepe-Like Layer Cake; p. 747)

MAY 25, 1975: "FOOD: ALL GOULASH," BY CRAIG CLAIBORNE. RECIPE ADAPTED FROM _THE CUISINE OF HUNGARY_," BY GEORGE LANG.

—1975

HIGH-TEMPERATURE ROAST LAMB

This technique was developed by a reader, Dorothy Moore, as an homage to Ann Seranne's Rib Roast of Beef on p. 519. The lamb is brought to room temperature, roasted at 500 degrees for a short period, and then left in the oven for a few hours to finish cooking. What's so great about this method—aside from the convenience of being able to roast the lamb far in advance—is that the meat rests while it finishes cooking, so that when you take it out of the oven, the meat is settled, ready for slicing and incredibly moist.

In Step 3, you are told to reheat the pan drippings and serve them as the sauce, which isn't a bad idea, but you can also make any kind of reduction sauce you'd like. I added wine to the drippings and reduced the mixture by half.

———

I small leg of lamb (about 6 pounds)
2 cloves garlic, cut into slivers
Salt and freshly ground black pepper
I bay leaf, broken
3 sprigs fresh thyme, chopped, or
    ½ teaspoon dried thyme
½ teaspoon dried rosemary
2 tablespoons olive oil
2 tablespoons dry vermouth

1. Heat the oven to 500 degrees. Place the lamb fat side up in a shallow roasting pan. Make several gashes in the fat and near the bone. Insert the slivers of garlic in the gashes. Rub the lamb all over with salt, pepper, the bay leaf, thyme, and rosemary. Add the oil and vermouth to the pan. (The lamb can be covered closely and refrigerated for several hours or overnight. However, it is best to let the lamb return to room temperature before putting it in the oven.)

2. Place the lamb in the oven. If you wish the lamb to be rare, bake for 15 minutes, then turn off the oven and let the lamb stand in the oven for 3 hours. Do not open the door at any time until the lamb is ready to be carved and served. If you wish the lamb to be medium-well, bake for 20 minutes before turning off the oven. Then, again without opening the door, let stand for 3½ hours. If you wish the lamb to be well-done, bake for 25 minutes and let stand in the oven for 3½ hours.

3. Transfer the lamb to a cutting board. Strain the pan liquid. Strain off most of the surface fat from the drippings. Reheat the drippings and serve with the lamb when carved.

SERVES 8 OR MORE

COOKING NOTE
Have the butcher remove and set aside the hipbone of the lamb: this is the upper bone that is attached to the main (straight) leg bone. This can also be done at home with a sharp knife: Cut away a layer of the top fat. Do not cut away all the fat, however—that's the good stuff, so leave a thin coating!

SERVING SUGGESTIONS
Chilled English Pea–Mint Soup (p. 162), Italian Roast Potatoes (p. 300), Pea Puree (p. 429; without the scallops), Butter-Braised Asparagus and Oyster Mushrooms with Peas and Tarragon (p. 262), Al Forno's Roasted Asparagus (p. 233), Rhubarb-Strawberry Mousse (p. 835), Rhubarb Orange (p. 864)

NOVEMBER 26, 1978: "THE EASIEST ROAST LAMB EVER," BY CRAIG CLAIBORNE WITH PIERRE FRANEY. RECIPE ADAPTED FROM DOROTHY MOORE OF QUOGUE, NEW YORK.

—1978

KÖNIGSBERGER KLOPSE (MEATBALLS IN CREAMY CAPER SAUCE)

———

½ pound ground pork
½ pound ground beef
½ pound ground veal
6 tablespoons unsalted butter
¾ cup finely chopped onion
½ teaspoon grated lemon zest
¾ cup fine fresh bread crumbs
½ cup heavy cream
I large egg, lightly beaten
4 anchovy fillets, chopped (about I tablespoon)
¼ cup finely chopped flat-leaf parsley
⅛ teaspoon freshly grated nutmeg
Salt and freshly ground black pepper
5 tablespoons all-purpose flour

3 cups beef broth

¾ cup dry white wine, preferably a Rhine wine

I cup sour cream

2 large egg yolks, lightly beaten

¼ cup fresh lemon juice

½ cup drained capers

Chopped dill

1. Put the meats into a bowl.

2. Heat 2 tablespoons butter in a skillet. Add the onion and cook, stirring, until wilted. Cool briefly, and add to the meats.

3. Add the lemon zest. Blend the bread crumbs and cream in a small bowl, and add to the meats. Add the lightly beaten whole egg, anchovies, chopped parsley, nutmeg, and salt and pepper to taste. (Do not add much salt, the anchovies are salty.) Blend the ingredients well. Shape into about 36 meatballs, each about 1 inch in diameter.

4. Melt the remaining 4 tablespoons butter in a saucepan. Add the flour, stirring with a wire whisk. When blended, add the broth, whisking rapidly, until thickened and smooth. Add the wine and salt and pepper to taste. Remove from the heat.

5. Arrange the meatballs in one layer in a large casserole. Pour the sauce over them. Bring to a boil, then reduce the heat and simmer for 20 minutes. Using a slotted spoon, remove the meatballs to a dish and keep warm. Strain the sauce if desired.

6. Blend the sour cream, egg yolks, and lemon juice in a small bowl. Stir this into the sauce and add the capers and salt and pepper to taste. Return the meatballs to the sauce and heat through.

7. Garnish with chopped dill and serve with buttered noodles or mashed potatoes.

SERVES 6

SERVING SUGGESTIONS

Carrot and Fennel Soup (p. 151), Janson's Temptation (p. 278), Florida Beets (p. 216), Shredded Brussels Sprouts with Bacon and Pine Nuts (p. 235), Noodles Romanoff (p. 311), Haricots Verts with Balsamic Vinaigrette (p. 231), Swedish Nut Balls (p. 694)

NOVEMBER II, 1979: "FOOD: NATIONALIZING THE MEATBALL," BY CRAIG CLAIBORNE WITH PIERRE FRANEY.

—1979

POLPETTE ALLA ROMANA (ROMAN-STYLE MEATBALLS)

Prosciutto really amplifies the flavors of these meatballs, and lots of liquid—milk and eggs—in the mixture keeps them light. (As long as you don't mush the balls together when shaping—and you won't do that, right? Because I'll lose sleep if you do. So don't!)

———

For the Meatballs

1¼ pounds ground beef

¼ pound slices prosciutto, finely chopped (about ¾ cup)

I cup fresh bread crumbs

½ cup whole milk

½ teaspoon finely minced garlic

3 tablespoons freshly grated Parmesan cheese

2 large eggs, lightly beaten

⅛ teaspoon freshly grated nutmeg

¼ cup finely chopped flat-leaf parsley

Salt and freshly ground black pepper

I tablespoon olive oil

For the Sauce

¼ cup olive oil, finely diced pancetta, diced bacon, salt pork, or ham fat

¼ cup finely chopped onion

¼ cup finely chopped carrot

¼ cup finely chopped celery

¼ cup finely diced zucchini

1½ pounds ripe tomatoes, peeled (see Cooking Note, p. 146) and cored, or 3 cups canned tomatoes

Salt and freshly ground black pepper

I tablespoon chopped basil

1. To make the meatballs, put the beef into a bowl, add the prosciutto, and blend.

2. Combine the bread crumbs and milk in another bowl and blend well. Let stand for a minute or so, and add to the beef. Add the garlic, grated cheese, eggs, nutmeg, and parsley. Add a little salt (the prosciutto is already salty) and pepper to taste. Blend the mixture well. Shape into about 36 meatballs, each about 1½ inches in diameter.

3. To prepare the sauce, heat the oil in a skillet. Add the onion, carrots, celery, and zucchini and cook, stirring often, until the onion starts to brown.

4. Put the tomatoes into a food processor or blender

and blend. Add to the vegetables and cook for about 10 minutes. Add salt and pepper to taste and the basil. Set aside.

5. To cook the meatballs, heat the tablespoon of olive oil in a large skillet. Add the meatballs a few at a time; do not crowd them. Brown them all over, turning often so that they cook evenly. When each batch is cooked, remove it and cook another, until all the balls are browned.

6. Add the meatballs to the sauce and simmer for about 15 minutes, turning the balls in the sauce occasionally.

SERVES 4 TO 6

COOKING NOTE

I find an icing spatula comes in handy when turning meatballs, because you can maneuver it into small spaces.

SERVING SUGGESTIONS

Raw Artichoke Salad with Cucumber (p. 173), Mezzaluna Salad (p. 185), Italian Roast Potatoes (p. 300), Soft Polenta (p. 556), Hazelnut Cheesecake (p. 753), Almond Granita (p. 731), Campton Place Buttermilk Chocolate Cake (p. 765)

NOVEMBER 11, 1979: "NATIONALIZING THE MEATBALL," BY CRAIG CLAIBORNE WITH PIERRE FRANEY.

—1979

✑ FILET DE BOEUF RÔTI (ROAST FILLET OF BEEF) WITH SAUCE BORDELAISE

———

One 3¾-pound center-cut beef fillet
3 tablespoons unsalted butter
Salt and freshly ground black pepper
¼ cup red wine vinegar
2 cups Sauce Bordelaise (recipe follows)

1. Heat the oven to 450 degrees. Tie the fillet crosswise in several places with kitchen string.

2. Melt 2 tablespoons butter in a shallow roasting pan in which the fillet will fit comfortably. Turn the fillet in the butter and sprinkle with salt and pepper to taste.

3. Turn the heat to high and cook until the butter starts to sizzle slightly. Put the pan in the oven and roast for 15 minutes. Turn the fillet and continue roasting for 5 minutes.

4. Reduce the oven heat to 415 degrees. Continue roasting until an instant-read thermometer, inserted in the thickest part, reads 125 degrees (for rare), 10 to 15 minutes. Remove the beef from the oven and let stand on a carving board, covered, for 20 minutes before carving.

5. Meanwhile, pour off the fat from the pan. Place the pan on the stove and add the red wine vinegar. Cook for about 1 minute, stirring to dissolve the brown particles clinging to the bottom and sides of the pan. Add the bordelaise sauce and stir. Put the sauce through a fine sieve, preferably one of the sort known in French kitchens as a chinois.

6. Pour the sauce into a small saucepan, heat briefly, and swirl in the remaining tablespoon of butter. Serve with the beef.

SERVES 12

SAUCE BORDELAISE (A RED WINE SAUCE)

3 tablespoons thinly sliced shallots
1 cup dry red wine, preferably a Bordeaux
2 cups Demi-Glace (recipe follows)

Combine the shallots and wine in a saucepan and bring to a boil. Cook over high heat until all the wine is evaporated. Add the demi-glace and simmer for about 2 minutes.

MAKES 2 CUPS

DEMI-GLACE (A BASIC MEAT GLAZE)

4 pounds veal bones, cracked
1½ cups coarsely chopped carrots
1½ cups coarsely chopped celery
1½ cups coarsely chopped onions
2 cloves garlic
1 medium tomato, coarsely chopped
6 sprigs parsley
2 bay leaves

½ teaspoon dried thyme
Salt
6 black peppercorns, crushed
3 quarts water

1. Heat the broiler. Put the veal bones in a roasting pan in one layer. Place them under the broiler and broil until browned, about 5 minutes. Turn the pieces and continue broiling for about 5 minutes.

2. Scatter the carrots, celery, onions, garlic, and tomato over the bones. Continue broiling for about 10 minutes.

3. Transfer the ingredients to a stockpot and add the parsley sprigs, bay leaves, thyme, salt to taste, the peppercorns, and water. Bring to a boil, skimming, then reduce the heat and simmer, skimming often, for 7 hours.

4. Strain the stock and discard the solids. There should be about 4½ to 5 cups. Put the stock in a saucepan, bring to a boil and continue cooking down for about 2 hours, or until reduced to 2 cups.

MAKES 2 CUPS

SERVING SUGGESTIONS
Rillettes de Canard (Duck Rillettes; p. 65), Chiffonade Salad (p. 173), Cheese Pudding Soufflés (p. 643), Saratoga Potatoes (p. 273), Apple Galette (p. 843)

MARCH 30, 1980: "FOOD: ANATOMY OF A BEEF FILLET," BY CRAIG CLAIBORNE WITH PIERRE FRANEY.

—1980

✎ CLEO'S DADDY'S BARBECUED RIBS

Cleo Johns was the owner of Cleo's La Cuisine Catering in Maplewood, New Jersey, a woman who described cooking as like "turning on a faucet." Cleo did not write down her recipes, but Betty Fussell, a *Times* contributor, did so for her after watching her make these ribs. Whether or not the ribs are just like Cleo's version, they're remarkable—not saucy, but crisp and chewy, as ribs should be. The barbecue sauce will be good and spicy, as long as you have the guts to add enough cayenne or Tabasco; it thickens and smooths after you add the pan drippings.

½ cup soy sauce
⅓ cup good wine vinegar
2 cloves garlic, finely chopped
¼ cup grated onion
2 racks lean spareribs

For the Barbecue Sauce
½ cup cider vinegar
¼ cup packed brown sugar
½ cup ketchup
2 tablespoons mustard
Freshly ground black pepper
Cayenne pepper or Tabasco sauce
2 tablespoons marinade
¼ to ½ cup pan drippings (from ribs)

1. Mix the soy sauce, vinegar, garlic, and onion. Rub each slab of ribs with the marinade, and let sit for at least 30 minutes, turning once or twice.

2. Heat the oven to 400 degrees. Remove the ribs from the marinade (reserve the marinade) and lay them meaty side up in a roasting pan. Bake the ribs for 1 hour, then turn the ribs and bake for 30 minutes longer.

3. Meanwhile, to make the sauce, mix together the vinegar, sugar, ketchup, and mustard, black pepper and cayenne pepper to taste, and 2 tablespoons marinade in a saucepan. Bring to a boil and cook for 15 to 20 minutes, until thick. Add the pan drippings and cook for another 10 minutes. Season to taste with cayenne.

4. Cut between every 2 or 3 ribs to serve as an entrée, or between every rib to serve as an hors d'oeuvre. Serve with the barbecue sauce on the side.

SERVES 8 AS A MAIN COURSE,
4 AS A FIRST COURSE

SERVING SUGGESTIONS
Patsy's Bourbon Slush (p. 32), Fresh Succotash (p. 275), Docks Coleslaw (p. 191), Spoonbread's Potato Salad (p. 288), Hoppin' John (p. 298), Old South Buttermilk Biscuits (p. 655), Jellied Strawberry Pie (p. 811), Buttermilk Pie (p. 859), Mississippi Pecan Pie (p. 820)

FEBRUARY 11, 1981: "CATERING, DOWN-HOME AND NATURAL," BY B. H. FUSSELL. RECIPE ADAPTED FROM CLEO'S LA CUISINE CATERING IN MAPLEWOOD, NEW JERSEY.

—1981

MADAME MOURIERE'S CASSOULET

Madame Mouriere, a terrific home cook in Quercy, France, also created the Tourtière (Apple, Prune, and Armagnac tart) on p. 827.

———

1 Confit de Canard (recipe follows)
2 pounds dried white beans (Great Northern or navy are excellent), rinsed and picked over
1 pound fresh pork rind or bacon, cubed
2 bay leaves
1 teaspoon dried thyme
1/2 pound carrots, peeled and cut into 1/2-inch-thick rounds
1 tablespoon salt
1/2 cup goose fat or 8 tablespoons (1 stick) unsalted butter, or as needed
2 1/2 pounds fresh all-pork garlic sausage (Polish or German sausage is fine)
1 pound medium onions (about 4), thinly sliced
Two 28-ounce cans imported plum tomatoes, with their juices
2 cloves garlic
2 cups fresh bread crumbs, blended with 2 cloves garlic, finely minced

1. Prepare the confit: this can be done weeks in advance or the same day if desired. To reduce the amount of time the dish takes, though, it is best to make it at least a day ahead.

2. The day before serving the cassoulet, prepare the beans. Put them in a Dutch oven or large saucepan, cover with cold water, and bring to a boil. Cover, remove from the heat, and let sit for 40 minutes.

3. Meanwhile, cover the fresh pork rind (or bacon) with cold water in another large saucepan and bring to a boil over high heat. Simmer for several minutes, then drain, rinse, and set aside. (This is done to remove the salt, which would have a toughening effect on the beans.)

4. By this time the beans should have swollen. Discard the liquid (to help make the beans more digestible), rinse the beans, and just cover them again with cold water. Add the bay leaves, thyme, and pork rind and bring to a boil over medium-high heat. Boil vigorously

for 45 minutes to 1 hour, or until the beans are quite well cooked but still a bit firm.

5. Add the carrots and additional boiling water if necessary and cook for 15 minutes, or just until the carrots are cooked. The mixture should be loose and not too dry. Remove from the heat, stir in the salt, and allow to cool to room temperature. Cover and refrigerate overnight.

6. To prepare the cassoulet, melt 3 tablespoons goose fat (or butter) in a very large skillet. Add the sausages, all in a single coil, if you can, and cook them over medium heat for about 6 minutes on one side, about 3 minutes on the other side. (Remember which side was cooked for the shorter time: when the cassoulet is assembled, you want to place the sausage with the less cooked side down so the remaining fat will soak into the bean mixture.) You need not prick the sausage. Remove the sausage from the pan and set aside.

7. Add an additional 3 tablespoons goose fat if necessary to the pan to cook the confit. If you made the confit ahead, let it come to room temperature to soften the fat, and remove all of the confit pieces, wiping off the fat as you remove them. Sauté the pieces of confit over medium-high heat until the skin is very crisp and turns a rich, deep brown; skim off the fat as necessary. The duck should cook for about 3 to 5 minutes on each side. Remove from the pan, drain, and set aside; set the pan, with the fat, aside.

8. Remove the beans from the refrigerator to come to room temperature.

9. Add 2 tablespoons goose fat if necessary to the skillet and cook the onions over high heat for about 5 minutes. Add the tomatoes, with the liquid, and a garlic clove and cook until the mixture is fairly dry, about 40 minutes. The onions should be a rich, deep red. Add to the bean and carrot mixture.

10. Heat the oven to 325 degrees. Remove the bones from the duck confit and cut or pull the duck into large chunks, without removing the skin.

11. Assemble the cassoulet in a large earthenware casserole: an oval casserole measuring 12 by 17 by 3 inches deep is a perfect size. Rub the inside of the casserole with the remaining garlic clove and discard the garlic. Layer in this order: Add a single layer of the bean mixture, using about a third of it. Cover this with the cut-up pieces of duck. Add a second layer of the bean mixture. Add the sausages in one layer, with the less-cooked side down. Add the last layer of beans.

Finally, add the bread crumb mixture. Be sure there is at least half an inch of growing space between the bread crumbs and the rim of the casserole.

12. Bake for 1½ to 2 hours, or until the crust is golden and firm. Serve immediately.

SERVES 10 TO 12

CONFIT DE CANARD (PRESERVED DUCK)

    1 duck (4 to 5 pound)
    2 tablespoons coarse sea salt
    ¼ teaspoon freshly ground black pepper
    3 cloves garlic
    3 whole cloves
    3 bay leaves
    2 teaspoons dried thyme
    4 cups rendered duck fat (see instructions below)
        or goose fat, or as needed

1. Cut the duck into serving pieces: 2 legs with thighs, 2 breast halves, 2 wings, and neck. Trim away any excess fat from the duck and from the cavity of the carcass, reserving it for rendering. Layer the duck pieces, in a large shallow bowl, sprinkling them with the salt and pepper. Add the garlic, cloves, bay leaves, and thyme, cover with plastic wrap, and refrigerate for 24 hours, turning the pieces occasionally.

2. Rinse the pieces to remove the salt and wipe dry with paper towels. Heat the duck fat in a very large pot just enough to melt it, and add the duck pieces, garlic, and herbs. (Preferably, the pot should be large enough to hold the pieces in one layer; use a copper pot if you have one—it will allow the duck to cook slowly and evenly.) Bring the fat almost to the boil, then quickly lower the heat to a gentle simmer and simmer slowly, uncovered, for 1½ hours. Do not allow the fat to boil, or the meat will be fried, not gently cooked. After 1½ hours, pierce the duck meat with a metal skewer. If the juice flows clear, the duck is cooked; if it flows red, continue cooking until it flows clear. The meat should be soft and not offer the least bit of resistance.

3. Remove the duck pieces and arrange them in a large round earthenware terrine, a large wide-mouth canning jar, or several jars. (If you will be using the confit right away or the next day, just cover and refrigerate.) To store the confit, strain the fat through a very fine strainer over the duck pieces. There should be enough fat to fully cover them. If not, add additional fat. Cover the terrine or jar(s) with a lid or plastic wrap. Refrigerate (or store in a very cool cellar) for several weeks before using. The confit should keep for several months as long as it is well covered with fat.

4. When ready to serve, allow the confit to stand at room temperature for an hour, then lift as many pieces as you need out of the fat.

5. To serve hot, broil the pieces or cook them in a very hot oven in a little of their own fat, or panfry them in a little of their own fat, until the skin is crisp and deep brown and the meat is heated through. Drain and serve. To serve at room temperature, brown as described, drain, and allow to cool. Cold duck confit is excellent with a green salad with a garlicky dressing.

MAKES 1 PRESERVED DUCK

HOW TO RENDER DUCK FAT

Combine any of the extra skin from the cut-up duck and all of the excess fat, including the fat in the cavity of the carcass and the visible and readily accessible fat just under the skin. You may not have enough fat from a single duck to preserve it; if necessary, add goose fat or a good-quality fresh lard.

To render the fat, combine it with ½ cup water in a heavy casserole and cook on top of the stove until all the fat is rendered. Stir frequently to prevent burning. When rendered, strain through a sieve and use; or freeze it for future use, like frying potatoes in the dead of winter when anything fried in duck fat sounds good.

Note: Goose fat can be rendered in the same way as duck fat. When roasting a duck or a goose, the fat can always be saved, after straining through cheesecloth, for use in cooking or in preparing a confit.

COOKING NOTES

You can skip preserving a duck and just buy duck confit, although that makes for a more expensive recipe. And while the method of preserving described here is classic, there is an exceptional recipe for duck confit in *Bouchon* by Thomas Keller with Jeffrey Cerciello.

I used—and recommend—navy beans.

I've included the recipe for rendering duck fat because it's always good to know how to do it, but rendering it isn't really necessary for this recipe, which uses so little of the fat. Buy the fat if you can, or just use butter. Plenty of duck and pork fat (from the duck confit and pork rind) end up in the cassoulet anyway.

SERVING SUGGESTIONS
Apple Tarte Tatin (p. 837) or Tartelettes aux Pommes Lionel Poilâne (p. 834), and a shot of Fernet Branca, then bed.

READERS
"The cassoulet is the best I have ever had. I make it at least once a winter and guests love it. I follow the recipe (using the pork rind) except that I use duck confit from the store—about 6 legs. Also, I use French garlic sausage that comes in a roll—I remove the casing, cut it into half-moons, and brown it in goose fat."

Stephen F. Patterson, Delray Beach, FL, letter

NOVEMBER 4, 1981: "HEARTY FARE OF FRANCE'S SOUTHWEST," BY PATRICIA WELLS. ADAPTED FROM JEANNE-MARIE MOURIERE.

—1981

⌒ BOBOTIE

Joseph Lelyveld, the Johannesburg bureau chief at the time this piece ran and later the executive editor of the *Times*, wrote that South African bobotie, a baked lamb dish hidden beneath a savory custard, is often compared with Greek moussaka (see p. 518 for a great version of that dish). However, he noted, "bobotie is usually less creamy and always spicier than its Hellenic analogue. Any reasonable palate, I think, would find it an altogether more interesting dish."

Lelyveld added that, "Most South African recipes now call for commercial curry powder in addition to onions, garlic, black pepper, raisins, and lemon leaves—bay leaves are regarded as a poor but acceptable substitute—to flavor the chopped lamb or beef, which was traditionally taken from leftover roasts. In the old days, the Malay cooks poured a light custard over the top and returned it to the oven until it was burnished to the appropriate color."

———

2 tablespoons olive oil
2 large onions, finely chopped

2 large cloves garlic, crushed
I tablespoon hot curry powder
I slice day-old white or brown bread
I cup whole milk
2 large eggs
I tablespoon sugar
I teaspoon salt
½ teaspoon freshly ground black pepper
½ teaspoon turmeric
Juice of I large lemon
3 tablespoons chopped bottled mango chutney
12 blanched whole almonds, chopped
½ cup raisins
4 strips of lemon zest
2 pounds ground lamb or beef
Hot cooked rice for serving
Stewed apricots for serving (optional)

1. Heat the oven to 350 degrees. Place a large skillet over medium-high heat and add the oil. Add the onions and garlic and lightly brown, about 10 minutes. Add the curry powder and cook gently for about 2 minutes.
2. Meanwhile, soak the bread in the milk, then firmly squeeze dry, saving the milk, and transfer to a large bowl.
3. Add the onion mixture to the bread, plus all the remaining ingredients except 1 egg. Mix well.
4. Spoon the mixture into an 8-inch square baking dish that has been rubbed with butter. Bake for 35 minutes.
5. Beat the remaining egg with the saved milk and pour over the top. Bake for 15 to 20 minutes longer, until the custard is set and the top a golden brown. Serve with rice and, if desired, stewed apricots.

SERVES 8

SERVING SUGGESTIONS
Lemon Syrup (p. 9), Salade à la Romaine (p. 171), Spicy Orange Salad Moroccan-Style (p. 181), Confit of Carrot and Cumin (p. 244), Sally Darr's Golden Delicious Apple Tart (p. 839), Pine Nut Cookies (p. 689), Moroccan Rice Pudding (p. 848)

DECEMBER 20, 1981: "BOBOTIE: SOUTH AFRICA'S INDIGENOUS CUISINE," BY JOSEPH LELYVELD. ADAPTED FROM BOSCHENDAL RESTAURANT IN CAPE TOWN, SOUTH AFRICA.

—1981

⤚ CHORESH QORMEH SABZI (GREEN HERB STEW)

A Persian Passover dish, this beef stew uses an unusual technique: you simmer onions and beef in a heavy pot without any additional liquid until the beef is tender. Separately, you cook down a mountain of chopped leeks, spinach, parsley, cilantro, and dill. Then, just before serving, you combine the two and fuse them with a shower of lemon juice.

———

¾ cup corn oil

2 large onions, thinly sliced

2½ to 3 pounds beef chuck or sirloin tips, trimmed of fat and cut into 1 to 1½-inch cubes

1 teaspoon salt, plus more to taste

¼ teaspoon ground white pepper, plus more to taste

1 medium leek

3 cups chopped flat-leaf spinach (about two 1-pound bunches)

2 cups chopped flat-leaf parsley (about 2 large bunches)

½ cup chopped cilantro (about 1 large bunch)

¾ cup chopped dill (about 1 large bunch)

Lemon juice to taste (from about 1 lemon)

Steamed white rice for serving

1. Heat half of the oil in a 4-quart Dutch oven or other stew pot. Add the onions and sauté over very low heat until just slightly brown. Add the beef and stir with the onions. Add the salt and pepper. Cover and let simmer gently but steadily over low heat for about 2 hours. Stir at intervals to prevent scorching and check to be sure there is enough liquid, adding water only if necessary.

2. While the beef is cooking, prepare the greens: wash the leek thoroughly and chop the white and green portions separately.

3. Heat the remaining oil in a deep skillet or wide saucepan. Add the white portion of the leek and sauté gently over medium heat for about 5 minutes, or until it begins to soften. Add the green portion of the leek and sauté for another 5 minutes, or until it begins to soften; the leeks should not take on color. Add the chopped spinach and sauté for 5 minutes, then add the parsley and sauté for 5 minutes. Add the cilantro and sauté for 5 minutes, and then add the dill and sauté for 5 minutes. Season to taste with salt and pepper. By this time, the mixture should be reduced to a near sauce but still be bright green. Set aside.

4. When the meat is thoroughly cooked, turn off the heat and let it settle. Skim the fat from the surface and discard. Stir in the green sauce and reheat together for a minute or so before serving. Adjust the seasonings, adding lemon juice to taste.

5. Serve the stew spooned over steamed rice.

SERVES 4

COOKING NOTES

The original recipe called for beef chuck, which wasn't available the day I went shopping, so I went with sirloin tips, and they worked out beautifully.

Stew meats cook at varying speeds—start checking the meat after 1 hour. My sirloin tips took the entire 2 hours.

I treated the spinach as if it were an herb and finely chopped it. When cooking the greens, you will need to adjust the heat to accommodate the moisture in the leaves. Spinach, for instance, throws off more water, so I cooked it at a slightly higher heat.

I added one step: skimming the fat from the stewed beef before combining it with the greens. If you make the stew over the course of 2 days, prepare the meat the first day and chill it in the refrigerator. The fat will rise to the top and harden, and the next day you can lift it off with a spoon. Then prepare the greens and combine with the gently reheated beef.

Mimi Sheraton wrote about this dish: "If not prepared for Passover, this stew can be seasoned with cumin, turmeric, powdered mustard, and other curry spices. At other times of year, Mrs. Amini also adds ½ cup large dried lima beans to the beef as it starts to cook." Sheraton also noted that the stew can be made with stewing lamb or veal.

SERVING SUGGESTIONS

Turkish Split-Pea Soup with Mint and Paprika (p. 140), A Perfect Batch of Rice (p. 316), Yogurt Rice (p. 356), Fresh Ginger Cake (p. 775), Sugared Puffs (p. 867), Pots de Crème (p. 815)

MARCH 31, 1982: "TWO PASSOVER FEASTS IN UNUSUAL STYLES," BY MIMI SHERATON. RECIPE ADAPTED FROM ILANA AMINI, A HOME COOK IN QUEENS, NEW YORK.

—1982

COLD BEEF WITH TARRAGON VINAIGRETTE

East and West agree that cold sliced beef is a revelation if you dress it with herbs and an acid (citrus or vinegar). For the East's version, Thai Beef Salad, see p. 543.

———

1½ pounds thinly sliced rare beef

For the Vinaigrette
1 clove garlic
Coarse salt
½ cup extra virgin olive oil
About 2 tablespoons tarragon vinegar (more or less to taste)
Freshly ground black pepper
2 tablespoons tarragon leaves

1 small red onion, thinly sliced
1 bunch watercress, trimmed and washed
1 cup cornichons

1. Cut the beef into thin strips and place in a large bowl.
2. To make the vinaigrette, using a mortar and pestle, pound the garlic into a puree with a little salt. Gradually add the oil and vinegar. Season to taste with pepper, and stir in the tarragon leaves.
3. Add the onion to the beef and pour on the dressing. Mix thoroughly.
4. Arrange the watercress around the edges of a serving dish. Mound the beef in the middle and decorate with the cornichons. Serve at room temperature.

SERVES 4

COOKING NOTES
For the beef, I broiled a T-bone steak (usually 1½ to 2 pounds) in a cast-iron skillet, 3 inches from the broiler flame, for 3 minutes per side.

Adjust the amount of vinegar to your liking. I thought the salad benefited from more vinegar.

SERVING SUGGESTIONS
Beet and Ginger Soup with Cucumber (p. 150), Ice-Cold Tomatoes with Basil (p. 234), Leeks Vinaigrette (p. 217), Sugar Snap Peas with Horseradish (served cold, p. 259), Couscous Salad (p. 321), Lemon Bars (p. 690), Fresh Raspberry (or Blackberry or Blueberry) Flummery (p. 824)

PERIOD DETAIL
In 1899, the *Times* published this recipe for "A Very Pretty Way to Eat Cold Boiled Beef" (from a 1734 cookbook by Mrs. Mary Kettilby):

"Slice it as thin as possible, slice also an onion or a shallot, and squeeze on it the juice of a lemon or two, then beat it between two plates, as you do cucumbers; when it is very well beaten and tastes sharp of the lemon, put it into a deep China dish—pick out the onion and pour on oil, shake in also some shred parsley, and garnish with sliced lemon; it is very savory and delicious."

AUGUST 12, 1984: "PUTTING TOGETHER SALADS FROM LEFTOVERS," BY MOIRA HODGSON.

—1984

SHEPHERD'S PIE WITH CURRIED MEAT

6 white potatoes (about 1½ pounds)
Salt
1 tablespoon peanut, vegetable, or corn oil
¾ cup finely chopped onion
1 tablespoon finely minced garlic
1½ tablespoons curry powder
1 teaspoon ground cumin
1 teaspoon ground coriander
2 pounds lean ground beef
1 cup crushed canned imported tomatoes
½ cup chicken broth
1 teaspoon sugar
Freshly ground pepper
2 cups cooked fresh or frozen green peas
½ cup hot whole milk, plus more if needed
3 tablespoons unsalted butter

1. Put the potatoes into a pot and add water to cover and salt to taste. Bring to a boil and cook for 20 to 30 minutes, until the potatoes are tender to the core when pierced with a fork.
2. While the potatoes cook, heat the oil in a large

skillet. Add the onions and garlic, and cook, stirring occasionally, until wilted. Add the curry powder, cumin, and coriander and cook briefly, stirring. Add the meat and cook, stirring down with the side of a heavy kitchen spoon to break up the lumps, until it's lost its raw color. Add the tomatoes, broth, sugar, and salt and pepper to taste and cook, stirring occasionally, for 20 to 30 minutes.

3. Heat the broiler. Drain the potatoes and put them through a food mill or a potato ricer back into the hot pot. Stir in the peas and heat briefly. Add the hot milk, 2 tablespoons butter, and pepper, preferably white, beating with a wooden spoon. If the mixture is too thick, add more hot milk.

4. Spoon the piping-hot curried meat into a 2½-quart baking dish (a soufflé-dish works well). Top with the hot mashed potatoes. Smooth over the top. Dot with the remaining tablespoon of butter.

5. Run the mixture under the broiler until the top is golden brown.

SERVES 4 TO 6

COOKING NOTE
You can prepare this dish through Step 2 in advance, then reheat the potatoes and meat before filling the baking dish.

SERVING SUGGESTIONS
Green Pepper Salad (p. 172), salad with Cream Dressing (p. 592), Fennel and Apple Salad with Juniper (p. 189), Chocolate Caramel Tart (p. 847), Brown Sugar Shortbread (p. 690), Frozen Meringue Velvet (p. 723)

AUGUST 19, 1984: "FOOD: BOTH TASTE AND PRICE ARE RIGHT," BY CRAIG CLAIBORNE WITH PIERRE FRANEY.

—1984

⌒ OSSO BUCO ALLA MILANESE

You could eat very well by learning how to broil steak and fish and to make three condiments: gremolata—a composite of lemon, parsley, and garlic (recipe follows), pesto (p. 614), and salsa verde (p. 484). Here, in osso buco, the gremolata reinvigorates your palate after each bite of the succulent veal.

¼ cup olive oil, plus more if needed
6 portions veal shank (about 6 pounds total)
¼ cup all-purpose flour
I cup finely chopped onion
½ cup finely chopped carrots
½ cup finely chopped celery
I large clove garlic, minced
I½ cups dry white wine
I½ cups peeled (see Cooking Note, p. 146), seeded, and chopped ripe tomatoes (canned Italian tomatoes, drained and chopped, can be substituted)
I¼ cups veal, beef, or chicken broth
½ teaspoon dried thyme
Salt and freshly ground black pepper
Gremolata (recipe follows)

1. Heat the oil in a heavy casserole large enough to hold the veal in a single layer. Dust the shank pieces with the flour and lightly brown on all sides over medium heat. (You may find the browning easier if you do not put all the shanks in the pot at once; add more oil as necessary if browning in batches.) Do not allow them to become dark or blackened. Remove the shanks from the casserole and lower the heat.

2. Heat the oven to 350 degrees. Add the onion, carrots, and celery to the casserole and sauté, until they begin to soften. Add the garlic and sauté for a minute longer. Add the wine and cook over medium-high heat, scraping the bottom of the pot, until all the brown bits clinging to it have dissolved. Stir in the tomatoes, broth, and thyme.

3. Return the shanks to the casserole, basting them with the sauce. Season with salt and pepper, cover, and bake for about 1½ hours, until the meat is tender when pierced with a fork. Baste the shanks several times during cooking.

4. Remove the shanks to a serving dish and keep warm. Taste the sauce and season with salt and pepper if necessary. If the sauce is too thin (it should be about the consistency of cream), place the pot on top of the stove and boil down the sauce for several minutes.

5. Pour the sauce over the shanks and sprinkle with a little of the gremolata. Pass the rest on the side.

SERVES 6

GREMOLATA

1 large clove garlic, very finely minced

Grated zest of 1 lemon

¼ cup finely minced flat-leaf parsley

Mix together all the ingredients.

MAKES ABOUT ¼ CUP

COOKING NOTE

Florence Fabricant advised, "For osso buco, have the butcher saw the veal into 2½- to 3-inch lengths so they average about a pound apiece. They should have a thin, transparent 'skin' wrapping the meat. Do not remove this membrane, because it holds the shanks together. If it has been removed, the meat should be tied with a string."

SERVING SUGGESTIONS

Potato Gnocchi (p. 340), Soft Polenta (p. 556), Steamed Spinach with Balsamic Butter (p. 226), Stewed Fennel (p. 245), Almond Custard Cake (p. 741), Cornmeal Biscotti (p. 696), Marcella's Pear Cake (p. 769), Bolzano Apple Cake (p. 783)

OCTOBER 27, 1985: "OSSO BUCO, THE CLASSIC ITALIAN 'STEW,' IS ON THE SCENE AGAIN," BY FLORENCE FABRICANT.

—1985

☙ CENTER-RING STRIP STEAK MARINATED IN SCOTCH WHISKEY

If New York strip steak isn't your favorite cut, try a porterhouse or T-bone.

———

For the Marinade

⅓ cup Scotch

¼ cup soy sauce

¼ cup packed brown sugar

2 tablespoons Dijon mustard

1 teaspoon Worcestershire sauce

1 onion, chopped

For the Steak

4 New York strip sirloin steaks

(approximately 12 ounces each)

1. Combine all the ingredients for the marinade in a container large enough to hold the steaks. Stir to dissolve the sugar. Place the steaks in the marinade and refrigerate, covered, overnight.

2. Heat the broiler. Remove the steaks from the marinade. Broil to desired doneness.

SERVES 4

SERVING SUGGESTIONS

Curried Zucchini Soup (p. 123), Baked Mushrooms (p. 212), Mashed Potatoes Anna (p. 294), Smoked Mashed Potatoes (p. 300), Fried Corn (p. 274), Chocolate Guinness Cake (p. 783), Chocolate Silk Pie (p. 838), Cherry and Coconut Brown Betty (p. 806)

APRIL 8, 1987: "AND NOW, IN THE CENTER RING, SPOTLIGHT'S ON CIRCUS COOKING" BY GLENN COLLINS. ADAPTED FROM GUNTHER GEBEL-WILLIAMS, A WILD ANIMAL TRAINER FOR THE RINGLING BROTHERS AND BARNUM & BAILEY CIRCUS.

—1987

☙ '21' CLUB HAMBURGER

It's probably not a coincidence that the last two economic booms were each marked by a burger made famous by ravenous, well-heeled diners. Because what, really, is more lavish than an outrageous burger? The '21' Club burger, the invention of Anne Rosenzweig, is gargantuan, 12 ounces of ground chuck, and is seasoned from the inside out, with a button of frozen herb butter tucked into the center that melts and trickles through the meat as it broils. The butter serves a secondary purpose, as well—because it starts out cold, it helps prevent the center of the burger from overcooking while the outside gets seared on a grill. Rosenzweig also paid close attention to the bread, which she rubbed with olive oil before toasting, and to the tomato and onion, which she soaked in olive oil, lemon juice, and basil before piling them atop the burger. (Her recipe also sternly commands, "serve tomato ketchup only on request"—so you can have your fancy burger, as long as you do it our way.)

This was clearly the rootstock for the more recent boom burger—the DB burger at DB Bistro Moderne in Midtown—a conglomeration of ground beef stuffed with shortribs, foie gras, and truffles.

———

8 tablespoons (1 stick) unsalted butter, softened

2 tablespoons finely chopped basil

1 tablespoon finely chopped thyme

1 tablespoon finely chopped flat-leaf parsley

¾ pound freshly ground Choice chuck, preferably with a 22% fat content

Salt and freshly ground pepper to taste

2 slices Italian peasant bread, about ½ inch thick and 5 inches in diameter

3 tablespoons olive oil

2 to 4 thin slices ripe tomatoes

2 thin slices red onion

2 teaspoons fresh lemon juice

1. Combine the butter, 1 tablespoon basil, the thyme, and parsley and blend well. Place the mixture on a rectangle of wax paper or aluminum foil and roll it into a sausage shape about 1 inch in diameter. Place in the freezer for an hour or longer, until it is frozen solid. (The butter can be used a portion at a time and refrozen.)

2. Heat a gas or charcoal grill to high. Shape the meat into a ball, without kneading. With your finger, make a partial indentation through the center of the ball. Shove 1 frozen tablespoon of butter into the center of the ball and press to close the opening. Flatten the meat into a patty about ¾ inch thick. Sprinkle on both sides with salt and pepper.

3. Place the meat on the grill and cook for 3 to 4 minutes, until it is well seared on one side. Turn the meat and cook for about 3 minutes longer, or to the desired degree of doneness.

4. Meanwhile, brush the bread slices on one side with 1 tablespoon olive oil. Place oiled side down on the grill and cook briefly, until lightly toasted. Turn and cook briefly on the second side.

5. Place the tomato and onion slices in a small bowl and sprinkle with the remaining 2 tablespoons oil, the lemon juice, salt and pepper to taste, and the remaining tablespoon basil. Toss briefly.

6. Place 1 slice of the warm grilled bread oiled side down on a dinner plate, place the hamburger in the center, and cover with the second slice of bread (oiled side up). Serve the tomato and onion slices on the side to be added to the hamburger as desired.

SERVES 1

SERVING SUGGESTIONS

Vermouth Cup (p. 15), French Fries (p. 292), Saratoga Potatoes (p. 273), Docks Coleslaw (p. 191), Kosher Pickles the Right Way (p. 608), Ice Cream Pie (p. 726)

JUNE 21, 1987: "FOOD; THE PERFECT HAMBURGER," BY CRAIG CLAIBORNE WITH PIERRE FRANEY. RECIPE ADAPTED FROM ANNE ROSENZWEIG THE CHEF AT THE '21' CLUB.

—1987

GIGOT À LA PROVENÇAL ET GRATIN DE POMMES DE TERRE (LEG OF LAMB WITH POTATO GRATIN)

This is the lamb analog to Mark Bittman's Fish Steamed over Vegetables and Fresh Herbs on p. 434. Here potatoes are partially cooked, sliced, and combined with milk, as you would for a gratin, but instead of roasting the leg of lamb in another pan, you simply plunk it on top of the gratin and put them both into the oven. The lamb juices seep into the gratin, and when you spread a bread crumb crust atop the lamb halfway through cooking it echoes the crisp top layer of the gratin beneath. Just don't try carving the lamb while it's still nestled in the gratin.

———

For the Gratin

4 pounds baking potatoes, peeled and very thinly sliced

2 teaspoons salt

4 cups whole milk

Freshly ground black pepper

A handful of flat-leaf parsley leaves, finely minced

6 large cloves garlic, finely minced

1 leg of lamb (about 6 to 7 pounds), at room temperature

Salt and freshly ground black pepper

For the Herb Crust

2 tablespoons finely minced thyme

2 tablespoons finely minced rosemary

2 cloves garlic, finely minced

¼ cup very fine fresh bread crumbs

1. To make the gratin, bring the potatoes, salt, and milk to a boil in a large saucepan over medium-high heat, stirring occasionally so the potatoes do not stick to the bottom of the pan. Reduce the heat to medium and cook, stirring from time to time, until the potatoes are tender, about 15 minutes. Season with pepper. Remove from the heat and set aside.

2. Heat the oven to 400 degrees. Combine the parsley and garlic and sprinkle half into a large oval gratin dish, measuring about 16 by 10 by 2 inches. Spoon the potato-and-milk mixture into the dish and sprinkle with the remaining parsley and garlic.

3. Carefully trim the fat from the lamb. Season with salt and pepper and place the lamb on top of the potatoes. Roast, uncovered, for about 1 hour (or 8 to 10 minutes per pound). Do not turn the lamb.

4. Meanwhile, combine the ingredients for the herb crust. After the lamb has roasted for about 45 minutes, sprinkle with the herb mixture. When the internal temperature, tested with an instant-read thermometer, reaches 130 degrees (for medium-rare), remove from the oven. Let rest for 20 minutes before serving.

5. To serve, carve the lamb into thin slices and arrange on warmed dinner plates or on a serving platter, with the potatoes alongside.

SERVES 8 TO 10

SERVING SUGGESTIONS

Sautéed Asparagus with Fleur de Sel (p. 241), Escarole with Pan-Roasted Garlic and Lemon (p. 248), Ratatouille Niçoise (p. 219), Licorice Ice Cream (p. 728), Chocolate Cake with Bay Leaf Syrup (p. 768), Fontainebleau (p. 829), Pruneaux du Pichet (Prunes in a Pitcher; p. 822)

SEPTEMBER 13, 1987: "FOOD: WHEN THINGS GO RIGHT," BY PATRICIA WELLS.

—1987

⌐ SAUSAGE, BEAN, AND CORN STEW

The ingredients make this the perfect bridge between summer and fall cooking.

————

1 pound small white navy (pea) beans, rinsed and picked over

1 teaspoon salt

6 coarse sweet Italian sausages (about 1½ pounds)

6 hot Italian sausages (about 1 pound)

2 onions (about 12 ounces), peeled and cut into 1-inch dice (2 cups)

2 carrots (about 6 ounces), peeled and cut into ½-inch dice (about 1 cup)

1½ cups sliced celery

3 cloves garlic, sliced (about 1½ tablespoons)

1 small jalapeño pepper, seeded and coarsely chopped (1 teaspoon; optional)

5 plum tomatoes (about 1 pound), cut into 1-inch pieces (about 2½ cups)

3 sprigs fresh thyme or 1 teaspoon dried thyme

4 ears corn, shucked and kernels removed (3 cups)

1. The beans do not need to be presoaked, provided they are started in cold water. Place them in a large saucepan, cover with 7 cups of cold water, and add the salt. Bring to a boil, then lower the heat, cover, and boil gently for 50 to 60 minutes. The beans should be just tender but still a bit firm.

2. Meanwhile, prick the sausages. Place a large saucepan over medium heat, add the sausages, and brown on all sides, about 10 minutes, turning once. Remove the sausages from the pan and set aside.

3. Add the onions, carrots, celery, garlic, and jalapeño, if using, to the saucepan and cook until lightly browned, 5 to 10 minutes. Return the sausages to the pan; set aside.

4. When the beans are cooked, drain and add them, along with the tomatoes and thyme, to the sausage mixture. Cover and cook for 10 minutes. By then, the beans should be tender and the mixture just slightly soupy. Set aside, ready to be reheated when needed. (The dish can be prepared to this point up to a day ahead.)

5. At serving time, slice the sausages, return them to the stew, and bring to a boil on top of the stove or, if

at the beach, on the grill. When it is boiling, add the corn kernels, return to a boil, and serve.

SERVES 6

COOKING NOTE
Jacques Pépin assured us that the sausages can be cut into chunks before or after cooking.

SERVING SUGGESTIONS
Pan con Tomate (p. 91), Green Pepper Salad (p. 172), Stuffed Tomatoes (p. 213), Fried Green Tomatoes (p. 212), Peach Salad (p. 805), Peach Balls (p. 804), Apple Galette (p. 843), Purple Plum Torte (p. 763)

SEPTEMBER 4, 1988: "FOOD: THE LAST PICNIC SHOW," BY JACQUES PÉPIN.

—1988

⌒ T-BONE STEAK WITH 6666 SOPPIN' SAUCE

_____

For the Sauce
One 16-ounce can tomato paste
2 teaspoons chili powder, plus more to taste
1½ teaspoons freshly ground black pepper
½ cup ketchup
½ teaspoon garlic salt
3 tablespoons Worcestershire sauce
1 cup water
⅓ cup white vinegar
⅓ cup fresh lemon juice (from about 2 lemons)
⅓ cup (5⅓ tablespoons) unsalted butter or margarine
¼ teaspoon cayenne pepper
⅓ cup honey
⅓ cup packed light brown sugar
½ teaspoon salt

For the Steaks
4 T-bone steaks, 1 inch thick
½ teaspoon garlic salt
½ teaspoon freshly ground black pepper

1. To make the sauce, combine all the ingredients in a saucepan and stir until blended. Bring to a boil, then reduce the heat to medium-low and simmer until

thick, about 1 hour. Remove from the heat. Set aside half the sauce for basting the steaks, reserve the rest for another use.
2. Heat a gas or charcoal grill, or heat the broiler. Season the steaks with the garlic salt and pepper. Place them on the grill or under the broiler. For medium-rare, cook the steaks for 10 minutes, brushing them occasionally with the barbecue sauce, then turn the steaks and cook for another 6 to 7 minutes.

SERVES 4

COOKING NOTE
The sauce recipe makes a very large amount. You can halve the recipe, but keep in mind that it will take less time to cook.

SERVING SUGGESTIONS
Docks Coleslaw (p. 191), Smoked Mashed Potatoes (p. 300), Red Velvet Cake (p. 757)

AUGUST 6, 1989: "FOOD; COME 'N' GET IT," BY RENA COYLE. RECIPE ADAPTED FROM PITCHFORK RANCH, GUTHRIE, TEXAS.

—1989

⌒ HIMMELREICH (ROASTED PORK WITH APRICOTS, APPLES, AND PRUNES)

This is one of the strangest recipes in the book. In the 1990s, German food hadn't been in style for at least two decades, meat cooked with dried fruits wasn't on many menus, and roasting meat in a plastic cooking bag certainly wasn't an everyday technique. For an outlier recipe, though, it's excellent. The juices from the fruit and pork meld inside that weird cooking bag (which is made of nylon, and so doesn't melt), and the pork steams as much as it roasts, yielding tender, lovely meat. Himmelreich means "kingdom of Heaven." I never pictured lavish pork dinners in paradise, but perhaps.

_____

1 tablespoon all-purpose flour
One 2-pound boneless pork butt roast
Salt and freshly ground black pepper
1 cup dried apricots

1 cup dried apple slices

1 cup pitted prunes

1 cup packed brown sugar

½ cup dry white wine

1. Heat the oven to 325 degrees. Dust the inside of an oven-cooking bag with the flour. Generously season the pork all over with salt and pepper. Place the pork and the dried fruits in the bag. Place the bag in a large shallow roasting pan. (The edges of the bag should not spill over the sides of the pan.) Sprinkle the brown sugar into the bag and pour in the wine. Tie the bag securely.

2. Using a fork, puncture 4 evenly spaced holes across the top of the bag. Roast for 1½ hours, or until the pork is cooked to a temperature of 170 degrees, measured on an instant-read thermometer.

3. Slit the bag open, being careful not to get burned by the escaping steam. Place the meat on a serving platter. Scatter the fruit around the roast. Season the cooking glaze with salt if needed, and spoon it over the meat and fruit.

SERVES 4 TO 6

COOKING NOTES

The original recipe called for rolled pork, which I took to mean loin, but most pork loin doesn't have enough fat to work well in a recipe like this. So I call for pork butt, a cut that comes from the shoulder and that's often used for barbecue.

Oven-cooking bags for roasting meat can be bought at most supermarkets.

VARIATION

Why not throw some thyme and sage into the bag along with the fruit?

SERVING SUGGESTIONS

Ralph Vetter's Sweet Potatoes with Lemon (p. 295), French Potato Salad (p. 277), Salade à la Romaine (p. 171), Anton Mosimann's Braised Brussels Sprouts in Cream (p. 232), Caramelized Endive (p. 238), Marcella's Pear Cake (p. 769), Chocolate Caramel Tart (p. 847), Dorie Greenspan's Sablés (p. 703)

READERS

"When I misplace [the recipe], I start to panic, so having it in book form would be neat."

Peter B. D'Esopo, Ramsey, NJ, letter

SEPTEMBER 30, 1990: "FOOD: WUNDERBAR!" BY DULCIE LEIMBACH. RECIPE ADAPTED FROM THE HEIDELBERG RESTAURANT IN STAMFORD, CONNECTICUT.

—1990

✐ VEAL SHANKS WITH GARLIC MASHED POTATOES

Emeril's cooking, pre-"Bam!" These shanks are everything you want from a braise—the meat slackened and silky, the flavors concentrated. The recipe is a little more complicated than the kind of food he later made on television. If you miss the showmanship of the later-period Emeril, you can always toss a few sausages to your dinner guests.

———

For the Shanks

½ cup Creole Seasoning (recipe follows)

¼ cup all-purpose flour

4 veal shanks, 1¼ inches thick (about 12 ounces each)

¼ cup olive oil

1 cup diced onion

1 cup diced carrots

1 cup diced celery

¼ cup diced green bell pepper

1 tablespoon minced jalapeño pepper

1 tablespoon minced garlic

1 cup peeled (see Cooking Note, p. 146), cored, seeded, and diced tomatoes

¾ cup dried navy beans, rinsed, picked over, and soaked in water overnight

¾ cup dried red beans, rinsed, picked over, and soaked in water overnight

Two 12-ounce bottles beer, preferably Dixie longnecks

3 cups veal broth

1 cup diced meat from smoked ham hocks

1 bouquet garni—4 sprigs parsley, 5 sprigs thyme, 2 sprigs oregano, 6 bay leaves, and 4 black peppercorns, tied in cheesecloth

½ teaspoon salt

½ teaspoon cracked black pepper

2 teaspoons hot pepper sauce

2 teaspoons Worcestershire sauce

For the Potatoes

12 medium red potatoes, scrubbed, and quartered

1 cup heavy cream

4 tablespoons unsalted butter

3 tablespoons roasted garlic (see Cooking Note)

1 teaspoon salt, or to taste

¼ teaspoon freshly ground white pepper

1. To prepare the shanks, combine 1 teaspoon Creole seasoning with the flour. Sprinkle about ¼ cup of the remaining seasoning on both sides of the veal shanks (reserve the remaining seasoning for another use). Dust the shanks with the flour mixture.

2. Heat 2 tablespoons olive oil in a 3-inch-deep 14-inch skillet or a Dutch oven over high heat. Add the shanks and brown well, about 3 minutes per side. Add the onion, carrots, celery, bell pepper, jalapeño, and garlic and cook for 3 to 4 minutes. Add the tomatoes and beans and cook for 2 minutes. Add the beer, 2 cups broth, the ham hock meat, bouquet garni, salt, and pepper and bring to a boil. Reduce the heat and simmer, uncovered, for 1 hour and 20 minutes. Add the remaining cup of broth, the hot pepper sauce, and Worcestershire sauce and cook until the meat is very tender, about 20 minutes longer.

3. Meanwhile, place the potatoes in a large pot, cover with water and season the water. Bring to a boil, then reduce the heat and simmer until the potatoes are tender. Drain, and return to the pot.

4. About 15 minutes before the shanks are done, place the pot of potatoes over medium-high heat, add the cream, and bring to a simmer. Add the butter, garlic, 1 teaspoon salt, and the pepper and bring to a boil. Reduce the heat to medium. With a potato masher, mash the potatoes over the heat until they are mashed but still lumpy and all of the cream is absorbed. Taste and adjust the seasoning if needed.

5. Place 1 shank on each of 4 plates, cover with sauce, and spoon the potatoes beside the shanks.

SERVES 4

CREOLE SEASONING

2½ tablespoons paprika

2 tablespoons salt

2 tablespoons garlic powder

1 tablespoon freshly ground black pepper

1 tablespoon onion powder

1 tablespoon cayenne pepper

1 tablespoon dried oregano

1 tablespoon dried thyme

Combine all the ingredients, mixing well. Store in an airtight container.

MAKES ABOUT ¾ CUP

COOKING NOTE

To make roasted garlic, heat the oven to 350 degrees. Wrap 2 heads of garlic, sprinkled with olive oil, in foil. Lay the foil packet on a baking sheet and roast until the garlic is very soft, 35 to 45 minutes.

SERVING SUGGESTIONS

Cauliflower Soup with Cremini Mushrooms and Walnut Oil (p. 149), Shredded Brussels Sprouts with Bacon and Pine Nuts (p. 235), Steamed Lemon Pudding (p. 849), Gooey Chocolate Stack (p. 778)

FEBRUARY 21, 1993: "FOOD: THE ENGAGIN' CAJUN," BY MOLLY O'NEILL. RECIPE ADAPTED FROM EMERIL LAGASSE, THE CHEF AND OWNER OF EMERIL'S IN NEW ORLEANS, LOUISIANA.

—1993

STEWED LAMB SHANKS WITH WHITE BEANS AND ROSEMARY

A wonderful dish that had its moment in the Provence period of the 1990s and deserves an encore.

————

8 meaty lamb shanks (about 1 pound each)

2 teaspoons salt, or more to taste

Freshly ground black pepper

2 teaspoons olive oil

5 large cloves garlic, minced

1 large onion, diced (¼-inch)

4 medium carrots, peeled and diced (¼-inch)

3 stalks celery, peeled and diced (¼-inch)

1 cup dry red wine

One 28-ounce can plum tomatoes in tomato puree

1 pound dried Great Northern beans,
    rinsed and picked over

8 cups chicken broth

3 sprigs rosemary

2 bay leaves

1. Season the shanks with the salt and pepper to taste. Heat the olive oil in a large heavy skillet over medium-high heat. Add as many shanks as will fit without crowding and brown well on all sides, about 10 minutes. Set the browned shanks aside and repeat with the remaining shanks, pouring off the fat between batches.

2. Add the garlic, onion, carrots, and celery to the skillet and sauté until softened, about 10 minutes. Pour in the wine and cook for about 2 minutes, scraping the bottom of the skillet with a wooden spoon to loosen any browned bits.

3. Transfer the vegetable and wine mixture to a large stockpot or Dutch oven. Add the tomatoes and use the back of a spoon to break them up into bite-sized chunks. Add the remaining ingredients, including the shanks, and bring to a boil. Reduce the heat and simmer, skimming as necessary, until the lamb and beans are very tender, 1½ to 2 hours. If the lamb is done before the beans, transfer the shanks to a platter and cover them with foil to keep them warm until the beans are done. (The dish can be prepared up to this point a day in advance and refrigerated. Remove from the refrigerator at least half an hour before reheating and serving.)

4. Skim off as much fat from the top of the liquid as possible. If you removed the shanks, return them to the pot and simmer over low heat until they are heated through. Use tongs to remove the shanks from the liquid, placing 1 shank on each of 8 plates. Season the bean mixture with additional salt if needed.

5. Using a slotted spoon, arrange some of the beans and vegetables around each shank. Spoon some of the liquid over and around the shanks.

SERVES 8

SERVING SUGGESTIONS
Butternut Squash Soup with Brown Butter (p. 156), Escarole with Pan-Roasted Garlic and Lemon (p. 248), Red Wine Ice Cream (p. 730), Lucas Schoormans's Lemon Tart (p. 857), Wine-Stewed Prunes and Mascarpone (p. 861)

OCTOBER 10, 1993: "ENTERTAINING: DINNER'S IN THE KITCHEN," BY MOLLY O'NEILL.

—1993

ROMAN LAMB

For a home cook in a nondescript town outside of Rome, Paola di Mauro has gotten her fair share of coverage in the *Times*. Following some leads I'd gotten from chefs, I thought I was blazing a trail when I wrote about her in 2001, but I was humbled to discover that Nancy Harmon Jenkins had written a feature on her seven years earlier. Di Mauro never mentioned it—and why should she have? The good news is: we now relish more of her exceptional recipes. See pp. 77 and 561.

————

2 tablespoons extra virgin olive oil

2¼ pounds young lamb—the leg or shoulder—
    bone-in, cut by the butcher, into 8 chunks,
    rinsed and patted dry

4 cloves garlic

Salt and freshly ground black pepper

1 tablespoon instant flour, like Wondra, or cake flour

¾ cup dry white wine

1 tablespoon coarsely chopped rosemary

4 anchovy fillets, coarsely chopped
3 tablespoons red wine vinegar

1. Heat the oven to 350 degrees. Heat the olive oil in a casserole or flameproof roasting pan large enough to hold all the pieces of lamb over medium-high to high heat. When the oil is almost smoking, add the lamb chunks and brown, turning frequently, for 10 to 15 minutes. Coarsely chop 2 garlic cloves and add to the lamb as it browns.

2. When all the lamb is browned, add salt and abundant pepper. Sprinkle the flour over the lamb pieces and turn them to mix in the seasoning. Add the wine. As soon as it starts to bubble, cover the pot (or pan) and roast in the oven for 30 minutes.

3. While the lamb is roasting, coarsely chop the remaining 2 garlic cloves. Using a mortar and pestle, pound them with the chopped rosemary into a coarse paste. Add the anchovies and continue pounding to make a fairly smooth paste. A tablespoon at a time, mix in the wine vinegar to make a smooth emulsion.

4. When the lamb has roasted for 30 minutes, remove it from the oven and pour the vinegar emulsion over the lamb pieces. Turn them to coat well with sauce. Return to the oven, uncovered, and roast for 30 minutes, or until the lamb is cooked, with no trace of red in the meat. Remove from the oven and let rest for 5 minutes.

5. Transfer the lamb to a heated serving platter. Bring the pan juices to a boil and cook rapidly for about 45 seconds, or just long enough to reduce juices and thicken them slightly. Add salt and pepper to taste. Pour the juices over the lamb and serve.

SERVES 4

SERVING SUGGESTIONS
Crostini Romani (p. 77) Potato, Shiitake, and Brie Gratin (p. 285), Squashed Tomatoes (p. 90), Baked Zucchini with Herbs and Tomatoes (p. 250), Pine Nut Cookies (p. 689), Revani Verrias (Semolina Cake; p. 788), Ricotta Kisses (p. 852)

MAY 11, 1994: "LESSONS FOR CHEFS IN THE OLD WAYS OF THE ITALIAN KITCHEN," BY NANCY HARMON JENKINS. RECIPE ADAPTED FROM PAOLA DI MAURO OF MARINO, ITALY.
—1994

⌒ THAI BEEF SALAD

What I like most about this recipe is that it challenges our notion of salad: there's hardly a leaf in sight. The dish is really just sliced beef dressed in a snappy marinade—but it radiates the freshness you expect in a salad.

———

I cup fresh lime juice (from about 8 large limes)
½ cup Asian fish sauce, preferably nam pla
I tablespoon sugar
2 teaspoons minced Thai chile or jalapeño pepper
2 small tomatoes, cored, seeded, and diced
2 small cucumbers, peeled, halved lengthwise, seeded, and diced
Two ¾-pound flank steaks
I cup mint leaves

1. Prepare a hot charcoal or gas fire. Combine the lime juice, fish sauce, sugar, and chile in a large bowl. Add the tomatoes and cucumbers and toss.

2. Grill the steaks, turning once, until medium-rare, about 3 to 5 minutes per side. Let rest for 5 minutes.

3. Slice the meat across the grain into thin slices. Add to the salad, add the mint leaves, and toss well. Serve at room temperature.

SERVES 8

SERVING SUGGESTIONS
Pork-and-Toasted-Rice-Powder Spring Rolls (p. 74), Clear Steamed Chicken Soup with Ginger (p. 145), Pad Thai–Style Rice Salad (p. 357), Mango Ice Cream (p. 729)

MAY 22, 1994: "EARLY-BIRD SPECIALS," BY MOLLY O'NEILL.
—1994

GRILLED LEG OF LAMB WITH MUSTARD SEEDS

This is the creation of Morley Safer, a correspondent for *60 Minutes*.

_____

Two 4-pound butterflied legs of lamb,
    trimmed of excess fat
Salt and freshly ground black pepper
¼ cup olive oil
5 tablespoons mustard seeds
I teaspoon ground cumin
I tablespoon finely chopped garlic
2 tablespoons chopped fresh rosemary
    or I tablespoon dried rosemary
4 sprigs fresh thyme or I teaspoon dried thyme
I teaspoon fennel seeds
2 bay leaves, crumbled
¼ cup fresh lemon juice
2 cups dry red wine
2 tablespoons unsalted butter
¼ cup finely chopped flat-leaf parsley

1. Lay the lamb out flat and sprinkle with salt and pepper on both sides. Put the oil in a baking dish large enough to hold the lamb. Add the lamb and sprinkle on both sides with the mustard seeds, cumin, garlic, rosemary, thyme, fennel seeds, bay leaves, lemon juice, and red wine. Turn and rub lamb so it is evenly coated with the ingredients.

2. Marinate the lamb in a cool place for 1 or 2 hours, or in the refrigerator up to 6 hours. If the lamb has been refrigerated, let it return to room temperature before cooking.

3. Heat a charcoal or gas grill or heat the broiler.

4. Remove the lamb from the marinade, and reserve the marinade. If using a grill lay the lamb on the grill. (You may have to do one leg at a time, depending on the size of your grill or broiler.) Or put the lamb in the broiler pan 4 to 5 inches from the heat. Cook, uncovered on the grill, or under the broiler, for 7 to 10 minutes. Turn and cook for 7 to 10 minutes on the second side for medium-rare. For medium or well-done meat, cook longer.

5. Meanwhile, bring the reserved marinade to a boil in a roasting pan large enough to hold the lamb and boil, stirring, until the liquid is reduced by half.

Remove from the heat and swirl in the butter and parsley.

6. Transfer the lamb to the marinade pan and keep warm; let rest 10 to 15 minutes.

7. Thinly slice the lamb against the grain and serve with the pan juices.

SERVES 10 TO 12

COOKING NOTE
You can halve this recipe and do just one leg of lamb.

SERVING SUGGESTIONS
Crostini with Eggplant and Pine Nut Puree (p. 78), Tomatoes Stuffed with Crab (p. 393), Haricots Verts with Balsamic Vinaigrette (p. 231), Mashed Potatoes Anna (p. 294), The Most Voluptuous Cauliflower (p. 241), Bolzano Apple Cake (p. 783), Chocolate Rum Mousse (p. 814)

OCTOBER 12, 1994: "CORRECTION: LEG OF LAMB THE MORLEY SAFER WAY." RECIPE ADAPTED FROM MORLEY SAFER, A CORRESPONDENT FOR *60 MINUTES*.

—1994

ORANGE-BRAISED SHORT RIBS WITH FENNEL AND OREGANO

The title of the story in which this recipe appeared was "Coaxing Flavor from Lesser Cuts." We've since learned that the flavor doesn't need to be coaxed; cuts like short ribs and shin and neck and tail are where all of beef's best flavor and succulence lies.

As in many recipes from Chris Schlesinger and John Willoughby, the formidable grilling duo who became popular in the 1990s, there was no such thing as too much flavor. While many cooks would now argue that short ribs should be left alone, I think Schlesinger and Willoughby were onto something. Well marbled short ribs shine when aggressively seasoned; the fat enriches and diffuses flavors like fennel, chiles, and mustard.

_____

4 pounds beef short ribs (about 4 inches long)
½ cup cracked fennel seeds
Salt and freshly ground black pepper
3 tablespoons vegetable oil

2 medium red onions, sliced into very thin rounds

¼ cup minced garlic

I to 2 teaspoons crushed red pepper flakes

I cup dry red wine

I cup beef broth

I cup orange juice

½ cup balsamic vinegar

½ cup ketchup

2 tablespoons whole-grain mustard

½ cup coarsely chopped oregano

1. Heat the oven to 350 degrees. Rub the ribs on all sides with the fennel seeds and salt and pepper. Heat the oil in a large Dutch oven or other heavy pot over medium-high heat until hot but not smoking. Add the ribs and brown well on all sides, 6 to 8 minutes per side. Remove the ribs and set aside.

2. Pour off all but about 2 tablespoons oil from the pot, and scoop out any remaining fennel seeds and discard. Add the onions and sauté, stirring occasionally, until wilted and shiny, 7 to 9 minutes. Add the garlic and red pepper flakes, and stirring frequently, for 2 minutes. Add the wine, broth, orange juice, and balsamic vinegar and bring just to a boil, stirring once or twice and scraping any browned bits from the bottom of the pot. Add the ribs, along with the ketchup, mustard, oregano, and salt and pepper to taste, and return to a boil. Skim any scum from the surface.

3. Cover the pot, place in the oven, and cook for 1 to 1½ hours, or until the meat is fork-tender (when you try to pick up the ribs with a fork, they should slip off the fork). Remove the ribs from the pot, skim any fat off the sauce, and cook the sauce over high heat until slightly thickened. Skim again.

4. Return the ribs to the sauce and serve.

SERVES 4

COOKING NOTE

Consider cooking the short ribs a day before serving: the flavors will improve and you'll have a chance to lift off all the fat that will rise and harden on the surface of the sauce when chilled.

SERVING SUGGESTIONS

Wilted Chard with Pickled Red Onion (p. 261), French Potato Salad (p. 277), Sweet Potato Cecelia (p. 276), Butterscotch Pudding (p. 851)

JANUARY 7, 1998: "COAXING FLAVOR FROM LESSER CUTS," BY JOHN WILLOUGHBY AND CHRIS SCHLESINGER.

—1998

TIBS

In this Ethiopian dish, marinated lamb cubes are seared in butter and seasoned with turmeric, garlic, and cardamom. The lamb is usually served with injera, the tangy, spongy, pancake-like bread of Ethiopia, and if you can find injera in an African market, you should. Otherwise, serve with another thin, tender flatbread.

———

2 pounds boneless lamb loin, cut into ½-inch cubes

I red onion, minced

I jalapeño pepper, seeded and minced

1¼ cups dry red wine

¾ pound (3 sticks) unsalted butter (to be seasoned and clarified, 3 tablespoons used for this recipe)

1½ teaspoons turmeric

I clove garlic, crushed

2 cardamom pods, crushed

2 tablespoons mild chili powder

Kosher salt and freshly ground black pepper

I tablespoon chopped rosemary

Injera, pita, or tortillas, for serving

1. Combine the lamb, onion, and jalapeño in a medium bowl. Add ¾ cup red wine and mix well. Cover and refrigerate for 1 to 2 hours.

2. Meanwhile, combine the butter, turmeric, garlic, and cardamom in a small saucepan and bring to a boil. Using a skimmer or large spoon, remove any impurities that rise to the surface. Carefully pour only the clarified butter into a clean container; discard the rest.

3. Combine 1 tablespoon clarified butter with the chili powder in a small saucepan over low heat and stir for about 1 minute, to toast the powder; do not allow to burn. Add the remaining ½ cup wine, remove the chili sauce to a serving bowl, and reserve.

4. Using a slotted spoon, remove the meat from the marinade and drain on paper towels; reserve the marinade. Heat a large cast-iron skillet over medium-high heat until very hot. Add 2 tablespoons clarified butter (reserve the remaining butter for another use), then add the lamb and sauté until seared on all sides. Add

the marinade and continue stirring until the lamb is cooked through, 2 to 3 minutes. Season with salt and pepper and the rosemary. Allow the liquid in the pan to reduce until slightly thickened.

5. Serve the lamb and pan juices in individual bowls, accompanied by bowls of the chili dipping sauce and injera, pita bread, or tortillas with which to scoop up the meat.

SERVES 4

SERVING SUGGESTIONS
Spicy Orange Salad Moroccan-Style (p. 181), Hoppers (without the egg; p. 349), Stuck-Pot Rice with Yogurt and Spices (p. 351), Ismail Merchant's Spinach Puree (p. 229), Tapioca Pudding (p. 798), Plum Fritters (p. 865)

JANUARY 21, 1998: "THE CHEF," BY MARCUS SAMUELSSON, THE EXECUTIVE CHEF AND CO-OWNER OF AQUAVIT IN NEW YORK CITY, WITH AMANDA HESSER.
—1998

↝ SPOON LAMB

Possibly the best recipe title ever.

––––––––

¹/₂ pound dried navy beans, rinsed and picked over

3 ounces (about 3 cups) dried porcini mushrooms

2 tablespoons extra virgin olive oil

1 boneless lamb shoulder roast (about 4¹/₂ pounds), well trimmed of fat and tied in 3 places with kitchen twine

2 medium onions, coarsely chopped

2 cloves garlic, smashed

2 tablespoons tomato paste

¹/₄ cup all-purpose flour

2 cups dry white wine

2 carrots, peeled and cut into 2-inch-long sticks

2 stalks celery, cut into 2-inch-long sticks

3 medium zucchini, cut into 2-inch-long sticks

3 leeks, white and pale green parts only, chopped and washed well

1 large turnip, peeled and diced (or 4 small turnips, peeled and cut lengthwise in half)

1 bouquet garni—4 sprigs parsley, 5 sprigs thyme, 6 bay leaves, and 4 black peppercorns, tied in cheesecloth

1 tablespoon crushed black peppercorns

3 whole cloves

5 cups lamb or beef broth

Salt to taste

1. Place the beans in a bowl, add water to cover by 2 inches, and set aside to soak for at least 4 hours. Place the mushrooms in a bowl, cover with warm water, and set aside to soak for at least 1 hour.

2. Heat the oven to 300 degrees. Heat the oil in the largest casserole you own over medium-high heat. Add the lamb and brown it on all sides. Remove it from the casserole and remove the string. If there are any burned bits left in the pot, wipe them out with a thick piece of wet paper towel.

3. Add the onions and garlic to the casserole and cook over medium heat until soft and starting to brown. Blend the tomato paste and flour together, and add to the casserole. Cook, stirring, for a few minutes, then stir in the wine. Add the remaining ingredients. Drain the beans and add them to the pot. Lift (don't drain, or any grit will end up in the mushrooms) the mushrooms from their soaking liquid and add them. Bring to a simmer.

4. Return the lamb to the casserole, cover, and place in the oven. Cook until the lamb is very tender, about 4 hours.

5. Serve directly from the casserole, or transfer to a serving dish, and serve with tablespoons—the lamb is so soft it can be pulled apart with a spoon. If desired, serve with mashed potatoes or couscous.

SERVES 8

COOKING NOTE
If using canned broth, use 4 cups broth and 1 cup water.

SERVING SUGGESTIONS
Soupe à l'Ail (Garlic Soup; p. 130), Watercress Salad (p. 171), Baked Mushrooms (p. 212), Shallot Pudding (p. 247), Roasted Cauliflower (p. 248), Barley Risotto (p. 327), Mashed Potatoes Anna (p. 294), Tangerine Sherbet (p. 734), Tourtière (p. 827), Coffee Caramel Custard (p. 849)

JANUARY 28, 1998: "GIVING DINNER A LONG, LAZY DAY IN THE OVEN," BY FLORENCE FABRICANT. RECIPE ADAPTED FROM ANTOINE BOUTERIN.
—1998

☞ COLORADITO (RED *MOLE* WITH PORK)

A red *mole* with pork, this coloradito comes from *The Food and Life of Oaxaca* by Zarela Martinez, the owner of the restaurant Zarela in Manhattan. The smooth red sauce, thickened with a brioche-like bread (Martinez suggests using challah), is sweet from the tomatoes and buttery from the almonds, and it has just a touch of heat, which seems to blossom with each bite. Martinez points out that in Oaxacan *mole*, the sauce, rather than the meat, is the focal point of the dish.

———

One 3-pound bone-in pork butt roast,
 trimmed of most but not all fat
1 head garlic, halved horizontally,
 plus 6 garlic cloves, minced
1 teaspoon black peppercorns, bruised,
 plus 5 black peppercorns
3 bay leaves
2 teaspoons salt, or to taste
10 to 12 cups water
4 dried ancho chiles, stems and seeds removed
4 dried guajillo chiles, stems and seeds removed
1 thick slice day-old challah or brioche
One 2-inch piece canela or 2 teaspoons ground cinnamon
5 whole cloves or 1/8 teaspoon ground cloves
1/4 cup lard or vegetable oil
1 small onion, coarsely chopped
3 medium ripe tomatoes, cored and coarsely chopped
1/3 small yellow plantain, peeled and chopped
 (about 1 cup)
12 sprigs thyme
6 sprigs oregano
3 tablespoons sesame seeds, toasted
1/4 cup raisins
3/4 cup blanched almonds, coarsely chopped
1 1/2 ounces Mexican chocolate (available at
 www.amazon.com), coarsely grated

1. Place the pork butt, head of garlic, bruised black peppercorns, bay leaves, and 1 teaspoon salt in a 5- to 6-quart pot. Add enough cold water to cover well and bring to a boil over high heat, then immediately reduce the heat to low. Remove any foam that collected on top. Simmer, partly covered, until the meat is tender, about 2 to 2 1/2 hours.

2. Lift out the pork, letting it drain well, and let cool to room temperature. Meanwhile, raise the heat to high and boil the broth until reduced to 7 cups. Strain the broth through a fine-mesh sieve, discarding the solids; let sit until the fat can be skimmed off (or refrigerate for several hours and then lift off the solidified fat). Reserve.

3. Remove and discard any visible fat from the pork butt. Pull the meat from the bones and carefully tear it into long shreds; refrigerate if not using at once.

4. Place the ancho and guajillo chiles in a bowl, pour over boiling water to cover, and let soak for 20 minutes. Drain and reserve.

5. Meanwhile, crush the bread to fine crumbs in a food processor. You should have about 1 cup. Set aside.

6. Using a spice/coffee grinder or a mortar and pestle, grind together the canela, cloves, and remaining 5 peppercorns. Set aside.

7. Heat half the lard in a medium skillet over medium heat until rippling. Add the ground spices and cook, stirring, just until fragrant, 1 to 2 minutes. Add the onion, minced garlic, tomatoes, plantain, thyme, oregano, sesame seeds, raisins, and almonds and cook, uncovered, stirring frequently, for 15 minutes. Remove from the heat.

8. Let the cooked mixture cool for about 10 minutes, then place half the mixture in a food processor with 1 cup of the reserved pork broth and half the drained chiles. Process to a smooth puree. Repeat with the remaining sauce mixture, another cup of pork broth, and the remaining chiles.

9. Heat the remaining lard in a large Dutch oven or deep skillet over medium-high heat until rippling. Add the pureed mixture, stirring well to prevent splattering. Stir in the remaining broth a little at a time. Cook, covered, stirring frequently, for 15 to 20 minutes, until the chiles lose the raw edge of their flavor. Stir in the bread crumbs and cook, stirring frequently, until the mixture is lightly thickened, about 10 minutes. Stir in the chocolate and cook, stirring constantly, until it is well dissolved. Add the remaining teaspoon of salt.

10. Stir in the shredded pork. Cook, partially covered, stirring occasionally, just until heated through, 7 to 10 minutes. Taste for seasoning.

SERVES 4 TO 6

SERVING SUGGESTIONS

La Paloma (p. 35), Ceviche with Mint and Mango (p. 417), Guacamole Tostadas (p. 67), Yogurt with Plantain and Mango (p. 290), the rice from Maida Heatter's Cuban Black Beans and Rice (p. 282), Lemon Lotus Ice Cream (p. 724), Key Lime Pie (p. 826), Salted Caramel Ice Cream (p. 733)

AUGUST 5, 1998: "BY THE BOOK: PRESERVING AN ANCIENT CUISINE," BY AMANDA HESSER. RECIPE ADAPTED FROM *THE FOOD AND LIFE OF OAXACA*, BY ZARELA MARTINEZ.

—1998

✎ MONTE'S HAM

At some point in your life, if it hasn't happened already, you'll be asked to bake a ham. Here's a simple recipe that will please the masses at a shower, brunch, or wake, and please yourself when you make a sandwich with the leftovers.

———

One 15-pound smoked ham (on the bone)
1 1/2 cups orange marmalade
1 cup Dijon mustard
1 1/2 cups packed brown sugar
1 rounded tablespoon whole cloves

1. Position a rack in the lower third of the oven and heat the oven to 300 degrees. Cut off the ham's tough outer skin and excess fat and discard. Put the ham in a large roasting pan. With a long sharp knife, score it, making crosshatch incisions all over the ham about 1/2 inch deep and 1 inch apart.

2. Roast the ham for 2 hours.

3. Meanwhile, stir together the orange marmalade, mustard, and brown sugar in a medium bowl.

4. Remove the ham from the oven, and increase the heat to 350 degrees. Stud the ham with the cloves, inserting one at the intersection of each crosshatch. Brush the entire surface of ham generously with glaze, reserving some of the glaze, and return to the oven. Cook for 1 1/2 hours more, brushing with glaze at least 3 times. Transfer the ham to a cutting board or platter and allow to rest for about 30 minutes.

5. Carve the ham and serve warm or at room temperature.

SERVES 30 OR MORE

COOKING NOTES

You can use any size ham, but you'll need to adjust the cooking time. A 9-pound ham took 2 hours and 40 minutes.

For Step 4, get out your asbestos hands—the ham is hot! You can put the cloves in before baking, but if you do, they may char by the time the ham is finished.

SERVING SUGGESTIONS

Moscow Mule (p. 20), Smoked Mashed Potatoes (p. 294), Stir-Fried Collards (p. 254), Old South Buttermilk Biscuits (p. 655), Bourbon Pecan Pie (p. 842)

READERS

"Every Wednesday I anxiously await the Dining Out section. I hope that you include a recipe for ham with a delicious sauce. The recipe/article appeared about 7 to 8 years ago. It was written by a man who said a friend had told him to buy the cheapest piece of ham he could purchase and coat it with the sauce. Guests loved his ham and were licking up the last bits with their finger. I followed the recipe and had the same success, but now I can't find the recipe in my pile of recipes I've cut out of the *NY Times*. Can you help me?"

Maria del Rio, e-mail

"We make three or four of these for our annual 4th of July party. People just cannot stay away from it.... We use bone-in half hams, which come as shank end or butt end, and average about 10 pounds.... After roasting for 2 hours, the oven is increased to 375 degrees instead of 350. This gives a more lacquered finish to the glaze, plus a slight carbonization of the corners of the scored squares of meat. People are shameless in ripping these morsels from the ham and vacuuming them into their mouths."

Reynold Weidenaar, New York, NY, e-mail

SEPTEMBER 30, 1998: "BY THE BOOK: *SAVEUR* WITH A TRULY AMERICAN SAVOR," BY SUZANNE HAMLIN. RECIPE ADAPTED FROM *SAVEUR COOKS AUTHENTIC AMERICAN*, RECIPE BY MONTE MATHEWS, AN ADVERTISING EXECUTIVE IN NEW YORK CITY.

—1998

BROILED LAMB LEG CHOPS ON EGGPLANT PLANKS WITH MINT-YOGURT SAUCE

In 1990, *The Thrill of the Grill* by two friends from New England, Chris Schlesinger and John Willoughby, opened up new opportunities for backyard cooks. Schlesinger, the chef and owner of East Coast Grill in Cambridge, Massachusetts, and Willoughby, then a writer for *Cook's Illustrated*, flouted the burger-and-dogs conventions that had dominated (and dulled) our outdoor pastime. They put rabbit and beef heart on the grill. They made banana-green mango chutney to go with grilled pork. On one page you found West Indies chicken, and on the next, Chilean hot *pebre* (a spicy condiment). The dishes they concocted were roused with chiles, vinegars, and loads of cilantro. Grilling had graduated from searing meat over an open flame to composing dishes with layers of smoke and spice and marinade.

But their indoor recipes were also distinctive for the way they layered powerful flavors (see p. 552 for another example) that could challenge your sense of proportion. The ¼ cup of coriander and pepper seasoning on the lamb, for instance, appears to be an outrageous amount, but don't be afraid of it: it's the perfect quantity. And the sweetened yogurt with mint may seem like something that would be better for breakfast (and it *would* be great with fruit), but it asserts itself well here, a beacon of tartness between the garlicky eggplant and heavily spiced broiled lamb.

———

1 cup plain whole-milk yogurt, preferably Greek-style

2 tablespoons honey

¼ cup roughly chopped mint

2 small eggplants

¼ cup olive oil

Kosher salt and freshly ground black pepper

1 tablespoon minced garlic

3 tablespoons cracked coriander seeds

Four 10-ounce lamb leg chops, ¾ to 1 inch thick
    (or substitute center-cut lamb leg steaks),
    trimmed of fat

1. Heat the broiler. Combine the yogurt, honey, and mint in a small bowl, mixing well. Set aside.

2. Trim the ends off the eggplants, then cut lengthwise into planks about ¾ inch thick. Brush the eggplant with the olive oil, sprinkle with salt and pepper to taste, and press the garlic onto one side. Place the planks garlic side down on a piece of aluminum foil. (If you have more than 8 eggplant slices, you can cook off the extra slices, brushed with more oil. No need to waste it.)

3. Combine the coriander and 1 tablespoon each salt and pepper and mix well. Press the mixture all over the lamb chops. Place the chops on the broiler pan and broil until they are well seared on one side, then turn and cook to the desired doneness, about 8 to 10 minutes total for medium-rare, depending on the thickness of the chops. To check for doneness, cut into one of the chops; when the center is slightly less done than you like it, remove the lamb from the heat. Place chops on a platter, cover with foil, and allow to rest while the eggplant cooks.

4. Lay the sheet of foil holding the eggplant on broiler pan and broil until well browned, very soft, and moist all the way through, about 4 minutes on the first side and 2 minutes on the second.

5. Place 2 eggplant planks on each plate, top with a lamb chop, and spoon a couple of tablespoons of yogurt sauce over the top.

SERVES 4

COOKING NOTES

Using a rich Greek yogurt like Fage Total makes a huge difference in the sauce. Do not get the low-fat variety.

I served the leftover yogurt sauce with roasted salmon and braised cabbage with apples.

The original recipe calls for 1 small eggplant—I changed this to medium because the lamb is pretty big and it's nice to have enough eggplant to go with every bite or two.

I reworked the garlic and eggplant as well. Originally, the garlic was pressed into both sides of the eggplant slices. Done this way, the garlic burns under the broiler. If you press it into just one side of the eggplant and broil the other side first, the garlic on the bottom gets a chance to soak up the juices and chars less when turned. And the side of the eggplant that gets cooked first soaks up some of the garlic juices once the eggplant is turned.

SERVING SUGGESTIONS
Roasted Feta with Thyme Honey (p. 92), Marina Anagnostou's Spanakopetes (Spinach Triangles; p. 63), Salade à la Grecque (p. 179), Flourless Apricot Honey Soufflé (p. 846), Hazelnut Baklava (p. 706)

MARCH 31, 1999: "CURING LAMB'S INFERIORITY COM-PLEX," BY JOHN WILLOUGHBY AND CHRIS SCHLESINGER.
—1999

ARNAKI ARAKA (LAMB WITH PEAS)

In most braised dishes, the vegetables and herbs are there to serve the meat, flattering it with sweetness and fragrance. But in this Greek dish, the lamb, scallion, and peas come together in equal proportions to produce a hearty and bright spring dish.

---

2 pounds boneless lamb shoulder, cut into 2-inch cubes

2 tablespoons unsalted butter

10 scallions, white parts and half of green parts, sliced into $\frac{1}{2}$-inch pieces

6 canned tomatoes, roughly chopped, plus 1 cup of the juice

1 teaspoon kosher salt, or more to taste

$1\frac{1}{2}$ pounds frozen green peas (about 4 cups)

$\frac{1}{2}$ cup chopped dill

Freshly ground black pepper

1. Pat the lamb dry with paper towels. Put it in a deep skillet over medium heat and cook for 5 minutes to remove excess moisture. Add the butter and scallions, stir, and cook until the scallions start to become translucent, about 5 minutes.
2. Add the tomatoes, tomato juice, and enough water to bring the liquid two-thirds of the way up the meat. Add the salt, cover, reduce the heat, and simmer for 30 minutes.
3. Turn the meat and continue to cook until it is tender but not falling apart, 30 to 50 minutes.
4. Add the peas and dill to the skillet and cook, covered, until the peas are tender, about 6 minutes. Season to taste with salt and pepper.

SERVES 6

SERVING SUGGESTIONS
Hummus bi Tahini (p. 68), Marina Anagnostou's Spanakopetes (Spinach Triangles; p. 63), Jean Yves Legarve's Spaghetti with Lemon and Asparagus Sauce (p. 319), Asparagus Mimosa (p. 258), Beet Tzatziki (p. 89), Cumin-Mustard Carrots (p. 237), Honey Spice Cookies (p. 685), Hazelnut Baklava (p. 706), Rhubarb Orange (p. 864)

APRIL 11, 1999: "GREEK FIRE," BY MOLLY O'NEILL. RECIPE ADAPTED FROM VEA KESSISSOGLOU, A HOME COOK FROM QUEENS, NEW YORK.
—1999

NORTH CAROLINA–STYLE PULLED PORK

Along with grunge and McMansions, the 1990s showcased long-form outdoor cooking, the time consuming, low-temperature style of grilling—i.e., barbecuing—that produces tender, fatty meats so wildly different from the charred steaks and chops of decades past. Barbecue requires attention, patience, and a willingness to have your hair smell like smoke for a few days. Which doesn't seem like much to ask if you want a pork shoulder to turn soft and buttery and its outer rim of fat to form a crust so hard it's like a porcelain shell.

---

1 bone-in pork shoulder roast (5 to 6 pounds)

$\frac{1}{4}$ cup Basic Rub (recipe follows)

4 cups hickory chips, soaked in cold water for 1 hour and drained

For the Vinegar Sauce

$1\frac{1}{2}$ cups cider vinegar

$\frac{1}{2}$ cup water

2 tablespoons sugar, or to taste

1 tablespoon crushed red pepper flakes

2 teaspoons salt, or to taste

$\frac{1}{2}$ teaspoon freshly ground black pepper

Hamburger buns or Kaiser rolls

1. Heat a grill, building the fire on opposite sides of the grill if using charcoal, or on one side or opposite sides if using gas. If using charcoal, every hour for the first

4 hours, add fresh coals and toss ½ cup wood chips on each mound of coals. If using gas, place the wood chips in a smoker box and heat until you see smoke (depending on the model of your gas grill, use all 4 cups at once or 1 cup every hour for first 4 hours).

2. Season the pork with the rub. Place the pork fat side up on the grill over a drip pan, away from the fire. Barbecue until nicely browned and cooked through, 4 to 6 hours, or until the internal temperature registers 195 degrees on an instant-read thermometer so that the meat will shred properly.

3. Meanwhile, combine the ingredients for the vinegar sauce in a bowl and whisk to mix. Add additional salt or sugar to taste, if desired.

4. Transfer the cooked pork to a cutting board, cover with foil, and let it rest until cool enough to handle, about 15 minutes.

5. Pull the meat into pieces, and discard the skin, bones, or fat. With your fingertips or a fork, pull each piece of pork into shreds about 2 inches long and ¼ inch wide. (Or finely chop the meat with a cleaver.) Transfer to a metal or foil pan and stir in 1 cup vinegar sauce, or enough to keep the meat moist and flavorful. Cover with foil and rewarm on the grill before serving.

6. Serve on hamburger buns with coleslaw and the remaining sauce on the side.

SERVES 10 TO 12

BASIC RUB FOR BARBECUE

½ cup kosher salt
½ cup sugar
½ cup ground black pepper
½ cup paprika

Combine ingredients in a bowl, and whisk them all together to mix. Store in an airtight jar.

MAKES 2 CUPS

COOKING NOTES
My pork shoulder weighed 8 pounds and took 5 hours to cook.

This is cooked using indirect heat. If the pork begins charring, move it farther away from the coals (or gas) or take it off the grill until the coals cool a bit. Remember, slow-and-steady is the secret of great barbecue.

SERVING SUGGESTIONS
Mint Julep (p. 24), Julia Harrison Adams's Pimento Cheese Spread (p. 64), Pickled Shrimp (p. 95), Summer Squash Casserole (p. 252), Gratin of Yams and Chipotle Cream (p. 291), Stewed Corn (p. 271), Docks Coleslaw (p. 191), Boston Baked Beans (p. 274), Jellied Strawberry Pie (p. 811), Bourbon Pecan Pie (p. 842), Buttermilk Pie (p. 859), Cashew Butterscotch Bars (p. 697)

MAY 26, 1999: "TIME AND SMOKE, THE SOUL OF BARBECUE," BY STEVEN RAICHLEN.

—1999

GRILLED HANGER STEAK

I included this recipe for anyone looking for basic steak grilling instructions—the recipe comes from Lobel's, a fourth-generation butcher shop on Madison Avenue. If you can grill a steak well, you hold the key to countless winning dinners.

Vegetable-oil cooking spray
1 hanger steak (about 2½ pounds), trimmed and center vein removed
Olive oil
Kosher salt and freshly ground black pepper

1. Prepare a charcoal or gas grill (set on high). Lightly spray the grill rack with cooking spray. The coals are hot enough for grilling when you can hold your palm 4 inches above them for only 3 seconds.

2. Brush the steak with olive oil and generously season both sides with salt and pepper. Gently press the salt and pepper into the meat.

3. Sear the meat for about 1 minute on each side, then grill for 12 to 15 minutes, depending on the thickness of the steak. Turn the steak frequently during grilling. If the thin end of steak cooks before the wider end is done, position the steak so that the thin end is on the edge of grill. Cook to desired doneness: a rare steak is done when an instant-read thermometer inserted in the center reads 130 degrees.

4. Transfer to a cutting board and let the steak rest for about 5 minutes before slicing.

SERVES 4

Roasted Squash Soup with Cumin (p. 147), Herbed French Fries (p. 292), Fresh Mushrooms Stewed with Madeira (p. 214), Spinach Roman-Style (p. 233), Poached Pears in Brandy and Red Wine (p. 832), Chocolate Pudding (p. 858), Coconut Pie (p. 801)

AUGUST 18, 1999: "BY THE BOOK: GOOD ADVICE, RIGHT FROM THE BUTCHER," BY AMANDA HESSER. RECIPE ADAPTED FROM *PRIME TIME: THE LOBELS' GUIDE TO GREAT GRILLED MEATS*, BY EVAN, LEON, STANLEY, AND MARK LOBEL.

—1999

MARINATED FLANK STEAK WITH ASIAN SLAW

An excellent Asian-ish recipe. Although the cup of basil may seem excessive, the hungry dressing eats it up.

For the Flank Steak
¼ cup rice wine vinegar
¼ cup soy sauce
1 tablespoon minced fresh ginger
1 tablespoon Asian sesame oil
1 tablespoon brown sugar
½ teaspoon crushed red pepper flakes
One 2-pound flank steak

For the Slaw
3 tablespoons peanut oil
1 shallot, minced
2 small bird or other hot chiles, seeded and minced
1 tablespoon fresh lime juice
1 teaspoon Asian sesame oil
¾ teaspoon kosher salt
3 cups very thinly sliced red cabbage
2 carrots, peeled and cut into fine julienne
2 scallions, thinly sliced
1 cup thinly sliced basil leaves

1. To prepare the steak, whisk together the vinegar, soy sauce, ginger, sesame oil, sugar, and pepper flakes. Place the steak in a large plastic bag or in a shallow baking dish. Pour the marinade over the steak and refrigerate for at least 6 hours, and up to 36 hours, turning occasionally.

2. To make the slaw, whisk together the peanut oil, shallot, chiles, lime juice, sesame oil, and salt in a medium bowl. Add the cabbage, carrots, and scallions, tossing well. Refrigerate for at least 1 hour.

3. When ready to cook, prepare a charcoal or gas grill or heat the broiler. Grill or broil the steak, turning once, until it reaches the desired doneness, about 5 minutes per side for medium-rare. Transfer to a cutting board and allow to rest for 10 minutes.

4. Meanwhile, toss the slaw with the basil, and place a mound of slaw on each of 4 plates. Thinly slice the steak on the diagonal, and drape over the slaw.

SERVES 4

SERVING SUGGESTIONS
Kaffir Lime Lemonade (p. 26), Pork Belly Tea Sandwiches (p. 88), Pad Thai–Style Rice Salad (p. 357), Lemon Lotus Ice Cream (p. 724), Sticky Rice with Mango (p. 861)

AUGUST 22, 1999: "FOOD: SLAW AND ORDER," BY MOLLY O'NEILL.

—1999

MALAYSIAN-INSPIRED PORK STEW WITH TRADITIONAL GARNISHES

As Chris Schlesinger and John Willoughby explained in the story accompanying this recipe, the pork cuts called for in the stew—Boston butt or picnic shoulder—are not what they seem. Boston butt has nothing to do with the rear end of a pig but is actually the shoulder; "Boston" refers to a packing method for the shoulders that was developed in Boston and involved the use of barrels called butts. And picnic shoulder doesn't come from the shoulder, but from the front leg; in the nineteenth century, this cut was cured and sold as picnic fare.

When we think of Southeast Asian food, we think of chiles, but here cayenne, a searing, one-dimension heat, offsets the warmer flavors of curry, ginger, soy, and basil.

3 tablespoons minced garlic

2 tablespoons curry powder

2 tablespoons ground cumin

I tablespoon paprika

I tablespoon cayenne pepper, or to taste

2 pounds boneless Boston butt or picnic shoulder,
cut into 1-inch cubes

Salt and freshly ground black pepper

5 tablespoons olive oil

2 red onions, thinly sliced

3 tablespoons minced fresh ginger

3 plum tomatoes, cored and cut into small dice

$\frac{1}{4}$ cup soy sauce

1$\frac{1}{4}$ cups unsweetened coconut milk

I cup dry white wine

$\frac{1}{4}$ cup roughly chopped basil

$\frac{1}{4}$ cup roughly chopped mint

$\frac{1}{4}$ cup roughly chopped cilantro

$\frac{1}{2}$ cup roughly chopped unsalted roasted peanuts

3 tablespoons fresh lime juice (from about 2 limes)

5 dashes Tabasco sauce, or to taste

I teaspoon brown sugar

1. Combine the garlic, curry powder, cumin, paprika,
and cayenne in a large bowl. Dry the pork cubes with
paper towels, sprinkle with salt and pepper, and toss
with the spice mix to coat.

2. Heat 3 tablespoons oil in a 5-inch-deep Dutch oven
or other heavy pot over medium-high heat until hot
but not smoking. Add the pork and brown well on all
sides, about 10 minutes. Transfer to a platter, and discard the oil in the pot.

3. Add the remaining 2 tablespoons oil to the pot and
heat over medium-high heat. Add the onions and sauté,
until golden brown, 11 to 13 minutes. Add the ginger
and tomatoes and sauté for 2 minutes more. Return
the meat to the pot, add the soy sauce, coconut milk,
and wine, and bring to a simmer. Skim any film off the
surface, then cover, reduce the heat to low, and cook
gently until the meat is very tender, 1 to 1$\frac{1}{2}$ hours.

4. Combine the basil, mint, cilantro, peanuts, lime,
Tabasco, and brown sugar in a small bowl and mix
well. Place a generous helping of stew in each bowl,
top with a couple tablespoons of the garnish, and serve
accompanied by rice.

SERVES 6

COOKING NOTE

When you're browning the pork and onions, make sure
you scrape up the pan drippings so they don't burn.

SERVING SUGGESTIONS

Mango Lassi (p. 27), Pork-and-Toasted-Rice-Powder
Spring Rolls (p. 74), Beef Satay with Peanut Sauce
(p. 66), Jasmine Tea Rice (p. 354), Basmati Rice with
Coconut Milk and Ginger (p. 339), Green Beans with
Coriander-Coconut Crust (p. 246), Mango Ice Cream
(p. 729), Coconut Rice Pudding with Lime Syrup (p.
846)

OCTOBER, 20, 1999: "ANATOMICALLY INCORRECT:
DECODING THE PIG," BY JOHN WILLOUGHBY AND
CHRIS SCHLESINGER.

—1999

WHITE VEAL STEW WITH MUSHROOMS, CORN, AND SHERRY

Your entire neighborhood will smell of sherry from this
brothy yet delicate stew. If anyone complains, invite
them over for a taste.

2 tablespoons unsalted butter

2 tablespoons vegetable oil, or as needed

2 pounds veal stew meat, cut into 1-inch cubes

Salt and freshly cracked white or black pepper

Approximately $\frac{1}{2}$ cup all-purpose flour

2 onions, cut into small dice

I tablespoon minced garlic

I pound white mushrooms, trimmed and quartered

I cup dry sherry

I cup corn kernels

2 cups veal or chicken broth

3 tablespoons thyme leaves

Rice or buttered noodles for serving

1. Place 1 tablespoon each butter and oil in a large
Dutch oven or other heavy pot and heat over medium
heat until the butter has just melted. Dry the veal
cubes with paper towels. Sprinkle them generously
with salt and pepper and dredge lightly in the flour,

shaking off any excess. Add half the veal to the pot in a single layer and brown lightly on all sides, about 4 to 5 minutes, removing the pieces to a platter as they are done. Add the remaining tablespoon each of butter and oil to the pot, let the butter melt, and brown the remaining veal. Transfer to a platter.

2. There should be about 2 tablespoons of fat remaining in the pot; add more if needed, or pour off any excess. Wipe out any scorched bits in the pot. Add the onions, and sauté, stirring occasionally, until they are translucent, about 7 to 9 minutes. Add the garlic, and sauté for 1 minute. Add the mushrooms and sauté, stirring frequently, for 5 minutes. Add the sherry and cook for 2 more minutes, stirring to dissolve any brown, crusty bits adhering to the pot.

3. Return the veal to the pot, add the corn and broth, and season to taste with salt and pepper. Bring to a boil, then reduce the heat to low and skim any film off the surface. Cover and simmer gently until the veal is fork-tender, about 1 to 1½ hours.

4. Skim any film off the surface of the stew. Taste and adjust the seasonings. Stir in the thyme.

SERVES 4 TO 6

SERVING SUGGESTIONS

Crostini with Eggplant and Pine Nut Puree (p. 78), Salad with French Dressing (p. 597), Artichoke Salad with Anchovy and Capers (p. 174), Bittersweet Chocolate Semifreddo (p. 727), Lucas Schoormans's Lemon Tart (p. 857), Pear Upside-Down Cake (p. 772)

NOVEMBER 10, 1999: "THE ARISTOCRAT OF MEATS DOES STEW DUTY," BY JOHN WILLOUGHBY AND CHRIS SCHLESINGER.

—1999

✍ OLIVER CLARK'S MEAT LOAF

This recipe seems to have been written by a mad chemist or a mouse, with tiny pinches of this and that all coming together to create a meat loaf like no other. A half teaspoon of onion powder, 2 tablespoons of whipped cream cheese—what will they do, you wonder, other than vex you as you measure them? But in the end, all the dribs and drabs coalesce into a tangy, juicy beef and pork meat loaf. The green pepper keeps

it moist and adds a dash of bitterness, the mushrooms give it depth, and the bacon on top never hurts.

The meat loaf was created by Oliver Clark, who Jonathan Reynolds, a *Times* food columnist, described as an "actor, cook, magician, mechanical-bank collector, folk-art enthusiast, and one of the all-time ten-best brilliant dinner guests." Most people see meat loaf as a dish to be thrown together at the last minute, but Clark treated it like delicate soufflé. He said to Reynolds, "Now listen to me, you must chop everything the same size as the ground beef so nothing stands out texturally." And he has you half-cook the bacon ahead of time to render the fat and prevent the meat loaf from getting greasy. The only detail he forgot to mention was how good the leftovers are as a sandwich between slices of rye bread.

———

¼ cup olive oil

4 cloves garlic, finely chopped

2 medium onions, finely chopped

Salt and freshly ground black pepper

1½ large Portobello mushroom caps, finely chopped

1 green bell pepper, cored, seeded, and finely chopped

2 pounds ground beef

1 pound ground pork or sausage meat

1 cup plain dry bread crumbs

½ teaspoon onion powder

1 teaspoon Dijon mustard

½ teaspoon Cajun seasoning

⅓ cup freshly grated Parmesan cheese

¼ cup ketchup

1 tablespoon mayonnaise

2 tablespoons whipped cream cheese

3 large eggs

½ pound bacon

1. Heat the oven to 350 degrees. Sauté the garlic and onions in 2 tablespoons of oil in a large skillet until the garlic is golden and the onions are translucent. Remove to a bowl. Add a dash of salt and pepper: it's important to season well here.

2. Place all the remaining ingredients except the eggs and bacon in a bowl. Paw at it with 2 forks, combining thoroughly but not overmixing. Mix in the eggs and the onions and garlic. Scrape the mixture into a large baking dish and shape into a loaf about 4 inches wide and 3 inches high.

3. Bake for 50 to 60 minutes.

4. Meanwhile, midway through the baking time, sauté the bacon in a large skillet over medium heat until pale, limp, and partially rendered, about 5 minutes. Adorn the meat loaf with it and finish cooking.

SERVES 8

COOKING NOTE

You can use regular cream cheese in place of whipped.

SERVING SUGGESTIONS

Iceberg Lettuce with Smoked Bacon and Buttermilk Dressing (p. 200), Mashed Potatoes Anna (p. 294), Spinach and Artichoke Casserole (p. 255), Sally Darr's Golden Delicious Apple Tart (p. 839), Reuben's Apple Pancake (p. 831), Blueberry Pie with a Lattice Top (p. 853)

OCTOBER 22, 2000: "MEAT LOAF: THE MUSICAL," BY JONATHAN REYNOLDS. RECIPE ADAPTED FROM OLIVER CLARK.

—2000

⌒ PORK AND SQUASH IN COCONUT MILK

With coconut milk, you get a flavorful broth and a thickening agent in one liquid. As Mark Bittman, whose recipe this is, pointed out, "Its full flavor ties together other flavors with little effort, which is one reason it's among the most important ingredients that have become widely available in the last five years." The milk's creamy sweetness is one reason I could eat this dish every day.

———

1 tablespoon light oil, like corn or canola
2 pounds boneless pork, preferably shoulder or spareribs, cut into 1-inch chunks
1 large onion, sliced
1 pound butternut squash or sweet potatoes, peeled and cut into 2-inch chunks
1 can unsweetened coconut milk (about 1½ cups)
2 to 3 tablespoons Asian fish sauce, or preferably nam pla, or soy sauce, or salt to taste

Juice of 1 lime, or more to taste
Chopped cilantro for garnish (optional)

1. Place the oil in a large skillet or casserole and turn the heat to medium-high. When the oil is hot, add the pork. Cook, without stirring, until the pork is nicely browned on one side, about 5 minutes.

2. Add the onion and stir. Cook, stirring occasionally, until the onion softens, about 5 minutes. Watch to make sure it doesn't burn. Add the squash, coconut milk, and 2 tablespoons fish or soy sauce (or a big pinch of salt) and stir. Bring to a boil. Turn the heat to low, cover, and simmer until the pork is tender but not dry, 30 to 40 minutes (if using pork loin, check after 20 minutes).

3. Uncover and taste the broth. If needed, add more fish or soy sauce or salt. If the mixture is too loose for your taste, raise the heat to high and reduce it until it thickens. Stir in the lime juice, garnish with the cilantro, if desired, and serve, with white rice if you like.

SERVES 4 TO 6

COOKING NOTES

I used pork loin and nam pla, Thai fish sauce. A fattier cut of pork is preferable because you want it to be chewy and moist. If you don't have fish sauce, buy some at a good supermarket or an Asian grocery store. It's a handy staple to have in your pantry.

I didn't find it necessary to add the last tablespoon of fish sauce, and I didn't reduce the brothy sauce, which I liked loose. If you reduce it, you should remove the pork and squash first so they don't overcook.

SERVING SUGGESTIONS

Kaffir Lime Lemonade (p. 26), Pork-and-Toasted-Rice-Powder Spring Rolls (p. 74), Beef Satay with Peanut Sauce (p. 66), String Beans with Ginger and Garlic (p. 260), Jasmine Tea Rice (p. 354), Glazed Mango with Sour Cream Sorbet and Black Pepper (p. 850)

JANUARY 31, 2001: "THE MINIMALIST: STOCK IN A NUTSHELL," BY MARK BITTMAN.

—2001

SEARED LOIN LAMB CHOPS WITH OLIVES AND SOFT POLENTA

A simple dish with each ingredient well deployed. The polenta is so good you might want to double it, and, as a green olive fan, I don't see why you couldn't use Lucques or Picholines in place of the black olives.

––––––––

8 thick-cut loin lamb chops (about 2½ pounds total), each tied with butcher's twine
1 cup coarsely chopped pitted black olives
¾ cup olive oil
Grated zest of 1 lemon
¼ teaspoon crushed red pepper flakes
Kosher salt and freshly ground black pepper
Soft Polenta (recipe follows)

1. Place the loin chops in a shallow dish. Combine the olives, oil, zest, and pepper flakes in a small bowl, and pour over the chops. Cover and refrigerate for at least 2 hours, and up to 24.
2. When ready to cook, remove the chops from the marinade and place on a plate. Transfer the marinade to a small saucepan and set aside. Prepare a charcoal or gas grill or heat the broiler.
3. Season the chops generously on both sides with salt and pepper. Grill or broil 4 inches from the heat, turning once, until the chops are very browned and have reached the desired doneness, 3 to 4 minutes per side for medium-rare.
4. Meanwhile, place the pan of marinade over medium heat and cook just until the oil bubbles.
5. Place a scoop of warm polenta on each of 4 plates and top with 2 chops. With a slotted spoon, remove the olives from the warmed marinade and scatter them over the chops (discard the marinade).

SERVES 4

SOFT POLENTA

4 cups water
1¼ teaspoons salt
1 cup yellow cornmeal

2 tablespoons unsalted butter
⅓ cup freshly grated Parmesan cheese

1. Combine the water and salt in a saucepan, and bring to a boil. Using a wooden spoon, gradually stir in the cornmeal. Reduce the heat to medium-low and cook, stirring, until the cornmeal is thick and just beginning to pull away from the sides of the pan as you stir, 20 to 25 minutes.
2. Stir in the butter and Parmesan cheese, and serve.

SERVES 4

SERVING SUGGESTIONS
Bagna Cauda (p. 58), Watercress Salad (p. 171), Steamed Fennel with Red Pepper Oil (p. 263), Asparagus alla Fontina (p. 222), Grapefruit Granita (p. 731), Wine-Stewed Prunes and Mascarpone (p. 861), Queen of Puddings (p. 866)

MARCH 18, 2001: "FOOD: ACCIDENTAL LAMB," BY MOLLY O'NEILL.

—2001

BRINED AND ROASTED PORK BELLY

––––––––

1¾ cups extra-fine sugar
2½ cups coarse sea salt, plus more for seasoning
12 juniper berries
12 whole cloves
12 black peppercorns
3 bay leaves
4 quarts plus 1 cup water
2½ pounds bone-in pork belly with skin
2 onions, chopped
Olive oil

1. Combine the sugar, salt, spices, and bay leaves in a large pot. Add the water and bring to a boil. Cool completely.
2. Transfer the brine to a large bowl and add the pork. Let stand, loosely covered, for 3 days in the refrigerator.
3. Heat the oven to 375 degrees. Place the onions in a roasting pan. Rinse the pork and score the skin with

a sharp knife. Place skin side up on the onions, rub the skin with a bit of olive oil, and season lightly with sea salt. Roast, uncovered, 1½ to 2 hours; do not let the pork skin burn. The skin should be crisp; if not, transfer the pork to a hot broiler.

4. Cut the pork into thick slices, and serve with the onions.

SERVES 4

SERVING SUGGESTIONS

Fennel and Apple Salad with Juniper (p. 189), Green Goddess Salad (p. 176), salad with Cream Dressing (p. 592), Sautéed Potatoes with Parsley (p. 283), Figs in Whiskey (p. 859), Poppy Seed Torte (p. 786), Raspberry Bavarian Cream (p. 807)

APRIL 25, 2001: "LUXURY CUT, SURPRISE SOURCE," BY WILLIAM L. HAMILTON. RECIPE ADAPTED FROM *THE WHOLE BEAST: NOSE TO TAIL EATING*, BY FERGUS HENDERSON.

—2001

PORK BRAISED IN MILK AND CREAM

I remember watching Gabrielle Hamilton make this dish in her kitchen at Prune in New York: a burnished golden custard billowed around the pork as it braised, nestling softened garlic cloves, wilted sage leaves, and curls of lemon peel within. My stomach growled and my heart pounded. This is love, I thought.

Commercial pork loin has become so lean that it's not worth your time cooking it. Only make this dish if you can get your hands on a pork loin from a small farm raising nice plump heritage pigs.

―――――

One 2-pound pork loin roast, seasoned to taste,
    larded with fatback (about 8 ounces), and tied
1 tablespoon chopped sage, plus 20 whole leaves
20 cloves garlic (from about 2 heads), lightly crushed,
    plus 1 tablespoon chopped garlic
Kosher salt and freshly ground black pepper
1 tablespoon olive oil
2 cups whole milk
2 cups half-and-half
2 cups heavy cream
3 lemons
3 tablespoons unsalted butter
Coarse salt

1. Place the pork in a container and rub all over with the chopped sage and chopped garlic. Cover and refrigerate overnight.

2. The next morning, bring the pork to room temperature. Scrape off and discard the sage and garlic. Generously season the pork with salt and pepper.

3. Heat the olive oil in a Dutch oven or other heavy casserole over medium-high heat. Add the pork loin and brown very well on all sides, about 20 minutes.

4. Meanwhile, combine the milk, half-and-half, and cream in a large saucepan and bring to a boil, then shut off the heat.

5. Using a vegetable peeler, remove the zest from the lemons in long strips. Set the zest aside, and reserve the fruit for another use.

6. When the pork is browned, transfer it to a plate and discard the fat in the pot. Reduce the heat to medium and add the butter to the pot. When it becomes foamy, add the garlic cloves and stir until lightly browned on the edges. Add the sage leaves and stir to coat. Put the pork back in the pot and pour in enough of the warm milk mixture to come halfway to two-thirds up the side of the pork. Bring to a simmer, add the lemon zest, and season to taste with salt. Partially cover and simmer until an instant-read thermometer registers 140 degrees, 15 to 30 minutes (cooking time will vary according to the shape of the roast and degree of browning). The liquid will form a skin and custard around the pork. Shut off the heat and allow to cool, then cover and refrigerate until shortly before serving.

7. When ready to serve, remove the pork from the milk mixture, place the pot over medium heat, and reduce the liquid to a soupy custard. Carve the pork into ⅛-inch-thick slices. When the liquid is still a little loose, return the sliced pork to the casserole, spoon the sauce on top, and allow the pork to heat through.

8. Serve, spooning some custard, lemon zest, and sage on top of the pork and sprinkling it with coarse salt.

SERVES 4

COOKING NOTE

It's best to have your butcher lard and tie the pork loin, but you can do it at home if you have a larding needle. Cut long thin strips of fatback (thin enough to fit in the larding needle), then push the larding needle through the pork loin from end to end. Remove the needle, pressing the lever that keeps the fat in the meat. Repeat in 4 or 5 more spots.

SERVING SUGGESTIONS

Bagna Cauda (p. 58), Fried Artichokes Azzurro (p. 229), Fresh Morel, Asparagus, and Sweet Pea Risotto (p. 327), Balducci's Tiramisù (p. 830), Ricotta Kisses (p. 852), Breton Butter Cake (p. 777)

MAY 9, 2001: "THE CHEF: A CREAMY CUSTARD HAS A MELLOWING EFFECT ON PORK," BY GABRIELLE HAMILTON WITH AMANDA HESSER.

—2001

ᘓ CRISPY CHICKPEAS WITH GROUND MEAT

A really fun dish to make. You think it's not working because the meat sweats out its moisture and the mixture gets soupy. Keep cooking. The liquid boils off, and when the meat and chickpeas begin browning and snapping, you know you're in for something good.

It's crucial to use a heavy pan so the beef and chickpeas cook evenly.

———

½ to 1 pound ground beef or other ground meat

4 cups freshly cooked or canned chickpeas (about one 28-ounce can), drained, 1 cup liquid reserved

2 teaspoons ground cumin

1 dried ancho or chipotle chile, soaked in warm water, stemmed, seeded, and minced, or 1 teaspoon pure chile powder

2 teaspoons minced garlic

Salt and freshly ground black pepper

1 tablespoon extra virgin olive oil

Minced cilantro for garnish (optional)

1. Turn the heat to high under a large deep skillet and add the meat a little at a time, breaking it into small pieces as you do. Stir and break up the meat a bit more, then add the chickpeas. Keep the heat high and continue to cook, stirring occasionally, until the chickpeas begin to brown and pop, 5 to 10 minutes. Don't worry if mixture sticks a bit, but if it begins to scorch, lower the heat slightly.

2. Add the cumin, chile, and garlic and cook, stirring, for about a minute. Add the reserved chickpea liquid and stir, scraping the bottom of the pan to loosen any browned bits. Season with salt and pepper, turn the heat to medium-low, and cook until the mixture is no longer soupy but not dry.

3. Stir in the olive oil, then taste and adjust the seasoning. Garnish with cilantro if you like, and serve immediately, with rice or pita bread.

SERVES 4

COOKING NOTES

This recipe isn't worth it unless you can get great ground beef (or pork). It's a super-simple dish, and you need the meat to have ample fat and flavor.

Mark Bittman suggests using "the smaller amount of meat for flavor and texture, the larger for bulk and protein." Is there any question? Use the smaller amount.

I ate this plain, without rice or pita. I didn't feel the need to add another starch, and since the dish doesn't have much cooking juice, there was no need for a mop.

Dried chipotles don't take well to soaking. I ended up just mincing mine, without soaking, and since the seeds were included, I added just half the pepper, which worked out perfectly.

SERVING SUGGESTIONS

Jennifer's Moroccan Tea (p. 33), Blood Orange, Date, and Parmesan Salad with Almond Oil (p. 199), Moroccan Rice Pudding (p. 848)

AUGUST 8, 2001: "THE MINIMALIST: CHICKPEAS, DRESSED UP TO SHOW OFF," BY MARK BITTMAN.

—2001

ᘓ BRAISED STUFFED BREAST OF VEAL

Like a good porchetta, stuffed veal breast is fragrant and buttery. And, like vitello tonnato, it's served cold.

I like the meat sliced extremely thin and paired with salsa verde (pureed parsley, garlic, capers, olive oil, and lemon juice—see p. 484 for a recipe).

---

1 head garlic

About 5 tablespoons extra virgin olive oil

Leaves from 2 large bunches Swiss chard, preferably white chard

Salt

1/4 pound prosciutto

1/4 cup freshly grated Parmesan cheese

Freshly ground black pepper

One 10- to 12-pound breast of veal, boned

4 sprigs thyme

2 tablespoons finely chopped flat-leaf parsley

2 carrots, peeled and quartered

2 onions, quartered

1 leek, white and pale green parts, quartered and washed well

1 stalk celery, quartered

About 3 quarts veal or chicken broth or water, or a blend

Herbed vinaigrette, salsa verde, or aioli (optional)

1. Heat the oven to 450 degrees. Rub the garlic with a little olive oil, wrap in foil, and roast until soft, about 30 minutes. Remove the garlic and reduce the oven temperature to 325 degrees.

2. Heat 3 tablespoons olive oil in a large saucepan. Add the Swiss chard, sprinkle with a little salt, and cook for a few minutes, turning with tongs, until wilted. Place in a colander and press out as much liquid as possible.

3. Finely chop the Swiss chard, then finely chop the prosciutto. Combine the chard, prosciutto, and cheese. Season with salt and pepper.

4. Use a sharp knife to remove excess fat from the surface of the veal. Turn boned side up and lightly score the surface of the veal in a crisscross pattern. Season with salt and pepper. Squeeze the garlic out of the cloves and mash. Spread on the meat. Spread with an even layer of the chard mixture. Strew with the thyme and parsley. Tightly roll up the slab of veal the long way. Use butcher's twine to tie the veal at 1 1/2-inch intervals, tucking in any stuffing that oozes out.

5. Heat 2 tablespoons oil in large deep casserole over medium heat. Cut the roast in half or thirds if necessary to fit in the casserole, and lightly brown on all sides, one section at a time if you have more than one. If the pot blackens, wash it after browning the veal. Return the meat to the pot.

6. Scatter the carrots, onions, leek, and celery over the veal. Add enough liquid to nearly cover the meat. Bring to a simmer on top of the stove, then place in the oven and cook for 2 1/2 to 3 hours, basting frequently, until the meat is fork-tender. Remove from the oven and allow to cool to room temperature in the liquid.

7. Remove the veal from the cooking liquid, reserving the liquid. Place the veal on a plate and wrap in foil; refrigerate overnight. Reduce the cooking liquid by half and skim off fat. Strain and freeze for another use.

8. To serve, snip and remove the twine from the veal. Slice the veal and arrange on a platter, with vinaigrette, salsa verde, or aioli alongside, if desired.

SERVES 10 TO 12

SERVING SUGGESTIONS
Claret Cup (p. 12), Caramelized Onion and Quark Dip (p. 84), Leeks Vinaigrette (p. 217), Herb Vinaigrette (p. 430), Aioli (p. 488), Salsa Verde (p. 484), Light Potato Salad (p. 301), Purple Plum Torte (p. 763), Summer Pudding (p. 847), Fresh Raspberry (or Blackberry or Blueberry) Flummery (p. 824)

AUGUST 22, 2001: "THE CHEF: TOM COLICCHIO," BY TOM COLICCHIO, THE CHEF AND OWNER OF CRAFT IN MANHATTAN, WITH FLORENCE FABRICAN.

—2001

VITELLO TONNATO

I love this dish for the mere fact that Italians take veal, one of the finest, most expensive meats, and disguise it with a sauce made with a can of tuna. Don't let that deter you: it's as special as blanquette de veau and as satisfying as a tuna sandwich.

A large trussed piece of veal, usually top round, is braised or poached, then cooled, sliced, and layered like a cake, its icing a lemony mayonnaise made with canned tuna, capers, and anchovies. It flunks in the visual appeal department, yet is one of the most delectable dishes I know.

1½ cups dry white wine

1 stalk celery, roughly chopped

1 medium onion, cut into quarters

1 carrot, peeled and roughly chopped

1 leek, white part only, chopped and washed well

4 sprigs marjoram

4 sprigs thyme

5 cloves garlic

One 2- to 2½-pound top round veal roast, tied
(it should be no thicker than 3 inches)

For the Sauce

2 large egg yolks, at room temperature

¼ teaspoon sea salt, or to taste

2¼ cups extra virgin olive oil

5 tablespoons freshly lemon juice (from about 2 lemons)

One 7-ounce can tuna packed in olive oil

5 anchovy fillets

3 tablespoons capers, drained

Thin slices of lemon, thinly sliced pitted black olives,
capers, flat-leaf parsley leaves, and/or anchovy fillets
for garnish

1. Put the wine, celery, onion, carrot, leek, marjoram, thyme, and garlic in a pot just large enough to hold the veal. Add 3 inches of water and bring to a boil. Add the veal and bring back to a boil, then immediately turn off the heat. Cover the pot and let the veal cool in its liquid, 2 to 3 hours.

2. While the veal cools, make the sauce: Whisk together the egg yolks and salt in a large bowl until pale yellow and the consistency of cream. Beginning a drop at a time, add 1¼ cups of the oil, whisking constantly. As the mixture thickens, you can add the oil more quickly. When it gets quite thick, whisk in 1 tablespoon lemon juice. Continue adding the oil until all of it has been absorbed and the mayonnaise is quite thick and shiny. Whisk in another tablespoon of lemon juice.

3. Drain the tuna and put it in a food processor, along with the anchovies, remaining cup of olive oil, remaining 3 tablespoons lemon juice, and the capers. Process until you have a creamy, uniformly blended sauce. Scrape the sauce into the bowl with the mayonnaise and fold to combine. Taste: it should be quite tangy and highly seasoned. Refrigerate until needed.

4. When the veal is completely cool, drain and slice ¹⁄₁₆ to ⅛ inch thick.

5. To assemble the dish, reserve ¾ cup sauce to serve alongside the veal. Smear the bottom of a large serving platter with some of the remaining sauce. Place a layer of veal slices on top, meeting edge to edge, without overlapping. Cover with sauce, then make another layer of meat and sauce. Repeat until all the meat is used, leaving yourself enough sauce to blanket the top layer. Cover with plastic wrap and refrigerate for at least 24 hours and up to 36 hours.

6. Bring the veal to room temperature before serving. Garnish with some or all of the suggested ingredients, and serve with the reserved sauce on the side.

SERVES 6 TO 8

SERVING SUGGESTIONS
Fried Olives (p. 87), Crostini with Eggplant and Pine Nut Puree (p. 78), Garden Minestrone (p. 118), No-Knead Bread (p. 670), Tomatoes Vinaigrette (p. 218), Raspberry Granita (p. 719), Plum Fritters (p. 865)

AUGUST 22, 2001: "FROM ITALY, A COOL SUMMER SECRET," BY AMANDA HESSER. VEAL PREPARATION ADAPTED FROM IL BUCO, SAUCE ADAPTED FROM *THE ESSENTIALS OF CLASSIC ITALIAN COOKING*, BY MARCELLA HAZAN.

—2001

✐ DIJON AND COGNAC BEEF STEW

"Long before there were antidepressants, there was stew," Regina Schrambling, a food writer and editor at the *Times*, wrote. Just a week after September 11, when so many people were turning to the stove as a way of dealing with the tragedy, Schrambling published a handful of recipes she'd been cooking in the aftermath, including this beef stew. "The food is not really the thing," she wrote. "It's the making of it that gets you through a bad time."

This stew is so good it could get you through anything. The mustard and Cognac form a silken cloak around each piece of beef, and the two mustards—Dijon and Pommery—are so pungent they make you tremble. Serve over buttered noodles.

———

¼ pound salt pork or bacon, diced

I large onion, finely diced

3 shallots, chopped

4 tablespoons unsalted butter, or as needed

2 pounds boneless beef chuck, cut into 1-inch cubes

2 tablespoons all-purpose flour

Salt and freshly ground black pepper

½ cup Cognac or other brandy

2 cups beef broth

½ cup Dijon mustard

¼ cup Pommery or whole-grain mustard

4 large carrots, peeled, halved lengthwise,
   and cut into half-moons

½ pound white mushrooms, stemmed and quartered

¼ cup dry red wine

1. Place the salt pork in a Dutch oven or other heavy pot over medium-low heat and cook until the fat is rendered. Remove the solid pieces with a slotted spoon and discard. Raise the heat, add the onion and shallots, and cook until softened but not brown, 10 to 15 minutes. Use a slotted spoon to transfer to a large bowl.

2. If necessary, add 2 tablespoons butter to the pot to augment the fat and increase the heat to medium-high. Dust the beef cubes with the flour and season with salt and pepper. Shake off any excess flour and place half the cubes in the pot. Cook until well browned, almost crusty, on all sides, then transfer to the bowl with the onions. Repeat with the remaining beef.

3. Add the Cognac to pot, and cook, stirring, until the bottom is deglazed and the crust comes loose. Add the broth, Dijon mustard, and 1 tablespoon Pommery mustard and whisk to blend, then return the meat and onion mixture to the pot. Lower the heat, partially cover the pot, and simmer gently until the meat is very tender, about 1½ hours.

4. Add the carrots and continue simmering for 30 minutes, or until tender.

5. Meanwhile, melt 2 tablespoons butter in a medium skillet over medium-high heat, and sauté the mushrooms until browned and tender.

6. Stir the mushrooms into the stew, along with the remaining 3 tablespoons Pommery mustard and the red wine. Simmer for 5 minutes, then taste and adjust the seasoning.

SERVES 4 TO 6

COOKING NOTES

The original recipe gave no alternative for salt pork. Since that can be hard to come by, I substituted bacon. A thick slice of pancetta would also do.

This stew freezes well. Thaw in the refrigerator, then reheat, covered, in a 250-degree oven.

I needed to add 2 tablespoons butter to the pot before browning the beef.

SERVING SUGGESTIONS

Seasoned Olives (p. 90), Fresh and Smoked Salmon Spread (p. 72), salad with Creamy Salad Dressing (p. 605), Mashed Potatoes Anna (p. 294), Haricots Verts with Balsamic Vinaigrette (p. 231), Shredded Brussels Sprouts with Bacon and Pine Nuts (p. 235), Baked Mushrooms (p. 212), Roasted Cauliflower (p. 248), Toasts with Chocolate, Olive Oil, and Sea Salt (p. 844), Marcella's Pear Cake (p. 769), Pierre Hermé's Chocolate Sablés (p. 704)

SEPTEMBER 19, 2001: "WHEN THE PATH TO SERENITY WENDS PAST THE STOVE," BY REGINA SCHRAMBLING.

—2001

⌒ SALTIMBOCCA

Most saltimbocca recipes instruct you to wrap the veal in the prosciutto, but the prosciutto gets too crisp and chewy. Here, tucked inside the veal, it seasons the meat and is protected by it.

———

8 thin slices prosciutto

4 small veal cutlets, pounded very thin

1½ tablespoons unsalted butter

1½ tablespoons olive oil

8 sage leaves

Sea salt

Splash of dry white wine (just a few drops)

1. Place 2 slices of prosciutto on each piece of veal so they hang over the ends and overlap in the middle. Fold each piece of veal in half, securing it with toothpicks in 2 places.

2. Heat the butter and olive oil in a medium nonstick pan until foamy. Add the veal packages and sage leaves and cook for about 1 minute on each side, turn-

ing once, until slightly brown. Season with salt as the packages cook, and sprinkle the white wine into the pan as they finish. Discard the sage and serve.

SERVES 4

SERVING SUGGESTIONS
Crostini Romani (p. 77), Italian Roast Potatoes (p. 300), Fried Artichokes Azzurro (p. 229), Baked Zucchini with Herbs and Tomatoes (p. 250), Yette's Garden Platter (p. 220), Panna Cotta (p. 840), Almond Granita (p. 731), Canestrelli (Shortbread from Ovada; p. 692)

DECEMBER 5, 2001: "A ROMAN MUSE FOR AMERICA'S GREAT CHEFS," BY AMANDA HESSER. RECIPE ADAPTED FROM PAOLA DI MAURO, A WINEMAKER AND HOME COOK IN MARINO, ITALY.

—2001

✑ CODA ALLA VACCINARA (OXTAIL BRAISED WITH TOMATO AND CELERY)

A dish found all over Rome. I love having to excavate the oxtails for their sweet, fat-rimmed nuggets of meat.

———

¼ pound thickly sliced pancetta, cut into ¼-inch dice

I carrot, peeled and finely diced

I small onion, finely diced

4 inner stalks celery, I finely diced, 3 sliced into 3-inch-long pieces

Extra virgin olive oil

3 pounds oxtails (trimmed weight), severed at the joints into pieces about 3 inches long

Sea salt or kosher salt and freshly ground black pepper

1½ tablespoons tomato paste

2 cups dry white wine

3 sprigs fresh marjoram or 1½ teaspoons dried marjoram

¼ teaspoon ground cloves

¼ teaspoon ground cinnamon

One 28-ounce can Italian tomatoes, drained

I. Combine the pancetta, carrot, onion, and diced celery in a Dutch oven or deep heavy casserole that can hold all the oxtails in one layer and add enough oil

to cover the bottom of the pot (about 3 tablespoons). Place the pot over medium heat and cook until the pancetta renders its fat, about 15 minutes.

2. Heat the oven to 325 degrees. Season the oxtails on all sides with salt and pepper, add to the casserole, and brown well on all sides, turning them only after they've browned. Using tongs, remove the oxtails from pan to a bowl. Set aside.

3. Add the tomato paste to the vegetables in the casserole and cook, stirring, until it caramelizes, about 2 minutes. Stir in the wine, bring to a boil, and cook for 3 minutes. Add the marjoram, cloves, cinnamon, and then the tomatoes, squishing them between your fingers into the pot.

4. Return the oxtails to the pot. The liquid should come one-third of the way up the ingredients; if necessary, add a little water. Bring the liquid to a boil, cover the pot, and place in the oven. Braise for 1½ hours, turning the oxtails now and then.

5. Add the remaining celery and continue cooking until the meat is tender and falling off the bone, 30 to 60 minutes longer. Remove the pot from the oven and let sit for 15 minutes, then add salt and pepper to taste.

6. Serve on a large platter or in shallow bowls, making sure everyone gets a bit of the pulpy sauce and celery.

SERVES 6

SERVING SUGGESTIONS
Puntarelle with Anchovies (p. 194), Red Wine Risotto (p. 346), Potato Gnocchi (p. 340), Roasted Cauliflower (p. 248), Licorice Ice Cream (p. 728), Whiskey Cake (p. 784), Olive Oil and Apple Cider Cake (p. 771)

JANUARY 27, 2002: "FOOD DIARY: WHEN IN ROME," BY AMANDA HESSER.

—2002

✑ RIB-EYE STEAKS WITH PEPPERED CRANBERRY MARMALADE AND SWISS CHARD

Steak is meant for the broiler or grill, so its glorious fat can pop all over the contained space of your (self-cleaning) oven or in the open space of the (self-cleaning) great outdoors. Only masochistic French chefs pan-sear steak: in Alain Ducasse's world, you should cook steak on your stovetop and the heat should be such that even a spatter guard is no match for the blobs of beef fat jumping around your kitchen.

But, then again, masochistic French chefs do come up with accompaniments like peppered cranberry marmalade textured with a matrix of shallots, celery, and onion, and for this, we should forgive them their stubbornness.

————

Two 1½-pound boneless rib-eye steaks, each about
     1½ inches thick, at room temperature
Salt
4 tablespoons unsalted butter
4 large cloves garlic, unpeeled, crushed
Freshly ground black pepper
2 sprigs thyme
Peppered Cranberry Marmalade (recipe follows)
Sautéed Swiss Chard (recipe follows)

1. Place a heavy sauté pan large enough to hold both steaks comfortably over medium heat. Stand the steaks up in the pan on the fatty side and cook until the fat has browned and most of it has been rendered into the pan.

2. Use tongs to turn the steaks onto a flat side, dust with salt, and cook until browned on the first side. Turn and cook on the second side until browned but still very rare. Pour off all but a couple of tablespoons of fat, and add the butter and crushed garlic. Cook, basting the steaks with the butter and fat, until cooked almost to the desired degree of doneness: for medium-rare, it will take about 5 minutes on each side.

3. Remove the pan from the heat, season the steaks with salt and pepper, and place a sprig of thyme on each. Set the pan aside—the steaks must rest in a warm place for at least 10 to 15 minutes. They can rest longer than that if placed in a very low (150-degree) oven after the first 10 minutes.

4. Cut the steaks into thick slices, trimming away excess internal fat. Divide among 4 warm dinner plates, and place a generous dollop of cranberry marmalade alongside each. Serve with the chard and remaining marmalade.

SERVES 4

PEPPERED CRANBERRY MARMALADE

1 cup cranberry juice
1 cup dried cranberries
½ cup cherry liqueur (not kirsch)
6 tablespoons sherry vinegar
1 tablespoon extra virgin olive oil
½ cup minced shallots
½ cup minced onion
½ cup minced celery
⅓ cup glace de viande or concentrated beef stock or
     Demi-Glace (see p. 528)
Salt and freshly ground black pepper

1. Place the cranberry juice in a saucepan and bring to a simmer. Add the cranberries and remove from the heat. Allow to plump for 40 minutes.

2. Drain the cranberries, reserving the juice. Place in a food processor with the liqueur and ¼ cup vinegar, and pulse until chopped.

3. Heat the oil in a 3-quart saucepan. Add the shallots, onion, and celery and cook over low heat until tender but not colored. Stir in ¼ cup of the reserved cranberry juice and the remaining 2 tablespoons vinegar and simmer until most of the liquid has evaporated. Stir in the cranberry mixture and simmer until thick, about 5 minutes.

4. Stir in the glace de viande, salt to taste, and a generous amount of pepper. Serve at once, or rewarm just before serving.

MAKES 2 CUPS

SAUTÉED SWISS CHARD

2 bunches Swiss chard, 1 red, 1 white
1½ cups chicken broth
2 large cloves garlic
2 tablespoons extra virgin olive oil
⅓ cup freshly grated Parmesan cheese
Salt and freshly ground black pepper

1. Trim the leaves from the chard stems. Coarsely chop the leaves and set aside. Cut the stems into pieces ½ inch wide and 2 inches long.

2. Place the stems in a saucepan with the chicken broth, bring to a simmer, and simmer for 10 minutes, or until tender. Drain the stems and set aside. (The broth can be reserved for another use.)

3. Impale the garlic cloves on a large cooking fork. Heat the oil in a large skillet. Add the chard leaves and stems and sauté, stirring with the fork, until the leaves have wilted. Toss with the cheese and add salt and pepper to taste.

SERVES 4

SERVING SUGGESTIONS
Tuna Tartare (p. 416), Golden Winter Puree (p. 235), The Most Voluptuous Cauliflower (p. 241), Lemon Cake (p. 781), Evelyn Sharpe's French Chocolate Cake (p. 752), Delicate Bread Pudding (p. 798)

FEBRUARY 27, 2002: "THE CHEF: STEAK WITH STYLE: EASY DOES IT," BY ALAIN DUCASSE WITH FLORENCE FABRICANT.

—2002

◢ VEAL CHOPS WITH SAGE

———

4 veal chops with fat on the edges, about ¾ inch thick, at close to room temperature
Sea salt and freshly ground black pepper
2 tablespoons unsalted butter
I tablespoon olive or vegetable oil
I2 large leaves sage

1. Season the veal chops on one side with a generous amount of salt and pepper. Place a sauté pan large enough to hold the chops in a single layer over high heat for a minute or two. Add the butter and oil and heat until the foam subsides. Carefully lay the veal chops seasoned side down in the pan. Season the other side of the chops with salt and pepper and scatter the sage leaves over them, pushing a few down into the bottom of the pan. Cook the chops for 2 to 3 minutes, until browned, then turn and cook on the other side for 2 minutes.
2. Transfer to a plate and garnish with the browned sage leaves.

SERVES 4

SERVING SUGGESTIONS
Crostini Romani (p. 77), Fried Olives (p. 87), Risotto with Lemon and Crème Fraîche (p. 345), Puntarelle

with Anchovies (p. 194), Figs in Whiskey (p. 859), Gooey Chocolate Stack (p. 778), Tortoni (p. 720)

SEPTEMBER 22, 2002: "FOOD DIARY: STOVE-TOP SEMINAR" BY AMANDA HESSER.

—2002

◢ LAMB IN MUSTARD-MASCARPONE SAUCE

I made this delicious beast of a recipe while watching the Super Bowl, a program well suited to short bursts of busywork. I prepped everything in advance, and then set my timer between tasks so I could simply run in to the kitchen, add an ingredient to the pot, stir, taste, and get back to the game.

Big recipes can easily take over your day—don't let them. Most can be adapted to your schedule, and this one, created by Karen MacNeil, the author of *The Wine Bible* and an owner of Fife Vineyards, is particularly forgiving. You can braise the lamb shanks up to 2 days in advance and then finish the sauce before serving.

Another good Super Bowl recipe—Carolina Chicken Bog—is on p. 491.

———

For the Braised Lamb
2 tablespoons vegetable oil
5 pounds lamb shanks, cut crosswise into 2- to 3-inch pieces (by the butcher)
½ stalk celery, coarsely chopped
I small onion, coarsely chopped
I carrot, peeled and coarsely chopped
I cup dry Marsala
3 cups chicken broth

For the Marinade
3 large cloves garlic, crushed
½ small onion, chopped
½ cup Dijon mustard
2 tablespoons minced rosemary
2 tablespoons dry Marsala
½ teaspoon cracked black pepper

For the Sauce and Garnish

1 tablespoon olive oil

4 ounces thinly sliced pancetta,
      cut into ¼-inch-wide strips

12 large shallots

One 6-inch branch rosemary

12 cloves garlic, crushed

1 tablespoon ground cumin

⅓ cup dry Marsala

¼ cup white wine vinegar

1 tablespoon sweet paprika

1 tablespoon tomato paste

½ cup mascarpone cheese

1. Up to 2 days before serving, heat the oil in a large Dutch oven over medium-high heat. In batches, brown the shanks on all sides; transfer to a platter. Add the celery, onion, and carrot to the pot and sauté for about 3 minutes. Add the shanks, Marsala, chicken broth, and enough water to cover and bring to a boil, then reduce the heat, cover, and simmer until the lamb is tender, 1 to 1½ hours. Cool, cover, and refrigerate.

2. About 2 hours before serving, scrape the fat off the top of the meat and discard. Remove the meat from the shanks, break it into 1-inch chunks, and return to the pot. Mix the marinade ingredients, add to the lamb and cooking liquid, and let stand at room temperature for 1 hour.

3. Heat the olive oil in a large deep skillet over medium-high heat and crisp the pancetta; remove to a bowl. Add the shallots and rosemary to the skillet and sauté until the shallots are browned. Set the shallots aside and discard the rosemary. Add the garlic and cumin and sauté for 3 minutes, then deglaze the pan with the Marsala and vinegar, boiling over medium heat until reduced to about ⅓ cup.

4. Add the lamb and cooking liquid and cook, stirring, for 5 minutes. Stir in the paprika and tomato paste and mix well. Stir in the shallots and simmer for 15 minutes.

5. Remove the lamb and shallots to a bowl and keep warm. Boil the liquid until thickened, about 10 minutes. Whisk in the mascarpone and add the lamb and shallots. Spoon over barley or couscous. Sprinkle with the crisp pancetta.

SERVES 6

SERVING SUGGESTIONS

Karen MacNeil serves the lamb with couscous or barley. A few more ideas: Chiffonade Salad (p. 173), Artichauts Vinaigrette (p. 225), Caramelized Endive (p. 238), Sugar Snap Peas with Horseradish (p. 259), Sautéed Potatoes with Parsley (p. 283), Mashed Potatoes Anna (p. 294), Pear Upside-Down Cake (p. 772), Tourtière (Apple, Prune, and Armagnac Tart; p. 827), Frozen Meringue Velvet (p. 723).

SEPTEMBER 29, 2002: "QUE SYRAH, SYRAH," BY JONATHAN REYNOLDS. RECIPE ADAPTED FROM KAREN MACNEIL, AUTHOR OF THE WINE BIBLE.

—2002

∾ BRISKET IN SWEET-AND-SOUR SAUCE

This brisket has become something of a classic. It's bad karma to use Diet Coke in place of Coke for this recipe—or any other.

———

For the Sauce

1 medium onion, quartered

One 2-inch piece fresh ginger, peeled

6 large cloves garlic

¼ cup Dijon mustard

½ cup dry red wine

1½ cups Coca-Cola or ginger ale

1 cup ketchup

¼ cup honey

¼ cup cider vinegar

¼ cup soy sauce

½ cup olive oil

¼ teaspoon ground cloves

1 tablespoon coarsely ground black pepper, or to taste

One 6- to 7-pound first-cut brisket, rinsed
      and patted thoroughly dry

1. Heat the oven to 350 degrees. Place all the sauce ingredients in a food processor and process until smooth.

2. Place the brisket fat side up in a heavy flameproof roasting pan just large enough to hold it, and pour the sauce over it. Cover tightly and bake for 2 hours.

3. Turn the brisket over and bake, uncovered, for 1 hour, or until fork-tender. Cool, then cover the brisket and refrigerate overnight.

4. The next day, heat the oven to 350 degrees. Transfer the brisket to a cutting board, cut off the fat, and slice with a sharp knife, against the grain, to the desired thickness. Remove any congealed fat from the sauce, set the pan over 2 burners, and bring to a boil. Taste the sauce to see if it needs reducing. If so, boil it down for a few minutes, or as needed.

5. Return the meat to the sauce and warm in the oven for 20 minutes.

SERVES 12

SERVING SUGGESTIONS
Caramelized Onion and Quark Dip (p. 84), Russ & Daughters' Chopped Chicken Liver (p. 82), Latkes (p. 280), Smoked Mashed Potatoes (p. 300), Barley Risotto (p. 327), Salade à la Romaine (p. 171), Revani Verrias (Semolina Cake; p. 788), Purple Plum Torte (p. 763)

NOVEMBER 27, 2002: "JUST RIGHT FOR THE FIRST NIGHT OF HANUKKAH," BY JOAN NATHAN. RECIPE ADAPTED FROM *LEVANA'S TABLE*, BY LEVANA KIRSCHENBAUM.

—2002

NEW YORK STRIP STEAK WITH HORSERADISH-MINT GLAZE

Bobby Flay, the chef who came up with this recipe, declared that by 2008, ancho chile powder—whose flavor he described as that of "a spicy raisin"—would be in everyone's pantry. Maybe it hasn't made it to everyone's pantry yet, but he was certainly on to something.

For the Glaze
3 tablespoons Dijon mustard
2 tablespoons honey
1 tablespoon prepared horseradish, drained
3 mint leaves, finely chopped
Kosher salt and freshly ground black pepper

For the Steaks
2 tablespoons coarsely ground black pepper
1/2 teaspoon ancho chile powder or
    crushed red pepper flakes
1 teaspoon kosher salt
2 New York strip steaks (10 ounces each)
2 tablespoons canola oil

1. To make the glaze, whisk together the mustard, honey, horseradish, and mint in a small bowl. Season with salt and pepper, and set aside.

2. Heat the oven to 425 degrees. Combine the black pepper, chile powder, and salt in a small bowl. Rub one side of each steak with the mixture.

3. Place a medium ovenproof sauté pan over high heat, add the oil and heat, until smoking. Place the steaks in the pan rub side down and sear for 35 to 40 seconds. Turn the steaks over, season with salt, and place the pan in the oven. Cook until the steaks are medium-rare, 8 to 10 minutes, brushing with the glaze during the last 2 minutes of cooking.

4. Remove the steaks from the oven and brush again with the glaze. Allow to rest for 5 minutes before serving.

SERVES 2

SERVING SUGGESTIONS
Fennel and Apple Salad with Juniper (p. 189), Chopped Salad with Lemon Zest Vinaigrette (p. 188), Broccoli Puree with Ginger (p. 253), Roasted Cauliflower (p. 248), Wilted Chard with Pickled Red Onion (p. 261), Fresh Corn Griddle Cakes with Parmesan and Chives (p. 294), Moroccan Rice Pudding (p. 848), Fresh Blueberry Buckle (p. 815)

FEBRUARY 12, 2003: "THE CHEF: BOBBY FLAY: A PRETTY PENNY'S WORTH OF PRIME BEEF," BY MATT LEE AND TED LEE. RECIPE ADAPTED FROM BOBBY FLAY, THE CHEF AND CO-OWNER OF MESA GRILL AND BOLO IN MANHATTAN.

—2003

PORK BURGERS

This is a true ham-burger: spicy, warm, and sloppy. Between bookends of toasted brioche lie dabs of aioli and romesco sauce, a cluster of arugula leaves, and a patty containing three forms of pork—ground pork, chorizo, and bacon—seasoned with cumin, chiles de árbol, and thyme.

––––––––

1½ teaspoons cumin seeds

Olive oil

¾ cup diced shallots

2 small dried chiles de árbol, or any dried chile, thinly sliced on the diagonal

Kosher salt

2 teaspoons thyme leaves

3 cups ground pork (about 1½ pounds)

½ cup Mexican chorizo, cut into small pieces

1 cup finely chopped applewood-smoked bacon (about ⅓ pound)

¼ cup roughly chopped flat-leaf parsley

Freshly ground black pepper

Aioli (p. 488) and Romesco Sauce (p. 610) or mayonnaise

6 brioche buns or floury hamburger buns

18 arugula leaves

1. Pour the cumin into a small pan, place over medium heat and cook, swirling the pan, until the seeds begin to toast. Coarsely pound the seeds in a mortar.

2. Cover the bottom of a medium sauté pan with a thick slick of oil, place over medium-low heat, and add the shallots. When the oil begins to sizzle, add the cumin and chiles. Stir, then season with salt. When the shallots become translucent, stir in the thyme leaves and turn off the heat.

3. Combine the pork, chorizo, and bacon in a bowl. Add the shallot mixture and parsley and season with salt and pepper. Using your hands, lift and fold the ingredients together until blended; do not overmix.

4. Cover the bottom of a medium sauté pan with a thin layer of oil and place over medium-high heat. Form the meat into 6 patties that will fit the buns; do not make them too thick. Cook the burgers until browned on the bottom. Turn them, basting with the fat in the pan. When they are browned on both sides, cut a slit in one patty to check for doneness—it should be only slightly pink.

5. Toast the insides of the buns in a pan with a little oil. Spread with aioli and romesco, if using, or mayonnaise. Lay a burger on each bun and top with the arugula leaves.

SERVES 6

COOKING NOTE

Use Mexican chorizo, which is a fresh sausage. Spanish chorizo is dry-cured and too firm for this dish.

SERVING SUGGESTIONS

Pickled Shrimp (p. 95), Fried Olives (p. 87), Beet Tzatziki (p. 89), Cucumbers in Cream (p. 225), Saratoga Potatoes (p. 273), Strawberry Sorbet (p. 732), Churros with Chocolate Sauce (p. 866)

MAY 21, 2003: "THE CHEF: SUZANNE GOIN: A PORK BURGER THAT DOES THE SALSA," BY AMANDA HESSER. RECIPE ADAPTED FROM SUZANNE GOIN, THE CHEF AND CO-OWNER OF LUCQUES AND A.O.C. IN LOS ANGELES, CALIFORNIA.

—2003

LAMB SHOULDER CHOPS WITH ANCHOVY AND MINT BUTTER

You can add almost any herb you like to the butter— sage, savory thyme, or marjoram, for instance.

––––––––

4 tablespoons unsalted butter, softened

2 tablespoons minced shallots

1 tablespoon chopped mint

4 anchovy fillets

4 lamb shoulder chops, ½ inch thick

Sea salt and freshly ground black pepper

4 lemon wedges

1. Combine the butter, shallots, mint, and anchovies in a small bowl. Using a fork, mash to a paste. Spoon the paste onto a square of plastic wrap and roll into a 3-inch-long log. Twist the ends to seal, and refrigerate for at least 20 minutes.

2. Meanwhile, heat the broiler with a rack positioned 4 to 6 inches from the flame. Season the lamb generously on both sides with salt and pepper. Place the lamb on the broiling pan and broil for about 2 minutes a side for rare, 3 minutes for medium-rare.

3. To serve, place a chop on each of 4 serving plates and top with a ½-inch-thick slice of anchovy butter and a wedge of lemon.

SERVES 4

If you prefer, you can cook the chops on a grill. Heat a charcoal or gas grill to medium-high, and grill the chops for 2 to 3 minute per side.

Carrot and Fennel Soup (p. 151), Soupe à l'Ail (Garlic Soup; p. 130), Barley Risotto (p. 327), Saratoga Potatoes (p. 273), Potato "Tostones" (Flattened Potatoes; p. 301), Stewed Fennel (p. 245), Zucchini and Vermouth (p. 227), Fresh Ginger Cake (p. 775), David Eyre's Pancake (p. 813), Raspberry Bavarian Cream (p. 807)

FEBRUARY 18, 2004: "A LITTLE FISH, MUCH MALIGNED," BY AMANDA HESSER.

—2004

～ TUSCAN-STYLE PORK SPARERIBS

I'm not sure how Worcestershire sauce and Tabasco figure into Tuscan cooking; Cesare Casella, a New York chef who moved here from Italy, has clearly taken up the time-honored immigrant tradition of adapting a cuisine in a new environment. But I have made this recipe a bunch of times—it's easy, and it's so pleasing to see how the components merge as if they were always meant to be one.

Serve the ribs and sauce in large shallow bowls, with beer and plenty of napkins on the side.

———

3 tablespoons minced garlic, plus 2 cloves garlic, sliced

3 tablespoons finely chopped sage

2 tablespoons finely chopped rosemary

1½ tablespoons coarse salt, plus more to taste

1 tablespoon freshly ground black pepper, or more to taste

1 tablespoon plus 2 teaspoons crushed red pepper flakes

7 pounds pork spareribs

3 tablespoons extra virgin olive oil, or as needed

Two 28-ounce cans tomatoes, with their juice

1½ tablespoons Worcestershire sauce

1½ tablespoons Tabasco sauce

2½ cups water

1 cup dry white wine

1. Combine the minced garlic, sage, rosemary, salt, black pepper, and 1 tablespoon crushed red pepper in a small bowl. Put the spareribs on a baking sheet and rub well with the spice mixture. Marinate in the refrigerator for at least 24 hours.

2. Heat the oven to 375 degrees. Arrange the ribs in a 12-by-16-inch roasting pan (use 2 pans if necessary) and roast uncovered for 1 hour, or until browned.

3. Turn the ribs over and roast for another hour. If the bottom of the pan begins to burn, add a small amount of water or olive oil.

4. Meanwhile, pour the olive oil into a large saucepan, add the sliced garlic and remaining tablespoon of crushed red pepper, and sauté over medium heat until the garlic begins to color. Add the tomatoes, Worcestershire sauce, Tabasco, and 1½ cups water, season with salt, and bring to a boil, then reduce to a simmer. As the tomatoes soften, break them up with a whisk and stir. Simmer the sauce, uncovered, for 30 minutes. Adjust the seasoning, and remove from the heat.

5. When the ribs have browned on both sides, pour the wine, remaining 1 cup water, and the tomato sauce over them. (If you've used 2 pans to roast the ribs, combine them all in one pan now.) Cover the pan with foil and roast for 40 minutes.

6. Remove the foil, skim off the excess fat, and roast uncovered for 20 minutes more. Cut into 4-rib sections.

SERVES 6

Stewed Corn (p. 271), Fried Green Tomatoes (p. 212), Italian Roast Potatoes (p. 300), Soft Polenta (p. 556), Strawberry Sorbet (p. 732), Blueberry Pie with a Lattice Top (p. 853), Canestrelli (p. 692)

MARCH 10, 2004: "THE CHEF: CESARE CASELLA; ONCE UPON A TIME IN THE ITALIAN WILD WEST," BY MATT LEE AND TED LEE. ADAPTED FROM CESARE CASELLA, CHEF AND OWNER OF BEPPE RESTAURANT IN NEW YORK CITY.

—2004

BRINE-CURED PORK CHOPS

Julia Reed developed this recipe for the *Magazine*, and it's one we should all dog-ear. "Soaking the chops for a day or two in a water bath with sugar, salt, and spices makes them much more tender and flavorful," she wrote, "but if you haven't planned ahead, much the same result can be achieved by rubbing them with salt and herbs and letting them sit at room temperature for a couple of hours." (Brush off the salt before grilling.)

_____

For the Brine
¾ cup kosher salt
⅔ cup sugar
4 quarts warm water
20 juniper berries
20 allspice berries
I teaspoon black peppercorns
4 bay leaves
3 sprigs thyme
3 sprigs marjoram

For the Chops
Six 1½-inch-thick center-cut rib or loin pork chops
Olive oil
Freshly ground black pepper
12 to 15 sprigs rosemary (optional)
Salt

1. To make the brine, dissolve the salt and sugar in the warm water in a large bowl. Lightly crush the juniper, allspice berries, and peppercorns with the bay leaves and herbs in a mortar. Add to the brine.

2. When the brine is cool, add the pork chops and completely submerge, putting weights on top of a plate if necessary. Refrigerate overnight.

3. Remove the chops from the brine about 2 hours before cooking, and dry with paper towels. Rub them with a bit of olive oil and pepper. (You can also perfume the meat at this point with a few sprigs of fresh rosemary, placed on top of and beneath the chops.) Allow the chops to come to room temperature.

4. Heat a charcoal or gas grill, or preheat 2 heavy skillets over medium-high heat. Grill the chops, partly covered if possible to control flaming, over medium-hot coals for about 4 minutes a side, or fry in the skillets, turning once. Place them on a warm platter, cover loosely with foil, and allow them to rest for about 10 minutes.

5. Sprinkle the chops with salt if needed.

SERVES 6

COOKING NOTE
Because the brine stiffens the pork's texture, the chops will feel firm even when cooked properly in the center. Keep an eye on them.

SERVING SUGGESTIONS
Smoked Mashed Potatoes (p. 300), Mushrooms with Manzanilla Sherry (p. 249), Butter-Braised Asparagus and Oyster Mushrooms with Peas and Tarragon (p. 262), Beets in Lime Cream (p. 230), Anton Mosimann's Braised Brussels Sprouts in Cream (p. 232), Leek and Shiitake Bread Pudding (p. 244), Swedish Ginger Cookies (p. 708), Spanish Cream (p. 802), Fruit Crostatas (p. 855)

MARCH 14, 2004: "FOOD: MAKING THE CUT," BY JULIA REED.
—2004

SHAKING BEEF

Like almost any stir-fry, shaking beef—the most popular dish at the Slanted Door in San Francisco—is a cinch to make: you toss garlic-infused beef cubes with sugar and salt, sear them in a vinegar-and-soy mixture, and send them to the table with salt, pepper, and lime. The challenge comes in browning the beef properly in a wok. "People think a wok is a big salad bowl with a flame under it," Charles Phan, the owner of the restaurant, told Mark Bittman. "They think you can throw all the ingredients in, toss them around, and you've got a stir-fry. But that's ridiculous. When you cook in a wok, you're not just looking to cook things—you want to give them what we call 'the breath of the wok,' the special taste that comes from being cooked over intensely high heat."

The best way to achieve this quality is to be bold with the heat and to work in batches. Bittman suggests 2 batches, but you may want to do 4 the first time round.

_____

1½ to 2 pounds beef tenderloin (filet mignon), trimmed
   of excess fat and cut into 1-inch cubes

2 tablespoons chopped garlic

2 tablespoons sugar

Salt and freshly ground black pepper

About 5 tablespoons neutral oil, like corn or canola

¼ cup rice wine vinegar

¼ cup rice wine or dry white wine

3 tablespoons soy sauce

1 tablespoon Asian fish sauce

1 red onion, thinly sliced

3 scallions, cut into 1-inch lengths

2 tablespoons unsalted butter

2 bunches watercress, trimmed and washed, or 1 head red
   leaf lettuce, separated into leaves, and washed

2 limes, cut into wedges

1. Toss the meat with the garlic, half the sugar, 1 tea-spoon salt, ¼ teaspoon pepper, and 1 tablespoon oil in a bowl and let marinate for about 2 hours. (Refrigerate if your kitchen is very warm.)

2. Meanwhile, combine the vinegar, remaining sugar, wine, soy sauce, and fish sauce in a bowl. Taste and add salt and pepper if necessary. Mix about 1 tablespoon salt and 1 teaspoon pepper in a small bowl.

3. Divide the meat into 2 portions, and do the same with the onion and scallions. Put a wok or a large skil-let over the maximum heat and add about 2 table-spoons oil. When the oil smokes, add half the meat in one layer. Let it sit until a brown crust forms, then turn to brown the other side; browning should take less than 5 minutes. Add half the onion and half the scallions and cook, stirring, for about 1 minute. Add half the vinegar mixture and shake the pan to release the beef, stirring if necessary. Add half the butter and shake the pan until the butter melts. Remove the meat, and repeat.

4. Serve the beef, drained of excess juices, over the watercress, passing the salt and pepper mixture and lime wedges at the table.

SERVES 4

COOKING NOTE
Phan uses beef tenderloin for this recipe. Feel free to swap it out for a cheaper cut like skirt steak.

SERVING SUGGESTIONS
Pork-and-Toasted-Rice-Powder Spring Rolls (p. 74), Pad Thai–Style Rice Salad (p. 357), Mi Quang (Rice Noodles with Shrimp, Herbs, and Fried Pork Rinds; p. 349), Tea Ice Cream (p. 717)

APRIL 21, 2004: "FROM OUT OF THE WEST, A WOK SLINGER, SEARING THE BEEF," BY MARK BITTMAN. ADAPTED FROM CHARLES PHAN, THE CHEF AT THE SLANTED DOOR IN SAN FRANCISCO.

—2004

⌒ BRAISED LAMB SHOULDER WITH SHEEP'S-MILK CAVATELLI

For the Lamb
10 garlic cloves, chopped

6 shallots, chopped

8 Thai or serrano chiles, chopped

2 tablespoons thyme leaves

Salt and freshly ground black pepper

¾ cup Armagnac or other brandy

½ cup plus 1 tablespoon olive oil

1 bone-in lamb shoulder roast, preferably organic
   (about 4 pounds)

For the Braising Vegetables
10 shallots, chopped

1 to 2 carrots, peeled and chopped

¼ cup chopped fresh ginger

1 fennel bulb, trimmed and chopped

4 stalks celery, chopped

1 head garlic, cut horizontally in half

6 cups chicken or lamb broth

2 tablespoons unsalted butter, cut into pieces

1 pound cavatelli

1½ cups heavy cream

½ pound semi-soft sheep's-milk cheese, like
   Tomme du Berger, cut into small pieces

A chunk of hard sheep's-milk cheese, like Ossau Vieille
   or P'tit Basque, for grating

1. To marinate the lamb, combine the garlic, shal-lots, chiles, thyme, a generous pinch each of salt and pepper, ¼ cup Armagnac, and ½ cup olive oil in a

blender and puree. Spread all over the lamb. Marinate, refrigerated, overnight.

2. To cook the lamb and vegetables, heat the oven to 250 degrees. Heat the remaining tablespoon of oil in a heavy skillet over high heat. Add the lamb and brown on all sides, about 10 to 15 minutes. Remove the lamb from the pan and pour off the fat. Add the shallots, carrots, ginger, fennel, celery, and garlic and cook until lightly browned. Deglaze the pan with the remaining 1/2 cup Armagnac, scraping up the browned bits, and pour the vegetables and liquid into a Dutch oven. Set the lamb on top, add the broth, and bring to a simmer.

3. Cover, place in the oven, and braise for 3 hours, or until the meat is tender and easily pulls away from the bone. Transfer the lamb to a dish and allow to cool.

4. Meanwhile, skim the fat from the cooking liquid (if you refrigerate the cooking liquid for 1 hour, or overnight, the fat will lift off in pieces). Strain out the vegetables, return the liquid to the pan and reduce by half over medium-high heat, about 25 minutes.

5. Separate the lamb into 8 portions. When the sauce is reduced by half, whisk in the butter pieces one at a time. Adjust the seasoning, return the lamb pieces to the pot, and baste with sauce to reheat.

6. Meanwhile, cook the cavatelli according to the package instructions; drain.

7. Warm the cream in a large pot over medium-low heat. Add the semi-soft cheese and stir until melted. Fold in the cavatelli.

8. To serve, divide the pasta among individual dishes, top with the lamb pieces, and spoon the sauce over the meat. Finish with grated sheep's-milk cheese.

SERVES 8

COOKING NOTE
You can use boneless lamb shoulder if you can't find bone-in.

SERVING SUGGESTIONS
Smoked Mackerel on Toasts (p. 80), Bagna Cauda (p. 58), Fried Artichokes Azzurro (p. 229), Eggplant Involtini (p. 256), Mushrooms with Manzanilla Sherry (p. 249), Steamed Fennel with Red Pepper Oil (p. 263), Puree of Peas and Watercress (p. 296), Reuben's Apple Pancake (p. 831), Lee's Marlborough Tart (p. 816), Marjolaine (Multilayered Chocolate and Praline Cake; p. 766), Marcella's Pear Cake (p. 769), Red Wine Ice Cream (p. 730)

NOVEMBER 7, 2004: "LAISSEZ-FARE," BY AMANDA HESSER. RECIPE ADAPTED FROM ZAK PELACCIO, THE CHEF AND OWNER OF 5 NINTH RESTAURANT IN NEW YORK CITY.

—2004

🖛 BORDER TOWN HUNTER'S STEW WITH ANTELOPE (OR VENISON), POBLANOS, PUMPKIN, AND HOMINY

If you can't get antelope or venison, use cubed pork shoulder and start checking it for doneness after 2 hours of simmering.

———

3 pounds antelope or venison stew meat, cut into 2-inch cubes
Kosher salt and freshly ground black pepper
2 tablespoons olive oil
2 medium onions, chopped
2 poblano chiles, chopped
6 cloves garlic, minced
1 small sugar pumpkin or 1 medium butternut squash, peeled and cubed (about 3 cups)
3 tablespoons New Mexico or ancho chile powder, or to taste
4 teaspoons dried oregano, preferably Mexican
2 bay leaves, preferably fresh
1 cinnamon stick
One 12-ounce bottle amber beer, such as Shiner Bock, Bohemia, or Dos Equis Amber
4 cups chicken broth, or more as needed
Two 15 1/2-ounce cans white hominy, drained and rinsed
Lime wedges for garnish

1. Season the meat generously with salt and pepper, and let stand for 30 minutes.

2. Heat the oil in a large Dutch oven or other heavy pot over medium-high heat until very hot but not smoking. Add the meat in batches (do not overcrowd the pot) and sear until well browned on all sides. Using a slotted spoon, transfer to a bowl.

3. Add the onions and chiles to the pan, reduce the heat to medium, and sauté until softened, about 5 minutes. Add the garlic and sauté for another 2 minutes. Add the pumpkin, chile powder, oregano, bay leaves, and cinnamon stick and sauté until the spices

thicken into a paste and coat the vegetables, about 2 minutes. Add the beer and stir well, scraping the bottom of the pot.

4. Return the meat to the pot and add the chicken broth and hominy. Bring to a boil, then reduce the heat to low and simmer, partially covered, until the meat is tender, 2 to 2½ hours. Add more stock or water if necessary to prevent the stew from becoming too thick.

5. Remove and discard the bay leaves and adjust the salt to taste. Serve garnished with wedges of lime.

SERVES 6 TO 8

SERVING SUGGESTIONS
Sweet-and-Spicy Pepper Stew (p. 247), Pineapple Carpaccio with Lime Sorbet (p. 842)

OCTOBER 19, 2005: "THE FALL COOK: THE WILD FLAVORS OF TEXAS HILL COUNTRY," BY PAULA DISBROWE.

—2005

⌒ MATT'S WHOLE BRISKET WITH TOMATO GRAVY

Matt is Matt Lee. He and his brother Ted, known around town as the Lee Brothers, have been a bright spot in the *Times* food sections for more than a decade. They've covered everything from food chemistry to the men who dig wine caves, but their culinary heart lies in the South, where they lived for a few years growing up. See the cheese straws on p. 79, and *The Lee Bros. Southern Cookbook*.

The sauce that cooks with this brisket is densely spiced, which makes it seem like a cross between tomato sauce and mole.

―――――――

¼ cup minced garlic (about 12 cloves)

2 tablespoons finely chopped rosemary

1 tablespoon kosher salt, plus more to taste

2 tablespoons freshly ground black pepper, plus more to taste

1 tablespoon crushed red pepper flakes

2 teaspoons brown sugar

1 tablespoon smoked paprika (pimentón) or hot paprika

One 8- to 9-pound trimmed whole brisket

¼ cup extra virgin olive oil

3 cups chopped yellow onions (about 2 large onions)

One 35-ounce can plus one 28-ounce can tomatoes (about 7 cups), with their liquid

1¼ cups fruity white wine

1. Heat the oven to 450 degrees. Combine the garlic, rosemary, salt, pepper, red pepper, brown sugar, and paprika in a small bowl. Place the brisket fat side up in a large deep roasting pan (about 13 by 16 inches) and rub all over with the mixture.

2. Roast the brisket, uncovered, for 20 minutes.

3. While the brisket cooks, pour the olive oil into a large saucepan over medium heat, add the onions, and sauté, stirring occasionally, until the onions soften, about 5 minutes. Add the tomatoes, and their liquid, and bring to a boil, then reduce to a simmer. Simmer uncovered, stirring occasionally, and breaking up the tomatoes with a spoon or whisk, for 10 minutes. Season to taste with salt and pepper and remove from the heat.

4. Remove the brisket from the oven and reduce the oven temperature to 325 degrees. Pour 1 cup wine and the tomato sauce over the brisket. Cover the pan as tightly as possible with foil and roast for 3½ hours, turning once at 2 hours and again at 3 hours, each time carefully replacing the foil.

5. Transfer the brisket to a platter. Allow the sauce to settle for a moment in the pan, then skim off the fat. Transfer the sauce and to a blender and puree until smooth, adding the remaining ¼ cup wine. Season to taste with salt and pepper.

6. Slice the brisket against the grain, starting from the thinnest end, into ¼-inch-thick slices. Serve with the sauce.

SERVES 10

COOKING NOTES

Matt Lee and Ted Lee explained, "A whole brisket is composed of two flat pieces of meat (typically sold separately as 'first cut' and 'second cut') sandwiched together with a layer of fat between them and with a thick layer of fat along one side. A 12-pound untrimmed whole brisket weighs about 8 pounds when trimmed. If purchasing the brisket untrimmed, trim the external fat to within ⅓ or ½ inch; also, excavate any large cavities of fat between the two layers."

You can cook this a day ahead, which makes both lifting the chilled fat off the top of the sauce and slicing the meat easier. Prepare it up through Step 4, then let it cool and refrigerate until the next day.

SERVING SUGGESTIONS
Latkes (p. 280), Smoked Mashed Potatoes (p. 300), Mezzaluna Salad (p. 185), Purple Plum Torte (p. 763), Buttermilk Pie (p. 859)

APRIL 12, 2006: "GOT A CROWD COMING OVER? THINK BIG CUTS OF MEAT," BY MATT LEE AND TED LEE.

—2006

⬅ STEAK AU POIVRE

Do use a variety of peppercorns—it will refresh your perspective on this dish. Spreading crushed peppercorns on steak always feels wrong and excessive, but the pepper mellows when seared. I promise.

———

2 tablespoons mixed peppercorns (such as long pepper, Pondicherry, cubeb, and Tasmanian black pepper)
4 strip steaks, 1½ inches thick (10 to 12 ounces each)
Kosher salt
1 to 2 tablespoons vegetable oil
1 large shallot, thinly sliced
⅓ cup Cognac or other brandy, plus additional for finishing the sauce
2 cups brown veal or beef broth
⅓ cup heavy cream
2 tablespoons green peppercorns in brine, drained and rinsed

1. Heat the oven to 400 degrees. Crush the peppercorns between two layers of a kitchen towel with a rolling pin. Season both sides of the steaks with salt and sprinkle evenly with the crushed pepper, pressing gently so that it adheres.

2. Set a large heavy sauté pan over medium-high heat and add 1 tablespoon oil. When the oil starts to smoke, add 2 of the steaks and sear until browned, about 2 minutes a side. Transfer to a rack set in a shallow roasting pan. Repeat with the remaining steaks, adding more oil to the pan if necessary. Set the sauté pan aside.

3. Put the steaks in the oven to finish cooking: for medium-rare meat, remove when the internal temperature registers 135 degrees on an instant-read thermometer, 10 to 12 minutes. Cover loosely with aluminum foil and let the meat rest for at least 5 minutes.

4. While the steaks are in the oven, set the sauté pan over low heat and add the shallot. Cook, stirring frequently, until lightly browned, about 3 minutes. Add the Cognac (be careful, as it may ignite) and boil until reduced by half, about 2 minutes. Add the broth, increase the heat to medium, and simmer until thickened and reduced by about half, 8 to 10 minutes. Remove from heat and stir in the cream and green peppercorns; season with salt if desired. Cover and keep warm.

5. When ready to serve, return the sauce to a bare simmer over medium heat and add a splash of Cognac. Spoon the sauce over the steaks.

SERVES 4

SERVING SUGGESTIONS
Mashed Potatoes Anna (p. 294), Haricots Verts with Balsamic Vinaigrette (p. 231), Wilted Chard with Pickled Red Onion (p. 261), Spinach with Sour Cream (p. 216), Apple Tarte Tatin (p. 837), Apple Galette (p. 843), Chocolate Pudding (p. 858)

PERIOD DETAIL
In 1879, a writer noted, "For seasoning a dish, or for perfecting a salad, the delicate aroma which freshly ground pepper gives, when once tried, will convince the most unimpassioned diner of the great difference between a fresh and a stale condiment."

MAY 7, 2006: "THE DISH: THE NEW STAPLES," BY MERRILL STUBBS.

—2006

✒ PORK AND WATERMELON SALAD

This dish captures just what diners wanted in the first years of the twenty-first century: a flavorful cut of meat (pork belly), braised and then paired with a bright, vigorously flavored salad (watermelon). Rich and crisp. Succulent and sharp. Evil and good.

This salad is the creation of Zak Pelaccio, an independent-minded young chef. After spending time in Southeast Asia, he came back to New York and opened a sophisticated restaurant with slacker décor in Williamsburg, Brooklyn—the restaurant-industry equivalent of an indie film. The food crowd took the bait, and Pelaccio, crowned the wunderkind of Williamsburg, soon moved to Manhattan, where he opened up two more very different places: 5 Ninth, an annoyingly popular restaurant with an ambitious menu, and Fatty Crab, a casual Southeast Asian spot that feels like a great strip-mall find in Los Angeles.

As you will see, Pelaccio likes his ingredients—plan a trip to an Asian market and make this with a friend who can help prep.

————

For the Pork Belly

3 pounds uncured pork belly, skin on
2 cups ketjap manis
6 tablespoons Chinese black vinegar
3 tablespoons dark soy sauce
3 tablespoons Asian fish sauce
Juice of 1 lime
Canola or peanut oil for deep-frying
Flour for dusting
Salt if needed

For the Watermelon Salad

One 5-pound watermelon
2 cups rice wine vinegar
1 cup water
3 shallots, thinly sliced
2 Thai chiles or 1 jalapeño pepper, thinly sliced
2 kaffir lime leaves
One 2-inch piece fresh ginger, peeled and thinly sliced
½ round (1 ounce) palm sugar or 2 tablespoons
    light brown sugar
1 tablespoon kosher salt

For the Dressing

1½ rounds palm sugar (3 ounces) or 6 tablespoons
    light brown sugar
1 cup rice wine vinegar
½ cup fresh lime juice (from about 4 limes)
One 6-ounce piece fresh ginger,
    peeled and sliced
6 cilantro roots with 1 inch of stems or
    12 cilantro stems, cleaned
2 garlic cloves, roughly chopped
¾ teaspoon kosher salt

For the Garnish

3 scallions, thinly sliced
1 cup torn Vietnamese coriander (rau ram)
    or cilantro leaves
1 cup torn Thai or regular basil leaves
Sesame seeds (optional)

1. To prepare the pork belly, using a sharp knife, crosshatch the pork belly skin, making cuts ½ inch apart. Place the pork belly in a baking dish. Combine the kerjap manis, vinegar, soy sauce, fish sauce, and lime juice and pour over the pork belly. Marinate, refrigerated, for 24 to 48 hours, turning several times.

2. Heat the oven to 275 degrees. Place the belly skin side up in a baking pan and add 2 cups of the marinating liquid and 2 cups water. The liquid should come halfway up the pork; if necessary add more water or use a smaller pan. Cover the pan with foil and bake until a skewer penetrates the belly with little or no resistance, 3 to 4 hours. Remove the pork from the liquid and let cool.

3. Meanwhile to make the salad, cut the watermelon flesh into 1-inch cubes (discard the seeds).Reserve the rind. Refrigerate the flesh until ready to use. With a sharp knife, remove the outer green skin from the rind. Dice the white rind into ½-inch cubes. Transfer to a heatproof bowl.

4. Combine the rice wine vinegar, water, shallots, chiles, kaffir lime, ginger, palm sugar, and salt in a medium saucepan and bring to a boil over medium-high heat. Cook until the sugar dissolves. Strain the liquid over the white rind. Let cool, then refrigerate for 1 hour.

5. To make the dressing, if using palm sugar, roughly crush it with a mortar and pestle, or place it in a plastic bag and crush with a hammer or heavy can. Combine

the sugar, vinegar, lime juice, ginger, cilantro, garlic, and salt in a blender and blend until smooth.

6. Slice the pork belly into 1-inch chunks, leaving the skin on. Heat 1 inch of canola oil to 375 degrees in a medium saucepan or a wok. Lightly dust the pork belly cubes with flour, shaking off the excess. Working in batches, deep-fry the pork belly until dark golden brown and crispy, 4 to 6 minutes. Transfer to a paper-towel-lined plate. Season with salt if necessary.

7. Toss the watermelon flesh in a bowl with just enough dressing to coat. Divide the pork among serving plates, and top with the watermelon flesh and a few cubes each of pickled rind. Drizzle additional dressing around the plates. Garnish with the scallions, coriander, basil, and sesame seeds, if using.

SERVES 8

SERVING SUGGESTIONS
Pork-and-Toasted-Rice-Powder Spring Rolls (p. 74), Mi Quang (Rice Noodles with Shrimp, Herbs, and Fried Pork Rinds; p. 349), Minced Fish Salad (p. 436), Mango Ice Cream (p. 729), Tapioca Flamingo (p. 810), Sticky Rice with Mango (p. 861)

AUGUST 16, 2006: "THE CHEF: ZAK PELACCIO: THE FRESHEST PRODUCE (AND DUCK TONGUES?)," BY MELISSA CLARK.

—2006

❧ HUNAN BEEF WITH CUMIN

Each bit of beef is wrapped in a musky veil of cumin, chiles, garlic, and sesame oil.

---

1 tablespoon Shaoxing wine or medium-dry sherry

1 tablespoon water

½ teaspoon salt

1 teaspoon light soy sauce

1 teaspoon dark soy sauce

1 tablespoon potato starch

¾ pound boneless short ribs or beef steak

¾ cup peanut oil

2 teaspoons minced fresh ginger

1 tablespoon finely chopped garlic

2 red chiles, seeded and finely chopped

2 to 4 teaspoons crushed red pepper flakes

2 teaspoons ground cumin

Salt

2 scallions, green parts only, thinly sliced

1 teaspoon Asian sesame oil

1. Mix the wine, water, salt, soy sauces, and potato starch in a medium bowl. Cut the beef across the grain into thin slices and add to the marinade, turning to coat.

2. Heat the oil over medium-high heat to about 275 degrees in a wok. Add the beef and stir gently for 2 to 3 minutes, then remove from the oil with a slotted spoon and drain well.

3. Pour off all but 3 tablespoons of the oil in the wok, and set over a high flame. Add the ginger, garlic, chiles, red pepper flakes, and cumin and stir-fry briefly until fragrant. Return the beef to the wok and stir well, seasoning with salt to taste. When the beef is sizzling and fragrant, add the scallion greens and toss briefly. Remove from the heat and stir in the sesame oil.

SERVES 2 TO 4—WITH A LOT OF SIDE DISHES

COOKING NOTES
You can use 2 teaspoons of either light or dark soy sauce if you don't have both.

If you can't find fresh red chiles, 2 small green jalapeños work just fine.

SERVING SUGGESTIONS
Oriental Watercress Soup (p. 111), Jasmine Tea Rice (p. 354), Spicy Cucumber Salad (p. 183), Sugar Snap Peas with Horseradish (p. 259), Lemon Lotus Ice Cream (p. 724)

MARCH 14, 2007: "EAT DRINK MAKE REVOLUTION: THE CUISINE OF HUNAN PROVINCE," BY ANNE MENDELSON. RECIPE ADAPTED FROM *REVOLUTIONARY CHINESE COOKBOOK*, BY FUCHSIA DUNLOP.

—2007

∽ NUECES CANYON CABRITO (GOAT TACOS)

Though goat is the world's most widely consumed meat, Americans are still just beginning to catch on. In 2008, Bill Niman, who founded the phenomenally successful meat company Niman Ranch, began raising and selling goats. The meat hasn't yet found its way to Stop & Shop, but it may soon enough: goat, when grilled slowly, turns smoky and sweet, its fat softened to a glaze. And it makes the best taco you've ever tasted.

———

One 3-pound cabrito (goat) hindquarter

½ teaspoon ground allspice

½ teaspoon ground cumin

Kosher salt and freshly ground black pepper

½ cup chopped cilantro

6 to 8 radishes, very thinly sliced

Corn tortillas, warmed

Tomato salsa

1. Season the cabrito with the allspice, cumin, and a generous amount of salt and pepper. Marinate at room temperature for 1 hour.
2. Build a wood fire in a grill and let it burn down to coals. Move about half of the coals to one side of the grill and maintain a small fire on the other side of the grill, so there will be additional hot coals to move under the goat as necessary. (Add more wood to the fire as needed.) Place the cabrito on the grill, about 8 inches above the coals. Grill for 1 to 3 hours (a longer grilling time creates a deeper smoky flavor and a crustier outer layer of meat), turning it every 20 minutes or so.
3. Heat the oven to 250 degrees. Wrap the grilled cabrito in foil, place in a roasting pan, and transfer to the oven. Cook for 2 to 3 hours, until the meat is falling off the bone. Remove the cabrito from the oven and let stand for about 15 minutes.
4. Using a fork, separate the meat from the bones and shred, reserving the juices in the foil packet. Place the shredded meat in a warmed serving dish and top with the juices, the cilantro, and sliced radishes. Serve the meat in warm corn tortillas, with salsa.

SERVES 4

COOKING NOTE
Goat can be ordered online at www.foxfirefarms.com and is sold in specialty and ethnic markets.

SERVING SUGGESTIONS
Moscow Mule (p. 20), La Paloma (p. 35), Wild Mushroom Quesadillas (p. 375), Tomatoes Vinaigrette (p. 218), Maida Heatter's Cuban Black Beans and Rice (p. 281), Beets in Lime Cream (p. 230), Grapefruit Fluff (p. 809), Caramel Custard (p. 836)

JUNE 17, 2007: "FOOD: THE WAY WE EAT: THE YEAR OF THE GOAT," BY PAULA DISBROWE.

—2007

∽ ROASTED MARROW BONES

Sometimes a dish resonates so strongly with food writers that everyone feels the need to pay homage to it. The recipe for these roasted marrow bones, which were made famous by Fergus Henderson, the father of the nose-to-tail cooking movement of the early 2000s and the owner of St. John Restaurant in London, was published in the *Times* by me in 2003, in 2004 by Jonathan Reynolds, and most recently, in 2007, by Mark Bittman. What's most remarkable is that each time the recipe (which also appears in Henderson's book *The Whole Beast*) appeared in the *Times*, it was different! Mine had more parsley and capers. Reynolds's version was heavy on oil. And Bittman's was somewhere in the middle, the most judicious balance of brine, oil, and lemon juice—and that's why I went with his.

———

8 to 12 center-cut beef or veal marrow bones, 3 inches long (3 to 4 pounds total)

1 cup tightly packed flat-leaf parsley leaves

2 small shallots, thinly sliced

2 teaspoons capers

1½ tablespoons extra virgin olive oil

2 teaspoons fresh lemon juice

Flaky sea salt

At least four ½-inch-thick slices crusty bread, toasted

1. Heat the oven to 450 degrees. Put the bones cut side up on a foil-lined baking sheet or in an ovenproof skillet. Cook until the marrow is soft and has begun

to separate from the bones, about 15 minutes. (Stop before the marrow begins to drizzle out.)

2. Meanwhile, combine the parsley, shallots, and capers in a small bowl. Just before the bones are ready, whisk together the olive oil and lemon juice, and drizzle the dressing over the parsley mixture until the leaves are just coated.

3. Put the roasted bones, parsley salad, salt, and toast on a large plate. To serve, scoop out the marrow, spread it on the toast, sprinkle with salt, and top with a bit of parsley salad.

SERVES 4

COOKING NOTE

Butchers and many supermarkets carry beef marrow bones, but veal marrow bones have to be ordered in advance from a butcher.

SERVING SUGGESTIONS

Potted Salmon (p. 388), Scotch Eggs (p. 62), Chestnut Soup (p. 133), Roasted Squab with Chicken Liver Stuffing (p. 454), Maida Heatter's Preheated-Oven Popovers (p. 657), Baked Mushrooms (p. 212), Delicate Bread Pudding (p. 798), Transparent Pudding (p. 805), Snow Pudding (p. 800)

OCTOBER 31, 2007: "THE MINIMALIST: A LITTLE BIT OF WORK AND A LOT OF SATISFACTION," BY MARK BITTMAN. RECIPE ADAPTED FROM FERGUS HENDERSON, THE OWNER OF ST. JOHN RESTAURANT AND AUTHOR OF THE *THE WHOLE BEAST: NOSE TO TAIL EATING.*

—2007

⌒ PORK ARROSTO WITH PRUNES AND GRAPPA

Put this in your dinner party rotation. The dish doesn't try too hard, but then brined pork, grappa, prunes, fresh herbs, and lemon don't have to.

For the Brine

1½ cups kosher salt

1⅓ cups sugar

8 cups water

One 4- to 5-bone center-cut pork loin roast
(3 to 5 pounds)

For the Spice Rub

2 cloves garlic, thinly sliced

1½ teaspoons fennel seeds

1 tablespoon thyme leaves

1 tablespoon rosemary leaves

10 sage leaves

1½ tablespoons kosher salt

1 tablespoon freshly ground black pepper

2 tablespoons olive oil

For the Prunes

1¾ cups pitted plump prunes

1½ cups water

½ cup sugar

Juice of 2 lemons

2 bay leaves

Pinch of cracked black pepper

¼ cup grappa

Salt

1. To brine the meat, bring the salt, sugar, and water to a boil in a large pot, stirring until the salt and sugar dissolve. Transfer to a heatproof container and cool completely.

2. Cover the pork with the brine and refrigerate for 45 minutes, then drain and pat dry.

3. Set an oven rack in the center position and heat the oven to 400 degrees. To make the spice rub, mix together the garlic, fennel seeds, thyme, rosemary, sage, salt, and pepper on a cutting board, and finely chop with a chef's knife. Pour the olive oil over the mixture. With your fingers pressing on the side of the knife, holding the knife at a slight angle, grind the herbs and spices by rocking the knife back and forth and pulling the mixture across the board. (Be careful not to cut yourself; the mixture is slippery.) Alternatively, grind the mixture in a mortar and pestle. The mixture should have the consistency of wet sand.

4. Rub the pork all over with the spice mixture and set in a roasting pan. Roast until the internal temperature registers 140 degrees on an instant-read thermometer for medium, between 1 and 1½ hours, depending on size. Let rest for 15 minutes.

5. Meanwhile, prepare the prunes: Combine the prunes, water, sugar, lemon juice, bay leaves, and black pepper in a medium saucepan, bring to a simmer, and simmer until the prunes just start to break apart, about 20 minutes. Add the grappa and simmer for 5 minutes

more. Season to taste with salt and remove from the heat.

6. Slice the pork into chops. Serve topped with the prune sauce.

SERVES 4 TO 5

COOKING NOTE

When you cook the prunes in Step 5, they will look like they're drowning in the liquid. Fear not: they'll eventually soak up the grappa, and the sauce will tighten once it sits for a bit.

SERVING SUGGESTIONS

Kir Royale 38 (p. 28), Ricotta Crostini with Fresh Thyme and Dried Oregano (p. 93), Fennel and Apple Salad with Juniper (p. 189), Risotto with Lemon and Crème Fraîche (p. 345), Red Wine Risotto (p. 346), The Most Voluptuous Cauliflower (p. 241), Steamed Fennel with Red Pepper Oil (p. 263), Sautéed Potatoes with Parsley (p. 283), Evelyn Sharpe's French Chocolate Cake (p. 752), Lucas Schoormans's Lemon Tart (p. 857)

JANUARY 6, 2008: "THE WAY WE EAT: THE GRAPES OF WRATH," BY ALEKSANDRA CRAPANZANO. RECIPE ADAPTED FROM *URBAN ITALIAN*, BY ANDREW CARMELLINI AND GWEN HYMAN.

—2008

⌒ COCIDO (CHICKPEA, SPARERIB, AND CHORIZO STEW)

Although the catch-all word for Spanish stew is now *cocido*, it used to be *olla poderida*: *olla* means "pot" and *poder* means "strength." This strong pot comes from Alexandra Raij, who was once the chef at Tía Pol, the best-food-per-square-foot Spanish restaurant in New York. Raij's stew braids together chickpeas, bacon, spareribs, and chorizo, and it is probably best eaten on the coldest day in January. (Don't plan any strenuous activities for after dinner.) Her fried chickpeas are on p. 88, and her rebujito, a refreshing cocktail, is on p. 38.

¾ pound (about 1½ cups) dried chickpeas, rinsed, picked over, and soaked overnight in water to cover by 2 inches

1 large leek

1½ pounds slab bacon, cut into 2 large pieces, rind peeled off

2 pounds baby back ribs, cut into individual ribs (each about 4 inches long)

1 small smoked ham hock (about 6 ounces), 2-ounce piece of serrano ham, or 2-ounce prosciutto end

1 medium yellow onion, unpeeled

½ bulb garlic (halved horizontally), unpeeled

1 carrot, peeled and cut in half

1½ teaspoons sweet Spanish smoked paprika (pimentón)

1 tablespoon plus ¾ teaspoon kosher salt, or more to taste

1 sprig fresh thyme or 1 teaspoon dried thyme

1 bay leaf

About 7½ cups water

¾ pound Spanish chorizo

Extra virgin olive oil for drizzling

Crusty bread for serving (optional)

1. Drain the chickpeas and place in a large stockpot. Keeping the root end intact, trim the leek of its roots and dark green leaves. Slice lengthwise in half, submerge in cold water, and rinse thoroughly. Add to the stockpot, along with the bacon, baby back ribs, ham hock, onion, garlic, carrot, paprika, salt, thyme, and bay leaf. Cover with water by 2 inches, about 6 cups, and bring to a boil, then reduce the heat to medium-low and simmer, partially covered, for 1 hour, occasionally skimming the foam.

2. Add 1 cup cold water to the stew and simmer, partially covered, for 45 minutes.

3. Add ½ cup cold water and the chorizo, return to a low simmer, and cook until all the ingredients are tender, about 30 minutes more.

4. Using a slotted spoon and kitchen tongs, carefully remove the meats, garlic, bay leaf, thyme sprig, onion, carrot, and leek from the pot; discard the ham hock, garlic, bay leaf, and thyme sprig, if you used one. When the remaining vegetables are cool enough to handle, peel the onion and puree in a blender with the carrot, leek, ¾ cup of the chickpeas, and 1 cup of the cooking liquid.

5. Cut the bacon into 2-inch pieces and the chorizo into 1-inch pieces. Return the meats and vegetable

puree to the stockpot and stir gently to combine. Reheat, and adjust the salt if necessary.

6. Ladle the stew into large soup plates and drizzle with extra virgin olive oil. If desired, serve with crusty bread for sopping up the sauce.

SERVES 4 TO 6

COOKING NOTES

If you haven't soaked the chickpeas overnight here's a quick cheat: place them in a pot, cover with 2 inches of cold water, and bring to a boil, then lower the heat, cover, and simmer for 15 minutes.

I think this stew is better the next day, after it's had time to relax. Overnight chilling also gives you a chance to remove the excess fat that rises to the top.

SERVING SUGGESTIONS

Sangria (p. 23), Pan con Tomate (p. 91), Catalan Tortilla with Aioli (p. 86), Chorizo Revueltos (Scrambled Eggs with Chorizo; p. 640), Spanish Cream (p. 802), Toasts with Chocolate, Olive Oil, and Sea Salt (p. 844)

|JANUARY 30, 2008: "ONE POT," BY ELAINE LOUIE. RECIPE ADAPTED FROM ALEXANDRA RAIJ, THE CO-OWNER OF TÍA POL IN NEW YORK CITY.

—2008

SHORT RIBS WITH COFFEE AND CHILES

These earthy, spicy short ribs could serve as a devastating rebuke to all the sweet, fatty short ribs of yore—but there's a place for both, namely at my table. I like this kind atop a pile of polenta.

———

2 tablespoons vegetable oil

4 large or 8 small beef short ribs

Salt and freshly ground black pepper

1 large carrot, peeled and chopped

1 large onion, chopped

3 cloves garlic, chopped

Pinch of sugar

1 dried pasilla chile, stemmed, seeded, and minced

1 dried chipotle chile, stemmed, seeded, and minced

1 cup dry red wine

1 cup strong coffee

1. Drizzle the oil into a heavy pot and brown the ribs well over medium heat, adjusting the heat as necessary to get a dark crust. Take your time, and season the ribs with salt and pepper as they cook. Remove them to a plate. (If there are burnt bits in the pot, wipe them out using a paper towel, then add 1 tablespoon oil and set on the stove again.) Turn the heat to low.

2. Add the carrot, onion, garlic, sugar, and chiles to the pot and cook, stirring occasionally, until the onions are soft, about 15 minutes.

3. Add the wine and coffee and reduce by about half over high heat. Return the ribs to the pot, cover, and cook over low heat (or in a 300-degree oven) for 2 to 3 hours, until very tender—beyond when the meat falls off the bone—turning every hour or so. Taste and adjust the seasoning.

SERVES 4 TO 8

COOKING NOTE

I added a carrot and a little sugar to the recipe.

SERVING SUGGESTIONS

Soupe à l'Ail (Garlic Soup; p. 130), Oyster Chowder (p. 159), Soft Polenta (p. 556), Larded Potatoes à la *New York Times* (p. 271), Watercress Salad (p. 171), Roasted Cauliflower (p. 248), Shredded Brussels Sprouts with Bacon and Pine Nuts (p. 235), Savory Bread Pudding (p. 242), Molasses Cup Cakes with Lemon Icing (p. 745), Polish Jewish Plum Cake (p. 769), Wine-Stewed Prunes and Mascarpone (p. 861)

PERIOD DETAIL

The first short ribs recipe I could find was in 1947, and they were braised rather joylessly with onion, garlic, bay leaf, and water.

FEBRUARY 13, 2008: "THE MINIMALIST: COAXING EXOTIC FLAVOR FROM FAMILIAR ELEMENTS," BY MARK BITTMAN.

—2008

⌒ SPRING LAMB SALAD WITH PEA SHOOTS AND SUGAR SNAP PEAS

Filled with nuance and hard-to-find specialty items, this salad recipe comes from a chef. So embark on it when you want to challenge yourself. You can make it in lots of stages, none very difficult.

---

1 tablespoon coriander seeds

1 tablespoon black peppercorns

1 side of a lamb belly

¾ cup kosher salt (Diamond Crystal, not Morton), plus more for seasoning

Grated zest of 1 orange

Grated zest of 1 lemon, preferably a Meyer lemon

6 cups plus 5 tablespoons extra virgin olive oil

15 cloves garlic, unpeeled

2 small shallots, thinly sliced

3 sprigs thyme

2½ tablespoons lemon juice, preferably Meyer lemon juice

Freshly ground black pepper

6 ounces soft goat cheese

½ cup crème fraîche

2 tablespoons finely chopped preserved lemon (flesh and rind), seeds removed

1 pound sugar snap peas

3 cups densely packed pea shoots

5 cups densely packed pea greens

30 small basil leaves, left whole, or 10 large basil leaves, thinly sliced

6 red shiso leaves, very thinly sliced (optional)

1. Toast the coriander seeds and black peppercorns in a small heavy skillet over medium heat for about 5 minutes, shaking occasionally, until fragrant and lightly browned. (Be careful not to burn them.) Let cool.

2. Coarsely crush the toasted spices using a spice/coffee grinder or mortar and pestle. Rub the lamb belly all over with the spices, salt, and citrus zests. Place in a baking dish, cover with plastic wrap, and refrigerate for at least 12 hours or overnight.

3. Remove the lamb belly from the refrigerator and heat the oven to 275 degrees. Heat 6 cups olive oil to 160 degrees in a heavy saucepan over medium-low heat. Turn off the heat, add the garlic, shallots, and thyme, and let the oil infuse for 20 minutes.

4. Meanwhile, wipe as much of the salt mixture off the lamb belly as you can; wipe out the baking dish and return the lamb belly to it. Discard the thyme sprigs and pour the infused oil, with the garlic and shallots, over the lamb belly. Cover the dish, place on a rimmed baking sheet, and cook in the oven for 3 to 4 hours, until a cake tester slides in and out of the belly with little resistance. Remove from the oven.

5. When it is cool enough to handle, remove the lamb belly from the oil (discard the oil), and gently slide out all of the bones. Put the belly on a baking sheet, cover with another baking sheet, and wrap the entire thing in plastic wrap. Place a weight on top and refrigerate for at least 6 hours, and up to 12 hours.

6. To prepare the rest of the salad, whisk together the lemon juice and remaining 5 tablespoons olive oil in a small bowl and season with salt and pepper. Set aside.

7. Using an electric mixer, whip the goat cheese in a bowl at medium speed for 2 minutes. Fold in the crème fraîche and preserved lemon, and set aside.

8. Blanch the sugar snaps in a large pot of boiling salted water for 30 seconds; drain and immerse in ice water. Drain well and set aside.

9. Thirty minutes before serving, thinly slice the lamb belly and bring it to room temperature.

10. Set a large heavy skillet over medium heat. Working in batches, add the slices of lamb belly and cook until browned and crisp on both sides, about 3 minutes per side. Drain on paper towels.

11. Toss the pea shoots, pea greens, and sugar snap peas with the dressing and season with salt and pepper to taste. Run a thick smear of the goat cheese mixture across the center of each plate and arrange some of the salad and 5 to 6 slices of lamb belly on top. Sprinkle with the basil and shiso, if using.

SERVES 8 TO 10 AS A FIRST COURSE OR LUNCH

COOKING NOTES

Lamb belly can be found at butcher shops and ethnic markets. If you can't find it, boneless lamb shoulder can be substituted (about 3 pounds). Salt the shoulder whole, then cut into large cubes, poach the cubes in oil, and break them into serving-sized pieces to fry.

Preserved lemons are available in Middle Eastern and specialty markets, or at www.kalustyans.com. To make your own, see p. 610 (you can omit the cardamom).

SERVING SUGGESTIONS

Rhubarb Bellini (p. 30), White Gazpacho with Almonds and Grapes (p. 137), Hearth's Fava Bean Salad (p. 202), Jean Yves Legarve's Spaghetti with Lemon and Asparagus Sauce (p. 319), Rhubarb-Strawberry Mousse (p. 835), Strawberry Ice Cream (p. 722)

MAY 4, 2008: "THE NEW STAPLES," BY MERRILL STUBBS. RECIPE ADAPTED FROM RESTO IN NEW YORK CITY.

—2008

⌒ EL PARIAN'S CARNE ASADA (GRILLED BEEF)

"If you were a woman living on a rancho in southern California in the nineteenth century, you would have found yourself short on 'me' time," Jennifer Steinhauer, the *Times* Los Angeles bureau chief, wrote. "There was corn to grind, butter to churn, candles to make, and piles of excessively long skirts to launder in streams. But the payoff for all this pastoral toil was the occasional feast of *carne asada*, meat grilled over a pit, yielding a tender, salty treat.

"Like many of the foodstuffs of early California, carne asada remains a vital player in kitchens here. This is in no small part thanks to the contributions of Mexican immigrants, who have added dimensions to its presentation and have spread the carnivorous love that is consummated between meat and an extremely hot grill."

This recipe comes from El Parian restaurant in Los Angeles (the sauce is from Diana Kennedy, the grande dame of Mexican cooking). Do your best to track down flap meat, a cut from the loin, which may require a few calls around to butcher shops. Mexican butcher shops tend to have it on hand.

---

2 tablespoons salt
¼ teaspoon freshly ground black pepper
¼ teaspoon garlic powder
2 pounds flap steak
2 limes, quartered
2 avocados, peeled, pitted, and thinly sliced
Cooked black beans for serving (optional)
I cup Oaxacan Chile Pasilla Sauce
   (recipe follows; optional)
About 12 small corn tortillas (optional)

1. Prepare a charcoal or gas grill. Combine the salt, pepper, and garlic powder in a small bowl.
2. When the grill is very hot, place the meat on the grill, fat side down. Sprinkle half of the salt mixture over the meat and cook until nicely browned, 6 to 9 minutes. Flip, sprinkle the remaining salt mixture over the meat, and cook for another 6 to 9 minutes, or until the internal temperature registers 140 degrees on an instant-read thermometer. Let rest for a few minutes.
3. Thinly slice the meat against the grain and serve with the lime wedges and avocado slices, and black beans, Oaxacan pasilla sauce, and tortillas if you choose.

SERVES 4 TO 6

OAXACAN CHILE PASILLA SAUCE

½ pound tomatillos, husked, rinsed, and quartered
3 large cloves garlic, unpeeled
I dried pasilla chile
½ teaspoon sea salt, or to taste

1. Place the tomatillo quarters in a medium saucepan and add enough water to cover them halfway. Cover and simmer over medium heat until very soft, about 10 minutes. Drain, reserving ½ cup of the cooking water (you may have slightly less—use what you have).
2. Set a cast-iron skillet over high heat. Add the garlic and roast, turning, until the skin has blackened on all sides, 8 to 10 minutes. Meanwhile, blacken the chile in the same skillet, 1 to 2 minutes per side. Remove from the pan.
3. Rinse the chile briefly in cold water, and break half of it into small pieces over a blender, removing the seeds and veins. (For intense heat, you can add the whole chile—but start with half and add more to taste.) Peel the garlic and add it to the blender, along with the reserved cooking liquid and ½ teaspoon salt. Blend until smooth. Add the cooked tomatillos and pulse briefly. The sauce should have a medium consistency. If it seems too thick, add more water; it will thicken as it sits. Taste and adjust the seasoning.

MAKES ABOUT I CUP

Pasilla chiles are available at www.kalustyans.com and some supermarkets.

The taco ingredients are listed as optional. I say they're mandatory, as is the accompanying cold beer.

Steinhauer wrote, "If you cannot find flap meat, substitute hanger or skirt steak and cook for about the same amount of time, or until it reaches 140 degrees."

If you don't have a grill, you can use a cast-iron skillet or grill pan. Turn on your hood fan!

SERVING SUGGESTIONS
A cold beer, and maybe Guacamole Tostadas (p. 67) and Mango Ice Cream (p. 729)

JULY 27, 2008: "THE WAY WE EAT: CARNE KNOWLEDGE," BY JENNIFER STEINHAUER. CARNE ASADA RECIPE ADAPTED FROM EL PARIAN IN LOS ANGELES; OAXACAN CHILE PASILLA SAUCE ADAPTED FROM *THE ART OF MEXICAN COOKING*, BY DIANA KENNEDY.

—2008

APPLE CITY WORLD-CHAMPION BABY BACK RIBS

For the Magic Dust Rub
2 tablespoons sweet Spanish smoked paprika (pimentón)
2 tablespoons kosher salt
1 tablespoon sugar
1½ teaspoons dry mustard
1 tablespoon chili powder
1 tablespoon ground cumin
1½ teaspoons freshly ground black pepper
1 tablespoon garlic powder
1½ teaspoons cayenne pepper

For the Ribs
Two 2- to 3-pound racks baby back ribs
Vegetable oil
2 tablespoons applewood dust or chips
1 cup apple cider or apple juice
1 cup water
1 teaspoon kosher salt

For the Barbecue Sauce
1 cup ketchup
2⅓ cups seasoned rice vinegar
1½ cups apple cider or apple juice
1¼ cups cider vinegar
1½ cups packed dark brown sugar
1¼ cups Worcestershire or soy sauce
2 teaspoons prepared Colman's mustard
3¼ teaspoons garlic powder
1¼ teaspoons freshly ground white pepper
1 teaspoon cayenne pepper
1⅓ cups minced cooked bacon
1⅓ cups finely grated peeled apples
1⅓ cups finely grated onions

1. Several hours, or at least 30 minutes before cooking, make the rub: Combine all the ingredients in a small bowl. Cut the racks of ribs in half, brush with oil, and sprinkle all sides with about 6 tablespoons of the magic dust.

2. Heat the oven to 300 degrees. Place a stovetop smoker or homemade smoker (see Cooking Note) on a burner. Place the wood dust on the bottom of the smoker, toward the center. Cover with the drip pan. Set the grate over the drip pan and place the ribs on the rack, cutting them as needed to fit in one layer. Cover with a lid or foil, making sure there is at least 1 inch between the lid and the ribs. Turn the heat to high. When smoke appears, lower the heat to medium-high and smoke for 35 minutes.

3. Meanwhile, make the barbecue sauce: Combine all the ingredients except the apples and onions in a medium pot and bring to a boil over medium-high heat. Stir in the apples and onions, reduce the heat, and simmer uncovered, stirring often, until slightly thickened, 15 to 20 minutes. Remove from the heat. (The sauce will keep for up to 2 weeks in the refrigerator.)

4. Line a large rimmed baking sheet with heavy-duty foil. Add the cider, water, and salt. Set a rack over the pan. Transfer the ribs to the rack and cook until the meat shrinks away from the ends and comes easily off the bone, about 1½ hours.

5. Brush the ribs on all sides with the barbecue sauce and cook for 15 minutes more. Serve with more sauce on the side.

SERVES 4 TO 6

Jill Santopietro noted, "Camerons stovetop smokers and ground wood chips can be purchased at many cooking stores or at www.cameronscookware.com. To make a smoker, line the inside of a large wok with heavy foil. Place the wood chips in the wok. Make a drip pan by placing a heavy piece of foil over both the chips and the bottom of the wok. (Make sure it doesn't rise up the sides.) Set a 10- to 11-inch round baking rack over the drip pan. Use another piece of heavy foil as a lid."

SERVING SUGGESTIONS

Ginger Lemonade (p. 26), Jay Grelen's Southern Iced Tea (p. 27), Spoonbread's Potato Salad (p. 288), Docks Coleslaw (p. 191), Watermelon and Tomato Salad (p. 197), Summer Pudding (p. 847), Brownies (p. 684)

SEPTEMBER 12, 2008: "THE WAY WE EAT: THANK YOU FOR SMOKING," BY JILL SANTOPIETRO. RECIPE ADAPTED FROM *PEACE, LOVE, AND BARBECUE*, BY MIKE MILLS AND AMY MILLS TUNNICLIFFE.

—2008

⌒ BACON EXPLOSION

In early 2009, the *New York Times* was briefly taken over by a college frat. . . .

———

2 pounds thick-sliced bacon

3 tablespoons Basic Rub for Barbecue (see p. 551)

1½ pounds Italian sausage, casings removed

¾ cup bottled barbecue sauce

1. Using 10 slices of bacon, weave a square lattice like that on top of a pie: Place 5 slices side by side on a large sheet of aluminum foil, sides touching. Place another strip of bacon across one end, perpendicular to the other strips. Fold the first, third, and fifth bacon strips back over this strip, then place another strip next to it. Unfold the first, third, and fifth strips, and fold back the second and fourth strips. Repeat with the remaining bacon until all 10 strips are tightly woven.

2. Heat the oven to 225 degrees or light a fire in an outdoor smoker. Place the remaining bacon in a large skillet and cook until crisp. Drain on paper towels.

3. Meanwhile, sprinkle the bacon weave with 1 tablespoon barbecue rub. Spread the sausage evenly over the bacon lattice, pressing it to the edges.

4. Crumble the fried bacon into bite-sized pieces. Sprinkle on top of the sausage. Drizzle with ½ cup barbecue sauce and sprinkle with another tablespoon of barbecue rub.

5. Very carefully separate the front edge of the sausage layer from the bacon weave and roll the sausage into a compact log. The bacon weave should stay where it is, flat. Press the sausage roll to remove any air pockets, and pinch together the seams and ends. Roll the sausage toward you, this time with the bacon weave, until it is completely wrapped. The roll should be 2 to 3 inches thick. Turn it so the seam faces down. Sprinkle with the remaining tablespoon of barbecue rub.

6. Place the roll on a baking sheet in the oven or in a smoker and cook until the internal temperature registers 165 degrees on an instant-read thermometer, about 1 hour per inch of thickness.

7. Glaze the roll with the remaining ¼ cup barbecue sauce. To serve, slice into ¼ to ½-inch rounds.

SERVES 10 OR MORE

SERVING SUGGESTIONS

Beer, Guacamole Tostadas (p. 67), Chocolate Quakes (p. 702)

JANUARY 28, 2009: "TAKE BACON. ADD SAUSAGE. BLOG," BY DAMON DARLIN. RECIPE ADAPTED FROM JASON DAY AND AARON CHRONISTER.

—2009

12 ∽ SAUCES, DRESSINGS, CONDIMENTS, RUBS, AND PRESERVES

- The golden era of marmalade: pumpkin, pineapple, quince, rhubarb, and lemon are common.

—1870s—

- Make-your-own Worcestershire Sauce (p. 589).

—1876—

- Dulce de Lece (p. 593), 125 years before Häagen-Dazs discovers it.

—1878—

- Tomato Figs (p. 591), sweetened sun-dried tomatoes, are a popular preserve, as is Tomato Jelly (p. 595).
- Americans know their way around ketchup, and mushroom ketchup is as common as tomato. Heinz Ketchup, introduced in 1876, eventually changes this.

—1880s—

- If you grow too much cabbage, you shred it and turn it into the pickle Chow-Chow (p. 593).

- Hollandaise is a fancy party sauce.

—1881—

- Smucker's is founded, and home preserving begins its shift from necessity to hobby.

—1897—

- Tartar Sauce (p. 595).

—1909—

- Harbinger of a grilling nation: Barbecue Sauce (p. 596).

—1939—

- The pickles decade.

—1940s—

- Spiced Hard Sauce (p. 604) harks back to British Colonial days.

—1966—

- Lorane Schiff's Pesto Genovese (p. 311) is the first pesto recipe to appear in the *Times*.

—1969—

- No savory dish can't be improved with a few dashes of Tabasco and Worcestershire sauce.

—1970s—

- We discover guacamole, then salsa, and, as a result, consume a whole lot of chips, garlic, and beer.

—1980s—

- Preserved lemons (p. 610) fascinate but never really catch on.

- Brie Butter with Fresh Bread (p. 605).

—1983—

- Dry rubs replace marinades.

—1990s—

- It's fashionable to make your own mayonnaise.

- Romesco Sauce (p. 610), a delicious tomato and bread sauce from Spain, emerges. Cooks wonder how they've lived this long without it.

—2002—

- Salsa verde replaces pesto in restaurants.

—2005—

- Homemade Butter and Buttermilk (p. 613).

—2007—

- Sriracha sauce makes a bid to become a mainstream condiment.

—2008—

12

～

SAUCES, DRESSINGS, CONDIMENTS, RUBS, AND PRESERVES

In some ways this is my favorite chapter in the book, because it gathers up all the kitchen's toothsome marginalia, the pungent sauces and rubs, the preserves and handmade condiments. These foods are like the invisible seam work underpinning a good dress, making it hang just so.

In addition to classics such as New England Grape Butter (p. 600) and Cream Dressing for Salad (p. 592), here are a few unusual gems, such as Tomato Figs (p. 591), made by cooking tomatoes in syrup and then drying them in the sun; Homemade Butter and Buttermilk (p. 613), whipped together in a mixer; and Worcestershire Sauce (p. 589), mixed up in a Mason jar.

You'll notice that there's a preponderance of nineteenth-century recipes in these pages: cooks then needed to store more food than we do and they were good at it, which made for recipes that lasted. I am indebted to Eugenia Bone, a preserves expert, who vetted (and often rewrote) the preserves and canning recipes—from the Rhubarb Marmalade on p. 589 to the Bread-and-Butter Pickles on p. 600—to make sure they were up to USDA safety standards. What's here includes just a sprinkling of jams and pickles and syrups; if you want to learn more about preserving food, pick up Bone's book *Well-Preserved*.

RECIPES BY CATEGORY

⌒ RHUBARB MARMALADE

2½ pounds rhubarb, trimmed
3 oranges
4½ cups sugar

1. Cut the rhubarb into ½-inch-thick slices; you need 10 cups. Peel the zest from the oranges with a vegetable peeler, and cut the zest into small pieces; you need ½ cup. Cut the pith from the oranges, then slice the oranges in half like a grapefruit. Remove and discard the seeds. Cut the orange pulp into small chunks; you need 2½ cups.

2. Combine the rhubarb, oranges, and orange zest in a large heavy enameled cast-iron or other nonreactive pot, add the sugar, and bring to a simmer. Cook, stirring occasionally so the fruit doesn't stick to the pan; you'll need to stir more often as the marmalade thickens. Skim the foam as needed. The marmalade is ready when a spoonful dropped onto a plate sets when cool.

3. Have ready 6 scalded half-pint jars and screw bands, with new lids (see Cooking Notes). Simmer the lids in hot water to soften the rubberized flange. Ladle the marmalade into the jars leaving ¼-inch headspace. Wipe the rims. Put the lids on and screw on the bands fingertip tight.

4. Place the jars on a rack in a big pot and add water until it is 2 to 3 inches over the jars. Cover the pot and bring to a boil over high heat, then lower the heat to medium and boil gently for 15 minutes. Remove the lid and then, after about 5 minutes, remove the jars. Allow the jars to cool, untouched, for 4 to 6 hours.

5. Check the seals, and store in a cool, dark place for up to a year. Refrigerate after opening.

MAKES ABOUT 6 HALF-PINTS

COOKING NOTES

Always use a heavy nonreactive pot for preserves. I like enameled cast-iron because it holds heat well and the preserves tend not to stick or burn so easily.

To scald preserving jars, simply dip the jars in boiling water.

To sterilize preserving jars, boil the jars in water to cover for 10 minutes.

"Fingertip tight" means the band is screwed on as tight as you can when screwing on a band using your fingertips—in other words, not super-tight.

When filling jars, if you can't completely fill the last jar, don't sweat it—just put that one in the fridge and use it up in a week or two.

To check the seal on a jar, remove the band and lift the jar by its thin lid. If it's sealed properly, it will hold.

To lessen the incidence of foam, add ½ teaspoon butter to the marmalade while it is cooking.

APRIL 16, 1876: "THE HOUSEHOLD."

—1876

⌒ WORCESTERSHIRE SAUCE

This is a fun recipe because you discover that the mysterious dark sauce you've been dousing on burgers and adding to Caesar salad and Chex Mix your whole life is actually easy to make at home.

The original Lea & Perrins, made in Worcester, England, was fermented and contained, according to Wikipedia, "malt vinegar, spirit vinegar, molasses, sugar, salt, anchovies, tamarind extract, onions, garlic, spice, and flavouring." Lea & Perrins' American version leaves out the malt vinegar and substitutes high-fructose corn syrup for the sugar. This version is better than both—it's sharp and peppery and much looser than commercial Worcestershire.

¼ pound shallots, chopped
2½ tablespoons ground allspice
1 tablespoon ground mace
2 teaspoons cayenne pepper
¼ nutmeg, grated
1 tablespoon plus ¾ teaspoon salt
One 2-ounce tin anchovy fillets, drained
6 tablespoons soy sauce
3 cups cider vinegar

1. Combine all the ingredients in a sterilized (see Cooking Notes, this page) 1-quart glass jar and screw the lid on tight. Refrigerate for 1 month, shaking the jar every other day or so.

2. Strain the sauce into another sterilized jar (or jars), and it's ready to use. Keep refrigerated.

MAKES 3½ CUPS

SEPTEMBER 10, 1876: "THE HOUSEHOLD."

—1876

JULY 8, 1877: "RECEIPTS FOR THE TABLE." RECIPE FROM *BUCKEYE COOKERY*.

—1877

∽ PLUM JAM

2¾ pounds plums, halved and pitted
½ cup water
1 cup sugar, or as needed

1. Place the plums and water in a medium saucepan, cover, and bring to a boil, then reduce the heat and simmer until the plums are soft. The time will depend on the ripeness and variety of the plums.

2. Press the plums through a sieve into a bowl to remove the skins. Measure the juice and pulp; you should have about 2¾ cups. Combine this with 1 cup sugar in a medium heavy enameled cast-iron or other nonreactive saucepan. (If you have a different amount of juice, adjust the sugar accordingly.) Bring to a simmer over medium heat and simmer, stirring occasionally, until the jam thickens. To test it, spoon a little onto a plate and let it cool: if it sets, it's ready.

3. Have ready 2 sterilized half-pint jars with screw bands and new lids (see Cooking Notes, p. 589). Simmer the lids in hot water to soften the rubberized flange. Ladle the marmalade into the jars, leaving ¼-inch headspace. Wipe the rims. Put the lids on and screw on the bands fingertip tight.

4. Place the jars on a rack in a big pot and cover with 2 to 3 inches of water. Cover the pot and bring to a boil over high heat, then lower the heat to medium and gently boil for 10 minutes. Remove the lid and then, after about 5 minutes, remove the jars. Allow the jars to cool, untouched, for 4 to 6 hours.

5. Check the seals, and store in a cool, dark place for up to a year. Refrigerate after opening.

MAKES 2 HALF-PINTS

COOKING NOTE
Slightly underripe plums will make the jam thicken faster than ripe plums (green skins are higher in pectin, the thickening polysaccharide in fruits). A combination of ripe and underripe is ideal.

∽ STRAWBERRY JAM

This recipe was presented as instructions for jam made with any kind of fruit. Notice that the proportions of fruit to sugar are 1 to ¾; most modern jam recipes are 1 to 1, a ratio that masks the flavor of the fruit with sweetness. Another reason to restore the original ratio, according to Eugenia Bone, the author of *Well-Preserved*, who vetted this recipe for me, is that the gelling success rate will be much higher.

2 pounds strawberries (about 2 quarts)
1½ pounds sugar (3 cups)

1. Place the strawberries in a medium heavy enameled cast-iron or other nonreactive saucepan and gently mash the fruit with a potato masher or fork. Start over low heat and as the strawberries release their juices, increase the heat until the liquid simmers. Cook for 15 minutes.

2. Stir in the sugar and continue simmering, skimming often. The jam is ready when spoonful dropped onto a plate firms up when cool.

3. Have ready 3 sterilized half-pint jars with screw bands and new lids (see Cooking Notes, p. 589). Simmer the lids in hot water to soften the rubberized flange. Ladle the jam into the jars, leaving ¼-inch headspace. Wipe the rims. Put the lids on and screw on the bands fingertip tight.

4. Place the jars on a rack in a big pot and cover with 2 to 3 inches of water. Cover the pot and bring to a boil over high heat, then lower the heat to medium and boil gently for 5 minutes. Remove the lid and then, after about 10 minutes, remove the jars. Allow the jars to cool, untouched, for 4 to 6 hours.

5. Check the seals, and store in a cool, dark place for up to a year. Refrigerate after opening.

MAKES 3 HALF-PINTS

COOKING NOTE

To lessen the incidence of foam, add ½ teaspoon of butter to the marmalade while it is cooking.

JULY 8, 1877: "RECEIPTS FOR THE TABLE." RECIPE FROM *BUCKEYE COOKERY.*

—1877

TOMATO FIGS

These are odd, and wonderfully so. You simmer tomatoes in a sugar syrup to candy them, dry them in the sun for 2 days, and then dust them with confectioners' sugar. The reader who contributed this recipe (several versions of which show up in the nineteenth-century archive) said their flavor "is nearly that of the best quality of fresh figs." I'd say they're just as great, but much more acutely sweet and assertive.

———

4 pounds small slightly underripe plum tomatoes
   (about 24 tomatoes)
1½ pounds granulated sugar (3 cups)
Confectioners' sugar

1. Core the tomatoes, then peel them by cutting a shallow X in their rounded end, dipping them in boiling water for 30 seconds, and slipping off the skins.
2. Place the tomatoes in a large heavy enameled cast-iron or other nonreactive saucepan, pour in the sugar, and bring to a simmer over medium heat, stirring to dissolve the sugar. Cook gently until the tomatoes are translucent on the edges and candied, 45 minutes to 1 hour.
3. Use a slotted spoon to lift the tomatoes from the syrup, lay them on a baking sheet, and let cool. Let the tomato syrup cool, then bottle it and keep refrigerated (for up to 3 months). Cover the tomatoes with another baking sheet and gently press on the top sheet to flatten the tomatoes and press out excess juices.
4. Brush a wire rack with oil and lay the tomatoes on it. Wrap the rack in cheesecloth (or if you have some other netting contraption to keep out flies, feel free to use it). Put the rack on a baking sheet and set it out in the sun for 2 days to dry the tomatoes, bringing them in at night.
5. Unwrap the tomatoes. Dust them with confectioners' sugar, tapping off the excess. You can store them between layers of wax paper in plastic containers or tins in a cool place for up to a month, or you can devour them right away.

MAKES 20 TO 24 TOMATO FIGS

COOKING NOTES

Check the weather before planning a batch. You'll need 2 straight sunny, nonhumid days to dry the tomatoes.

Select slightly underripe tomatoes, which hold up better when simmered.

SERVING SUGGESTIONS

Eat the figs like candy. My sister, Rhonda, who also made them, served them with a platter of cheeses. Use the leftover syrup for sprinkling on ice cream. Or add it to salad dressings. Brush it between layers of cake. Sprinkle a few drops into a vodka cocktail. Slip some into the broth you use to braise short ribs.

JULY 22, 1877: "RECEIPTS FOR THE TABLE."

—1877

TOMATO KETCHUP

If you don't love the pungency of Worcestershire and Tabasco, this may not be your thing. For everyone else, this is your dream ketchup and hot sauce rolled into one. First, you're slapped by cayenne, then numbed with clove, then shaken back awake with mustard vinegar. It's masochistic, and invigorating. And the dish is the perfect accompaniment to a lamb burger.

Not that that's what Mrs. William Craren, the author of this recipe, had in mind for it. Everyone in the late nineteenth century had a recipe for "catsup," and many versions ended up in the paper. Most were variations on the same theme—tomatoes boiled down with spices such as nutmeg, clove, cayenne, and pepper, then finished with vinegar. With Mrs. Craren's recipe, you end up with a sauce that's dark, incisive, and a little looser than Heinz.

I did not provide canning instructions here because the recipe doesn't contain enough vinegar or onion to be considered safe by today's standards, but I didn't want to fiddle with the flavor, which is terrific as is. So make this and keep it in your fridge. It doesn't yield much anyhow—a few barbecues, and it'll be gone. (For a larger amount, simply double or triple the recipe.)

---

4 pounds tomatoes, peeled, cored, and sliced

About I tablespoon kosher salt

I small onion, finely chopped

3 tablespoons cider vinegar (5% acidity)

2 teaspoons dry mustard

1½ teaspoons ground cloves

½ teaspoon cayenne pepper, less if you don't like heat

¾ teaspoon freshly ground black pepper

I teaspoon freshly grated nutmeg

1. Layer the tomatoes in a bowl with a sprinkling of salt. Using a potato masher, lightly squash them. Cover and let sit out overnight.

2. The next day, pass the tomatoes and juices through the finest plate of a food mill. Measure the juices and pulp. You should have about 6 cups. Pour into a medium heavy enameled cast-iron or other nonreactive pot, bring to a boil over medium-high heat, and reduce the juices by half.

3. Add the onion, vinegar, and mustard and boil for 30 minutes, stirring occasionally.

4. Add the cloves, cayenne, and black pepper and continue cooking for a few minutes, until the ketchup is a consistency that you like. Stir in the nutmeg. Add more salt if needed.

5. Ladle the ketchup into a jar and let cool, then seal and refrigerate. (The ketchup will keep for a month.)

MAKES I CUP

COOKING NOTE

If you want a smoother sauce, pass the finished ketchup through a food mill.

PERIOD DETAILS

Another common condiment of the time was "tomato soy," which combined tomatoes, vinegar, sugar, and cloves, cooked down to a thick sauce. (The proportions: 16 pounds tomatoes, 1 quart vinegar, 3½ pounds sugar, and 1 ounce cloves.)

In the nineteenth century, *Times* recipes were lumped into a weekly Sunday column called "The Household" that often contained domestic remedies as well. This one appeared a few recipes away from the following entry:

To Rid a Dog of Fleas: Wash him thoroughly with common soft soap, such as they use onboard ships; or place him on a newspaper and rub Persian Insect powder well over him, and the fleas will drop out on the paper and die almost immediately. This method is also effective with cats.   —Bow Wow."

AUGUST 26, 1877: "THE HOUSEHOLD." RECIPE SIGNED MRS. WILLIAM CRAREN.

—1877

∽ CREAM DRESSING FOR SALAD

Many old school dressings were as hearty as mud. You didn't so much dress a lettuce leaf, you clobbered it, which meant a salad could not only fill you up but make you want to lie down. This egg-and-cream-thickened dressing is relatively light, and incredibly delicious.

Although it's still too hefty for sweet, fragile lettuces, it's endlessly handy. I used it on arugula, romaine hearts, and seeded and slivered black tomatoes; as a sauce with roasted lamb; to bind a salad of roasted chicken and arugula; and with arugula and artichoke hearts. And then it was gone. If you've never made a cooked dressing before, it's a treat. As you whisk the dressing, it foams and thickens, like warm pudding.

---

3 large eggs

6 tablespoons heavy cream

3 tablespoons unsalted butter, melted

I teaspoon salt

I teaspoon Colman's prepared mustard

½ teaspoon freshly ground black pepper

¼ cup cider vinegar

Whisk together the eggs, cream, butter, salt, mustard, and pepper in the top of a double boiler set over medium heat. Once the mixture is warm, whisk in the vinegar and continue to cook, whisking. After a few minutes, the mixture will foam and then quickly thicken; it's done when it's the thickness of crème anglaise. Be careful not to curdle it: pull it on and off the heat as you go if necessary. Let cool. The dressing keeps, refrigerated, for up to a week.

MAKES ABOUT I CUP

APRIL 7, 1878: "THE HOUSEHOLD." RECIPE SIGNED NELLIE.

—1878

➥ BORDEAUX JELLY

Wine jellies (which are more Jell-O than jelly) tend to be found chopped into Lilliputian cubes, speckling the edge of a dessert plate as an adornment to pies, cakes, or confections. Here, however, you end up with a mold too large, bouncy, and boozy to serve as a sidelight. Yet I wasn't quite sure I had the nerve to serve the jelly as is—it's wonderfully intense, but it needs a counterpoint so it doesn't become too monotonous. I suggest Sour Cream Ice Cream (p. 730), Lindy's Cheesecake (p. 759), Chamomile and Almond Cake (p. 786), or New Jersey Blancmange (p. 797).

———

I (750-ml) bottle dry red wine, preferably Bordeaux
6 tablespoons Cognac or other brandy
Juice of I lemon
I cup plus I tablespoon sugar
Two $\frac{1}{4}$-ounce packets powdered gelatin,
    dissolved in 2 tablespoons water

Bring the wine, Cognac, lemon, and sugar to a boil in a medium saucepan. Add the gelatin and stir until dissolved. Pour into a round (or any shape you like) mold. Let cool to room temperature, then refrigerate overnight.

MAKES ABOUT 5 CUPS

COOKING NOTE
You can halve the recipe if you don't want to be eating wine jelly for the next 2 weeks.

MAY 11, 1879: "RECEIPTS FOR THE TABLE." RECIPE SIGNED LE DOCTEUR DE M.

—1879

➥ DULCE DE LECE [SIC]

"This is a Spanish sweetmeat, and can be used as a sauce for pudding, or can be spread on bread for children," wrote B. C. Orange, a reader who contributed this recipe in 1879. B. C. Orange, you were *way* ahead of your time!

———

4 cups whole milk
2 cups sugar
I teaspoon ground cinnamon
I teaspoon all-purpose flour

Whisk together the milk, sugar, cinnamon, and flour in a medium heavy saucepan. Bring almost to a boil, then reduce the heat and cook at a slow simmer, stirring every 10 minutes or so, until the mixture thickens and turns a leathery brown, 2 to 3 hours. It's done when a spoonful dropped onto a plate sets up like jelly.

MAKES ABOUT 3 CUPS

COOKING NOTE
In the beginning, the mixture has a tendency to boil over. Keep the heat low and keep an eye on it. If it boils up, whisk it back down.

DECEMBER 14, 1879: "RECEIPTS FOR THE TABLE." RECIPE BY B. C. ORANGE.

—1879

➥ CHOW-CHOW

A classic chow-chow—a pickled vegetable relish—with an emphasis on clove, the trademark flavor of the 1880s.

———

4 cups sliced cabbage (about $\frac{1}{4}$ head)
2 cups sliced green tomatoes
2 cups sliced onions
6 cups sliced Kirby cucumbers (about 8 cucumbers)
$\frac{1}{4}$ cup sliced red and green bell peppers
$\frac{1}{4}$ cup kosher salt
I $\frac{1}{2}$ teaspoons black peppercorns

1¼ teaspoons celery seeds

1¼ teaspoons whole cloves

1 teaspoon mustard seeds

1 teaspoon dry mustard

1½ teaspoons turmeric

½ cup packed dark brown sugar

¼ cup grated fresh horseradish

4 cups cider vinegar (5% acidity)

1. Set a large plastic or other nonreactive strainer over a bowl and add the cabbage, tomatoes, onions, cucumbers, and peppers. Toss with the salt, cover, and let stand in a cool place overnight.

2. The next day, discard the drained-off liquid. Transfer the vegetables to a large enameled cast-iron or other nonreactive pot, add the spices, sugar, and horseradish, and pour in the vinegar. Bring to a boil and cook for 20 minutes. The cabbage and onions should be tender but not falling apart. Continue cooking if needed. If not, remove from the heat.

3. Have ready 10 sterilized half-pint jars with screw bands and new lids (see Cooking Notes, p. 589). Simmer the lids in hot water to soften the rubberized flange. Ladle the chow-chow into the jars, leaving ½-inch headspace. Remove any air bubbles trapped in the jars by running a sterilized butter knife between the sides of the jars and the chow-chow. Wipe the rims. Put the lids on and screw on the bands fingertip tight.

4. Place the jars on a rack in a big pot and cover with 2 to 3 inches of water. Cover the pot and bring to a boil over high heat, then lower the heat to medium and boil gently for 10 minutes. Remove the lid and then, after about 5 minutes, remove the jars. Allow the jars to cool, untouched, for 4 to 6 hours.

5. Check the seals, and store in a cool, dark place for up to a year. Refrigerate after opening.

MAKES 10 HALF-PINTS

COOKING NOTES

I quartered the original recipe. Old canning recipes were not meant to be a soul-replenishing weekend project, but were regarded as a necessity to carry you and your seven children through a long, barren winter, and so the amounts involved were often colossal.

SERVING SUGGESTIONS

North Carolina–Style Pulled Pork (p. 550), the '21'

Club Hamburger (p. 536), French Fries (p. 292), and other barbecue foods.

OCTOBER 3, 1880: "RECEIPTS."

—1880

⌒ HORSERADISH SAUCE

This republished recipe from Mary Lincoln, presumably conceived before she lost her mind, is one of a handful of recipes from First Families and their cooks that have been printed in the *Times*. See Huguenot Torte, served in the White House during Martin Van Buren's presidency, on p. 750; Roman Punch, on p. 12; and Nancy Reagan's Monkey Bread, on p. 669.

This is essentially whipped cream seasoned with salt, pepper, and horseradish, which means its moussey texture conceals a good punch of flavor. You'll want to eat it with a spoon. By yourself. I make a similar sauce to serve with smoked salmon, although I add fresh herbs and capers to it. Keep it chilled, or the horseradish will cause the cream to weep.

————

1 cup heavy cream

½ teaspoon salt

½ teaspoon freshly ground black pepper

3 tablespoons prepared horseradish
(drained a little if watery)

Watercress for garnish

Whip the cream until it holds soft peaks. Fold in the salt, pepper, and horseradish. Serve in a shallow dish, garnished with watercress, if desired.

MAKES ABOUT 2 CUPS

SERVING SUGGESTIONS

Use in cold roast beef sandwiches, or serve with smoked salmon, Braised Stuffed Breast of Veal (p. 558), leftovers from High-Temperature Roast Lamb (p. 526), or Ann Seranne's Rib Roast of Beef (p. 519).

APRIL 11, 1897: "SOME SEASONABLE RECEIPTS: HOT CROSS BUNS FOR GOOD FRIDAY—MAKING OF EASTER EGGS—JOLLY BOYS AND TWISTERS." RECIPE ADAPTED FROM MARY LINCOLN.

—1897

TOMATO JELLY

This is essentially tomato aspic. Served with cold meats, this jelly, the story said, "will prove both decorative and tasty." If you suffer from aspicaphobia, a common affliction, keep in mind that vegetable aspics shouldn't be lumped with meat aspics; while the latter bring to mind bones and marrow and gelatinous substances, the former are just your favorite vegetables, seasoned and mixed with gelatin. How bad could that be?

———

4 cups chopped tomatoes
⅓ cup chopped onion
1¼ cups water
Salt and freshly ground black pepper
Paprika
Worcestershire sauce
One ¼-ounce packet powdered gelatin

1. Combine the tomatoes, onion, and 1 cup water in a saucepan and bring to a boil, then reduce the heat and simmer for 10 minutes. Strain into a bowl. Season generously with salt, pepper, paprika, and Worcestershire sauce.
2. Pour the remaining ¼ cup water into a small bowl and sprinkle the gelatin over the top. Let sit for 5 minutes.
3. Stir the gelatin into the tomato mixture until fully dissolved. Pour into a 9-inch pie plate or other mold and let cool, then refrigerate until set.
4. To unmold, dip the bottom of the pie plate in a bowl of hot water, then flip the tomato jelly onto a cutting board. Finely chop and pile into a bowl. Serve as a condiment.

MAKES 2 CUPS

COOKING NOTE
I used a pie plate to mold the jelly because I was in a summer house when I made it, and my selection of molds was boring at best. Pull down that mold you've been using for decoration, dust it off, and make it proud with some aspic.

SERVING SUGGESTIONS
Serve with Roast Chicken Salad (p. 492), leftover High-Temperature Roast Lamb (p. 526), Cold Beef with Tarragon Vinaigrette (p. 534), Elizabeth Frink's Roast Lemon Chicken (p. 478).

OCTOBER 6, 1907: "TURTLE AND PARTRIDGE FIND MANY PATRONS."

—1907

RAVIGOTE FROIDE (HERBED MAYONNAISE WITH CORNICHONS)

Ravigote and tartar sauce (see this page) are very similar except that ravigote is more about herbs (parsley and tarragon) and tartar is more about pungency (capers and shallots).

———

½ cup mayonnaise
2 tablespoons chopped flat-leaf parsley
1 tablespoon chopped tarragon
2 tablespoons finely chopped cornichons

Stir together the mayonnaise, parsley, tarragon, and cornichons. You're done.

MAKES ABOUT ¾ CUP

SERVING SUGGESTIONS
Use ravigote as you would tartar sauce, with chilled lobster and shrimp, fried oysters, or soft-shell crabs. I also like ravigote with sliced cold chicken and lamb.

MAY 23, 1909: "SECRETS OF FRENCH COOKING," BY LAURA A. SMITH.

—1909

TARTAR SAUCE

What's great about this tartar sauce is that instead of the usual arrangement—capers and shallots lost in a sea of mayonnaise—here there are so many capers and shallots that the mayonnaise merely dresses them.

———

½ cup mayonnaise

2 tablespoons chopped capers

2 tablespoons finely chopped shallots

Stir together the mayonnaise, capers, and shallots.

MAKES ¾ CUP

SERVING SUGGESTIONS
Serve with Crab Cakes Baltimore-Style (p. 407), or
Deep-Fried Soft-Shell Crabs (p. 398).

MAY 23, 1909: "SECRETS OF FRENCH COOKING," BY
LAURA A. SMITH.

—1909

☙ BARBECUE SAUCE

————

8 tablespoons (1 stick) unsalted butter, melted

1 teaspoon dry mustard

Dash of cayenne pepper

1 teaspoon Tabasco sauce

2 tablespoons ketchup

2 tablespoons fresh lemon juice

2 tablespoons cider vinegar

½ teaspoon onion salt

½ teaspoon garlic salt

1 tablespoon tomato sauce

2 tablespoons finely chopped flat-leaf parsley

¼ cup water

Combine all the ingredients in a bowl, blending well.

MAKES ENOUGH TO BASTE 2 CHICKENS OR
PROPORTIONATE QUANTITIES OF MEAT

JANUARY 8, 1939: "IN HARLEM NEW FRONTIERS AWAIT THE
GOURMET," BY AUGUST LOEB.

—1939

☙ SCHRAFFT'S MINT SAUCE

Schrafft's, a popular restaurant in New York City,
served this sauce with lamb, but it's not the kind of
mint sauce you're picturing. Here the emphasis is
divided between orange and mint, with a background
scent of currants. I served this with High-Temperature
Roast Lamb on p. 526, cold and sliced. But I'd also
happily eat it spread on toast with salted butter.

————

ORIGINAL RECIPE
"At Schrafft's mint will come to the table chaperoned
by currant jelly. Into a glassful of the jelly, two tablespoons of grated orange rind and six of finely cut mint
leaves are gently folded to complete a trinity of color,
flavor and fragrance as sweet as a Spring morning."

MAKES 1 CUP

COOKING NOTE
I took a "glassful of the jelly" to mean 1 cup.

MARCH 17, 1940: "VICTUALS AND VITAMINS," BY
KILEY TAYLOR.

—1940

☙ SAUCE SUPRÊME

This eggy, boozy sauce, adapted from Schrafft's restaurant in New York City, was supposed to be served with
blueberry waffles, but it would go well with almost any
dessert. It is nearly the same as the Foamy Sauce on p.
603, but I included them both because this one contains an important distinguishing ingredient: salt.

————

2 large eggs, separated

5 tablespoons light brown sugar

1 cup heavy cream

3 tablespoons rum

¼ teaspoon salt

1. Whisk together the egg yolks and ¼ cup sugar in a
large bowl until thickened. Whip the egg whites with

the remaining tablespoon of sugar in another bowl until they form stiff peaks. Whip the cream in another bowl until it also holds stiff peaks.

2. Fold the whites into the yolks, followed by the cream. Fold in the rum and salt, blending well. The sauce will keep in the fridge for up to a week.

MAKES ABOUT 6 CUPS

SERVING SUGGESTION

If you'd like to serve this with waffles, try the Amazing Overnight Waffles on p. 642.

JULY 7, 1940: "VICTUALS AND VITAMINS," BY KILEY TAYLOR. RECIPE ADAPTED FROM SCHRAFFT'S RESTAURANT IN NEW YORK CITY.

—1940

FRENCH DRESSING

The classic proportions, in case you don't already know them.

———

I clove garlic
¼ teaspoon salt
Freshly ground black pepper
½ teaspoon Colman's prepared mustard
I tablespoon red wine vinegar
3 tablespoons olive oil
Lettuce, including some watercress

Rub a salad bowl with the garlic clove. Add the salt, pepper to taste, and mustard. Stir in the vinegar until the mixture is smooth. Gradually whisk in the olive oil until thick, shiny, and emulsified. Adjust the seasoning.

MAKES ¼ CUP

COOKING NOTE

After the dressing is made, Kiley Taylor, a *Times* columnist, instructs you to add lettuce, "washed and dried and chilled," to the dressing and turn and toss "until each sprig glistens. And be sure to put in some watercress."

VARIATION

For sauce vinaigrette, Taylor said to replace the red wine vinegar with 2 teaspoons cider vinegar and 1 teaspoon tarragon vinegar and add chopped pickles and green pepper (no amounts given) and 1 teaspoon each chopped parsley and chives.

APRIL 13, 1941: "VICTUALS AND VITAMINS: THE QUESTION OF OIL AND VINEGAR," BY KILEY TAYLOR.

—1941

GREEN MAYONNAISE

If you're using store-bought mayonnaise—I used Hellmann's—season it with lemon juice before adding the herbs. If you'd like to make your own mayonnaise, there's an excellent recipe on p. 465.

———

I tablespoon thinly sliced chives
I tablespoon finely chopped tarragon
I½ tablespoons finely chopped flat-leaf parsley
I teaspoon finely chopped chervil
I teaspoon finely chopped dill
About ½ cup mayonnaise
Lemon juice to taste (if using store-bought mayonnaise)
Salt

Combine the herbs in a bowl. Add the mayonnaise (blended with lemon juice if using store-bought) a little at a time, tasting as you go, until you have something you like. Season with salt if needed.

MAKES ¾ CUP

SERVING SUGGESTIONS

Spread on sandwiches, dollop on a warm, ripe tomato half, or use as a dipping sauce for artichokes and asparagus.

APRIL 13, 1941: "VICTUALS AND VITAMINS: THE QUESTION OF OIL AND VINEGAR," BY KILEY TAYLOR.

—1941

⤙ SLICED GREEN TOMATO PICKLES

2½ pounds medium green tomatoes

6 tablespoons kosher salt

2 cups cider vinegar (5% acidity)

¾ cup granulated sugar

½ cup packed dark brown sugar

2 tablespoons mustard seeds

I teaspoon celery seeds

1½ teaspoons turmeric

2¼ pounds onions, sliced

2 large green bell peppers, cored, seeded, and chopped

I hot red chile, chopped

1. Slice the tomatoes into wedges (8 to 10 per tomato). Toss with the salt in a bowl, cover, and let stand in a cool place overnight.

2. Bring the vinegar, sugars, mustard seeds, celery seeds, and turmeric to a boil in a large enameled cast-iron or other nonreactive pot. Add the onions and cook for 5 minutes. Add the tomatoes and peppers and bring to a boil, then reduce the heat and simmer for 5 minutes, stirring often.

3. Have ready 12 sterilized half-pint jars with screw bands and new lids (see Cooking Notes, p. 589). Simmer the lids in hot water to soften the rubberized flange. Ladle the pickle into the jars leaving ½-inch headspace. Remove any air bubbles trapped in the jars by running a sterilized butter knife between the sides of the jars and the pickles. Wipe the rim. Put the lids on and screw on the bands fingertip tight.

4. Place the jars on a rack in a big pot and cover with 2 to 3 inches of water. Cover the pot and bring to a boil over high heat, then lower the heat to medium and boil gently for 10 minutes. Remove the lid and then, after about 5 minutes, remove the jars. Allow the jars to cool, untouched, for 4 to 6 hours.

5. Check the seals, and store in a cool, dark place for up to a year. Refrigerate after opening.

MAKES 12 HALF-PINTS

SEPTEMBER 19, 1944: "NEWS OF FOOD: GREEN TOMATOES PUT TO GOOD USE IN MAKING OF PICKLES AND RELISHES," BY JANE HOLT.

—1944

⤙ PICKLED WATERMELON RIND

The rind is to the flesh of a watermelon as mace is to nutmeg—it retains the crispness of the flesh, but it has a tart vegetal flavor. Here the rind is suspended in a sweet and tart syrup, infused with allspice, cloves, cinnamon, and lemon zest.

This recipe was part of a story geared toward city dwellers who didn't have the space necessary to make large batches of pickles and preserves. Jane Nickerson, the *Times* columnist who wrote the story, made the still-valid point that pickling and preserving can be done in small batches so the work is more like darning a sock than sewing a pleated skirt.

------

3 pounds watermelon rind (from a medium watermelon)

6 cups cold water

¼ cup canning salt

I tablespoon allspice berries

I tablespoon whole cloves

2 tablespoons broken cinnamon sticks

½ cup water

1½ cups cider vinegar (5% acidity)

2 cups light corn syrup

1½ cups sugar

Zest of ½ lemon—removed in strips with a vegetable peeler

1. Cut the watermelon rind into large pieces. Use a vegetable peeler to remove the green skin. Use a spoon to scoop out any remaining pink flesh. Cut the rind into 1-inch squares and measure: there should be about 8 cups.

2. Mix the cold water with the salt in a bowl large enough to hold the rind. Add the rind and allow to stand overnight.

3. Drain and rinse the rind. Place in a large saucepan, cover with water, and bring to a simmer. Simmer until tender, 8 to 10 minutes. Drain.

4. Tie the spices in a piece of cheesecloth. Combine the spices, ½ cup water, vinegar, corn syrup, sugar, and lemon zest in a large enameled cast-iron or other nonreactive saucepan and bring to a boil. Add the watermelon rind and simmer until translucent, about 45 minutes. Remove the spice bag.

5. Have ready 5 sterilized half-pint jars with screw bands and new lids (see Cooking Notes, p. 589).

Simmer the lids in hot water to soften the rubberized flange. Pack the pickle into the jars and cover with the syrup, leaving ½-inch headspace. Remove any air bubbles trapped in the jars by running a sterilized butter knife between the sides of the jars and the pickles. Wipe the rim. Put the lids on and screw on the bands fingertip tight.

6. Place the jars on a rack in a big pot and cover with 2 to 3 inches of water. Cover the pot and bring to a boil over high heat, then lower the heat to medium and boil gently for 10 minutes. Remove the lid and then, after about 5 minutes, remove the jars. Allow the jars to cool, untouched, for 4 to 6 hours.

7. Check the seals, and store in a cool, dark place for up to a year. Refrigerate after opening.

MAKES ABOUT 5 HALF-PINTS

COOKING NOTE
Do not process a half-packed jar, or you risk compromising the seal. If your rind doesn't fit evenly into jars, fill up as many as you can, and eat the remaining rind—problem solved!

SERVING SUGGESTIONS
Mint Julep (p. 24), North Carolina–Style Pulled Pork (p. 550), Old South Buttermilk Biscuits (p. 655), Summer Squash Casserole (p. 252), Fresh Succotash (p. 275), Docks Coleslaw (p. 191), Buttermilk Pie (p. 859)

JULY 17, 1946: "NEWS OF FOOD: PICKLING AND PRESERVING IN SMALL LOTS NOW ECONOMICAL FOR CITY HOUSEWIFE," BY JANE NICKERSON.

—1946

⌒ BRANDIED PEACHES

Canning fruit, like many domestic arts, has traveled the diminishing path from a technique universally practiced to a craft reserved for those with the luxury of time. But time is all we have, and I vote for spending that time eating delicious food.

The time it takes to can a few peaches will be rewarded with hours of eating well. Think of it this way: if you choose to watch a rerun of *Friends* rather than whip up some canned peaches one night this summer, in the middle of February you'll find yourself eating Chunky Monkey for dessert when you could be indulging in a bowl of juicy peaches, lightly glazed in syrup.

Many of the traditional modes of canning peaches—peach jam, peach chutney, canned peach halves—are still common today. Brandied peaches, however, which were popular as far back as the nineteenth century, are now a relic of old cookbooks. It's time to rectify this historical misjudgment: brandied peaches not only taste better than other canned peaches—with each bit of sweetness, you get a little zing—they're remarkably handy. For a simple dessert, I like to spoon the peaches into small bowls and splash them with cream. You can also blend them into ice cream, add them to a drink, or slip a few into a sauce for pork.

When I tasted a batch of these with Eugenia Bone, the author of *Well-Preserved*, she said, "Can't you see people having them after some continental-style dinner in Westport?" It's true: they're boozy and restrained, and they'd go perfectly with chintz.

———

3 pounds ripe peaches
3 cups water
3 cups sugar
About ½ cup brandy

1. Bring a large pot of water to a boil. Using the tip of a paring knife, make a shallow X in the bottom of each peach. Add the peaches a few at a time to the boiling water and cook for 1 minute, then plunge into a bowl of ice water. Peel the peaches, then pit and quarter them.

2. Combine the 3 cups water and sugar in a large pot and bring to a boil, stirring to dissolve the sugar. Add the peaches and cook until just soft (time will depend on the ripeness of the fruit).

3. Have ready 2 scalded pint jars with screw bands and new lids. (To scald, see Cooking Notes, p. 589.) Simmer the lids in hot water to soften the rubberized flange. Using a slotted spoon, gently pack the peaches into the jars.

4. Boil the poaching syrup until it thickens slightly, then spoon it over the fruit, filling the jars three-quarters full. Remove any air bubbles trapped in the

jars by running a sterilized butter knife between the sides of the jars and the peaches. Pour in enough brandy to fill the jars, leaving ½-inch headspace. Wipe the rims. Put the lids on and screw on the bands fingertip tight.

5. Place the jars on a rack in a big pot and cover with 2 to 3 inches of water. Cover the pot and bring to a boil over high heat, then lower the heat to medium and gently boil for 20 minutes. Remove the lid and then, after about 5 minutes, remove the jars. Allow the jars to cool, untouched, for 4 to 6 hours.

6. Check the seals, and store in a cool, dark place for up to a year. Refrigerate after opening.

MAKES 2 PINTS

COOKING NOTES

Three pounds of peaches yielded 1 quart of brandied peaches. The recipe can be doubled, tripled, even sextupled!

If there's no brandy in your house, substitute bourbon, rum, or an eau-de-vie.

SERVING SUGGESTIONS

Keep the canning syrup simple, and get creative once you open the jar. Slice the peaches and arrange them between layers of a cake. Douse them with cream and accompany with ginger cookies. Add some to your granola for a breakfast of champions.

AUGUST 18, 1946: "PUTTING UP PEACHES," BY JANE NICKERSON.

—1946

BREAD-AND-BUTTER PICKLES

The molasses turns the pickles the color of stained wood, which may needlessly alarm anyone who grew up on the golden green kind. If you want them golden, use regular sugar.

———

4 cups thinly sliced Kirby cucumbers (about 2 pounds)
2 cups sliced onions
¼ cup kosher salt
Ice cubes

2 cups white vinegar (5% acidity)
¾ cup molasses or 1½ cups sugar
2 teaspoons celery seeds
2 teaspoons mustard seeds
1½ teaspoons turmeric

1. Combine the cucumbers, onions, and salt in a large bowl and stir to mix. Cover with ice cubes and refrigerate for 4 to 8 hours. Drain.

2. Combine the vinegar, molasses, celery seeds, mustard seeds, and turmeric in a large pot, bring to a boil, and boil gently for 10 minutes. Add the cucumbers and onions, and slowly bring to a boil again.

3. Have ready 3 sterilized pint jars with screw bands and new lids (see Cooking Notes, p. 589). Simmer the lids in hot water to soften the rubberized flange. Pack the pickles into the jars and cover with the pickling solution, leaving ½-inch headspace. Remove any air bubbles trapped in the jars by running a sterilized butter knife between the sides of the jars and the pickles. Wipe the rims. Put the lids on and screw on the bands fingertip tight.

4. Place the jars on a rack in a big pot and cover with 2 to 3 inches of water. Cover the pot and bring to a boil over high heat, then lower the heat to medium and gently boil the jars for 10 minutes. Remove the lid and then, after about 5 minutes, remove the jars. Allow the jars to cool, untouched, for 4 to 6 hours.

5. Check the seals, and store in a cool, dark place for up to a year. Refrigerate after opening.

MAKES 3 PINTS

AUGUST 28, 1946: "NEWS OF FOOD: HOW TO SELECT VEGETABLES FOR PICKLING, AND SOME TIPS ON CANNING THEM AT HOME," BY JANE NICKERSON.

—1946

NEW ENGLAND GRAPE BUTTER

Among common American grape varietals, the Concord is probably the most peculiar, a "slipskin"—its tart covering acts like a separate shell encasing the fragrant pulp and seeds, so with a gentle pinch, you can pull the skin from the fruit. In a perfect world, the grape would lose its seeds as well, and you'd just eat the fragrant pulp. However, the Concord became popular not because it's easy to eat, but because it was one of the few varieties that could survive New England's harsh winters. It was bred for hardiness in the nineteenth century by Ephraim Wales Bull, a farmer outside of Boston, who, despite honors from the Boston Horticultural Society, apparently never felt he got the credit he deserved. His tombstone bears the inscription "He sowed—others reaped."

Concords are best pressed into juice or cooked. As Jane Nickerson, the columnist who wrote the piece, noted, grape butter is a good use of the fruit because it's "easiest to make and useful in these days of high prices for dairy butter." Grape butter is a little thicker than jelly, and it's hard to ruin.

———

Concord grapes stemmed
Sugar

1. Place the grapes in a sturdy pot, large enough that the grapes come just halfway up the sides. Add cold water to barely cover the bottom of the pot, place over medium heat, and cook until the skins pop and the pulp starts to break down. Let cool slightly.

2. Pass the grapes and liquid through the finest plate of a food mill. Measure the liquid and pulp. Clean the pot and add the grape juice and pulp. Add half as much sugar. Place over medium heat, bring to a simmer, and simmer, stirring occasionally, until the mixture is thick enough to spread. As it gets closer to being done, turn the heat down to avoid scorching the butter. The thicker the butter gets, the greater the chance it will scorch. Test it by spooning a small amount onto a plate and letting it cool: it should be a little stiffer than jelly.

3. Have ready 1 sterilized half-pint jar with a screw band and new lid for every 1½ pounds of grapes (see Cooking Notes, p. 589). Simmer the lids in hot water to soften the rubberized flange. Spoon the butter into the jars, leaving ¼-inch headspace. Use a sterilized butter knife to remove any air bubbles that may have become trapped in the jars. Wipe the rims. Put the lids on and screw on the bands fingertip tight.

4. Place the jars on a rack in a big pot and cover with 2 to 3 inches of water. Cover the pot and bring to a boil over high heat, then lower the heat to medium and gently boil the jars for 10 minutes. Remove the lid and then, after about 5 minutes, remove the jars. Allow the jars to cool, untouched, for 4 to 6 hours.

5. Check the seals, and store in a cool, dark place for up to a year. Refrigerate after opening.

COOKING NOTES

This recipe can be prepared with any amount of grapes. I started with 1½ pounds. After the initial cooking and straining, this yielded 3 cups of juice. I added 1½ cups of sugar to the juice. Once reduced and thickened, this made about 1¼ cups of grape butter.

Fruit butters are best cooked in a heavy pot, such as enameled cast-iron, to reduce the risk of scorching.

Fruit butter is ready when it mounds on a spoon and when a ring of liquid does not separate around the edge of the butter.

PERIOD DETAIL

The 1947 grape crop was a whopper, according to Nickerson's article. California produced 3,000,000 tons of grapes, 600,000 tons of which were eaten fresh. You would think that with huge growth in the wine industry over the most recent decade, those numbers would be much greater today, but the total grape harvest in 2005, another record year, was just 4,300,000 tons.

OCTOBER 4, 1947: "NEWS OF FOOD: THIS IS THE SEASON FOR GRAPES, AND CROPS ON EAST, WEST COASTS MAY BREAK RECORDS," BY JANE NICKERSON.

—1947

SAUCE RÉMOULADE (FOR SHRIMP)

———

¼ cup Creole mustard
2 tablespoons chopped cornichons, or other sour pickles
¾ cup French dressing
2 tablespoons chopped scallions
2 tablespoons prepared horseradish
    (drained a little if watery)
⅛ teaspoon cayenne pepper

Mix all the ingredients thoroughly. Chill and use to dress shrimp for a first course. Garnish with lettuce.

MAKES 1 CUP

Serve with shrimp, of course, and with Fried Green Tomatoes (p. 212) or Deep-Fried Soft-Shell Crabs (p. 398).

NOVEMBER 16, 1947: "FOOD: CREOLE FLAVOR," BY JANE NICKERSON.

—1947

⌒ TOMATO PRESERVES

Time has a way of winnowing recipes, leaving behind the forlorn and ill-conceived, those requiring pot-washing marathons. And because time doesn't look back, great foods occasionally get lost along the way. But, really, how could we have let tomato preserves slip away?

A few years ago, I began spotting *marmellata di pomodori*, tomato marmalade, a seemingly exotic novelty from the land of culinary wisdom in New York restaurants and shops. It seemed so perfectly Mediterranean, emitting warmth, intensity, and the promise of a lifestyle we will never have. Only we didn't actually need to import it, because we had already done so long ago.

"Americans were big preservers," said Stephen Schmidt, a culinary historian and the author of the forthcoming book *Dessert in America*. Homemakers going back to the eighteenth century put up tomatoes in syrup, then served them on their own with custard or as a condiment for desserts like sago pudding, a tapioca-like dish. Later came tomato jelly and jam (sometimes called marmalade). These tomato recipes, which appeared in many cookbooks, including *The Virginia House-Wife* and *The Fannie Farmer Cookbook*, often contained lemon or ginger, and the preserves in syrup were sometimes made with yellow tomatoes. "One of the criteria for these preserves was for the syrup to be clear," Schmidt said. "That was a point of pride. Women clarified the sugar before making the preserve." (Clarifying is no longer necessary now that sugar is commercially produced.)

In 1948, the heyday of canned foods and the sunset of tomato jelly and preserves, Jane Nickerson wrote up this recipe, which could have been dated a century earlier. You begin by peeling tomatoes and simmering them whole in a syrup scented with lemon, cloves,

cinnamon, and slivers of fresh ginger. The tomatoes tint the syrup the color of embers and, if cooked correctly (that is, gently), never become part of it. Instead you simmer until the tomatoes' flesh brightens and becomes translucent at the edges. Then you pack them into jars and cover them with the syrup. They are sublime looking and tasting: tender like a plum, with a concentrated, persistent fragrance like jasmine.

Not every fruit can be made into a preserve. You need a fruit whose structure is strong enough to withstand the long simmering. Tomatoes are perfect because they have a firm flesh that likes to soak up syrup and spices, and juice that readily thickens.

The best tomatoes for this recipe are firm plum tomatoes—Nickerson even called for slightly under-ripe fruit—but you can use almost any type. Just avoid mushy, soggy heirlooms, which would be pointless here (and generally).

As with some of the other preserve recipes in this book, the quantities are dependent on the number of tomatoes you want to preserve. Seven pounds will yield approximately 8 pints of preserves. But you can use any amount you like—it's all about proportions.

———

Small slightly underripe plum tomatoes

For Each Pound of Cored and Peeled Tomatoes
¾ pound sugar (1½ cups)
3 whole cloves
1 cinnamon stick
¼ lemon, thinly sliced, seeds discarded
One ¼-inch slice peeled fresh ginger

1. Core the tomatoes, then skin them by cutting a shallow X in their rounded ends and dipping them in boiling water for 30 seconds. Peel. If the tomatoes are large, slice them in half across the middle and remove their seeds. Weigh the tomatoes, then measure the sugar and spices.
2. Leave tomatoes that are smaller than an egg whole; if they're larger, thickly slice them. (If using round tomatoes, cut the halves into thick wedges.) Arrange the tomatoes and sugar in layers in a deep heavy pot (enameled cast-iron works best). Cover and let stand overnight—no need to refrigerate.
3. The next day, tie the spices in a square of cheesecloth. Add the spice bag to the tomatoes, along with the sliced lemon and ginger and bring to a simmer

over medium heat. Cook, stirring occasionally, until the tomatoes have become slightly translucent and the syrup is thick and beginning to gel—it's ready when a spoonful dropped onto a plate sets when cool. Don't boil the syrup, or the tomatoes will fall apart. If the tomatoes become translucent before the syrup thickens, remove them from the pan with a slotted spoon and reduce the syrup over medium-high heat until thickened, then return the tomatoes to the syrup and bring to a boil. Remove from the heat, remove the spice bag, and skim off the foam.

4. Have ready 1 scalded half-pint jar with a screw band and new lid for every cup of preserve. (To scald, see Cooking Notes, p. 589.) Simmer the lids in hot water to soften the rubberized flange. Using a slotted spoon, fill the jars three-quarters full with tomatoes and lemons (or save the lemons to eat separately), then cover the tomatoes with syrup leaving 1/4-inch headspace. Remove any air bubbles trapped in the jars by running a sterilized butter knife between the sides of the jars and the preserves. Wipe the rims. Put the lids on and screw on the bands fingertip tight.

5. Place the jars on a rack in a big pot and cover with 2 to 3 inches of water. Cover the pot and bring to a boil over high heat, then lower the heat to medium and boil gently for 20 minutes. Remove the lid and then, after about 5 minutes, remove the jars. Allow the jars to cool, untouched, for 4 to 6 hours.

6. Check the seals, and store in a cool, dark place for up to a year. Refrigerate after opening.

I POUND TOMATOES MAKES I CUP

COOKING NOTES

This is best made with at least 3 pounds of tomatoes. Using level pounds makes the math easier. Buy the smallest plum tomatoes you can find so you can leave them whole.

The tomatoes can easily burn, as I learned. Once most of the liquid cooks off, stay close to the stove, and stir gently now and then to prevent the tomatoes from sticking and caramelizing.

If you don't have cheesecloth, a tea ball works well for holding the spices.

If you cut the tomatoes into wedges, they may fall apart during cooking. No worries, your preserve syrup may not be clear, but it will taste just as good.

SERVING SUGGESTIONS
Spoon this onto toasted country bread, spread with European butter or fresh ricotta. Finish with a pinch of fleur de sel. Or spread on a corn-bread biscuit with a thin slice of country ham.

AUGUST I, 1948: "COUNTRY PRESERVES," BY JANE NICKERSON. RECIPES BY RUTH P. CASA-EMELLOS, THE HEAD OF THE *NEW YORK TIMES* TEST KITCHEN.

—1948

⌒ FOAMY SAUCE

What this recipe produces is at first neither foamy nor sauce-like. But foamy sauce is what the mixture becomes when you spoon it on top of a warm pudding and the tight bond of meringue, whipped cream, and brandy slowly dissolves into a creamy, foamy river of sauce.

————

I large egg, separated
1/2 cup confectioners' sugar
3/4 cup heavy cream
1/2 teaspoon vanilla extract, or brandy, sherry, or rum to taste

Beat the egg white in a medium bowl until it's stiff. Gradually add the sugar and beat until the mixture forms stiff peaks. Beat the egg yolk and fold it into the meringue. Whip the cream to soft peaks, then fold into the meringue. Add the vanilla.

MAKES ABOUT 2 CUPS

SERVING SUGGESTIONS
Spoon this over Aztec Hot Chocolate Pudding (p. 855) or Indian Pudding (p. 809).

DECEMBER 12, 1948: "CHRISTMAS SAUCES," BY JANE NICKERSON. RECIPE ADAPTED FROM RUTH P. CASA-EMELLOS, THE HEAD OF THE *NEW YORK TIMES* TEST KITCHEN.

—1948

✎ SPICED HARD SAUCE

Hard sauce is really just sweetened and spiced butter. Pass it at the table with a warm pudding or cake (such as the Indian Pudding on p. 809 or Mary Ann's Fruitcake—warmed—on p. 660) so when guests shave off a slice of sauce, they can watch it collapse over the dessert.

———

12 tablespoons (1½ sticks) unsalted butter, softened
1 cup confectioners' sugar
½ teaspoon ground cinnamon
½ teaspoon freshly grated nutmeg
1 teaspoon bourbon, rum, or vanilla extract

Cream the butter with an electric mixer in a medium bowl. Gradually beat in the sugar, cinnamon, and nutmeg and continue whipping until very light. Add the bourbon. Chill until firm.

MAKES ABOUT 1 CUP

PERIOD DETAIL
In a story from 1880, when a female writer took a tour of Delmonico's kitchen, she wrote that she was "amazed at a man who patiently turns the handle of something which looks like a churn. 'What might that be?' he is asked. 'Hard sauce,' is the reply. 'Fifty pounds of the best fresh butter, about the same of sugar, and a pound of nutmeg, with four quarts of lemon-juice; it takes three hours hard working; the boss do say he is going to run her by machinery, and I wish he would,' and the hard-sauce compounder wipes his forehead."

DECEMBER 11, 1966: "SEASON FOR SWEETS," BY CRAIG CLAIBORNE.

—1966

✎ FLORENCE LA GANKE'S THREE-DAY MARMALADE

Florence La Ganke, a food editor for the *Cleveland Plain Dealer*, published this marmalade recipe in 1929 in *Patty Pans*, a cookbook for children. The recipe resurfaced half a century later, when it was printed in a cookbook intended for people with small kitchens, called *Claustrophobic Cooking*. Marmalade can be prepared surprisingly easily in a tiny space if you use La Ganke's method, which involves the use of a knife, a single pot, a wooden spoon, and a jar.

———

1 grapefruit
1 orange
1 lemon
Sugar

1. On the first day, slice the fruit as thin as possible; discard the ends and remove the seeds. Barely cover with cold water in a china or enamel bowl. Leave overnight at room temperature, covered.
2. On the second day, put the mixture in a medium heavy enameled cast-iron or other nonreactive saucepan, bring to a boil, and boil for 30 minutes. Cover and leave at room temperature overnight.
3. On the third day, measure the fruit mixture and return to the pan. Add an equal amount of sugar (decrease the amount by half a cup overall if you prefer a tart marmalade). Cook over low heat, stirring frequently to prevent burning. After 45 minutes, test on a cold saucer for thickness. If it is still runny, cook a little longer. The marmalade will take on a dark golden color as it cooks longer.
4. Have ready 5 sterilized half-pint jars with screw bands and new lids (see Cooking Notes, p. 589). Simmer the lids in hot water to soften the rubberized flange. Spoon the marmalade into the jars, leaving ¼-inch headspace. Remove any air bubbles trapped in the jars by running a sterilized butter knife between the side of the jars and the marmalade. Wipe the rims. Put the lids on and screw on the bands fingertip tight.
5. Place the jars on a rack in a big pot and cover with 2 to 3 inches of water. Cover the pot and bring to a boil over high heat, then lower the heat to medium and boil gently for 10 minutes. Remove the lid and then, after about 5 minutes, remove the jars. Allow the jars to cool, untouched, for 4 to 6 hours.
6. Check the seals, and store in a cool, dark place for up to a year. Refrigerate after opening.

MAKES 5 HALF-PINTS

COOKING NOTE

I had 4 cups of fruit mixture and used 3½ cups sugar, which made a pleasantly tart marmalade. The original recipe yielded 1 pint. This may be because citrus fruits were smaller then. My batch made 2½ pints.

JANUARY 31, 1974: "A WOMAN WHO LEARNED TO COOK HER WAY OUT OF TIGHT SPOTS," BY CRAIG CLAIBORNE. RECIPE ADAPTED FROM FLORENCE LA GANKE.

—1974

CREAMY SALAD DRESSING

Explaining the difference between what the French call dressing—a standard vinaigrette—and French dressing, Craig Claiborne and Pierre Franey wrote, "What Americans call 'French dressing' is a creamy concoction which coats the greens in a way that the basic French dressing does not. It is made of oil, vinegar, a trifling amount of egg yolk, plus a touch of heavy cream to thin it. It is, in fact, like a mayonnaise. The heavy cream tends to give a smoothness to the dressing, and it also prevents the dressing from 'breaking down' or separating once it is made."

---

1 large egg yolk
2 teaspoons Dijon or Düsseldorf mustard
Tabasco sauce
½ teaspoon finely chopped garlic
Salt and freshly ground black pepper
1 teaspoon vinegar
½ cup peanut, vegetable, or corn oil
2 teaspoons fresh lemon juice
1 teaspoon heavy cream

Beat the egg yolk, and add 1 teaspoon of it to a bowl (discard the rest). Whisk in the mustard, a dash or two of Tabasco, and the garlic. Season with salt and pepper. Add the vinegar and whisk vigorously to blend. While whisking, gradually add the oil, beating until thickened and well blended. Add the lemon juice. Beat in the heavy cream. At this point you should taste the salad dressing. Add more of the following to taste: salt, pepper, mustard, or lemon juice.

MAKES ABOUT ¾ CUP

APRIL 30, 1978: "FOOD: COATING THE GREENS," BY CRAIG CLAIBORNE WITH PIERRE FRANEY.

—1978

SIMPLE COOKED TOMATO SAUCE

6 ripe tomatoes
4 tablespoons unsalted butter
Salt and freshly ground black pepper

1. Cut an X in the bottom of each tomato. Put enough water to cover the tomatoes in a pot and bring to a boil. Turn off the heat, drop the tomatoes in, and let stand for 1 minute. Drain the tomatoes, rinse under cold water, and peel off the skins.
2. Coarsely chop the tomatoes and put them, juice and all, into a saucepan. Bring to a boil and cook down, stirring often, until reduced by a third or half. If you like a smoother sauce, pass the tomatoes and juice through a food mill.
3. Turn off the heat, stir in the butter until all is well blended, and season with salt and pepper. The sauce keeps in the fridge for up to a week; it can also be frozen for up to 3 months.

MAKES ABOUT 2 CUPS; SERVES 2 TO 4

AUGUST 21, 1983: "THE SEASON OF VEGETABLE EXTRAVAGANCE: EXPLOITING THE RICH DIVERSITY OF SHAPES," BY ROBERT FARRAR CAPON.

—1983

BRIE BUTTER WITH FRESH BREAD

If all goes well, you will experience bliss. If your Brie is at all bitter (make sure you remove every last bit of the rind), you will experience slightly bitter Brie butter.

½ pound Brie

8 tablespoons (1 stick) unsalted butter, softened

¼ cup dry white wine

Sea salt

1 loaf bread

1. Remove the rind from the cheese and bring to room temperature.

2. Blend the Brie with the butter and wine in a food processor until very smooth. Season to taste with salt. Spoon the cheese into a crock and chill to firm up.

3. Serve with sliced bread.

MAKES 1½ CUPS

VARIATION

Bryan Miller, a *Times* food writer and former restaurant critic, included this alternative: "This compound butter can be made with any combination of cheese and liquid—another possibility is Cheddar and beer, a kind of Welsh rarebit butter. It will last a long time and freezes well."

OCTOBER 23, 1983: "TAILGATE FEASTS," BY BRYAN MILLER.

—1983

✎ CRANBERRY CHUTNEY

Cardamom, honey, and apricots give this chutney a sweet, exotic flavor without overriding the tartness of the cranberries.

———

1 cup orange juice

One 12-ounce bag (3 cups) fresh cranberries

1 juice orange, halved, seeded, and finely chopped (skin and all)

1 tart apple, cored and chopped

12 dried apricots, chopped

Approximately 1¼ cups honey

½ teaspoon ground cardamom

1. Place the orange juice, cranberries, and chopped orange in a saucepan, bring to a boil, and cook over medium heat until the berries begin to pop.

2. Add the apple, apricots, 1¼ cups honey, and the cardamom and cook for 10 to 20 minutes, until

reduced a bit and more of a uniform sauce, as opposed to fruit and liquid. Adjust the sweetness if desired.

MAKES ABOUT 6 CUPS; SERVES 8 TO 10

NOVEMBER 25, 1987: "THE NO-PANIC, COOK-IN-A-DAY THANKSGIVING MEAL PLAN," BY FLORENCE FABRICANT.

—1987

✎ SCHRAFFT'S HOT FUDGE

Schrafft's, a candy company that opened in 1861 and had a restaurant in New York City, finally shared its recipe for hot fudge an arbitrary 127 years later. As it turns out, it's actually two recipes in one. I first followed the original instruction, which said to cook the fudge sauce to 220 degrees. But if you do this, you no longer have sauce, you have caramelized fudge candy. I poured the hot mixture onto a baking sheet, and once it cooled and firmed up, I snipped it into pieces and ate it as candy. (I recommend trying this.) Then I remade the recipe, this time cooking the mixture to a tamer 150 degrees, which produces a glossy, limpid sauce.

———

2 tablespoons unsweetened cocoa powder

¼ cup sugar

¾ cup heavy cream

½ cup light corn syrup

1 ounce semisweet chocolate, chopped

1 tablespoon salted butter

A few drops of malt or cider vinegar

½ teaspoon vanilla extract

1. Mix the cocoa, sugar, and ¼ cup heavy cream in a heavy saucepan until smooth. Stir in the remaining ½ cup cream, the corn syrup, chocolate, butter, and vinegar and bring to a boil, stirring. Boil over medium heat for 7 to 8 minutes, until smooth and glossy, or until the mixture reaches 150 degrees on a candy thermometer.

2. Remove from the heat, stir in the vanilla, and allow to stand for about 3 minutes before serving.

MAKES 1 SCANT CUP

Strawberry Ice Cream (p. 722), Tea Ice Cream (p. 717), Sour Cream Ice Cream (p. 730)

JUNE 15, 1988: "SCHRAFFT'S HOT FUDGE, TO MAKE AT HOME." RECIPE ADAPTED FROM SCHRAFFT'S RESTAURANT IN NEW YORK CITY.

—1988

JOHN BERWALD'S DRY RUB

There is nothing exotic or esoteric about this recipe, and that's why it's great. It's a straight-shooting rub that's spicy but not unbearably so and would make any grilling fanatic happy. It comes from John Berwald, a former art gallery owner who started Armadillo Willy's Real Texas BBQ, a chain on the West Coast.

I spread about 1/2 cup of the rub on a rack of baby back ribs, laid the ribs on a baking sheet lined with foil, and baked them for 3 hours at 225 degrees. They were superb, and they didn't lack the smoke or crispness you get from the grill (though that wouldn't have hurt).

————

1/2 cup packed brown sugar
1/2 cup salt
1/2 cup freshly ground black pepper
1/2 cup paprika
2 tablespoons garlic powder
2 tablespoons onion powder
I tablespoon cayenne pepper

Combine all the ingredients and stir well. Rub the mixture on beef, poultry, and pork before barbecuing. It keeps indefinitely, tightly sealed.

MAKES ABOUT 2½ CUPS (ENOUGH FOR ABOUT 6 BRISKETS)

JULY 3, 1988: "SAVORING BARBECUE," BY MARIAN BURROS. RECIPE ADAPTED FROM JOHN BERWALD.

—1988

RHUBARB-GINGER COMPOTE

You might have read the title of this recipe and thought, oh, I've made that, but chances are you haven't. First of all, this is not a dessert sauce. Second, it's exceptionally good, much better, in my view, than most rhubarb and ginger recipes. The compote (the English language's horrible word, not mine) seems at once sweet and savory. You almost want to put it on ice cream, but then you find yourself thinking of fatty pork belly, and then toast, and then cheese, and finally salmon. Most savory rhubarb sauces aren't quite good enough to make that critical leap from brief fascination to enduring standby. This one does.

————

2 teaspoons olive oil
2 shallots, minced
2 cloves garlic, minced
2 tablespoons grated fresh ginger
2 cups water
I cup sugar
4 cups 1/4-inch-thick slices trimmed rhubarb
2 tablespoons plus 2 teaspoons rice wine vinegar
1/8 teaspoon salt
Freshly ground black pepper

1. Heat the olive oil in a medium saucepan over medium heat. Add the shallots and garlic and cook until softened, about 2 minutes. Add the ginger and cook, stirring, for 45 seconds. Add the water and sugar and bring to a boil, then reduce the heat so that the liquid barely simmers. Add the rhubarb and cook, without simmering, until the rhubarb is tender but still whole, 8 to 10 minutes.

2. Using a slotted spoon, remove the rhubarb to a bowl. Bring the liquid to a boil over medium heat. Cook, adding the juices that accumulate from the rhubarb (you will need to do this several times), until reduced to 1 cup, 30 to 40 minutes. It's done when it starts to bubble up the sides of the pan. Set aside to cool.

3. Stir the vinegar, salt, and pepper to taste into the reduced liquid. Stir in the rhubarb. Serve, or store in the refrigerator.

MAKES 2½ CUPS

MAY 15, 1994: "RHUBARB BITES," BY MOLLY O'NEILL.

—1994

⌘ KOSHER PICKLES
THE RIGHT WAY

If you've never pickled before, this is a great warm-up recipe because it doesn't involve boiling vinegar and hot-packing and all that. You just brine the cucumbers with a few aromatics and wait until they're pickled to your liking. Salted pickles won't store as long as those cured with vinegar, but these are so addictive they won't last long anyway.

———

1/3 cup kosher salt

I cup boiling water

2 pounds small Kirby cucumbers, washed and
    cut into halves or quarters

5 cloves garlic or more, smashed

I large bunch dill, with flowers, or 2 tablespoons
    dried dill plus I teaspoon dill seeds, or
    I tablespoon coriander seeds

1. Combine the salt and boiling water in a large bowl, stir to dissolve the salt. Add a handful of ice cubes to cool down the mixture, then add all the remaining ingredients. Add cold water to cover. Use a plate slightly smaller than the diameter of the bowl and a small weight to hold the cucumbers under the water. Set aside at room temperature.

2. Begin sampling the cucumbers after 2 hours if they are quartered, 4 hours if they are halved. In either case, it will probably take from 12 to 24 hours, or even 48 hours, for them to taste "pickley" enough to suit your taste. When they are, refrigerate them, still in the brine. The pickles will continue to ferment as they sit, more quickly at room temperature, more slowly in the refrigerator.

**MAKES ABOUT 32 PICKLE QUARTERS
(OR 16 HALVES)**

SEPTEMBER 13, 1995: "PICKLES: HOLDING THE COOKING, CANNING, VINEGAR, AND SUGAR," BY MARK BITTMAN.

—1995

⌘ HOLIDAY CRANBERRY
CHUTNEY

Although we may like traditional English-style chutneys, the message they convey isn't optimistic. There is a suggestion that whatever you're eating the chutney with isn't good enough on its own, that it needs this aggressively spiced condiment to mask its dullness. So why not rethink chutney, and employ it as it's used in Indian cooking, to complement an already full-flavored main dish? If your Thanksgiving turkey is boring, no chutney—not even this delicious one—can save it!

The chutney, which comes from the novelist Lee Smith, uses a smart technique: the fresh cranberries are added in three stages, so some berries are completely broken down while others are plump and full with juice. And the other fruits—raisins, apricots, lemons, oranges, and apple—act as a sweet counterbalance to the tart berries.

———

1/2 cup cider vinegar

2 1/4 cups packed light brown sugar

3/4 teaspoon curry powder

1/2 teaspoon ground ginger

1/4 teaspoon ground cloves

1/4 teaspoon ground allspice

1/2 teaspoon ground cinnamon

1 1/2 cups water

2 lemons, zest finely grated, white pith discarded,
    and fruit cut into sections

2 navel oranges, zest finely grated, white pith discarded,
    and fruit cut into sections

I tart apple, peeled, cored, and coarsely chopped

Two 12-ounce bags (6 cups) fresh cranberries

1/2 cup golden raisins

1/2 cup dried apricots

1/2 cup chopped pecans

1. Combine the vinegar, sugar, curry, ginger, cloves, allspice, cinnamon, and water in a large saucepan and bring to a boil, stirring until the sugar is dissolved, about 3 minutes. Add the lemon zest and lemon sections, orange zest and orange sections, and apple, reduce the heat, and simmer for 10 minutes.

2. Add 3 cups cranberries, the raisins, and apricots and simmer, stirring occasionally, until thickened, about 35 minutes.

3. Add another 2 cups cranberries and simmer for 10 more minutes.

4. Add the remaining cup of cranberries and the pecans and simmer the mixture for 15 minutes longer. Pour the chutney into a bowl and let cool. Refrigerate overnight (or for up to 2 weeks) before using.

MAKES 6 CUPS

SERVING SUGGESTIONS

Serve this with Roasted Brine-Cured Turkey (p. 474) or Slow-Roasted Duck (p. 475).

READERS

"Besides using it instead of 'regular' cranberry sauce, I have used leftovers as a filling for crumb bar cookies."
Sherine Levine, Brooklyn, NY, letter

DECEMBER 22, 1996: "BELLE LETTERS," BY MOLLY O'NEILL. RECIPE ADAPTED FROM LEE SMITH, AUTHOR OF *THE CHRISTMAS LETTERS*.

—1996

⌐ SWEET-AND-PULPY TOMATO KETCHUP

Andrew Smith, author of *Pure Ketchup*, tells us that the word "ketchup" means any sauce made from a single ingredient that is spiced. It derives from the Chinese *ke-tsiap*, fermented fish sauce, a variation of which the British discovered in Indonesia in the seventeenth century. They began making the sauce with their own ingredients—like anchovies, mushrooms, and spices—eventually expanding the ingredients and definition of the sauce.

Commercial tomato ketchup arose from the thrift of tomato canneries. Irregular or damaged tomatoes unfit for canning were used to make a ketchup so cheap and convenient that by the end of World War II home production had almost died out.

This ketchup is a convincing antidote to the commercial stuff—it has texture, a nod to sweetness, and a bright infusion of spices that are steeped in the ketchup rather than cooked until they have nothing left to say.

———

10 medium ripe tomatoes, peeled (see Cooking Note, p. 146), cored, and quartered
2 medium onions, minced
2 red chiles, seeded and minced
1½ teaspoons kosher salt
½ cup sugar
½ cup cider vinegar (5% acidity)
1 teaspoon paprika
1 teaspoon prepared horseradish
½ teaspoon black peppercorns
½ teaspoon allspice berries
½ teaspoon celery seeds
½ teaspoon ground cinnamon
½ teaspoon ground mace
½ teaspoon chopped fresh ginger
½ teaspoon chopped garlic
½ teaspoon whole cloves

1. Place the tomatoes in a large pot and simmer over low heat, stirring frequently, until they're soft. Press the tomatoes through a coarse sieve into a bowl; discard the seeds.

2. Combine the tomatoes, onions, and chiles in a large heavy pot, bring to a boil over high heat, and reduce until slightly thickened, about 10 minutes.

3. Reduce the heat to medium-low, add the salt, sugar, vinegar, paprika, and horseradish, and stir until the sugar is dissolved. Simmer, stirring occasionally to prevent scorching, until the ketchup is slightly looser than bottled ketchup, about 2½ hours.

4. Combine the peppercorns, allspice, celery seeds, cinnamon, mace, ginger, garlic, and cloves in a square of cheesecloth and tie it closed with kitchen string. Add to the ketchup and continue simmering, stirring to prevent scorching until thickened and no longer drippy, about 25 minutes. Remove the spice bag and discard.

5. Ladle into jars and let cool, then seal, and keep refrigerated. The ketchup will keep for up to a month.

MAKES 1½ CUPS

COOKING NOTE

The ketchup can be used immediately, but it improves

with 2 to 3 weeks' rest, it can also be frozen for up to 6 months.

OCTOBER 22, 1997: "ADVENTUROUS CHEFS POUR THE GLORY BACK INTO THE KETCHUP BOTTLE," BY AMANDA HESSER. RECIPE ADAPTED FROM *PURE KETCHUP*, BY ANDREW SMITH.

—1997

PRESERVED LEMONS WITH CARDAMOM AND BAY LEAVES

If you're planning to make a tagine, you may want to start 14 days ahead of time—seriously—by preparing these preserved lemons. Store-bought preserved lemons, if you can find them at all, are rarely anything you actually want to eat. The traditional recipe for preserved lemons is monastic: lemons, salt, and nothing else. *Times Magazine* food columnist Molly O'Neill's is more enthusiastic, with bay leaves and cardamom added for depth. You can dice them up to go with roasted chicken or grilled lamb or use them in O'Neill's Asparagus and Bulgur with Preserved-Lemon Dressing on p. 190 or her Fettuccine with Preserved Lemon and Roasted Garlic on p. 335.

6 medium lemons, scrubbed

½ cup kosher salt

1 tablespoon cardamom pods

3 bay leaves

1 cup fresh lemon juice (from about 4 lemons), more if needed

1. Cut the lemons lengthwise into quarters, leaving them attached at one end. Rub the flesh with a little of the salt. Place 1 tablespoon salt in the bottom of a sterilized wide-mouth quart jar or 2 sterilized wide-mouthed pint jars (see Cooking Notes, p. 589). Place the lemons in the jar alternately with the remaining salt, cardamom pods, and bay leaves, pressing on the lemons to fit them snugly into the jar(s). Pour in enough lemon juice to cover the lemons. Put on the lid(s) and screw on the band(s).

2. Refrigerate, shaking the jar(s) daily, for 2 to 3 weeks before using. Covered with liquid and tightly sealed,

preserved lemons will keep for several months in the refrigerator.

MAKES 6 PRESERVED LEMONS

COOKING NOTES

Because lemons vary in size, you may need more than 1 jar (I did), and if you do, you'll need more juice to fill up the jar—I needed the juice of 12 more lemons.

Over time, you may see some white residue on the lemons. It's OK: it's just a precipitate of salts, oil, and whatever is drawn from the pith by the salt.

You can leave out the cardamom and bay leaves if you want a classic preserved lemon.

MARCH 7, 1999: "FOOD: CURIOUS YELLOW," BY MOLLY O'NEILL.

—1999

ROMESCO SAUCE

Romesco, the pesto of Spain, is a synthesis of the best local ingredients: tomatoes, chiles, garlic, olives, nuts, and wine vinegar. Each is first elevated: the tomatoes and garlic are roasted. The chiles are soaked. The olives are made into oil. The nuts are toasted. Then they are all blended together into a puree, which can be coarse or silky, depending how you like it.

I've had the sauce in many versions, sometimes loose and sweet, sometimes thickened with bread. Once it was served alongside mayonnaise with fat, firm asparagus. Another time it was spooned over braised cod. And in several instances, it was dolloped onto a salad of frisée with black olives, white beans, and slivers of salt cod.

In and around Barcelona, they eat romesco with grilled calçots, a wintered-over onion. You can grill spring onions instead.

5 baseball-sized ripe tomatoes, cored and halved

8 large cloves garlic, unpeeled

Olive oil

Sea salt

⅓ cup blanched whole almonds

10 blanched whole hazelnuts

1 dried ancho chile pepper, soaked in
    very hot tap water for 20 minutes
2 jarred piquillo peppers
Aged sherry vinegar
Dry red wine, preferably from Priorat or Rioja

1. Heat the oven to 400 degrees. Place the tomatoes, cut side up, and garlic cloves in a medium roasting pan. Sprinkle with olive oil and season with salt. Roast for 15 minutes.

2. Reduce the oven heat to 350 degrees and roast the tomatoes for another 60 to 75 minutes until shriveled and concentrated. The garlic should be soft after 20 minutes; remove it and let cool.

3. Meanwhile, coat a small sauté pan with $1/8$ inch of olive oil and place over medium heat. When the oil shimmers, add the almonds and hazelnuts and cook until toasted a golden brown, about 2 minutes. Remove and cool on paper towels.

4. Remove the seeds from the ancho chile and discard. Scrape the thin layer of flesh from the skin. Place this pulp, along with the tomatoes, nuts, and piquillo peppers in a food processor. Squeeze the garlic from its skin and add it. Pulse a few times to blend and then, leaving the processor on, pour olive oil through the feed tube in a thin stream. The sauce should become thick and creamy, like a mayonnaise; about 1 cup oil should be enough. To sharpen it, season with salt and add a tablespoon or two of vinegar and red wine.

MAKES ABOUT 2 CUPS

COOKING NOTE
Jarred fire-roasted piquillo peppers are available at www.tienda.com and many gourmet markets.

SERVING SUGGESTIONS
Romesco is delicious with any roasted or grilled fish and vegetables. Or serve with grilled spring onions: Brush with olive oil, season with salt, and grill until charred and soft, or roast in a 350-degree oven; peel to the tender part.

JULY 14, 2002: "FOOD DIARY: UNDER THE SPANISH SUN," BY AMANDA HESSER. RECIPE ADAPTED FROM BILL DEVIN, AN EXPAT WHO LIVED IN SPAIN.

—2002

⌒ KATTA SAMBOL

A Sri Lankan condiment built for cast-iron stomachs.

————

2 tablespoons Maldives fish flakes or small dried shrimp,
    soaked in warm water for 10 minutes and drained
10 small red chiles, or to taste, halved
1 shallot, thinly sliced
Sea salt

With a mortar and pestle, pound together the fish, chiles, shallot, and a pinch of salt. Taste and adjust the chiles and salt as needed; the mixture should be hot, fishy, and slightly salty. Serve as a condiment.

MAKES ABOUT $1/3$ CUP

COOKING NOTE
Fish flakes and dried shrimp are sold in Asian markets.

SERVING SUGGESTIONS
Hoppers (Coconut Crepes; p. 349), Tuna Curry (p. 435)

OCTOBER 13, 2004: "JUST OFF INDIA, KISSED BY EUROPE," BY AMANDA HESSER.

—2004

⌒ GRAPEFRUIT AND MEYER LEMON MARMALADE

Preserves would seem a difficult food to make distinctive, yet June Taylor, a preserves expert in Berkeley, California, manages to make hers unforgettable. They are unlike any commercial preserves, not simply because she uses esoteric fruits like bergamots, Kadota figs, and Santa Rosa plums—virtually all of them organic—but also because she cooks them in a way that underlines their individual essence. Her silver lime and ginger marmalade has a sting to it; her grapefruit and Meyer lemon marmalade is bright, concentrated, and vigorously bitter.

Taylor prepares her jams in small batches in large pots so they cook rapidly and reach the gel point before they taste cooked. She uses only the fruit's natural pectin and incorporates sugar not as a crutch but a tool to bring out the nuances in the fruit's flavor. Christine Ferber, a French preserves maker, wrote in her book *Mes Confitures* that jams should be 65 percent sugar. Taylor's jams are about 20 percent; her marmalades are about 50 to 60 percent.

For this marmalade, she includes grapefruit rind and both the flesh and squares of Meyer lemon rind, so when you eat the marmalade, she said, "you get a burst of Meyer lemon." Taylor stirs in water, lemon juice, and a jelly bag filled with the grapefruit and lemon membranes (for extracting pectin) and simmers the mixture.

Marmalade is the most difficult of the preserves, Taylor said, because you must balance so many things at once: acid, sugar, pectin, and water. In the final stage, you want the marmalade to cook quickly— about 30 minutes is ideal—so the water evaporates and the flavor crystallizes in a fresh state.

When the marmalade is ready, Taylor works at a table covered with jars, fresh from the oven. "Hot jar, hot product, work fast, don't take phone calls," Taylor said.

————

5 pounds grapefruit (about 5 grapefruits), rinsed

1 pound Meyer lemons or small regular lemons (about 5 lemons), rinsed

2½ cups water

½ cup fresh lemon juice

2½ pounds (5 cups) sugar

1. Remove the grapefruit zest with a vegetable peeler. Cut the zest into ⅛-inch-wide slivers; stop when you have ¾ cup, and discard the rest. Slice off the ends of the grapefruit and the remaining grapefruit pith. Remove the grapefruit segments by using a sharp paring knife to slice between the membranes—reserve the membranes. Stop when you have 5 cups of segments.
2. Cut the ends off the Meyer lemons, deep enough so you can see the flesh. Cut off the remaining peel and reserve it. Remove the segments of lemon, reserving the membranes. Cut the lemon peel into ½-inch squares. Cut the segments crosswise into ¼-inch pieces. Put the membranes from the grapefruit and Meyer lemons in a jelly bag and tie with kitchen twine.
3. Combine the grapefruit segments, grapefruit zest, lemon segments, lemon peel, and jelly bag in a wide deep enameled cast-iron or other nonreactive pot.

Add the water and the lemon juice, bring to a simmer, and simmer until the grapefruit peel is tender, 25 to 30 minutes. Let cool.
4. Working over a bowl in your sink, squeeze the liquid from the jelly bag: keep squeezing and wringing it out until you extract ⅓ to ½ cup of pectin—the creamy white substance. Add the pectin and sugar to the pot. Attach a candy thermometer to the pot, place over high heat, and boil, stirring now and then and skimming off the foam, until the marmalade reaches 220 degrees or passes the gel test. It's ready when a spoonful dropped onto a plate sets up when cool.
5. Have ready 6 sterilized half-pint jars with screw bands and new lids (see Cooking Notes, p. 589). Simmer the lids in hot water to soften the rubberized flange. Spoon the marmalade into the jars, leaving ¼-inch headspace. Remove any air bubbles trapped in the jars by running a sterilized butter knife between the sides of the jars and the marmalade. Wipe the rims. Put the lids on and screw on the bands fingertip tight.
6. Place the jars on a rack in a big pot and cover with 2 to 3 inches of water. Cover the pot and bring to a boil over high heat, then lower the heat to medium and boil gently for 10 minutes. Remove the lid and then, after about 5 minutes, remove the jars. Allow the jars to cool, untouched, for 4 to 6 hours.
7. Check the seals, and store in a cool, dark place for up to a year. Refrigerate after opening.

MAKES 6 HALF-PINTS

FEBRUARY 13, 2005: "THE WAY WE EAT: JELLY'S LAST JAM," BY AMANDA HESSER. RECIPE ADAPTED FROM JUNE TAYLOR, THE OWNER OF JUNE TAYLOR JAMS IN BERKELEY, CALIFORNIA.

—2005

⌁ RANCH DRESSING

————

1 cup mayonnaise, preferably homemade (p. 465)

½ cup buttermilk

¼ cup buttermilk powder

Salt and freshly ground black pepper

¼ cup chopped chives or flat-leaf parsley

Put the mayonnaise, buttermilk, and buttermilk powder in a medium jar with a tight-fitting lid. Sprinkle with a little salt and lots of pepper. Add the chives if you like, put the lid on, and shake vigorously for 30 seconds or so. Taste and adjust the seasoning. Use immediately, or store in the refrigerator for a few days; it will keep longer without herbs.

MAKES 2 CUPS

COOKING NOTE
Buttermilk powder can be found in the baking aisle of many grocery stores. I didn't believe Mark Bittman when he wrote this in his story, but it's true.

OCTOBER 25, 2006: "THE MINIMALIST: THE WELL-DRESSED SALAD WEARS ONLY HOMEMADE," BY MARK BITTMAN.

—2006

CLEMENTINE PEPPERCORN GLAZE

This may be used in place of the glaze for Monte's Ham on p. 548.

———

1½ cups packed light brown sugar
2 clementines, stemmed if necessary, quartered, skin left on
2 fresh green serrano chiles or 1 jalapeño chile, stemmed, seeded, and coarsely chopped
2 tablespoons white wine vinegar
1 tablespoon plus 1 teaspoon crushed red peppercorns or peppercorn blend
1 tablespoon Dijon mustard
½ teaspoon ground cinnamon, preferably freshly ground

Combine all the ingredients in a food processor and pulse until the chiles are reduced to tiny green flecks. Transfer to a jar with a tight-fitting lid and store in the refrigerator until needed. Making the glaze a day in advance allows flavors to bloom and thickens the glaze, which makes it easier to apply.

MAKES 1¾ CUPS, ENOUGH FOR A WHOLE HAM

DECEMBER 20, 2006: "FANFARE FOR THE CITY HAM" BY MATT LEE AND TED LEE.

—2006

HOMEMADE BUTTER AND BUTTERMILK

As Daniel Patterson, a chef and contributor to the *Times*, summed it up: to make butter, all you do is "Beat cream until it curdles, expel liquid, and presto: butter." And oh, is it extraordinary, especially with some flaky sea salt and a crust of bread. The buttermilk doesn't have the tang or sloppy thickness of the commercial kind; homemade, it's elegant and a little creamy.

———

6 cups organic heavy cream
Sea salt (optional)

1. Leave the cream out of the refrigerator for a little while first (it works best when it's around 50 degrees). Fill a mixer bowl with the cream, insert the whisk attachment, and be sure to cover the bowl with plastic wrap, or it will look as if a milk truck exploded in your kitchen. Turn the mixer on medium-high, and then do that thing professional cooks live in fear of being yelled at for: overwhip the cream! As you peer through the spattered plastic, you will see the cream thickening and getting progressively more yellow. This will take several minutes—when it starts to look like a solid mass of golden pebbles, it's almost done. After another minute or so, the mixer will start pelting the plastic with liquid. That's your cue to turn it off. Quickly.
2. Two more easy steps will bring you to butter nirvana: Set a strainer over a bowl and empty the contents of the mixer bowl into the strainer. The white liquid that drains into the bowl below is real buttermilk, nothing like the cultured processed stuff that goes by the same name. Its sweet, delicate flavor is great in shakes, oatmeal, and soups or even in coffee or tea.
3. Let the butter drain for a few minutes. Then comes the fun part: kneading the butter. This will push out much of the buttermilk and consolidate the remaining liquid and fat. Taste as you go—you will notice the flavor getting less diluted, the texture more lush and velvety. After about 5 minutes, you should be done. If you want salted butter, you can mix in some sea salt. Transfer to an airtight container and refrigerate.

MAKES ABOUT 16 OUNCES (2 CUPS) EACH OF BUTTER AND BUTTERMILK

JULY 1, 2007: "THE WAY WE EAT: CURD MENTALITY," BY DANIEL PATTERSON.

—2007

GREEN TOMATO AND LEMON MARMALADE

Green tomatoes are lemony, so this is like a double lemon marmalade with an underlying vegetal aroma, courtesy of the tomatoes.

———

1 lemon, thinly sliced and seeded
2¼ pounds green tomatoes (about 5 large tomatoes), cored and thinly sliced
3¼ cups sugar
¼ cup water
2 tablespoons fresh lemon juice
Pinch of salt

1. Bring the lemon slices to a boil in a pot of water. Drain.
2. Combine the lemon slices and all the remaining ingredients in a medium heavy enameled cast-iron or other nonreactive pot and bring to a simmer, stirring to dissolve the sugar. Cook at a bare simmer until the tomatoes and lemon slices are translucent and the syrup thickens, 1 to 1½ hours. Cool completely. Store in a refrigerator for up to a month.

MAKES 1¾ CUPS

AUGUST 22, 2007: "A GOOD APPETITE: SO MANY TOMATOES TO STUFF IN A WEEK," BY MELISSA CLARK.

—2007

LAST-OF-THE-SUMMER PESTO

A more intensely bonded, more modern oil-based pesto than the one on p. 311.

———

½ cup pine nuts
¾ cup extra virgin olive oil
4 ounces basil, stemmed (about 5 cups loosely packed leaves)
2 cloves garlic, coarsely chopped
½ teaspoon salt, or to taste

1. Heat a small skillet over medium heat. Add the pine nuts and toast them, shaking the pan and stirring, until golden brown all over, about 3 minutes. Pour the nuts onto a plate to cool.
2. Combine the nuts and all the remaining ingredients in a blender and puree until smooth, stopping occasionally to scrape down the sides with a spatula and work the basil toward the blade. Use immediately, or store in the refrigerator for up to a week; or freeze for up to 6 months.

MAKES ABOUT 1 CUP

OCTOBER 10, 2007: "A GOOD APPETITE: THE URBAN FARMER'S AUTUMN RITUAL," BY MELISSA CLARK.

—2007

FRESH RICOTTA

By 2008, asking a home cook to make dinner every night was out of the question, but asking him to make his own crème fraîche or butter (see p. 613)—anything elemental or artisanal—was somehow reasonable. Homemade ricotta, then, had a ready audience. As it turns out, ricotta is much more rewarding to make than crème fraîche, because it goes through a vast transformation from milk to curd. As Julia Moskin, a *Times* food writer explained, all you need to do is "apply heat and little bit of acid to milk—whether grass-fed, organic, or supermarket—and it separates with startling obedience into curds and whey. The 'cheesemaker' has only to stand there with a ladle, a colander and some cheesecloth."

Pure and bouncy, the ricotta's flavor comes in the finish, although you'll want to include some salt, either sprinkled on top or added in abundance to whatever you're pairing the ricotta with. I spread it on my morning toast with fig jam and a pinch of fleur de sel. Andrew Carmellini, one of the New York City chefs Moskin interviewed for her story, serves ricotta mixed with fresh thyme and dried oregano atop grilled country bread that has been brushed with olive oil and seasoned with salt—see p. 93.

————

2 quarts whole milk

2 cups buttermilk

1. Line a wide sieve or colander with cheesecloth, folded so that it is at least 4 layers thick, and set it over a bowl. Pour the milk and buttermilk into a heavy pot and attach a candy thermometer to the pot. Set the pot over high heat and cook, stirring frequently; scrape the bottom of the pot occasionally to prevent scorch-ing. As the milk heats, curds will begin to rise and clump on the surface. Once the mixture is steaming, stop stirring. When the mixture reaches 170 degrees, the curds and whey will separate. (The whey will look like cloudy gray water underneath a mass of thick white curds.) Immediately turn off the heat, and gently ladle the curds into the sieve.

2. When all the curds are in the sieve and the dripping has slowed (about 5 minutes), gently gather the edges of the cloth and twist to bring the curds together; do not squeeze. Let drain for 15 minutes more. Discard the whey.

3. Untie the cloth and pack the ricotta into airtight containers. Refrigerate and use within 1 week.

MAKES ABOUT 2 CUPS

MAY 28, 2008: "SUDDENLY, RICOTTA'S A BIG CHEESE," BY JULIA MOSKIN. RECIPE ADAPTED FROM *MICHAEL CHIAREL-LO'S CASUAL COOKING*, BY MICHAEL CHIARELLO.

—2008

- The era of crullers, jolly boys, twisters, and moonshines—doughnuts!
- German Toast (p. 621), a lighter-weight cousin to French toast.

—1870s—

- Uptown breakfast: poached eggs with wine sauce.
- Griddle cakes abound: buckwheat cakes, flannel cakes, Johnnycakes (p. 622) and snow pancakes (actually made with snow).

- Omelet with Asparagus (p. 624).

—1879—

- Worker's breakfast: chipped beef, veal, or lamb on toast.

—1880s—

- Milk toast and cream toast.

—1880—

- An omelet made with apples is sometimes called a friar's omelet.

- Scrambled eggs are jazzed up with dried mushrooms and caraway (see p. 624) and with ham and anchovies (p. 624).

—1900s—

- The first IHOP opens in Toluca Lake, California.

—1958—

- Obsession with coffee cake.

—1960s—

- Eggs Benedict starts its long run as a brunch star.

—1967—

- Weekend breakfast: pancakes.

—1980s—

- Bagels go mainstream.

- Heavenly Hots (p. 634): pancake and crepe unite in a pillowy disk.

—1987—

- Game changer: the frittata eases the anxiety of cooks who can't roll an omelet.
- Muffin tops—first a food, later a fashion problem.

—1990s—

- Blue period: first someone has the horrible idea of removing the yolks from omelets, then someone else convinces people to start the day with protein shakes.

- Fage Greek yogurt is first imported, and it changes granola with yogurt forever.

—2001—

- Bill Granger's Scrambled Eggs (p. 640).

—2002—

- Poached Scrambled Eggs (p. 645).

—2006—

- Breakfast pizza on both coasts—Morandi in New York City and Big Sur Bakery in California (see p. 646).

—2009—

13

‿

BREAKFAST AND BRUNCH

Breakfast has changed more than any other meal over the past century and a half. When the *Times* started publishing recipes in the 1850s, breakfast looked more like dinner. A typical breakfast might have included hashed beef or lamb, potatoes, johnnycakes, eggs, and fried smelts. There were pancakes too, including a variation called "snow pancakes," in which a few heaping tablespoonfuls of "dry snow" were folded into the batter before it was ladled onto a griddle.

In the late nineteenth century, Americans began laying off meat as European-style coffee and sweet treats such as coffee cakes and pastries started infiltrating the morning meal.

But it was the late 1930s when Sunday breakfast changed from a meal focused on sustenance to a culinary spectacle called brunch. "Sunday breakfast has, in fact, become so important in the modern scheme of things," Jane Holt, a *Times* reporter, wrote in 1941, "and such flights of fancy have been taken from the traditional cereal, bacon and eggs, and toast, that it becomes impossible to draw a line between where breakfast ends and lunch begins—a dilemma that resulted in the coining of 'brunch' to cover borderline cases." Among the flights of fancy Holt discussed were kidneys and mushrooms and cocktail frankfurters with pineapple sauce. And you can thank me for not including them.

Over the decades, as breakfast became less like dinner and more like lunch, some great cooks have continued to return to eggs, pastry, and pancakes, making tiny adjustments in a tireless effort to perfect them. This chapter contains some extraordinary examples of these classic breakfasts, including Molly Katzen's Amazing Overnight Waffles (p. 642), Bill Granger's Scrambled Eggs (p. 640), and Daniel Patterson's Poached Scrambled Eggs (p. 645).

RECIPES BY CATEGORY

GERMAN TOAST

The *Times*'s food coverage started to take off in the 1870s, and the fervor of people's responses seemed to take the editors by surprise. "During the past week, we have received upward of two hundred letters from correspondents in various parts of the country, containing receipts or questions for the 'Household' columns," the editors wrote, with evident exasperation. "We have made the best selection we could from them, and must beg the indulgence of correspondents whose letters we are not able to acknowledge this week." Among the recipes chosen were an apple tart scented with rosewater, queen pudding, eggplant gratin, eggs with anchovy sauce, orange pudding, Welsh rarebit, and this one for German toast, which is like deconstructed French toast. You first dip the bread in milk, then coat it in egg before frying it and dusting it with sugar. Milk soaks into the bread more quickly than an egg-and-milk mixture and its moisture causes any excess egg coating the bread to slip off, leaving just a thin sheath. After a quick trip to a hot griddle, you end up not with a rich, heavy toast but a crisp shell encasing a soft belly of milk-soaked bread. I'm a convert.

––––––––

2 cups whole milk

4 large eggs

Butter for the griddle or pan

Twelve ½- to ¾-inch-thick slices bread

Sugar for sprinkling

1. Heat the oven to 200 degrees. Pour the milk into a wide shallow bowl and beat the eggs in a similarly sized bowl; set both near the griddle or stove.

2. Heat a griddle or place a large nonstick pan over medium-high heat, and butter the surface of the griddle. Working quickly, dip the slices of bread in batches, first in the milk, then in the egg, set on the griddle, and brown on both sides. Transfer to a baking sheet and keep warm in the oven until all the slices are cooked; don't stack them. Sprinkle with sugar just before serving.

SERVES 4

COOKING NOTES

The best bread for this is a crusty Pullman loaf with a loose, airy center (airier than pain de mie) so the edges remain firm and the center fluffy. In a pinch, any good sandwich bread will do.

Do not dip the bread in the milk ahead of time or allow it to soak in the milk, or it might fall apart.

You can sprinkle regular sugar on top; I like infusing sugar with other flavors. Blend 1 cup sugar with a spent vanilla bean, and let it sit in a jar for a week. Or zest a lemon, rub the zest into 1 cup sugar, and let sit for a few hours before using.

DECEMBER 19, 1875: "THE HOUSEHOLD." RECIPE SIGNED CHRISTMAS.

—1875

CALLIE'S DOUGHNUTS

These cinnamon-scented cake doughnuts incorporate both sour milk and regular whole milk—"sweet milk" in nineteenth-century parlance—in the dough, which keeps them light and downy.

––––––––

1¼ to 1½ cups whole milk

1 teaspoon cider vinegar

4 cups all-purpose flour

¾ cup sugar

1 teaspoon cream of tartar

¾ teaspoon baking soda

½ teaspoon ground cinnamon

1½ teaspoons salt

2 large eggs

Peanut oil for deep-frying

Confectioners' sugar or cinnamon sugar

1. Mix together ¾ cup milk and the vinegar in a medium bowl; let sit until curdled, about 5 minutes.

2. Combine the flour, sugar, cream of tartar, baking soda, cinnamon, and salt in a large bowl. Make a well in the center of the dry ingredients. Beat the eggs into the milk mixture, then pour into the well. Add ½ cup more milk and begin stirring, incorporating the flour mixture from the edges, until all the flour is incorporated and the mixture is smooth. You want the texture

to be somewhere between batter and dough; add up to another ¼ cup milk if it's too dry.

3. Heat 3 inches of peanut oil to 365 degrees in a deep heavy pot, or test by dropping a bread crumb in the oil; if it browns in 30 seconds, the oil is ready. Using two soupspoons, drop the dough by tablespoonfuls into the oil. Make sure you don't crowd the pot—you want the doughnuts to cook quickly—and adjust the heat from batch to batch as needed. Let the doughnuts brown on the bottom, then turn and brown the other side, 2 to 3 minutes total. Drain on a baking sheet lined with paper towels. Dust with confectioners' sugar (or roll in cinnamon sugar).

MAKES 24 TO 30 DOUGHNUTS

SERVING SUGGESTION
Honey-Orange Smoothie (p. 29)

FEBRUARY 27, 1876: "RECEIPTS FROM CORRESPONDENTS." RECIPE SIGNED CORNELIA.

—1876

⌇ JOHNNYCAKE

Johnnycake, a cornmeal flatbread, can easily be sodden, but these are at once lacy like Swedish pancakes and gritty like good corn bread. I could eat them by the dozen. Serve them with syrup for breakfast, or as a side dish with roasted chicken.

———

3 cups whole milk

I tablespoon cider vinegar

I teaspoon baking soda

2 large eggs

8 tablespoons (I stick) unsalted butter, melted

I tablespoon sugar

I teaspoon salt

2½ cups cornmeal

Butter and syrup or honey for serving

1. Mix the milk and vinegar in a bowl and let sit until it curdles, about 5 minutes. Whisk the baking soda into the milk.

2. Beat the eggs in a large bowl, then whisk in the milk mixture, butter, sugar, and salt. Whisk in the

cornmeal. The batter will seem very loose, but it will thicken as it sits. Let rest for 1 hour, whisking every 30 minutes.

3. Heat a large nonstick pan or griddle over medium-high heat. (No greasing is necessary.) Whisk the batter, fill a ¼-cup measure halfway with it, and gently drop the batter into the pan—it should sizzle and bubble and spread into a thin round cake. Add more cakes to the pan, being careful not to crowd them. Cook until browned, 30 to 60 seconds, then flip and brown on the other side. Adjust the heat as you go so the cakes brown quickly without burning. Serve the cakes with butter and syrup as you cook them, or keep them warm on a heatproof platter in a 175-degree oven.

MAKES ABOUT 4 DOZEN CAKES

COOKING NOTES
I used Quaker Oats cornmeal, which is bright yellow and coarse.

This makes a large amount—you can halve it easily.

It will take a few tries before you get the hang of cooking the cakes. The cornmeal sinks to the bottom of the batter, so you need to whisk the mixture every few minutes for your cakes to have the right mix of liquid and cornmeal. Also, because the cakes are so thin, you need the thinnest-possible flexible spatula to turn them. Slide it halfway under the cake, then lift it up and gently set the cake back down on its other side. Then pat yourself on the back.

MARCH 17, 1878: "THE HOUSEHOLD: RECEIPTS FOR THE TABLE." RECIPE SIGNED GEORGIE L.W.

—1878

⌇ EGGS À LA LAVALETTE

If you're an egg-white-omelet eater, run away quickly. Eggs à la Lavalette are for egg fanatics (a similar recipe that appeared in 1897 was called "eggs for epicures"). Poached in heavy cream, this dish is the savory equivalent of floating island and is as sublime, in my opinion, as eggs en cocotte. Use the best eggs and cream you can get hold of.

———

Heavy cream (at least I cup)

2 large eggs

Salt and freshly ground black pepper
2 slices country bread, toasted

1. Fill a very small shallow flameproof baking dish (or tiny skillet) with ¼ inch of cream. Bring to a boil over medium heat.

2. Meanwhile, crack the eggs into a bowl. When the cream is about to boil, gently slide the eggs into the cream. They should be almost covered by it; if not, add more cream. Simmer the cream, spooning it over the yolks, until the whites are just set but the yolks are still runny, 2 to 3 minutes. Season with salt and pepper. Serve directly from the dish, setting it on a potholder on a plate, or carefully transfer to a shallow bowl. Garnish with the toast.

SERVES 1

COOKING NOTES

I used a 5-inch-diameter cast-iron pan.

The recipe can be doubled or quadrupled, using a larger pan.

PERIOD DETAIL

Modern food pages aren't nearly as captivating as those from the nineteenth century. Often printed under the rubric "The Household," the *Times* columns contained a random blend of reader recipes, food prices, and advice ranging from tips on personal hygiene to how to mend rugs. On the day this recipe ran, the editors listed the foods available in New York City markets—potatoes from Bermuda, strawberries, gooseberries, cherries, Spanish mackerel, weakfish, porgies, cod, soft-shell crabs, spring lamb, and peaches from Florida—and gave instructions for pressing seaweed for decoration and removing skin blemishes by burning them off with "lunar caustic," a method described as "somewhat painful" but "worth the experiment." Jane Brody, the *Times*'s personal health columnist, would not approve.

JUNE 2, 1878: "THE HOUSEHOLD: RECEIPTS FOR THE TABLE." RECIPE SIGNED CHESTNUT-STREET.

—1878

⌒ AN OMELET

The culinary rift between France and America apparently began not with *le burger* but *l'omelet*. In 1881, a Frenchman wrote to the "Household" editors:

I look over a great many cook-books to instruct myself, and to see how the great American people are to be advised as to the making of an omelet, and I am made very unhappy. I see the reason why I so rarely eat a good omelet. There are two little words—which always come in—which destroy such pleasures as one ought to get from an omelet. These very bad words are "or milk." "Or milk" is the extinguisher of the omelet. The receipts are generally beautiful as far as they go, but they always say— add a little water "or milk." I say never use water "or milk," because the "or milk"—which must be, I suppose, a peculiar kind of milk, converts a soft, light omelet into the toughest leather. No "or milk" in an omelet if you please, or the future of this great country is lost.

This Frenchman must have missed the recipe contributed to the *Times* two years earlier by another of his countrymen, who was equally passionate about the proper way to make this unprepossessing breakfast, without milk, of course.

ORIGINAL RECIPE

"It is an easy thing to do, and not often well done. I think the trouble lies in the fact that most cooks overbeat their eggs. A simple omelet is not a soufflé. Break all your eggs in one plate; stir rather than beat up the whites and yolks; to each three eggs you use, put in a teaspoonful of cold water; I do not like milk; salt and pepper your eggs moderately (American cooks use too much pepper); take some parsley and chop it; let the parsley be fine-fine (American cooks never chop parsley fine enough), put two ounces of sweet butter in your pan; lard for an omelet is an abomination; when your butter is very, very hot, pour in your eggs; just as soon as it is cooked on one side, not crisp, turn quickly and cook on the other side; double it over when you serve it, on a very hot plate; the cold water in the eggs makes the omelet light and moist."

APRIL 13, 1879: "RECEIPTS FOR THE TABLE." RECIPE SIGNED A LITTLE VACHETTE.

—1879

OMELET WITH ASPARAGUS

20 thin asparagus spears, wild asparagus if you can get it
8 large eggs
1 tablespoon whole milk
Salt
1 tablespoon unsalted butter

1. Use the top 3 inches of the asparagus spears; reserve the rest for another use. Bring a pot of salted water to a boil. Add the asparagus tips and blanch until crisp-tender. Drain and transfer to a bowl of ice water. Drain again. Finely chop.
2. Whisk together the eggs and milk in a bowl. Season with salt. Add the chopped asparagus.
3. Melt the butter in a large nonstick pan over medium heat. Add the egg mixture and cook until set on the bottom and nearly cooked in the center. Carefully lift one edge of the omelet and fold it over the center of the omelet, as if you were folding a letter, then fold the remaining third on top.

SERVES 3 TO 4

SERVING SUGGESTIONS
Rhubarb Bellini (p. 30), Green Goddess Salad (p. 176)

JUNE 22, 1879: "USEFUL FAMILY HINTS." RECIPE SIGNED MISS GEORGIE D.

—1879

EGGS WITH MUSHROOMS AND CARAWAY

1 ounce (about 1 cup) dried chanterelles, porcini, or morels
2 tablespoons unsalted butter
½ teaspoon caraway seeds, lightly crushed
Salt
5 large eggs, beaten
Buttered toast, preferably rye, for serving

1. Soak the mushrooms in hot water for 20 minutes. Lift the mushrooms from the liquid, leaving any grit behind (reserve the liquid for another use, such as soup or risotto, if desired) and pat dry. Roughly chop the mushrooms.
2. Melt the butter in a medium skillet, preferably non-stick, over medium heat. Add the mushrooms and cook until they've released most of their moisture, are lightly browned and starting to crisp. Season with the caraway and salt to taste. Reduce the heat to medium-low, then pour in the eggs and cook, stirring to gather the eggs toward the center of the pan. Pull the pan off the heat about 30 seconds before the eggs are cooked to the desired doneness. Serve with toast.

SERVES 2 TO 4

SERVING SUGGESTION
Bloody Mary (p. 21)

JANUARY 12, 1902: "A NEW MUSHROOM RECIPE."

—1902

EGGS ELI

A century ago, the *Times* ran a story on ways to cook eggs for breakfast on Easter Sunday. According to the unnamed writer, the challenge a cook faces in disguising the flavor of eggs "is a puzzle that adds years to his age unless inspiration or accident brings a happy solution." He apparently never experienced the delight of eggs with truffles or, for that matter, of eggs and bacon. Three decades later, Marcel Boulestin's book *Eggs* would come to the aid of anyone still befuddled by egg cookery, and by 2000, eggs had inspired so many recipes that Marie Simmons's cookbook *The Good Egg* ran to 464 pages.

In the article, one solution was offered by John W. Keller, a former city commissioner. His Eggs Eli involved rubbing a chafing dish with a garlic clove, then scrambling eggs in it with a mash of Virginia ham and anchovies—just the kind of robust, unfussy dish you might find today on the brunch menu at Prune in the East Village. (Though Keller, a Yale dropout, added, "Serve on a Yale blue dish.")

Among the story's other overstrenuous ideas for masking the dread flavor of eggs were poached eggs topped with a hops-scented béchamel, President Taft's campfire omelet (fried trout, salt, and pepper), and the Colony Club's Eggs Suffragette, a twist on deviled eggs that incorporated anchovies (see p. 52; the dish didn't hasten women's suffrage, however). Delmonico's restaurant, on the other hand, was lambasted for having "failed to evolve any novelty" on the egg front.

Most inventive of all was Mark Twain's Eggs à la Canton, Williamsport, Trout Run, and Way Stations, which instructed you to: "Divest two genuine eggs of shell and claws, being careful to avoid breaking same. If you break 'em, begin again at the top of the recipe and proceed anew. Lay the plumage and cackle on one side, roll the remainder very thin, add baking powder, and boil in a pudding bag over a slow fire for a week. Tie with baby ribbons and serve cold."

———

1 clove garlic

2 tablespoons unsalted butter

8 large eggs, beaten

1 tablespoon finely minced anchovy

3 tablespoons finely minced Virginia ham
    or other smoked ham

Rub the inside of a large skillet with the garlic clove. Place over medium-high heat and add the butter. When it's nice and foamy, pour in the eggs. Sprinkle the anchovy and ham over the eggs, then begin scrambling them, stopping when they're done to your liking.

SERVES 4

APRIL 4, 1909: "WAYS OF COOKING EGGS." RECIPE BY JOHN W. KELLER.

—1909

⌇ SHAD ROE SCRAMBLE

Surf 'n' turf eggs, a forgotten East Coast specialty.

———

½ pair shad roe

1 tablespoon fresh lemon juice

1½ teaspoons salt

3 large eggs

3 tablespoons whole milk

¼ teaspoon freshly ground black pepper

2 tablespoons unsalted butter or bacon fat

2 tablespoons chopped flat-leaf parsley

1. Bring a small saucepan of water to a boil. Add the

roe, lemon juice, and 1 teaspoon salt and simmer for 5 minutes. Drain and let the roe cool enough to handle.

2. Remove the outer membrane from the roe and discard.

3. Beat the eggs with the milk in a bowl. Add the pepper, the remaining ½ teaspoon salt, and the roe, broken into small pieces.

4. Melt the butter in a medium nonstick skillet over medium heat. Add the egg mixture and scramble to your liking. Sprinkle with the parsley.

SERVES 4

APRIL 22, 1946: "NEWS OF FOOD; SHAD AGAIN IN LIBERAL SUPPLY HERE—A WELCOME SUBSTITUTE FOR SCARCE MEAT," BY JANE NICKERSON.

—1946

⌇ FRESH PLUM KUCHEN

A hearty, crackly-topped cake, inlaid with plums. Serve it for breakfast or dessert.

———

For the Cake

1½ cups sifted all-purpose flour

2 teaspoons baking powder

½ teaspoon salt

¼ cup sugar

¼ cup vegetable shortening

1 large egg

⅓ cup whole milk

Grated zest of 1 lemon

Melted butter for brushing

For the Topping

⅓ to ½ cup sugar

½ teaspoon ground cinnamon

1½ teaspoons all-purpose flour

8 small ripe plums, halved and pitted

1 large egg yolk

2 tablespoons heavy cream

Heavy cream, for serving

1. To make the cake, heat the oven to 400 degrees. Sift together the flour, baking powder, salt, and sugar into a bowl. Add the shortening and cut in using a pastry

blender or your fingertips, until the mixture resembles coarse cornmeal.

2. Beat the egg, milk, and lemon zest together. Add to the flour mixture, stirring just until blended.

3. Press the dough into a greased 8-inch square baking pan. Brush the surface with melted butter.

4. To make the topping, mix the sugar (exact amount depends on the sweetness of the plums), cinnamon, and the 1½ teaspoons flour. Arrange the plums cut side up on the dough. Sprinkle the sugar mixture over the fruit.

5. Blend the egg yolk with the cream and drizzle over the fruit. Bake for 35 minutes, covered for the first 15 minutes of baking. Serve warm, with cream.

SERVES 6 TO 8

JULY 21, 1947: "NEWS OF FOOD; FRESH PLUM KUCHEN A TASTY SUMMER DISH SERVED WARM WITH CREAM FOR DESSERT," BY JANE NICKERSON.

—1947

THE NEXT SIX RECIPES OFFER INDISPENS-ABLE BASICS ON COOKING EGGS.

SHELL-COOKED EGGS

Large eggs, at room temperature

Bring enough water to cover the eggs to be cooked to a rapid boil in a saucepan. Place each egg on a spoon and lower it into the water. Reduce the heat until the water barely simmers; cook the eggs to desired doneness. For soft-cooked eggs, leave in the water from 3 to 4½ minutes. For hard-cooked, leave in the water for 9 minutes, then drain immediately and plunge the eggs into cold water; this causes a jacket of steam to form between the egg and the shell, facilitating peeling.

COOKING NOTE
Craig Claiborne added; "Eggs cooked in this fashion for exactly 6 minutes are called eggs mollets. The white is set and firm and the yolks remain liquid. They are used in much the same way as poached eggs."

MARCH 23, 1958: "FRAGILE—HANDLE WITH CARE," BY CRAIG CLAIBORNE.

—1958

SCRAMBLED EGGS

6 large eggs, at room temperature
2 tablespoons unsalted butter
2 tablespoons heavy cream
Salt

1. Break the eggs into a small bowl and beat until well mixed but not frothy.

2. Melt the butter in a skillet or the top of a double boiler and add the eggs. Place the skillet over low heat or the double boiler top over boiling water and cook, stirring constantly, until the eggs begin to set. Add the cream and continue stirring until the desired degree of firmness. Correct the seasoning with salt and serve immediately.

SERVES 2 TO 3

VARIATIONS
Craig Claiborne noted; "Tarragon, chives, parsley, and chervil complement the flavor of scrambled eggs. Garnishes include sautéed mushroom caps, anchovy fillets, and chicken livers."

MARCH 23, 1958: "FRAGILE—HANDLE WITH CARE," BY CRAIG CLAIBORNE.

—1958

FRIED EGGS

Unsalted butter or bacon fat
Large eggs, at room temperature

1. Melt enough butter or bacon fat in a heavy skillet to cover the bottom.

2. Break the eggs into a small bowl and slip them carefully into the pan. Cook over low heat, basting the eggs with the hot fat, until the whites are set. If the eggs are to be cooked on both sides, turn with a pancake turner.

VARIATION
Craig Claiborne added, "The most famous fried egg dish, other than plain fried eggs, is the French spe-

cialty fried eggs *au beurre noir*. Eggs are fried in butter and transferred to a warm serving dish. A little additional butter is added to the pan and cooked quickly until dark brown. A few drops of vinegar are added for each egg and the mixture is poured over the eggs. Each egg is garnished with ½ teaspoon of capers."

MARCH 23, 1958: "FRAGILE—HANDLE WITH CARE," BY CRAIG CLAIBORNE.

—1958

✑ POACHED EGGS

_____

1 tablespoon vinegar
1 teaspoon salt
Large eggs, at room temperature

1. Bring 4 cups water to a rolling boil and add the vinegar and salt. Immediately reduce the heat.
2. Break the eggs one at a time into a small bowl, then slip them gently into the water. Let the eggs steep until the white is firm.
3. Using a slotted spoon or spatula remove the eggs and drain on absorbent paper. Trim with a knife or cookie cutter. Serve topped with butter or a sherry and cheese sauce.

COOKING NOTE

Craig Claiborne wrote, "Eggs may be poached in advance and reheated briefly in boiling salted water for about 30 seconds just before serving. This is advantageous if a quantity of eggs are to be poached for special occasions." I'd use simmering, not boiling water, though.

MARCH 23, 1958: "FRAGILE—HANDLE WITH CARE," BY CRAIG CLAIBORNE.

—1958

✑ PLAIN OMELET

_____

3 large eggs, at room temperature
1 tablespoon cold water
Salt
1 tablespoon unsalted butter

1. Break the eggs into a small bowl, add the water, season with salt, and beat until light and foamy.
2. Place an omelet pan over moderate heat. Flick a drop of water into the pan; if it skitters about and disappears almost at once, the pan is ready. Swirl the butter around in the pan, and pour the eggs into the pan. Shake the pan with your left hand, using fore-and-aft motion; with your right hand stir in a circular motion with a fork.
3. Change your left hand position, to hold the handle with your palm turned upward. Raise the skillet to a 45-degree angle. Using a fork, roll the omelet from the top down; turn onto a warm plate held in your right hand. Garnish as desired.

SERVES 1

MARCH 23, 1958: "FRAGILE—HANDLE WITH CARE," BY CRAIG CLAIBORNE.

—1958

✑ BAKED OR SHIRRED EGGS

_____

Unsalted butter
Large eggs, at room temperature

Melt 1 teaspoon of butter in each individual ramekin (any small heatproof dish). Break 1 or 2 eggs into each dish and bake in a moderate oven (350 degrees) for 10 to 12 minutes, until the white is milky and still creamy.

MARCH 23, 1958: "FRAGILE—HANDLE WITH CARE," BY CRAIG CLAIBORNE.

—1958

✑ DANISH PASTRY

As Craig Claiborne pointed out, we call this pastry Danish, and the Danes call it *wienerbrod*, or Vienna bread. Somehow I doubt the Viennese call it American pastry to complete the loop, although I wish they would. Danish differs from puff pastry in that it's leavened with yeast.

_____

Approximately 4¾ cups sifted flour
1 teaspoon salt
¾ pound (3 sticks) unsalted butter, softened
1½ packages (scant 1½ tablespoons) dry yeast
1¼ cups whole milk, warmed
¼ cup sugar
2 large eggs
Choice of fillings (recipes follow)

1. Measure ⅓ cup flour and the salt onto a board or into a bowl. Add the butter and chop the flour and butter together with a pastry blender or 2 knives.

2. Roll the mixture between two sheets of waxed paper into a 12-by-6-inch rectangle. Chill.

3. Sprinkle the yeast over the warm milk and let stand until the yeast becomes foamy and the mixture has cooled.

4. Add the sugar and 1 lightly beaten egg to the yeast. Stir in the remaining flour (4⅓ cups or so) gradually, mixing with a wooden spoon until a soft dough is formed.

5. Turn the dough onto a floured work surface and knead until it is smooth. Roll the dough on a generously floured board into a 14-inch square. Place the butter-flour mixture on one half of the dough and fold the other half of the dough over it. Press around the edges to seal.

6. Pat the dough with a rolling pin and then roll it out into a paper-thin sheet. Fold the sheet of dough into thirds like a business letter. Repeat the patting, rolling, and folding process 3 times. If the butter mixture softens and begins to ooze out upon rolling, chill the dough before continuing.

7. Cut the finished dough into 3 equal portions. Roll and shape into envelopes, combs, and crescents and fill as described below. (Save any trimmings and stack them neatly to preserve the pastry layers; chill and use to make additional pastries.)

8. Place the pastry shapes on lightly greased baking sheets. Set them aside to rise until half doubled in size.

9. While the pastries are rising, heat the oven to 400 degrees. Brush the envelopes and crescents with the remaining egg, lightly beaten and diluted with a teaspoon or two of water. Bake on the lower shelf until brown, about 20 minutes. Cool on racks.

10. If desired, ice the crescents and envelopes with confectioners' icing made by mixing 1 cup confectioners' sugar with about 1 tablespoon whole milk and ½ teaspoon vanilla extract.

MAKES 2 DOZEN PASTRIES

VANILLA CREAM FILLING

½ cup whole milk
1 tablespoon all-purpose flour
1 large egg yolk
1 tablespoon sugar
½ teaspoon vanilla extract

1. Mix all the ingredients except the vanilla in the top of a double boiler. Cook the mixture over boiling water, stirring constantly, until thick. Cool the mixture, stirring occasionally.

2. Stir in the vanilla.

MAKES ENOUGH FOR 8 PASTRIES

ALMOND PASTE FILLING

¾ pound blanched almonds (about 2¼ cups)
½ cup sugar
1 large egg

Grind the almond with the sugar in a food processor. Transfer to a bowl, fold in the egg by hand, and mix until smooth.

MAKES ENOUGH FOR 8 PASTRIES

PRUNE FILLING

½ cup pureed prunes
¾ cup ground almonds
1 teaspoon grated orange zest

Mix all the ingredients together.

MAKES ENOUGH FOR 8 PASTRIES

CHEESE FILLING

1 cup creamed cottage cheese
1 large egg, well beaten
1 tablespoon sugar
1 tablespoon unsalted butter, melted
Pinch of salt

Pinch of freshly grated nutmeg
Pinch of ground ginger

Blend all the ingredients thoroughly.

MAKES ENOUGH FOR 8 PASTRIES

SHAPING PASTRIES

Envelopes

1. Roll 1 portion of the dough into a long strip about 5 inches wide and ¼ inch thick. Trim the edges to make it 4 inches wide and cut it into 4-inch squares.
2. Spread the center of each square with 1 tablespoon of filling. Fold all 4 corners into the center, and press down.

Cockscombs

1. Roll 1 portion of the dough into a strip about 5 inches wide and ¼ inch thick.
2. Place a strip of filling about ½ inch in diameter down the center and fold the dough over it. Press around the edges and trim evenly.
3. Sprinkle with sugar and chopped almonds and cut into 4-inch lengths. Gash side of each piece 4 times, cutting in about ¾ inch toward the filling.

Crescents

1. Roll 1 portion of the dough into a strip about 5 inches wide and ¼ inch thick. Trim the edges to make it about 4 inches wide. Cut into 2 squares, and then cut into triangles.
2. Place 2 teaspoons filling on the wide side of each triangle and roll up, twisting the ends if necessary to cover the filling.

SERVING SUGGESTION
A café au lait.

JANUARY 11, 1959: ". . . AND A CUP OF COFFEE," BY
CRAIG CLAIBORNE.

—1959

⌒ FYRSTEKAKE (ROYAL CAKE)

Indulge yourself with this fragrant and crumbly Scandinavian breakfast bar—filled with cardamom-infused almond paste—and repent with Mark Bittman's Coconut Oat Pilaf on p. 647.

———

For the Filling
1¼ cups sifted confectioners' sugar
¾ teaspoon ground cardamom
½ teaspoon ground cinnamon
1 large egg white
About 6 tablespoons water
1¼ cups blanched almonds, finely ground

For the Cake
2¼ cups sifted all-purpose flour
2 teaspoons baking powder
½ teaspoon salt
¾ cup sugar
12 tablespoons (1½ sticks) unsalted butter
1 large egg yolk
2 tablespoons whole milk

1. Heat the oven to 300 degrees. To prepare the filling, mix together the confectioners' sugar, cardamom, cinnamon, egg white, and 2 tablespoons water in a bowl. Fold in the ground almonds. Continue adding water, 1 tablespoon at a time until the mixture forms a spreadable paste.
2. To prepare the cake, sift together the flour, baking powder, salt, and sugar. Add the butter and cut it in until mixture has the consistency of coarse crumbs. Beat the egg yolk with the milk, add to the flour mixture, and blend well.
3. Press two-thirds of the dough into the base of a 13-by-9-by-2-inch baking pan. It should be about ¼ inch thick. Spread with the filling.
4. Roll the remaining dough into a ⅛-inch-thick rectangle roughly the same dimensions as the pan. With a pastry cutter or knife, cut into ½-inch-wide strips. Place crisscross fashion over the filling to make a simple lattice.
5. Bake for 45 minutes, or until browned on top. Cool, then cut into 2-by-1-inch bars.

MAKES 54 BARS

If rolling and shaping dough makes you nervous, you can skip the lattice and just crumble the pastry on top.

PERIOD DETAIL

In 1960, three well-regarded hostesses were asked for their menus for Christmas brunch.

June Platt, cookbook author

Baked foie gras [from a can] with toasts
Champagne
Pineapple ice meringue

Evelyn Patterson, cookbook writer and owner of a cooking school

Ripe persimmons or broiled grapefruit with sherry
Sweetbreads on fried toast
Croissants
Banket [puff pastry roll filled with almond paste]

Helen Worth, cookbook writer and owner of a cooking school

Orange and lemon punch
Chicken sticks [deep-fried chicken wings]
Crusty cornmeal [baked polenta]
Panned apples
Platter of kumquats and assorted cheeses

DECEMBER 8, 1963: "CHRISTMAS SPICE," BY CRAIG CLAIBORNE.

—1963

SOUR CREAM COFFEE CAKE

A great coffee cake should have on interior that's sweet and dewy, and a sugary top that's as crusty as Robert Frost. This recipe, which appeared in Craig Claiborne's annual "Four Favorites" column, more than meets the challenge.

Early "coffee cakes" were made with coffee. Stephen Schmidt, a food historian and the author of the forthcoming *Dessert in America*, said such coffee cakes were "part of the Victorian fashion for dark-colored fruited, spiced cakes." If you're curious about this style, see the Wedding Cake on p. 743. "Coffee cakes" designed to be eaten with coffee appeared toward the end of the nineteenth century and were typically made with rich yeast doughs, although now we tend to call these kinds of breakfast breads Danishes. By the 1960s, many coffee cakes, like this one, were leavened with baking soda and baking powder, making them easier to toss together if an impromptu visitor arrived.

———

2 cups all-purpose flour
1 teaspoon baking powder
1/4 teaspoon salt
1/2 pound (2 sticks) unsalted butter, softened
2 cups plus 4 teaspoons sugar
2 large eggs
1 cup sour cream
1/2 teaspoon vanilla extract
1 cup (about 4 ounces) chopped pecans
1 teaspoon ground cinnamon

1. Heat the oven to 350 degrees. Grease and flour a Bundt pan or 9-inch tube pan. Sift the flour with the baking powder and salt.
2. Cream the butter in a large bowl. Add 2 cups sugar gradually, beating until very light and fluffy. Beat in the eggs one at a time, beating very well. Fold in the sour cream and vanilla. Fold in the flour mixture.
3. Combine the remaining 4 teaspoons sugar, pecans, and cinnamon.
4. Place about one-third of the batter in the prepared pan. Sprinkle with three-quarters of the pecan mixture. Spoon in the remaining batter. Sprinkle with the remaining pecans. Bake for 50 to 60 minutes, or until a skewer or knife inserted in the center of the cake comes out clean. Cool on a rack until cool enough to touch, then unmold the cake, or the edges will get mushy.

SERVES 12

COOKING NOTES

This can be made in either a Bundt pan or a tube pan. If you use a Bundt pan, the cake will be more architectural, but once you turn out the cake, you'll lose the great crust that formed on top. If you use a tube pan, you can serve it crust side up, but the cake won't look as handsome.

You might want to toast the pecans to intensify their flavor before adding them to the batter.

JANUARY 7, 1968: "FOUR FAVORITES," BY CRAIG CLAIBORNE.

—1968

DOROTHY JEWISS'S COFFEE CAKE

If you like watching a batter come together in your mixing bowl, you'll love this one, which develops into a silky, golden mass. Out of the oven, the cake is light and springy and rather sweet. For a sterner cake, reduce the sugar in the topping to ¼ cup.

———

2 cups all-purpose flour

1 teaspoon baking powder

1 teaspoon baking soda

¼ teaspoon salt

8 tablespoons (1 stick) unsalted butter, softened

1½ cups sugar

2 large eggs

1 cup sour cream

2 teaspoons vanilla extract

⅓ cup chopped pecans

1 teaspoon ground cinnamon

1. Heat the oven to 325 degrees. Grease a 9-inch square baking pan. Sift together the flour, baking powder, baking soda, and salt.
2. Using a mixer or beating by hand, beat the butter and 1 cup sugar together in a large bowl until fluffy. Beat in the eggs one at a time. Stir in the sour cream and vanilla. Stir the flour mixture into the batter until it is smooth.

3. Spoon half the batter into the pan. Combine the remaining ½ cup sugar, the pecans, and cinnamon and sprinkle two-thirds of it over the batter. Top with the remaining batter and sprinkle with the remaining pecan mixture.
4. Bake until a toothpick inserted in the center of the cake comes out almost clean, 40 to 50 minutes. Serve warm.

SERVES 9

COOKING NOTE
In Step 3, use a spoon dipped in water to spread the top layer of batter, or it will be impossible to nudge the batter to the edges of the pan.

NOVEMBER 24, 1968: "TO GRANDMOTHER'S HOUSE," BY JEAN HEWITT. RECIPE ADAPTED FROM DOROTHY JEWISS, A HOME COOK IN WINCHESTER CENTER, CONNECTICUT.

—1968

LAURA GOODENOUGH'S APPLE COFFEE CAKE

A moist, tall cake, threaded with cinnamon-bound apples. You may recognize the proportions which have appeared in various cake recipes for decades—it is the pound cake of coffee cakes.

———

3 to 5 apples, peeled, cored, and sliced ⅛ inch thick (4 cups)

2 cups plus 5 tablespoons sugar

5 teaspoons ground cinnamon

3 cups all-purpose flour

1 tablespoon baking powder

1 teaspoon salt

1 cup vegetable oil

4 large eggs, lightly beaten

¼ cup orange juice

1 tablespoon vanilla extract

Whipped cream for serving

1. Heat the oven to 375 degrees. Grease a 10-inch tube pan. Combine the apples, 5 tablespoons sugar, and cinnamon; set aside.

2. Sift the flour, the remaining 2 cups sugar, baking powder, and salt into a bowl. Make a well in the center and pour in the oil, eggs, orange juice, and vanilla. Beat with a wooden spoon until well blended.

3. Spoon one-third of the batter into the prepared pan. Make a ring of half the apple mixture, drained of any excess moisture on top, taking care not to let the apple mixture touch the sides of the pan. Spoon another one-third of the batter over. Make a ring of the remaining apples and top with remaining batter.

4. Bake until a skewer or knife inserted in the center of the cake comes out clean, 60 to 70 minutes. Cover the top with aluminum foil if it begins to overbrown.

5. Allow the cake to cool to lukewarm in the pan, then turn out onto a serving plate. Serve warm, with whipped cream.

SERVES 10

COOKING NOTE

Use a flavorful apple such as Honeycrisp, Winesap, or Braeburn. You can also make the recipe with peaches or plums.

NOVEMBER 24, 1968: "TO GRANDMOTHER'S HOUSE," BY JEAN HEWITT. RECIPE ADAPTED FROM LAURA GOODENOUGH, A HOME COOK IN WINCHESTER CENTER, CONNECTICUT.

—1968

MAIDA'S BLUEBERRY CRUMB CAKE

I love that food writers had become such affectionate fans of Maida Heatter's baking that they began to use only her first name, as we now might refer to Marcella, Alice, and Julia. One of the reasons people love Heatter is her perfectionism. She obsesses so you don't have to. Craig Claiborne wrote about the time that, after turning in a cookbook, Heatter discovered that her oven temperature was 25 degrees off. She told her publisher to hold the manuscript and promptly retested all the recipes.

2 cups blueberries
Dry bread crumbs

2⅓ cups all-purpose flour
1 teaspoon ground cinnamon
1¼ cups sugar
8 tablespoons (1 stick) unsalted butter
2 teaspoons baking powder
½ teaspoon salt
1 teaspoon vanilla extract
1 large egg
½ cup whole milk
Finely grated zest of 1 lemon
½ cup finely chopped walnuts

1. Pick over and wash the berries. Drain in a sieve and turn them onto a towel in a single layer. Pat dry with a second towel and set aside to dry thoroughly.

2. Heat the oven to 375 degrees. Butter a 9-inch-square baking pan and dust with dry bread crumbs. Combine ⅓ cup flour, the cinnamon, and ½ cup sugar in a small bowl. Cut in 4 tablespoons of the butter until the mixture resembles coarse crumbs. Set aside.

3. Sift together the remaining 2 cups flour, the baking powder, and salt. Place the blueberries in a bowl and sprinkle with 1½ tablespoons of the dry ingredients. Toss gently. Set aside.

4. Beat the remaining 4 tablespoons butter with the remaining ¾ cup sugar in a large bowl with a hand mixer (or in a mixer fitted with a paddle) until light and fluffy. Beat in the vanilla and egg until the mixture is light and fluffy. Stir in the remaining dry ingredients alternately with the milk, starting and ending with the dry ingredients. Stir in the zest.

5. Spoon the stiff batter over the blueberries and, with a rubber spatula, fold until just mixed. Turn into the prepared pan. Sprinkle with the nuts and then the cinnamon topping.

6. Bake for 50 minutes, or until done. Cool on a rack in the pan for 30 minutes.

7. Loosen the sides of the cake with a knife, place a large sheet of foil over the cake, and invert onto a rack. Place a cake plate over the cake and invert again so that the crumb side is up.

SERVES 9 TO 12

JUNE 10, 1973: "OUR TRUE BLUE BERRY: NATIVE DELIGHTS," BY JEAN HEWITT. RECIPE ADAPTED FROM MAIDA HEATTER, THE COOKBOOK AUTHOR.

1973

KATHARINE McCLINTON'S FOURSOME PANCAKES

Mix sour cream and cottage cheese into pancakes, and you give them character. Fold in egg whites, and you give them wings. And if you stir Cognac into the maple syrup that's poured over the downy pancakes, you get a breakfast you will never forget.

———

1 cup sour cream
1 cup cottage cheese
¾ cup all-purpose flour
1½ teaspoons sugar
¾ teaspoon kosher salt
2 teaspoons vanilla extract
4 large eggs, separated
Butter for cooking the pancakes
Maple syrup
Cognac (optional)

1. Combine the sour cream, cottage cheese, flour, sugar, salt, vanilla extract, and egg yolks in a large bowl and beat with an electric mixer to blend thoroughly.
2. Beat the whites until they hold stiff peaks, and fold them into the batter.
3. Heat a griddle and lightly butter it. Ladle on about ⅓ cup of batter for each pancake. Cook until browned on one side. Turn and cook on the other side. Transfer to a platter and keep warm in a 175-degree oven. Continue ladling the batter and cooking until all the batter is used. Be sure to stir the batter from the bottom as it is used so that it maintains its consistency.
4. Serve with maple syrup, laced, if desired, with Cognac to taste.

MAKES 16 TO 20 PANCAKES

SERVING SUGGESTIONS
Serve with Spiced Hard Sauce (p. 604) or Sauce Suprême (p. 596) and Honey-Orange Smoothie (p. 29).

FEBRUARY 3, 1980: "FOOD: PANCAKES ON THE REBOUND," BY CRAIG CLAIBORNE WITH PIERRE FRANEY. RECIPE ADAPTED FROM READER KATHARINE McCLINTON.
—1980

KATHLEEN CLAIBORNE'S HOT CAKES

In 1980, Craig Claiborne and Pierre Franey were cautiously bullish about pancakes in their Sunday food column, noting that there was "a time a couple of decades ago when pancakes were a staple of this country's diet, as much a part of the breakfast table as ham or bacon and eggs; then they almost disappeared. But the correspondence that has reached our desk within recent months indicates that pancakes may be making some small comeback. More and more readers seem to be asking for recipes." And yet, they hedged—"We do not predict a tidal wave in the popularity of pancakes . . ."—before providing a few recipes, including this marvelously light cornmeal pancake from Claiborne's mother, Kathleen.

The method is nothing very promising. First you pour boiling water over a cornmeal mixture, which thickens to the consistency of library paste. But if you keep whisking the batter, it eventually loosens, and it is further lightened—and this is the key—when you fold in whipped egg whites. If you don't have a griddle, use a large nonstick frying pan or a well-seasoned cast-iron skillet. I made smaller cakes than the original recipe instructed—a scant ¼ cup batter rather than the ⅓ cup recommended. They get crisper edges and are easier to flip.

———

½ cup cornmeal
1 tablespoon sugar
½ teaspoon salt
1 cup boiling water
2 large eggs, separated
1 cup all-purpose flour
1 tablespoon baking powder
1 cup whole milk
¼ cup peanut, vegetable, or corn oil
Syrup, preserves, jams, or jellies for serving

1. Combine the cornmeal, sugar, and salt in a small saucepan. Pour the boiling water over, stirring constantly with a whisk, making sure to get all the lumps in the corners. Cook over medium heat, stirring, for 1 to 2 minutes. The mixture will begin to coalesce and then suddenly will stiffen. Don't fret. Scrape the mix-

ture into a mixing bowl, and let sit for a few minutes to cool, whisking it every now and then.

2. Whisk in the egg yolks. Sift together the flour and baking powder and stir it into the batter; it will get very lumpy and impossibly thick. Add the milk and oil and whisk until smooth.

3. Beat the egg whites until stiff and fold them into the batter.

4. Lightly oil a griddle and heat it to medium-high; you want the pancakes to brown in less than 1 minute. Ladle on about ¼ cup of the batter for each pancake. Cook until browned on one side: bubbles will rise to the surface, and when they begin popping and the edges begin to dry, it's a sign that the pancakes are brown beneath. Turn and cook on the other side, less than 1 minute. Transfer to a platter and keep warm in a 175-degree oven. Continue ladling and cooking until all the batter is used. Serve with syrup, preserves, jams, or jellies.

MAKES ABOUT 20 PANCAKES

SERVING SUGGESTION
Serve these with Spiced Hard Sauce (p. 604).

FEBRUARY 3, 1980: "FOOD: PANCAKES ON THE REBOUND," BY CRAIG CLAIBORNE AND PIERRE FRANEY. RECIPE ADAPTED FROM KATHLEEN CLAIBORNE.

—1980

⌒ HEAVENLY HOTS

Sometimes the name of a dish is irresistible: Ratatouille. Financiers. Mooncakes. Oysters Rockefeller. Fallen soufflé. Anything confited. And my recent favorite, *pudding chômeur* (biscuit dough baked in maple syrup and cream—a delight that Canadians have been keeping to themselves), which translates to "unemployed-person pudding." When I began work on this book and several readers wrote in about heavenly hots, there was no question—I *had* to try a recipe with that name.

Although heavenly hots sound like a late-night cable offering, they're nothing more salacious than pancakes. Once you make them, you'll understand the name: they are so feathery, creamy, and tangy—so

heavenly—that you find yourself unable to let them cool at all before devouring them.

Heavenly hots clarify what's wrong with other pancakes—namely, that most of them are god-awful: doughy, heavy thuds in our bellies. You always think they're a great idea until about ten minutes after you've eaten them.

What makes the hots so heavenly is that they ignore all the classic ratios of flour to sugar to eggs (sorry, Michael Ruhlman!). They're made with low-gluten cake flour and just enough of it to lash the batter of sour cream, sugar, and salt into fragile cakes.

The only problem with heavenly hots is that your first batch is likely to be a wash. The batter is very loose and it produces pancakes—some might call them blini—that are about as sturdy as wet tissue paper. You need to take deep breaths when it's time for flipping, and you need to let the hots know you're the boss. Timid jabs with a spatula will not end well.

Heavenly hots were popularized at the Bridge Creek Restaurant in Berkeley, but the original recipe came from Bob Burnham, a chef who once worked for John Hudspeth, later the owner of Bridge Creek. Burnham served a sugarless version like blini, with caviar. At Bridge Creek, they were breakfast, served in stacks and doused with maple syrup—"real maple syrup," Hudspeth said, "which was unusual in Berkeley at the time." They're the kind of recipe that makes an impression. Hudspeth named his company Heavenly Hots, Inc., and Marion Cunningham, the author of *The Fannie Farmer Cookbook*, and a friend of Hudspeth, included the hots in *The Breakfast Book*.

———

4 large eggs
½ teaspoon salt
½ teaspoon baking soda
¼ cup cake flour
2 cups sour cream
3 tablespoons sugar
Vegetable shortening for cooking the pancakes
Maple syrup or honey

1. Whisk together all the ingredients (except the vegetable shortening and syrup) in a large bowl, beating until smooth. This can also be done in a blender. Chill the batter overnight. (The batter will keep, refrigerated, for up to 1 week.)

2. The next day, heat a griddle or large skillet over medium-high heat. Beat the batter again until smooth. Lightly coat the griddle or skillet with shortening. Drop small spoonfuls (I used ¾ tablespoon) of batter onto the griddle, making sure that when they spread out, they measure less than 3 inches in diameter. When a few bubbles appear on top of the pancakes and the bottoms are browned, turn and cook the second side briefly—you don't want to cook the pancakes all the way through, because you want them to remain creamy in the center. Transfer to a platter and keep warm in a 175-degree oven. Repeat with the remaining batter.

3. Serve with syrup or honey.

MAKES 50 TO 60 SMALL PANCAKES

COOKING NOTES

Don't cook the pancakes all the way through. You want the center to be a pocket of cream.

The pancakes are so fragile that it may take a few tries to flip them. I used the thinnest, most flexible spatula I own, wedged it halfway under each pancake, letting the other half hang, then turned my wrist and gently laid the cake down on its other side. I recommend this over more aggressive flipping, which will tear the pancakes.

VARIATION

Substitute light brown sugar for the sugar and full-fat Greek yogurt for the sour cream.

SERVING SUGGESTIONS

A light maple syrup or acacia honey served on the side, or better yet a sprinkling of lemon zest sugar or cinnamon sugar. Also, Mango Lassi (p. 27).

MARCH 1, 1987: "FOOD: FEAST BEFORE FAST," BY JOANNA PRUESS. RECIPE ADAPTED FROM MARION CUNNINGHAM AND THE BRIDGE CREEK RESTAURANT IN BERKELEY, CALIFORNIA.

—1987

↪ JORDAN MARSH'S BLUEBERRY MUFFINS

Mashing some of the blueberries before adding them to the batter and building the batter on a sturdy foundation of butter makes for muffins that are as delicate as baby birds. As Andrea Estes, a reporter, once wrote in the *Boston Globe*, "For decades, any decent downtown shopping trip ended at Jordan Marsh, where the promise of a sugar-crusted blueberry muffin could make annoying children angelic."

————

2 cups all-purpose flour
½ teaspoon salt
2 teaspoons baking powder
8 tablespoons (1 stick) unsalted butter, softened
1¼ cups plus 1 tablespoon sugar
2 large eggs
½ cup whole milk
2 cups blueberries, rinsed and picked over

1. Heat the oven to 375 degrees. Grease 12 large muffin cups. Sift together the flour, salt, and baking powder.
2. Cream the butter and 1¼ cups sugar in a large bowl until light. Add the eggs one at a time, beating well after each addition. Add to the flour mixture alternately with the milk, beating just until smooth.
3. Crush ½ cup blueberries with a fork, and mix into the batter. Fold in the remaining whole berries.
4. Fill the muffin cups with batter. Sprinkle the remaining tablespoon of sugar over the tops of the muffins. Bake until a toothpick inserted in the center comes out clean, about 30 minutes. Cool for 30 minutes before removing from the pan.
5. Store, uncovered, or the muffins will be too moist the second day—if they last that long.

MAKES 12 MUFFINS

READERS

"[T]here are two sacred things in my life (and kitchen). My mother's seventy-five-year-old rusted vegetable peeler, which I use religiously, and my blueberry muffin recipe. Both items look like they need to be tossed, but they contain my very soul."

Suzanne Casden-Borriello, Woodmere, NY, letter

JUNE 13, 1987: "DE GUSTIBUS: THE BATTLE OVER BLUE-BERRY MUFFINS," BY MARIAN BURROS. RECIPE ADAPTED FROM JORDAN MARSH, A DEPARTMENT STORE IN NEW ENGLAND.

—1987

LIDIA BASTIANICH'S SWISS CHARD AND SCALLION FRITTATA

While frittatas are usually served warm here, Lidia Bastianich, the restaurateur, cookbook author, and cooking show host, reminded us that in Italy they are often eaten at room temperature. This frittata, layered with greens, garlic, and ricotta, is allowed to cool, wrapped in wax paper, and refrigerated until you're ready to eat.

Bastianich also introduced a smart technique: half the eggs are poured into the hot pan and allowed to set, establishing a crisp foundation for the rest of the eggs and the filling.

This frittata would also make a fine lunch. Slice and serve between thin slices of focaccia with the Mezzaluna Salad (p. 185) on the side.

———

1 pound Swiss chard

¼ cup olive oil

2 cloves garlic, lightly crushed

Salt and freshly ground black pepper

8 scallions, cut into ¼-inch-wide slices

1 cup ricotta cheese

8 large eggs, lightly beaten

1. Heat the oven to 350 degrees. Remove the leaves from the chard (reserve the ribs and stems for another use). Wash and dry the leaves and cut them into ½-inch-wide strips.

2. Heat 3 tablespoons oil in a 12-inch ovenproof nonstick skillet over medium-high heat and sauté the garlic until golden-brown. Add the chard and salt and pepper to taste, cover, and cook over medium heat until the chard is wilted, 1 to 2 minutes. Discard the garlic and transfer the chard to a bowl.

3. Cook off any excess liquid left in the pan, then add the scallions and sauté until wilted, 1 to 2 minutes. Pour off any liquid that has accumulated in the bowl

of chard, then add the scallions to the chard. Mix in the ricotta and half of the eggs.

4. Heat the remaining tablespoon of oil in the skillet over medium heat. Add the remaining eggs and allow to set on the bottom. Add the vegetable mixture, spreading it evenly. Cook, uncovered, over low heat until the frittata browns lightly on the bottom, 3 to 5 minutes.

5. Transfer the skillet to the oven and cook until the frittata is set but not dry, about 10 minutes. Let cool.

6. Transfer the frittata to a plate, cover with wax paper, and refrigerate. (The frittata can be made up to a day in advance.) To serve, cut into thin wedges.

SERVES 6

JUNE 2, 1991: "A DAY AT THE BEACH," BY MARK BITTMAN. RECIPE ADAPTED FROM LIDIA BASTIANICH.

—1991

POACHED EGGS WITH DATE-CHORIZO PASTE

This is a dish I had at Arzak, a three-star restaurant in San Sebastián, Spain. The flavors—eggs, chorizo, and bread—are routine in Spanish cooking, but in the hands of the right chef, they sparkle (and cost a lot more). The egg was poached sous vide with goose fat and truffle oil. The bread was reduced to crumbs and mixed with ham and olive oil, then spooned onto the plate like a relish next to the egg. The chorizo was pureed with dates, which subdued its sharpness and gave the resulting orange paste a deep, tantalizing sweetness. This sauce was spooned in a straight line on the plate.

The poached egg preparation turned out to be easy to replicate in a home kitchen. I substituted butter for goose fat and, following a hint from the chef, Juan Arzak, let the eggs sit in little plastic-wrapped packages of truffle oil and salt for 2 days before poaching them (you may own a sous-vide machine; I don't). The paste was a matter of balancing acidity and sweetness, adding a touch of vinegar and sugar syrup as I pureed the dates and chorizo in the food processor.

The bread sauce would turn this dish into a project; serving toasted country bread sprinkled with great olive oil on the side, I decided, would be a saner alternative.

A single bite will tell you that it's the date paste that makes this dish. If you want to take a shortcut, a little dab of the paste rubbed on a hard-boiled egg wouldn't be a bad idea. In fact, it was a fantastic discovery, worth traveling to Spain to learn.

Medjool dates are available at markets with a good dried fruit selection.

————

Unsalted butter, softened

White truffle oil

Fine sea salt

6 large eggs

¼ cup sugar

¼ cup water

½ cup Medjool dates, pitted and coarsely chopped

¾ cup skinned, thinly sliced Spanish chorizo

3 tablespoons rice wine vinegar

Freshly ground black pepper

2 tablespoons extra virgin olive oil,
    plus more for the bread

6 thick slices rustic bread

Coarse salt

1. Two days before serving, prepare the eggs: For each egg, lay out a 12-inch square of plastic wrap. Generously grease it with butter and sprinkle with truffle oil and salt. Crack an egg in the center of each square, then quickly collect the edges of the plastic wrap, twist the ends of wrap tightly, and tie with kitchen string. Refrigerate for 2 days.

2. Combine the sugar and water in a small saucepan and bring to a boil, stirring to dissolve the sugar. Let cool.

3. Combine the dates, chorizo, vinegar, and 2 tablespoons of the sugar syrup in a food processor, season with pepper, and puree until smooth, scraping down the sides of the bowl with a spatula. The mixture should be thick but not stiff. Pulse in the olive oil, and then water, a tablespoon at a time, as needed. Taste and adjust the seasoning.

4. Put the paste on a large square of cheesecloth. Wrap it into a ball and squeeze with your hands over a bowl. (This is messy and time-consuming, but it strains out any chewy pieces of chorizo and makes the paste markedly smoother.)

5. Bring a medium saucepan of water to a simmer. Using a slotted spoon, gently add the egg packages to the water. Simmer for 3½ minutes, for a runny yolk.

6. Meanwhile, toast the bread.

7. When the eggs are done, transfer the packages to paper towels to drain. Place 1 package on each of 6 plates and cut open at the top with scissors. Carefully remove the plastic wrap, making sure all the oil stays on the plate. Sprinkle each egg with coarse salt and spoon a little date-chorizo paste around it. Sprinkle olive oil on the toasts, and serve with the eggs.

SERVES 6 FOR BRUNCH OR AS A FIRST COURSE

JANUARY 12, 2000: "SURPRISE FROM A 3-STAR TABLE," BY AMANDA HESSER. RECIPE ADAPTED FROM ARZAK IN SAN SEBASTIÁN, SPAIN.

—2000

⌒ SPICED PUMPKIN OATMEAL

————

¼ teaspoon ground allspice

¼ teaspoon freshly grated nutmeg

½ teaspoon ground cinnamon

⅛ teaspoon ground ginger

¼ cup packed brown sugar

1 cup canned pumpkin puree

4½ cups low-fat milk or water

1½ cups steel-cut oats

¾ teaspoon salt

Warm applesauce (optional)

Chopped apples (optional)

Apple cider syrup (optional)

1. Toast the allspice, nutmeg, cinnamon, and ginger in a large saucepan over low heat, stirring occasionally, until fragrant, about 2 minutes. Stir in the brown sugar, then add the pumpkin and stir to combine. Add the milk, raise the heat, and bring to a simmer. Stir in the oats and simmer over medium heat until tender but not mushy, about 25 to 30 minutes.

2. Stir in the salt. Serve with applesauce, apples, and syrup, if desired.

SERVES 6

JANUARY 3, 2001: "OATMEAL THAT ISN'T FOR URCHINS," BY MELISSA CLARK. RECIPE ADAPTED FROM OLIVES NY IN NEW YORK CITY.

—2001

SCRAMBLED EGGS WITH TOAST AND BACON

7 large eggs
Freshly ground white pepper
¼ cup cold heavy cream

I once got the hardship assignment of having Daniel Boulud prepare me breakfast, lunch, and dinner. This is what he made for breakfast—a display of how a great chef can turn the most basic of basics into gastronomic bliss.

He cracked seven room-temperature eggs into a sieve set over a bowl and began whisking. "What's very important," he said, "is to strain them, so you remove what makes the coagulation lumpy. It should be smooth." The eggs streamed from the sieve into the bowl, and he seasoned them with salt and white pepper. Then he placed them over a pan of simmering water and began gently rocking the eggs back and forth in the bowl with a spoon.

The bowl heated slowly, and he stirred and stirred and looked bored. I thought he might start whistling. The eggs lost their shine and thickened like pastry cream. When tiny curds began to form, he returned to his whisk and increased the pace, all the while keeping the heat as low as possible. When the mixture began to look creamy, like polenta, he began adding chunks of cold Échiré butter. One tablespoon, then two, each getting absorbed in the mix. Next came the finishing touch: off the heat, he held the bowl close to his stomach and whisked in large spoonfuls of cold heavy cream, "to stop the cooking," he said.

As promised, there wasn't a single lump. Just creamy egg pudding with tiny soft curds. Boulud resisted the temptation to plop on a dollop of caviar. Instead, he had toasted some bread crumbs in a pan with butter and salt and piled them into a small round dish. He'd also cut bacon on a meat slicer. Some slices he baked flat; others he wrapped around dowels and baked into thin, salty coils, as fragile as icicles.

I sprinkled the bread crumbs on the eggs like cheese on pasta and nibbled on the bacon. It was a little like eating soufflé and pudding at once, the eggs delicate and lovely, the crumbs offering up faint crunch.

------

6 paper-thin slices bacon (sliced like prosciutto)
3 slices day-old white bread, crusts removed
5 tablespoons unsalted butter, preferably French
Fine sea salt

1. Heat the oven to 350 degrees. Line a baking sheet with parchment paper and arrange the bacon on top. Cover with another piece of parchment, then top with another baking sheet, to keep the bacon flat.

2. Bake until the bacon is browned and crisp, about 15 minutes. Drain on paper towels and place on a serving plate. Keep warm.

3. Rip the bread into pieces and pulse in a food processor until coarse crumbs form. Melt 3 tablespoons butter in a large skillet over medium heat. Stir in the crumbs and sauté until toasted to a hazelnut color. Season with salt and place in a serving bowl. Set in a warm spot.

4. Add water to the bottom of a double boiler and bring to a steady light simmer. Crack the eggs into a fine sieve set over the top of the double boiler and, using a whisk, work the eggs thoroughly through the sieve. Season generously with salt and pepper. Place the pan with the eggs over the bottom pan (with about 1 inch of clearance between it and the water). Using a wooden spoon, stir the eggs constantly. If they begin to coagulate, lower the heat. It should take about 5 minutes for a light film to form on the bottom and sides of the pan. Keep stirring. When small curds appear, whisk the mixture until it is thick like pudding.

5. Remove the top pan and whisk in the remaining 2 tablespoons butter; the eggs should smooth out. Whisk in the cream 1 tablespoon at a time until the texture is like a creamy polenta. If the eggs are runny, place the pan briefly back over the hot water and stir until they have thickened. Taste and adjust the seasoning. Pour the eggs into serving dishes. Serve with the bacon, and sprinkle with the bread crumbs.

SERVES 2

COOKING NOTE
You may need to go to a specialty market to get the bacon sliced like prosciutto.

SERVING SUGGESTION
Bloody Mary (p. 21)

APRIL 8, 2001: "FOOD: HOW TO: COOK THE BASICS LIKE DANIEL BOULUD," BY AMANDA HESSER. RECIPE ADAPTED FROM DANIEL BOULUD, THE OWNER AND CHEF AT DANIEL AND OTHER RESTAURANTS IN NEW YORK CITY.

—2001

MORNING BREAD PUDDING

One year for Christmas, my sister, Rhonda, made a strata (baked eggs and bread). Hers was actually more flan than strata, with caramel on the bottom and a filling of bread that had been soaked overnight in egg and milk. It was baked and then inverted like an upside-down cake. Everyone loved it, but the holidays passed, and the recipe vanished.

This was my attempt to replicate it, which resulted in a dish that's more like a cross between a tarte Tatin and a moist, delicate bread pudding. I swirled a caramel around the base of a pie dish as you would for flan, then filled the bottom of the pan with thick slices of challah. I could have used any kind of bread—the Italian sweet bread panettone would be delicious, as would walnut bread or even plain country bread—but I like the feathery interior and shiny crust of challah.

Then I whisked together eggs, sugar, and a little mascarpone cheese, adding milk a little at a time, as you would oil to a salad dressing. I also whisked in a few drops of almond extract (and, later, just before baking, sprinkled chopped toasted almonds over the top, for a little crunch). I poured this mixture over the bread in the pie dish, making sure every piece was saturated, and let it rest overnight in the refrigerator. That extra time seems to meld the bread with the pudding, so that when it bakes it is light, moist, impossibly fluffy.

The next morning all I needed to do was slide the pie dish into a hot oven. Then I inverted it onto a serving plate. The caramel soaked through the edges and formed a dark sauce that ran around the plate. It was like syrup on French toast, without any of the cloying qualities of syrup.

A spoonful of fromage frais or fromage blanc, both of which are weepy and loose, works here much the way crème fraîche does on tarte Tatin. It eases the richness of the pudding with a rousing touch of acidity.

¾ cup plus 2 tablespoons sugar

6 tablespoons unsalted butter

12 to 15 slices brioche or challah (all should be about ½ inch thick and about 3 inches round; cut accordingly)

8 large eggs

¼ cup mascarpone cheese

1 cup whole milk

¼ teaspoon almond extract

¼ cup coarsely chopped toasted almonds

About ¾ cup fromage frais or fromage blanc for serving

1. Combine ¾ cup sugar and the butter in a small heavy saucepan and place over medium-low heat. The butter will melt and the sugar will dissolve, then the mixture will boil for a few minutes and begin to brown. Adjust the heat and stir occasionally with a wooden spoon so it browns evenly. When it's a dark brown, remove from the heat and pour into a 9-inch ceramic or Pyrex pie dish. Swirl the caramel around the base and 1 inch up the sides of the dish. Place the dish in the refrigerator and chill until the caramel is cold.

2. Place the heel of bread in the center of the pie dish (or 2 slices stacked on top of each other). Arrange the remaining slices, standing them against one another, around the center. They should fill the pie dish snugly.

3. Whisk together the eggs, the remaining 2 tablespoons sugar, and mascarpone cheese in a large bowl until very smooth. Add the milk and almond extract. Pour this over the bread, making sure to saturate all of it. Cover with plastic wrap and refrigerate overnight.

4. In the morning, take the pie dish out of the refrigerator and discard the plastic wrap. Heat the oven to 375 degrees.

5. Bake the pudding for 15 minutes. Sprinkle the almonds over the pudding and continue baking until moist but not wet in the center, about 15 to 20 minutes more. Remove from the oven and run a knife around the edges of the dish, loosening the bread from the sides. Place a serving plate over top of the dish (bottom side up) and, using pot holders, hold the pudding over the sink and, in a single fluid motion, holding it away from your body, invert the plate. Lift off the pie dish. Scrape any extra caramel from the pie dish over the pudding.

6. To serve, cut into wedges at the table and spoon a healthy dollop of fromage frais onto each plate.

SERVES 6

I served this with Winter Fruit Salad (p. 850). Other possibilities: a glass of tangerine juice, scented with fresh mint and just a splash of Champagne. Perhaps a few crisp slices of Irish bacon, to give the meal the contrast of sweetness and salinity. A cup of milky coffee (warm whole milk and whisk it so it's frothy but not too hot) never hurts.

DECEMBER 19, 2001: "THE LAST GIFT OF THE MORNING,"
BY AMANDA HESSER.

—2001

BILL GRANGER'S SCRAMBLED EGGS

This dish made Bill Granger, a young cook with a small restaurant in Sydney, famous. After cooking these eggs, for which no adjective is adequate, a friend summed them up as "fried cream." I'd say that's exactly right; the eggs are there just to bind the cream as you cook it.

No one who's serious about food goes to Sydney without stopping in at Bills Café for his scrambled eggs. R. W. Apple Jr., the *Times* correspondent and legendary gourmand, was a regular, and on one of his visits, he had the foresight to secure the recipe for the rest of us. I've included an ingredient list to make shopping and assembling the dish easier, but I've left Apple's artful recipe instructions, which he wove into his story about Granger.

½ tablespoon unsalted butter
Pinch of salt
½ cup heavy cream, at room temperature
2 large eggs, at room temperature

"Mr. Granger uses a nonstick pan and the merest sliver of butter (¼ ounce), a pinch or two of salt, no water, and ½ cup of cream with 2 eggs. The eggs have a soft, mousse-like texture, not the slightest bit rubbery, with unusually large curds. Not surprisingly, they are divinely creamy, but they are also as light as the breath of an angel.

"Melt the butter over high heat, whisk the other ingredients together in a bowl, pour them into the pan, and—summon your courage. Do nothing for 20 seconds, except maybe cross your fingers. Then stir very slowly with a wooden spoon, folding the rim of the egg mixture toward the center. Don't churn away like a cement mixer. Pause for another 20 seconds, then repeat the gentle stirring-and-folding process. Take the pan off the flame, allowing the residual heat in the pan to complete the cooking. Finally, give the eggs one last easy swirl.

"The additional liquid represented by the cream slows down the cooking, reducing the prospects of overcooking. But there is a limit to the amount the eggs can absorb; research by the food scientist Harold McGee suggests that Mr. Granger is pushing the limit hard. Overcooking is a disaster, resulting in either a leathery texture or solid lumps floating in watery liquid.

"Serve with thick toast."

SERVES 1, MAYBE 2

JANUARY 9, 2002: "THE EGG MASTER OF SYDNEY," BY
R. W. APPLE JR. RECIPE ADAPTED FROM BILL GRANGER,
THE OWNER OF BILLS CAFÉ IN SYDNEY, AUSTRALIA.

—2002

CHORIZO REVUELTOS (SCRAMBLED EGGS WITH CHORIZO)

Revueltos are a Spanish form of scrambled eggs and, in my view, are the best way to scramble eggs. The eggs are cracked directly into the pan and cooked rapidly over high heat while you break them up and swirl them around, gathering threads of white and yolk and, in this recipe, bits of chorizo. Revueltos make a fine breakfast and an even better first course for dinner. The fat in the chorizo has a way of making the eggs taste creamy without the need for any cream.

1½ ounces mild Spanish chorizo, thinly sliced,
    cut crosswise into half-moons
1 tablespoon olive oil
6 large eggs, cracked into a bowl
Coarse sea salt

1. Spread the sliced chorizo over the bottom of a large nonstick skillet and place over medium-high heat. When the chorizo begins to sizzle, add the olive oil to the pan. Pour in the eggs, then, using a wooden spoon, very quickly stir the eggs, breaking the yolks and turning the eggs over and over again, until just barely cooked, lifting the pan off the heat halfway through. It will take less than a minute.

2. Pour onto a serving dish, sprinkle with sea salt, and serve.

SERVES 2 FOR BREAKFAST OR AS A FIRST COURSE

COOKING NOTES

If you want to serve 4, it's best to repeat the recipe in the same pan, or use 2 pans at once.

To make the recipe less stressful, I have you crack the eggs into a bowl and then pour them into the hot pan. If you prefer to crack them into the pan, go for it.

VARIATIONS

Revueltos can be made with almost anything, but they are best with drier ingredients (i.e., not tomatoes or peppers). Try rock shrimp, sautéed ramps, cured ham, or sautéed mushrooms. And don't use too much of any of them—revueltos are best when the added flavors merely scent the eggs.

SERVING SUGGESTIONS

Pan con Tomate (p. 91), Potato, Ham, and Piquillo Pepper Croquetas (p. 94), Rabbit Soup with Garlic, Peppers, and Chorizo (p. 152), Lightly Smoked Salt Cod Salad (p. 437), Churros with Chocolate Sauce (p. 866)

MARCH 6, 2002: "TRULY SPANISH CHORIZO, IN AMERICA AT LAST," BY AMANDA HESSER; AND FEBRUARY 6, 2005: "THE ARSENAL," BY AMANDA HESSER.

—2002

☞ "BREAKFAST" SHRIMP AND GRITS

There's no reason to limit this Low Country dish to breakfast. Shrimp and grits makes an enviable lunch or dinner, which is how I ate it. The grits portion is an excellent recipe itself and should probably become your go-to grits method, to be used with this or any other accompaniment.

———

For the Grits
3 1/2 cups water
3/4 cup grits
1/4 teaspoon salt
6 ounces cheddar cheese, grated (about 1 1/2 cups)
3 tablespoons unsalted butter

For the Shrimp
4 tablespoons unsalted butter
3/4 cup chopped onion
1/2 cup chopped green bell pepper
2 cloves garlic, minced
1 cup diced ripe tomatoes with a little of their juice (chopped canned tomatoes are preferable to less-than-perfect fresh tomatoes)
1/2 teaspoon dried thyme
1 tablespoon all-purpose flour
1 pound medium to large shrimp, shelled, shells reserved for stock
1/2 to 1 cup shrimp stock (see Cooking Note)
1 tablespoon tomato paste
1/3 cup heavy cream
2 teaspoons Worcestershire sauce
2 dashes Tabasco
Salt
2 tablespoons chopped flat-leaf parsley

1. To make the grits, bring the water to a boil in a medium saucepan and stir in the grits. Reduce the heat to low, cover, and cook for 15 to 20 minutes, until the grits are tender and the water has been absorbed. Remove from the heat, add the salt, cheese, and butter, and stir until the cheese is melted. Keep warm.

2. To make the shrimp, melt the butter in a large skillet over medium heat. Add the onion, pepper, and garlic and sauté until softened, about 3 minutes. Add the tomatoes, with their juice, and thyme, bring to a simmer, and cook for 2 to 3 minutes. Sprinkle with the flour and stir well. Add the shrimp and stir constantly until they begin to turn pink, about 2 minutes.

3. Add 1/2 cup stock and cook for 2 to 3 minutes more. Add the tomato paste and stir until blended. Add the cream, Worcestershire, and Tabasco, and more stock

if needed to make a spoonable sauce that generously coats the shrimp. Heat thoroughly, being careful not to let it come to a boil. Taste for salt.

4. Place a portion of grits in the center of each plate and spoon the shrimp over or around it. Sprinkle with the parsley.

SERVES 4 FOR BREAKFAST OR AS A LIGHT LUNCH OR FIRST COURSE

COOKING NOTES

You can have your fish guy shell the shrimp and save the shells for you—or just do it yourself, it's only 1 pound.

I added, as I often find I need to with recipes calling for Tabasco, more than what's called for.

Shrimp cook very quickly—it's better to take them off the heat when they're underdone and have to finish them later. If you overcook them, you're doomed.

The recipe offered this method for making shrimp stock: Combine the reserved shrimp shells and 2 cups water and boil until the liquid is reduced by half. Strain.

SERVING SUGGESTION
Bloody Mary (p. 21)

AUGUST 18, 2002: "FOOD: BIGHEARTED SHRIMP," BY JULIA REED.

—2002

◦ AMAZING OVERNIGHT WAFFLES

Like a warm pretzel, these waffles have the consummate balance of sweetness, yeast, and salinity. They're the work of Mollie Katzen, one of America's most successful cookbook writers of the 1980s and '90s. If you make the waffles, you'll understand her success.

2 cups all-purpose flour
1 teaspoon active dry yeast
1 tablespoon sugar
$1/2$ teaspoon salt
2 cups whole milk

1 large egg, lightly beaten
6 tablespoons unsalted butter, melted,
    plus butter for the waffle iron
Nonstick cooking spray

1. Combine the flour, yeast, sugar, and salt in a bowl. Whisk in the milk until blended. Cover the bowl tightly with plastic wrap and let stand overnight at room temperature. (If the room is warmer than 70 degrees, refrigerate.)

2. In the morning, heat the waffle iron. Beat the egg and melted butter into the bowl of batter; the batter will be quite thin. Spray the hot waffle iron with nonstick spray, and rub on a little butter with a paper towel or piece of bread. For each waffle, add just enough batter to cover the cooking surface—like icing on a cake. Cook the waffle until crisp and brown but not too dark, 2 to 3 minutes. Serve hot with toppings.

MAKES 3 TO 12 WAFFLES, DEPENDING ON THE KIND OF WAFFLE IRON YOU USE (BELGIAN OR STANDARD)

COOKING NOTES

I used a 1961 Westinghouse waffle iron and the recipe made 12 thin waffles.

I did my very best to rid this book of all "nonstick spray," and yet here it is (it makes a few other appearances, but let's not discuss the details). I grudgingly admit that it's helpful for evenly, sparingly coating the iron. Butter, of course, is still needed, for flavor.

SERVING SUGGESTION
Serve these with Sauce Suprême (p. 596).

OCTOBER 9, 2002: "BREAKFAST AS THE NEW CURE-ALL," BY ALEX WITCHEL. ADAPTED FROM *MOLLIE KATZEN'S SUNLIGHT CAFÉ*, BY MOLLY KATZEN.

—2002

MISSISSIPPI PANCAKES

In Mississippi they know how to make a feathery pancake.

———

    2 large eggs
    I cup whole milk
    2 tablespoons vegetable oil
    3 tablespoons unsalted butter, melted
    I ¼ cups all-purpose flour
    I tablespoon baking powder
    I tablespoon sugar
    ½ teaspoon salt

1. Place a nonstick griddle or skillet over medium heat. Beat the eggs in a large bowl until light and foamy. Add the milk, oil, and butter.
2. Sift together the dry ingredients into another bowl, then beat them into the liquid ingredients with a whisk.
3. When the griddle is hot, pour in about ¼ cup batter for each pancake, leaving space between. Flip when the batter bubbles and continue cooking for about a minute. Serve immediately.

MAKES ABOUT 20 PANCAKES

SERVING SUGGESTIONS
Honey-Orange Smoothie (p. 29), Mango Lassi (p. 27)

DECEMBER 4, 2002: "WITH PANCAKES, EVERY DAY IS SUNDAY," BY LUCIAN K. TRUSCOTT IV.

—2002

CHEESE PUDDING SOUFFLÉS

Many steps, many rewards. You end up with individual soufflés, each as light as a dandelion puff and suffused with onion and garlic. These are ideal for both brunch and as a first course for dinner. Plan them for a party, because you can make them, up to the point of the second baking, before everyone arrives. And don't be shy with the cayenne. Onion and garlic grow more beguiling when stoked with a little heat.

———

    4 tablespoons unsalted butter
    ¼ cup all-purpose flour
    I ½ cups whole milk, slightly warmed
    I teaspoon salt, or to taste
    2 sprigs thyme
    I medium onion, diced
    ½ cup thinly sliced scallions, including
        a bit of the green part
    ½ cup thinly sliced garlic
    ½ teaspoon freshly ground black pepper, or to taste
    Pinch of cayenne pepper
    ½ cup grated Gruyère cheese
    3 large eggs, separated
    ⅓ cup heavy cream

1. Melt 3 tablespoons butter in a saucepan over medium-low heat. Add the flour and cook for a few minutes, stirring constantly. Pour in the milk a little at a time, whisking after each addition until smooth. Add ½ teaspoon salt and the thyme sprigs, reduce the heat to very low, and cook, stirring frequently, until the sauce is medium thick, 10 to 15 minutes. Let cool to room temperature, and remove the thyme.
2. Melt the remaining tablespoon of butter in a large skillet over medium heat. Add the onion and cook until translucent, about 5 minutes. Add the scallions, garlic, the remaining ½ teaspoon salt, and ¼ cup water, reduce the heat, and cook until the garlic is soft and the water is nearly evaporated, about 10 minutes; add more water if necessary to keep the vegetables from browning. Set aside to cool.
3. Puree the onion mixture in a food processor. Add the sauce, black pepper, cayenne, and Gruyère and process until blended. Taste and adjust the seasoning—it should be fairly highly seasoned. Add the egg yolks and process until blended. Transfer to a large bowl.
4. Heat the oven to 400 degrees. Generously butter six 6-ounce ramekins or custard cups. Beat the egg whites in a medium bowl until they form soft peaks, and gently fold them into the cheese mixture. (Do not overfold.)
5. Spoon the mixture into the ramekins and place them in a baking pan. Add enough boiling water to come halfway up the sides of the ramekins. Bake until the soufflés are puffed and light golden brown, 20 to 30 minutes. Carefully remove the ramekins from the water bath.

6. When the soufflés have cooled for 10 minutes, unmold them by running a paring knife around the edges, inverting each soufflé into the palm of your hand, and placing it in a shallow baking dish, top side up. They can now be held at room temperature for a few hours. (They can also be held in the refrigerator, covered in plastic wrap, overnight.)

7. When ready to serve, heat the oven to 425 degrees. If they've been refrigerated, bring the soufflés to room temperature. Pour the cream over and around the soufflés. Bake until the cream is hot and bubbling and the soufflés are puffed up again, about 6 to 8 minutes. Serve with the hot cream.

SERVES 6 FOR BRUNCH OR AS A FIRST COURSE

COOKING NOTE

In Step 2, I added 3 more tablespoons water after the initial 10 minutes of cooking the garlic.

FEBRUARY 16, 2003: "PREP SCHOOL," BY JULIA REED. RECIPE ADAPTED FROM *CHEZ PANISSE CAFÉ COOKBOOK* BY ALICE WATERS AND THE COOKS OF CHEZ PANISSE.

—2003

⌢ BOILED EGGS

Julia Moskin, a *Times* food writer, laid down these rules for boiling eggs that produce "consistently excellent results."

————

ORIGINAL RECIPE

"Place the eggs in a single layer in a heavy saucepan and cover with cold water by at least 1 inch. Add a teaspoon of salt. Leaving the pan uncovered, turn the heat to high. As soon as the water comes to a boil, turn off the heat and cover. After 10 minutes, remove the cover and run cold water over the eggs for 1 minute. (For firmer yolks, leave the eggs to cool in the water for up to 2 hours.) Refrigerate for up to 1 week.

"To peel, gently tap each egg against the counter, turning to make a crackle pattern. Start peeling at the broad end, where there is an air pocket. For the best flavor, eggs, once peeled, should be used within a few hours."

APRIL 9, 2003: "HOW TO BOIL AN EGG: SO SIMPLE, BUT NOT EASY," BY JULIA MOSKIN. RECIPE ADAPTED FROM *COOKS ILLUSTRATED.*

—2003

⌢ HAZELNUT-LEMON-RICOTTA PANCAKES

Notes from my recipe playbook: here I essentially fused the lemon-ricotta pancakes from the Four Seasons in New York City with the hazelnut waffles served downtown at Balthazar—and I did so by taking a recipe for cottage cheese pancakes from *Joy of Cooking* and adding ricotta, lemon zest, hazelnuts, and more salt.

————

Grated zest of 2 lemons
1/3 cup sugar
I cup all-purpose flour
1/2 cup finely ground toasted hazelnuts
2 teaspoons baking powder
1/2 teaspoon baking soda
I teaspoon kosher salt
I cup whole milk
3 tablespoons unsalted butter, melted, plus
    butter for cooking the pancakes
2 large eggs, separated
I teaspoon vanilla extract
I cup ricotta cheese, drained of any liquid
Honey

1. The day before, rub together the lemon zest and sugar in a bowl. Cover and set aside at room temperature.

2. The next day, make the pancakes: Mix the flour, lemon sugar, hazelnuts, baking powder, baking soda, and salt in a bowl. Whisk the milk, butter, egg yolks, vanilla, and ricotta in another bowl. Fold this into the dry ingredients.

3. Whip the egg whites just until stiff, then fold them into the batter.

4. Heat a pancake griddle. Lightly coat the surface with butter, then use a 1/4-cup measure to scoop the batter and cook, in batches, until the pancakes appear dry around the edges, about 3 minutes, then flip them and cook for another minute or two. Serve with honey.

NOVEMBER 6, 2005: "THE WAY WE EAT: CITRUS MAXIMUS," BY AMANDA HESSER. FOUNDATION OF THE RECIPE ADAPTED FROM *THE ALL NEW ALL PURPOSE JOY OF COOKING*.

—2005

⌒ POACHED SCRAMBLED EGGS

Daniel Patterson, the chef and owner of Coi in San Francisco and an occasional columnist for the *Times Magazine*, came up with this recipe in an attempt to find a low-stress egg dish. "What would happen," he wrote, "if I beat the eggs before putting them in the water? I expected that they would act much as the intact eggs did and bind quickly, but I did not expect them to set into the lightest, most delicate scrambled eggs imaginable."

————

4 large eggs

Fine sea salt and freshly ground black pepper

2 tablespoons extra virgin olive oil or melted butter
   (optional)

1. Crack each egg into a medium-mesh sieve set over a bowl, letting the thin part of the white drain away, then transfer the remaining yolk and white to a small bowl. Beat the eggs vigorously with a fork for 20 seconds. Don't add salt. (The grains of salt would tear the structure of the eggs, causing them to disintegrate on contact with the water.)

2. Set a medium saucepan filled with 4 inches of water over moderate heat. Put a strainer in the sink—line it with cheesecloth if you have it. When the water is at a low boil, add a few large pinches of salt, then stir in a clockwise direction to create a whirlpool. Pour the eggs into the moving water, cover the pan, and count to 20. Almost instantly, the eggs will change from translucent to opaque and float to the surface in gossamer ribbons.

3. Turn off the heat and uncover the pan. While holding back the eggs with a spoon, pour off most of the water through the strainer. Gently slide the eggs into the strainer and press them lightly to expel any excess liquid. Let them sit there for a minute while you get bowls or remove bread from the toaster.

4. Scoop some eggs into each bowl, season with salt and pepper, and drizzle with a fresh and vibrant green olive oil or melted butter if desired.

SERVES 2

COOKING NOTE

Patterson instructs you to strain the egg whites, an odd step, but as he explained, the thicker parts of the whites are higher in protein and help bind the eggs in the simmering water. The loose whites dilute the thick whites' strength, so it's best to strain them out. Fresh eggs have less loose whites, so use fresh ones!

SERVING SUGGESTIONS

Serve with smoked paprika (pimentón), piment d'Espelette, or a spoonful of crème fraîche and a dollop of caviar.

JANUARY 8, 2006: "THE WAY WE EAT: WHICH CAME FIRST?" BY DANIEL PATTERSON.

—2006

⌒ BUTTERY POLENTA WITH PARMESAN AND OLIVE-OIL-FRIED EGGS

This is the kind of dish that will be good no matter who makes it, as long as he follows the directions and doesn't skimp on the butter. But its presentation—yellow on white on yellow, blob on blob on blob—separates the stylist from the functionalists. Someone like Suzanne Goin, the chef at Lucques in Los Angeles, would plate it in such a way that you'd be rapturous before even tasting it. Kenny Shopsin, the famously sloppy king of diner food in New York, would toss it onto the plate in a heap, and you'd probably avert your eyes. Which are you?

————

5 cups chicken broth or water

1½ cups polenta (not quick-cooking),
   coarse cornmeal, or corn grits

¾ teaspoon salt

4 tablespoons unsalted butter

¼ teaspoon freshly ground black pepper,
    plus more to taste

One 1-ounce chunk Parmesan cheese

2 tablespoons olive oil

8 large eggs

Coarse sea salt

1. Bring the broth to a simmer in a large pot. Stir in the polenta and salt. Simmer, stirring frequently, until thickened to taste, 10 to 20 minutes. Stir in the butter and pepper; cover the pot to keep warm.

2. Using a vegetable peeler, slice the cheese into slivers. Or grate it on the largest holes of a box grater.

3. Heat 1 tablespoon olive oil in a large skillet until very hot. Fry 4 eggs until their edges are crisp and the yolks still runny. Transfer to a warm plate. Repeat with the remaining oil and eggs.

4. Spoon the polenta into 4 shallow bowls, shower with the cheese, and top with the fried eggs. Garnish with coarse salt and more pepper.

SERVES 4

FEBRUARY 7, 2007: "A GOOD APPETITE; A MORNING MEAL BEGS TO STAY UP LATE," BY MELISSA CLARK.

—2007

⌒ SOFT SCRAMBLED EGGS WITH PESTO AND FRESH RICOTTA

Melissa Clark designed this recipe to serve just one—a knowing choice, because you won't want to share this with anyone.

_____

½ tablespoon unsalted butter

3 large eggs

Pinch of salt

Freshly ground black pepper

1 tablespoon freshly grated Parmesan cheese (optional)

1 heaping tablespoon pesto, homemade (p. 614) or
    store-bought, or more to taste

3 tablespoons fresh ricotta cheese, broken up into clumps

1. Melt the butter in a medium skillet, preferably well-seasoned cast-iron or nonstick over medium-high

heat. Beat the eggs with the salt, pepper to taste, and, if using, Parmesan cheese. Pour the eggs into the pan, swirl, and turn the heat to low. Using a heatproof rubber spatula, stir the eggs constantly until very loosely set and slightly runnier than you like them.

2. Remove the pan from heat and drizzle the pesto on the eggs. Give the eggs one more gentle stir—enough to finish cooking them and to distribute the pesto in dark green streaks. Scatter the ricotta on eggs and drizzle with more pesto if desired. Serve at once.

SERVES 1

SERVING SUGGESTION
Rhubarb Bellini (p. 30)

OCTOBER 10, 2007: "A GOOD APPETITE; THE URBAN FARMER'S AUTUMN RITUAL," BY MELISSA CLARK.

—2007

⌒ BREAKFAST PIZZA

Pizza for breakfast, but a big step up from the leftovers-in-college kind. Christine Muhlke, a *Times Magazine* columnist and food editor, called this pizza "a life-changing pie of bacon, eggs, and cheese that will make scallion skeptics rethink that '70s garnish."

_____

Pizza dough (p. 377)

For the Topping

6 slices bacon

½ cup freshly grated Parmesan cheese

2 cups grated mozzarella cheese (about 8 ounces)

6 large eggs

Freshly ground black pepper

2 tablespoons minced flat-leaf parsley

2 tablespoons minced chives

2 scallions, thinly sliced

1 shallot, minced

1. One hour before baking, place the dough in a warm spot. Adjust the oven rack to the lowest position and set a pizza stone on it. Heat the oven to 500 degrees.

2. Fry the bacon in a large skillet over medium-high heat until crisp. Drain on a paper-towel-lined plate, then roughly chop.

3. Dip your hands and a ball of dough into flour. Divide dough in half. On a lightly floured countertop, pat the dough into a disk with your fingertips, then drape the dough over your fists and carefully stretch it from beneath to form a 12-inch circle.

4. Generously dust the surface of a pizza peel or large inverted baking sheet with flour and place the stretched dough on it. Sprinkle the dough with half of the Parmesan, mozzarella, and bacon. Crack 3 eggs on top and season with salt and pepper.

5. Shake the pizza peel slightly to make sure the dough is not sticking. Carefully lift any sections that are sticking and sprinkle a bit more flour underneath, then slide the pizza directly onto the baking stone in one quick forward-and-back motion. Bake for 8 to 10 minutes, rotating the pizza after 5 minutes. When the crust is golden, the cheese is melted, and the egg yolks are cooked, use the peel to transfer the pizza to a cutting board. Sprinkle half of the parsley, chives, scallions, and shallot on top. Let cool for 2 minutes, then slice and serve immediately. Prepare the second pizza in the same way.

MAKES TWO 12-INCH PIZZAS

AUGUST 10, 2008: "THE WAY WE EAT: WOOD-FIRED," BY CHRISTINE MUHLKE. RECIPE ADAPTED FROM BIG SUR BAKERY, IN BIG SUR, CALIFORNIA.

—2008

∽ COCONUT OAT PILAF

2 tablespoons peanut oil or unsalted butter

1½ cups steel-cut oats (not rolled), rinsed and drained

1 tablespoon minced or grated fresh ginger

1 tablespoon mustard seeds (brown or black is fine)

3 cardamom pods

1 or 2 dried red chiles, like Thai (optional)

Salt and freshly ground black pepper

2½ cups water

½ cup grated unsweetened dried coconut

½ cup chopped cilantro, mint, scallions, or flat-leaf parsley, or a combination

1. Put the oil or butter in a pot with a tight-fitting lid over medium-high heat. When the oil is hot or the butter melts, add the oats and ginger and stir until coated. Add the spices and a pinch each of salt and pepper; stir until fragrant, just a minute or two.

2. Gradually stir in the water—be careful, some of the oats may hop out of the pan. Bring to a boil, then reduce the heat to medium-low so the mixture gently bubbles. Cook, undisturbed, until most of the water has been absorbed and holes begin to appear on the surface, 5 to 7 minutes. Cover, remove from the heat, and let sit for at least 10, or up to 20, minutes.

3. Meanwhile, toast the coconut in a skillet over medium-low heat, shaking the pan and stirring until it is toasted and fragrant, several minutes (watch carefully so that it does not burn).

4. Toss the coconut and cilantro into the oats, fluffing the mixture with a fork. Taste and adjust the seasoning, and serve hot or at room temperature.

SERVES 4

COOKING NOTES
If you want a lot of coconut flavor, you can double the coconut.

Go light on the scallions, if using; you don't want them to upstage the other herbs.

SERVING SUGGESTIONS
Mango Lassi (p. 27), Honey-Orange Smoothie (p. 29)

FEBRUARY 18, 2009: "THE MINIMALIST: YOUR MORNING PIZZA," BY MARK BITTMAN.

—2009

• Mrs. Miriam Hill's potato bread recipe runs in the *Times*.

—1854—

• Rolls called whigs and gems are wildly popular.

—1870s—

• Rusks have their moment; three recipes for them are published in the *Times*, two for soft fluffy rolls (p. 652), the other one for dried rusks.

—1877—

• A recipe for Astor House Rolls shows up in the *Times* (p. 652), while the recipe for Parker House Rolls is eventually printed three times.

—1878—

• Brioche (p. 653).

—1880s—

• Samuel Bath Thomas opens a bakery in New York and begins selling English muffins.

—1880—

• Hot Cross Buns (p. 654).

—1890s—

• Wonder Bread begins to be made by the Taggart Baking Company in Indianapolis.

—1921—

• Cornell Bread (p. 658) is conceived.

—1930—

• Bisquick is introduced, lowering peoples' baking IQs.

—1931—

• A good recipe for Crumpets (p. 654) comes out of nowhere.

—1939—

• Old South Buttermilk Biscuits (p. 655).

—1949—

• Baking from scratch—what's that?

—1950s—

• Maida Heatter's Preheated-Oven Popovers (p. 657) are part of a story with three popover recipes.

—1966—

• We look to Europe for pastries and sweet breads, like Christmas Stollen (p. 657).

—1970s—

• Bernard Clayton writes *The Breads of France*.

—1978—

• The artisan bread revolution begins.

—1980s—

• Steve Sullivan opens Acme Bread Company in Berkeley, California.

—1983—

• *The Italian Baker*, a seminal book by Carol Field, is published.

—1985—

• Petits Pains au Chocolat à l'Ancienne (p. 664).

—1988—

• Nancy Silverton opens La Brea Bakery in Los Angeles, and the world falls in love with olive bread.

—1989—

• The year of the scone.

—1990—

• Florence Fabricant writes about Classic Ciabatta (p. 665), but it won't become popular for another decade.

—1992—

• Sullivan Street Bakery opens in New York City, introducing people to filone, meter pizza, and pane Pugliese.

—1994—

• Baking stones become popular, while bread machine sales grow 320 percent since 1993.

—1997—

• Americans discover baguettes, but most of those produced here are dense, flavorless wands.

• But restaurants still think it's OK to put zucchini bread in the bread basket.

14

BREADS AND BAKING

RECIPES BY CATEGORY

⌒ RUSKS

Rusks—dry, leftover country bread—are an ingredient you come across in European peasant cooking, where they are used to thicken soups and stews and given to teething babies. This recipe's title may be a misnomer, because dry rusks are certainly not what you end up with here. Instead, you have tender and airy potato rolls, the ideal landing pad for a shaving of salted butter.

———

1 medium white potato, boiled, peeled, and mashed

2¼ cups whole milk

1 envelope active dry yeast

6 to 7½ cups all-purpose flour

2 teaspoons kosher salt

5 tablespoons plus 1 teaspoon sugar

4 tablespoons unsalted butter, softened

1 large egg

1 teaspoon freshly grated nutmeg

1. Combine the mashed potato, 2 cups milk, the yeast, and 3 cups flour in a large bowl, mixing well. Cover and let rise in a cool place until doubled in size, 2 to 3 hours. (You can also leave the starter in the fridge overnight.)

2. Stir the salt, 5 tablespoons sugar, the butter, egg, nutmeg, and 2½ cups flour into the starter. When it's too stiff to stir, turn out onto a floured work surface and knead until a smooth, pliant dough forms, about 10 minutes. The dough will be sticky and you'll need to add up to 2 cups more flour as you go—add it in small amounts. Place in a clean bowl and let rise, covered, until doubled, 1 to 1½ hours.

3. Punch down the dough and turn it out onto a floured work surface. Using a pastry cutter or sharp knife, cut off large-egg-sized pieces of dough, shape them into loose rounds and lay smooth side up on a large baking sheet. The rounds should just touch each other. Continue until the baking sheet is full or you've run out of dough; if you have leftover dough, shape it into a single round and bake separately. Loosely cover the baking sheet and let rise until almost doubled, 30 minutes to 1 hour.

4. Heat the oven to 400 degrees. Dissolve the remaining 1 teaspoon sugar in the remaining ¼ cup milk. Brush the top of each rusk with this mixture. Bake until golden brown and cooked through and a rusk sounds hollow when tapped on the bottom, about 20 minutes.

MAKES ABOUT 2½ DOZEN ROLLS

COOKING NOTES

Let's do away with a bread-baking myth: bread dough does not need to rise in a warm place. In fact, it prefers cooler temperatures, which allow more time for the flavors to develop. Slower proofing also gives you more control over the baking schedule. If you're not ready to shape the dough, you can place it in the fridge, where the rising will slow to a crawl.

To shape rolls, follow the instructions of Nancy Silverton in her book *Breads from the La Brea Bakery*: "Shape the dough into balls by cupping your hand lightly around the dough and rounding it against the friction of the work surface to form a smooth bun. Begin slowly and increase speed as the ball becomes tighter and smoother. Use as little flour as possible to prevent sticking."

SERVING SUGGESTION
Tomato Jelly (p. 595)

APRIL 29, 1877: "RECEIPTS FOR THE TABLE." RECIPE SIGNED AUNT ADDIE.

—1877

⌒ ASTOR HOUSE ROLLS

The sturdier, WASP-ier cousin to the soft urbane Parker House roll (for which the *Times* ran a recipe in 1877). Astor House rolls have a fluffy interior concealed beneath an appropriately (upper) crusty exterior, qualities that make them excellent for toasting. I've eaten the rolls for breakfast, halved and toasted, and variously spread with butter, fig jam, or pot cheese.

———

1 packet active dry yeast

½ cup lukewarm water

About 6 cups all-purpose flour, or more as needed

4 teaspoons kosher salt

1 tablespoon sugar

3 tablespoons unsalted butter, softened

2 cups whole milk scalded and cooled to lukewarm

7 tablespoons plus 1 teaspoon cold unsalted butter

1. Dissolve the yeast in the lukewarm water and let stand until foamy. Put 5 cups flour in a large bowl (you can use a mixer with a dough hook if you want) and make a well in the center. Add the yeast mixture, salt, sugar, softened butter, and milk and stir, slowly incorporating the flour from the sides. Then stir and beat the mixture until a ball of dough has formed. Pour the dough and any remaining flour onto a work surface and gradually knead in the remaining 1 cup flour.

2. Put the dough in a clean bowl, cover, and let rise until light and fluffy and almost doubled.

3. Punch down the dough and knead until it is smooth and elastic, about 10 minutes—you should need very little, if any, extra flour for this step. Return to the bowl, cover, and let rise until in size doubled.

4. Punch down the dough and divide into 22 pieces. Shape each piece into a tight round (see Cooking Notes, p. 652), keep the other pieces covered with plastic wrap while you work. Beginning with the first round, flatten each roll, seam side up, to ½-inch thick. Place 1 teaspoon butter in the center, lift one edge of the dough, and pull it up and over the butter, forming a turnover-shaped roll, and pinch the edges firmly closed to seal in the butter. Arrange rolls 3 inches apart on nonstick baking sheets (or baking sheets covered with parchment). Cover loosely with plastic wrap and let rise until almost doubled, about 1 hour.

5. Heat the oven to 425 degrees.

6. Bake until the rolls are puffed, golden, and cooked through, about 16 minutes. Cool on baking racks.

MAKES 22 ROLLS

OCTOBER 27, 1878: "USEFUL HINTS FOR HOUSEKEEPERS." RECIPE SIGNED LILLIE.

—1878

⌒ BRIOCHE

This recipe produces a wet, buttery dough that likes to stick to your counter. A trick for handling sticky doughs is to chill them and let the dough rise in the refrigerator. It'll take longer, but it also gives you more control over the schedule.

When it's time to shape the rolls, use a pastry scraper to lift the dough from the counter if needed, and work quickly (do your best to resist adding more flour). Bread doughs are much more cooperative when you show them who's boss.

About 7 cups plus 5½ tablespoons all-purpose flour

2 teaspoons active dry yeast

6 tablespoons lukewarm water

3½ teaspoons kosher salt

¾ pound (3 sticks) unsalted butter, softened

½ cup whole milk

10 large eggs

1. Combine ¾ cup plus 1½ tablespoons flour, the yeast, and water in a medium bowl and mix until smooth. This is the starter. Cover and let rise in a cool place until doubled in size, about 3 hours. (You can put it in the fridge overnight.)

2. Scrape the starter into the bowl of a stand mixer, preferably fitted with a dough hook (or do by hand in a large bowl with a wooden spoon and elbow grease). Add the salt, butter, milk, 9 eggs, and 5 cups flour. Mix until all the flour has been incorporated, then run the mixer on low to knead the dough. (If doing this by hand, scrape the dough onto a floured work surface and knead it.) Knead, adding up to 1½ cups more flour as needed, until the dough is smooth and elastic, 5 to 8 minutes; work quickly.

3. Shape the dough into a loose round and set it smooth side up in an oiled bowl. Cover and let rise in a cool place until doubled, about 2 hours.

4. Punch down the dough and knead it a few times, then return it to the bowl. Cover, place in the fridge, and let rise again until doubled, about 4 hours.

5. Scrape the dough onto a floured work surface and shape into a smooth ball. Let rest for 10 minutes.

6. Butter a large baking sheet. Divide the dough into 18 pieces. Shape each piece into a round (see Cooking Notes, p. 652); try to avoid adding excess flour. Arrange 3 inches apart on the buttered baking sheet. Cover loosely with plastic wrap and let rise until almost doubled, about 1 hour.

7. Heat the oven to 400 degrees. Whisk the remaining egg in a small bowl. Brush the top of each roll with beaten egg. Bake until a roll sounds hollow when tapped on the bottom, 20 to 25 minutes. Transfer the rolls to baking racks to cool.

FEBRUARY 13, 1881: "RECEIPTS." RECIPE SIGNED CUISINIÈRE DE LA CAMPAGNE.

—1881

✐ HOT CROSS BUNS

Hot cross buns, traditionally made for Good Friday, were thought to be a good luck charm. People would preserve old buns, sometimes hung in the window, from year to year to prevent misfortunes (and collect dust).

———

I cup whole milk, scalded

I tablespoon unsalted butter, softened

¾ cup plus I tablespoon sugar

½ teaspoon salt

I teaspoon active dry yeast

3 tablespoons water

3½ cups all-purpose flour, plus more for kneading

⅛ teaspoon ground cinnamon

⅛ teaspoon freshly grated nutmeg

½ cup dried currants

I large egg

1. Mix together the milk, butter, ¼ cup sugar, and salt in a large bowl (you can use a stand mixer fitted with a dough hook, if you want). Let the mixture cool to lukewarm.

2. Meanwhile, dissolve the yeast in lukewarm water and let stand until foamy.

3. Add the yeast mixture to the milk, and stir in 2 cups flour. Cover and let rise until the sponge is foamy and doubled in bulk.

4. Blend ½ cup sugar with the cinnamon, nutmeg, and currants and stir into the dough, along with the egg. Beat in the remaining 1½ cups flour until a stiff dough forms. Then knead with the dough hook, or turn the dough out onto a lightly floured board and knead by hand, until smooth and elastic, about 10 minutes. Put the dough in a clean bowl, cover, and let rise until doubled in size, 1 to 2 hours.

5. Punch down the dough and turn out onto a floured work surface. Cut into 24 pieces. Shape the pieces into tight round balls (see Cooking Notes, p. 652) and set 3 inches apart on ungreased baking sheets. Cover loosely with plastic wrap and let rise until puffed but not quite doubled, about 1 hour. Dissolve the remaining 1 tablespoon sugar in the remaining 2 tablespoons water.

6. Heat the oven to 350 degrees.

7. Using a sharp paring knife dipped in flour, cut a cross in the top of each roll. Bake for 20 minutes. Brush with the sugar glaze and bake until brown and shiny, 2 to 5 minutes more; the rolls should sound hollow when tapped on the bottom. Cool on baking racks.

APRIL 11, 1897: "SOME SEASONABLE RECEIPTS: HOT CROSS BUNS FOR GOOD FRIDAY—MAKING OF EASTER EGGS—JOLLY BOYS AND TWISTERS."

—1897

✐ CRUMPETS

From the 1930s through most of the 1940s, America's buoyant food culture sank. You can blame the war, but I prefer to blame newspaper editors. During these decades, the *Times*, like many of its competitors, filled its food pages with press releases from the government. The releases, which were often tied to crop reports, were written by government nutritionists and home economists who promoted surplus foods, offering "economical," "practical," and "healthy" recipes to journalists around the country. The *Times* happily complied.

Occasionally, however, a perfectly good recipe would slip through the weave of propaganda, such as the one for these crumpets, which appeared in an article encouraging the use of cornmeal, wheat, and graham flour.

———

I teaspoon sugar

½ teaspoon salt

3 tablespoons unsalted butter, melted

2 cups whole milk, scalded

I teaspoon active dry yeast

3 cups all-purpose flour

Softened butter for greasing the griddle and the rings

1. Blend the sugar, salt, butter, and milk in a bowl. Let the mixture cool to lukewarm.

2. Stir the yeast into the milk mixture until dissolved.

Beat in the flour. Cover and let rise in a cool place until doubled in size.

3. Heat a griddle over medium heat, and have ready some 3-inch baking rings (without bottoms). Ideally, you'll have enough to fill the griddle surface. (If you don't have baking rings, don't worry, you can shape the crumpets in a free-form manner; or if you have rings but in another size, that's fine too, though you may need to adjust the cooking time.) Butter the insides of the rings using a basting brush.

4. Brush the surface of the griddle with butter and arrange the rings on it. Spoon enough dough into each ring to cover the base by ¼ inch. You'll need to nudge the dough to the edges of each ring, and the best way to do this is to use the basting brush, because the butter will prevent the dough from sticking to the brush. (If not using rings, do your best to make ¼-inch-thick rounds about 3 inches in diameter.) Cook until the bottoms are crisp and lightly browned, about 2 minutes. You'll know they're getting close when the butter on the sides of the rings begins to bubble and sizzle. Remove the rings, turn the crumpets, and brown the other side. Cool on a baking rack.

MAKES 16 TO 18 CRUMPETS

SERVING SUGGESTION
Strawberry Jam (p. 590)

JULY 23, 1939: "HOT BREAD FOR HOT DAYS," BY AMY LYON SCHAEFFER. RECIPE ADAPTED FROM THE U.S. BUREAU OF HOME ECONOMICS.

—1939

☞ BANANA TEA BREAD

This is a simple tea bread with extraordinary banana flavor. My friend Meg Hourihan's family has made this recipe for fifty years, although they cut back the flour to 1⅓ cups and the shortening to ¼ cup. Recently Meg began using butter in place of the shortening and mixing the dough by hand instead of using a mixer, with excellent results. Play around and see which way you like it best.

———

1¾ cups sifted flour
2 teaspoons baking powder

¼ teaspoon baking soda
½ teaspoon salt
⅓ cup vegetable shortening
⅔ cup sugar
2 large eggs, well beaten
1 cup mashed ripe bananas (2 to 3)

1. Heat the oven to 350 degrees. Grease an 8½-by-4½-by-3 inch loaf pan. Sift together the flour, baking powder, soda, and salt.

2. Beat the shortening in a large bowl until creamy; you can do it by hand or with a hand mixer. Gradually add the sugar and continue beating until light and fluffy. Add the eggs and beat well. Add the flour mixture alternately with the bananas, a small amount at a time, beating after each addition until smooth.

3. Turn the dough into the prepared pan and bake until a toothpick inserted in the center comes out almost clean, 50 to 60 minutes. Let the bread cool slightly, then remove from the pan and let cool completely on a baking rack.

MAKES 1 LOAF

SEPTEMBER 14, 1947: "FOOD: BANANAS—COOKED," BY JANE NICKERSON.

—1947

☞ OLD SOUTH BUTTERMILK BISCUITS

"The cooking of the South is as mysterious as that of Tibet to most Yankees," Jane Nickerson, a *Times* columnist, wrote. And so, to enlighten her Yankee readers, Nickerson presented a menu of fried chicken, gravy, and these superb biscuits.

A fluffy angel biscuit made with White Lily flour this is not. Nickerson proclaimed tall, plump biscuits a Yankee fantasy and said that Southern biscuits should be small, flat, and crisp, "peeling off into little layers of deliciousness." That's exactly what these are.

———

2 cups sifted all-purpose flour
1 teaspoon salt
½ teaspoon baking soda
1 teaspoon baking powder

4 tablespoons vegetable shortening (see Cooking Notes)

¾ cup buttermilk, or more as needed

Whole milk for brushing (optional)

1. Heat the oven to 500 degrees. Grease a baking sheet. Sift together the dry ingredients twice into a bowl. Cut in the shortening with a pastry blender or 2 knives until the mixture resembles coarse cornmeal.

2. Add enough buttermilk to produce a soft dough, and stir until the mixture forms a ball. Knead lightly in the bowl until the dough holds together, about 30 seconds.

3. Turn the dough out onto a lightly floured board and roll to ¼ inch thick. Cut out biscuits with a small biscuit cutter and put on the greased baking sheet. If a glazed surface is desired, brush the tops with milk.

4. Bake until golden brown, about 12 minutes. Serve warm.

MAKES 1 TO 2 DOZEN BISCUITS, DEPENDING ON THE SIZE OF YOUR BISCUIT CUTTER

COOKING NOTES

I could only find low-fat buttermilk, so I added 2 more tablespoons shortening (6 total).

My biscuit cutter is 3 inches in diameter, so the recipe yielded just 12 biscuits.

SERVING SUGGESTIONS

My husband, Tad, and I once stayed at the Soniat House, an elegant small hotel in New Orleans's French Quarter. Every morning, the kitchen delivered a basket of hot biscuits, very much like these, with a cube of cold sweet butter and strawberry preserves, a silver pot of coffee, and fresh-squeezed orange juice. I don't think I've had a better breakfast. However, if you'd like to serve the biscuits with lunch or dinner, think about North Carolina–Style Pulled Pork (p. 550), Chicken Betty's Fried Chicken and Gravy (p. 462), Julia Harrison Adams's Pimento Cheese Spread (p. 64), Iceberg Lettuce with Smoked Bacon and Buttermilk Dressing (p. 200), Spoonbread's Potato Salad (p. 288), and Red Velvet Cake (p. 757).

FEBRUARY 27, 1949: "SOUTHERN FRIED CHICKEN," BY JANE NICKERSON.

—1949

⌒ BOSTON BROWN BREAD

Not something you come across much these days, but not a bad recipe to have on your culinary bench. Boston brown bread leads with sweetness and finishes with a pleasant nutty, caramel flavor.

———

1 cup yellow cornmeal

1 cup rye flour

1 cup whole wheat flour

2 teaspoons baking soda

1 teaspoon salt

2 cups buttermilk

¾ cup molasses

1 cup raisins

1. Combine the cornmeal, flours, soda, and salt in a large bowl. Mix together the buttermilk, molasses, and raisins. Add to the dry ingredients, mixing well.

2. Divide the batter between 2 well-greased 1-quart pudding molds or No. 2½ (3½-cup) cans; or use 3 No. 2 (2½-cup) cans. Cover with the greased mold covers or can lids and then with aluminum foil.

3. Place the molds on a rack in a large pot and add enough hot water to come halfway up the sides of the molds. Cover and cook at a gentle simmer for 3 hours, replenishing the water as necessary. Transfer to baking racks to cool; unmold when completely cool.

MAKES 2 TO 3 LOAVES; SERVES 12 TO 18

COOKING NOTE

I had neither a pudding mold nor a can, so I used a 3-quart stainless steel bowl, which produced a bread that looked like a large brown button.

DECEMBER 27, 1964: "READERS' CHOICE," BY CRAIG CLAIBORNE.

—1964

MAIDA HEATTER'S PREHEATED-OVEN POPOVERS

The popover is a culinary marvel, a loose batter that, with the aid of a hot oven, expands like a golden cumulus cloud, producing a crisp, hollow pastry with a soft, eggy interior. While the mixture is very similar to crepe batter, when you confine it to deep narrow muffin-like molds, the surface of the batter sets and the air is trapped inside, so that the pastry has nowhere to go but up and out, creating a gravity-defying bubble.

Popovers, so named for the way the batter often rises up and over the sides of its molds, grew out of English Yorkshire pudding, except that the former is mostly made with butter and the latter with meat drippings. Early recipes for Yorkshire pudding call for pouring the batter into a shallow baking dish set under mutton or beef roasting on a spit. (Another batter-based cousin is Toad in the Hole, whose pudding is embedded with sausage.)

There is little consensus on popover technique. Some recipes call for putting the buttered molds in the oven as it heats, then adding the batter later. Others instruct you to pour the batter into the popover molds and place them in a cold oven. Maida Heatter, the cookbook author whose recipe this is, has you preheat the oven and place the filled molds into it, as you would a cake.

The best part of making popovers is their ease. As long as you can use a measuring cup and turn on your oven, you'll soon be an expert.

___

6 large eggs
2 cups whole milk
6 tablespoons unsalted butter, melted
2 cups sifted all-purpose flour
1 teaspoon salt

1. Heat the oven to 375 degrees. Generously butter ten 4-ounce custard cups. Arrange the cups on a baking sheet.
2. Beat the eggs lightly in a bowl, and add the milk and butter. Gradually stir in the flour and salt. Beat just until mixture is smooth; do not overbeat. If the mixture is not smooth, strain it. Pour the mixture into a pitcher and then into the custard cups, filling the cups almost to the top.

3. Bake for 50 minutes. Do not open the oven door while the popovers bake. After 50 minutes, cut several slits in the top of each popover and return to the oven for 5 to 10 minutes. Immediately remove the popovers from the cups.

MAKES 10 POPOVERS

COOKING NOTE
Special pans that look like extra-deep muffin pans have been created for popovers, but finding room for one in your cabinet is like trying to store a tuba. I use a regular muffin pan, and well-buttered ramekins also work.

AUGUST 15, 1966: "READERS POP OFF ABOUT POPOVERS," BY CRAIG CLAIBORNE. RECIPE ADAPTED FROM MAIDA HEATTER.

—1966

CHRISTMAS STOLLEN

Many people wrote to me about this recipe, as well as one called John Clancy's Dresden Stollen. I made both. Clancy stollen partisans: I'm sorry. This stollen won me over, and I urge you to try it too! This stollen is so moist and fragrant, it tastes as if it contains almond paste.

___

For the Stollen
²/₃ cup whole milk, scalded
²/₃ cup sugar
³/₄ teaspoon salt
8 tablespoons (1 stick) unsalted butter, cut into pieces, plus butter for brushing
2 tablespoons vegetable shortening
2 packages active dry yeast
¹/₄ cup warm water
2 large eggs, lightly beaten
¹/₂ teaspoon ground cinnamon
¹/₈ teaspoon ground mace
¹/₈ teaspoon ground cardamom
3¹/₂ to 4¹/₂ cups all-purpose flour
1 cup diced mixed candied fruits
¹/₄ cup raisins
¹/₂ cup chopped pecans

For the Frosting

2 tablespoons unsalted butter, softened

Approximately 1 cup confectioners' sugar

1½ teaspoons light corn syrup

1 teaspoon water

¼ teaspoon vanilla extract

Pecan halves for decorating

1. To make the stollen, pour the milk into a large bowl (see Cooking Notes), add the sugar, salt, butter, and shortening and stir to melt the butter and dissolve the sugar. Let cool to lukewarm.

2. Dissolve the yeast in the warm water, let stand until foamy. Add to the milk mixture, then beat in the eggs, cinnamon, mace, and cardamom and enough flour to make a soft dough that can be kneaded.

3. Turn the dough onto a lightly floured board and knead until smooth. Knead in the candied fruits, raisins, and chopped nuts until evenly distributed.

4. Place the dough in a greased bowl, cover, and let rise until doubled in size, about 2½ to 3 hours.

5. Punch down the dough, turn out onto a floured work surface, and roll into an oval 12 by 18 inches. Fold the dough over lengthwise so that the two edges do not quite meet. Place on a greased baking sheet, cover, and let rise in a warm place until just doubled in size, about 1 to 2 hours; don't let it overrise.

6. Heat the oven to 400 degrees. Bake the stollen for 10 minutes. Reduce the oven temperature to 350 degrees and bake until the stollen sounds hollow when tapped on the bottom, about 25 minutes longer. Brush the stollen with butter, and set on a rack.

7. To make the frosting, cream the butter and sugar together in a bowl until light and fluffy. Beat in the corn syrup, water, and vanilla. Spread over the warm stollen and decorate with pecan halves.

MAKES 1 STOLLEN; SERVES 8 TO 10

COOKING NOTES

I made the dough in a stand mixer with a dough hook.

I used candied cherries, citron, and orange peel, a great combination.

DECEMBER 6, 1970: "CHRISTMAS SCENE-STEALER," BY CRAIG CLAIBORNE. RECIPE ADAPTED FROM DAVID DUGAN, A RETIRED BAKER IN NORTH CALDWELL, NEW JERSEY.

—1970

⌒ CORNELL BREAD

Cornell bread was created in the 1930s by Clive M. McKay, a professor at the university. His bread, a white sandwich loaf enriched with soy flour, dry milk, and wheat germ, was promoted for its healthfulness, and it became a staple in New York bakeries. It's a good-tasting loaf—nutty and a little sweet—and its crumb is peppered with tiny holes.

———

3 cups lukewarm water

2 packages active dry yeast

2 tablespoons honey

Approximately 6 cups unbleached bread flour, such as Hecker's

½ cup full-fat soy flour

¾ cup nonfat dry milk

3 tablespoons wheat germ

4 teaspoons salt

2 tablespoons vegetable oil

Melted butter for brushing (optional)

1. Place the water, yeast, and honey in the bowl of a stand mixer or another large bowl and stir to mix. Let stand until foamy, about 5 minutes.

2. Sift together the flour, soy flour, and dry milk. Stir in the wheat germ.

3. Add the salt to the yeast mixture, then stir in half to three-quarters of the flour mixture, so that the batter has a consistency that can be beaten. Beat for 2 minutes with an electric mixer (preferably with a paddle attachment), or about 75 strokes by hand. Add the oil and work in the remainder of the flour mixture, adding extra flour if needed to form a dough.

4. Turn the dough out onto a floured board and knead for 10 minutes, or until smooth and elastic. Place in a greased bowl and grease the top of the dough lightly. Cover and let rise in a warm place until almost doubled in size, about 45 minutes.

5. Punch down the dough, fold over the edges, and turn upside down in the bowl. Cover and let rise for 20 minutes longer.

6. Turn the dough out onto a board. Divide into 3 parts. Form into balls, cover, and let stand for 10 minutes.

7. Grease three 8½-by-4½-by-3-inch loaf pans. Roll

out 1 ball into a rectangle twice as big as the loaf pans. Fold the long sides into the center, and fold the short ends into the center. Pinch to seal the seams, and fit, seams down, into a greased pan. Repeat with the other 2 balls.

8. Cover the pans and let the dough rise in a warm place until doubled in bulk, about 45 minutes.

9. Heat the oven to 350 degrees. Bake the loaves for 50 to 60 minutes; cover with foil if the tops begin to overbrown. The bread is done when it sounds hollow when tapped on the bottom. For a soft crust, brush the tops with melted butter. Cool on a rack in the pans for 10 minutes, then remove from the pans.

MAKES 3 LOAVES

COOKING NOTE

In Step 3, you may need to add up to 1 cup flour. The dough won't entirely lose its stickiness—if you work quickly (or better yet, chill it, too) it will be easier to deal with.

SERVING SUGGESTIONS

Brie Butter (p. 605), Green Tomato and Lemon Marmalade (p. 614)

FEBRUARY 20, 1972: "THE DO-GOOD LOAF," BY JEAN HEWITT. RECIPE ADAPTED FROM DR. CLIVE M. MCKAY, A PROFESSOR AT CORNELL UNIVERSITY.

—1972

⌒ CHALLAH

This über-challah came from Sarah Schecht, a home cook in Bensonhurst with a gift for bread making. In the article by Craig Claiborne, a friend of Schecht's described the loaf as if it were a magical visitor that rode in on the north wind: "Her challah has a texture to rival that of the finest spongecakes. It is airborne, light as a zephyr, delicate as eiderdown."

The recipe, which Claiborne wrote out in great detail, creates a soft, velvety dough—and so much of it that it recalls the *I Love Lucy* episode in which Lucy's bread shoots out of the oven and pins her against the kitchen cabinets. But what a beautiful loaf you get! Schecht's shaping technique, which sounds nightmarishly finicky—you must braid eight strands of dough—is easy once you get going and makes for an intricately woven, cinnamon-scented loaf the size of a skateboard. Plenty to eat fresh, and plenty for French toast later.

———

About 9 cups sifted unbleached all-purpose flour, plus flour for kneading
2 packages active dry yeast
2½ cups lukewarm water
½ teaspoon baking powder
½ teaspoon ground cinnamon
I tablespoon salt
I teaspoon vanilla extract
4 large eggs
¾ cup corn oil or clarified unsalted butter
¾ cup plus ⅛ teaspoon sugar
I tablespoon sesame or poppy seeds

1. Place 6 cups flour in a large bowl and make a well in the center. Stir the yeast into 1 cup lukewarm water in a small bowl until dissolved, and let stand until foamy. Add this to the well. Using a fork, stir, gradually incorporating one-quarter of the flour—no more—into the yeast mixture. Set the bowl in a warm place and let stand for 45 to 50 minutes.

2. Sprinkle the baking powder, cinnamon, and salt over the flour mixture. Add the vanilla, 3 eggs, the oil, and ¾ cup sugar. Add the remaining 1½ cups lukewarm water and blend again, first using a fork and then your hands. Gradually add 2 cups flour, kneading for about 10 minutes. If the dough is still too sticky, add up to a cup more flour. The dough is ready when it doesn't stick to your hands.

3. Shape the dough into a rough ball, cover, and let stand for 20 minutes.

4. Turn the dough out onto a lightly floured board and knead for about 5 minutes, adding a little flour to the board as needed to prevent sticking. Set the dough in a floured bowl and lightly coat in flour. Cover and let stand for 30 minutes.

5. Turn the dough onto a work surface and knead briefly. Cut off one-eighth of the dough and knead quickly, then shape into a ball, flour lightly, and let rest briefly. Repeat with the remaining 7 pieces. Using your hands, roll each ball into a 12- to 15-inch-long rope.

6. Align the ropes vertically, side by side. Gather the

top ends together, one at a time, pinching to seal. Separate the ropes in the center, 4 to a side. Braid them as follows: Bring the outer right rope over toward the center next to the inside rope on the left. Bring the outer left rope over toward the center next to the inside rope on the right. Repeat this process until the loaf is braided. As the last ropes are brought over, pull and stretch them a bit as needed. Gather the bottom ends of the braid and pinch them together.

7. Generously oil or butter the bottom and sides of a large baking sheet. Carefully lift the braided loaf onto the baking sheet. Cover the loaf with a kitchen towel and place in a warm spot until doubled in size, about 45 minutes.

8. Heat the oven to 325 degrees. Beat the remaining egg with the remaining ⅛ teaspoon sugar. Brush the loaf with the egg glaze and sprinkle with the sesame seeds. Bake until puffed and golden, about 1 hour. Cool on a rack.

MAKES 1 HUGE LOAF

COOKING NOTES

When braiding the loaf, spread the strands like wings so you're bringing them across the dough rather than down through it. You'll get a more tightly braided loaf this way.

I find with sweet doughs, the first time you knead them, they get smooth after about 7 minutes, then, when you keep going, they get sticky again. Work through this unexpected discouragement, because the dough will turn smooth again—really smooth—a few minutes later.

This dough is particularly sticky; resist the temptation to keep adding flour. It's better to move quickly, keep kneading, and use a pastry scraper to help lift the dough. (Chilling it will also help, if you have the time to do so.)

When shaping the dough into strands, add as little flour as possible, because you need the tension between the counter and the dough to stretch it into taut strands. And when rolling the strands, don't press outward—focus the pressure down on the dough and move from the center to the sides. The strands will lengthen much more easily this way.

Remove any extra racks from your oven so the bread has plenty of room to expand.

READERS

Schecht's daughter wrote, "We were always proud of her great cookies, cakes, chicken dishes, etc.—most of all the challah. Craig Claiborne made her day. He came to her apartment in Brooklyn in August of '76. I was there—he watched her make her favorite dishes and then, of course, the N.Y. *Times* celebrated her by printing her recipes. . . . Thanks again. Love to all who still care to appreciate home cooking and baking."

Rosalyn Sandberg, Miami, FL, letter

APRIL 28, 1976: "SORCERY FROM AN OVEN IN BENSONHURST: CHALLAH AT ITS BEST," BY CRAIG CLAIBORNE. RECIPE ADAPTED FROM SARAH SCHECHT.

—1976

🖙 MARY ANN'S FRUITCAKE

Save your easy skepticism—fruitcake can be excellent. You will love this one, which ran in the *Times* at least three times and was reprinted in two of Craig Claiborne's cookbooks. I learned the story behind the recipe from Jean C. LaCamera, a reader in New Haven, Connecticut. In the 1950s, her husband's aunt in Cincinnati took in Mary Ann, a college student who couldn't get home to Mississippi for Thanksgiving. As a thank-you for her hospitality, Mary Ann's mother sent the aunt pecans and this fruitcake recipe. For decades, the LaCameras baked the cake every holiday season, making just one tweak to the ingredient list: the original called for lemon extract; they replaced it with Grand Marnier.

LaCamera sent the recipe to Claiborne in fall 1976, and he printed it that December. "Mr. Claiborne gave me one shot at immortality!" LaCamera wrote to me. "And I'm everlastingly and deeply grateful to the staff of the *New York Times*—*all* of them—not just on Wednesday morning!" For the recipe itself, it was a long journey home—turns out Mary Ann (whose last name I never learned) and Claiborne were from the same small town in Mississippi: Indianola.

———

1 pound golden raisins
1 pound pecans, broken
3 cups sifted all-purpose flour
1 teaspoon salt

1 pound unsalted butter, softened

2 cups sugar

6 large eggs, separated

1 teaspoon baking soda

1 tablespoon warm water

¼ cup Grand Marnier

Cognac or rum (optional)

1. Heat the oven to 250 degrees. Butter a 10-inch tube pan. Sprinkle liberally with flour and shake out the excess. Combine the raisins and pecans in a large bowl. Sprinkle the flour and salt over all and toss until thoroughly blended. Set aside.

2. Place the butter in the bowl of a stand mixer. Start beating and gradually add the sugar. Cream the mixture well, and add the egg yolks one at a time, beating constantly. Blend the baking soda and water and add it, beating. Beat in the Grand Marnier. Pour this mixture into the nut mixture and blend together with your hands.

3. Beat the whites until stiff, and fold them in with your hands. Continue folding until the whites are not apparent.

4. Spoon and scrape the mixture into the prepared pan, smoothing the top with a spatula. Bake for 2 to 2¼ hours, or until the cake is puffed above the pan and nicely browned on top. If the cake starts to brown too soon, cover with aluminum foil. Remove the cake from the pan shortly after it is baked: tapping the bottom of the cake pan with a heavy knife will help loosen it.

5. Store the cake in the refrigerator for at least 10 days before serving. If desired, add an occasional touch of cognac or rum to the cake as it stands. Keep it tightly covered and refrigerated until ready to serve.

MAKES ONE 10-INCH CAKE

COOKING NOTES

In Step 2, when you're mixing together the wet and dry ingredients, the batter will seem a little hopeless. Use a stiff spatula or wooden spoon and keep at it, and the batter will come together eventually.

I like to sprinkle a little brandy on the cake before serving for a little zing.

To remove the cake from the pan, cut a piece of parchment to fit on the top, then find a friend or family member to help you invert the cake. The parchment gives you something to hold on to as you tip the pan.

READERS

"This beloved recipe is the only thing I bake—it is for family and friends at holiday time! I bake ahead of time, wrap in foil, refrigerate and add a tablespoonful of the liquor 2 or 3 times before gifting."

Isobel Perry, Rye, NY, letter

DECEMBER 5, 1976: "HAPPY PUDDING! MERRY FRUIT-CAKE!" BY CRAIG CLAIBORNE WITH PIERRE FRANEY. RECIPE ADAPTED FROM JEAN C. LACAMERA, A READER FROM NEW HAVEN, CONNECTICUT.

—1976

⌒ AN INCREDIBLE DATE-NUT BREAD

Rita Alexander, a neighbor of Craig Claiborne, used this cake as an example of a great food gift at the holidays. It's also not a bad gift for yourself. The impossibly springy cake has a crisp top and is filled with moist dates and raisins. A brushing of whiskey syrup (2 tablespoons sugar dissolved in 2 tablespoons whiskey) on the top is my own variation—perhaps an obvious idea, but I'm laying claim to it.

Perplexed by Step 2, in which you're instructed to pour boiling water over baking soda and mix it into the dried fruit, I e-mailed Harold McGee, a *Times* food columnist and the author of *On Food and Cooking*. "My guess is that the baking soda step is a quick way of hydrating and softening the fruit, and probably turns the date bits into mush, which would help moisten the cake more than discrete pieces [of dates]," he wrote. (The alkali in baking soda can break down cell walls in fruit.) McGee also noted that baking soda helps cakes brown, and the cake emerges from the oven dark and tawny.

———

1 cup diced pitted dates

¾ cup raisins

¼ cup golden raisins

1 teaspoon baking soda

1 cup boiling water

8 tablespoons (1 stick) unsalted butter, softened

1 cup sugar

1 teaspoon vanilla extract

1 large egg

1⅓ cups sifted all-purpose flour

¾ cup walnuts, broken into small pieces

1. Heat the oven to 350 degrees. Butter a 9-by-5-by-3-inch loaf pan. Line the bottom with a rectangle of wax paper. Butter the rectangle and sprinkle with flour; shake out the excess flour.

2. Put the dates and raisins in a medium bowl. Dissolve the baking soda in the boiling water and pour it over the date mixture.

3. Cream together the butter and sugar in a large bowl. Beat in the vanilla and egg. Add the flour and mix well. Add the date mixture including the liquid. Add the walnuts.

4. Pour the mixture into the prepared pan and smooth the top. Place in the oven and bake for 50 to 70 minutes, or until the top of the cake is dark brown and a knife inserted in the center comes out clean. Let cool for about 3 to 5 minutes, then unmold onto a rack, remove the paper, and let cool.

MAKES 1 LOAF

DECEMBER 7, 1977: "FOOD GIFTS YOU CAN MAKE AT HOME," BY CRAIG CLAIBORNE. RECIPE ADAPTED FROM RITA ALEXANDER.

—1977

⌒ AN HONEST LOAF OF FRENCH BREAD

This is a terrific bread recipe—carefully structured and succinct, so there's no risk of failure.

———

1⅛ teaspoons active dry yeast

¼ cup lukewarm water

1 cup cold water

2 tablespoons unsalted butter

3½ cups all-purpose flour

1 teaspoon salt

1. Blend the yeast with the lukewarm water in a small bowl. Stir to dissolve the yeast, and let stand until foamy.

2. Combine the cup of cold water with the butter in a saucepan and heat slowly until the butter melts (a thermometer is not essential, but the best temperature for this is 95 to 110 degrees).

3. Add the flour and salt to the container of a food processor. Blend the flour and salt by activating the motor on and off briefly 3 times. With the lid and motor off, add the dissolved yeast mixture. With the lid and motor off, add the dissolved butter mixture. Blend until the dough becomes a ball and clears the side of the container, about 5 to 10 seconds.

4. Lightly flour a clean surface and turn the dough out onto it. With floured fingers, knead the dough quickly and gently. This is primarily for shaping the dough. Do not add an excess of flour at any time. Shape the dough into a ball.

5. Put the ball of dough in a lightly buttered bowl. Cover with a clean cloth and place the bowl in a warm place. Let stand until doubled in bulk, 30 to 40 minutes. The time will vary depending on the temperature around the bowl.

6. Turn the dough out onto a lightly floured surface and knead briefly. Shape into a ball and return the dough to the bowl. Cover and let stand for about 30 to 60 minutes, until doubled in bulk.

7. Turn the dough out onto a lightly floured surface. Roll into a loose ball; let sit for 5 minutes.

8. Turn the dough seam side up and flatten with your fingers into a rough rectangular shape. Fold one-third of the dough toward the center of the rectangle, then roll up like a jelly roll. Transfer the loaf to a baking sheet with the seam on the bottom and the ends folded under. The dimensions of the loaf at this time should be approximately 13½ inches long, 3½ inches wide, and 2 inches high. Cover with a clean cloth and return to a warm place. Let stand for 15 to 30 minutes, until doubled in bulk.

9. As the dough rises, heat the oven to 450 degrees. Using a knife with a razor-sharp edge or an old-fashioned razor blade, make 3 parallel, diagonal gashes in the top of the dough. Immediately place the pan in the oven and add 4 ice cubes to the floor of the oven. Bake for 5 minutes, and add 4 more ice cubes as before. Turn the pan on which the bread bakes so that the loaf bakes evenly. Bake for 10 minutes (making for a total of 15 minutes baking time), and reduce the oven heat to 400 degrees. Bake for 15 to 20 minutes longer. Transfer the bread to a rack and let stand until cooled.

The recipe called for 1½ envelopes of yeast, which is an unnecessarily whopping amount. I cut it back to 1⅛ teaspoons.

When kneading, try to add as little additional flour as possible. Chilling the dough makes it easier to handle.

PERIOD DETAIL

In this story, Craig Claiborne and Pierre Franey noted that they'd recently been "pondering and writing about the wondrous avenues that food processors have opened to the home cook."

FEBRUARY 26, 1978: "FRENCH BREAD WITHOUT TEARS," BY CRAIG CLAIBORNE WITH PIERRE FRANEY.

—1978

SHIRLEY ESTABROOK WOOD'S ZUCCHINI BREAD

In the oven, this bread rises like St. Peter's Dome. Behold it while it lasts.

Approximately 1¼ pounds zucchini
1½ cups sugar
¾ cup unsalted butter, melted
3 large eggs
3 cups all-purpose flour
1 teaspoon baking soda
¼ teaspoon baking powder
1½ teaspoons salt
1 teaspoon ground cinnamon
¾ cup chopped walnuts
2 teaspoons vanilla extract

1. Heat the oven to 350 degrees. Peel and grate the zucchini. There should be 2 cups. Set aside.
2. Combine the sugar and butter in the bowl of a stand mixer fitted with a paddle attachment (or use a large bowl and a hand mixer). Start beating, and add the eggs one at a time.
3. Sift together the flour, baking soda, baking powder, salt, and cinnamon. Add this mixture gradually to the butter mixture while beating. The batter will be quite thick. Fold in the zucchini, walnuts, and vanilla.
4. Lightly oil a 9-by-5-by-3-inch loaf pan and pour in the batter. Place in the oven and bake for 60 to 80 minutes, or until the bread pulls away from the sides of the pan. Remove from the pan to a wire rack. Let cool before slicing.

MAKES I LOAF; SERVES 10

JANUARY 4, 1981: "FOOD: GARDEN-VARIETY CAKES AND BREADS," BY CRAIG CLAIBORNE WITH PIERRE FRANEY. RECIPE ADAPTED FROM SHIRLEY ESTABROOK WOOD, A HOME COOK AND FRIEND OF CLAIBORNE'S.

—1981

PANETTONE

If everyone knew how easy panettone, the classic Italian fruit brioche, is to make, they'd bake it all the time. I had my doubts about the recipe because it calls for 3 envelopes of yeast, and my only complaint about Craig Claiborne's cooking is that his bread recipes often contain too much yeast. But it turns out you need the yeast to give the dough a punchy lift in the oven. This panettone, which is much more a cross between a soufflé and bread, somehow manages to be both buttery and airy, so it has the richness of Danish pastry and the lightness of a cotton ball.

3 envelopes active dry yeast
⅓ cup warm water
¼ cup sugar
½ cup raisins
½ cup diced candied citron
1 tablespoon dark rum
8 large egg yolks
1 teaspoon vanilla extract
Grated zest of 1 lemon
½ teaspoon salt
8 tablespoons (1 stick) unsalted butter, softened
1½ cups all-purpose flour
4 tablespoons unsalted butter, melted

1. Put the yeast and water in a small bowl, add 1 teaspoon of the sugar, and stir to dissolve the yeast. Set aside in a warm place until it foams.

2. Combine the raisins, citron, and rum in a small bowl. Set aside until ready to use.

3. Rinse a large bowl with hot water. Drain and dry thoroughly. Add the egg yolks and the remaining sugar. Beat with a wire whisk until pale yellow. Beat in the vanilla, lemon zest, and salt. Add the yeast mixture and beat, then add the softened butter about a tablespoon at a time. Beat well. Add the flour and beat briskly for 2 to 3 minutes. You may need to switch to a wooden spoon to do this.

4. Scrape down the sides of the bowl, letting the dough rest in the center. Cover and let stand in a warm place for about 60 to 75 minutes, until doubled in bulk.

5. Meanwhile, heat the oven to 400 degrees. Butter a 6- to 7-cup fluted mold.

6. Punch down the dough. Drain the raisins and citron and knead them briefly into the dough. (This can also be done with a wooden spoon.)

7. Turn the dough into the prepared mold. Brush the top with melted butter and place the mold in the oven. Bake for 10 minutes, and reduce the oven heat to 325 degrees. Continue baking, basting often with more melted butter, until the bread is golden brown and sounds hollow when tapped on the crust, about 40 minutes longer. Let cool in the mold.

MAKES 1 LOAF

COOKING NOTES
You need really fresh candied citron and good raisins—it's worth going out of your way for them.

I baked the panettone in a tall narrow 6-cup ceramic soufflé mold, which worked well.

APRIL 5, 1981: "AN ITALIAN TREAT FOR EASTER SUNDAY," BY CRAIG CLAIBORNE WITH PIERRE FRANEY.

—1981

↶ PETITS PAINS AU CHOCOLAT À L'ANCIENNE (OLD-FASHIONED BREAD AND CHOCOLATE ROLLS)

These soft milk rolls wrapped around a bar of chocolate are the storied *goûter de quatre heures*, or afternoon snack, of urban French children. Less fortunate kids from the provinces had to make do with toasted country bread spread with salted butter or crème fraîche and sprinkled with grated chocolate.

If you've never had a proper petit pain au chocolat, do make these. Eat them fresh, when they've cooled just enough so you can hold them. Each bite is chewy, crisp, and suffused with the hope of finding a pocket of warm chocolate.

———

½ cup whole milk, heated until lukewarm, plus
   1 tablespoon milk for brushing
½ cup lukewarm water
1 tablespoon sugar
1 teaspoon active dry yeast
2¼ to 2½ cups unbleached all-purpose flour
1 teaspoon salt
6 ounces bittersweet chocolate,
   cut into 8 equal portions

1. Combine the lukewarm milk, water, sugar, yeast, and 1 cup flour in a large bowl (see Cooking Notes) and stir until thoroughly blended. Set aside until foamy, about 5 minutes.

2. Add the salt to the yeast mixture, then add the remaining flour little by little until the dough is too stiff to stir. Place the dough on a lightly floured work surface and begin kneading, adding additional flour if the dough is too sticky. Knead until the dough is smooth and satiny, about 10 minutes.

3. Place the dough in a bowl, cover with plastic wrap, and let rise at room temperature until doubled in bulk, about 1 hour, or in the fridge for 2 to 3 hours.

4. Punch down the dough and let rise again, covered, until doubled in bulk, about 1 hour at room temperature, or in the fridge for at least 2 hours.

5. Divide the dough into 8 equal portions. On a lightly floured board, roll each portion into a loose ball; let sit for 5 minutes.

6. Turn each ball seam side up and roll into a 6-by-4-inch rectangle. Place a portion of chocolate in the center of each rectangle. First fold over the ends, then the sides, pinching the dough together to make a neat package. Arrange the rolls pinched side down on an ungreased baking sheet. Cover with a flour-dusted tea towel (don't use plastic wrap, which will stick) and allow to rest at room temperature for about 30 minutes, or in the fridge for 1 hour.

7. Heat the oven to 400 degrees. Brush the rolls

with milk and bake until golden brown, about 20 to 25 minutes. Some of the chocolate should leak out of the dough during baking. Serve warm or at room temperature.

MAKES 8 ROLLS

COOKING NOTES

I made the dough in a mixer fitted with a dough hook, scraping down the dough occasionally and kneading it on medium speed for 5 minutes.

I let the dough rise in the refrigerator, which takes longer but makes it easier to work with.

If you're serving these for breakfast, prepare up through Step 4 the night before and let the dough rise overnight in the refrigerator.

SEPTEMBER 25, 1988: "FOOD: TIME FOR SNACKS," BY PATRICIA WELLS.

—1988

CLASSIC CIABATTA

There have been many terrific bread-baking books, but none has been as groundbreaking as Carol Field's *The Italian Baker*, published in 1985. Field wrote about pane Pugliese and pizza bianca long before anyone ever heard of Jim Lahey, the owner of New York City's Sullivan Street Bakery, who popularized them. Lahey didn't go to Rome to learn the techniques until ten years later.

Field took home bread baking beyond generalized European "country" breads and, by focusing on Italy, told a fascinating story about Italian baking traditions, introducing readers not only to regional breads, but also to recipes from tiny villages. I've made countless breads from her book, all of them with great success.

Ciabatta, which comes from around Lake Como in northern Italy, is named for its shape—it resembles an old slipper. Made with a very wet dough and very little yeast, it rises slowly and won't budge much, so rather than shape it, you cut it and stretch it.

———

For the Starter
¼ teaspoon active dry yeast
¼ cup warm water

¾ cup tepid water
2½ cups unbleached all-purpose flour

For the Dough
1 teaspoon active dry yeast
5 tablespoons warm water
1 tablespoon olive oil
1 cup plus 3 tablespoons tepid water
3¾ cups unbleached flour
1 tablespoon salt
Cornmeal for dusting

1. To make the starter, stir the yeast into the warm water in a large bowl or the bowl of a stand mixer and let stand until foamy, about 10 minutes.
2. Stir in the tepid water. Then add the flour a cup at a time, beating by hand or with an electric mixer to form a sticky dough. Place in a lightly oiled bowl, cover with plastic wrap, and set aside in a cool place to rise until tripled in volume, 6 to 24 hours. (The starter can be made in advance and once risen, refrigerated until ready to use.)
3. To make the dough, mix the yeast with warm water in the bowl of a stand mixer fitted with a paddle. Let stand until foamy, about 10 minutes.
4. Add the oil, starter, and a little of the tepid water to the yeast mixture and start mixing at very slow speed, gradually adding the rest of the tepid water until the ingredients are well blended. Mix the flour with the salt, add, and mix for 2 to 3 minutes.
5. Attach the dough hook to the mixer and mix for 2 minutes at low speed, then for 2 minutes at medium speed. Scoop the dough out onto a floured work surface and knead briefly. The dough should be very moist and elastic.
6. Place the dough in a lightly oiled bowl, cover with plastic wrap, and set aside to rise until doubled, 1½ to 2 hours. The dough should still be sticky but full of air bubbles.
7. Place dough on a well-floured work surface and cut into 4 equal portions. Roll each into a cylinder, then stretch the cylinders into rectangles about 4 by 10 inches.
8. If you can bake the bread on a baking stone, generously flour 4 pieces of parchment paper and place each shaped loaf seam side up on a sheet of paper. Otherwise, oil a baking sheet, dust it with flour and cornmeal, and place the loaves on the baking sheet. Cover

the loaves loosely with damp tea towels and allow to rise about 2 hours, until doubled.

9. Heat the oven to 425 degrees, with a baking stone (if you have one) on a rack in the lower third of the oven. Dust the stone with cornmeal. Gently roll the breads from the parchment onto the stone so the seams are down and the floured sides are up. Otherwise, simply place the baking sheet with the breads in the oven. Bake until the breads are golden brown, about 30 minutes, spraying them with water a few times during the first 10 minutes. Cool on racks.

MAKES 4 SMALL LOAVES

PERIOD DETAIL

With its wet dough and long rising times, this is clearly the precursor to the No-Knead Bread on p. 670.

FEBRUARY 12, 1992: "DE GUSTIBUS: SO WHAT IF IT LOOKS LIKE AN OLD SHOE? CIABATTA IS LOVED," BY FLORENCE FABRICANT. RECIPE ADAPTED FROM *THE ITALIAN BAKER*, BY CAROL FIELD.

—1992

make a soft but not sticky dough. Shape the dough into a ball.

3. Butter a large bowl, place the dough in the bowl, and cover with a kitchen towel. Let rise until doubled in bulk, 1 to 1½ hours.

4. Grease 2 baking sheets. Punch down the dough and divide into 12 equal pieces. Shape 1 piece of dough into a ball. Press about 1½ teaspoons of the cheese into the center and seal firmly around the cheese, forming the dough back into a ball. Repeat with the remaining dough and cheese. Divide the rolls between the baking sheets. Cover with kitchen towels and let rise for 30 to 60 minutes.

5. Heat the oven to 350 degrees. Bake until the rolls are nicely browned, about 25 minutes, rotating the baking sheets halfway through the cooking time. Serve the rolls warm, passing honey to drizzle over them.

MAKES 12 ROLLS

NOVEMBER 26, 1995: "FOOD: SWEET TIDINGS" BY MOLLY O'NEILL.

—1995

PISTACHIO-HONEY ROLLS STUFFED WITH BLUE CHEESE

—————

1 package active dry yeast

1½ cups warm water

4½ cups all-purpose flour, plus more if needed

2 teaspoons kosher salt

1 teaspoon ground cardamom

½ teaspoon ground mace

½ cup honey, plus more for serving

2 tablespoons unsalted butter, melted and cooled

½ cup shelled pistachios, chopped

6 tablespoons cold Saga Blue cheese

1. Place the yeast and water in a large bowl and stir until the yeast is dissolved. Let stand until foamy, about 5 minutes.

2. Stir 2 cups flour into the yeast mixture. Stir in the salt, cardamom, and mace. Stir in the honey, butter, and pistachios. Gradually add 2 more cups flour; the dough should become too difficult to stir. Turn the dough out onto a floured surface and knead until smooth, about 10 minutes, adding enough flour to

CREAM SCONES

It's hard to believe that the shaggy lump of dough this recipe produces will ever transform into anything edible, but magical things happen in the oven. The dough coheres, the sugar and salt flavors polarize, and springy, moist scones rise up from the heaps on the baking sheet.

As Molly O'Neill pointed out in her article, "Sugar and shape are the only differences between biscuits and scones, though socially they are worlds apart." Scones, she added, are usually sweet and triangular, while biscuits are unsweetened and round.

—————

2 cups all-purpose flour

⅓ cup sugar

1 tablespoon baking powder

½ teaspoon salt

1¼ to 1½ cups heavy cream, plus more
    for brushing the scones

1. Position a rack in the top third of the oven and heat the oven to 400 degrees. Thoroughly combine

the flour, sugar, baking powder, and salt in a large bowl. Make a well in the center of this mixture, add 1¼ cups cream, and stir the dry ingredients into the wet ingredients with a fork. Work quickly, stirring as little as possible, until a soft, shaggy dough forms. Add more cream a tablespoon at a time if the dough seems too dry.

2. Divide the dough into 8 pieces and place on an ungreased baking sheet, allowing at least 2 inches between the scones. Brush the top of each with heavy cream, and bake until golden, about 15 minutes. Transfer to a wire rack to cool.

MAKES 8 LARGE SCONES

COOKING NOTE
In Step 2, I used 2 tablespoons cream.

READERS
"Not only amenable to additions such as zest or fruit, they're so easy, so light, so delicious. I now can't imagine using any other scone recipe."
Barbara Zimmerman, Mount Holly, NJ, letter

MAY 31, 1998: "FOOD: JAM SESSION," BY MOLLY O'NEILL.
—1998

PAIN D'EPICES

This recipe from François Payard, the owner of pâtisserie shops in New York, Japan, and Korea, fuses the finest details from three types of cakes—honey, fruit, and spice—to produce something that humbles them all.

———

2 cups nuts, preferably a mix of sliced almonds, slivered almonds, skinned pistachios, skinned hazelnuts, walnut halves, and pine nuts
1 cup dried fruit cut into ¼-inch dice, preferably equal amounts of apricots, figs, prunes, and dates
¼ cup raisins
¼ cup golden raisins
Finely grated zest of 1 lemon
Finely grated zest of 1 orange
4 teaspoons baking soda

1 teaspoon pastis or other anise-flavored liqueur
¼ teaspoon ground cinnamon
¼ teaspoon freshly grated nutmeg
¼ teaspoon ground cloves (optional)
Pinch of salt
1¾ cups water
1 cup pine honey or other strong-flavored honey
¾ cup sugar
2 tablespoons dark rum
2 pieces star anise, tied in a square of cheesecloth
3 cups all-purpose flour, sifted

1. Heat the oven to 350 degrees. Butter 4 aluminum foil baby loaf pans, each 5¾ inches by 3¼ inches by 2 inches. Dust with flour and tap out the excess. Place the pans on a baking sheet.

2. Combine the nuts, diced fruit, raisins, lemon zest, and orange zest in a large bowl and mix well. Add the baking soda, pastis, cinnamon, nutmeg, cloves, and salt. Stir to mix.

3. Combine the water, honey, sugar, rum, and star anise in a medium saucepan, bring to a boil over medium heat, and immediately remove from the heat. Remove and discard the star anise. Pour the liquid into the bowl of fruit and nuts, and stir gently. Let the mixture rest for 5 minutes, stirring occasionally.

4. Add the flour, stir well, and let rest for 2 or 3 minutes.

5. Divide the batter among the pans; the pans will be about three-quarters full. Place the baking sheet in the oven. Bake until a knife inserted in the center of the cakes comes out with the tiniest bit of moist batter at the tip, 35 to 45 minutes. (Check the cakes after 20 minutes of baking; if at any time the cakes appear to be browning too quickly, cover them loosely with a tent of aluminum foil.) Transfer the cakes to a rack and cool to room temperature.

6. Unmold the cakes and wrap in plastic wrap. The cakes are best after ripening for 3 days at room temperature. (If sealed airtight, they may be frozen for a month.) To serve, cut into thin slices.

MAKES 4 SMALL LOAVES

COOKING NOTES
If you can't buy skinned pistachios or hazelnuts, using ones with the skins won't ruin the cake.

The worst thing you can do to this cake is overbake it. Keep a close eye on it toward the end of baking.

If the cake begins to dry out after a day or two, brush it with rum and wrap it in plastic wrap.

OCTOBER 14, 1998: "THE CHEF," BY FRANÇOIS PAYARD WITH DORIE GREENSPAN.

—1998

SAGE BISCUITS

There is no historical significance to these biscuits—except that Molly O'Neill used the recipe as a way of demonstrating what she saw as a comeback for the herb—I just liked them. O'Neill describes sage's aroma as "hinting at camphor and musk, with a tart, astringent finish." Great qualities, it turns out, when folded into biscuit batter.

———————

2 cups all-purpose flour

2 teaspoons baking powder

1/2 teaspoon baking soda

I teaspoon salt

6 tablespoons chilled, unsalted butter, cut into 1/2-inch cubes

1/4 cup chopped sage

3/4 cup plus I tablespoon buttermilk

I tablespoon unsalted butter, melted

1. Heat the oven to 450 degrees. Sift together the flour, baking powder, baking soda, and salt into a bowl. Cut in the cold butter until the mixture resembles coarse meal. Stir in the sage. Stir in the buttermilk until the dry ingredients are just moistened.

2. Lightly flour your hands and gather the dough into a ball. Lightly flour a work surface and place the dough on it. Using your hands, form the dough into a square about 1/2 inch thick and roughly 7 inches by 7 inches. Cut the dough into 9 squares and transfer them to a baking sheet.

3. Brush the tops with the melted butter and bake until golden brown, 12 to 14 minutes. Serve warm.

MAKES 9 BISCUITS

NOVEMBER 14, 1999: "FOOD: SAGE ADVICE," BY MOLLY O'NEILL.

—1999

RAISIN PECAN BREAD

Although this recipe didn't make it into the *Times* until 2000, I think of it as being from precisely 1993, when I was in college and thinking about becoming a bread baker. I drove from Boston to New York to go on a bakery crawl in the city—who doesn't have fond memories of their college bakery crawl?—and came across raisin-pecan rolls in every top bakery from Tom Cat to Eli's.

This excellent recipe turns out loaves that look and taste professionally made. Plumping the raisins in hot water and grinding some of the pecans make for a dense, nutty, sweet bread.

———————

For the Poolish (Starter)

3/4 cup plus 2 tablespoons room-temperature water

3/4 teaspoon crumbled cake yeast

2 cups organic white flour with retained germ

For the Bread

2 cups raisins

2 cups boiling water

3 cups lightly toasted pecan halves

2 tablespoons turbinado sugar, such as Demerara or Sugar in the Raw

1 1/2 cups water just slightly warmer than room temperature

I tablespoon crumbled cake yeast

1/2 cup Poolish (above)

4 1/4 cups unbleached all-purpose flour

2 teaspoons fine sea salt

1. To prepare the poolish, combine the water and yeast in a 1-gallon plastic container and stir until the mixture is milky and foamy and the yeast is fairly dissolved. Stir in the flour until just combined. Cover and leave at room temperature for 5 hours. (The poolish can be refrigerated for up to 48 hours. Bring to room temperature before using.)

2. To make the bread, combine the raisins and boiling water in a bowl and let stand for 10 minutes.

3. Combine 1/2 cup pecan halves and sugar in a food processor and pulse until the pecans are very finely ground. Set aside. Thoroughly drain the raisins and set aside.

4. Place the warm water and yeast in a large bowl (see

Cooking Notes). Break the poolish into small pieces with your hands or a wooden spoon and add it to the bowl. Stir until fairly dissolved. Stir in the flour, ground pecans, and salt. Stir until combined.

5. Turn the dough out onto a lightly floured surface and knead for 10 minutes. Slowly begin to fold in the raisins and the remaining pecan halves a little at a time. Return the dough to the bowl, cover with a tea towel, and let rise until doubled in bulk, 1 to 2 hours, or let rise in the refrigerator, about 4 hours.

6. Gently turn the dough out onto a lightly floured surface and cut into 3 equal pieces. Form into loose rounds. Leave the dough on your work surface and cover with a tea towel. Let rest for 10 minutes.

7. Gently shape each piece into a short log and place the logs on a baking sheet lined with parchment paper. Cover with the tea towel and let rise until the loaves just hold a fingerprint when lightly pressed, 30 minutes to 1 hour.

8. Heat the oven to 375 degrees. Have a plant sprayer full of fresh water ready. Using a single-sided razor at a 30-degree angle, slash the loaves diagonally with two 3-inch slashes each.

9. When the oven is hot, spray it thoroughly with water and immediately put in the bread and close the door. Spray the oven (not the bread) again 2 more times during the first 5 minutes of baking. Bake until the bread is very brown and sounds hollow when the bottom is tapped, 25 to 30 minutes more. Remove the loaves from the oven and cool them on a wire rack.

MAKES 3 LOAVES

COOKING NOTES

The bread freezes well, so eat one loaf and freeze the others.

The dough can be made in a stand mixer fitted with a dough hook. If so, knead for 5 minutes in the mixer, and finish kneading by hand for a minute or two.

If you don't have white flour with retained germ for the poolish, you can add 1 tablespoon wheat germ to 2 cups regular all-purpose flour. It's not ideal but is an acceptable substitute.

APRIL 23, 2000: "FOOD: BY BREAD ALONE," BY MOLLY O'NEILL. RECIPE ADAPTED FROM ALISON PRAY AND MATT JAMES, THE OWNERS OF THE STANDARD BAKING COMPANY IN PORTLAND, MAINE.

—2000

⌒ NANCY REAGAN'S MONKEY BREAD

Monkey bread, the epitome of 1970s baking, was apparently a regular on the TV trays of the Reagan White House. The loaf, a ring of small rolls baked together in a tube pan, is meant to be pulled apart with your fingers, like a monkey would do.

———

1 package active dry yeast

1 cup lukewarm whole milk

3 large eggs

3 tablespoons sugar

2 teaspoons salt

4 to 5 cups all-purpose flour

12 tablespoons (1½ sticks) unsalted butter, softened

8 tablespoons (1 stick) unsalted butter, melted

1. Butter and flour a 4-cup or larger ring mold or tube pan. Whisk the yeast with the milk in a large bowl. Whisk in 2 of the eggs, then whisk in the sugar, salt, and 4 cups flour, switching to a wooden spoon when the dough gets stiff. Stir in the softened butter and knead the dough in the bowl until it comes together in a ball.

2. Turn the dough out onto a work surface and knead until it forms an elastic ball, sprinkling with and working in up to 1 cup more flour to keep dough from getting sticky. Place the dough in a clean bowl and cover with plastic wrap. Let rise in a warm place until doubled in size, 1 to 1½ hours.

3. Pour the melted butter into a small bowl. Punch down the dough and turn out onto a lightly floured work surface. Roll the dough into a log and cut into 28 equal pieces. Shape each piece into a ball, dip in melted butter, and place in the prepared pan, staggering the pieces in 2 layers. Cover loosely with plastic wrap and let rise in a warm place until doubled in size, about 30 minutes.

4. Heat the oven to 375 degrees. Beat the remaining egg and lightly brush over the top of the bread. Bake until the top is nicely browned and dough is cooked through, 25 to 30 minutes. Test by turning out the loaf onto a rack; the bottom and sides should be nicely browned. Turn upright on another rack and let cool slightly before serving.

COOKING NOTES

I doubled the salt. Sorry, Nancy.

When putting the balls of dough into the pan, place them seam side up so when you invert the loaf, the smooth sides will be visible.

The monkey bread I grew up with was sweet. Each ball of dough was dipped first in butter, then in cinnamon sugar, before being added (along with raisins) to the tube pan. We ate it on Christmas morning. You can easily adapt this recipe if you want a sweet version.

SERVING SUGGESTIONS

A friend insists that monkey bread must be served with fried chicken. See pp. 462 and 490 for inspiration.

FEBRUARY 23, 2003: "FOOD: JUST SAY DOUGH," BY MICHAEL BOODRO. RECIPE ADAPTED FROM NANCY REAGAN AND REPRINTED FROM THE 1985 *AMERICAN CANCER SOCIETY COOKBOOK.*

—2003

NO-KNEAD BREAD

I'm not sure this Jim Lahey recipe needs an introduction. After it was published in Mark Bittman's column, it inspired a tsunami of internet chatter, stayed on the *Times*'s most-emailed list for weeks, and became the foundation for Lahey's first book, *My Bread: The Revolutionary No-Work, No-Knead Method.* It is easily the most famous recipe ever to run in the *Times.*

If you happened to be living in Siberia at the time, this recipe revolutionized home bread baking, because it does not require kneading or a baking stone, and mostly because it yields a loaf that looks and tastes in every way as if it were made by an artisan baker with a wood-fired oven.

The dough, which is a very wet dough (42 percent water), is fermented for up to 18 hours, which gives it time to develop both flavor and elasticity. It is then loosely shaped and baked in a hot covered pot, which creates a steamy environment, just the right conditions to produce a rustic, crackly crust. The best part? It's fun to make.

3 cups all-purpose or bread flour, plus more for dusting
$1/4$ teaspoon instant yeast
$1^{1}/4$ teaspoons salt
$1^{1}/2$ cups plus 2 tablespoons cool water
Cornmeal or wheat bran as needed

1. Combine the flour, yeast, and salt in a large bowl. Add the water and stir until blended; the dough will be shaggy and sticky. Cover the bowl with plastic wrap. Let the dough rest for at least 12 hours, preferably 18, at warm room temperature, about 70 degrees. The dough is ready when its surface is dotted with bubbles.

2. Lightly flour a work surface and place the dough on it; sprinkle it with a little more flour, and fold it over on itself once or twice. Cover loosely with plastic wrap and let rest for about 15 minutes.

3. Using just enough flour to keep the dough from sticking to the work surface or to your fingers, gently and quickly shape the dough into a ball. Generously coat a cotton towel (not terry cloth) with flour, wheat bran, or cornmeal, put the dough seam side down on the towel, and dust with more flour, bran, or cornmeal. Cover with another cotton towel and let rise for 2 to $2^{1}/2$ hours. When it is ready, the dough will be more than doubled in size and will not readily spring back when poked with a finger.

4. At least 30 minutes before the dough is ready, heat the oven to 450 degrees. Put a 6- to 8-quart covered heavy pot (cast iron, enamel, Pyrex, or ceramic) in the oven as it heats.

5. When the dough is ready, carefully remove the pot from the oven. Lift off the top towel, slide your hand under the bottom towel, and turn the dough over into the pot, seam side up; it may look like a mess, but that is OK. Shake the pot once or twice if dough is unevenly distributed; it will straighten out as it bakes.

6. Cover with the lid and bake for 30 minutes, then remove the lid and bake another 15 to 30 minutes, until the loaf is beautifully browned. Cool on a rack.

MAKES ONE $1^{1}/2$-POUND LOAF

NOVEMBER 8, 2006: "THE MINIMALIST: THE SECRET OF GREAT BREAD: LET TIME DO THE WORK," BY MARK BITTMAN. RECIPE ADAPTED FROM JIM LAHEY, THE OWNER OF SULLIVAN STREET BAKERY IN NEW YORK CITY.

—2006

CHALLAH REVISITED

B & R Artisan Bread, a bakery with a devoted following in Framingham, Massachusetts, occupies a storefront that was for decades a Jewish bakery well known for its challah. "The baker, he actually mispronounced it," Michael Rhoads, the owner of B & R, said. "He called it 'holly,' not 'challah.' So all of his old customers come in and ask for holly bread." Rhoads, who is known for his crisp baguettes and rustic pain levain, is not a challah maker, but when I asked him to come up with a modern interpretation of a challah recipe that had run in the *Times* in 1976 (see p. 659), he was delighted: the perfect excuse to finally master it.

Rather than improve the loaf, he rethought its construction. Most challah contains fat added directly to the dough. Rhoads chose to use butter as you would in puff pastry, chilling it and layering it in, "so you get these really eye-popping layers from the braid," he said. "It will be more of an after-meal challah than a before-meal." Rhoads's version is stunning, a peony of challahs, with petals of sweet, puffy dough, braided and shaped in a taut circle. The perfect any-time-of-day holly.

———

10½ ounces (about 2 cups plus 1½ tablespoons)
    all-purpose flour
1¼ ounces (about 2½ tablespoons) sugar
0.15 ounce (about 1½ teaspoons) kosher salt
0.15 ounce (about 1½ teaspoons) active dry yeast
2 large eggs
10 tablespoons (1¼ sticks) unsalted butter
¼ cup plus 1½ teaspoons lukewarm water
Confectioners' sugar

1. About 9 hours before baking, combine the flour, sugar, salt, yeast, eggs, 2 tablespoons butter, and water in the bowl of a stand mixer fitted with dough hook. Mix for 5 minutes at medium speed, or until the dough forms a smooth ball. Cover the bowl with plastic wrap and refrigerate for 6 to 8 hours.
2. Using a rolling pin, flatten the dough into an oval, then roll it into a 5-by-9-inch rectangle. Put on a baking sheet and freeze for 30 minutes.
3. Set the remaining butter at room temperature for a few minutes. Using a rolling pin, flatten the butter between sheets of wax or parchment papers into a 4-by-5-inch rectangle. If it is too soft, refrigerate for 5 minutes. Remove the dough from the freezer. Lay the butter on one end of the dough. Cut the dough in half. Place the half without butter on top of the other half and gently press on the edges to seal. Roll into a 6-by-12-inch rectangle. Fold into thirds, like a business letter. Cover with plastic and chill for 20 minutes.
4. Roll the dough into an 8-by-10-inch rectangle. Trim the edges to make it neat; reserve the trimmings. Slice the rectangle lengthwise into nine ½-inch-wide strips. Group the strips into 3 groups of 3. Gather the tops of the strands in each group and pinch to seal. Braid each group separately, and pinch the ends to keep each braid intact. Using the 3 braids, create 1 large ring on a baking sheet, then pinch the braids together.
5. Roll the trimmings out ⅛ inch thick and, using cookie cutters, cut out 3 pretty shapes. Lay the shapes over the seams between the 3 braids and press gently. Brush the ring with water. Loosely cover with plastic wrap and let rise until almost doubled in size, about 1 hour.
6. Heat the oven to 375 degrees. Bake the loaf for 10 minutes, then reduce the temperature to 325 degrees and bake for 10 minutes more, or until golden and an instant-read thermometer inserted into the center of the loaf reaches 180 degrees. Cool on the pan, then dust with confectioners' sugar.

MAKES 1 LOAF

COOKING NOTE
If you don't own a good kitchen scale, now is the time to buy one. I use a My Weigh KD7000 scale, which is available at www.oldwillknottscales.com.

SEPTEMBER 28, 2008: "RECIPE REDUX: 1976: CHALLAH," BY AMANDA HESSER. RECIPE ADAPTED FROM MICHAEL RHOADS, THE OWNER OF B & R ARTISAN BREAD IN FRAMINGHAM, MASSACHUSETTS.

—2008

⌒ SPELT-FLOUR CRACKERS

These crackers are so hard and so smooth, tapping on one sounds like flicking a porcelain plate.

———————

¼ teaspoon salt
½ cup cold water
1½ cups white spelt flour, plus more for dusting
Flaky sea salt, fennel seeds, caraway seeds, or
    kalunji seeds (optional)

1. Heat the oven to 350 degrees. Dissolve the salt in the cold water in a medium bowl. Stir in the spelt flour until combined. Knead the dough a few turns, until a ball forms.

2. Flour an overturned 12-by-17-inch baking sheet and roll out the dough on top of it, using as much flour as needed to prevent sticking, until the dough covers the sheet from edge to edge. Using a spray bottle filled with water, spray the dough to give it a glossy finish. Prick the dough all over with a fork. If you choose, sprinkle with sea salt or seeds. For neat crackers, score the dough into grids.

3. Bake until the dough is crisp and golden and snaps apart, 15 to 25 minutes. (Check after 10 minutes to make sure it does not overcook.) Break into pieces and serve.

MAKES 1 LARGE CRACKER SHEET

COOKING NOTES

White spelt flour is available at most Whole Foods markets and health food stores, and at www.kingarthurflour.com.

Kalunji seeds, also known as chernushka seeds, are available from www.kalustyans.com.

SERVING SUGGESTIONS

Feta Spread (p. 71), Fresh and Smoked Salmon Spread (p. 72), Cheese Ball with Cumin, Mint, and Pistachios (p. 85), The Best Spinach Dip, with Chipotle and Lime (p. 90), Olive Oil–Tuna Spread with Lemon and Oregano (p. 95)

NOVEMBER 30, 2008: "THE WAY WE EAT: GRAIN EXCHANGE," BY HEIDI JULAVITS. RECIPE ADAPTED FROM ELI WINOGRAD AT HUNGRY GHOST BREAD IN NORTHAMPTON, MASSACHUSETTS.

—2008

—1860s—
- Cookies are referred to as jumbles, and they can come in almost any form.

—1870s—
- Chocolate caramels (at least ten recipes are published during this period; see p. 683) provide pleasure—and dental issues.

—1877—
- Gingersnaps (p. 679).

—1910—
- Oatmeal macaroons.

—1930s—
- Ruth Wakefield invents the Toll House cookie, aka the chocolate chip cookie.

—1943—
- Brownies emerged from the nest three decades earlier, but the recipe finds its wings this year.

—1946—
- William Greenberg Jr. Desserts opens in New York City; it becomes famous for its Sand Tarts (p. 688).

—1949—
- Party Balls (p. 685): think Rice Krispies treat meets molasses cookie.

—1950s—
- A cookie is still spelled cooky.

—1960s—
- Rum Balls (p. 687), because there isn't enough rum in the cocktails.

—1969—
- Cookie Monster makes his debut on *Sesame Street*; in 2006, record levels of childhood obesity will cause him to stop scarfing down so many cookies on the show.

—1970s—
- No school lunch is complete without an oatmeal raisin cookie.

—1977—
- The first Mrs. Fields cookie store opens.

—1980s—
- The bar cookie decade.

—1991—
- Ben & Jerry's introduces Chocolate Chip Cookie Dough ice cream.

—1993—
- We are so devoted to Italy that we abandon soft chewy cookies for hard, brittle biscotti.

—2000—
- Miniature madeleines, the shell-shaped French cakes, become *the* petit four at Manhattan restaurants.

—2008—
- Caramels covered in chocolate and sprinkled with sea salt obsess everyone, including the Obamas.

—2009—
- French sandwich-style macaroons rivet bakers and eaters alike, a trend launched by Parisian pastry king Pierre Hermé.

- David Leite deconstructs the chocolate chip cookie and rebuilds it into the platonic version (p. 709).

15

❧

COOKIES AND CANDY

The nineteenth century was a good time for someone with a sweet tooth, as you will see from the number of candy and cookie recipes in this chapter. Commercial candy making was just taking off, which is why by the early twentieth century, the candy recipes are replaced by more and more cookies—bars, macaroons, nut balls, quakes, crisps, and sablés, to name a few. And, of course, there is the indominable chocolate chip cookie invented in the 1930s, but repeatedly tweaked by absolutely everyone (myself included) in the search for Toll House perfection (see pp. 706 and 709).

RECIPES BY CATEGORY

∽ BUTTERSCOTCH

Not for those with a lot of fillings! (If you have a lot of fillings, you've probably had enough butterscotch anyway.) For the rest of you, what bliss—butterscotch is a form of slow and steady gratification. You get the sweet butter flavor you want, and the hard, chewy candy draws out the pleasure. Here, a "gill" (½ cup) of molasses adds a mineral dimension to the whole.

––––––––

½ pound (2 sticks) unsalted butter
1 cup plus 2 tablespoons light brown sugar
½ cup unsulphured molasses
½ teaspoon salt
Fleur de sel or Maldon sea salt for sprinkling (optional)

1. Butter a 9-by-13-inch baking pan. Combine the butter, brown sugar, molasses, and salt in a medium heavy saucepan and attach a candy thermometer to the pan. Bring to a boil, stirring to dissolve the sugar, and boil until the mixture registers 255 degrees. Remove from the heat and pour into the buttered pan, tilting the pan so the butterscotch spreads evenly. Let stand until the butterscotch has firmed up and is cool enough to touch.

2. Use buttered scissors to cut the butterscotch into ¾-inch squares (first cut into ¾-inch-wide strips, then cut the strips into squares). Wrap the squares individually in wax paper or layer between sheets of wax paper in an airtight container.

MAKES ABOUT 12½ DOZEN CANDIES

COOKING NOTE

When cutting the butterscotch, if it becomes too firm, slip it back into the baking pan and warm in a 250-degree oven until it's soft enough to cut.

DECEMBER 31, 1876: "THE HOUSEHOLD: RECEIPTS FOR THE TABLE." RECIPE SIGNED SARAH.

—1876

∽ GINGERSNAPS

Rarely does a cookie recipe give you the satisfaction of pounding the dough. Here you can do it with reckless abandon—in fact, Lillie, who contributed the recipe to the *Times*, instructed you to "beat hard with a rolling pin, which will make it crisp when baked."

––––––––

1 cup unsulphured molasses
8 tablespoons (1 stick) unsalted butter, cut into chunks
Scant ¼ cup packed dark brown sugar
3 tablespoons ground ginger
1 teaspoon ground cinnamon
¼ teaspoon cayenne pepper
Large pinch of salt
½ teaspoon baking soda
4 cups all-purpose flour

1. Warm the molasses, butter, and brown sugar in a large saucepan over medium-low heat, stirring occasionally until the butter is melted. Pour into a large bowl and stir until smooth.

2. Whisk the ginger, cinnamon, cayenne, salt, baking soda, and ¼ cup flour in a small bowl. Stir this into the butter mixture. Start whisking in the remaining 3 ¾ cups flour until the dough is too heavy for a whisk; switch to a wooden spoon and continue working in the flour until the dough is a cohesive lump and begins to pull away from the sides of the bowl.

3. Scrape the dough out onto a lightly floured work surface and knead for a minute or two. Then pound the dough flat with a rolling pin, using a few stern whacks. Continuing with the rolling pin, pound it into a rectangle. Fold the dough into thirds, like a business letter, turn it 90 degrees, and repeat the pounding, shaping and folding 10 times. Divide the dough into 2 pieces, shape each half into a disk, and wrap in plastic wrap. Chill in the refrigerator for at least 4 hours, and up to 24 hours.

4. Heat the oven to 350 degrees. Line 2 baking sheets with parchment paper. Using one half of the dough at a time, working on a barely floured work surface, roll out the dough as thin as possible, 1/16 to ⅛ inch thick. Cut out the cookies using a 2½-inch round cookie cutter and transfer to the parchment-lined baking sheets, spacing them an inch apart.

5. Bake until just browning on the edges, 8 to 10 minutes; turn the baking sheets 180 degrees after 4 minutes. Transfer the cookies to racks to cool. Repeat until the remaining dough has been used; reroll the scraps of dough to make more cookies.

MAKES ABOUT 6 DOZEN COOKIES

JANUARY 14, 1877: "RECEIPTS FOR THE TABLE." RECIPE SIGNED LILLIE.

—1877

⌒ MOLASSES CANDY

Molasses candy would be good enough on its own, but here you get the glow of lemon too. This is a soft and airy confection, more like taffy than hard candy.

Make this with a friend: it's an adventure. The original instructions say that after you cook the molasses mixture, you cool it enough to handle and then "pull it white," which means pulling and stretching the warm, silky, utterly gorgeous brown mass like a piece of taffy until you've lightened the color and tightened the texture.

Referring to the candy-pulling instructions in Bruce Weinstein's *The Ultimate Candy Book*, my friend Merrill and I attacked the mass with my two-year-old kids, who were the perfect height: they held on to the candy mass while we stretched it upward. When you pull candy, you're simply stretching it and folding it over itself, again and again. At first the molasses mixture is like molten copper with a satin sheen. It's soft and loose, and as you pull it, the color whitens and the layers collapse, creating thin striations of brown. Over time, the candy becomes stickier and more difficult to stretch. We spread our palms with soft butter and pulled the candy one last time into long, thin, 1/2-inch-diameter strands, then, using buttered scissors, snipped the strands into 1-inch pieces—pieces of candy.

-----

2 cups unsulphured molasses

1 1/2 teaspoons cider vinegar

1/4 cup sugar

1/2 tablespoon unsalted butter, plus more for the baking sheet and your hands

1/2 teaspoon baking soda, dissolved in 2 teaspoons hot water

1 1/2 teaspoons lemon extract or essence

1. Butter a 9-by-13-inch baking dish. Combine the molasses, vinegar, sugar, and butter in a deep heavy saucepan and attach a candy thermometer to the pan. Bring to a boil, stirring to dissolve the sugar, and cook until the mixture reaches 255 degrees. Remove from the heat and, wearing an oven mitt on your stirring hand, stir in the dissolved baking soda and the lemon extract. Pour the mixture into the buttered dish and let stand until set up but still pourable, about 10 minutes.

2. Butter a baking sheet, or if you have a marble or granite countertop, butter a 15-inch-square area. Pour the molasses mixture onto the sheet or countertop. Lightly butter your hands and start folding the molasses mixture onto itself by lifting the corners and bringing them up onto the middle of the taffy. Continue folding the corners onto the center until the taffy can be gathered into a ball, about 3 minutes. The taffy is now ready to be pulled. (If your hands are small, you can divide the ball into 2 or 3 pieces before you begin to pull the candy.)

3. Holding the ball of candy with both hands, pull it into a rope about 2 feet long, twisting the rope as you pull. Bring the ends of the rope together, creating a 1-foot rope, then pull this rope to a length of 2 feet or more, twisting it as you pull. Bring the ends together again, and repeat the process until the taffy becomes golden and very hard to pull, about 10 minutes.

4. Divide the pulled candy into 4 pieces. Roll or pull each piece into a rope about 1/2 inch in diameter. Cut each rope into bite-sized pieces with buttered scissors. Wrap the cooled pieces individually in wax paper, or layer them between sheets of wax paper, and store them in an airtight container at room temperature for up to 3 weeks.

MAKES ABOUT I POUND

COOKING NOTE

As you pull the candy, focus on using your fingertips, which will help keep the ropes of candy evenly shaped.

AUGUST 12, 1877: "THE HOUSEHOLD: RECEIPTS FOR THE TABLE." RECIPE SIGNED MOLLIE; PULLING INSTRUCTIONS ADAPTED FROM *THE ULTIMATE CANDY BOOK*, BY BRUCE WEINSTEIN.

—1877

CREAM CHOCOLATES

Once you get the hang of preparing the filling—which requires boiling milk and sugar to the soft-ball stage and then beating it in a mixer—these chocolates are easy and fun to make. After cooking the first batch, I decided to add peppermint to the filling for a Peppermint Patty–like candy. Feel free to skip this variation and stick to the plain vanilla filling.

———

2 cups sugar
½ cup whole milk
1 tablespoon vanilla extract
½ teaspoon peppermint extract (optional)
6 ounces 72% (or higher) cacao chocolate

1. Line a baking sheet with parchment paper. Combine the sugar and milk in a small heavy saucepan, attach a candy thermometer to the pan, and bring to a boil over medium-high heat. Boil until the mixture reaches 235 to 240 degrees.
2. Pour the hot mixture into the bowl of a mixer fitted with a whisk (or use a hand mixer) and beat until the mixture thickens, about 10 minutes, adding the vanilla and peppermint, if using, halfway through. Stop when the mixture is thick enough to shape.
3. Form the sugar mixture into small gumball-sized drops, and set on the parchment-lined baking sheet to cool.
4. Melt the chocolate in a double boiler or in the microwave. Using a fork, dip the sugar balls a few at a time into the chocolate, roll to lightly coat, and return to the parchment to cool and set. Then coat once more with chocolate.

MAKES ABOUT 50 CHOCOLATES

COOKING NOTE
When in doubt, make the cream balls smaller than you think. You want to really taste the chocolate.

SEPTEMBER 2, 1877: "RECEIPTS FOR THE TABLE," RECIPE SIGNED CALIFORNIA.

—1877

JUMBLES

Jumbles were early cookies, many examples of which were uninspiring lumps of dough. But these jumbles are champs: crisp and buttery and trilling with freshly grated nutmeg.

———

1¾ cups all-purpose flour
1 teaspoon freshly grated nutmeg
Large pinch of salt
½ pound (2 sticks) unsalted butter, softened
1 cup sugar
1 teaspoon baking soda, dissolved in
    a scant teaspoon of hot water
½ cup sour cream
1 large egg, lightly beaten

1. Whisk together the flour, nutmeg, and salt in a small bowl.
2. In the bowl of a stand mixer fitted with a paddle (or in a bowl with a hand mixer), beat the butter and sugar until light and fluffy. Add the baking soda mixture and sour cream and beat until blended. Beat in the egg. With the mixer on low speed, gradually add the flour and beat just until the dough clings together. Refrigerate the dough, covered, until chilled.
3. Heat the oven to 350 degrees. Line 2 baking sheets with parchment paper. Drop the dough by rounded teaspoonfuls onto the baking sheets, 2 inches apart. Bake until the cookies are golden brown on the edges, about 12 minutes. Transfer to racks to cool.

MAKES ABOUT 5 DOZEN COOKIES

JANUARY 13, 1878: "RECEIPTS FOR THE TABLE." RECIPE SIGNED MOLLIE.

—1878

MACAROONS

These are unlike any macaroons I've tasted. Flat and shiny, with a crackled surface, they're crisp on the perimeter, chewy in the center—the ideal cookie. Because I ground the almonds in a food processor, not a nut grinder, the texture was pleasantly pebbly.

———

½ pound blanched almonds, finely ground

Grated zest of 1 lemon

2½ cups confectioners' sugar

3 large egg whites, lightly beaten

1. Position an oven rack on the bottom shelf and pre-heat the oven to 300 degrees. Line 2 baking sheets with parchment paper. Blend the ground almonds and lemon zest in a bowl. Mix in the sugar, then stir in the whites.

2. Drop the macaroon batter by teaspoonfuls onto the baking sheets, keeping them 2 inches apart. Bake until golden on the edges, about 20 minutes. (You can bake them darker, but the texture will change; try it and see what you prefer.)

3. Let the macaroons cool on the baking sheets, then pluck them off. Store in an airtight tin.

MAKES 40 TO 45 MACAROONS

COOKING NOTES

Grinding the almonds together with the lemon zest will infuse the citron flavor more deeply into the cookies.

The flavor of the cookies improves after a day or two.

I used these to make the powdery macaroon coating for the Tortoni on p. 720.

MARCH 31, 1878: "RECEIPTS FOR THE TABLE." RECIPE SIGNED M. A.

—1878

⌒ PEPPERMINTS

Peppermints were a popular European candy by the mid-nineteenth century. "Brandy balls," a sweet made with peppermint and cinnamon—"all the spices that warm the tongue, like brandy does," explained Francine Sagan, a food historian—were sold on the street in London in the 1850s.

But until Wrigley's spearmint gum was introduced in America in 1893 and peppermint LifeSavers appeared on the market about a decade later, mint candy was something that was made at home. It was one of those things, like recaning a chair or boning a leg of lamb, that every woman seemed to know how

to do. A recipe for peppermints that ran in the *Times* in 1879 is a surprise in that it actually gives precise measurements for all of the ingredients, which was not always the case with the paper's nineteenth-century recipes.

Without candy-making expertise, however, I quickly ran into trouble: I boiled a pound of sugar and a little water for 5 minutes, at which point the mixture began to caramelize. Off the heat, I added peppermint extract and followed the instructions to beat the mixture until it thickened. But even if I'd beaten it with an airplane propeller, the mixture had determined to remain loose and glistening, so I gave up and poured the caramelized sugar onto a greased baking sheet.

Cooled, the candy looked like a shiny amber ink blot, attractive but not terribly promising. Then I tasted a piece and suddenly understood why you'd want to make candy at home. The caramelization of the sugar gave the candy an unexpected buttery flavor and bitterness, and the peppermint was profuse and alive in a way that you never find in store-bought candy.

To fix up the recipe into one that was less shards and more candy drops, I turned once again to Bruce Weinstein's excellent *The Ultimate Candy Book* for help in writing a modern version. The proportions and method are based on his recipe for lemon drops.

————

1 cup sugar

⅓ cup light corn syrup

½ cup water

1 teaspoon peppermint extract

Confectioners' sugar for dusting (optional)

1. Lightly oil a large baking sheet and line it with parchment paper. Oil the parchment.

2. Combine the sugar, corn syrup, and water in a medium heavy saucepan and bring to a boil over medium heat, stirring until the sugar is completely dissolved. Attach a candy thermometer to the side of the pan and cook, without stirring, until the syrup reaches 300 degrees. Immediately remove the pan from the heat and allow the syrup to cool to 270 degrees, then stir in the peppermint extract.

3. Pour teaspoonfuls of the hot syrup onto the prepared baking sheet, spacing them ½ inch apart (transferring the hot syrup to a Pyrex measuring cup with a spout makes shaping the candies much easier.) Let cool.

4. When the candies are completely cool, peel them off the parchment. Wrap each piece in wax paper, or toss them all in confectioners' sugar. Store in an airtight container at room temperature for up to 2 months.

MAKES 30 TO 36 CANDIES

COOKING NOTES

Boyajian makes excellent extracts. Their peppermint extract is $5 for a 1-ounce bottle at www.amazon.com—you may also find it in specialty markets.

The candies should be kept between layers of wax paper in an airtight tin.

In addition to snacking on these mints, you can crush the candy and sprinkle the peppermint dust over chocolate ice cream and use the snippets to decorate cakes.

FEBRUARY 23, 1879: "RECEIPTS FOR THE TABLE." RECIPE SIGNED G. PARTS OF THE RECIPE ADAPTED FROM *THE ULTIMATE CANDY BOOK*, BY BRUCE WEINSTEIN.

—1879

CHOCOLATE CARAMELS

4½ ounces bittersweet chocolate, chopped (about 1 cup)

1 cup whole milk

1 cup unsulphured molasses

1 cup sugar

3 tablespoons unsalted butter

1 teaspoon vanilla extract

1. Butter an 8-inch-square baking dish. Combine the chocolate, milk, molasses, sugar, and butter in a heavy saucepan, attach a candy thermometer to the pan, and cook over medium heat, stirring constantly with a wooden spoon, until the mixture reaches 245 degrees; scrape the bottom of the pan with the spoon to make sure the mixture doesn't stick and burn.

2. Remove from the heat and, wearing an oven mitt, add the vanilla to the hot mixture. Quickly pour the mixture into the buttered baking dish.

3. When the caramel is cool enough to handle, transfer it to a cutting board. With a buttered chef's knife (or scissors), cut into ½-inch-wide strips, then cut crosswise into ¾-inch pieces.

4. When they are completely cool, wrap the caramels individually in wax paper, or layer between sheets of wax paper in an airtight container. Store in a cool place.

MAKES 80 TO 100 PIECES

COOKING NOTES

If the caramel hardens too much to cut it, slip it back into the baking dish and into a 200-degree oven to soften.

If you like a firm caramel, bring the mixture to 250 degrees in Step 1.

MARCH 6, 1881: "RECEIPTS." RECIPE SIGNED FANNY.

—1881

CHARLESTON COCONUT SWEETIES

These coconut meringues crackle and grow hollow in the oven, leaving you with a sweet fragile shell and a chewy coconut center.

½ cup coconut water (not milk—from a fresh coconut or a store-bought coconut water drink, like Zico)

3 cups sugar

½ cup water

4 large egg whites

Pinch of salt

2 cups grated fresh (or frozen) unsweetened coconut

1. Arrange the racks in your oven to accommodate 3 baking sheets and heat the oven to 400 degrees. Line 3 baking sheets with parchment paper. Combine the coconut water, 2 cups sugar, and water in a small heavy saucepan, attach a candy thermometer to the pan, and bring to a boil. Cook until the mixture registers 250 degrees. Remove from the heat and let cool for a few minutes.

2. Meanwhile, in a mixer fitted with a whisk attachment, beat the egg whites with the salt until foamy. Add the remaining 1 cup sugar a little at a time, beating until a glossy, elastic meringue forms.

3. With the mixer running, pour in the hot syrup in a thread-like stream as close to the sides of the bowl as

possible to avoid the whisk. Some syrup will get thrown up on the sides of the bowl; this is fine. Keep beating after all the syrup is added to cool the mixture slightly. 4. Fold in the coconut. Drop the mixture by table-spoonfuls onto the parchment-lined baking sheets, about 2 inches apart. Place the baking sheets in the oven and turn off the heat. Leave the candies in the oven until completely cool (overnight is easiest).

MAKES 40 TO 50 SWEETIES

COOKING NOTE

See p. 247 for instructions on opening a coconut. To grate the meat, press pieces of coconut through the grating disk of your food processor, or use the large holes on a hand grater.

OCTOBER 16, 1883: "RECEIPTS." RECIPE SIGNED YADIS—THE LIVE OAKS.

—1883

◢ PRALINES

———

2 cups packed and lightly mounded light brown sugar
1 cup whole milk
Large pinch of salt
1/8 teaspoon cream of tartar
2 tablespoons unsalted butter
1 cup pecan halves

1. Line 2 baking sheets with parchment paper and butter the paper. Combine the brown sugar, milk, salt, and cream of tartar in a heavy saucepan and attach a candy thermometer to the pan. Bring to a gentle boil and cook, stirring frequently with a whisk, "until a fine thread of [the syrup] spun from a spoon and blown with the breath will wave and bend, but not break," or until it reaches 245 degrees on the candy thermometer. It may take up to 30 minutes to reach this point. 2. Off the heat, stir in the butter. Pour the mixture into a mixer fitted with a paddle attachment (or use a hand mixer and a large bowl) and beat until it thickens enough to leave a ribbon trail when the beater is lifted. Stir in the pecans. 3. Working quickly so the mixture doesn't harden, drop the pralines by tablespoonfuls onto the baking sheets. Let cool completely.

MAKES ABOUT 3 DOZEN PRALINES

COOKING NOTES

Be careful when cooking the syrup, because it boils over easily and froths when stirred. I suggest wearing an oven mitt, standing back from the saucepan, and using a whisk to stir, because it helps the syrup boil more calmly.

Don't make the pralines any larger than a table-spoonful, or they'll be sugar bombs.

NOVEMBER 14, 1937: "THE HOUSEWIFE WELCOMES A BUMPER NUT CROP," BY EDDA MORGAN.

—1937

◢ BROWNIES

I made many brownie recipes in an effort to find the best one to include in this book. There was a delicious, elemental one from 1913 that didn't call for vanilla or salt, a ten-step monster from 1985 that produced a fine chocolaty square; and a few more recent examples, including Katherine Hepburn's recipe and one by a French pastry chef that was like a souffléd brownie. In the end, though, I settled on this unadorned version, with classic proportions of butter, sugar, eggs, flour, and chocolate, which I believe is the best kind of brownie: a little buttery, a little bitter, a little salty, but mostly about the chocolate. These brownies also exhibit my favorite brownie detail, a shiny, chewy crackled surface.

This recipe ran close to the holidays in the middle of World War II and was highlighted as a sweet that traveled well as a care package for soldiers.

———

1/4 pound semisweet or bittersweet chocolate
8 tablespoons (1 stick) unsalted butter
2 large eggs
1 cup sugar
1/2 cup sifted all-purpose flour
1/2 cup chopped nuts
1 teaspoon vanilla extract
1/4 teaspoon salt

1. Heat the oven to 350 degrees. Butter an 8-inch-square baking pan and line the base with parchment.

2. Melt the chocolate and butter in a saucepan over low heat. Remove from the heat.

3. Beat the eggs with the sugar until the sugar is mostly dissolved, and add to the chocolate mixture. Add the other ingredients and mix well. Pour the batter into the prepared pan and smooth the top.

4. Bake until a toothpick inserted in the center comes out almost, but not quite, clean, about 25 minutes. Let cool for a few minutes, then invert the brownie onto a rack, remove the parchment, and turn it right side up. When cool, cut into 16 squares.

MAKES 16 BROWNIES

COOKING NOTE

You might laugh at the size of these brownies, which are 2-inch squares—brownie "bites" by today's standard. Cut them larger at your (waistline's) peril.

NOVEMBER 14, 1943: "GIFTS FOR THE ABSENT ONES," BY JANE HOLT.

—1943

❧ HONEY SPICE COOKIES

When I first made these cookies, I liked their crisp bottoms and pillowy interiors but was ambivalent about the flavor. Firmly stuck between sweet and savory, they needed a swing vote. So for the next batch, I sprinkled a little sea salt on a few of them and some raw sugar on others, and after a short stay in the oven, I had two very different cookies that I was crazy about. The ones with salt became a neatly formed biscuit suited to British cheeses. The ones with sugar became a lovely tea cookie, firm and fragrant, but not too sweet. Make the batch half sweet and half savory, and you'll get plenty of both.

———

2⅓ cups sifted all-purpose flour

1 teaspoon baking soda

½ teaspoon ground cinnamon

¼ teaspoon ground cloves

¼ teaspoon ground allspice

8 tablespoons (1 stick) unsalted butter, softened

½ cup mild honey (such as clover or orange blossom)

1 large egg

Flaky sea salt and/or coarse raw sugar, such as Sugar in the Raw, for sprinkling

1. Sift together the flour, baking soda, cinnamon, cloves, and allspice.

2. Beat the butter in a large bowl until soft. Beat in the honey. Add the egg and mix well. Add the flour mixture, mixing until blended. Chill for at least 3 hours.

3. Heat the oven to 350 degrees. Grease 2 baking sheets, or use nonstick sheets.

4. Roll the dough out on a lightly floured board to about 1/16 inch thick. Cut out cookies with a 2-inch round cutter and place 2 inches apart on the cookie sheets. Sprinkle the tops with salt or sugar (or sprinkle half with salt and half with sugar).

5. Bake until lightly browned on the bottoms, 6 to 8 minutes, turning the pans around halfway through. Transfer to racks to cool.

MAKES ABOUT 6 DOZEN COOKIES

COOKING NOTES

The flavor of these cookies improves with time. Try to wait at least 2 days, if you can.

The original recipe called for fortified margarine, which I don't even want to know exists. I changed it to butter.

OCTOBER 25, 1948: "NEWS OF FOOD: 350 KINDS OF CHEESE—3 TO 4 TONS OF IT—ALWAYS ARE ON HAND AT BROOKLYN STORE," BY JANE NICKERSON.

—1948

❧ PARTY BALLS

I can't say the name of this recipe out loud without cracking a smile. Clearly whoever named Rice Krispies Treats missed an opportunity.

I'd argue that party balls are a superior variation on popcorn balls because they're crackly rather than gooey, and because the molasses gives them a little austerity.

For a modern take on the party ball, see p. 708.

———

½ cup light corn syrup

½ cup molasses

1 teaspoon cider vinegar

2 tablespoons unsalted butter, plus

    softened butter for shaping

5½ cups rice cereal (like Rice Krispies)

1. Combine the corn syrup and molasses in a medium saucepan, attach a candy thermometer to the pan, and bring to a boil, stirring only enough to prevent burning, to a temperature of 240 degrees. Remove from the heat and stir in the vinegar and butter.

2. Place the cereal in a large buttered bowl, pour in the syrup, and stir well with a wooden spoon. Coat your palms with softened butter, form the mixture into balls (you'll need to press the mixture firmly), and place on a greased baking sheet to cool. (Or press into a shallow greased baking pans and cut into bars when cool.)

MAKES TWENTY 2-INCH BALLS

COOKING NOTES

If shaping the balls by hand, you'll need to wash and rebutter your hands occasionally.

I love this detail, which was added at the bottom of the original recipe: "While balls are still soft, a small birthday candle may be inserted into each, if desired."

VARIATION

Make the balls small enough to pop into your mouth, and sprinkle each with a little Maldon sea salt. Serve, with a knowing wink, at a dinner party.

PERIOD DETAIL

A cookbook the *Times* published in 1875 included a nearly identical recipe that called for popcorn rather than cereal.

JULY 9, 1949: "NEWS OF FOOD: MOLDS USED FOR HOME-FREEZING OF 'POPSICLES' NOW SERVE AS MASKS FOR YOUNGSTERS' DISHES," BY JANE NICKERSON.

—1949

⌒ SPRINGERLE COOKIES

Springerle are hard anise-flavored tea cookies, roughly the same shape and color as mahjong tiles. Craig Claiborne wrote that the name springerle "derives from the old German word for a band or grouping of animals, such as a *sprung* of reindeer."

The tops of classic springerle have beautiful shapes pressed into the dough with carved wood boards or rolling pins, much like old butter molds. "There are many shapes and sizes of springerle boards," Claiborne continued, "all of them with intaglio designs. Some of the designs are of human figures, others merely geometric studies. Human likenesses include various characters from fairy tales and nursery rhymes, witches on broomsticks, knights in full armor, and extravagantly caparisoned beldames."

Springerle are true outliers in the cookie world. The dough is chilled overnight, and after the cookies are pressed with the intricately carved boards, they are left out overnight before they are baked. When the cookies finally get in the oven, they aren't allowed to brown, but merely dry. And then the springerle schoolmarms recommend that you don't eat them for another week (or three) to allow the flavor to develop.

But what you end up with is worth it all: a beautiful cookie that sings with anise and calls out for teatime.

———

4 cups sifted all-purpose flour

1 teaspoon baking powder

½ teaspoon salt

4 large eggs

2 cups sugar

1 teaspoon grated lemon zest

3 tablespoons anise seeds

1. Sift together the flour, baking powder, and salt.

2. Place the eggs, sugar, and lemon zest in the bowl of a mixer fitted with a paddle (or mix in a large bowl with a hand mixer) and beat for 5 minutes at medium speed. Reduce the speed to low and beat in the flour mixture, one half at a time, just until a dough forms (you may not need to add it all). Refrigerate the dough, covered, overnight.

3. Line 2 baking sheets with parchment paper, and sprinkle the paper with the anise seeds. On a generously floured work surface, roll out the dough into a shape resembling that of your springerle board and ⅝ inch thick. If you don't have a springerle board (or rolling pin), just roll out the dough into a ⅝-inch-thick square. Press a springerle board on top (or roll a springerle rolling pin over the dough), bearing down

firmly to leave clear-cut designs. (Without the board or rolling pin, just leave your springerle patternless.)

4. With a floured knife, cut the cookies apart, following the lines of the designs (they're usually square or rectangular). Arrange the cookies on the prepared sheets, on top of the anise seeds. Let stand overnight, uncovered, at room temperature.

5. Heat the oven to 325 degrees. Bake the cookies until thoroughly dried but not at all colored, 13 to 15 minutes. Transfer to racks to cool.

MAKES ABOUT 3 DOZEN COOKIES

COOKING NOTE

Springerle molds are usually available on eBay—but you can also go patternless.

NOVEMBER 30, 1958: "THE SEASON FOR SPRINGERLE," BY CRAIG CLAIBORNE. RECIPE ADAPTED FROM CRISCO KITCHENS.

—1958

✑ FINNISH BRIDAL COOKIES

Thin, sweet, and buttery—use a tart jam for contrast.

––––––––––

8 tablespoons (1 stick) unsalted butter, softened
½ cup Vanilla Sugar (recipe follows)
¾ cup all-purpose flour
1 large egg white, stiffly beaten
About ⅓ cup thick jam or marmalade

1. Heat the oven to 375 degrees. In a mixer fitted with a paddle (or in a bowl with a hand mixer), beat the butter with the vanilla sugar until very light and fluffy. Add the flour and beat until smooth. Fold in the beaten egg white.

2. Drop the dough by rounded half teaspoonfuls onto ungreased cookie sheets, 1½ inches apart. Bake for 8 minutes, or until light brown around the edges (rotate the cookie sheets from front to back after 4 minutes). Remove the cookies and cool on a rack.

3. Spread the flat bottoms of half the cookies with the jam or marmalade. Cover with the remaining cookies to make little jam sandwiches.

MAKES ABOUT 2 DOZEN SANDWICH COOKIES

VANILLA SUGAR

Slit one-quarter of a vanilla bean open. Place in a covered jar with ½ cup sugar. Let stand for 3 to 4 days before using. (You can then remove the bean and reuse it to make more vanilla sugar—it's the gift that keeps on giving.)

MAY 23, 1962: "FOOD NEWS: COOKED BIRD IS IN THE BAG." RECIPE ADAPTED FROM *EUROPEAN DESSERTS FOR AMERICAN KITCHENS*, BY ELAINE ROSS.

—1962

✑ RUM BALLS

What to have after cocktails and a meal of sherry-soaked 1960s dishes? Rum balls!

––––––––––

½ pound walnuts (about 2 cups), finely ground
½ pound bittersweet chocolate, finely grated
½ cup sugar
3 large egg whites, lightly beaten
About 5 tablespoons rum
4 to 6 ounces (about 1 cup) chocolate shot

1. Mix together the nuts, chocolate, sugar, and half the egg whites in a bowl. Add enough rum to moisten the mixture so that it comes together when pinched. Refrigerate the mixture until chilled. Refrigerate the remaining egg whites.

2. Line a baking sheet with parchment paper. Shape the mixture into 1-inch balls. Roll the balls in the remaining egg white and then in the chocolate shot. Set on the lined baking sheet and allow to dry. Store in a covered tin in the refrigerator. (The rum balls will keep for a week or two; let come to room temperature before serving.)

MAKES ABOUT 2½ DOZEN BALLS

COOKING NOTES

If you're concerned about the use of uncooked egg whites, skip this recipe.

I'm not a fan of chocolate shot—aka chocolate sprinkles or jimmies—so I used unsweetened grated coconut. You could also substitute cacao nibs, lightly crushed.

DECEMBER 22, 1968: "SUGARPLUM TIME," BY JEAN HEWITT.

—1968

SAND TARTS (PECAN SANDIES)

A good sand tart, like this beauty from the Madison Avenue pastry shop William Greenberg Jr. Desserts, explodes in your mouth as if tripwired.

———

6 ounces (about 1½ cups) pecans
1 pound lightly salted butter, softened
1 cup sugar, plus extra for sprinkling
1 large egg
1½ teaspoons vanilla extract
4½ cups all-purpose flour

1. Using a Mouli grater, the fine plate of a meat grinder, or a food processor, grate the pecans; you should have about 2½ cups fluffy ground pecans. Do not use a blender.
2. In a mixer fitted with a paddle (or in a bowl with a hand mixer), beat the butter and sugar together until very light and fluffy. Beat in the egg and vanilla. Fold in the nuts. Stir in the flour. Divide the dough in two, wrap well, and chill.
3. Heat the oven to 325 degrees. Line 2 baking sheets with parchment paper.
4. Roll one half of the dough between sheets of wax paper to ¼ inch thick. Peel off the wax paper, then, using a 1½-inch round cutter, cut out cookies and arrange them 1 inch apart on the baking sheets. Gather up the scraps of dough into a ball, chill, and roll again. Repeat until all the dough has been used. Sprinkle the cookies with sugar.
5. Bake for 15 to 20 minutes, or until the bottoms are lightly browned; the tops will remain pale. Cool on a rack.
6. Dip the cooled cookies in sugar, and store in a sealed container.

MAKES ABOUT 8 DOZEN COOKIES

COOKING NOTES

Pecan sandies always taste better after a day or two, so make them and hide them.

Be gentle with the dough, and you'll be rewarded.

MARCH 29, 1971: "CAKES DECORATED WITH ARTISTIC FLAIR," BY JEAN HEWITT. RECIPE ADAPTED FROM WILLIAM GREENBERG JR. DESSERTS IN NEW YORK CITY.

—1971

SPICE KRINKLES

Krinkles are cookies that are cracked or wrinkled on the surface—which means every little crevice adds texture to the cookie. These krinkles have the bonus of being both wrinkled and chewy.

———

12 tablespoons (1½ sticks) unsalted butter, softened
1 cup packed light brown sugar
1 large egg, lightly beaten
¼ cup molasses
2¼ cups all-purpose flour
2 teaspoons baking soda
2 teaspoons ground cinnamon
2 teaspoons ground ginger
¾ teaspoon ground cloves
¼ teaspoon salt
2 tablespoons granulated sugar

1. In a mixer with a paddle attachment (or in a bowl with a hand mixer), beat the butter and brown sugar until light and fluffy. Beat in the egg and molasses. Sift together the remaining ingredients except the granulated sugar and stir into the dough. Wrap the dough in wax paper and chill for at least 2 hours, or as long as overnight.
2. Heat the oven to 375 degrees. Pull or cut off pieces of dough and form into balls the size of walnuts. Dip the tops in the sugar and set 3 inches apart on ungreased baking sheets.
3. Bake until set but not hard, 8 to 10 minutes. For a festive look, the cookies can be decorated while hot from the oven by pressing each one with a wooden butter print mold (see Cooking Note). Cool on a rack.

MAKES 36 TO 40 COOKIES

In the last step, you're instructed to press the tops of the warm cookies with a "wooden butter print mold." As I doubt you have a collection of these, you can use the bottom of an etched tumbler or patterned dish— or even just the tines of a fork.

DECEMBER 9, 1973: "HOLIDAY FARE: FOR A TRADITIONAL OPEN HOUSE," BY JEAN HEWITT. RECIPE ADAPTED FROM *FANNY PIERSON CRANE RECEIPTS*.

—1973

PINE NUT COOKIES

———

8 tablespoons (1 stick) unsalted butter, softened
1 cup sifted all-purpose flour
½ cup sugar
1 large egg yolk
1 teaspoon vanilla extract
½ cup toasted pine nuts

1. Heat the oven to 300 degrees. Butter and flour 2 baking sheets. In a mixer fitted with a paddle (or in a bowl with a hand mixer), beat the butter and sugar until light and fluffy. Beat in the egg yolk, vanilla, and flour. Mix in the nuts.
2. Drop the batter a teaspoon or so at a time onto the prepared baking sheets. Bake until pale golden, 20 to 25 minutes. While still hot, remove with a spatula to a rack and let cool.

MAKES ABOUT 2½ DOZEN COOKIES

READERS

"Did you know that the *Times* also published recipes on a roll of paper towels . . . at least twenty-five years ago? I received a roll as a gift from a visiting Boston friend. I make an exciting 'variation' of a cookie recipe that appeared on that roll of paper towels imprinted with '*NY TIMES* Recipes.'"

For Booth's variation, she uses Wondra flour in place of the all-purpose flour and bakes the cookies on parchment-paper-lined baking sheets. She presses the delicate dough into a teaspoon, unmolds it onto the baking sheets, and makes a crosshatch pattern on top of each one with a fork dipped into water.

Lila Booth, Blue Bell, PA, e-mail

DECEMBER 7, 1977: "FOOD GIFTS YOU CAN MAKE AT HOME," BY CRAIG CLAIBORNE. RECIPE ADAPTED FROM RITA ALEXANDER, A FRIEND AND NEIGHBOR OF CLAIBORNE.

—1977

FLORENTINES WITH GINGER

Wafer-thin almond and ginger cookies, whose bottoms are spread with a thin layer of chocolate.

———

¾ cup heavy cream
4 tablespoons unsalted butter
¾ cup sugar
1¾ cups grated or finely chopped almonds
⅓ cup all-purpose flour
6 tablespoons finely chopped candied ginger
¼ pound semisweet chocolate, chopped

1. Heat the oven to 350 degrees. Line 2 baking sheets with Silpats or other silicone baking mats or with parchment. If using parchment, brush with oil.
2. Combine the cream, butter, and sugar in a heavy saucepan. Bring to a boil, stirring until the sugar is dissolved and all the ingredients are well blended. Fold in the almonds, flour, and candied ginger and simmer for a minute to cook the flour. Remove from the heat.
3. Drop the batter about a tablespoon at a time onto the baking sheets, spacing the mounds 3 inches apart. Bake until golden on the edges and cooked in the center, 10 to 12 minutes. Remove from the oven and let cool briefly. (If the cookies become too cool, they will stick to the pans.)
4. Brush your thinnest spatula with oil, and use it to remove the cookies racks to cool.
5. When the cookies are thoroughly cool, melt the chocolate in a double boiler or in the microwave. Use a spatula to spread a little chocolate over the bottom of each cookie, and let stand upside down until the chocolate is set.

MAKES 2½ DOZEN COOKIES

COOKING NOTE

The almonds and ginger must be finely chopped to keep the cookies delicate—do this in a blender.

SEPTEMBER 23, 1979: "FOOD: A DESSERT THAT'S PUREED AND SIMPLE," BY CRAIG CLAIBORNE WITH PIERRE FRANEY.

—1979

∽ LEMON BARS

Usually very little creativity is expended on the lemon bar. Not so here. These have a whiff of coconut, and a core like pecan pie, all concealed by a sheath of lemon icing.

———

1½ cups all-purpose flour

3 tablespoons granulated sugar

¼ teaspoon salt

8 tablespoons (1 stick) unsalted butter

3 large eggs

1½ cups lightly packed dark brown sugar

¾ cup chopped pecans

¾ cup shredded, unsweetened coconut

1½ teaspoons vanilla extract

2¾ cups confectioners' sugar

Grated zest of 2 lemons

¼ cup fresh lemon juice

1. Heat the oven to 350 degrees. Mix together the flour, sugar, and salt in a bowl. Mix in the butter until the mixture resembles coarse meal.

2. Press into a 12-by-18-inch baking pan. Bake until golden, 15 to 20 minutes.

3. Mix the eggs with the brown sugar, pecans, coconut, and vanilla. Pour over the partially baked pastry and bake for 20 to 30 minutes longer, or until the topping is firm. Remove from the oven.

4. Mix together the confectioners' sugar, lemon zest, and juice until smooth. Spread over the bars. Let cool.

5. Cut into 1-by-1½-inch bars. (The bars can be frozen.)

MAKES 80 BARS

COOKING NOTE

The bars are better the next day, after the layers have settled and firmed.

NOVEMBER 2, 1983: "DESSERT PARTY: A FEAST OF SUMPTUOUS TREATS," BY MARIAN BURROS. RECIPE ADAPTED FROM WORD OF MOUTH, A CATERING COMPANY AND TAKE-OUT SHOP IN NEW YORK CITY.

—1983

∽ BROWN SUGAR SHORTBREAD

What is shortbread but butter and sugar met by a little flour? The brown sugar contributes caramel flavor, the salt contrast, and the almonds unnecessary but entirely welcome richness. This is a cookie for cookie purists, and it comes from the master of culinary purity, Alice Waters.

———

½ pound (2 sticks) unsalted butter, softened

⅔ cup packed light brown sugar

2 cups all-purpose flour

⅛ teaspoon salt

½ cup toasted unblanched almonds, coarsely chopped

1. In a mixer fitted with a paddle (or in a bowl with a hand mixer), beat the butter and sugar until light and fluffy. Add the flour and salt and blend by hand until the dough is kneadable. Knead the nuts into the dough. Gather the dough into 2 balls, wrap in wax paper, and chill thoroughly.

2. Heat the oven to 300 degrees. On a lightly floured board, roll both halves of the dough into neat 8-inch circles, about ⅓ inch thick or slightly less. Place the circles on a buttered baking sheet and deeply score each one into 8 wedges. Prick the wedges decoratively with a fork.

3. Bake until lightly browned and cooked through, about 30 minutes. Remove from the oven and let the shortbread cool on the sheets.

4. Cut into wedges and serve alone or with fresh cherries.

MAKES 16 SHORTBREAD WEDGES

JUNE 29, 1986: "STAR-SPANGLED PICNIC," BY CRAIG CLAIBORNE. RECIPE ADAPTED FROM ALICE WATERS.

—1986

MAIDA HEATTER'S RUGELACH (WALNUT HORNS)

Maida Heatter, the grand dame of home baking, is responsible for a number of terrific recipes in this book, including the Cuban Black Beans and Rice on p. 281 and the Preheated-Oven Popovers on p. 657. Like many of her fans, I adore her recipes not because they're particularly surprising or inventive, but because they work so seamlessly. Heatter has thought of every detail so you don't have to. Take Step 1 in this recipe: she knows the dough has a tendency to creep up on the beaters, so she tells you to scrape it off and finish adding the flour by hand. Tough dough averted.

The first batch, before you find your bearings with the dough, may be hard on the eyes. Mine resembled an explosion of cinnamon sugar and pastry dough. But the rugelach improved with each batch, and they certainly tasted perfect, so light and unbelievably buttery, with crisp little walnuts and chewy currants.

———

For the Pastry
½ pound (2 sticks) unsalted butter, softened
½ pound cream cheese, at room temperature
½ teaspoon salt (optional)
2 cups sifted all-purpose flour

For the Filling
½ cup plus 2 tablespoons sugar
1 tablespoon ground cinnamon
3 tablespoons unsalted butter, melted
¾ cup dried currants or raisins
1¼ cups walnuts, finely chopped

For the Glaze
1 egg yolk, beaten with 1 teaspoon water

1. Prepare the pastry the night before you are ready to bake: Put the butter, cream cheese, and salt into the large bowl of a mixer. Beat on medium, then high speed, until the mixture is creamy and smooth. Then beat on low speed while gradually adding the flour. If the dough starts to overly coat the beaters, scrape it off the beaters and continue adding the flour, stirring it in with your hands until thoroughly and evenly blended. The dough will be extremely sticky.

2. Scrape the dough off your hands and fingers. Rinse, wash, and dry your hands. Turn the dough out onto a well-floured board. Flour your hands and gather the dough into a short sausage shape. Cut this into 3 pieces of equal size. Flatten each piece slightly, forming it into a disk, and wrap in plastic wrap. Refrigerate overnight.

3. When ready to bake, heat the oven to 350 degrees. Line 2 baking sheets with aluminum foil. Combine the sugar and cinnamon for the filling and set aside.

4. Place 1 disk of dough on a floured pastry cloth. Hammer the dough firmly with a rolling pin to soften it slightly; do not let it become warm. Quickly roll out the dough, turning it occasionally, with the floured rolling pin into a circle about 12 inches in diameter. Don't worry about a slightly uneven edge. Using a pastry brush, brush the dough with a tablespoon of the melted butter. Sprinkle the dough all over with one-third of the cinnamon-sugar mixture. Sprinkle with one-third of the currants and one-third of the walnuts. Roll the rolling pin lightly over the top to press the filling slightly into the dough.

5. Using a long sharp knife, cut the circle into 12 pie-shaped wedges. Roll up each wedge jelly-roll fashion, rolling from the outside toward the point. Do not be dismayed if some of the filling falls out. Place the rolls point side down about 1 inch apart on one foil-covered cookie sheet. Repeat with a second ball of dough and then a third, filling and rolling each as indicated.

6. Brush the top of each walnut horn lightly and evenly with the glaze. Bake for 30 minutes. Preferably at mid-point during the baking, reverse the sheets top to bottom and front to back, to ensure even browning. When the horns are cooked, remove them with a metal spatula and transfer them to racks to cool.

MAKES 3 DOZEN COOKIES

COOKING NOTES
The dough is so soft it feels like wet cold cream. When rolling it out, be generous with the flour and work quickly. If you have a rimless baking sheet, roll out the dough on it and place the sheet in the fridge to chill the dough again before forming the rugelach.

You can skip the glaze. It doesn't add much curb appeal, and that will save you a step.

MAY 22, 1988: "FOOD: EASY DOES IT," BY CRAIG CLAIBORNE WITH PIERRE FRANEY. RECIPE ADAPTED FROM MAIDA HEATTER.

—1988

╼ CANESTRELLI (SHORTBREAD FROM OVADA)

A flat round cookie that's a little nutty, a little salty, and not too sweet. Use these as the bookends of an ice cream sandwich filled with chocolate or honey ice cream.

———

1 ½ cups unbleached all-purpose flour
½ cup semolina flour
½ pound (2 sticks) lightly salted butter, softened
½ cup sugar

1. Heat the oven to 325 degrees. Sift together the flour and semolina and set aside.
2. Place the butter in the bowl of a mixer fitted with a paddle (or mix in a bowl with a hand mixer) and beat on high speed for 1 minute, then add the sugar and continue beating until light and fluffy. Lower the speed of the mixer and add the flour mixture a cup at a time, scraping down the walls of the bowl and beating until the ingredients are just blended. Be careful not to overmix, because the semolina, which is high in gluten, can toughen the canestrelli. The dough will be somewhat crumbly.
3. Press the dough together into a ball, place on a lightly floured surface or wax paper, and roll it out ¼ inch thick. Cut the dough into small round shapes. (I use a juice glass with a 2-inch-diameter rim.)
4. Using a metal spatula, transfer the canestrelli to ungreased baking sheets, placing them an inch apart. Prick them all over with the tines of a fork, making a design of your choice. If you cannot get all of the dough into the oven at once, wrap the extra dough in wax paper and refrigerate in the meantime.
5. Bake for 15 to 20 minutes, or until the cookies begin to blush with color. Remove from the baking sheets with a metal spatula and cool on racks. (The cookies can be stored for up to 2 weeks in an airtight tin.)

MAKES ABOUT 3 DOZEN COOKIES

AUGUST 27, 1989: "FOOD: DISTINCTIVE ITALIAN FARE: LIGURIA," BY JOHN MARTIN TAYLOR. RECIPE ADAPTED FROM *COUNTRY HOST COOKBOOK*, BY RONA DEME.

—1989

╼ RUTH'S OATMEAL CRISPS

This is a great example of the power of shortening and salt in cookies. Butter would be too heavy and the cookies wouldn't be quite as crisp and chewy, and without the salt, they would be too sweet. This recipe won the cookie contest at the 1966 Kentucky State Fair; Ruth is a friend of the winner, Martha Adkins.

———

1 ½ cups sifted all-purpose flour
1 teaspoon baking soda
1 teaspoon salt
1 cup vegetable shortening
1 cup granulated sugar
1 cup packed light brown sugar
2 large eggs
1 teaspoon vanilla extract
3 cups oats (not quick-cooking)
1 cup chopped pecans
1 cup golden raisins

1. Heat the oven to 350 degrees. Line 2 baking sheets with parchment paper. Sift together the flour, baking soda, and salt.
2. Beat the shortening and sugars in a large bowl just enough to blend well. Add the eggs and vanilla and beat until thoroughly mixed. Add the oats and mix again. Add to the flour mixture, mixing well. Stir in the nuts and raisins.
3. Drop the dough by tablespoonfuls onto the parchment-lined baking sheets, 1 ½ inches apart. Bake until golden brown, 12 to 15 minutes. Transfer to racks to cool.

MAKES ABOUT 5 DOZEN COOKIES

AUGUST 30, 1989: "STATE FAIRS FANCIER, BUT THE LURE IS STILL THAT BLUE RIBBON," BY MOLLY O'NEILL. RECIPE ADAPTED FROM MARTHA ADKINS OF LOUISVILLE, KENTUCKY, WINNER OF THE 1966 ARCHWAY COOKIE CONTEST AT THE KENTUCKY STATE FAIR.

—1989

⌒ ENGLISH GINGERSNAPS

A crisp, direct hit of ginger, just as you'd want. Gingersnaps get better with time and can be kept for at least a month.

———————

2 cups sifted all-purpose flour
I teaspoon baking soda
¹/₂ teaspoon salt
I¹/₂ teaspoons ground ginger
I teaspoon ground cloves
¹/₂ teaspoon ground cinnamon
8 tablespoons (I stick) unsalted butter, softened
I cup sugar
I large egg
I teaspoon white vinegar
¹/₄ cup unsulphured molasses

1. Sift together the flour, baking soda, salt, ginger, cloves, and cinnamon.
2. In the bowl of a mixer fitted with a paddle (or in a bowl with a hand mixer), beat the butter for a minute, then add the sugar and continue beating until light and fluffy. Beat in the egg, vinegar, molasses, and flour mixture. Refrigerate the dough, covered, until chilled.
3. Heat the oven to 325 degrees. Shape the dough into balls 1 inch in diameter and place 1 inch apart on ungreased baking sheets. Slightly flatten the balls with the wet tines of a fork, then press again to make a crosshatch pattern. The cookies should be about ¹/₂ inch high.
4. Bake for 14 to 18 minutes—14 for a soft center, 18 for a crisp cookie. Let the cookies cool on the baking sheets for 5 minutes, then remove them with a spatula and cool on racks.

MAKES ABOUT 5 DOZEN COOKIES

DECEMBER 6, 1992: "COOKIES FOR EATING AND GIVING AS CHRISTMAS GIFTS," BY MOIRA HODGSON.

—1992

⌒ ENGLISH TEA CART WAFERS

This is the kind of recipe—a delicate sandwich cookie spread with jam and dipped in chocolate—that takes a few times to perfect. The first time, you'll be so thrilled that you survived all the spreading, dipping, and layering that you'll proclaim them the best cookies you've ever eaten. And they are great. But the truth is that the first time you make them, you'll probably get a proportion wrong: the chocolate overdipped, the cookies too large—something. And each time thereafter you'll refine your technique, until your cookies are so dainty and wonderful, you'll think about selling them. My crash-course advice is to keep the cookies as narrow as a finger and the layers of jam and chocolate as thin as possible.

———————

For the Cookies
¹/₂ pound (2 sticks) cool lightly salted butter,
    cut into chunks
²/₃ cup sugar
2 large egg yolks
I teaspoon vanilla extract
2¹/₄ cups sifted all-purpose flour
¹/₄ teaspoon baking powder

For the Chocolate Glaze
2 ounces semisweet chocolate
2 teaspoons unsalted butter
¹/₄ cup sugar
2 tablespoons water

¹/₄ cup raspberry preserves

1. Heat the oven to 375 degrees. Line a baking sheet with parchment paper. To make the cookies, beat together the butter and sugar in a large bowl. Add the egg yolks and vanilla and beat until smooth. Combine the flour and baking powder, and stir into the butter mixture.
2. Place the dough in a cookie press fitted with a 1-inch bar cookie disk with 3 stripes. Press out the dough 3 inches long and 2 inches apart. (If you don't have a cookie press, use a pastry bag fitted with a ¹/₂-inch plain round tip and pipe 3-inch-long stripes on the parchment, 2 inches apart.)

3. Bake until set but not brown, 5 to 8 minutes, turning the pan back to front halfway through baking. Transfer the cookies to a rack to cool.

4. Combine the glaze ingredients in a double boiler over low heat and stir frequently until the chocolate is melted and the sugar has dissolved. Dip each end of half of the wafers in the glaze. Return to the rack to dry.

5. Gently spread the raspberry preserves on the flat side of the undipped wafers. Top each wafer with a chocolate-dipped wafer to make a sandwich. Handle very carefully. (The cookies can be stored in an airtight tin in a cool place for up to 3 weeks; do not freeze.)

MAKES ABOUT 2 DOZEN COOKIES

DECEMBER 13, 1992: "FOOD: SWEET DREAMS," BY MOLLY O'NEILL.

—1992

⌐ SWEDISH NUT BALLS

Molly O'Neill's mother made these cookies for the holidays, as did my own mother. They keep well for weeks—as long as you hide them.

———

½ pound (2 sticks) cold lightly salted butter, cut into chunks
1¾ cups confectioners' sugar
2 cups all-purpose flour
Large pinch of salt
1 teaspoon vanilla extract
1 cup finely ground pecans

1. Heat the oven to 325 degrees. Line 2 baking sheets with parchment. Beat together the butter and ¾ cup of the confectioners' sugar in a bowl. Add the flour, salt, vanilla, and ground pecans. Stir to combine.

2. Shape the dough into balls, using a slightly rounded teaspoon for each, and place 2 inches apart on the parchment-lined baking sheets. Bake until the edges turn gold, about 20 minutes. Transfer the cookies to a rack to cool. (The cookies can be frozen in an airtight container, with wax paper between each layer, for up to 6 months. Defrost for 30 minutes.)

3. Just before serving, place the remaining cup of confectioners' sugar in a plastic bag. Add several cookies and shake gently to dust with sugar. Repeat with the remaining cookies.

MAKES 4 TO 5 DOZEN COOKIES

DECEMBER 13, 1992: "FOOD: SWEET DREAMS," BY MOLLY O'NEILL.

—1992

⌐ CRANBERRY PISTACHIO BISCOTTI

If the 1970s were the decade of oatmeal cookies and the 1980s the decade of bar cookies, the 1990s were definitely the decade of biscotti. This recipe is clearly a derivative—a delicious, acceptable derivative—of the austere almond originals found in Tuscany.

———

1¾ cups unbleached all-purpose flour
¼ teaspoon fine sea salt
1 teaspoon baking powder
¼ cup mild extra virgin olive oil
¾ cup sugar
2 teaspoons vanilla extract
Scant ½ teaspoon almond extract
2 large eggs
½ cup dried cranberries
1½ cups shelled unsalted pistachios

1. Position a rack in the center of the oven and heat the oven to 350 degrees. Spray a baking sheet with nonstick baking spray (to anchor the parchment), and line with parchment paper. Whisk together the flour, salt, and baking powder in a small bowl.

2. Beat the olive oil and sugar together in the bowl of a mixer (or in a bowl with a hand mixer). Add the vanilla and almond extracts and eggs, beating until completely blended. Beating on low speed, gradually add the flour mixture. Slowly beat in the cranberries and pistachios.

3. Divide the dough in half. Form each half into a log about 12 inches long and 2 inches wide on the baking sheet, spacing the logs about 4 inches apart. (The

dough will be very sticky; to make it easier to form the logs, rinse your hands in cool water.) Bake for about 35 minutes, or until the logs are light brown. Remove from the oven and reduce the heat to 275 degrees. Let the logs cool on the baking sheet for 10 minutes.

4. With a long metal spatula, remove the logs to a cutting board. Use a long sharp knife to cut the logs on the diagonal into ¾-inch-thick slices. Stand the slices upright on the baking sheet and return to the oven for 8 to 9 minutes, until they are light brown. Transfer to a rack to cool. (Layered between sheets of wax paper in a tin, the biscotti can be stored at room temperature for up to 2 weeks.)

MAKES 3 DOZEN BISCOTTI

NOVEMBER 1, 1995: "GIFTS TO MAKE AT HOME," BY SUZANNE HAMLIN.

—1995

❧ PEPPER-CUMIN COOKIES

"Just as good needs evil to seem really, really good, and darkness exists only when contrasted with light," Molly O'Neill, the *Times* columnist, wrote, "discrete taste sensations require their opposites in order to be more fully realized." Here, the sugar brings out the best in the salt and pepper, as the lemon zest does with the cumin.

———

2 cups all-purpose flour
6 tablespoons sugar
1 teaspoon kosher salt
2 teaspoons grated lemon zest
1 teaspoon black peppercorns, cracked
1 teaspoon cumin seeds, cracked
½ pound (2 sticks) unsalted butter, cut into pieces and softened slightly
1 teaspoon vanilla extract

1. Heat the oven to 350 degrees. Line 2 baking sheets with parchment paper. Put the flour, sugar, salt, lemon zest, cracked peppercorns, and cumin in a food processor and pulse to combine. Add the butter and vanilla and pulse until the mixture just forms a dough.

2. Transfer the dough to a work surface. Shape into 1-inch balls and place them 2 inches apart on the parchment-lined baking sheets. Flatten each cookie with the palm of your hand to ¼ inch thick.

3. Bake until lightly browned, about 15 minutes. Remove from the pans and place them on a rack to cool.

MAKES ABOUT 2½ DOZEN COOKIES

DECEMBER 1, 1996: "SUGAR AND SPICE," BY MOLLY O'NEILL.

—1996

❧ COCOA CHRISTMAS COOKIES

A recipe headnote is designed to entice and to inform, so I'm going to inform you of one drawback of these cookies: they're ugly. No, they're really ugly, a chocolate dab topped with straggly ribbons of lemon icing. The good news is they're delicious, and that lemon icing is a crucial counterpoint to the sweet spiced cookie.

———

4 cups all-purpose flour
1 cup unsweetened cocoa powder, preferably Valrhona, Callebaut, or Droste
1½ tablespoons baking powder
2 teaspoons ground cinnamon
½ teaspoon freshly grated nutmeg
½ teaspoon ground cloves
½ teaspoon salt
1½ cups plump, moist raisins, coarsely chopped
1 tablespoon orange juice
¾ pound (3 sticks) unsalted butter, softened
1¼ cups granulated sugar
2 large eggs, at room temperature
1 teaspoon vanilla extract
1 cup apricot jam
¼ cup whole milk, at room temperature
1½ cups lightly toasted walnuts, coarsely chopped
1½ cups confectioners' sugar
3 tablespoons fresh lemon juice

1. Whisk together the flour, cocoa, baking powder, cinnamon, nutmeg, cloves, and salt in a large bowl;

set aside. Combine the raisins and orange juice in a small bowl; reserve.

2. In a mixer fitted with a paddle attachment (or in a bowl with a hand mixer), beat the butter and granulated sugar together until creamy. Add the eggs one at a time, beating for 1 minute on medium speed after each addition. Beat in the vanilla, jam, and milk. Reduce the speed to low and gradually add the flour mixture, beating only until it is incorporated. Stir in the nuts and the reserved raisins and juice. Cover the dough tightly with plastic wrap and chill for at least 2 hours, or for as long as 2 days.

3. Heat the oven to 350 degrees. Line 2 baking sheets with parchment, or use nonstick sheets. Using a tablespoon of dough for each cookie, roll the dough between your palms to form walnut-sized balls, and place on the baking sheets, 1½ inches apart.

4. Bake for 10 to 12 minutes, until the tops look dry; the tops may crack, which is fine. Transfer the cookies to a rack.

5. While the cookies are baking, make the glaze: Combine the confectioners' sugar and lemon juice in a small bowl and whisk until smooth. After the cookies have cooled for a few minutes, dip their tops into the glaze, and place them on a rack to cool to room temperature. (The cookies can also be painted with the glaze using a fine pastry brush.)

MAKES ABOUT 7 DOZEN COOKIES

DECEMBER 16, 1998: "THE CHEF: OF SICILIAN CHRISTMAS EVES PAST AND FUTURE," BY ALFRED PORTALE AND FLORENCE FABRICANT.

—1998

CORNMEAL BISCOTTI

Generally I don't believe biscotti should contain butter or fat of any kind, because it makes the texture of the finished cookie too dense and too soft, but I'm willing to accept these biscotti as the sole exception. Classic biscotti are as hard as shale; these are crumbly and coarse from the cornmeal. A Spartan amount of sugar and rosemary gives them a pleasant muskiness. Most biscotti recipes instruct you to serve the cookies with vin santo, a sweet dessert wine, but because

the cookies themselves are usually so sweet, it ends up being a sickening combination. Not so here.

½ cup coarsely chopped blanched almonds
¼ cup coarsely chopped skinned hazelnuts
4 tablespoons unsalted butter
1 tablespoon minced rosemary
1½ tablespoons finely grated orange zest
1 cup all-purpose flour
½ cup coarse yellow cornmeal
½ cup sugar
1 teaspoon baking soda
1 teaspoon anise seeds
3 large eggs
1 tablespoon water

1. Heat the oven to 350 degrees. Spread the nuts out on a rimmed baking sheet and toast them in the oven, stirring occasionally, until lightly golden around the edges, about 6 to 8 minutes. Let cool on a rack. (Keep the oven on.)

2. Melt the butter in a small saucepan over medium-high heat. Turn off the heat and add the rosemary and orange zest. Let cool.

3. In the bowl of a mixer fitted with a paddle attachment, beating at low speed, mix together the flour, cornmeal, sugar, baking soda, and anise seeds (or mix by hand in a bowl with a wooden spoon). Add 2 eggs one at a time, mixing well after each addition. Add the cooled melted butter and mix to combine. Stir in the nuts. Let the dough rest for 5 minutes.

4. Line a baking sheet with parchment. Form the dough into a log 2 inches wide and place it on the baking sheet. Mix the remaining egg with the water in a small bowl. Brush this wash over the log, then bake the log until it is a deep golden brown, about 30 minutes. Let cool on a rack. Reduce the oven temperature to 200 degrees.

5. Using a serrated knife, slice the log on a diagonal into ¼-inch-wide pieces. Arrange the biscotti on 2 parchment-lined baking sheets and dry them in the oven until crisp, 40 minutes to 1 hour. Let cool on a rack.

MAKES ABOUT 2½ DOZEN COOKIES

I'd add a large pinch of sea salt to the flour mixture in Step 3.

A glass of vin santo.

The first biscotti recipe to appear in the *Times* was published in 1970. The recipe, a classic nut-and-anise-flavored cookie, came from Mrs. August Sebastiani, who also contributed the malfatti recipe on p. 313.

APRIL 21, 1999: "THE CHEF," BY CLAUDIA FLEMING WITH MELISSA CLARK.

—1999

CASHEW BUTTERSCOTCH BARS

I never thought I'd recommend a recipe containing butterscotch chips, but I'm open to change. Are you?

The recipe comes from Amy Scherber, the owner of Amy's Bread and one of New York City's finest bread bakers. If you've had semolina bread with fennel seeds and golden raisins, she is the one who created it.

½ pound (2 sticks) plus 5½ tablespoons
    unsalted butter, softened

¾ cup plus 2 tablespoons packed light brown sugar

1¾ teaspoons kosher salt

2½ cups all-purpose flour

One 10-ounce bag butterscotch chips,
    preferably Hershey's

½ cup plus 2 tablespoons light corn syrup

5½ teaspoons water

2½ cups salted cashew pieces

1. Center a rack in the oven and heat the oven to 350 degrees. Butter a 13-by-18-inch rimmed baking sheet, including the sides. In a mixer fitted with a paddle, beat ½ pound plus 2 tablespoons butter and the brown sugar together (or mix in a bowl with a rubber spatula) until smooth. Stir the salt into the flour, then add the flour to the butter and sugar mixture and mix until the dough is well combined but still crumbly (if the dough is mixed until a ball forms, the crust will be tough).

2. Pat the dough—don't pack it!—evenly into the bottom of the buttered pan. Bake for 5 minutes. With a fork, prick the dough deeply all over, return the pan to the oven, and bake until the dough is lightly browned, dry, and no longer soft to the touch, 10 to 15 minutes. Transfer to a cooling rack (leave the oven on).

3. Combine the remaining 3½ tablespoons butter, the butterscotch chips, corn syrup, and water and cook in a large saucepan over medium heat, stirring constantly, until the butter and butterscotch chips are melted, about 5 minutes. Pour the topping over the crust, using a spatula to spread it evenly all the way to the corners. Sprinkle the cashew pieces on top, pressing down lightly.

4. Bake until the topping is bubbly and the cashews are lightly browned, 12 to 16 minutes. Transfer to a rack and cool completely before cutting into 2-by-3-inch bars.

MAKES 3 DOZEN BARS

Bar cookies emerged sometime in the 1930s. Although brownies already existed, Laura Shapiro, a food historian, wrote in an e-mail: "Cookie bars in the form we know them appear in the first *Joy of Cooking* (1931), including 'Almond and Date Squares,' 'Brownies or Fudge Squares,' and—ta da! 'Date Bars,' two versions but both made the way we do now and rolled in confectioners' sugar." Also in 1931, Irma Rombauer made "Quick Caramel Squares"—a cake baked in a "shallow greased pan" and iced, then cut into squares.

SEPTEMBER 22, 1999: "THE CHEF: A COOKIE THAT TRANSCENDS THE AGES," BY AMY SCHERBER WITH DORIE GREENSPAN.

—1999

CLASSIC FINANCIERS (BUTTERY ALMOND CAKES)

The financier is a tiny almond cake that is leavened with egg whites, moistened with browned butter, and baked in small shallow molds. Such simplicity is deceiving: a great financier is springy, damp, and nutty, with an exterior that's as crisp as an eggshell. The shape may be round in some pastry shops, rectangular in others, but the base is rarely anything but almond. It has been that way for more than a century.

In *Memorial Historique de la Pâtisserie*, published in 1890, Pierre Lacam wrote that the financier was created by a baker named Lasne, whose bakery on the Rue St.-Denis was near the Bourse, the financial center of Paris. Presumably the rich little cake was named for the rich financiers who frequented his bakery. The cake was baked in rectangular molds the shape of gold bars.

Nick Malgieri, the director of the baking program at New York's Institute for Culinary Education, said a similar cake, made with nuts, egg whites, and brown butter, existed even before that. It was made, he said, by nuns of the Order of the Visitation and was called a *visitandine*. It's possible that the baker Lasne simply altered the shape and the name of the cake to flatter his clientele.

The recipe has withstood the test of time, despite a lack of notice from cookbook authors. There is no mention of the financier in *Le Cordon Bleu at Home* or *La Varenne Pratique*, two of the leading encyclopedic French cookbooks. Nor is it in Lindsey Shere's *Chez Panisse Desserts*, which is populated with French desserts that are largely underappreciated in America. And the financier earns just a vague definition in some editions of *Larousse Gastronomique*.

---

9 tablespoons unsalted butter

1¼ cups confectioners' sugar, plus (optional) for dusting

¾ cup almond flour or ½ cup unbleached whole almonds

¼ cup all-purpose flour

1 tablespoon plus 2 teaspoons cake flour

1 teaspoon baking powder

Pinch of salt

4 large egg whites, at room temperature

1 teaspoon vanilla extract

1. Generously butter twelve 2-by-4-inch (measured at the top) rectangular financier molds. Refrigerate. Heat the butter in a small pan over medium-low heat, occasionally swirling, until it begins to brown, about 5 minutes. Set aside.

2. Sift the sugar over the almond flour in a medium

bowl. Or, if using whole almonds, process them with the sugar in a food processor until mostly fine, then transfer to a bowl. Add both flours, baking powder, and the salt and gently whisk to combine. Add the egg whites one at a time, whisking just to combine. Do not overwork, or the cakes will be tough.

3. Add the vanilla to the butter. In a steady stream, whisk the butter into the flour mixture. Cover with plastic wrap and refrigerate for 3 hours.

4. Heat the oven to 375 degrees. Set the molds on a baking sheet. Spoon the batter into a pastry bag that has a ¼-inch round tip, and pipe into the molds, filling them halfway. Bake for 18 to 20 minutes, until browned and springy. Remove from oven and cool for 2 minutes before unmolding, then cool completely on a rack.

5. Serve plain or dusted with confectioners' sugar, or rewarm and serve with ice cream.

MAKES 12 SMALL CAKES

COOKING NOTES

A few steps make or break these little cakes. The first, browning the butter, is what defines the financiers' flavor and adds depth to the almonds. You need to heat the butter over medium-low heat until it begins to brown and smell nutty. It is best to do this slowly and to keep a careful eye on it. Once butter begins to brown, it burns easily. Remove it the moment it turns the color of a chestnut. Undercooking it is equally damaging, for then it would lack—*mon Dieu!*—the necessary aroma.

The second trick is to mix the batter as little as possible. It should be stirred until just blended. If you stir too much, the gluten in the flour will get overworked and the cakes will be tough.

The batter then has to rest before baking. A few hours in the refrigerator, and the flavors will harmonize and the batter will firm, making it easier to pipe into the molds.

The one decision you need to make regards texture. If you use almond flour, the cake will be finer but denser. If you grind the almonds, it will be coarser and rustic. I prefer grinding my own. Somehow the roughness of home-ground almonds and flecks of almond skin in the finished cakes give them a kind of soulful intensity that you find in Parisian pastries.

Financiers must be eaten on the day they're baked.

NOVEMBER 24, 1999: "THE PASTRY CHEF'S RICH LITTLE SECRET," BY AMANDA HESSER. RECIPE ADAPTED FROM FRANÇOIS PAYARD, THE CHEF AND OWNER OF PAYARD PÂTISSERIE IN NEW YORK CITY.

—1999

PETIT BEURRE COOKIES

I first encountered this cookie at Jean Georges, the 4-star restaurant in New York. The cookie was 2 inches in diameter, about as thick as a plate, and the color of sand. It was perched on a neat circle of raspberries.

Anticipating something crisp, I struck it with my fork, and it fractured without a problem. But I felt as if I had stabbed at air. It wasn't until I tried to scoop up a piece that things really got strange. Everywhere I touched the cookie, it fell apart. When I finally got the cookie into my mouth, the mere pressure of my teeth dragging it off my fork caused it to collapse into a million sweet, buttery crumbs. Poof! It was gone.

After that, I tried to keep each piece intact long enough to figure out what it was made of. Did it contain meringue? Was it made with low-gluten White Lily flour, rendering it lighter than air? It yielded no clues.

Eventually, I got hold of the recipe, which essentially asks you to bind butter together with cookie crumbs. First a standard almond cookie dough is mixed, shaped into a cookie the size of a Frisbee, and baked. That's the warm-up.

Then that large, tasty cookie is smashed to bits. Very fine bits, which are mixed with a lot more butter and whirled in a mixer until they are as light and fluffy as whipped butter. This mixture is spread onto a baking sheet and chilled. Hours later, cookies are cut from it and baked. After they emerge from the oven, filling your house with the aroma of sweet butter, you put the cooled cookies—still on the baking sheet—in the refrigerator until they're cold. (Chilling them makes lifting them possible.)

Whoever spent hours figuring out this method was an ingenious person, but he or she would have benefited from more fresh air. Vongerichten came across the original recipe in *Nouvelle Cuisine Bourgeoise pour la Ville et pour la Campagne*, a nineteenth-century cookbook by Urbain Dubois. It does work at home, but you might save it for when you are feeling patient

and steady of hand. The rewards are worth every careful step.

Forget everything you know about cookie baking. Get a scale (you need precision) and a paper-thin flexible spatula, and do not veer from the instruction. This is no time to toss in some chopped chocolate.

———

1/2 pound all-purpose flour
3 ounces almond flour (from 3 ounces slivered almonds—see Cooking Note)
2¾ ounces confectioners' sugar
10 ounces (2½ sticks) unsalted butter, softened

1. Heat the oven to 325 degrees. In the bowl of a mixer fitted with a paddle (or in a bowl with a hand mixer), mix the two flours, confectioners' sugar, and 6½ ounces butter on medium-low speed until a dough forms.
2. Transfer to a baking sheet and roll out 1/8 inch thick. The shape of the dough does not matter, but smooth the edges for even browning. Bake until barely golden brown at the edges, 25 to 35 minutes; be careful not to overbake. Remove from the oven and cool completely.
3. Using your fingers, crumble the dough into fine crumbs, and place in the mixer bowl (or another large bowl). Using the paddle (or hand mixer), mix in the remaining 3½ ounces butter, beating at medium speed. The mixture will gather into small pieces and, after a few minutes, will change to a dough, pulling away from the sides of the bowl. Continue to mix until the mixture becomes fluffy and creamy like whipped butter; this may take an additional 5 minutes.
4. Line a baking sheet with plastic wrap. Using a rubber spatula, transfer the dough to the sheet and spread into a thick oval. Cover with plastic wrap and use a rolling pin to roll the mixture to about 1/3 inch thick. Chill until firm, about 1 hour.
5. Heat the oven to 350 degrees. Line a baking sheet with parchment paper. Using a 3-inch round cookie cutter, cut circles from the chilled dough. Transfer to the baking sheet, spacing the cookies at least 2 inches apart. (Scraps of dough may be rerolled and chilled to make additional cookies.)
6. Bake until the edges are golden brown, 7 to 10 minutes. Remove from the oven and cool on the baking sheet, then transfer the baking sheet to the refrigerator; allow the cookies to become well chilled.

7. Fifteen minutes before serving, use a thin flexible spatula to remove the cookies from the sheet. The chilled cookies can be placed atop a circle of raspberries or other berries. If desired, garnish each plate with a scoop of ice cream.

MAKES 10 TO 12 COOKIES

COOKING NOTE

Almond flour can be purchased or prepared by pulverizing blanched almonds with some of the sugar in a food processor. Avoid overprocessing the almonds into a paste.

SERVING SUGGESTIONS

These cookies are best made for a party and served with something like Tea Ice Cream (p. 717) or Blueberry Ice Cream (p. 726). I might spread lightly sweetened crème fraîche on each plate and top it with berries and then a petit beurre. It's not a cookie you'd serve on its own, unless you're alone, in which case all foods are fair game.

JULY 19, 2000: "HOW THE COOKIE SHOULD CRUMBLE," BY AMANDA HESSER. RECIPE ADAPTED FROM JEAN GEORGES IN NEW YORK CITY.

—2000

ENGLISH TOFFEE

This is a Victorian candy, which Dorie Greenspan, who wrote about it, described as "a cross between peanut brittle and caramel."

———

½ pound (2 sticks) unsalted butter

1½ cups sugar

3 tablespoons light corn syrup

3 tablespoons water

2 cups (about 12 ounces) almonds or other nuts, toasted and chopped

¾ pound semisweet chocolate, melted

Sea salt (optional)

1. Lightly butter a 12-by-18-inch rimmed baking sheet and line with foil; butter the foil. Have ready 2 large cutting boards or pieces of cardboard covered with parchment or wax paper.

2. Melt the butter in a large heavy saucepan. Remove from the heat and stir in the sugar, corn syrup, and water. Attach a candy thermometer to the pan and cook over medium-high heat, stirring occasionally, until the mixture reaches 300 degrees. Remove from the heat, stir in 1 cup chopped nuts, and quickly pour into the foil-lined pan, spreading the mixture with the back of a spoon or offset spatula to fill the pan.

3. When the candy is just firm enough to handle, turn out onto one parchment-covered surface, peel off the foil, and allow to cool completely.

4. Wipe the top of the candy with a damp paper towel to remove excess butter, and allow to dry.

5. Use a small offset spatula to spread half the chocolate quickly over the candy. Scatter half of the remaining nuts over the chocolate. Cover with parchment or wax paper, place the second parchment-covered surface on top, and turn the candy over onto the second surface. Remove the top board and paper. Quickly spread the candy with the remaining chocolate, sprinkle with sea salt, if using, and scatter on the remaining nuts. Refrigerate for 20 minutes to set the chocolate.

6. Break the candy into 2-inch pieces and pack into a container with a tight-fitting top, using parchment or wax paper to separate the layers. (The candy will keep at cool room temperature for up to 1 week.)

MAKES ABOUT 3 POUNDS

COOKING NOTES

Greenspan urged readers to buy a candy thermometer before attempting this recipe: "For toffee, the recommended thermometer is the type that looks like a ruler—long and flat, with the mercury tube in the center and the readouts printed on either side. Most important, the ruler-type thermometer has little feet that raise the mercury bulb above the bottom of the pan, so you get an accurate reading of the contents."

I like a little flaky sea salt, such as Maldon or fleur de sel, sprinkled on the toffee right after it's spread with chocolate.

DECEMBER 13, 2000: "CRUNCH, CRUNCH: THE HOLIDAY APPROACHES," BY DORIE GREENSPAN. RECIPE ADAPTED FROM CHOCOLATE, BY NICK MALGIERI.

—2000

⌇ TWO-DAY MADELEINES WITH BROWN BUTTER

Madeleines are often a beginning baker's fantasy of what great baking is about. So if you've never made them before, go ahead. You'll be surprised by how easy they are, and it's hard not to feel triumphant as their famous "hump" rises in the oven. (You don't have to take 2 days to make these, but the resting time improves both the flavor and the rise.)

―――――――

7 tablespoons unsalted butter
5 large eggs
½ cup plus 3 tablespoons sugar
1¼ cups unbleached all-purpose flour
Large pinch of sea salt
1 teaspoon baking powder
Grated zest of 1 lemon

1. Melt the butter in a small pan over medium heat, and cook until it begins to smell nutty and turns brown. Strain through a fine sieve into a bowl.
2. Beat the eggs and sugar in the bowl of a mixer fitted with the whisk (or in a bowl with a hand mixer), until fluffy. Remove the bowl from the mixer and sift the flour, salt, and baking powder over the eggs. Fold together with a spatula. Pour in the butter and lemon zest and fold together.
3. Spoon the batter into a pastry bag fitted with a small (about ¼-inch) round tip. Refrigerate for at least 2 hours, or overnight.
4. Heat the oven to 375 degrees. Generously butter and flour a madeleine pan (small or large molds). Pipe batter into the molds so they are three-quarters full.
5. Bake until the madeleines form humps and are nut brown around the edges, 6 to 8 minutes (1 to 3 minutes longer if using large molds). Remove from the oven and bang the pan on a countertop to release the madeleines. Carefully lift out any that stick. Wrap in a napkin to keep warm. Repeat with the remaining batter.

MAKES ABOUT 5 DOZEN SMALL MADELEINES

VARIATION
After adding the butter in Step 2, you could fold in any number of flavors, like ½ cup finely chopped nuts, the grated zest of an orange, ½ cup grated coconut, or 1 teaspoon ground cardamom.

APRIL 18, 2001: "WHEN A SWEET NOTHING BECOMES REALLY SOMETHING," BY AMANDA HESSER. RECIPE ADAPTED FROM NICOLE KAPLAN, THE PASTRY CHEF AT ELEVEN MADISON PARK IN NEW YORK.

—2001

⌇ MAPLE SHORTBREAD BARS

As I was testing recipes for this book, I often discovered that readers would recommend more than one recipe from the same story. (Both this recipe and the Dijon and Cognac Beef Stew on p. 560, each of which was recommended by several readers, came from the same Regina Schrambling piece, "When the Path to Serenity Wends Past the Stove.") This made me suspect that the popularity of the recipes has a lot to do with the story itself—that if people really like a story, they're more inclined to try the recipes. Which led me to worry that I might have overlooked a number of excellent recipes simply because the accompanying stories weren't that interesting. You'll have to let me know.

―――――――

For the Crust
2 cups all-purpose flour
½ cup sugar
½ teaspoon salt
½ pound (2 sticks) unsalted butter, well chilled

For the Filling
1½ cups packed light brown sugar
⅔ cup real maple syrup
2 large eggs
4 tablespoons unsalted butter, melted
1 teaspoon vanilla extract
1 teaspoon maple extract
½ teaspoon salt
2 cups (about 8 ounces) chopped pecans

1. Heat the oven to 350 degrees. To make the crust, combine the flour, sugar, and salt in a bowl. Slice the butter, and cut it into the flour mixture with a pastry blender or 2 knives until the mixture is crumbly. Press onto the bottom and ½ inch up the sides of a 9-by-13-inch baking pan.

2. Bake for 15 to 25 minutes, or until the edges begin to brown. Cool on a rack. (Leave the oven on.)

3. For the filling, combine all the ingredients except the pecans in a bowl and mix until smooth. Pour into the cooled crust. Distribute the nuts evenly over the top. Bake until the filling is set, about 30 minutes. Cool on a rack before cutting into bars.

MAKES 2 DOZEN BARS

COOKING NOTES

The crust is crumbly and difficult to work with. You may want to chill the dough for a few minutes before pressing it into the baking pan.

Maple extract is an odd bird—dark as tar and fairly bitter—but don't be discouraged. It gives the sweet filling something to stand up to.

SEPTEMBER 19, 2001: "WHEN THE PATH TO SERENITY WENDS PAST THE STOVE," BY REGINA SCHRAMBLING. RECIPE ADAPTED FROM *THE NEW CARRYOUT CUISINE*, BY PHYLLIS MÉRAS WITH LINDA GLICK CONWAY.

—2001

⌒ CHOCOLATE QUAKES

These cookies, sometimes called krinkles, are dusted with confectioners' sugar before baking, so when they expand in the oven, their domed surfaces crack, making them look like ice-covered earth after a frost heave.

———

3 tablespoons unsalted butter, melted

$1/2$ cup granulated sugar

1 large egg

$1/2$ teaspoon vanilla extract

3 tablespoons unsweetened cocoa powder, preferably Dutch-process

$1/2$ cup all-purpose flour

$1/2$ teaspoon baking powder

$1/8$ teaspoon salt

$1/4$ cup finely ground pecans or almonds

$1/4$ cup semisweet chocolate chips

About $3/4$ cup confectioners' sugar

1. In a mixer fitted with a whisk (or in a bowl with a hand mixer), beat the butter, granulated sugar, egg,

and vanilla on low speed until pale yellow in color and thickened, about 1 minute. Sift the cocoa, flour, baking powder, and salt into the bowl and mix on low speed until incorporated. Fold in the nuts and chocolate chips. Cover and chill until the dough is firm enough to handle, about 1 hour.

2. Heat the oven to 350 degrees. Line 2 baking sheets with parchment paper or foil. Place the confectioners' sugar in a medium bowl.

3. Form the chilled dough into 1-inch balls, place in the confectioners' sugar, and roll to coat completely. Place on the baking sheets, leaving about 2 inches between the cookies. Bake for 12 minutes, or until the cookies are puffed and the surfaces have cracked; the centers will appear underdone. Remove from the oven and let sit for 5 minutes, then transfer to a rack to cool completely.

MAKES 20 TO 24 COOKIES

COOKING NOTE

Use the best cocoa powder you can find.

FEBRUARY 6, 2002: "THIS TIME, CHOCOLATE TAKES A POWDER," BY REGINA SCHRAMBLING. ADAPTED FROM *GOT MILK? THE COOKIE BOOK*, BY PEGGY CULLEN.

⌒ BUCKWHEAT COOKIES

These will cause you to pause and ponder what you seek in a cookie. If the answer is chocolate, move along to another recipe. If it's engaging flavor and not too much sugar, you have found the holy grail. These cookies, which are great with tea, taste like sweet wet stone—in a good way, I promise.

Buckwheat flour is available at www.arrowheadmills .com. (For a similarly reserved cookie, see the Honey Spice Cookies on p. 685.)

———

1 cup buckwheat flour

1 cup all-purpose flour

$2/3$ cup sugar

$1/2$ teaspoon salt

$1/2$ teaspoon baking powder

$1/2$ pound (2 sticks) unsalted butter, cut into cubes

2 large egg yolks, beaten

1. Heat the oven to 325 degrees. Put the dry ingredients in a food processor and pulse once or twice to mix. Add the butter and pulse about 15 times, until pea-sized pieces form. Add the egg yolks and pulse 8 times, or until the dough just comes together. (Alternatively, combine the dry ingredients in a bowl and stir with a whisk to mix. Beat the butter in a bowl until fluffy, and add the egg yolks. Beat in the dry ingredients in 2 batches, scraping down the sides of the bowl between additions.)

2. Form tablespoons of dough into balls and place 1½ inches apart on ungreased baking sheets. Use a fork to press the dough into ⅜-inch-thick rounds.

3. Bake for 15 to 20 minutes, until golden around the edges. Cool on a rack.

MAKES ABOUT 6 DOZEN COOKIES

SEPTEMBER 1, 2004: "TEMPTATION; THE COOKIES THAT SIMPLY WOULD NOT GO FOR A RIDE," BY MELISSA CLARK. RECIPE ADAPTED FROM ELENA ROVERA, A FOUNDER OF CASCINA DEL CORNALE, A MARKET AND RESTAURANT NEAR ALBA IN ITALY.

—2002

⌒ DORIE GREENSPAN'S SABLÉS

Dorie Greenspan, an expert baker and cookbook author, has written cookbooks with Julia Child, Daniel Boulud, and Pierre Hermé, and over the years has perfected her ability to glean tips from such masters. Greenspan's remarkably good sablés (so called for their sand-like texture—*sable* means "sand" in French), for instance, were formulated after years of studying other pastry chefs. She liked the homespun quality of Paris baker Lionel Poilâne's sablés and the delicacy of Alsatian pastry chef André Lerch's. From Poilâne, she learned to leave the dough elemental, and from Lerch, she discovered that using confectioners' sugar keeps the dough tender and allows the sugar to provide the necessary "sand" in the crumb.

½ pound (2 sticks) unsalted butter (preferably high-fat, like Plugrá), softened
½ cup granulated sugar
¼ cup sifted confectioners' sugar
½ teaspoon salt, preferably sea salt

2 large egg yolks, preferably at room temperature
2 cups all-purpose flour

For the Decoration (Optional)
1 egg yolk
Crystal or dazzle sugar

1. In a mixer fitted with a paddle attachment (or in a bowl with a hand mixer), beat the butter at medium speed until it is smooth and very creamy. Add the sugars and salt and beat until smooth and velvety, not fluffy and airy, about 1 minute. Reduce the mixer speed to low and beat in the egg yolks, beating until well blended.

2. Turn off the mixer and pour in the flour. Drape a kitchen towel over the mixer and pulse the mixer about 5 times at low speed for 1 to 2 seconds each time. Take a peek: if there is still a lot of flour on the surface of the dough, pulse a couple of more times; if not, remove the towel. Continuing at low speed, mix for about 30 seconds more, just until the flour disappears into the dough and the dough looks uniformly moist. If you still have some flour in the bottom of the bowl, stop mixing and use a rubber spatula to work it into the dough. (The dough will not come together in a ball—and it shouldn't. You want to work the dough as little as possible. What you're aiming for is a soft, moist, clumpy dough. When pinched, it should feel a little like Play-Doh.)

3. Scrape the dough onto a work surface, gather it into a ball, and divide it in half. Shape each piece into a smooth log about 9 inches long (it's easiest to work on a piece of plastic wrap and use the plastic to help form the log). Wrap the logs well and chill them for at least 2 hours. (The dough can be refrigerated for up to 3 days or frozen for up to 2 months.)

4. When ready to bake, center a rack in the oven and heat the oven to 350 degrees. Line a baking sheet with a silicone baking mat or parchment paper. If desired, to decorate the edges of the sablés, whisk the egg yolk until smooth. Place 1 log of chilled dough on a piece of wax paper and brush it with yolk (the glue), then sprinkle the entire surface of the log with coarse sugar. Trim the ends of the roll if they are ragged and slice the log into ⅓-inch-thick cookies.

5. Place the rounds on the baking sheet, leaving an inch of space between the cookies, and bake for 17 to 20 minutes, rotating the baking sheet at the halfway point. When properly baked, the cookies will be

light brown on the bottom, lightly golden around the edges, and pale on top. Let the cookies rest for 1 or 2 minutes before carefully lifting them onto a rack with a wide metal spatula. Repeat with the remaining log of dough. (Make sure the sheet is cool before baking the second batch.)

MAKES ABOUT 50 COOKIES

VARIATIONS

Lemon Sablés: Before mixing the butter and sugar together, pour the sugar into a bowl and add the grated zest of 1 to 1½ lemons. Work the zest and sugar together with your fingertips until the mixture is moist and aromatic, then cream the butter with it.

Parmesan Sablés: Replace the sugars with ¾ cup very finely grated Parmesan added to the beaten butter. A few grains of fleur de sel can be gently pressed into the top of each sablé before the baking sheet is slipped into the oven.

NOVEMBER 7, 2004: "COOKIE MASTER," BY JULIA MOSKIN. RECIPE ADAPTED FROM DORIE GREENSPAN.

—2004

⌣ PIERRE HERMÉ'S CHOCOLATE SABLÉS

Pierre Hermé, the world's most famous pastry chef, is best known for his macaroons, but these sablés aren't too shabby either. Luckily for us, Dorie Greenspan, a food writer who's an exceptional baker herself, teamed up with Hermé for two books, *Desserts* and *Chocolate Desserts*, recording many of his sweet gems. Greenspan, according to the accompanying article by Julia Moskin, said these sablés are "the most important innovation in cookies since Toll House."

"They are definitely sablés," Moskin wrote, "but also very American in their explosive crunch and addictive combination of salt, chocolate, and the caramel warmth of brown sugar."

——————

1¼ cups all-purpose flour
⅓ cup Dutch-process cocoa powder
½ teaspoon baking soda

11 tablespoons unsalted butter, softened
⅔ cup packed light brown sugar
¼ cup granulated sugar
½ teaspoon fleur de sel or ¼ teaspoon fine sea salt
1 teaspoon vanilla extract
5 ounces bittersweet chocolate, chopped into chip-sized bits

1. Sift the flour, cocoa, and baking soda together.
2. Put the butter in the bowl of a mixer fitted with a paddle attachment (or mix in a bowl with a hand mixer) and beat at medium speed until soft and creamy. Add the sugars, salt, and vanilla and beat for another 1 or 2 minutes. Reduce the speed to low and add the dry ingredients, mixing only until the dry ingredients are incorporated (the dough may look crumbly). For the best texture, work the dough as little as possible. Toss in the chocolate; mix to incorporate.
3. Turn the dough out onto a work surface and divide in half. Working with one half at a time, shape the dough into a log that is 1½ inches in diameter. (As you're shaping the log, flatten it once or twice and roll it up from one long side to the other, to make certain you haven't got an air channel.) Wrap the logs in plastic wrap and chill them for at least 1 hour. (Wrapped airtight, the logs can be refrigerated for up to 3 days or frozen for 1 month.)
4. Center a rack in the oven and heat the oven to 350 degrees. Line 2 baking sheets with parchment paper. Working with a sharp thin-bladed knife, slice the logs of dough into ½-inch-thick rounds. (If any of the cookies break, squeeze the broken-off bit back onto the cookie.) Place the cookies on the parchment-lined sheets, leaving an inch of space between them. Bake the first sheet for 12 minutes. The cookies will not look done, nor will they be firm, but that is the way they should be. Transfer the sheet to a rack and let the cookies rest, on the sheet, until they are only just warm. Repeat with the second sheet of cookies.

MAKES ABOUT 3 DOZEN COOKIES

NOVEMBER 7, 2004: "COOKIE MASTER," BY JULIA MOSKIN. RECIPE ADAPTED FROM PIERRE HERMÉ AND DORIE GREENSPAN.

—2004

LEMON GUMDROPS

4 packets powdered gelatin

1 cup water

2½ cups sugar

Juice of 1 lemon

Grated zest of 1 orange

3 drops yellow food coloring

1. Butter an 8-inch square baking dish. Dissolve the gelatin in ½ cup water and let stand for 5 minutes.

2. Combine 2 cups sugar and the remaining ½ cup water in a medium saucepan and bring to a boil, stirring constantly and washing down the sides of the pan several times with a pastry brush that has been dipped in cold water to prevent crystallization. Add the gelatin and continue boiling and stirring until the mixture thickens, about 15 minutes.

3. Add the lemon juice and orange zest and boil for 5 more minutes. Stir in the food coloring. Pour the mixture into the prepared dish and let set up for about 1 hour.

4. Put the remaining ½ cup sugar in a shallow bowl. Butter a large chef's knife and your fingers. Cut the lemon gel into ½-inch squares and coat with the sugar.

MAKES 256 GUMDROPS

DECEMBER 18, 2005: "THE WAY WE EAT: FREE RANGING," BY AMANDA HESSER. RECIPE ADAPTED FROM *MAKING GREAT CANDY*, BY LAURA DOVER DORAN.

—2005

SALTED BUTTER CARAMELS

Great-tasting candy is much easier to make than it might seem. Getting it to look perfect is the difficult part. As long as you don't mind aesthetic imperfections, all you need to do is buy a good candy thermometer and get boiling. You'll have candy made sooner than you can bake a batch of cookies.

1⅓ cups heavy cream

2 cups sugar

½ cup light corn syrup

⅓ cup honey

6 tablespoons unsalted butter, cubed

1 teaspoon vanilla paste or extract

1 tablespoon fleur de sel or sea salt

1½ pounds bittersweet chocolate, finely chopped (optional)

1. Line an 8-inch square baking pan with aluminum foil, letting it extend over the sides. Grease with vegetable oil. Pour the cream into a heavy 4-quart saucepan. Attach a candy thermometer to the pan, and bring to a boil. Add the sugar, corn syrup, and honey, and stir constantly with a wooden spoon until the mixture comes to a boil. Cook, stirring occasionally, until the mixture reaches 257 degrees, 15 to 30 minutes.

2. Remove the pan from the heat and, with oven mitts on, stir in the butter, vanilla, and 2 teaspoons salt. Pour into the prepared pan.

3. If you are not coating the caramels in chocolate, let cool slightly and then sprinkle with the remaining teaspoon of salt. When the caramel is completely cool, coat a cutting board and the blade of a large chef's knife with vegetable oil. Invert the caramel onto the cutting board, peel off the foil, and invert again. Cut the caramel into eight 1-inch-wide strips; then cut each strip into ½-inch pieces.

4. To coat the caramels with chocolate, melt the chocolate in a double boiler (temper the chocolate if you want the coating to have polish; directions can be found at www.baking911.com). Using a fork to hold the caramels, dip them one at a time into the chocolate and set them on a rack to cool. As you go, after dipping 4 caramels, sprinkle each with a little of the remaining teaspoon of salt. Transfer to parchment paper to set up.

MAKES 128 CARAMELS

PERIOD DETAIL

This was the moment for salt, butter, and caramel. The three came together in another form—ice cream—a year after this recipe appeared; see p. 733. By 2008, the trio went mainstream, showing up as a Häagen-Dazs flavor (salted caramel ice cream), at Starbucks (salted caramel hot chocolate), and in Walmart (as boxed chocolates).

DECEMBER 18, 2005: "THE WAY WE EAT: FREE RANGING," BY AMANDA HESSER. RECIPE ADAPTED FROM *TRUFFLES, CANDIES, AND CONFECTIONS*, BY CAROLE BLOOM.

—2005

✑ FLAT-AND-CHEWY CHOCOLATE CHIP COOKIES

Everyone declares his chocolate chip cookies the best, right? I fell into that trap too. I mean, I *really* fell into that trap. Not only did I claim that these cookies were the best flat-and-chewy version around, I noted that I'd worked with my colleague Jill Santopietro on the recipe for six months. The ink on the recipe was not yet dry when the complaint e-mails began rolling in. One particularly memorable one came from a woman who said making the cookies was the first time she and her child had baked together and that I'd ruined the magical once-in-a-lifetime-moment with salty cookies!

It's true that these cookies contain more salt than the average cookie, but that's intentional. The extra salt counteracts—and complements—the sugar, butter, and richness of the chocolate. What I didn't realize was that the salt I'd used to test the recipes, Diamond Crystal kosher salt, is less salty tasting than the other major brand, Morton, which is iodized. So please use Diamond. They *are* terrible when made with Morton!

Also, to guard against anyone who rounds their tablespoons, I've changed the measurement to "1 scant tablespoon" salt.

Again, if you get the salt right, these truly are the best flat-and-chewy chocolate chip cookies, so don't listen to what David Leite says on p. 709. . . .

———

2 cups all-purpose flour

1¼ teaspoons baking soda

1 scant tablespoon Diamond Crystal kosher salt

½ pound (2 sticks) unsalted butter, softened

1½ cups packed light brown sugar

¼ cup granulated sugar

2 large eggs

1 tablespoon vanilla extract

2 cups (about 12 ounces) chopped bittersweet chocolate (chunks and shavings)

2 cups (about 8 ounces) chopped toasted walnuts (optional)

1. Sift together the flour, baking soda, and salt.

2. In the bowl of a mixer fitted with a paddle (or in a bowl with a hand mixer), beat the butter and sugars until fluffy, 3 minutes. Add the eggs one at a time, then add the vanilla. Add the flour mixture all at once and blend until a dough forms. Fold in the chocolate and walnuts. Refrigerate the dough until chilled, preferably overnight.

3. Heat the oven to 325 degrees. Line 2 baking sheets with parchment paper or Silpats or other silicone baking liners. Roll 2½-tablespoon lumps of dough into balls, place 3 inches apart on the baking sheet, and flatten to ½-inch-thick disks. (Chill the remaining dough between batches.)

4. Bake until the edges are golden brown, 14 to 16 minutes. Let cool slightly on the baking sheets, then transfer to a rack.

MAKES 30 TO 35 COOKIES

JANUARY 22, 2006: "THE ARSENAL," BY AMANDA HESSER.

—2006

✑ HAZELNUT BAKLAVA

———

For the Nut Filling

2 cups (about 8 ounces) skinned hazelnuts

1 cup (4 ounces) slivered almonds

1½ tablespoons sugar

1 teaspoon ground cinnamon

¼ teaspoon ground cloves

⅛ teaspoon salt

For the Pastry

One 1-pound package frozen phyllo dough, defrosted

1½ cups warm clarified butter

For the Honey Syrup

1¼ cups sugar

¾ cup water

⅓ cup honey

2 strips lemon zest—$\frac{1}{2}$ inch wide by 2 inches long

1 teaspoon fresh lemon juice

1 teaspoon rosewater

1 teaspoon orange-flower water

1 cinnamon stick

3 whole cloves

$\frac{1}{8}$ teaspoon salt

1. Heat the oven to 350 degrees. To make the filling, pulse together the hazelnuts, almonds, sugar, cinnamon, cloves, and salt in a food processor until the nuts are finely ground.

2. Unfold the phyllo dough on a large work surface. With a sharp knife, slice the stack of dough crosswise in half, forming two 9-by-12-inch rectangles. Cover entirely with 1 or 2 damp dish cloths.

3. With a pastry brush, generously brush the bottom of a 9-by-12-inch baking pan with clarified butter. Carefully place 1 phyllo sheet in the pan (it should just fit) and brush with butter. Repeat with 7 more phyllo sheets, brushing each sheet with butter. (Keep the unused phyllo covered as you work.) Sprinkle about one-third of the filling evenly over the top layer. Repeat the layering process with 6 more sheets of phyllo, brushing each sheet with butter. Sprinkle another one-third of the filling evenly over the top layer. Repeat the layering process with another 8 sheets of phyllo, buttering each sheet. Sprinkle the remaining filling over the phyllo. Cover with 2 more sheets of phyllo, leaving the top layer unbuttered.

4. Place your palms in the center of the top of the baklava and gently move your hands in an outward sweeping motion, flattening and smoothing the pastry. Brush an additional $\frac{1}{4}$ cup melted butter evenly over top layer.

5. Using a sharp-pointed knife, carefully slice the baklava into 2-inch-wide diagonal strips. Repeat in the opposite direction, forming a diamond pattern. Bake the baklava until golden and flaky, 50 to 60 minutes, rotating the pan as necessary to ensure even baking.

6. Meanwhile, combine all the honey syrup ingredients in a medium heavy saucepan, bring to a boil, stirring occasionally, and cook until the sugar has completely dissolved, about 5 minutes. Transfer the syrup to a bowl and refrigerate, stirring occasionally, until cool. Once it has cooled, strain the syrup into a liquid measuring cup.

7. While the baklava is still very hot, pour the cooled syrup into the cracks between the diamond-shaped pieces; reserve about 3 tablespoons syrup. Drizzle the reserved syrup evenly over the top of the baklava. Let cool on a wire rack for 2 hours, then cover with foil and let sit for at least 4 hours, or overnight, before serving.

MAKES ABOUT 2½ DOZEN PIECES

COOKING NOTE

Rosewater and orange-flower water are available in Middle Eastern markets.

MARCH 29, 2006: "TO LURE THE FRENCH, DON'T BE TOO SWEET," BY MELISSA CLARK. RECIPE ADAPTED FROM PÂTISSERIE MALIKA IN PARIS.

—2006

ALMOND-LEMON MACAROONS (ALMENDRADOS)

These look like little almond buttons, yet are soft inside, like almond paste dampened with lemon.

———

2 cups (about 12 ounces) blanched whole almonds, plus about 30 almonds for decoration

1 cup sugar

1 large egg

Finely grated zest of 1 lemon

1. Grind the 2 cups almonds very fine in a food processor. Add $\frac{3}{4}$ cup sugar, the egg, and lemon zest and pulse to make a cohesive dough. Transfer to a medium bowl, cover, and refrigerate for at least 12 hours.

2. Heat the oven to 350 degrees. Line a baking sheet with parchment paper or a Silpat or other silicone baking liner. Place the remaining $\frac{1}{4}$ cup sugar in a small bowl.

3. Pinching off pieces of dough about the size of a walnut, roll them into balls, then roll in the sugar. Gently press an almond point first into the top of each cookie, so that half the almond can be seen, and arrange the cookies 1 inch apart on the baking sheet.

4. Bake until the cookies have the barest hint of color but are still soft, 10 to 12 minutes. (The cookies must be soft when removed from the oven or they will be

too hard when they cool.) Transfer to racks, to cool completely. Store in an airtight container.

MAKES ABOUT 2½ DOZEN COOKIES

MARCH 28, 2007: "FOR A SWEETER PASSOVER, OLD AND NEW SEPHARDIC DELIGHTS," BY JOAN NATHAN. RECIPE ADAPTED FROM *DULCE LO VIVAS*, BY ANA BENSADÓN.

—2007

❧ SWEDISH GINGER COOKIES

You can't find a simpler recipe, nor one that will provoke as much conversation once you reveal that the richness and moisture come from bacon fat. Do not use fancy bacon: Oscar Mayer is the only way to go. And eat them up quickly—this won't be a problem—as they're best fresh.

———

¾ cup bacon fat (rendered from about
   1½ pounds bacon)
1 cup sugar, plus more for coating the cookies
¼ cup unsulphured dark molasses
1 large egg
2 cups all-purpose flour
2 teaspoons baking soda
1 teaspoon ground ginger
1 teaspoon ground cloves
1 teaspoon ground cinnamon
¾ teaspoon salt

1. In a mixer fitted with a paddle attachment (or in a bowl with a hand mixer), mix all the ingredients until blended. Refrigerate the dough until chilled.
2. Heat the oven to 350 degrees. Roll the dough into small gum-ball-sized balls, dip in sugar, put 2 inches apart on ungreased baking sheets, and flatten with your fingers to 1- to 2-inch disks. Bake until dark brown, 10 to 12 minutes. Transfer to a rack to cool.

MAKES ABOUT 80 COOKIES

COOKING NOTE
If making these by hand—which is easy—first blend the sugar and molasses, then add the bacon fat and egg. Finally, mix together the dry ingredients and fold them into the wet bacon fat mixture.

APRIL 8, 2007: "LET'S EAT," BY CATHY HORYN.

—2007

❧ CARAMELIZED BROWN BUTTER RICE KRISPIES TREATS

Less gooey, more composed than the childhood kind. If you want the latter, use 12 ounces of marshmallows.

———

½ pound (2 sticks) salted or unsalted butter,
   preferably cultured
One 10½-ounce bag marshmallows
⅛ teaspoon salt if using unsalted butter
One 12-ounce box Rice Krispies cereal

1. Line an 11-by-17 inch rimmed baking sheet with parchment paper or wax paper, or butter it well. Melt the butter in a large pot, over medium-low heat. It will melt, then foam, then turn clear golden, and finally start to turn brown and smell nutty. Watch closely and stir often.
2. When the butter is evenly browned, stir in the marshmallows, and the salt if using unsalted butter. Cook, stirring often, until the marshmallows melt and the mixture turns pale brown, then stir constantly until lightly browned but not dark, 3 to 5 minutes.
3. Turn off the heat, add the cereal, and mix well, preferably with a silicone spoon or a spatula. Scrape into the prepared pan and press down lightly. If necessary, butter your hands to press the mixture flat. Let cool, and cut into squares or bars.

MAKES 40 TREATS

OCTOBER 31, 2007: "GOOD TASTE TAKES A HOLIDAY," BY JULIA MOSKIN. RECIPE ADAPTED FROM COLIN ALEVRAS, THE CHEF AT THE TASTING ROOM IN NEW YORK CITY.

—2007

❧ WHITE BARK BALLS

If Party Balls (p. 685), and Caramelized Brown Butter Rice Krispies Treats (above) married and had a baby, it would be a White Bark Ball.

———

1 1/2 cups Rice Krispies

1 cup crunchy peanut butter

1 cup confectioners' sugar

2 tablespoons unsalted butter, softened

3/4 pound white chocolate

Colored sugar for sprinkling (optional)

1. Combine the Rice Krispies, peanut butter, confectioners' sugar, and butter in a medium bowl, and mix until very well combined. Firmly compress into balls 1 1/2 inches in diameter. Place on a baking sheet, cover, and refrigerate until well chilled, at least 4 hours, or overnight.

2. Line a baking sheet with wax paper. Melt the white chocolate in a double boiler over medium-low heat, stirring until completely smooth. Pour the chocolate into a wide shallow bowl. Working quickly, in small batches, roll the chilled balls in the chocolate, turning gently with a fork. Transfer to wax paper. If desired, sprinkle the tops of the cookies with colored sugar.

3. Place the baking sheet in the refrigerator long enough for the chocolate to become firm, 30 minutes to 1 hour, then transfer the balls to an airtight container. (The balls can be stored in a cool place for up to 3 days or refrigerated for up to 3 weeks.)

MAKES ABOUT 3 DOZEN BALLS

COOKING NOTE

If you're into the current fondness for contrasting flavors, then add a pinch of salt to the Rice Krispies mixture in Step 1, and sprinkle the finished balls with a little coarse sea salt at the end of Step 2.

DECEMBER 19, 2007: "IN THE KITCHEN OF LONG AGO, WITH GRANDMA," BY JENNIFER STEINHAUER. RECIPE ADAPTED FROM ISABELLE STEINHAUER.

—2007

↬ CHOCOLATE CHIP COOKIES

"Too bad sainthood is not generally conferred on bakers, for there is one who is a possible candidate for canonization," wrote David Leite. "She fulfills most of the requirements: (1) She's dead. (2) She demonstrated heroic virtue. (3) Cults have been formed around her work. (4) Her invention is considered by many to be a miracle. The woman: Ruth Graves Wakefield. Her

contribution to the world: the chocolate chip cookie." Sometime in the 1930s, Wakefield added chopped chocolate to a cookie recipe and changed baking forever.

And so, more than seventy years after Wakefield's culinary eureka, Leite researched some of New York's best chocolate chip cookies (an arduous task, clearly). He talked to Maury Rubin at City Bakery; Jacques Torres, the chocolate maker; Dorie Greenspan, the baking writer; and Shirley Corriher, a food science expert, among others, to divine the essential parts of great chocolate chip cookie.

Leite learned that 24 to 36 hours resting time for the dough allows the liquid ingredients to be fully absorbed, making for a more richly flavored cookie. Baking large—5- to 6-inch—cookies gives them three textures, from crisp on the perimeter to chewy to gooey in the center. The ratio of chocolate to dough should be 40 to 60. And you must add a generous portion of salt to the dough to give the cookies "dimension."

Leite's impressive recipe incorporates all these principles—and draws heavily on one of Jacques Torres's recipes.

———

1 3/4 cups plus 2 tablespoons (8 1/2 ounces) cake flour

1 2/3 cups (8 1/2 ounces) bread flour

1 1/4 teaspoons baking soda

1 1/2 teaspoons baking powder

1 1/2 teaspoons coarse salt

2 1/2 sticks (10 ounces) unsalted butter, softened

1 1/4 cups (10 ounces) packed light brown sugar

1 cup plus 2 tablespoons (8 ounces) granulated sugar

2 large eggs

2 teaspoons natural vanilla extract

1 1/4 pounds bittersweet chocolate disks or fèves, at least 60 percent cacao content (see Cooking Note)

Sea salt

1. Sift the flours, baking soda, baking powder, and salt into a bowl.

2. In the bowl of a mixer fitted with a paddle (or in a bowl with a hand mixer), beat the butter and sugars together on medium speed until very light, about 5 minutes. Add the eggs one at a time, mixing well after each addition. Stir in the vanilla. Reduce the speed to low, add the dry ingredients, and mix until just combined, 5 to 10 seconds. Drop in the chocolate pieces and incorporate them without breaking them. Press a

sheet of plastic wrap against the dough and refrigerate for 24 to 36 hours. (The dough can be used in batches, and it can be refrigerated for up to 72 hours.)

3. When ready to bake, heat the oven to 350 degrees. Line a baking sheet with parchment paper or a Silpat or other silicone baking mat.

4. Scoop six 3½-ounce mounds of dough (the size of generous golf balls) onto the baking sheet, making sure to turn any chocolate pieces that are poking up horizontally; it will make for a more attractive cookie. Sprinkle lightly with sea salt and bake until golden brown but still soft, 18 to 20 minutes. Transfer the sheet to a rack for 10 minutes, then slip the cookies onto another rack to cool a bit more. Repeat with the remaining dough, or reserve the dough, refrigerated, for baking the next day.

5. Eat warm, with a big napkin.

COOKING NOTE

Leite noted, "Disks are sold at Jacques Torres Chocolate; Valrhona fèves, oval-shaped chocolate pieces, are at Whole Foods." If you can't find chocolate disks or fèves, just chop up 1¼ pounds of chocolate, use the chunks, shards and all, and your cookies will turn out fine. Believe me!

MAKES 1½ DOZEN LARGE COOKIES

JULY 9, 2008: "PERFECTION? HINT: IT'S WARM AND HAS A SECRET," BY DAVID LEITE. RECIPE ADAPTED FROM JACQUES TORRES.

—2008

↞ BROWN BUTTER PEACH BARS

Christine Muhlke, who replaced me as the food editor at the *Times Magazine*, has a knack for identifying signposts at the nexus of food and style. One week it's the Crop Mob a group of young volunteer farmers. The next it's Japanese paper bowls she spotted in Paris. In this story, Muhlke visited Big Sur Bakery, a recent glimmer of culinary light on California's Highway 1.

———

For the Jam
1 cup sugar
Grated zest and juice of 2 oranges
½ vanilla bean, split
4 cups diced (½-inch) unpeeled peaches
    (about 2 pounds peaches)

For the Crust
½ pound (2 sticks) unsalted butter
½ cup confectioners' sugar, sifted
1½ cups all-purpose flour

For the Filling
3 large eggs
1 cup sugar
Grated zest of 2 oranges
¾ cup plus 2 tablespoons all-purpose flour
½ vanilla bean, split
10 tablespoons (1¼ sticks) unsalted butter

1. To make the jam, mix together the sugar and orange zest and juice in a 3-quart pot, using a wooden spoon. Using a paring knife, scrape the seeds from the vanilla bean, and add the vanilla bean and seeds to the pan. Attach a candy thermometer to the pot, bring to a boil over medium heat, and cook for a few minutes, until the mixture reaches 220 degrees.

2. Add the peaches and boil, stirring occasionally, until the peaches turn into a thick jam and the thermometer returns to 220 degrees, 35 to 45 minutes. Wear long oven mitts, as the jam can splatter. When the jam begins to stick to the bottom of the pan, it's nearly there. Transfer the jam to a baking pan to cool. Remove the vanilla bean.

3. To prepare the crust, melt the butter in a saucepan over medium-high heat, stirring frequently. Cook until the white milk solids start to brown and smell nutty, 5 to 10 minutes. Strain through a fine sieve set over a heatproof container. Freeze the butter until solid.

4. Mix together the confectioners' sugar and flour in a large bowl. Scoop the chilled brown butter into the flour mixture and, using a pastry cutter, blend until crumbly. Transfer the mixture to a 9-by-13-inch baking pan and firmly pat it evenly over the bottom of the pan. Refrigerate for 30 minutes.

5. Adjust an oven rack to the middle position and heat the oven to 375 degrees. Bake the crust until golden, 18 to 20 minutes. Let cool. (Leave the oven on.)

6. To make the filling, whisk together the eggs, sugar, zest, and flour in a large bowl.

7. Scrape the seeds from the vanilla bean, and place the seeds, vanilla bean, and butter in a small sauce-

pan. Cook over medium-high heat until the butter melts and the white milk solids start to brown and smell nutty; strain through a fine sieve. Remove the vanilla bean. Carefully add the brown butter to the egg and flour mixture, whisking until the butter is incorporated.

8. To assemble the bars, spread half of the filling over the baked crust. Spoon large dollops of the peach jam over the filling; reserve a quarter of the jam. Pour the remaining brown butter filling over the peach jam, and finish by spooning smaller dollops of the reserved jam over the top. Bake until the filling is golden brown, 25 to 30 minutes. Cool completely. Cut into bars.

MAKES 2 DOZEN BARS

AUGUST 10, 2008: "THE WAY WE EAT: WOOD-FIRED," BY CHRISTINE MUHLKE. RECIPE ADAPTED FROM BIG SUR BAKERY IN BIG SUR, CALIFORNIA.

—2008

✑ BUTTERY FRENCH TV SNACKS (CROQ-TÉLÉ)

These pyramid-shaped cookies are not only France's delicious little version of a TV snack (epitomizing the difference between the French and Americans: fragile and buttery versus filling and salty), they are surprisingly malleable! The first time I made them, I decided to have my two-year-old twins help me. The loose and granular dough, much of which ended up permanently wedged into the grooves of the kitchen floor, was eventually shaped into pointy mounds and laid on a baking sheet set on the floor, only to be smashed flat when my son fell on top of the baking sheet. Turns out you can shape and reshape the cookie dough, and it still turns out well.

———

¾ cup blanched whole almonds or hazelnuts, lightly toasted

½ cup sugar

½ teaspoon kosher or flaky sea salt (if using fine sea or table salt, use ⅜ teaspoon)

1 cup all-purpose flour

7 tablespoons cold unsalted butter, cut into ½-inch pieces

1. Position 2 oven racks in the top and bottom thirds of the oven. Heat the oven to 325 degrees. Line 2 baking sheets with parchment paper. Grind the nuts, sugar, and salt to a fine meal in a food processor.

2. Beat the flour and butter together in the bowl of a mixer fitted with a paddle attachment (or in a bowl with a hand mixer) on low speed until the texture is sandy. Add the nut mixture and mix until the dough starts to form small lumps, then keep mixing until the dough just holds together when pinched between your fingers. (Do not use wet fingers: the cookies will collapse.)

3. Pinch off about a teaspoon of dough, place it in the palm of your hand, and, with your fingertips, pinch and press the dough together until the cookie has a flat bottom and pointed top, like a rough pyramid. The cookies need not be perfectly smooth or equal in size. Place on the parchment-lined sheets and shape more cookies, spacing them about 1 inch apart.

4. Bake for about 15 minutes, rotating the baking sheets halfway through. The cookies should be turning golden brown on the edges. Cool on the sheets for 5 minutes, then transfer to racks and cool completely. (The cookies can be stored in an airtight container for up to 1 week.)

MAKES 2 TO 3 DOZEN COOKIES

COOKING NOTE

"Butter is like the concrete you use to pour the foundation of a building," Anita Chu, the author of both this recipe and *Field Guide to Cookies*, said. "So it's very important to get it right: the temperature, the texture, the aeration." The butter should be creamed for at least 3 minutes—a process that creates the air bubbles that expand in the oven and leavens the cookies. It's a good tip to remember for all baking.

DECEMBER 17, 2008: "BUTTER HOLDS THE SECRET TO COOKIES THAT SING," BY JULIA MOSKIN. RECIPE ADAPTED FROM *FIELD GUIDE TO COOKIES*, BY ANITA CHU, WHO ADAPTED IT FROM ARNAUD LARHER, A PASTRY CHEF IN PARIS.

—2008

- The first hand-crank ice cream maker is invented.

—1840s—

- Despite serious technical challenges, people persevere and make frozen treats.

—1870s—

- Granita was not invented in 1990, friends! See Raspberry Granita (p. 719).

—1895—

- The first Dairy Queen opens in Joliet, Illinois.

—1940—

- Velvets are frozen meringue and cream— a great ice cream cheat if you don't own an ice cream maker (see p. 723).

—1950s—

- Mister Softee is founded by William and James Conway, who drive an ice cream truck around West Philadelphia.

—1956—

- Soufflé 2.0: the frozen soufflé (p. 725).

—1970s—

- Steve Herrell comes up with the concept of à la carte "mix-ins" in ice cream at his shop, Steve's Ice Cream, in Somerville, Massachusetts.

—1973—

- Ice Cream Pie (p. 726).

—1975—

- Ben & Jerry's is founded in Burlington, Vermont.

—1978—

- First TCBY opens in Little Rock, Arkansas.

—1981—

- The era of the luxury sorbet—berries with herbal infusions, cocoa, passion fruit, sour cream.

—1990s—

- Jon Snyder founds Il Laboratorio del Gelato on Manhattan's Lower East Side and kicks off a gelato craze.

—2002—

- Mario Batali's Otto Enoteca Pizzeria opens in Manhattan and instantly becomes more famous for its olive oil gelato dusted with sea salt than for its pizza.

—2003—

- The first Pinkberry hits Los Angeles, and teens line up by the hundred for plain and green tea "frozen yogurt."

—2005—

- The Van Leeuwen Artisan Ice Cream truck starts puttering around New York City's SoHo district, selling ice creams with painstakingly sourced ingredients such as red currants from the Hudson Valley and pistachios from the slopes of Mount Etna.

—2008—

- Sherbet makes a comeback.

—2009—

- Restaurant pastry chefs start serving super-smooth ice cream made in a Pacojet, which scrapes and churns frozen custard at high speeds.

16

❧

FROZEN DESSERTS

As someone who eats ice cream nearly every day, I'm an enthusiastic proponent of making it yourself. With a reliable machine, it couldn't be easier. Much of the work is simply stirring; only a few recipes require you to simmer custard on the stove. Cooks from the nineteenth century seemed to share my zeal—there were dozens and dozens of frozen desserts in the archives, including a few unexpected discoveries. If you thought Italian granita was created in 1995, see the Raspberry Granita from 1895 on p. 719. (A century later, ideas for granita expanded to include grapefruit [p. 731], almond [p. 731], and clove [p. 727].) And I highly recommend you try the Tea Ice Cream (p. 717) from 1877, which is made with green tea.

Citrus sherbets went in and out of vogue, as you'll see from the 1946 Lime Sherbet (p. 722) and the 2009 Tangerine Sherbet (p. 734)—and the absence of sherbets in between. And the range of flavors we experimented with grew in recent years. In the past decade, you can find licorice (p. 728), star anise (p. 728), and even red wine (p. 730).

The best part of making ice cream is that, unlike most desserts, it keeps for weeks. And while friends seem to appreciate anything homemade these days, there's something about home-fashioned ice cream and sorbets that induces astonishment among guests, who've become all too accustomed to Häagen-Dazs. Someone needs to start a make-at-home movement, and if it has to be me, fine!

RECIPES BY CATEGORY

ORANGE ICE

I think of this as a timeless children's dessert. A simple flavor that's not quite sorbet, not quite shaved ice, but somewhere in between—an icy hillock that can be slowly excavated with a small spoon.

————

5 oranges

3 cups fresh orange juice (from about 9 oranges total, including the ones for zesting)

1 tablespoon fresh lemon juice

1 cup confectioners' sugar

1 cup water

1. Using a sharp paring knife, thinly pare the zest from the oranges and place in a bowl. Add the orange juice, lemon juice, sugar, and water and stir to dissolve the sugar. Let sit for 1 hour.

2. Strain the juice, pour into an ice cream maker, and freeze according to the manufacturer's instructions. Then pack into a container and freeze until ready to serve.

MAKES ABOUT 1 QUART

MAY 6, 1877: "RECEIPTS FOR THE TABLE." RECIPE SIGNED AUNT ADDIE.

—1877

TEA ICE CREAM (A MASSACHUSETTS RECEIPT)

This is one of the best ice creams I've ever made. The original called for "old Hyson tea," which is a green tea. Use any tea you like. I made it with jasmine silver tip from the Rare Tea Company (www.rareteacompany.com), a gorgeous tea with glimmers of green tea flavor.

————

¼ cup high-quality green or other tea leaves

4 cups heavy cream

4 large eggs

1 cup sugar

Pinch of salt (optional)

1. Combine the tea and 2 cups heavy cream in a double boiler and scald the cream (heat it until the cream is steaming and bubbles form around the edges). Turn off the heat and let steep for 10 minutes.

2. Strain the cream, return to the double boiler, and add the remaining 2 cups heavy cream. Scald again.

3. Whisk together the eggs and sugar in a large bowl until pale yellow and fluffy. Slowly whisk in the hot cream, followed by the pinch of salt, if using. Let cool, then chill overnight.

4. The next day, whisk the cream mixture, pour it into an ice cream maker, and freeze according to the manufacturer's instructions. Then pack the ice cream into a container and freeze until ready to serve.

MAKES ABOUT 1½ QUARTS

COOKING NOTES

Many desserts from this period were oversweetened. This ice cream called for ¾ pound of sugar, about 1½ cups; I reduced it to 1 cup.

I added the pinch of salt—all desserts benefit from a little salt, which amplifies flavors.

The ice cream base separates when chilled overnight, so make sure you whisk it together again before adding it to your ice cream maker.

PERIOD DETAIL

In addition to offering bits of dubious advice, "The Household" column also ran reader queries. Pet birds were of particular interest. On the day the column ran this ice cream recipe, it also published these squawks for help:

"What will relieve a pet parrot (gray) that is troubled with what appears to be cramps, causing it at times to fall from its perch, evidently in much pain."

"What to do for an afflicted canary-bird. The top of his head and back of his neck are entirely bare of feathers; he is not moulting, and there is no appearance of feathers dropping out, they seem to disappear; otherwise he seems perfectly well, and sings all the time."

JUNE 16, 1878: "THE HOUSEHOLD: RECEIPTS FOR THE TABLE." RECIPE SIGNED A.C.L.

—1878

⌒ NESSELRODE PUDDING

Chestnut puddings of this era were often called Nesselrode, after Count Nesselrode, a Russian diplomat who negotiated the Treaty of Paris. None of the sources I found explain why he became associated with chestnuts—for all we know, he may not have even liked them. This version is more ice cream than pudding. The original recipe called for folding the egg whites and cream into the ice cream base and then freezing it in a mold, but I found that the ice cream turned icy in the freezer. So now you fold the egg whites and cream into the ice cream as it's churning.

———

¼ cup raisins

¼ cup finely chopped candied citron

¼ cup dried currants

1¼ cups maraschino liqueur

24 peeled chestnuts (see Cooking Notes) or
    vacuum-packed peeled chestnuts

1 cup plus 2 tablespoons sugar

½ vanilla bean, split, seeds scraped out and reserved

1 cup whole milk

2 cups heavy cream

3 large egg yolks

3 large eggs, separated

1. Combine the raisins, citron, currants, and 1 cup maraschino liqueur in a small bowl. Cover and let sit overnight.

2. Meanwhile, combine the chestnuts, vanilla seeds, sugar, and the remaining ¼ cup maraschino liqueur in a food processor. Puree the mixture until smooth, scraping down the sides of the bowl with a rubber spatula as needed.

3. Scrape the puree into a medium heavy saucepan. Add the milk and 1 cup heavy cream and whisk until smooth. Set over medium heat and bring to a simmer. Lightly whisk the egg yolks in a bowl. Whisk 1 cup of the hot milk mixture into the egg yolks, then whisk this mixture into the remaining milk. Stir constantly with a wooden spoon over medium-low heat until the mixture thickens enough to coat the back of the spoon. Make sure you don't overcook it, or you'll have scrambled eggs. Adjust the heat as necessary and go slowly. Pour the mixture into a clean bowl, set the bowl in a bowl of ice water, and let cool, stirring occasionally, then cover and refrigerate overnight.

4. The next day, drain the raisin mixture and add the fruit to the ice cream base. Pour into an ice cream maker and freeze according to the manufacturer's instructions.

5. Meanwhile, when the ice cream is almost done, whip the egg whites until they hold stiff peaks. Add to the ice cream in the machine, and continue churning. Whip the remaining heavy cream until it holds stiff peaks and add to the ice cream. Continue churning until the ice cream is ready. Scrape the ice cream into a container and freeze until ready to serve.

MAKES 1½ TO 2 QUARTS

COOKING NOTES

You can freeze this in a mold if you like. To unmold, dip the base in warm water, dry it, and invert onto a plate.

This recipe is a two-day process. Do up through Step 3 the first day and finish the pudding the following day.

To boil chestnuts, bring a large pot of water to a boil. Cut an X in the rounded side of each chestnut. Add the nuts to the boiling water and cook until tender, about 15 minutes. Drain. When the chestnuts are cool enough to handle, peel off their shells as well as the light brown skin that sticks to the nut.

PERIOD DETAIL

Later, the essential Nesselrode flavors—chestnuts, raisins, brandy—would be made into pies. During the 1940s, Hortense Spier, the owner of Hortense Spier Pies in New York, became well known for her Nesselrode dessert, which she sold to restaurants around the city.

JULY 6, 1879: "RECEIPTS FOR THE TABLE." RECIPE ADAPTED FROM *ANNE BOWMAN'S NEW COOKERY-BOOK.*

—1879

☙ PINEAPPLE SHERBET

---

1 large very ripe pineapple, trimmed, peeled,
    cored, and cut into chunks
1 tablespoon powdered gelatin
¼ cup cold water
1¾ cups warm water
1¼ cups sugar
3 tablespoons fresh lime juice, or to taste
    (from about 2 limes)
Pinch of salt

1. Place the pineapple chunks in a food processor and pulse until the pineapple is broken down to small, coarse bits but is not pureed. Measure out 4 cups pineapple.
2. Sprinkle the gelatin over the ¼ cup cold water in a large bowl. Let soften for 5 minutes.
3. Add the 1¾ cups warm water, 4 cups pineapple, and the sugar to the gelatin mixture and stir until both the sugar and gelatin are dissolved. Add half the lime juice and the salt. Chill thoroughly.
4. Pour the pineapple mixture into an ice cream maker and freeze according to the manufacturer's instructions; add the remaining lime juice if desired, halfway through.

MAKES ABOUT 2 QUARTS

VARIATION

In Step 3, combine the sugar and water in a saucepan. Bring to a boil, add 4 bruised kaffir lime leaves, and shut off the heat. Let cool until just warm, remove the kaffir lime leaves, and add the sugar syrup and pineapple to the gelatin mixture.

APRIL 10, 1881: "VARIOUS COOKING RECEIPTS: HOW MISS PARLOA PREPARES SOME POPULAR DISHES." RECIPE REPRINTED FROM THE *HARTFORD EVENING POST*.

—1881

☙ RASPBERRY GRANITA

"A few years ago, the making of frozen desserts was considered to be so difficult and delicate an operation that their accomplishment was, as a rule, relegated to the skilled caterer or French cook," said the *Times* writer in an article on frozen desserts. But now, he claimed, a good ice cream maker "is rapidly becoming a necessary factor in every well-ordered kitchen." The article included recipes for frappes, Pomona ice (orange and apple), cherry ice, milk sherbet, custard ice cream, and this delicious granita.

Of the granita, which the writer recommended for garden parties, he said, "This is a favorite dessert with all who have tried it and deserves a prominent place in the list of frozen dainties." I couldn't agree more. A nice touch is the last step, in which fresh raspberries are folded into the icy granita shortly before serving.

---

4 cups water
2 cups sugar
Juice of 3 small lemons, or to taste
11 cups (about 5½ pints) raspberries

1. Combine the water and sugar in a large saucepan and bring to a boil, stirring to dissolve the sugar, then reduce the heat and cook at a low boil for 15 minutes. Remove from the heat, stir in the lemon juice (to taste) and 8 cups raspberries and stir until the raspberries just begin to break down. Let cool. Taste, adding more lemon juice as desired. If the mixture is too sweet, dilute with a little water.
2. Pour the mixture into a lasagna pan or similar wide shallow pan (large enough so the raspberry mixture isn't more than an inch or two deep, yet small enough to fit in your freezer), and freeze for 1 hour. Use a sturdy fork to stir up the frozen bits, and continue doing this every 30 minutes or so, until the granita is just shards of raspberry ice. (It will hold overnight, so you can take a break and finish it in the morning if needed.)
3. Thirty minutes before serving, fold in the remaining 3 cups raspberries, and return to the freezer.

SERVES 8 TO 12

COOKING NOTES

This makes a lot of granita, maybe more than you need (and raspberries can be expensive), but the recipe can easily be halved.

I served this in plain glass tumblers. It's also good with fresh cream poured on top!

JULY 28, 1895: "FROZEN TABLE DAINTIES: AUGUST DESSERTS SHOULD BE ICED CREAMS, FRUITS, AND SYRUPS."

—1895

⌒ TORTONI

Figuring out the route a recipe took to get from, say, the Alps two centuries ago to your dinner table in Vermont is a bit like tracking a scent in the woods: there are moments of baying enthusiasm followed by dead ends and whimpering. Tortoni, a frozen mousse speckled with crushed macaroons, is no exception. It's usually attributed to Giuseppe Tortoni, whose Café Tortoni in Paris was known for its ices and ice creams (and also for its clientele, which included Balzac and Maupassant). Tortoni, also called biscuit tortoni, became the rage in mid-nineteenth-century Paris, then wended its way to America, where it found a ravenous following as a street cart and restaurant treat before evaporating from our culinary memory sometime in the early twentieth.

At least, I think that's what happened. Everyone I talked to about tortoni pointed me to Robin Weir, acknowledged as the foremost expert on ice cream. When I reached him in England, I asked if he could tell me about tortoni's history. "Absolutely not!" he bellowed. Weir and his wife, Caroline, have an ice cream book—*Ice Creams, Sorbets and Gelati* (then in the works, now published)—that apparently reveals a whole new history of tortoni. "You will be absolutely riveted by it," he promised, adding, "you will have a hard time finding any information about tortoni, since it took us four years." Whimper!

If you've never had tortoni, you're in for a delight. It's ice cream's fantasy of ice cream: scented with almonds and sometimes with rum, its airy mousse is uninhibited by gravity yet also a tiny bit chewy. The differences between ice cream and tortoni lie in the techniques of their making. Ice cream is made by blending rich materials—cream and sugar and sometimes eggs—and then churning air into the heavy mixture with an ice cream maker. With tortoni, the technique is deconstructed. In the following version, air is whipped into egg whites and yolks, and the mousse is bolstered by the addition of a hot sugar syrup. More air is whipped into cream, and the two mousses are folded together, then poured into a mold

lined with crushed macaroons. (This tortoni is unusual in that the crushed macaroons aren't mixed into the mousse and it doesn't contain alcohol or fruit.) Because tortoni has so much air and elasticity to it, the mixture never hardens like ice cream when it freezes, and when it melts, it gets fluffy rather than soupy.

———

12 almond macaroons (you can use
    coconut macaroons in a pinch)
¾ cup sugar
¾ cup water
3 large eggs, separated
1 teaspoon vanilla extract
2 cups heavy cream

1. Heat the oven to 250 degrees. Break the macaroons into pieces and toast them on a baking sheet until golden, dry, and crumbly, about 10 minutes. Let cool.
2. Grind the macaroons to fine crumbs in a food processor. You need about 1 cup.
3. Combine the sugar and water in a small heavy saucepan, attach a candy thermometer to the pan, and bring to a boil, stirring to dissolve the sugar. Cook until the syrup reaches 230 degrees.
4. Meanwhile, whip the whites in a mixer fitted with a whisk until they form firm peaks. Whip the yolks by hand until fluffy, then fold into the whites.
5. When the sugar syrup is ready, turn on the mixer to medium speed and slowly pour in the syrup in a fine thread; try to pour the syrup between the side of the bowl and the whisk so the whisk doesn't fling the syrup all over the sides of the bowl and your counter. Be patient: you don't want the eggs to cook—they should become mousse-like. Reduce the speed to low and whip until the mixture cools to room temperature. Mix in the vanilla.
6. Whip the cream to soft peaks, and fold it into the egg mixture.
7. Line the base of a 2-quart soufflé dish or other mold with parchment. Spoon half the macaroon crumbs into the mold. Cover with the mousse. Top with the remaining crumbs. Cover the dish with plastic wrap and freeze overnight.
8. To unmold, dip the base of the dish in a bowl of hot water, just long enough to warm the edges of the mousse. Run a thin knife around the edges of the mold, dry the base of the mold, and invert onto a plate, discard the parchment paper. Cut into wedges.

SERVES 8

COOKING NOTES

I made a fortunate mistake when I first tried this recipe. I hadn't bought enough cream and had just 1⅓ cups, so I used ⅔ cup sour cream to make up the difference. This added a lovely tang to the sweet, chewy frozen mousse.

Tortoni is often frozen in small cups the size of a cupcake paper. This one is frozen in a large mold, then sliced.

SEPTEMBER 11, 1898: "WOMEN HERE AND THERE."

—1898

BAKED ALASKA

Don't bother making your own ice cream or sponge cake for this one. Buy a sponge cake that you can freeze, and keep a stock of your favorite ice cream flavor. Then, as long as you have some eggs in the house, you're ready to impress with this Everest of desserts. And if you really want to make a statement, you can douse it with rum and light it on fire before whisking it to the table (though you should keep in mind that "maker of flaming meringues" could end up on your tombstone).

_____

1 pint ice cream (flavor of your choosing)
1 store-bought sponge cake layer
4 large egg whites
⅛ teaspoon cream of tartar
1 teaspoon vanilla extract
¼ cup confectioners' sugar, plus more for dusting

1. Pack the ice cream into a mold—any shape you like (I used a round stainless steel bowl). Freeze.
2. Heat the oven to 500 degrees. Trim the sponge cake so it's the same shape and size as the base of your ice cream mold—this will be the bed on which the ice cream sits. It should be no more than 1 inch thick. (Reserve the trimmings for another use, like snacking.) Lay the sponge cake base in a small baking pan.
3. Whip the egg whites in a large bowl until frothy. Add the cream of tartar, vanilla, and confectioners' sugar and continue whisking until the whites hold firm peaks.

4. Dip the base of the ice cream mold in warm water, then unmold the ice cream onto the sponge cake base. Working quickly, cover the ice cream and cake base with the meringue—treat it like icing. Dust with confectioners' sugar. Slide the baking dish into the oven and bake just until the meringue begins to toast and brown, 2 to 3 minutes. Serve immediately.

SERVES 6

JULY 4, 1909: "DELICIOUS DISHES FOR SUMMER." SOME PROPORTIONS AND INSTRUCTIONS COME FROM THE BAKED ALASKA RECIPE IN "NEWS OF FOOD; BRAVE COOK FIRST PUT ICE CREAM IN OVEN AND NOW THE RESULT IS BAKED ALASKA," BY JANE NICKERSON, AUGUST 4, 1949.

—1909

BROWN SUGAR ICE CREAM

Get ready for an intense, fleecy ice cream.

_____

One 1-pound box dark brown sugar
¼ cup water
3½ cups whole milk
5 large eggs
Pinch of salt
2 cups heavy cream, whipped to soft peaks
1 cup pecans, lightly toasted and finely chopped

1. Moisten the brown sugar with the water in a large saucepan. Bring to a boil over medium-high heat, stirring just until the sugar is dissolved, and cook until the water boils off and the sugar begins to caramelize and darken like a chestnut, about 5 minutes. Let cool for 15 minutes.
2. Meanwhile, pour the milk into a medium saucepan and heat over medium-high heat until bubbles form around the edges of the pan. Lightly beat the eggs in a bowl. Whisk in a little hot milk, then whisk this mixture into the remaining milk. Cook, stirring constantly, over medium-low heat until the mixture thickens enough to coat the back of a spoon, 10 to 15 minutes. Transfer the custard to a bowl.
3. Whisk the caramel into the custard and add the salt. Let cool, then chill overnight.
4. The next day, pour the custard into an ice cream maker and begin freezing according to the manufac-

turer's instructions (see Cooking Notes). When the ice cream begins to firm up, fold in the whipped cream and pecans and continue churning until it's done. Pack the ice cream into a container and freeze until ready to serve.

MAKES 2½ TO 3 QUARTS

COOKING NOTES

This makes more than most ice cream makers can hold, so you may need to churn the ice cream (and whipped cream and pecans) in two batches.

I added 3 more eggs than the original recipe called for, because modern eggs seem to have less binding strength, and it takes more of them to thicken a custard.

Whipping the cream before adding it to the churning ice cream gives it extra air and creaminess—a great trick.

MARCH 13, 1910: "NEW DISHES FOR EPICURES."

—1910

STRAWBERRY ICE CREAM

Jane Holt, a food writer for the *Times* in the 1940s, quoted Dr. William Butler, an English physician, on strawberries: "Doubtless God could have made a better berry. But doubtless God never did." The strawberry's beauty is on full display here, embellished with a pillowy ice cream.

I quart ripe strawberries, washed and hulled
I cup sugar
I tablespoon fresh lemon juice
A few grains of salt
2 cups heavy cream

1. Force the berries through a colander into a bowl. Add the sugar, lemon juice, and salt and refrigerate until chilled.
2. Whip the cream until it holds soft peaks. Fold into the strawberry mixture. Chill the mixture overnight.
3. The next day, pour the mixture into an ice cream maker and freeze according to the manufacturer's instructions. Pack the ice cream into a container and freeze until ready to serve.

MAKES ABOUT I QUART

PERIOD DETAIL

In 1877, Aunt Addie, a frequent contributor, shared a recipe for strawberry ice cream that included maraschino (the spirit, not the cherries) and cochineal (a red dye derived from a Central American insect) for extra color. Otherwise the same method was used—folding whipped cream into the ice cream base just before freezing.

MAY 25, 1941: "FOR STRAWBERRY ADDICTS," BY JANE HOLT.

—1941

LIME SHERBET

½ teaspoon powdered gelatin
2 cups whole milk
½ cup sugar
½ cup corn syrup
½ cup fresh lime juice (about 4 limes)
Pinch of salt

1. Soften the gelatin in ¼ cup milk in a small cup. (Then warm in the microwave to help it fully dissolve.)
2. Combine the gelatin mixture, the remaining 1¾ cups milk, sugar, corn syrup, lime juice, and salt in a large bowl and stir until the sugar is fully dissolved.
3. Pour the mixture into an ice cream maker and freeze according to manufacturer's instructions. Spoon the sherbet into a freezer container and freeze until ready to serve.

MAKES ABOUT I QUART

SEPTEMBER 1, 1946: "FLAVORED WITH LIMES," BY JANE NICKERSON.

—1946

COUPE LENA HORNE (COFFEE ICE CREAM SUNDAE)

The name of this coffee-colored sundae, a shout-out to the singer Lena Horne, who died in 2010, had unfortunate racial overtones, but I included the dish because it's a worthy historical snapshot, and because it's very good.

Don't sweeten the whipped cream: it should contrast with the ice cream. The crème de cacao wraps the dessert with notes of caramel. This may not be what you serve at your next dinner party, but it's the perfect dessert for family—it reminds you of what you used to think fancy food was.

––––––––

1 quart coffee ice cream
½ cup heavy cream, whipped to soft peaks
½ cup crème de cacao

Place the ice cream in parfait glasses, top with the cream, and add the crème de cacao.

SERVES 6

PERIOD DETAIL
Two years after this recipe appeared, the *Times* ran a similar recipe for Moscow Embassy Punch, which was ice cream doused with coffee. The modern manifestation of these ideas is affogato, or espresso poured over vanilla gelato, a dessert popular in Italian restaurants.

AUGUST 10, 1947: "SIMPLE FARE—FOR GOURMETS," BY JANE NICKERSON. RECIPE ADAPTED FROM TOWN PENGUIN, A RESTAURANT IN NEW YORK CITY.

—1947

FRUIT MARLOW

The frozen cousin to ambrosia. Make this with your kids—they'll love it.

––––––––

½ pound (24) marshmallows
¼ cup water
2 cups canned crushed pineapple or
    2 cups pureed bananas
2 tablespoons fresh lemon juice
1 cup heavy cream, whipped to soft peaks

1. Put the marshmallows and water in a double boiler and cook, covered, stirring occasionally until the marshmallows are melted. Transfer to a bowl.

2. Blend the fruit and lemon juice into the marshmallow mixture. Chill thoroughly.
3. Fold the whipped cream into the marshmallow mixture. Pour into an ice cream maker and freeze according to the manufacturer's instructions. Pack the ice cream into a container and freeze until ready to serve.

SERVES 6 TO 8

PERIOD DETAIL
The three other ice cream recipes in this article called for ingredients we'd find intolerable today: an orange coconut ice cream made with evaporated milk, apricot ice cream with sweetened condensed milk, and peach ice cream containing vanilla pudding mix. Thankfully, cooking with processed foods—which took hold for decades in most American kitchens—lasted just a few years in the *Times*: from the end of the war until the early 1950s.

JUNE 6, 1948: "FRUIT-FLAVORED ICE CREAMS," BY JANE NICKERSON. RECIPE BY RUTH P. CASA-EMELLOS, THE HEAD OF THE *TIMES* TEST KITCHEN.

—1948

FROZEN MERINGUE VELVET

This and Dick Taeuber's Cordial Pie on p. 817 were clearly separated at birth. Velvets are beautiful frozen mousses, often infused with a light or dark spirit, that can be made without an ice cream maker. Another example is the Tortoni on p. 720.

––––––––

1 cup chopped or diced candied fruit
⅓ cup maraschino liqueur
1⅔ cups sugar
½ cup water
6 large egg whites
1¾ cups coarsely chopped toasted hazelnuts or
    a combination of almonds and pistachios
4 cups heavy cream, whipped to soft peaks

1. Combine the candied fruit and maraschino liqueur in a small bowl and let marinate until ready to use.
2. Combine the sugar and water in a saucepan and attach a candy thermometer to the pan. Bring to a boil, stirring to dissolve the sugar, then lower the

heat to medium-low to low and cook until the syrup reaches 236 degrees.

3. Meanwhile, beat the egg whites in a mixer fitted with a whisk, until they form stiff peaks. Add the syrup to the egg whites in a fine stream while beating—try to pour it between the side of the bowl and the whisk so it doesn't fly around the bowl. Continue beating until the meringue forms stiff peaks. Refrigerate until chilled.

4. Add the nuts to the marinated fruit, and fold into the meringue.

5. Fold in the whipped cream, blending the two mixtures well. Pack into a container and freeze.

MAKES ABOUT 3 QUARTS

JUNE 7, 1959: "SWEETS FOR SUMMER," BY CRAIG CLAIBORNE.

—1959

☙ LEMON LOTUS ICE CREAM

My friend Narcissa Titman insisted I try this ice cream—her family has been making it for decades. It's the kind of recipe that shouldn't work, as milk and lemon are naturally opposed. Sugar acts as the mediator, allowing the cream to stay rich and moussey and the lemon to blaze alongside.

———

4 lemons
2 cups sugar
4 cups heavy cream (see Cooking Notes)
2 cups whole milk

1. Cut 1 lemon into paper-thin slices. Remove the seeds from the slices and cut the slices in half to resemble half moons.

2. Squeeze the juice of the remaining 3 lemons and combine with the sugar in a medium bowl. Add the lemon slices. Stir until all the sugar is dissolved, then refrigerate for at least 2 hours, or, preferably, overnight.

3. Whisk the cream and milk into the lemon mixture, then pour into an ice cream maker and freeze according to the manufacturer's instructions. Pack the ice cream into a container and freeze until ready to serve.

MAKES ABOUT 2½ QUARTS

COOKING NOTES
The lemon must be sliced paper-thin, or you'll get hard lemon chips in your ice cream. Use a mandoline if you have one.

Narcissa recommends using half heavy cream, half light cream, which makes it, she says, less "gummy."

VARIATION
Make this with Meyer lemons!

JULY 2, 1961. I COULD NOT FIND THE TITLE OR AUTHOR, BUT THE SAME RECIPE POPPED UP ON AUGUST 23, 1976, IN AN ARTICLE TITLED "HEATED DEBATE OVER KITCHEN GRAMMAR," BY CRAIG CLAIBORNE.

—1961

☙ MRS. FOSTER'S FROSTY LIME PIE

When the lime filling freezes, it turns crystalline, which adds texture to the pie—a little like bubbles in bathwater.

———

For the Graham Cracker Crust
1¼ cups graham cracker crumbs
¼ cup superfine sugar
4 tablespoons unsalted butter, softened

For the Filling
5 large eggs, separated
¾ cup superfine sugar
2 teaspoons grated lime zest
⅔ cup strained fresh lime juice (from about 6 limes)
⅛ teaspoon salt

For the Topping
1½ cups heavy cream, whipped to soft peaks
Thin lime slices or fresh strawberries
Sugar if using lime slices

1. Heat the oven to 350 degrees. To make the crust, place the graham cracker crumbs and sugar in a bowl. Add the butter and work with a wooden spoon (or your fingers) to blend well.

2. Press the mixture evenly into a 9-inch pie plate with your fingertips (or use an 8-inch pie plate to press

down the mixture). Bake for 10 minutes. Cool to room temperature. (Leave the oven on.)

3. To make the filling, beat the egg yolks in the top of a double boiler over medium heat until very thick (they should register 165 degrees on an instant-read thermometer). Gradually beat in ½ cup sugar and continue beating until the mixture is very pale and thick and forms a rope when dropped from the beater. Stir in the lime zest and juice and cook over simmering water, stirring, until the mixture coats the back of the spoon; do not allow to boil. Pour the mixture into a large bowl and let cool to room temperature.

4. When the yolk mixture is at room temperature, beat the egg whites with the salt in a large bowl until soft peaks form. Gradually beat in the remaining ¼ cup sugar until the meringue is stiff and shiny. Stir one-third of the meringue into the cooled yolk mixture. Fold in the remaining meringue mixture until evenly distributed.

5. Turn the filling into the graham cracker crust and bake for 15 minutes, or until lightly tinged with brown. Cool.

6. Chill the pie in the refrigerator, then transfer to the freezer. Once it is frozen, cover with plastic wrap.

7. Remove the pie from the freezer 10 minutes before serving. Cover with the whipped cream and garnish with lime slices dipped in sugar or fresh strawberries.

SERVES 8 TO 10

COOKING NOTES

Raymond A. Sokolov, who wrote about this pie, added that the "pie will keep frozen 2 to 3 weeks. If a sweeter pie is desired, cut down the lime juice to ½ cup. Extra pie can be refrozen. If desired, the pie can be well chilled and served without freezing."

Press the crust as thin as possible, because once the pie is frozen, a thick crust will make it very difficult to cut.

JULY 11, 1971: "BAKE A PIE TO BEAT THE HEAT," BY RAYMOND A. SOKOLOV. RECIPE ADAPTED FROM PEARL FOSTER OF MR. AND MRS. FOSTER'S PLACE IN NEW YORK CITY.

—1971

✐ FROZEN LEMON SOUFFLÉ

6 large eggs, separated
6 large egg yolks
1¾ cups plus 2 teaspoons sugar
¾ cup fresh lemon juice (from about 3 lemons)
Grated zest of 1 lemon
½ cup heavy cream
Whipped cream for garnish (optional)
Candied flowers for garnish (optional)

1. Select a deep skillet into which a 2-quart bowl fits comfortably. Add enough water to come up around the sides of the bowl without overflowing. Remove the bowl and start heating the water in the skillet.

2. Drop the egg yolks and 1½ cups sugar into the bowl and beat with a whisk or hand mixer until light and lemon colored. Add the lemon juice. When the water is boiling, set the bowl in the skillet and continue beating until the egg mixture is like a very thick, smooth, and creamy custard, 5 to 10 minutes. (The temperature of the egg mixture at this point should be about 120 to 140 degrees on an instant-read thermometer.)

3. Scrape the mixture into another bowl and stir in the lemon zest. Let cool, then chill thoroughly.

4. Prepare a 1½-quart soufflé dish: Tear off a length of wax paper that will fit around the outside of the dish, adding an inch or two for overlap. Fold the wax paper lengthwise into thirds. Wrap it around the soufflé dish so it extends about 2 inches above the rim, making sure that it overlaps itself at the end by at least 1 inch; secure it with string or paper clips.

5. Beat the heavy cream in a small bowl, and when it starts to thicken, add 2 teaspoons sugar. Continue beating until stiff. Fold this into the egg yolk mixture.

6. Beat the egg whites in a large bowl. When they start to mound, add the remaining ¼ cup sugar, beating constantly. Continue beating until the whites are stiff. Fold them into the soufflé mixture.

7. Pour the mixture into the prepared dish and place in the freezer. Let stand for at least 5 hours, or overnight, until frozen.

8. Remove the wax paper. Decorate the soufflé if desired with whipped cream, piped out of a pastry tube, and candied flowers.

SERVES 8

OCTOBER 20, 1974: "FOOD: AH, LEMON SOUFFLÉ," BY
CRAIG CLAIBORNE WITH PIERRE FRANEY.

—1974

ICE CREAM PIE

There are a few versions of ice cream pie, none of
them very complicated. Some are nothing more than
ice cream pressed in layers in a pie dish, frozen again,
and sliced. Others include a crust. Occasionally there
are garish toppings. This one is fun to make because
rather than pressing a cookie crust into the pie dish,
you fill the dish with a chocolate soufflé mixture and
let it rise in the oven, then fall as it cools and firms.
Then you pile the soufflé shell with ice cream and nuts
and chill before serving. *Et voilà*—a children's birthday
party dessert that you'll be happy to eat too!

———

2 teaspoons unsalted butter, softened

2 tablespoons graham cracker crumbs

One 6-ounce package (1 cup) semisweet chocolate chips

4 large eggs, separated

Pinch of salt

¼ cup sugar

½ teaspoon vanilla extract

¼ teaspoon almond extract

1 pint chocolate or vanilla ice cream

¼ cup chopped walnuts

1. Heat the oven to 350 degrees. Generously grease a
9-inch pie plate with the butter. Coat the sides and
bottom of the pie plate with the crumbs; set aside.

2. Melt the chocolate in the top of a double boiler over
hot, not boiling, water (or melt them in the microwave). Remove from the heat.

3. Beat the egg whites with the salt in a mixer fitted
with a whisk (or in a large bowl with a hand mixer)
until foamy. Gradually beat in 2 tablespoons sugar, and
continue beating until the whites are stiff and glossy.

4. Beat the egg yolks with the remaining 2 tablespoons
sugar in another large bowl until thick and lemon colored. Stir in the vanilla, almond extract, and melted
chocolate until well blended. Carefully fold in the egg
whites. Fill the pie plate with the mixture.

5. Bake for 15 minutes. Set on a rack and cool for

about 2 hours. As the soufflé mixture cools, it will sink
in the center to form a shallow shell.

6. Fill the shell with spoonfuls of ice cream and sprinkle with the nuts. Freeze until firm, at least 1 hour.

SERVES 6 TO 8

JUNE 8, 1975: "FOOD: FOR HIS SWEET TOOTH," BY
JEAN HEWITT.

—1975

BLUEBERRY ICE CREAM

I love that when you taste this ice cream it's not immediately clear that it contains blueberries. The lemon
gives the ice cream a sharp, high pitch and a soft, buttery texture.

———

1 pint blueberries

¾ cup sugar

¾ cup water

¼ cup fresh lemon juice

1 cup heavy cream

1. Heat the blueberries in a heavy saucepan, stirring
occasionally, until they break down and yield their
juice, 10 to 15 minutes.

2. Meanwhile, dissolve the sugar in the water in
another pan and simmer over low heat for 10 to 15
minutes, or until you have a thin syrup. Cool.

3. Puree the blueberries in a food processor. Transfer
to a bowl and add the lemon juice. Mix in the cooled
syrup. Add the cream and mix well. Chill overnight.

4. The next day, pour the blueberry mixture into an
ice cream maker and freeze according to the manufacturer's instructions. Pack the ice cream in a container
and freeze until ready to serve.

MAKES ABOUT 1 QUART

AUGUST 7, 1988: "BLUEBERRIES: BEYOND JUST CREAM," BY
MOIRA HODGSON.

—1988

CLOVE GRANITA

This granita was meant to be an accompaniment to poached pears. And you should feel free to pursue that idea—a great recipe for Poached Pears in Brandy and Red Wine is on p. 832. But I loved this recipe so much on its own that I kept it that way. Clove's aroma is wonderful but monolithic; it needs to be surrounded with richer and brighter flavors, like the light brown sugar and balsamic vinegar here.

———

3 cups water
25 whole cloves
I cup packed light brown sugar
I tablespoon balsamic vinegar

1. Combine the water, cloves, and brown sugar in a saucepan and bring to a boil, stirring to dissolve the sugar. Reduce the heat and simmer for 15 minutes. Let cool.
2. Remove the cloves with a slotted spoon, and stir in the vinegar. Pour the mixture into a shallow metal pan and place in the freezer. Freeze, stirring with a fork every 20 minutes, until firm but not frozen solid, about 2 hours. Then cover and keep frozen until ready to serve. Stir up with a fork before spooning into bowls.

SERVES 4

SEPTEMBER 25, 1994: "PEARS, AN APOLOGIA," BY MOLLY O'NEILL.

—1994

BITTERSWEET CHOCOLATE SEMIFREDDO

———

¾ cup egg whites (from about 5 large eggs)
1½ cups sugar
Pinch of salt
10 ounces bittersweet chocolate, chopped, plus 2 ounces chocolate shavings for garnish
6 tablespoons unsalted butter
1¾ cups heavy cream
3 tablespoons dark rum
I cup unblanched whole hazelnuts

1. Combine the egg whites, sugar, and salt in the top of a double boiler, attach a candy thermometer to the pan, and cook, whisking continually, until the mixture registers 140 degrees. Transfer the mixture to the bowl of a mixer fitted with a whisk and whip on high speed until the meringue is completely cooled, 20 to 25 minutes.
2. Meanwhile, heat the oven to 400 degrees. Combine the chocolate and 4 tablespoons butter in the top of a double boiler set over barely simmering water and heat, stirring occasionally, until the chocolate melts and the mixture is smooth. Remove from the heat and set aside.
3. Whip the cream with the rum in a large bowl until soft peaks form. Cover and refrigerate.
4. Place the hazelnuts on a baking sheet and roast until the skins crack and the nuts are lightly browned, about 10 minutes. Rub the nuts in a towel to remove the skins. Transfer the nuts to a food processor, add the remaining 2 tablespoons butter, and process until a smooth paste is formed.
5. Line a 9-by-5-inch loaf pan with plastic wrap. Combine the melted chocolate and hazelnut paste in a large bowl. Fold in the whipped cream. Fold in one-quarter of the meringue, then fold in the remainder. Scrape the mixture into the prepared pan, cover with plastic wrap, and freeze overnight.
6. To serve, remove the top sheet of plastic wrap, invert the semifreddo onto a platter, and peel away the remaining plastic wrap. Slice into ½-inch-thick slices and garnish with chocolate shavings.

SERVES 16

COOKING NOTE
To make chocolate shavings, use a vegetable peeler to shave slivers of chocolate from a bar.

FEBRUARY 8, 1998: "FOOD: DESSERT IN VENICE," BY MOLLY O'NEILL. RECIPE ADAPTED FROM VINCENT SCOTTO, THE CHEF AT FRESCO IN NEW YORK CITY.

—1998

☞ LICORICE ICE CREAM

When I ordered this ice cream at the restaurant Gary Danko in San Francisco, I expected an anise-alcohol-infused ice cream. But I was in for a surprise. The flavor was not boozy. It did not tingle on my tongue. It did not taste of candy or of anisette. It was pure, clean, and herbal, with a base of cream to bend and soften any sharp edges.

When I asked Danko, the chef, how it was made, he laughed lightly, as if embarrassed that he was stumping me with something as simple as ice cream. The licorice flavor does not come from any of the usual suspects, but from licorice root—yes, the plant—bought in a health food store. And because there is no anisette, there is no alcohol. You won't miss it.

————

3 cups heavy cream

1½ cups whole milk

½ vanilla bean, split

½ cup chipped licorice root (see Cooking Notes)

10 large egg yolks

1 cup sugar

½ teaspoon kosher salt

1. Combine 1½ cups cream, the milk, and vanilla bean in a large saucepan, and bring almost to a boil over medium heat. Remove from the heat, stir in the licorice root, cover, and let steep for 20 to 25 minutes.
2. Combine the egg yolks, sugar, and salt in a heavy saucepan, and mix with a whisk until well combined. Strain the licorice and vanilla bean from the milk mixture and whisk the milk into the egg yolk mixture. Place over medium heat, and cook stirring constantly, until the mixture is lightly thickened and coats the back of the spoon. Remove from the heat and whisk in the remaining 1½ cups heavy cream. Strain, cool, and refrigerate overnight.
3. Pour the mixture into an ice cream maker and freeze according to the manufacturer's directions. Pack the ice cream in a container and freeze until ready to serve. Serve about 2 scoops a person.

MAKES ABOUT 1½ QUARTS

COOKING NOTES

Licorice root is sold in health food stores as licorice root bulk tea or chipped licorice; it resembles wood chips. Do not buy licorice root sticks, which are difficult to cut.

In the years since I first wrote about this ice cream, Yogi Tea (www.yogiproducts.com) has come out with licorice tea, in bags. You can use 3 licorice tea bags instead of the licorice root.

MARCH 22, 2000: "TEMPTATION: LICORICE TASTE, IN A PURE FORM," BY AMANDA HESSER. RECIPE ADAPTED FROM GARY DANKO, THE CHEF AND OWNER OF GARY DANKO IN SAN FRANCISCO.

—2000

☞ CANTALOUPE–STAR ANISE SORBET

A good sorbet should taste like an extraction of its main ingredients, and nothing else. It should be gutsier than ice cream, and purer; its flavors don't have to compete with aerated cream. Cantaloupe has a fragrant but thin flavor and needs something more robust to bolster it. Star anise does the trick, lingering on your palate long after the cantaloupe has swept past.

————

2 very ripe cantaloupes, peeled, seeded, and cut into large chunks

12 star anise

¾ cup sugar

1 cup water

¼ cup light corn syrup

1. Puree the cantaloupe until smooth in a food processor. This should yield at least 4 cups.
2. Combine 4 cups cantaloupe puree, the star anise, sugar, water, and corn syrup in a large saucepan, place over medium-low heat, and stir just until the sugar is dissolved. Remove from the heat and let infuse for at least 2 hours at room temperature.
3. Strain through a fine sieve, pressing out as much juice as possible. Pour into an ice cream maker and freeze according to the manufacturer's instructions. Pack the sorbet into a container and freeze until ready to serve.

JULY 19, 2000: "IMPROVING ON NATURE: THE SMALL MIR-ACLE OF SORBET," BY AMANDA HESSER. RECIPE ADAPTED FROM SONO IN NEW YORK CITY.

—2000

✐ BLACKBERRY ICE CREAM WITH CANDIED LEMON ZEST

————————

2 lemons
1½ cups sugar
1 cup water
1 quart blackberries
1 tablespoon créme de cassis
1½ cups heavy cream

1. With a vegetable peeler or paring knife, remove the zest from the lemons in long strips and finely chop. Squeeze ¼ cup juice from the lemons.
2. Combine ½ cup sugar and the water in a medium saucepan and bring to a boil, swirling the pan to dissolve the sugar. Add the lemon zest and boil over medium-high heat until the lemon zest is translucent and the syrup forms big, sticky bubbles that cover the surface, 20 to 30 minutes.
3. Strain the syrup into a bowl. Reserve the syrup for another use (for example, lemonade or sorbet). Let the zest cool and dry in the sieve.
4. Puree the blackberries in a food processor. Push the pulp through a sieve placed over a large bowl to remove the seeds. Add the remaining 1 cup sugar, cassis, lemon juice, and cream and whisk until blended. Stir in the lemon zest. Cover and refrigerate until thoroughly chilled, preferably overnight.
5. Pour the mixture into an ice cream maker and freeze according to the manufacturer's instructions. Transfer to a container and freeze until ready to serve.

APRIL 1, 2001: "THE GOOD LIFE: PORCH SONG," BY MARIALISA CALTA. RECIPE ADAPTED FROM *THE FEAR-RINGTON HOUSE COOKBOOK*, BY JENNY FITCH.

—2001

✐ MANGO ICE CREAM

This ice cream couldn't be easier to make—put it at the top of your recipe life list. After pureeing some sweet mangoes, you blend them with milk, a little sugar, and a lump of crème fraîche, and you are well on your way to bliss. The ice cream is sweet and tangy, with all the fullness of a custard ice cream.

————————

1¼ cups whole milk
⅔ cup sugar
3 medium to large ripe mangoes
1 cup crème fraîche

1. Pour the milk into a saucepan and bring to a boil over medium heat. Pour the milk into a bowl with a spout, and stir in the sugar until it is dissolved. Let cool.
2. Peel the mangoes and remove the flesh from the seeds. Process the flesh in a food processor until smooth.
3. Add about 2 cups mango puree (reserve the extra for another use) to the milk, along with the crème fraîche; stir until completely blended. Pour into an ice cream maker and freeze according to the manufacturer's instructions. Pack the ice cream into a container and freeze until ready to serve.

PERIOD DETAIL
By the turn of the twenty-first century, even the humblest foods were getting a thorough examination. As I wrote when I reviewed *Mediterranean Street Food*, by Anissa Helou, which contained this recipe, "There is a certain absurdity in a cookbook about Mediterranean street food. You imagine the author tracking down a vendor of fried-pork sandwiches, cornering him on the fine points of a recipe that has never been recorded, and then going home and writing a recipe so that it can be prepared in a nonstick pan for a family of four and served on a pretty ceramic platter." And yet I loved Helou's book and its recipes; other good street food books and restaurants would follow.

SEPTEMBER 18, 2002: "BY THE BOOK: GLOBAL STREET FARE IS ALIVE WITH FLAVOR," BY AMANDA HESSER. RECIPE ADAPTED FROM *MEDITERRANEAN STREET FOOD* BY ANISSA HELOU.

—2002

⌁ RED WINE ICE CREAM

Putting red wine in ice cream is like inserting the principal in a classroom. The cream perks up, the spices sing, and a sudden sense of peace and order takes over the ice cream.

————

2 (750-ml) bottles full-bodied red wine,
    like cabernet sauvignon
2 cinnamon sticks
1/2 teaspoon black peppercorns
2 cups whole milk
2 cups heavy cream
1 1/4 cups sugar
9 large egg yolks
1/4 teaspoon kosher salt
1/8 teaspoon vanilla extract

1. Pour the wine into a large pot and bring to a simmer. Add the cinnamon sticks and peppercorns and simmer until the wine is reduced to 1 cup (it should take about 1 hour).
2. Combine the milk, cream, and half of the sugar in a large saucepan, bring to a boil, and turn off the heat.
3. Whisk together the yolks and remaining sugar in a medium bowl. Temper the yolks by gradually whisking about 1 cup of the hot milk into the yolks, then add this to the pan with the remaining milk. Stir in the salt and vanilla. Whisk in the reduced wine. Set the pan over a bowl full of water and ice to cool.
4. Strain the chilled ice cream base through a fine-mesh strainer, then pour into an ice cream maker and freeze according to the manufacturer's instructions. Transfer the ice cream to a container and freeze for at least 2 hours before serving.

SERVES 8

NOVEMBER 7, 2004: "LAISSEZ-FARE," BY AMANDA HESSER. RECIPE ADAPTED FROM KAREN DEMASCO, THE PASTRY CHEF AT CRAFT, IN NEW YORK CITY.

—2004

⌁ SOUR CREAM ICE CREAM

Much of the flavor of industrial ice cream is masked under a suffocating layer of sweetness. Taste this invigorating version, and you'll see what I mean.

————

1/2 cup sugar
1/4 cup water
2 cups whole-milk sour cream
I cup nonfat yogurt
1/4 teaspoon salt
Fresh berries for serving (optional)

1. Combine the sugar and water in a small saucepan and heat over low heat, stirring, until the sugar has dissolved. Allow to cool, about 15 minutes.
2. Combine the sour cream, yogurt, and salt in a large bowl. Pour in the cooled syrup in a thin stream while whisking. When it is well incorporated, transfer to a container with a tight-fitting lid and refrigerate for at least 4 hours, or, preferably, overnight.
3. Pour the sour cream mixture into an ice cream maker and freeze according to the manufacturer's instructions. Transfer to a container with a tight-fitting lid and freeze for at least 2 hours before serving.
4. Remove the ice cream from the freezer 10 minutes before serving. Serve with fresh berries, if desired.

MAKES 1½ PINTS

AUGUST 10, 2005: "ICE DREAMS, CRYSTALLIZING," BY MATT LEE AND TED LEE.

—2005

⌁ PISTACHIO GELATO

Gelato, as Jill Santopietro, a *Times* writer, explained, "has less cream, less butterfat to bind to air molecules, and, therefore, less air than American ice cream. A small cup of gelato typically weighs the same as a cup of ice cream double its size."

This intense pistachio gelato, made with milk, is Sicilian in style. Varieties made with eggs or eggs and some cream can be found farther north. Santopietro warned readers to prepare themselves for a drab green dessert, "the correct color of authentic pistachio gelato."

For a nonfrozen pistachio dessert, see p. 806.

----

4 cups whole milk

2 tablespoons cornstarch

1/4 teaspoon kosher salt

I cup sugar

2 cups toasted unsalted pistachios, finely ground

1. Pour 3 tablespoons milk over the cornstarch in a small bowl and whisk until smooth.

2. Bring the remaining milk to just below a boil in a heavy saucepan over medium heat. Whisk in the salt, sugar, and cornstarch mixture and continue whisking until the sugar has dissolved, about 8 minutes. Transfer the pan to an ice bath, a bowl of ice and water, and cool, stirring occasionally. When cool, stir in the pistachios and refrigerate overnight.

3. Strain the mixture, pressing on the nuts to release all the liquid. Pour into an ice cream maker and freeze according to the manufacturer's instructions. Serve immediately, or pack the gelato into a container and freeze until ready to serve.

MAKES I QUART

NOVEMBER 6, 2005: "THE DISH: MOLTO PISTACHIO," BY JILL SANTOPIETRO.

—2005

☞ GRAPEFRUIT GRANITA

You go to New York's 4-star fixture Masa for the sushi, not the fruit, but after a twelve-course raw-fish extravaganza there one afternoon, the recipe I wanted to take home with me was the one for this grapefruit granita—a mash-up that's gentle on the Sauternes and sings with yuzu, a brightly aromatic citrus fruit. The icy shards mingle with tender sections of grapefruit.

----

2 cups fresh red or pink grapefruit juice

(from about 3 grapefruits), strained

I cup Sauternes or Champagne

1 1/2 teaspoons sugar, or to taste

I large red or pink grapefruit

I tablespoon Grand Marnier

Grated zest of I yuzu or 2 limes

1. Combine the juice and Sauternes in a medium bowl. Add the sugar and stir until dissolved. Pour into an 8-by-10-inch baking pan. Place in the freezer for several hours, or until completely frozen.

2. Meanwhile, peel and segment the grapefruit, discarding the membrane (see p. 809 for instructions). Cut each segment into quarters.

3. Scrape the granita with a thin-tined fork to create loose crystals. Transfer to a large airtight container. Stir in the grapefruit segments. Freeze again.

4. To serve, divide the granita among 6 dessert bowls. Pour 1/2 teaspoon Grand Marnier over each and sprinkle with the zest.

SERVES 6

COOKING NOTE

Yuzu can be found in Asian grocery stores; you may want to call ahead.

NOVEMBER 27, 2005: "FOOD: EAT, MEMORY: THE IDEOLOGY OF TASTE," BY ROY BLOUNT JR. RECIPE ADAPTED FROM MASA IN NEW YORK CITY.

—2005

☞ ALMOND GRANITA

With granita, there is no need for a machine, just a spoon, a freezer, and some elbow grease for breaking the ice sheets into fine crystals. At A Voce, in New York, where the almond granita was created, it's served cushioned between crackly layers of crushed amaretti.

----

14 ounces almond paste, broken into pieces

4 cups water

2 1/4 cups whole milk

Pinch of ground cinnamon

About 20 amaretti cookies, crushed into

small pieces and crumbs

1. Combine the almond paste, water, and milk in a large saucepan. Set over medium heat; as it warms, use the back of a spoon or a potato masher to crush

and dissolve the paste. When the mixture begins to steam—before it boils—take it off the heat.

2. Let the mixture cool slightly, then carefully whiz with an immersion blender until the paste is fully incorporated (or pour into a regular blender and blend well). Pour into a cheesecloth-lined sieve set over a bowl. Let drain completely, without pressing on the solids.

3. When the milk mixture is cool, add the cinnamon. Pour into a shallow baking pan and freeze. Check after about 30 minutes; when it begins to get icy, use the back of a large spoon to press down on the mixture and break it into pieces. Repeat several times over the next 2 hours, until the granita is fully frozen but broken into shards.

4. To serve, place 1½ tablespoons crushed amaretti cookies in the bottom of each glass, followed by a serving of granita, and top with 2 more tablespoons crushed cookies.

SERVES 8

JULY 16, 2006: "THE ARSENAL," BY AMANDA HESSER. RECIPE ADAPTED FROM A VOCE IN NEW YORK CITY.

—2006

STRAWBERRY SORBET

This strawberry sorbet comes from Ruth Rogers and the late Rose Gray, the owners of the River Café in London. It's as brilliant as it is unconventional: a whole lemon (rind and all) is ground up, sweetened with crushed strawberries, and then enlivened with some fresh lemon juice. The resulting sorbet is wildly bright and jungly. (If you like its flavor, then make the Raspberry Granita on p. 719 next.)

———

1 lemon, halved, seeded, and roughly chopped
2 cups sugar
2 pounds strawberries, washed and hulled
Juice of 1 to 2 lemons

1. Place the chopped lemon and sugar in a food processor and pulse until combined. Transfer to a bowl.

2. Puree the strawberries in the food processor, and add to the lemon mixture, along with the juice of 1 lemon. Taste and add more juice as desired. The lemon flavor should be intense but should not overpower the strawberries.

3. Pour the mixture into an ice cream maker and freeze according to the manufacturer's instructions. Pack into a container and freeze until ready to serve.

MAKES 1½ QUARTS

JULY 16, 2006: "THE ARSENAL" BY AMANDA HESSER. RECIPE ADAPTED FROM *LONDON RIVER CAFÉ COOK BOOK*, BY RUTH ROGERS AND ROSE GRAY.

—2006

CHERRY SPUMONI

Denise Landis, whose ice cream recipe this is, is the unsung hero of the Dining section. Every week since 1989, the *Times* food writers and editors have sent her batches of recipes—often with panicked pleas to have them back in twenty-four hours—and she takes these scribblings and tests them and shapes them into something that you and I could make for dinner.

Landis is a writer too, and for a few years, she had a *Times* column called "Test Kitchen," for which she'd test-drive cookware and appliances. This recipe comes from a column on ice cream makers. (She preferred the Salton Big Chill ice cream maker.) Ordering the cherry concentrate is worth it—the resulting ice cream has depth and waves of rich cherry flavor.

———

¾ cup whole milk
¾ cup sugar
⅛ teaspoon salt
¾ cup half-and-half
1½ cups heavy cream
1 teaspoon vanilla extract
1 teaspoon almond extract
3 tablespoons tart cherry concentrate
½ cup packed frozen pitted tart (sour) or sweet cherries, defrosted, or canned pitted tart or sweet cherries (do not use fresh fruit)
6 tablespoons slivered or sliced blanched almonds
6 tablespoons chopped semisweet chocolate or chocolate chips

1. Place the milk in a small heavy saucepan and heat over medium heat until bubbles just begin to form

around the edges of the pan. Remove from the heat, add the sugar and salt, and stir until dissolved. Add the half-and-half, heavy cream, vanilla, almond extract, and cherry concentrate and mix well. Transfer to a bowl and set in an ice water bath until cool, about 10 minutes.

2. Coarsely chop the cherries, and press them between paper towels to remove excess liquid. Add to the chilled milk mixture.

3. Pour the mixture into an ice cream maker and begin freezing according to the manufacturer's instructions. When the ice cream has begun to thicken, after about 10 minutes, add the almonds and chopped chocolate. Continue freezing until done. Pack into a container and freeze until ready to serve.

MAKES 1½ QUARTS

COOKING NOTE
Tart cherry concentrate is available from www.tartissmart.com; (509)488-1049.

AUGUST 16, 2006: "TEST KITCHEN: CHURNING OUT ICE CREAM TILL THE SUNDAE AFTER NEXT," BY DENISE LANDIS.
—2006

☞ SALTED CARAMEL ICE CREAM

This ice cream comes from Nicole Kaplan, one of the most talented pastry chefs in New York City. Kaplan's style is understated. She never grasps for attention with cascading garnishes or esoteric flavors, she just takes flavors we all love and makes them better than we thought possible. See her Two-Day Madeleines with Brown Butter on p. 701.

If you can't get enough of salt and caramel, try the Salted Butter Caramels on p. 705.

————

1¼ cups sugar
2 teaspoons light corn syrup
2 cups heavy cream, preferably organic
2 cups whole milk
10 large egg yolks
½ teaspoon fleur de sel, plus more for serving

1. Place ¾ cup sugar and the corn syrup in a large heavy saucepan and cook over medium-high heat—do not stir—to a dark caramel, swirling as it begins to brown to distribute the sugar. Carefully pour in the cream, then slowly add the milk. The caramel will harden; don't panic. Bring to a boil, then reduce the heat and simmer, stirring, just until the caramel has dissolved. Remove from the heat.

2. Whisk together the remaining ½ cup sugar, egg yolks, and fleur de sel in a large bowl. Whisk a little caramel cream into the egg mixture to temper it, then pour the egg mixture into the remaining caramel cream and mix. Strain through a fine-mesh sieve into a bowl. Refrigerate until thoroughly chilled, or, preferably, overnight.

3. Pour the mixture into an ice cream maker and freeze according to the manufacturer's instructions. Pack the ice cream in a container and freeze until ready to serve.

4. Serve the ice cream sprinkled with fleur de sel.

MAKES ABOUT 1 QUART

COOKING NOTE
This makes a mean milk shake—just combine with whole milk in a blender and whiz away—my kids and I have even made it with great success in their toy blender.

OCTOBER 8, 2006: "THE WAY WE EAT: SALT WITH A DEADLY WEAPON," BY CHRISTINE MUHLKE. RECIPE ADAPTED FROM NICOLE KAPLAN, THE PASTRY CHEF AT ELEVEN MADISON PARK, NEW YORK.
—2006

☞ ALMOND AND BUTTERMILK SORBET

————

⅓ cup fresh lemon juice
1¼ cups sugar
¼ cup light corn syrup
½ cup unblanched whole almonds
2 cups buttermilk, shaken to blend
½ teaspoon almond extract

1. Combine the lemon juice, 1 cup sugar, and the corn syrup in a small saucepan, place over medium-low heat, and simmer until the sugar is dissolved. Cool to room temperature.

2. Meanwhile, place the almonds in a small dry skillet over medium heat. Shake until the nuts are fragrant and evenly toasted, about 2 minutes. Transfer to a plate to cool.

3. Put the almonds and the remaining ¼ cup sugar in a food processor or blender and process to a powder; set aside.

4. Stir the cooled lemon syrup, buttermilk, and almond extract together in a bowl. Refrigerate until well chilled.

5. Transfer the buttermilk mixture to an ice cream maker and freeze according to the manufacturer's instructions. Pack the sorbet into a container and freeze until ready to serve.

6. Serve the sorbet in small bowls, with the almond and sugar topping.

MAKES ABOUT I QUART

JUNE 6, 2007: "THE MINIMALIST; IN PARIS, BRINGING VEGETABLES OUT TO PLAY," BY MARK BITTMAN. RECIPE ADAPTED FROM *VEGETABLE HARVEST*, BY PATRICIA WELLS.

—2007

VANILLA PLUM ICE

I vanilla bean
¼ cup plus 3 tablespoons sugar
½ cup dry white wine
¼ cup water
1½ pounds ripe plums, pitted and chopped
Salt
Small sprigs mint for garnish

1. Split the vanilla bean lengthwise, scrape out the seeds, and place the bean and seeds in a small saucepan. Add the sugar, white wine, and water and bring to a boil, stirring constantly until the sugar dissolves. Steep over low heat for 5 minutes, then cool completely; remove the vanilla bean.

2. Combine the plums, cooled syrup, and a dash of salt in a blender and puree. Strain through a fine-mesh sieve set over a baking dish.

3. Put the mixture in the freezer and scrape with a fork every 15 to 20 minutes, as it chills, until the texture is light and fluffy. Serve in small bowls, garnished with mint.

SERVES 8

AUGUST 26, 2007: "THE INDUSTRY: CHILL SEEKERS," BY MATT LEE AND TED LEE.

—2007

TANGERINE SHERBET

Bright and peppy tangerine meets languorous cream and it's love at first sight.

½ teaspoon powdered gelatin
About 2 teaspoons water
2¼ pounds tangerines
½ cup sugar
¼ teaspoon salt
½ cup very cold heavy cream

1. Drop the gelatin and water into a small saucepan and turn your back on it. Strip the zest from 2 tangerines with a Microplane or a zester, or, if you aren't that kind of person, a regular potato peeler. Toss the zest into a bowl (if you used a potato peeler, give it a rough chop first), and squeeze in enough juice from the tangerines, even the naked ones, to make 1½ cups, removing any seeds.

2. Remembering the saucepan, put a little heat under it until the gelatin starts to look smooth, not grainy. Stir in the sugar, salt, and juice and zest and turn up the heat, letting it come to something like the temperature of your finger. Stir to make sure the sugar is dissolved, then chill in the refrigerator.

3. When the juice mixture is cold, strain out the zest and toss the juice into the tank of your ice cream maker, along with the cream (which should be cold too). Do whatever you usually do with your ice cream maker until you have a creamy sherbet. With luck, you will have an extra hour to chill the sherbet before serving it. Tiny spoons will make it last longer, but not much longer. You might think about making twice as much.

MAKES 3 TO 4 CUPS

JANUARY 4, 2009: "COOKING WITH DEXTER: ORANGE GENIUS" BY PETE WELLS. RECIPE ADAPTED, WITH SIGNIFICANT LIBERTIES, FROM *CHEZ PANISSE FRUIT*, BY ALICE WATERS AND THE COOKS OF CHEZ PANISSE.

—2009

- Tipsy cake, sometimes called tipsy squire, a brandy-soaked sponge cake topped with almond custard sauce, is popular.

—1870s—

- Silver cake (without yolks) and gold cake (with yolks).

- Angel Food Cake (p. 742), back when it was enjoyed for its miraculous texture rather than for being low-fat.

—1880—

- Wedding cakes are dark spice cakes interlaced with dried fruit (see p. 743).

—1890s—

- Devil's food cakes (p. 744) infiltrate angel food turf.

—1940s—

- Jane Nickerson predicts that cheesecakes will become as popular as brownies, and she is right.

- Ice boxes are new(ish), so it's time to make ice-box cake (p. 746)!

—1948—

- Harry Rosen opens Junior's in Brooklyn. The restaurant will become famous for its cheesecake (p. 771).

—1950—

- *Times* food writers promote European multi-layered cakes made with pancakes or crepes, such as Baumkuchentorte (p. 747) and Laggtarta (p. 750).

—1960s—

- If you aren't eating Black Forest cake (p. 754), you're settling into carrot cake with cream cheese icing.

—1970s—

- Bakers decide to call cakes "tortes," and "decadent" and "chocolate" become inseparable.

—1980s—

- Marian Burros publishes the first version of Purple Plum Torte (p. 763), the most popular recipe ever from the *Times*. The recipe will run in various forms eleven more times.

—1983—

- Rose Levy Beranbaum writes *The Cake Bible*. People feel bad about their now-dowdy-seeming homespun cakes.

—1988—

- The first flourless chocolate cake recipe appeared in the *Times* in 1969 (p. 752), but the cake has its moment in this decade.

—1990s—

- Sylvia Weinstock, a cake baker who wears remarkably large glasses, starts making elaborate wedding cakes that bridezillas all over New York City must have.

- Magnolia Bakery opens in Manhattan's Greenwich Village, selling OK cupcakes. They unwittingly start a revolution.

—1996—

- Done with baroque chocolate cakes, people return to simple pour-and-stir batters and straightforward ganache.

—2000s—

- Food Network premieres *Ace of Cakes*, a show about a cake baker.

—2006—

17

CAKES

RECIPES BY CATEGORY

✑ SOUR-MILK CAKE

Unassuming yet wickedly good, this sour-milk cake has a thin, crisp top and a gauzy bottom. It's best eaten the day you bake it, but it will keep for a day or two.

The original recipe instructed you to "spice to taste." I added cinnamon and nutmeg, which were lovely if perhaps a little tame. Feel free to get crazy with your spice rack—and send me the results! (You can find me on Twitter and Facebook.)

Sour-milk cakes showed up in the latter half of the nineteenth century because baking soda—then a fairly new leavening—needs an acid to react with and create the carbon dioxide bubbles that lift the cake. As the cake bakes, the center of the batter bubbles and froths in a mildly alarming way. Fear not: the cake settles toward the end of baking.

———

1/2 cup raisins, chopped

2 cups plus 1 teaspoon all-purpose flour

1 teaspoon baking soda

Pinch of salt

3/4 teaspoon ground cinnamon

1/4 teaspoon freshly grated nutmeg

1 teaspoon vinegar (any kind will work)

1 cup whole milk

8 tablespoons (1 stick) unsalted butter, softened

1 cup sugar

1 large egg

1. Heat the oven to 350 degrees. Butter an 8-inch round cake pan and line the bottom with parchment. Toss the raisins with 1 teaspoon flour. Mix the remaining 2 cups flour with the baking soda, salt, cinnamon, and nutmeg. Stir the vinegar into the milk in a small bowl.

2. In a mixer fitted with a paddle (or in a large bowl with a hand mixer), beat the butter and sugar until very light and fluffy. Add the egg and blend. Alternately add the milk and flour mixture in 2 additions, each ending with the flour. Fold in the raisins.

3. Pour the batter into the prepared pan and level the top. Bake until a toothpick inserted in the center comes out clean, 35 to 40 minutes. Let cool for 10 minutes on a rack, then unmold and finish cooling on a rack.

SERVES 6 TO 8

FEBRUARY 27, 1876: "RECEIPTS FROM CORRESPONDENTS." RECIPE SIGNED A.P.

—1876

✑ ALMOND CUSTARD CAKE

Find a flower or berries to lay on top of this cake, which compensates for its rather ragged look with the fragrance of lemon, butter, and almonds. As the cake's icing is more of a nut paste, you could also swirl on a top layer of whipped cream, if looks are your thing.

———

For the Cake

1/2 pound (2 sticks) unsalted butter, softened

2 cups sugar

5 large eggs

1 cup whole milk

Grated zest of 2 lemons

3 1/4 cups plus 3 tablespoons all-purpose flour

2 teaspoons baking powder

For the Custard

1 cup sour cream

3/4 cup sugar

3 cups (about 1 pound) unblanched whole almonds, finely chopped

1 teaspoon vanilla extract

1. To make the cake, heat the oven to 350 degrees. Butter three 9-inch round cake pans. Line the bottoms with parchment, and flour the sides of the pans. In a mixer fitted with a paddle (or in a bowl with a hand mixer, or enthusiastically by hand), beat the butter and sugar until very light. Beat in the eggs one at a time. Add the milk and lemon zest and blend until smooth. Combine the flour and baking powder, and fold into the batter just until smooth.

2. Divide the batter evenly among the 3 pans. Bake until a toothpick inserted in the center of the cakes comes out clean, 25 to 30 minutes. Let the cakes cool in their pans on a rack, then unmold.

3. When the cakes are cool, prepare the custard: Beat together the sour cream and sugar in a bowl until

the sugar is fully dissolved. Fold in the almonds and vanilla.

4. Spread one-third of the custard over one cake layer. Top with another layer, spread it with custard, and top with the third layer. Spread the remaining custard on the top layer. Find a pretty flower to garnish the cake.

SERVES 12

COOKING NOTE

Warning: you need 3 cake pans to make this! And why deprive yourself of 3-layer cakes? Go out and buy those pans once and for all.

MAY 6, 1877: "RECEIPTS FOR THE TABLE." RECIPE SIGNED AUNT ADDIE.

—1877

↩ ANGEL FOOD CAKE

A 1947 recipe for angel food cake noted that "frosting is neither customary nor necessary" for the cake. I leave it up to you. A mound of whipped cream topped with berries never hurt anyone.

———

1 cup cake flour
1 teaspoon baking powder
1¼ cups sugar
10 large egg whites
Pinch of salt
1 teaspoon almond extract

1. Heat the oven to 350 degrees. Sift together the flour, baking powder, and ½ cup plus 2 tablespoons sugar 3 times.
2. In a mixer fitted with a whisk (or in a bowl with a hand mixer), beat the egg whites with the salt until foamy. Add the remaining ½ cup plus 2 tablespoons sugar a few tablespoons at a time, and continue beating until the whites hold soft peaks. Fold in half of the dry ingredients until smooth; repeat with the remaining flour. Fold in the almond extract.
3. Scrape the batter into an ungreased 10-inch tube pan. Bake until a cake tester inserted in the center of the cake comes out clean, 20 to 30 minutes. Remove the cake from the oven and invert the pan; if it has

feet, let the pan rest on the feet. If not, set the tube on top of an empty wine bottle. Let the cake cool completely upside down.

4. To remove the cake from the pan, run a long thin knife around the sides and center tube to loosen the cake. Invert onto a cake plate.

SERVES 10

JULY 25, 1880: "RECEIPTS." RECIPE SIGNED A.

—1880

↩ FILBERT TORTE

The original recipe for this hazelnut (filbert) layer cake was written as a single sentence and ended with "ice with maraschino icing"—as if we all had one ready-mixed in the icehouse. It was one of many old recipes that I was tempted to toss for their lack of detail, but, as was often the case, a little re-engineering paid off. This is one of my favorite cakes in the book. It's a little austere, being more woodsy and boozy than sweet.

For a recipe with similar structure—airy layers separated by icing—see Bosiljka Marich's Serbian Torte on p. 751.

———

For the Cake
1¾ cups (about 7 ounces) unblanched hazelnuts
2 teaspoons orange-flower water
2¼ cups confectioners' sugar
8 large eggs, separated
½ cup all-purpose flour

½ cup apricot or peach jam
1 tablespoon water

For the Icing
3 large egg whites
¾ cup sugar
⅓ cup light corn syrup
⅛ teaspoon salt
1 tablespoon maraschino liqueur or kirsch

1. To make the cake, heat the oven to 350 degrees. Butter three 9-inch round cake pans. Line the bottoms with parchment and butter the parchment. Grind the

hazelnuts as fine as possible in a food processor. Add the orange-flower water and pulse a few times.

2. Transfer the nuts to a large bowl and stir in the sugar. Fold in the egg yolks, and then the flour.

3. Beat the whites in a mixer fitted with a whisk (or in a bowl with a hand mixer) until they hold soft peaks, then fold them into the nut mixture. Divide the batter among the cake pans and spread it evenly.

4. Bake until the cakes are lightly browned on top and spring back when touched, about 20 minutes. Let cool on a rack, then unmold.

5. Warm the jam with the water in a small saucepan or in the microwave, stirring until smooth. Place 1 cake layer on a cake plate. Brush generously with a third of the jam. Repeat with the remaining layers, stacking them as you go.

6. To prepare the icing, combine the egg whites, sugar, corn syrup, and salt in the top of a large double boiler over medium heat. Using a hand mixer, beat the mixture until the meringue forms dense, shiny peaks. Remove from the heat and fold in the liqueur. Let cool, then ice the cake. (You will have ½ to 1 cup leftover icing, for which I'm sure you will find another use.)

SERVES 8

COOKING NOTES

The only sane way to prepare the icing is with an electric hand mixer. If you don't have one—and I don't—you will have to whisk the whites in a double boiler over simmering water for 12 to 15 minutes. Your arms don't want to do this.

Maraschino liqueur's flavor is a cross between grappa and kirsch, with a little more sweetness. It has a peppery edge and a smattering of floral cherry. It's worth seeking out at better liquor stores. You can use the rest of the bottle for making batches of the Improved Holland Gin Cocktail on p. 39 and the Frozen Meringue Velvet on p. 723.

Before you start fantasizing about eating this, make sure you have three 9-inch cake pans at your disposal. If not, call your neighbor or head to the store.

Orange-flower water is available in Middle Eastern markets and online at www.amazon.com.

JANUARY 15, 1882: "RECEIPTS." RECIPE BY ADOLPHE WURTH, THE CHEF AT DELMONICO, 26TH STREET SOCIÉTÉ CULINAIRE. RECIPE FOR THE MARASCHINO ICING ADAPTED FROM *BIRTHDAY CAKES*, BY KATHRYN KLEINMAN.

—1882

∽ WEDDING CAKE, THE DELMONICO RECEIPT

Wedding cakes have come a long way from the Roman days, when the cakes were broken over the bride's head (Congratulations! Bonk!). Today's elegant lemon-berry-fondant affairs would flop more than break, and they'd really mess up the bride's hairdo. The *Times* published at least half a dozen wedding cake recipes in the nineteenth century, none of which you'd ever find at a modern wedding. They were essentially heavily spiced one-layer fruitcakes. When an Englishwoman wrote to the *Times* about how she missed the tiered wedding cakes back home, she caused a minor kerfuffle. A New York reader responded by sending in not one but two wedding cake recipes, one from Delmonico's, a top restaurant of the period, and one from a Southern plantation, along with an indignant riposte: "English cooks may make their wedding cake in tiers; that is a matter of taste and custom; but I know that no wedding cake of which I have ever eaten from a London baker, and I have tasted a good many of them in a considerable residence over there, excels those which have been made here in New York in private kitchens." Unsurprisingly, both recipes the reader sent in were heavily spiced one-layer fruitcakes.

And yet, the whole episode made no sense, as dark cakes (often called groom's cakes) and fruitcakes (bride's cakes) were common at English weddings. This British tradition of fruitcakes—"symbols of fertility and prosperity," according to Carol Wilson, who wrote about wedding cakes for *Gastronomica* in 2005—traveled here on the merchant routes to America.

This recipe from Delmonico's is like a cross between panforte (Italy's chewy and heavily spiced fruit disk) and fruitcake. There's barely any batter, just enough to bind the fruit. I love it in thin slivers carved off the round and served with milky sweetened Earl Grey tea.

4½ cups (about 1½ pounds) raisins, chopped

3 cups dried currants

½ pound (about 2 cups) candied citron, finely chopped

½ pound (about 1½ cups) dried figs, finely chopped

1½ cups almonds, chopped

2 cups all-purpose flour

2 tablespoons ground cinnamon

1 tablespoon ground mace

1 tablespoon ground cloves

½ pound (2 sticks) unsalted butter, softened

One 1-pound box dark brown sugar

½ cup unsulphured molasses

5 large eggs

¼ cup brandy

¼ cup dry sherry

1. Heat the oven to 325 degrees. Butter two 9-inch springform pans and line the bottoms with parchment. Butter the parchment and flour the pans. Combine the raisins, currants, citron, figs, and almonds in a large bowl.

2. Place ¾ cup flour in a small saucepan and cook over medium-low heat, stirring often, until it begins to smell toasted, then pour over the fruit and toss to coat. Combine the remaining 1¼ cups flour with the cinnamon, mace, and cloves in another bowl.

3. In a mixer fitted with a paddle (or in a large bowl with a hand mixer), beat the butter with the brown sugar and molasses. Beat in the eggs one at a time, then beat in the brandy and sherry. Gradually blend in the flour just until incorporated. Pour the batter over the fruit and fold until completely blended.

4. Divide the batter between the prepared pans and spread it to the edges, smoothing the tops. Bake until a toothpick inserted in the center comes out clean, about 1 hour and 10 minutes. Let cool on racks for 10 minutes, then remove the cakes from the pans and let cool completely on the racks.

MAKES TWO 9-INCH CAKES, EACH SERVING 12

COOKING NOTES

This makes 2 cakes. Both are better the second day, once they've had time for the flavors to harmonize. I'd recommend brushing the cakes with brandy, wrapping them in plastic wrap, and letting them sit for a day. They can also be wrapped and frozen.

One unusual step involves toasting the flour, which gives it a nutty flavor—it's also a technique used with rice flour in Asian cooking (see the Pork-and-Toasted-Rice-Powder Spring Rolls on p. 74).

If you have sweet rather than dry sherry in the house, go ahead and use it. The dry is not worth a trip to the store.

FEBRUARY 5, 1893: "TWO FAMOUS RECEIPTS: HOW TO MAKE WEDDING CAKE IN THE NORTH AND IN THE SOUTH."

—1893

☞ DEVIL'S FOOD CAKE

Devil's food cake is essentially an angel food cake made less virtuous with the addition of sinful chocolate, butter, and egg yolks. It's fun to make by hand because you count your strokes as you beat the mixture: 50 after adding each portion of sugar and 50 again after folding in the rest of the ingredients. This kind of incidental exercise is why people didn't use to go to the gym. (Whenever people ask my mother, a lifelong size 4, what her secret is, she always says, "I clean my house, I cook, and I rake the yard." And she always bakes from scratch, with her bowl and handy wooden spoon.)

———

For the Cake

2 cups sifted cake flour

1 teaspoon baking soda

¼ teaspoon salt

8 tablespoons (1 stick) unsalted butter or
    ½ cup vegetable shortening

1¼ cups granulated sugar or packed brown sugar

3 large egg yolks, beaten until very thick and
    lemon colored

2 to 3 ounces unsweetened chocolate, melted

1 cup whole milk

1 teaspoon vanilla extract

For the Frosting

¾ pound cream cheese, at room temperature

8 tablespoons (1 stick) unsalted butter, softened

3 tablespoons heavy cream

Grated zest of 1 lemon

3 tablespoons fresh lemon juice

2 cups confectioners' sugar, sifted

1. To make the cake, heat the oven to 350 degrees. Grease two 3-inch-deep 9-inch round cake pans or three 8-inch pans. Sift the flour, baking soda, and salt together twice.

2. Beat the butter in a large bowl with a wooden spoon until smooth and pliable. Gradually add the sugar, in 4 to 6 additions: begin with 2 tablespoons and increase somewhat; after each addition, beat 50 strokes. When all the sugar has been added, scrape down the sides of the bowl and spoon. Beat 50 strokes more.

3. Add the eggs yolks and beat in thoroughly. Beat in the melted chocolate. Add about one-quarter of the

flour mixture and stir, not beat, until just blended, no more. Then add one-third of the milk, and stir, not beat, until blended. Repeat until all the flour mixture and milk are added. Add the vanilla. Finally, scrape down the bowl and spoon and stir the mixture a final 50 strokes.

4. Pour the batter into the prepared pans. Bake until a toothpick inserted in the center comes out clean and dry, about 20 minutes (if using 3 pans, start checking after 12 minutes). Let cool in the pans on a rack for 5 minutes, then turn out onto racks and turn right side up to cool completely.

5. To make the frosting, combine the cream cheese and butter in a mixer fitted with a paddle (or mix in a bowl, with a hand mixer) and beat until light and fluffy, about 2 minutes. Add the cream, lemon zest, and juice and blend well, scraping down the sides of the bowl as needed. Add the sugar in 3 stages, blending well after each addition. If the frosting is too loose, chill in the refrigerator for 15 minutes before frosting the cake.

6. To frost the cake, slice 1 cake layer on a cake plate. Cover the top with a generous layer of frosting. Lay the second layer on top, then frost the top and sides.

SERVES 10

COOKING NOTES

The recipe didn't come with a frosting. For those who don't already have a favorite, I've adapted a cream cheese frosting from Carole Bloom's *The Essential Baker* (cutting out the vanilla, reducing the sugar to 2 cups, and adding 3 tablespoons lemon juice and the zest of 1 lemon).

Various ingredient alternatives were offered. I used butter, regular sugar, and 3 ounces of chocolate, and my cake turned out swell. Also, I used two 9-inch cake pans with removable bases (they make it much easier to get the cake out!).

SEPTEMBER 29, 1947: "NEWS OF FOOD: TIPS OFFERED ON PREPARATION OF CAKES—GOOD SUPPLY OF SUGAR IS SPUR TO BAKING," BY JANE NICKERSON.

—1947

∽ MOLASSES CUP CAKES WITH LEMON ICING

These might not be quite as popular with the kids as chocolate ones loaded up with jimmies, but you can tell them these are more subtle, and I'm sure they'll appreciate that.

_____

For the Cupcakes
2 cups sifted all-purpose flour
2 teaspoons baking powder
1/2 teaspoon baking soda
1 1/2 teaspoons ground cinnamon
1/4 teaspoon salt
1/2 cup vegetable shortening
1/2 cup sugar
1/2 cup unsulphured molasses
1 large egg
1/2 cup whole milk
Grated zest of 1 lemon

For the Icing
6 tablespoons unsalted butter, softened
2 1/4 cups confectioners' sugar, sifted
About 2 teaspoons whole milk
    or heavy cream
3/4 teaspoon lemon extract

1. To make the cupcakes, heat the oven to 350 degrees. Line 12 cupcake molds with cupcake papers. Sift together the flour, baking powder, baking soda, cinnamon, and salt.

2. Melt the shortening in a small pan over low heat (or in a bowl in the microwave); transfer to a bowl and let cool.

3. Add the sugar, molasses, and egg to the shortening; beat well. Add the milk in 2 additions, alternating with the flour mixture. Add the lemon zest. Pour the batter into the cupcake papers, filling them three-quarters full.

4. Bake until a toothpick inserted in the center of a cupcake comes out clean, about 16 minutes. Cool the cupcakes in the pan for 10 minutes, then turn out onto a rack to cool.

5. To make the icing, in a mixer fitted with a whisk (or in a bowl with a hand mixer) beat the butter until light and fluffy. Gradually add the sugar, beating well.

Add enough milk to make the mixture the right consistency for spreading. Beat in the lemon extract.

6. When the cupcakes are cool, spread the tops with the icing.

MAKES 12 CUPCAKES

APRIL 20, 1948: "NEWS OF FOOD: VARIETY OF NEWER USES FOR MOLASSES DESCRIBED IN FREE BOOKLET, WITH PICTURES," BY JANE NICKERSON. RECIPE ADAPTED FROM *BRER RABBIT'S NEW ORLEANS MOLASSES RECIPES*.

—1948

↶ CHOCOLATE ICE-BOX "CAKE"

This cake was surely served at countless birthday parties in your youth. And if it wasn't, here's your chance to catch up on forgone pleasures—this one a "cake" made of store-bought chocolate wafers and whipped cream. After 3 hours of chilling, the wafers soften on the edges but still have a nice little crunch in the middle.

————

1¼ cups heavy cream
¼ cup sugar
¾ teaspoon vanilla extract
24 chocolate wafer cookies

1. Whip the cream with the sugar until it holds stiff peaks. Fold in the vanilla. Spread each of the wafer cookies with ¼ inch of whipped cream, piling one on top of the other. Press gently together. (I did this in stacks of 8 so it was manageable.) Lay the stacks on their sides on a serving platter, to make one long log. Frost the top and sides with the remaining whipped cream. Refrigerate for 3 hours.

2. Slice the "cake" diagonally to serve.

SERVES 6

JULY 8, 1948: "NEWS OF FOOD: CANNED MUSHROOM PRODUCT SEEMS TO PRESERVE FLAVOR OF FRESH FUNGUS," BY JANE NICKERSON.

—1948

↶ ALLEGRETTI CHIFFON CAKE

If a recipe appeared in the *New York Times* but was not generated by the paper's staff, does it qualify for inclusion? I couldn't resist this recipe, recommended by a reader, that came from an advertisement for Wesson oil. "[T]he talk of the party! Extra-light! Extra-luscious!" the ad exclaims. It's like angel food cake only richer, the ad promised. In fact, that's just about right. The cake is flecked with chocolate and scented with vanilla and orange zest.

————

For the Cake
1 cup plus 2 tablespoons cake flour
¾ cup plus 2 tablespoons sugar
1½ teaspoons baking powder
½ teaspoon salt
¼ cup vegetable oil
2 large egg yolks
6 tablespoons cold water
1 teaspoon vanilla extract

1½ tablespoons grated orange zest
½ cup egg whites (from about 4 eggs)
¼ teaspoon cream of tartar
1½ ounces bittersweet chocolate, grated

For the Icing
3 tablespoons vegetable shortening or
    unsalted butter, softened
1 large egg yolk
2 tablespoons heavy cream, or as needed
2 cups sifted confectioners' sugar
1 teaspoon vanilla extract

1½ ounces bittersweet chocolate
¼ teaspoon vegetable oil

1. To make the cake, heat the oven to 325 degrees. Butter a 9-by-5-inch loaf pan and line the bottom with parchment paper. Sift together the flour, sugar, baking powder, and salt into a large bowl. Make a well in the center and add the oil, egg yolks, water, vanilla, and orange zest. Beat with a wooden spoon until smooth.

2. In a mixer fitted with a whisk (or in a bowl with a hand mixer), beat the egg whites with the cream of tartar until they hold stiff peaks. Fold in the flour

mixture just until blended. Add the grated chocolate and fold again, just a few times. Pour the batter into the loaf pan.

3. Bake until the top springs back when lightly touched, 50 to 55 minutes. Turn the pan upside down to cool, resting the edges on 2 other pans; let hang free of the table. When cooled, loosen the sides with a spatula, or run a thin knife around the sides, turn the pan over, and hit the edge sharply on the table to loosen the cake. Turn right side up and place on a serving platter.

4. To make the icing, in a mixer fitted with a whisk (or in a bowl with a hand blender), cream the shortening. Beat in the egg yolk. Add the cream, confectioners' sugar, and vanilla; beat well. Add more cream if needed.

5. Ice the top and sides of the cake.

6. Melt the chocolate with the oil in a double boiler (or in the microwave); cool slightly. Drizzle over the top of the cake, letting it trickle down the sides.

SERVES 8 TO 10

COOKING NOTE
Eat within a day—the cake is excellent fresh, but dries out quickly.

MAY 8, 1949. RECIPE ADAPTED FROM AN ADVERTISEMENT FOR WESSON OIL.

—1949

CECILY BROWNSTONE'S CHIFFON ROLL

Cecily Brownstone, a food writer for the Associated Press for forty years, was well known for her love of Country Captain (see p. 455), but she should have been knighted for this vanilla-scented cake.

———

1 cup sifted cake flour
3/4 cup granulated sugar
1 1/2 teaspoons baking powder
1/2 teaspoon salt
1/4 cup corn oil
3 large eggs, separated
6 tablespoons water

1 teaspoon vanilla extract
1/4 teaspoon cream of tartar
Confectioners' sugar for dusting
Whipped cream for serving
Fresh berries for serving

1. Heat the oven to 350 degrees F. Lightly grease a 10-by-15-inch jelly-roll pan. Line with parchment paper and grease the paper. Sift the flour, sugar, baking powder, and salt into a deep bowl. Make a well in the center and add, in the order listed, the oil, egg yolks, water, and vanilla. Beat with a spoon until smooth.

2. In a mixer fitted with a whisk (or in a bowl with a hand mixer), beat the egg whites and cream of tartar until the egg whites form stiff peaks. Gently fold in the flour mixture until well blended. Scrape the mixture into the prepared pan.

3. Bake until the cake springs back when lightly touched, or for about 12 minutes. Turn out onto a kitchen towel covered with confectioners' sugar. Peel off the parchment paper. Starting at one end, roll up in the towel, and let cool.

4. Unroll, and spread the cake with whipped cream and strawberries (or any desired filling). Roll up and wrap firmly in wax paper. Chill for about 1 hour, or until ready to slice and serve. Serve sprinkled with confectioners' sugar.

SERVES 10 TO 12

MAY 14, 1959: "DINNER MENUS AND RECIPES OFFERED FOR THE WEEKEND."

—1959

BAUMKUCHENTORTE (CREPE-LIKE LAYER CAKE)

German baumkuchentortes are typically a foot high (this one is 3 to 4 inches high) and look like a stack of crepes. You get this effect by beating together a beautiful yellow, moussey batter, then adding it to a springform pan a few tablespoonfuls at a time and setting it under the broiler to toast. As each layer browns, you add a fresh layer to broil, until you have two dozen or so layers. Make this on a cool day when you don't mind standing by the broiler.

You can ice the cake with the chocolate ganache

frosting, or just dust the top with confectioners' sugar and serve with whipped cream. Each slice is extraordinary looking, like fine layers of sand and earth.

For the Cake
I pound unsalted butter, softened
1⅔ cups sugar
1½ cups cornstarch
Pinch of salt
¾ cup plus 2 tablespoons all-purpose flour
8 large eggs, separated
2 tablespoons rum

For the Frosting (optional)
¼ pound bittersweet chocolate, chopped
2 tablespoons heavy cream
I tablespoon cold water

Confectioners' sugar for dusting
   (if not making the frosting)

1. To make the cake, set the oven rack at least 6 inches from the broiler heating element. Heat the broiler. Line the base of a 9-inch springform pan with parchment paper. Butter the paper.

2. Beat the butter and sugar in a large bowl (use a hand mixer if you don't want to do it by hand) until light and fluffy. Gradually add the cornstarch, salt, flour, and egg yolks. Add the rum.

3. Beat the egg whites until they hold stiff peaks, then fold them into the batter.

4. Using the back of a spoon, spread a wafer-thin layer of batter (about 2½ tablespoons) in the springform pan and broil until lightly toasted, about 1 minute. Spread another wafer-thin layer of batter over the top and broil until lightly browned—it will take slightly less time to cook each layer as the cake gets taller and thus closer to the broiler). Repeat the process until all the batter has been used. There should be about 25 to 35 layers. Let cool.

5. To make the optional frosting, melt the chocolate in a double boiler. Remove from the heat, add the cream and water, and mix well.

6. Frost the top of the cake if desired, or simply dust with confectioners' sugar.

SERVES 8

COOKING NOTE
The trick to this recipe is not overcooking the layers—it's better to undercook them slightly to keep them moist. Fortunately, you have 25 to 35 layers to get the hang of it.

DECEMBER 6, 1962: "SECRET OF FESTIVE CAKE'S SUCCESS IS PATIENCE," BY NAN ICKERINGILL.

—1962

⌒ DE LUXE CHEESECAKE

Yes, there are a lot of cheesecakes in this book, but I couldn't resist this one: when was the last time anyone had the guts to call a recipe "de luxe"? And it's the *New York Times*, after all, so cheesecake is a hometown creation (the signature cream cheese foundation of the New York–style cheesecake was served at Reuben's Restaurant a century ago). There were countless noteworthy cheesecake recipes in the archives: cheesecakes with a sweet bottom layer and a tangy top; fluffy, crustless cheesecakes made with cornstarch; and cheesecakes singing with mocha; as well as this one—an early inductee in the cheesecake pantheon when Craig Claiborne chose it for his annual "Four Favorites" list of the year's most popular recipes. It's so old school it has a pastry crust.

The De Luxe is totally unlike its tasty but hefty counterparts, being light, downy, and judiciously sweetened. It's also assembled in an unusual way. First you pat a butter crust, scented with lemon zest, into the pan and bake it. Then you pat the rest of the crust onto the sides (a pain in the neck, but worth it). You beat the hell out of the filling so it's well aerated, pour it into the unbaked/baked crust, and then watch it emerge from the oven like a soufflé that gently sinks upon itself. The pastry and filling fuse in the oven, and when you unmold the cake, the pastry looks like the rind on an aged Reblochon.

The weird but amusing part of the recipe comes in the glaze, for which you're instructed to cook frozen strawberries in cherry juice, thicken the sauce with cornstarch, and then pour it over the cake. Steeling yourself to pour is difficult—it feels like dumping grated Velveeta atop a beautifully made pizza dough, and your arm refuses to move.

But the glaze can also be made with fresh strawberries or another fruit, like blackberries. If using strawberries, quarter them, combine with ½ cup sugar, and let macerate for an hour. Then you can either spoon the berries directly over the cake, or proceed with Step 8 in the recipe. If you're feeling more ambitious, candy some thin slivers of Meyer lemon zest, or simmer some blueberries in a little sugar and grappa for a minute—both would be excellent counterpoints to the cake.

For the Crust

I cup all-purpose flour
¼ teaspoon sugar
I teaspoon grated lemon zest
8 tablespoons (I stick) unsalted butter
I large egg yolk, lightly beaten
¼ teaspoon vanilla extract

For the Filling

Five 8-ounce packages cream cheese, at room temperature
¼ teaspoon vanilla extract
I teaspoon grated lemon zest
1¾ cups sugar
3 tablespoons all-purpose flour
¼ teaspoon salt
5 large eggs
2 large egg yolks
¼ cup heavy cream

For the Glaze

Two I-pound packages frozen whole strawberries, thawed
Cherry juice or water
2 tablespoons cornstarch

1. To prepare the crust, heat the oven to 400 degrees. Combine the flour, sugar, and lemon zest in a bowl. Cut in the butter until the mixture is crumbly. Add the egg yolk and vanilla; mix. (If when pressed between your thumb and forefinger, the dough doesn't hold together, add 1 tablespoon ice water and mix once more.)

2. Gently and patiently pat one-third of the dough over the bottom of a 9-inch springform pan. Bake for about 6 minutes, or until golden. Let cool. Increase the oven heat to 475 degrees.

3. Butter the sides of the pan and pat the remaining dough around the sides to a height of 2 inches.

4. To prepare the filling, beat the cream cheese in a large bowl until fluffy. Add the vanilla and lemon zest.

5. Combine the sugar, flour, and salt. Gradually blend into the cheese mixture. Beat in the eggs and egg yolks one at a time, and then the cream, beating well.

6. Pour the mixture into the pan. Bake for 8 to 10 minutes. Reduce the oven heat to 200 degrees. Bake for 1½ hours longer, or until set. Turn off the heat. Allow the cake to remain in the oven with the door propped open with a wooden spoon for 30 minutes.

7. Cool the cheesecake completely on a rack. Chill.

8. To prepare the glaze, drain the strawberries very well, reserving the juice. Add enough cherry juice to the strawberry juice to measure 2 cups.

9. Pour the juices into a small pan and slowly mix in the cornstarch. Gradually bring to a boil, stirring, and cook for 2 to 3 minutes, or until translucent and thick. Cool, and then chill.

10. Fold in the strawberries into the glaze. Spread atop the chilled cake.

SERVES 8

COOKING NOTES

The crust dough was dry, so I added 1 tablespoon ice water to it to bring it together—a good trick for a dry crust. The dough is challenging to "pat out"—you have to do a little at a time with small pats. But for all of its demands, the crust is worth the trouble, because the prebaking means the bottom crust doesn't get soggy once the filling is added.

If you do make the glaze, half the amount would be plenty.

The cherry juice I used was unsweetened, so I added 3 tablespoons sugar.

When slicing the cake, it helps to use a knife that you've run under hot water (and wiped dry).

PERIOD DETAIL

In 1947, food columnist Jane Nickerson, who was usually fairly stodgy, earned herself some cool-hunting cred when she wrote: "If we're to judge by the comments of readers that reach this department, cheese cake will some day rival apple pie and ice cream as a leading American dessert."

DECEMBER 29, 1963: "THE READERS CHOOSE," BY CRAIG CLAIBORNE.

—1963

HUGUENOT TORTE
(APPLE AND PECAN TORTE)

When I first tasted Huguenot torte, a recipe that ran in the *Times* in 1965, I had but one thought: why isn't everyone making this weekly? The torte is easy to assemble, goes on a transformative journey as it cooks, and pleases everyone who tastes it.

The silky apple-and-pecan-flecked batter billows in the oven and then, just when it seems like it may spill over the sides of its pan, begins retracting until it sinks all the way down into itself like a crater. You'll get past the slight appearance problem when you taste the warm cake: the brown crust is like the ideal macaroon and the center has the gooey, custard-like texture of a proper pecan pie.

The torte's dense, meringuey look probably contributes to the misconception that it was brought over from France by the Huguenots, or French Protestants, who fled to South Carolina seeking religious freedom in the seventeenth century. John Martin Taylor, a cookbook author and culinary historian, points out that the use of baking powder for leavening is the first indication that the dish is not French. Instead, he said, the torte descends from a more recent Midwestern dessert called Ozark pudding. Huguenot torte, Taylor said, first showed up in print in 1950 in *Charleston Receipts*, a successful community cookbook in which the torte recipe was attributed to Evelyn Anderson Florance (then Mrs. Cornelius Huguenin). In the 1980s, Taylor tracked down Florance in a nursing home and discovered that she'd eaten Ozark pudding on a trip to Galveston, Texas, in the 1930s. After fiddling with the recipe, she renamed it Huguenot torte after Huguenot Tavern, a restaurant she made desserts for in Charleston. The tavern became known for the torte.

The *Times* recipe came from *The First Ladies Cook Book*, where it's featured in the chapter on Martin Van Buren—a historical impossibility, as the dessert was created 100 years after his term. It could easily have gone in the chapter on Harry Truman, who, it turns out, was fond of Ozark pudding.

---

2 large eggs
1/2 teaspoon salt
1 1/2 cups sugar
1 cup peeled, cored, and chopped tart cooking apples

1 cup coarsely chopped pecans
1 teaspoon vanilla extract
1/4 cup all-purpose flour
2 1/2 teaspoons baking powder
1 cup heavy cream, flavored with 1 teaspoon almond extract, barely sweetened, and whipped to soft peaks

1. Heat the oven to 325 degrees. Grease a baking pan about 8 by 12 inches or 9 by 9 inches and at least 2 inches deep. Beat the eggs and salt in a bowl with a rotary beater until light and fluffy. Gradually beat in the sugar.
2. Fold in the apples and pecans with a rubber spatula. Add the vanilla, flour, and baking powder. Pour into the baking pan.
3. Bake for 45 minutes, or until sunken and crusty. Serve warm or chilled, with whipped cream.

SERVES 8

VARIATION

The recipe calls for apples and pecans; you could also use pears and hazelnuts, or even black walnuts.

COOKING NOTE

The original recipe said that the torte could be served chilled, but I liked it best warm and cut into squares. It has so much sticky sugar in it that when it's cold, you have to do battle to cut it. Either way, I suggest adding little or no sugar to the accompanying whipped cream—in fact, I'd fold in some crème fraîche.

JULY 14, 1965: "*FIRST LADIES COOK BOOK* CONTAINS TIPS ON THE CARE AND FEEDING OF PRESIDENTS," BY CRAIG CLAIBORNE. RECIPE ADAPTED FROM *THE FIRST LADIES COOK BOOK*, BY MARGARET BROWN KLAPTHOR.

—1965

LAGGTARTA
(PANCAKES LAYERED
WITH STRAWBERRIES)

Giant, crisp pancakes layered with pureed strawberries and served with fresh strawberries and whipped cream. What's not to like?

For other pancake-style cakes, see the Gâteau de Crepes on p. 785 and the Baumkuchentorte on p. 747.

---

3 large eggs

I cup granulated sugar

I cup cake flour

I teaspoon baking powder

8 tablespoons (I stick) unsalted butter

I cup thick applesauce, preferably homemade

1/3 cup pureed strawberries or raspberries

Confectioners' sugar for dusting

Sweetened strawberries or blueberries for serving

Sweetened whipped cream for serving

1. Heat the oven to 425 degrees. Beat the eggs and sugar together in a bowl with a mixer on high speed until lemon yellow and quite thick.

2. Sift the flour and baking powder together. Use a rubber spatula to fold them into the egg mixture with a gentle motion: cut through the center of the mixture, then around the bottom of the bowl, then draw the spatula up and out.

3. To clarify the butter, heat it in a small pan over very low heat until the milk solids drop to the bottom of the pan. Let it cool slightly, then gradually add the clear yellow liquid to the batter, folding it in with the spatula. Discard the white milk solids.

4. Grease an 8- or 10-inch griddle or ovenproof non-stick skillet and heat in the oven. Pour and spread about 2/3 cup batter onto the 8-inch griddle or pan or about 1 cup batter onto the 10-inch griddle or pan. Bake for 5 minutes, or until lightly browned. Loosen the edges and bottom of the cake layer with a spatula and gradually ease out onto a rack. Clean the griddle thoroughly, regrease, and heat before repeating with more of the batter. Continue until all the batter is used.

5. Combine the applesauce with the pureed berries in a bowl. Spread between the cake layers, stacking them carefully. Sprinkle the top with confectioners' sugar. Serve with berries and whipped cream.

SERVES 6 TO 8

NOVEMBER 12, 1967: "SWEDEN'S FRYING-PAN CAKE," BY CRAIG CLAIBORNE.

—1967

✏ BOSILJKA MARICH'S SERBIAN TORTE

This is a fantastic little cake, layers of lemon and almond meringue iced with chocolate. There's just one annoying detail: you need 4 pans to make it. But if you don't happen to have the pans, you can just pipe the batter into 9-inch circles on parchment-lined baking sheets.

———

10 large eggs, separated

1 3/4 cups sugar

1/4 cup zwieback crumbs or fine dry bread crumbs

I teaspoon grated lemon zest

1/4 cup fresh lemon juice

1/2 pound (about 1 1/2 cups) blanched almonds, very finely ground

3 ounces unsweetened chocolate, melted

1/2 pound (2 sticks) unsalted butter, softened

3/4 cup toasted sliced almonds

1. Heat the oven to 350 degrees. Grease four 9-inch round cake pans and line the bottoms with parchment paper or unglazed brown paper; butter the paper. Beat the egg whites in a mixer fitted with a whisk (or in a large bowl with a hand mixer) until they hold stiff peaks. Gradually beat in 1 cup sugar. Fold in the crumbs, zest, and juice. Fold in the ground almonds.

2. Divide the mixture among the prepared pans. Bake for 15 to 20 minutes, or until faintly browned. Cool on a rack.

3. Lightly beat the egg yolks in the top of a double boiler, then add the remaining 3/4 cup sugar and cook over hot water, whisking constantly, until the sugar dissolves and the mixture thickens. Do not allow to boil, or it will curdle.

4. Remove from the hot water and beat in the chocolate, then gradually beat in the butter. Refrigerate until the mixture reaches spreading consistency.

5. Use the chocolate mixture to fill and frost the torte. Garnish the sides of the torte with the sliced almonds, pressing them gently. Refrigerate until firm before serving.

SERVES 10

I ground the almonds in a small food processor, which did a decent job, but the almonds were more pebbles than powder. For a finer texture, use a nut grinder or a blender. Or add some of the sugar to the nuts in the food processor; just be careful not to let the mixture turn to a paste.

When icing the cake, the easiest way to place the next layer on top is to invert it onto the iced layer, then peel off the parchment.

You probably won't need all the sliced almonds for garnishing the cake, but it helps to have a full handful when pressing them onto the sides. If this seems too tedious or wasteful, reduce the amount of almonds and simply sprinkle them on top of the cake.

JULY 27, 1969: "NUTS OVER CHOCOLATE," BY JEAN HEWITT.

—1969

EVELYN SHARPE'S FRENCH CHOCOLATE CAKE

As far as I could determine, this is the first flourless chocolate cake to appear in the *Times*. Earlier than you'd think, right? Like many "flourless" chocolate cakes, it does contain a smidgen of flour—a tablespoon.

---

1 pound semisweet or bittersweet chocolate, chopped

10 tablespoons (1¼ sticks) salted butter, softened

1 tablespoon all-purpose flour

1 tablespoon sugar

4 large eggs, separated

Whipped cream for garnish

1. Heat the oven to 425 degrees. Line the base of an 8-inch springform pan with parchment paper. Melt the chocolate in the top of a double boiler over hot, not boiling, water (or in the microwave). Remove the melted chocolate from the heat and stir in the butter, flour, and sugar.

2. Beat the yolks lightly and gradually whisk into the chocolate mixture.

3. Beat the whites in a mixer fitted with a whisk (or in a large bowl with a hand mixer) until they hold a definite shape but are not dry. Fold into the chocolate mixture. (Overbeating or underbeating will ruin the cake.) The beaten egg whites should be folded smoothly, quickly, and easily into the chocolate mixture.

4. Pour into the prepared pan and bake for 15 minutes. Turn off the heat, prop open the oven door with the handle of a wooden spoon, and allow the cake to cool slightly in the oven.

5. The cake is best served warm. Garnish with whipped cream and serve in small pieces. It is rich.

SERVES 10

COOKING NOTES

The original recipe called for Maillard's Eagle sweet chocolate, but I changed this to semisweet or bittersweet; I prefer the latter.

The second time I made the recipe, I had only salted butter in the house, and the cake was even better, with a hint of salinity underlining the bitterness and sweetness of the chocolate. I changed the recipe accordingly.

As an alternative to whipped cream, fold some crème fraîche into the whipped cream. This creates a cream with more heft and tang, a more formidable pairing with the intense cake.

When slicing the cake, use a knife that you've run under hot water (and dried).

SEPTEMBER 7, 1969: "HANDLE WITH CARE," BY JANE HEWITT. RECIPE ADAPTED FROM EVELYN SHARPE.

—1969

TEDDIE'S APPLE CAKE

For reasons that elude me, cakes are reputed to require long hours in the kitchen, when anyone who actually makes cakes knows that cookies are the true time suck. Cookies require measuring out portions and multiple batches. Cakes get mixed up and go into the oven all at once. The most complaisant ones even cool in their pans and require no icing.

All of which is why if you look back in the *Times* archives at recipes from thirty or more years ago, when most people cooked every day, there were many more cake recipes. Cake was a staple you whipped up every couple of days, after the previous one had vanished into crumbs.

Teddie's apple cake is a typical standby of the period. None of the ingredients are difficult to find—most are probably already in your pantry. Based on oil rather than butter, the cake has a light, airy crumb that's delicious while it lasts, with walnuts, raisins, and slivers of apple threaded through the cinnamon-scented cake. There is no icing, and no need for it.

When I asked readers for their favorite recipes from the *Times*, this one was near the top, with thirty-seven votes. Like many of the most recommended recipes, it shares three qualities: ease, good flavor, and someone's name in its title. Unfortunately, I still have no idea who Teddie is.

———

3 cups all-purpose flour

1 teaspoon salt

1 teaspoon ground cinnamon

1 teaspoon baking soda

1½ cups peanut, vegetable, or corn oil

2 cups sugar

3 large eggs

1 teaspoon vanilla extract

3 cups peeled, cored, and thickly sliced apples

1 cup chopped walnuts

1 cup raisins

Vanilla ice cream for serving (optional)

1. Heat the oven to 350 degrees. Butter and flour a 9-inch tube pan. Sift together the flour, salt, cinnamon, and baking soda.

2. Beat the oil and sugar together in a mixer with a paddle (or in a bowl with a hand mixer) for 5 minutes. Add the eggs and beat until the mixture is creamy. Stir in the dry ingredients. Add the vanilla, apples, walnuts, and raisins and stir until combined.

3. Turn the batter into the prepared pan. Bake for 1 hour and 15 minutes, or until a toothpick inserted in the center comes out clean. Cool in the pan before turning out.

4. Serve with vanilla ice cream, if desired.

SERVES 8

COOKING NOTES

If mixing the batter in a mixer, use a paddle attachment and turn the speed to low once you add the flour mixture, or the texture of the cake will be tough. Even better, mix the rest by hand.

The recipe called for Red Delicious or McIntosh apples, but I'd recommend a variety that's brighter in flavor and firmer in texture, such as a Honeycrisp, Macoun, or Granny Smith.

The apple slices can be halved if you want a more uniform texture.

This cake can be eaten at any time of day, including breakfast. If you serve it for dessert, the recipe suggested a scoop of vanilla ice cream on the side. I prefer to whip ½ cup of heavy cream to soft peaks, then fold in crème fraîche to taste.

READERS

"I most recently baked this cake for Thanksgiving 2004. There was a small piece left over and several days later (it keeps beautifully), I wrapped it in aluminum foil and took it to NYC for my son and daughter-in-law. He took it from me and started looking around his kitchen. When I questioned him, he said he had to hide it from his wife."

Rochelle Rogers-Lippin, Huntington, NY, letter

SEPTEMBER 30, 1973: "JUST DESSERTS," BY JEAN HEWITT. RECIPE BY TEDDIE.

—1973

HAZELNUT CHEESECAKE

With one deft addition—hazelnuts—a cheesecake became this engaging treat. Without any crust to speak of, just a dusting of graham cracker crumbs, this is really more like a cream cheese flan. The ground hazelnuts fuse with the sugar, the edges turn macaroon-chewy, and the center, with all those nuts, becomes rich like a bon-bon's filling.

———

1½ cups (about 8 ounces) blanched hazelnuts or
    blanched almonds

⅓ cup graham cracker crumbs

Four 8-ounce packages cream cheese, at room temperature

½ cup heavy cream

4 large eggs

1¾ cups sugar

1 teaspoon vanilla extract

1. Because of the importance of oven temperature, the nuts must be toasted well in advance of proceed-

ing with the recipe. If they are not already toasted, heat the oven to 400 degrees. Place the nuts on a baking sheet or in a skillet and bake, stirring often, until nicely browned. Remove them and let cool.

2. When ready to make the cheesecake, heat the oven to 300 degrees. Butter a round cake pan that is 8 inches wide and 3 inches deep (or use a 9-inch round cake pan); do not use a springform pan. Sprinkle with the graham cracker crumbs and shake the crumbs around the bottom and sides until coated. Shake out the excess crumbs.

3. Place the cooled nuts in a blender or food processor and blend. If you want a crunchy texture, blend them until coarse-fine. If you want a smooth texture, blend them until they are almost paste-like.

4. Place the cream cheese, cream, eggs, sugar, and vanilla in the bowl of mixer fitted with a whisk (or mix in a bowl with a hand mixer). Start beating at low speed, and as the ingredients blend, increase the speed to high. Continue beating until thoroughly blended and smooth. Add the nuts and continue beating until thoroughly blended. Pour and scrape the batter into the prepared pan; shake gently to level the mixture.

5. Set the pan inside a slightly wider pan and pour boiling water into the larger pan to a depth of about $\frac{1}{2}$ inch. Do not let the sides of the cheesecake pan touch the sides of the larger pan. Set the pans thus arranged inside the oven and bake for $1\frac{1}{2}$ hours. Turn off the oven and let the cake sit in the oven for 1 hour longer.

6. Lift the cake out of its water bath and place it on a rack. Let stand for at least 2 hours.

7. Place a round cake plate over the cake and carefully turn both upside down to unmold the cake. Serve lukewarm or at room temperature.

SERVES 12

COOKING NOTE
When slicing the cake, use a knife that you've run under hot water (and dried).

SEPTEMBER 1, 1974: "FOOD: HAZELNUT MAKES THE DIFFERENCE: THE ULTIMATE CHEESECAKE," BY CRAIG CLAIBORNE WITH PIERRE FRANEY.

—1974

∽ BLACK FOREST CAKE

For the Chocolate Sponge Cake
6 large eggs
1 cup sugar
$\frac{1}{2}$ cup plus 3 tablespoons all-purpose flour
6 tablespoons unsweetened cocoa powder
$\frac{1}{4}$ cup cornstarch
3 tablespoons unsalted butter, melted

For the Assembly
$\frac{1}{2}$ cup plus 1 tablespoon sugar
1 cup water
2 thin orange or lemon wedges
One 1-pound can sour cherries in syrup
One 15-ounce can dark sweet cherries in syrup
$\frac{1}{3}$ cup kirsch
3 ounces bittersweet chocolate, chopped
3 cups heavy cream
3 drops vanilla extract
Grated chocolate

1. To make the cake, heat the oven to 375 degrees. Butter a 10-by-2-inch round cake pan. Sprinkle the inside with flour and shake the flour around until the bottom and sides are well coated. Shake out any excess flour.

2. Put the eggs into a double boiler, set over medium heat, and whisk vigorously by hand or with a hand mixer while adding the sugar. Then beat constantly for about 5 minutes, until the eggs are lukewarm.

3. Remove the top of the double boiler from the heat and beat on high speed until the mixture is thick, mousse-like, and at room temperature. To test, run a spatula through the mass: if it is ready, the spatula will leave a track.

4. Combine the flour, cocoa, and cornstarch and sift together 2 or 3 times. Fold the mixture into the batter, using a wooden spoon or spatula. Fold in the butter, and pour the mixture into the prepared pan.

5. Bake for 25 minutes, or until the cake pulls away from the sides of the pan. Turn the cake out onto a rack to cool.

6. When ready to assemble the cake, combine $\frac{1}{2}$ cup sugar and the water in a saucepan. Add the orange or

lemon wedges and bring to a boil. Simmer for about 3 minutes, then let the syrup cool. Discard the wedges.

7. Drain both cans of cherries, keeping them separate, and set aside. Combine the kirsch with ⅔ cup of the sugar syrup. Set aside.

8. Melt the chocolate in a double boiler (or in the microwave). When it is melted, gradually stir in 3 tablespoons of the remaining sugar syrup; set aside.

9. Whip the cream to firm peaks. Beat in the remaining tablespoon of sugar and the vanilla. Fold 1½ cups of the whipped cream into the chocolate mixture. Set the remaining whipped cream aside.

10. Place the cake on a flat surface and, holding a knife parallel to the bottom of the cake, slice the cake into thirds. Place the bottom layer on a serving plate and brush with some of the kirsch mixture. Add about half the chocolate mixture to the layer and smooth it over. Cover with the top cake layer, but place it bottom side up. Brush with syrup and add the remaining chocolate mixture, smoothing it over the cake. Using a pastry tube, pipe 3 rings of whipped cream on the cake: one in the center, another around the rim, and another in between those two. Arrange the sour cherries in the center and between the middle and outer rings.

11. Top with the final layer of cake. Brush it with the remaining syrup. Add the remaining whipped cream to the top, saving enough cream to make 13 rosettes on top of the cake and smooth the whipped cream over the top and sides of the cake. Using a pastry bag fitted with a No. 4 star pastry tube, pipe 12 rosettes, equally spaced, around the upper edge of the cake. Make 1 rosette in dead center. Garnish each rosette with a dark sweet cherry. Garnish the top with grated chocolate. Hold in the refrigerator until ready to serve.

SERVES 12

COOKING NOTES

The ingredient list called for canned cherries in syrup. Obviously, pitted fresh cherries cooked in syrup would be better. To make your own, combine 1 cup water and 1 cup sugar in a medium sauce pan. Bring to a boil, stirring to dissolve the sugar. Add 2 cups pitted cherries and simmer until the cherries just begin to soften, 5 to 8 minutes. If you can, make one batch of sweet cherries and one batch of sour cherries, using 1 cup cherries for each.

This recipe takes an army of minions to construct. Minionless, I skipped making the rosettes of whipped cream.

The addition of lemons to the syrup in Step 6 is a nice touch—I used Meyer lemons.

FEBRUARY 9, 1975: "FOOD: PRIDE OF THE FOREST," BY CRAIG CLAIBORNE WITH PIERRE FRANEY. RECIPE ADAPTED FROM ALBERT KUMIN, PASTRY CHEF AT THE CULINARY INSTITUTE OF AMERICA.

—1975

⌒ HEAVENLY CHOCOLATE ROLL

This pillowy chocolate-and-coffee-scented cake, which you pave with whipped cream and roll up like a sleeping bag, is similar in structure to Cecily Brownstone's Chiffon Roll on p. 747, except hers is scented with vanilla and is blond.

---

6 large eggs, separated, at room temperature

¾ cup granulated sugar

6 ounces semisweet chocolate, chopped

3 tablespoons cold strong coffee

Pinch of salt

Cocoa powder for dusting

1¼ cups heavy cream

2 tablespoons confectioners' sugar (optional)

½ teaspoon vanilla extract

1. Heat the oven to 350 degrees. Grease a 10-by-15-inch jelly-roll pan, line with parchment paper, and grease the paper. Beat the egg yolks in a mixer fitted with a whisk (or in a large bowl with a hand mixer) until creamy. Gradually beat in the sugar until the mixture is very thick and light in color.

2. Meanwhile, place the chocolate and coffee in the top of a double boiler and melt over hot, not boiling, water.

3. Stir the melted chocolate into the yolk mixture.

4. Beat the egg whites with the salt in a clean mixer bowl with the clean whisk (or in a clean bowl with clean beaters) until stiff but not dry. Carefully fold the whites into the chocolate mixture. Spread the mixture evenly in the prepared pan with a rubber spatula.

5. Bake for 15 minutes. Set the pan on a rack, cover the top of the cake with a damp kitchen towel, and allow to cool to room temperature, at least 1 hour.

6. Sift a layer of cocoa evenly over a piece of wax paper that is slightly larger than the jelly-roll pan. Turn the pan and cake upside-down onto the wax paper. Lift off the pan and carefully remove the parchment paper on top.

7. Beat the heavy cream with the confectioners' sugar, if desired, and vanilla until thick. Spread over the chocolate roll. Using the wax paper underneath as a guide, roll up the cake like a jelly roll and slide seam down onto a board or platter. Rolling from a long side gives an elegant, slender roll that can be cut into 12 to 16 small slices. Rolling from the short side produces a shorter, fatter roll and bigger slices. Chill for several hours before serving.

SERVES 12 TO 16

JUNE 8, 1975: "FOOD: FOR HIS SWEET TOOTH," BY JEAN HEWITT.

—1975

✑ MOCHA CHEESECAKE

This is the most ridiculously rich cake I've ever made. Assuming no one would want to eat such decadence, no matter how good it tasted, I put it in the "no" pile. My husband, though, thought it was a life-altering success and was outraged when, to make room in the fridge, I threw out the last piece. To save our marriage, and to throw a bone to the hedonists and cardiologists of the world (hi!), I've included it.

———

1 cup graham cracker crumbs

5 tablespoons unsalted butter

1 cup plus 2 tablespoons granulated sugar

Three 8-ounce packages cream cheese, at room temperature

2 large eggs

1/2 pound semisweet chocolate, melted and cooled

2 tablespoons heavy cream

1 cup sour cream

1/2 cup cooled double-strength espresso (1/4 cup ground espresso beans plus 3/4 cup water, brewed in a coffee maker) or 1/4 cup cooled coffee plus 1/4 cup dark rum

1 teaspoon vanilla extract

Chocolate curls for garnish (optional)

1 tablespoon confectioners' sugar, mixed with 1 tablespoon unsweetened cocoa powder, for garnish (optional)

1. Heat the oven to 350 degrees. Combine the graham cracker crumbs with the butter and 2 tablespoons sugar, blending thoroughly with your fingers. Press the mixture firmly and smoothly into the bottom of an ungreased 9-inch springform pan.

2. Put the cream cheese in the bowl of a mixer fitted with a whisk (or mix in a bowl with a hand mixer). Add the remaining 1 cup sugar, then add the eggs and start beating on low speed. Continue beating until smooth and well blended, increasing the mixer speed as necessary, but cautiously, to prevent splattering. Add the chocolate along with the heavy cream and mix until blended. Add the sour cream. Pour in the cooled espresso (or the coffee and rum). Add the vanilla extract and beat until well blended.

3. Pour and scrape the batter into the prepared pan. Bake for 45 minutes, or until puffed at the sides. The center will remain somewhat soft but will become firm on cooling. Let the cake cool on a rack for several hours.

4. Remove the sides of the pan. Garnish, if desired, with chocolate curls and sprinkle, if desired, with the confectioners' sugar and cocoa.

SERVES 12

COOKING NOTES

As with any cheesecake recipe, it's important that the cream cheese is fully at room temperature; otherwise, you'll end up with small beads of cream cheese that never fully blend into the batter.

When slicing the cake, use a knife that you've run under hot water (and dried).

MARCH 17, 1976: "MOCHA CHEESECAKE TO SATISFY A NEW YORKER'S SOUL," BY CRAIG CLAIBORNE.

—1976

RED VELVET CAKE

Craig Claiborne was forcibly introduced to this dish after he published a recipe for red velvet cake and was flooded with letters from readers touting their own, better versions. This one came from Carolyn A. Knutsen of Long Island. I never made Claiborne's earlier recipe, but Knutsen's is brilliant—moist, dense, and flush with cocoa.

_____

For the Cake
½ cup vegetable shortening
1½ cups sugar
2 large eggs
2 to 4 tablespoons unsweetened cocoa powder
1½ ounces red food coloring
1 teaspoon salt
1 teaspoon vanilla extract
1 cup buttermilk
2½ cups sifted all-purpose flour
1 tablespoon cider vinegar
1 teaspoon baking soda

For the Icing
10 tablespoons (1¼ sticks) unsalted butter, softened
4 cups sifted confectioners' sugar
6 tablespoons heavy cream
2 teaspoons vanilla extract
Pinch of salt

1. To make the cake, heat the oven to 350 degrees. Butter and flour two 9-inch round cake pans; shake out the excess flour. In the bowl of a mixer fitted with the whisk (or in a large bowl with a hand mixer) beat the shortening and sugar until light and fluffy. Add the eggs one at a time, beating well after each addition. Beat for 1 minute on medium speed.

2. Blend the cocoa and red food coloring to make a paste. Add this and the salt to the creamed mixture. Blend the vanilla and buttermilk. Alternately add this and the flour to the creamed mixture, beating constantly. Blend the vinegar and soda and beat this in.

3. Divide the cake batter between the prepared pans. Bake until a toothpick inserted in the center of the cake comes out clean, about 25 minutes. Cool the cakes in the pans on a rack, then turn out.

4. To make the icing, in a mixer fitted with a whisk (or use a large bowl and a hand mixer), cream the butter. Gradually add the confectioners' sugar, alternating with the heavy cream. Add the vanilla and salt and continue beating until smooth and light.

5. Spread the icing between the cake layers and on the top and sides.

SERVES 10

APRIL 25, 1977: "DE GUSTIBUS: RED VELVET CAKE RETURNS; TOMATO PASTE LINGERS ON," BY CRAIG CLAIBORNE. CAKE RECIPE ADAPTED FROM CAROLYN A. KNUTSEN, A READER FROM KINGS POINT, NEW YORK; ICING RECIPE ADAPTED FROM RHONDA THOMSON, MY SISTER.

—1977

LINDY'S CHEESECAKE

Joan Nathan, a frequent contributor to the _Times_ food pages and an expert on Jewish cooking, told me that Lindy's, the New York restaurant, didn't invent its famous cheesecake but acquired it by cunningly poaching the pastry chef from Reuben's Restaurant in Manhattan. Reuben's was the first place to make cheesecake with cream cheese rather than cottage cheese—a detail that came to define New York cheesecake, and that earned them a gold medal at the 1929 World's Fair. (Too bad they didn't think to give their pastry chef a raise to keep him.)

When Lindy's closed in 1969, Leo Lindemann, the owner, refused to give Craig Claiborne the cake recipe. But Lindemann was not the only one who possessed it. His pastry chef (not the same one from Reuben's, obviously) wound up at a restaurant in Las Vegas, where the cake again besotted everyone. Guy Pascal, who ran the Vegas kitchen, asked the pastry chef for the recipe but came up empty-handed. So, over the course of weeks, according to the story Claiborne wrote about this recipe, Pascal made mental notes of the ingredients the pastry chef was using when making the cheesecake. Then, to reverse-engineer the proportions, he checked the ingredients orders against the number of cakes produced. Clever! This is what he came up with.

_____

½ cup fine cake crumbs or graham cracker crumbs

Three 8-ounce packages cream cheese,
    at room temperature

Grated zest of 2 lemons

Grated zest of 1 orange

1 teaspoon vanilla extract

½ cup heavy cream

¾ cup plus 2 tablespoons sugar

4 large eggs

2 tablespoons sour cream

¼ cup half-and-half

1. Heat the oven to 375 degrees. Generously butter an 8-inch springform pan. Sprinkle the inside with the crumbs, then shake out excess crumbs.

2. Add the cream cheese to the bowl of a mixer fitted with a whisk (or mix in a bowl with a hand mixer). Add the grated zests and vanilla, beating. Gradually add the heavy cream and sugar, beating constantly on medium speed. The important thing to avoid in making this recipe is beating on very high speed; that would incorporate air into the cheesecake and make the cake rise like a soufflé. Add the eggs one at a time, beating well after each addition. Beat in the sour cream and half-and-half.

3. Pour the mixture into the prepared pan and smooth the surface. Set the pan in a larger pan and pour boiling water around it. Place in the oven and bake for 1¼ hours or until the center does not quiver when the pan is shaken. Remove from the water bath and let stand on a rack for about 10 minutes, then invert and unmold while hot. Let stand until cool.

SERVES 8 TO 12

COOKING NOTE
When slicing the cake, use a knife that you've run under hot water (and dried).

MAY 18, 1977: "IS CHEF PASCAL'S CHEESECAKE LINDY'S LONG-KEPT SECRET?" BY CRAIG CLAIBORNE.

—1977

✑ WALNUT CAKE WITH CHOCOLATE WALNUT BUTTERCREAM

One of Craig Claiborne's greatest skills was beguiling his subjects into surrendering the secrets to their best recipes. And so we have David Eyre's Pancake (p. 813), Maria Tillman Jackson Rogers's Carrot Cake (p. 761), and Julia Harrison Adams's Pimento Cheese Spread (p. 64).

But Claiborne didn't always succeed. For a walnut cake recipe from a pastry shop in East Hampton, he and Pierre Franey trailed the owner like hounds on a scent, but they were outfoxed. "Well, two summers ago the shop closed and the owner-cook retired," they wrote. "Once more we pleaded for her recipe. No dice, she said. She did, however, offer us a clue. She said the basic cake recipe could be found on the back of a box of cake flour and that the frosting was a simple chocolate buttercream. The cake on this page is a result of our experiments. It may not quite measure up to the manna that came out of our friend's oven, but it is a reasonable—and delicious—facsimile."

The Almond Cake on p. 777 is a replica version of a cake from an East Hampton pastry shop that also denied my mother-in-law the recipe. (Perhaps the walnut cake shop's competitor?) And the Gâteau de Crepes on p. 785 is my likeness of the Mille Crepes at Lady M, a pastry shop on the Upper East Side that also refused to divulge its recipe. Perhaps the CIA should start recruiting in bakeries.

———

For the Cake
½ pound (2 sticks) unsalted butter

2 cups sugar

3 cups sifted cake flour, plus 1 tablespoon unsifted flour

1 tablespoon baking powder

¼ teaspoon salt

1 cup whole milk

1 teaspoon vanilla extract

½ teaspoon almond extract

2 cups broken walnuts

4 large eggs

For the Buttercream
¼ pound unsweetened chocolate, chopped

4 large egg yolks

½ cup sugar

¼ teaspoon salt

2 tablespoons very strong coffee

½ pound (2 sticks) unsalted butter

I cup broken walnuts

12 large walnuts for garnish

1. To make the cake, heat the oven to 350 degrees. Lightly butter and flour two 9-by-5-inch loaf pans. Cut the butter into cubes and add to the bowl of a mixer fitted with a paddle (or mix in a bowl with a hand mixer). Beating on medium speed, gradually add the sugar and then beat for at least 10 minutes.

2. Sift together the 3 cups flour, the baking powder, and salt. Combine the milk with the vanilla and almond extracts. Toss the broken walnuts with the remaining tablespoon of unsifted flour.

3. Add the eggs one at a time to the creamed mixture, beating well after each addition. Alternately add the flour mixture and milk to the creamed mixture, beating well after each addition. Add the floured walnuts and beat on low speed until well blended.

4. Spoon and scrape the batter into the prepared pans. Put the pans in the oven and bake for 50 minutes or until a needle inserted in the center of the cakes comes out clean. Let the pans cool on a rack for 10 minutes. Turn the cakes out onto the rack, turn right side up, and let cool.

5. To make the buttercream, set a bowl in a pot of simmering water (or use a double boiler). Add the chocolate and heat, stirring often, until the chocolate is melted and smooth. Remove from the heat.

6. Combine the yolks, sugar, and salt in another bowl. Set the bowl in the pot of simmering water and beat the yolk mixture rapidly with a wire whisk or a hand mixer until the mixture forms a "ribbon"; that is to say, until it is thickened and falls in a "ribbon" when the beater is held up. Remove from the heat.

7. Spoon and scrape the chocolate into the yolk mixture. Mix in the coffee. Return the bowl to the simmering water and continue beating for 5 minutes. Gradually beat in the butter, bit by bit.

8. Remove the bowl from the heat and continue beating for 5 to 7 minutes in a cool place until the mixture thickens slightly and becomes spreadable. Beat in the broken walnuts. Continue beating with a wooden spoon until the buttercream becomes somewhat lighter. Let cool until spreadable.

9. Spread the top of each cake with half the buttercream. Garnish the top of each cake with 6 walnuts.

MAKES 2 CAKES, EACH SERVING 8

COOKING NOTES

Yes, do beat the butter and sugar for 10 minutes in Step 1! As I learned from a story by *Times* writer Julia Moskin, all the air in a cake is added when you beat the butter. (Baking powder helps the air in cake batter expand, but it can't create air bubbles.)

The recipe calls for "broken walnuts." I took this to mean walnut halves, placed in a plastic bag and lightly crushed with a rolling pin, so you end up with a mix of pea-sized pieces and small flakes.

You may notice the walnuts aren't toasted. If you'd like them toasted, go ahead. But I liked the sweetness of the untoasted nuts.

APRIL 20, 1980: "FOOD: A REASONABLE FACSIMILE OF A FAVORITE CAKE," BY CRAIG CLAIBORNE WITH PIERRE FRANEY.

—1980

LORA BRODY'S CHOCOLATE CHERRY TORTE

This is the kind of cake you'd find in a pâtisserie, with defined layers of chocolate cherry cake, almond paste, and a flawless glassy top.

———

For the Cake

3 tablespoons fine fresh bread crumbs

One 24-ounce jar pitted sour or Morello cherries

6 ounces semisweet chocolate, chopped

12 tablespoons (1½ sticks) unsalted butter, softened

⅔ cup granulated sugar

3 large eggs

I teaspoon vanilla extract

½ teaspoon almond extract

½ cup ground almonds

⅔ cup all-purpose flour

2 tablespoons confectioners' sugar

½ pound almond paste

For the Glaze

½ cup heavy cream

2 teaspoons instant espresso coffee

½ pound semisweet chocolate, chopped

Candied flowers for decoration (optional)

1. To make the cake, heat the oven to 350 degrees. Butter a 9- or 10-inch springform pan. Add the bread crumbs and shake to coat the inside. Shake out the excess. Drain the cherries well and set them aside.

2. Put the chocolate in a double boiler and melt over barely simmering water, stirring occasionally. (Or melt it in the microwave.) Remove from the heat.

3. Put the butter and sugar into a food processor or mixer and blend until light and creamy. Add 2 of the eggs, one at a time, blending well after each addition. Blend in the vanilla and almond extracts. Add the chocolate and mix gently (if using a food processor, turn it on and off to blend). Mix in the almonds and flour. Mix in the remaining egg.

4. Pour and scrape the batter into the prepared pan. Smooth the top with a rubber spatula. Arrange the cherries, close together, in concentric circles, working from the outside to the center. The entire surface should be covered with cherries. As you add the cherries, press them gently into the batter so that just a small portion of the top of each one shows. If the surface of the cake is uneven, smooth it out with a wet rubber spatula. There may be a few cherries left over, which may be put to another use.

5. Place the cake in the oven and bake for 50 minutes to 1 hour. Take care not to overbake; the cake will look dry on top but should be quite moist inside. Let cool on a rack.

6. Put a length of wax paper on a flat surface. Sprinkle with the confectioners' sugar. Work the almond paste with your hands to make a flat round cake. Place it on the wax paper and turn it in the sugar. Cover with another sheet of wax paper. Roll out the almond paste into a circle the diameter of the top of the cake and about ¹⁄₁₆ inch thick. Peel off the top layer of wax paper. If the round of almond paste tears, you can patch it.

7. Cut the almond paste into a round to fit the top of the cake exactly. Any scraps of almond paste can be recycled or used to fashion decorations for the top of the cake. Cover the cake with the almond-paste

round. Place the cake on a rack and place the rack on a sheet of wax paper to catch the drippings.

8. To make the glaze, put the cream in a saucepan and add the coffee. Bring to a slow boil. Add the chocolate and stir gently until the chocolate is melted and smooth. If there are any lumps, put the sauce through a fine strainer. Let the glaze cool briefly, until it is spreadable.

9. Pour a thin layer of chocolate glaze over the cake, spreading it smooth with a spatula. The glaze should cover the bottom and sides of the cake. Chill the cake briefly, then add a second coating of glaze.

10. Decorate the top of the cake, if desired, with candied flowers such as roses or violets or with almond paste cut into decorative shapes. This cake will keep for 2 days in a cool place; it can be refrigerated, but this will dull the cake's gloss.

SERVES 8 TO 12

COOKING NOTES

Make sure you roll the almond paste until it's no thicker than ¹⁄₁₆ inch, or it will be difficult to cut through.

For a less sweet cake, use bittersweet chocolate.

JULY 20, 1980: "FOOD: THE ART OF THE TORTE," BY CRAIG CLAIBORNE WITH PIERRE FRANEY. RECIPE ADAPTED FROM LORA BRODY, A COOKING TEACHER AND FOOD WRITER.

—1980

⌒ MRS. RAYMOND SCHENK'S PUMPKIN CAKE

A lot of people told me about this cake, and now I understand why. It doesn't try to solve world problems, it just sticks to what it does well—giving pumpkin a sense of purpose after Thanksgiving and satisfying our innate hankering for sweet spiced cakes.

———

3 cups all-purpose flour

2 teaspoons baking powder

2 teaspoons baking soda

2 teaspoons ground cinnamon

1 teaspoon salt

2 cups sugar

1¼ cups peanut, vegetable, or corn oil

1½ cups pumpkin puree, homemade or store-bought

4 large eggs

½ cup raisins

½ cup golden raisins

1 cup chopped walnuts or pecans

1. Heat the oven to 350 degrees. Grease a 10-inch tube or Bundt pan. Sift together the flour, baking powder, baking soda, cinnamon, and salt.

2. Place the sugar, oil, and pumpkin puree in a mixer fitted with a paddle (or mix in a large bowl with a hand mixer) and beat well on medium speed. Add the eggs one at a time, beating well after each addition. Sift and fold the dry ingredients into the batter. Stir in the raisins and nuts.

3. Pour into the prepared pan. Bake until a cake tester inserted in the center comes out clean; start checking the cake after 1 hour. Let cool slightly in the pan before turning out onto a rack to cool completely.

SERVES 12

COOKING NOTE

If using a dark-coated nonstick Bundt pan, turn down your oven 10 degrees and start checking the cake for doneness after 50 minutes. It will take less time to cook.

OCTOBER 29, 1980: "Q & A."

—1980

☙ MARIA TILLMAN JACKSON ROGERS'S CARROT CAKE

Eating this cake is startling, because we're so used to carrot cake being a leaden, nut-strewn mass. This one's as light as cotton.

The recipe comes from *My Mother Cooked My Way Through Harvard with These Creole Recipes*, by Mrs. Walter Tillman and Oscar A. Rogers. A reader wrote to tell me that Rogers went on to become a minister, a dean at Jackson State University, and the president of Claflin College.

For the Cake

Approximately 1 pound carrots

2 cups all-purpose flour

2 teaspoons baking powder

2 teaspoons baking soda

2 teaspoons salt

2 cups granulated sugar

1½ cups corn or peanut oil

4 large eggs

½ cup coarsely chopped pecans

For the Frosting

2 cups confectioners' sugar

Two 8-ounce packages cream cheese, at room temperature

4 tablespoons unsalted butter, softened

2 teaspoons vanilla extract

1. To make the cake, heat the oven to 325 degrees. Lightly oil three 9-inch round cake pans. Line the bottoms with circles of parchment; oil the paper. Trim, scrape, and grate the carrots, then measure them; there should be about 3 cups. Set aside.

2. Sift together the flour, baking powder, baking soda, and salt.

3. Combine the sugar and oil in mixer fitted with a paddle (or mix in a large bowl with a hand mixer). Start beating and add the eggs one at a time, beating well after each addition. Add the dry ingredients while beating. Add the grated carrots and nuts and blend well.

4. Pour the batter into the prepared pans. Place in the oven and bake until the cakes spring back when pressed with your finger, about 45 minutes. Turn the cakes onto racks and let cool, then remove the parchment paper.

5. To make the frosting, sift the confectioners' sugar into the bowl of a mixer fitted with a paddle (or mix in a large bowl with a hand mixer). Add the cream cheese, butter, and vanilla. Beat until smooth and creamy.

6. Fill and frost the cake.

SERVES 10

COOKING NOTES

I doubled the cream cheese in the frosting, so if it seems different from the original, that's because it is! The frosting is also more plentiful and less sweet.

Before you get going, you should know that you'll need three 9-inch round cake pans. Several other recipes in this chapter call for the same, so if you don't already have them, I think it's time to splurge.

JANUARY 4, 1981: "FOOD; GARDEN-VARIETY CAKES AND BREADS," BY CRAIG CLAIBORNE. RECIPE ADAPTED FROM *MY MOTHER COOKED MY WAY THROUGH HARVARD WITH THESE CREOLE RECIPES* BY MRS. WALTER TILLMAN AND OSCAR A. ROGERS.

—1981

⌒ MISSISSIPPI MUD CAKE

This is really a Mississippi "Mutt" Cake, as Craig Claiborne and Pierre Franey came up with it by crossbreeding a bunch of recipes sent in by readers. A chocolate cake is baked, then covered with marshmallows and sent back to the oven until the marshmallows melt across the cake's surface. Finally, the cake is topped with a cocoa and pecan icing. Claiborne and Franey included a marshmallow recipe, should you wish to make them from scratch.

For the Cake
1/2 pound (2 sticks) unsalted butter, softened
2 cups sugar
4 large eggs
1 1/2 cups all-purpose flour
1/3 cup unsweetened cocoa powder
1 cup coarsely chopped pecans
1 teaspoon vanilla extract
3 cups miniature marshmallows or large marshmallows cut into 1/2-inch pieces (store-bought, or see recipe that follows)

For the Icing
1/2 pound (2 sticks) unsalted butter
One 1-pound box confectioners' sugar
1/3 cup unsweetened cocoa powder
1 cup coarsely chopped pecans
1/2 cup evaporated milk

1. To make the cake, heat the oven to 350 degrees. Butter a 9-by-13-inch baking pan. Add a little flour and shake it around to coat the bottom and sides of the pan. Shake out the excess. Beat the butter and sugar in a mixer (or in a large bowl with a hand mixer) until creamy. Add the eggs one at a time, beating thoroughly after each addition.

2. Sift together the flour and cocoa. Fold this into the creamed mixture. Add the chopped nuts and vanilla. Beat well.

3. Spoon the mixture into the prepared pan and smooth it over. Place in the oven and bake for 30 to 35 minutes.

4. Remove from the oven and sprinkle the top with the marshmallows. Return to the oven and bake for about 10 minutes, or until the marshmallows are melted and starting to brown. Remove from the oven and let cool in the pan on a rack for about 30 minutes.

5. To make the icing, melt the butter in a saucepan. Remove from the heat.

6. Sift together the confectioners' sugar and cocoa. Stir this into the butter, along with the nuts and milk. Spread this over the cake and let stand until thoroughly cooled. Cut into slices and serve.

SERVES 12

MARSHMALLOWS

1/4 cup cornstarch
1/3 cup confectioners' sugar
1 packet powdered gelatin
1/3 cup water
2/3 cup granulated sugar
1/2 cup light corn syrup
1/4 teaspoon salt
1 teaspoon vanilla extract

1. Sift together the cornstarch and confectioners' sugar. Lightly butter an 8-inch square baking pan and sprinkle with 1 tablepoon of the cornstarch mixture. Tilt the pan in all directions to coat the bottom and sides. Do not shake out the excess.

2. Blend the gelatin with the water in a small saucepan and let soak for 5 minutes. Add the granulated sugar and stir over low heat until the gelatin and sugar dissolve.

3. In a mixer, combine the gelatin mixture, corn syrup, salt, and vanilla and beat on high speed for 15 minutes, until peaks form.

4. Spread the gelatin mixture over the bottom of the prepared pan and smooth the top. Let stand for 2 hours, or until set.

5. With a wet knife, cut the marshmallow mixture into quarters and loosen around the edges. Sprinkle the remaining cornstarch mixture on a baking sheet and invert the marshmallows onto it. Cut each quarter into pieces, and roll each in the cornstarch and sugar mixture.

6. Place the marshmallows on a rack and cover with paper towels. Let stand overnight to dry the surface slightly. Store airtight; the marshmallows will keep for a month.

MAKES ABOUT 3 DOZEN MARSHMALLOWS

AUGUST 23, 1981: "FOOD: THOSE EARTHLY DESSERTS," BY CRAIG CLAIBORNE WITH PIERRE FRANEY. MARSHMALLOW RECIPE ADAPTED FROM *BETTER THAN STORE-BOUGHT*, BY HELEN WITTY AND ELIZABETH SCHNEIDER COLCHIE.

—1981

LORA BRODY'S BÊTE NOIRE (INTENSE CHOCOLATE CAKE)

Lora Brody, a cookbook author, suggests serving this cake either warm with crème anglaise or at room temperature with whipped cream.

———

½ cup water

1⅓ cups sugar

½ pound unsweetened chocolate, finely chopped

¼ pound semisweet chocolate, finely chopped

½ pound (2 sticks) unsalted butter,
  cut into small pieces and softened

5 extra-large eggs, at room temperature
  (about 1 cup whites plus the yolks)

1. Heat the oven to 350 degrees. Butter a 9-inch round cake pan and place a neat circle of parchment or wax paper in the bottom, covering it completely. If wax paper is used, butter it; if parchment is used, it is not necessary to butter it.

2. Combine the water with 1 cup sugar in a 2-quart heavy saucepan; a copper pan is ideal for this. Attach a candy thermometer to the pan, bring to a boil over high heat, and cook for about 4 minutes, or to a temperature of 220 degrees.

3. Remove the saucepan from the heat and immedi-ately add the chocolate, stirring until it is melted and smooth. The mixture may "seize," but that is all right; it will blend when the butter is added. Immediately start adding the butter, stirring gently until all of it is used.

4. Place the eggs and the remaining ⅓ cup sugar in the bowl of a mixer fitted with a whisk (or mix in a large bowl with a hand mixer). Start beating on high speed and continue until the yolks are quite thick, pale yellow, and tripled in volume. This may take about 15 minutes. (It may be useful to place a dishcloth over the mixer and bowl to prevent splattering.)

5. Reduce the mixer speed to low. Add the chocolate mixture, mixing only until it is fully incorporated. Do not overbeat—this would cause air bubbles to form.

6. Spoon and scrape the mixture into the prepared cake pan. Set the pan in a slightly larger pan and pour boiling water around it. Do not allow the sides of the pans to touch. Place in the oven and bake for 25 minutes. Insert the sharp point of a knife into the center of the cake; if it comes out clean, the cake is done. If it does not come out clean, continue baking for up to 10 minutes longer. Do not cook longer than a total of 35 minutes. Let cool in the pan for 10 minutes.

7. Run a sharp knife around the edges of the cake and unmold onto a cookie sheet; remove the paper. Invert a serving plate over the cake and turn it right side up onto the serving plate. Serve warm or at room temperature.

SERVES 6 TO 8

MARCH 13, 1983: "FOOD: A FANCY BOTH BITTER AND SWEET," BY CRAIG CLAIBORNE WITH PIERRE FRANEY.

—1983

PURPLE PLUM TORTE

This is both the most often published and the most requested recipe in the *Times* archives. By my count, Marian Burros (who was given the recipe by Lois Levine, with whom Burros wrote *Elegant but Easy*) ran the recipe in the paper twelve times. And when I asked readers for recipe suggestions for this book, 247 people raved about the torte. The torte happily lives up to its billing: crusty and light, with deep wells of slackened, sugar-glazed plums.

I've thought a lot about why this torte struck such a chord with people: the answer, I think, is that it's a nearly perfect recipe. There are only eight ingredients, all of which, except for the plums, you probably already have in your kitchen. There are just four steps, most of which are one sentence long. You need no special equipment, just a bowl, a wooden spoon, and a pan. The batter is like pancake batter, which most everyone is comfortable making. And baked plums are sweet and tart, making the flavor more complex and memorable than a hard-hitting sweet dessert.

It also freezes well.

"A friend who loved the tortes said that in exchange for two, she would let me store as many as I wanted in her freezer," Burros wrote one year when she ran the recipe. "A week later, she went on vacation for two weeks and her mother stayed with her children. When she returned, my friend called and asked, 'How many of those tortes did you leave in my freezer?'

"'Twenty-four, but two of those were for you.'

"There was a long pause. 'Well, I guess my mother either ate twelve of them or gave them away.'"

In later versions of the recipe, Burros cut back the sugar to ¾ cup—feel free to if you like—and added variations, such as substituting blueberries or apples and cranberries for the plums (I haven't tried either, but Burros was a fan). She jumped the shark, in my view, though, when she created low-fat variations with mashed bananas and applesauce. While I respect her enthusiasm for innovation, this is one recipe that needs no improvement.

––––––––

I cup all-purpose flour

I teaspoon baking powder

Large pinch of salt

I cup sugar, plus I tablespoon, or more or less, depending on the tartness of the plums

8 tablespoons (I stick) unsalted butter, softened

2 large eggs

12 purple plums, halved and pitted

2 teaspoons fresh lemon juice, or more or less, depending on the tartness of the plums

I tablespoon ground cinnamon

1. Heat the oven to 350 degrees. Sift the flour with the baking powder and salt.

2. Cream 1 cup sugar and the butter in a large bowl with a hand mixer (or in a mixer) until light in color. Add the dry ingredients and then the eggs.

3. Spoon the batter into an ungreased 9-inch springform pan. Cover the top of the batter with the plum halves, skin side up. Sprinkle with the remaining tablespoon of sugar and the lemon juice, adjusting to the tartness of the fruit. Sprinkle with the cinnamon.

4. Bake until the cake is golden and the plums are bubbly, 45 to 50 minutes. Cool on a rack, then unmold.

SERVES 8

COOKING NOTE

I like this best with oval Italian plums, available in early fall.

READERS

"Not only is it delicious, it is also simple. It has served me as an impromptu dessert on numerous occasions (even in the winter, one almost always has apples and frozen cranberries in the house). I have served it with ice cream, sorbet, whipped cream, yogurt, sour cream, crème fraîche, Barbados Cream (à la Nigella), or crème anglaise—depending on the particular torte, my mood, and what I have on hand. And yes, I *did* laminate it!" [Presumably, the recipe, not the cake.]

Donna L. Boies, Washington, D.C., letter

"I make a dozen every fall and store in the freezer just as she recommends. I also sometimes instead use peaches, mango, blueberries. I add ½ tsp. of vanilla and the grated rind of 1 small lemon to the dough."

Frances Gordon, Atlantis, FL, letter

"In August and September of each year I make at least 2 cakes a week. They freeze very well and cheer me up during the dark winter months."

Dagmar Greve, New York, NY, letter

"The only change I have made over the years is to add a teaspoon of almond extract. The combination of the almond flavoring with the purple plums is ethereal."

Nancy Denburg, e-mail

SEPTEMBER 21, 1983: "FOOD NOTES," BY MARIAN BURROS.

—1983

CAMPTON PLACE BUTTERMILK CHOCOLATE CAKE

Beneath a frosting so silky and delicate that it floats across your palate is a cake that reminds me of the moist, light soil lying beneath moss.

For the Cake
5 ounces unsweetened chocolate, chopped
12 tablespoons (1½ sticks) unsalted butter
1½ cups buttermilk
5 large eggs, separated
1½ cups sugar
1¼ cups all-purpose flour
½ teaspoon baking soda

For the Frosting
¾ pound semisweet chocolate, chopped
½ cup warm water
1 cup sugar
¾ pound (3 sticks) unsalted butter, softened
5 large egg yolks

1. To make the cake, heat the oven to 350 degrees. Butter two 9-by-2-inch round cake pans. Line the bottom of each pan with parchment paper cut to fit neatly. Butter the paper. Sprinkle the inside of the pans with flour and shake out the excess.
2. Combine the chocolate and butter in a heavy saucepan. Place the pan in a larger saucepan of simmering water and heat, stirring, just until the butter and chocolate are melted and blended. Off the heat, gradually beat in the buttermilk. Set aside to cool.
3. Beat the egg yolks and sugar in a mixer with a paddle (or in a large bowl with a hand mixer) until thickened and lemon colored. Gradually add the chocolate mixture, stirring. Set aside.
4. Sift together the flour and baking soda. Set aside.
5. Beat the egg whites in a clean mixer bowl with a whisk (or in a large bowl with clean beaters) until they are stiff but not dry. Fold into the chocolate mixture. Sift the flour mixture over the chocolate batter, folding it in. Pour and scrape equal amounts into the prepared cake pans.
6. Place in the oven and bake for 30 minutes, or until a cake tester, or a toothpick, comes out clean. Place

the cakes on a rack and let stand for about 10 minutes. Invert the cakes onto a rack and let cool.
7. Meanwhile, to prepare the frosting, put the chocolate in a large bowl. Combine the water and sugar in a saucepan and bring to a boil. When the sugar is dissolved, pour this over the chocolate, stirring until smooth and about as thick as mayonnaise. If the mixture seems too stiff, add a little more water. Cover with plastic wrap and let cool to room temperature.
8. Put the butter in a large bowl and beat until smooth. Add the yolks one at a time, beating. Gradually fold in the chocolate mixture, until just blended.
9. Place 1 cake layer on a cake plate and spread the top generously with frosting. Top with the second layer. Spread the top and sides with the remaining frosting, smoothing it as you go along.

SERVES 12

COOKING NOTE
The frosting is beautiful to work with: after generously frosting the cake, you'll still have about ¾ cup left over. I don't need to tell you what to do with it. Although, Craig Claiborne noted, "If you wish to spread the chocolate frosting a little further, you may slice each layer through the center to make 2 rounds. Place one round at a time on a flat surface, frost it, add a second layer, more frosting, and so on until all the layers have been added. Frost the cake on the top and around the sides before cutting."

JULY 15, 1984: "FOOD: FLOWING WITH BUTTERMILK," BY CRAIG CLAIBORNE WITH PIERRE FRANEY. RECIPE ADAPTED FROM BRADLEY OGDEN, CHEF AT THE CAMPTON PLACE HOTEL IN SAN FRANCISCO.

—1984

PANFORTE (TRADITIONAL SIENESE FRUITCAKE)

Panforte, from Siena, in Tuscany, is like fruitcake with the texture of nougat. It's dense and densely spiced, and one of my favorite holiday desserts, because with it, you get the intense punctuation you want after a titanic meal.

This recipe comes from *The Italian Baker*, one of the

most important baking books of the twentieth century. Carol Field unearthed the breads of small villages across Italy, the ciabatta, pane Pugliese, pizza bianca, and rosemary breads that we've since come to regard as everyday loaves. Panforte hasn't yet become a household staple, but it should.

———

1 cup unblanched whole hazelnuts

1 cup blanched whole almonds

1 cup coarsely chopped candied orange peel

1 cup finely chopped candied citron

1 teaspoon grated lemon zest

½ cup unbleached all-purpose flour

1 teaspoon ground cinnamon

¼ teaspoon ground coriander

¼ teaspoon ground cloves

¼ teaspoon freshly grated nutmeg

Pinch of white pepper

¾ cup granulated sugar

¾ cup honey

2 tablespoons unsalted butter

Confectioners' sugar for dusting

1. Heat the oven to 350 degrees. Butter a 9-inch springform pan, line the bottom and sides with parchment paper, and butter the paper. Toast the hazelnuts on a baking sheet in the oven until the skins pop and blister, 10 to 15 minutes. Rub the skins from the hazelnuts in a kitchen towel.

2. Meanwhile, toast the almonds on a baking sheet until very pale golden, 10 to 15 minutes. Remove from the oven and let cool. Reduce the oven temperature to 300 degrees.

3. Chop the almonds and hazelnuts very coarsely. Mix the nuts, orange peel, citron, lemon zest, flour, cinnamon, coriander, cloves, nutmeg, and pepper thoroughly in a large bowl.

4. Combine the granulated sugar, honey, and butter in a heavy saucepan and attach a candy thermometer to the pan. Cook over low heat, stirring constantly, until the syrup registers 242 to 248 degrees (a little of the mixture will form a ball when dropped into cold water). Immediately pour the syrup into the fruit mixture and stir quickly until thoroughly blended, then immediately pour into the prepared pan and smooth the top with a spatula. The batter will become stiff and sticky very quickly, so you must work fast.

5. Bake for 40 minutes. The panforte won't color or seem very firm even when ready, but it will harden as it cools. Cool on a rack until the cake is firm to the touch.

6. Remove the sides of the pan and invert the cake onto a sheet of wax paper. Peel off the parchment paper. Dust heavily with confectioners' sugar.

SERVES 10

VARIATION

To make Panforte Scuro (dark), add 2 ounces dried figs, coarsely chopped, and 1 to 2 tablespoons unsweetened cocoa powder.

DECEMBER 8, 1985: "BAKING: AROMATIC ACTIVITY FOR THE SEASON," BY FLORENCE FABRICANT. RECIPE ADAPTED FROM *THE ITALIAN BAKER*, BY CAROL FIELD.

—1985

⌐ MARJOLAINE (MULTILAYERED CHOCOLATE AND PRALINE CAKE)

Marjolaine, a hazelnut cake layered with rum cream and praline, had its moment during the 1980s fascination with French pâtisserie. No dessert with seventeen steps is going to endure through the ages as a go-to classic, but it would be a shame to skip past this recipe. All the effort and layering make for one spectacular cake, the kind you can peel away level by level with your fork.

Two recipes for the cake ran around the same time—one by Raymond A. Sokolov and this one by Patricia Wells, both frequent *Times* contributors. Figuring out which one to make was a Sophie's choice, and both looked great, but I didn't want to err with a recipe that takes a day to make. I finally chose Wells's because it seemed to have more complex flavor (and crème fraîche in the ingredient list didn't hurt). You can check out Sokolov's online. I was pleased with my decision: Wells's is extraordinary.

Still, making it is a nearly insane test of willpower and endurance. It's not difficult—as always, Wells's instructions are precise and helpful—it's just that the baking and layering takes all day. I started at breakfast and finished just in time for cocktails.

Marjolaine is actually better the next day: it mellows and relaxes and becomes not five desserts in one, but one.

———

For the Praline Powder
I cup unblanched whole almonds
I cup confectioners' sugar

For the Chocolate Cream
2 cups crème fraîche
15 ounces bittersweet chocolate,
    broken into pieces

For the Pastry Cream
8 large egg yolks
I cup sugar
½ cup unbleached all-purpose flour
2½ cups whole milk
10 ounces (2¼ sticks) unsalted butter, softened

For the Cake
I cup unblanched whole hazelnuts
¾ cup sugar
10 large egg whites
¼ cup unbleached all-purpose flour

For the Rum Cream
2 cups Pastry Cream (above)
I tablespoon vanilla extract
I tablespoon rum

For the Praline Cream
2 cups Pastry Cream (above)
2 cups Praline Powder (above)

1. To prepare the praline powder, heat the oven to 300 degrees. Spread the almonds on baking sheet and bake until fragrant and light brown, about 10 minutes. Remove from the oven and let cool.

2. Oil a baking sheet with a light vegetable oil. Combine the almonds and sugar in a heavy saucepan. Cook, stirring constantly, over medium heat until the sugar begins to melt. The mixture will go through several stages, from a dry blend to one where the sugar forms little bubbles the size of peas. Continue cooking, stirring constantly so all of the sugar clinging to the almonds melts, until the mixture turns dark brown and

syrupy and the nuts make a popping sound. The whole process will take about 5 minutes.

3. Quickly pour the mixture onto the oiled baking sheet. The mixture will harden to almond brittle. When the praline is cool, break it into pieces. Grind it to a fine powder in a food processor. (The praline can be made weeks in advance and refrigerated or frozen in an airtight container.)

4. To prepare the chocolate cream, bring the crème fraîche to a boil in a medium saucepan. Remove from the heat and whisk in the chocolate piece by piece until it is completely melted and blended. Set aside until cool and thick. It should have the consistency of a thick, spreadable frosting. (This can be made as much as 3 days in advance and refrigerated. If it hardens, reheat it gently, beating until it reaches the proper consistency.)

5. To prepare the pastry cream, using a whisk (or a mixer fitted with a whisk), beat the egg yolks and sugar in a large bowl until thick and lemon colored. Gently whisk in the flour.

6. Bring the milk to a boil in a large heavy saucepan. Whisk one-third of the hot milk into the egg mixture, then pour the egg mixture into the remaining milk. Boil, stirring constantly, over medium-high heat until thickened, about 2 minutes. (You have to whisk really hard to keep it from lumping; and you do need to cook it for a full 2 minutes, so take the pan on and off the heat as you go.) Transfer to a bowl, lay a piece of plastic wrap on the surface of the cream, and let cool.

7. Beat the butter in a bowl until soft and creamy. When the pastry cream is completely cool, whisk in the butter. (The pastry cream can be made up to 3 days in advance and kept refrigerated.)

8. To prepare the cake, heat the oven to 300 degrees. Heavily butter 2 jelly-roll pans, measuring about 14 by 10 by 1 inch. Line them with parchment paper and butter and flour the paper. (If you don't have jelly-roll pans, use 2 large baking sheets.)

9. Spread the hazelnuts on another baking sheet and roast until fragrant and lightly browned, about 10 minutes. Remove from the oven and rub the warm nuts in a dish towel to remove as much skin as possible. Cool, then finely grind them with ¼ cup sugar in a food processor.

10. Beat the egg whites in a mixer fitted with a whisk (or in a large bowl with a hand mixer) until they begin to stiffen. Slowly add the remaining ½ cup sugar, mix-

ing until the whites form stiff but not dry peaks. Fold in the flour and the hazelnut mixture. Spread the batter evenly in the prepared pans (or spread into 14-by-10-by-1-inch rectangles on the baking sheets).

11. Bake until the cakes are thoroughly browned, 25 to 30 minutes. Remove the cakes from the oven and invert them onto racks. Cover each cake with a damp towel and let stand for several minutes, then remove the parchment paper while the cakes are still warm. Let cool completely.

12. At least 24 hours, but no more than 3 days before serving, assemble the marjolaine: Cut each cake lengthwise in half and trim as needed into 4 equally sized rectangles. Divide the pastry cream in half. Blend the vanilla extract and rum into one portion of the pastry cream. Blend the praline powder into the remaining pastry cream. (Mix the praline cream just before assembling the cake, because the flavor will fade if mixed up in advance.) The chocolate and pastry creams should be chilled but spreadable.

13. Place 1 cake layer on a large rectangular serving platter. Spread a little less than half the chocolate cream on the cake. Refrigerate until firm, about 10 minutes.

14. Cover the chocolate cream with the second cake layer. Spread with all of the praline cream and refrigerate until firm, about 15 minutes.

15. Top the praline cream with the third cake layer. Spread with all of the rum cream and refrigerate until firm, about 15 minutes.

16. Top the rum cream with the fourth cake layer. Frost the top and sides of the cake with the remaining chocolate cream. Refrigerate for 15 minutes, then cover with plastic wrap. Refrigerate for 1 to 3 days before serving.

17. Remove the cake from the refrigerator 15 minutes before serving, then cut into thin slices.

SERVES 16 TO 20

COOKING NOTE
To save a step, you can use blanched hazelnuts for the cake and just toast them before grinding.

SEPTEMBER 13, 1987: "FOOD: WHEN THINGS GO RIGHT," BY PATRICIA WELLS.

—1987

⌒ CHOCOLATE CAKE WITH BAY LEAF SYRUP

This is vintage Tom Colicchio, back when he was at Mondrian.

———

For the Bay Leaf Syrup
I cup sugar
I cup water
I vanilla bean, split, seeds scraped out and reserved
12 fresh bay leaves (available at specialty food stores)

For the Chocolate Cake
12 tablespoons (1½ sticks) unsalted butter, plus 1 tablespoon for greasing the pan
15 ounces bittersweet chocolate
6 large eggs, separated
¾ cup sugar
I cup almond flour (available at specialty food stores) or 1 cup ground almonds (about ¼ pound unblanched whole almonds)

I cup heavy cream
6 fresh bay leaves

1. To make the syrup, combine the sugar and water in a small saucepan. Add the vanilla bean and seeds and bay leaves and bring to a boil, stirring to dissolve the sugar. Lower the heat and simmer until the liquid is reduced to about 1 cup, 15 to 20 minutes. Cool, strain, and set aside.

2. To make the cake, heat the oven to 375 degrees. Grease a 9-inch springform pan with 1 tablespoon butter. Place the remaining 12 tablespoons butter and 12 ounces chocolate in the top of a double boiler. Heat over barely simmering water, stirring occasionally, until the butter and chocolate melt.

3. Beat the egg yolks and ½ cup sugar in a mixer fitted with a whisk (or a large bowl with a hand mixer) until the mixture thickens and is pale yellow in color. Add the melted chocolate mixture and mix well. Fold in the almond flour.

4. Beat the egg whites with the remaining ¼ cup sugar in a clean mixer bowl with the clean whisk (or in a large bowl with clean beaters) until they hold stiff peaks. Fold into the egg yolk mixture. Pour the batter into the prepared pan.

5. Chop the remaining chocolate into coarse chunks, about ½ to 1 inch. Scatter randomly over the batter. Bake for 25 to 30 minutes, or until the cake feels firm to the touch. Let cool on a rack.

6. To make the whipped cream, combine the heavy cream with 1 tablespoon of the bay leaf syrup in a bowl and beat until firm peaks form.

7. Remove the cake from the pan and slice into 6 wedges. Pool a few tablespoons of the bay leaf syrup on each of 6 dessert plates. Place a slice of cake on each plate. Add a dollop of the bay leaf whipped cream, and garnish each with a bay leaf.

SERVES 6

OCTOBER 14, 1990: "FOOD: IT'S THYME FOR DESSERT," BY KAREN MACNEIL. RECIPE ADAPTED FROM TOM COLICCHIO, THE CHEF, AND SUSIE DAYTON, THE PASTRY CHEF, AT MONDRIAN IN NEW YORK CITY.

—1990

✑ MARCELLA'S PEAR CAKE

½ cup fine dry bread crumbs

2 large eggs

¼ cup whole milk

1 cup sugar

Tiny pinch of salt

1½ cups all-purpose flour

2 pounds ripe Bosc pears

2 tablespoons unsalted butter

1. Position a rack in the upper third of the oven and heat the oven to 350 degrees. Butter a 9-inch-round cake pan and sprinkle with the bread crumbs. Turn the pan upside down and tap it or shake it lightly to get rid of all the loose crumbs. Beat the eggs and milk together in a bowl. Add the sugar and salt and continue beating until well combined. Add the flour, mixing thoroughly.

2. Peel the pears, slice in half, and scoop out the seeds and core. Cut lengthwise into thin slices. Add to the bowl, mixing well; the batter will be very thick.

3. Spoon the batter into the pan, leveling it off with the back of a spoon or a spatula. Dot the surface with the butter. Bake for 45 minutes, or until the top is lightly golden. Cool slightly on a rack.

4. Remove the cake from the pan as soon as it is cool and firm enough to handle. Serve warm or at room temperature.

SERVES 10

APRIL 28, 1991: "FOOD: NIGHT OF THE LONG KNIVES," BY WILLIAM GRIMES. RECIPE ADAPTED FROM MORE CLASSIC ITALIAN COOKING, BY MARCELLA HAZAN.

—1991

✑ POLISH JEWISH PLUM CAKE

In the Northeast, at least, from late September to late October, you can readily find olive-shaped purple Italian plums. They hold up well when cooked, tend not to release too much juice—a boon to bakers of cakes and tarts—and they sink into cakes, like encased jewels.

Laura Goodenough's Apple Coffee Cake (p. 631), which ran in the *Times* in 1968, in a story by Jean Hewitt, is very similar to this one. The oil and orange juice foundation makes for a beautiful cake that has become an American classic.

---

3 cups all-purpose flour

1 tablespoon baking powder

½ teaspoon salt

1½ to 2 pounds Italian plums

1½ teaspoons ground cinnamon

1½ cups granulated sugar

4 large eggs

1 cup vegetable oil

½ cup orange juice

1 teaspoon vanilla extract

Confectioners' sugar for dusting

1. Heat the oven to 350 degrees. Grease a 10-inch Bundt or tube pan and dust with flour. Sift together the flour, baking powder, and salt.

2. Halve the plums (quarter them if large), and remove the pits. You will need 4 cups sliced plums. Place in a large bowl and sprinkle with the cinnamon and ¼ cup sugar.

3. Beat the eggs in a large bowl. Gradually add the remaining 1¼ cups sugar, the oil, orange juice, and

vanilla. Add the dry ingredients to the egg mixture, beating just until combined.

4. Pour one-third of the batter into the prepared pan. Layer with one-third of the plums. Repeat 2 more times, ending with plums. Bake for 65 to 75 minutes, or until golden on top and a toothpick inserted into the center of the cake comes out clean. Let sit for 15 minutes on a rack.

5. Run a knife around the cake to loosen it, and unmold onto a plate. Sprinkle with confectioners' sugar and serve.

SERVES 12

SEPTEMBER 23, 1992: "JEWISH FOOD TRADITIONS LINGER IN A POLAND BEREFT OF JEWS," BY JOAN NATHAN.

—1992

☞ TAILLEVENT'S CHOCOLATE CAKE WITH PISTACHIO SAUCE

A recipe from one of the world's great restaurants, Taillevent in Paris, and one of the best food books ever written, *The Food Lover's Guide to Paris*, by Patricia Wells.

When I made these cakes—they're individual cakes, despite the recipe title—I thought the individual portions seemed stingy. But the bitty cakes turned out to be so rich I couldn't finish a single serving.

———

For the Cake

4½ ounces bittersweet chocolate, chopped

6 tablespoons confectioners' sugar

6 tablespoons unsalted butter, softened

2 large eggs, separated

For the Sauce

½ cup roasted pistachios

1 cup sugar

1 large egg, separated

2 cups whole milk

3 large egg yolks

1. To make the cake, melt the chocolate in a small saucepan over very low heat. Add ¼ cup sugar and the butter and stir until melted. Whisk in the egg yolks. Attach a candy thermometer to the side of the

pan and cook, stirring constantly, until the mixture reaches 160 degrees. Set aside to cool for 10 minutes.

2. Beat the egg whites in a mixer fitted with a whisk (or in a bowl with a hand mixer) until stiff. Add the remaining 2 tablespoons sugar and beat until the whites are glossy. Whisk one-third of the egg whites into the chocolate mixture, then fold in the remaining whites.

3. Rinse four 4-ounce molds (ramekins or tartlet pans work) with water; do not dry. Divide the chocolate mixture among the molds. Refrigerate for 24 hours.

4. Meanwhile, to make the sauce, remove as much skin as possible from the pistachios. Rinse quickly with boiling water, drain, and then remove as much of the remaining skin as possible. Place the nuts in a food processor and pulse until finely ground. Add ⅓ cup sugar and the egg white and process until the mixture forms a paste.

5. Place 3 tablespoons of the pistachio paste in a medium saucepan (save the rest for another use), add the milk, and bring to a boil over medium heat. Remove from the heat and let steep for 5 minutes.

6. Strain the milk through a fine-mesh sieve into another medium saucepan; set aside.

7. Whisk together the egg yolks and the remaining ⅔ cup sugar in a bowl until thick and light. Whisk in half the strained milk, then whisk the mixture back into the remaining milk. Cook the sauce over low heat, stirring constantly, until thick enough to coat the back of a spoon; do not let it come to a boil. (This may take longer than you expect, as much as 20 minutes.) Refrigerate for 24 hours.

8. To serve, spoon a pool of sauce onto the center of each of 4 plates. Run the tip of a small knife around the inside edges of the molds, dip them briefly in a bowl of hot water, and invert them onto the plates. Let the cakes warm up for a minute or two before serving.

SERVES 4

COOKING NOTES

If you buy good-quality shelled pistachios, you can skip Step 4.

It's difficult to remove the cakes from their molds or ramekins without mashing in an edge or two. Serve them as if the flaws were intended. Or make the cakes using small cake rings: lay 4 small pieces of parchment on a baking sheet, place the rings on top, and fill the rings with the batter. To unmold, dip a knife in hot water, dry it, run it around the sides of the rings to loosen, and invert the cakes onto plates and peel back the parchment.

Do not use low-fat milk for the sauce—it needs the fat for texture and also to temper the sugar.

FEBRUARY 12, 1995: "FOOD: DANGER: CHOCOLATE AHEAD," BY MOLLY O'NEILL. RECIPE ADAPTED FROM *THE FOOD LOVER'S GUIDE TO PARIS*, BY PATRICIA WELLS.

—1995

JUNIOR'S CHEESECAKE

A true New York–style cheesecake—creamy rather than fluffy. The secret lies in the single egg which just holds together the heavy cream and cream cheese. Unlike most cheesecakes, this one is not baked in a water bath, and yet its texture is creamy even at the edges.

Cheesecakes originated in Central and Eastern Europe, where they were made with cottage or farmers' cheese and set on a zwieback crust. The hop and skip to cream cheese and graham crackers, the food writer Joan Nathan says, was made early in the twentieth century with the birth of Breakstone's, which commercialized cream cheese, and Kraft, which sold both cream cheese and graham crackers. Junior's, the Brooklyn restaurant where this cheesecake become famous, opened in 1950.

———

¼ cup graham cracker crumbs

¾ cup plus 2 tablespoons sugar

3 tablespoons sifted cornstarch

30 ounces (3¾ large packages) cream cheese, at room temperature

1 large egg

½ cup heavy cream

¾ teaspoon vanilla extract

1. Heat the oven to 350 degrees. Generously butter an 8-inch springform pan. Lightly coat the bottom of the pan with the graham cracker crumbs, and refrigerate the pan.

2. Combine the sugar and cornstarch in a mixer fitted with a paddle (or mix in a large bowl with a hand mixer). Beat in the cream cheese. Beat in the egg.

Slowly drizzle in the heavy cream, beating constantly. Beat in the vanilla.

3. Pour the batter into the prepared pan. Bake until the top is golden, 40 to 50 minutes. Cool in the pan on a wire rack for 3 hours.

SERVES 8 TO 10

COOKING NOTE

When slicing the cake, use a knife that you've run under hot water (and dried).

OCTOBER 11, 1996: "HARRY ROSEN IS DEAD AT 92: JUNIOR'S RESTAURANT FOUNDER," BY ERIC ASIMOV. RECIPE ADAPTED FROM *NEW YORK COOKBOOK*, BY MOLLY O'NEILL.

—1996

OLIVE OIL AND APPLE CIDER CAKE

A dense, gently perfumed cake. Have it for breakfast or with tea. You must use good olive oil (I've used Capezzana and Manni); the flaws of an inferior oil—namely bitterness and insipidity—would be very much on display.

———

8 apples, peeled, cored, and quartered

1 cup apple cider

3 cups unbleached all-purpose flour

1½ teaspoons baking powder

¼ teaspoon kosher salt

5 large eggs

1½ cups sugar

1 cup high-quality extra-virgin olive oil

1 cup heavy cream, whipped with 1 tablespoon sugar (optional)

1. Place the apples and ½ cup apple cider in a small saucepan, cover, and bring to a boil. Lower the heat and simmer for 10 minutes, or until the apples are falling apart. Remove from the heat and mash the apples with a fork to make a coarse applesauce. Let cool.

2. Heat the oven to 325 degrees. Brush a Bundt pan or 10-inch tube pan with a light coating of olive oil. Dust the pan with flour and tap out any excess. Combine

the flour, baking powder, and salt in a bowl; set aside. Stir together the remaining ½ cup cider and ½ cup of the applesauce.

3. Whip the eggs with the sugar in a mixer fitted with a paddle attachment (or in a large bowl with a hand mixer) until tripled in volume, about 8 minutes. Fold in one-third of the dry ingredients until just combined. Fold in half of the cider-applesauce mixture. Gently fold in the olive oil, deflating the batter as little as possible. Alternate the remaining dry ingredients and the cider mixture, ending with dry ingredients.

4. Gently pour the batter into the prepared pan. Bake for 1 hour and 10 minutes, or until a toothpick inserted in the center of the cake comes out clean. Put the cake on a rack to cool for 10 minutes, then unmold and let cool on a rack.

5. Serve with the remaining cider-applesauce and whipped cream, if desired.

SERVES 12

COOKING NOTE

Have fun with Step 3, but beat it in a mixer—watching the eggs and sugar turn thick, yellow, and silky is a beautiful process, and doing it by hand is not.

OCTOBER 12, 1997: "LOVE, ITALIAN STYLE," BY MOLLY O'NEILL. RECIPE ADAPTED FROM JOANNE KILEEN AND GEORGE GERMON, THE OWNERS OF AL FORNO IN PROVIDENCE, RHODE ISLAND.

—1997

⌒ PEAR UPSIDE-DOWN CAKE

Sometimes you read a recipe title and immediately have a clear picture in your head of how it will turn out. And sometimes you're way off, as I was with this pear upside-down cake. I saw the molasses and ginger and dark brown sugar prominent among the ingredients, but I still expected the cake to turn out light and buttery yellow, like most pear upside-down cakes. This one is as dark as night, the pears sunk into the top like slivers of moon. The rich, dense cake is reminiscent of a gingersnap and is a memorable, if unorthodox, counterpoint to the pears.

The cake is best eaten within a day of baking. And

don't skip the accompaniment of rum-spiked whipped cream.

———

11 tablespoons unsalted butter
5 small ripe Bartlett pears, peeled, cored, and quartered
2 tablespoons fresh lemon juice
¼ cup granulated sugar
6 tablespoons Poire Williams (pear eau-de-vie)
1 cup all-purpose flour
1 tablespoon ground ginger
1 teaspoon ground cinnamon
¼ teaspoon ground cloves
¼ teaspoon freshly grated nutmeg
¼ teaspoon salt
¼ cup packed dark brown sugar
3 large eggs
½ cup unsulphured molasses
2 tablespoons grated ginger
    (from a 4-inch piece of fresh ginger)
1 teaspoon baking soda
2 tablespoons boiling water
Rum-scented whipped cream (see Cooking Notes)
    or rum-raisin ice cream for serving

1. Butter a 9-inch cake pan with 1 tablespoon butter; set aside. Toss the pears with the lemon juice; set aside.

2. Melt 2 tablespoons butter in a large sauté pan over medium-high heat. Sprinkle with 2 tablespoons sugar. Add the pears, cut side down, in a single layer, and cook until browned on all sides, 6 to 8 minutes; gently move them around in the pan as they cook so they brown evenly. Transfer to a plate.

3. Add the Poire Williams to the pan, and sprinkle with the remaining 2 tablespoons granulated sugar. Cook, stirring, until reduced to a syrup, about 1 minute.

4. Pour the syrup into the cake pan, coating the bottom. Place the pears in the cake pan, cut side down, arranging them in a single layer (there may be a few leftover slices).

5. Heat the oven to 350 degrees. Whisk together the flour, ginger, cinnamon, cloves, nutmeg, and salt in a medium bowl.

6. In the bowl of a mixer fitted with a paddle attachment (or in a bowl with a hand mixer), beat the remaining 8 tablespoons butter until fluffy. Add the brown sugar, and beat on medium-high speed for 3

minutes. Add the eggs and continue beating to combine. Add the molasses and fresh ginger. Gradually add the flour mixture.

7. Combine the baking soda and boiling water in a small bowl, beating with a fork. Add to the batter and mix well. Pour the batter into the cake pan over the pears.

8. Bake for 25 minutes. Lower the heat to 325 degrees and bake for an additional 15 to 20 minutes, until the cake springs back when touched in the center. Remove from the oven and cool for 1 hour.

9. Invert the cake onto a serving plate. Serve with rum-spiked whipped cream or rum-raisin ice cream.

SERVES 10

COOKING NOTES

I used just 3 pears; buy 4 if they're on the small side.

The pears only lightly browned when sautéed, which didn't seem to hurt the cake.

To make rum-scented whipped cream, beat 1 cup heavy cream until it holds soft peaks. Add 2 tablespoons confectioners' sugar and whisk until the sugar is dissolved. Then beat in 1 to 2 tablespoons dark rum, as desired.

DECEMBER 17, 1997: "HOLIDAY TASTES FROM THE OLD CHATHAM INN," BY R. W. APPLE JR. RECIPE ADAPTED FROM MELISSA KELLY, THE CHEF AT THE OLD CHATHAM SHEEP-HERDING COMPANY INN IN CHATHAM, NEW YORK.

—1997

WARM SOFT CHOCOLATE CAKE

If you dined in New York in the late 1990s, you probably ate dozens of these fragile chocolate bombs. The small plump cakes cook on the outside, creating a bouncy cake-like shell, while the inside remains loose chocolate custard, waiting to spill out on your plate as soon as you plunge your greedy fork into its side. Jean-Georges Vongerichten, the chef whose recipe this is, served it with coconut sorbet.

8 tablespoons (1 stick) unsalted butter
¼ pound bittersweet chocolate
2 large eggs
2 large egg yolks
¼ cup sugar
2 teaspoons all-purpose flour

1. Heat the oven to 450 degrees. Butter and lightly flour four 4-ounce molds, custard cups, or ramekins. Tap out the excess flour. Gently heat the butter and chocolate together in a double boiler or a small saucepan until the chocolate is almost completely melted.

2. While the chocolate mixture is heating, beat the eggs, yolks, and sugar in a bowl with a whisk or electric mixer until light and thick.

3. Beat the melted chocolate and butter together. While it is still warm, pour into the egg mixture, then quickly beat in the flour until combined.

4. Divide the batter among the molds. (At this point, you can refrigerate the desserts for several hours; bring to room temperature before cooking.) Put on a baking sheet.

5. Bake the cakes for 12 minutes; the centers will still be quite soft, but the sides will be set. Invert each mold onto a plate, and let sit for about 10 seconds, then unmold by lifting up one corner of the mold; the cake will fall out onto the plate. Serve immediately.

SERVES 4

PERIOD DETAIL

Although it feels as though food trends come and go dizzyingly fast, Florence Fabricant wrote a story called "The Cakes That Take New York Erupt with Molten Chocolate" in 1991, but Vongerichten's recipe, which launched the trend, didn't appear until 1997. The cake kicked around in numerous restaurants until 2009, when Domino's pizza chain introduced its Chocolate Lava Crunch Cake. Trend over.

DECEMBER 24, 1997: "THE CHEF," BY JEAN-GEORGES VONGERICHTEN WITH MARK BITTMAN.

—1997

COCONUT LOAF CAKE

This recipe began my lasting obsession with pastry chef Pierre Hermé's work—I love his use of daring yet understated flavors, his confidence that you'll notice his ingenuity without him underlining it with antennae-like garnishes. These traits have since built the Parisian pastry chef an empire of shops around the globe.

Hermé's work has been translated and brought to an American audience by Dorie Greenspan, who is the modern-day Maida Heatter. Like Heatter, Greenspan is both a passionate baker and an exceptional recipe writer. Note how in this cake recipe you're on Step 4 before you begin mixing the cake batter. Greenspan spends four steps making sure you've prepared your pans and ingredients so there are no unpleasant surprises along the way.

———

I ½ cups finely grated unsweetened dried coconut, plus extra for the pan (available at health food and specialty stores)

I ½ cups sugar

I ½ cups all-purpose flour

2 tablespoons ground coriander

I teaspoon baking powder

9 tablespoons unsalted butter, softened

3 large eggs, at room temperature

¼ cup powdered milk

¾ cup whole milk

¼ cup water

¼ cup white rum

1. Combine the coconut with 1 tablespoon sugar in a food processor and pulse until the coconut is pulverized but still powdery and dry. Set aside.
2. Center a rack in the oven and heat the oven to 350 degrees. Butter an 8½-by-4½-by-2½-inch loaf pan, dust the interior with grated coconut, and tap out the excess.
3. Sift together the flour, coriander, and baking powder.
4. In a mixer fitted with a paddle (or in large bowl with a hand mixer), beat the butter at medium-high speed until creamy, then slowly add 1 cup plus 3 tablespoons sugar. While beating, add the eggs one at a time, scraping down the sides of the bowl as necessary. Reduce the mixer speed to low. One at a time, add the ground coconut, powdered milk, and whole milk, beating only until each addition is incorporated.
5. Divide the flour mixture into two batches. With a rubber spatula, gently fold in first one batch and then the other; the batter should be smooth and thick. Immediately spoon the batter into the prepared pan.
6. Place the pan on 2 baking sheets, one on top of the other, or on an insulated baking sheet. Bake until the cake is golden brown and split down the center, about 70 to 80 minutes. To test whether the cake is done, insert a long thin knife into the center; it should come out dry and crumb-free. If the cake appears to be browning too quickly, cover loosely with a foil tent after the first 30 minutes of baking.
7. Meanwhile, prepare a simple syrup. Combine the remaining ¼ cup sugar with the water in a small saucepan, place over medium heat, and stir until the sugar is dissolved. Remove from the heat and add the rum. Let cool to room temperature.
8. Place a rack on a sheet of wax paper. When the cake is done, release it from the pan and turn it right side up on the rack. While it is still hot, brush the rum syrup over the top and sides of the cake.
9. To serve, cut the cake into thin slices. If desired, toast them lightly.

SERVES 8

JUNE 3, 1998: "EN ROUTE: FRANCE; A KITCHEN EMPEROR WHO MARSHALS NAPOLEONS" BY AMANDA HESSER. RECIPE ADAPTED FROM *DESSERTS BY PIERRE HERMÉ*, BY PIERRE HERMÉ AND DORIE GREENSPAN.

—1998

PAPA'S APPLE POUND CAKE

Just before baking this delicious loaf cake, you arrange apple pieces in two tidy rows down the center, like a spine. And as it bakes, they sink into the top of the batter.

———

I ⅓ cups raisins

I tablespoon plus 2½ teaspoons dark rum

2 Fuji apples, peeled and cored

I cup plus 3 tablespoons all-purpose flour

¼ teaspoon baking powder

8½ tablespoons unsalted butter, softened

1⅓ cups confectioners' sugar

3 large eggs, at room temperature

¼ cup apricot jam, melted and still warm

1. Center a rack in the oven, and heat the oven to 350 degrees. Butter and flour an 8-by-4-by-2½-inch loaf pan. Line the pan with parchment paper, allowing an extra inch or two to drape over the ends. (This will allow the finished cake to be lifted from the pan before serving.)

2. Bring a small pan of water to a boil, add the raisins, and boil for 1 minute. Drain and repeat the process. Drain the raisins well a second time and place in a small bowl with 1 tablespoon of rum; stir and set aside.

3. Cut 1 apple into 12 wedges; set aside. Cut the other into 8 wedges, then cut each wedge crosswise in half; set aside. Sift the flour and baking powder together; set aside.

4. Working in a mixer with a paddle (or by hand in a bowl with a rubber spatula), beat the butter until it is smooth. Slowly add 1 cup confectioners' sugar and beat until creamy. Add the eggs one at a time, beating until well blended. Fold in the flour mixture just until blended. Fold in the raisins.

5. Spoon half the batter into the prepared pan and smooth the top. Lay the 12 apple wedges down the center of the pan so their sides touch and the domed side of each wedge is on top. There will be a thin strip of exposed batter on either side of the row. Spoon the rest of the batter over and around the apples, and again smooth the top. Arrange the halved apple wedges in a single row down each long side of the pan, pressing the center-cut sides of the apples against the sides of the pan, so there are 2 rows of apple wedges with their points toward the center of the pan and exposed batter in the center. Gently push the apples into the batter, leaving the tops of the apples exposed. The mixture in the center of the pan will be slightly lower than the sides. Let rest for 10 minutes.

6. Place the pan in the oven and bake for 10 minutes. Using a sharp knife, cut a slit down the center of the batter to help it rise evenly. Continue to bake until a knife inserted into the cake comes out clean, another 40 to 50 minutes. Remove the pan from the oven, and gently brush the warm apricot jam over the hot cake. Allow the glaze to dry for 5 minutes.

7. Meanwhile, combine the remaining 2½ teaspoons rum and ⅓ cup confectioners' sugar in a small pan, stir well, and warm over low heat for a minute. Brush this icing over the dried apricot glaze and return the pan to the turned-off oven just until the icing is dry, about 2 minutes. Place the cake on a rack and cool to room temperature. To keep the cake moist, leave it in its pan until serving time.

8. To remove the cake from the pan, lift it by the edges of the parchment paper, carefully remove the paper, and transfer to a platter. Cut into slices to serve.

SERVES 6 TO 8

NOVEMBER 11, 1998: "THE CHEF," BY FRANÇOIS PAYARD WITH DORIE GREENSPAN.

—1998

FRESH GINGER CAKE

This dish is well known among dessert fanatics— a fragrant, spicy cake as dark as tar. David Lebovitz, the pastry chef and blogger (www.davidlebovitz.com), whose recipe it is, also created the spectacular Sugared Puffs on p. 867.

1 cup mild molasses

1 cup sugar

1 cup peanut oil

2½ cups all-purpose flour

1 teaspoon ground cinnamon

½ teaspoon ground cloves

½ teaspoon freshly ground black pepper

1 cup water

2 teaspoons baking soda

¼ pound fresh ginger, peeled, sliced, and finely chopped

2 large eggs, at room temperature

1. Position a rack in the center of the oven and heat the oven to 350 degrees. Line a 9-inch round cake pan with 3-inch-high sides or a 9½-inch springform pan with a circle of parchment paper. Mix together the molasses, sugar, and oil in a large bowl. Sift together the flour, cinnamon, cloves, and black pepper.

2. Bring the water to a boil in a small saucepan. Stir in the baking soda, then mix into the molasses mixture. Stir in the ginger. Gradually whisk the dry ingredients into the batter. Add the eggs and continue mixing until everything is thoroughly combined.

3. Pour the batter into the prepared cake pan. Bake for about 1 hour, until the top of the cake springs back lightly when pressed or until a toothpick inserted into the center comes out clean. If the top of the cake browns too quickly before the cake is done, drape a piece of foil over it. Cool the cake for at least 30 minutes in the pan on a rack.

4. Run a knife around the edges of the cake to loosen it from the pan. Invert the cake onto a rack, and peel off the parchment paper.

SERVES 10

PERIOD DETAIL

A related version of this cake actually appeared decades earlier, in *Economy Gastronomy* by Sylvia Vaughn Thompson, published in 1963.

NOVEMBER 3, 1999: "BY THE BOOK: SIMPLE AND SWEET FROM A MASTER BAKER," BY AMANDA HESSER. RECIPE ADAPTED FROM *ROOM FOR DESSERT*, BY DAVID LEBOVITZ.

—1999

⌒ CRANBERRY UPSIDE-DOWN CAKE

This cake floats like a butterfly and stings like a bee. And it was the smart, understated punctuation to a Thanksgiving dinner at Alice Waters's house in 1999. Many upside-down cakes are too sweet. This one commits no such crime. The key ingredient is a judicious amount of brown sugar, which plays off the tart cranberries and helps form a rich caramel sauce that seeps into the cake.

———

For the Topping

4 tablespoons unsalted butter

¾ cup packed brown sugar (I used light brown sugar)

9 ounces (about 2¼ cups) fresh cranberries

¼ cup fresh orange juice

For the Batter

1½ cups all-purpose flour

2 teaspoons baking powder

¼ teaspoon salt

8 tablespoons (1 stick) unsalted butter, softened

1 cup sugar

1 teaspoon vanilla extract

2 large eggs, separated

½ cup whole milk

¼ teaspoon cream of tartar

Sweetened whipped cream flavored with orange liqueur, for serving

1. To prepare the topping, melt the butter in a 9-inch round cake pan over low heat. Add the brown sugar and stir until it dissolves, swirling the pan to coat the bottom. When the sugar starts to caramelize, remove the pan from the heat and allow to cool.

2. Combine the cranberries and orange juice in a small bowl and toss to coat the berries well. Spread the berries evenly in the pan, and sprinkle with any juice remaining in the bowl. Set the pan aside.

3. To prepare the batter, heat the oven to 350 degrees. Sift together the flour, baking powder, and salt.

4. In a mixer fitted with a paddle (or in a bowl with a hand mixer), beat the butter with the sugar until pale, light, and fluffy. Add the vanilla, then beat in the egg yolks one at a time, scraping the bowl once or twice. Add the flour mixture alternately with the milk, ending with the dry ingredients.

5. Whisk the egg whites with the cream of tartar in a clean mixer bowl with a whisk (or in a bowl with clean beaters) just until stiff enough to hold a slight peak. Fold the whites into the batter in 3 additions. Spoon the batter into the prepared pan and spread it evenly over the cranberries.

6. Bake until the top is browned and the cake pulls away slightly from the edges of the pan, 30 to 45 minutes. Let the cake cool for 15 minutes before turning it onto a cake plate.

7. Serve with slightly sweetened whipped cream flavored with orange liqueur.

SERVES 8

COOKING NOTE

You need a solid cake pan; pans with a removable bottom or springform pans will not work on the stovetop because the butter will seep through. But if these are what you have, to get around the problem without going out and buying a new pan, prepare the sugar and cranberries in a small saucepan. Line your cake pan with aluminum foil, then proceed. There is no need to grease the foil (or the pan)—the batter does not stick.

NOVEMBER 17, 1999: "NEW AMERICAN TRADITIONS: IN A BERKELEY KITCHEN, A CELEBRATION OF SIMPLICITY," BY R. W. APPLE JR. RECIPE ADAPTED FROM ALICE WATERS, THE OWNER OF CHEZ PANISSE IN BERKELEY, CALIFORNIA.

—1999

☙ BRETON BUTTER CAKE

This recipe comes from Gabrielle Hamilton, a chef beloved for her tiny restaurant, Prune, which led other restaurateurs to the frontier of the East Village. As a child, Hamilton spent a fair amount of time in Brittany, where she was introduced to kouign amann, or Breton butter cake, a flaky, buttery dessert scented with orange-flower water.

Having spent months on her own recipe, Hamilton put it on the Prune menu and served it, she said, "just as in France, cut in a slice and put on a plate. No mint sprig. No ice cream. No ridiculous embellishment."

"And you know what?" she continued, "Nobody ordered it."

But once she began serving it with a glass of Muscat de Beaumes-de-Venise, orders flew out of the kitchen.

1⅛ teaspoons active dry yeast

⅔ cup water

¾ teaspoon orange-flower water, plus more for sprinkling

1⅓ cups all-purpose flour

2 tablespoons cake flour

⅛ teaspoon coarse salt

12 tablespoons (1½ sticks) cold unsalted butter, preferably French

¾ cup sugar, plus more for the pie plate and top of cake

1½ tablespoons unsalted butter, melted

1. Combine the yeast with the water and orange-flower water in a small bowl. Let sit until bubbly.

2. Combine the flours, salt, and yeast mixture in a large bowl and stir until a dough forms. Scrape the dough onto a lightly floured surface and knead it until smooth. Butter a large bowl and add the dough. Cover and let rise in a warm place until doubled, 30 to 60 minutes.

3. Place the dough in the refrigerator to firm up, about 30 minutes.

4. On a lightly floured surface, pound the cold butter into a 5-inch square. Cover with plastic wrap and let come almost to room temperature; it should have an icing-like texture.

5. On a lightly floured surface, roll out the dough into a 10-inch disk. Place the butter on top and fold the dough up and around it to cover. Working quickly, roll out the dough so that it is 2 feet long and 1 foot wide. Using a pastry brush, brush off excess flour. Sprinkle the dough with 3 tablespoons sugar, and fold into thirds, as if folding a business letter. Turn 90 degrees, sprinkle with 3 tablespoons sugar, and roll out to 2 feet long and 1 foot wide again; fold into thirds. Repeat 2 more times, scraping up any sticky areas; avoid using too much flour.

6. Butter and sugar a 9-inch glass pie plate. Place the dough in the plate, tucking the corners under. Let rise in a warm place until soft and puffy, 1 to 2 hours.

7. Heat the oven to 425 degrees. Brush the surface of the dough with the melted butter, and sprinkle with a generous amount of sugar and a little orange-flower water. Bake until risen and golden brown, 25 to 30 minutes. If the top browns before the bottom, cover with foil. The bottom should be hazelnut brown. Remove from the oven, slice, and serve warm.

SERVES 8

APRIL 4, 2001: "THE CHEF: GABRIELLE HAMILTON," BY GABRIELLE HAMILTON WITH AMANDA HESSER.

—2001

☙ ALMOND CAKE

I learned this recipe from my mother-in-law, Elizabeth Friend. She'd discovered the cake at a bakery in East Hampton, and when the bakery was closing, she made her move, buttonholing the owners for the recipe. They turned her down flat. Undeterred, she set out to re-create the recipe herself. Elizabeth's cake rises and then, near the end of its time in the oven, exhales dramatically and sinks in the center. "You open the oven door," Elizabeth said, "and it looks great. And two minutes later, it's Grand Canyon department." Thankfully, she was never able to remedy this because, in fact, the "problem" makes the cake superbly dense and buttery in the center, which everyone loves and remembers.

I've made this cake more times than any other recipe in this book, because it travels well and improves with time. I call it my "thank-you cake," because I've sent it as a gift to countless friends and colleagues.

I cup sour cream, at room temperature

I teaspoon baking soda

2 cups sifted all-purpose flour

½ teaspoon kosher salt

½ pound (2 sticks) unsalted butter, softened

1½ cups granulated sugar

One 7-ounce tube almond paste

4 large egg yolks, at room temperature

I teaspoon almond extract

Confectioners' sugar for dusting

1. Heat the oven to 350 degrees. Butter a 9-inch springform pan. Line the bottom with parchment paper; butter the paper. Mix together the sour cream and baking soda in a small bowl. Sift the flour and salt together.

2. Cream the butter and sugar in a food processor, until pale and fluffy. Pull the almond paste into small pieces and add it, a little at a time, to the butter mixture, pulsing until very smooth. Add the egg yolks one at a time, mixing until incorporated. Blend in the almond extract and sour cream mixture.

3. Using a rubber spatula, transfer the batter to a bowl. Fold in the flour mixture until the batter is smooth and there are no bits of flour left.

4. Scrape the batter into the prepared pan and spread evenly. Bake for 50 to 60 minutes. It is done when you press the top and it springs back and it shrinks from the sides of the pan. Remove from the oven and place on a rack to cool in the pan.

5. When ready to serve, remove the sides of the pan, sift confectioners' sugar on top of the cake, and slice into wedges.

SERVES 10

READERS

"It came out amazingly well, and I was thrilled to find people asking me for the recipe, something that continues to this day. You may rest assured that you and your article are always credited when I pass the recipe along. (Up until that time, I had always worn a rather bemused expression when I saw people in my office exchanging recipes. Now I find myself trading them like baseball cards.) Since then, I must have made the cake twenty five to thirty times."

Gary Welch, e-mail

AUGUST 12, 2001: "FOOD DIARY: AMATEUR NIGHT," BY AMANDA HESSER. RECIPE ADAPTED FROM ELIZABETH FRIEND, MY LATE MOTHER-IN-LAW.

—2001

⌒ GOOEY CHOCOLATE STACK

Three disks of cocoa meringue buffeted by chocolate cream.

---

6 large eggs, separated

1⅓ cups granulated sugar

5 tablespoons unsweetened cocoa powder

I teaspoon red wine vinegar

2 tablespoons all-purpose flour

1⅓ cups whole milk

1⅓ cups heavy cream

¼ pound bittersweet chocolate, melted

I teaspoon vanilla extract

About 2 tablespoons confectioners' sugar

2 tablespoons chopped unsalted pistachios

1. Heat the oven to 250 degrees. Line 3 baking sheets with parchment, and draw an 8-inch circle on each. Whisk the egg whites in a mixer (or in a large bowl with a hard mixer) until they hold stiff peaks. Add 1 cup sugar a spoonful at a time, beating well after each addition. Sprinkle 3 tablespoons cocoa and the vinegar on top, and fold in gently but firmly.

2. Divide the meringue among the 3 circles, spreading evenly. Bake for 1 hour, then turn off the oven. Leave the meringues in it to cool.

3. Beat the egg yolks and the remaining ⅓ cup sugar together in a large bowl. Add the remaining 2 tablespoons cocoa and the flour, whisking well. Warm the milk and cream in a saucepan until bubbles form around the edges. Whisking, pour this into the egg yolks and sugar. Then pour everything back into the saucepan, and, stirring constantly, bring to a boil. When the mixture has thickened, take it from the heat and stir in the melted chocolate and vanilla. Transfer to a bowl and sift a layer of confectioners' sugar over the top to keep the surface from forming a skin. Let cool completely.

4. To assemble the stack, place a meringue disk on a plate and spread with a layer of chocolate cream (¼ to ½ inch thick), then layer, finishing with cream. (Reserve any leftover cream for another use.) Scatter the pistachios on top. Slice into wedges to serve.

SERVES 10

COOKING NOTE

It's best to assemble this dessert shortly before you serve it. If you need to make the components in advance, leave the cooked meringues uncovered at room temperature and keep the filling refrigerated. Assemble no more than 1 hour before serving.

JANUARY 9, 2002: "CULINARY CRITIQUE: SEX AND THE KITCHEN," BY AMANDA HESSER. RECIPE ADAPTED FROM *HOW TO BE A DOMESTIC GODDESS*, BY NIGELLA LAWSON.

—2002

⌒ AMAZON CAKE (COCOA CAKE)

You know how you occasionally forget until the last minute that you were supposed to bring a dish to the potluck or bake a cake for your kid's school thing? This is the cake for those moments. It will take you longer to think of another cake than it will take to get this one in the oven. Will it be the best cake ever? No. But it will be very good and it will be homemade. And it will show that you care, even though you kind of forgot.

1½ cups all-purpose flour
⅓ cup unsweetened cocoa powder
1 teaspoon baking soda
1 cup granulated sugar
½ teaspoon salt
5 tablespoons corn oil
1 cup cold water
1½ teaspoons vanilla extract
1 tablespoon cider vinegar
Confectioners' sugar for dusting

1. Heat the oven to 350 degrees. Grease a 9-inch round cake pan. Whisk together the flour, cocoa, baking soda, sugar, and salt.

2. Whisk together the oil, water, vanilla, and vinegar in a large bowl. Whisk in the dry ingredients, blending until completely lump-free. Pour into the prepared pan and bake for 30 to 35 minutes, or until the top springs back when pressed gently.

3. Cool on a rack before removing from the pan and dusting with confectioners' sugar (or frosting, if desired).

SERVES 6 TO 8

READERS

"I use cold coffee instead of water and add a bit of fresh-ground black pepper, about half a grind of the mill. For me this takes longer to bake (would the coffee make a difference?), about 45 to 50 minutes. I like to sift powdered sugar through a round paper doily to make a lacy design on top (this has to be done just before serving, or the moist cake will absorb the sugar) and serve the cake with sweetened whipped cream flavored with vanilla and Cognac."

Robert Croskey, e-mail

"Here's why I love this recipe and make it frequently. First of all, it makes an excellent chocolate cake—black-brown, moist, tender, with excellent keeping qualities. Second, it is a total snap to make. You can do it in four minutes from start to finish. No need to let butter come to room temperature; no oddball ingredients; no beating (in fact, the only appliance you use for this recipe is the oven, not even the refrigerator). It is made with common, long-life pantry ingredients, so you will never find yourself in the mood to make it but without an ingredient. You don't even have to flour the pan. Third, it never sticks to the pan. Period. Four, for a cake, it's pretty healthy. No eggs or butter, cocoa instead of hard chocolate. Five, double the recipe and use an old *Time-Life* frosting trick, and you have the world's best and easiest chocolate layer cake." [See p. 744 or 751 for other frostings that work well with the cake.]

Laura E. Perry, e-mail

FEBRUARY 6, 2002: "THIS TIME, CHOCOLATE TAKES A POWDER," BY REGINA SCHRAMBLING. RECIPE ADAPTED FROM *CAFÉ BEAUJOLAIS*, BY MARGARET FOX AND JOHN S. BEAR.

—2002

LEMON-ALMOND BUTTER CAKE

Regina Schrambling, a food editor and writer at the *Times*, aptly described this cake as "the ultimate citrus tart, without the heartbreak of piecrust."

Making lemon curd is fun, and if you have the time, I recommend doing so, but for a shortcut, you can use store-bought.

———

For the Lemon Curd
Grated zest and juice of 2 lemons
¾ cup plus 2 tablespoons sugar
4 extra-large eggs
6 tablespoons unsalted butter, cubed

For the Cake
9 tablespoons unsalted butter, softened
I cup plus I tablespoon all-purpose flour
I teaspoon baking powder
½ teaspoon kosher salt
I cup plus I to 2 tablespoons sugar
2 extra-large eggs
½ cup ground toasted almonds
2 tablespoons toasted sliced almonds

½ cup heavy cream
I tablespoon almond liqueur (optional)

1. To make the lemon curd, combine the zest, juice, sugar, and eggs in a heatproof bowl and beat well. Add the butter, place over a saucepan of simmering water, and cook, stirring constantly with a rubber spatula or wooden spoon, until the mixture thickens into curd, about 5 minutes.
2. Strain into a bowl and press plastic wrap onto the surface to keep a skin from forming. Refrigerate until cool, at least 1½ hours.
3. To make the cake, heat the oven to 350 degrees. Grease a 9-inch springform pan with 1 tablespoon butter, and dust with 1 tablespoon flour, shaking out the excess. Sift together the remaining 1 cup flour, the baking powder, and salt.
4. In a mixer fitted with a paddle (or in a bowl with a hand mixer), beat the remaining 8 tablespoons butter and 1 cup sugar until light and fluffy. Mix in the dry ingredients.
5. Whisk the eggs in a bowl until they start to foam. Do not overbeat, or the cake will be tough. Add the eggs and ground almonds to the batter, and mix well.
6. Scrape the batter into the prepared pan. Drop 8 tablespoons of the lemon curd around the perimeter of the batter, leaving a 1-inch border and taking care to space the drops evenly. Drop 3 to 4 tablespoons curd onto the center of the batter. (Refrigerate the remaining curd for another use.) Sprinkle the cake with the toasted almonds and 1 to 2 tablespoons sugar, depending on taste.
7. Bake until the cake is toasty brown on top and a toothpick inserted into the cake (not curd) comes out clean, 35 to 40 minutes. Let cool on a rack for 10 minutes, then remove the sides of the pan and cool completely.
8. Whip the cream, with the almond liqueur if using, to soft peaks. Present the cake at the table, and offer the whipped cream on the side.

SERVES 8

MARCH 27, 2002: "NOT THE USUAL CHEF ON THE SHELF," BY REGINA SCHRAMBLING. RECIPE ADAPTED FROM *IN THE HANDS OF A CHEF*, BY JODY ADAMS.

—2002

CHOCOLATE DUMP-IT CAKE

When I was growing up, my mother baked this cake for my birthdays. Now I make it for my husband's and children's birthdays. "Dump-it" doesn't have quite the appeal of "galette" or "confit," but it candidly lays out the cake's virtue. This moist, bouncy chocolate cake is the easiest one you'll ever make: you mix the batter in a saucepan, stirring in one ingredient after the other, and when it's glassy and smooth, you dump the batter into the cake pan and slide it in the oven. The icing is similarly economical: you blend melted chocolate chips with sour cream and slather it on the cake.

————

For the Cake

2 cups sugar

¼ pound unsweetened chocolate, chopped

8 tablespoons (1 stick) unsalted butter

1 cup water

2 cups all-purpose flour

2 teaspoons baking soda

1 teaspoon baking powder

1 teaspoon salt

1 cup whole milk

1 teaspoon cider vinegar

2 large eggs

1 teaspoon vanilla extract

For the Icing

1½ cups Nestlé's semisweet chocolate chips

1½ cups sour cream, at room temperature

1. To make the cake, heat the oven to 375 degrees. Place a baking sheet on the lowest rack to catch any drips when the cake bakes on the middle rack. Mix together the sugar, unsweetened chocolate, butter, and water in a 2- to 3-quart saucepan, place over medium heat, and stir occasionally until all of the ingredients are melted and blended. Remove from the heat and let cool slightly.

2. Meanwhile, sift together the flour, baking soda, baking powder, and salt. Stir together the milk and vinegar in a small bowl (it will curdle, but that's OK). Grease and flour a 9-inch tube pan.

3. When the chocolate has cooled a bit, whisk in the milk mixture and eggs. In several additions, and with-

out overmixing, whisk in the dry ingredients. When the mixture is smooth, add the vanilla and whisk once or twice to blend.

4. Pour the batter into the tube pan. Bake until a skewer inserted in the center comes out clean, about 30 to 35 minutes. Let the cake cool for 10 minutes, then remove from the pan and set on a rack. (This can be tricky; the cake is heavy and likes to break in half—if someone is around to help, enlist him.) Let cool completely.

5. To make the icing, melt the chocolate chips in a double boiler, then let cool to room temperature. Stir in the sour cream ¼ cup at a time until the mixture is smooth.

6. You can ice the cake as is, or cut it in half so that you have 2 layers, and fill and ice it. There will be extra icing whether you have 1 or 2 layers. My mother always uses it to make flowers on top. She makes a small rosette, or button, then uses toasted sliced almond as the petals, pushing them in around the base of the rosette.

SERVES 10

MAY 12, 2002: "FOOD DIARY: PERSONAL BEST," BY AMANDA HESSER. RECIPE ADAPTED FROM JUDITH HESSER.

—2002

LEMON CAKE

Imagine the taste of lemon cake, then multiply that flavor by three, and you'll have a faint idea of the piercing resonance in this cake. There's lemon zest creamed with the butter, lemon juice combined with buttermilk as the liquid, and a lemon syrup doused on the finished cake.

If you were a fan of Maida Heatter's East 62nd Street Lemon Cake, which ran in 1970 (seventeen readers recommended it), you'll be happy to know that this recipe has nearly the same proportions: a tiny bit more salt, less baking powder, buttermilk instead of milk, and lemon juice added to the batter. While I love Heatter's recipe, I thought this one was more lemony and moist. I hope you'll agree.

————

For the Cake

3 cups all-purpose flour

1/2 teaspoon baking powder

1/2 teaspoon baking soda

I teaspoon kosher salt

1/2 pound (2 sticks) unsalted butter, softened

2 cups sugar

4 extra-large eggs, at room temperature

1/3 cup grated lemon zest (from 6 to 8 large lemons)

1/4 cup fresh lemon juice

3/4 cup buttermilk, at room temperature

I teaspoon vanilla extract

For the Lemon Syrup

1/2 cup sugar

1/2 cup fresh lemon juice (from about 2 lemons)

For the Lemon Glaze

2 cups confectioners' sugar, sifted

3 1/2 tablespoons fresh lemon juice

1. Heat the oven to 350 degrees. Grease and flour two 8 1/2-by-4 1/4-by-2 1/2-inch loaf pans, and line the bottoms with parchment paper. Sift together the flour, baking powder, baking soda, and salt.

2. Beat the butter and sugar in a mixer fitted with a paddle (or in a large bowl with a hand mixer) for about 5 minutes, or until light and fluffy. Mixing at medium speed, add the eggs one at a time, and then the lemon zest.

3. Combine the lemon juice, the buttermilk, and vanilla in a bowl. Add the flour and buttermilk mixtures alternately to the butter and sugar mixture, beginning and ending with flour.

4. Divide the batter evenly between the pans and smooth the tops. Bake for 45 minutes to 1 hour, until a cake tester comes out clean.

5. Meanwhile, to make the lemon syrup, combine the sugar and lemon juice in a small saucepan and cook over low heat, stirring, until the sugar dissolves. Remove from the heat.

6. When the cakes are done, let them cool for 10 minutes, then remove the parchment and invert them onto a rack set over a tray. Spoon the lemon syrup over the cakes. Let cool completely.

7. To make the glaze, combine the confectioners' sugar and lemon juice in a bowl, mixing with a whisk until

smooth. Pour over top of the cakes, and allow the glaze to dribble down the sides.

MAKES 2 CAKES, EACH SERVING 8 TO 10

JUNE 4, 2003: "THE 3 THAT MAKE A KITCHEN COMPLETE," BY AMANDA HESSER. RECIPE ADAPTED FROM *BAREFOOT CONTESSA PARTIES!*, BY INA GARTEN.

—2003

⌒ NEW ENGLAND SPIDER CAKE

This is my favorite kind of recipe—there are no thorny passages, and there's a surprising trick. After mixing up what is essentially a sweetened cornmeal batter, you scrape it into a hot cast-iron skillet, then pour cold cream into the very center of the cake. The cream tears through the batter, creating a web of rivulets spreading out from the center. As the cake bakes, this layer of cream thickens like custard, and the edges of batter pushed up against the skillet get firm and crisp, so the finished cake contains a spectrum of textures.

Jonathan Reynolds, a food columnist for the *Times Magazine*, offered up this cake in a story on breakfast. He wrote, "This substantial one-skillet meal will get your kids to school happier than they've ever been, and you happy only if they've left some behind." It's a hearty way to begin the day, and, I'd argue, a gratifying way to end it.

———

2 cups whole milk

4 teaspoons white vinegar

I cup all-purpose flour

3/4 cup yellow cornmeal

3/4 cup sugar

1/2 teaspoon baking soda

1/2 teaspoon salt

2 large eggs

2 tablespoons unsalted butter

I cup heavy cream

1. Heat the oven to 350 degrees. Combine the milk and vinegar in a bowl and set aside to sour.

2. Combine the flour, cornmeal, sugar, baking soda,

and salt in a medium bowl. Whisk the eggs into the soured milk. Stir into the dry ingredients.

3. Melt the butter in a 12-inch cast-iron skillet. Pour in the batter. Pour the cream into the center, do not stir, slide the skillet into the oven, and bake until golden brown on top, about 45 minutes. Let cool for 5 to 10 minutes, then slice into wedges and serve warm.

SERVES 10

COOKING NOTE

It's important not to bake this too long. The cake should still feel soft but bouncy in the center when you remove it from the oven.

PERIOD DETAIL

An almost identical recipe appeared in *The White House Cookbook* published in 1935.

MARCH 7, 2004: "WAKE-UP CALL," BY JONATHAN REYNOLDS.

—2004

BOLZANO APPLE CAKE

Mark Bittman, the *Times* food columnist, described this cake as a "perfect clafoutis." But that doesn't do justice to the cake's fragrance and delicacy. A pile of wafer-thin apples is lashed together with a vanilla-speckled batter that, once cooked and settled, yields a strata of fruit. When done properly, the center is dewy and the edges like dry leaves.

---

8 tablespoons (1 stick) unsalted butter,
 plus more for greasing the pan

2 large eggs

1 cup granulated sugar

1 vanilla bean, split, seeds scraped out and reserved

1¼ pounds (3 to 4 small to medium)
 Granny Smith apples

½ cup all-purpose flour

2 teaspoons baking powder

½ cup whole milk, at room temperature

Confectioners' sugar for dusting

1. Heat the oven to 375 degrees. Line the base of an 8-inch springform pan with parchment, then smear the bottom and sides with a thick layer of butter. Dust with flour, turn the pan over, and tap lightly to remove excess flour. Melt the butter in a small saucepan. Set aside.

2. Beat together the eggs and half the sugar in a bowl. Continue to beat while slowly adding the remaining sugar until thick; the batter should form a ribbon when dropped from a spoon. Add the vanilla seeds to the batter, and add the bean to the melted butter.

3. Peel, quarter, and core the apples, then trim the ends and thinly slice.

4. Remove the vanilla bean from the butter and stir the butter into the batter. Combine the flour and baking powder, and stir into the batter alternately with the milk. Stir in the apples, coating every piece with batter. Pour the batter into the pan, using your fingers to pat the top evenly.

5. Bake for 25 minutes, then rotate the pan. Bake for about 25 minutes more, or until the cake pulls away from the sides of the pan and is brown on top; a thin-bladed knife inserted into the center will come out clean when it is done. Cool for 30 minutes on a rack.

6. Remove the sides of the pan, cut the cake into wedges, and sprinkle with confectioners' sugar. Serve warm.

SERVES 6 TO 8

COOKING NOTE

You can blend the batter in a mixer, but I like to do it by hand. There's not much batter, so it's easy to handle, and it's satisfying to form the cake on your own.

SEPTEMBER 22, 2004: "THE CHEF: SCOTT CARSBERG: SEATTLE-GROWN, ITALIAN-FLAVORED," BY MARK BITTMAN. RECIPE ADAPTED FROM SCOTT CARSBERG, THE CHEF AND OWNER OF LAMPREIA IN SEATTLE, WASHINGTON.

—2004

CHOCOLATE GUINNESS CAKE

In this Nigella Lawson recipe, chocolate and Guinness briefly fuse in a magical way. The austere caramel flavor of the beer and the cocoa-flavored batter seem so serious, so right together. But eat the cake right away. By morning, the energy is gone, the crumb spongy and misbegotten, like most mornings after too much Guinness.

The froth-like topping is classic Lawson—easy to make and amusing.

_____

For the Cake
I cup Guinness stout
10 tablespoons (1¼ sticks) unsalted butter
¾ cup unsweetened cocoa powder
2 cups superfine sugar
¾ cup sour cream
2 large eggs
I tablespoon vanilla extract
2 cups all-purpose flour
2½ teaspoons baking soda

For the Topping
1¼ cups confectioners' sugar
One 8-ounce package cream cheese, at room temperature
½ cup heavy cream

1. To make the cake, heat the oven to 350 degrees. Butter a 9-inch springform pan and line the bottom with parchment paper. Combine the Guinness and butter in a large saucepan and place over medium-low heat until the butter melts, then remove from the heat. Add the cocoa and sugar and whisk to blend.
2. Combine the sour cream, eggs, and vanilla in a small bowl; mix well. Add to the Guinness mixture, whisking. Add the flour and baking soda, and whisk until smooth.
3. Pour into the buttered pan and bake until risen and firm, 45 minutes to 1 hour. Place the pan on a rack and cool completely in the pan.
4. To make the topping, using a food processor or by hand, mix the confectioners' sugar to break up any lumps. Add the cream cheese and blend until smooth. Add the heavy cream and mix until smooth and spreadable.
5. Remove the sides of the pan and place the cake on a platter or cake stand. Ice the top of the cake only—so that it resembles a frothy pint of Guinness.

SERVES 12

COOKING NOTE
I used "extra stout" Guinness.

DECEMBER 8, 2004: "AT MY TABLE: A FEAST FOR A HOLI-DAY, OR EVERYDAY EXULTING," BY NIGELLA LAWSON.

—2004

⌒ WHISKEY CAKE

This now rarely seen cake was a popular recipe among *Times* readers in the nineteenth century. Back then, it was called Tipsy Cake.

_____

For the Cake
Fine dry bread crumbs for dusting the pan
1½ cups all-purpose flour
I teaspoon baking powder
½ teaspoon salt
8 tablespoons (I stick) unsalted butter
1¼ cups sugar
Grated zest of I lemon
2 teaspoons vanilla extract
4 large eggs

For the Whiskey Syrup
½ cup sugar
⅓ cup water
½ cup bourbon

1. To make the cake, heat the oven to 350 degrees. Butter a Bundt pan and dust with bread crumbs. Sift together the flour, baking powder, and salt.
2. In a mixer fitted with a paddle (or in a bowl with a hand mixer), beat the butter, sugar, and lemon zest until fluffy and fragrant. Beat in the vanilla and 2 eggs. Add the remaining eggs, and beat again. Add half the flour mixture and mix on low speed until just incorporated. Add the remaining mixture and mix again until almost smooth, then mix with a rubber spatula until smooth.
3. Scrape the batter into the Bundt pan. Bake until a toothpick inserted into the center comes out clean, 30 to 35 minutes.
4. Meanwhile, to make the syrup, combine the sugar with the water in a saucepan. Bring to a boil, stirring to dissolve the sugar, and cook until the bubbles grow

small and make fine snapping sounds, about 3 minutes. Remove from the heat and let cool. Stir in the whiskey.

5. When the cake is done, let it cool for a few minutes, then unmold onto a serving plate with a lip. (The whiskey may pool at the base.) Pierce the top of the cake in about 20 places with a skewer, then pour the whiskey syrup over it.

6. Once the cake is cool, cover with plastic wrap. This cake is best served the next day.

SERVES 10

JANUARY 30, 2005: "THE ARSENAL," BY AMANDA HESSER.

—2005

⌒ GÂTEAU DE CREPES

I thought I'd found the best cake in New York City. The Mille Crepes, sold at Lady M Cake Boutique on East 78th Street, was made up of twenty (as opposed to a thousand) lacy crepes separated by clouds of whipped-cream-lightened pastry cream and had a top layer that was spread with sugar and caramelized like crème brûlée. A fork plunged into a slice slid like a shovel through fresh snow. You got a whiff of smoky sugar, then layer after silky-sweet layer.

The owner of Lady M, however, wasn't at all enthusiastic about handing over his recipe; I was on my own. But nothing makes you want to master a twenty-layer cake more than a flat rejection. With a little sleuthing, I figured out the layered crepe cake wasn't something new. I opened *Joy of Cooking*, and right among the pancake recipes is one for crepe cake, made with a dozen crepes layered with lemon sauce. A similar version, layered with whipped cream and jam, called *gâteau de crepes*, appears in *Larousse Gastronomique*. As the book explains, filled layers of crepes is an age-old concept.

The top-secret Mille Crepes could be mine after all. I used the crepe recipe from *Joy of Cooking*, the vanilla pastry cream from *Desserts by Pierre Hermé*, by Hermé and Dorie Greenspan, and my own whipped cream. My gâteau de crepes didn't look quite as neat as the Mille Crepes, but it was charming the way the sagging roof of an old cottage is, and darn tasty.

For the Crepe Batter
6 tablespoons unsalted butter
2 cups whole milk
6 large eggs
1 1/2 cups all-purpose flour
5 tablespoons sugar
Pinch of salt

For the Vanilla Pastry Cream
2 cups whole milk
1 vanilla bean, split, seeds scraped out and reserved
6 large egg yolks
1/2 cup sugar
1/3 cup cornstarch, sifted
3 1/2 tablespoons unsalted butter, cut into small cubes

For Assembly
Corn oil
2 cups heavy cream
1 tablespoon granulated sugar, or more for brûléeing
3 tablespoons kirsch
Confectioners' sugar for dusting (optional)

1. The day before, make the crepe batter and pastry cream. To make the batter, cook the butter in a small pan until brown like hazelnuts. Set aside. Heat the milk in another small pan until steaming; allow to cool for 10 minutes.

2. In a mixer fitted with a whisk (or in a bowl with a hand mixer), beat together the eggs, flour, sugar, and salt on medium-low speed. Slowly add the hot milk and browned butter. Pour into a container with a spout, cover, and refrigerate overnight.

3. To make the pastry cream, combine the milk, vanilla bean, and seeds in a saucepan and bring to a boil. Set aside for 10 minutes; remove the bean.

4. Fill a large bowl with ice and water and set aside a small bowl that can hold the finished pastry cream and be placed in this ice bath. Whisk together the egg yolks, sugar, and cornstarch in a medium heavy pan. Gradually whisk in the hot milk, then place the pan over high heat, bring to a boil, whisking vigorously, and whisk until thickened, 1 to 2 minutes. Press the pastry cream through a fine-mesh sieve into the small bowl.

5. Set the bowl in the ice bath and stir until the temperature reaches 140 degrees on an instant-read thermometer. Stir in the butter. When completely cool, cover and refrigerate.

6. The next day, assemble the cake: Bring the batter to room temperature. Line a baking sheet with parchment. Place a nonstick or seasoned 9-inch crepe pan over medium heat. Swab the surface with oil, then add about 3 tablespoons batter and swirl to cover the surface. Cook until the bottom just begins to brown, about 1 minute, then carefully lift an edge and flip the crepe with your fingers. Cook on the other side for no longer than 5 seconds. Flip the crepe onto the baking sheet, and repeat until you have 20 perfect crepes.

7. Pass the pastry cream through a sieve once more. Whip the heavy cream with the sugar and kirsch. (It won't hold peaks.) Fold it into the pastry cream.

8. Lay 1 crepe on a cake plate. Using an icing spatula, completely cover with a thin layer of pastry cream (about ¼ cup). Cover with a crepe and repeat to make a stack of 20, with the best-looking crepe on top. Chill for at least 2 hours.

9. Set the cake out for 30 minutes before serving. If you have a blowtorch for crème brûlée, sprinkle the top crepe with 2 tablespoons sugar and caramelize with the torch; otherwise, dust with confectioners' sugar. Slice.

SERVES 10

MAY 15, 2005: "THE WAY WE EAT: BUILDING A MODERN, MULTISTORIED DESSERT," BY AMANDA HESSER. RECIPE FOR BATTER ADAPTED FROM *THE ALL NEW ALL PURPOSE JOY OF COOKING*, BY IRMA S. ROMBAUER, MARION ROMBAUER BECKER, AND ETHAN BECKER; RECIPE FOR PASTRY CREAM ADAPTED FROM *DESSERTS BY PIERRE HERMÉ*, BY PIERRE HERMÉ AND DORIE GREENSPAN.

—2005

POPPY SEED TORTE

Hovering above this dense and nutty cake is a fragile layer, like a veil of poppy seed meringue.

———

1½ cups poppy seeds

1 teaspoon baking powder or 3 tablespoons potato starch

6 large eggs, separated, at room temperature

1 cup granulated sugar

1 teaspoon vanilla extract

7 tablespoons unsalted butter, melted and cooled

Confectioners' sugar for dusting

1. Heat the oven to 300 degrees. Grease a 9-inch springform pan and line the bottom with parchment paper. Using a spice/coffee grinder, grind the poppy seeds, in batches, for about 20 seconds. (The seeds will become slightly sticky.) Combine with the baking powder in a large bowl.

2. In a mixer fitted with the paddle (or in a bowl with a hand mixer), beat the egg yolks until slightly thickened. Slowly add the sugar and vanilla. Slowly pour in the butter, then add the poppy seed mixture. Beat until combined. Return the mixture, which will be very thick, to the large bowl.

3. Using a clean bowl and a whisk, beat the egg whites until they form soft peaks. Fold them into the batter, and pour it into the prepared pan. Bake for 50 to 60 minutes, or until a toothpick inserted into the center comes out fairly dry.

4. Cool the cake on a rack for at least an hour before unmolding. Dust with confectioners' sugar before serving.

SERVES 12

APRIL 9, 2006: "EAT, MEMORY: GHOSTS OF PASSOVERS PAST," BY ANNA WINGER.

—2006

CHAMOMILE AND ALMOND CAKE

Don't eat this cake alone—it needs an accompaniment like Lemon Lotus Ice Cream (p. 724) or Tangerine Sherbet (p. 734) to spar with its captivating but intense herbal flavor.

———

¼ cup toasted sliced almonds

3½ tablespoons chamomile tea leaves

1 cup plus 2 tablespoons blanched whole almonds

¾ cup granulated sugar

Large pinch of salt

4 large eggs, 1 separated

Grated zest of 1 lemon

3 tablespoons cornstarch

¼ teaspoon baking powder

4 tablespoons unsalted butter, melted

Vegetable oil

Confectioners' sugar for dusting

1. Heat the oven to 320 degrees. Butter a 9-inch round cake pan, then dust with flour. Shake out excess flour. Sprinkle the sliced almonds over the bottom of the pan.

2. Grind the tea, whole almonds, sugar, and salt into a paste in a food processor. If the mixture is too dry, add the egg white and process to form a paste; otherwise, add the white at the end of processing.

3. Transfer the almond paste to a mixer fitted with a paddle attachment (or use a large bowl and a hand mixer). Add the egg yolk and 1 egg and beat on medium-low speed for 1 minute. Add another egg and beat for another minute. Add the last egg and the lemon zest and beat on medium speed for 5 minutes.

4. Using as few strokes as possible, fold in the cornstarch and baking powder with a rubber spatula until mostly combined. Pour in the melted butter a little at a time, folding just until combined. Do not overmix.

5. Pour the batter into the cake pan and bake until the top is just set, 35 to 40 minutes. Let cool for 3 minutes.

6. Lightly grease a cake plate. Turn the cake out onto the plate. Cool fully, then cover with foil until ready to serve.

7. Dust with confectioners' sugar just before serving.

SERVES 12

DECEMBER 17, 2006: "FOOD: THE WAY WE EAT: STEEP INCREASE," BY DANIEL PATTERSON. RECIPE ADAPTED FROM *AROMA*, BY MANDY AFTEL AND DANIEL PATTERSON.

—2006

☙ PEANUT BUTTER CUPCAKES WITH MILK CHOCOLATE FROSTING

The frosting is so silky and good you'll want to use it to frost other cakes, like the Angel Food Cake on p. 742.

For the Cupcakes
3 cups cake flour
1 tablespoon baking powder
¼ teaspoon salt
12 tablespoons (1½ sticks) unsalted butter, softened
1½ cups granulated sugar
½ cup packed light brown sugar
1 cup creamy peanut butter, preferably Skippy
4 large eggs
1 cup whole milk

For the Frosting
3 cups confectioners' sugar
Pinch of salt
⅔ cup unsweetened natural cocoa powder
¾ pound (3 sticks) unsalted butter, softened
1½ teaspoons vanilla extract
6 tablespoons whole milk

Chocolate flakes or sprinkles (optional)

1. To make the cupcakes, heat the oven to 350 degrees. Line two 12-cup muffin tins with paper cups. Sift together the cake flour, baking powder, and salt.

2. In a mixer fitted with paddle (or in a large bowl with a hand mixer), beat the butter and sugars on low speed to combine, then beat on high speed until fluffy, about 5 minutes. Mix in the peanut butter, then beat in the eggs one at time. On low speed, alternately add the flour mixture and milk to the batter in 3 parts.

3. Fill the baking cups ¾ full with batter. Bake until a toothpick inserted in the center comes out clean, 17 to 19 minutes. Cool on a rack.

4. To make the frosting, sift together the confectioners' sugar, salt, and cocoa powder.

5. In a mixer fitted with a paddle attachment (or in a large bowl with a hand mixer), beat the butter until smooth. On low speed, slowly add the cocoa mixture. Add the vanilla, then add the milk a little at a time, beating until the frosting reaches a spreadable consistency.

6. Frost the cooled cupcakes. If you choose, decorate with chocolate flakes or sprinkles.

MAKES ABOUT 2 DOZEN CUPCAKES

NOVEMBER 11, 2007: "THE WAY WE EAT: THE HOLLYWOOD DIET," BY JENNIFER STEINHAUER. RECIPE ADAPTED FROM VANILLA BAKE SHOP IN SANTA MONICA, CALIFORNIA.

—2007

REVANI VERRIAS (SEMOLINA CAKE)

For another cake doused with liquor, see the Whiskey Cake on p. 784.

———

For the Syrup
3 cups water
1 1/2 cups sugar
1 cinnamon stick
1 tablespoon Cognac or other brandy

For the Cake
2 cups coarse semolina
1 tablespoon baking powder
1/2 pound (2 sticks) unsalted butter, softened
1 1/2 cups sugar
6 large eggs, separated, at room temperature
1 tablespoon Cognac or other brandy
1 tablespoon orange juice
1/2 cup finely ground blanched almonds

1. To make the syrup, bring the water and sugar to a boil in a medium saucepan, stirring to dissolve the sugar. Add the cinnamon stick and Cognac and simmer over medium heat until reduced by half, about 15 minutes. Let cool; discard the cinnamon.

2. To make the cake, heat the oven to 350 degrees. Butter a 10-inch springform pan. Sift together the semolina and baking powder.

3. In a mixer fitted with a whisk (or in a large bowl with a hand mixer), beat the butter until creamy. Gradually add the sugar, then add the egg yolks one at a time, beating well after each addition. Beat in the Cognac and orange juice. With the mixer on, sprinkle in the semolina mixture and then the almonds, mixing well. Transfer to a large bowl.

4. Whisk the egg whites to soft peaks in a clean mixer bowl with a clean whisk (or in a large bowl with clean beaters), then fold into the batter until combined. Pour into the prepared pan. Bake until golden and a thin, spongy layer has formed on top, about 45 minutes. Transfer to a rack.

5. Gently score the cake: Draw a sharp knife across the top of the cake, cutting through the spongy top layer, and then score diagonally to form diamonds. Pour the syrup over the cake. Serve warm or at room temperature.

SERVES 8 TO 12

COOKING NOTE
Coarse semolina is available at www.kalustyans.com.

JUNE 8, 2008: "THE WAY WE EAT: THE FRENCH CONNECTION," BY ALEKSANDRA CRAPANZANO. RECIPE ADAPTED FROM *THE FOOD AND WINE OF GREECE*, BY DIANE KOCHILAS.

—2008

EVEN-GREATER AMERICAN POUND CAKE

This is a burly cake that is, indeed, more buttery and fragrant than any pound cake I know.

———

Nonstick cooking spray with flour
12 tablespoons (1 1/2 sticks) cool unsalted butter, cut into 6 pieces
1/2 cup vegetable shortening
3 cups sugar
1 tablespoon vanilla extract
1/4 teaspoon almond extract
1/3 cup canola oil
2 large egg yolks
5 large eggs
2 2/3 cups all-purpose flour, preferably bleached
1/4 cup potato starch (or additional flour)
1 teaspoon baking powder
1 teaspoon salt
1/4 cup buttermilk
1/2 cup heavy cream

1. Place a rack in the lower third of the oven and heat the oven to 350 degrees. Spray a 10-inch tube pan or Bundt pan very well with cooking spray. In a mixer (or in a large bowl with a hand mixer), beat the butter at medium speed until smooth. Add the shortening and mix until fluffy, about 3 minutes. Add the sugar and mix until smooth; touch the outside of the bowl to make sure the ingredients are still cool. If not, place the bowl in the freezer for 5 minutes.

2. Mix in the extracts. A little at a time, mix in the oil. At the lowest speed, mix in the egg yolks. One at a time, mix in the eggs.

3. Whisk the flour, potato starch, baking powder, and salt in a bowl for a minute until well blended. At the lowest speed, mix a third of the flour mixture into the butter mixture. Mix in a third of the buttermilk. Repeat until everything is incorporated, scraping down the bowl at least once.

4. Whip the cream in a chilled bowl until soft peaks form. Mix a quarter of the whipped cream into the batter, then fold in the remainder just until combined. Pour the batter into the prepared pan. From a height of 4 inches, drop the pan on the counter to knock out bubbles. Smooth the top.

5. Bake until a toothpick inserted into the center comes out clean, 65 to 70 minutes. Cool in the pan on a rack for 10 minutes. Invert the cake onto the rack to finish cooling.

SERVES 12

COOKING NOTE

Shirley Corriher, whose recipe this is, published this cake twice in the *Times*. In the other version, she added 1 teaspoon almond extract and the grated zest of 1 lemon. I recommend adding both.

OCTOBER 22, 2008: "SOME HEAVY READING, RECIPES INCLUDED," BY JULIA MOSKIN. RECIPE ADAPTED FROM *BAKE WISE*, BY SHIRLEY O. CORRIHER.

—2008

- Sago soup, or tapioca simmered in spiced sweet wine, is common, as are wine jellies (like Jell-O).

- Lots of readers send in recipes for vinegar pie, sometimes called Jenny Lind pie, a pie that gives your palate a lashing with vinegar and spices.
- People can't get enough of cornmeal and molasses: Indian pudding (p. 809) is a fixture in the food pages.

- Ofenschlupfer (p. 804), one of many bread puddings in an era that includes cabinet pudding and Captain Mondaygoes, delicate bread pudding and scrap pudding.
- Long before cruise ships took Baked Alaska (p. 721) hostage, it was a lovable dessert.
- Bavarian creams (p. 807) are like panna cotta with a few more frills, from pastry chefs up north in Germany.
- Tapioca Flamingo (p. 810)—fruit, tapioca, and whipped cream layered in a glorious pile.
- Flaming desserts wake up a dinner party!
- David Eyre's Pancake (p. 813).
- Trend alert: crepes! The Magic Pan, a creperie, expands.
- Pots de crème (p. 815) replace diner-style pudding.
- *Maida Heatter's Book of Great Desserts* is published. The world is a better place.
- Coeur à la Crème (p. 864), a lovely fresh cream made with ricotta and egg yolks, would still be popular if cooks hadn't insisted on making it in single-use heart-shaped molds.
- Apple tart (see p. 843) starts making its move to defeat apple pie.
- Apple tart gets support from Tarte Tatin (p. 837) in its quest.
- Panna cotta (p. 840) replaces crème brûlée, excising the egg yolks and using gelatin for a wobbly texture.
- A recipe for Queen of Puddings (p. 866) runs in the the *Magazine*, but it had its heyday in the 1870s.

—1870s—
—1877—
—1880s—
—1882—
—1909—
—1910s—
—1949—
—1950s—
—1966—
—1970s—
—1975—
—1978—
—1980s—
—1990s—
—2007—

- The prevalence of île flottante and snow eggs (p. 800) makes one thing clear: home cooks have a lot of leftover egg whites lying around.

- Oh how people love lemon meringue pie!
- But even more, they love to eat milk Jell-O, better known as blancmange (see p. 797).

- Dessert carts zip around fancy restaurants.

- Crème brûlée (see p. 844) sheltered by a layer of caramelized sugar, replaces pots de crème.

- Claudia Fleming, the pastry chef at Gramercy Tavern, becomes known for her chocolate and caramel tart sprinkled with sea salt (p. 847).

18

PIES, TARTS, AND OTHER DESSERTS

As I tested recipes for this book, I often hopped around in time and course, from 1962 to 1875 to 2008, from desserts to hors d'oeuvres to breads. As a result, I wasn't always sure what shape a large chapter such as this was going to take. So when I finally pulled the dessert recipes together, I was stunned and delighted by their breadth and originality. There are puddings, and bread puddings; a betty, a buckle, a charlotte, and flummery; and pies and all manner of tarts, of course. But there are also plenty of sleepers, such as Fontainebleau (p. 829), a tangy and sublime yogurt mousse that shares DNA with the more familiar Coeur à la Crème (for which an excellent recipe is on p. 864); Delicate Bread Pudding (p. 798), whose name says it all; Peach Balls (p. 804), fried-rice croquettes stuffed with slivers of peach; and Rum Omelet (p. 808), which is like a soufflé that's first sautéed and then flambéed—what could be more fun to make?

If you simply choose among the apple dishes, you can trace a memorable journey—one that begins, say, with the baked Apple Dumplings (p. 807) and ends with Apple Snow (p. 808), a fluffy meringue mousse, by way of Reuben's Apple Pancake (p. 831), a caramelized crepe, and an Apple Galette (p. 843) that is the most carefully constructed apple tart you'll ever make.

You'll enjoy the chapter most if you alternate making a dessert you know about with one you've never heard of. Happy exploring!

RECIPES BY CATEGORY

⌒ NEW JERSEY BLANCMANGE

In the nineteenth century, people had a more robust appetite for food with unusual textures. Pickled oysters were a common snack, and you could find the occasional brain fritter and kidney omelet. But nothing got cooks more excited than a chance to entomb a favorite food in jelly. Into a preserve went perfectly unsuspecting ham, pineapple, calf's foot, sole, even a chicken or two. And then there was milk. Sweetened with sugar, lemon, almond, cinnamon, and sometimes chocolate, milk was ideal for pouring into molds and serving for dessert as a beloved dish called blancmange, which means "white food." After being tapped out of its mold, blancmange is gorgeous and subdued, like a piece of carved ivory. In those days, form trumped delicacy. In 1877, the *Times* ran a recipe for Fairy Apples, which were egg-shaped and made with half sherry-flavored blancmange and half pink rosewater-scented blancmange.

Blancmange is mentioned in *The Canterbury Tales* and, according to *The First Ladies Cook Book*, was a favorite of Andrew Jackson. And the dessert, which remained popular in Britain long after it died away here, had its pop-culture epiphany when it played tennis in a *Monty Python* episode.

This New Jersey blancmange appeared in the *Times* at the height of blancmange mania. Like many recipes then, it was noncommittal about measurements and ingredients. You could use milk or cream and flavor it with peach water or almond.

For a story I was doing about the recipe, I asked Karen DeMasco, then the pastry chef at Craft, to make a few variations, some with all milk, some with a mix of milk and cream, and some with less gelatin. As we tasted them, going from the all-milk version to the half-gelatin one, we retraced the evolution toward panna cotta, which is made primarily with cream but is looser and lighter, more custard than sculpture. The full-gelatin milk blancmange was as savory as a rubber ball—it didn't so much melt in your mouth as ricochet around inside it.

You can't argue with history, but you can alter it for the modern palate, which is what DeMasco and I did with the New Jersey blancmange. We cut back the gelatin slightly and intensified the aromatics, and then DeMasco created a nifty port sauce, infused with pep-percorns and star anise, to accompany it. The resulting blancmange is still firm and a little odd, but delightful.

---

3 cups rich whole milk with a layer of cream
   (or use half milk, half cream)
5 tablespoons sugar
2½ teaspoons powdered gelatin
½ teaspoon kosher salt
Grated zest of 1 lemon
1 cinnamon stick
½ teaspoon almond extract

1. Combine the milk, sugar, gelatin, salt, zest, and cinnamon in a medium saucepan and slowly bring to a boil, whisking to dissolve the sugar and gelatin. As soon as bubbles form on the milk, remove from the heat. Strain into a bowl, and stir in the almond extract.

2. Pour into six 4- to 6-ounce ramekins or bowls. Chill until firm, 2 to 3 hours.

3. Dip the bowls in warm water to loosen, and unmold onto plates. Serve each with a spoonful of port sauce (see Cooking Notes), if desired.

SERVES 6

COOKING NOTES

Blancmange can be set in any small molds, including bowls or ramekins.

For DeMasco's port sauce: Combine 2 cups port, ¾ cup sugar, 1 teaspoon black peppercorns, 1 star anise, and 1 wide strip lemon peel in a small saucepan, bring to a boil, and boil until reduced and syrupy. Strain and let cool. (Makes about ¾ cup.)

Most blancmange recipes from this time called for milk. Use the richest milk you can buy—something like Ronnybrook. If you can only get ordinary milk, mix in some cream.

PERIOD DETAIL

Blancmanges were sometimes thickened with isinglass, a collagen harvested from the swimbladders of sturgeon (and later cod). Until commercial gelatins, derived from animals' bones and connective tissue, were produced, another common thickener was Irish moss, which grows on rocks along the East Coast.

MARCH 19, 1876: "THE HOUSEHOLD." RECIPE SIGNED O.H. RECIPE IMPROVEMENTS AND PORT SAUCE ADAPTED FROM KAREN DEMASCO, THE PASTRY CHEF AT CRAFT IN NEW YORK CITY.

—1876

DELICATE BREAD PUDDING

In these delicate and unassuming little puddings, the bread rises to the top, leaving a layer of silky custard below. Surround the puddings with a moat of the lively orange sauce.

———

For the Puddings
25 ounces brioche, sliced
4 cups whole milk, at room temperature
3 large eggs, separated
$\frac{1}{2}$ cup sugar
Pinch of salt
1 teaspoon vanilla extract

For the Sauce
$\frac{1}{2}$ cup sugar, or more to taste
Grated zest and juice of 1 large orange,
    or more juice to taste
1 cup water
$\frac{1}{2}$ cup dry white wine or cherry or plum eau-de-vie

1. To make the puddings, heat the oven to 350 degrees. Butter six 10-ounce ramekins. Combine the brioche and milk in a saucepan and let sit for 10 minutes.
2. Place the saucepan over medium-high heat, and when bubbles form around the edges of the milk, remove from the heat.
3. In a mixer fitted with a paddle (or in a bowl with a hand mixer), beat together the egg yolks and sugar until light and pale. Lightly beat the hot bread mixture into the eggs. It will break up into chunks, but don't let it turn to mash.
4. Whisk the whites with the salt in the clean mixer bowl (or a large bowl) until they hold soft peaks. Beat in the vanilla. Fold the whites into the bread mixture. Ladle the pudding mixture into the ramekins. Set the ramekins in a baking dish just large enough to hold them, and pour enough boiling water into the dish to come halfway up the sides of the ramekins.
5. Bake the puddings until a cake tester inserted in the center comes out clean, 25 to 35 minutes. Remove from the water bath.
6. While the puddings bake, make the sauce: Combine the sugar, orange zest, orange juice, and water in a small saucepan, bring to a boil, and cook for 5 minutes. Remove from the heat and stir in the white wine. Taste and adjust the orange juice and sugar, if desired.
7. To serve, invert the puddings into shallow bowls, and spoon a little sauce over and around each.

SERVES 6

JANUARY 7, 1877: "THE HOUSEHOLD: RECEIPTS FOR THE TABLE." RECIPE SIGNED GOOD HOUSEKEEPER.

—1877

TAPIOCA PUDDING

My sister, Rhonda, who has also made this dish, calls it "a cloud in a casserole dish."

———

5 tablespoons small tapioca pearls (not instant)
4 cups whole milk
4 large eggs, separated
2 large egg yolks
$\frac{1}{4}$ teaspoon salt, plus a pinch
Grated zest of 1 lemon
$\frac{1}{2}$ cup heavy cream
$\frac{1}{4}$ dry cup sherry
$\frac{1}{2}$ cup plus 3 tablespoons sugar

1. The day before, combine the tapioca and milk in a medium saucepan. Let sit overnight in the fridge to soften the tapioca.
2. The next day, place the saucepan over medium-high heat and bring to a boil. Whisk the 6 egg yolks in a small bowl. Slowly whisk in some of the hot milk mixture to temper the eggs, then pour this mixture back into the saucepan and stir until thickened. This may happen right away. If not, cook over low heat; do not let the mixture boil. It's done when it's thick enough to coat the back of the spoon. Let cool for 15 minutes.
3. Heat the oven to 450 degrees. Stir $\frac{1}{4}$ teaspoon salt, lemon zest, cream, sherry, and $\frac{1}{2}$ cup sugar into the pudding; blend until the sugar is dissolved. Whisk the egg whites with a pinch of salt until they hold soft

peaks, then beat in the remaining 3 tablespoons sugar and continue beating until the mixture is meringue-like. Fold the whites into the pudding.

4. Pour the pudding into a 2-quart baking dish. Bake until warmed through and lightly toasted on top, about 5 minutes.

SERVES 6

PERIOD DETAIL
Another popular nineteenth-century use for tapioca pearls was "sago soup." Sago, or tapioca, was simmered in wine, sugar, and spices—the same way we now treat poached pears—and served as a hot or cold soup.

JANUARY 28, 1877: "RECEIPTS FOR THE TABLE." RECIPE SIGNED AMANDA C.

—1877

⌇ RICE CROQUETTES

An excellent dessert for people who don't have a real sweet tooth—these fried rice balls are fragrant and crisp, with just a hint of sugar.

In the ingredient list, I included the option of either fine dry bread crumbs or panko, Japanese bread crumbs. Panko, which I prefer for its jagged texture, can be found in Japanese grocery stores and better supermarkets. It works well as a coating for the croquettes.

————

½ cup plus 1½ tablespoons jasmine rice
1½ cups whole milk
1 tablespoon unsalted butter
¼ cup plus 1 teaspoon granulated sugar
Grated zest of ½ lemon
3 large egg yolks, lightly beaten
2 large eggs
½ cups fine dry bread crumbs or panko (see headnote)
About 6 cups vegetable or canola oil for deep-frying
Confectioners' sugar for dusting

1. Combine the rice, milk, and butter in a medium saucepan and bring to a boil. Reduce the heat to a simmer and cook, uncovered, until the rice is tender, about 15 minutes.

2. Butter a small baking sheet or baking dish. Stir the sugar and lemon zest into the rice, followed by the egg yolks. Cook, stirring, over low heat until the mixture thickens. Pour the mixture onto the prepared baking sheet or into the baking dish, and let cool. Chill in the fridge.

3. Form the rice into small balls, using a scant table-spoon of rice for each. You should have 30 to 35 balls. Set aside in a plate. Beat the eggs in a shallow dish; pour the bread crumbs into another shallow dish. Pour the oil into a large deep heavy saucepan—it should be at least 2 inches deep—and place over medium-high heat. The oil is ready when it's at 355 degrees.

4. When the oil is ready, dip the rice balls—in batches—first in the eggs (draining off as much as possible) and then the bread crumbs, and carefully lower into the oil. Fry until nut brown, about 1 minute. The balls should be toasted on the outside but still creamy inside. Adjust the heat and cooking time as needed. As the croquettes finish frying, transfer them to a paper-towel-lined baking sheet. Dust with confectioners' sugar before serving.

MAKES 30 TO 35 CROQUETTES

FEBRUARY 18, 1877: "RECEIPTS FOR THE TABLE." RECIPE SIGNED AUNT ADDIE.

—1877

⌇ STRAWBERRY SHORTCAKES

I'm not one for fluffy shortcakes. I want a cake with oomph and character, and that's just what you get with these wonderful dense, faintly salty shortcakes. They must be eaten warm, so get everything else—the strawberries, the cream—ready before popping the shortcakes into the oven. You can either pour or whip the cream. If it's grocery store cream, I whip it; if it's rich, grassy cream from a local farm, I pour it.

————

2 quarts strawberries, hulled
¼ cup sugar, or more to taste
4 cups heavy cream
4 cups all-purpose flour
1 tablespoon baking powder
1 teaspoon salt
8 tablespoons (1 stick) unsalted butter, cut into cubes,
    plus 3 tablespoons unsalted butter, softened

1. Halve or quarter the strawberries, depending on size. Toss with the sugar in a bowl and let macerate for about 30 minutes. Taste and add more sugar if needed.

2. Whip 2 cups of the cream to soft peaks; chill it.

3. Heat the oven to 400 degrees. Line a baking sheet with parchment paper. Pulse together the flour, baking powder, and salt in a food processor. Add the cubed butter and pulse until pebbly.

4. Scrape the mixture into a bowl. Add the remaining 2 cups cream and use a fork to gently mix it together. When the dough is blended but still shaggy, turn it out onto a floured work surface and, using a rolling pin, gently flatten it into a ¾-inch-thick square.

5. Use a 3-inch round biscuit cutter to cut the dough into circles. Lay the circles 2 inches apart on the parchment-lined baking sheet. Bake until puffed, browned on the edges, and cooked through, 12 to 16 minutes. Transfer to baking racks to cool.

6. To serve, split the biscuits in half and butter each half with the softened butter. Lay each pair of halves in a shallow dish, spoon on some strawberries and juices, and top with whipped cream.

SERVES 8 TO 10

COOKING NOTE

If you don't have a biscuit cutter, use a tumbler, or just cut the dough into 3-inch squares.

MAY 13, 1877: "RECEIPTS FOR THE TABLE." RECIPE SIGNED AUNT ADDIE.

—1877

✎ SNOW PUDDING

Snow pudding, a soul mate of floating island and snow eggs—all are puffs of meringue setting sail on lakes of custard—has gone the way of the dodo. But my two-year-old twins would like to revive it. When they tasted this pudding, their eyes lit up, thrilled by their uncertainty about whether they were supposed to drink or chew.

———

For the "Snow"
1 envelope powdered gelatin
1 cup boiling water
1 cup sugar
Juice of 1 lemon
2 large egg whites

For the Custard
2 cups whole milk
5 large egg yolks
¼ cup sugar
½ teaspoon vanilla extract

1. To make the snow, place the gelatin in a medium bowl, pour the water over it, and stir until dissolved. Stir in the sugar and lemon juice and, again, stir until dissolved. Set the bowl in a larger bowl filled with ice water and stir the mixture until it begins to thicken and gel.

2. Pour the gelatin mixture into the bowl of a mixer fitted with a whisk. Add the egg whites and beat until the mixture turns white and then slowly thickens—it will nearly grow out of the bowl. Stop beating when it's like a dense, shiny meringue, 5 to 10 minutes. Leave the "snow" in the bowl.

3. To make the custard, pour the milk into a medium saucepan and heat over medium-high heat until bubbles form around the edges. Meanwhile, whisk together the egg yolks, sugar, and vanilla in a medium bowl. Gradually whisk the hot milk into the egg yolk mixture. Pour this mixture back into the saucepan and cook over medium heat, stirring constantly, until it's thick enough to coat the back of a spoon.

4. To serve, divide the custard among 6 wide shallow bowls. Top each with a dollop of "snow."

SERVES 6

MAY 25, 1877: "THE HOUSEHOLD: RECEIPTS FOR THE TABLE." RECIPE SIGNED LILLIE.

—1877

✎ CHOCOLATE ECLAIRS

Eclairs are no harder to make than iced cupcakes, and they float free of cupcakes' baggage of trend-dom.

———

For the Eclairs

4 tablespoons unsalted butter

1 cup water

1 cup all-purpose flour

1 teaspoon sugar

¼ teaspoon salt

4 large eggs, separated

¼ teaspoon baking soda, dissolved in ½ teaspoon water

For the Filling

3 cups whole milk

6 large egg yolks

3 tablespoons sugar

3 tablespoons all-purpose flour

3 ounces bittersweet chocolate, melted

For the Glaze

2½ ounces unsweetened chocolate, chopped

½ cup sugar

3½ tablespoons water

1. To make the éclairs, melt the butter in the water in a medium saucepan over medium heat. Combine the flour, sugar, and salt, and when the butter is melted and the liquid is hot, add the flour mixture to the saucepan and beat with a wooden spoon until the dough is smooth and releases from the sides of the pan, about 4 minutes. (You may need to take the pan on and off the heat to avoid burning it.) Let cool for 10 minutes.

2. Whisk the egg yolks in a bowl until thickened. Whisk the egg whites until frothy. Beat the yolks and whites into the dough a little at a time, alternating yolks and whites. The whites will break the dough apart, so be patient and keep beating; the dough will come back together. After the eggs are incorporated, beat in the baking soda mixture. Cover the pan and let rest for 1 hour.

3. Heat the oven to 400 degrees. Line a baking sheet with parchment; butter the parchment. Using a pastry bag fitted with a ¼-inch plain tip, pipe the dough onto the parchment in strips 4 inches long by 1 inch wide; keep them at least 2 inches apart. You should have about 12 éclairs.

4. Bake until puffed, lightly browned, and completely cooked through, about 20 minutes. If they're not dry in the center, they'll deflate once out of the oven. Transfer to a baking rack to cool.

5. To make the filling, heat the milk in a medium saucepan over medium-high heat until bubbles form around the edges. Whisk together the egg yolks, sugar, and flour in a medium bowl until smooth. Slowly whisk in the hot milk, then pour the mixture back into the saucepan, bring it to a boil, whisking constantly, and boil, whisking, for 1 minute. Cook until thickened, like pudding. Whisk in the melted chocolate. Pour into a bowl, lay a piece of plastic wrap on the surface of the filling, and let cool.

6. To make the glaze, melt the chocolate in the top of a double boiler over hot, not simmering, water. When the chocolate is melted, stir in the sugar and water. It will look seized and gritty; forge ahead! It will unseize when the sugar dissolves. Place the pan over direct heat and stir briskly with a whisk for a few seconds, until the mixture becomes very smooth and only slightly thickened. Add a little water to thin if necessary.

7. To assemble the éclairs, fill a pastry bag fitted with a ¼-inch plain tip with the filling. Using the pastry bag tip, puncture a hole in the end of each éclair and slowly and gently fill the éclair with the cream. Use a spoon to spread a thin layer of chocolate glaze on top of each éclair. (Alternatively, slice the éclairs lengthwise in half, like a hot dog roll. Fill the bottom halves with pastry cream. Dip the exterior of the top halves in the glaze and replace on the bottom halves.)

MAKES ABOUT 12 ÉCLAIRS

SEPTEMBER 2, 1877: "RECEIPTS FOR THE TABLE." RECIPE SIGNED CALIFORNIA. SOME TECHNIQUE AND PROPORTIONS COME FROM *LA VARENNE PRATIQUE*, BY ANNE WILLAN, AND *MAIDA HEATTER'S BOOK OF GREAT CHOCOLATE DESSERTS*, BY MAIDA HEATTER.

—1877

⌒ COCONUT PIE

This is a complete redefinition of coconut pie, which is usually a tsunami of sugar flecked with bits of coconut. The filling here, textured with freshly grated coconut, is so light it's almost fragile. And before you even get to the filling, you're met by a thin, lemony stratum of meringue. Could there be a more perfect combination?

———

Cream Cheese Pastry (p. 843)

2 cups whole milk

I cup grated fresh coconut (frozen is fine)

1/2 cup plus 2 tablespoons sugar

2 large eggs, separated

2 large egg yolks

1/2 cup confectioners' sugar

3 tablespoons fresh lemon juice

1. Place a baking sheet on the middle oven rack and heat the oven to 400 degrees. Place the pastry dough between 2 sheets of lightly floured plastic wrap. Roll out to a 12-inch circle, about 1/8 inch thick, and fit into a 9-inch pie pan. Trim the extra dough. Prick the dough with a fork, lay a piece of parchment over the dough, and add rice, dried beans, or pie weights. Loosely cover the rim of the pan with aluminum foil so the crust doesn't brown too quickly.

2. Set the pie plate on the baking sheet in the oven and bake for 15 minutes. Remove the parchment and weights and bake until the dough is dry in the center, 5 to 7 minutes longer. Let cool. Reduce the oven heat to 350 degrees.

3. Heat the milk in a small saucepan over medium-high heat, until bubbles form around the edges. Remove from the heat and whisk in the coconut and sugar. Lightly beat the 4 egg yolks in a bowl. Whisk a little hot milk into the yolks, then whisk the yolk mixture into the milk.

4. Pour the coconut filling into the crust. Set the pie on the baking sheet in the oven and bake (again, with foil around the edges) until the custard is just set, about 30 minutes. Remove from the oven. Increase the oven heat to 450 degrees.

5. In a mixer fitted with a whisk (or in a bowl with a hand mixer), beat the whites until frothy. Gradually beat in the confectioners' sugar and beat until the whites are firm and shiny. Whisk in the lemon juice. Spread the meringue over the pie (I like to make a smooth, flat layer), making sure it touches the pastry all around. Place in the oven and bake until the meringue is toasted on the edges, 4 to 5 minutes.

SERVES 8

APRIL 7, 1878: "THE HOUSEHOLD: RECEIPTS FOR THE TABLE." RECIPE SIGNED BROOKLYN COOK.

—1878

✐ SPANISH CREAM

Serve this two-layer custard, half pudding, half fluffy custard, with the Cherry Bounce (p. 13) or Fresh Raspberry Flummery (p. 824). And if you want to do a custard taste test, try the blancmange on p. 797 and the panna cotta on p. 840.

---

4 cups whole milk

2 envelopes powdered gelatin

4 large eggs, separated

6 tablespoons sugar

I teaspoon vanilla extract

Pinch of salt

1. Pour 1 cup milk into a small bowl and sprinkle the gelatin on top. Let sit for 10 minutes to soften.

2. Bring the remaining 3 cups milk to a simmer in a medium saucepan. Stir in the gelatin mixture until dissolved. Beat the egg yolks and sugar in a small bowl until light and pale. Whisk in a little of the hot milk mixture to temper the yolks, then pour this mixture back into the milk and whisk to blend. Cook over medium heat, stirring constantly, until the mixture thickens slightly. Stir in the vanilla and remove from the heat.

3. Whisk the egg whites with a pinch of salt until they hold soft peaks. Fold the whites into the custard, making sure they're thoroughly dispersed. Ladle the cream into ten 8-ounce ramekins, filling them three-quarters full. Chill.

SERVES 10

APRIL 7, 1878: "THE HOUSEHOLD: RECEIPTS FOR THE TABLE." RECIPE SIGNED MRS. H.

—1878

✐ HUNTINGTON PUDDING

The nineteenth-century home cook couldn't get enough of meringue. It topped puddings. It was used to bind cookies. It formed the base of icings. It found its way into charlottes and chiffons.

Here the meringue, which buzzes with lemon, is what makes this odd but pleasing dish. You whip the egg whites with sugar until they form long elastic peaks, sharpen the meringue with lemon juice, and pile it on top of an unsweetened rice pudding that's scented with the lemon's zest and thickened with the egg yolks. The layers are drawn together as irresistibly as the opposites in a romantic comedy. The pudding is creamy and perfumed with lemon, the topping tangy and sweet with a thin, toasty shell. As you taste the sweet and savory mix, you'll wonder if dessert's evolution into uniformly sweet concoctions hasn't been a terrible mistake.

_____

2 cups whole milk

$^{1}/_{2}$ cup long-grain white rice, like jasmine

2 large eggs, separated

1 tablespoon unsalted butter

Grated zest and juice of 1 lemon

$^{1}/_{2}$ cup sugar

1. Combine the milk and rice in a double boiler and barely simmer, covered, until the rice is just tender, 25 to 30 minutes.

2. Remove the rice from the heat and stir in the egg yolks, butter, and lemon zest. Pour into a 1- to 1$^{1}/_{2}$-quart soufflé or baking dish.

3. Beat the egg whites to a stiff froth in a medium bowl. Gradually beat in the sugar and beat until the whites are shiny and elastic. Fold in the lemon juice. Spread this on top of the rice pudding in a big pouf.

4. Heat the broiler, with a rack low enough so the meringue will be at least 4 inches from the flame. Broil the pudding until the meringue is toasted a nut brown. The pudding can be served right away or at room temperature. When serving, scoop downward to make sure each person gets both rice and meringue.

SERVES 4

COOKING NOTE

Use a Meyer lemon (usually available from November through February) if possible—it's more fragrant and less tart.

PERIOD DETAIL

During this week in April 1879, the editor of "The Household" reported that the *Times* had received more than 200 letters with recipes from readers around the country.

APRIL 6, 1879: "RECEIPTS FOR THE TABLE." RECIPE SIGNED MADGE.

—1879

ORANGE MARMALADE PUDDING

This is a sweet bread-and-custard pudding that's split through the middle with a layer of bright and bitter marmalade.

_____

2 teaspoons unsalted butter

$^{1}/_{2}$ cup sugar

4 large eggs, separated

1 cup whole milk

1 cup fine fresh bread crumbs

$^{2}/_{3}$ cup orange marmalade

Heavy cream for serving

1. Heat the oven to 350 degrees. In a mixer fitted with a paddle (or in a large bowl with a hand mixer), beat the butter and sugar until blended. Beat in the egg yolks. Stir in the milk and bread crumbs.

2. Beat the whites in a clean mixer bowl with a whisk (or in a large bowl with clean beaters) until they hold soft peaks. Fold into the milk mixture.

3. Spread one-quarter of the pudding in a 1$^{1}/_{2}$-quart soufflé mold or baking dish. Drop one-third of the marmalade in spoonfuls on top, doing your best to spread it around without combining the layers. Repeat, ending with the pudding mixture. Bake until just set, about 40 minutes.

4. Serve the pudding while still warm. Unmold the pudding (by placing a deep serving platter on top and inverting it), or simply spoon it out. Pour a little cool cream on top.

SERVES 6

MAY 15, 1881: "RECEIPTS." RECIPE SIGNED COMMON SENSE IN THE HOUSEHOLD.

—1881

⌐ PEACH BALLS

Doughnuts, which became hugely popular in the nineteenth century, have stuck around ever since. I can't understand why these peach balls—a sliver of preserved peach nestled in a fried ball of sweetened rice—didn't follow the same trajectory. They are a testament to the value of letting salinity and sweetness duel on the tongue. The rice is cooked with a generous amount of salt, some sugar is stirred in, and then the balls are coated in powdered saltine crackers and fried. When they come out of the hot oil as peach balls, they're remarkably good, but it's the confectioners' sugar, sifted on top, that makes the recipe sublime.

I used the Brandied Peaches on p. 599 as the peach filling, but any preserved peach will do, as long as it doesn't come out of a can. If you're making the recipe in the summer, you can use a very ripe fresh peach.

This recipe was one of dozens by Juliet Corson, a contributor to "The Household." In Corson's column, seasonal cooking was the theme. She also operated a one-woman cookbook industry and headed a cooking school on St. Mark's Place. Among her many recipes that appear in this book are Watercress Salad (p. 171), Asparagus Salad (p. 214), Lobster Bisque I (p. 108), and Clam Chowder (p. 107).

———

½ cup basmati or jasmine rice

½ teaspoon kosher salt

2 tablespoons sugar

¼ teaspoon freshly grated nutmeg

1 large egg yolk

¾ cup fine saltine cracker crumbs

2 large eggs

Eight ¾-inch slivers of peach (fresh, brandied, or otherwise home-preserved)

About 4 cups canola oil for deep-frying

Confectioners' sugar for dusting

1. Bring 2 cups water to a boil in a small saucepan. Add the rice and salt, cover the pan, turn the heat to low, and simmer until the rice begins to burst, 16 to 18 minutes.

2. Drain the rice, then return it to the pan. Stir in the sugar, nutmeg, and egg yolk. Place the pan over low heat and stir with a wooden spoon until the mixture begins to thicken slightly, 2 to 3 minutes. Remove from the heat and let cool enough to handle.

3. Have a bowl of water near your work space. Spread the cracker crumbs in a wide shallow bowl. Beat the eggs in another bowl. Wet your hands, then scoop up a golf-ball-sized lump of rice into your palm, shape it into a loose ball, and hollow out the center. Lay a piece of peach in the hollow and enclose it with rice; the peach should not be visible. Lay the ball in the dish of cracker crumbs, and make 7 more balls in the same way.

4. When all are formed, roll the balls in the crumbs, then dip them into the beaten egg, rolling very gently and quickly, and then lay them again in the crumbs and lightly coat.

5. Pour 2 inches of oil into a medium heavy saucepan and place over medium-high heat. The oil is ready when it browns a piece of cracker (or bread) in 30 seconds. Use a slotted spoon to lower the peach balls into the hot oil; fry just 2 at a time, because it's easier to control the heat. The balls are cooked when the coating is a deep golden brown, about 2 minutes. Drain on paper towels.

6. Serve piled on a dish and dusted with confectioners' sugar.

MAKES 8 PEACH BALLS

FEBRUARY 12, 1882: "HINTS FOR THE HOUSEHOLD: HOW TO PREPARE A GOOD FAMILY DINNER," BY JULIET CORSON.

—1882

⌐ OFENSCHLUPFER (ALMOND BREAD PUDDING)

This is one of several bread puddings in this chapter—turns out there's a reason it's so timeless. It's good! While it's a dish that would seem to transcend class divisions, variations in the ingredients suggest otherwise. Those made simply with stale bread (or cake) and milk and eggs, or bread and fruit, were called cabinet pudding or poverty pudding. The fancier folk came up with Queen of Puddings (topped off with jam and meringue, p. 866), Delicate Bread Pudding (made with fine bread crumbs, p. 798), and this Almond Bread Pudding (infused with pricey almonds).

A 1910 recipe noted that if you got tired of your

bread pudding leftovers (something I'm not sure is possible), you could always dip slices of it in confectioners' sugar and deep-fry them.

———

For the Pudding
½ loaf stale Pullman (sandwich) bread,
    cut into ½-inch-thick slices
¼ pound (about ¾ cup) blanched almonds,
    finely ground in a food processor
Grated zest of 1 lemon
1 teaspoon ground cinnamon
8 large eggs
½ cup plus 2 teaspoons sugar
4 cups whole milk

For the Sauce
1 teaspoon cornstarch, dissolved in ½ cup water
2 tablespoons currant jelly
2 tablespoons sugar
2 cups water

1. Heat the oven to 350 degrees. Butter a large baking dish. Cut the bread slices in half and lay them like fallen dominos in the baking dish. They should just fill it. Combine the ground almonds with the lemon zest and cinnamon. Sprinkle over the bread.
2. Whisk together the eggs, sugar, and milk in a large bowl. Pour over the bread, lifting the layers with your fingers so the liquid gets between the slices. Press lightly on the bread to make sure it soaks up the liquid.
3. Bake the pudding until set, about 30 minutes.
4. Meanwhile, to make the sauce, combine the cornstarch mixture, currant jelly, sugar, and water in a small saucepan, bring to a boil, and stir until lightly thickened. Remove from the heat.
5. Serve the pudding warm, drizzled with a little currant sauce.

SERVES 6

COOKING NOTE
Do not use commercial sandwich bread for this (or any other bread pudding) recipe, or the texture and flavor will disappoint. A handmade loaf of white Pullman bread, or one from a good bakery, works well.

JUNE 11, 1882: "HINTS FOR THE HOUSEHOLD."

—1882

⤫ PEACH SALAD

This dessert salad was a revelation for me—I discovered that you don't need pastry dough or cobbler or shortcakes to make peaches a full-fledged dessert. You just slice the peaches and toss them with a sweet dressing that makes them taste richer and brighter (a similar apple salad, dressed with cinnamon and sherry, was also common at the time). You may find the dressing too sweet, so start with less sugar and add more as you like.

———

4 ripe peaches, pitted and cut into quarters
6 tablespoons sugar
¼ cup dry Madeira
1 teaspoon fresh lemon juice
¼ teaspoon ground cinnamon
Freshly grated nutmeg to taste
Heavy cream for serving

1. Place the peaches in a serving dish, preferably wide and shallow.
2. Whisk together the sugar, Madeira, lemon juice, cinnamon, and nutmeg in a bowl until the sugar is dissolved. Pour over the peaches, and toss gently. Serve with a pitcher of chilled cream.

SERVES 6

JULY 30, 1893: "THE LUSCIOUS PEACH IS WITH US."

—1893

⤫ TRANSPARENT PUDDING

The recipe says this tart "will cut light and clear." It's not exactly transparent, but it has luminescence and tastes like a butter tart. One of the variations offered in the original recipe was to add candied orange peel—sprinkle a few tablespoons chopped peel into the crust along with the custard.

———

8 large eggs
1 cup plus 3 tablespoons sugar
½ pound (2 sticks) unsalted butter, cut into pieces

Lots of freshly grated nutmeg

6 ounces puff pastry (or 1 sheet Pepperidge Farm
    puff pastry)

1. Place a baking sheet on the middle oven rack and heat the oven to 350 degrees. Beat the eggs in a medium saucepan. Add the sugar and butter and warm gently over medium-low heat, stirring constantly. Season generously with nutmeg (start with ½ teaspoon). Once the butter is melted, increase the heat to medium and continue stirring until the mixture thickens enough to coat the back of the spoon, 5 to 10 minutes. Set the pan in a bowl of ice water to stop the cooking, and let the custard cool a bit while you prepare the pastry.

2. Roll out the puff pastry as thin as possible, 1/16 to 1/8 inch. Line a 9-inch pie plate with it, trimming the edges. Press to secure the dough to the edges of the pie plate.

3. Pour the slightly cooled custard into the crust. Place the pie on the baking sheet in the oven and bake until the custard is just set, 25 to 30 minutes.

SERVES 8

DECEMBER 25, 1895: "PUDDINGS OF OUR FATHERS."

—1895

PISTACHIO CREAM

Serve in tiny portions for a brief and wonderfully intense moment with the pistachio.

———

6 large egg yolks

3 tablespoons sugar

1 ounce (about ¼ cup) raw pistachios,
    very finely ground in a food processor

3/8 teaspoon orange-flower water

Pinch of salt

4 cups heavy cream

1. Beat the egg yolks and sugar in a medium bowl until light. Beat in the pistachios, orange-flower water, and salt.

2. Heat the cream in a medium saucepan over medium-high heat until bubbles form around the edges. Slowly whisk about ½ cup of the hot cream into the egg yolks, then add this mixture to the remaining cream, whisking constantly. Place over low heat and cook, stirring constantly, until thickened, 5 to 7 minutes; do not let the mixture boil.

3. Pour the cream into 4 ramekins or small glasses. Cover with plastic wrap and chill until cold.

SERVES 6

COOKING NOTE

Raw pistachios and orange-flower water are available at Middle Eastern grocery stores and specialty supermarkets.

MAY 28, 1899: "QUAINT OLD-TIME RECEIPTS."

—1899

CHERRY AND COCONUT BROWN BETTY

Among the family of buckles, crisps, crumbles, and slumps, brown Betty is the lean and thrifty cousin, as it relies on nothing more than bread crumbs and sugar for its infrastructure. Here the bread crumbs soak up the cherry juices and help the layers latch together. And the sugar helps all the flavors blossom. You can, of course, improve this brown Betty in a million ways: you can add vanilla, use brioche crumbs rather than regular white bread, or slip in some lemon zest for more fragrance. But should you?

———

4 cups halved and pitted cherries

¾ cup sugar

½ cup grated fresh coconut (frozen coconut also works;
    if using sweetened coconut, reduce the sugar to
    ½ cup)

2 cups fresh bread crumbs

Heavy cream for serving

1. Heat the oven to 350 degrees. Butter an 8-inch square baking dish. Spread 1 cup cherries in the base of the dish. Sprinkle with 2 tablespoons sugar, 2 tablespoons coconut, and ½ cup bread crumbs. Repeat 3 times. Cover the baking dish with foil.

2. Bake until the cherry juices bubble and candy a bit on the edges, about 1 hour.

3. Remove the foil and place the dish under the broiler to toast the top layer, 1 to 3 minutes. Serve warm, passing a pitcher of chilled cream at the table.

SERVES 6

JUNE 26, 1910: "NEW DISHES FOR SUMMER."

—1910

RASPBERRY BAVARIAN CREAM

The lovely, sophisticated, and even a trifle bouncy precursor to Jell-O fluff.

———

1½ tablespoons powdered gelatin
¼ cup cold water
⅓ cup boiling water
1 cup raspberry juice (see Cooking Note)
⅓ cup plus 2 tablespoons sugar
2 cups heavy cream, whipped to soft peaks

1. Sprinkle the gelatin over the cold water in a small bowl. Let sit for 5 minutes.

2. Add the boiling water and stir until the gelatin is dissolved. Add the raspberry juice and sugar and stir until the sugar is dissolved. Chill the raspberry mixture until it begins to firm up, about 1 hour.

3. Fold the whipped cream into the raspberry mixture. Pour into a 1½-quart soufflé dish or charlotte mold. Chill until set.

4. You can serve the cream directly from the dish. Or, to unmold, set the dish in a bowl of hot water for a minute, then tap it out onto a plate.

SERVES 6

COOKING NOTE
Raspberry juice is made by pureeing raspberries in a food processor, then straining the liquid. You'll need about 4 cups raspberries to yield 1 cup juice.

JULY 17, 1910: "SOME WARM WEATHER RECEIPTS."

—1910

APPLE DUMPLINGS

These dumplings, which are baked on top of sliced apples, will remind you of a scone or biscuit. I love that you add no sugar to the apples, no embellishments to the dumplings. This dessert is about the fruit and the lightness of your touch with the dumpling dough. No pressure.

———

2 small tart apples, like Macoun, peeled,
    halved, cored, and thinly sliced
1 cup all-purpose flour
½ cup cake flour
½ teaspoon salt
1 tablespoon baking powder
¼ cup vegetable shortening
½ cup plus 1 tablespoon whole milk
Sugar and heavy cream for serving or
    Spiced Hard Sauce (p. 604)

1. Heat the oven to 400 degrees. Butter 6 English muffin rings (or 4-inch tart rings or tartlet pans) and set on a buttered baking sheet (no need to butter the baking sheet if using tart pans). Fill the rings with the apple slices—better to be scant than overflowing.

2. Sift together the flours, salt, and baking powder twice. Pour into a bowl. Add the shortening and, using a pastry blender or your fingertips, work the shortening into the flour until it forms coarse pebbles. Add the milk and lightly mix the dough until it just holds together and no longer has dry patches.

3. Drop the dough on top of the apples in each muffin ring, spreading it to the edges as best as you can. Bake until the dough is golden on top and cooked through, about 20 minutes.

4. To serve, invert each dumpling into a shallow serving bowl, so the apples are on top. Serve sprinkled with sugar and cream, or serve with hard sauce.

SERVES 6

NOVEMBER 12, 1911: "TIMELY HINTS ABOUT THE HOUSEHOLD."

—1911

⌒ RUM OMELET

This omelet is really more of a sautéed soufflé—cooked until crisp on the bottom, then flipped and crisped on the other side. Just before serving, you douse it with rum and light it on fire, basting the omelet for a few exciting moments until the flames die. It's a dramatic dessert—and even more of an eye-opener if you make it before you've had your morning coffee.

_____

3 large eggs, separated
1 tablespoon granulated sugar
Kosher salt
Grated zest of 1 lemon
2 tablespoons unsalted butter
1 cup confectioners' sugar
2 tablespoons dark rum

1. Whisk together the egg yolks and sugar in a large bowl.
2. Beat the whites with a pinch of salt in a medium bowl until they hold soft peaks. Add the lemon zest and continue beating until firm. Fold the whites into the yolk mixture.
3. Place an 8-inch nonstick skillet over medium-high heat. Add 1 tablespoon butter, and when it's foamy, pour in the egg mixture. Cook until the mixture is golden brown on the bottom.
4. Meanwhile, melt the remaining tablespoon of butter in another nonstick skillet. Invert this pan over the omelet, then quickly flip the omelet, so it lands in the freshly buttered pan. Cook over medium heat until the bottom is golden brown and crisp and the omelet is just cooked through. Remove from the heat.
5. Dust the top of the omelet heavily with confectioners' sugar. Pour the rum on top and, using a long match or lighter, carefully light the rum. Let it cook, shaking the pan and spooning it over the omelet, until the flame dies out. Serve immediately.

SERVES 4

NOVEMBER 8, 1914: "WHAT EVERY WOMAN WANTS TO KNOW."

—1914

⌒ APPLE SNOW

Apple snow is as fun to make as it is peculiar. It's not quite floating island, and not quite apple mousse (p. 816). You whip up a meringue and slowly beat in apple puree. As you whisk it, the mixture lightens in both color and texture until it's like, well, snow. There have been at least half a dozen recipes for apple snow in the _Times_, some with less egg, some with more. One contains the unforgiving instruction, long before electric mixers were invented, to "beat for three-quarters of an hour without stopping." That is one way to get arms like Madonna's.

Apple snow needs an accompaniment. You can serve it with whipped cream or custard. Some recipes suggest ladyfingers, though any thin, crisp cookie will do (try the Gingersnaps on p. 679). This recipe calls for jelly too. Any flavor that goes with apples will work—I used peach and ginger jelly, and I'd happily try it with lemon marmalade or a wine jelly.

_____

3 large tart apples, cored and quartered
3 large egg whites
½ cup confectioners' sugar, or to taste
1 cup Custard (p. 800)
½ cup jelly

1. Place the apple quarters in a medium saucepan, add just enough water to cover, and bring to a boil over medium-high heat. Reduce the heat and simmer until the apples are totally soft, 5 to 10 minutes. Drain off the liquid, and pass through a food mill or sieve into a bowl. (Alternatively, peel the apples before boiling and puree in a food processor.) You need 1 cup apple puree.
2. In a mixer fitted with a whisk (or in a large bowl with a hand mixer), whip the egg whites until foamy, then begin adding the sugar a little at a time, beating until the whites are firm and shiny. With the mixer on high speed, begin adding the apple puree a few spoonfuls at a time. The mixture will transform from foamy to dense and will nearly grow out of the bowl. Once all the apple puree is added, taste the "snow" and add more sugar if needed.
3. Serve a large dollop of the apple snow set on a small pool of custard in each bowl. Spoon a little jelly around the edges.

NOVEMBER 15, 1914: "APPLES DESERVE THE ATTENTION OF THE WISE HOUSEKEEPER, FOR THEY ARE INEXPENSIVE."

—1914

GRAPEFRUIT FLUFF

This grapefruit fluff was like a shining beacon in the sea of dull and sometimes abominable food served in the 1940s. (I moved right on by the Date Ice-Box Pudding made with evaporated milk and the Fruit Turnovers that called for canned fruit.) This fluff is joyful, an adult ice cream sundae—to eat it, you pierce a crisp, sugary snowcap to land your spoon first on a layer of warm, floppy meringue, then a layer of vanilla ice cream, and finally a well of tart and boozy slivers of grapefruit.

As you can see by the ingredient list, you can make this on the spur of the moment. You probably already have everything in your pantry and fridge.

———

2 pink grapefruits
1/4 cup brandy or kirsch
2 large egg whites
Pinch of salt
1/2 cup sugar
4 large scoops vanilla ice cream

1. Halve the grapefruits. Using a small sharp paring knife or one of those nifty grapefruit knives, remove the grapefruit segments and place them in a bowl. Then gently remove the membrane from the grapefruit halves and discard it. You will be left with 4 hollowed-out grapefruit halves. Reserve them.
2. Pour the brandy over the grapefruit segments. Chill for 1 hour.
3. When ready to serve, heat the broiler with an oven rack about 6 inches from the heating element. In a mixer fitted with a whisk (or in a bowl with a hand mixer), whip the egg whites with the salt until foamy. Gradually add the sugar, beating until the whites are firm and shiny.
4. Spoon the grapefruit segments into the reserved grapefruit halves. Arrange them in a baking pan on a layer of ice (this helps steady them and also keeps the cool part cool). Add a large scoop of ice cream to

each, and flatten the ice cream to make room for the meringue. Dollop the meringue on top. Place under the broiler and toast the meringue until a hazelnut brown, about 1 minute. Transfer the grapefruits to shallow bowls, and serve!

JANUARY 12, 1941: "VICTUALS AND VITAMINS," BY KILEY TAYLOR. RECIPE ADAPTED FROM MAURICE GONNEAU, THE EXECUTIVE CHEF AT THE PARK LANE AND THE CHATHAM IN NEW YORK CITY.

—1941

INDIAN PUDDING

This crude yet lovable New England classic is good when served with the Spiced Hard Sauce on p. 604, even better with sweetened whipped cream or ice cream, and sublime served with all three.

———

4 cups whole milk
1/3 cup yellow cornmeal
1/2 teaspoon salt
1/2 teaspoon ground ginger
1/2 teaspoon ground cinnamon
1/3 to 1/2 cup unsulphured molasses (to taste)
Spiced Hard Sauce (p. 604), sweetened whipped cream, or ice cream for serving

1. Heat the oven to 350 degrees. Mix 1/2 cup milk with the cornmeal in a small bowl. Scald the rest of the milk by bringing it almost to a boil in a large saucepan. Stir in the moistened cornmeal and all the other pudding ingredients. Simmer, stirring often, until the cornmeal is cooked and the pudding has thickened like polenta about 20 minutes.
2. Pour into a greased 8-inch square baking dish. Cover and bake for 1½ hours; the pudding should still be loose on top but firm underneath. Serve with hard sauce, whipped cream, or ice cream.

DECEMBER 30, 1945: "ALL FROM THE OVEN," BY JANE NICKERSON.

—1945

⌒ STRAWBERRY CHARLOTTE

Strawberry charlotte, a chiffon-like mousse set in a fanciful mold, belongs to the indulgent family of charlottes made with whipped cream and egg whites. Apple charlotte, which belongs to the more healthful line of the tribe, is a baked mold of bread and sweetened apples. Attributed to Carême, the well-known nineteenth-century French chef, mousse-like charlottes were held together with gelatin and often set in molds lined with ladyfingers. This strawberry charlotte forgoes the ladyfingers; the result is a lot like a buoyant whipped panna cotta. In fact, if you poured the charlotte into smaller molds and called it panna cotta, you'd never know it came from 1947.

1½ envelopes powdered gelatin
¼ cup cold water
½ cup boiling water
¾ cup sugar
1 tablespoon fresh lemon juice
1 cup crushed or sieved strawberries, plus (optional)
    sweetened crushed berries for serving
3 large egg whites, beaten to stiff peaks
1 cup heavy cream, whipped to soft peaks
A handful of whole strawberries with stems attached,
    for garnish

1. Soften the gelatin in the cold water in a bowl, about 5 minutes. Add the boiling water and stir until the gelatin is dissolved. Add the sugar, lemon juice, and 1 cup strawberries. Let cool, then chill until starting to set.
2. Whip the gelatin mixture until somewhat fluffy. Fold in the egg whites and then the cream. Pour into a 1-quart mold and refrigerate until firm, about 2 hours.
3. Turn out of the mold and decorate with a few whole berries. Serve plain, or with the sweetened crushed strawberries as a sauce.

SERVES 8

JUNE 8, 1947: "STRAWBERRY DESSERTS," BY JANE NICKERSON.

—1947

⌒ TAPIOCA FLAMINGO

In 1951, 1.5 million pounds of tapioca spilled into the East River one morning when a pier holding a shipment from Brazil collapsed. The headline in the *Times*: "Tapioca à la East River." It wasn't the first time that the flavorless pudding base—the powder, or granular "pearls," of dried cassava root—made headlines. Before World War II, the tapioca that Americans consumed came from Java; when the Japanese invaded the island, the supply was cut off.

During the war, the *Times* food reporters treated lists of scarce ingredients like casualty reports from the front, and they kept close tabs on the tapioca situation. General Foods came up with a substitute made from sorghum, called Minute Dessert, which the *Times* declared an acceptable but inferior substitute. To pudding makers across America, relief came at last in 1947, when the United States began importing tapioca from Brazil—a turn of events that set the stage for the drama on the pier.

Today tapioca pudding is usually a creamy blend of tapioca pearls, milk, sugar, and vanilla. But until just after the war, tapioca was customarily a blend of the pearls, cooked in water or fruit juice, and fresh fruit, served with whipped cream. *Times* recipes in this vein go back to 1876.

In 1949, the exotically named Tapioca Flamingo appeared in the paper. It built on the old-style fruit-and-tapioca recipes by making one layer with half of the tapioca-and-fruit mixture and a second layer by combining the rest with whipped cream. It's a delicious combination and pretty too, with bits of strawberry suspended in the clear pink jelly and a pouf of cream and jelly on top. It was so good, in fact, that the editors couldn't resist running the same recipe again two years later during a record strawberry harvest.

----

1 pound strawberries, hulled
1 cup sugar
About 2 cups pineapple juice or water
⅓ cup quick-cooking tapioca
Scant ½ teaspoon kosher salt
½ cup heavy cream, whipped to soft peaks

1. Lightly crush the strawberries in a bowl. Add the sugar and let stand for at least 30 minutes.

2. Set a strainer over a bowl and drain the strawberries. Set them aside. Add enough pineapple juice (or water) to the strawberry juice to make 3 cups total.

3. Mix together the juice, tapioca, and salt in a saucepan and bring to a full boil, stirring constantly, then and pour into a bowl. (The mixture will be thin; do not overcook.)

4. Fold the drained strawberries into the tapioca mixture. Cool, stirring occasionally. The mixture will thicken as it cools.

5. When the tapioca mixture is cool, divide half of it among 4 coupe glasses or bowls. Chill the glasses and the remaining tapioca mixture.

6. Fold the cream into the remaining tapioca mixture, then pile lightly into the glasses.

SERVES 4

COOKING NOTES

Today most people prefer their tapioca on the looser side. If you're in that camp, add 1/4 cup more juice or water to the tapioca cooking liquid and 1/4 cup more cream to the topping.

If you like a tidier presentation, the strawberries can be cut into small pieces rather than crushed.

MAY 29, 1949: "FOOD; STRAWBERRIES OFF THE VINE," BY JANE NICKERSON.

—1949

⌒ JELLIED STRAWBERRY PIE

If you're serving this to friends, call it "strawberry pie." If to enemies, call it "jellied pie," which sounds revolting—but, thankfully, isn't.

———————

For the Flaky Pastry
1 cup plus 1 tablespoon sifted all-purpose flour
1/2 teaspoon salt
6 tablespoons vegetable shortening
3 tablespoons ice water

For the Filling
1 envelope powdered gelatin
1/4 cup cold water
4 cups strawberries
3/4 to 1 cup sugar

2/3 cup boiling water
1 tablespoon fresh lemon juice

1/2 to 1 cup heavy cream, whipped to soft peaks

1. To make the flaky pastry, heat the oven to 425 degrees. Combine the flour and salt in a bowl. With a pastry blender or knives, cut in the shortening until the mixture looks like coarse cornmeal. Add the water a few drops at a time, mixing lightly with a fork until all the flour is moistened. Gather the dough into a ball.

2. On a lightly floured work surface, roll out the dough to a circle 1/8 inch thick and about 12 inches in diameter. Line a 9-inch pie pan with the pastry. Trim the dough to 1/2 inch beyond the rim; roll under the edges, and crimp. Prick the dough all over with a fork. Lay a piece of parchment over the dough and fill with rice, dried beans, or pie weights.

3. Bake for 10 minutes, then remove the pie weights. Continue baking until the pastry is lightly browned on the edges and dry in the center, 12 to 15 minutes. Remove from the oven and let cool completely.

4. To make the filling, soften the gelatin in the cold water, about 5 minutes.

5. Meanwhile, chop 1 1/2 cups berries and puree in a blender or food processor. Chill the remainder.

6. Dissolve the sugar in the boiling water in a medium bowl. Add the gelatin and stir until dissolved. Add the pureed berries and lemon juice. Chill until the mixture begins to set, about 1 hour.

7. Fold the reserved whole berries into the gelatin mixture. Turn into the pie shell and chill until firm. Garnish the pie with whipped cream.

SERVES 6 TO 8

COOKING NOTE

The recipe said to "garnish" with the whipped cream. I used 2/3 cup heavy cream, sweetened it with 1 1/2 tablespoons of sugar, and spread the whipped cream over the entire top, so the pie looked like a smooth white button with crimped edges.

VARIATION

Try it with blueberries or blackberries!

JULY 13, 1958: "BAKE A BERRY PIE," BY CRAIG CLAIBORNE.

—1958

⌘ BANANA MERINGUE STEAMED CUSTARD

This custard is cooked, rather unusually, on top of the stove.

––––––––

For the Custard
2 large eggs
I large egg yolk
6 tablespoons sugar
$\frac{1}{8}$ teaspoon salt
2 cups whole milk
I teaspoon vanilla extract
$\frac{1}{4}$ teaspoon grated lemon zest
I banana, thinly sliced

For the Meringue
I large egg white
Pinch of salt
2 tablespoons sugar
$\frac{1}{4}$ teaspoon vanilla extract

1. To make the custard, butter six 4-ounce ramekins. Whisk together the eggs and yolk in a bowl. Whisk in the sugar, salt, milk, vanilla, and lemon zest. Pour an equal amount of the mixture into each ramekin.

2. Place a rack in the bottom of a baking pan and arrange the ramekins on it. Pour hot water around the cups to come halfway up the sides, and cover tightly with aluminum foil. Place over medium heat and simmer for 12 to 15 minutes; do not let the water boil. When the custards are done, a knife inserted 1 inch from the rim of a ramekin should come out clean. Transfer the ramekins to a baking sheet.

3. To make the meringue, heat the oven to 450 degrees. Beat the egg white with the salt in a bowl until soft peaks form. Gradually beat in the sugar and vanilla, and beat until stiff.

4. Top each of the custards with banana slices and cover with meringue. Bake until the meringue is toasted, about 5 minutes.

SERVES 6

MARCH 3, 1960: "NEW MENUS ARE OFFERED HOME COOK."
—1960

⌘ LEMON CHEESE PIE

This is a hybrid pie—lemon meringue crossed with cheesecake. The secret is the fat—cream cheese is rich and adds depth to a lean, abrupt flavor like lemon. You still enjoy the creaminess of the cheese, but the lemon keeps the feeling featherweight. Best of all is the crust, which seems like it's doing nothing but holding up the filling, and yet offers its own discreet measure of fragrance and salinity.

––––––––

For the Crust
I cup sifted all-purpose flour
$\frac{1}{2}$ teaspoon salt
$\frac{1}{3}$ cup vegetable shortening
I large egg, lightly beaten
I teaspoon grated lemon zest
I tablespoon fresh lemon juice

For the Filling
I $\frac{1}{4}$ cups sugar
$\frac{1}{4}$ cup cornstarch
I cup water
I teaspoon grated lemon zest
$\frac{1}{3}$ cup fresh lemon juice (from about 2 lemons)
2 large eggs, separated, yolks lightly beaten
$\frac{1}{4}$ pound cream cheese, at room temperature

1. To make the crust, heat the oven to 400 degrees. Sift the flour and salt into a bowl. Cut in the shortening until the mixture resembles fine oatmeal. Combine the egg with the lemon zest and juice, sprinkle over the flour mixture, and mix lightly with a fork until the dough holds together.

2. On a lightly floured surface, roll out the dough to an 11-inch round. Fit it into a deep 9-inch pie pan and flute the edges. Prick the surface thoroughly with a fork and bake for 12 to 15 minutes. Cool completely.

3. To make the filling, combine 1 cup sugar with the cornstarch in a heavy saucepan. Add the water, lemon zest, juice, and egg yolks, and stir until smooth. Cook, stirring, without boiling, until thick. Remove from the heat and blend in the cream cheese. Let cool.

4. Beat the egg whites until soft peaks form. Gradually beat in the remaining $\frac{1}{4}$ cup sugar until stiff. Fold into the lemon mixture, and turn into the pie shell.

5. Chill thoroughly before serving.

SERVES 8

COOKING NOTES

The dough is very soft; do your best not to overwork it.

This is an exceptionally thrifty recipe—there's no leftover dough!

NOVEMBER 18, 1963: "FOOD NEWS: LEMONS."

—1963

ZABAGLIONE

Classic zabaglione always has the same proportions of egg, sugar, and Marsala—the ones you find here.

———

6 large egg yolks
6 tablespoons sugar
⅔ cup dry Marsala or Madeira

1. Beat the egg yolks in the top of a double boiler or a heatproof bowl. Gradually add the sugar and wine. Place over boiling water and beat vigorously until the custard foams up and begins to thicken.
2. Serve immediately, in warm sherbet glasses or dessert dishes.

SERVES 4 AS A DESSERT, 6 AS A SAUCE

COOKING NOTES

If you've never made zabaglione before, when you heat the mixture in the double boiler, it will foam right away, but you won't be near the finish line until the foam gets dense. I like to move the pan on and off the heat (by lifting the top pan out of the double boiler), because zabaglione changes rapidly and will scramble the instant it gets too hot. Best to play it safe.

Small Italian macaroons make a good accompaniment for zabaglione. I served this in small glass bowls with the Almond-Lemon Macaroons on p. 707.

Zabaglione can be used as a custard sauce to accompany warm desserts such as Steamed Lemon Pudding (p. 849) and Apple Dumplings (p. 807).

DECEMBER 12, 1963: "FESTIVE HOLIDAY DINNERS CALL FOR TRADITIONAL HOT DESSERT," BY JEAN HEWITT.

—1963

DAVID EYRE'S PANCAKE

Craig Claiborne described making the acquaintance of this oven-baked pancake, "in the handsome, Japanese-style home of the David Eyres in Honolulu," as if he had met Grace Kelly. "With Diamond Head in the distance, a brilliant, palm-ringed sea below, and this delicately flavored pancake before us, we seemed to have achieved paradise."

Life was good if you were a food writer in the 1960s. Mistakes (Claiborne doubled the butter in his recipe) passed without a public shaming in the paper's corrections column or the blogosphere. A few weeks later, he simply mentioned airily, "The food editor was in such reverie on his return from Hawaii he did not notice the gremlins in his measuring spoons."

Forty years later, readers are still making the pancake with no less bliss. It appears on a dozen blogs, embellished with family stories and photos and new-and-improved versions of the recipe. (Eyre, by the way, said he got his from the *St. Francis Hotel Cookbook*, published in 1919, but his calls for more flour and egg. Both belong to a family of oven-baked pancakes called German pancakes or Dutch babies.)

What keeps cooks faithful to one recipe is often some confluence of ease and surprise. Eyre's pancake possesses both. A batter of flour, milk, eggs, and nutmeg is blended together, then poured into a hot skillet filled with butter and baked. Anyone confused? I didn't think so.

The surprise comes at the end, when you open the oven door to find a poufy, toasted, utterly delectable-looking pancake. It soon collapses as you shower it with confectioners' sugar and lemon juice, slice it up and devour it. It's sweet and tart, not quite a pancake and not quite a crepe. But lovable all the same.

———

⅓ cup all-purpose flour
½ cup whole milk
2 large eggs, lightly beaten
Pinch of freshly grated nutmeg
4 tablespoons unsalted butter
2 tablespoons confectioners' sugar
Juice of ½ lemon

1. Heat the oven to 425 degrees. Combine the flour, milk, eggs, and nutmeg in a bowl. Beat lightly. Leave the batter a little lumpy.

2. Melt the butter in a 12-inch skillet with a heatproof handle. When it is very hot, pour in the batter. Bake for 15 to 20 minutes, until the pancake is golden brown.

3. Sprinkle with the sugar and return briefly to the oven. Sprinkle with lemon juice, and serve with jelly, jam, or marmalade.

SERVES 2 TO 4

COOKING NOTE

Don't overmix the batter, or the pancake will be tough—a few lumps are fine.

This is the moment to call your well-seasoned cast-iron skillet into service.

PERIOD DETAIL

In 1881, the *Times* ran a recipe for a lemon-scented baked "omelet soufflé," a kindred spirit to the oven-baked pancake, and, for that matter, the soufflé. It's clear we like lemons, eggs, and puffy things fresh from a hot oven.

READERS

"So many of us eat essentially the same foods, over and over, each day for breakfast. It was for me, a young man in my first apartment, a revelation when Craig Claiborne introduced a Breakfast Pancake on April 10, 1966. I still have the page out of the magazine I tore out and saved. I have prepared his recipe at least 500 times since, first in a cast-iron skillet and in recent years in a paella pan. Being impatient, 20 minutes was too long to wait for it to bake, so I have inched up the temperature over the years and enjoy a pancake that creeps up over the edge of the pan and browns along the edges in less than 10 minutes of baking. His original recipe calls for sprinkling lemon juice and powdered sugar on the baked pancake, but up here in the north woods, maple syrup is the finishing touch. Sometimes I sauté thin apple slices sprinkled with a bit of sugar before pouring the batter in the pan for a variation on the original recipe."

Roland Krause, Harbor Springs, MI, letter

"Surely a golden thread through my life. . . . My memory is of jumping up and making it then and there.

Once I passed through Honolulu and phoned David Eyre, the address blazed from the directory: No. 1 Diamond Head Drive. When I thanked him for all the lovely Sunday mornings, he remarked that I wasn't the first to call, either. Later I moved to Indonesia, where Sundays were so different from L.A.; without even noticing, I forgot both pancake and recipe. Years later, a friend sent me a copy of a cooking magazine with recipes from readers. A woman from the Midwest sent an "oven pancake," which she said had a man's name but she never learned it. There it was and I felt that golden thread connecting my two lives, then (L.A.) and now (Jakarta)."

Loura White, letter

APRIL 10, 1966: "PANCAKE NONPAREIL," BY CRAIG CLAIBORNE. RECIPE ADAPTED FROM DAVID EYRE.

—1966

⌒ CHOCOLATE RUM MOUSSE

Note the cool technique, which reminds me a little of that used for the Salmon Mousse on p. 394. You add the milk and gelatin to the blender, then gradually drop in all the ingredients, which include ice cubes. So it's like a smoothie, except that the result is less annoyingly virtuous.

¼ cup cold whole milk

1 envelope powdered gelatin

¾ cup milk, heated to a boil

6 tablespoons dark rum

1 large egg

¼ cup sugar

⅛ teaspoon salt

1 cup semisweet chocolate chips

2 cups heavy cream

2 ice cubes

1 teaspoon vanilla extract

1. Put the cold milk and gelatin in the blender and blend at low speed to soften the gelatin. Add the boiling milk and blend until the gelatin dissolves. If gelatin granules cling to the sides of the container, use a rubber spatula to push them down. When the gelatin is dissolved, add the rum, egg, sugar, and salt. Turn the

control to high speed and add the chocolate chips. Blend until smooth.

2. Add 1 cup cream and the ice cubes. Continue blending until the ice is liquefied. Pour into parfait or wineglasses and chill.

3. Add the vanilla to the remaining cup of cream and whip until stiff. Top the mousse with the whipped cream.

SERVES 8

COOKING NOTE
Feel free to use better quality chocolate.

JULY 31, 1966: "PLURAL OF MOUSSE," BY JANE HEWITT.

—1966

◤ FRESH BLUEBERRY BUCKLE

A buckle is a low-lying cake that's threaded with fruit, veiled with streusel, and baked in a dish. The name comes from its buckled surface. Here the soft cake cushions a layer of fresh blueberries and a cardamom-scented topping that's crackly like a crust of ice.

––––––––

8 tablespoons (1 stick) unsalted butter, softened
1 cup sugar
1 large egg
½ teaspoon vanilla extract
1⅓ cups all-purpose flour
1 teaspoon baking powder
Rounded ¼ teaspoon salt
⅓ cup whole milk
2 cups blueberries
½ teaspoon ground cardamom
¼ teaspoon freshly grated nutmeg
Whipped cream for serving

1. Heat the oven to 375 degrees. Butter a 9-inch square baking dish. In a mixer fitted with a paddle (or in a bowl with a hand mixer), beat half the butter with half the sugar until light and fluffy. Beat in the egg and vanilla.

2. Sift together 1 cup flour, the baking powder, and salt. Add alternately with the milk to the creamed mixture, starting and ending with the dry ingredients.

Pour into the baking dish and pour the blueberries over it.

3. Combine the remaining sugar, ⅓ cup flour, cardamom, and nutmeg in a bowl. Using a pastry blender or 2 knives, cut in the remaining butter until the texture is that of coarse cornmeal.

4. Sprinkle over the blueberries and bake for 40 to 50 minutes. Cool slightly before serving with whipped cream.

SERVES 6 TO 8

COOKING NOTES
This is best served warm. If you make the buckle in advance, you can reheat it in a 175-degree oven for 20 minutes.

I grated my own nutmeg and ground my own cardamom—and if you have these spices whole, I recommend you do the same. The fragrance is much more pervasive.

I've doubled this recipe with no problems.

JULY 21, 1967: "WEEKEND MENUS: LAMB CHOPS AND BLUEBERRY BUCKLE."

—1967

◤ POTS DE CRÈME

Orange custards baked—if you have them—in tiny ceramic pots. If you don't have them, just dig out your smallest ramekins.

––––––––

2 cups heavy cream
4 large egg yolks
5 tablespoons sugar
½ teaspoon salt
1 tablespoon grated orange zest
2 tablespoons Grand Marnier
Candied violets (optional)

1. Place the cream in a saucepan and bring it almost but not quite to a boil.

2. Meanwhile, beat the yolks, sugar, and salt in the top of a double boiler until light and lemon colored. Gradually add the cream to the yolks, stirring with a whisk.

3. Place the double boiler pan on top of its water-filled base and place over low heat. Stir with a wooden spoon until the custard thickens and coats the spoon. Immediately set it in a basin of cold water to stop the cooking action.

4. Stir in the grated orange zest and Grand Marnier. Pour the custard into individual pots de crème or custard cups and chill thoroughly.

5. Garnish each crème with a candied violet, if desired.

SERVES 4 TO 6

DECEMBER 27, 1970: "FLAVORSOME FOUR," BY CRAIG CLAIBORNE.

—1970

MADELEINE KAMMAN'S APPLE MOUSSE

If you're looking for an elegant and not-too-taxing dessert to make for a fall dinner, this is it. The citrus analog of this recipe is Lemon Mousse for a Crowd, p. 861; the simplicity analog is Apple Snow on p. 808.

———

3 pounds McIntosh apples (about 6 to 8 large)

½ cup water

½ cup sugar

Grated zest of ½ lemon

⅛ teaspoon salt

2 tablespoons unsalted butter

A ½-inch piece cinnamon stick

3 to 4 tablespoons Calvados or other apple brandy

1 cup heavy cream

3 glacé orange slices, halved (optional)

1. Peel, core, and slice the apples into a heavy saucepan. Add the water, sugar, lemon zest, and salt, cover tightly, and cook, stirring once or twice to prevent sticking, until the apples are soft, about 10 minutes.

2. Add the butter and cinnamon stick and cook uncovered, stirring occasionally, until the mixture is very thick and reduced to about 2 cups, about 35 minutes. Cool and chill at least 4 hours.

3. Remove the cinnamon stick and stir in the Calvados. Whip the cream until it is thick but not quite stiff

enough to form peaks. Fold into the chilled applesauce and chill again.

4. Decorate the mousse with the glacé orange slices, if using.

SERVES 4 TO 6

MARCH 5, 1972: "THE FRUITS OF WINTER," BY RAYMOND A. SOKOLOV. RECIPE ADAPTED FROM MADELEINE KAMMAN, A COOKING TEACHER AND THE AUTHOR OF *THE NEW MAKING OF A COOK* AND OTHER COOKBOOKS, IN BOSTON, MASSACHUSETTS.

—1972

STRAWBERRY SOUP

———

1 quart strawberries, hulled and sliced

2 tablespoons dry white wine

¼ cup confectioners' sugar, or to taste

1 cup plain yogurt

1. Place the strawberries and wine in a blender and blend until smooth. Force the mixture through a sieve to strain out the seeds.

2. Return the puree to the blender, add the sugar and yogurt, and blend until mixed. Chill briefly before serving in chilled soup bowls.

SERVES 4

COOKING NOTE

It may seem like an unnecessary extra step to push the strawberries through a sieve after pureeing them in a blender, but you get a much smoother mixture.

Use a Greek yogurt like Fage (full fat).

JULY 29, 1973: "ELEGANCE SANS EFFORT," BY JEAN HEWITT.

—1973

LEE'S MARLBOROUGH TART

I'm not sure who Lee is but her (or was it his?) unusual tart—a sherry-and-cinnamon-infused apple custard topped with toasted meringue—is an excellent antidote to French apple tarts. Mind you, if you're eating so many French apple tarts that you're sick of them, you must be doing something right.

———

French Pie Pastry (p. 825)

2 medium McIntosh apples, peeled, cored, and thinly sliced

1 tablespoon water

1 tablespoon brown sugar

$1/8$ teaspoon ground cinnamon

$1/2$ cup granulated sugar

$2/3$ cup heavy cream

Grated zest and juice of 1 large lemon

$1/4$ cup dry sherry or Madeira

3 large eggs, well beaten

3 large egg whites

$1/3$ cup confectioners' sugar

1. Heat the oven to 400 degrees. Line a 9-inch pie pan with the pastry: Roll it as thin as you can, and trim and crimp the edges. Refrigerate until ready to fill.

2. Place the apples and water in a small saucepan, cover, and simmer until the apples are falling apart, about 20 minutes. Add the brown sugar and cinnamon and mix well. Transfer $1/2$ cup of this applesauce into a bowl. Any extra makes a nice little snack for yourself.

3. Add the sugar, cream, lemon zest and juice, sherry, and eggs. Mix well and pour into the pie shell.

4. Bake for 15 minutes. Reduce the oven temperature to 325 degrees and bake for 20 to 30 minutes longer, or until the filling is set and golden. Cool to room temperature.

5. Heat the oven to 350 degrees. Beat the egg whites in a mixer fitted with a whisk (or in a bowl with a hand mixer) until frothy. Gradually beat in the confectioners' sugar, and continue beating until the mixture is thick and glossy. Pile the meringue on top of the pie, making sure that it touches the pastry edge all around. Use the back of a spoon to make swirls and peaks on the surface. Bake for 15 minutes, or until lightly browned.

SERVES 8

SEPTEMBER 30, 1973: "JUST DESSERTS," BY JEAN HEWITT.

—1973

⌒ DICK TAEUBER'S CORDIAL PIE

In January 1970, the *Times* published a recipe for brandy Alexander pie. It was an unassuming confection: a graham cracker crust filled with a wobbly, creamy mousse that contained enough alcohol to make your neck wobbly too. Later that year, Craig Claiborne, the food editor, declared it one of the paper's three most-requested dessert recipes (the other two were cheesecake and pots de crème, p. 815) and ran it again. By rights, that should have been the recipe's swan song.

But thanks to Dick Taeuber, a Maryland statistician, the pie lived on. Taeuber discovered that you could use a simple formula to make the pie in the flavor of almost any cocktail you wanted (3 eggs to 1 cup cream to $1/2$ cup liquor). Among the ones he came up with were the Fifth Avenue (apricot brandy and dark crème de cacao), the Shady Lady (coffee-flavored brandy and Triple Sec), and Taeuber's favorite, the Pink Squirrel (crème de almond and white crème de cacao). Each pie had a corresponding crust made with graham cracker, gingersnaps, or chocolate cookie crumbs. Taeuber sent Claiborne a letter including ten variations on the pie. By the time Claiborne responded and said he wanted to run his recipes, Taeuber was up to twenty. In 1975, Claiborne renamed it Dick Taeuber's Cordial Pie and published it once more, this time with all twenty variations in a chart. (The complete chart follows.)

Calling it a cordial pie doesn't quite capture its punch or proof. Booze pie would be more to the point—it's not the kind of thing to serve for a children's birthday party. "I kept going, and in 1978, I think, it was up to fifty variations," said Taeuber, now seventy-three and retired. "I mailed Craig a copy just for information. He put a note in his food column that I had copies available if anybody wanted to send me a quarter and a self-addressed envelope. The quarter was so I could pay for the postage. Everyone sent a quarter and a stamp." The note came out on a Monday. By Friday, Taeuber had 1,200 requests. And then the pie went into a twenty-eight-year hibernation.

———

For the Crust

1½ cups cookie crumbs (graham cracker, chocolate wafer, or gingersnaps)

4 tablespoons unsalted butter, melted (5⅓ tablespoons if using graham cracker crumbs)

For the Filling

½ cup cold water

1 envelope powdered gelatin

⅔ cup sugar

⅛ teaspoon salt

3 large eggs, separated

½ cup liqueurs or liquor, as directed in chart (see below)

1 cup heavy cream

Food coloring (optional)

1. To make the crust, heat the oven to 350 degrees. Combine the crumbs with the butter. Press into a 9-inch pie pan, and bake for 10 minutes. Cool.

2. To make the filling, pour the cold water into a saucepan, sprinkle the gelatin over it, and let soften, about 5 minutes. Add ⅓ cup sugar, the salt, and egg yolks. Stir to blend. Place over low heat and stir until the gelatin dissolves and the mixture thickens. Do not boil! Remove from the heat.

3. Stir the liqueurs or liquor into the mixture. Then chill until the mixture starts to mound slightly when dropped from a spoon.

4. Beat the egg whites in a medium bowl until stiff, then add the remaining ⅓ cup sugar and beat until the peaks are firm. Fold the meringue into the thickened gelatin mixture.

5. Whip the cream to soft peaks, then fold into the mixture. Add food coloring if desired. Turn the mixture into the crust. Add a garnish, if desired (see the chart). Chill for at least several hours, or overnight.

SERVES 6

COOKING NOTES

The filling is made by folding whipped egg whites into a base thickened with egg yolks and gelatin. Be careful not to chill the base too much, or the filling will be lumpy.

The filling will be fluffier if you let the egg whites come to room temperature before whipping.

Chocolate shaved into curls with a vegetable peeler was once a classy garnish. Why not?

AUGUST 3, 1975: "FOOD: PIE, SPIKED," BY CRAIG CLAIBORNE WITH PIERRE FRANEY. RECIPE ADAPTED FROM RICHARD C. TAEUBER, A READER FROM COLLEGE PARK, MARYLAND.

—1975

	LIQUOR	CRUST	GARNISH
	(Equal parts unless otherwise noted; ½ cup total)	(Graham cracker can be used for any)	
1. Brandy Alexander	Cognac, dark crème de cacao	Graham cracker	Chocolate curls
2. Chocolate Mint	White crème de menthe, dark crème de cacao	Chocolate cookie	Chocolate curls
3. Grasshopper	White crème de menthe, green crème de menthe	Chocolate cookie	
4. Eggnog	Rum	Gingersnap	Nutmeg
5. Banana Mint	Crème de banane, white crème de menthe	Graham cracker	

	LIQUOR	CRUST	GARNISH
	(Equal parts unless otherwise noted; ½ cup total)	(Graham cracker can be used for any)	
6. Pink Squirrel	Crème de almond, white crème de cacao	Graham cracker	
7. Brown Velvet	Triple Sec, dark crème de cacao	Chocolate cookie	
8. Irish Coffee	Irish whiskey; use double-strength coffee in place of water	Graham cracker	
9. Golden Dream	Galliano, Cointreau; use ¾ cup orange juice in place of water, and add 2 tablespoons grated orange zest	Graham cracker	Toasted coconut
10. Midnight Cowboy	Chocolate mint, brandy	Chocolate cookie	
11. Italian Mousse	Chocolate mint, vodka	Chocolate cookie	
12. Fifth Avenue	Apricot brandy, dark crème de cacao	Chocolate cookie	
13. Raspberry Alexander	3 ounces raspberry brandy, 1 ounce white crème de cacao	Graham cracker	
14. Blackberry Alexander	3 ounces blackberry brandy, 1 ounce white crème de cacao	Graham cracker	
15. Banana Chocolate Cream	Crème de banane, white crème de cacao	Chocolate cookie	
16. George Washington	Chocolate mint, cherry brandy	Chocolate cookie	
17. Shady Lady	Coffee-flavored brandy, Triple Sec; use coffee in place of water	Chocolate cookie	
18. Chéri-Suisse	Chéri-Suisse (cherry chocolate)	Chocolate cookie	
19. Vandermint	Vandermint (chocolate mint)	Chocolate cookie	
20. Sabra	Sabra (orange chocolate)	Chocolate cookie	

🍂 MISSISSIPPI PECAN PIE

This pecan pie stands out because its filling is properly rich but not as gooey as most pecan pies. It's as light as pudding. If you can buy good pastry dough, save yourself some time and buy it, but please do not use one of those loathsome premade crusts. Pecan pies need a sturdy and flavorful crust to contrast with the intense filling.

As the pie bakes, the center fluffs up into a dome and then gradually deflates. It's done when the center wobbles no more than the outer edges when the pan is shaken.

Pastry for a 10-inch pie (see Cooking Notes)

1¼ cups dark corn syrup

1 cup sugar

4 large eggs

4 tablespoons unsalted butter, melted

1½ cups (about 6 ounces), chopped pecans

1 teaspoon vanilla extract

2 tablespoons dark rum

1. Heat the oven to 350 degrees. On a lightly floured surface, roll out the pastry to a 12-inch circle, about ⅛ inch thick. Fit it into a 10-inch pie pan. Trim the edges and crimp the border.
2. Combine the corn syrup and sugar in a saucepan and bring to a boil. Cook, stirring, just until the sugar is dissolved. Remove from the heat.
3. Beat the eggs in a bowl, and gradually add the syrup, beating. Add the remaining ingredients. Pour the mixture into the pie shell. Bake for 50 minutes to 1 hour, or until the pie is set—and it's set when the center wobbles in sync with the outer edges. Cool on a rack.

SERVES 8

COOKING NOTES

I didn't have a 10-inch pie pan, so I used a 10-inch tart pan instead—it worked beautifully.

A great recipe for cream cheese pastry can be found on p. 843. You want a pastry that is firm and buttery but not too sweet, because the pecan filling is intensely sweet.

🍂 CHOCOLATE MOUSSE

This is quintessential Craig Claiborne: a well-conceived version of a classic that you'll be proud to have made despite having dirtied eighty-seven bowls in the process. I served this with fanfare, in a footed glass charlotte dish.

½ pound semisweet or bittersweet chocolate

6 large eggs, separated

3 tablespoons water

¼ cup sweet liqueur, such as Chartreuse, amaretto, mandarine, or Grand Marnier

2 cups heavy cream
6 tablespoons sugar
Whipped cream for garnish
Grated chocolate for garnish

1. Cut the chocolate into ½-inch pieces and place in a saucepan. Set the saucepan in a pan of hot, almost boiling, water and cover. Let melt over low heat.

2. Put the yolks in a heavy saucepan and add the water. Place the saucepan over very low heat and beat vigorously and constantly with a wire whisk. Experienced cooks may do this over direct low heat; it may be preferable, however, to use a metal disk such as a Flame-Tamer to control the heat. In any event, when the yolks start to thicken, add the liqueur, beating constantly. Cook until the sauce achieves the consistency of a hollandaise or a sabayon, which it is. Remove from the heat.

3. Add the melted chocolate to the sauce and fold it in. Scrape the sauce into a bowl.

4. Beat the cream until stiff, adding 2 tablespoons sugar toward the end of beating. Fold this into the chocolate mixture.

5. Beat the whites until soft peaks start to form. Beat in the remaining ¼ cup sugar and continue beating until stiff. Fold this into the mousse. Spoon the mousse into a crystal bowl and chill until ready to serve.

6. To serve, garnish with whipped cream and grated chocolate.

SERVES 12

READERS

"Smooth, rich, foamy, delicious. I served this at a bridal shower for the first time some twenty years ago and I can still recall the wonderful flavor."

Carol Neely, letter

FEBRUARY 20, 1977: "FOOD: THE NE PLUS ULTRA MOUSSE," BY CRAIG CLAIBORNE WITH PIERRE FRANEY.

—1977

✎ CREPES SUZETTE

Crepes Suzette, which bring to mind dusty velvet banquettes and menus the size of shutters, are actually an exquisite dessert—lacy crepes nestled in a citrus butter and flamed with Cognac. Making the recipe is a bit like running in an Ironman competition. There will be some setbacks and readjustments, but you'll end with renewed respect for the underlying discipline. Or so I hope.

The best part is that you can make the crepes and crepe butter in advance, take time to recover, and then march back into the kitchen to tackle the dessert once more and carry it, flaming, to the table.

————

For the Crepes
1 cup all-purpose flour
2 small eggs
1¼ to 1½ cups whole milk
1½ teaspoons sugar
2 tablespoons unsalted butter, melted
1½ teaspoons vanilla extract
½ teaspoon salt

For the Crepe Butter
12 sugar cubes
1 to 2 oranges
½ pound (2 sticks) unsalted butter, softened
¼ cup sugar
1 tablespoon fresh lemon juice
1 tablespoon Grand Marnier

For Flaming
1 tablespoon sugar
¼ to ⅓ cup Cognac (plus or including, if desired, a little maraschino liqueur, kirsch, and/or Grand Marnier)

1. To prepare the crepe batter, place the flour in a bowl and make a well in the center. Add the eggs and, while stirring with a wire whisk, add ½ cup milk. Beat to make as smooth as possible. Add more milk to make the batter the consistency of heavy cream. Put the mixture through a fine sieve. (Or it may be blended.) Pour back into the bowl and stir in the sugar, butter, vanilla, and salt. Let rest for 2 hours.

2. To cook the crepes, rub the bottom of a crepe pan (4-, 5-, 6-, or 7-inch diameter) with a piece of paper towel that has been dipped in melted butter. This is necessary for the first crepe but probably unnecessary after the first crepe has been made if the crepe pan is properly cured. Place the pan over medium-high heat. Spoon 2 to 4 tablespoons of the crepe batter into the hot pan, depending on the size of the pan, and quickly

swirl the pan around this way and that until the bottom is evenly coated. The crepe should be quite thin. Cook briefly until the crepe sets and starts to brown lightly on the bottom. Using as spatula, turn the crepe in the skillet and cook briefly on the other side without browning. Turn out onto wax paper. A properly made crepe, held up to the light, looks like lace. Continue cooking until all the batter is used.

3. When all the crepes are made, heat the oven to 400 degrees. To prepare the crepe butter, rub the sugar cubes all over the skin of 1 orange, then squeeze the orange and save the juice (you need ½ cup, so squeeze the second orange if necessary). Place the sugar lumps between sheets of wax paper and crush them with a rolling pin. Spoon or pour the sugar into a bowl and add the butter, sugar, lemon juice, ½ cup orange juice, and Grand Marnier. Beat to blend well, preferably with an electric mixer.

4. Smear the unbrowned side of each crepe with a teaspoon or so of the crepe butter and fold once in half, then again to make a triangle. Rub the bottom of a large ovenproof skillet with the remaining crepe butter. Arrange the crepes in the skillet, overlapping slightly, and sprinkle the tablespoon of sugar over all. Place in the oven and bake for 5 minutes.

5. Place the pan over an open flame, such as a gas burner or the burner of a chafing dish. Sprinkle the Cognac over the crepes and carefully ignite; allow the spirit to cook off for 10 to 20 seconds. Ladle the sauce over the crepes until the flame dies.

MAKES 18 TO 24 CREPES; SERVES 6

COOKING NOTES

In Step 1, you're given the option of using a blender to make the batter smooth—use it.

I used a 5½-inch crepe pan, which made the perfect size crepe.

If you can, use a steel crepe pan rather than nonstick. The crepe batter needs something to grab onto so it gets lacy and crisp.

As you cook the crepes, lay them out on a baking sheet to cool. If you stack them, they'll steam and lose all traces of texture.

Rubbing the orange with the sugar cubes is a perverse and tedious step, but it works to infuse the sugar with the oils from the zest.

MARCH 6, 1977: "FOOD: THE LEGENDARY CREPES SUZETTE," BY CRAIG CLAIBORNE WITH PIERRE FRANEY.

—1977

✎ PRUNEAUX DU PICHET (PRUNES IN A PITCHER)

Pruneaux du pichet, a name that sounds better in French, is credited to Fernand Point, the chef at the Pyramide Restaurant in Vienne, a town outside Lyon. Point supposedly created the dessert for one of his regulars, the Aga Khan the Third. "On one occasion," Craig Claiborne wrote, "the Aga Khan offered Mr. Point a splendid terra-cotta pitcher, or *pichet*, ornamented with Islamic motifs. In return, Mr. Point, perhaps the most celebrated chef of this century, created a dessert for the Aga Khan. He invariably served it in the pitcher. It is surprisingly simple but delicious. Nothing but prunes cooked in port wine and Bordeaux."

For a newer take on this combination, see the Wine-Stewed Prunes and Mascarpone on p. 861.

———

36 to 40 plump, soft prunes

2 cups port

2 cups Bordeaux or other dry red wine

½ vanilla bean, split

1 cup sugar

1 cup heavy cream

1. Place the prunes in a bowl and add the port. Let stand until the prunes have softened, about 24 hours.

2. Pour the prunes and port into a saucepan and add the Bordeaux, vanilla bean, and sugar. Stir. Bring to a boil, reduce the heat, and simmer for about 30 minutes. The sauce should be on the syrupy side.

3. Cool, and chill well. It will become more syrupy. Remove the vanilla bean, and serve with the heavy cream on the side.

SERVES 6 TO 8

COOKING NOTE

Pruneau d'Agen, a large and luscious prune found in high-end grocery stores, works best.

MAY 2, 1977: "DE GUSTIBUS: FROM LA PYRAMIDE, THE APO-
THEOSIS OF THE PRUNE," BY CRAIG CLAIBORNE. RECIPE
ADAPTED FROM *MA GASTRONOMIE*, BY FERNAND POINT.

—1977

FORGET-IT MERINGUE TORTE

Meringue has long been a by-product of other desserts, an economical way to use up leftover egg whites. Lemon meringue pie is a kind of finger exercise for the thrifty baker (see p. 833 for a great one), while meringue cookies and macaroons (p. 681) tend to be provoked more by guilt than by ambition.

This meringue torte from the 1970s—an almond-scented meringue cake piled with whipped cream—is a more inspired enterprise. The dessert is reminiscent of Pavlova (p. 826), except that it's baked in a tube pan and comes out more like a cake. Or, as Craig Claiborne and Pierre Franey, who got the recipe from Molly Chappellet, an owner of Chappellet Vineyards in the Napa Valley, described it, "When the meringue comes from the oven, it looks like a disaster."

And it does—like a saggy, toasted marshmallow shaped like a tire. But its cosmetic failings can all be tidied up with whipped cream and a boozy raspberry sauce. The unusual part of the recipe is all the time the dish spends in the oven. The night before serving, you plop the meringue into the tube pan, slip it into a 425-degree oven, and turn off the heat. Then you promise yourself not to peek until morning, at which point it's done, earning its full name: Forget-It Meringue Torte.

I have made this countless times, always to raves.

1½ cups egg whites (from 9 to 11 eggs)
¼ teaspoon cream of tartar
3 cups plus 1 tablespoon sugar
1 teaspoon vanilla extract
½ teaspoon almond extract
1 cup heavy cream
Three 10-ounce packages frozen raspberries, defrosted,
    or 1 quart fresh raspberries
2 tablespoons kirsch or framboise liqueur

1. Heat the oven 425 degrees. Butter an angel food cake pan with a removable bottom. In a mixer on medium speed, beat the egg whites until frothy. Add the cream of tartar. With the mixer on high speed, gradually add 2½ cups sugar. Add the vanilla and almond extracts and beat to stiff, glossy peaks.

2. Spoon the meringue into the buttered pan. Level the top. Place in the oven and turn off the heat. Do not open the door until the oven is cool. The torte will look messy, but do not worry.

3. Push up the removable bottom of the pan. Cut away the top crust; reserve the crust and any crumbs. Unmold the cake onto a plate. Whip the cream with 1 tablespoon sugar, then ice the cake with it. Chop the reserved crust to make crumbs, then sprinkle them around the sides and top of the cake, pressing gently.

4. Combine the raspberries, the remaining ½ cup sugar, and kirsch in a bowl. Stir until the sugar is dissolved. Serve the cake sliced, with the sauce spooned on the side.

SERVES 12

COOKING NOTES

The original recipe calls for kirsch, sugar, and frozen raspberries. Feel free to use fresh ones if they're in season.

This dessert is best made on a dry day. Humidity will turn the torte into a sticky, droopy mess. I've tried it.

APRIL 2, 1978: "FOOD: OVERNIGHT SUCCESS," BY CRAIG
CLAIBORNE WITH PIERRE FRANEY. RECIPE ADAPTED FROM
MOLLY CHAPPELLET, AN OWNER OF CHAPPELLET
VINEYARDS IN NAPA VALLEY, CALIFORNIA.

—1978

RUM PUMPKIN CREAM PIE

Although I have not found a store-bought pastry crust that doesn't fill me with gloom, if you have, you can certainly use it for this simple, delicious pie. The filling is creamy and deceivingly light, and the rum hovers above it like a fragrant halo.

For the Pastry Shell
1½ cups sifted all-purpose flour
1 teaspoon kosher salt

½ cup plus 1 tablespoon vegetable shortening
(or 5 tablespoons unsalted butter and
¼ cup lard)
3 to 4 tablespoons ice water

For the Filling
1½ cups canned pumpkin puree
¾ cup sugar
½ teaspoon salt
½ teaspoon grated fresh ginger
½ teaspoon freshly grated nutmeg
3 large eggs
1 cup whole milk
¼ cup dark rum
¾ cup heavy cream

For the Whipped Cream
½ cup heavy cream
2 tablespoons sugar
1 tablespoon rum
½ teaspoon grated fresh ginger

1. To make the pastry dough, sift the flour and salt into a bowl. Work in the shortening with a pastry blender or 2 knives until the mixture resembles coarse cornmeal. Sprinkle with the ice water, 1 teaspoon at a time, mixing thoroughly with a 2-pronged fork after each addition. When all the flour is moistened, gather the dough into a ball and chill for at least 1 hour.

2. Heat the oven to 425 degrees. On a floured surface, roll out the dough into a circle about ⅛ inch thick and about 1½ inches larger than the pie plate. Line a 9-inch pie plate with the pastry, trim the excess dough, and flatten the edges.

3. Lay a piece of parchment over the dough and fill with rice, dried beans, or pie weights. Bake for 10 minutes. Remove the parchment and weights, and bake until the pastry is dry on the bottom, another 5 minutes. Let cool.

4. To make the filling, combine the pumpkin, sugar, salt, ginger, and nutmeg in a bowl. Mix the eggs, milk, rum, and cream in another bowl. Pour the egg mixture into the pumpkin mixture. Pour the pumpkin mixture into the prepared pie shell.

5. Bake for 10 minutes. Reduce the heat to 350 degrees. Bake for 30 to 35 minutes longer, until just set in the center (test by gently shaking the pan). Cool on a rack.

6. To make the topping, whip the cream in a small bowl, gradually adding the sugar, to soft peaks. Fold in the rum and ginger.

7. Slice the pie and serve garnished with dollops of whipped cream.

SERVES 8

COOKING NOTE
You can use almost any pastry for the crust—butter, shortening, even gingersnap. If you elect to make the crust given here, you can prepare it in a food processor. Combine all the dry ingredients in the work bowl and pulse a few times. Then pulse in the shortening (or whatever fat you're using) until the mixture resembles coarse crumbs. Very quickly pulse in the water. The dough is ready when you pinch a small amount between your thumb and forefinger and it sticks together.

PERIOD DETAIL
In the story accompanying this recipe, Craig Claiborne wrote that, according to the American Spice Trade Association, the most common spice in American households at the time was pepper. The next two were dehydrated onion and garlic. It's no coincidence that these three spices are the primary seasonings in Mrs. Dash, which was introduced in 1981.

MARCH 12, 1979: "DEGUSTIBUS: ON SPICES AND SPIRITS," BY CRAIG CLAIBORNE.

—1979

FRESH RASPBERRY (OR BLACKBERRY OR BLUEBERRY) FLUMMERY

Dictionary writers are not kind to flummery. The pudding is referred to as "bland custard" and "a sort of pap." *Webster's* says an alternative meaning is "something insipid, or not worth having."

Nearly 400 years ago, flummery was a Welsh specialty of oatmeal, boiled until dense—and indeed a sort of pap. As this specialty shockingly fell from favor cooks gave the name flummery to puddings firmed up with almonds and gelatin. By the time flummery reached America, it had been transformed into a pure, delicately set fruit stew that was popular for about five minutes in the 1980s. It is made by gently breaking down the fragile berries with heat and sugar, fortifying them with a little cornstarch, and then drenching the pudding with cool, fresh cream at the table. (Flummery appears to be a close relative of *rote grütze*—"red grits"—a German berry stew.) Had we stuck with "red grits," we might still know the dish.

Pour on the cream at the table so your guests can enjoy the web of cream streaming through the lustrous red pudding.

————

I quart raspberries or other berries
I cup sugar
½ cup water
2 tablespoons cornstarch
3 tablespoons cold water or milk
Juice of ½ lemon
Heavy cream for serving

1. Combine the berries, sugar, and water in a saucepan and cook over low heat, stirring, until the mixture is liquid.
2. Strain the pulp through a fine sieve. Pour the strained liquid into a saucepan. Bring to a boil.
3. Meanwhile, blend the cornstarch with the cold water or milk. Stir this into the boiling berry liquid. Add the lemon juice. Simmer for 1 minute. Serve with heavy cream.

SERVES 6 TO 8

VARIATION
Flummery can be made with any berry. Blackberries and blueberries are especially good. A blackberry version that ran in the *Times* just a month before this one included ¼ cup more sugar, ½ cup less water, and nutmeg and salt as seasonings.

JULY 16, 1980: "THE DELIGHTS OF THAI COOKERY IN A CONNECTICUT FIREPLACE," BY CRAIG CLAIBORNE. RECIPE ADAPTED FROM THE FAMILY RECIPE OF NANCY AND ROBERT CHARLES OF WALLINGFORD, CONNECTICUT.

—1980

⌇ TARTE AUX POMMES (FRENCH APPLE TART)

I like how Claiborne and Franey instruct you to use the apple trimmings in the base of the tart. No waste!

————

French Pie Pastry (recipe follows)
5 unblemished firm tart-sweet cooking apples, such as McIntosh or Granny Smith
½ cup sugar
2 tablespoons unsalted butter
⅓ cup clear apple jelly

1. Heat the oven to 400 degrees. Roll out the pastry and line an 11-inch pie tin, preferably a quiche tin, with it.
2. Peel the apples and cut them into quarters. Cut away and discard the cores. Trim off and reserve the ends of the apple quarters. Chop these pieces. There should be about ½ cup. Cut the quarters lengthwise into slices. There should be 5 cups sliced apples.
3. Scatter the chopped apple ends over the pie shell. Arrange the apple slices overlapping in concentric circles, starting with the outer layer and working to the center. Sprinkle the apples with the sugar and dot with the butter.
4. Place the pie in the oven and bake for 15 minutes. Reduce the oven heat to 375 degrees and continue baking until the apples are tender and golden brown on the tips, about 25 minutes.
5. Meanwhile, heat the apple jelly over low heat, stirring, until melted.
6. Brush the top of the hot apple tart with the jelly. Serve hot or cold.

SERVES 6 TO 8

FRENCH PIE PASTRY (CROUSTADE)

12 tablespoons (1½ sticks) cold unsalted butter
1½ cups all-purpose flour
2 tablespoons sugar
2 to 3 tablespoons ice water

Cut the butter into small cubes and add them to a food processor. Add the flour and sugar. Start processing while gradually adding the water. Add only enough water so that the dough holds together and can be shaped into a ball. Gather the dough into a ball. Wrap it in wax paper and refrigerate for at least 30 minutes.

MAKES ENOUGH PASTRY FOR A 1-CRUST PIE

AUGUST 31, 1980: "FOOD: THE CRUSTY DIFFERENCE," BY CRAIG CLAIBORNE WITH PIERRE FRANEY.

—1980

☙ PAVLOVA

This tremendous pile of meringue, fruit, and whipped cream was supposedly created in Australia in the '20s to celebrate a visit by the acclaimed Russian ballerina Anna Pavlova. However, New Zealand, ever the feisty underdog, maintains that Pavlova—the dessert, not the dancer—was its invention.

————

3 large egg whites
¾ cup plus 2 tablespoons sugar
¼ teaspoon salt
1 teaspoon white wine vinegar
½ teaspoon vanilla extract
1 teaspoon cornstarch
4 kiwis
¾ cup heavy cream

1. Heat the oven to 250 degrees. Butter an 8- or 9-inch springform pan. Line the bottom with parchment or wax paper. Butter the paper. Dust the bottom and sides of the pan with flour; shake out the excess flour. Beat the whites in a medium bowl until frothy. Continue beating while gradually adding ¾ cup sugar and the salt. Add the vinegar and vanilla extract and continue beating until the meringue is stiff.

2. Sift the cornstarch over the meringue and fold it in with a rubber spatula. Scrape the meringue into the prepared pan and smooth it over. Make a slight indentation extending from the center of the meringue out to about 1 inch from the sides of the pan. Build up the sides of the meringue slightly. The indentation will hold when the meringue is baked.

3. Place the pan in the oven and bake for 30 minutes.

Turn off the heat and let the meringue rest in the oven for 1 hour. Cover and let stand until thoroughly cool.

4. Unmold the meringue. Peel the kiwis. Cut 1 of them into 10 slices. Garnish the rim of the meringue with the slices.

5. Cut the remaining kiwis lengthwise into quarters. Cut the quarters crosswise into 1-inch pieces. Put the fruit in a bowl and add 1 tablespoon sugar. Stir until the sugar dissolves. Spoon this into the center of the meringue.

6. Whip the cream until frothy, and add the remaining tablespoon of sugar. Continue beating until stiff. Use a pastry bag and tube to pipe the whipped cream over the fruit. Or use a spatula to cover the fruit-filled meringue with the cream.

SERVES 6 TO 8

COOKING NOTES
Don't make Pavlova on a humid day, or it'll just be floppy.

If kiwis are out of season, use another juicy fruit, like peaches or plums, or berries. Pavlova is also delicious with passion fruit.

DECEMBER 21, 1980: "FOOD; DOING THE MERINGUE," BY CRAIG CLAIBORNE WITH PIERRE FRANEY.

—1980

☙ KEY LIME PIE

Adjusted for northerners, the recipe calls for regular limes. By all means use key limes if you can get them.

————

For the Graham Cracker Crust
1½ cups graham cracker crumbs
¼ cup sugar
¼ cup finely chopped almonds
4 tablespoons unsalted butter, melted

For the Pie Filling
6 large egg yolks
One 14-ounce can (about 1¼ cups)
   sweetened condensed milk
2 teaspoons grated lime zest
¾ cup fresh lime juice (from about 6 limes)

For the Meringue

6 large egg whites

I cup sugar

½ teaspoon cream of tartar

1. To make the crust, heat the oven to 375 degrees. Combine the crumbs, sugar, almonds, and butter in a bowl. Blend well. Use the mixture to line the bottom and sides of a 9-inch pie plate.

2. Bake for 8 to 10 minutes. Remove the crust to a rack and let cool. Reduce the oven heat to 350 degrees.

3. To make the filling, beat the yolks in a bowl. Pour in the condensed milk, stirring constantly. Add the lime zest and juice.

4. Pour the mixture into the crumb crust. Place the pie in the oven and bake for 15 minutes. Transfer to a rack and let cool.

5. To make the meringue, beat the egg whites until frothy in a large bowl. Gradually add the sugar and cream of tartar, beating constantly until soft peaks form. Continue beating until stiff.

6. Spread the meringue over the pie, being sure to cover the filling all the way to the edges of the crust. Bake for 5 to 6 minutes, or until the meringue is nicely browned. Removed to a rack to cool, then refrigerate. Serve chilled.

SERVES 8

COOKING NOTES

Craig Claiborne suggested this topping alternative: "If you prefer, you may ignore the meringue and spread the pie, once baked and cooled, with a layer of sweetened whipped cream." I'd use unsweetened whipped cream.

The filling will still be quite jiggly in the center when the pie is ready to come out of the oven.

FEBRUARY 1, 1981: "SWEET SOLUTIONS TO A TART PROBLEM," BY CRAIG CLAIBORNE.

—1981

⌐ TOURTIÈRE (APPLE, PRUNE, AND ARMAGNAC TART)

The assembly of this tart from Southwest France reminded me of making a bed. You lay down layer upon layer of clean white phyllo, stretching and pulling it to keep it flat. You finish each layer with a promising splash of sugar and Armagnac. After a while, you add the apples and prunes, and then get back to layering the phyllo until everything is tucked in snugly.

---

2 pounds Golden Delicious apples (about 7)

1½ cups granulated sugar

¼ cup water

½ pound prunes, pitted and quartered (about I cup)

½ cup Armagnac or rum

About ½ pound phyllo dough

Approximately I tablespoon peanut oil

2 tablespoons confectioners' sugar

1. To prepare the tourtière, you will need a large, round, shallow baking pan: a 16-inch paella pan is perfect. (I used a 14-inch braising pan.) Peel the apples, quarter them, and slice very thin.

2. Stir together the apples, ½ cup sugar, and water in a medium saucepan and cook over medium-high heat, stirring occasionally until quite dry, about 20 minutes. Set aside.

3. Meanwhile, combine the prunes with the Armagnac and allow them to macerate while the apples cook.

4. Heat the oven to 350 degrees. Unfold the phyllo dough, dampen a large cloth towel, and drape it over the phyllo to prevent it from drying out.

5. Drain the prunes and combine them with the cooked apples; reserve the Armagnac.

6. To assemble the toutière, using a pastry brush, lightly oil the bottom and sides of the baking pan. Center 1 sheet of phyllo dough in the pan and sprinkle generously with sugar and Armagnac. Do this 3 more times, until you have used 4 sheets of phyllo. Spoon the apple-and-prune mixture in a single layer on top of the dough, covering the pastry. (Be sure to keep the unused phyllo dough covered as you work.)

7. Continue with the rest of the phyllo dough, layering it sheet by sheet, covering each sheet with a sprinkling of sugar and a sprinkling of Armagnac, until you have

used all the sugar, Armagnac, and dough. Use about 10 sheets, or layers, in all.

8. Trim off any overhanging pastry from the edges so they are even, and sprinkle the trimmings on top of the last layer of pastry.

9. Place the tourtière in the oven and bake for 30 minutes, then reduce the oven temperature to 300 degrees and cook for an additional hour.

10. Just before serving dust the tourtière with confectioners' sugar. Serve hot, at room temperature, or gently reheated, cut into wedges.

SERVES 10

COOKING NOTES

Patricia Wells, who wrote about this tart, noted "that tourtière is usually made with homemade strudel-like dough. The phyllo works well as a compromise."

If you can find prunes from Agen, use them. They're softer and more luscious than other varieties. Accordingly, they're more expensive.

NOVEMBER 4, 1981: "HEARTY FARE OF FRANCE'S SOUTHWEST," BY PATRICIA WELLS. RECIPE ADAPTED FROM JEANNE-MARIE MOURIERE.

—1981

❧ MRS. HOVIS'S HOT UPSIDE-DOWN APPLE PIE

Architecturally this pie is like a tarte Tatin, but it differs tremendously in flavor. The apples roast in a bath of butter, brown sugar, and lemon zest, and are finished with bourbon, so the fruit turns mahogany brown, its juices thicken, and the whole tart is perfumed with lemon and whiskey—dessert and digestif in one.

For the Short Butter Crust
2 cups unbleached all-purpose flour
1/2 pound (2 sticks) unsalted butter, cut into small pieces and chilled
5 to 6 tablespoons ice water

For the Filling
8 tablespoons (1 stick) unsalted butter, melted
1 cup packed dark brown sugar

1 tablespoon grated lemon zest
2 tablespoons arrowroot
4 or 5 apples (about 2 pounds), such as Granny Smith
2 tablespoons bourbon

1. To make the crust, put the flour in a bowl and add the butter pieces. Work the flour and butter together with your fingers or a pastry blender until well blended. Gradually sprinkle the mixture with the ice water, using only enough so that the dough holds together and can be formed into a ball. Shape the dough into a ball and flatten slightly. Wrap closely in plastic wrap and refrigerate until ready to use.

2. To make the filling, pour the melted butter into a baking dish or skillet about 1½ to 2 inches deep and 12 inches in diameter (the dish might also be rectangular). Sprinkle evenly with the brown sugar, grated lemon zest, and arrowroot.

3. Peel the apples and cut away any blemishes. Quarter the apples and cut away the cores. Cut the quarters lengthwise in half. Arrange the apple pieces in neat concentric circles over the brown sugar mixture. Sprinkle the bourbon over the apples.

4. Roll out the dough on a lightly floured surface into a circle about 13 inches in diameter. Carefully place the dough on top of the apples. Trim the dough to 1/2 inch beyond the edges of the baking dish or skillet, and gently fold over the edges toward the center, pressing down lightly all around so that the apples are totally covered with dough. If you're planning to serve this warm, cover closely with plastic wrap and refrigerate until ready to bake.

5. When ready to bake, heat the oven to 400 degrees. Place the pie in the oven and bake until the crust is golden brown and the apples are tender, 45 to 55 minutes. Remove to a rack and let cool briefly.

6. Run a knife around the inside rim of the pie. Place a large dish over the pie. Quickly invert the pie onto the plate. Serve hot or at room temperature.

SERVES 12

COOKING NOTE

Rolling out the dough between layers of flour-dusted plastic wrap makes transferring the dough to the tart easier—just peel back the top layer of plastic wrap and invert the dough onto the apples, then peel back the remaining plastic wrap and discard it.

FEBRUARY 15, 1984: "OLD LINEN, FINE CHINA, AND
CAROLINA SOUL," BY CRAIG CLAIBORNE. RECIPE ADAPTED
FROM MRS. HOVIS, WHOEVER SHE WAS.

—1984

❧ FONTAINEBLEAU

Fontainebleau is much like coeur à la crème (see p. 864 for a superb recipe), in which ricotta or another fresh cheese is blended with whipped cream and whipped egg whites, then drained to condense it. But this is made with yogurt, which means you end up with a lighter, tangier, and much silkier featherbed of cream. (It may even be marginally healthier, if you care.)

———

2 cups plain low-fat yogurt

¾ cup sugar

2 cups heavy cream

3 large egg whites

Fruit sauce (see p. 864 or 823) or
  fresh berries, for serving

1. Line a 6-cup perforated mold or 2 or more smaller perforated molds with cheesecloth. Combine the yogurt and all but 2 tablespoons of the sugar in a bowl.
2. Whip the cream until stiff, and fold into the yogurt mixture.
3. Whip the egg whites until stiff, add the remaining 2 tablespoons sugar, and whip until glossy, another 20 seconds. Fold the egg whites into the yogurt mixture.
4. Transfer the mixture to the lined mold(s) and place in a bowl to catch the liquid that will drain off. Cover and refrigerate for 24 hours, discarding the liquid from time to time. The cheese should become fairly firm and dry, almost like whipped cream cheese.
5. To serve, unmold the Fontainebleau onto a platter and surround with a colorful fresh fruit sauce or fresh berries.

SERVES 8 TO 10

COOKING NOTES
When you drain the yogurt mixture, it will give off a lot of liquid. I poured it off three times, for a total of about 1½ cups of liquid.

I reduced the sugar from 1 cup in the original recipe to ¾ cup to emphasize the tanginess of the yogurt.

I don't have a perforated mold, so I lined a fine-mesh sieve with cheesecloth and set it over a bowl—not as pretty, but it worked just fine.

This is one recipe for which low-fat yogurt is acceptable.

MAY 6, 1984: "ENTERTAINING ABROAD/FRANCE: WEEKENDS IN THE DORDOGNE," BY PATRICIA WELLS. RECIPE ADAPTED FROM ISABELLE D'ORNANO, A DIRECTOR OF SISLEY COSMETICS, IN PARIS, FRANCE.

—1984

❧ TARTE AUX FRUITS (FRUIT OR BERRY TART)

If you've always wanted to make a fruit tart that looks like it came from a Parisian pâtisserie, this is it. If you've always wanted to make a fruit tart that looks like it came from a Roman bakery, move on to p. 855.

———

Baked Tart Shell (recipe follows)

Pastry Cream (recipe follows)

2 to 3 pints raspberries, strawberries, or blueberries,
  or 2 to 3 cups other fresh fruit, peeled and pitted
  as necessary (enough berries or fruit to completely
  cover the pastry cream)

¼ cup apricot, strawberry, raspberry,
  or other preserves (optional)

2 tablespoons water (optional)

1. If you used a removable-bottom pan for the tart shell, remove the rim from the shell. Fill the tart shell with the pastry cream and smooth the top. Garnish the top of the pastry cream by placing the berries or cut fruit as close together as possible to completely cover the cream. The tart may be served as is or it may be glazed.
2. If you desire to glaze the berries or fruit, combine the preserves with the water in a small saucepan. Bring to a boil, stirring. Put the mixture through a sieve to remove the seeds. Dip a pastry brush into the glaze and brush the tops of the berries or fruits with it.

SERVES 6 TO 8

BAKED TART SHELL

2 cups all-purpose flour
1/4 teaspoon salt (if desired)
2 tablespoons sugar
12 tablespoons (1 1/2 sticks) very cold unsalted butter
2 large egg yolks
2 to 4 tablespoons ice water

1. Place the flour, salt, and sugar in a food processor. Cut the butter into small pieces and add it. Add the yolks. Blend briefly, and gradually add the water. Add only enough water so the dough pulls away from the sides of the container. *Alternatively*, put the flour, salt, and sugar in a bowl. Cut the butter into small pieces and add it. Using your fingers or a pastry blender, cut in the butter until the mixture has the texture of coarse cornmeal. Beat the yolks and 2 tablespoons water together and add, stirring quickly with a fork. Add more water if necessary to make a dough that will hold together and can be shaped into a ball.

2. Gather the dough into a ball, wrap in wax paper, and chill for 1 hour. (This dough may also be frozen for later use.)

3. Heat the oven to 400 degrees. Roll out the dough and use it to line a 10-inch pan, preferably with a removable bottom. Line the dough with wax paper and add enough dried peas, beans, or specially made aluminum pellets to prevent the shell from buckling.

4. Place a baking sheet in the oven and let it heat for 5 minutes. Place the pastry shell on the baking sheet and bake for 20 minutes. Remove the dried peas, beans, or pellets and wax paper. Reduce the oven heat to 375 degrees. Continue baking for 15 minutes, or until the tart shell is golden brown on the bottom. Remove and let cool.

MAKES ONE 10-INCH TART SHELL

PASTRY CREAM (CRÈME PÂTISSIERE)

1 1/2 cups whole milk
1/2 cup heavy cream
4 large egg yolks
1/2 cup sugar
3 tablespoons cornstarch
1 teaspoon vanilla extract

1. Blend 1 cup of the milk and the cream in a saucepan and bring to a boil.

2. As the mixture is heating, put the egg yolks and sugar into a bowl and beat until pale yellow. Add the cornstarch and beat well. Add the remaining 1/2 cup milk and beat until blended.

3. When the milk and cream mixture is at the boil, remove from the heat. Add the yolk mixture, beating rapidly with a wire whisk. Return to the heat and bring to a boil, stirring constantly with the whisk. When thickened and at the boil, remove from the heat and add the vanilla. Let cool, stirring occasionally. Refrigerate until needed.

MAKES ABOUT 2 1/4 CUPS

COOKING NOTE
For the glaze, use apricot preserve for light fruits such as peaches, and berry preserves for darker fruits like strawberries or blueberries.

SEPTEMBER 16, 1984: "FOOD: WORTH REPEATING," BY CRAIG CLAIBORNE WITH PIERRE FRANEY.

—1984

⌘ BALDUCCI'S TIRAMISÙ

This tiramisù, which comes from two 1980s food icons, the gourmet store Balducci's and the pastry chef Giuliano Bugialli, has a few unconventional details. The mascarpone is lightened with egg whites and infused with Triple Sec, in addition to the usual brandy. The tiramisù is too soft to hold a shape, as it usually does, and instead happily slumps on the serving plate like an English confection. And it's showered with chopped chocolate, not cocoa, which gives the dessert a textural tension that I love.

24 Italian ladyfingers (see Cooking Note)
1 cup espresso, cooled
6 large eggs, separated
3 tablespoons sugar
1 pound mascarpone
2 tablespoons Marsala
2 tablespoons Triple Sec
2 tablespoons brandy

1 teaspoon orange extract
½ pound bittersweet chocolate, chopped

1. Dip 12 ladyfingers quickly in the espresso. Arrange on a flat serving platter (or in a gratin dish) in a row.
2. Beat the yolks with the sugar in a large bowl until pale. Add the mascarpone, liqueurs, and extract and stir to mix thoroughly.
3. Beat the whites until stiff but not dry. Fold into the mascarpone mixture.
4. Spread half of the mascarpone mixture on top of the ladyfingers. Sprinkle with half of the chopped chocolate.
5. Dip the remaining ladyfingers in the remaining espresso. Repeat the layering with the ladyfingers and remaining mascarpone mixture. Sprinkle with the remaining chocolate.
6. Cover lightly with foil and refrigerate for at least 1 hour, or as long as overnight (but it is best to make the dish about 6 hours before serving).

SERVES 8 TO 10

COOKING NOTE
Marian Burros, who wrote the story, said, "Italian ladyfingers, which are drier and larger than the American version, are preferable. They are available at many Italian specialty markets. If American ladyfingers are substituted, you will need about one-fourth more of them, and they should be toasted at 375 degrees for about 15 minutes to dry them out before you prepare the recipe."

MARCH 6, 1985: "WHAT'S TIRAMISÙ? WELL, IT DEPENDS . . . ," BY MARIAN BURROS. RECIPE ADAPTED BY NINA BALDUCCI FROM A RECIPE TAUGHT TO HER BY GIULIANO BUGIALLI.

—1985

☞ REUBEN'S APPLE PANCAKE

Although Reuben's Restaurant in New York was known for its cheesecake (see p. 757 for the saga of the cook who tried to reverse-engineer the dish), the *Times* focused on Reuben's apple pancake. When the restaurant closed in 1966 after sixty years, no one outside its kitchen had any idea how to replicate its buttery, caramelized crepe, whose singed and rumpled edges belied its remarkable flavor.

Marian Burros, the dogged and beloved *Times* food writer, was not about to live without tasting that pancake again. She called Arnold Reuben Jr., the son of the restaurant's owner, for help. He warned her it wouldn't be easy and gave her the ingredients and a few tips, but not much else. Burros headed to the kitchen. "Five pancakes, 30 eggs, 2½ pounds of butter, and 5 cups of sugar later, I understood what he meant," Burros wrote. What follows is the result of her hard work.

What Burros figured out was that you need to cook the apple-and-raisin-flecked batter in butter to create a pancake, then shower it with sugar and flip it, and repeat this sugaring and flipping twice, for a total of *three* times.

A mini-scandal occurred in 2001, when Jonathan Reynolds, another *Times* food columnist, ran the recipe without crediting Burros. "My own newspaper!" Burros later lamented in her book, *Cooking for Comfort*. But then she wrote, "I confess, it offered a slight improvement that was not spelled out in my version: how to flip a 12-inch pancake easily. And it took advantage of a nonstick skillet, a piece of equipment that was not available in 1986."

Burros also added one last tweak in her book, suggested to her by Libby Hillman, a cookbook author who, years before, had actually watched a cook at Reuben's prepare the pancake: a last-minute flambéing with rum to maximize the caramelization of the sugar on the edges of the pancake. I've added all of these upgrades to the Cooking Notes.

———

1 large green apple
2 tablespoons raisins
Scant ½ cup plus 1½ tablespoons sugar
½ teaspoon ground cinnamon
3 large eggs
½ cup whole milk
½ cup all-purpose flour
⅛ teaspoon vanilla extract
About 8 tablespoons (1 stick) unsalted butter

1. Heat the oven to 400 degrees. Peel, quarter, and core the apple. Slice into ¼-inch-thick quarter-moon-shaped slices. Place in a bowl with the raisins, 1½

tablespoons sugar, and the cinnamon. Mix well. Cover and allow to macerate for at least 24 hours, longer if possible. Stir occasionally.

2. Beat the eggs with the milk in a small bowl. Beat in the flour and vanilla to make a smooth batter.

3. Heat 2 tablespoons butter in a well-seasoned 8-inch French steel skillet or nonstick skillet with sloping sides and a long handle until it sizzles. Add the drained apples and raisins and cook over medium heat, stirring, for about 5 minutes, until the apples soften.

4. Add another 2 tablespoons of butter and melt it. Pour in the batter evenly and cook over medium-high heat, pulling the cooked sides of the pancake away from the edges and allowing the batter to flow under and cook. Keep lifting with the spatula to keep it from sticking.

5. When the pancake begins to firm up, sprinkle one-quarter to one-third of the remaining $\frac{1}{2}$ cup sugar evenly over the top. Add another few tablespoons of butter, slipping it underneath the pancake. Then flip the pancake and cook, allowing the sugar to caramelize. When it begins to brown, sprinkle the top with another quarter to third of the sugar. Add more butter if needed. Flip the pancake again and allow the sugar to caramelize on the bottom.

6. Sprinkle another quarter to third of the sugar on top. Add more butter to the pan if needed. Flip the pancake once again and continue caramelizing.

7. Sprinkle the top lightly with sugar and place in the oven for 20 minutes to caramelize further.

SERVES 2

COOKING NOTES

A nonstick skillet is easier to deal with.

To flip the pancake, follow these instructions from Reynolds's 2001 article: "Place a cookie sheet over the pan and invert the pancake onto it. Return the pan to the heat and add 2 tablespoons butter, swirling to coat. Slide the pancake back into the pan to cook the other side. Repeat, each time you flip the pancake."

To flambé the pancake, skip Step 7. Instead, sprinkle the pancake with $\frac{1}{4}$ cup rum and light with a long match (standing back). When the flames die, bring the pancake forth, beaming with pride.

JANUARY 11, 1986: "DE GUSTIBUS: RE-CREATING REUBEN'S LEGENDARY APPLE PANCAKE," BY MARIAN BURROS. RECIPE ADAPTED FROM ARNOLD REUBEN OF REUBEN'S RESTAURANT.

—1986

◠ POACHED PEARS IN BRANDY AND RED WINE

I often find red wine too commanding with pears. I liked the clear, warm touch of brandy here.

———

1 (750-ml) bottle dry red wine
1 cup brandy
1 cup sugar
$\frac{1}{4}$ of a whole nutmeg
2 cinnamon sticks
Zest of 2 oranges—removed with a vegetable peeler and thinly sliced
$\frac{1}{4}$ cup fresh lemon juice
8 medium Bosc or Anjou pears (about 6 ounces each)

1. Combine the wine, brandy, sugar, nutmeg, cinnamon sticks, and orange zest in a large pot and bring to a boil over medium-high heat, then reduce the heat and simmer for 20 minutes, stirring occasionally.

2. Meanwhile, fill a large bowl with water and add the lemon juice. Peel the pears and trim the bottoms so they will stand up. Put them in the water until ready to use.

3. Stand the pears on their trimmed bases in a saucepan large enough to hold them in one layer. Pour the syrup over the pears and simmer, covered, until the pears are tender but still firm; depending on the ripeness of the pears, this will take 10 to 15 minutes. Transfer the pears to a serving dish.

4. Reduce the syrup over high heat to 1 to $1\frac{1}{2}$ cups. Pour the syrup over the pears and chill until ready to serve, basting occasionally. Baste again just before serving.

SERVES 8

OCTOBER 26, 1986: "THE MENUS," BY ANNE DE RAVEL.

—1986

✑ CHEZ PANISSE MEYER LEMON MERINGUE PIE

Just what you expect from a Chez Panisse lemon meringue pie—a crust that's flakier than most, a filling that's lighter than most, and the presence of a once-esoteric fruit, the lovely Meyer lemon.

The Meyer lemon is thought to be a cross between either a lemon and an orange or a lemon and a mandarin orange. It looks like a small lemon with a taut orange-yellow skin. The fruit's lemony sharpness is softened with a beguiling sweetness and perfume that's both floral and herbaceous, a little like rosemary. Returning to a regular tart lemons after a Meyer is like chugging jug wine after sipping a glass of Pétrus.

The first Meyer lemon tree was brought to the United States from China in 1908 by Frank N. Meyer, an influential plant explorer for the Department of Agriculture. Meyer had discovered it as a potted plant in Beijing and introduced it here as an ornamental that became a backyard staple in the West. It might have caught on in kitchens earlier, had it not been for a virus called tristeza (Portuguese for "sadness") that spread among the trees in the 1940s. California agriculture officials, concerned that the virus would be transmitted to larger citrus groves, banned the Meyer in many citrus-growing areas. By 1970, the University of California at Riverside had developed a tree that could withstand the disease, which it called the Improved Meyer Lemon. It wasn't until the late 1990s that the Meyer became popular among chefs, and now, of course, you find it everywhere, in sparkling juices, in olive oils, and even in jams (see p. 611).

———

½ recipe Lindsey Shere's Flaky Piecrust (recipe follows)

For the Filling

2 Meyer lemons or other large lemons

2 large eggs

3 large egg yolks

6 tablespoons sugar

3 tablespoons salted butter, cut into 3 pieces

3 tablespoons unsalted butter, cut into 3 pieces

For the Meringue

3 large egg whites, at room temperature

¼ teaspoon cream of tartar

1. Roll the pastry into a 12-inch circle, ⅛ inch thick, and fit gently into a 9-inch pie pan. Trim the edges to ½ inch beyond the rim, fold under, and crimp or pinch to make a decorative edge. Prick the bottom with a fork. Freeze the shell for 20 to 30 minutes.

2. To prepare the filling, grate the zest from the lemons into a small bowl. Strain in the lemon juice, then press through as much lemon pulp as possible.

3. Beat the eggs, yolks, and sugar in a heavy nonreactive saucepan until just mixed. Stir in the lemon juice and pulp, then the 6 tablespoons butter. Cook over low to medium heat, stirring constantly, until the mixture comes together and thickens enough to coat the spoon. Remove from the heat and allow to stand for 5 minutes, then whisk briefly to smooth. Set aside.

4. Heat the oven to 375 degrees. Line the frozen shell with aluminum foil and weight with rice, dried beans, or pie weights. Bake for 20 minutes, or until set and dry looking. Remove the weights and foil, turn the heat down to 350 degrees, and continue baking until the shell is golden brown, about 12 to 15 minutes. Set aside to cool slightly. (Leave the oven on.)

5. Spread the filling in the shell. Bake for 5 to 10 minutes, or until the filling is just set. Remove the pie, and turn the oven up to 375 degrees.

6. To make the meringue, beat the egg whites in a medium bowl until frothy. Add the cream of tartar and continue beating until rounded peaks form. Beat in the sugar and vanilla.

7. Spread the meringue over the filling, making sure it meets the edges of the crust to make a seal. Swirl in a design with a knife or spatula. Bake for about 10 minutes, or until the meringue is lightly browned. Allow to cool completely, 1 to 2 hours; do not refrigerate.

SERVES 6

LINDSEY SHERE'S FLAKY PIECRUST

2 cups unbleached all-purpose flour

⅜ teaspoon salt

⅛ teaspoon sugar

5 tablespoons salted butter, cut into several pieces

6½ tablespoons unsalted butter, cut into several pieces

3 tablespoons vegetable shortening

3 tablespoons ice water (a bit more or less
   may be needed)

1. Mix the flour, salt, and sugar. Using a food processor, a pastry blender, or your fingertips, cut the salted butter into the dry ingredients until the mixture resembles cornmeal. Add the unsalted butter and shortening and cut them in until the lumps are the size of peas.

2. If you have been using a processor, transfer the mixture to a large bowl. Sprinkle on the ice water a little at a time and toss with a fork until the mixture comes together in lumps and holds together when pressed. If necessary, add more ice water, sparingly. Avoid kneading the dough.

3. Gather the dough into 2 balls, wrap each tightly in plastic wrap, and chill for at least 4 hours. You can freeze half the dough for another time; it will keep, well wrapped, in the freezer for up to a month.

MAKES ENOUGH PASTRY FOR TWO 9-INCH
SINGLE-CRUST PIES

COOKING NOTE
The crust is extremely delicate. As you roll it out, you have to keep reassembling and patching it.

VARIATION
To make Key Lime or Lime Meringue Pie, substitute the zest of 2 limes for that of the lemons and 6 tablespoons lime juice plus 1 tablespoon water for the lemon juice.

PERIOD DETAIL
We now know to be careful with custards and meringues, but before we understood the causes of salmonella, "Poisoned by Lemon Pie" was a recurring headline in the *Times*. There were tales of whole families falling ill, bakers being arrested, and suspect copper pans. If only people had known to use eggs from a good local farm, to keep them cool, and not to let their pies sit out in the sun.

JULY 5, 1987: "FOOD: AMERICAN PIE," BY LESLIE LAND.
RECIPE ADAPTED FROM LINDSEY SHERE, THE PASTRY CHEF
AT CHEZ PANISSE.

—1987

☙ TARTELETTES AUX POMMES LIONEL POILÂNE (INDIVIDUAL APPLE TARTS)

If you've ever waited in line for one of these tartelettes on rue du Cherche-Midi in Paris, you'll find this recipe an impressive replica.

––––––

Flaky Sweet Pastry Dough (recipe follows)
4 Golden Delicious or Granny Smith apples
4 tablespoons unsalted butter
¼ cup granulated sugar
I egg, beaten
I tablespoon light brown sugar

1. Divide the dough into 4 equal portions. On a flour-dusted surface, roll each portion into a 6-inch circle. Place the circles of dough on a baking sheet and refrigerate until ready to bake.

2. Peel and core the apples, then cut them each into 12 wedges (an apple corer and slicer can be used for this). Heat the butter until hot but not smoking in a large skillet over medium-high heat. Add the apples, sprinkle with the granulated sugar, and sauté until lightly browned, about 15 minutes. Remove from the heat.

3. Heat the oven to 425 degrees. Remove the pastry from the refrigerator and spoon the apples into the center of the prepared pastry rounds, dividing them evenly. Fold the edges of the dough up over the apples to form a 1-inch border. Brush the border with the beaten egg.

4. Bake until golden, 20 to 25 minutes. Sprinkle the apples with the brown sugar and serve warm or at room temperature.

MAKES 4 INDIVIDUAL TARTS

FLAKY SWEET PASTRY DOUGH (PÂTE BRISÉE)

I to 1¼ cups all-purpose flour (not unbleached)
7 tablespoons unsalted butter, cut into pieces and chilled
2 teaspoons sugar
⅛ teaspoon salt
3 tablespoons ice water

1. Place 1 cup flour, the butter, sugar, and salt in a food processor and process just until the mixture resembles coarse crumbs, about 10 seconds. Add the water and slowly pulse just until the pastry begins to hold together, about 6 to 8 times. Do not let it form a ball.

2. Turn the pastry out onto wax paper and flatten into a circle. If the dough is excessively sticky, sprinkle it with several tablespoons of flour. Wrap in the wax paper and refrigerate for at least 1 hour.

MAKES ENOUGH PASTRY FOR FOUR 6-INCH OR EIGHT 4-INCH TARTLETTES OR 1 LARGE TART

SEPTEMBER 25, 1988: "FOOD: TIME FOR SNACKS," BY PATRICIA WELLS. RECIPE ADAPTED FROM LIONEL POILÂNE, THE OWNER OF BOULANGERIE POILÂNE IN PARIS.

—1988

➥ RHUBARB-STRAWBERRY MOUSSE

So many rhubarb and strawberry desserts focus on the tartness of the fruit; this one focuses on a lavish kirsh-infused mousse. The rhubarb and strawberries stain the mousse pink and create a lush bank of flavor along a river of cream.

––––––

1¼ pounds rhubarb, trimmed and finely diced
1 cup sliced strawberries
1 cup sugar
2 tablespoons kirsch
¼ cup cold water
1 tablespoon powdered gelatin
2 cups heavy cream

1. Combine the rhubarb, strawberries, and sugar in a 2-quart heavy saucepan and simmer for 20 minutes, or until the rhubarb is soft. Let cool.

2. Pour two-thirds of the cooled mixture into a blender. Add the kirsch and puree; set aside.

3. Pour the cold water into a small saucepan and sprinkle the gelatin over the top. Allow to soften for 10 minutes.

4. Heat the gelatin over low heat until it has completely dissolved. Stir into the rhubarb puree. Stir in the remaining cooked rhubarb mixture.

5. Whip the heavy cream until stiff, and fold into the rhubarb mixture. Chill for several hours.

SERVES 8 TO 10

MAY 31, 1989: "RHUBARB: A TART TASTE OF SPRING," BY OLWEN WOODIER. RECIPE ADAPTED FROM MALLARDS RESTAURANT AT ARROWWOOD.

—1989

➥ TAILLEVENT PEAR SOUFFLÉ

The pear eau-de-vie blazes through the soufflé, cutting a trail of happiness.

––––––

2¼ cups sugar
3⅓ cups water
8 ripe Bartlett or Anjou pears
¼ cup pear eau-de-vie
1½ tablespoons unsalted butter
8 large egg whites

1. Combine 1⅓ cups sugar with 3 cups water in a saucepan, bring to a simmer, and cook until the sugar dissolves. Remove from the heat.

2. Peel, core, and quarter the pears. Place them in the saucepan, adding a little more water if necessary, so they are just covered with syrup. Simmer gently until the pears are tender, 12 to 15 minutes. Remove from the heat and drain; discard the syrup.

3. Dice 8 of the pear quarters; set aside. Puree the rest in a food processor. Return the puree to a saucepan and cook until it is reduced to 2 cups (measure it). Remove from the heat.

4. Dissolve ⅔ cup of the remaining sugar in ⅓ cup water in a saucepan and cook over medium-high heat, without stirring, until the syrup turns a light golden caramel.

5. Wearing an oven mitt to protect your hand and forearm, pour the hot caramel into the warm pear puree and stir. Add the eau-de-vie.

6. Heat the oven to 475 degrees. Butter eight 8-ounce ramekins and dust them with the remaining ¼ cup sugar. Divide the diced pears among them. (The soufflé base and ramekins can be prepared a day ahead to this point.)

7. Beat the egg whites until they hold firm peaks but are still creamy. Fold into the pear puree. Spoon the mixture into the prepared ramekins.

8. Bake for 8 to 10 minutes, until the soufflés are puffed and nicely browned. Serve at once.

SERVES 8

OCTOBER 29, 1989: "RISING TO THE OCCASION: SIMPLE SOUFFLÉS," BY FLORENCE FABRICANT. RECIPE ADAPTED FROM TAILLEVENT RESTAURANT IN PARIS.

—1989

❧ CARAMEL CUSTARD

You might not think too deeply about custard as you happily dig into a cupful, but Joan Acocella, the dance critic, has. She wrote in the *Times*:

> Of all the psychologically resonant foods—oysters (success), raw carrots (virtue), grapes (peel me a grape)—the one your mother would most approve of is custard. Or perhaps not your mother, but the Platonic-absolute mother, the mother of our imaginings, for custard is everything life would have been for us if only the perfect mother had arranged it: soft, unresisting, with no nasty surprises. No one should ever put things in custard—raisins or nuts or bits of glacé, whatever. In a custard, nothing should ever bump up against your spoon or cause you to ask, What's that? A custard should harbor no mysteries. It should be one long, yellow sameness.

After I devoured a batch of this caramel custard, I began pondering what made it so much better than others. It contains lots of eggs, and their flavor really comes through. The custard is just barely sweet, which makes you appreciate the character of the milk and eggs and the bitterness of the sugar. And the custard also challenges Acocella's theory of sameness: this pudding has three distinct regions—the top and sides "cure" in the caramelized sugar; the center is a soft, silky pudding; and the bottom is a thin crust. But can't we agree to disagree? I like Acocella's ideas, and I like this custard.

The recipe offers you the option of making individual custards in ramekins—don't. A single large custard is more dramatic and easier to make: who wants to swirl hot caramel into 6 small ramekins?

———

1¼ cups sugar
2½ tablespoons water
3¾ cups whole milk
1 vanilla bean or 1½ teaspoons vanilla extract
5 large eggs
4 large egg yolks

1. Bring ½ cup sugar and the water to a boil in a small heavy saucepan, slowly swirling the pan by its handle until the sugar has dissolved completely and the liquid is perfectly clear. Continue to boil, swirling the pan frequently, until the sugar turns a caramel brown, about 3 to 5 minutes. Immediately pour the hot caramel into a 1½-quart charlotte mold or wide soufflé dish and turn in all directions to film the bottom and sides. (If desired, individual ramekins may be used. When the sugar is caramelized, pour into 6 individual ramekins and swirl to coat as above.) Set aside until ready for use.

2. Position a rack in the lower third of the oven and heat the oven to 350 degrees. Heat the milk to a simmer in a small heavy saucepan. Remove from the heat. Slit the vanilla bean, if using, with a knife and scrape the seeds into the milk. Add the bean to the milk and allow to steep for 10 minutes. Strain and discard the bean.

3. Meanwhile, beat the eggs and yolks in a large bowl with a wire whisk or electric mixer. Gradually beat in the remaining ¾ cup sugar. When the mixture is light and foamy, beat in the milk in a very thin stream; beat in the vanilla extract, if using. Strain through a fine-mesh sieve into the prepared mold.

4. Set the mold in a roasting pan just large enough to accommodate it. Pour in enough boiling water to come halfway up the side of the mold. Bake for 40 to 50 minutes, or until a knife comes out clean when stuck in the center of the custard. Check the water from time to time to make sure it never comes to a boil; adjust the heat if necessary. This will ensure a smooth custard.

5. To serve warm, let the custard settle for 10 minutes in a pan of cold water. Turn a warm serving dish upside down over the custard, then reverse to unmold. To

serve cold, let cool to room temperature; chill for several hours, then unmold.

SERVES 6 TO 8

COOKING NOTES

In Step 1, make sure you take the sugar to a nice copper brown—you want it to be bitter, sweet, and toasty.

Wear an oven mitt when you're swirling the sugar around the charlotte mold (or soufflé dish): you want the caramelized sugar to spread up the sides of the mold, but you don't want it to splash out and burn your hand.

FEBRUARY 17, 1991: "THE WORLD IS MY CUSTARD," BY JOAN ACOCELLA. RECIPE ADAPTED FROM JULIA CHILD'S *THE FRENCH CHEF*.

—1991

☞ APPLE TARTE TATIN

This Molly O'Neill recipe taught me the secret of tarte Tatin. The conventional thinking has always been that the more butter, the better. In fact, more butter makes for a heavy tarte and slows down the caramelization of the apples because you have to cook off the water in the butter before the sugar can work its magic. O'Neill puts the sugar in the bottom of the pan, followed by the apples and then the butter. The butter melts slowly as the apples warm up. And the sugar gets a head start on caramelizing.

With this recipe and others, O'Neill helped to carry forward a revolution in popular thinking about French food that began when Patricia Wells published *Bistro Cooking* in 1989. Wells's book suggested that French food didn't have to be fussy—that, in fact, what most French people ate was in the same casual vein as Americans' meat and potatoes. Bistros began opening in American cities, and tarte Tatin became the hallmark recipe of the bistro movement. It was close enough to apple pie not to frighten timid diners. And it was the dream dessert for busy restaurateurs. It could be made far ahead of time, and its free-form construction allowed bistros without a trained pastry chef to get by.

These qualities also make it a great dessert for home

cooks. There is no pinching of the crust's edges. The single crust goes on last, and is simply laid on top of the apples like a blanket, the edges folded back loosely. As O'Neill observed, tarte Tatins are like snowflakes: each one emerges differently. All you really need to make a great tarte Tatin, then, is enthusiasm and a good tarte Tatin pan which you can find in a high-end cookware store—or even just a skillet.

————

8 large Granny Smith apples
2 tablespoons fresh lemon juice
¾ cup sugar
4 tablespoons unsalted butter
½ recipe Tarte Tatin Pastry (recipe follows)
Crème fraîche for serving (optional)

1. Peel, quarter, and core the apples. Place in a large bowl and toss with the lemon juice. Set aside.
2. Place the sugar in a 10-inch skillet or tarte Tatin pan over low heat. When some of the sugar begins to melt, begin stirring with a wooden spoon until all the sugar is melted and begins to turn a pale golden color.
3. Remove the pan from the heat. Begin arranging the apple pieces in the skillet, rounded side down, in concentric circles, fitting them as close together as possible. Fill the center with 2 or 3 apple pieces, as needed. Arrange the remaining pieces, rounded side up, in concentric circles on top of the first layer, filling in the gaps. Cut the butter into small pieces and scatter over the apples.
4. Place the pan over medium heat and cook until the sugar turns a deep caramel color and the juices released from the apples are nearly evaporated, about 15 to 20 minutes. Remove from the heat.
5. Position a rack in the bottom third of the oven and heat the oven to 375 degrees. Flour a work surface and a rolling pin well. Divide the dough in half (you can freeze the extra dough). Pat the dough into a disk with your hands. Roll the dough into a circle that is almost ¼ inch thick, flouring the surface under the dough and the rolling pin frequently to prevent sticking.
6. Carefully place the pastry round over the fruit in the skillet. Trim the dough to ½ inch larger than the skillet. Tuck the overhanging dough in around the fruit. Bake until the crust is golden brown, about 25 to 30 minutes. Remove from the oven and let rest for 10 minutes.

7. Run a small sharp knife around the edges of the tarte to loosen. Place a large plate or platter over the skillet. Using 2 kitchen towels, hold the plate and skillet together and carefully but quickly invert the tarte onto the plate. Let stand for a few minutes to cool slightly. Cut into wedges and serve with crème fraîche, if desired.

SERVES 8

TARTE TATIN PASTRY

2 cups all-purpose flour
1 teaspoon salt
½ pound (2 sticks) unsalted butter,
    cut into small pieces and chilled
1 large egg yolk, whisked together with
    2 tablespoons water

1. Combine the flour and salt in a large bowl. Add the butter and rub the flour and butter together between your fingers until most of the butter is incorporated and only pea-sized pieces remain. Add the egg yolk mixture and stir until the dough begins to come together.

2. Use your hands to gently press the dough into a ball. Cover and refrigerate until firm but not hard, about 30 minutes (if making ahead, let the dough stand at room temperature until pliable but still cold). Do not roll out until just before the tarte Tatin's fruit is finished cooking.

MAKES ENOUGH PASTRY FOR 2 TARTES TATIN

NOVEMBER 28, 1993: "FOOD: EASY AS TARTE TATIN," BY MOLLY O'NEILL.

—1993

☞ ROSH HASHANAH PLUM PIE

————

8 tablespoons (1 stick) unsalted butter or margarine
¾ cup sugar
Pinch of salt
2 large eggs, separated
Grated zest of ½ lemon

1 tablespoon fresh lemon juice
1½ cups all-purpose flour
2 pounds Italian plums or apricots

1. Heat the oven to 400 degrees. Combine the butter, ¼ cup sugar, the salt, yolks, lemon zest, and juice in a food processor and pulse a few times, scraping down the sides once or twice. Add the flour and process just until well blended.

2. Turn the dough out, and press it into the bottom and up the sides of a 9-inch fluted tart pan with a removable bottom, flouring your fingers if necessary. It should be about ⅛ inch thick on the bottom and sides. (You may have some leftover dough; don't use it all if you don't have to.)

3. Bake until the dough is dry on the bottom and just beginning to turn golden, about 10 minutes. Transfer to a rack, and lower the oven heat to 350 degrees.

4. Cut the plums (or apricots) in half, and remove the pits. Place on the crust with the cut side up. Sprinkle the fruit with ¼ cup sugar. Bake for 30 minutes.

5. Beat the egg whites in a medium bowl until frothy. Add the remaining ¼ cup sugar and beat until the whites form firm but elastic peaks.

6. Spoon the meringue on the top of the tart, spreading it to the edges. Lower the oven heat to 325 degrees and bake for about 15 minutes more, or until the top is golden.

SERVES 6

COOKING NOTE
If the plums don't fit lying flat, lay them on their sides and arrange them in concentric circles as you would for an apple tart.

AUGUST 31, 1994: "IN ISRAEL, DIVERSITY OVER ROSH HA-SHANAH," BY JOAN NATHAN.

—1994

☞ CHOCOLATE SILK PIE

The "silk" is a result of the butter and eggs fusing late in the mixing, which makes the filling slippery. I like the pie in bird-like portions, and cool but not chilled.

————

12 tablespoons (1½ sticks) unsalted butter, softened

1¼ cups sugar

¼ teaspoon kosher salt

1 teaspoon vanilla extract

1 teaspoon brandy (optional)

¼ pound unsweetened chocolate, melted

3 large eggs

Chocolate Crumb Crust (recipe follows)

1. In a mixer fitted with a paddle (or in a bowl with a hand mixer), beat the butter and sugar until light and fluffy. Mix in the salt, vanilla, and brandy, if using. Add the chocolate and mix well. Add the eggs one at a time, mixing well after each addition.

2. Scrape the filling into the pie shell, and sprinkle the crumb mixture reserved from the crust over the top. Refrigerate for at least 2 hours to set.

SERVES 10

CHOCOLATE CRUMB CRUST

1½ cups chocolate wafer crumbs (from about 30 cookies)

⅓ cup sugar

7 tablespoons unsalted butter, melted

1. Heat the oven to 350 degrees. Combine the chocolate crumbs and sugar in a bowl. Add the butter and stir until well mixed. Reserve ½ cup of the mixture for garnishing the pie. Press the remaining mixture evenly over the bottom and up the sides of a 9-inch pie plate.

2. Bake for 8 minutes. Let cool.

MAKES ONE 9-INCH CRUST

COOKING NOTE

Because of a shopping oversight, I didn't have enough chocolate crumbs for the crust, so I supplemented with gingersnap cookies. This combination was so good that next time, I'd do half chocolate, half gingersnap crumbs. I might also toss in a little cayenne or lemon zest.

SEPTEMBER 10, 1995: "RICH AND RICHER," BY MOLLY O'NEILL.

—1995

⌣ SALLY DARR'S GOLDEN DELICIOUS APPLE TART

What's interesting about this tart is that the apples have the same relationship with sugar that a potato does with salt. The sugar is added judiciously as a seasoning for the apples, rather than the customary blanketing.

Also, the crust is treated much differently than most tart doughs, which are handled gingerly. Here, it's folded over itself to produce layers like puff pastry. It's become my go-to tart crust.

———

Tart Pastry (recipe follows), chilled

4 to 5 Golden Delicious or Cortland apples

⅓ cup plus 1 tablespoon sugar

6 tablespoons unsalted butter, cut into thin slices

¼ cup apricot or other jelly

2 tablespoons dark rum

1. Remove the dough from the refrigerator and set aside for 10 minutes to soften slightly, so it is easy to handle.

2. On a lightly floured surface, roll out the dough into a 13-inch circle. Fit the dough into a 10-inch tart pan with a removable bottom, pressing the dough gently into place. Prick the bottom with a fork and cover with plastic wrap. Chill for 1 hour.

3. Heat the oven to 425 degrees, and place a baking sheet on the lowest oven rack to catch any drippings. Take the pastry shell from the refrigerator.

4. Core, peel, and halve the apples. With the flat side of each half apple down, cut crosswise into thin slices. Fan them in concentric circles in the tart shell, reserving 6 to 10 slices for the center of the tart. Sprinkle the apples with the sugar and dot with the butter.

5. Bake until the crust is brown and the apples lightly caramelized, about 1 hour. Remove the tart from the oven and set on a rack to cool to room temperature. Remove the sides of the pan.

6. Melt the apricot preserves with the rum in a saucepan, stirring until the mixture is smooth, about 5 minutes. Strain the glaze through a fine-mesh sieve and brush over the tart.

SERVES 8

TART PASTRY

1 cup all-purpose flour

1 tablespoon sugar

Pinch of kosher salt

8 tablespoons (1 stick) unsalted butter,
   thinly sliced and chilled

3 to 4 tablespoons ice water

1. Combine the flour, sugar, and salt in a medium bowl. Add the butter and cut in with a pastry blender or 2 forks until the mixture resembles small pebbles. Stir in just enough of the ice water so the dough forms a rough ball.

2. Place the dough on a lightly floured surface and push the dough with the heels of your hands into a 6-by-4-inch rectangle. Fold up the bottom one-third of the rectangle, then fold the top one-third down, as if folding a business letter. Turn the dough 90 degrees and repeat, rolling out the dough to a 6-by-4-inch rectangle and refolding. Cover with plastic wrap and chill for 1 hour.

MAKES ENOUGH PASTRY FOR A 10-INCH TART

COOKING NOTES

Folding the pastry over itself creates a flaky crust, a cross between tart dough and puff pastry. This recipe is the closest I've ever gotten to replicating the tart crusts you find in France.

If there's not enough room in the pan for your apples to fan, don't worry: as the slices cook, they'll soften and fall against one another.

The third time I made this tart, I glazed it with a combination of blood orange marmalade and rum— and I'd happily repeat this the fourth time!

SEPTEMBER 17, 1995: "AN APPLE TODAY," BY MOLLY O'NEILL. RECIPE ADAPTED FROM *NEW YORK COOKBOOK* BY MOLLY O'NEILL.

—1995

PANNA COTTA

This is one of the first recipes I tested for this book, and it set the bar extremely high for desserts. "Excellent. A perfect recipe," I wrote in my notes. I've made it many times since.

———

1 cup plus 2 tablespoons heavy cream

½ cup sugar

3 tablespoons cold water

1 envelope powdered gelatin

1⅔ cups buttermilk

⅛ teaspoon kosher salt

Fresh fruit for garnish

1. Place the cream and sugar in a medium saucepan and heat over medium heat until the sugar dissolves, about 7 minutes.

2. Meanwhile, place the water in a small bowl and sprinkle the gelatin over it. Let stand for 5 minutes.

3. Stir the gelatin into the warm cream until dissolved. Stir in the buttermilk and salt and remove from heat.

4. Ladle the mixture into six 6-ounce ramekins. Refrigerate, loosely covered, until set, at least 2 hours.

5. To unmold, run the tip of a small knife around the edges of the ramekins to loosen the panna cotta, and unmold onto individual plates. Let stand until almost at room temperature, about 1 hour. Surround with fruit and serve.

SERVES 6

COOKING NOTES

To unmold, dip the ramekins in a bowl of hot water for 30 seconds, then dry the bottoms of the ramekins before inverting onto serving plates and tapping out the panna cotta.

For serving, I brought ½ cup sugar and ½ cup water to a boil in a small saucepan, added 1 cup blueberries and 1 star anise pod, turned off the heat, and let the mixture steep for 20 minutes (remove the star anise before serving the sauce).

MAY 17, 1996: "FOOD: BABY FOOD," BY MOLLY O'NEILL. RECIPE ADAPTED FROM GRAMERCY TAVERN IN NEW YORK CITY.

—1996

⌒ APPLE CRUMB PIE

Stacie Pierce, then the pastry chef at Union Square Café, dissected the traditional apple crumb pie and fixed each of its failings before reassembling the whole into an exceptional pie. Pierce blind-baked the crust, so there's no gummy layer of uncooked dough lurking at the bottom of the pie. She cooked the apples in a sauté pan so they were tender but still held their form, and she thickened the pan juices so there would be no danger of a wet pie filling. Lastly, she used a vanilla bean, rather than extract, to scent the apples, so the vanilla flavor was pervasive and intoxicating.

I know what you're thinking: that such fussiness moots the whole point of a crumb pie—its tossed together ease. But Pierce's method allows you to make each component in stages, so the parts are done a day in advance and then the pie is just assembled and baked on the day you want to eat it. What you sacrifice in ease, you gain back in convenience (and a sense of triumph).

———

For the Crust
1 cup unbleached all-purpose flour
Pinch of kosher or sea salt
8 tablespoons (1 stick) cold unsalted butter
2 to 2½ tablespoons ice water

For the Topping
1 cup unbleached all-purpose flour
½ cup packed dark brown sugar
2 teaspoons ground cinnamon
8 tablespoons (1 stick) cold unsalted butter

For the Filling
1 cup sugar
2 teaspoons ground cinnamon
5 tablespoons unsalted butter
3 pounds McIntosh apples, peeled, cored, and cut into
    1-inch dice (8 to 9 cups)
1 vanilla bean, split
¼ cup unbleached all-purpose flour
Squeeze of lemon juice

1. To make the crust, combine the flour and salt in a medium bowl. Cut the butter into small cubes and add to the flour mixture. Using a pastry blender or your fingertips, cut or blend the butter into the flour until pea-sized pieces are formed. Add just enough ice water so the dough can be formed into a ball. Do not overwork, or the crust will be tough. Wrap the dough in plastic wrap and chill for at least 1 hour.

2. Meanwhile, make the topping: Combine the flour, brown sugar, and cinnamon in a medium bowl. Cut the butter into small pieces and add to the flour mixture. Using a pastry blender or your fingertips, work the butter into the flour mixture until lumps about the size of hazelnuts are formed. Refrigerate until needed.

3. On a lightly floured surface, roll out the dough to an 11-inch circle, ⅛ inch thick. Press into a 9-inch pie pan, and trim the excess dough; crimp the edges to make a border. Prick the bottom of the pie shell with a fork, and refrigerate or freeze to set the crust.

4. Position a rack in the lower third of the oven and heat the oven to 350 degrees. Line the dough with foil, fill with rice, dried beans, or pie weights, and bake for 15 minutes. Remove the weights and foil and continue baking for about 15 minutes, or until the crust just begins to brown. Remove from the oven and let cool. (Leave the oven on.)

5. To make the filling, combine the sugar and cinnamon. Melt the butter in a large skillet or sauté pan over medium heat. Add the diced apples and sugar mixture. With a small knife, scrape the seeds from the vanilla bean into the apple mixture; discard the bean. Cook the apples, stirring, for about 5 minutes, or until the edges just begin to soften. Add the flour and continue to cook, stirring, until the flour is completely absorbed, about 2 to 3 minutes. Remove from the heat and add lemon juice to taste.

6. Add the cooked apple mixture to the pie shell, mounding it high in the center. Cover with the crumb topping. Bake in the oven until the crumbs are lightly browned, 30 to 40 minutes. (If the crust starts getting too dark, cover it with a band of aluminum foil.) Serve warm.

SERVES 8

COOKING NOTE
You may find that you don't need all the topping. If so, reserve it for another use—a pear crumble, perhaps.

OCTOBER 8, 1997: "THE CHEF," BY MICHAEL ROMANO WITH AMANDA HESSER. RECIPE ADAPTED FROM STACIE PIERCE, THE PASTRY CHEF AT UNION SQUARE CAFÉ IN NEW YORK CITY.

—1997

⌇ BOURBON PECAN PIE

Tart Pastry (p. 840)
1 1/2 cups (about 6 ounces) pecans
3 large or extra-large eggs
1/2 cup packed dark brown sugar
1 cup dark corn syrup
1/4 teaspoon salt
6 tablespoons unsalted butter, melted
1 teaspoon vanilla extract
2 tablespoons bourbon
1 tablespoon all-purpose flour
Whipped cream, crème fraîche, or
    vanilla ice cream for serving

1. On a lightly floured surface, roll out the pastry dough to a 12-inch round. Fit it into a 9-inch pie plate, and trim the excess dough. Refrigerate while you prepare the filling.

2. Position a rack in the lower third of the oven and heat the oven to 350 degrees. Spread the pecans on a baking sheet and roast them for about 7 minutes, until toasted. Remove them from the baking sheet, and cool. Raise the oven temperature to 450 degrees.

3. Beat the eggs lightly in a large bowl. Whisk in the brown sugar and corn syrup. Whisk in the salt, butter, vanilla, and bourbon. Mix the flour with the pecans, and stir in.

4. Prick the bottom of the pastry all over with a fork. Pour the filling into the crust, and put the pan on a baking sheet. Place in the oven, reduce the temperature to 350 degrees, and bake for 35 to 40 minutes, until the filling is puffed and firm. Check after 20 minutes; if the crust is browning too quickly, loosely drape a piece of aluminum foil over the edges. Remove to a rack.

5. Serve warm or at room temperature, with whipped cream, crème fraîche, or vanilla ice cream.

SERVES 8

NOVEMBER 19, 1997: "IT'S O.K. TO BUY A CRUST—REALLY," BY SUZANNE HAMLIN.

—1997

⌇ PINEAPPLE CARPACCIO WITH LIME SORBET

A trendy dish that deserved its moment. Let's not allow it to go the way of raspberry coulis.

2/3 cup water
2/3 cup sugar
Finely grated zest of 1/2 lime
2/3 cup fresh lime juice (from 5 or 6 limes)
2/3 cup whole milk
1 pineapple
3 tablespoons canned unsweetened coconut milk
1/4 cup large crystal sugar
Salt, preferably fleur de sel, or coarse salt,
    crushed in a mortar and pestle
Freshly ground black pepper, preferably Sarawak

1. Combine the water and sugar in a medium saucepan and bring to a boil, stirring to dissolve the sugar. Immediately remove from the heat, and cool the syrup to room temperature.

2. Whisk together the sugar syrup, zest, lime juice, and milk. Transfer to an ice cream maker and freeze according to the manufacturer's instructions.

3. Pack the sorbet into an airtight container, and store it in the freezer until serving.

4. Trim and peel the pineapple. Halve it from blossom to stem, and remove the core. Cut half of the pineapple into slices, as thin as you can make them. Divide the slices among 6 large dinner plates, arranging them in a single layer on each plate.

5. Cut the remaining pineapple into chunks, place in a blender or food processor, add the coconut milk, and puree until the mixture is smooth and very bubbly.

6. Quickly pour the puree over the pineapple slices. Sprinkle each plate with 2 teaspoons crystal sugar, a pinch of salt, and a little black pepper. Place a scoop of the lime sorbet in the center of each plate, and serve immediately.

SERVES 6

JUNE 3, 1998: "EN ROUTE: FRANCE: A KITCHEN EMPEROR WHO MARSHALS NAPOLEONS," BY AMANDA HESSER. RECIPE ADAPTED FROM *DESSERTS BY PIERRE HERMÉ*, BY PIERRE HERMÉ AND DORIE GREENSPAN.

—1998

⌒ APPLE GALETTE

Rose Levy Beranbaum, the author of the best-selling *The Cake Bible* and *The Pie and Pastry Bible* (from which this recipe comes), may be the most meticulous cook who ever lived. To her, baking is about as whimsical and improvisational as building a rocket ship. Sizes are measured to the quarter inch, temperatures set to the precise degree, and quantities weighed to the hundredth of an ounce.

The pastry dough in this recipe took her several years and more than fifty attempts to perfect. It is as soft and velvety as an old cotton sheet. For the apple galette, the pastry is rolled into a 16-inch disk, lined with paper-thin slices of tart apple, sprinkled with sugar, and baked on a baking sheet. It's as thin as tarte flambée and has more flavor than an apple pie five times as thick.

_____

Cream Cheese Pastry (recipe follows)
4 Granny Smith apples, peeled, cored,
    and sliced ⅛ inch thick
2 teaspoons fresh lemon juice
Approximately 2 tablespoons whole milk
¼ cup sugar
2 tablespoons unsalted butter
½ cup apricot preserves
1 tablespoon apricot eau-de-vie or Calvados
    (or other apple brandy)

1. Set a rack on the lowest oven shelf and heat the oven to 400 degrees. Place the pastry dough between 2 sheets of lightly floured plastic wrap and roll out ⅛ inch thick. Using a cardboard template as a guide, cut a 16-inch circle. Transfer to a 12- to 14-inch pizza pan or an inverted baking sheet.
2. Sprinkle the apple slices with the lemon juice. Arrange the slices on the dough, overlapping them in concentric circles, starting from the outer edge of the dough (¾ inch from the edge), cored sides facing toward the center. Fold the border of dough over the apples, pleating it. Brush the rim with the milk. Sprinkle the apples and rim with the sugar. Dot the apples with the butter.
3. Bake for 40 minutes, or until the apples are tender when pierced and the dough is crisp. Cool the tart on the pan on a rack until warm.

4. Bring the apricot preserves to a boil in a saucepan over medium-low heat; strain. Stir in the liquor, and brush onto the apples.

SERVES 8

CREAM CHEESE PASTRY

8 tablespoons (1 stick) unsalted butter
1⅓ cups plus 4 teaspoons pastry flour
¼ teaspoon salt
3 ounces cream cheese
1½ tablespoons ice water
1½ teaspoons cider vinegar

1. Cut the butter into ¾-inch cubes. Wrap in plastic wrap and freeze for 30 minutes. Place the flour and salt in a large freezer bag and freeze for 30 minutes.
2. Place the flour mixture in a food processor and process for a few seconds to combine. Cut the cream cheese into 3 or 4 pieces, add to the flour, and process for 20 seconds. Add the frozen butter and pulse until none of the butter pieces are larger than a pea. Add the water and vinegar and pulse until the butter is the size of small peas. (The mixture will not hold together.)
3. Spoon the mixture into a freezer bag. Knead it in the bag until it holds together in one piece and feels slightly stretchy. Remove from the bag, wrap in plastic wrap, and flatten into a disk. Refrigerate for at least 45 minutes, or preferably, overnight.

MAKES ENOUGH DOUGH FOR A 14-INCH GALETTE

READERS

"In the 1950s, we were with a young couple of German background who served us a memorable pastry. The wife mentioned cream cheese in the pastry. This was the first time since that occasion when I found the cream cheese pastry recipe. This galette was so perfect and delicious that we took pictures of it and have made it many times since."

Sarah D. Rosen, Hughsonville, NY, letter

DECEMBER 16, 1998: "BY THE BOOK: A BAKING BIBLE, INSTALLMENT NO. 2," BY AMANDA HESSER. RECIPE ADAPTED FROM *THE PIE AND PASTRY BIBLE*, BY ROSE LEVY BERANBAUM.

—1998

JUDSON GRILL'S BERRY CLAFOUTIS WITH CRÈME FRAÎCHE

---

2 large eggs

⅓ cup granulated sugar

½ vanilla bean, split, seeds scraped out and reserved

3 tablespoons all-purpose flour

Pinch of salt

⅓ cup whole milk

⅔ cup crème fraîche, or ⅓ cup heavy cream, whipped to soft peaks

½ pint raspberries

½ pint blackberries

1 tablespoon confectioners' sugar, plus extra for dusting

1. Heat the oven to 375 degrees. Lightly grease a 10-inch nonstick cake pan. Whisk the eggs and sugar in a bowl until frothy. Mix in the vanilla seeds, flour, and salt. Stir in the milk and half of the crème fraîche.

2. Pour one-third of the batter into the pan. Bake the cake for 3 minutes to set.

3. Spread two-thirds of the berries in the pan and pour the remaining batter over. Return to the oven and bake for about 15 minutes, until starting to brown at the edges and puffy in the center. Let cool for 20 minutes.

4. Mix the remaining crème fraîche with the confectioners' sugar.

5. Dust the clafoutis with confectioners' sugar. Serve cut in wedges, with the crème fraîche and remaining berries on the side.

SERVES 4 TO 6

AUGUST 22, 1999: "FOOD: RECIPES FROM RESTAURANTS THAT BUY FROM AN ORGANIC FARM," BY FLORENCE FABRICANT.

—1999

TOASTS WITH CHOCOLATE, OLIVE OIL, AND SEA SALT

I first had this treat late one night at a tapas bar in Barcelona. The woman behind the bar set down a small plate, then explained apologetically, "This is not our normal dessert. Our pastry chef is on vacation." Moments later, I was very glad he was.

The bread was toasted on the edges and warmed until the chocolate was as soft as cream. The olive oil, like a good brandy, lingered with each bite, and the crystals—sea salt—cracked under my teeth, an echo to the crisp bread.

Combining bread and chocolate is never a bad idea. In France, the original pain au chocolat is said to have been a baguette wrapped around a bar of chocolate, a treat bakers made for children (see p. 664 for a recipe). Good dark chocolate has bitter and acidic elements, as does good bread. In the kitchen, they are drawn to each other. They also couldn't be easier to combine, especially in this recipe, where the four ingredients—bread, chocolate, olive oil, and sea salt—are left in their raw state, with just a dash of heat to encourage them to mingle.

Eight ¼-inch-thick baguette slices

8 thin 1-inch squares best-quality bittersweet chocolate

Extra virgin olive oil for sprinkling

Coarse sea salt for sprinkling

1. Heat the oven to 350 degrees. Lay the bread slices on a baking sheet. Lay a chocolate square on top of each. Sprinkle with a little olive oil and sea salt.

2. Bake until the chocolate is molten but not seeping through the bread, about 3 to 5 minutes. The bread should crisp slightly but not toast. Sprinkle with a little more olive oil and salt, and serve immediately.

SERVES 4

OCTOBER 13, 1999: "TEMPTATION: A CHILD'S TREAT, GROWN UP," BY AMANDA HESSER.

—1999

LE CIRQUE'S CRÈME BRÛLÉE

Although crème brûlée recipes have popped up in the *Times* since at least 1954 (crème brûlée with peaches), the dessert wasn't declared a trendy item until 1984. And that was a sad moment for the egg custard with the sugar roof, because it unleashed a stampede of cooks anxious to muck it up with green tea and chocolate mint. One restaurant, in Los Angeles, even baked it in a tostada.

Le Cirque's recipe is just as it should be, cream thickened and flavored with eggs and fresh vanilla bean. In a crème brûlée, you want layers of temperature: a hot crisp sheath of caramelized sugar, a warm custard beneath it, and cool custard at the bottom.

———

4 cups heavy cream
1 vanilla bean, split, seeds scraped out and reserved
Pinch of salt
8 large egg yolks
¾ cup plus 2 tablespoons granulated sugar
½ cup packed light brown sugar

1. Heat the oven to 300 degrees. Place eight 6-ounce ramekins in a roasting pan. Combine the cream, vanilla bean and seeds, and salt in a saucepan set over low heat and warm for 5 minutes.
2. Gently whisk the egg yolks and granulated sugar in a large bowl. Gradually pour in the hot cream and stir gently to combine. Strain the custard into a pitcher; discard the vanilla bean and use a spoon to skim off any bubbles on the surface of the custard.
3. Pour the custard into the ramekins, filling them almost to the rim. Place the roasting pan in the oven and carefully pour warm water into the pan until it reaches halfway up the sides of the ramekins. Loosely cover the pan with aluminum foil. Bake until set, 1 to 1¼ hours. Remove the ramekins from the water bath and allow to cool.
4. Cover the ramekins individually and refrigerate for at least 3 hours, or for up to 2 days.
5. When ready to serve, heat the broiler (see Cooking Note). Uncover the ramekins and place them on a baking sheet. Top each with 1 tablespoon brown sugar and, using a metal spatula or your finger, spread the sugar evenly over the custards. Broil the custards about 4 inches from the heating element until the sugar browns and caramelizes, 30 seconds to 1 minute.

SERVES 8

COOKING NOTE
Use a blowtorch, if you have one, to caramelize the sugar on top of the custard in Step 5.

OCTOBER 17, 1999: "FOOD: CODDLED EGOS," BY MOLLY O'NEILL. RECIPE ADAPTED FROM *NEW YORK COOKBOOK*, BY MOLLY O'NEILL.

—1999

❧ SAFFRON PANNA COTTA

———

3½ cups heavy cream
¾ cup sugar
Grated zest of 1 lemon
Large pinch of saffron threads (60 to 65), pounded with a mortar and pestle
1 envelope powdered gelatin plus 1 teaspoon, softened in ¼ cup cold water
1 cup whole milk

1. Chill six 8-ounce ramekins or dessert cups. Combine the heavy cream, sugar, lemon zest, and saffron threads in a medium saucepan and bring to a boil, stirring gently, then remove from the heat. Let steep for 15 minutes to develop flavor and color.
2. Stir the gelatin into the cream mixture until it's dissolved. Strain the cream through a fine-mesh sieve or chinois into a bowl, and stir in the milk. Pour the mixture into the chilled ramekins or dessert cups. Chill before serving.

SERVES 6

OCTOBER 27, 1999: "THE MIDAS SPICE: FROM FLOWER TO SAFFRON," BY AMANDA HESSER. RECIPE ADAPTED FROM BABBO IN NEW YORK.

—1999

COCONUT RICE PUDDING WITH LIME SYRUP

The lime syrup is so sharp it's like a bolt of lightning that illuminates the delicacy of the rice pudding.

———

1¼ cups granulated sugar
½ cup water
4 limes
¾ cup Japanese short-grain (sushi) rice
3 cups whole milk
3 cups canned unsweetened coconut milk
1 vanilla bean, split, seeds scraped out and reserved
1 teaspoon salt
2 tablespoons crushed palm sugar
  or brown sugar

1. Set a small pot of water on to boil. Combine ½ cup sugar and the ½ cup water in a separate pot, and bring to a boil. Cook for a few seconds, until the sugar dissolves; reduce the heat to low.
2. Zest the limes, and blanch the zest in the boiling water for 10 seconds, no more; drain in a strainer and plunge into ice water to chill. Drain and set aside.
3. Juice the limes and add the juice to the sugar syrup; cook over medium heat, stirring only occasionally, until the syrup darkens and thickens, about 20 minutes. Cool, then stir in the lime zest. Set aside.
4. Put the rice in a deep bowl and run cold water over it, stirring with your hand. Drain and repeat until the excess starch has been removed and the water runs clear.
5. Combine the milk and coconut milk in a wide, deep, heavy saucepan and turn the heat to medium-high. Add the vanilla bean seeds, along with the rice, the remaining ¾ cup sugar, and salt. When the liquid begins to boil, adjust the heat so that it bubbles steadily but not vigorously; if at any point the mixture browns, turn the heat down a little more. Stir occasionally at first, then more and more frequently, until the mixture becomes thick and much like oatmeal, 20 to 25 minutes total.
6. Spoon the rice pudding into 6 ramekins and cool to room temperature. (You can refrigerate these for up to a day, but bring to room temperature before serving.)
7. Sprinkle the top of each pudding with 1 teaspoon palm sugar. Use a propane torch or run under a hot broiler until the sugar bubbles and begins to burn. Serve drizzled with lime syrup.

SERVES 6

COOKING NOTES
You may find blanching the lime zest in Step 2 tedious, but the process sets the zest's color beautifully.

FEBRUARY 23, 2000: "THE CHEF: TADASHI ONO," BY TADASHI ONO WITH MARK BITTMAN.

—2000

FLOURLESS APRICOT HONEY SOUFFLÉ

———

¼ cup Demerara sugar (or other raw sugar), for sprinkling
1 cup whole milk
3 large eggs, separated
Sea salt
3 tablespoons honey
1 cup dried Turkish apricots
3 tablespoons Sauternes or other white dessert wine
2 large egg whites
1 tablespoon confectioners' sugar
1½ tablespoons finely chopped almonds
Vanilla or almond ice cream for serving (optional)

1. Generously butter a 1½-quart soufflé dish. Sprinkle the Demerara sugar into the dish, tilting so that the sugar coats bottom and sides. Place in the refrigerator.
2. Heat the milk in a small pan over medium-high heat until bubbles form around the edges; remove from the heat and let cool slightly.
3. Place the egg yolks, a pinch of salt, and the honey in a medium bowl and whisk until light and fluffy. Very slowly whisk one-third of the milk into the yolks, then add this mixture back to the pan. Stirring constantly, cook over medium-low heat, until the mixture thickens enough to coat the back of the spoon. Strain into a bowl and let cool.
4. Combine the apricots and Sauternes in a small pan, bring to a boil, and stir. Shut off the heat and let cool.
5. Heat the oven to 400 degrees and place a baking sheet on bottom rack. Puree the egg mixture and apricots in a blender or food processor. Transfer to a medium bowl.

6. Remove the soufflé dish from the fridge. Place the egg whites, a pinch of salt, and the confectioners' sugar in bowl and whisk until fairly stiff peaks form. Using a rubber spatula, add about one-third of the egg whites to the apricot mixture and fold until combined. Add the apricot mixture to the remaining egg whites and fold together until mixed well, being careful not to overmix.

7. Spoon this mixture into the soufflé dish. Sprinkle the almonds on top. Place on the baking sheet and bake for 17 to 20 minutes, until risen but still a little wobbly when shaken. Remove from the oven and serve immediately, plunging 2 large spoons into the center to lift out pieces. Serve with ice cream, if desired.

SERVES 4

MARCH 8, 2000: "THE MODERN SOUFFLÉ: BASTION OF STRENGTH," BY AMANDA HESSER.

—2000

✎ SUMMER PUDDING

No tricks here: excellent fruit with just enough bread for the pudding to hold its shape, and just enough sugar to remind you it's a dessert. Jane Grigson knew what she was doing.

———

2 pounds (about 7 cups) mixed raspberries, blackberries, and currants (or blueberries)
⅔ cup superfine sugar
About 1½ pounds good-quality white bread (unsliced)
Heavy cream, for serving

1. Combine the berries and sugar in a bowl. Cover and let macerate at room temperature for 1 hour.
2. Transfer the berry mixture to a large saucepan, place over medium heat, and bring to a boil. Reduce the heat to low and simmer gently to allow the fruit to release its juices, about 2 minutes. Remove from the heat.
3. Cut the bread into ¼-inch-thick slices; remove the crusts. Cut a circle of bread to fit the bottom of a 5-cup bowl. Cut enough slices of bread into triangles to fit around the sides of the bowl, leaving no gaps. Reserve ¼ cup of the berries and juice for garnish; cover and refrigerate. Pour half the remaining berries and juice into the bread-lined bowl. Place a slice of bread over the fruit, and top with the remaining (unreserved) berries and juice.
4. Cut enough slices of bread to make a layer completely covering the top of the bowl. Top with a plate that fits snugly in the bowl. Weight with a heavy can and place in the refrigerator for 24 to 72 hours.
5. To serve, remove the plate and run a thin knife around the sides of the bowl to loosen the pudding. Invert a large serving plate over the top of the bowl, then turn the plate and bowl over. Remove the bowl. Garnish the pudding with the reserved berries and juice.

SERVES 8 TO 10

COOKING NOTE
I made two small changes when I tested this recipe. You are supposed to set aside ¼ cup berries for a garnish, but that seemed pointless to me. The beautiful mound of fruit needs no garnish, just a rim of good cream poured around it. And I didn't macerate the fruit for 24 hours as instructed; I did it for just 1 hour, and that was plenty.

MARCH 22, 2000: "THE WORLDLY PLEASURES OF NURSERY PUDDINGS: IN ENGLAND, THERE WILL ALWAYS BE WHIM WHAM AND APPLE DAPPY," BY R. W. APPLE JR. RECIPE ADAPTED FROM JANE GRIGSON.

—2000

✎ CHOCOLATE CARAMEL TART

This tart made Claudia Fleming, the pastry chef who came up with it, famous. It inspired pastry chefs all over the country to begin using salt as a pivotal flavor in desserts; and it made a whole lot of diners happy at the end of their meal at Gramercy Tavern.

———

For the Chocolate Dough
8 tablespoons (1 stick) salted butter, softened
½ cup plus 1 tablespoon confectioners' sugar
¼ cup unsweetened cocoa powder
1 large egg yolk
¾ teaspoon vanilla extract
1¼ cups all-purpose flour

For the Caramel Filling

2 cups sugar

¼ cup corn syrup

8 tablespoons (1 stick) unsalted butter

½ cup heavy cream

2 tablespoons crème fraîche

For the Chocolate Glaze

3½ ounces extra-bittersweet chocolate, finely chopped

½ cup heavy cream

Fleur de sel

1. To prepare the chocolate dough, combine the butter, confectioners' sugar, and cocoa in a mixer fitted with a paddle (or use a bowl and a hand mixer), and beat until smooth. Add the egg yolk and vanilla and beat until blended. Sift the flour over the mixture and beat on low speed until combined.

2. Scrape the dough onto a sheet of plastic wrap and shape into a disk. Wrap and chill until firm, at least 1 hour, or for up to 3 days.

3. Heat the oven to 350 degrees. On a lightly floured surface, roll the dough into an 11-inch circle. Transfer to a 10-inch tart pan, fitting it into the pan. Line the crust with foil and fill with rice, dried beans, or pie weights.

4. Bake for 15 minutes. Remove the foil and weights and bake until the pastry is dry and set, another 10 to 15 minutes. Transfer to a rack to cool.

5. To prepare the caramel filling, bring the sugar and corn syrup to a boil in a large saucepan. Cook, stirring occasionally, until the mixture is a deep caramel color. Off the heat, carefully (the mixture will bubble) whisk in the butter, cream, and crème fraîche until smooth. Pour the hot caramel into the tart shell and allow to cool and set, at least 30 minutes.

6. To prepare the chocolate glaze, place the chocolate in a bowl. Bring the cream to a boil in a small saucepan. Pour over the chocolate and whisk until the chocolate has melted and the mixture is smooth. Pour the glaze over the tart, tilting the tart for even coverage. Allow the glaze to set for at least 1 hour.

7. Sprinkle the tart with a few granules of fleur de sel before serving.

SERVES 10 TO 12

COOKING NOTE

Like most tarts, this can be prepared in stages, so don't feel like it has to be a consuming project. Make the crust in the morning, the filling in the afternoon, and the glaze just before dinner.

AUGUST 30, 2000: "THERE'S A NEW FLAVOR IN TOWN AND IT'S . . . SALT: DESSERT TRADITIONS GO OVER THE SHOULDER," BY AMANDA HESSER. RECIPE ADAPTED FROM CLAUDIA FLEMING, THE PASTRY CHEF AT GRAMERCY TAVERN IN NEW YORK CITY.

—2000

☙ MOROCCAN RICE PUDDING

⅔ cup blanched whole almonds

1 cup very hot water

2 cups water

2¼ cups medium- or short-grain rice

½ cup confectioners' sugar, or more to taste

2 cinnamon sticks

5⅓ tablespoons (⅓ cup) unsalted butter

½ teaspoon coarse salt

¾ teaspoon almond extract

8 cups whole milk

⅓ cup ground pistachios

⅓ cup shredded unsweetened coconut

⅓ cup orange-flower water (optional)

1. Place half the almonds in a food processor, add ½ cup very hot water, and process until liquid. Press the mixture firmly through a sieve into a large saucepan. Place the pulp in the sieve back in the food processor, add the remaining almonds and ½ cup very hot water, and liquefy again. Press through the sieve into the saucepan. Discard the pulp.

2. Add the 2 cups water to the almond milk and bring to a boil. Sprinkle in the rice and sugar and add the cinnamon sticks, half the butter, the salt, almond extract, and 4 cups milk. Bring to a boil, then reduce the heat, cover, and simmer gently until the rice is almost cooked through, about 30 minutes, adding more milk if necessary.

3. Continue cooking the rice, adding more milk as it is absorbed, and stirring often, until thick and velvety but loose. Taste for sweetness: it should be barely sweet; add more sugar if necessary.

4. Continue cooking for another 15 minutes, stirring constantly to prevent the rice from burning. Stir in the remaining butter. Pour into a large serving bowl, and sprinkle with the pistachios and coconut. Pass the orange-flower water for people to add on their own, if desired. (The pudding may also be left to cool and served at room temperature.)

SERVES 12

PERIOD DETAIL

Rice pudding, like bread pudding, goes back forever. Most older recipes were prepared simply, perfumed with lemon or cinnamon, thickened with egg, and baked. So-called "French rice pudding" called for grinding the rice before adding it to the milk.

MARCH 28, 2001: "HOME IS WHERE THE PARTY IS," BY AMANDA HESSER. RECIPE ADAPTED FROM *COUSCOUS AND OTHER GOOD FOOD FROM MOROCCO,* BY PAULA WOLFERT.

—2001

☞ COFFEE CARAMEL CUSTARD

Three of my favorite food words, all in one title.

_____

1¼ cups sugar

A few drops of fresh lemon juice

⅓ cup water

2½ cups heavy cream

½ vanilla bean, split

7 large egg yolks

1 tablespoon instant espresso powder, dissolved in ¼ cup hot water

Sea salt

½ teaspoon vanilla extract

A dark bitter, only faintly sweet, chocolate for shaving

1. Heat the oven to 350 degrees. In a deep heavy pot (at least 8 quarts), mix together the sugar, lemon juice, and water. Cook until the sugar dissolves and begins to darken; do not stir. Continue caramelizing until the sugar turns a dark amber color and begins to smoke. When it gets just a touch darker, remove it from the heat and immediately add the cream. The mixture will steam violently and bubble up; don't be alarmed.

2. Add the vanilla bean. Protecting your stirring hand with an oven mitt, stir the mixture with a wooden spoon over low heat until the hardened caramel is fully dissolved and the mixture has stopped bubbling. Remove from the heat, and remove the vanilla bean.
3. Whisk the egg yolks in a medium bowl, then add the warm caramel cream a little at a time, whisking continuously so the yolks don't curdle. Then whisk in the espresso, a large pinch of salt, and the vanilla extract. Pour the custard into a large measuring cup or pitcher, then pour into six 6-ounce ramekins.
4. Put the ramekins in a deep baking dish. Fill the dish with enough warm water to reach halfway up the sides of the ramekins. Cover the pan tightly with aluminum foil. Bake until the custards are just barely set, about 35 to 45 minutes. They should still be jiggly in the center.
5. Remove the custards from the water bath and set on a rack to cool, then chill, covered, until ready to serve.
6. To serve, shave a few curls of chocolate over each custard (this can be done with a vegetable peeler).

SERVES 6

MAY 27, 2001: "FOOD DIARY: A TASTE TEST," BY AMANDA HESSER. RECIPE ADAPTED FROM *ROOM FOR DESSERT,* BY DAVID LEBOVITZ.

—2001

☞ STEAMED LEMON PUDDING

What begins as a uniform batter separates in the oven. Down sinks a light spongy cake and up rises a tart lemon curd. To serve the puddings, I spooned loosely whipped cream into shallow bowls and laid the puddings in the center of the cream, like eggs sunny-side up.

_____

1 tablespoon unsalted butter, softened

¾ cup plus 2 tablespoons sugar

5 tablespoons all-purpose flour

Finely grated zest of 2 lemons

3 large eggs, separated

1 cup buttermilk

¼ cup fresh lemon juice

1 pint blueberries (optional)

⅔ cup heavy cream, whipped to soft peaks (optional)

1. Heat the oven to 375 degrees. Butter six 4-ounce ramekins, or place 6 foil muffin cups in a muffin tin and butter them. Dust each with 1 teaspoon sugar, shaking out any excess.

2. Mix the remaining ¾ cup sugar with the flour and lemon zest in a small bowl. Lightly beat the egg yolks in a large bowl, and stir in the buttermilk and lemon juice.

3. Whip the egg whites until softly peaked. Whisk the sugar mixture into the buttermilk mixture. Fold in the beaten egg whites in thirds.

4. Spoon the batter into the ramekins or muffin cups. Place in a baking pan and add enough hot water to the pan to come halfway up the sides of the ramekins or tin. Cover the pan with foil.

5. Bake for about 15 minutes, until the batter begins to puff. Remove the foil and bake for another 15 minutes or so, until the tops begin to brown and are springy to the touch. A little cracking is fine.

6. Remove from the oven, and serve warm. (If you make the pudding in advance, allow it to cool and unmold to serve at room temperature, or reheat in a warm water bath and serve warm.) Fresh blueberries and whipped cream can be served alongside.

SERVES 6

AUGUST 8, 2001: "THE CHEF: TOM COLICCHIO," BY TOM COLICCHIO WITH FLORENCE FABRICANT. RECIPE ADAPTED FROM KAREN DEMASCO, THE PASTRY CHEF AT CRAFT IN NEW YORK CITY.

—2001

WINTER FRUIT SALAD

This makes for a good dessert, but you could also eat it for breakfast.

———

5 cups water

1¼ cups sugar

3 star anise

1 plump vanilla bean, split

Two 2-inch-long strips lemon zest (removed with a vegetable peeler), preferably from a Meyer lemon

3 firm Bosc pears

1 firm tart apple

8 dried Turkish apricots, cut in half

4 dried figs, quartered

1. Pour the water into a medium saucepan, add the sugar, star anise, vanilla bean, and lemon zest, and bring to a boil, stirring, until all the sugar is dissolved. Then shut off the heat.

2. Meanwhile, peel and core the pears and apple. Thinly slice lengthwise and place in a large heatproof bowl. Add the apricots and figs.

3. Pour the hot sugar syrup over the top, making sure all the fruit is covered. Cover the bowl with plastic wrap, and poke a few holes in the plastic to allow the steam to escape. Chill overnight in the refrigerator.

4. The next day, using a slotted spoon, ladle the fruit into a serving bowl and serve.

SERVES 6

DECEMBER 19, 2001: "THE LAST GIFT OF THE MORNING," BY AMANDA HESSER.

—2001

GLAZED MANGO WITH SOUR CREAM SORBET AND BLACK PEPPER

The Pepper-Cumin Cookies on p. 695 would make a fine companion to this dessert.

———

2 large ripe but not soft mangoes

4 tablespoons unsalted butter

⅓ cup sugar

⅓ cup fresh lemon juice (from about 2 lemons)

Freshly ground black pepper

Sour Cream Sorbet (recipe follows)

1 teaspoon coarsely ground black pepper

1. Peel the mangoes. Cut them horizontally in thirds, leaving the pit in the middle section. Place each portion without pit cut side down on a work surface and, with a large knife, cut into 8 slices perpendicular to the cutting board. Gently push down on the slices so they spread out and overlap slightly.

2. Sliver enough of the mango flesh left around the pits to make ½ cup; set aside.

3. Heat the broiler. Butter a baking sheet large enough to hold the mangoes in a single layer.

4. Melt the butter in a large nonstick skillet. Use a spatula to place the sliced mango thirds in the pan so they keep their shape. Cook over medium heat until warmed through and lightly browned on the edges, about 5 minutes, sprinkling with 2 tablespoons sugar and basting with the pan juices.

5. With a spatula, transfer the mangoes to the baking sheet (set the skillet aside). Place under the broiler, and broil until the edges just start to color, 2 to 3 minutes. Do not overcook. Set aside.

6. Add the remaining sugar to the juices in the skillet and cook over medium heat until the juices start to caramelize. Add the lemon juice and continue to cook, stirring, until the sauce is amber colored. Season lightly with pepper. Spoon over the mangoes.

7. Place a sliced caramelized mango third in each of 4 shallow soup plates. Scatter the mango slivers around. Top each with a large scoop of sour cream sorbet, sprinkle ¼ teaspoon coarse pepper on top, and serve at once.

SERVES 4

SOUR CREAM SORBET

    I cup sugar
    ¾ cup water
    I pint sour cream
    I ½ teaspoons finely grated lime zest
    3 tablespoons fresh lime juice (from about 2 limes)

1. Combine the sugar and water in a saucepan and simmer until the sugar dissolves. Remove from the heat and let cool.

2. Whisk the sour cream in a large bowl until smooth. Gradually whisk in the cool sugar syrup. Whisk in the lime zest and juice. Refrigerate until cold.

3. Transfer the mixture to an ice cream maker and freeze according to the manufacturer's instructions. Pack into a container and freeze until ready to serve.

MAKES I QUART

COOKING NOTE
I dropped the passion fruit sauce that was in the original recipe, because it didn't add that much and because

I thought a third component to the recipe would deter too many cooks. If you want to make it, you can find it at www.nytimes.com.

MARCH 27, 2002: "THE CHEF: ALAIN DUCASSE: COOL, HOT, AND EXOTIC," BY ALAIN DUCASSE WITH FLORENCE FABRICANT.

—2002

⌇ BUTTERSCOTCH PUDDING

Karen DeMasco, the pastry chef at Craftbar, gave butterscotch pudding some gentility. She cut out the cornstarch, which so many recipes call for—cornstarch is just a cheat's shortcut to thickening, and a sure way to get a sticky pudding—reduced the sugar, and added more salt. Her pudding is light and milky, like a good panna cotta, and as intense as a caramel.

The salt in her recipe plays with your head, flickering over your palate like candlelight. The pudding is salty, you think. No, no, it's just rich and sweet. I must taste it again to see.

Once when I made this, I let the pudding come to room temperature, then thinly paved the top with chilled crème fraîche, completely covering the pudding. That way, in every bite you got a temperature contrast and the right amount of tangy cream.

———

    I cup whole milk
    2 cups heavy cream
    ¼ cup packed dark brown sugar
    ¾ cup granulated sugar
    ¼ cup water
    6 large egg yolks, at room temperature
    I teaspoon kosher salt
    I teaspoon vanilla extract
    Crème fraîche for serving

1. Heat the oven to 300 degrees. Warm the milk, cream, and brown sugar in a medium pan, stirring to dissolve the sugar. Remove from the heat.

2. Meanwhile, mix together the granulated sugar and water in a deep heavy pan, place over medium heat, and bring to a boil, stirring to dissolve the sugar. Then monitor closely, swirling the pan so the syrup cooks evenly, until the syrup is a very light golden caramel.

Remove it from the heat. Put on oven mitts and slowly whisk about a cup of the milk mixture into the caramel; it will bubble up violently. Stir until smooth. Add this to the rest of the milk.

3. Lightly beat the egg yolks in a bowl. Ladle some of the milk mixture into the eggs, whisking, to temper them. Add the eggs to the milk and whisk to combine. Stir in the salt and vanilla, and strain.

4. Pour the custard into 4 crème brûlée dishes or 8-ounce ramekins. Place the dishes in a baking pan and pour enough boiling water to come halfway up the sides of the dishes. Cover the pan tightly with aluminum foil. Bake for 15 minutes, then carefully lift up the aluminum foil to let out some steam. Reseal the pan, turn it 180 degrees, and continue baking, checking every 10 minutes. The pudding is done when the sides are set but the center is still wobbly when you shake the dish, about 25 to 35 minutes longer.

5. Remove from the water bath and let cool to room temperature, then chill. Serve with a dollop of crème fraîche atop each pudding.

SERVES 4

APRIL 2, 2003: "TEMPTATIONS: A DUET OF PUDDINGS, PLAYING TASTE NOTES THAT TEASE," BY AMANDA HESSER. RECIPE ADAPTED FROM KAREN DEMASCO, THE PASTRY CHEF AT CRAFT AND CRAFTBAR IN MANHATTAN.

—2003

☞ RICOTTA KISSES (BACI DI RICOTTA)

Featherweight like a good gougère, creamy and puffy like an exceptional soufflé, these kisses are the lightest, tidiest, most delicious doughnuts I've ever made. The night I prepared them, I laid them before our three guests, and the entire batch vanished in five minutes.

———

1 cup ricotta
2 large eggs
½ cup Italian 00 flour (see Cooking Notes)
1½ teaspoons baking powder
Pinch of salt
½ teaspoon ground cinnamon
1 tablespoon superfine sugar
½ teaspoon vanilla extract
Vegetable oil for frying
2 teaspoons confectioners' sugar

1. Combine the ricotta and eggs in a medium bowl and mix until smooth. Add the flour, baking powder, salt, cinnamon, sugar, and vanilla. Mix to make a smooth batter.

2. Fill a wide shallow skillet with about ¾ inch of oil. Heat over medium-high heat until a bit of batter sizzles when dropped in. Drop rounded teaspoons of batter into the pan, 5 or 6 at a time. When the batter puffs and the undersides turn golden brown, after about 1 minute, flip the kisses and allow to brown again for about 1 more minute. Transfer the kisses to paper towels to drain, and continue until all the batter is used.

3. Pile the kisses in a rough pyramid on a serving plate. Sift the confectioners' sugar through a small fine-mesh sieve evenly over the baci. Serve immediately.

MAKES ABOUT 30 KISSES; SERVES 6

COOKING NOTES
I used regular unbleached all-purpose flour and it worked just fine. Be careful not to overmix the batter. Italian 00 flour is sold in specialty food markets and at King Arthur Flour online, www.kingarthurflour.com.

My batch of doughnuts, after browning on their bottom sides, flipped over on their own, a phenomenon I cannot explain but greatly appreciated.

MAY 14, 2003: "AT MY TABLE: A CARNIVORE FINDS JOY, MEATLESSLY," BY NIGELLA LAWSON.

—2003

☞ CARAMELIZED CHOCOLATE BREAD PUDDING

Suzanne Goin, the chef at Lucques and A.O.C. in Los Angeles, is best known for her Mediterranean-style cooking. But she still makes some of the recipes she learned growing up in Los Angeles, including this caramelized chocolate bread pudding, which has been in her repertory since she was sixteen. When she worked at Chez Panisse after college, it was a favorite for staff parties. In those days, she made it with Pepperidge Farm bread. Now she uses brioche.

But, unlike most bread puddings, this is not really about the bread. "I hate bread pudding that's all bread," Goin told me, "I like it to be about the custard."

Goin first chops some chocolate and places it in the bottom of a deep casserole. Then she butters five thick slices of brioche and layers them over the chocolate. Next she pours over a simple custard made with extra egg yolks and cinnamon.

As it bakes, a custard forms under the bread, and the bread acts more like a top crust. To close the deal, Goin sprinkles sugar on top and then sears the bread with a blowtorch to make it crisp and caramelized. It's a smart touch if you have the gear. Otherwise, simply eat it as is; a broiler would curdle the delicate custard.

If you have a fondness for layer cakes, tiramisù, or any other stratified desserts, this will be a high point in your dessert life. As Goin said, "The custardy part stays vanilla, but then when you get to the bottom of the dish, you get this little chocolate reward."

———————

Five to six ½-inch-thick slices brioche

About 3 tablespoons unsalted butter, softened

4 large eggs

3 large egg yolks

2 cups heavy cream

1¾ cups whole milk

⅔ cup packed light brown sugar

2 teaspoons vanilla extract

¾ teaspoon ground cinnamon

½ teaspoon freshly grated nutmeg

½ teaspoon kosher salt

¼ pound bittersweet chocolate, chopped

1 tablespoon Demarara or other raw sugar (optional)

1. Heat the oven to 325 degrees. Place a large roasting pan in the oven and bring a kettle of water to a boil. Generously butter the brioche slices on one side; cut in half diagonally. Whisk together the eggs, egg yolks, heavy cream, milk, brown sugar, vanilla, cinnamon, nutmeg, and salt in a large bowl.

2. Sprinkle the chocolate in a large (3-quart) casserole that's at least 3 inches deep. Lay the slices of bread butter side up over the chocolate, overlapping them like fish scales. Use just enough bread to cover all the chocolate. Pour the custard on top, making sure to soak all the bread.

3. When the kettle comes to a boil, place the casserole in the roasting pan in the oven, and pour enough boiling water into the roasting pan to come halfway up the sides of the casserole. Bake until the custard is just set, 40 to 60 minutes, depending on the dimensions of the casserole. The pudding is done when the bread in the center rises up and is bouncy to the touch. Remove from the oven, lift the pudding out of the water bath, and let cool slightly; the pudding should be served warm, not hot.

4. If you have a kitchen blowtorch, sprinkle the raw sugar over the top of the pudding, and use the torch to lightly caramelize the sugar. If not, skip this step (the broiler would curdle the custard).

SERVES 6

JUNE 18, 2003: "THE CHEF: SUZANNE GOIN: BREAD PUDDING LAYERED WITH RICH SURPRISES," BY AMANDA HESSER. RECIPE ADAPTED FROM SUZANNE GOIN, THE CHEF AND CO-OWNER OF LUCQUES AND A.O.C. IN LOS ANGELES.

—2003

✑ BLUEBERRY PIE WITH A LATTICE TOP

Blueberries are the ideal fruit for pies. While other berries fall apart when heat is applied, blueberries puff up and stiffen, and if the heat is steady, they sometimes pop and wilt, never dissolving, just losing shape like a dead tire. Because blueberries don't have a ton of juice, they're easier to handle. All you need is a little flour or cornstarch to thicken the juices and help hold the fruit together just long enough to go from slicing to a plate.

As I discovered when I tried to work up the ideal blueberry pie, the crust is worth a few minutes of consideration. Cultivated blueberries do not have a great deal of acidity, so placing them amid a heavy shortening crust will only weaken their character. I found that a butter crust, only lightly sweetened, worked best. This crust isn't flaky, but it is delicate with a richness that comes through more in flavor than in heft.

I grated lemon zest and folded it into the sweet pastry to add a little fragrance, something that will seep into your consciousness as you eat. It's important to add salt to the pastry, to underline this aroma, and to be light on the sugar, so that the pastry does not disappear against the filling. When you bake the pie, place it on a rack near the floor of the oven so that the bottom bakes through and does not become gummy.

I roll out my pastry between two layers of plastic wrap, as follows: Place a layer on the counter and flour it generously, then put the dough in the center, flour it, and cover with a second layer of plastic. This way, the rolling pin never touches the dough, and the dough, pressed between plastic, splits less at the edges. Keep in mind that as you roll out the dough, you will occasionally need to peel back the plastic and reflour some parts.

This method also makes transferring the dough to the pan much easier. When the dough is thin enough for molding, simply peel back the top layer of plastic, and invert the dough into the pie dish or tart pan. Peel off the other layer of plastic, and you're ready to begin crimping.

For the Pastry

2 cups all-purpose flour

²/₃ cup confectioners' sugar

¹/₂ teaspoon kosher salt

¹/₈ teaspoon baking powder

12 tablespoons (1¹/₂ sticks) unsalted butter,
    cut into small cubes

1¹/₂ tablespoons grated lemon zest

1 large egg yolk, plus 1 more if needed

2 tablespoons heavy cream

For the Filling

5 cups blueberries

3 tablespoons cornstarch

³/₄ cup sugar

2 tablespoons fresh lemon juice

¹/₄ teaspoon kosher salt

Whipped cream for serving

1. To make the pastry, combine the flour, confectioners' sugar, salt, and baking powder in a 1-gallon plastic bag. Wrap the butter cubes in plastic wrap. Place both in the freezer for at least 30 minutes.

2. Pour the contents of the flour bag into a food processor and pulse a few times. Add the butter and pulse until the mixture is reduced to flakes. Add the lemon

zest, 1 egg yolk, and the heavy cream and pulse 5 times. The dough is ready if it holds together when you press the mixture between your thumb and index finger; if necessary add another egg yolk.

3. Pour the mixture onto a countertop. Using the heel of your hand, smear the dough bits until they cohere. Form into 2 balls, one slightly smaller than the other, and flatten each into a disk. Cover with plastic wrap and chill for at least 3 hours.

4. To make the filling, mix together the blueberries, cornstarch, sugar, lemon juice, and salt in a large bowl.

5. Roll out the larger disk of dough between 2 sheets of floured plastic wrap. When it is ¹/₈ inch thick, remove the top layer of plastic and invert the dough into a pie dish. Peel off the plastic, gently lift the edges of the dough, and press it into the dish, without stretching it. Chill.

6. Roll out the other disk of dough ¹/₈ inch thick. Slice into ¹/₂-inch-wide strips. Chill the strips on a baking sheet.

7. Remove the pie shell from the refrigerator and pour the berry mixture into it. Arrange the strips of pastry in a lattice pattern on top (see Cooking Note). Cut the overhang of dough to ³/₄ inch, then roll it up and over the lattice edge, making a neat rounded border. Crimp the border. Chill the unbaked pie while you heat the oven to 400 degrees.

8. Bake the pie until the filling bubbles at the edges and the crust is golden brown, 40 to 45 minutes. Check after 20 minutes; if the crust is browning too quickly, cover the edges with a round band of aluminum foil. Place the baked pie on a rack and let cool to room temperature.

9. Serve with huge dollops of whipped cream.

SERVES 8

COOKING NOTE

In Carole Bloom's *The Essential Baker* (an excellent source for classic recipes), she includes these instructions for a woven lattice crust: "place half of the pastry strips evenly spaced across the pie, leaving at least an inch of space between them. Carefully fold back every other strip to the center and place a pastry strip across the pie perpendicular to the first strips. Unfold the pastry strips and fold back the strips that weren't folded the first time. Place another pastry strip across the pie, leaving at least an inch of space between the strips. Repeat this process until the top is covered with lattice."

JULY 2, 2003: "THREE CHEERS FOR THE RED, WHITE, AND BLUEBERRY," BY AMANDA HESSER.

—2003

AZTEC HOT CHOCOLATE PUDDING

Like a chocolate version of sticky toffee pudding, but much more nuanced. In each bite, you get a burn from the chile, the scent of cinnamon, and the warmth of rum. The pudding looks like tar and is best eaten straight from the oven, because as it cools, it tightens and takes on the consistency of tar, too. Serve with unsweetened whipped cream.

————

1 cup all-purpose flour
2 teaspoons baking powder
1/2 teaspoon baking soda
Pinch of salt
1 teaspoon ground cinnamon
1/4 teaspoon pure chile powder
1 cup superfine sugar
1/2 cup unsweetened cocoa powder
1/2 cup whole milk
1 teaspoon vanilla extract
1/4 cup corn oil
3/4 cup water
1/2 cup packed dark brown sugar
1/4 cup dark rum
Vanilla ice cream for serving (optional)

1. Heat the oven to 350 degrees. Butter a 2-quart baking dish or soufflé dish. Combine the flour, baking powder, baking soda, salt, cinnamon, chile, superfine sugar, and 1/4 cup cocoa powder in a large bowl. Mix the milk, vanilla, and oil in a small bowl. Pour into the flour mixture and stir to make a thick, smooth batter. Spoon the batter into the baking dish and smooth the top.
2. Pour the water into a small pan, set over high heat, and bring to a boil. Combine the remaining 1/4 cup cocoa with the brown sugar in a small bowl, making

sure there are no lumps. Spread evenly across the batter. Pour the boiling water over it, and then the rum.
3. Bake the pudding until the top is a bubbling sponge but the center is still wobbly and liquid, about 30 minutes. To serve, spoon out portions that include some of the top and chocolate sauce beneath. If desired, accompany with vanilla ice cream.

SERVES 4

COOKING NOTE
You can use any chile powder you like—ancho, chipotle, you name it.

OCTOBER 15, 2003: "AT MY TABLE: THE MILD AND THE FIERY: SWEET HARMONY," BY NIGELLA LAWSON.

—2003

FRUIT CROSTATAS

The Italian form of tartlettes, which mostly means you don't have to be so precise in shaping them. In keeping with the rustic, free-form theme, these are baked directly on a baking stone.

————

1 cup all-purpose flour
1/2 cup pastry flour
4 teaspoons sugar
1/2 teaspoon fine sea salt
6 tablespoons high-fat (European-style) unsalted butter, cut into 6 pieces and chilled
4 to 5 tablespoons ice water
Blueberry or Blackberry Filling with Lemon Curd (recipe follows)
Confectioners' sugar, whipped cream, or heavy cream for serving

1. Combine the flours, sugar, and salt in a food processor and pulse to combine. Scatter the butter over the surface of the flour and pulse until the butter pieces are no longer visible, 5 to 10 pulses of 10 seconds or so each.
2. Turn the mixture into a bowl, and sprinkle with 1/4 cup ice water. Toss lightly with your fingertips. Gather the dough together, and squeeze a small portion with

your fingers. If the dough feels dry, add another table-spoon of water and toss to combine.

3. Turn the dough onto a work surface, press together firmly, and pat into a disk. Cut into 6 wedges. Roll each wedge into a ball, flatten slightly, and wrap in plastic wrap. Refrigerate for at least 30 minutes, or up to 24 hours.

4. Place an oven rack in the lowest position and top with a large baking stone. Set the oven to 450 degrees and let heat for 1 hour while you prepare the crostatas. Cut six 8-inch-square sheets of aluminum foil.

5. Working with 1 piece of dough at a time, flour the top and bottom lightly and roll into a thin 8-inch round. Transfer the round to a square of foil. Spoon 1½ to 2 tablespoons of the curd into the center, leaving a 2-inch periphery free. Mound ½ cup fruit in a circle on top of the curd. (Use all the filling for the 6 crostatas.) Fold the edges of the dough over to support the filling. If using the blackberry filling, sprinkle the crostata with 1 tablespoon sugar. Place the crostata on a baking sheet and put in the refrigerator. Continue forming tarts with the remaining dough and fruit filling. Refrigerate the crostatas for at least 20 minutes.

6. Slide 2 or 3 crostatas onto the baking stone. Bake until the dough is dark golden brown, 15 to 20 minutes. Remove and cool on a rack for 10 minutes. Repeat with the remaining crostatas.

7. Sprinkle with confectioners' sugar, or add a dollop of whipped cream or a few tablespoons of chilled heavy cream to each serving.

MAKES 6 INDIVIDUAL TARTS

BLUEBERRY OR BLACKBERRY FILLING WITH LEMON CURD

For the Lemon Curd
1 large egg
2 large egg yolks
½ cup sugar
⅓ cup fresh lemon juice (from about 2 lemons; grate the zest first)
Finely grated zest of 1 lemon
1 tablespoon cold unsalted butter, cut into 2 pieces
Pinch of salt
3 tablespoons heavy cream

For the Blueberries
3 pints blueberries
3 tablespoons cornstarch
6 tablespoons sugar
¼ cup fresh lemon juice
Pinch of salt

For the Blackberries
2 pints blackberries
¼ cup cornstarch
6 tablespoons sugar

1. Place a small conical stainless steel strainer over a 2-cup glass measuring cup, and set aside. Whisk the egg, yolks, and sugar together in a small heavy non-reactive saucepan. Add the lemon juice and whisk to combine. Add the zest, butter, and salt. Place the pan over medium heat and cook, stirring constantly with a wooden spoon, until the mixture is shiny, opaque, and thick enough to coat the back of the spoon, 5 to 10 minutes. Do not boil. Remove from the heat and stir in the cream. Strain immediately into the measuring cup, cover, and refrigerate until ready to use.

2. For blueberry crostatas, place half the blueberries in a medium saucepan. Add the cornstarch and sugar and stir well. Add the lemon juice and salt. Cook over medium heat, stirring constantly, until the blueberries give up their juices, thicken, and simmer a bit. The compote will be very thick. Remove from the heat and stir in the remaining blueberries. Cool.

3. For blackberry crostatas, place the blackberries in a large bowl, sprinkle with the cornstarch, and toss to combine.

MAKES ENOUGH FILLING FOR 6 CROSTATAS

SEPTEMBER 15, 2004: "LATE-SUMMER SWEETNESS, ARISING," BY KAY RENTSCHLER.

—2004

POACHED PEARS WITH ASIAN SPICES

In one go, Mark Bittman, who wrote this recipe for his "The Minimalist" column, solves two problems with poached pears. First, he makes the point that since most supermarket pears are hard and unripe, poaching them is the best solution. (It is.) Second, he releases the poached fruit from its traditional—and now clichéd—accompaniment of red wine and cinnamon. This recipe does contain cinnamon, but its aroma derives more from star anise, ginger, and clove.

I served these with the Almond Cake on p. 777.

2½ cups sugar

3 star anise

5 slices fresh ginger

2 whole cloves

1 cinnamon stick

5 cups water

4 firm Anjou pears

1. Combine the sugar, spices, and water in a medium saucepan (large enough to accommodate the pears upright) and turn the heat to high. Peel the pears, leaving the stems on, then core them from the bottom (see Cooking Notes).

2. Lower the pears into the water, and adjust the heat to a gentle simmer. Cook the pears, turning them every 5 minutes or so, until they meet little resistance when prodded with a thin-bladed knife, usually 10 to 20 minutes. Turn off the heat, and cool the pears in liquid.

3. Place the pears on serving plates. (At this point, they can also be covered and refrigerated up to a day; they should be brought to room temperature before serving.) Reduce the poaching liquid to about a cup (it can also be stored for a day), then spoon a little over each pear before serving.

SERVES 4

COOKING NOTES

Bittman said that reducing the liquid is optional—but I think it's worth doing. Turn the heat up and boil the liquid; 10 to 15 minutes of reducing concentrates the flavors marvelously.

One instruction I suggest changing is carving the core from the bottom of the pear. This task, along with coring Brussels sprouts and peeling chestnuts, should be banned by the Geneva Convention. Simply use a melon baller to remove the stem, then score the indentation left from the melon baller with a paring knife. Guests can carve around the core as they eat. If they are unable to do so, put them on dish duty.

VARIATION

Bittman called for bronze-colored Bosc pears and suggested Anjou pears as an alternative. Anjou are the way to go. He also suggested: "a few slices of ginger, a couple of star anise pieces and cloves, a cinnamon stick, a couple of branches of bruised lemongrass (or a handful of lemongrass trimmings), a split vanilla pod." I'm definitely trying the lemongrass version next.

SEPTEMBER 22, 2004: "THE MINIMALIST," BY MARK BITTMAN.

—2004

✒ LUCAS SCHOORMANS'S LEMON TART

There is no lemon custard in this ingenious tart. Instead, a cushion of almond frangipane fills the crust and serves as a cradle for a delightfully assertive lemon confit and vanilla-scented syrup. The dessert was created by Lucas Schoormans, an art dealer and talented home baker in Manhattan.

For the Lemon Confit

4 lemons, thinly sliced, ends and seeds discarded

1 cup sugar

1 vanilla bean, split, seeds scraped out and reserved

For the Pastry Dough

2 cups all-purpose flour

½ cup plus 1 tablespoon sugar

¼ teaspoon salt

6 tablespoons cold unsalted butter

3 large egg yolks

For the Frangipane

11 tablespoons unsalted butter, softened

⅔ cup ground almonds

2 tablespoons all-purpose flour

½ cup sugar

Grated zest of 1 lemon

2 large eggs

1. To make the lemon confit, place the sliced lemons in a bowl and cover with boiling water. Steep for 4 to 8 hours.

2. Drain the lemons, place in a saucepan, and cover with cold water. Simmer gently until the lemon rind is just softened, about 5 minutes. Let cool, then drain the lemons again, reserving 1 cup of the cooking liquid.

3. Return the lemon slices and reserved liquid to the pan and add the sugar and vanilla bean and seeds. Simmer for 5 minutes.

4. Use tongs or a slotted spoon to transfer the slices to a rack to cool. Return the pan with the liquid to the stove, bring to a boil, and cook until thick and reduced to about ⅔ cup. Discard the vanilla bean. Set aside.

5. To make the pastry dough, pulse together the flour, sugar, and salt in a food processor. Add the butter and pulse until the butter pieces are no larger than peas. Add the yolks and pulse until you have a dough that just pulls away from the sides of the bowl; add a tablespoon or two of water if necessary. Form the dough into a disk, wrap in plastic, and refrigerate for 30 minutes.

6. Remove the bottom from an 11-inch tart pan and place it on a work surface. Put two-thirds of the dough on top, and using a floured rolling pin, roll the dough over the tart pan bottom to cover it. Using a knife, trim the excess dough (reserve it). Lift up and place the bottom back in the tart ring. Using your fingers, break off bits of the remaining dough and press them onto the sides of the pan to cover. Roll the pin over the top of the pan to trim. Refrigerate for 15 minutes.

7. Heat the oven to 400 degrees. Cover the dough with parchment paper, weight down with rice, dried beans, or pie weights, and bake until the edges of the crust are just browned, 10 to 15 minutes. Take out of the oven and remove the parchment and weights.

8. To make the frangipane, in the bowl of a mixer (or in a bowl with a hand mixer), beat the butter until light and fluffy. Beat in the almonds and flour. Beat in the sugar and zest. Beat in the eggs one at a time.

9. Scrape the frangipane into the baked crust and return to the oven. Bake until the filling is browned and firm to the touch, about 20 minutes. Transfer to a rack.

10. Lay the lemon slices over the top of the tart. Gently reheat the lemon syrup and pour over the tart. The tart can be served chilled or at room temperature.

SERVES 10

OCTOBER 3, 2004: "KITCHEN VOYEUR: TART DEALER," BY JONATHAN REYNOLDS. RECIPE ADAPTED FROM LUCAS SCHOORMANS, AN ART DEALER IN NEW YORK CITY.

—2004

CHOCOLATE PUDDING

When I set out to find the ideal chocolate pudding, I gathered a handful of recipes, including this one, which comes from Dorie Greenspan, author of *Paris Sweets*. But I didn't try Greenspan's at first. It seemed too involved for something as simple as chocolate pudding. So I put it aside.

I had a mental picture of what a great chocolate pudding should taste like. It should be light and not overly sweet. It should have elasticity yet not be too sticky. Above all, it should taste of good-quality chocolate. I tried recipes from a bunch of cookbooks, but they came out too sweet or, if they worked, were more pot de crème than pudding.

So I began working on my own recipe, using milk instead of cream, less sugar, a combination of eggs and cornstarch—for richness and elasticity—and cooking it on the stove. But mine never achieved the right balance of lightness and decadence.

Going through my original notes, I came across Dorie Greenspan's recipe. In it were all the elements I had been aiming for, plus a stroke of genius: the pudding is pulsed in the food processor in the last step, suffusing it with air and making a rich treat that's light in spirit.

2¼ cups whole milk

6 tablespoons sugar

2 tablespoons unsweetened cocoa powder

2 tablespoons cornstarch

¼ teaspoon salt

1 large egg

2 large egg yolks

5 ounces bittersweet chocolate, melted and still warm

2 tablespoons unsalted butter, cut into 4 pieces, softened

1 teaspoon vanilla extract

Heavy cream for serving

1. Bring 2 cups milk and 3 tablespoons sugar to a boil in a saucepan.

2. While the milk is heating, toss the cocoa, cornstarch, and salt into a food processor and pulse to blend; turn the ingredients out onto a sheet of wax paper. Place the egg, egg yolks, and remaining 3 tablespoons sugar in the work bowl and process for 1 minute. Scrape down the sides of the bowl and add the remaining 1/4 cup milk. Process for a few seconds, then return the dry ingredients to the bowl and pulse just until blended.

3. With the machine running, slowly pour in the hot milk, processing to blend. The mixture will be foamy, but the bubbles will disappear when the pudding is cooked. Pour the mixture into the saucepan and cook over medium-high heat, stirring constantly, for about 2 minutes, or until the pudding thickens. (The pudding should not boil.) Scrape the pudding into the processor, add the chocolate, butter, and vanilla, and pulse until evenly blended.

4. Pour the pudding into 6 individual bowls or 1 large bowl. Chill for at least 4 hours.

5. Serve plain or topped with heavy cream, whipped or not.

SERVES 6

DECEMBER 5, 2004: "THE ARSENAL," BY AMANDA HESSER. RECIPE ADAPTED FROM *PARIS SWEETS*, BY DORIE GREENSPAN.

—2004

FIGS IN WHISKEY

The novelist James Salter, who mentioned this recipe in an essay on French food, described the figs as "marvelously plump and tender, bathed in a smooth, faintly alcoholic liquid." To get the recipe from a restaurant in southwestern France, Salter gave the chef a pair of drugstore reading glasses.

1 package (about 14 ounces) dried figs,
    Turkish or Greek seem best
2 cups sugar
1 1/2 cups Scotch whiskey

ORIGINAL RECIPE

"Boil the figs for 20 minutes in about a quart of water in which the sugar has been dissolved. Allow to cool until tepid. Drain half the remaining water or a bit more, and add the Scotch. Allow to steep a good while in a covered bowl before serving."

SERVES 6

JANUARY 2, 2005: "EAT, MEMORY: MICHELIN MAN," BY JAMES SALTER. RECIPE ADAPTED FROM LA RIPA RESTAURANT IN PLAISANCE, FRANCE.

—2005

BUTTERMILK PIE

As buttermilk pie bakes, its tangy custard splits into two levels—smooth, butter yellow pudding on the ground floor, and a frothy mezzanine. If you want to whip this up with some homemade buttermilk, see p. 613.

6 tablespoons unsalted butter, softened
1 cup sugar
2 large eggs, separated
3 tablespoons all-purpose flour
1 tablespoon fresh lemon juice, or more to taste
1/2 teaspoon freshly grated nutmeg
1/4 teaspoon salt
1 cup buttermilk, at room temperature
One 8-inch deep-dish piecrust, blind-baked until very
    lightly browned (see French Pie Pastry, on p. 825)

1. Position a rack in the middle of the oven and heat the oven to 350 degrees. In mixer fitted with a whisk (or in a bowl with a hand mixer), mix the butter and sugar until well blended. Add the egg yolks and mix well. Add the flour, lemon juice to taste, nutmeg, and salt. Add the buttermilk in a thin stream, mixing until blended.

2. Whisk the egg whites in a large bowl until they form soft peaks. Pour about 1/4 cup of the buttermilk mixture into the egg whites and fold gently to combine. Pour the egg white mixture into the remainder of the buttermilk mixture and fold gently until just combined. The mixture will be somewhat lumpy.

3. On a lightly floured surface, roll out the dough to ⅛ inch thick. Press into a deep 8-inch pie pan (or a standard 9-inch pie pan), and trim the excess dough; flute or fold, and press the edges to make a border. Prick the bottom of the pie shell with the tines of a fork, and refrigerate or freeze briefly to set the crust.

4. When the crust has set, line the dough with foil or parchment, fill with pie weights or dried beans, and bake for 15 minutes. Remove the weights and foil, and continue baking for about 15 minutes, or until the crust just begins to brown. Remove from the oven and cool.

5. Pour the filling into the baked pie shell. Bake until the filling is lightly browned and barely moves when the pie is jiggled, 40 to 45 minutes. (If you added more than 1 tablespoon of lemon juice, it may take longer for the pie to brown; bake for 5 to 10 minutes longer if necessary.) If the edges of the crust brown too quickly, cover with foil.

6. Cool on a rack, and serve warm or at room temperature. Refrigerate leftovers.

SERVES 6 TO 8

COOKING NOTE
Robert Stehling, the Charleston chef whose recipe this is, came up with a clever stand-in for a cooling rack: 3 chopsticks, set a few inches apart on a countertop.

AUGUST 31, 2005: "A SOUTHERN SLEEPER, TART AND LIGHT," BY MATT LEE AND TED LEE. RECIPE ADAPTED FROM ROBERT STEHLING, THE CHEF AT THE HOMINY GRILL IN CHARLESTON, SOUTH CAROLINA.

—2005

JEAN HALBERSTAM'S DEEP-FRIED PEACHES

While David Halberstam was famous for his exhaustively researched books on sports and the conduct of the Vietnam War, his wife, Jean, had an equally imposing reputation among their friends for her cooking. For years, until his death in 2007, David wrote big books, Jean cooked big feasts, and they lived and dined happily in New York and Nantucket.

If you wanted to capture the essence of summer in a chrysalis, these peaches, encased in a fragile fritter shell, would do the trick.

————

1½ cups all-purpose flour
Pinch of salt
1½ tablespoons olive oil
2 large eggs, separated
¾ cup very cold water
2 tablespoons brandy
4 ripe peaches
Fresh lemon juice
2 large egg whites
2 pounds Crisco or other vegetable shortening
1 cup sugar

1. Mix the flour and salt in a large bowl. Form a well and stir in the oil and egg yolks. Add the cold water little by little, stirring until all the flour is incorporated. Add the brandy and stir for 10 minutes, or until the batter is smooth and a bit thicker. Let the batter rest in the fridge for at least 2 hours.

2. Skin the peaches by dropping them in boiling water for 5 to 10 seconds and plunging them immediately into ice water. Peel off the skin, then sprinkle the peaches with lemon juice to prevent browning.

3. When the batter is ready, beat the 4 egg whites stiffly. Stir one-quarter of the egg whites into the batter to lighten it, then gently fold in the rest.

4. Heat the shortening to 360 degrees in a large deep pot. Cut the peaches in half and remove their pits. Dip them in the batter, a few at a time, and fry in the hot oil until golden, 30 to 90 seconds per side. (Don't put all the peaches in at once, or the oil temperature will drop too much.) As soon as the peaches are golden, remove them to drain on a rack or paper towels, and quickly roll them in the sugar to coat completely. Serve right now!

SERVES 8

SEPTEMBER 4, 2005: "KITCHEN VOYEUR: THE ORIGINAL 'UNORIGINAL,'" BY JONATHAN REYNOLDS. RECIPE ADAPTED FROM JEAN HALBERSTAM.

—2005

LEMON MOUSSE FOR A CROWD

Lemon wrapped in a cloud. The Apple Snow on p. 808 and Madeleine Kamman's Apple Mousse on p. 816 are like-minded in their pursuit of ethereally light fruit desserts.

I cup egg whites (from 6 to 8 large eggs)

2 cups confectioners' sugar

½ cup fresh lemon juice (from 2 large lemons)

I cup light corn syrup

3 cups heavy cream

1. Bring 2 inches of water to a boil in the bottom of a double boiler. Combine the egg whites, sugar, and lemon juice in the top of the double boiler. Place over the boiling water and, with a large balloon whisk, whisk the egg whites vigorously until smooth, airy, and very thick, about 5 minutes. Add the corn syrup and whisk just until smooth, then transfer to a large bowl. Cover and refrigerate for about 1 hour.

2. Remove the beaten whites from the refrigerator and add the heavy cream. Using an electric mixer, whisk until thick enough to hold stiff peaks, about 2 minutes.

3. Place in dessert cups or bowls, cover, and refrigerate for 15 minutes to 1 hour before serving.

SERVES 18 TO 24

MAY 24, 2006: "FEED ME: LAUGH AND YOUR GUESTS WILL LAUGH WITH YOU," BY ALEX WITCHEL. RECIPE ADAPTED FROM WILLIAM POLL IN NEW YORK CITY.

—2006

STICKY RICE WITH MANGO

If there were one dessert in this chapter that I'd like to have in my fridge every day, this is it.

1½ cups Thai sticky rice (kao niow) or
    broken jasmine rice

1½ cups canned unsweetened coconut milk

3 tablespoons sugar

½ teaspoon salt, or more to taste

2 to 4 ripe mangoes, depending on size,
    peeled, pitted, and sliced

1. Rinse the rice, then soak it in water to cover for at least 1 hour, or for up to 24.

2. Drain the rice, wrap it in cheesecloth, and place in a steamer over boiling water. Steam for about 30 minutes, until tender. Transfer to a bowl and set aside to cool for half an hour or so.

3. Gently warm the coconut milk in a pan with the sugar and salt, just until they are dissolved.

4. Pour half the coconut milk mixture over the still-warm sticky rice and stir well to combine. Transfer the sweetened rice to individual serving bowls and top with the remaining coconut milk. Add the mango slices, and serve.

SERVES 4

MAY 31, 2006: "THE MINIMALIST: STICKY RICE TAKES A TURN AS DESSERT," BY MARK BITTMAN.

—2006

WINE-STEWED PRUNES AND MASCARPONE

For the 1.0 version of this dish, see Pruneaux du Pichet on p. 822.

I pound pitted prunes (about 40)

1¼ cups sugar

2 cinnamon sticks

2½ cups dry red wine

Two 8-ounce containers mascarpone

1. Combine the prunes, sugar, cinnamon, and wine in a pot and set over medium-high heat. When the mixture boils, reduce to a simmer and cook for 45 minutes, or until the liquid has turned to syrup. Remove from the heat, and let stand for at least 15 minutes.

2. Spread a mound of mascarpone on each serving plate, top with 6 prunes, and drizzle with some syrup. Serve immediately.

SERVES 6

MAY 31, 2006: "WHY NOT RELAX BEFORE DINNER, TOO?"
BY DANA BOWEN. RECIPE ADAPTED FROM FRANK
CASTRONOVO AND FRANK FALCINELLI.

—2006

STRAIGHT-UP RHUBARB PIE

Anne Dimock, the author of *Humble Pie*, a lucid and thoughtful treatise on the round fruit-filled pastry, has an elegiac and even melancholy temperament. She writes that "the natural habitat for pies has changed, shrunk, disappeared," and when we met, she told me, "There is a threshold for the number of pies you can make at once before their greatness is compromised. For me, it's eight. After eight, they taste fine, but all the little things that you might be proud of are lost."

Dimock grew up in a family of pie makers in Madison, New Jersey. There were four apple trees in the backyard, and five children. Come August, when the fruit began dropping, the baking of a hundred pies would commence. Each would be frozen to last through the winter. During these early years, Dimock was just an apprentice, although, she writes, her opinions were already forming: "My mother insisted that each pie contain a full cup of sugar, and although I knew that was too much, I dutifully scooped and leveled and poured oceans of sugar upon fleets of pies."

She continued to bake pies, but it took decades before she became a "Pie Maker"—a person whose pies are inseparable from her identity. "Each Pie Maker is called to a particular type of pie," she writes. "It is a deeper, more profound relationship than a favorite pie or one's specialty. It is closer to destiny or fate."

Dimock says that Pie Makers usually receive the calling in their mid-thirties. She was thirty-six when she and her husband moved to Minnesota, and they inherited thirty rhubarb plants from their house's previous owner. "I came to rhubarb the same way my mother came to apple—out of utility and thrift," she says.

This is the fundamental misunderstanding about most pies: they are rarely just about generosity. They are a way to salvage fruit before it rots, a way to compose the forlorn, to conceal its problems and polish it with crust.

There is little about pie that Dimock hasn't considered. She has sized up potential love interests by how they dig in: "You don't need me to tell you what to stay away from—the ones who don't say anything, the ones who don't chew, the ones who ask for a second slice before thanking you for the first, the ones who use a spoon. You already know what you're in for with them." A man who digs out the filling, she warns, reveals a propensity to lie, while one who starts eating his slice somewhere other than the point shows curiosity and liveliness.

With rhubarb as her muse, Dimock set out to mend her mother's sweetening errors. She came up with a foolproof formula: for every cup of sliced rhubarb, there should be ¼ cup sugar and 1 tablespoon flour. For the crust, she relies on what she calls "the golden ratio" of 3 parts flour to 1 part shortening. The top is marked with 8 razor-thin vents. Her rhubarb pie is the best I've ever tasted.

———

For the Crust
2 cups all-purpose flour (see Step 1)
½ teaspoon salt
2 teaspoons sugar
⅔ cup plus 2 tablespoons vegetable shortening
About 6 tablespoons ice water

For the Filling
5 cups sliced rhubarb (1½ to 2 pounds)
1¼ cups sugar
5 tablespoons all-purpose flour
¼ teaspoon ground cinnamon
1½ tablespoons unsalted butter

1. To make the crust, heat the oven to 425 degrees. Before measuring the flour, stir it to leaven with air, and then measure out the 2 cups. Combine the flour, salt, and sugar in a large bowl and fluff with a fork. Cut in the shortening with a fork or pastry blender. Stop as soon as the sheen of the shortening disappears and the mixture is a bunch of coarse pieces. Sprinkle a tablespoon of water at a time over the dough, lifting and tossing it with the fork. When it begins to come together, gather the dough, press it into a ball, and then pull it apart; if it crumbles in your hands, it needs more water. (It's better to err on the side of too wet than too dry.) Add a teaspoon or two more water, as needed.

2. Gather the dough into 2 slightly unequal balls, the larger one for the bottom crust and the smaller one

for the top. Flatten the larger ball, re-forming any frayed edges with the sides of your hand. Dust with flour and roll the dough, starting from the center and moving toward the edges. Take a knife or thin spatula and quickly work its edge between the crust and the countertop, then lift the dough to the side; dust the dough and countertop with flour. Roll again until the diameter is an inch or 2 larger than that of a 9-inch pie pan. Lay the rolling pin a third of the way from one of the edges, roll the crust onto the pin, and then unroll the crust into the pie pan and press it into place. Place in the freezer.

3. To make the filling, blend the rhubarb, sugar, flour, and cinnamon in a large bowl. Pour into the crust-lined pie pan. Dot with the butter.

4. Roll out the top crust. Dab the rim of the bottom crust with water to create a glue, then place the top crust over the rhubarb; trim, seal, and cut several steam vents.

5. Bake for 15 minutes; reduce the temperature to 350 degrees and bake for 25 to 30 minutes more, or until a bit of pink juice bubbles from the vents in the crust. Remove from the oven and place on a rack to cool. Serve warm or at room temperature.

SERVES 8

COOKING NOTE

Anne Dimock's secret ingredient is "Extra Fancy Vietnamese Cassia Cinnamon," available from Penzeys Spices, www.penzeys.com.

JUNE 25, 2006: "THE WAY WE EAT: CIRCULAR THINKING," BY AMANDA HESSER. RECIPE ADAPTED FROM ANNE DIMOCK, THE AUTHOR OF *HUMBLE PIE*.

—2006

⌒ BANANA CREAM PIE

———

For the Graham Cracker Crust
1¼ cups graham cracker crumbs
    (about 10 or 11 whole crackers)
1 teaspoon sugar
4 tablespoons unsalted butter, melted

For the Pastry Cream
1⅔ cups whole milk
¼ cup plus 3 tablespoons sugar
½ vanilla bean, split, seeds scraped
    out and reserved
3 tablespoons cornstarch
1 large egg
2 large egg yolks
1½ tablespoons unsalted butter

For Assembly
1½ cups heavy cream
¼ cup crème fraîche
3½ medium bananas, sliced into
    ⅜-inch-thick rounds

1. To make the crust, heat the oven to 325 degrees. Combine the crumbs and sugar in a bowl. Add the butter and mix, first with a fork, then with your fingers, until the crumbs are moistened. Pour the mixture into a 9-inch pie pan and use a flat-bottomed cup to press the crumbs evenly over the bottom; press it up the sides with your fingers. The edges of the shell will be crumbly.

2. Bake until lightly browned, 9 to 10 minutes. Cool completely.

3. To prepare the pastry cream, combine the milk, ¼ cup sugar, and the vanilla bean and seeds in a medium saucepan and bring to a simmer over medium heat. Sift the remaining 3 tablespoons sugar together with the cornstarch. Whisk together the egg and yolks in a large bowl.

4. When the milk comes to a simmer, discard the vanilla bean. Add the cornstarch mixture to the eggs and whisk until well combined. While whisking, slowly pour in about one-quarter of the milk. Transfer this mixture to the saucepan, set over low heat, and simmer, whisking constantly, until it reaches the consistency of thick pudding. (Be careful not to curdle the eggs.)

5. Remove from the heat and stir in the butter until incorporated. Pour into a shallow bowl, place plastic wrap directly on the surface, and chill.

6. To assemble, using an electric mixer or a whisk, whip the heavy cream and crème fraîche into peaks. Transfer the pastry cream to a large bowl and whisk until smooth. Fold in ½ cup of the whipped cream. Line the bottom of the pie crust with a layer of bananas. Fold the remaining bananas into the pastry cream, then

spoon it evenly into the crust. Mound the remaining whipped cream on top, swirling it decoratively. Chill, and serve within 24 hours.

SERVES 8

JANUARY 14, 2007: "THE WAY WE EAT: L.A.'S TOP BANANA," BY JENNIFER STEINHAUER. RECIPE ADAPTED FROM CLEMENTINE IN LOS ANGELES.

—2007

RHUBARB ORANGE

It may seem wrongheaded to add citrus to already tart rhubarb, but it won't once you taste it.

————

14 ounces rhubarb, trimmed

1 blood or navel orange

2 vanilla beans

3 tablespoons Demerara sugar (or other raw sugar)

⅔ cup crème fraîche

1. Heat the oven to 300 degrees. Cut the rhubarb into 2- to 2½-inch pieces and place in a medium bowl. Finely grate the zest of half the orange over the rhubarb, and then squeeze the juice of the whole orange into the bowl. Split the vanilla beans, scrape out the seeds, and place both in the bowl. Add the sugar and stir to combine.

2. Pour the rhubarb into a baking dish and arrange the pieces so that they lie flat. Bake for 15 to 20 minutes. Remove the vanilla beans. Serve with the crème fraîche.

SERVES 4

APRIL 29, 2007: "THE STALK OF THE TOWN," BY AMANDA HESSER. RECIPE ADAPTED FROM *ITALIAN TWO EASY: SIMPLE RECIPES FROM THE LONDON RIVER CAFÉ*, BY ROSE GRAY AND RUTH ROGERS.

—2007

COEUR À LA CRÈME WITH RHUBARB SAUCE

Seeing ricotta only as a filling would be to miss the point. Unlike cream, which can flatten a dish, or grated cheese, which can weigh it down, ricotta has a way of complementing other flavors without masking them. It is a muse for the plain-food set—and a reminder that restraint has its merits.

A few years ago, at a dinner party, my friend Narcissa Titman spooned out fluffy dollops of this coeur à la crème, a throwback I'd read about but never encountered. Whole-milk ricotta, whipped egg whites, whipped cream, and the tiniest bit of sugar come together in a cream that's as light as goose down yet substantial enough to call dessert. Gentle waves of flavor were all the intensity this perfectly plain dessert would ever need.

Narcissa got the recipe from her friend Betty Kramer; Betty no longer recalls where she discovered it. I added the rhubarb sauce. If you don't have heart molds, just use a wide shallow sieve.

For coeur à la crème's frenemy, see the Fontainebleau on p. 829.

————

1 pound whole-milk ricotta

3 tablespoons confectioners' sugar

½ teaspoon vanilla extract

1 cup heavy cream

3 large egg whites

Pinch of salt

4 cups chopped rhubarb (about 8 stalks)

⅓ cup granulated sugar

1 whole clove

¼ cinnamon stick

1. Line two 7-inch-wide perforated ceramic heart-shaped molds or a shallow 8-inch round sieve with 4 layers of cheesecloth that have been rinsed in cold water and wrung out.

2. Using the back of a spoon, press the ricotta through a fine-mesh sieve into a bowl. Stir in the confectioners' sugar and vanilla. Whip the cream and fold it into the ricotta mixture. Whip the egg whites with the salt until stiff, then fold them into the ricotta as well.

3. Fill the lined mold or sieve with the ricotta mixture, making sure you don't flatten or mush it. Fold the

excess cheesecloth over the ricotta. Place on a tray or in a bowl and refrigerate overnight to drain.

4. The next day, combine the rhubarb, sugar, clove, and cinnamon in a small saucepan. Cover and simmer over medium heat until the pieces of rhubarb are soft but still intact, 5 minutes. Let cool.

5. To serve, unmold the ricotta cream onto a platter and pass it along with the rhubarb sauce.

SERVES 6

MAY 13, 2007: "THE WAY WE EAT: THE CHEESE STANDS ALONE," BY AMANDA HESSER. RECIPE ADAPTED FROM NARCISSA TITMAN AND BETTY KRAMER.

—2007

CRUNCHY NOODLE KUGEL À LA GREAT-AUNT MARTHA

Melissa Clark has written nearly twenty cookbooks and has collaborated with chefs such as Claudia Fleming (see p. 696) and Daniel Boulud on yet more cookbooks. A few years ago, the *Times* hired Clark to write a weekly cooking column, "A Good Appetite." Clark's cooking is larded with smart details that make her recipes distinctive yet inclusive. Her spinach dip on p. 90 is deepened with smoked paprika; her pea pancakes are sweetened with a puree of sugar snap peas; and, here, her noodle kugel is brilliantly reconstructed by spreading the noodles on a baking sheet, so that everyone gets plenty of crisp bits.

_____

I cup raisins
Sherry or orange juice
I pound egg noodles
6 tablespoons unsalted butter, cut into pieces
4 large eggs
3 cups cottage cheese
I cup sour cream
⅓ cup sugar
I teaspoon ground cinnamon
Grated zest of I lemon
Pinch of salt

1. Put the raisins in a microwave-safe bowl or a small saucepan and cover with the sherry. Heat in the

microwave oven or on the stovetop until the liquid is steaming hot (about 1½ minutes in the microwave, or 3 minutes on the stove). Let cool while you prepare the kugel mixture.

2. Heat the oven to 400 degrees. Butter an 11-by-17-inch jelly-roll pan. Cook the noodles according to the package directions. Drain well, immediately return the noodles to the pot, and add the butter. Toss until the butter melts.

3. Whisk together the eggs, cottage cheese, sour cream, sugar, cinnamon, lemon zest, and salt in a large bowl. Drain the raisins and add to the bowl, along with the buttered noodles. Mix well.

4. Spread the mixture in the prepared pan and smooth the top. Bake until the top is crusty and golden, 25 to 35 minutes. Serve warm or at room temperature.

SERVES 12

SEPTEMBER 12, 2007: "A GOOD APPETITE: EXTRA CRUNCH FOR THE KUGEL," BY MELISSA CLARK.

—2007

PLUM FRITTERS

These fritters look as if little plum bombs had exploded in hot oil, but man, are they good—sugar and fried dough crisply wrapping a jammy interior.

_____

I cup all-purpose flour
½ teaspoon kosher salt
½ cup plus I tablespoon sugar
3 large eggs, separated
½ cup ice water
2½ tablespoons plum brandy (or other eau-de-vie)
I teaspoon ground cinnamon
Canola oil or vegetable shortening for deep-frying
6 small ripe plums, halved and pitted

1. Mix together the flour, salt, and 1 tablespoon sugar in a bowl. Make a well in the center and add the egg yolks and ice water. Gradually blend the liquid into the flour mixture until almost smooth. Stir in the plum brandy. Chill for 30 minutes.

2. Combine the cinnamon with the remaining ½ cup sugar in a wide shallow bowl. Whip the egg whites to soft peaks.

3. Fold the whipped egg whites into the batter. Heat 2 inches of oil in a large heavy saucepan over medium-high heat; it's hot enough when it quickly browns a small drop of batter. Working in batches, coat the plum halves in the batter, then fry in the oil until puffed and golden, turning once. If you have one, use a splatter guard to prevent the juices from splattering. Using a slotted spoon, transfer the fritters to the bowl of cinnamon sugar, roll them in the sugar, and then set on a plate lined with paper towels. Eat warm or at room temperature.

MAKES 12 FRITTERS; SERVES 4 TO 6

SEPTEMBER 16, 2007: "THE WAY WE EAT: BLESS THIS MESS," BY AMANDA HESSER.

—2007

⌒ QUEEN OF PUDDINGS

This bread pudding spread with jam and crowned with meringue was created for Queen Victoria by her cooks, and now you may make it for yourself.

————

1½ cups plus 1 teaspoon sugar

4 cups whole milk

Pinch of salt

Finely grated zest of 2 lemons

6 tablespoons unsalted butter

½ pound slightly stale white bread, cut into ½-inch cubes (7 to 8 cups)

4 large eggs, separated

4 large egg yolks

3 tablespoons apricot jam

½ teaspoon fresh lemon juice

½ teaspoon vanilla extract

1. Stir together ½ cup sugar, the milk, salt, lemon zest, and butter in a medium pot. Bring to a boil, then turn off the heat, cover, and let steep for 30 minutes.
2. Butter a 9-inch square baking pan or a 2-quart gratin dish. Lay the bread cubes evenly over the bottom.
3. Beat the 8 egg yolks in a medium bowl. Stir in 1 cup of the warm milk, then pour the tempered yolks into the remaining milk. Pass the liquid through a sieve onto the cubes of bread. Push down on the cubes to submerge them, and let soak for 20 to 60 minutes.
4. Heat the oven to 350 degrees. Put the baking pan of soaking bread in a larger baking pan and add enough hot water to the larger pan to come halfway up the sides of the smaller one. Bake until the bread cubes bounce back when pressed with your finger, 25 to 30 minutes. Remove from the oven, and let rest in the water bath. (Keep the oven on.)
5. Warm the jam in a small saucepan, and spread it over the baked custard.
6. In a mixture fitted with a whisk attachment (or in a bowl with a hand mixer), beat the egg whites on low speed until foamy. Beat in the lemon juice and vanilla, and gradually increase the speed to high. When the whites form very soft peaks, add 1 cup sugar, a little at a time, beating until glossy, stiff peaks form.
7. Cover the jam with dollops of meringue, then sprinkle with the remaining 1 teaspoon sugar. Bake until the meringue peaks are lightly browned, 15 to 20 minutes. Cool completely, then refrigerate. Serve chilled.

SERVES 6

NOVEMBER 18, 2007: "FOOD: THE WAY WE EAT: THE SWEET HEREAFTER," BY CHRISTINE MUHLKE. ADAPTED FROM LOST DESSERTS, BY GAIL MONAGHAN.

—2007

⌒ CHURROS WITH CHOCOLATE SAUCE

These Spanish doughnuts are like thinner, crisper crullers—almost all shell and no interior, like a muffin top.

————

For the Chocolate Sauce

1 cup heavy cream

6 ounces bittersweet chocolate, finely chopped

1 tablespoon unsalted butter, softened

1 teaspoon bourbon

For the Churros

½ teaspoon ground cinnamon

¾ cup sugar

6 tablespoons unsalted butter

1 cup whole milk

1 teaspoon kosher salt

1 cup all-purpose flour

2 large eggs, lightly beaten

8 cups peanut oil, for deep-frying

1. To make the chocolate sauce, heat the cream in a medium saucepan until small bubbles form around the edges. Remove from the heat. Add the chocolate to the hot cream and let sit for 5 minutes, then stir until smooth. Stir in the butter and then the bourbon. Cover and keep warm.

2. To make the churros, combine the cinnamon and sugar in a shallow pan; set aside. Melt the butter with the milk and salt in a small saucepan over medium heat, and bring to a boil. Add the flour and cook, stirring constantly, until a dough forms and pulls away from the sides of the pan, about 30 seconds. Remove from the heat and cool for 3 minutes, then stir the eggs into the batter until smooth. Fill a pastry bag fitted with a large star tip with the batter.

3. Meanwhile, heat about 3 inches of oil to 350 degrees in a medium pot. Holding the pastry bag several inches above the oil, squeeze out the batter and snip it with kitchen shears when it reaches 4 inches long. Fry the churros in batches, turning once, until deep golden brown, about 4 minutes. Using a slotted spoon, transfer to a paper-towel-lined plate to drain. While they are still hot, roll in the cinnamon sugar. (The churros can be made ahead and kept warm in a low-temperature oven.) Serve with the chocolate sauce.

MAKES ABOUT 16 CHURROS

OCTOBER 5, 2008: "THE WAY WE EAT: FRY, BABY," BY KELLY ALEXANDER. RECIPE ADAPTED FROM WATTS GROCERY IN DURHAM, NORTH CAROLINA.

—2008

SUGARED PUFFS

These puffs were inspired by Maida Heatter's Preheated-Oven Popovers on p. 657. David Lebovitz, a cookbook author and blogger (www.davidlebovitz .com), took Heatter's batter, added more sugar and more salt, and then, after baking, brushed the popovers with butter and dipped them in cinnamon sugar.

"It's like a cinnamon doughnut," he said. "Who needs the fried and all the inside? You want the crunch." That's exactly what you get: a crisp, fragrant swell of pastry, pebbled with sugar: part soufflé, part doughnut, part cinnamon toast. As with Heatter's popovers, all you need is a blender and a tiny pulse of ambition, and you'll have a new favorite dessert.

—————

For the Puffs

2 tablespoons unsalted butter, melted

3 large eggs, at room temperature

1 cup whole milk

1 1/2 teaspoons sugar

1 teaspoon salt

1 cup all-purpose flour

For the Sugar Coating

2/3 cup sugar

1 teaspoon ground cinnamon

4 tablespoons unsalted butter, melted

1. To make the puffs, heat the oven to 400 degrees. Liberally butter a nonstick popover pan or a muffin pan with 1/2-cup molds. Put the melted butter, eggs, milk, sugar, and salt in a blender and whiz for a few seconds. Add the flour and whiz for 5 to 8 seconds, just until smooth.

2. Divide the batter among 8 or 9 greased molds, filling each half to three-quarters full. Bake for 35 minutes, or until the puffs are deep brown.

3. Remove from the oven and wait a few minutes until cool enough to handle, then remove the puffs from the pan. You may need a small knife to help pry them out.

4. To make the coating, mix the sugar and cinnamon in a medium bowl. Thoroughly brush each puff all over with melted butter, then dredge in the cinnamon sugar to coat completely. Let cool on a baking rack.

MAKES 8 TO 9 PUFFS (8 IN A POPOVER PAN, 9 IN A MUFFIN PAN)

MARCH 15, 2009: "RECIPE REDUX, 1966: MAIDA HEATTER'S POPOVERS," BY AMANDA HESSER. RECIPE ADAPTED FROM DAVID LEBOVITZ, THE AUTHOR OF ROOM FOR DESSERT AND THE GREAT BOOK OF CHOCOLATE, AMONG OTHER TITLES.

—2009

MENUS

To help you navigate the book and to give you some ideas for how to cook from it, I've assembled these menus. Some are related to holidays, some to time periods, and others to special occasions. For big holidays or groupings like Thanksgiving and Southern food, I've simply listed all the recipes I thought were relevant to the grouping rather than arranging them in menus. Happy party planning!

Nineteenth Century
Claret Cup
Potted Salmon
Asparagus Salad
Epigram of Lamb
Green Pea Fritters
Astor House Rolls
Almond Custard Cake

Salted and Deviled Almonds
Palestine Soup
Collared Pork
Watercress Salad
Fresh Mushrooms Stewed with
  Madeira
Maître d'Hôtel Potatoes
Gingersnaps
Delicious Milk Punch

Early Twentieth Century
Vermouth Cassis
Eggs Suffragette
Raw Artichoke Salad with
  Cucumber
Roast Quail with Sage Dressing
Fried Radishes
Apple Dumplings *or* Apple Snow

Vermouth Cup
Eggs Louisiana
Artichoke Salad with Anchovy
  and Capers
Chicken à la Marengo
Saratoga Potatoes
Baked Alaska

1960s
Málaga Gazpacho
Paella
Lemon Lotus Ice Cream

Leeks Vinaigrette
Boeuf Bourguignon I *or* II
Chocolate Mousse

Bagna Cauda
Lorane Schiff's Pesto Genovese
Chicken Canzanese
Tomatoes Vinaigrette
Zabaglione

1970s
Rillettes de Canard
Artichokes Croisettes
Sole Grenobloise
Cucumbers in Cream

Frozen Lemon Soufflé *or*
  Crepes Suzette

Onion Rings
Cream of Carrot Soup
High-Temperature Roast Lamb
Noodles Romanoff
Lindy's Cheesecake *or* Forget-It
  Meringue Torte

1980s
Alice Waters's Baked Goat
  Cheese with Salad
Madame Mouriere's Cassoulet
Crisp Potato Crowns
Tarte aux Pommes *or* Tourtière

Janice Okun's Buffalo Chicken
  Wings
'21' Club Burger
Key Lime Pie

Mint Julep
Stuffed Clams
Paul Prudhomme's Cajun-Style
  Gumbo
Brown Sugar Shortbread *or*
  Lemon Bars

1990s

Kaffir Lime Lemonade

Fried Zucchini Blossoms

Yellow Pepper Soup with Paprika
Mousse

Seared Tuna in Black Pepper
Crust

Ice-Cold Tomatoes with Basil

Green Lentils with Roasted Beets
and Preserved Lemon (at room
temperature)

Pineapple Carpaccio with Lime
Sorbet *or* Pepper-Cumin
Cookies

———

Toasts with Walnut Sauce

Mezzaluna Salad

Conchiglie Al Forno with
Mushrooms and Radicchio

Bittersweet Chocolate
Semifreddo *or* Panna Cotta

———

Cucumber–Goat Cheese Dip with
Radishes and Scallions

Roast Chicken with Bread Salad

Shredded Brussels Sprouts with
Bacon and Pine Nuts

Fresh Ginger Cake *or* Olive Oil
and Apple Cider Cake

———

Kir Royale 38

Fresh and Smoked Salmon
Spread

Butternut Squash and Cider Soup

Stewed Lamb Shanks with White
Beans and Rosemary

Caramelized Endive

Fennel, Orange, Watercress, and
Walnut Salad

Warm Soft Chocolate Cake

Thanksgiving

DRINKS

The Normandy

HORS D'OEUVRES

Spiced Pecans

Pickled Shrimp

Cheese Straws

Pork-and-Toasted-Rice-Powder
Spring Rolls

SOUPS

Cream of Carrot Soup

Carrot and Fennel Soup

Creamy Curried Sweet Potato
Soup

Butternut Squash and Cider Soup

Roasted Squash Soup with
Cumin

Butternut Squash Soup with
Brown Butter

TURKEY

Roasted Brine-Cured Turkey with
Wild Mushroom Stuffing

Roasted Brine-Cured Turkey
with Shiitake and Lotus Seed
Stuffing

Turducken

VEGETABLES

Holiday Cranberry Chutney

Cranberry Chutney

Baked Mushrooms

Fresh Mushrooms Stewed with
Madeira

Creamed Onions

Braised Red Cabbage with
Chestnuts

Red Cabbage Glazed with Maple
Syrup

Anton Mosimann's Braised
Brussels Sprouts in Cream

Shredded Brussels Sprouts with
Bacon and Pine Nuts

Brussels Sprouts "Slaw" with
Mustard Butter

Golden Winter Puree

James Beard's Pureed Parsnips

Cumin-Mustard Carrots

Confit of Carrot and Cumin

Savory Bread Pudding

Shallot Pudding

Stewed Fennel with Red
Pepper Oil

Roasted Cauliflower

Ratatouille with Butternut Squash

Wilted Chard with Pickled Red
Onion

Sugar Snap Peas with Horseradish

String Beans with Ginger and
Garlic

POTATOES

Gratin of Yams and Chipotle
Cream

Sweet Potato Cecelia

Candied Sweet Potatoes

Sautéed Potatoes with Parsley

Sweet Potato Casserole

Ralph Vetter's Sweet Potatoes
with Lemon

Sweet Potatoes Anna

Mashed Potatoes Anna

Madame Laracine's Gratin
Dauphinois

STUFFINGS

Corn Bread Stuffing

Porcini Bread Stuffing

Wild Mushroom Stuffing

Shiitake and Lotus Seed Stuffing

BREADS

Astor House Rolls

Old South Buttermilk Biscuits

Sage Biscuits

Maida Heatter's Preheated-Oven
Popovers

DESSERTS

Teddie's Apple Cake

Bolzano Apple Cake

Lee's Marlborough Tart

Apple Crumb Pie

Tarte aux Pommes

Sally Darr's Golden Delicious
Apple Tart

Apple Galette

Mrs. Raymond Schenk's Pumpkin
Cake

Cranberry Upside-Down Cake

Mississippi Pecan Pie

Bourbon Pecan Pie

Rum Pumpkin Cream Pie

Christmas

DRINKS

Swedish Glögg
Eggnog
Blender Eggnog
Tom and Jerry
Cranberry Liqueur
Kumquat-Clementine Cordial
Grapefruit Wine
Hot Buttered Rum
Holiday Punch
The Normandy

HORS D'OEUVRES

To Sugar or Crystallize Pop-Corn
Nicole Kaplan's Gougères
The Spice Boys' Cheese Ball
Cheese Straws
Hot Cheese Olives
Seasoned Olives
Spiced Pecans
Fresh and Smoked Salmon
  Spread
Pickled Shrimp

SOUPS

Chestnut Soup
Cream of Carrot Soup
Carrot and Fennel Soup
Butternut Squash and Cider
  Soup
Roasted Squash Soup with
  Cumin
Butternut Squash Soup with
  Brown Butter
Creamy Curried Sweet Potato
  Soup

SALADS

Watercress Salad
Diane Forley's Arugula Salad with
  Artichoke, Ricotta Salata, and
  Pumpkin Seeds
Fennel and Apple Salad with
  Juniper

MAIN COURSE

Ann Seranne's Rib Roast of Beef
Horseradish Sauce

Slow-Roasted Duck
Choucroute à l'Alsacienne
Crown Roast of Lamb
Roasted Brine-Cured Turkey with
  Wild Mushroom Stuffing

VEGETABLES

Holiday Cranberry Chutney
Cranberry Chutney
Fried Radishes
Florida Beets
Spinach with Sour Cream
Leeks Vinaigrette
Mushrooms Stuffed with Duxelles
  and Sausage
Mushrooms with Manzanilla
  Sherry
Anton Mosimann's Braised
  Brussels Sprouts in Cream
Brussels Sprouts "Slaw" with
  Mustard Butter
Shredded Brussels Sprouts with
  Bacon and Pine Nuts
Red Cabbage Glazed with Maple
  Syrup
Braised Red Cabbage with
  Chestnuts
Golden Winter Puree
James Beard's Pureed Parsnips
The Most Voluptuous Cauliflower
Roasted Cauliflower
Savory Bread Pudding
Leek and Shiitake Bread Pudding
Shallot Pudding
Escarole with Pan-Roasted Garlic
  and Lemon
Cumin-Mustard Carrots
Caramelized Endive
String Beans with Ginger and
  Garlic
Wilted Chard with Pickled Red
  Onion

POTATOES

Sweet Potato Cecelia
Candied Sweet Potatoes
Sweet Potato Casserole
Gratin of Yams and Chipotle
  Cream

Ralph Vetter's Sweet Potatoes
  with Lemon
Sweet Potatoes Anna
Mashed Potatoes Anna
Sautéed Potatoes with Parsley
Madame Laracine's Gratin
  Dauphinois

STUFFINGS

Corn Bread Stuffing
Porcini Bread Stuffing
Wild Mushroom Stuffing
Shiitake and Lotus Seed Stuffing

BREADS

Astor House Rolls
Old South Buttermilk Biscuits
Sage Biscuits
Maida Heatter's Preheated-Oven
  Popovers

DESSERTS

Poached Pears in Brandy and Red
  Wine
Poached Pears with Asian Spices
Clove Granita
Panforte (Traditional Sienese
  Fruitcake)
Teddie's Apple Cake
Bolzano Apple Cake
Lee's Marlborough Tart
Tarte aux Pommes
Sally Darr's Golden Delicious
  Apple Tart
Apple Galette
Apple Crumb Pie
Pear Upside-Down Cake
Cranberry Upside-Down Cake
Mrs. Raymond Schenk's Pumpkin
  Cake
Rum Pumpkin Cream Pie
Mississippi Pecan Pie
Bourbon Pecan Pie
Fresh Ginger Cake
Whiskey Cake
Figs in Whiskey
Wine-Stewed Prunes and
  Mascarpone
Black Forest Cake

Walnut Cake with Chocolate
    Walnut Buttercream
Lora Brody's Bête Noire
Chocolate Rum Mousse
Red Wine Ice Cream
Almond Granita

Gingersnaps
English Gingersnaps
Spice Krinkles
Honey Spice Cookies
Pine Nut Cookies
Swedish Nut Balls
Florentines with Ginger
Cranberry Pistachio Biscotti
Pepper-Cumin Cookies
Cocoa Christmas Cookies
English Toffee
Molasses Candy
Chocolate Caramels
Pralines
Party Balls
Rum Balls
Peppermints

Christmas Stollen
Panettone
Mary Ann's Fruitcake
An Incredible Date-Nut Bread

German Toast
Callie's Doughnuts
Fyrstekake (Royal Cake)
Winter Fruit Salad
Spiced Pumpkin Oatmeal
Morning Bread Pudding
David Eyre's Pancake
Heavenly Hots

Russ & Daughters' Chopped
    Chicken Liver
The Minimalist's Gravlax
Matzoh Ball Soup
Matt's Whole Brisket with
    Tomato Gravy

Brisket in Sweet-and-Sour Sauce
Elizabeth Frink's Roast Lemon
    Chicken
Roast Chicken with Bread Salad
Sautéed Potatoes with Parsley
Latkes
Saratoga Potatoes
Mashed Potatoes Anna
Potato "Tostones"
Teddie's Apple Cake
Junior's Cheesecake
Poppy Seed Torte
Chamomile and Almond Cake
Cranberry Pistachio Biscotti
Maida Heatter's Rugelach
Dorie Greenspan's Sablés
Challah
Challah Revisited

James Beard's Champagne Punch
Buckwheat Blini with Crème
    Fraîche and Caviar
Cromesquis d'Huîtres à la Sauce
    Tartare (Fried Oysters with
    Creamy Tartar Sauce)
Lobster Bisque or Spaghetti with
    Caviar, Scallions, and Chopped
    Egg
Filet de Boeuf Rôti (Roast Fillet
    of Beef) with Sauce Bordelaise
    or Roast Lobster with Vanilla
    Sauce
The Most Voluptuous Cauliflower
Taillevent's Chocolate Cake with
    Pistachio Sauce or Gâteau de
    Crepes

Hoppin' John

Ginger Cordial
Oriental Watercress Soup
Clams in Black Bean Sauce
Warm Eggplant Salad with
    Sesame and Shallots
Chilled Sesame Spinach
Stir-Fried Collards

Spicy Cucumber Salad
Chinese Pork Balls
Chinese Barbecued Spareribs
Takeout-Style Sesame Noodles
Chinese-Style Steamed Black Sea
    Bass
Hunan Beef with Cumin
Lee Lum's Lemon Chicken
Hot Pepper Shrimp
Tea Ice Cream
Poached Pears with Asian Spices

Rhubarb Bellini
Monte's Ham
Sautéed Potatoes with Parsley
Asparagus Mimosa
Hot Cross Buns
Charleston Coconut Sweeties
Party Balls

Faki (Greek Lentil Soup)
Matzoh Ball Soup
Red Lentil Soup with Lemon
Spicy Orange Salad
    Moroccan-Style
Haricots Verts with Balsamic
    Vinaigrette
Moroccan Carrot Salad
Confit of Carrot and Cumin
Rachel's Green Beans with Dill
String Beans with Ginger and
    Garlic
Sugar Snap Peas with
    Horseradish
Sautéed Potatoes with Parsley
Potato "Tostones"
Sautéed Asparagus with Fleur de
    Sel
Al Forno's Roasted Asparagus
Artichauts Vinaigrette
Warm Eggplant Salad with
    Sesame and Shallots
Sweet-and-Sour Salmon in
    Almond Prune Sauce
Sole Grenobloise
Brisket in Sweet-and-Sour
    Sauce

Matt's Whole Brisket with
  Tomato Gravy
Iraqi Grape Leaves Stuffed with
  Lamb, Mint, and Cinnamon
Choresh Qormeh Sabzi (Green
  Herb Stew)
Roman Lamb
Arnaki Araka (Lamb with Peas)
High-Temperature Roast Lamb
  with Schrafft's Mint Sauce
Moroccan Chicken Smothered in
  Olives
Poached Pears in Brandy and Red
  Wine
Macaroons
Charleston Coconut Sweeties

Rosh Hashanah
Fried Chickpeas
Moroccan Tomato Soup
Ismail Merchant's Very Hot
  Chicken Soup
Turkish Split-Pea Soup with Mint
  and Paprika
Winter Borscht
Carrot and Fennel Soup
Raw Artichoke Salad with
  Cucumber
Warm Eggplant Salad with
  Sesame and Shallots
Moroccan Carrot Salad
Confit of Carrot and Cumin
Braised Red Cabbage with
  Chestnuts
Couscous Salad
Bulgur Salad with Pomegranate
  Dressing and Toasted Nuts
Barley Risotto
Potted Salmon
Joyce Goldstein's Pickled
  Salmon
Salmon and Beet Tartare
Epigram of Lamb
Arnaki Araka (Lamb with Peas)
Brisket in Sweet-and-Sour Sauce
Matt's Whole Brisket with
  Tomato Gravy
Roasted Squab with Chicken
  Liver Stuffing

Chicken Paprikash
Roast Chicken with Bread Salad
James Beard's Chicken with 40
  Cloves of Garlic
Moroccan Chicken Smothered in
  Olives
Huguenot Torte (Apple and
  Pecan Torte)
Teddie's Apple Cake
Purple Plum Torte
Polish Jewish Plum Cake
Rosh Hashanah Plum Pie
Plum Fritters
Olive Oil and Apple Cider
  Cake
Ginger Cake
Pear Upside-Down Cake
Bolzano Apple Cake
Poppy Seed Torte
Apple Dumplings
Apple Snow
Tarte aux Pommes
Crunchy Noodle Kugel à la
  Great-Aunt Martha
Honey Spice Cookies
Spice Krinkles
Maida Heatter's Rugelach
Challah
Challah Revisited

July 4
Patsy's Bourbon Slush
Jay Grelen's Southern Iced Tea
North Carolina–Style Pulled
  Pork
Docks Coleslaw
Fried Green Tomatoes
Fresh Succotash
Pickled Watermelon Rind
Buttermilk Pie
Chocolate Chip Cookies

The Bone
Ginger Lemonade
Chicken Betty's Fried Chicken
  and Gravy
Spoonbread's Potato Salad
Iceberg Lettuce with Smoked
  Bacon and Buttermilk Dressing

Ice-Cold Tomatoes with Basil
Rachel's Green Beans with Dill
Old South Buttermilk Biscuits
Bread-and-Butter Pickles
Even-Greater American Pound
  Cake
Red Velvet Cake

Labor Day
Peach Bowl
Claret Cup
Vermouth Cup
Grilled Onion Guacamole
Pamela Sherrid's Summer Pasta
Char-Grilled Tuna with Toasted
  Corn Vinaigrette and Avocado
  Salad
Stewed Corn
Jean Halberstam's Deep-Fried
  Peaches
Blueberry Pie with a Lattice Top

Super Bowl
The Bone
Pickled Shrimp
Bacon Explosion
Rosa de la Garza's Dry Chili
Carolina Chicken Bog
Green Goddess Salad
Cashew Butterscotch Bars

Valentine's Day
Improved Holland Gin
  Cocktail
Ricotta Crostini with Fresh
  Thyme and Dried Oregano
Beet and Ginger Soup with
  Cucumber
Braised Duck Legs with Pinot
  Noir Sauce
Madame Laracine's Gratin
  Dauphinois
Evelyn Sharpe's French
  Chocolate Cake

Cocktail Party for 10
Sangria
Rebujito
Sir Francis Drake

Potato, Ham, and Piquillo Pepper
    Croquetas
Pan con Tomate
Seasoned Olives
Fried Sage Leaves
Fried Chickpeas
Fried Olives
Catalan Tortilla with Aioli
Goat's-Milk Cheese, Buttered
    Brown Bread, and Salted
    Onion

Cocktail Party for 20
The Vesper
Junipero Gibson with Pickled
    Red Onion
Eggs Suffragette
Salted and Deviled Almonds
Caramelized Bacon
Caramelized Onion and
    Quark Dip
Smoked Mackerel on Toasts

Special-Occasion Cocktails
Park Avenue Cocktail
Nicole Kaplan's Gougères
Rillettes de Canard
Buckwheat Blini with Crème
    Fraîche and Caviar

Cocktails with Close Friends
Fino sherry
Roasted Feta with Thyme Honey
Marina Anagnostou's
    Spanakopetes

Picnic
Ginger Lemonade
Jay Grelen's Southern Iced Tea
Scotch Eggs
Roast Chicken Salad
Clementine's Tuna-Macaroni
    Salad
Orzo with Pine Nuts and Basil
Brie with Herbs in Bread
Pickled Shrimp
Watermelon and Tomato Salad
Haricots Verts with Balsamic
    Vinaigrette

Four-Bean Salad
Brownies
Lemon Bars

Food That Travels Well
Olive Oil–Tuna Spread With
    Lemon and Oregano
Feta Spread
Cheese Ball with Cumin, Mint,
    and Pistachios
Beet Tzatziki
Parmesan Crackers
Rillettes de Canard
Carrot Salad
Caponata
Golden Winter Puree
Summer Squash Casserole
Ratatouille with Butternut
    Squash
Boston Baked Beans
Candied Sweet Potatoes
Ralph Vetter's Sweet Potatoes
    with Lemon
Light Potato Salad
Lasagna
Boeuf Bourguignon I *and* II
Carbonnades à la Flamande
Moussaka
Sausage, Bean, and Corn Stew
Dijon and Cognac Beef Stew
Turkey with Noodles
    Florentine
Luxury Chicken Potpies
Georgia Pecan Turkey Salad
Any cookie, bar, or pie

Make-Ahead Dinner Party
Rillettes de Canard
Butternut Squash and Cider
    Soup
Dijon and Cognac Beef Stew
Mashed Potatoes Anna
Frozen Lemon Soufflé

———

Seasoned Olives
Catalan Tortilla with Aioli
Gazpacho
Grilled Leg of Lamb with Mustard
    Seeds

Baked Zucchini with Herbs and
    Tomatoes
Pretty much any dessert

Dinner for 2
Hearth's Fava Bean Salad
Spicy Lemony Clams with Pasta
Saffron Panna Cotta

Ambitious Dinner Party
Improved Holland Gin Cocktail
Nicole Kaplan's Gougères
Yellow Pepper Soup with Paprika
    Mousse *or* Diane Vreeland's
    Salade Parisienne
Halibut with Parsley-Shellfish
    Sauce
Beet Tartare
Crepes Suzette

Weekend Brunch
Honey-Orange Smoothie
Heavenly Hots
Crisp bacon
Caffè latte

Winter Brunch
Amazing Overnight Waffles
Bill Granger's Scrambled Eggs
Brioche
Winter Fruit Salad
Grapefruit and Meyer Lemon
    Marmalade

Summer Brunch
Peach Salad
Soft Scrambled Eggs with Pesto
    and Fresh Ricotta
Cream Scones *with* Strawberry
    Jam

Family Breakfast
Sour Cream Coffee Cake
Jordan Marsh's Blueberry
    Muffins

Southern Brunch
Bloody Mary
"Breakfast" Shrimp and Grits

Eggs à la Lavalette
Old South Buttermilk Biscuits
with Strawberry Jam

Italian

Ricotta Crostini with Fresh
Thyme and Dried Oregano
Zuppa di Funghi Siciliana
Potato Gnocchi
Italian Beef Stew with Rosemary
Red Wine Ice Cream

Crostini Romani
Red Wine Risotto
Coda alla Vaccinara
Spinach Roman-Style
Marcella's Pear Cake

Rhubarb Bellini
Fried Olives
Spicy Lemony Clams with Pasta
Pork Braised in Milk and Cream
Salade à la Romaine
Tortoni *or* Ricotta Kisses *or*
Almond Granita

Bagna Cauda
Parmesan Crackers
Lorane Schiff's Pesto Genovese
Braised Ligurian Chicken
Bittersweet Chocolate
Semifreddo

Crostini with Eggplant and Pine
Nut Puree
Fried Artichokes Azzurro
Corn and Yellow Tomato Risotto
with Shrimp
Sea Bass in Grappa
Raspberry Granita

Shaved Artichoke Salad with
Pine Nuts and Parmesan
Tuscan-Style Pork Spareribs
Eggplant Involtini
Italian Roast Potatoes
Escarole with Pan-Roasted Garlic
and Lemon
Panna Cotta

Asparagus alla Fontina
Polpette alla Romana
Mezzaluna Salad
Zabaglione *with* Pine Nut
Cookies *or* Canestrelli

Caesar Salad
Lasagna
Balducci's Tiramisù

Spanish

Rebujito
Fried Chickpeas
Pan con Tomate
Potato, Ham, and Piquillo Pepper
Croquetas
Marmitako *or* Cocido
Toasts with Chocolate, Olive Oil,
and Sea Salt

Chorizo Revueltos *or* Gazpacho
Sauteed Cod with Potatoes in
Chorizo-Mussel Broth
Churros with Chocolate Sauce

Catalan Tortilla with Aioli *or*
Fried Eggplant with Salmorejo
Sauce
Mushrooms with Manzanilla
Sherry
Paella
Caramel Custard

Brandade (Salt Cod Mousse) *or*
Lightly Smoked Salt Cod
Salad
White Gazpacho with Almonds
and Grapes
Eldorado Petit's Fried Noodles
with Garlic Mayonnaise *and*
roasted fish or shellfish

Fancy French

Kir Royale 38
Nicole Kaplan's Gougères
Coquilles St.-Jacques *or* Potage
Parisien with Sorrel Cream *or*
Pointe d'Asperge

Filet de Boeuf Rôti with Sauce
Bordelaise
The Most Voluptuous Cauliflower
or Cassolette of Morels, Fiddleheads, and Asparagus *or* Maître
d'Hôtel Potatoes
Taillevent's Chocolate Cake
with Pistachio Sauce *or* Crepes
Suzette

French Bistro

Leeks Vinaigrette
Boeuf Bourguignon
Madame Laracine's Gratin
Dauphinois
Salade à la Romaine
Evelyn Sharpe's French
Chocolate Cake *or*
Chocolate Rum Mousse

Alice Waters's Baked Goat
Cheese with Salad
Madame Mouriere's Cassoulet
Apple Tarte Tatin *or* Apple
Galette

Soupe à l'Ail
Artichauts Vinaigrette
Fricassee of Chicken with
Tarragon
Sautéed Potatoes with Parsley *or*
Mashed Potatoes Anna
Sautéed Asparagus with Fleur de
Sel
Breton Butter Cake *or* Chocolate
Eclairs

Rillettes de Canard
Soupe à la Bonne Femme *or* Jean
Yves Legarve's Spaghetti with
Lemon and Asparagus Sauce
Sole Grenobloise
Sautéed Potatoes with Parsley *or*
Mashed Potatoes Anna
Butter-Braised Asparagus and
Oyster Mushrooms with Peas
and Tarragon
Frozen Lemon Soufflé *or* Coeur à
la Crème with Rhubarb Sauce

German

Arundel (Sausages in Ale)
Pork Chops with Rye Bread
    Stuffing
Himmelreich (Roast Pork with
    Apricots, Apples, and Prunes)
Königsberger Klopse (Meatballs
    in Creamy Caper Sauce)
Wilted Red Cabbage Salad
Braised Red Cabbage with
    Chestnuts
Cabbage and Potato Gratin with
    Mustard Bread Crumbs
Potato Salad with Beets
Sautéed Potatoes with Parsley
Black Forest Cake
Baumkuchentorte
Laura Brody's Chocolate Cherry
    Torte
Ofenschlupfer (Almond Bread
    Pudding)
Spice Krinkles
Gingersnaps
Honey Spice Cookies
German Toast
Fresh Plum Kuchen

Middle Eastern

Jennifer's Moroccan Tea
Seasoned Olives
Hummus bi Tahini
Beet Tzatziki
Moroccan Carrot Salad
Roasted Carrot and Red Lentil
    Ragout
Green Lentils with Roasted Beets
    and Preserved Lemon
Eggplant Gratin with Saffron
    Custard
Yogurt Rice
Couscous Salad
Bulgur Salad with Pomegranate
    Dressing and Toasted Nuts
Iraqi Grape Leaves Stuffed with
    Lamb, Mint, and Cinnamon
Choresh Qormeh Sabzi (Green
    Herb Stew)
Arnaki Araka (Lamb with
    Peas)

Crispy Chickpeas with Ground
    Meat
Moroccan Chicken Smothered
    in Olives
Almond and Buttermilk Sorbet
Moroccan Rice Pudding
Flourless Apricot Honey Soufflé

Indian

Aloo Kofta
Green Beans with Coriander-
    Coconut Crust
Mulligatawny Soup
Manjula Gokal's Gujarati Mango
    Soup
Baked Goan Fish with Fresh
    Green Chile Chutney
Crab and Coconut Curry
Ceylon Curry of Oysters
Bombay Curry
Bademiya's Justly Famous Bombay
    Chile-and-Cilantro Chicken
Sweet (or Savory) Lassi
Mango Lassi
Mango Ice Cream

Southeast Asian

Kaffir Lime Lemonade
Pad Thai–Style Rice Salad
Hoppers (Coconut Crepes)
Fresh Salmon and Lime Cakes
Tuna Curry
Minced Fish Salad (Koy Pa)
Jean-Georges Vongerichten's
    Crab Salad
Mi Quang (Rice Noodles with
    Shrimp, Herbs, and Fried Pork
    Rinds)
Thai Sole Chowder with Lima
    Beans and Corn
Laotian Catfish Soup
Pork-and-Toasted-Rice-Powder
    Spring Rolls
Chicken with Lime, Chile and
    Fresh Herbs
Southeast Asian Chicken Two
    Ways
Pho Bo (Hanoi Beef Soup)
Shaking Beef

Thai Beef Salad
Pork and Squash in Coconut
    Milk
Malaysian Pork Stew with
    Traditional Garnishes
Coconut Rice Pudding with Lime
    Syrup
Sticky Rice with Mango
Glazed Mango with Sour Cream
    Sorbet and Black Pepper
Cantaloupe–Star Anise Sorbet
Pineapple Carpaccio with Lime
    Sorbet
Poached Pears with Asian Spices

New England

Clam Chowder
Oyster Chowder
Lobster Bisque I *and* II
Butternut Squash and Cider Soup
Basic Corn Chowder
Docks Coleslaw
Red Cabbage Glazed with Maple
    Syrup
James Beard's Pureed Parsnips
Stewed Corn
Boston Baked Beans
Fresh Succotash
Corn Bread Stuffing
Macaroni with Ham and Cheese
Lobster Roll
Deviled Crabs
Stuffed Clams
Clambake in a Pot
Spicy New England Pot Roast
Ann Seranne's Rib Roast of Beef
Meat and Spinach Loaf
Sour-Milk Cake
Molasses Cup Cakes with Lemon
    Icing
Maida's Blueberry Crumb Cake
Teddie's Apple Cake
Sally Darr's Golden Delicious
    Apple Tart
Mrs. Raymond Schenk's Pumpkin
    Cake
Cranberry Upside-Down Cake
New England Spider Cake
Blueberry Ice Cream

Indian Pudding
Blueberry Pie with a Lattice Top
Molasses Candy
Brown Sugar Shortbread
Maple Shortbread Bars
Ruth's Oatmeal Crisps
Maida Heatter's Preheated-Oven
 Popovers
Boston Brown Bread
Johnnycake
New England Grape Butter
Cranberry Chutney
Holiday Cranberry Chutney
Spiced Hard Sauce

Southern
Mint Julep
Jay Grelen's Southern Iced Tea
Patsy's Bourbon Slush
Eggs Louisiana
Ramos Gin Fizz
Sazerac
The Spice Boys' Cheese Ball
Caramelized Bacon
Cheese Straws
Pickled Shrimp
Julia Harrison Adams's Pimento
 Cheese Spread
Okra Soup with Beef (and
 Oysters)
Paul Prudhomme's Cajun-Style
 Gumbo
Fried Green Tomatoes
Florida Beets
Fried Corn
Candied Sweet Potatoes
Sweet Potato Casserole
Hoppin' John
Pan-Barbecued Shrimp
Chicken Betty's Fried Chicken
 and Gravy
Turducken
Georgia Pecan Turkey Salad
Carolina Chicken Bog
North Carolina–Style Pulled
 Pork
Cleo's Daddy's Barbecued Ribs
Apple City World-Champion
 Baby Back Ribs

Red Velvet Cake
Maria Tillman Jackson Rogers's
 Carrot Cake
Mrs. Foster's Frosty Lime Pie
Key Lime Pie
Coconut Pie
Strawberry Charlotte
Jellied Strawberry Pie
Lemon Cheese Pie
Mississippi Pecan Pie
Bourbon Pecan Pie
Buttermilk Pie
Charleston Coconut Sweeties
Pralines
Sand Tarts (Pecan Sandies)
Old South Buttermilk Biscuits
Nancy Reagan's Monkey Bread
Mississippi Pancakes
Chow-Chow
Barbecue Sauce
Sliced Green Tomato Pickles
Pickled Watermelon Rind
Brandied Peaches
Bread-and-Butter Pickles
Sauce Rémoulade (for Shrimp)

Latin American
La Paloma
Guacamole Tostadas
Grilled Onion Guacamole
Black Bean Soup with Salsa and
 Jalapeño Corn Bread Muffins
Pumpkin–Black Bean Soup
Tortilla Soup
Maida Heatter's Cuban Black
 Beans and Rice
Ceviche with Mint and Mango
Fish Tacos
Yucatán Fish with Crisp Garlic
Shrimp in Green Sauce
Staff Meal Chicken with Salsa
 Verde
Rosa de la Garza's Dry Chili
Coloradito
Nueces Canyon Cabrito
El Parian's Carne Asada
Aztec Hot Chocolate Pudding
Churros with Chocolate Sauce
Dulce de Lece

Vegetarian
Eggplant Involtini
Curried Root Vegetable Stew
 with Dumplings
Takeout-Style Sesame Noodles
Pasta with Yogurt and Caramel-
 ized Onions, from Kassos
Spaghetti with Fried Eggs and
 Roasted Peppers
Fettuccine with Preserved Lemon
 and Roasted Garlic
Swiss Chard Casserole with
 Farfalle and Cheeses
Cremini Mushroom Pasta with
 Wilted Arugula, Goat Cheese,
 and Extra Virgin Olive Oil
Cucumber Risotto with Yellow
 Peppers and Herbs
Trenette, Fagliolini, e Patate al
 Pesto
Pamela Sherrid's Summer Pasta
Conchiglie Al Forno with
 Mushrooms and Radicchio
Spaghettini with Vegetables and
 Pepper Vodka Sauce
Jean Yves Legarve's Spaghetti with
 Lemon and Asparagus Sauce
Ed Giobbi's Sweet Red Pepper
 Sauce for Pasta
Manicotti with Ricotta Cheese
Mrs. Sebastiani's Malfatti
Lorane Schiff's Pesto Genovese

Kids' Birthday Party
Sweet-and-Salty Popcorn with
 Orange Blossom Honey
Caramelized Bacon
Macaroni with Ham and Cheese
Breaded Chicken Breasts with
 Parmesan Cheese
Fresh Succotash
Party Balls
Chocolate Dump-It Cake

Dinner on a Moment's
Notice
Pasta with Vodka
Spaghetti with Fried Eggs and
 Roasted Peppers

The Minimalist's Paella
Pasta with Fast Sausage Ragu
Salmon and Tomatoes in Foil
Shrimp in Green Sauce
Sea Bass in Grappa
Grilled Hanger Steak
Breaded Chicken Breasts with
    Parmesan Cheese
Butternut Squash and Cider
    Soup
Red Lentil Soup with Lemon
Speedy Fish Stew with Orange
    and Fennel
Steamed Lemon Pudding
Brownies
Panna Cotta
David Eyre's Pancake
Coupe Lena Horne
Grapefruit Fluff
Peach Salad
Poached Pears in Brandy and
    Red Wine
Carmelized Brown Butter Rice
    Krispies Treats

Freezing-Cold Out
Mushrooms Stuffed with Duxelles
    and Sausage
Dijon and Cognac Beef Stew
Sautéed Potatoes with Parsley
Salade à la Romaine
Aztec Hot Chocolate Pudding

Sweltering Hot
Tom's Chilled Cucumber Soup
Salade Niçoise
Raspberry Granita

Dinner on the Deck
Mezzaluna Salad
Hot Penne with Chilled Tomato
    Sauce and Charred Tuna
Fruit Crostatas

———

Pork Burgers
Light Potato Salad
Watermelon and Tomato Salad
Coconut Pie

———

'21' Club Hamburger
Spoonbread's Potato Salad
Docks Coleslaw
Chez Panisse Meyer Lemon
    Meringue Pie

Afternoon Tea
Cream Scones
Strawberry Jam
Banana Tea Bread
Crumpets
Two-Day Madeleines with
    Brown Butter
Chocolate Eclairs
An Incredible Date-Nut Bread
Shirley Estabrook Wood's
    Zucchini Bread
Onion Rings
Welsh Rarebit
Cheese Crusts
Scotch Woodcock
Open-Faced Tomato Sandwich

Movie Snacks
Sweet-and-Salty Popcorn with
    Orange Blossom Honey

To Sugar or Crystallize Pop-Corn
Spiced Pecans
Salted and Deviled Almonds
Saratoga Potatoes
Maple Shortbread Bars
Buttery French TV Snacks
Butterscotch
Chocolate Caramels

Bake Sale
Brownies
Lemon Bars
Brown Butter Peach Bars
Caramelized Brown Butter Rice
    Krispies Treats
Brown Sugar Shortbread
Cashew Butterscotch Bars
Flat-and-Chewy Chocolate Chip
    Cookies
Chocolate Chip Cookies
Chocolate Quakes
Almond-Lemon Macaroons
Ruth's Oatmeal Crisps
English Gingersnaps
Straight-Up Rhubarb Pie
Apple Crumb Pie
Papa's Apple Pound Cake
Teddie's Apple Cake
Even-Greater American
    Pound Cake
Peanut Butter Cupcakes with
    Milk Chocolate Frosting
Molasses Cup Cakes with Lemon
    Icing

SOURCES

AMAZON

www.amazon.com
Go-to for all variety of ingredients, from dried lotus seeds to hickory chips for barbecuing.

Applewood dust or chips
Candied citron
Candied ginger
Candied orange peel
Candied pineapple
Ceylon tea
Chinese egg noodles
Cinnamon syrup
Clear apple jelly
Crème de banana
Dark soy sauce
Dried lotus seeds
Dried shrimp
Elderberry or raspberry syrup
Fermented black beans
Fish sauce, Thai and Vietnamese
Hickory or oak chips
Ketjap manis
Kombu
Licorice root
Maple extract
Matcha
Mirin
Oyster Sauce
Palm Sugar
Peppermint extract (Boyjian's)
Rice powder
Sambal oelek
Shrimp paste
Sour or morello cherries (jarred)
Sriracha
Sticky rice
Tart cherry concentrate
Thai or Lao sticky rice
Vanilla paste
White Miso
Yuzu Juice

ASTOR WINES & SPIRITS

www.astorwines.com;
212-674-7500; 399 Lafayette
Street, New York NY 10013
Solid selection of high and low, plus a ready-to-help staff.

Amaretto
Apricot eau-de-vie
Aquavit
Cassis syrup
Cherry liqueur
Cointreau
Crème de cacao (white and brown)
Galliano
Green crème de menthe
Pepper vodka
Stolichnaya Gold vodka
Dry Swiss Wine (Fendant or Neuchâtel)

BENTON'S SMOKY MOUNTAIN COUNTRY HAMS

www.bentonshams.com;
423-442-5003
Slow-cured country hams, prosciutto, and bacon

BOB'S RED MILL NATURAL FOODS

www.bobsredmill.com;
800-349-2173
Bob's Red Mill produces a wide variety of organic and whole-grain products, from flours to baking mixes and grains, including a full line of gluten-free products.

Almond flour
Buckwheat flour
Rye flour
Semolina flour
Soy flour, full-fat
Tapioca, small pearl

CALIFORNIA CAVIAR

www.californiacaviar.com;
415-921-1226
In addition to sustainable domestic caviars, California Caviar sells smoked salmon, truffles, and crème fraîche.

CHEFSHOP

www.chefshop.com;
800-596-0885
Producer-driven sustainable ingredients, including Italian salt-packed anchovies, French le Puy lentils, and a large selection of dry goods.

Caper berries
Le Puy lentils
Marrow beans
Recca salt-packed anchovies
White verjus

D'ARTAGNAN

www.dartagnan.com;
800-327-8246
The best source for foie gras, game, truffles, pâté, sausage, smoked meats, and organic poultry.

Demi-glace
Duck
Piegeon
Quail
Quail eggs
Rabbit
Sweetbreads
Venison stew meat

EARTHY DELIGHTS

www.earthy.com; 800-367-4709
A favorite among chefs, Earthy offers the freshest mushrooms, as well as mushroom powder, and other wild-harvested items. They also offer

cheeses, vinegars, and other hard-to-find ingredients.

Chanterelle mushrooms
Dried morel mushrooms
Dried porcini mushrooms
Fiddlehead ferns

FORMAGGIO KITCHEN

www.formaggiokitchen.com;
888-212-3224; 244 Huron Avenue,
Cambridge MA 02138

A Cambridge, Massachusetts, institution for over 30 years, Formaggio Kitchen specializes in fine imported cheeses, jams, coffee, wine, and these delicate dried plums from the Aquitaine region of France.

Pruneaux d'Agen

GUITTARD CHOCOLATE COMPANY

www.guittard.com; 800-468-2462

Guittard has been making quality chocolate since the nineteenth century.

72% cacao bittersweet chocolate
Nocturne 91% cacao extra dark bar

IGOURMET

www.igourmet.com;
877-446-8763

Igourmet is the Amazon.com of food, with a beautiful store of high-end, gourmet, and imported food products.

Almond oil
Chestnuts
Cotija cheese
Creole mustard
Fleur de sel
Fromage blanc
Hazelnut oil
Kefalotyri cheese
Lingonberry preserves
Maldon sea salt
Matcha (green tea powder)
Mexican chocolate
Oaxaca cheese
Pepitas
Peppadew peppers
Pistachio oil
Tasso ham
Walnut oil
White truffle oil
Whole-grain Meaux mustard

K&L WINE MERCHANTS

www.klwines.com; 877-559-4637;
3005 El Camino Real, Redwood
City CA 94061

K&L stocks wines from around the world at competitive prices; it has a knowledgeable staff and comprehensive website.

Absinthe
Absolut citron vodka
Appleton Estate V/X rum
Bacardi Gold Label rum
Baker's 107-proof rum
Chartreuse
Cruzan 5-year-old rum
Deluxe bourbon
Fino sherry
Ginger beer
Grappa
Haitian white rum
Herradura Hacienda del Cristero
    tequila blanco
Holland gin
Italian vermouth
Luxardo maraschino liqueur
Madeira
Manzanilla sherry
Marsala
Ouzo
Poire Williams
Sauternes
Shaoxing wine
Spanish brandy
Tio Pepe dry sherry
Triple Sec

KALUSTYAN'S

www.kalustyans.com;
800-352-3451; 123 Lexington
Avenue, New York NY 10016

Kalustyan's seems to have every ingredient ever created, with a focus on Indian, Middle Eastern, and Asian goods. Most of their stock is available online, but stopping by the store is always a promising adventure.

Chana dal
Chickpea flour
Coarse semolina
Coconut: chips, desiccated,
    unsweetened, and shelled whole
Coconut oil
Dates, Deglect Noor and Medjool
Dhana dal
Fenugreek seeds
Fresh curry leaves
Galangal

Ghee
Harissa
Indian pickles
Jarred and canned grape leaves
Jasmine tea pearls
Kaffir lime leaves
Kalunji seeds
Mango pulp (Alphonso)
Mustard oil
Orange flower water
Pappadum
Pasilla chile, dried
Pomegranate molasses
Preserved lemons
Red lentils
Rosewater
Sichuan peppercorns
Tamarind concentrate
Thai bird chiles
Urad dal
White spelt flour

KEGWORKS

www.kegworks.com;
877-636-3673

KegWorks will help you set up a well-stocked bar, with a large selection of bartending tools and premium bitters and syrups.

Falernum
Orange bitters
Peychaud bitters

KING ARTHUR FLOUR

www.kingarthurflour.com;
800-827-6836

This Vermont company makes high-quality all-natural flours and mixes and supplies hard-to-find baking ingredients.

Bittersweet chocolate disks or fèves
Italian "00" flour

LA TIENDA

www.tienda.com;
888-331-4362

La Tienda imports high-quality Spanish and Latin ingredients, including Serrano ham, sausages, smoked paprika, and tuna packed in olive oil.

Fideos
Fire-roasted piquillo peppers
Chorizo, Mexican and Spanish
Saffron
Serrano ham
Smoked pork chops and loin
    (lomo)

Spanish smoked paprika
(pimentón)
Tuna packed in olive oil

LOBEL'S
www.lobels.com; 877-783-4512
Top-quality prime and Wagyu beef, lamb, veal, Berkshire pork, pork belly, and sausages, and personal service from the Lobel family.

THE MEADOW
www.atthemeadow.com;
888-388-4633
This Portland, Oregon, shop specializes in artisan salt from around the world, orange flower water, chocolate, and local and European wines. They also have a terrific selection of bitters and syrups.

MELISSA'S
www.melissas.com;
800-588-0151
Melissa's is the largest distributor of specialty produce in the United States, with a vast selection of exotic fruits and vegetables, Latin ingredients, and chiles.

Bay leaves, fresh
Cipollini onions
Italian prune plums
Key limes
Lemongrass
Meyer lemons
New Mexico chiles, dried
Okra
Plantains
Serrano chiles
Sorrel
Tomatillos

MING'S PANTRY
www.mingspantry.com;
866-646-4266
Ming's Pantry is Chef Ming Tsai's online store and a fantastic resource for Asian ingredients, like Chinese vinegars—including black and rice vinegars—and cooking wines.

MOZZARELLA COMPANY
www.mozzco.com; 800-798-2954
This artisanal cheese company just outside Dallas makes excellent mozzarella and Latin cheeses like queso blanco (panela).

MURRAY'S CHEESE
www.murrayscheese.com;
888-692-4339
This New York City cheese shop stocks an incomparable selection of cheeses—from ricotta to Comté—from around the world.

NUTS ONLINE
www.nutsonline.com;
800-558-6887
Roasted or raw, salted or unsalted, nuts and dried fruit by the pound. They carry exceptional figs, raw cashews, and Turkish apricots.

PENZEYS SPICES
www.penzeys.com; 800-741-7787
Penzeys carries whole and ground chiles, dried herbs, spices, and many spice blends.

Ancho chile powder
Ancho chiles, dried
Cardamom pods
Filé powder
Chipotle chiles, dried
Guajillo chiles, dried
Chiles de árbol, dried
Hungarian paprika
Vietnamese cassia cinnamon

PETROSSIAN
www.petrossian.com;
800-828-9241
Stocks all grades of caviar as well as pike, trout, and salmon roe—also sustainable varieties.

Black caviar
Osetra Caviar

PIMENTO WOOD
www.pimentowood.com;
612-868-5375
Pimento wood sticks and chips for barbecuing and jerk cooking.

RUSS & DAUGHTERS
www.russanddaughters.com;
800-787-7229
A purveyor of caviar, whitefish roe, and smoked and cured salmon and herring, and a New York City institution.

Golden whitefish caviar
Salmon caviar
Smoked mackerel
Smoked trout
Trout caviar

SAVANNAH BEE COMPANY
www.savannahbee.com;
800-955-5080
Savannah sells a wide range of artisan honeys from orange blossom to tupelo to sourwood.

SID WAINER & SON
www.sidwainer.com;
888-743-9246
A nearly century-old specialty-foods company based in New Bedford, Massachusetts, and a great source for hard-to-find seasonal produce, some of which they grow themselves.

Lemon thyme
Lovage
Mâche
Mung bean sprouts
Pea greens and shoots
Romano beans
Shiso leaves

SMUCKER'S
www.onlinestore.smucker.com;
800-742-6729
Smucker's now owns White Lily and sells this beloved brand's delicate, low-protein flour through their website.

VANNS SPICES
www.vannsspices.com;
800-583-1693
Vanns offers custom spice blends and all-natural herbs and rubs, including grains of paradise and asafoetida.

ZINGERMAN'S
www.zingermans.com;
888-636-8162
This quirky Ann Arbor, Michigan, store sources fresh-baked breads, cheeses, varietal coffee, estate bottled olive oils, salt-packed capers, and many other products from around the world.

CREDITS

Chapter 1: Drinks, Cocktails, Punches, and Glögg

1948: PEACH BOWL

Adapted from *American Wines*, by Tom Marvel and Frank Schoonmaker. New York: Duell, Sloan & Pearce (1941).

1958: GIN RICKEY

Adapted from *The Fine Art of Mixing Drinks*, by David A. Embury. New York: Doubleday (1948)

1984: HOT BUTTERED RUM

Adapted from *Rum Yesterday and Today*, by Hugh Barty-King and Anton Massel. London: Heinemann (1983).

1987: MINT JULEP

Adapted from *The Williamsburg Art of Cookery or, Accomplish'd Gentlewoman's Companion: Being a Collection of upwards of Five Hundred of the most Ancient & Approv'd Recipes in Virginia Cookery*, by Helen Bullock. Williamsburg, VA: Colonial Williamsburg Foundation (1985).

1989: SWEET (OR SAVORY) LASSI

Adapted from *Classic Indian Cooking*, by Julie Sahni. New York: Morrow (1980).

1999: JAMES BEARD'S CHAMPAGNE PUNCH

Adapted from *Champagne Cocktails*, by Anistatia Miller, Jared Brown, and Don Gatterdam. New York: Morrow (1999).

Chapter 2: Hors d'Oeuvres, Snacks, and Small Dishes

1998: FRESH AND SMOKED SALMON SPREAD

Adapted from *Le Bernardin Cookbook: Four Star Simplicity*, by Maguy Le Coze and Eric Ripert. New York: Broadway (1998).

1999: TOASTS WITH WALNUT SAUCE

Adapted from *Recipes from Paradise*, by Fred Plotkin. Boston: Little, Brown (1997).

2002: CROSTINI WITH EGGPLANT AND PINE NUT PUREE

Adapted from *Local Flavors*, by Deborah Madison. New York: Broadway (2002).

2006: BEET TZATZIKI

Adapted from *Spice: Flavors of the Eastern Mediterranean*, by Ana Sortun. New York: Morrow (2006).

2007: SQUASHED TOMATOES

Adapted from *Flavors of Puglia*, by Nancy Harmon Jenkins. New York: Broadway (1997).

2008: OLIVE OIL–TUNA SPREAD WITH LEMON AND OREGANO

Adapted from *Patricia Wells's Trattoria*, by Patricia Wells. New York: Scribner (1999).

2008: PICKLED SHRIMP

Adapted from *Frank Stitt's Southern Table*, by Frank Stitt. New York: Artisan (2004).

Chapter 3: Soups

1974: SOUPE À L'OIGNON GRATINÉE

Adapted from *Gastronomie Pratique*, by Ali-Bab. Paris: Flammarion (1993).

1977: FAKI (GREEK LENTIL SOUP)

Adapted from Vilma Liacouras Chantiles, author of *The Food of Greece*. New York: Atheneum (1975).

1980: CURRIED ZUCCHINI SOUP

Adapted from *Gad Zukes*, by the Allentown, Pennsylvania, Branch of the American Association of University Women. Copyright date unknown.

1994: WHITE GAZPACHO WITH ALMONDS AND GRAPES

Adapted from *From Tapas to Meze*, by Joanne Weir. Berkeley: Ten Speed Press (2004).

1996: ISMAIL MERCHANT'S VERY HOT CHICKEN SOUP

Adapted from *The Whole World Loves Chicken Soup*, by Mimi Sheraton. New York: Warner Books (2000).

1997: TURKISH SPLIT-PEA SOUP WITH MINT AND PAPRIKA

Adapted from *Kitchen Conversation*, by Joyce Goldstein. New York: Morrow (1997).

1998: CREAMY FARRO AND CHICKPEA SOUP

Adapted from *Mediterranean Grains and Greens*, by Paula Wolfert. New York: Morrow (1998).

1999: PHO BO (HANOI BEEF SOUP)

Adapted from *Simple Art of Vietnamese Cooking*, by Binh Duong and Marcia Kiesel. New York: Prentice Hall Press (1991).

1999: CLEAR STEAMED CHICKEN SOUP WITH GINGER

Adapted from *A Spoonful of Ginger*, by Nina Simonds. New York: Stewart Tabori Chang (1999).

2000: POTAGE PARISIEN WITH SORREL CREAM

Adapted from *Café Boulud Cookbook*, by Daniel Boulud and Dorie Greenspan. New York: Scribner (1999).

2003: MANJULA GOKAL'S GUJARATI MANGO SOUP

Adapted from a recipe by Manjula Gokal in *From Curries to Kebabs*, by Madhur Jaffrey. New York: Clarkson Potter (2003).

2003: PASTA AND BEAN SOUP

Adapted from *Tom Valenti's Soups, Stews, and One-Pot Meals*, by Tom Valenti. New York: Scribner (2003).

Chapter 4: Salads

1983: ALICE WATERS'S BAKED GOAT CHEESE WITH SALAD

Adapted from *The Chez Panisse Menu Cookbook*, by Alice Waters. New York: Random House (1995).

2000: DIANE VREELAND'S SALADE PARISIENNE

Adapted from *How to Do It*, by Elsa Maxwell. Boston: Little, Brown (1957).

2000: AVOCADO AND BEET SALAD WITH CITRUS VINAIGRETTE

Adapted from *The Chez Panisse Café Cookbook*, by Alice Waters. New York: Morrow (1999).

Chapter 5: Vegetables

2000: GREEN BEANS WITH CORIANDER-COCONUT CRUST

Adapted from *Raji Cuisine: Indian Flavors, French Passion*, by Raji Jallepalli. New York: Morrow (2000).

2001: ZUCCHINI WITH CRÈME FRAÎCHE PESTO

Adapted from *The Crème Fraîche Cookbook*, by Sadie Kendall. Atascadero, CA: Ridgeview (1989).

2002: FRIED EGGPLANT WITH SALMOREJO SAUCE

Adapted from *¡Delicioso!: The Regional Cooking of Spain*, by Penelope Casas. New York: Knopf (1996).

2006: WILTED CHARD WITH PICKLED RED ONION

Adapted from *Vegetarian Cooking for Everyone*, by Deborah Madison. New York: Broadway (1997).

2007: ZUCCHINI CARPACCIO WITH AVOCADO

Adapted from *Vegetable Harvest*, by Patricia Wells. New York: Morrow (2007).

2008: STEAMED FENNEL WITH RED PEPPER OIL

Adapted from *A Platter of Figs and Other Recipes*, by David Tanis. New York: Artisan (2008).

Chapter 6: Potatoes, Corn, and Legumes

1979: BLENDER CORN PUDDING

Adapted from *Ale-Wives to Zucchini*, by the Southampton Historical Society. Southampton, NY (1976).

1993: DRUNKEN BEANS

Adapted from *The New Texas Cuisine*, by Stephan Pyles. New York: Doubleday (1993).

1998: GREEN LENTILS WITH ROASTED BEETS AND PRESERVED LEMON

Adapted from *Vegetarian Cooking for Everyone*, by Deborah Madison. New York: Broadway (1997).

1998: YOGURT WITH PLANTAIN AND MANGO

Adapted from *Madhur Jaffrey's World Vegetarian*, by Madhur Jaffrey. New York: Clarkson Potter (1999).

1999: BAKED CHICKPEAS

Adapted from *The Basque Kitchen*, by Gerald Hirigoyen. New York: Morrow (1999).

1999: MASHED POTATOES ANNA

Adapted from *A Passion for Potatoes*, by Lydie Marshall. New York: Morrow (1992).

2001: PUREE OF PEAS AND WATERCRESS

Adapted from *The Loaves and Fishes Cookbook*, by Anna Pump. New York: Macmillan (1987).

2007: POTATO "TOSTONES" (FLATTENED POTATOES)

Adapted from *Recipes: A Collection for the Modern Cook*, by Susan Spungen. New York: Morrow (2005).

Chapter 7: Pasta, Rice, Grains, and Stuffings

1982: PASTA WITH VODKA

Adapted from *Italian Cooking in the Grand Tradition*, by Jo Bettoja and Anna Maria Cornetto. New York: Dial Press (1982).

2001: PASTA WITH YOGURT AND CARAMELIZED ONIONS, FROM KASSOS

Adapted from *The Glorious Foods of Greece*, by Diane Kochilas. New York: Morrow (2001).

2007: SAVORY RICOTTA PUDDING

Adapted from *Sunday Suppers at Lucques*, by Suzanne Goin. New York: Knopf (2005).

2007: YOGURT RICE

Adapted from *Grains, Greens, and Grated Coconuts*, by Ammini Ramachandran. Birmington, IN: iUniverse (2007).

2008: RICE AND PEAS (JAMAICAN RICE WITH COCONUT AND RED BEANS)

Adapted from *Jerk: Barbecue from Jamaica*, by Helen Willinsky. Berkeley: Crossing Press (1990).

Chapter 9: Fish and Shellfish

1997: NINA SIMONDS'S BROILED HALIBUT WITH MISO GLAZE

Adapted from *A Spoonful of Ginger*, by Nina Simonds. New York: Knopf (1999).

2000: FRESH SALMON AND LIME CAKES

Adapted from *Flavours*, by Donna Hay. New York: Morrow (2003).

2002: GRILLED MOROCCAN SARDINES

Adapted from *The Moroccan Collection*, by Hilaire Walden. London: Hamlyn (1998).

2003: SWEET-AND-SOUR SALMON IN ALMOND PRUNE SAUCE

Adapted from *Delights from the Garden of Eden*, by Nawal Nasrallah. Bloomington, IN: Author House (2003).

2006: SCANDINAVIAN SEAFOOD SALAD

Adapted from *Aquavit: And the New Scandinavian Cuisine*, by Marcus Samuelsson. New York: Houghton Mifflin Harcourt (2003).

2006: FRIED MUSSELS WITH ALMOND-GARLIC SAUCE

Adapted from *Spice: Flavors of the Eastern Mediterranean*, by Ana Sortun. New York: Morrow (2006).

2007: OVEN-ROASTED BRANZINO WITH HAZELNUT PICADA

Adapted from *The Zuni Café Cookbook*, by Judy Rodgers. New York: Norton (2002).

Chapter 10: Poultry and Game

2000: STEAMED AND CRISPED DUCK

Adapted from *Classic Chinese Cuisine*, by Nina Simonds. Boston: Houghton Mifflin (2003).

2002: BRAISED DUCK LEGS WITH PINOT NOIR SAUCE

Adapted from *BayWolf Restaurant Cookbook*, by Michael Wild and Lauren Lyle. Berkeley: Ten Speed Press (2004).

2002: MOROCCAN CHICKEN SMOTHERED IN OLIVES

Adapted from *Mediterranean Cooking*, by Paula Wolfert. Rev. ed. New York: Ecco (1999).

Chapter 11: Beef, Veal, Lamb, and Pork

1949: EISENHOWER'S STEAK IN THE FIRE

Adapted from *What's Cooking on Governors Island*. Compiled by Members of St. Cornelius Altar Guild. Third Ed. New York (1949).

1998: COLORADITO (RED *MOLE* WITH PORK)

Adapted from *The Food and Life of Oaxaca*, by Zarela Martinez. New York: Wiley (1997).

1999: GRILLED HANGER STEAK

Adapted from *Prime Time: The Lobels' Guide to Great Grilled Meats*, by Evan, Leon, Stanley, and Mark Lobel. New York: Wiley (1999).

2001: BRINED AND ROASTED PORK BELLY

Adapted from *The Whole Beast*, by Fergus Henderson. New York: HarperCollins (2004).

2001: VITELLO TONNATO

Sauce adapted from *The Essentials of Classic Italian Cooking*, by Marcella Hazan. New York: Knopf (1992).

2002: BRISKET IN SWEET-AND-SOUR SAUCE

Adapted from *Levana's Table*, by Levana Kirschenbaum. New York: Abrams (2002).

2007: HUNAN BEEF WITH CUMIN

Adapted from *Revolutionary Chinese Cookbook*, by Fuchsia Dunlop. New York: Norton (2007).

2007: ROASTED MARROW BONES

Adapted from *The Whole Beast*, by Fergus Henderson. New York: HarperCollins (2004).

2008: PORK ARROSTO WITH PRUNES AND GRAPPA

Adapted from *Urban Italian*, by Andrew Carmellini and Gwen Hyman. New York: Bloomsbury USA (2008).

2008: EL PARIAN'S CARNE ASADA

Sauce adapted from *The Art of Mexican Cooking*, by Diana Kennedy. New York: Bantam (1989).

2008: APPLE CITY WORLD-CHAMPION BABY BACK RIBS

Adapted from *Peace, Love, and Barbecue*, by Mike Mills and Amy Mills Tunnicliffe. Emmaus, PA: Rodale Books (2005).

Chapter 12: Sauces, Dressings, Condiments, Rubs, and Preserves

1997: SWEET-AND-PULPY TOMATO KETCHUP

Adapted from *Pure Ketchup*, by Andrew Smith. Washington, DC: Smithsonian (2001).

2008: FRESH RICOTTA

Adapted from *Michael Chiarello's Casual Cooking*, by Michael Chiarello with Janet Fletcher. San Francisco: Chronicle Books (2002).

Chapter 13: Breakfast and Brunch

2002: AMAZING OVERNIGHT WAFFLES

Adapted from *Mollie Katzen's Sunlight Café*, by Mollie Katzen. New York: Hyperion (2002).

2005: HAZELNUT-LEMON-RICOTTA PANCAKES

Foundation of the recipe adapted from *Joy of Cooking*, by Irma S. Rombauer. Marion Rombauer Becker, and Ethan Becker. New York: Scribner (2006).

Chapter 14: Breads and Baking

2003: NANCY REAGAN'S MONKEY BREAD

Adapted from Nancy Reagan, printed in *The American Cancer Society Cookbook*, by Anne Lindsay. New York: Hearst (1985).

Chapter 15: Cookies and Candy

1877: MOLASSES CANDY

Pulling instructions adapted from *The Ultimate Candy Book*, by Bruce Weinstein. New York: Morrow (2000).

1879: PEPPERMINTS

Adapted from *The Ultimate Candy Book*, by Bruce Weinstein. New York: Morrow (2000).

1973: SPICE KRINKLES

Adapted from *Fanny Pierson Crane: Her Receipts*, by Mary Donovan et al. Montclair, NJ: Montclair Historical Society (1972).

1989: CANESTRELLI (SHORTBREAD FROM OVADA)

Adapted from *Country Host Cookbook*, by Rona Deme. New York: Quick Fox (1980).

2000: ENGLISH TOFFEE

Adapted from *Chocolate*, by Nick Malgieri. New York: Morrow (1998).

2001: MAPLE SHORTBREAD BARS

Adapted from *The New Carryout Cuisine*, by Phyllis Méras with Linda Glick Conway. Boston: Houghton Mifflin (1986).

2002: CHOCOLATE QUAKES

Adapted from *Got Milk? The Cookie Book*, by Peggy Cullen. San Francisco: Chronicle Books (2000).

2005: LEMON GUMDROPS

Adapted from *Making Great Candy*, by Laura Dover Doran. New York: Lark Books (2001).

2007: ALMOND-LEMON MACAROONS (ALMENDRADOS)

Adapted from *Dulce lo Vivas*, by Ana Bensadón. Miami: Planeta Publishing (2006).

2008: BUTTERY FRENCH TV SNACKS (CROQ-TÉLÉ).

Adapted from *Field Guide to Cookies*, by Anita Chu. Philadelphia: Quirk Books (2008).

Chapter 16: Frozen Desserts

1879: NESSELRODE PUDDING

Adapted from *Anne Bowman's New Cookery-Book*, by Anne Bowman. London: Routledge (date unknown).

2001: BLACKBERRY ICE CREAM WITH CANDIED LEMON ZEST

Adapted from *The Fearrington House Cookbook*, by Jenny Fitch. Chapel Hill, NC: Ventana (1987).

2002: MANGO ICE CREAM

Adapted from *Mediterranean Street Food*, by Anissa Helou. New York: Morrow (2002).

2006: STRAWBERRY SORBET

Adapted from *London River Café Cook Book*, by Ruth Rogers and Rose Gray. London: Ebury Press (1996).

2009: TANGERINE SHERBET

Adapted, with significant liberties, from *Chez Panisse Fruit*, by Alice Waters. New York: Morrow (2002).

Chapter 17: Cakes

1882: FILBERT TORTE

Icing adapted from *Birthday Cakes*, by Kathryn Kleinman. San Francisco: Chronicle Books (2004).

1948: MOLASSES CUP CAKES WITH LEMON ICING

Adapted from *Brer Rabbit's New Orleans Molasses Recipes*. Penick and Ford (1948).

1965: HUGUENOT TORTE

Adapted from *The First Ladies Cookbook*, by Margaret Brown Klapthor. New York: Parents' Magazine Press (1975).

1981: MARIA TILLMAN JACKSON ROGERS'S CARROT CAKE

Adapted from *My Mother Cooked My Way Through Harvard with These Creole Recipes*, by Mrs. Walter Tillman and Oscar A. Rogers. Hattiesburg: University and College Press of Mississippi (1972).

1985: PANFORTE (TRADITIONAL SIENESE FRUITCAKE)

Adapted from *The Italian Baker*, by Carol Field. New York: Morrow (1985).

1991: MARCELLA'S PEAR CAKE

Adapted from *More Classic Italian Cooking*, by Marcella Hazan. New York: Random House (1995).

1995: TAILLEVENT'S CHOCOLATE CAKE WITH PISTACHIO SAUCE

Adapted from *The Food Lover's Guide to Paris*, by Patricia Wells. 4th ed. New York: Workman (1999).

1996: JUNIOR'S CHEESECAKE

Adapted from *New York Cookbook*, by Molly O'Neill. Reprint. New York: Workman (1992).

1998: COCONUT LOAF CAKE

Adapted from *Desserts by Pierre Hermé*, by Pierre Hermé and Dorie Greenspan. Boston: Little, Brown (1998).

1999: FRESH GINGER CAKE

Adapted from *Room for Dessert*, by David Lebovitz. New York: Morrow (1999).

2002: GOOEY CHOCOLATE STACK

Adapted from *How to Be a Domestic Goddess*, by Nigella Lawson. New York: Hyperion (2001).

2002: AMAZON CAKE

Adapted from *Café Beaujolais*, by Margaret Fox and John S. Bear. Berkeley: Ten Speed Press (1984).

2002: LEMON-ALMOND BUTTER CAKE

Adapted from *In the Hands of a Chef*, by Jody Adams. New York: Morrow (2002).

2003: LEMON CAKE

Adapted from *Barefoot Contessa Parties!* by Ina Garten. New York: Clarkson Potter (2001).

2005: GÂTEAU DE CREPES

Batter adapted from *Joy of Cooking*, by Irma S. Rombauer, Marion Rombauer Becker, and Ethan Becker. New York: Scribner (2006).

Pastry cream adapted from *Desserts*, by Pierre Hermé and Dorie Greenspan. Boston: Little, Brown (1998).

2006: CHAMOMILE AND ALMOND CAKE

Adapted from *Aroma*, by Mandy Aftel and Daniel Patterson. New York: Artisan (2004).

2008: REVANI VERRIAS (SEMOLINA CAKE)

Adapted from *The Food and Wine of Greece*, by Diane Kochilas. New York: St. Martin's Griffin (1993).

2008: EVEN-GREATER AMERICAN POUND CAKE

Adapted from *BakeWise*, by Shirley O. Corriher. New York: Scribner (2008).

Chapter 18: Pies, Tarts, and Other Desserts

1877: CHOCOLATE ECLAIRS

Some technique and proportions adapted from *LaVarenne Pratique*, by Anne Willan; New York: Crown (1989) and from *Maida Heatter's Book of Great Chocolate Desserts*, by Maida Heatter; Random House (1995).

1977: PRUNEAUX DU PICHET (PRUNES IN A PITCHER)

Adapted from *Ma Gastronomie*, by Fernand Point. New York: Xs Books (1989).

1991: CARAMEL CUSTARD

Adapted from *The French Chef Cookbook*, by Julia Child. Reprint. New York: Knopf (2006).

1995: SALLY DARR'S GOLDEN DELICIOUS APPLE TART

Adapted from *New York Cookbook*, by Molly O'Neill. Reprint. New York: Workman (1992).

1998: PINEAPPLE CARPACCIO WITH LIME SORBET

Adapted from *Desserts by Pierre Hermé*, by Pierre Hermé and Dorie Greenspan. Boston: Little, Brown (1998).

1998: APPLE GALETTE

Adapted from *The Pie and Pastry Bible*, by Rose Levy Beranbaum. New York: Scribner (1998).

1999: LE CIRQUE'S CRÈME BRÛLÉE

Adapted from *New York Cookbook*, by Molly O'Neill. Reprint. New York: Workman (1992).

2007: RHUBARB ORANGE

Adapted from *Italian Two Easy: Simple Recipes from the London River Café*, by Rose Gray and Ruth Rogers. New York: Clarkson Potter (2006).

2007: QUEEN OF PUDDINGS

Adapted from *Lost Desserts*, by Gail Monaghan. New York: Rizzoli (2007).

PHOTO CREDITS

INDEX

Note: Page numbers in **boldface** type refer to recipes themselves.

Amanda Hesser has designed a seventeenth-century-style herb garden at a French chateau, developed the Twitter app Plodt, and appeared in *Julie & Julia*, playing herself. She began her career as a kitchen runner and bread truck driver in college, then picked grapes in France, made pretzels in Germany, and cleaned rabbits in Italy. As a longtime staffer at the *New York Times*, Hesser has written more than 750 stories, created the columns Food Diary and Recipe Redux, and was the food editor at the *Times Magazine*, where she launched T Living. She has written the award-winning books *Cooking for Mr. Latte* and *The Cook and the Gardener* and edited the essay collection *Eat, Memory*, based on a column she conceived for the *Times Magazine*. She is also the cofounder of food52.com. Hesser lives in Brooklyn with her husband, Tad Friend, and their two children.

HANDY SUBSTITUTIONS AND TIPS

1 cup buttermilk (aka sour milk) = 1 scant cup whole milk + 1 tablespoon white (or cider) vinegar

1 cup crème fraîche = 1 scant cup heavy cream + 1 tablespoon buttermilk (blended at room temperature, covered, and allowed to rest for 24 hours)

1 teaspoon baking powder = $\frac{1}{4}$ teaspoon baking soda + $\frac{1}{4}$ teaspoon cornstarch + $\frac{1}{2}$ teaspoon cream of tartar

1 cup sifted cake flour = $\frac{3}{4}$ cup sifted bleached all-purpose flour + 2 tablespoons cornstarch

.6 ounces fresh or compressed yeast = $2\frac{1}{4}$ teaspoons active dry yeast

4 sheets leaf gelatin = one $\frac{1}{4}$-ounce envelope powdered gelatin

1 cup brown sugar = 1 cup granulated white sugar + 3 tablespoons molasses (or, in a pinch, honey)

1 ounce semisweet chocolate = 1 scant ounce unsweetened chocolate + 1 tablespoon sugar

1 teaspoon chopped fresh herbs = $\frac{1}{2}$ teaspoon dried herbs

1 teaspoon dried whole spice = 1 teaspoon ground spice (generally, give or take a pinch)

1 cup corn syrup = 1 cup brown rice syrup (or agave nectar, though you may want to cook it down to thicken it slightly)

When measuring liquid, always set the measuring cup on a flat surface—if you hold it in the air, you inevitably tip it slightly.

When measuring flour, first whisk the flour (in the bag or container). Never pack it into a measuring cup. Drop scoops of flour into the measuring cup until the flour rises above the rim of the cup. Then use the straight, dull side of a knife to sweep across the rim of the measuring cup to level the flour. This is called the "dip-and-sweep" method. I use it for all dry ingredients.

Buy a scale! You won't regret it. I like the My Weigh KD-7000.